VATICAN ARCHIVES

VATICAN ARCHIVES

AN INVENTORY AND GUIDE TO HISTORICAL DOCUMENTS
OF THE HOLY SEE

Francis X. Blouin, Jr.

GENERAL EDITOR

Leonard A. Coombs
ARCHIVIST

Elizabeth Yakel
ARCHIVIST

Claudia Carlen, IHM
HISTORIAN

Katherine J. Gill
HISTORIAN

New York   Oxford
OXFORD UNIVERSITY PRESS
1998

Oxford University Press

Oxford   New York
Athens   Auckland   Bangkok   Bogotá   Bombay
Buenos Aires   Calcutta   Cape Town   Dar es Salaam
Delhi   Florence   Hong Kong   Istanbul   Karachi
Kuala Lumpur   Madras   Madrid   Melbourne
Mexico City   Nairobi   Paris   Singapore
Taipei   Tokyo   Toronto   Warsaw

and associated companies in
Berlin   Ibadan

Published by Oxford University Press, Inc.,
198 Madison Avenue, New York, New York 10016

Library of Congress Cataloging-in-Publication Data

Vatican Archives : an inventory and guide to historical documents of
the Holy See / Francis X. Blouin, Jr., general editor; Leonard A.
Coombs, archivist, Elizabeth Yakel, archivist; Claudia Carlen,
historian, Katherine J. Gill, historian.
p.   cm.
Includes bibliographical references and index.
1. Archivio vaticano—Catalogs. 2. Catholic Church—History—Sources—
Bibliography—Catalogs. 3. Church history—Sources—Bibliography—
Catalogs. I. Blouin, Francis X. II. Archivio vaticano.
CD 1586 1998 016.282—dc21 97-29248 CIP
ISBN 0-19-509552-9

Printing (last digit): 9 8 7 6 5 4 3 2 1

Printed in the United States of America
on acid-free paper

Contents

Agencies and Collections

Introduction

THE HISTORICAL DOCUMENTATION GENERATED BY THE HOLY SEE over the course of its history constitutes one of the most important sources for research on the history of Christianity, the history of the evolution of the modern state, the history of Western culture and institutions, the history of exploration and colonization, and much more. Though important, it has been difficult to grasp the extent of this documentation. This guide represents the first attempt to describe in a single work the totality of historical documentation that might properly be considered Vatican archives.

Although there are Vatican archival records in a number of repositories that have been included in this publication, this guide is designed primarily to provide useful information to English-speaking scholars who have an interest in using that portion of the papal archives housed in the Vatican Archives or Archivio Segreto Vaticano (ASV). As explained more fully below, it the result of a project conducted by archivists and historians affiliated with the University of Michigan. The project, initiated at the request of the prefect of the ASV, focused on using modern computer database technology to present information in a standardized format on surviving documentation generated by the Holy See. This documentation is housed principally in the ASV but is also found in a variety of other repositories. This guide is, in essence, the final report of the results of this project. What follows is a complete printout of the database that was constructed.

The database structure used in compiling the information was predicated on principles that form the basis for the organization of the archives of most modern state bureaucracies (e.g., provenance). Fundamentally, that is, one cannot understand the true nature of archival material unless one understands the administrative divisions, functions, and processes of the organization that generated those archives. Thus, the conceptual framework for this guide is based on the organizational structure of the Holy See.

Historically, the Holy See (also called the Apostolic See) has functioned in several different capacities, leading to a very complicated structure of congregations, commissions, offices, and so forth; it is the central government of the Roman Catholic church; it has functioned as a royal court; it served until 1870 as the civil government of the Papal States; it has functioned since 1929 as the civil government of Vatican City. Numerous offices have been established and abolished over the years to meet the needs of these different functions. This guide presents a brief history of each of these various offices and then links each office or agency to its extant records.

The administration of the Holy See has a history that is long, complex, and for the early years not fully known. The extant records of the papacy reflect two general periods of development. The first, from the medieval period through the mid-sixteenth century, and the second from the mid-sixteenth through the early twentieth century. The latter part of the twentieth century saw further changes.

During the first period, the affairs of the Holy See were handled primarily by the Apostolic Chancery. As the Chancery became busier, other offices and specialized subdepartments were developed at various times. Among these were the Apostolic Camera and the Datary. Toward the end of this period, special commissions of cardinals began to be created to handle the ever-increasing number and complexity of questions to be examined. The first of these commissions with a permanent character was the Congregation of the Inquisition, set up by Paul III in 1542. This was followed by others.

In 1588 Sixtus V organized the extant commissions or congregations and established additional bodies. Sixtus's Curia was made up of fifteen congregations, each charged with part of the governance of the church and its holdings. This action is considered the origin of the modern Roman Curia. In addition to the congregations, the Curia contained several other bodies, which over time became grouped into the Tribunals of Justice (the Roman Rota, Apostolic Camera, and Signature of Justice), Tribunals of Favor (the Signature of Favor, Apostolic Datary, and Apostolic Penitentiary), and Tribunals of Expedition (the Apostolic Chancery, Secretariat of Briefs, Secretariat of State, and Secretariat of Memorials).

As time passed and the requirements of the church changed, new congregations and other offices were created and old agencies were abolished (or suppressed, in the language of the church). The Curia was reformed and reorganized by Pius X in 1908. By this time, the agencies of the curia were grouped into three divisions: congregations (administrative), tribunals (judicial), and offices (ministerial). In 1967 Paul VI extensively reformed the Curia by creating five main divisions: the Secretariat of State, congregations, tribunals, secretariats (ecumenical offices), and offices. John Paul II, in 1988, once again modified the Curia.

As the administration of the Holy See evolved, so too did the role of the pope. The papacy developed a royal presence during the Middle Ages. A royal court of the pope took definite form at the time of papal residence in Avignon, France (1305–1377). The court comprised the offices of the papal chapel and the papal household. The court maintained its general form until the pontificate of Paul VI, who extensively reshaped the court, abolishing many of the trappings of royalty, in 1968.

The States of the Church, also known as the Papal States, took shape as a region under the civil control of the papal court during the Middle Ages. The pope's authority over the territory rose and fell with the political fortunes of the various powers interested in Italy, but in the sixteenth century the Papal States became fixed as a territory in central Italy, from Bologna and Ferrara in the north to Terracina in the south. (Noncontiguous areas of the Papal States included Pontecorvo and Benevento in Italy and Avignon and the county of Venaissin in France.) The Papal States controlled this territory until the era of the French Revolution. From 1798 until 1814, the territory was first divided between the Roman and Cisalpine republics, then between the Kingdom of Italy and a restored Papal States, and finally between the Kingdom of Italy and the region around Rome, which was annexed to France. In 1814 the Papal States were restored to previous boundaries. Except for a period of republican rule in 1849, they survived intact until 1860. The papacy ruled this territory, which was a source of significant wealth for the work of the church. Administration of these lands and their inhabitants required all the accoutrements of government. Just as the spiritual power of the pope required an extensive bureaucracy in support, so too did his temporal power require a civil bureaucracy not unlike others of the states of Europe.

By the mid-nineteenth century, the political forces interested in a united kingdom in Italy gained considerable strength backed by effective armed force. In 1860 the armies of Pius IX (1846–1878) were defeated and all papal lands with the exception of those in Rome and its vicinity were annexed to the new kingdom of Italy. For the next ten years Pius IX accepted the protection of a French garrison. But with the outbreak of the Franco-Prussian War, the French withdrew and unification forces occupied Rome itself. On September 20, 1870, the remainder of the Papal States was annexed to Italy, and the pope's civil authority came to an end. The pope took refuge in the Vatican and considered himself a prisoner. The matter was resolved when the Vatican City was established as a sovereign state, under the terms of the Lateran Treaty of 1929, for the purpose of assuring the independence of the popes. The state continues to have a government separate from the administration of the Catholic church, but because of the state's small size, the civil government of the state requires only a small administrative structure.

The bulk of the archives of the Holy See pertain to the latter periods of this history, that is, from the sixteenth century to the present. Moreover, as a result of the growing bureaucracy of the Curia, the court, and the Papal States, the records in the archives are divided and organized according to the activities and functions of the particular congregations, offices, tribunals, colleges, and so forth. These sorts of divisions are characteristic of archives generated by modern bureaucratic organizations.

This guide provides a comprehensive overview of extant historical documentation generated by the Holy See since the ninth century. Most previous guides have quite rightly emphasized the great holdings of medieval and Renaissance records in the Vatican Archives, such as the *Vatican Registers* and the contents of the original cabinets or "armaria." This guide has a different point of departure; it is organized around the bureaucratic structure of the Holy See from the time of its establishment under Sixtus V and is thus divided into the following sections: Part 1, College of Cardinals; Part 2, Papal Court; Part 3, Roman Curia (Congregations, Offices, and Tribunals); Part 4, Apostolic Nunciatures, Internunciatures, and Delegations; Part 5, Papal States; Part 6, Permanent Commissions; and Part 7, which includes miscellaneous official material and separate collections of personal papers and organizational records. The organization of the first six sections reflect this post-1588 conception of the bureaucratic structure of the Holy See, though earlier material is included. In general the holdings and structure of the records generated by the Holy See in these more recent centuries are not as well known as those for the late medieval period. The seventh section lists some official records series that the project staff could not match with the the specific offices and agencies that form the bureaucratic framework of the previous six. This seventh section also includes listings of personal papers of individuals acquired by Vatican archival repositories. Though designated personal papers, many of these collections have material that shed light on the official work of the Holy See. Also listed in this section are collections of records of institutions separate in organization from the Holy See but formed for a religious purpose. These institutions include religious orders, confraternities, and particular churches.

ALL RECORDS GENERATED AFTER JANUARY 22, 1922, ARE CLOSED TO RESEARCH IN THE VATICAN ARCHIVES AND IN OTHER VATICAN REPOSITORIES. Therefore, the agencies created by the curial reforms of the Second Vatican Council and the reforms of Paul VI and John Paul II have not been incorporated into this guide. Moreover, the structure of the government of the state of Vatican City created at the time of the Lateran Treaty of 1929 has not been incorporated into the guide.

THE ARCHIVIO SEGRETO VATICANO

Over the years, the growth and complexity of an archive generally relates in an organic way to the development of the institution that generates the records in the course of its business. This kind of relationship is certainly evident in the records extant in the Vatican Archives. The name *Archivio Segreto* was to imply private rather than secret. It is derived from its organizational antecedent the Bibliotheca Secreta, which was an area in the then new Vatican Library that was to hold working documents of the church that were accessible only to officials.

In order to understand the holdings of the ASV, it is necessary to have a sense of its history and its relationship to particular events in the history of the Holy See. In the brief overview that follows, three periods are of particular importance: first, the early centuries of the church; second the organizational reforms of Sixtus V and the reorganization of the Roman Curia; and third, the tumultuous events of the nineteenth century, which had a direct effect on the nature and content of the archival collections.

Early Centuries. In his guide to the ASV, Rev. Leonard Boyle, OP, points out that even the earliest popes retained letters, acts of martyrs, and other significant documents in a scrinium or chartarium.[1] Since the popes in these earliest centuries of the church did not have a permanent residence, the collected documents were simply handed from pope to pope. By 649, it is apparent that these collections had found a permanent home in the Lateran Palace in Rome. By the eleventh century, the collection is known to have been moved to the slope of the Palatine Hill near the Arch of Titus in the Roman Forum. Most of these early records were on delicate papyrus and have long since disintegrated.

Innocent III (1198–1216) was the first pope to recognize the need for a regularized form of record keeping. Copies of letters sent were entered by hand in great registers. This action inaugurated the *Vatican Registers*, still among the most important records of the archives. This series is one of the principal sources for documents on the papacy between the years 850 and the reorganization of the papacy in 1588. From the perspective of the history of the nature of documentation, the *Vatican Registers* are important in that they were regular in format and durable.

Moreover, during this period the papacy began to grow to the point that distinct offices began to emerge and keep records on a regular basis. The Apostolic Camera, the Chancery, the Datary, various secretaries, and the Roman Rota, all have their origins in this period of growth. This organizational framework was not nearly as extensive or formal as that implemented by Sixtus V.

During the period prior to 1588, there were likely many other kinds of documents that constituted the archives. However, during the Middle Ages, particularly after Innocent IV (1243–1254), the popes moved around a great deal. In 1245, Innocent IV is known to have taken a part of the archives with him to the Council of Lyon, after which the records remained for a while stored in the monastery at Cluny. Benedict XI (1303–1304) had the archives placed in Perugia. Clement V (1305–1314) then had the archives placed in Assisi where they remained until 1339, when Benedict XII (1334–1342) had them sent to Avignon.

The archives remained in Avignon during the time of the Great Schism. Once the difficulties were resolved, Martin V (1427–1431) had the records transported by boat and wagon to Rome, where they were temporarily housed in S. Maria Sopra Minerva, then established in his family palace (Colonna) in central Rome. Though important

[1]L. E. Boyle, *A Survey of the Vatican Archives and of its Medieval Holdings* (Toronto, 1972), p. 7.

historical records were returned to Rome at this time, including the *Vatican Registers*, the Avignon material, the paper registers known as the *Avignon Registers*, were not incorporated into the ASV until 1783.[2]

The travels of significant records of the papacy attest to the rather informal administrative structure that characterized the Holy See during the first fifteen centuries of its history. Records were moved around as needed by the various popes. Moreover, not all popes felt compelled to leave all their documents for their successors because of what Owen Chadwick calls the "family nature of papal government." It was not uncommon for popes to draw their assistants from trusted members of their families. At the death of a pope, then, the papers might be transferred to the family's archives rather than be kept centrally within an administrative division of the Holy See. Some of these materials, such as those from the Borghese, the Barberini, and the Chigi families have come to the ASV and the Vatican Library as personal family donations. Their presence as private manuscripts attests to this widespread practice even into the late seventeenth century.[3]

Reforms of Sixtus V. The founding of the Vatican Library under Nicholas V (1447–1455), marked the first step in bringing some control over the many volumes and documents in papal collections and in papal offices. Under Sixtus IV (1471–1484), specific quarters were established to house the great manuscript volumes and papers that would form the nucleus of the Vatican Library. At the same time he set aside a space called the Bibliotheca Secreta, which was to house documents of archival value. Documents considered of particular importance relating to privileges, grants, and claims were sent to the impenetrable and nearby Castel S. Angelo. Part of these documents form the current series in the ASV designated *Archivum Arcis*.

Throughout the sixteenth century efforts were made to bring together various collections of documents, including those of the Apostolic Camera, some which remained in private hands. In 1565, Pius IV (1559–1565) issued a brief that called for a search through papal offices as well as throughout all the Papal States for records and documents generated by the work of his predecessors.

By the late sixteenth century the church, in the aftermath of the Protestant Reformation and the resulting Council of Trent, was resolved to affect internal reform of its own institution and to standardize its practices and dogma in a way that would define what, in fact, Catholicism was in the face of strong Protestant challenges. As a part of this overall effort, Sixtus V (1585–1590) instituted a sweeping reform of the central administration of the church. In 1588, he created fifteen permanent congregations of cardinals, six to administer secular administration and nine to oversee spiritual affairs. His arrangement remained largely intact until the reforms of 1908, though some would argue that it was only as a result of the Second Vatican Council that the basic structure was changed. Though no direct link between the initiative of Sixtus V and the formal establishment of the Vatican Archives can be established, it seems clear that the emerging bureaucracy needed a place to deposit its inactive records.

The records generated by these new congregations were the result of standardization of procedures. The resulting files or dossiers were then clearly the records of the individual congregations and would not travel with individual prefects or administrators. These records then constituted the first components of the archives of the newly

[2]Boyle, *Survey*, pp. 8–11. See also relevant sections in J. N. D. Kelly, *Oxford Dictionary of Popes* (Oxford, 1986).

[3]O. Chadwick, *Catholicism and History: The Opening of the Vatican Archives* (Cambridge, 1978), p. 10.

established administrative structure of the church. Since so many records have survived, clearly each congregation took responsibility for caring for its inactive files.

It comes as no surprise, then, that in 1610, Paul V (1605–1621) called for the return of archival material relating to the papacy. In December 1611 he prepared rooms in the Belvedere palace in the Vatican to receive the archives. Six months later an archivist was appointed. At about the same time Paul V formally divided the library and the archives into two separate institutions with separate administrations. Over the subsequent forty-five years, documents and registers began to arrive at the new archive. All the holdings of the old Bibliotheca Secreta were transferred. The *Vatican Registers* and other documents of great importance were transferred from the Castel S. Angelo, including the records of the Council of Trent. Financial documents from the Apostolic Camera were also received.

As the records arrived, they were placed in a series of eighty cabinets or armaria. Over the years specific documents became associated with their specific cabinet numbers. These eighty cabinets remain the organizational framework for these early records that are considered the "original Vatican Archives."[4]

In 1656, Alexander VII (1655–1667) ordered that within the Secretariat of State, individual secretaries could no longer keep inactive files. They were required to transfer the records to the archives. This new authority established the archives as a central depository within the Vatican for inactive records. Over the successive centuries, a variety of departments in addition to that of the Secretariat of State have chosen to deposit records with the ASV. However, it is important to note that not all have chosen to do so. There remain throughout the Vatican several archival collections under an administration wholly separate from the ASV. To the extent possible, they are noted in this guide at the appropriate sections.

Chadwick emphasizes that this new central archive "owed nothing to the notion of helping scholars to write history. It was a business transaction intended to make the administration more efficient."[5] In fact, the archives was a closed institution open only to those in the administration of the Curia who had need to consult the records. Because of its close association with the business of the church during its early existence, the ASV grew further apart from the library and in essence was a division of the Secretariat of State.

Nineteenth Century. As a result of three events, the nineteenth century was an exceptionally noteworthy period for the ASV. The first arose from the ambition of Napoleon to consolidate the archives of his empire in Paris. The second was a direct result of the establishment of a unified Italian state and the effective removal of all temporal power from the pope. Third, perhaps in reaction to the second, was the formal opening of the archives for research use.

The first events surround the transport of the archives to Paris. While the territorial ambitions of Napoleon Bonaparte are well known, his ambitions for a consolidated archive for his empire are often ignored. However, he did envision that the greatest art, manuscripts, and archives of his empire would be brought eventually to Paris. He planned a great central archive to be built in Reims (he later decided on Paris), where the archives of European capitals would be brought together. In December 1809, shortly after he arrested and imprisoned Pius VII (1800–1823), he dispatched one of his generals to Rome with instructions to bring to Paris the whole of the Vatican Archives.

[4]Boyle, *Survey*, pp. 10–11.
[5]Chadwick, *Catholicism*, p. 9.

The shipments via wagon began in 1810 and continued through 1813. In all, 3,239 chests arrived in Paris with very few lost. The inventory prepared by French archivists counted more than 102,435 registers, volumes, or bundles. The great central archives building was never realized, so the archives were stored in the Archives Nationales at the Palais Soubise.

With the defeat of Napoleon in 1814, the newly established authorities immediately ordered the archives returned to the Vatican. However, that was easier said than done. Napoleon had expended an enormous sum to transport the load to Paris. Defeated France did not have the resources to return the archives. There are many stories and legends about the fate of the archives during the years between the order for their return and the arrival in Rome of the last of the chests in December 1817.

Because of the costs involved, some analysis was apparently done on the relative importance of various records in the archives. The responsibility for managing this operation was assigned to Count Giulio Ginnasi, with Marino Marini in charge of the actual work with the documents. In 1816 Ercole Consalvi, cardinal secretary of state, wrote to various congregations asking that they "specify what material formerly in their custody might be abandoned in Paris and, presumably, destroyed."[6] Those deemed of lesser importance were separated and may have been sold for scrap paper. Other parts of the archives—particularly many of the records of the Holy Office pertaining to the Inquisition—though considered by some of major importance, were deliberately destroyed by the papal commissioners dispatched to oversee the transfer and eager to see the legacy of the Inquisition extinguished. Some chests were sent via ship and suffered water damage. Other material, considered unimportant or damaged, never left Paris and remains in the Archives Nationales.[7]

In any case 3,239 chests were used to get the archives to Paris but only 2,200 were used for their return, and these arrived over an extended period of time. As the material began to arrive in Rome, many of the congregations were upset with what was returned and what was not. Their complaints resulted in the replacement of Ginnasi. John Tedeschi notes that added work needed to be done; this was financed by the sale of some of the registers of the Holy Office.[8] However, in all probably about one-third of the material sent was lost. Losses were particularly great among the records of the Apostolic Datary and the Holy Office. Tedeschi notes that "among the untold treasures that perished in Paris were the youthful writings of Tommaso Campanello and the defense testimony of Giordano Bruno."[9]

With the incorporation of the Papal States into the new kingdom of Italy in 1870, documents of a civil nature identified in the ASV were transferred to the newly established Archivio di Stato di Roma. The division of the records in the archives was hasty and not always precise. As a result, records series for some congregations or offices are found in both archives. See, for example, entries in this guide for the Roman Rota and the Signatura Iustitiae. Particularly problematic are the financial records of the Apostolic Camera. Initially most of the cameral records were transferred. However, the Camera at times served both the temporal and spiritual interests of the pope. In 1918–1919 a significant portion of the cameral records was returned to the Vatican. Nev-

[6]J. Tedeschi, "A 'Queer Story': The Inquisitorial Manuscripts" in *Treasures of the Library, Trinity College Dublin*, edited by P. Fox (Dublin, 1986), p. 67. See also J. Tedeschi, "La dispersione degli archivi della inquisizione romana," *Rivista di storia e letteratura religiosa* 9 (1973): 298–312.

[7]Boyle, *Survey*, p. 85. Chadwick, *Catholicism*, pp. 16–17.

[8]Tedeschi, "Queer Story," p. 68.

[9]Tedeschi, "Queer Story," p. 68.

ertheless material for the Camera is still found in both archival institutions.[10]

A third event marks the transformation of the archives from an agency of institutional service to a research repository. On January 1, 1881, Leo XIII (1878–1903) opened the Archivio Segreto Vaticano to research use. He argued that the best defense for the church in addressing the charges of its critics would be to open the archives for the world to see. The church, Leo believed, had nothing to fear from a true history written from the actual sources. Documents created up to 1815 were made available. Scholars had no access to inventories or finding aids but rather had to rely on assistance from the staff archivists. But the archives were opened upon application. The archives then served for the first time as a center for research as well as a center for the administration of the inactive records of the Holy See.[11]

THE BROADER CORPUS OF DOCUMENTATION OF THE HOLY SEE

Not all papal documentation is found in the ASV. Partly as a result of historical forces and partly as a result of administrative convenience, the historical documentation of the Holy See is spread among a variety of repositories. In describing the locations of the various institutions that house such documents, it is important to make one distinction at the start. There is a great body of papal material found in most archives of the world. These documents are for the most part either documents received in an official capacity by an institution or government or manuscripts purchased by collectors and deposited in an archival repository or library.

This guide is concerned only with papal documentation generated by the Holy See that was intended to be retained within the offices of the Holy See. The principal repository for this material is the Archivio Segreto Vaticano. However, archival materials from the Holy See exist in a number of archival repositories. As a result of the division of the archives in 1870, the Archivio di Stato di Roma contains a huge collection of records regarding the civil administration of the Papal States. This guide integrates civil administrative material in the ASV and major civil administrative series (prior to 1870) in the Archivio di Stato di Roma.

Furthermore, as noted above, many other congregations maintain their own archives. Those whose records are described in this guide to the same level as the descriptions for series in the ASV are as follows:

1. The historical archives of the Congregazione per l'evangelizzazione dei popoli, formerly and popularly known as the Congregation "De Propaganda Fide." This is the congregation of the Curia that has responsibility for the missions of the church. The holdings of the historical archive of the Propaganda Fide are listed in this guide in the section "Roman Curia: Congregations." The archive is located in the historic headquarters of the congregation on the Piazza di Spagna in central Rome (address: Piazza di Spagna 48, 00187 Rome).

2. The archive of the Reverenda fabbrica di San Pietro. The Fabbrica is the agency of the church that was responsible for the construction of St. Peter's Basilica. It now has responsibility for the maintenance of the building among other duties. The holdings of this archive are listed in this guide in the section "Roman Curia: Congregations." The archive is located in a series of rooms within the basilica itself (address: Fabbrica di San Pietro, 00120 Vatican City).

There are many other congregations that maintain their own historical archive but

[10]Boyle, *Survey*, pp. 12, 42, 48, 91, 94.

[11]Chadwick, *Catholicism*, pp. 102–109.

whose holdings were not included in this survey and guide.[12] Among those are the following that are known to have important holdings:

1. The Archive of the Sezione dei rapporti con gli Stati, formerly the Congregation for Extraordinary Ecclesiastical Affairs. This congregation is described in the guide in the section "Roman Curia: Congregations." Founded in 1814, the archive is therefore primarily a nineteenth-century collection of documents concerning a wide range of topics relating to the worldwide interests of the Holy See (address: Palazzo Apostolico, 00120 Vatican City).

2. The Archive of the Congregazione per il culto divino e la disciplina dei sacramenti, formerly the Congregation of Rites. This congregation is described in the guide in the section "Roman Curia: Congregations." It has responsibility for administering the process for determining the saints of the church. The holdings in its archive date from its founding in 1588. However a substantial portion of its records have been deposited in the ASV. Others can be found in the Bibliothèque Nationale in Paris. The archive is located just outside St. Peter's Square in Rome (address: Piazza Pio XII, 00193 Rome).

3. The Archive of the Penitenzieria (Paenitentiaria) apostolica. This office predates the reform of Sixtus V and is described in this guide in the section "Roman Curia: Tribunals." (The name of this office was historically spelled Poenitentiaria, which spelling is used elsewhere in this guide.) It has had responsibilities for matters of conscience, certain questions regarding marriage, and for certain dispensations. Its archive spans most of its history with records as early as 1409 and on through the nineteenth century (address: Via della Conciliazione 34, 00193 Rome).

4. The Archive of the Ufficio delle celebrazioni liturgiche del Sommo Pontifico, formerly Prefect for Apostolic Ceremonies (Prefettura delle ceremonie pontificie). This office has responsibility for arranging ceremonies, for example, for the consecration of bishops and for the reception of foreign sovereigns and ambassadors. This agency is described in the section "Papal Court." Its small archive includes material from the fifteenth century onward (address: Palazzo Apostolico, Loggia I del Cortile di S. Damaso, 00120 Vatican City).

5. The Archive of the Congregation for the Doctrine of the Faith, formerly known as the Holy Office. This archive is not open for consultation (address: Palazzo del S. Uffizio, Piazza S. Uffizio 11, 00120 Vatican City).

It is useful at this point to recall that the pope is and has always been the bishop of Rome. As such, the archive of the diocese of Rome, while pertaining to a local diocese, does have a special relationship with the general records of the Holy See. The archive of the diocese of Rome is located in the offices of the Vicariato next to the basilica of St. John Lateran (address: Palazzo Lateranense, Piazza S. Giovanni in Laterano 6, 00184 Rome).

In addition to the archives within the Holy See, there is significant papal archival material in three repositories not connected with the Vatican. These holdings have been incorporated into the structure of this guide and described in connection with their appropriate offices.

1. At Trinity College Dublin there is a collection of Lateran Registers and of registers from the Holy Office (address: College Street, Dublin 2, Ireland).

2. At the Archives Nationales, Paris, there is a collection of registers from the Camera, from the Congregation of Bishops and Regulars, and a few volumes from

---

[12]L. Pásztor, *Guida delle fonti per la storia dell'America Latina negli archivi della Santa Sede e degli archivi ecclesiatici d'Italia* (Vatican City, 1970) pp. 305–355.

other offices. These were left behind when the bulk of the ASV holdings were returned (address: CARAN, 60 rue des Francs-Bourgeois, 75141 Paris, France).

3. At the Bibliothèque Nationale, Paris, there is a series of printed records from the Congregation of Rites (address: 58 rue de Richelieu, 75002 Paris, France).

THE VATICAN ARCHIVES PROJECT OF
THE UNIVERSITY OF MICHIGAN

The idea for the Vatican Archives project arose from my own questions as a first-time user of the various sources in the index rooms of the ASV. At the invitation of the Prefect of the archives, Rev. Josef Metzler, OMI, and assisted by Msgr. Charles Burns of the archives staff, a group under the auspices of the Bentley Historical Library of the University of Michigan was brought together to consider the applicability of standardized descriptive techniques to the existing access system at the Vatican Archives and to the access systems at related repositories holding Vatican archival material.[13] The purpose of this project has been to make the organization of extant papal archives better understood among scholars whose primary language is English and to explore the use of computerbased technology to achieve this end.

A user normally begins using the ASV by visiting the index room of the archives, where there are three categories of finding aids that together are known as the numbered "indici" to the collections. First, there are the modern indici (numbered 1000 and above), which have been prepared over the past eighty years or so. These are modern access tools to most of the major series in the archives. They resemble modern provenance-based finding aids found in all major archives. Those in the ASV reflect extraordinary scholarship on the part of the archives staff and are exceptionally valuable tools. As noted in specific sections of this guide, there are some modern indici, not numbered, which for one reason or another are kept in reserve at the reference desk.

Second, there are indici (numbered up to 999) that were, for the most part, prepared prior to the opening of the archives for research in 1881. These fall into two subcategories. (1) There are several summary registers and inventories that were selected by the ASV staff and pulled from the stacks and placed in the Index Room to serve users as indici to the collections. In most cases these particular indici were prepared at the same time as the records themselves and were designed for administrative retrieval of particular records series. Written in diverse hands and often of unpredictable format, these can be much more difficult to use. Because there have been many changes in the archives over the years, most notably the losses during the Napoleonic era, many of these older indices are inaccurate with regard to the current contents and organization of the record series they purport to describe. However, these may provide the only evidence of documents that no longer exist. (2) There are some early inventories of documents prepared by early archivists. Particularly important are those that list the contents of the original cabinets or armaria of the ASV.

Third, there are a variety of specialized indices that are not provenance-based but rather reflect the interests or the energies of a particular archivist in relation to particular documents or subjects. The most important of these is the Schedario Garampi, pre-

[13]See the following correspondence: Prefect to F. Blouin, Dec., 11, 1986; Prefect to Harold Williams, Jan. 22, 1989; Agreement, F. Blouin and Prefect, May 20, 1991; Prefect to F. Blouin, June 10, 1991; F. Blouin to Prefect, May 9, 1994; Prefect to F. Blouin, June 1, 1994; F. Blouin to Prefect, June 11, 1996; Prefect to F. Blouin, June 15, 1996. These documents are located in the administrative files, Bentley Historical Library, University of Michigan. See *L'Attivita della Santa Sede 1989* (Vatican City, 1990), p. 1398.

pared in the late eighteenth century by Giuseppe Garampi, which presents a sometimes chronological listing of select documents in the "miscellaneous cabinets" of the archives. There are many others as well. These specialized indexes rarely indicate indexing criteria nor do they indicate if they cover all or part of a series.

Another important group of access tools are various published works in many languages that explore a particular dimension of the archives. These publications fall into a number of categories. First, there are the major studies of particular records series in the archives such as Katterbach on the supplications, Hoberg on the Rota, or Pásztor on the Fondo Moderno.[14] Second, there are the major national guides that highlight documents in a variety of series that cover a specific country, done under a variety of auspices. These point to specific material of a particular national interest.[15] Third, there are many editions of particular documents or sets of documents. These are directed in some cases toward analysis and publication of specific items or more general descriptions of major documents relating to a particular subject area.[16] Some of these items are in the index room of the ASV or in a separate room in the ASV devoted to related printed works.

As noted above, proper administrative practice required the development of inventories and indexes to record series. These access tools were created at the same time as the documents themselves. Many of these are located in the stacks as part of the records series to which they pertain and are not considered by the ASV to be official "indici." These particular indici were created to facilitate administrative retrieval. These can be a chronological listing of items received or an alphabetical listing by correspondent or diocese. In some cases this kind of material has been pulled from the stacks and placed in the Index Room for the convenience of researchers. The protocol books for the Congregation of Bishops and Regulars and those for the Fondo Moderno of the Secretariat of State are examples. These are in the Index Room but are not part of the numbered indici.

A researcher who arrives at the ASV is presented with an array of items designed to provide access to specific archival material. While a list of the indici is available, there has been no overall schema readily apparent to the user to give that user a sense of the entire archives and how the various levels or groups of finding aids fit. At that most general level of inquiry, that of a general inventory, a standardized system assembled

---

[14]For example, see B. Katterbach, "Päpstliche Suppliken mit der Klausel der sola Signatura," *Römische Quartalschrift für christliche Altertumskunde und für Kirchengeschichte* 31 (1923): 185–196, and *Inventario dei registri delle suppliche* (Vatican City, 1931); H. Hoberg, "Die Protokollbücher der Rotanotare von 1464 bis 1517," *Zeitschrift der Savigny-Stiftung für Rechtsgeschichte. Kanonistische Abteilung* 39 (1953): 177–227, and "Die 'Admissiones' des Archivs der Rota," *Archivalische Zeitschrift* 50–51 (1955): 391–408; and L. Pásztor, "La Segretaria di Stato di Pio IX durante il triennio 1848–1850," *Annali della Fondazione italiana per la storia amministrativa* 3 (1966): 308–365.

[15]See W. H. Bliss, C. Johnson, and J. A. Twemlow, eds., *Calendar of Entries in the Papal Registers Relating to Great Britain and Ireland: Calendar of Papal Letters* (London, 1893–); P. Lacacheux and G. Mollat, eds., *Lettres secrètes et curiales du pape Urbain V (1362–1370) se rapportant à la France,* (Paris, 1902–1955); and the many publications in the *Bibliothèque des Écoles Françaises d'Athènes et de Rome,* 3d ser., *Registres et lettres des papes du XIVe siècle.*

[16]See, for example, B. Barbiche, "Les 'scriptores' de la chancellerie apostolique sous le pontificat de Boniface VIII (1295–1305)," *Bibliothèque de l'École des Chartes,* 128 (1970): 114–187; and D. Conway, "Guide to Documents of Irish and British Interest in the Fondo Borghese," *Archivium hibernicum* 23 (1960): 1–147 and 24 (1961): 31–102. See also P. O. Kristeller, *Iter Italicum,* Vol. 6 (London, 1992), and P. Carucci and R. Santoro, eds., *Le fonti archivistiche,* vol. 1 of *La Rivoluzione Francese (17871799): Repertorio delle fonti archivistiche e delle fonti a stampa conservate in Italia e nella Città del Vaticano,* (Rome, 1991).

via a structured database seemed to hold the greatest potential for organizing and presenting relevant information. A structure would be designed to receive information on the ASV and then to receive information on Vatican materials located in other Vatican and related repositories.

The University of Michigan group approached the problem rooted in a fundamental sense of what in fact an archival collection is. This basic idea was stated best in a report of the Association of Canadian Archivists:

> Archives are chiefly the non-current substantive records of the institutions or individuals they document. Administrative records are created in the first instance to serve a specific purpose. Once that purpose has been accomplished, they may have a secondary value as reference material, and later historical source material. Their usefulness is enhanced if the relationship to the original transaction remains apparent.[17]

It was this latter relationship that was particularly difficult to determine in the current access system at the ASV. In order to realize the full potential of the finding aids in the ASV, it seemed essential to clearly present to the user the essence of this fundamental relationship between the Vatican as an organization and the documents that it had generated over a period of a thousand years. Because of the diversity of subject matter covered in the records of the ASV, a thorough subject guide would be extremely difficult to achieve in a reasonable amount of time. Therefore, the relationships between the function of the office, the activities devised to carry out that function, and the records that result, are of critical importance toward an understanding of the nature of the material. Thus, if a user understands the role of an agency and the activities of its offices, one can anticipate the range of subject matter covered in its activities.

Published guides have been the traditional vehicle through which this relationship has been presented.[18] Comprehensive guides to the ASV do exist but none of these is nearly complete nor is any specifically or completely based on the fundamental relationship between the organization and the records generated.[19] The staff of the Bentley Library at the University of Michigan designed a provenance-based system that would answer the following three basic questions: (1) what is the Vatican and what administrative agencies have formed the organization of the Vatican over time?, (2) which of those agencies have deposited records in the archives and which have not?, and (3) for those records that have been deposited in the archives, what are the characteristics of the record series and what sorts of finding guides exist both within the archives collection and outside it? The responses to these not insignificant questions would then be assembled into a computer database. At this point the idea of using the computer was less important than a clear sense of the relationships to be described and the level of description to be attained. It was therefore essential to define a specific layer of description to be done, to be sure that all materials in the various archival collections were visited, and then to be completely consistent in all work subsequently done. This consistency, which is essential to any guide, becomes vital to an electronic-based system.

The project that resulted from this proposition has been divided into two phases. The first was designed to build the basic structure of the database to include every record series housed in the ASV and related repositories. This was successfully completed in

[17]*Canadian Archives: Report to the Social Sciences and Humanities Research Council of Canada* (Ottawa, 1980), p. 16.

[18]J. Favier, *Les Archives Nationales: État général des fonds* (Paris, 1978–). P. d'Angiolini and C. Pavone, *Guida generale degli Archivi dei Stato Italiani* (Rome, 1981–).

[19]Boyle, *Survey.* L. Pásztor, *Guida delle fonti.* K. A. Fink, *Das Vaticanische Archiv: Einführung in die Bestände und ihre Erforschung* (Rome, 1951).

the spring of 1991. The second phase was designed to enhance the descriptive structure in a way that would provide some analysis of various dimensions of the archival holdings. This phase was completed in 1995.

The first phase of the project was launched in the fall of 1989. Two members of the University of Michigan project staff spent eleven months at the Vatican surveying the entire holdings of the ASV and creating a hierarchical structure for recording the information. At the same time two other staff members worked in Ann Arbor to research the evolution of the administrative functions of the Holy See from the medieval period through the twentieth century. The system then devised (essentially modern descriptive archival methods) links a sense of the Holy See as an organization with the records produced by that organization over time. This approach then required the preparation of two separate databases that eventually were linked. This work then provided the model for subsequent work at the Archives of the Propaganda Fide, the Archives of the Reverenda Fabbrica di San Pietro, the Archivio di Stato di Roma, Trinity College, the Archives Nationales, and the Bibliothèque Nationale.[20]

At one level, the staff prepared histories of each department or agency of the Holy See that was were identifiable through standard sources on the history of the papacy and of the church.[21] More than 450 agencies that functioned between the years 800 and 1960 were identified. While the histories for the most part have been drawn from general secondary sources, in those cases where the agency was particularly important or unusually complicated, the staff consulted the original bulls to clarify function, purpose and organizational evolution.[22] The emphasis in the agency histories is on function and competencies. Archival access is based on the assumption that if a user understands the function of an agency, the method of its operation, and the types of documents it generates, then that user can predict what sort of topics might be covered in those records.

[20]See L. Coombs, "A New Access System for the Vatican Archives," *American Archivist* 52 (1989): 538–546; F. Blouin, "A Case for Bridging the Gap: The Significance of the Vatican Archives Project for International Archival Information Exchange," *American Archivist* 55 (1992): 182–191; E. Yakel, "Pushing MARC-AMC to its Limits: The Vatican Archives Project," *American Archivist* 55 (1992): 192–201; and F. Blouin, "The Historian, the Archivist, and the Vatican Archives: A Case Study in Collaboration in the Age of Information Technology," *Archivi & computer* 2 (1993): 75–88.

[21]For example, G. Moroni, *Dizionario di erudizione storico-ecclesiastica* (Venice, 1840–1861); N. del Re, *La curia romana: Lineamenti storico-giuridici*, 3d ed. (Rome, 1970); J. N. D. Kelly, *Oxford Dictionary of Popes* (Oxford, 1986); L. von Pastor, *The History of the Popes from the Close of the Middle Ages*, translated and edited by F. I. Antrobus et al. (St. Louis, 1891–1953); P. Prodi, *The Papal Prince*, translated by S. Haskins (Cambridge, 1987); and M. G. P. Ruggiero, *La Reverenda Camera Apostolica e i suoi archivi* (Rome, 1987). Also important to a work of this sort were articles in the *Catholic Encyclopedia*, the *New Catholic Encyclopedia*, and the *Enciclopedia cattolica*. We also used various editions of the *Annuario Pontificio*.

[22]For 440–1740, *Magnum Bullarium Romanum: Bullarum Privilegorum ac Diplomatum Romanorum Pontificum Amplissima Collectio* (Graz, 1964–1965); reproduction of the edition published in 1733–1762. For 1740–1758, *Magnum Bullarium Romanum: Bullarum Privilegiorum ac Diplomatum Romanorum Pontificum Amplissima Collectio: Benedicti Papae XIV Bullarium* (Graz, 1966); reproduction of the edition published in Rome in 1746–1757. For 1758–1835, Magnum *Bullarium Romanum: Continuatio* (Graz, 1963–1964); reproduction of the edition published in Rome 1835–1857. For 1831–1846, *Acta Gregorii Papae XVI: Scilicet Constitutions, Bullae, Litterae Apostolicae, Epistolae* (Rome, 1901–1904). For 1846–1878, *Pii IX Pontificis Maximi Acta* (Graz, 1971); reproduction of the edition published in Rome, 1854–1878. For 1878–1903, *Leonis XIII Pontificis Maximi Acta* (Graz, 1971); reproduction of the edition published in Rome, 1881–1905. For 1903–1908, *Pii X Pontificis Maximi Acta* (Graz, 1971); reproduction of edition published in Rome, 1905–1914. For the recent period, *Acta Apostolicae Sedis*.

There exists an enormous body of scholarship on the history of the agencies of the Holy See, particularly for the Roman Curia. To digest and present the various interpretations of the role and function of the important agencies of the Holy See was far beyond the scope of this project. The histories presented in this guide are essentially official histories drawn from the documents that have authorized the creation or the refinement of a particular office. Users of this guide should be aware that the official documents to not always reflect or indicate the full history of a particular era in the evolution of an office. Users are encouraged to probe the broader corpus of research on the history of those particular divisions that are of interest. Some bibliographic pointers exist within the histories of the more complex agencies. However, those citations are by no means exhaustive.[23]

At a second level, the project staff at the Vatican worked through every shelf in the ASV to identify specific record series. These are clearly identifiable units composed of related material usually generated by a single organizational entity and usually as a result of a specific function or transaction. Our challenge was to make a census of the holdings of the archives using standardized descriptive fields. Because of the vastness of the task we emphasized only general descriptive attributes and did not emphasize the content of the particular series. In the ASV approximately eleven hundred series were identified. To assemble the information the project staff then entered basic descriptive data in USMARC-AMC format for each of the record series (United States Machine Readable Cataloging-Archival and Manuscripts Control—note that with the integration of formats the term AMC is no longer used). The basic USMARC record for an archival record series includes the following types of information: (1) name of the organization generating the particular record series, (2) name of the particular record series, (3) the inclusive dates of the series, (4) bulk in linear meters, (5) basic information on the way the series is organized, (6) information on the scope and content of the material in the series, (7) the existence of any finding aids or indexes to the particular series, and (8) various index terms.[24]

In 1991, this database was loaded into the archives and manuscripts section of the Research Libraries Information Network (RLIN), the principal database of the Research Libraries Group, located in Mountain View, California, to assist scholars who have an interest in locating historical documentation generated by the Holy See. The information regarding the ASV contained in this guide has been available to scholars through the RLIN network since 1991. Although some additions and corrections continue to be made, it is very important to note that no provision has been made for the maintenance of this database. The condition and definition of the series that constitute the holdings of the various repositories continue to evolve. The ASV itself will likely at some point develop a system of description that will be detailed and

[23]An important place to start for early archival material is T. Frenz, *Papsturkunden des Mittelalters und der Neuzeit* (Stuttgart, 1986). This work has been translated into Italian by S. Pagano and is titled *I documenti pontifici nel medioevo e nell'eta moderna* (Vatican City, 1989).

[24]The Vatican Archives Project relied considerably upon S. Hensen, *Archives, Personal Papers, and Manuscripts: A Cataloging Manual for Archival Repositories, Historical Societies and Manuscript Libraries*, 2d ed. (Chicago, 1989). MARC-AMC data was entered on site using the MicroMARC:amc program developed at Michigan State University. There are several sources of information on the MARC format in archival settings. Among the most useful is R. Smiraglia, ed., *Describinq Archival Materials: The Use of the MARC-AMC Format* (New York, 1990). This was discussed at a conference held at the Pierpont Morgan Library in New York City on November 6–7, 1992. Funded by the Homeland Foundation of New York the conference brought together scholars who use the Vatican Archives and archivists who understand the technology involved in database design. A review of the proceedings by D. Bearman appears in *Archives and Museum Informatics* 6.4 (Winter 1992): 5–6.

current. Because of this inevitable evolution, some of the specific data in the RLIN version will need to be withdrawn.[25]

At this point, the database is available at most major research libraries in the United States and selected European libraries. The best point of entry is to call up the master record (ID VATV878-A), which explains the structure of the information in RLIN. The database offers the following advantages to users who wish to explore this information: (1) it is possible to explore the links and cross references in a more direct way; (2) the relationship between the record series and the agencies that generated those series is presented in a more layered hierarchy; (3) it is possible to limit searches by a specific date or a specific set of inclusive dates; (4) there is the possibility for limited subject and geographical based searches; and (5) there is the limited possibility for form and genre searching. At this writing, scholars are best advised to consult the database with the assistance of a reference librarian. However, it is possible to obtain individual request accounts for the RLIN network. Researchers interested in such accounts should consult a librarian at an RLG member institution.

The database and now this guide will assist users of the various archives in determining what agencies of the Holy See existed over time, which of those agencies generated records that survive today in the ASV and elsewhere, what kinds of records were generated, and how best to locate material in a particular record series through existing published and unpublished finding aids.

In order to accomplish the core of this work, the prefect of the ASV extended to the project staff the extraordinary privilege of access to the stacks of the ASV. The logic of the placement of material on the shelves of the stacks proved particularly helpful in reconstructing the relationships required in the dual-tiered database. The stacks of the ASV contain nearly 20 linear kilometers of records dating from about 850 through to the late twentieth century (materials generated after 1922 are closed to research). As has been noted, the archival holdings of the congregation "de Propaganda Fide" and of the Fabbrica di San Pietro lie outside the ASV. Because of the particular historical importance of these two offices, their holdings were incorporated into the structure of the database at the same level as applied to the ASV. Project staff were given access to the stacks of these repositories as well. At the archives of the Propaganda Fide, however, access to unprocessed material was limited.

Also, because of the importance of the Papal States to the Holy See, the project staff incorporated existing descriptive information on the holdings of the Archivio di Stato di Roma that pertain to the government of the Papal States up until their demise as an arm of the Holy See in 1870. Citations used to describe records from the Archivio di Stato come from the Archivio di Stato di Roma section, by Edvige Aleandri Barletta and Carla Lodolini Tupputi, of the *Guida Generale degli Archivi di Stato Italiano*, edited by Piero D'Angiolini and Claudio Pavone (Rome, 1986). The project staff is grateful to the Italian Ministry of Cultural Affairs (Beni culturali) for permission to quote extensively from this guide for this purpose.

A second phase of the project was devoted to specific analytical work. This work focused on three particularly complex areas. First, the traditional application of the USMARC format simply notes whether or not finding aids exist. Because of the complex structure of extant inventories, protocol books and traditional indices at

[25]The Research Libraries Group is a consortium of more than one hundred research libraries. Its purpose is to foster cooperative work among those institutions to improve access to information resources. Its major contribution has been the formation of the RLIN computer network that links information on the holdings of all the member institutions as well as of certain specialized collections. The Vatican data falls into this latter category.

the ASV, the decision was made to include extensive analytical work on the nature of existing finding aids. Second, because the nature of records in the archives is not always clear from the title, work was done to present some sense of the scope and content of select records series. Third, many aspects of the ASV have been studied intensively by scholars around the world since it was opened for research in 1881. As a result, there is a huge bibliography that addresses particular aspects of one or another records series. We were able to identify a considerable selection of the relevant titles. The selection focuses on books and articles which have specific information on the organization or the content of particular series. The *Bibliografia dell'Archivio Vaticano* (6 vols.) provides the most comprehensive bibliographic overview of scholarship which draws from the holdings of the ASV.[26] However, a truly definitive bibliography would be difficult to assemble.

ACKNOWLEDGMENTS

A great number of individuals and institutions were of enormous help in formulating the project and in helping the work to completion. The idea for this project first emerged as the result of a short research trip to Rome funded by the Horace H. Rackham School of Graduate Studies at the University of Michigan. Once the idea took hold, the Office of the Vice President for Research at the University of Michigan provided a grant to test the proposed methodology among the diplomatic holdings of the ASV. Support for the first phase of the project was provided by the Getty Grant Program with matching funds from the National Endowment for the Humanities, a federal agency. Support for the second phase of the project was provided by the Lilly Endowment, Inc., The Andrew W. Mellon Foundation, and the National Endowment for the Humanities. At the start of the second phase, the Homeland Foundation of New York provided funding for a conference at the Pierpont Morgan Library in New York City that drew together archivists who are familiar with database construction and scholars who use the ASV. Final editing of the work was funded jointly by the American Friends of the Vatican Library and the Homeland Foundation. To these offices and foundations we submit this final report of our work with a profound sense of gratitude.

Deborah Marrow and Jack Meyers at the Getty Grant Program; Jane Rosenberg, George Farr, Jeff Field, and Barbara Paulson at the NEH; Edward Queen and Fred Hofheinz at the Lilly Endowment; Richard Ekman at the Andrew W. Mellon Foundation; Msgr. Eugene Clark and Patricia Donahoe at the Homeland Foundation; Msgr. Francis Canfield and the members of the board of the American Friends of the Vatican Library were all of enormous assistance in helping to focus and sharpen the thrust of what at the start seemed an overwhelming project.

The project staff proved a team in the truest sense of the term. Each member brought a particular expertise without which the project could not have succeeded.

Elizabeth Yakel, currently a doctoral student at the University of Michigan and formerly the archivist for the Archdiocese of Detroit, compiled the basic MARC record for each of the series in the ASV and for the Archives of the Propaganda Fide. Her clear

[26]There is a vast amount of scholarship based on the holdings of the Vatican Archives. G. Batelli has assembled a substantial number of the titles in his *Bibliografia dell'Archivio Vaticano* (Vatican City, 1962–). This set of bibliographies organizes the titles by series consulted in the Vatican Archives, so it is possible for a user to easily identify works based on series of particular interest. Note that the first four volumes were published by the Vatican Archives and the most recent two were published by the Vatican Library. Batelli continues to work on this bibliography.

sense of fundamental archival principles and their application to the complexities of the Vatican Archives was the critical factor in the ability of the project staff to complete the work thoroughly and in a timely manner. Her intelligent applications of the spirit as well as the letter of the USMARC-AMC format have resulted in a comfortable integration of the Vatican archival material into a database designed for modern archival records.

Leonard Coombs, associate archivist at the Bentley Historical Library at the University of Michigan, had charge of the database itself. He reviewed all entries before entering the information to be sure they were in a consistent form. He carefully determined the strategies for entering the information first in a personal computer and later into the mainframe computer of the Research Libraries Group. He prepared many of the agency histories and worked with Sr. Carlen in all phases of this work. Moreover he determined the structure of the indices and the choice of the index terms. In all this he worked steadily and patiently as the project began and grew. The printed version of the database required another intensive round of checking and standardizing of the information gathered. The careful attention to consistency in presentation that characterizes this volume is another of his fine accomplishments.

Sr. Claudia Carlen, IHM, has devoted a significant portion of her sixty-five years of service in the Catholic church to the study of papal documents. For this project she conducted painstaking research on the histories of the most complex agencies of the Holy See through the standard sources and through the appropriate papal bulls. She also prepared histories of the various individuals and families who deposited private papers in the ASV. Her combination of experience and persistence was the prime factor in the completeness of the histories contained herein.

Katherine Gill, now assistant professor of history at the Yale Divinity School, served as principal historical adviser to the project. She advised on the scope and content of particular series in the ASV as well as on the structure of the most complex parts of the ASV holdings. As a graduate of the Scuola vaticana di paleografia, diplomatica e archivisitica, she had a thorough knowledge of the types of documents in the archives. A specialist in medieval history, she had an extraordinary ability to comfortably read sample documents. Her understanding of the complexities of the archives as well as her interest in communicating the results of this project to the scholarly community that makes use of these archival materials was important to this overall effort.

The project gained much from the dedication of those who worked in a supporting role. At the Bentley Library, Thomas Powers worked on the initial pilot project and helped develop the basic argument that modern archival descriptive principles would prove useful in this work. This project generated complex administrative demands and resulted in a very complex text. Diane Hatfield patiently coped with the administrative challenges and Kimberlee Mayer worked carefully with the text. Linda Powers assisted with the greatest care in the preparation of the bibliography, data entry, and in the adaptation of the information on records in the Archivio di Stato di Roma. Lisa Gibbon assisted with the use of Latin titles and terms. Ben Alexander helped in the initial surveys. The members of the Bentley Library Administrative Committee, Bill Wallach, Marjorie Barritt, Nancy Bartlett, and Thomas Powers, helped keep the core work of the Bentley Library running smoothly as this project progressed.

Many individuals and institutions were of great help, most importantly, at the Archivio Segreto Vaticano. Rev. Josef Metzler, OMI, prefect, first suggested and encouraged the need for a comprehensive view of extant papal documentation. He launched our efforts to seek outside funding to accomplish his vision. Throughout the ten years of our work on this project he was always encouraging and appreciative of our work. He encouraged its appearance in both digital and printed form. We are particularly grateful for the privileges he extended that facilitated this work beyond measure. We hope this work will serve as an appreciation for his interest in making the research resources of the Archivio Segreto Vaticano accessible to scholars worldwide. Project staff always appreciated conversations with other members of the staff of the archives, most notably Germano Gualdo and Msgr. Charles Burns. Mr. Saveri and his staff in the reading room were unfailingly helpful in the many requests a work of this kind entails.

At the Archives of the Propaganda Fide, Rev. P. Sarkis Tabar was extraordinarily helpful in the early stages of our survey work. We only regret that he had moved on before the project work at that archives could be completed. At the Propaganda Fide, Mr. Giovanni Fosci and his assistants were always ready to retrieve what was needed.

At the Archives of the Reverenda Fabbrica di San Pietro, Rev. Anthony Ward was most generous with his time and provided important information on that extraordinary collection.

At the University of Michigan, John D'Arms, Raymond Grew, and Alfred Sussman provided critical advice as this project took its initial form. Sidney Fine, chair, and Farris Womack, Walter Harrison, James J. Duderstadt, John D'Arms, Gilbert Whitaker, and Robert Warner, members of the Executive Committee of the Bentley Historical Library, were a source of constant encouragement as the project took shape and developed. In the provost's office, Mary Ann Swain, John D'Arms, and the late Susan Lipschutz, to whom I reported in succession over the life of this project, were extremely supportive of this effort. At the School of Information, Dean Daniel Atkins and my faculty colleagues were helpful in the conceptualization of this effort.

At the American Academy in Rome, Sophie Consagra, then president in the New York office, saw the need for this work and was particularly important in helping identify a community of scholars who could verify the significance of the project and validate its methodology. At the Academy itself, Jim Melchert, then professor in charge, and Darby Scott, professor of classical studies, welcomed this project to the academy in its early stages. Members of the staff including Pina Pasquantonio and Pat Weaver helped facilitate two periods of residence. Christina Heumer, librarian at the Academy, was helpful as well. Also in Rome Carl Nylander of the Swedish Academy and of the Unione was particularly encouraging as this project became a real possibility.

At the Italian Academy for Advanced Studies in America at Columbia University, Maristella Lorch and Andrea Bartoli extended several invitations to lecture and explore these ideas with interested scholars and archivists. I am particularly grateful to the Academy, to Elaine Sloan and Patricia Molholt at the Columbia University Library, and to Jonathan Cole, provost of Columbia University, for the invitation to be in residence at Columbia for two months, which provided time away to focus on the preparation of this work for publication.

At the Ministero per i Beni Culturali e Ambientali, Maria Pia Rinaldi-Muriani was particularly helpful. At the Archivio di Stato di Roma, Lucio Lume and Maria Grazia Ruggiero were generous with their time and interest in the dimension of this work that touched on the holdings of the Archivio di Stato di Roma. Also in Rome, Elio and Carla Lodolini, both distinguished archivists, were particularly helpful.

In Paris, Paule Rene-Bazin extended an invitation to me to lecture on this project at the Stage Technique Internationale at the Archives Nationales. Conversations with Bernard Barbiche, Olivier Gyotjenin, and Bruno Delmas at the École Nationales des Chartes in Paris were very helpful. Olivier Poncet at the École Française de Rome offered several helpful suggestions and assisted in the preparation of the list of the ASV indici. The staffs of the Bibliothèque Nationale and of the Archives Nationales were of great assistance in working with their respective papal holdings. I am also grateful to the staff of the Manuscripts Division of the Library at Trinity College Dublin, who facilitated a brief but efficient visit.

At the North American College in Rome, I am very grateful to Rev. Charles Kosanke and Rev. Steven Raica, who on several occasions hosted me as a guest of the college during stays in Rome. The College provided a perfect environment for learning more about aspects of the organization of the Holy See.

Many others were interested in this work and offered very sage advice. They include Luciano Amenti, Rudolph Arnheim, Melissa Bullard, Francesca Consagra, Margaret Child, Steven Hensen, David Bearman, Herbert Bloch, James O'Toole, Hope Mayo, Richard Szary, Robert Brentano, Lawrence Dowler, Luciana Duranti, George Fletcher, Marion Matters, Mary McLaughlin, Avra Michaelson, Laurie Nussdorfer, Elizabeth O'Keefe, Paul Oskar Kristeller, Rev. John O'Malley, SJ, Kathleen Roe, Nancy Siraisi, Jonathan Spence, Anne Van Camp, the late Alan Tucker, Kathleen Weil-Garris Brandt, Christine Weideman, and Richard Wilson.

I am grateful to the Medieval Institute at the University of Notre Dame for an invitation to lecture on this topic before an audience particularly familiar with the complexities of the organization of the Holy See. The Divinity School at Yale University kindly made space available for research materials assembled to support the work of Katherine Gill. At Yale, Joanna Webber, Paul Dover, Jennifer Andersen, and Janet Robson assisted Professor Gill in various facets of her work.

This work required access to a wide variety of publications. Three libraries and their superb staffs were very helpful in this effort. The Theological Collection of Sacred Heart Seminary (Detroit) and The Papal Collection of Marygrove College Library (Detroit) were very helpful in their support of the work of Sr. Claudia Carlen. The extensive material on the Vatican among the vast holdings of the University Library of the University of Michigan were invaluable.

The publication of this report was unforeseen in the initial stages of the project. I am grateful to Oxford University Press for agreeing to take on this text in its entirety and in its complexity. Claude Conyers, Jeff Edelstein, and Marion Osmun proved superb editors. The initial destination for this information was the database of the Research Libraries Group (i.e., RLIN). I am grateful to Jim Mahalko, president, and to all the staff for their interest in receiving this information. I am particularly grateful to the programming staff who downloaded the information in a way that facilitated an easy transition from database to standard book format. Also I extend appreciation to Frederick Honhart of Michigan State University who made his MicroMARC software available to us for initial preparation of the information for inclusion in RLIN.

In the final editing stages, Daniel Williman of the faculty of Classics at the State University of New York at Binghamton agreed to review the entire sections on the Curia Romana. His deep knowledge of history of the Holy See prior to the Council of Trent was particularly helpful. He suggested many revisions of our presentation of these early documents that have added precision and clarity to that portion of this work. I am particularly grateful to him for this assistance.

The Vatican Library is administratively separate from the Vatican Archives. Rev. Leonard Boyle, OP, prefect of the library, through his general commitment to enhance the presence of the Vatican as a central locus for scholarship, was a constant source of encouragement and inspiration at every stage of this work. His own work on the holdings of the archives stands as the critical point of entry for any student interested in the medieval holdings of the archives. We can only hope that this project is a worthy complement to that extraordinary book. Also at the library, Paul Weston was always available to consider matters relating to the structure of the database and its compatibility with efforts under way to create a comprehensive database for the holdings of the Vatican Library.

In the final stages of the project my wife, Joy, took on the task of reading through the entire manuscript of this work. Her characteristic careful attention to the work saved it from many errors and inconsistencies. I am grateful to her, to Ben, and to Tiffany for their appreciation of a project that, at times, was all consuming.

Despite the enormous amount of assistance and support received for this work, there will be inevitable errors for which I bear full responsibility. The idea behind this work was to push a framework for understanding the total corpus of documentation generated by the Holy See. Scholars have had need for such an overview. The purpose of this work is to provide as accurate a survey as possible of surviving papal archival material. Yet surely there are entries in this work that will need revision as the process of description of these enormously complex archival holdings continues to evolve.

—Francis X. Blouin, Jr.
Ann Arbor, Michigan
June 1996

How to Use This Book

THIS GUIDE WAS PREPARED BY HISTORIANS AND ARCHIVISTS affiliated with the Vatican Archives Project of the University of Michigan at the invitation of the prefect of the Archives, who was consulted at every stage of this work. This project could not have been accomplished without important special permissions granted the project staff by the prefect. Because of the press of other responsibilities, the staff of the ASV did not participate in this project in any official way, though many members of the staff were helpful in answering a variety of questions. As a result, users of this guide should be aware that while this work was authorized by the prefect, it is not an official inventory of the archives, though it was the hope of the prefect that this work might form the basis for an official inventory at some point in time. This guide is in essence the product of a research effort to understand the evolution of the corpus of papal documentation and the various extant instruments that assist in utilizing that documentation. Members of the project staff surveyed every shelf of the ASV, therefore what follows does represent a complete overview of the holdings of the ASV as seen by the project staff during the academic year 1989–1990 (with a brief follow-up visit in 1993) when the inventory was done. In 1990 and in 1993 a similar inventory of the Archives of the Propaganda Fide was completed. In 1994 a survey was conducted of the holdings of the Archives of the Fabbrica. In 1996 surveys were conducted of the materials in Paris and Dublin.

In using this guide, it is important to note that this is an archival guide. In order to realize the full potential of the information contained therein, it is important for the user to enter into an archival mindset. The introduction to this volume provides a historical and analytic framework for the entries in the guide. It is particularly important to read this introduction. Users unfamiliar with archival access frequently expect specific subject access to the material contained in the archives. Scholars used to libraries are familiar with searching subject lists and terms. The search process in an archive is more like the process of searching an office directory to find the individual in an organization whose responsibilities bear most closely to the kind of information desired. That is, one needs to read historical accounts to learn the nature of the function and activity of a given office. Then, based on that background, the user can start to predict where particular kinds of information might have been kept and the types of activities that were performed. This can then be used in conjunction with information in the series listings such as dates and types of documentation. For example, we know that in the seventeenth century the Datary had responsibility for various kinds of appointments to offices in the Vatican administration. We also know that documents labeled "consensus" pertain to this function. So we can predict that in that series, there will be the kind of information relating to the process of application for positions.

The entries in this guide are of two types designed to facilitate archival thinking about the documentation of the Holy See:

1. Agency Histories. The histories appear at the beginning of various sections and provide background on the office, agency, institution, family, or person that generated the documentation listed for that section. The history is designed to provide a user with basic elements of structure and function. When one agency was disbanded and another substituted, that information is noted to the extent that project staff was able to trace such relationships. Each entry presents the following fields:

Name of Agency: The name is usually in Latin unless the only authority for the name of the agency is in Italian. Agency names are indexed in the rear of the guide by their commonly cited names in Italian, Latin, and English.

History: The agency histories in this guide are designed to provide a brief overview of the structure and function of an office over time. The histories are drawn from general secondary sources and from the official bulls and other documents that mark official notice of change or direction. Often added to the agency history note is information about other agencies that contain records related to the particular agency under consideration.

References: For some of the most important agencies of the Holy See, there is a substantial body of scholarship and in some of those cases, there is some disagreement over the precise role and function of a particular office. The agency histories in this guide provide a basic historical background but do not attempt to present a complete historiography. References, where provided, are designed to point users toward the broader corpus of historical scholarship regarding particular offices. These entries are, however, only selective.

2. Series Descriptions. The series descriptions are the descriptions of the records generated by a particular agency. The project staff made every effort to determine what record series were most appropriate to each particular agency. Nearly all series consulted were assigned to a particular agency. Some of the assignments, particularly in Part 7 of the guide, are tentative. When series appeared to contain records created by more than one agency a cross-reference was provided. In some cases despite the best efforts of the project staff, series could not be assigned to particular agencies. These are noted in the miscellaneous section in Part 7.

It is difficult to define the word *series* in the context of this work. It is best to think of a series in this case as a discreet physical unit of documentation that was generated in the course of carrying out an activity or group of activities. In some cases, like the Datary *Supplications*, the series is composed of a series of volumes in chronological order, each of which is similar in form to the other. In other cases, such as the nunciature material of the Secretariat of State, a series is a known grouping of records that is in fact composed of several subseries. Also in some cases, a set of series identified separately in the guide is also known as a single entity. The *Fondo Moderno* of the Secretariat of State is an example of this. It is noted as a single series but in addition its four components are noted separately as series. When this occurs it is clearly noted. There are yet other cases where "series" are merely miscellaneous groups of somewhat related material brought together physically on particular shelves in the stacks. These cases, too, are specifically noted.

The structure of these records is as follows:

Name of series: To determine the name of the series the project staff first consulted the series list in the Index Room of the ASV or other repository. If the series had an official designation, that designation was assigned to the series. If the series did not appear in the list in the Index Room, the staff determined the title of the series from the labeling on the spines of the volumes or from the boxes or buste. If that could not be determined, the project staff assigned a title to the series. These supplied titles are clearly noted in brackets in the entry. In some cases, the project staff encountered miscellaneous material on a shelf that had no official designation. These were assigned the title *Miscellanea*, with a designation of the location of the material in 1990. These miscellaneous materials were found in two areas of the archives, the Scaffale di Ferro (SF), which is a two-story area of metal shelving placed in rooms that at one time were used as a picture gallery, and the Soffittone (V), which is the attic of the Belvedere. Series are listed alphabetically by title within each agency. Titles are for the most part in Italian or Latin. If a title was found in both languages we used the Latin. For the series in Dublin, the titles are in English; those in Paris are in French. They are not grouped by repository.

For series in the ASV, titles were often transcribed from the spines of volumes or from handwritten labels on boxes or buste. In this process we often encountered a mixture of languages, unusual abbreviations, and idiosyncratic, wrong, or antiquated spellings. Every effort was made to transcribe these as we found them.

In this guide series titles always appear in italics when found in the body of the descriptive texts. This is designed to facilitate location in this volume. Among the indexes in the back of this guide there is a complete aphabetical listing of the series that are listed in this volume along with their numerical designation in this guide.

Database ID: The information contained in this guide exists in database form and is accessible in the RLIN database of the Research Libraries Group (U.S.A.). This database is accessible through major colleges and universities in the United States and in the United Kingdom. The specific database ID will get a user to the comparable record in RLIN.

Inclusive Dates: Inclusive dates include the earliest document in the series and the latest document. In many cases, there is a stray early document that leads to a conclusion that a given series seems to cover a longer period than in fact is the case. In this case there can be two date designations: inclusive dates that give the entire chronological range and bulk dates that give the researcher the dates from which most of the materials originate. When this was evident to the project staff, it was also noted in the organizational note. When we were not sure of a date it is in brackets. A date in brackets with a question mark, for example, [18—?], means that we are not even sure of the century. When there is no question mark, for example, [18—], it means that we are sure of the century but not of the exact years. We did note the existence of material generated after 1922 even though under current Vatican policy, that material remains closed to research use. Note that a chronological index is provided in the back of this guide that facilitates locating those series containing material created during a particular century.

Bulk: To as great an extent as possible the project staff attempted to measure the amount of material in a collection in terms of linear meters. This was done by measuring the amount of shelf space taken up by the series. This only measures the width of the collection. Some series are composed of rather small volumes. In other cases the series is rather tall. That dimension was not taken into consideration. We also present the number of volumes, boxes, cassette, pacchi, and/or buste in this entry. In cases where there is a notation of number of volumes, it should be noted that it is not uncommon in the ASV for a number to be assigned to more than one volume (e.g., 109a, 109b, 109c). In these cases we have noted that a collection has, for example, 467 numbered volumes. That means that volume 467 is the last volume in the series.

Because of skipped numbers, missing volumes or multiple numbers, this may not be an accurate representation of the actual number of volumes in the series. The measurement in linear meters is a better indication of bulk.

Organization: The organization field gives the researcher three types of information. First, there is an indication of how the material divides within the series. It is here that subseries are noted, often with inclusive dates. In some cases where the series is a true miscellany, select items are listed. Second, a note may be given concerning how materials are filed within a series or subseries, for example, alphabetical or chronological. Third, there are notes concerning missing volumes, numbering irregularities, and so forth. Organizational information is not given for material generated after 1922.

In the ASV when we listed titles of individual volumes, boxes, or buste, titles were often transcribed from the spines of volumes or from handwritten labels on boxes or buste. We often encountered a mixture of languages; unusual abbreviations; and idiosyncratic, wrong, or antiquated spellings. Every effort was made to transcribe these as we found them.

Scope: The purpose of the scope note is to give some indication of the contents of the series. Scope was a secondary concern of this project. Scope information was derived from a number of sources and by observation in some cases. The bibliographical references with each series often will provide additional information on a specific series.

References: References fall into two categories. The brief citations in the reference section are to several standard guides to the ASV and to other collections of papal documentation. The brief citations are designed to indicate to the user of this guide the extent to which a series has been generally known to have existed. If there is no reference listed for a particular series, then it is one that has not been noted in these standard sources. In addition, in this section there can be more specific references to particular articles or books that relate to the series. These entries are not comprehensive bibliographies. Note in particular that some of these citations are not complete particularly for those items that are part of large series of publications. The bibliographic entries in this guide have been designed to provide enough essential information on a given work so that a user can consult an online bibliographic utility to obtain full cataloging and/or citation information.

The four standard guides to the Vatican Archives are L. E. Boyle, *A Survey of the Vatican Archives and of Its Medieval Holdings* (Toronto, 1972); L. Pásztor, *Guida delle fonti per la storia dell'America Latina negli archivi della Santa Sede e negli archivi ecclesiastici d'Italia* (Vatican City, 1970); L. Pásztor, *Guida delle fonti per la storia dell'Africa a Sud del Sahara negli archivi della Santa Sede e negli archivi ecclesiastici d'Italia* (Zug, 1983); and K. A. Fink, *Das Vaticanische Archiv Einführung in die Bestände und ihre Erforschung* (Rome, 1951). Also important for its list of recent holdings of the ASV is T. Natalini, S. Pagano, and A. Martini, eds., *Archivio segreto vaticano,* (Florence, 1991). A valuable earlier survey is L. Macfarlane, "The Vatican Archives: With Special Reference to Sources for British Medieval History," *Archives* 4 (1959): 29–44, 84–101. In addition to these standard general works, there are guides for specialized aspects of the documentation for the Holy See that are referred to in the reference notes: For the Propaganda Fide: N. Kowalsky and J. Metzler, *Inventory of the Historical Archives of the Congregation for the Evangelization of Peoples or "de Propaganda Fide,"* 3d enl. ed. (Rome, 1988). For the series that remain in Paris: J. Favier, *Les Archives Nationales: État General des Fonds,* (Paris, 1978–), and J. Favier, *Les Archives Nationales: État General des Inventaires,* (Paris, 1985–). For the material in the Archivio di Stato di Roma: P. d'Agiolini and C. Pavone, *Guida generale degli*

Archivi dei Stato Italiani (Rome, 1981–), and A. Lodolini, *L'archivio di Stato di Roma: Epitome d'una guida degli archivi dell'amministrazione dello Stato Pontificio* (Rome, 1960).

Finding Aids: Every effort has been made by project staff to locate and describe all known inventories and indici for the various series described in this guide. This is particularly true for material in the ASV, the Propaganda Fide, the Fabbrica, Trinity College, and the Archives Nationales. For material in the Archivio di Stato di Roma we relied on the descriptions of the finding aids as presented in the D'Angiolini/Pavone guide. In the finding aids section we have listed all official indices and inventories prepared by the staffs of each repository. For the ASV, we have also made every attempt to locate and describe those inventories and descriptions that have been prepared by scholars not affiliated with the archives. These are published for the most part and copies of many, but not all of these are located in the index room of the ASV. In addition, at the ASV there are several inventories that have been prepared by staff, but for one or another reason are not located in the index room of the ASV. These are noted where they were seen by project staff.

This section also includes information about those indexes that were generated at the time when the records were created. These in some cases are located with publicly available indici and in other cases with the records series themselves in the stacks of the particular archival institution. In addition to identifying finding aids, we have also presented an analysis of the sources identified by explaining limitations, strategies for use, and degree of completeness.

When an entry contains no finding aid entry, that is an indication that no inventory was located by the project staff.

Notes: The note field is to provide a variety of information. In some cases this relates to the provenance of a collection. In others it may indicate that a portion of the collection appears on microfilm or the like. To provide information on the continuity in record keeping, the note field also informs the user when a series has a direct predecessor series or a specific successor series.

Location: The location field indicates where the records are physically located.

There are several caveats to remember as you use this guide:

1. Access to material in Vatican repositories, even before 1922, may be problematic in those cases where no finding aids exist. Not all material in the repositories examined has been fully processed and the lack of a numbered ASV indice is an indication of this.

2. Users will very likely find variations and changes in the status of some of the series since the preparation of this guide. This is particularly true of the material in the Datary series, but also with the various groupings that we called miscellanea.

3. A few books and articles listed in the references section within the series descriptions and in the bibliography could not be verified in standard bibliographical sources, although their existence was noted through photocopies, detached parts, or consultation with other researchers. These titles are listed along with a note to that effect.

4. In a few cases the names of particular congregations or offices appear in another agency's history but do not appear in the general index to agencies listed in this guide. In those cases we simply could find no records or information about that particular congregation or office.

5. In many cases we present the history of an agency and then note that no records for that agency could be located. This means that during the course of our survey of the ASV, the Fabbrica, the Propaganda Fide, and the *Guida generale* of the Archivio di

Stato di Roma, we could not locate any records that were clearly generated by that agency. We stop short of saying that records do not exist. In some cases they may be subsumed by other series. This is particularly true in the series of the nunciatures. In other cases there may indeed be no records. Readers are urged to read the agency histories carefully.

6. Because of the international nature of the institutions and holdings described in this guide, we have freely used words from Italian, Latin, and in some cases French. We have not italicized these words unless they appear in a formal title of a published work or document.

7. As with all complex organizations, the Holy See has changed over time. To the extent possible we have tried to incorporate information relating to predecessor and successor offices. We have also tried to the same extent to link record series to antecedents and subsequent series.

8. As with most offices, the filing system for documents in Vatican offices was not perfect. Occasionally items are misfiled or deposited with offices that in retrospect may seem inappropriate. It is therefore useful to have a sense of all documentation that existed for a particular date. This guide contains chronological indexes for that purpose. It is also possible to conduct a chronological search in the RLIN database from which this guide has been derived. Note also that dates of dossiers can be deceiving in that often earlier supporting documentation can be attached to the particular document from which the date of the dossier has been determined.

9. Where we know microfilm copies exist, we have so noted that information. However, we did not do a complete survey of all microfilm copies that exist for the documents described in this guide. Researchers should consult the repositories directly for information.

It is important to note that access to archives of the Holy See (including the ASV) is a privilege granted upon application to the prefect. It is essential to write a letter in advance of a visit that states the purpose of the research and the series to be consulted. It is also important to have a signed response in hand prior to arrival at a Vatican archival repository. The State Archives of Rome is an agency of the Italian State. An exchange of letters is advisable at state archives as well.

VATICAN ARCHIVES

PART 1

College of Cardinals

THE COLLEGE OF CARDINALS (COLLEGIO DEI CARDINALI) WAS originally made up of the rectors of the parish churches in Rome. In the eleventh century the Sacred College achieved institutional form when popes assigned to it administrative as well as liturgical functions and elevated non-Romans to the cardinalate. In 1059 Nicholas II gave the cardinals the right to elect popes. The cardinals formed the Sacred College after 1150, with a dean who is bishop of Ostia and a camerlengo or property administrator (not the camerlengo of the Camera Apostolica). In 1179 the college became the exclusive electors of the pope.

The consistorium began in the eleventh century as an administrative body for the church, made up exclusively of cardinals. With the reorganization of the Holy See in 1588, the administrative structure became more formally organized, divided into separate congregations. These bureaucratic divisions, which formed the Roman Curia, were headed by committees of cardinals. The congregations assumed much of the administrative work formerly done by the consistorium.

The consistorium now functions as the solemn assembly of all cardinals present in Rome, presided over by the pope. It considers certain of the gravest matters concerning the government of the church. It also considers the creation of cardinals, the announcement of holy years, and the canonization of saints. The Congregatio Consistorialis, a division of the Curia Romana, prepares matters for consideration by the consistorium. As a connection with its origins, each cardinal is assigned a church in Rome as a titular parish.

The college has functioned as a single unit. Therefore in this section there are no subdivisions. What follows is a list of extant records series for the college.

References. G. Alberigo, *Cardinalato è collegialità: Studi sull'ecclesiologia tra l'XI e il XIV secolo* (Florence, 1969). C. G. Fürst, *Cardinalis: Prolegomena zu einer Rechtsgeschichte des römischen Kardinalskollegiums* (Munich, 1967). H. W. Klewitz, "Die Entstehung des Kardinalskollegiums," *Zeitschrift der Savigny-Stiftung für Rechtsgeschichte. Kanonistische Abteilung* 25 (1936): 115–221. S. Kuttner, "Cardinalis: The History of a Canonical Concept," *Traditio* 3 (1945): 129–214. Ch. Lefebvre, "Les origines et la rôle du Cardinalat au moyen âge," *Apollinaris* 41 (1968): 59–70. G. Mollat, "Contribution à l'histoire du Sacré Collège de Clément V à Eugène IV," *Revue d'histoire ecclésiastique* 46 (1951): 22–112, 566–594. R. Ritzler, "Per la storia dell'Archivio del Sacro Collegio," in *Mélanges Eugène Tisserant* (Vatican City, 1964), vol. 5, pp. 330–338. J. B. Sägmüller, *Die Thätigkeit und Stellung der Cardinäle bis Papst Bonifaz VIII* (Freiburg, 1896).

RECORDS. Records of the College of Cardinals consist of the following series.

1.1 Atti di sede vacante

[DATABASE ID: VATV10104-A]
Inclusive Dates: 1676–1846.
Bulk: .5 linear m. (6 vols.).
Organization: Chronological, except vol. 1.
Scope: This series is a collection of atti written during vacant sees: vol. 2, 1676; vol. 3, 1689, 1691, 1700, 1721, 1724, 1730; vol. 4, 1823; vol. 5, 1829–1830; and vol. 6, 1846. Volume 1 is entitled "Index 1829 sede vacante protocolo dei fascicoli."
Location: Archivio Segreto Vaticano.

1.2 Camerarius

[DATABASE ID: VATV10106-A]
Inclusive Dates: 1623–1659 (bulk 1650–1659).
Bulk: .1 linear m. (2 vols.).
Scope: This series contains records of tax payments by dioceses to the College of Cardinals. Diocesan names are noted in margins.
Location: Archivio Segreto Vaticano.

1.3 Camerlengato sede vacante

[DATABASE ID: VATV10107-A]
Inclusive Dates: 1769, 1823, 1829, 1846.
Bulk: 2 linear m. (26 vols.).
Organization: There are two subseries: 1. Camerlengato, vols. 1–24; —2. Passaporta, vols. 25–26.
Scope: This series contains files of the camerlengo dealing with in-house problems during vacant sees, including how to get food for the papal household and take care of the conclave, payment of employees, minor political issues, and so forth. In titolo 17 there are copies of eighteenth-century documents that describe how the Holy See operates during a vacant see and details the functions of the camerlengo, particularly regarding precedents for powers. The passaporta are the forms issued to allow entry and exit from the papal palace and indicate the passage of a variety of people.
Location: Archivio Segreto Vaticano.

1.4 Computisteria mandati estinti dei pagamenti sul conto corrente

[DATABASE ID: VATV10074-A]
Inclusive Dates: 1857–1900.
Bulk: 1 linear m. (14 vols.)
Organization: Chronological.
Scope: This series contains records of payments (obbligazione, giustificazione, etc.) to the College of Cardinals.
Location: Archivio Segreto Vaticano.

1.5 Conclavi

[DATABASE ID: VATV10103-A]
Inclusive Dates: 1585–1846.
Bulk: 12 linear m.
Organization: Series are organized by pope: Urban VIII, 1 vol.; —Innocent X, 1 vol.; —Clement IX, 3 vols.; —Clement X, 1 vol.; —Innocent XI, 2 vols.; —Alexander VIII, 6 vols. and 1 packet; —Innocent XII, 3 vols.; —Clement XI, 4 vols.; —Innocent XIII, 5 vols.; —Benedict XIII, 10 vols.; —Clement XII, 12 vols.; —Benedict XIV, 4 vols.; —Clement XIII, 12

vols.; —Clement XIV, 14 vols.; —Pius VI, 6 vols.; —Pius VII, 15 vols.; —Pius VIII, 8 vols.; —Leo XII, 11 vols.; —Gregory XVI, 4 vols.; —Pius IX, 1 vol.
Scope: The materials are diverse within this series, for example, the first volume of Clement XIII is entitled *Per la morte di Clement XIII: Relazione delle feste e regali fatti all'imperadore e gran duca di Toscana biglietti di Monsignore Magiordomo risguardati i regali sua fogli sopra il trattamento del gran duca di Toscana del Conte d'Almada trattamento del gran maestro di Maltae Repubblica di Lucca.* There are many incoming letters relating to the death of the particular pope. This correspondence relates to other similar material found in the records of the office of the Secretariatus Status.

There is additional conclave material located in a different section of the stacks of the ASV (in 1990 this material was shelved on SF/72). The relationship of this additional material to the *Conclavi* series is unclear. The additional material is as follows: Clement XIV, 2 vols.; —Pio VII, 2 vols.; —Leone XII, 1 vol.; —Clement XIII, 1 vol.; —Clemente XII e Benedetto XIV, 1 vol.; —Relativi di diverse conclavi, 1 vol.
References: Fink, p. 66; Boyle, p. 83. Ottavio Pio Conti, *Origine, fasti e privilegi degli avvocati consistoriali: memorie storiche* (Rome, 1898). B. Katterbach, "Archivio Vaticano," in *Enciclopedia italiana* (Rome, 1929), vol. 4, pp. 88–90.
Location: Archivio Segreto Vaticano.

1.6 Conclavi: [Historical Studies]

[DATABASE ID: VATV10112-A]
Inclusive Dates: 1464–1758.
Bulk: 1 linear m.
Organization: Five subseries: Conclavi, 1585–1758; —Conclavi, 1663; —Conclavi di Papi (Alexander VIII), 1691; —Leone X, Clement VIII, Paolo V, Gregorio XV [Histories of Papacies], 1513–1623; —Conclavi, Pio II, Innocenti X, 1464–1655.
Scope: These are handwritten histories of selected conclaves and papacies.
Location: Archivio Segreto Vaticano.

1.7 Littere post obitum Innocenti IX: Exemplum litterarum sacra collegio

[DATABASE ID: VATV10102-A]
Inclusive Dates: 1585–1592.
Bulk: .2 linear m. (2 vols.).
Organization: Innocent IX, 1591–1592; —Gregory XIV, Sixtus V, Urban VII, Innocent IX, 1585–1591. Each volume is arranged chronologically.
Scope: This series is composed of letters written after the death of popes to kings, dukes, bishops, abbots, governors of papal states, and the like to express mourning and to conduct business. Many are copies or abbreviated copies of letters, signed by three cardinals designated to issue papal bulls in the absence of a pope. There are some miscellaneous documents regarding the papal army.
Location: Archivio Segreto Vaticano.

1.8 Mandatorum

[DATABASE ID: VATV10108-A]
Inclusive Dates: 1710–1895.
Bulk: .5 linear m. (7 vols.).
Organization: Chronological.

Scope: These volumes record money sent to the depositorius and deposited at the Sacred College to be allocated to heirs or to pay for services rendered.

Location: Archivio Segreto Vaticano.

1.9 [Miscellanea SF/80]

[DATABASE ID: VATV10111-A]

Inclusive Dates: ca. 1676–1900.

Bulk: 3 linear m. (35 vols.).

Scope: This miscellany is a collection of a variety of volumes that include (numbers provided by project staff): 1. Computisteria, affari dei quindenni; —2. Giustificationi dei pagamenti e carte diverse; —3. Computisteria; —4. Giustificationi; — 5. Carte diverse; —6. Questione se gli emi. diaconi possono essere camerlenghi; —7. Obbligatione degli spendizionieri dei vescovi; —8. Foglie di prezenza dei cardinale dei Concistoriale; —9. Deputa sopre gli affari della soppressa Compagna di Gesù, 1774; —10. Commissione per monumento Pius IX; —11. Affari diverse; —12. Campo di Santa Lucia nel territorio della Tolfa spettante al Collegio; —13. Posizione sul marchesate di Castiglione del Lago e chiusi; —14. Carte legale; —15. Constitutions, 1833 (printed); —16. [Letterbook; — copies of letters and responses from princes, dukes, bishops, and other dignitaries], 1676–1786.

Note: This is a true miscellany and does not have an official designation by the ASV. The title was assigned by the project staff based on the location of the material in 1990.

Location: Archivio Segreto Vaticano.

1.10 Notitiae ecclesiarum per liber taxarum ordinariarum

[DATABASE ID: VATV10105-A]

Inclusive Dates: ca. 1600–1799.

Bulk: .5 linear m. (5 vols. and 1 packet).

Organization: Alphabetical.

Scope: This series contains notes on payments by selected (primarily French and Italian) monasteries and dioceses, with cross references to other registers with more information.

Location: Archivio Segreto Vaticano.

1.11 Registro dei pagamenti (Camerlengo)

[DATABASE ID: VATV10113-A]

Inclusive Dates: 1895–1900.

Bulk: 1 vol.

Organization: Chronological.

Scope: Registers of payment by the camerlengo to papal officials.

Location: Archivio Segreto Vaticano.

1.12 Riforma dei funerali cardinali

[DATABASE ID: VATV10109-A]

Inclusive Dates: ca. 1825.

Bulk: .3 linear m. (3 vols.).

Location: Archivio Segreto Vaticano.

1.13 Scrutinio per la morte de Benedetto XIV: Accessus et voti scrutinari

[DATABASE ID: VATV10110-A]

Inclusive Dates: 1758.

Bulk: .1 linear m. (1 vol.).

Location: Archivio Segreto Vaticano.

PART 2

The Papal Court

WITH THE GROWTH OF THE HOLY SEE IN PRESTIGE AND POWER, THE papacy, by the fourteenth century, began to resemble a royal court. The court was composed of the papal chapel and the papal household. The court persisted in this form up until the reforms of Paul VI in 1968.

The papal chapel includes the Sacred College of Cardinals and other dignitaries who have a right to participate with the pope in solemn liturgical ceremonies. The chapel originated in 1305 with the removal of the papal court to Avignon. Out of necessity, ceremonies formerly celebrated in various basilicas were then conducted in the papal chapel. This practice continued when the court returned to Rome in 1377. In 1968 the papal chapel was reorganized by Paul VI, eliminating honorary offices and hereditary titles.

The papal household consisted of laymen and ecclesiastics who had recognized functions as determined by protocol in the papal residence. The household dates back as early as the eighth century. In that period it included the officers of the chancery and others. By the thirteenth century the household included the officers of the Camera as well as the chancery officers and others. During the Avignon period (1306–1376) the household developed the membership that it kept for centuries afterward. In the fifteenth century, the household took form as an Italian Renaissance court and kept that form until 1968, when it was reformed by Paul VI, eliminating honorary offices and hereditary titles. In its new form it is made up of persons helping the pope govern as head of the church and the Vatican City State.

Before the reforms of Paul VI, the household had a very complex structure, based on orders of precedence. The major offices in the household can be divided into four groupings. First, the palatine cardinals were cardinals assigned to the personal service of the pope. Second, the noble privy antechamber was made up of three parts: (1) the palatine prelates, who were the most important officials of the household, including the majordomo of His Holiness, master of the chamber, auditor of His Holiness, and master of the sacred palace; (2) the participating privy chamberlains; and (3) the master of the sacred hospice. A third group was the participating privy chamberlains of sword and cape. Within the groups of participating privy chamberlains and participating privy chamberlains of sword and cape were many individual offices and titles. In this guide, these offices are more fully described in the sections for the Famiglia della Santità di Nostro Signore, which follow the entries for the Capella. A fourth group were the many other lower-ranking officers in the household.

The papal chapel and the papal household each comprised a variety of separate offices. They are identified and described in this section along with the extant records associated with each office.

2.1 CAPELLA PONTIFICIA
[DATABASE ID: VATV218-A]

2.1.1 Cappella musicale pontificia
[DATABASE ID: VATV098-A]

The Schola Cantorum was formed in early times and reorganized by Gregory I (590–604). It was suppressed by Urban V (1362–1370), then revived by Gregory XI (1371–1378). It has undergone several reorganizations and changes of name since that time.

Those interested in music in the papal court should consult the Fondo Cappella Sistina in the Vatican Library. This collection includes not only the series listed below, but also an extensive collection of music manuscripts from the Cappella Sistina and the Cappella Giulia.

Reference. R. Elze, "Die päpstliche Kapelle im 12. und 13. Jahrhundert," *Zeitschrift der Savigny-Stiftung für Rechtsgeschichte. Kanonistische Abteilung* 36 (1950): 145–204.

RECORDS. Records of the office consist of the following series.

2.1.1.1 Libri di entrata e di uscita
[DATABASE ID: VATV40059-A]
Inclusive Dates: 1600–1897.
Bulk: 230 vols.
Organization: Chronological.
Scope: These are the administrative records of the Camerlengato of the Capella Sistina.
Finding Aids: This series forms part of the *Fondo Cappella Sistina* of the Vatican Library. BAV indice 216, ff. 116–147, contains a listing of each volume in the series noting the name of the camerlengo and the inclusive dates. Also in the index, ff. 149–154 is an alphabetical listing of each camerlengo noting dates of service and relevant volumes. On ff. 155–159 there is a chronological listing noting each camerlengo and relevant volumes.
Location: Biblioteca Apostolica Vaticana.

2.1.1.2 Diari
[DATABASE ID: VATV40060-A]
Inclusive Dates: 1535–1897.
Bulk: 299 vols.
Organization: Chronological.
Finding Aids: This series forms part of the *Fondo Cappella Sistina* of the Vatican Library. BAV indice 216 (ff. 1–39) lists each volume with inclusive dates along with the name of the compiler of the volume. The indice (ff. 45–84) also contains an alphabetical index to the compilers of the various volumes. There is also ff. 85–92, a chronological list that gives year, name of compiler, and volume number, and there is an alphabetical list (ff. 95–111) with years served and related volume numbers.
Location: Biblioteca Apostolica Vaticana.

2.1.2 Collegio degli avvocati del Sacro concistoro
[DATABASE ID: VATV096-A]

In 598 seven defenders of the church were appointed. In 1340 the defenders were more formally organized. In 1471 their number was increased to twelve. Their duties in early times included the defense of cases treated in Consistory. After the establishment of pontifical tribunals they postulated the pallium for metropolitans, archbishops, and bishops and promoted causes of beatification and canonization. From 1587 the college held the office of rector of the University of Rome. In later years their duties included the defense and prosecution of those accused of crimes before the courts of the Holy See, the pleading of matrimonial cases before ecclesiastical tribunals, and consultation in disciplinary procedures against lawyers of the Rota. The members of the college were also members of the papal chapel.

RECORDS. No records for this college were located.

2.1.3 Collegio dei patriarchi, arcivescovi e vescovi, assistenti al soglio
[DATABASE ID: VATV092-A]

Bishops are found with this title as early as the eleventh century. By 1555–1559 they formed a college. The members of the college were also members of the papal chapel.

RECORDS. No records for this college were located.

2.1.4 Collegio dei procuratori dei Sacri palazzi apostolici
[DATABASE ID: VATV097-A]

The origin of the procurators goes back at least to 1130, date of the first certain reference. They were organized into a college in 1340. Their duties included the defense of cases coram sanctissimo and the gratuitous defense of the poor. In 1934 their right to plead causes before the Rota was confirmed. The members of the college were also members of the papal chapel.

RECORDS. No records for this college were located.

2.1.5 Commendatore di S. Spirito
[DATABASE ID: VATV095-A]

In 1515 the administration of the hospital of Santo Spirito in Sassia was transformed into a prelacy, and the title of the administrator was changed from preceptor to commendator. The commendatori were members of the papal chapel.

RECORDS. No records for this office were located.

2.1.6 Mazzieri pontifici
[DATABASE ID: VATV099-A]

The mazzieri (mace-bearers) belong to the Pontifical Chapel and are so called because of the silver mace that they would bear in papal chapels, consistories, papal functions, ordination of bishops, and functions of the College of Cardinals during the vacancy of the Holy See. Some authorities state that they date back to at least the twelfth century.

Eugenius IV confirmed their statutes in 1437; these were updated by Paul V on January 12, 1617. Nine in number, they were named by the pope on the recommendation of the maggiordomo and constituted a college with its own president, dean, and secretary.

The mazzieri were originally bodyguards of the pope. They were once called servientes armorum, or halberdiers. Their college was eliminated by Paul VI in 1968.

RECORDS. Records of the college consist of the following series.

2.1.6.1 Collegio dei mazzieri
[DATABASE ID: VATV10313-A]
Inclusive Dates: 1437–1968.
Bulk: .3 linear m. (3 vols. and 1 busta).
Organization: The Registri dei riparti constitute the three volumes.; —There is a label, "Eugenio Papa quarto in anno salutis MCCCXXXVII Statuta Officii Serventium Armorum"; —[one section is post-1922].
Scope: The registri contain lists of the mazzieri. The busta holding the statutes says "statuto del Collegio dei mazzieri creato sotto il pontificio di Eugenio Papa IIII nel 1437."
Reference: Natalini et al., p. 272.
Location: Archivio Segreto Vaticano.

2.1.7 Principi assistenti al soglio
[DATABASE ID: VATV093-A]

The title was used prior to the fourteenth century. By 1503–1513 the title was shared by the heads of the Orsini and Colonna families, as representatives of the Roman nobility.

RECORDS. No record series for this office were located.

2.1.8 Protonotari apostolici
[DATABASE ID: VATV094-A]

Notarii in Urbe were appointed in the third or fourth century. In the fifth century they formed a college. By 590–604 the head was the primicerius notariorum and the assistant the secundicerius. Their functions included legations and visits, investigations of processes, drawing up of council acts and letters in the Apostolic Chancery, reports to the pope, and the preparation of decisions. In the fourteenth century, a distinction appears between the seven protonotaries and the apostolic notaries. The number of protonotaries was increased to twelve in 1583 and reduced to seven in 1838. The importance of the protonotaries had diminished greatly by the time of the French Revolution. In the nineteenth century protonotaries had authority to draw up and certify documents and to act as referees for the Signatura Gratiae and Signatura Iustitiae. Their duties were redefined in 1853, 1905, and 1934.

RECORDS. Records of the college consist of the following series.

2.1.8.1 Collegio dei protonotarii apostolici
[DATABASE ID: VATV10164-A]
Inclusive Dates: ca. 1585–1902.
Bulk: 3 linear m. (24 buste).
Organization: Subseries include: Lauree: documenti riguardanti i laureandi e anche attentati per laureati per commissionem, 1585–1902 (buste 1–9); —Notariati (buste 10–12); —Varia (buste 13–15); —Eredità di Pio IX (busta 16); —Concilio Vaticano (buste 17–18); —Giuramenti (buste 19–20); —Amministrazione (busta 21); —Diritti e privilegi (busta 22); —Cappelle Pontificie, ca. 1735–1876 (busta 23); —Protonotari Onorari (busta 24).
References: Fink, pp. 130–131; Boyle, p. 96; Pásztor (1970), p. 197.
Finding Aids: ASV Indice 1064 provides a general list of materials in each busta.
Location: Archivio Segreto Vaticano.

2.1.8.2 Protonotari
[DATABASE ID: VATV10163-A]
Inclusive Dates: 1600–1903.
Bulk: 2.5 linear m. (68 vols.).
Organization: Subseries include (numerical designation provided by project staff): 1. Registrum doctorum utriusque juris in Urbe collegialiter laureatorum vigore indulti felicis recordationis Urbani Pp. VIII; —2. Registro delle concessioni degli uffizi de Protonotariati Apostolici Partecipanti, cioé delle supliche e delle procure a prenderne il possesso, come de Memoriali per averne o differirne l'abito; —3. Resignationes officii protonotariatus et subrogationes; —4. Registrum concessionum titulorum protonotariorum Apostolicorum honoris nuncupatorum ac Supranumerariorum iuxta constitutionem Pii Pp. VII . . . , 1818; —5. Expeditiones Bullarum ecclesiarum et abbatiarum consistorialium; —6. Divisiones emolumentorum Collegii pro expeditione ecclesiarum et abbatiarum Consistorialium; —7. Registro delle divisioni degli minuti servizii, spettanti al Collegio degli Ill.mi Signori Protonotari Apostolici Partecipanti . . . ; —8. Memoriae, Expeditiones, Divisiones, Quietantantiae; —9. Declarationes privilegiorum . . . ; —10. Matricula Protonotariorum Apostolicorum honorariorum creatorum a Collegio . . . ; —11. Matricula doctorum per commissionem creatorum a Collegio . . . ; —12. Registrum notitium per commissionem expeditorum per Collegium; —13. Legitimatationes factae ab Ill.mo Collegio.
Note: Volume 67 is miscellanea; volume 68, titled *De Protonotari Apostolici Partecipanti*, is a printed work (first 11 pages are missing). The volumes are not in chronological order.
Scope: This series appears to be a miscellany of what was left of the college. Note that there are some servitia minuta records here.

References: Fink, pp. 130–131; Boyle, p. 96; Pásztor (1970), p. 197.

Finding Aids: ASV Indice 1064 provides information on the first sixty-six volumes in this series. The index entries include: the volume number, inclusive dates, pagination, exact title, and sometimes an annotation regarding the content. Since the volumes are not in chronological order, this index is of particular importance.

Location: Archivio Segreto Vaticano.

2.2 FAMIGLIA DELLA SANTITA DE NOSTRO SIGNORE

[DATABASE ID: VATV219-A]

2.2.1 Auditor SSmi Domini Nostri Papae

[DATABASE ID: VATV102-A]

The auditor served as secretary of the commission established by Innocent XI (1676–1689) to provide the pope with information on individuals recommended for episcopal appointment. Later the position received judicial power in civil and criminal cases. The auditor also had jurisdiction over disputed claims, until 1831, when it was restricted to assisting in the examination of episcopal candidates for Italy. (See the Tribunal dell'auditor sanctissimi.) The office was abolished in 1903, but under Benedict XV (1914–1922) it was reorganized and united with that of the secretary pro tempore of the Supreme Tribunal of the Signature.

References. Fink, pp. 144–145; Pásztor (1970), pp. 185–194; Boyle, p. 99; Natalini et al., p. 275.

RECORDS. Records of the office consist of the following series.

2.2.1.1 Carte senza data

[DATABASE ID: VATV10156-A]
Inclusive Dates: ca. 1700–1899.
Bulk: .5 linear m. (3 scatole).
Organization: Two subseries: 1. Carte senza data (2 scatole); —2. Carte senza data (con nome dei Papi da Pio VII-Pio IX) (1 scatola).
Scope: Carte senza data seem to be letters and miscellaneous printed materials supporting petitions, with possibly some position papers drawn up by referendari. Box 3 seems to consist entirely of officially drawn up responses to petitions.
Location: Archivio Segreto Vaticano.

2.2.1.2 Cause e posizione: Stampati

[DATABASE ID: VATV10158-A]
Inclusive Dates: 1816–1860.
Bulk: .5 linear m. (5 scatole).
Organization: Chronological.
Scope: These are printed copies of positions that relate to materials in other series. They seem to involve cases with bishops, and the like.
Location: Archivio Segreto Vaticano.

2.2.1.3 Cause, posizioni e lettere

[DATABASE ID: VATV10155-A]
Inclusive Dates: 1793–1898.
Bulk: 32 linear m.
Organization: There are four subseries: Cause, posizioni e lettere, 1793–1898 (chronological); —Pio VII, 1800–1823 (lettere, alphabetical); —Eredità, Conte Venansio Corsidoni, 1887, 1 box; —Elenco-Posizioni, 1821–1862, 1 box.
Scope: Though the subseries are for the most part chronological, there are some discrepancies. For example, in Cause, posizione e lettere (1845–1846), the file contains materials from 1843. Inside many boxes, material is tied in bundles with a label reading "Cause e posizioni," or simply "posizioni," even the boxes labeled "lettere." Some of the posizioni are numbered, the indices to these are in subseries 4, Elenco-Posizioni.
Finding Aids: Subseries 4, Elenco-Posizione, contains two folders of indices arranged chronologically (folder 1, 1821–1839; folder 2, 1840–1862). The box label only refers to folder 2 (Elenco-Posizione, 1840–1862). These indices provide primarily name access to some of the numbered posizioni and some sections of the unnumbered posizioni. The indexes are not consistent. It is sometimes difficult to locate the exact box to which an index refers. Subseries 2, Pio VII lettere, has some partial indices to the letters in some boxes.
Auditor SSmi Domini Nostri Papae series *Registrum rescritti*, *Registrum rescritti: Rescripta*, and *Registrum rescritti: Reiecta*, all described separately, can be used as partial name indexes to supplicants in this series. However, for the most complete coverage, the actual letters should be reviewed.
Location: Archivio Segreto Vaticano.

2.2.1.4 [Miscellanea SF/350]

[DATABASE ID: VATV10145-A]
Inclusive Dates: 1687–1902.
Bulk: 1 linear m.
Scope: This miscellany includes: Per diocesi, 1885–1890, 1 vol.; —Minute dei decreti di diverse diocesi, 2 vols. (vol. 1, 1895–1896, vol. 2, da ordinare senza data); —Nomine vescovi e affari riguardanti le sedi vescovili (da ordinare senza data), 1 vol.; —Posizioni sospese, 1884–1902, 1 vol.; —Requisiti de concorrenti ai vescovati dello stato ecclesiastico, 1795–1800, 1 vol.; —Congregazione Accademia di Santa Cecilia, 1839, 1 vol.; —Carte da sistemare riguardanti i Consistori, 1687–1867, 1 vol.; —Signore Ecclesiastica, Lettere pastorali ed altri stampe riguardanti le diocesi, ca. 1870–1899, 3 vols.
Note: This is a true miscellany and is without an official ASV designation. The title was assigned by the project staff based on the location of the material in 1990.
Location: Archivio Segreto Vaticano.

2.2.1.5 [Miscellanea SF/367]

[DATABASE ID: VATV10160-A]
Inclusive Dates: 1803–1933.
Bulk: 3 linear m. (13 boxes, 1 bundle, and 20 printed vols.)
Organization: This miscellany includes (numerical designations assigned by project staff): 1. Giornali: Giornale di Roma (selected issues), 1859, 1866–1867, and altri giornali (selected issues), 1842–1909, 1 box; —2. Lettere e biglietti, 1830–1833, 1 box; —3. Governo Italiano: debito publico, 1820–1870, 2 boxes; —4. [1 series, post-1922]; —5. Registro ed

Ipoteche, 1803–1815, and Codice civile: Disposizioni preliminari, 1 box; —6. Ricevute e spese, 1815–1848, 2 boxes; ; —7. Ricevute, 1830–1845, 1 box; —8. Ricevute e sussidi, 1835–1861; —9. Propaganda: Piano di regolamento e corrispondenza, 1858–1863, 1 box; —10. Università Israelitica e catecumeni a Roma, 1844–1845; —11. Bolle e brevi, 1817–1864; —12. Editti, Republica Romana, 1847–1848; —13. [Miscellaneous printed works, e.g. Pope Pius IX, Acta and various diocesan synodal acta, ca. 1850–1903].

Note: This is a true miscellany of material. It was located at the time of this survey in SF/367. The series title was assigned by project staff. There is no official ASV designation for this material.

Location: Archivio Segreto Vaticano.

2.2.1.6 Nomine dei vescovi
[DATABASE ID: VATV10147-A]
Inclusive Dates: 1814–1869.
Bulk: 1 linear m. (8 vols.).
Organization: Three subseries: Nomine dei vescovi, 1816–1869, 5 vols.; —Nomine dei vescovi ed altri affari, Regno delle due Sicilie, 1814–1829, 2 vols.; —Nomine dei vescovi, Stato Pontificio ed altri Stati, 1814–1830, 1 vol. The subseries are chonological.
Scope: These are printed copies of propositions for the Consistory.
Location: Archivio Segreto Vaticano.

2.2.1.7 Notificazioni e editti: Stampati
[DATABASE ID: VATV10159-A]
Inclusive Dates: 1708–1926.
Bulk: 1 linear m. (7 scatole).
Organization: Chronological.
Scope: These are announcements of decisions.
Location: Archivio Segreto Vaticano.

2.2.1.8 Posizioni del consistoro
[DATABASE ID: VATV10146-A]
Inclusive Dates: 1820–September 1908.
Bulk: 11 linear m. (64 vols.).
Organization: Chronological.
Scope: Earlier volumes contain only written position papers, later volumes contain drafts and printed position papers.
Reference: Pásztor (1970), p. 193–194.
Location: Archivio Segreto Vaticano.

2.2.1.9 Registrum rescritti
[DATABASE ID: VATV10149-A]
Inclusive Dates: 1782–1809, 1814–1869.
Bulk: 3 linear m. (63 vols.).
Organization: Chronological.
Scope: Registers contain abbreviated copies of accepted petitions to the pope. These registers can be used as a partial index to people in the *Udienza* series (described below) for those petitions that were granted by the pope.
Reference: Pásztor (1970), p. 193.
Finding Aids: Each volume contains a good index, primarily to persons, but also listing organizations, offices, and types of rescritti. In using the index, it should be noted, however, that if separate years are bound together, each year will be paginated and indexed separately. Pásztor cites three series as

possible indices to the *Reg. rescritti*, these are: *Informazioni* (or *Registrum rescritti: Informazioni*); *Registrum rescritti: Reiecta*; and *Registrum rescritti: Rescripta*. These series are described below. A brief investigation did not find these particularly effective.

Location: Archivio Segreto Vaticano.

2.2.1.10 Registrum rescritti: Informazioni
[DATABASE ID: VATV10152-A]
Inclusive Dates: 1800–1809, 1814–1871.
Bulk: 1.5 linear m. (48 vols.).
Organization: The series is chronological by year and then alphabetical by name, institution, or office.
Scope: This series identifies where a supplication was sent for further information. If a supplication was rejected after more information was received, the entry is marked with an "R." Registers are very difficult to read, and neither dates nor persons match those that appear in the *Reg. rescritti*, although Pásztor cites this series as a possible index to the *Reg. rescritti*.
Reference: Pásztor (1970), p. 193.
Location: Archivio Segreto Vaticano.

2.2.1.11 Registrum rescritti: Reiecta
[DATABASE ID: VATV10151-A]
Inclusive Dates: 1795–1809, 1814–1871.
Bulk: 2 linear m. (53 vols.).
Organization: The series is chronological by year and then alphabetical by name, institution, or office.
Scope: These registers index entries of the year, date, name, and type of request rejected (i.e., lectum). This series can be used as a partial index to petitioners in the *Udienza* series. Pásztor cites this series as a possible index to the *Reg. rescritti* series, but it is not particularly effective for that purpose.
Reference: Pásztor (1970), p. 193.
Location: Archivio Segreto Vaticano.

2.2.1.12 Registrum rescritti: Rescripta
[DATABASE ID: VATV10150-A]
Inclusive Dates: 1800–1809, 1814–1871.
Bulk: 1.5 linear m. (49 vols.).
Organization : Chronological.
Scope: Although Pásztor cites these as a possible index to the *Registrum rescritti*, a brief investigation indicated that this was not a reliable index to the *Reg. rescritti* even though it often lists the same people and occasionally places, but cites a different month, for example, Accademia pittore et sculpture de Luca is listed in *Reg resc.* on July 7 and in *Reg. resc.: Rescripta* on August 7.
Reference: Pásztor (1970), p. 193.
Location: Archivio Segreto Vaticano.

2.2.1.13 Rescritti
[DATABASE ID: VATV10162-A]
Inclusive Dates: 1800–1870.
Bulk: .5 linear m. (5 scatole).
Organization: Chronological.
Scope: Notices of the persons discussed in the *Rescritti* can be found in the *Registrum rescritti*, *Registrum rescritti: Reiecta*, and the *Registrum rescritti: Rescripta*.
Location: Archivio Segreto Vaticano.

2.2.1.14 Ristretti d'udienze
[DATABASE ID: VATV10161-A]
Inclusive Dates: 1800–1867.
Bulk: .5 linear m. (4 scatole)
Organization: Chronological.
Scope: Box 1 has a chronological list of uditori. These may be notes for udienze.
Location: Archivio Segreto Vaticano.

2.2.1.15 Sez. Segretaria del Consistoro: Carte varie
[DATABASE ID: VATV10148-A]
Inclusive Dates: ca. 1800–1890.
Bulk: 1 linear m. (9 vols.).
Scope: These may be incoming requests for bishoprics.
Location: Archivio Segreto Vaticano.

2.2.1.16 Suppliche
[DATABASE ID: VATV10154-A]
Inclusive Dates: 1607–1809, 1812–1872 (bulk 1782–1809, 1812–1857).
Bulk: 23 linear m.
Organization: The series is chronological; however, for each year there may be four or five boxes. The suppliche are not organized chronologically within a given year, that is, it is likely that a researcher will find supplications from January in box 4 of 1822, and so forth.
Scope: These are supplications (written by professional supplication writers) and sometimes with supporting and/or printed documents. They were used to prepare official petitions probably to the pope.
Finding Aids: There is no one complete, official index to this series. However, three Auditor SSmi Domini Nostri Papae series, *Registrum rescritti*, *Registrum rescritti: Reiecta*, and *Registrum rescritti: Rescripta*, all described separately, list the names of people, and occasionally institutions, who made supplications and when these supplications were offered. If the researcher is looking for a certain person, these might assist in isolating a date. Even taken together these should not be considered a complete list of supplicants. The *Udienze* Giornale and the *Registrum rescritti: Informazioni* do not act as successful indexes to this series.
Location: Archivio Segreto Vaticano.

2.2.1.17 Udienze
[DATABASE ID: VATV10153-A]
Inclusive Dates: 1795–1809, 1814–1879.
Bulk: 99 linear m.
Organization: This series is chronological by date of the audience. There is no particular order to petitions within each audience. The final four boxes are out of chronological order and are entitled as follows: Udienza-Generale, Aprile-Maggio 1815; —Udienza-Generale, 1815–1816; —Giornale delle Udienze, 1815–1833; —Giornale delle Udienze, [1835–1848].
Scope: These are petitions perhaps as drawn up by the referendari. If accepted, there is a scrap of paper stating the terms of the favor either at the beginning of the bundle for the audience or tucked in the position paper done by the referendi.
Reference: Pásztor (1970), p. 192.
Finding Aids: There is no comprehensive index to this series. The Udienze can be accessed by a person's name by using a combination of three other Auditor SSme Domini Nostri

Papae series: *Registrum rescritti*, *Registrum rescritti: Reiecta*, and *Registrum rescritti: Rescripta*. These series are described separately. The Giornale at the end of the *Udienze* series and the separate series *Registrum rescritti: Informazioni* cannot be used nearly as successfully as indexes of the *Udienze*.
Location: Archivio Segreto Vaticano.

2.2.2 Cappellani secreti
[DATABASE ID: VATV125-A]

Chaplains in the papal household are found from the eleventh century. Their duties included sacred functions, the divine office, chant, and assisting the pope in the settling of various questions. They sometimes acted as legates and handled different items of business. The Roman Rota has its origin in the Cappellani papae, Auditores generales curiae domini papae, or Cappellani papae et apostolicae sedis Auditores causarum Sacri Palatii apostolici. From the end of the sixteenth century the chaplains have been divided into privy chaplains and common chaplains. The privy chaplains render the pope confidential services and assist him in sacred functions.

RECORDS. No records for this office were located.

2.2.3 Confessore della famiglia pontificia
[DATABASE ID: VATV127-A]

The origins of this office are unclear. In 1762 the office was reserved to the Order of Servites of Mary. The confessor was a member of the papal household.

RECORDS. No records for this office were located.

2.2.4 Cubicularii Honoris
[DATABASE ID: VATV116-A]

The origins of this office are unclear.

RECORDS. No records for this office were located.

2.2.5 Cubicularii Honoris ab Ense et Lacerna
[DATABASE ID: VATV118-A]

No certain information is available for this office before 1555. The chamberlains were assigned duty in the Throne Room and in other functions according to orders from their two superiors: the major-domo for all functions not connected with the Antecamera, and the maestro di camera for the others.

RECORDS. No records for this office were located

2.2.6 Cubicularii Honoris Extra Urbem
[DATABASE ID: VATV117-A]

These were first appointed by Pius VI (1775–1799).

RECORDS. No records for this office were located.

2.2.7 Cubicularii Intimi ab Ense et Lacerna
[DATABASE ID: VATV107-A]

This office was in existence by 1555. This title was held by the foriere maggiore, the praefectus stabuli, and the praefectus tabellariorum.

RECORDS. No records for this office were located.

2.2.8 Cubicularii Intimi seu Secreti
[DATABASE ID: VATV114-A]

These officials are found from the period 1623–1644. For service in the Antecamera they were subject to the maestro di camera, and for other functions they depended on the major-domo.

RECORDS. No records for this office were located.

2.2.9 Cubicularii Intimi seu Secreti ab Ense et Lacerna
[DATABASE ID: VATV115-A]

This office was established during the period 1623–1644. These cubicularii were appointed to replace the privy chamberlains participating when they were unable to perform their functions.

RECORDS. No records for this office were located.

2.2.10 Cubicularii Segretari Partecipanti
[DATABASE ID: VATV105-A]

Cubicularii (syncelli), who render private and personal services to princes, are found as early as the period 440–461. From the fourteenth century, these cubicularii presented all personal petitions to the pope and pressed for answers, which were signed by the first cubicularius. By the sixteenth century a distinction was made between chamberlains participating at the holy table and those not participating. The number and duties of the chamberlains have varied under the different popes.

RECORDS. No records for this office were located.

2.2.11 Eleemosinarius Secretus
[DATABASE ID: VATV128-A]

The practice of distributing alms to the poor goes back to early times. This office was first organized in 1271–1276. In 1409 the scope and procedure of the Almonry were determined. Its work increased greatly in the fifteenth and succeeding centuries. In the twentieth century the almoner supervised or administered certain schools and charitable institutions. In 1968 Paul VI renamed the office Almoner of His Holiness (alternate English name: Privy Almoner).

Reference: M. Piccialuti, *La carità come metodo di governo: Istituzioni caritative a Roma dal pontificato di Innocenzo XII a quello di Benedetto XIV* (Turin, 1994).

RECORDS. Records of the office consist of the following series.

2.2.11.1 Registri
[DATABASE ID: VATV10200-A]
Inclusive Dates: 1714–1969.
Bulk: 4.5 linear m. (109 numbered volumes).
Organization: Subseries, buste, numbers, and titles include: 1–15. Registri mastri Elemosineria apostolica, 1714–[post-1922]; —16. Conto cassa Basilica S. Marco del Can. Luigi Oreste Borgia; —17–19. Conto cassa con l'Amministrazione dei beni della S. Sede; —20. Sussidi monacande; —21. Rilasci-pensioni; —22. [1 subseries post-1922]; —23. Mastrino S. Caterina; —24. Libro di metodo di contabilita, 1837–[19—]; —25. Rendita; —26. Ex-impiegati civili pontifici; —27. Mastro scuole; —28–30. Doti conseguite sui fondi della Segreteria dei brevi; —31–33. Mastro zoccolette; —34. Rubrica generale assegni e sussidi fissi; —35. Protocollo generale, 1835; —36–37. Mastro pia casa di ricovero sordomute anziane; —38–39. Archivio pia casa sordomute anziane; —40. Informazioni; —41–43. Soldati; —44. Sussidi extra; —45. Sussidi mensili e periodici, 1922; —46–49. Sussidi vari fissi; —50. Monasteri sussidi; —51–55. Mastro Immacolata concezione e S. Luigi Gonzaga, 1857–[post-1922]; —56. Ex-militia pontifici; —57. Sussidi ex-impiegati; —58. Rubrica ex-impiegati; —59. Rubrica zoccolette; —60. Titolì; —61. Conto cassa con l'Amministrazione dei beni della Santa Sede, 1889–1890; —62. [1 subseries post-1922]; —63. Copia lettere, 1877–1883; —64. Libro istrumenti pubblici zoccolette Roma; —65. Registro infermi, visita S. Eustacio; —66. Ruolo della visita di visitatori Medici, ca. 1726; —67. Registro patenti levatrici; —68. Ruolo dei ministri, 1843; —69. Distribuzione millini, ca. 1750; —70. Ospizio S. Luigi, giornale 1834; —71–74. Libri conti correnti; —75. Caporale e vedove; —76. Protocollo corrispondenza; —77. Scuole. Rubrica; —78. Ex-impiegati, ex-militari, rubrica pasquale-natale; —79. Scadenze; —80. Ospizio della SS. Concezione e di Luigi Gonzaga, ca. 1906; —81. Negative; —82. Rubrica; —83. Rubricella; —84. Rubricella, libro mastro, A; —85. Rubricella, libro mastro, B; —86. Rubricella; —87. Rubricella del libro mastro, 1874; —88. Rubricella del libro mastro, lettere I; —[1 subseries post-1922]; —90. Sussidi fuori Roma, 1922–[post-1922]; —91. [1 subseries post-1922]; —92. Sussidi fissi; —93. Assegni, rubrica; —94–95. Rubrice; —[2 subseries post-1922]; —98. Verbali, ca. 1915; —99. Pagamenti, 1818–1852; —[1 subseries post-1922]; —101. Conservatorio dei SS. Clemente e Crescentino, archivio vol. 1; —102–103. Ospizio SS. Concezione e San Luigi Gonzaga, archivio vols. 1–2; —104–105. Archivio vols. 1–2; —106. [1 subseries post-1922]. Numbers given above refer to the current enumeration of the buste.
Scope: There may be some records of visitations within the series. See vols. 65 and 66, Protocol vol.35, and Rubrics vols. 34 and 78–95.
Reference: Natalini et al., p. 270.
Finding Aids: A prospectus to this series is available at the desk in the ASV main reading room. The prospectus is not a formal finding aid and must be used in consultation with the

archives staff. This prospectus gives a brief summary of the collection, which forms the basis for the organizational note above. The prospectus lists buste numbers, location or type of business, and number of buste concerning each entry.

Location: Archivio Segreto Vaticano.

2.2.11.2 Servizio assistenziale del Santo Padre
[DATABASE ID: VATV10199-A]

Inclusive Dates: 1881–1968.

Bulk: 20 linear m. (142 numbered buste).

Organization: Subseries include: Immacolata concezione e S. Luigi, buste 1–27; —Varie, buste 28–42 and 138–142; —Santa Caterina, buste 43–45; —Sordomuti, buste 46–49; —Maestre Pie Filippine, buste 53–54; —Scuola Arco dei Ginnasi, buste 53–54; —Scuola Nostra Signora di Lourdes, busta 55; —Scuola Regina Pacis, busta 56; —Scuole Dipendenti, buste 57–58; —Divina Providenza, buste 59–64; —Zoccolette, buste 65–89; —Sussidi Fissi, buste 90–105; —Spese e sussidi per mese, buste 106–137; —Miscellaneous, [post 1922], buste 138–142.

References: Natalini et al., p. 270.

Finding Aids: A prospectus to this series is available at the desk in the ASV main reading room. The prospectus is not a formal finding aid, and must be used in consultation with the archives staff. This prospectus provides a very brief summary of contents, as presented in the organizational note above. The prospectus lists buste numbers, place, and number of buste in each location.

Location: Archivio Segreto Vaticano.

2.2.12 Forerius Major
[DATABASE ID: VATV108-A]

This title originated in the fifteenth century. The forerius major was responsible for overseeing buildings, water supply, and furnishings of the papal palace. One of the privy chamberlains of sword and cape participated in this responsibility. The office was eliminated by Paul VI in 1968.

RECORDS. No records for this office were located in the ASV.

2.2.13 Gendarmeria pontificia
[DATABASE ID: VATV123-A]

The Gendarmeria pontificia was established in 1849 under the name Regiment of Pontifical Infantry, to succeed the Pontifical Carabineers. In 1850 the name was changed to Gendarmeria. The Gendarmeria was organized in one regiment, with three squadrons located in Rome, Ancona, and Bologna. It was dependent in part on the Ministero delle armi and in part on the Ministero dell'interno. Later the Gendarmeria was dependent on the secretary of state. Beginning in 1929 it was dependent on the governor of the State of Vatican City, the president of the Pontifical Commission for the State of Vatican City.

RECORDS. Records of the office consist of the following series.

2.2.13.1 Gendarmeria
[DATABASE ID: VATV20134-A]

Inclusive Dates: 1816–1870.

Bulk: 566 buste and 1 rubricella.

Organization: Subseries are: Comando, 1816–1870, 293 buste; —Protocollo segreto, 1851–1860, 13 buste and 1 rubricella; —Corrispondenza, 1866–1870, 16 buste; —Miscellanea di rapporti politici, 1819–1870, 244 buste. The Miscellanea was formerly called Gendarmeria, rapporti politici.

References: D'Angiolini, pp. 1158–1159; Lodolini (1960), p. 209.

Finding Aids: Summary inventories exist for most of this series.

Location: Archivio di Stato di Roma.

2.2.14 Guardia palatina d'onore
[DATABASE ID: VATV120-A]

This office was established in 1851 through the fusion of the Milizia urbana and the Guardia civica scelta. The guard provided voluntary service for the protection of the pope and his residence. Before 1870 it was also assigned watch-duties in the city of Rome and military operations in wartime. The guard was greatly reduced in size after 1870. The guard was dependent directly on the secretary of state, and was at the disposition of the maestro di camera. The Honor Guard took orders from the esente of the noble guards. The guard was abolished by Paul VI in 1970.

RECORDS. Records of the office consist of the following series.

2.2.14.1 [Archivio]
[DATABASE ID: VATV10237-A]

Inclusive Dates: 1851–1970 (bulk 1851–1928).

Bulk: 101 linear m.

Organization: This miscellany includes (numerical designations supplied by project staff): 1. Effettivi; —2. Domande in Corso o Sospeso; —3. Posizioni personali ed ausiliari; —4. Ufficiali-Anziani-Allievi-Muscanti; —5. Ufficio di Mons. Cappellano-Domande non ascolte; —6. Ufficio di Mons. Cappellano-Dimessi; —7. Segreteria; —8. Comando Guardia Palatina; —9. Posizioni personali, I Serie; —10. Posizioni personali, II Serie; —11. Domande d'Ammissione; —12. Rapporti dei Servizi Anticamera; —13. Ordine del Giorno, 1851–[post-1922]; —14. Presenze; —15. Registro mandati di pagamento, 1862–1904; —16. Servizi mancanza e punizioni; —17. Protocolli, 1851–[post-1922]; —18. Amministrazione; —19. Miscellaneous financial records.

Subseries 1, 3–6, and 11 are alphabetical. Subseries 12, 13, and 15–17 are chronological.

Note: This series does not have a designated title in the ASV. Project staff assigned the title *Archivio*.

Reference: Natalini et al., p. 272.

Finding Aids: A brief prospectus to the first eleven subseries is available at the desk in the main ASV reading room. The prospectus is not a formal finding aid and must be used in consultation with the archives staff. The prospectus gives a scant outline of what alphabetical letters or types of material can be found in some boxes. There is better access to some subseries than others. No dates are included in this prospectus.

Location: Archivio Segreto Vaticano.

2.2.15 Guardia svizzera pontificia
[DATABASE ID: VATV119-A]

Swiss soldiers were found in the service of the Holy See as early as the fourteenth century, but the Swiss Guard was organized by Julius II in 1506 It has been disbanded and reorganized at various times since then. Its duties include the protection of the pope and the guarding of the Sacred Palaces. The guard receives orders from the major-domo.

RECORDS. No records for this office could be located in the ASV.

2.2.16 Guardie nobili pontificia
[DATABASE ID: VATV111-A]

This group was founded in 1801 under the title Noble Bodyguard of His Holiness, replacing the Knight Guardians of His Holiness, who were disbanded in 1798 when the French occupied Rome. The guard was subject to the secretary of state for organization and administration, but for daily duty it was subject to the major-domo and the maestro di Camera. It was renamed Honor Guard of His Holiness by Paul VI in 1968.

RECORDS. Records of the office consist of the following series.

2.2.16.1 [Archivio]
[DATABASE ID: VATV10238-A]
Inclusive Dates: 1801–1970 (bulk 1823–1919).
Bulk: 46 linear m.
Organization: Materials are grouped in rough chronological segments as follows: Parte Ia, 1801–1840; —Parte IIa, 1826–1860 (primarily 1840–1850); —Parte IIIa, 1821–1870 (primarily 1850–1870); —Parte IVa 1866–1920 (primarily 1871–1900); —Parte Va, 1841–1915; —Parte VIa 1846–[post-1922]; —Parte VIIa 1851–[post-1922].
Within each parte cited above some of the following subseries generally occur: Regolamento disciplina; —Individuali ammessi; —Individuali non ammessi; —Amministrazione; —Spedizioni; —Missioni; —Ordini del giorno; —Consiglio di guerra; —Contratti; —Visite di Sovrani e Capi di Stato; —Viaggi di Sua Santita; —Servizi; —Carteggio; —Consiglio parziale.
In addition to the subseries cited, the following are at the end of the collection: Servizio in Palazzo, 1817–[post-1922]; —Rapporti di Scuderia, 1816–1880; —Decreti del Consiglio, [ca. 18—]; —Estratti and other miscellaneous financial records, [18—]–[19—]. There are also photographs.
Note: This series does not have a formal title designation by the ASV. The title *Archivio* was assigned by the project staff.
Reference: Natalini et al., p. 272.
Finding Aids: There is a prospectus to the initial seven "Parti" of this series available at the desk in the main ASV reading room. The prospectus is not a formal finding aid, and must be used in consultation with the archives staff. This pros-

pectus lists the subseries (buste) in each parte according to current buste numbers and provides a brief synopsis of the business and some inclusive dates.

Location: Archivio Segreto Vaticano.

2.2.17 Magister Sacri Hospitii
[DATABASE ID: VATV104-A]

The Magister Sacri Hospitii is responsible for the solemn reception of reigning sovereigns and heads of state visiting the pope. Since 1811 this office has been conferred on members of the Ruspoli family, who succeeded the Conti family, which had ceased to exist.

Note: See papers of the Ruspoli family listed in the section "Miscellaneous Official Materials and Separate Collections: Individual and Family Papers."

RECORDS. No records for this office were located in the ASV.

2.2.18 Magister Sacri Palatii
[DATABASE ID: VATV103-A]

The origins of this office go back to Honorius III (1216–1227). Originally reserved for Dominicans, one member of the order was chosen to serve as regent in the Faculty of Theology in the Studium Palatii. When the school ceased, the regent became Theologian of the Pope and had special duties, such as that of designating the preachers for papal chapels, examining their sermons, and studying theological questions. From 1515 to 1925 this official gave the imprimatur for books published in Rome and was president of the College of Theologians. After 1925 this official served as confidential theologian of the pope. In 1968 the office was renamed doctor theologus by Paul VI.

RECORDS. No records for this office were located in the ASV.

2.2.19 Magistri Caeremoniarum S.R.E. et Sedis Apostolicae
[DATABASE ID: VATV113-A]

This is an office with ancient origins that are not precisely known. The position was quite prominent by the year 1400. Responsibilities included direction of sacred ceremonies, episcopal consecrations, and abbatial blessings that took place in Rome. The office was attached to the Congregatio Ceremonialis.

RECORDS. No records for this office could be located in the ASV.

2.2.20 Notai dell'auditor sanctissimi
[DATABASE ID: VATV744-A]

This tribunal was a preliminary step in applying to the Signature of Grace. It was abolished in 1809, reestablished in 1814, then finally abolished in 1831.

RECORDS. Records of the office consist of the following series.

2.2.20.1 Notai dell'auditor sanctissimi
[DATABASE ID: VATV20060-A]
Inclusive Dates: 1759–1831.
Bulk: 158 vols.
Scope: Eighteenth century, 122 vols.; —Nineteenth century, 36 vols.
References: D'Angiolini, p. 1128; Lodolini (1960), p. 60.
Finding Aids: There is a summary inventory and an alphabetical index of notai (also an inventory of notai of the Tribunale dell'auditor camerae).
Location: Archivio di Stato di Roma.

2.2.21 Pontificiae Aulae Orator
[DATABASE ID: VATV126-A]

The title and office go back to Paul IV (1555–1559). Before that time the procurators general of the four mendicant orders preached in turn on Sundays in Advent and Lent. Beginning in 1743, under Benedict XIV, this office was reserved to the Order of Friars Minor Capuchins.

RECORDS. No records for this office were located in the ASV.

2.2.22 Praefectus Cubiculi Secreti Pontificis
[DATABASE ID: VATV101-A]

Under Gregory I (590–604) this office was held by the secundicerius (see history for the Protonotari apostolici for information about that office). Under Pius II (1458–1464) the incumbent was called magister aulae. Under Adrian VI (1522–1523) the title was principale di camera. From 1550, under Julius III, the title maestro di camera was in general use, along with that of cubiculi praefectus. Duties included authority over all matters relating to the daily personal service of the pope, especially the regulation of papal audiences. The office was eliminated by Paul VI in 1968.

RECORDS. No records for this office were located in the ASV.

2.2.23 Praefectus Palatii Apostolici
[DATABASE ID: VATV100-A]

Shortly after 1410 the government of the Sacred Palace was separated from the Apostolic Camera and turned over to the prefect of the Sacred Palace. Under Urban VIII (1623–1644) the title was changed to major-domo. In addition to the administration of the Sacred Palace, the major-domo's duties included acting as governor of the Conclave. Between 1878 and 1891, responsibility for administration of the Sacred Palace was transferred from this office to the Prefecture of the Sacred Apostolic Palaces. This office was eliminated by Paul VI in 1968. See also the history for the Tribunale del prefetto dei palazzi apostolici.

References. Fink, p. 139; Boyle, p. 99; Natalini et al., p. 273. E. Dante, *Catalogo dell'Archivio della Prefettura delle Ceremonie Apostoliche* (1956) [this title was noted but not verified by project staff].

In addition to the records listed below, series listed with another agency relate directly to this agency and should be consulted. See Papal Court (Cappella Pontificia) series *Mazzieri pontifici, Collegio dei mazzieri.*

RECORDS. Records of the office consist of the following series.

2.2.23.1 Amministrazioni
[DATABASE ID: VATV247-A]
Inclusive Dates: 1599–1923.
Bulk: 84 linear m.
Organization: 1,080 numbered and 54 unnumbered volumes. Major subseries are as follows: I. Castel Gandolfo, ca. 1808–1870 (no. 1–74); —II. Iura, 1599–1870 (no. 75–354); —III. Corpi militari, [19— ?]–1923 (no. 355–367); —IV. Scuole, ca. 1800–1850 (no. 368–373); —V. Musei, fabbriche, acque, 1820–1923 (no. 374–396b); —VI. Personaggi, ca. 1800–1870 (no. 397–401); —VII. Bilanci, 1658–1908 (no. 402–1027); —VIII. Inventari, 1520–1858 (no. 1028–1080). Subdivisions of the subseries are as follows:
Subseries I. Castel Gandolfo, contains the following Titoli (1–9) and divisions: Chiese parrochiale, ca. 1808–1870 (no. 1–5); —Palazzo apostolico (no. 6–8); —Acque (no. 9); —Magistratura governativa (no. 10–14); —Magistratura communale (no. 15–35); —Scuole (no. 36); —Opere pie (no. 37–41); —"manca"; —Miscellanea (no. 42); —Affitti (no. 45); —Atti civili e criminale (no. 61–62); —Prefettura, 1849–ca. 1900 (no. 65–74).
Subseries II. Iura, contains the following subdivisions: 75. Processo Phifer-Probstat, 1725; —76–80. Atti civili; —81. Prefettura. Atti criminali; —82–99, 159–199. Manuali civili, 1630–1650 and 1634–1778 (for Manuali 1779–1831 see note regarding unnumbered volumes below); —100–153. Atti civili, 1648–1718; —154. Liber sententiarum, 1661–1770; —155. Liber recusationum, 1774–1788; —156. Libro d'anni, 1789; —157–158. Liber actum civilium, 1628, Giornale udienze civile, 1843–1869; —200–201. Cause varie, 1733, Manuale atti volontari, 1617–1619; —202–204, 211–223. Atti civili, Attestati, 1700–1843; —205–210. Citazioni originali; —224–242. Cause civili, 1859–1868; —243–244. Atti di volontaria giurisdizione, 1850–1870; —245–246. Sentenze civili, 1828–1870; —247–260. Atti civili e criminali, 1623–1823; —261–322. Processi criminali, 1599–1907; —323–331. Carteggio governativo, 1728–1864; —332–354. Carte varie, 1732–1870.
Unnumbered volumes all refer to titoli II "Iura" and are as follows: [Account book], ca. 1600; —Case (con Rubricelle di nome), 1651–1658; —Rubricella Manuale cum Broliardo (alternatively identified as Rubricelle Istromentum in 1781 and Registri di Atti Civii is sometimes written on the spine after 1816), 1779–1831. These are unnumbered but should be inserted in the S.P.A. *Amministrazioni* after no. 199.
Subseries III. Corpi Militari contains information on the following: Gendarmeria pontificia; —Guardia d'onore palatina; —Guardia svizzera; —Truppe pontificia di cavalleria.
Subseries IV. Scuole, ca. 1800–1850 (no. 368–373).
Subseries V. Musei, fabbriche, acque includes the following: 374. Ruolo, 1824–1832; —374. Musei e gallerie, 1831; —

376. Proposta di lavoro nell'Arcibasilica lateranense; —377–380. Conto cassa, 1891–1923; —383–384. Restauro prospetto palazzo Cancelleria; —385–386. Cappella Sistina; —387–388. Basilica di S. Agnese fuori le Mùre; —389. Musei e gallerie, registro di esito, 1827; —390. Musei, etc. Fedi di versamento, etc., 1813–1905; —391–392. Musei pontificie, giustificazioni, 1892–1905; —393. Acqua Pia, Gallerie in Castel Gandolfo; —394. Descrizione del Giardino Vaticano, 1824; —395. Acqua Paola, tasse, 1840; —396a. Acqua Felice, 1848–[18—]; —396b. Musei, registro di quietanza, 1820–1822.

Subseries VI. Personaggi, includes: 397. Paolo Angelucci. —398. Augosto Baviera; —399. Giuseppe Collina; —400. Carlo Lenti; —401. Banchieri (includes Rothschild Freres, Paris).

Subseries VII. Bilanci, 1658–1908 (no. 402–1027).

Subseries VIII. Includes: 1028. Inventario di S. Stefano de'Mori, 1667; —1029. Inv. della sacrestia di S. Pietro (fr. Ambrogio Ganducci), [17—]; —1030. Libro . . . della Cera per servizio de Sac. Palazzo nel Pontificato di Papa Paolo terzo, 1540–1542; —1031. Palazzo pontificio a Castel Gandolfo; —1032. Floreria S.P.A., 1724; —1033. Floreria e palazzo al Quirinale, 1730; —1046. Inv. della Chiesa di S. Marta, 1667 and 1694; —1066. Inv. dei Giardino al Quirinale, 1841; —1067. Inv. dei giardino al Vaticano, 1841; —1073. Inv. oggetti vecchi al Vaticano, 1841; —1076. Inv. 1741; —1080. Inv. dell'Archivio del Sacro Palazzo Apostolico, [17—?].

Note: Nos. 402–422 and nos. 424–457 are missing. Subseries II also seems to pertain primarily to Castel Gandolfo.

Finding Aids: ASV Indice 1063 (by Antonio Luciani) provides a general introduction to the history and functions of the Sacro Palazzo Apostolico (S.P.A.) and its officers. Notes on the S.P.A. Amministrazioni appear on p. 56 and 94 and an inventory of this series begins on p. 95. This inventory groups the Amministrazioni by titoli and type and generally lists the type of volume (e.g. atti, manuale, processi criminali, etc.) and the inclusive dates. For selected titoli, such as the Musei, fabbriche, acque and the Inventari, individual volumes are listed with their current volume numbers, titles, and inclusive dates. Indice 1063 also includes a brief bibliography (of works dating between 1829 and 1972) where more in-depth information on the organization and function of the Papal States and the papal household can be located. The books and articles cited solely treat the Sacro Palazzo Apostolico in a brief fashion, if at all, and do not mention any particular fondi identified in the database as part of the S.P.A.

Within the series *Amministrazioni*, no. 1080 is an (eighteenth-century?) "Inventario dell'Archivio del Sacro Palazzo Apostolico." Although this does not reflect the current arrangement of any particular S.P.A. series as it exists today, it does provide a historical perspective on the archive.

Location: Archivio Segreto Vaticano.

2.2.23.2 Certificati

[DATABASE ID: VATV10357-A]

Inclusive Dates: 1839–1935.

Bulk: 8 linear m.

Organization: Chronological.

Scope: These appear to be certificates not only that work has been done, but also that the laborer has been paid. The years on the volumes reflect the date of the certification, not the actual work (which may have been up to three years earlier).

These cover work in the papal palace, the garden, and the Cappella pontificia (May 19, 1852) and include everything from setting up for ceremonies to landscaping.

Location: Archivio Segreto Vaticano.

2.2.23.3 Computisteria

[DATABASE ID: VATV10316-A]

Inclusive Dates: 1611–1928.

Bulk: 445 linear m. (6,103 numbered buste).

Organization: Buste enumeration and titles are: 1–145. Ammissioni e filze dei participanti nei ruoli del S.P.A., 1706–1909; —146–471. Mandati spediti da/a Mons. Tesoriere, 1672–1798; —472–499. Giustificazioni di pagamenti (a firma Nerli), 1657–1676; —500–514. idem (Paravicini), 1676–1690; —515. idem (Nerli), 1689–1691; —516–542. idem (Monthione); —543. idem (Monthione-Collicola), 1716; —544. idem (Collicola), 1717; —545–554. idem (Lelmi), 1718; —555–566. idem (Lombardi), 1725–1729; —567–574. idem (Minucci), 1730–1737; —575. idem (Morgani), 1737; —592–651. Pagamenti del Depositario generale della reverenda Camera apostolica, 1748–1798; —652–801. Monte di pietà, 1656–1795; —802–906. Pagamenti fatti dal dispensiere (Mansueti), 1669–1772; —908–953. idem (Bergondi), 1774–1798; —954–982. Spese per alloggi; —983–1030. Pagamenti diverse; —1031–1159. Pranzi fatti alla camera segreta, villeggiature, funzioni; —1160–1453. Giustificazioni del libro mastro; filze di conti e giustificazioni; —1454–1472. Musei e gallerie; —1473–1477. idem Restauri; —1478. Creditori; —1479–1480. Ottavario dei SS. Apostoli Pietro e Paolo; —1481. Assegni e pensioni; conti a parte; —1482–1495. Assegni e pensioni, 1823–1838; —1496–1502. Liquidazione di creditori arretrati, 1838; —1503–1508. Conto a parte. Esecuzione di lavori arretrati. Conto e giustificazioni, 1839–1908; —1509–1513. Dipartimenti, giustificazioni, conti, etc., 1839, Tome I. Foriere maggiore; —1514–1515. idem T. II, Cavallerizzo maggiore; —1516–1517. idem T. III, Maestro di casa; —1518. idem T. IV, Computisteria; —1519. idem T. V, Sagristia; —1520. idem T. VI, Guardia nobile; —1521. idem T. VII, Guardia svizzera; —1522. idem T. VIII, Musei e gallerie; —1523. idem T. IX, Prev.vo generale; —1524–1525. Assegni a vedove familiari del S.P.A.; —1526–1533. Dipartimenti, giustificazioni, conti, etc., 1840 (Foriere maggiore); —1534–1537. idem (Maestro di casa); —1538. idem (Guardia nobile); —1540. idem (Musei e gallerie); —1541. idem (Prev.vo. generale); —[4 no. post-1922]; —1546–2577. Dipartimenti, giustificazioni, conti, etc., 1841–1900 (as above, organized by year and then broken down by office); —2578–2620. Guardia nobile (1870–1909); —2621–2639. Guardia svizzera; —2640–2654. Gendarmeria; —2655–2672. Guardia palatina; —2674–2682. Conti a parte, giustificazioni; —3001–3291. Registri di partecipazioni a Mons. Tesoriere; —3601–3714. Ruolo permanenti e addizionali; —3715–3736. Ordini; —3737–4649. Mandati; —4650–4953. Mandati estinti; —4954–5009. Mandati estinti, ca. 1911–[post-1922]; —5010. Aggiunti, 1628; —5011. Inventario di Robbe di Floreria; —5012. Registro di quadri che si piglano al S.P., 1624–1644; —5017–5063. Rincontro, 1621–1758; —5224–5252. Registri d'ordini, 1647–1779; —5294–5302. Istrumenti diversi, 1611–1841; —5345–6103. Dipartimento, conti, giustificazioni (organized as above according to year and major sections, e.g., Foriere maggiore, Cavallerizzo maggiore, Maestro di casa, etc.), 1891–[post-1922].

Scope: The most interesting items seem to be after inventory 1063 ceases: no. 5011–5012, and Istrumenti no. 5294–5302. In the Indice 1063 p. 58 there is a note: "va inserito qui un fascicolo con gli ordini per la fabbrica di S. Maria Maggiore, autografo di Gian Lorenzo Bernini = 490 b = 272 + Guidi."

Finding Aids: ASV Indice 1063 provides a general introduction to the history and functions of the Sacro Palazzo Apostolico and its officers. Indice 1063 also includes a brief bibliography (of works dating between 1829 and 1972) where more in-depth information on the organization and function of the Papal States and the papal household can be located. A brief introduction and an inventory of the S.P.A. *Computisteria* nos. 1–4953 appears between pages 57 and 93 of Indice 1063. Entries delineate the different types of material in these buste (cf. above), for example, mandate, giustificazioni, dipartimenti, and so forth, and usually indicate the inclusive dates. The Indice does not cover later records in this series that include inventories and istromenti.

Location: Archivio Segreto Vaticano.

2.2.23.4 Prefettura

[DATABASE ID: VATV10356-A]

Inclusive Dates: 1833–1949.

Bulk: 21 linear m.

Organization: The series includes: Participazioni, 1838–1876, 4 boxes; —Gite, pranze, e rinfrischo di Sua Santità, 1831–1868, 10 boxes; —Candalora, 1833–1874, 3 boxes; —Trastevere, 2 boxes; —Piazza Mastai (scuola diretta dalle Agostiniani), 1 box; —Tasse, 1 box; —Gendarmeria palatino, 1 box; —Palazzo Belvedere, 1 box; —Vestiario, 1 box; —Documenti importanti riguardano il Maestro di Casa ed impiegati, 1 box; —Protocolli, 1895–[post-1922].

Location: Archivio Segreto Vaticano.

2.2.23.5 Protocolli

[DATABASE ID: VATV10315-A]

Inclusive Dates: 1832–1928.

Bulk: 6 linear m.

Organization: There are 123 volumes numbered 156–279; they can be considered the final subseries of the Sacro Palazzo Apostolico (S.P.A.) *Titoli.*

Scope: The *Protocolli* registers give a good overview of the types of business handled by the S.P.A. The *Protocolli* contain detailed notes on correspondence received and sent by the office of the S.P.A. Entries in the *Protocolli* indicate: the date of presentation, the date of receipt, the receiver, a protocol number, summaries of the object of business and the response, and where in the archives the letters were filed. It could not be determined if or how these could be used to access letters in the other S.P.A. series.

Finding Aids: ASV Indice 1063 provides a general introduction to the history and functions of the Sacro Palazzo Apostolico and its officers. Indice 1063 also includes a brief bibliography (of works dating between 1829 and 1972) where more in-depth information on the organization and function of the Papal States and the papal household can be located. On page 55, ASV Indice 1063 provides a brief overview of the *Protocolli.* The dates now reflected from the actual *Protocolli* are slightly different from those listed in Indice 1063.

Location: Archivio Segreto Vaticano.

2.2.23.6 Titoli

[DATABASE ID: VATV10314-A]

Inclusive Dates: ca. 1741–1958.

Bulk: 45 linear m. (279 buste).

Organization: Subseries are (numerical designation supplied by project staff): 1. Sua Santità, ca. 1741–[post-1922], 9 buste; —2. Sacro collegio; —3. Nunziature apostoliche; —4. Sacre congregazioni (titoli II–IV in 1 busta); —5. Cappella pontificia, 3 buste; —6. Famiglia pontificia, ca. 1823–1922, 56 buste; —7. Segreterie palatine, ca. 1833–1903, 1 busta; —8. Corpi militari palatini, ca. 1821–1912, 31 buste; —9. Monumenti, ca. 1820–1917, 14 buste; —10. Fabbriche ed acque, 11 buste; —11. Sacre funzioni, ca. 1816–[post-1922], 16 buste; —12. Sovrani e personaggi, 1819–[post-1922], 1 busta; —13. Miscellanea, ca. 1830–1900, 9 buste; —14. Protocolli, 1832–1928 (see previous record).

Finding Aids: ASV Indice 1063 provides a general introduction to the history and functions of the Sacro Palazzo Apostolico (S.P.A.) and its officers. Indice 1063 also includes a brief bibliography (of works dating between 1829 and 1972) where more in-depth information on the organization and function of the Papal States and the papal household can be located. An inventory of the S.P.A. *Titoli* appears between pages 8 and 54 in Indice 1063. Entries proceed busta by busta. At best, Indice 1063 provides detailed access by calendaring each fascicolo and indicating the type of document (bull, brief, chirografo, motu proprio, etc.), the date, and a brief synopsis of the business. Other entries in Indice 1063, however, simply indicate the general subject of materials in the buste and do not mention any dates. Although the bulk of the S.P.A. *Titoli* dates from the nineteenth and twentieth centuries, earlier materials can be located throughout this series. Note also that Indice 1063, p. 5, says that no. 4946 is "Registro delle Congregazioni del S.P.A." This is incorrect.

Location: Archivio Segreto Vatican.

2.2.24 Praefectus Sacrarii Apostolici

[DATABASE ID: VATV106-A]

Until the fourteenth century this office was often united with other functions. Beginning with Innocent VI in 1352 it was chosen from the Order of the Hermits of St. Augustine. Beginning with Alexander VI (1492–1503) it was turned over exclusively to the Augustinians. In 1929 Pius XI named the office sacristan vicar general for the Vatican City. Paul VI dropped the name *sacristan* from the vicar general's title in 1968.

RECORDS. No records for this office were located in the ASV.

2.2.25 Praefectus Stabuli

[DATABASE ID: VATV109-A]

The prior stabuli is mentioned as early as 590. The present title goes back to 1334–1342. Superintendent of the palace stables has shared, since 1832, in the administration of the Sacred Palace. This official was one of the privy chamberlains of sword and cape participating.

RECORDS. No records for this office were located in the ASV.

2.2.26 Praefectus Tabellariorum
[DATABASE ID: VATV110-A]

In ancient times this official was known as the praefectus cursus publici. The title probably was in use as early as the period 1585–1590. The office was responsible for the postal service, extraordinary couriers, pilot carriages, and teams of horses. This official was one of the privy chamberlains of sword and cape participating. This office eliminated by Paul VI in 1968.

RECORDS. No records for this office were located in the ASV.

2.2.27 Tribunale del prefetto dei palazzi apostolici
[DATABASE ID: VATV768-A]

This tribunal had civil and criminal jurisdiction over the papal household. It was suppressed during the French regime, 1809–1814. Its civil jurisdiction was suppressed in 1832.

RECORDS. Records of the office consist of the following series.

2.2.27.1 Tribunale del prefetto (o maggiordomo) dei palazzi apostolici
[DATABASE ID: VATV20239-A]
Inclusive Dates: 1715–1869 (bulk 1814–1869).

Bulk: 1,595 vols., 1 busta, and 1 rubrica.
References: D'Angiolini, pp. 1199–1200; Lodolini (1960), p. 119.
Finding Aids: Inventory, 1971.
Location: Archivio di Stato di Roma.

2.2.28 Tribunale dell'auditor sanctissimi
[DATABASE ID: VATV870-A]

This tribunal was a preliminary step in applying to the Signature of Grace. It was abolished by the French regime in 1809, reestablished in 1814, and finally abolished in 1831. See also the history for the office of the auditor sanctissimi.

RECORDS. Records of the office consist of the following series.

2.2.28.1 Tribunale dell'auditor sanctissimi (uditore del papa)
[DATABASE ID: VATV20059-A]
Inclusive Dates: 1676–1809 and 1814–1831.
Bulk: 30 vols., 22 buste, and 6 registri.
Reference: D'Angiolini, pp. 1127–1128, 1202.
Finding Aids: Inventory, 1970.
Location: Archivio di Stato di Roma.

PART 3

Roman Curia

THE ADMINISTRATION OF THE HOLY SEE HAS A HISTORY THAT IS LONG, complex, and for the early years not fully known. The extant records of the papacy reflect two general periods of development. The first, from the medieval period through the mid-sixteenth century, and the second from the mid-sixteenth century through the early twentieth century. Later organizational reforms are reflected in records currently closed to research use.

During the first period, the affairs of the Holy See were handled primarily by the Apostolic Chancery. As the Chancery became busier, other offices and specialized subdepartments were developed at various times. Among these were the Camera Apostolica and the Datary. Toward the end of this period, special commissions of cardinals began to be created to handle the ever-increasing number and complexity of questions to be examined. The first of these commissions with a permanent character was the Congregation of the Inquisition, set up by Paul III in 1542. This was followed by others.

In 1588 Sixtus V organized the extant commissions or congregations and established additional bodies. Sixtus's Curia was made up of fifteen congregations, each charged with part of the governance of the church and its holdings. This action is considered the origin of the modern Roman Curia. In addition to the congregations, the Curia contained several other bodies that over time became grouped into the Tribunals of Justice (the Rota Romana, Camera Apostolica, and Signatura Iustitiae), Tribunals of Favor (the Signatura Gratiae, Dataria Apostolica, and Poenitentiaria Apostolica), and Tribunals of Expedition (the Cancellaria Apostolica, Secretaria Brevium, Secretariatus Status, and Segretaria dei Memoriali).

As time passed and the requirements of the church changed, new congregations and other offices were created, and old agencies were abolished (or suppressed, in the language of the church).

The Curia was reformed and reorganized by Pius X in 1908. By this time, the agencies of the curia were grouped into three divisions: congregations (administrative), tribunals (judicial), and offices (ministerial). This guide uses these divisions of 1908 as a way to divide information on the extant historical records of the Curia. A few older agencies, such as the Audientia Litterarum Contradictarum, do not fit neatly into these categories and are placed with Curia offices.

In 1967 the Curia was extensively reformed by Paul VI, into five main divisions: the Secretariat of State, congregations, tribunals, secretariats (ecumenical offices), and offices. John Paul II, in 1988, once again modified the Curia.

Because the reforms of Paul VI and John Paul II will not be reflected in archives available to scholars in the near future, they are not described in this guide.

References. G. Barraclough, *Public Notaries and the Papal Curia: A Calendar and a Study of a Formularium Notariorum Curie from the early years of the Fourteenth Century* (London, 1934). J. F. D'Amico, *Renaissance Humanism in Papal Rome: Humanists and Churchmen on the Eve of the Reformation* (Baltimore, 1991). A. Haine, *Synopsis S.R.E. Cardinalium Congregationum* (Louvain, 1857). R. von Heckel, "Die Organisation der kurialen Behörden und ihr Geschäftsgang," in *Magister Heinrich der Poet in Würzburg und die römische Kurie*, by H. Grauert (Munich, 1912), pp. 206–229, 487–493. K. Jordan, "Die päpstliche Verwaltung im Zeitalter Gregors VII," *Studi Gregoriani per la storia di Gregorio VII e della riforma gregoriana* 1 (1947): 111–135. J. P. Kirsch, "Andreas Sapiti, ein englischer Prokurator an der Kurie im 14. Jahrhundert," *Historisches Jahrbuch* 14 (1893): 582–603. T. M. Ortolan, "Cour romaine," in *Dictionnaire de théologie catholique* (Paris, 1923), vol. 3, cols. 1931–1983. P. Partner, *The Papal State under Martin V: The Administration and Government of the Temporal Power in the Early 15th Century* (London, 1958). P. Prodi, *The Papal Prince: One Body and Two Souls: The Papal Monarchy in Early Modern Europe*, translated by S. Haskins (Cambridge, 1987). N. del Re, *La curia romana: lineamenti storico-giuridici*, 3d ed. (Rome, 1970). G. Stangler, *Matthias Corvinus und die Renaissance in Ungarn 1458–1541* (Vienna, 1982). A. M. Stickler, *Historia iuris canonici latini institutiones academicae*, vol. 1, *Historia fontium* (Turin, 1950).

3.1 CONGREGATIONS

3.1.1 Congregatio Ceremonialis

[DATABASE ID: VATV018-A]

There is some disagreement as to the origin of this congregation. Some trace its origin to the cardinalatial commission appointed by Gregory XIII, as early as 1572, to reform the ceremonies of the papal chapel (that group of official and ceremonial personages attending the pope in certain solemn functions). There is some indication that this commission was absorbed by the new Congregation of Rites and Ceremonies established by Sixtus V with his constitution *Immensa aeterni Dei* (Jan. 22, 1588).

Though documentation is lacking, presumably about 1601 Clement VIII decreed that the Congregation of Ceremonies be a separate department in order to regulate the ceremonies to be observed in the papal chapel and pontifical court. The curial reform of 1908 left the Congregation of Ceremonies relatively untouched. Pius X's constitution *Sapienti consilio* (Jun. 29, 1908) merely reaffirmed its traditional functions. This legislation was included in the Code of Canon Law in 1917.

During its history as a separate congregation, it had authority to regulate all papal ceremonies in the pontifical court (aula) and papal chapel (cappella papale) and functions performed by cardinals outside the pontifical court; to communicate instructions to legates of the Holy See for the proper procedure in transacting affairs of their missions; to instruct newly promoted cardinals on etiquette to be followed in their new position; to settle questions of procedure or protocol among cardinals or ambassadors to the Holy See; and to direct solemn reception by the pope of heads of state, prime ministers, and ambassadors. In 1924 a special commission was annexed to the congregation for handling general protocol and pontifical ceremonies.

In 1967 the Congregation of Ceremonies was suppressed and its functions transferred to the Prefecture of the Apostolic Palace (now the Prefecture of the Pontifical Household).

Reference. E. Dante, *Catalogo dell'Archivio della Prefettura delle Ceremonie Apostoliche* (1956) [this title was noted but not verified by project staff].

RECORDS. No records for this congregation were located.

3.1.2 Congregatio Concilii

[DATABASE ID: VATV011-A]

Shortly after the closing of the Council of Trent on December 4, 1563, Pius IV (1559–1565) appointed a commission of cardinals (Dec. 30, 1563) to ensure the application of the council's disciplinary decrees. With the motu proprio *Alias Nos nonnullas* (Aug. 2, 1564), he formally recognized this commission and established it as a permanent congregation called Congregatio super Executione et Observantia Sacri Concilii Tridentini et Aliarum Reformationum. From the beginning it was commonly known as the Congregatio Concilii.

Pius V (1566–1572) ratified the congregation's functions, extended them to include the interpretation of the conciliar decrees, even in judicial processes, and changed the congregation's name to Congregatio Cardinalium Concilii Tridentini Interpretum (May 1567).

Sixtus V (1585–1590), with the apostolic constitution *Immensa aeterni Dei* (Jan. 22, 1588), confirmed the congregation, defined its functions more clearly, increased its faculties, declared that the interpretation of the Tridentine decrees relating to dogmas of faith was to be reserved to himself while that of disciplinary decrees would be left to the interpretation of this congregation, and formally named it the Congregatio pro Interpretatione et Executione Concilii Tridentini.

Gregory XIV (1590–1591), with the brief *Ut securitati* (Feb. 22, 1591), empowered the congregation to interpret all the disciplinary orders of the Council of Trent, to handle all cases relating to those orders, and to publish their own decrees in the name of the pope. By the end of the sixteenth century the congregation's faculties had increased to include interpretative power, administrative power, judicial power, and beneficent power. This was the high point of the Congregation of the Council.

Because of the almost limitless scope of its original purpose and the ever-changing character of the needs of the church, the function of the Congregation of the Council was constantly revised, usually with increased responsibility. It gradually absorbed four other lesser congregations that, although autonomous by design, operated almost as its subsidiaries. All were suppressed before or by the curial reform of 1908. The four congregations are noted here but their history is presented and records described at their appropriate place in the alphabetical listing among the congregations in this section of the guide.

1. The Congregatio super Residentia Episcoporum was instituted by Urban VIII in 1636 and revitalized by Benedict XIV with the constitution *Ad universae christianae* (Sep. 3, 1746). After suppression in 1908 its functions were transferred to the Consistorial Congregation.

2. The Congregatio Iurisdictionis et Immunitatis Ecclesiasticae, instituted by Urban VIII in 1620, *vivae vocis oraculo* (i.e., issued orally rather than in written form), was eventually united by Leo XIII (1878–1903) to the Congregation of the Council (1879).

3. The Congregatio super Statu Ecclesiarum was established by Benedict XIV with the constitution *Decet Romanum Pontificem* (Nov. 23, 1740). Pius X trans-

ferred its functions to the Consistorial Congregation (constitution *Romanis Pontificibus*, Dec. 17, 1903).

4. The Congregatio super Revisione Synodorum Provincialium was created by Pius IX (1846–1878), *vivae vocis oraculo* (Jun. 3, 1849).

Under the reorganization of the Curia by Pius X, with the constitution *Sapienti consilio* (Jun. 29, 1908), the transformation of the Congregation of the Council was so complete that its original purpose was scarcely discernible, and its title had only historical significance. The reorganization also united to the Congregation of the Council the Congregatio Lauretana, but the latter was quietly suppressed in 1917.

The functions assigned to this congregation varied over time. From the beginning (1564), the Congregation of the Council was charged with caring for the practical implementation of the disciplinary decrees of the Council of Trent. This was followed by interpretation of the decrees (1567). Then it was charged with examining the decrees of the provincial councils. The congregation also had the responsibility for examining the reports of the state of the dioceses, which the bishops presented to the Holy See on the occasion of their ad limina visits. The congregation would respond to their questions and needs and would watch vigilantly over the discipline of the clergy and the faithful (1600).

Since the conciliar decrees touched almost every ecclesiastical discipline, the congregation was obliged before long to be concerned with the rights and duties of bishops, priests, chapters, benefices, ecclesiastical goods, Mass stipends, matrimonial cases, and other affairs, and with granting dispensations, indults, and privileges. Pius X changed all this with his curial reform of 1908.

The Congregation of the Council no longer had authority to legislate or to render judgment on questions relating to the sacraments; could no longer issue decrees regarding the validity of marriage or of ordination; nor issue decrees on daily communion. These were now in the hands of the Congregatio de Disciplina Sacramentorum. The Congregation of the Council was no longer to be concerned with the duties of bishops or with the reports (relatio status) given by them. *Sapienti consilio* assigned these to the Congregatio Consistorialis. The Congregatio Negotiis Religiosorum Sodalium Praeposita would pronounce on the validity or invalidity of religious profession. The Congregation of the Council would no longer have jurisdiction to try cases by judicial process; these cases were to be handed over to the tribunal of the Rota Romana.

Sapienti consilio (Jun. 29, 1908) charged the Congregation of the Council with the entire discipline of the secular clergy and the faithful of the Latin rite. It gave it the task of fostering observance of the commandments of Christian life and the precepts of the church, exclusive authority in matters pertaining to the duties of parish priests and canons, and authority to dispense in appointments reserved to bishops.

It was empowered to govern all pious sodalities (except Third Orders, secular institutes, and Catholic Action associations); to handle administration and alienation of church property, all cases involving pious legacies, Mass stipends, diocesan taxes, immunities, and precedence (except for rights of the Congregatio Ceremonialis and the Congregatio Negotiis Religiosorum Sodalium Praeposita). It was charged with regulating the holding of plenary and provincial councils and meetings of bishops as well as approving their decrees and pronouncements except in countries subject to the Congregation for the Propagation of the Faith.

Pius XI's motu proprio *Orbem catholicum* (Jun. 29, 1923) established two special offices attached to the Congregation of the Council: Pastoral Activity and Catechesis, and Administration of Ecclesiastical Property.

Paul VI's constitution *Regimini Ecclesiae universae* (Aug. 15, 1967) completely reorganized the Congregation of the Council, giving it the new name Congregatio pro Clericis and defining it as having authority over all matters affecting clergy who exercise their apostolate in a diocese as well as over their pastoral ministry and functions. In 1973 Paul VI annexed the International Office for Catechetics to the Congregation for the Clergy. In 1988 John Paul II added to it the Pontifical Commission for the Preservation of the Artistic and Historic Patrimony of the Church.

In general, much of what one finds in the various series of the congregation consists of decrees, deliberations, and supporting material concerning problematical cases (positiones). In addition, as the records reflect, the congregation undertook (1) the examination of reports of diocesan synods; (2) the soliciting and review of episcopal diocesan visits (relationes ad limina); (3) the enforcement of episcopal residence; (4) clerical reform; (5) review of issues concerning worship and the administration of the sacraments; (6) surveillance of popular piety, morality, and religious rebelliousness; and (7) decisions and dispensations involving marriage disputes. The concerns of the Congregation of the Council extended into almost all aspects of religious, social, and family life. The records of the synods and the relationes ad limina are especially useful to historians of art, popular piety, and social life. The abundance of material relative to marriage offers promising sources to historians of family life, economics, and gender relations.

Note: The Congregation for the Clergy maintains its own archives located in Rome (address: Piazza Pio XII 3, 00193 Rome). These archives were not examined by the project staff.

In addition to the records listed below, series listed with other agencies relate directly to this agency and should be consulted. See Miscellaneous official series

Miscellaneorum armarium X and *Miscellaneorum armarium* XIII.

References. For a general introduction to the historical records of this congregation, see W. Henkel, "Das Inventar des 'Fondo Concili' im Archiv der Konzilskongregation," *Annuarium Historiae Conciliorum* 15 (1983): 430–451. There is a geographic index to the *Fondo Concili* volumes discussed by Henkel at the end of this article.

La sacra Congregazione del Concilio: Quarto centenario della fondazione, 1564–1964, studi e ricerche (Vatican City, 1964) has several articles that are relevant, including F. Chiappa-Freddo, "L'Archivio della Sacra Congregazione del Concilio," pp. 395–422; R. Creytens, "La giurisprudenza della S.C. del Concilio nella questione della clausura delle monache (1564–1576)," pp. 563–597; C. Lefebvre, "La S. Congrégation du Concile et le Tribunal de la S. Rote Romaine à la fin du XVI siècle," pp. 163–177; G. Palazzini, "I poteri straordinari" [pagination not verified by project staff]; G. Papa, "Il cardinale Antonio Carafa, prefetto della S. Congregazione del Concilio," pp. 384–392; N. del Re, "I cardinali prefetti della S. C. del Concilio dalle origini ad oggi (1564–1964)," pp. 265–307; F. Romita, "Le origini della S.C. del Concilio," pp. 13–50; C. Varsanyi, "De competentia et procedura S.C. Concilii ab origine ad haec usque nostra tempora," pp. 51–161.

P. Caiazza, "L'archivio storico della Sacra Congregazione del Concilio: Primi appunti per un problema di riordinamento," *Ricerche di storia sociale e religiosa* 42 (1992): 7–24. Catholic Church, Congregatio Concilii, *Thesaurus resolutionum Sacrae Congregationis Concilii* (Rome, 1739–1963). A. Hackenberg, "Zu den ersten Verhandlugen der S. Congregatio Cardinalium Concilii Tridentini Interpretum (1564–1568)," in *Festschrift zum elfhundertjahrigen Jubiläum des Deutschen Campo Santo in Rom* (Freiburg, 1897) [this title was noted but not verified by project staff]. C. Monson, *Disembodied Voices: Music and Culture in an Early Modern Italian Convent* (Berkeley, 1995). P. Palazzini, "L'atto di consegna dell'Archivio della S. Congregazione del Concilio nella 1626 tra i due segretari: Fagnani e Paolucci," in *Miscellanea Antonio Piolanti* (Rome, 1963), vol. 2, pp. 239–257. G. Poggiani, *Julii Pogiani Sunensis: Epistolae et orationes*, edited by A. M. Graziani (Rome, 1756–1762). P. Prodi, *Il cardinale Gabriele Paleotti (1522–1597)* (Rome, 1959–1967). R. Robres Lluch and V. Castell Maiques, "La visita 'ad limina' durante el Pontificado de Sixto V (1585–1590): Datos para una estadística general: Su complimiento en Iberoamerica," *Anthologica annua* 7 (1959): 147–213. V. Rodrigues Valencia, "La diócesis de Buenos Aires y la Santa Sede en los últimos años del patronato español," *Anthologica annua* 9 (1961): 817–833. S. Tromp, "De manuscriptis acta et declarationes antiquas S. Congregationis Concilii Tridentini continentibus," *Gregorianum* 38 (1957): 481–502; 39 (1958): 93–129.

RECORDS. Records of the congregation consist of the following series.

3.1.2.1 Archivio segreto: Varia

[DATABASE ID: VATV10088-A]

Inclusive Dates: 1700–1890.

Bulk: 1 linear m. (11 bundles).

Organization: Chronological by case.

Scope: These are incoming correspondence from dioceses regarding nominations for offices, territorial questions, and the like.

Location: Archivio Segreto Vaticano.

3.1.2.2 Concilia provincialia

[DATABASE ID: VATV40038-A]

Inclusive Dates: 1564–1961.

Bulk: 12.5 linear m. (104 scatole).

Organization: Alphabetical by place.

Reference: Pásztor (1970), p. 154.

Finding Aids: ASV indice 1173, pp. 27–38, provides an index to the series noting the geographical locations covered by each scatola, the nature of the documentation, and some indication of the date of the material.

Note: Vols. 1, 3–6, 8–9, 11–15, 17–19, 21, 23–25, 27–31, 33–34, 36, 39–40, 43–47, 52–53, 54A, 55, 55 II, 57–60, 62–66, 69–70, 72–78, 81–89, 91–100, 101 I, 101 II, and 104 are available on microfilm. ASV indice 1173, appendix not paginated, indicates which scatole in this series have been filmed.

Location: Archivio Segreto Vaticano

3.1.2.3 De regularibus non alienandis

[DATABASE ID: VATV10293-A]

Inclusive Dates: 1610–1660.

Bulk: 2 linear m.

Scope: These documents appear to be correspondence to the Congregatio Concilii, perhaps supplications.

Location: Archivio Segreto Vaticano.

3.1.2.4 [Decizione, suppliche]

[DATABASE ID: VATV10195-A]

Inclusive Dates: 1713–1870.

Bulk: 3 linear m.

Organization: Buste are numbered 21 and 28–52. Nos. 28–52 are chronological, 1713–1870. No. 21 is for the year 1853.

Scope: These appear to be printed and written requests to the congregation as well as printed decisions of the congregation.

Note: This series was transferred from the Archivio di Stato di Roma in 1920. The title for the series was assigned by the project staff. There is no official ASV designation for the series.

Location: Archivio Segreto Vaticano.

3.1.2.5 Libri decretorum

[DATABASE ID: VATV40039-A]

Inclusive Dates: 1573–1805.

Bulk: 29.5 linear m. (292 vols.).

Organization: Chronological. The series as described contains 267 numbered volumes. However, 25 numbers are divided (A and B) into two actual volumes. There are therefore 292 actual volumes.

References: Pásztor (1970), p. 150. G. Palazzini, "I poteri straordinari," in *La sacra Congregazione del Concilio: Quarto centenario della fondazione, 1564–1964, studi e ricerche* (Vatican City, 1964) [this title was noted but not verified by project staff]. S. Pallottini, *Collectio Omnium Conclusionum ed Resolutionum quae in Causis Propositis apud Sacram Congregationem Cardinalium S. Concilii Tridentini Interpretum Prodierunt, ab eius Institutione Anno MDLXIV ad Annum MDCCCLX* (Rome, 1867–1893). G. Papa, "Il cardinale Antonio Carafa, prefetto della S. Congregazione del Concilio," in *La sacra Congregazione del Concilio: Quarto centenario della fondazione, 1564–1964, studi e ricerche,* 384–392 (Vatican City, 1964).

Finding Aids: ASV indice 1173, pp. 14–24, lists each volume in the series with inclusive dates, number of fogli in the volume, and the presence and completeness of any index in the volume.

Note: Vols. 1–67 (1573–1717) are available on microfilm. ASV indice 1173, appendix not paginated, indicates what has been filmed.

Location: Archivio Segreto Vaticano.

3.1.2.6 Libri litterarum
[DATABASE ID: VATV40040-A]
Inclusive Dates: 1564–1903.
Bulk: 2.8 linear m. (40 vols. or buste).
Organization: Chronological.
Scope: Volume 28 of this series contains records of the Congregazione dei Seminari, which was instituted by Benedict XIII.
References: Pásztor (1970), p. 151. A. Parisella, "Liber Litterarum—Sacrae Congregationis Concilii," in *La sacra Congregazione del Concilio: Quarto centenario della fondazione, 1564–1964, studi e ricerche* (Vatican City, 1964), pp. 451–476.
Finding Aids: ASV indice 1173, pp. 12–14, lists each volume/busta in the series. It notes the number of fogli in each and whether an index exists for the volume/busta and the degree to which the index is complete. Among the series listed for the Congregatio Concilii is *Parva regesta varia*. Within that series is one volume, Parvum regestum S. Congregationis super seminariis (1727–1735), that pertains to this series.
Note: Vols. 1–25 (1564–1720) are available on microfilm. ASV indice 1173, appendix not paginated, indicates what has been filmed.
Location: Archivio Segreto Vaticano.

3.1.2.7 Libri litterarum visitationum sacrorum liminum
[DATABASE ID: VATV40041-A]
Inclusive Dates: 1587–1881.
Bulk: 3.5 linear m. (48 vols.).
Organization: Chronological, though some volumes overlap in years.
References: Pásztor (1970), p. 153. H. Crovella, "De Libro Visitationum Sacrorum Liminum," in *La sacra Congregazione del Concilio: Quarto centenario della fondazione (1564–1964), studi e ricerche* (Vatican City, 1964), pp. 423–446.
Finding Aids: ASV indice 1173, pp. 24–26, lists each vol-

ume and provides inclusive dates, the number of fogli, and an indication of the presence and completeness of an index in each volume.

Among the series listed for the Congregatio Concilii are the *Parva regesta delle VV.WW.LL.* Within that series the Riposte, 1744–1885 (4 vols.) serve as an index to this series. The Riposte are located in the index room of the ASV.

Location: Archivio Segreto Vaticano.

3.1.2.8 Miscellanea
[DATABASE ID: VATV40042-A]
Inclusive Dates: 1340 (copy)–1801.
Bulk: 1.5 linear m. (31 vols. or buste).
Organization: This series is divided into three main groupings: Codices externi; —Codices de Immunitate ecclesiastica; —Codices varii.
Finding Aids: ASV indice 1173, pp. 39–40, provide a listing of each volume with some indication of the content and inclusive dates of the material.
Location: Archivio Segreto Vaticano.

3.1.2.9 [Miscellanea: Buste, scatole e volumi]
[DATABASE ID: VATV10289-A]
Inclusive Dates: 1574–1930.
Bulk: 38 linear m.
Organization: Among the material in this series are: Archivum: Varia (Antigua/alfabetica), 1574–1874; —Plurium diocesium de Taxis Cancell., 1651; —Thesaurus alphabetice; —Archivum: Cause per summaria precum, 1862–1918; —Archivum: Lauretana, ca. 1856–1908; —Archivum facoltà a stampa (fuori protocolli); —Archivum: Tasse di curia; —Archivum: Conferenza regionali; —Archivum: Causae; —Registro delle patenti Loreto, 1840–1904; —"Ordenaciones y Aranzelde la reformacion del Tribunal de la Nunciatura de España," 1611; —Avvocati, ca. 1892–1907; —Cause; —Litterae visitationum SS. Liminum, 1836–1848; —Ristretti delle relazioni dei vescovi, 1775–1785. 3 vols. (a–z); —Prelatura Bussa, Instituta dalla Bona Memoria Mons. Giovanni Battista Bussi, ca. 1735–1798; —Nulliatus matrimonii, ca. 1738–1884; —Resoconti amministrazioni, 1863–1908; —Ricevute dell'amministrazione dei beni della Santa Sede; —Spese; —[2 series post-1922].
Note: This is a true miscellany with no official ASV designation. The title was assigned by the project staff.
Scope: Nulliatus matrimonii includes the 1818 nullification of the marriage of Louis Bonaparte and Hortense de Beauharnais (in buste on one side of the aisle and in boxes formerly marked "Carte Sciolte" on the other).
Location: Archivio Segreto Vaticano.

3.1.2.10 [Miscellanea: Volumi]
[DATABASE ID: VATV10288-A]
Inclusive Dates: 1565–1730.
Bulk: 3 linear m.
Organization: Volume contents designations include: Processus di Busato, ca. 1700, 2 vols.; —Malta, 1701–1704, 1 vol.; —Religiosi, 1726, 1 vol.; —de Celebratione Missae; —de Reform, 1660, 1 vol.; —de Conservatoribus, 1660, 1 vol.; —Liber informationum, 1587, 1 vol.; —Processus, Borgo St. Domini, 1615, 1 vol.; —Processus informationis, 1574; —Processus (misc.), ca. 1662–1730; —Processus (Aquilan.),

1721, 1 vol.; —Gratia scritte della S.C. Concilio, 1696–1710, 1 vol.; —Iurisdictionis, 1565–1587, 1 vol.; —Seraphini liber, 1 vol.; —Tract. di Election., 1 vol.

Note: This is a true miscellany with no official ASV designation. The title was assigned by the project staff.

Scope: This series includes printed processus and some information on monasteries.

Location: Archivio Segreto Vaticano.

3.1.2.11 Parva regesta delle positiones
[DATABASE ID: VATV40043-A]
Inclusive Dates: 1668–1847.
Bulk: 11 linear m. (156 vols.).
Organization: Chronological. There are three volumes for 109.
Finding Aids: ASV indice 1173, pp. 2–6, gives a list of each volume and inclusive dates.
Note: These registers are located in the index room of the ASV.
Location: Archivio Segreto Vaticano.

3.1.2.12 Parva regesta delle VV.SS.LL.
[DATABASE ID: VATV40044-A]
Inclusive Dates: 1709–1885.
Bulk: .75 linear m. (16 vols.).
Organization: This series divides into three subseries: Attestati, 1709–1874 (10 vols.); —Riposte, 1744–1885 (4 vols.); —Risposte nullius, 1742–1863 (2 vols.).
Finding Aids: ASV indice 1173, p. 6, provides a list of each volume with inclusive dates.
Note: These registers are located in the index room of the ASV.
Location: Archivio Segreto Vaticano.

3.1.2.13 Parva regesta varia
[DATABASE ID: VATV40045-A]
Inclusive Dates: 1646.
Bulk: .5 linear m. (13 vols.).
Organization: This is a miscellany of material and includes: Parvum regestum archivi secreti, 1828–1869 (1 vol.); —Regestum appellationum, 1646–1674 (1 vol.); —Vacchette dei memoriali, 1737–1755 (2 vols.); —Regestum "Nihil transeat," 1815–1864 (1 vol.); —Vacchetta dei fogli di udienza, 1739 (1 vol.); —Regestum super resignatione beneficiorum, 1732–1734, (1 vol.); —Parvum regestum S. Congregationis super seminariis, 1727–1735 (1 vol.); —Parva regesta decretorum S. Congregationis super residentia episcoporum, 1708–1843 (5 vols.).
Finding Aids: ASV indice 1173, pp. 6–7, contains a listing for each volume in the series with inclusive dates.
Note: These registers are located in the index room of the ASV.
Location: Archivio Segreto Vaticano.

3.1.2.14 Positiones
[DATABASE ID: VATV10211-A]
Inclusive Dates: 1564–1922.
Bulk: 788 linear m. (3096 vols. and buste.).
Organization: Volumes are numbered 1–271 (1564–1677) and organized by the sessio and caput numbers as topics were divided in the Council of Trent.

A second numbering system, no. 1–2255, spans 1678–1911. Volumes in this section are initially organized chronologically by the date of the meeting (1678–1822). From 1823–1911, the series remains chronological but materials of each meeting are organized alphabetically by diocese.

References: Pásztor (1970), pp. 149–150; Pásztor (1983), pp. 170–171.

Scope: This very large series is composed mainly of records generated by the meetings of the congregation and includes reports received.

Finding Aids: ASV Indici 910–924, "Fondo Storico della S. Congregazione del Concilio-Positiones: Rilevazione," by Dom Domenico Troiani, F.D.P., is a detailed index to the first seventy-five volumes in the first section. These indici proceed page by page in each volume, copying at least the name of the diocese under consideration and sometimes a lengthy excerpt of the particular position. At the end of the reiteration of each volume, there is an alphabetical index to all dioceses and the like in that volume. At the end of each index volume there is a general index to places, dioceses, religious orders, congregations, and monasteries in that particular index volume. This index leads you to the annotated entry in the index, which leads you back to the original volume.

ASV Indice 1173 (pp. 41–55) lists each volume of the *Positiones* with inclusive dates 1912–1922.

The *Protocolli* and *Rubricelle* series listed among the series of the Congregatio Concilii are located in the index room of the ASV and serve as an index to the *Positiones.* The protocollo provides the diocese from which a request was made, the date, name of the petitioner, dispatch of the request, and a sense of the resolution. The form of the protocolli is consistent from 1847 to 1916. They are organized by number. The rubricelle provide an alphabetical index to the protocolli.

For the period 1668 to 1847, the series *Regestum parvum decretorum* is useful. They are alphabetical indexes to the Positiones with a brief indication of the matter of the request. After 1847 the function was taken over by the *Rubricelle.* The first six volumes of this series (1668–1681) are chronological. Sometime during 1681 the system was changed to be alphabetical.

Pásztor notes that in the series *Parva regesta varia,* two volumes are useful as indexes to select portions of the *Positiones:* Regestum "Nihil transeat" (1815–1864) and Vacchetta dei fogli di udienza (1739).

P. Caiazza, "L'archivio storico della Sacra Congregazione del Concilio: Primi appunti per un problema di riordinamento," *Ricerche di storia sociale e religiosa* 42 (1992): 7–24. Caiazza provides a good overall introduction to the archives of the entire Congregazione del Concilio, both in the ASV and at the Congregation per il Clero. He also provides a brief "Indice topografico del fondo."

There appear to be no internal indexes within the individual buste.

Location: Archivio Segreto Vaticano.

3.1.2.15 Positiones: Archivi secreti
[DATABASE ID: VATV10083-A]
Inclusive Dates: 1814–1900.
Bulk: 9 linear m.
Organization: Two series: Chronological, 1814–1857, 25 vols.; —Alphabetical, then semi-chronological, with cases grouped together, 60 vols.

Scope: Incoming letters.

Reference: Pásztor (1970), p. 154 (referred to by Pásztor as *Archivum secretum* or *S.C. Concilii Positiones Archivi Secreti*).

Finding Aids: Listed among the series for the Congregatio Concilii is the series *Parva regesta varia*. One volume in that series, Parvum regestum archivi secreti, 1826–1869, serves as an index to this series. The volume is located in the Index Room of the ASV.

Location: Archivio Segreto Vaticano.

3.1.2.16 Positiones et resolutiones ad dubia

[DATABASE ID: VATV10291-A]

Inclusive Dates: 1650–1667.

Bulk: 1 linear m. (11 vols.)

Organization: Volumes numbered 2–12 originally part of the Archivio SS. Giovanni e Paolo.

Reference: Pásztor (1970), p. 148 (footnote 2).

Location: Archivio Segreto Vaticano.

3.1.2.17 Protocolli

[DATABASE ID: VATV40046-A]

Inclusive Dates: 1833–1922.

Bulk: 6 linear m. (86 vols.).

Organization: Chronological.

Scope: These index the Congregatio Concilii series *Positiones*.

Finding Aids: ASV index 1173, pp. 8–10, lists each volume by date and its corresponding volume in the series *Rubricelle*. The ten *Protocolli* volumes 1833–1846 are brief descriptions of correspondence and are not as useful as the later volumes.

Note: These registers are located in the index room of the ASV.

Location: Archivio Segreto Vaticano.

3.1.2.18 Regesta litterarum super residentia episcoporum

[DATABASE ID: VATV40047-A]

Inclusive Dates: 1635–1908.

Bulk: .4 linear m. (6 vols.).

Organization: Chronological.

Reference: Pásztor (1970), p. 155.

Finding Aids: ASV indice 1173, p. 27, lists each volume and provides inclusive dates and number of fogli. None of these volumes has an internal index.

Among the series listed for the Congregatio Concilii is the *Parva regesta varia*. Among those regesta is the subseries Parva regesta decretorum S. Congregationis super Residentia Episcoporum, 1708–1843 (5 vols.), which serves as an index to the *Regesta litterarum super residentia episcoporum*.

Note: These five volumes are located in the index room of the ASV.

Location: Archivio Segreto Vaticano.

3.1.2.19 Relationes: Visita ad limina

[DATABASE ID: VATV10089-A]

Inclusive Dates: 1588–1901.

Bulk: 118 linear m. (894 numbered vols.).

Organization: These are alphabetical by diocese (and sometimes by country) and chronological within each diocese.

Scope: These appear to be incoming correspondence and reports concerning ad limina visits. The kind of information found in these reports includes: geographical information, descriptions, size of towns and parishes, annual income of diocese or churches, benefices, dedication of churches, physical condition of churches, conditions of seminaries, monasteries of nuns and monks. There is sometimes discussion of the bishop's role in the governance of various institutions. The series has some unexpected additions including correspondence from China (originally addressed to the Propaganda Fide) dating between 1611 and 1808. There is a U.S. diocese listed here (Pittsburgh) as well as many Latin American dioceses.

Note: Vols. 3, 8, 16, 34, 40A–B, 50–51, 66, 70A–B, 104, 118, 124, 136A, 137, 138, 141, 156, 168A–B, 176A–B, 178A–B, 187A, 193A–B, 203, 215, 243A–B, 245A–C, 251A–B, 252, 258A–B, 287 (part), 307, 310B, 311, 321, 352, 354, 367, 375A, 376, 395, 402, 410, 434A, 448, 454, 456A–B, 457,465A, 509A–B, 517A–B, 570A–B, 579–580, 581A–B, 580, 592, 595, 611A–B, 618A–C, 645B (part), 645C, 656, 728, 743A, 751, 756, 771A–B, 797A, 799, 810A–B, 814, 819A, 820A–B, 832A–B, 842–843, 847, 851A, and 891 are available on microfilm.

References: Pásztor (1970), pp. 151–152; Pásztor (1983), p. 173; Boyle, p. 86. Pásztor and Boyle refer to this series as *Relationes diocesium*. Its full title is *Archivio Segreto del Vaticano, Archivio della Sacra Congregazione del Concilio, Relazioni dei vescovi dopo le visite ad limina: Venezia* [this title was noted but not verified by project staff].

P. Rabikauskas, *Relationes status dioecesium in magno ducatu Lithuanie* (Rome, 1971–1978). This work provides Latin transcriptions of documents from the Vatican Archives, including the *Relationes: Visita ad limina*, and the Propaganda Fide Archives, with analytic biographical and bibliographical notes (particularly to other transcriptions) and notes of the volume and folio numbers, when appropriate. There is a note indicating if the document is an original or a copy, and there are cross-references to the ASV and APF archives when documents appear in both places. Transcribed documents can be found in this series under Vilnensis, Samogitien, and Mednicensis.

Finding Aids: ASV Indice 1140 briefly identifies which dioceses (and occasionally countries) are represented in each volume. The names of dioceses are in Latin and Italian.

Among the series listed for the Congregatio Concilii, two subseries of the *Parvum regesta delle VV.SS.LL.* contain indexes to the *Relationes*: the Attestati, 1709–1874 (9 vols.), are alphabetical by diocese; the Riposte nullius, 1742–1863 (2 vols.), are very brief and similar to the Attestati. These subseries are located in the Index Room of the ASV.

Location: Archivio Segreto Vaticano.

3.1.2.20 Rubricelle

[DATABASE ID: VATV40048-A]

Inclusive Dates: 1847–1922.

Bulk: 2 linear m. (66 vols.).

Organization: Chronological.

Scope: These index the Congregatio Concilii series *Positiones*.

Finding Aids: ASV index 1173, pp. 8–10, lists each volume by date and indicates its corresponding volume in the protocolli series.

Note: These rubricelle are located in the index room of the ASV.

Location: Archivio Segreto Vaticano.

3.1.2.21 [Supplicationes]
[DATABASE ID: VATV10290-A]

Inclusive Dates: 1664–ca. 1801.

Bulk: 27 linear m. (127 buste).

Scope: These are supplications for prebends, indulta (to get benefices), and even at the end of no. 125 a "Nulliatus professionis."

Note: This series has no official ASV designation. The title was supplied by project staff.

Location: Archivio Segreto Vaticano.

3.1.2.22 Synopsis resolutionum
[DATABASE ID: VATV40049-A]

Inclusive Dates: [17—]–[17—].

Bulk: .3 linear m. (5 vols.).

Organization: There are three subseries: Synopsis variarum resolutionum e selectioribus decretis S. Congregationis collecta per materias ordine alfabetico disposita a R. P. fratre Thoma de Villanova a S. Nicolao Carmelita Discalceato (2 vols., alphabetical); —a second copy of the preceding synopsis (2 vols., alphabetical); —a third copy of the synopsis that includes decreti from the Sacred Congregation of the Council 1722–1764 (this was in two volumes but only the first volume survived and is dated 1639–1722).

Finding Aids: ASV index 1173, pp. 7–8, lists each volume in the series.

Note: These volumes are located in the index room of the ASV.

Location: Archivio Segreto Vaticano.

3.1.2.23 Visite apostoliche
[DATABASE ID: VATV10157-A]

Inclusive Dates: 1571–1803.

Bulk: 7 linear m. (120 vols.).

Organization: Chronological except vols. 119 (Grosseto, 1576) and 120 (Ljubljana, Slovenia, 1620), which are out of chronological order.

Scope: This series consists primarily of visits within the Papal States with the exception of Ljubljana, Slovenia, found in the final volume.

Note: Vols. 16, 45, 72, 82, 89, 91, 92–93, 104, and 106 are available on microfilm.

References: Boyle, p. 86; Pásztor (1970), p. 153. (This series is referred to by Boyle and Pásztor as *Visitationes apostolicae.*)

Finding Aids: ASV Indice 1154, by Giuseppina Roselli, provides a volume-by-volume listing of this series, with the year and date of the visit, the visitor, often the notary, occasionally the deputy visitor, and perhaps a note concerning a brief resulting from the visit or an annotated list of other documents in the file. Indice 1154 also contains three useful appendices: (1) an index to names and places, (2) a chronological list of visits, and (3) an alphabetical list of places with inclusive dates and the volume number.

A series of ASV prospetti indici in a folder entitled "Visite apostoliche: Vescovi e Regolari e Concilio" are available on request at the desk in the main ASV reading room. This is not a formal ASV index and must be used in consultation with a member of the ASV staff. These prospetti indici include a "C" Prospetto numerico to the *Visite apostoliche* (which is completely superseded by Roselli's Indice 1154) that provides a numerical index to the Vescovi e Regolari, *Visite* 1–17, indicating

the current volume number, the location visited, and the year of the visit. There are two other prospetti: "A" Prospetto cronologico and "B" Prospetto alfabetico. These chronological and alphabetical prospetti provide integrated lists of apostolic visits from Congregatio Vescovi e Regolari series *Visite apostoliche,* Congregatio Concilii series *Visite apostoliche* (this series), and Congregatio Visitationis Apostolicae series *Visite apostoliche.* Visits in the Congregatio Concilii series are identified by a C and the busta number.

Location: Archivio Segreto Vaticano.

3.1.2.24 Vota
[DATABASE ID: VATV10292-A]

Inclusive Dates: 1675–1694.

Bulk: .5 linear m. (9 vols.).

Organization: Chronological.

Reference: Pásztor (1970), p. 148 (footnote 2).

Location: Archivio Segreto Vaticano.

3.1.3 Congregatio Consistorialis
[DATABASE ID: VATV003-A]

This congregation derives its name from the Consistory, or College of Cardinals, since its chief duty has been to prepare matters, by examination and discussion, for the Consistory.

Among the congregations founded by the constitution *Immensa aeterni Dei* (Jan. 22, 1588), Sixtus V gave third place to the Congregatio pro Erectione Ecclesiarum et Provisionibus Consistorialibus. The congregation was charged with preparing acts requiring decision for the formal approval of the cardinals. A second task assigned to it was transacting all business that related to the governance of the dioceses not under the Congregation of the Propagation of the Faith. Its name was changed twice almost immediately, first to Congregatio Rebus Consistorialibus Praeposita, and then more simply to Congregatio Consistorialis.

Gregory XIV (constitution *Onus apostolicae servitutis,* May 15, 1591) specifically charged the congregation with handling the informative process on the moral and intellectual qualifications of candidates for vacant episcopal sees and bringing the results of the individual inquiries before the commission of cardinals, leaving it to the pope to pronounce on the matters definitively. Shortly after the death of its founder, the Consistorial Congregation began to decline in importance as many of its original functions were assigned to other departments.

The Congregatio Examinis Episcoporum was established by Clement VIII in 1592 with the task of defining and researching the qualifications of candidates for episcopal sees.

The Congregatio super Residentia Episcoporum was established by Urban VIII in 1636 to regulate the residency of bishops for their pastoral work.

Innocent XI (1676–1689) instituted the Congregazione sopra l'Elezione dei Vescovi, which, after various modifications, fell into disuse. The congregation was reestablished by Benedict XIV (constitution *Ad apostolicae servitutis*, Oct. 17, 1740) under the name Congregatio Particularis super Promovendis ad Archiepiscopatus et Episcopatus, absorbing all the functions assigned to Clement VIII's earlier Congregatio Examinis Episcoporum; it was reactivated for the third time by Leo XIII's constitution *Immortalis memoriae* (Sep. 21, 1878), which conferred on it the same functions but limited its task to the appointment of bishops for the dioceses of Italy. In 1900 it assumed the name Commissio Cardinalitia de Eligendis Episcopis Italiae, but was suppressed by Pius X in 1903.

The Congregatio Extraordinaria Praeposita Negotiis Ecclesiasticis Orbis Catholici (constitution, Pius VII, Jun. 18, 1814) had already assumed the appointment of bishops for episcopal sees outside of Italy and in missionary territory. Thus it was inevitable that the original congregation would fall into disuse with the passage of time.

The successive institution of these similar congregations had absorbed every function that had originally been given to the Consistorial Congregation. There remained for it no other task, in definition, than that of receiving the names of bishops-designate, preparing their acts for the secret Consistory, and examining requests for the imposition of the pallium and some purely honorary privileges.

Pius X's apostolic letter *Romanis Pontificibus* (Dec. 17, 1903) stated that henceforth the procedure for electing bishops for all countries, except those subject to the Congregation for the Propagation of the Faith, or to the Congregation for Extraordinary Ecclesiastical Affairs, or where the election of bishops was regulated by constitutions or concordats, should be transacted by the Congregation of the Holy Office, not only for Italy, but for other countries as well. The same document suppressed Leo XIII's congregation of 1878 and transferred its functions to the Congregation of the Holy Office, giving it exclusive authority over everything relating to the development and promotion of bishops.

Pius X's motu proprio *Sacrae Congregationi* (May 26, 1906) suppressed the Congregatio super Disciplina Regulari and the Congregatio de Statu Regularium Ordinum. The latter had been reestablished by Pius IX in 1847. Its faculties were later transferred to the Congregation of Bishops and Regulars. With the suppression of that congregation on November 3, 1908, these functions were again transferred to the Consistorial Congregation.

With the reorganization of the Roman Curia by Pius X's *Sapienti consilio* (Jun. 29, 1908), the appointment of bishops was returned to the original congregation that was now formally named the Consistorial Congregation; responsibility for diocesan government was also re-turned to it. Pius X's reform of 1908 also transferred the functions of the Congregatio super Statu Ecclesiarum to the Consistorial Congregation.

The actual authority of the Consistorial Congregation is identical in substance with that stated in its original objectives: bishops and dioceses. It is clear that the original document intended to give to the congregation complete authority over all that related to a diocese as a juridical institution, including its establishment and conservation. Thus, the power of electing bishops, and of controlling the seminaries so intimately connected with the future of the dioceses, would rest with this congregation.

This authority included supervision of bishops in regard to the fulfillment of their duties, review of bishops' reports on the state of their churches, announcements of apostolic visitations, review of those previously made, and, with the approval of the pope, prescription of necessary or opportune remedies. The congregation also issued invitations to bishops to assist at solemn canonizations or other solemn pontifical ceremonies. It also took on the supervision of all that concerned government, discipline, temporal administration, and studies in seminaries. The congregation was given the power to settle whatever doubts might arise regarding the authority of each of the Roman Congregations.

With *Cum omnes catholicos* (Aug. 15, 1912), Pius X entrusted to the Consistorial Congregation spiritual assistance to emigrants. However, the care of seminaries, which *Sapienti consilio* had assigned to it in 1908 as an integral part of diocesan government, was taken from it by Benedict XV's motu proprio *Seminaria clericorum* (Nov. 4, 1915).

In 1942 Pius XII formally placed the Society of the Apostolate of the Sea under the direction of this congregation; his constitution *Exsul familia* (Aug. 1, 1952) gave it responsibility for the spiritual care of emigrants belonging to the Latin rite; Paul VI's motu proprio *Pastoralis migratorum cura* (Aug. 15, 1969) expanded these responsibilities. Paul VI's apostolic constitution *Regimini Ecclesiae universae* (Aug. 15, 1967) changed the name of the congregation to Congregatio pro Episcopis, extended its authority to cover all matters relating to the holding of particular councils and those relating to episcopal conferences except in places subject to the Congregation for the Eastern Churches and the Congregation for the Evangelization of the Nations (Propaganda Fide). It also formally attached to the congregation the commissions for emigration, for the apostolate of the sea, of the air, and of nomads.

NOTE ON THE RECORDS OF THE CONGREGATIO CONSISTORIALIS

In their regular meetings the College of Cardinals, together with the pope, considered important issues of diplomacy, policy, protocol, self regulation, patronage, canonization, and cult. In consistory also major ecclesiastical benefices were conferred. In the sixteenth century, when consistory records become more numerous, the consistory met every week or ten days. Accounts and diaries of consistory meetings, both those kept for official and for private purposes, together with other records pertaining to consistory business, are not concentrated in a single place, but can be found in various series of the ASV, in the manuscript collection of the BAV, and elsewhere. G. Gualdo, in his *Sussidi per la consultazione dell'Archivio Vaticano*, new ed. (Vatican City, 1989), provides the best overview of the records of the archives of the Congregatio Consistorialis together with valuable information about the location of consistory material in other places.

Records of the consistories are located principally in three Congregatio Consistorialis series: the *Acta camerarii*, kept under the direction of the camerarius; the *Acta vicecancellarii*, kept under the aegis of the vicecancellarius; and the *Acta miscellanea*. For the early sixteenth century there are some gaps, but from volume 2 of the *Acta camerarii* they are complete and increasingly clear and informative. Barbara Hallman notes that the *Acta camerarii* and the *Acta vicecancellarii* record the same consistories with slightly different perceptions of the events (*Italian Cardinals, Reform, and the Church as Property* [Berkeley, 1985], p. 4).

L. Pásztor, in his article, "Le cedole concistoriali," *Archivum Historiae Pontificiae* 11 (1973): 209–268, provides important information regarding the internal working of the Consistory and related offices, which clarifies the nature and purpose of two major forms of documentation produced from the fifteenth century: the consistorial cedole and contracedole. According to Pásztor, at least from the fifteenth century concistorial cedole transmitted decisions regarding the conferral of major ecclesiastical benefices to the curial officials who redacted the relevant bulls. Though the term cedola only appears at the end of the fifteenth century, this type of document existed earlier. There were two types of cedole: one emanated in the name of the pope, the other in the name of a cardinal. The *Acta consistorialia* furnishes the first information about cedole concistoriali and the texts of the first. (Note that *Acta miscellanea* 60 contains minutes of consistorial cedole, 1534–1559, and actually belongs with similar volumes in the records of the Secretaria Brevium.)

In the concistorial acts in 1421 we find for the first time the figure of the cardinale ponente or presenting cardinal, the cardinal who presented candidates for appointment. According to Pásztor, the role of the presenting cardinal becomes clearer in 1428 and from this time onward the name of the cardinal who had proposed the provision or appointment becomes more frequent in acti. With a cedole the cardinal notified the Cancelleria of the provision granted on the basis of his proposal.

However, this official recommendation or certificate (the cedola) of the proposing cardinal was not enough to attain a bull of provision. A cedola had to be confirmed by the vice-chancellor in a document called controcedola concistoriale.

See Pásztor's Appendix (pp. 246–256) for some samples of cedole and contracedole, some of which were found in the Congregatio Consistorialis series *Acta miscellanea* but many of which are located in other series of the Vatican Archives or in manuscript collections of the Vatican Library. See Pásztor, pp. 256–268, for a good, concise introduction to cedole and controcedole and a useful overview of the locations of cedole consistoriale in the ASV, most of which are in series related to the Secretaria Brevium and the Cancellaria Apostolica.

Note: The records of the Congregatio Consistorialis are collectively considered the records of the "Consistorium." When citing records of this congregation, the series title should always be preceded by that word as, for example, *Consistorium: Sedi titolari.*

In addition to the records listed below, series listed with other agencies relate directly to this agency and should be consulted. See Miscellaneous official series *Miscellaneorum armarium XII* and *Miscellaneorum armarium XIII*, and Collegio dei cardinali series *Camerarius* and *Notitiae ecclesiarum per liber taxarum ordinariarum.*

References. A good introduction and general overview of the College of Cardinals is provided by John F. Broderick in his "The Sacred College of Cardinals: Size and Geographical Composition (1099–1986)," *Archivum Historiae Pontificiae* 25 (1987): 7–47. Broderick gives useful, often descriptive, bibliographic references in his footnotes. His article makes use of some of the principal published sources that have relied heavily on the consistory material in the Vatican Archives; for example, Ludwig von Pastor, *The History of the Popes from the Close of the Middle Ages*, translated and edited by F. I. Antrobus et al. (London, 1891–1953); Heinrich Finke, ed., *Acta Concillii Constanciensis* (Münster, 1896–1928); and Konrad Eubel, *Hierarchia catholica medii et recentioris aevi, sive Summorum pontificum, S.R.E. cardinalium, ecclesiarum antisitum series* (Münster, 1913–1978). More recently, Barbara McClung Hallman has made good use of the consistorial *Acta camerarii, Acta miscellanea, Acta vicecancellarii* and consistory material in *Armaria XL–XLII* in her study of 102 cardinals and their financial strategies (1510–1559) in *Italian Cardinals, Reform, and the Church as Property* (Berkeley, 1985).

G. Alberigo, *Cardinalato e collegialità: studi sull'ecclesiologia tra l'XI e il XIV secolo* (Florence, 1969). D. Bouix, *Tractatus de Curia Romana seu de cardinalibus, romanis congregationibus, legatis, nuntiis, vicariis, et protonotariis apostolicis* (Paris, 1859). C. G. Fürst, *Cardinalis: Prolegomena zu einer Rechtsgeschichte des römischen Kardinalskollegiums* (Munich, 1967). S. Kuttner, "Cardinalis: The History of a Canonical Concept," *Traditio* 3 (1945): 129–214. Ch. Lefebvre, "Les origines et le rôle du Cardinalat au moyen âge," *Apollinaris* 41 (1968): 59–70. P. Partner, *The Pope's Men: The Papal Civil Service in the Renaissance* (Oxford, 1990). L. Pásztor, "Le cedole concistoriali," *Archivum historiae pontificiae* 11 (1973): 209–268. R. Ritzler, "Per la storia dell'Archivio del Sacro Collegio," in *Mélanges Eugène Tisserant* (Vatican City, 1964), vol. 5, pp. 300–338. J. B. Sägmüller, *Die Thätigkeit und Stellung der Cardinäle bis Papst Bonifaz VIII* (Freiburg, 1896). M. Tangl, *Die päpstlichen Kanzleiordnungen von 1200–1500* (Innsbruck, 1894). T. Vanyo, "Das Archiv der Konsistorialkongregation," in *Leo Santifaller Festschrift* (Vienna, 1950), pp. 151–179.

RECORDS. Records of the congregation consist of the following series.

3.1.3.1 Acta camerarii

[DATABASE ID: VATV257-A]

Inclusive Dates: 1489–1866.

Bulk: 4 linear m. (61 numbered volumes).

Organization: Three chronological series: vols. 1–41, 1503–1798; —vols. 42–48, 1541–1600; —vols. 49–61, 1800–1866. Indices are often in the front or back of volumes.

Note: This record series forms a part of the *Fondo concistoriale* described separately among the record series of this congregation.

Scope: These are for the most part the camerlengo's minutes of consistorial decisions. Acording to Boyle, the *Acta* contain official notes of questions treated in secret, public, or semi-public meetings of the Consistory, and in "general" and "particular" assemblies. Much of the business is financial and relates to the provision of major benefices controlled by the College of Cardinals and the allotment of pensions or subventions. B. M. Hallman, in her *Italian Cardinals, Reform, and the Church as Property* (Berkeley, 1985), uses this series to show how Italian cardinals received incomes from many and often foreign benefices and also how cardinals were able to confer on members of their households funds from benefices (pp. 98–100), to award their friends and servants with pensions (pp. 107–109), and to transfer ecclesiastical benefices to heirs (p. 121). The series contains copies of many materials and relates to other Congregatio Consistorialis (*Fondo concistoriale*) series, particularly *Consistorium secretum in . . .* and *Acta concistoriale.*

References: Fink, p. 61; Pásztor (1970), pp. 131–133; Pásztor (1983), pp. 162–163; Boyle, pp. 81–82. W. M. Brady, *The Episcopal Succession in England, Scotland, and Ireland,* A.D. *1400–1875: With Appointments to Monasteries and Extracts from Consistorial Acts Taken from mss. in Public and Private Libraries in Rome, Florence, Bologna, Ravenna and Paris* (Rome, 1876–1877). R. Ritzler, "Die archivalischen Quellen der 'Hierarchia catholica,'" in *Miscellanea archivistica Angelo Mercati* (Vatican City, 1952), pp. 51–74. R. Ritzler, "Per la storia dell'Archivio del Sacro Collegio," in *Mélanges Eugène Tisserant* (Vatican City, 1964), vol. 5, pp. 300–338.

Finding Aids: See A. Mercati, "Schedario Garampi, Registri Vaticani, Registri Lateranensi, Rationes Camerae, Inventario del Fondo Concistoriale," vol. 1 of *Sussidi per la consultazione dell'Archivio Vaticano* (Rome, 1926), pp. 203–206. This work provides a brief introduction to the *Fondo concistoriale* and then a volume-by-volume listing of the initial forty-eight volumes in this series with variations in title, inclusive dates, and occasional contents annotations.

Indici 716–718, "Registro dei Concistori 1800–1875," provide partial access to materials in this series for the period 1800–1866. These chronological indici list the year, month, day, diocese, and usually the person in question and are linked to the *Acta camerarii* by noting the date and finding the appropriate entry in the series or noting the diocese and locating the diocese in the index within the actual volume, if it has one.

Location: Archivio Segreto Vaticano.

3.1.3.2 Acta Congregationis Consistorialis

[DATABASE ID: VATV265-A]

Inclusive Dates: 1584–1809, 1816–1908.

Bulk: 36 linear m. (349 numbered volumes).

Organization: Chronological by year with limited indices at the beginning of each year. Note that there are variant titles on some of the spines of the volumes, including "Erectionis novi episcopatus . . ." and "Processus."

Scope: This series concerns consistorial provisions and decisions. It is also useful for other incidental information like papal elections, curial appointments, the creation of legatine commissions, etc. Earlier volumes record the decisions of the Consistory. Later volumes contain more information including letters regarding cases and the like and have more of a rough-draft quality.

Note: The series includes several maps.

References: Fink, pp. 61–62; Pásztor (1970), pp. 140–142; Pásztor (1983), pp. 166–169; Boyle, p. 87. Scope note is taken directly from MacFarlane, pp. 92–93. R. Ritzler, "Intorno al 'Liber Diurnus,'" *Miscellanea Franciscana* 42 (1942): 77–82.

Finding Aids: ASV Indici 707–713 provide a variety of access points to the *Acta Congregationis Consistorialis.* Indici 707–709, entitled "Index Actorum Sacra Congregationis Consistorialis," cover the following years: 707 (1593–1806), 708 (1700–1868), and 709 (1869–1906). It should be noted that these do not index the entire series and on examination the indices appear to have inconsistent coverage at some points. Indici 707–709 are arranged chronologically by year and then alphabetical by diocese within a given year. No. 707 provides the most information, listing year, diocese, an abbreviated note of actions taken by consistory, the exact date of the decision, a reference number to the case, and sometimes the cost levied. No. 708 only notes the year, diocese, and action, and 709 only notes the year, diocese, and reference number. Indici 710 (1627–1806), 711 (1700–1869), and 712 (1869–1906) are entitled "Index Actorum Sacra Congregationis Consistorialis, I. Materiae" and provide access to the series through type of action taken in Consistory. These also demonstrate the wide variety of business of the Consistory, that is, Admissiones articulorum pro coadjutoria episcopalia, Commende, Secularizzationi, and so forth. These indices are also arranged chronologically and then alphabetically by action.

ASV Indice 713, entitled "Index Decretorum: Index generalis Actorum Sacrae Congregationis Consistorialis" (1700–1823), duplicates some, but not all, of the information found in Indici 707–712. This index is divided into three parts: (1) chronological then alphabetical by diocese (as 707, 708, and 709), (2) chronological and then alphabetical by type of action "Materiae" (as in indices 710, 711, and 712), and (3) an alphabetical index to diocese and type of action but without dates.

Location: Archivio Segreto Vaticano.

3.1.3.3 Acta consistorialia
[DATABASE ID: VATV260-A]
Inclusive Dates: 1498–1895.
Bulk: 14 linear m. (231 numbered volumes).
Organization: Four subseries: Acta consistorialia, 1498–1644, 1 vol.; —Acta consistorialia, 1517–1629, 10 vols.; —Acta consistorialia, 1657–1668, 1 vol.; —Acta consistorialia, 1644–1895. 219 vols. Each series is chronological by Consistory meeting. Note that series 2 and 3 usually have indices at the beginning to dioceses and monasteries.
Note: This series forms part of the *Fondo concistoriale* described separately among the record series of this congregation.
Scope: This series consists of propositions, allocutions, and decrees of the Consistorial Congregation and of the Congregatio de Propaganda Fide. Boyle and Pásztor designate this series as: *Atti, copie* and *serie regolare*—Proceedings (complete?), which deal with the assignments of office, taxation, provisions, and grants of favor. In the mid-seventeenth century, printed documents began to appear. This series seems to be an amplification of Congregatio Consistoriale series *Consistoria secretum in* . . . and relates to the *Acta camerarii* and the *Acta miscellanea*. This series contains printed copies of the decisions and some supporting documents. Letters often give greater detail concerning the people or places involved in the discussions.
References: Fink, p. 61; Boyle, p. 83, Pásztor (1983), pp. 184–185.
Finding Aids: ASV Indici 716, 717, and 718, entitled "Registro dei Consistori," provide access to this series. The indices are arranged chronologically by consistory meeting and then list the dioceses involved and often the person under consideration.
Location: Archivio Segreto Vaticano.

3.1.3.4 Acta miscellanea
[DATABASE ID: VATV259-A]
Inclusive Dates: 1333–1809.
Bulk: 6 linear m. (100 vols.).
Scope: The series consists primarily of extracts from, or copies of, *Acta camerarii* and *Acta vicecancellarii* (both series described in this section), with some minutes of consistorial acts. It contains information on provisions but also can be used as a diary of Curia activities. Some volumes are indexed.

Volumes are widely different in character. Some record only decisions or selected decisions and others provide in-depth accounts of consistory proceedings. Volume 70 contains a selection of materials from 1333 regarding the Consistory, including who attended meetings, synopsis of orations by legates, and so forth. MacFarlane notes that the earliest volumes of this series (though mostly copies) are particularly valuable for medieval consistorial provisions.

The examples edited or noted by L. Pásztor in his "Le cedole conscistoriali," *Archivum Historiae Pontificiae* 11 (1973): 246–268, suggest that many of the cedole, controcedole, and related documents concern the provision of bishops with dioceses and their incomes or the transfer of bishops from one diocese to another. Pásztor also edits documents concerning the erection or establishment of dioceses and the appointment of cardinals and bishops to the role of administering and receiving income from monasteries and churches.

Note: This series is a part of the *Fondo concistoriale* described separately among the records of this congregation. Vol. 1 is available on microfilm.
References: Fink, p. 61; Pásztor (1970), pp. 138–139; Pásztor (1983), pp. 165–166; Boyle, p. 82; MacFarlane, p. 92. R. Ritzler, "Die archivalischen Quellen der 'Hierarchia catholica'," in *Miscellanea archivistica Angelo Mercati* (Vatican City, 1952), pp. 51–74. R. Ritzler, "Die bischöflichen Informativprozesse in den "Processus Consistoriales" im Archiv des Kardinalskollegs bis 1907," *Römische historische Mitteilungen* 2 (1957–1958): 204–220. R. Ritzler, "Per la storia dell'Archivio del Sacro Collegio," in *Mélanges Eugène Tisserant* (Vatican City, 1964), vol. 5, pp. 300–338.
Finding Aids: A. Mercati, "Schedario Garampi, Registri Vaticani, Registri Lateranensi, Rationes Camerae, Inventario del Fondo Concistoriale," vol. 1 of *Sussidi per la consultazione dell'Archivio Vaticano*, (Rome, 1926), pp. 207–213. This volume provides a volume-by-volume listing of exact titles, inclusive dates, and occasionally brief contents annotations for volumes 1–94.

ASV Indice 288, p. 242 (olim. 230) gives an itemized contents list of no. 60 of the *Acta miscellanea*.
Location: Archivio Segreto Vaticano.

3.1.3.5 Acta varie di diverse anni
[DATABASE ID: VATV10117-A]
Inclusive Dates: 1868–1896.
Bulk: 1 vol.
Organization: Chronological and alphabetical by diocese.
Scope: These are miscellaneous materials relating to the Acta.
Location: Archivio Segreto Vaticano.

3.1.3.6 Acta vicecancellarii
[DATABASE ID: VATV258-A]
Inclusive Dates: 1498–1632.
Bulk: 1 linear m. (18 numbered volumes).
Organization: Chronological.
Scope: This series consists of the vice-chancellor's minutes of consistorial business.
Note: This series forms part of the *Fondo concistoriale* described separately among the records of this congregation.
References: Fink, p. 61; Pásztor (1970), pp. 139–140; Pásztor (1983), p. 166; Boyle, p. 82; MacFarlane, p. 92. R. Ritzler, "Die archivalischen Quellen der 'Hierarchia catholica'," in *Miscellanea archivistica Angelo Mercati* (Vatican City, 1952), pp. 51–74. R. Ritzler, "Die bischöflichen Informativprozesse in den "Processus Consistoriales" im Archiv des Kardinalskollegs bis 1907," *Römische historische Mitteilungen* 2 (1957–58): 204–220. R. Ritzler, "Per la storia dell'Archivio del Sacro Collegio," in *Mélanges Eugène Tisserant* (Vatican City, 1964), vol. 5, pp. 300–338.
Finding Aids: A. Mercati, "Schedario Garampi, Registri Vaticani, Registri Lateranensi, Rationes Camerae, Inventario del Fondo Concistoriale," vol. 1 of *Sussidi per la consultazione dell'Archivio Vaticano*, (Rome, 1926), pp. 206–207. This volume provides a volume-by-volume listing with exact titles, inclusive dates, and occasional contents annotations.
Location: Archivio Segreto Vaticano.

3.1.3.7 Affari pendenti

[DATABASE ID: VATV10116-A]

Inclusive Dates: 1815–1871.

Bulk: 2 linear m. (18 vols.).

Organization: Chronological with case numbers assigned. Each case is grouped by diocese but these are chronological.

Reference: Pásztor (1970), p. 143.

Finding Aids: ASV Indici 714 and 715, entitled "Ricorsi e cause Concistoriali non risoluti (ossia Affari Pendenti)," provide partial access to this series. Indice 714, which covers the years 1818–1847, is organized chronologically and then lists dioceses alphabetically within a given year. The diocese is listed with its case number. Indice 715 covers the years 1848–1875 and again is organized chronologically with dioceses listed alphabetically within each year. In addition to the information given in indice 714, indice 715 includes the type of action taken, which acts as a brief case summary.

Location: Archivio Segreto Vaticano.

3.1.3.8 Allocutiones e provisiones

[DATABASE ID: VATV10118-A]

Inclusive Dates: 1867–1890.

Bulk: .15 linear m. (3 vols.).

Organization: Chronological.

Scope: Beneficial material.

Location: Archivio Segreto Vaticano.

3.1.3.9 Atti e miscellanea

[DATABASE ID: VATV10115-A]

Inclusive Dates: ca. 1815–1893.

Bulk: .5 linear m. (4 boxes).

Organization: Two series: Miscellanea, 1815–1877, 3 boxes (inside posizioni 1–31); —Atti, 1878–1893, (includes 1 vol., chronological).

Scope: Records contain information on diocesan affairs, for example, establishment, changes, promotions, and so forth. There is a history of the Concistoriale with information on functions and processes followed by the congregation.

Reference: Pásztor (1970), pp. 143–144.

Location: Archivio Segreto Vaticano.

3.1.3.10 Avvocati

[DATABASE ID: VATV10131-A]

Inclusive Dates: 1520–1867 (bulk 1740–1867).

Bulk: 5 linear m. (25 vols. and 33 scatole).

Organization: Fifteen subseries with the following contents designations: Apostolicae concessiones, 1560–1764, 1 vol.; —Processus pro admissione, 1520–1807, 8 vols.; —Intimationes, 1710–1794, 1 vol.; —Statuta, 1744, 1 vol.; —Jura et privilegia, 1566–1785, 2 vols. (Tom. I, 1566–1775 and Tom. II, 1567–1785); —Ius antianità, 1620–1784, 1 vol.; —Registri Camerariatus, 1597–1774, 3 vols.; —Libro del Camerlengato del collegio degli avvocati concistoriali, 1849–1870, 1 vol.; —Dissertationi, 1745–1786, 1 vol.; —Acta consistorialia (tom. I) . . . orationes in consistorio habitas ab ejus advocatis pro criminalibus . . . pro beatificatione et canonizatione . . . pro cardinalitiae dignitatis . . . , 1600–1781; —Mandata ad petenda palia, Tom. II and Tom. III, 1701–1817; —Regestum pallium, 1700–1807, 1 vol.; —

Divisiones, 1601–1800, 1 vol.; —Theses permissu rectoris archig., 1539–1801, 1 vol.; —[Corrispondenza] AA–AO, [18—], 33 scatole.

Reference: O. P. Conti, *Origine, fasti e privilegi degli avvocati concistoriali: Memorie storiche* (Rome, 1898).

Location: Archivio Segreto Vaticano.

3.1.3.11 Cappellani militari

[DATABASE ID: VATV10458-A]

Inclusive Dates: ca. 1926–1937.

Bulk: .25 linear m. (3 scatole).

Location: Archivio Segreto Vaticano.

3.1.3.12 Cedulae et controcedulae

[DATABASE ID: VATV10130-A]

Inclusive Dates: 1700–1760, 1814–1907.

Bulk: .5 linear m. (32 buste).

Organization: Chronological.

Scope: These cedulae are entitlements beginning "Hodie in consistorio . . ." (what) benefice available, per obitum (how), or per resignationem, etc. (which belonged to whom), then there is information regarding to whom it is going, plus their titles and credentials.

Location: Archivio Segreto Vaticano.

3.1.3.13 Cedularum et rotulorum

[DATABASE ID: VATV10123-A]

Inclusive Dates: 1504–1879 (bulk 1504–1809).

Bulk: 4 linear m. (61 vols.).

Organization: Several roughly chronological series.

Scope: These are registers of distribution payments from the taxes paid by bishops, abbots, and other religious officials upon election, and expenses of the Sacred College. Numbers 29–48 are duplicate volumes for the years 1565–1821.

MacFarlane notes that there are many gaps in this series that prevent it from being as useful as it might be, since what has survived contains valuable and precise dates of the elections and deaths of popes and cardinals. Only the first volume is pre-Reformation.

References: Fink, p. 64; Pásztor (1970), p. 134; Boyle, p. 83; MacFarlane, p. 93. R. Ritzler, "Per la storia dell'Archivio del Sacro Collegio," in *Mélanges Eugène Tisserant* (Vatican City, 1964), vol. 5, pp. 300–338.

Finding Aids: ASV Indice 1121 lists the volume numbers and gives inclusive dates of each one. The index also has brief notes on accounting methods.

Location: Archivio Segreto Vaticano.

3.1.3.14 Collezione bolle e breve apostolici

[DATABASE ID: VATV10456-A]

Inclusive Dates: ca. 1676–1843.

Bulk: .4 linear m. (6 vols.).

Scope: The titles on the spines of these volumes are misleading. Volume one contains bulls and briefs, but these bound copies appear to be almost minutes or presentation copies with mistakes. Volume 6 contains pastoral letters, relazioni, voti, lists of "Chiese patriarcali residenziali" and a "Catalogus Abbatorum et aliorum jurisdictionem quasi episcopalem habentium."

Location: Archivio Segreto Vaticano.

3.1.3.15 Concistori: Propositiones
[DATABASE ID: VATV10453-A]
Inclusive Dates: 1808–1840.
Bulk: 1.5 linear m. (29 vols.).
Organization: Chronological.
Scope: "Propositiones" is written in pencil on the front covers, except for vol. 29, which says "Uditore."
Location: Archivio Segreto Vaticano.

3.1.3.16 Consistorium secretum in . . .
[DATABASE ID: VATV10114-A]
Inclusive Dates: 1740–1806, 1814–1907.
Bulk: 6 linear m.
Organization: Three subseries: Consistorium secretum in Quiriniale, 1740–1870; —Consistorium secretum in Vaticano, 1870–1896; —Acta Consistorialia, 1896–1907. These series are chronological, usually with brief indices (to diocese or monastery) both at the beginning or end of each volume and incomplete indices after each meeting.
Note: This series forms part of the *Fondo concistoriale* described separately among the records series of this congregation.
Scope: These documents are a very formal record of decisions made by the Consistory, handwritten in ornate calligraphy, regarding offices, taxes, renovation of churches, and so forth. There are some opening speeches by the pope, for example, 1833. This series appears to be an archival copy of the Congregatio Consistorialis, *Acta consistorialia.* Perhaps it was the copy for the pope since Boyle and Pásztor refer to this series as "Libretti del Papa." This series is designated by Boyle and Pásztor as the *Archivio del Sostituto del Concistoro.* They identify its three subseries as Libretti del Papa, Atti (copie et serie regolari), and Varia. In addition to the *Acta consistorialia,* this series relates to other Congregatio Consistorialis series including the *Acta camerarii* and *Acta miscellanea.*
References: Boyle, p. 83; Pásztor (1983), pp. 184–185. L. Pásztor, "Il Sostituto del Concistoro e il suo archivio," *Archivum historiae pontificiae* 5 (1967): 355–372.
Finding Aids: ASV Indici 716–718, "Registro del Concistorio," provide access to this series. These indici, arranged chronologically, give the year, month, and day of the meeting then list the dioceses involved and usually the subject (person) under consideration.
Location: Archivio Segreto Vaticano.

3.1.3.17 Consistorium secretum in . . . : Acta
[DATABASE ID: VATV10459-A]
Inclusive Dates: 1700–1953.
Bulk: 6 linear m.
Organization: Chronological.
Scope: These are formal copies of the acta but the writing is crossed out on each one.
Location: Archivio Segreto Vaticano.

3.1.3.18 Decreta Congregationis Consistorialis
[DATABASE ID: VATV261-A]
Inclusive Dates: 1648–1701.
Bulk: 1 vol.
Location: Archivio Segreto Vaticano.

3.1.3.19 Fondo concistoriale
[DATABASE ID: VATV256-A]
Inclusive Dates: 1409–1907.
Bulk: 31 linear m.
Organization: The *Fondo concistoriale* is as well known as a whole as it is known by the six specific records series that are its parts: *Acta camerarii,* 1489–1866, 4 linear m.; —*Acta vicecancellarii,* 1498–1632, 1 linear m.; —*Acta miscellanea,* 1333–1809, 6 linear m.; —*Acta consistorialia,* 1498–1895, 14 linear m.; —*Consistorium secretum in . . . ,* 1740–1907, 6 linear m.; —*Processus consistoriales,* 1563–1906, 32 linear m. Each of these records series is listed separately among the series descriptions for the Congregatio Consistorialis.
Scope: The *Fondo concistoriale* is composed of materials from the Archivum sacri collegii cardinalium and the Archivio del Sostituto.
The Consistory was the regular assembly of the cardinals under the presidency of the pope, with its normal and extraordinary business, including the collation of reserved major benefices, at least three centuries before the Congregatio Consistorialis came into existence to exercise the residues of the Consistory's functions. This is why some records and copies here are older than the congregation.
References: Fink, p. 61; Pásztor (1970), pp. 127–144; Boyle, pp. 80–83.
Finding Aids: A. Mercati, "Schedario Garampi, Registri Vaticani, Registri Lateranensi, Rationes Camerae, Inventario del Fondo Concistoriale," vol. 1 of *Sussidi per la consultazione dell'Archivio Vaticano* (Rome, 1926), pp. 203–219.
Location: Archivio Segreto Vaticano.

3.1.3.20 Juramenta fidelitatis et professionis fidei
[DATABASE ID: VATV270-A]
Inclusive Dates: 1654–1904.
Bulk: 3 linear m. (28 vols.).
Organization: Alphabetical by diocese and then chronological within each diocesan listing. Volumes are usually indexed at the beginning.
Scope: These appear to be episcopal professions of faith.
References: Fink, p. 65; Pásztor (1970), p. 136; Boyle, p. 87.
Location: Archivio Segreto Vaticano.

3.1.3.21 [Miscellanea SF/72]
[DATABASE ID: VATV10460-A]
Inclusive Dates: ca. 1430 (copy)–1898.
Bulk: 5 linear m.
Organization: Volumes/buste titles or contents include: Indice generale delle chiese, ca. 1644–1881, 1 vol.; —Collezzione di bolle e notizie diverse alcune appartenenti anche alle materie concistoriali, 1538 (copy)–1807, 10 vols. (vol. I–IX, XI); —Decreta Sacrae Congregationis Rebus Consistorialibus Praeposita, pars prima, 1593–1690, 1 vol.; —Collectio veterum decretorum Consistorialium (outside title), contains Decreta Sacrae Congregationis Rerum Consistorialium, 1595–1697, and Intimationes et resolutiones Sacrae Congregationis Consistorialis, tom. 2, 1687–1731; —Collezioni di risoluzioni ecclesiastiche (3 vols.: vol. 1, 1795–1797, includes catechisms; vol. 2, 1801–1802, concerns China and India; vol. 3 concerns the Propaganda Fide and S. Officii); —Miscellanea II, 1558 (copy)–1719, 1 vol.; —[Miscellanea], ca. 1818–1847, 1 vol.; —Miscellanea [pastorali, beatificazione e canoniz-

zazione], ca. 1850–1864, 1 vol.; —Miscellanea [pastorali, acta, allocutiones], 1860–1869, 1 vol.; —Gallia moderna, 1802–1807, 1 vol.; —Miscellanea promovendorum (notizie vari per li promovendi alle catedrali) (includes formularies), ca. 1639–1768; —Repertorium Rerum Consistorialium, (tom. II), ca. 1678–1792 = Miscellanea rerum consistorialium tom. II, ca. 1678–1792; —Stati di chiese catedrali, 1665–1825; —Episcopatus, tituli, diaconiae aliaque officia, 1768 (contains information from 1659–1889); —Archiepiscopi et episcopi regulares creati a Clemente Papa XI, 1772, 1 vol.; —Tasse del Sacro Collegio, 1430 (copy)–1777, 2 vols.; —Concistoriale (list of benefices?), 1676–1689, 1 vol.; —Index abbatiarum et monasteriorum quibus provisum fuit in Consistoriis Secretis, 1644–1814, 1 vol.; —Viaggio di Papa Pio VI nell'anno 1782, 1 vol.; —Status ecclesiarum collationis apostolicae, 1644–1834 (contains inside Pensiones reservatae super mensis cathedralium liberae collationis), 1 vol.; —Repertorium nonnullarum rerum Consistorialium notabilium, 1763 (contains information copied from 1370) = Miscellanea rerum consistorialium I; —Coadjutores et suffraganei, 1644–1797 (f. 252 coadjutoriae monasteriorum); —Notitia episcopatuum Universalis Ecclesie, 1198 (copy)–1650; —Concordato, 1818, 3 vols. (numbered 2–4); —Busta marked "L," containing bolle and breve, [14—]–[15—]; —Sudunen, Memorie dell'Abbazia Concistoriale di Monastero di S. Maurizio Agauni dell'ordine dei Canonici Regolari di S. Agostino, congregazio Lateranense, 1784–1820; —Acta, 1668–1679, 4 vols. (numbered II–IV); —Epistolae regiae: Nominationes, proesentationes, supplicationes, 1686–1790 (concerns Gallia, Sardegna, Portogallo, Anglia, Hispania, Polonia); —Chiavari, ca. 1889–1898, 2 buste; —Uditore del Papa, 1807–1841, 1 box; —2 Scatole miscellanea, [18—]; —Indice.

The following items within this miscellany may relate to the Collegio dei cardinali series: Conclavi:. Clemente XIV, 2 vols.; —Pio VII, 2 vols.; —Leone XII, 1 vol.; —Clemente XIII, 1 vol.; —Clemente XII e Benedetto XIV, 1 vol.; —Relativi di diverse conclavi, 1 vol.

Reference: Pásztor (1983), p. 185, "Varia." This "Varia" cited by Pásztor could be either of the following two volumes identified above: Decreta Sacrae Congregationis Rebus Consistorialibus Praeposita pars prima, 1593–1690 (1 vol.) or Collectio veterum decretorum Consistorialium (outside title), contains Decreta Sacrae Congregationis Rerum Consistorialium, 1595–1697.

Finding Aids: The shelf label in this range serves as a partial index to six identifiable volumes on these shelves: Collezzioni di bolle e notizie diverse Tom. I and II; Miscellanea Promovendorum; Gallia Moderna, 1802–1807; Miscellanea rerum consistorialium I (Repertorium nonnullarum rerum Consistorialium); and Miscellanea rerum consistorialium II (Repertorium rerum Consistorialium, Tom. II). This label is generally organized according to the type of material or business.

Note: This is a true miscellany that in 1990 was located in SF/72. There is no official ASV designation for this material. The title was assigned by project staff.

Location: Archivio Segreto Vaticano.

3.1.3.22 [Miscellanea SF/73]
[DATABASE ID: VATV10455-A]
Inclusive Dates: ca. 1645–1899.
Bulk: 3.5 linear m.

Organization: This miscellany includes: Risoluzioni della Congregazione concistoriale, 1645–1681, 4 vols.; —Acta, 1655–1759, 4 vols. (vol. 1, 1655–1662; vol. 2, Diversi, 1670–1674; vol. 3, 1710–1715, 1730–1733; vol. 4, 1758–1759); —Abbatia Nullius di Ferentillo, ca. 1800, 4 vols.; —Sutrin, Processus Inquisitionis super erectione concathedralis e sedis episcopalis Bracenen, 1820, 1 vol.; —Congregationes Consistorialis, 4 vols.; —Proviste di chiese, 1871–1899, 3 buste; —Atti (miscellanea), 2 linear m. (unorganized); —Scatole, ca. 1800 (miscellanea).

Some of this material was transferred from the Archivio di Stato di Roma in 1920.

Note: This is a true miscellany that in 1990 was located in SF/73. It has no official ASV designation. The title was assigned by the project staff.

Location: Archivio Segreto Vaticano.

3.1.3.23 [Miscellanea SF/184 + SF/185]
[DATABASE ID: VATV10136-A]
Inclusive Dates: 1700–1953.
Bulk: 2 linear m.

Organization: Series/Items include: Regestra matrimonialium, 1890–1897, 1 vol.; —Regestra beneficialium, 1897, 1 vol.; —Provisiones, 1900–1907, 1 vol.; —[Miscellaneous Bulls and briefs, some Acta consistorium secretum], 1700–1879, 2 boxes; —Suppliche di coadiutore, 1700–1870, 6 buste; —Decreti consistoriali-titoli cardinalizii, ca. 1900; —Consistorio pubblico e segreto (noti-minute); —[1 series post-1922].

Note: This is a true miscellany that in 1990 was located in SF/184 or SF/185. There is no official ASV designation for this series. The title was assigned by project staff based on its location in 1990.

Location: Archivio Segreto Vaticano.

3.1.3.24 Monumenta Lusitaniae e tabularii Vaticanis
excerpta quorum hic exhibetur
[DATABASE ID: VATV10121-A]
Inclusive Dates: 1216 (copy)–1846.
Bulk: 1 vol. and 1 folder.
Organization: Chronological, index at beginning of the volume.

Scope: Volume 1 contains copies of documents from papal registers concerning Portugal (1216–1569). Documents primarily concern episcopal affairs and the royal family.

Location: Archivio Segreto Vaticano.

3.1.3.25 Ponenze, stampate
[DATABASE ID: VATV10133-A]
Inclusive Dates: 1911–1944.
Bulk: 4 linear m.
Organization: Chronological.

Scope: Printed matter. Perhaps these are summaries of cases for consultation in Consistory.

Location: Archivio Segreto Vaticano.

3.1.3.26 Positiones Congreg. Em. Capitum Ordinum
[DATABASE ID: VATV268-A]
Inclusive Dates: 1656–1861.
Bulk: 7 linear m. (78 vols.).
Organization: Chronological. Most volumes are indexed at beginning according to diocese. Note that there is a variant

title, *Cong Em Ordine Priorum in quibus nonnulla de quindenniis in. . . .*

Scope: These are petitions relating to the wide variety of matters to be decided by the Consistory regarding the establishment of dioceses, special provisions to dioceses and abbacies, and business regarding the papal (Sistine) chapel.

References: Fink, p. 65; Pásztor (1970), pp. 133–134; Pásztor (1983), p. 163; Boyle, p. 87.

Location: Archivio Segreto Vaticano.

3.1.3.27 Praeconia et propositiones
[DATABASE ID: VATV269-A]

Inclusive Dates: 1658–1907.

Bulk: 13 linear m. (170 vols.).

Organization: Organized into three subseries: Praeconia et propositiones, 1658–1823, 21 chronological vols.; —Propositiones ecclesiarum, 1818–1866, 1893–1895, 12 chronological vóls.; —Propositio, ca. 1850–1907, 137 chronological and/or alphabetical vols.

Scope: These are consistorial nominations of candidates to fill vacancies in church offices. Most volumes are indexed by diocese.

References: Fink, p. 65; Boyle, p. 87; Pásztor (1970), pp. 137–138; Pásztor (1983), p. 165.

Location: Archivio Segreto Vaticano.

3.1.3.28 [Processus]
[DATABASE ID: VATV10122-A]

Inclusive Dates: 1690–1870.

Bulk: 5 linear m. (7 vols.).

Organization: Chronological.

Scope: This series deals primarily with elections in monasteries and dioceses.

Note: This series has no official ASV designation. The title was supplied by project staff.

Location: Archivio Segreto Vaticano.

3.1.3.29 Processus consistoriales
[DATABASE ID: VATV262-A]

Inclusive Dates: 1563–1809, 1814–1906.

Bulk: 32 linear m. (300 numbered volumes).

Organization: Chronological by year. Each volume is arranged by case number. Many volumes are indexed at the beginning.

Note: This series forms part of the *Fondo concistoriale*, which is described separately among the record series of this congregation.

Scope: Boyle notes that these are original records of all informative processes (i.e., investigations into priests and parishes) conducted outside the Roman Curia with respect to the provision of bishops. The series also includes copies of informative processes conducted within the curia itself. The originals of these processes are located in Dataria Apostolica series *Processus datariae.* (Copies of the processes conducted outside the Roman Curia are also there.)

References: Fink, pp. 62–64; Pásztor (1970), pp. 135–136; Pásztor (1983), pp. 163–165; Boyle, p. 83. R. Ritzler, "Die bischöflichen Informativprozesse in den "Processus Consistoriales" im Archiv des Kardinalkollegs bis 1907," *Römische historische Mitteilungen* 2 (1957–1958): 204–220.

Finding Aids: ASV Indice 1045 provides an inventory of current holdings giving the volume number and inclusive dates. Then it continues with a cumulative, alphabetical list of dioceses, and occasionally country, appearing in volumes 1–249, giving the diocese, year, volume, and page number on which the diocese is mentioned. Also, there is an unnumbered index volume at the end of the series.

Location: Archivio Segreto Vaticano.

3.1.3.30 Processus erectionum in episcopatum San Deodati (Lucerna)
[DATABASE ID: VATV10119-A]

Inclusive Dates: 1717.

Bulk: 1 vol.

Scope: The volume is labeled "In causa nullius San Deodati."

Location: Archivio Segreto Vaticano.

3.1.3.31 Registri mandatorum et nominationum ad pensiones
[DATABASE ID: VATV10120-A]

Inclusive Dates: 1614–1804.

Bulk: .25 linear m. (3 vols.).

Organization: The volumes are: Liber primus registri mandatorum et nominationum ad pensiones Pauli Papi V, 1614–1617; —Regestrum nominatorum et mandatorum Clement XIV, 1771–1772; —Nominationes ac mandata, Pius PP VII, 1803–1804. Volumes are chronological.

Scope: These are payments for offices (mandatum, nominationum, etc.). If the action was *motu proprio* it is noted in the upper left. The record lists the type of payment and a summary of the actions taken.

Location: Archivio Segreto Vaticano.

3.1.3.32 Relationes
[DATABASE ID: VATV10213-A]

Inclusive Dates: 1908–1941.

Bulk: 23 linear m. (242 numbered boxes in the regular series and appendice numbered 1–7).

Organization: Both the regular series and the appendices are alphabetical by diocese. The appendice cover the years 1911–[post-1922]. Each diocese has been assigned a number (posizione).

Finding Aids: ASV Indice 1169, "Congregatio Consistorialis: Relationes," is a photocopy of an older handwritten index to the *Relationes.* It also contains three newly typed appendices that will be described below. The index is organized according to the Latin name of the diocese. This is followed by the name of the diocese in its national language. The brief entries in this index provide the years of *Relationes* represented for each diocese, the posizione of each diocese ("Inter." nos. 1–960), and the box (scatole, "sect." nos. 1–242) number in which specific *Relationes* can be located. The years of the relationes represented in the series are indicated under the Latin name of the diocese; all are in the twentieth century. The underlining of some dates indicates that those relationes are closed for research.

ASV Indice 1169 contains three newly typed appendices. The first is labeled "Appendice" and contains more recent additions to the relationes from selected dioceses. Additions date from 1911 on. This appendix follows the form established by the main body of the index: alphabetical by the name of the diocese in Latin, the name in the national language, the years of the relationes under the Latin name, and a posizione number. The second appendix is called "Cappellani militari" and contains only the names of Italian dioceses. Each of the dioceses is followed by an Arabic numeral that may be the posizione and a Roman numeral that may be the scatola number. A third appendix is identified as "Vescovo dell'Esercito e dell'Armata." This is also a list of Italian dioceses, which appears to be followed by a posizione number (in Arabic numerals) and a box or scatola number, also in Arabic numerals. Numerical designations and names of dioceses differ from those in the previous sections of this index.

Location: Archivio Segreto Vaticano.

3.1.3.33 Sedi titolari
[DATABASE ID: VATV10134-A]
Inclusive Dates: 1910–1948.
Bulk: 2 linear m.
Organization: Alphabetical by see.
Scope: These are documents granting titular sees.
Location: Archivio Segreto Vaticano.

3.1.3.34 Titoli
[DATABASE ID: VATV10454-A]
Inclusive Dates: ca. 1935–1960.
Bulk: 1 linear m. (sciolti).
Location: Archivio Segreto Vaticano.

3.1.4 Congregatio de Auxiliis Divinae Gratiae
[DATABASE ID: VATV900-A]

In 1597 Clement VIII appointed the Congregatio de Auxiliis Divinae Gratiae to settle the contemporary dispute over the relationship between actual grace and free will. This controversy between the Jesuits and Dominicans had reached a fresh stage when the Jesuit theologian, Luis de Molina, published his *Concordia liberi arbitrii cum gratiae donis* (1588).

Among others, the Dominican theologian, Domingo Bañez, attacked Molina's teaching, and the controversy became so heated between the two orders that Clement VIII brought the matter to Rome. In November 1597 he established the congregation to resolve the differences by examining the theology involved. The congregation reported for the first time on March 19, 1598, recommending that the circulation of Molina's book be forbidden and that ninety propositions from it be condemned. The pope, however, declined to approve the recommendation.

Influences on both sides prevented a calm evaluation of the controversy. After numerous sessions without essential change, the pope decided to convene a new commission and to have the theologians of both orders debate the issues. These debates began on March 20, 1602, but Clement died on March 4, 1605, without having promulgated a decision.

After the brief pontificate of Leo XI (Apr. 1–24,

1605), Paul V was elected pope (May 16, 1605). He had the debates resumed on September 14, 1605. The last discussion took place on March 1, 1606, ending the series of eighty-five sessions and forty-seven debates. On August 28, 1607, the pope convened the congregation at the Quirinal for the last time. He then declared that the Dominican position was far from Calvinistic, and that the Jesuits in holding their view were not Pelagians. Both orders were commanded to await the final decision of the Holy See; theologians were forbidden to accuse each other of heresy. On September 5, 1607, these decisions were remitted by letter to the generals of the two orders. Paul V judged that, given the situation, a doctrinal decision would be inopportune at that time. No decision on the matter was ever made.

With an edict of the Roman Inquisition of December 1, 1611, Paul V forbade the publication of books on the subject of efficacious grace without the authorization of the Holy See. This decree was confirmed by Urban VIII on May 22, 1625, and again on August 1, 1641. The prohibition was renewed by Innocent X (decree Apr. 25, 1654) and successively by Innocent XII on January 28 and February 6, 1694.

RECORDS. Records of the congregation consist of the following series.

3.1.4.1 Archivio
[DATABASE ID: VATV10392-A]
Inclusive Dates: 1588–1743.
Bulk: 2 linear m. (23 vols.).
Organization: Subseries volume enumeration and contents include: vols. 1–6., Acta (presentation copy); —vols. 11–13, writings by both Catholics and heretics concerning Molinism; —vols. 15–16., writings of the Jesuits versus Molina (rough copy).
Scope: The 1588 document is in vol. 21. This Congregatio was concerned with the Molinist controversy over freedom of the will. The series contains various writings from both the Catholic and non-Catholic viewpoints on grace and free will, primarily from the pontificates of Clement VIII (1592–1605) and Paul V (1605–1621). The title page of volume 1 (a presentation copy) reads: "Acta Sacrae Congregationis a Clemente Papa VIII instituta super controversia de viribus liberi arbitrii in statu naturae lapsae et de auxiliis gratiae divinae circa doctrinam P. Ludovici Molina et Societ. Iesu. opera et studio P. Gregorii Nunnii Coronel Lusitani ordinis Eremit. S. Augustini qui suit unus et duobus eiusdem Congregationis secretariis descripta cum originalibus collata et in VI. Tomos redacta. Joanni Baptistae Confalerio Custodi Archivi Arcis S. Angeli. Iussu. Smi. D. Nri. Urbani Papae VIII assignata. Eiusdemque inscriptionibus atque Indicibus locupletata tandem ab eodem in Armario IX. ord. p. ut et ibidem asseruarentur collocata. Anno domini MDCXXVIII. men. Iulii."
Note: Vols. 16–23 were presented to the ASV by the president of the parliament of Paris in the nineteenth century (cf. note on inside cover of vol. 16).
Location: Archivio Segreto Vaticano.

3.1.5 Congregatio de Disciplina Sacramentorum
[DATABASE ID: VATV010-A]

This congregation was established by Pius X with his motu proprio *Sapienti consilio* (Jun. 29, 1908) to regulate the discipline of the seven sacraments in the Latin church. It was the only new congregation in his reorganization of the Roman Curia. The numerous and important duties assigned to it had formerly been divided among other congregations, tribunals, and offices. These were the Congregation of the Holy Office, Congregation of the Council, Congregation of Rites, the Datary, and the Penitentiary.

Because of the many functions assigned to it, the new congregation was divided into three sections: (1) matrimonial dispensations (except those involving the Pauline privilege, mixed religion, or disparity of worship, which three areas were the province of the Congregation of the Holy Office); (2) all matters regarding matrimony except dispensations from impediments; and (3) all matters of discipline relating to the other six sacraments and dispensations in such matters. When any of the above matters required judicial process, they were to be handed over to the tribunal of the Roman Rota.

The function of the congregation was limited in relation to both persons and places; its authority was not to extend to areas assigned to the Congregation of the Propagation of the Faith or to members of religious orders. In the case of matrimony, however, the authority of the congregation was to be universal in regard to place. The Congregation for the Discipline of the Sacraments has no authority in matters touching on any of the Eastern rites or members thereof, even if such matters be of a mixed nature.

As the title indicates the new congregation was to deal with the discipline of the sacraments. Questions of doctrine were to be decided by the Congregation of the Holy Office, while those concerning the ceremonies to be observed in the administration and reception of the sacraments were to be settled by the Congregation of Rites. Within the province of the Congregation for the Discipline of the Sacraments were dispensations in the external forum (i.e., matters affecting the public welfare of the church and its members) in the impediments of matrimony, previously the function of the Datary; those in the internal forum (i.e., matters affecting the private spiritual good of individuals) belonged to the Tribunal of the Penitentiary.

The text of *Sapienti consilio* is very explicit: "To this congregation is assigned the entire legislation concerning the discipline of the seven sacraments, without prejudice to the authority of the Congregation of the Holy Office according to the provisions defined, and of the Congregation of Rites regarding ceremonies to be observed in the performance, administration, and reception of the sacraments, which were hitherto decided or granted by other congregations, tribunals, or offices of the Roman Curia."

The congregation also has specific responsibility for all those matters connected with the discipline of matrimony, such as dispensations in the external forum, sanationes in radice, dispensations super rato, the separation of married couples, the restitution of birthright or legitimation of children. In addition the congregation has responsibility for the discipline of the other sacraments, such as candidates for orders, without prejudice to the right of the Congregation for the Affairs of Religious to regulate ordinations of religious; dispensations concerning the place, time, and conditions for the reception of the sacrament, and other matters of a similar nature.

On July 11, 1975, Pope Paul VI suppressed the Congregation for the Discipline of the Sacraments and the Congregation for Divine Worship and united their functions in a new Congregation for the Sacraments and Divine Worship (apostolic constitution *Constans nobis*). By autograph letter of April 5, 1984, John Paul II reestablished them as separate congregations, but four years later (Jun. 28, 1988) his apostolic constitution *Pastor bonus* reunited them again as the Congregation for Divine Worship and the Discipline of the Sacraments.

References. Fink, p. 121; Natalini et al., p. 270.

RECORDS. Records of the congregation consist of the following series.

3.1.5.1 Ufficio: Buste numerate
[DATABASE ID: VATV10534-A]
Inclusive Dates: 1928–1954.
Bulk: Extent unavailable.
Location: Archivio Segreto Vaticano.

3.1.5.2 Ufficio I
[DATABASE ID: VATV10528-A]
Inclusive Dates: 1908–1948.
Bulk: ca. 52 linear m.
Organization: Two subseries: Cases 1–7300, 1908–[post-1922]; —[1 subseries post-1922].
Scope: These appear to be requests for permission to take the sacraments privately.
Finding Aids: There are several internal indices shelved with the series that may be useful in locating materials in this series. These are organized alphabetically by petitioner with diocese and case number noted.
Location: Archivio Segreto Vaticano.

3.1.5.3 Ufficio II: Busta da verificari
[DATABASE ID: VATV10529-A]
Inclusive Dates: 1920–1926.
Bulk: 3.5 linear m. (19 buste).
Finding Aids: There are several internal indices shelved with the series that may be useful in locating materials in this series. These are organized alphabetically by petitioner with diocese and case number noted.
Location: Archivio Segreto Vaticano.

3.1.5.4 Ufficio II: Commissione
[DATABASE ID: VATV10533-A]
Inclusive Dates: 1926–1965.
Bulk: about 100 linear m.
Note: L'Attività della Santa Sede (1990) noted that in April 1990 the Congregazione per il Culto Divino e la Disciplina dei Sacramenti transferred 530 cassette from *Ufficio II: Commissione* dating from 1956 to 1965 to the ASV.
Location: Archivio Segreto Vaticano.

3.1.5.5 Ufficio II: Directe
[DATABASE ID: VATV10531-A]
Inclusive Dates: 1908–1946.
Bulk: about 28 linear m.
Finding Aids: There are several internal indices shelved with the series that may be useful in locating materials in this series. These are organized alphabetically by petitioner with diocese and case number noted.
Location: Archivio Segreto Vaticano.

3.1.5.6 Ufficio II: Plenaria
[DATABASE ID: VATV10532-A]
Inclusive Dates: 1909–1947.
Bulk: about 28 linear m.
Finding Aids: There are several internal indices shelved with the series that may be useful in locating materials in this series. These are organized alphabetically by petitioner with diocese and case number noted.
Location: Archivio Segreto Vaticano.

3.1.5.7 Ufficio III
[DATABASE ID: VATV10535-A]
Inclusive Dates: 1909–1945 (bulk 1909–1930).
Bulk: 102 linear m.
Finding Aids: There are several internal indices shelved with the series that may be useful in locating materials in this series. These are organized alphabetically by petitioner with diocese and case number noted.
Location: Archivio Segreto Vaticano.

3.1.6 Congregatio de Propaganda Fide
[DATABASE ID: VATV016-A]

The "Propaganda," as it is generally known, serves what the Holy See considers its mission territories. The idea of a special congregation for missionary affairs seems to have originated with Ramón Lull, a Franciscan tertiary, who in the thirteenth century petitioned Celestine V (1294) and later Boniface VIII (1294–1303) to establish such a body. In 1567 Jean Vendville (later a bishop) revived the idea proposing that the pope institute a congregation for the conversion of the Greeks, another for alleviating the conditions of Christian captives among the Muslims, and a third for the Christian apostolate.

In 1568, at the urging of the Jesuit general Francis Borgia, Pius V (1566–1572) did establish two temporary commissions for the propagation of the faith: one for countries inhabited by Protestants, the other for non-Christian lands. The second commission began to meet immediately but ceased to function in 1569. There is no record of any activity on the part of the first.

In 1573 Gregory XIII (1572–1585) instituted a provisional Congregatio de Rebus Graecorum and assigned to it the duty of maintaining and propagating the Catholic faith among the Christians of the East. Clement VIII (1592–1605), who had in 1594 set up a special congregation for the missions in Abyssinia and a year later one for the Italo-Greeks, on August 11, 1599, created a new congregation that he explicitly called Congregatio de Propaganda Fide but almost immediately changed to Congregatio super Negotiis Sanctae Fidei et Religionis Catholicae. This, in fact, restored the original commission of Pius V and became a central authority for the missions, having a function corresponding to that of the Congregation for the Propagation of the Faith to be founded later.

During the pontificate of Clement VIII (1592–1605) four proposed organizations were considered: (1) a congregation of cardinals for the propagation of the faith; (2) an organization to solicit financial support for the missions; (3) a publishing house to print Christian literature; and (4) a seminary for the training of missionaries.

In 1599 Clement VIII established a so-called synodal congregation for handling missionary affairs, but after some years it ceased to exist. It was not until January 6, 1622, that a central missionary organization of permanent status was established. This formal action was confirmed by Gregory XV's bull *Inscrutabili divinae* (Jun. 22, 1622). The creation of the Congregation de Propaganda Fide marked a new era in mission history and was an important step in wresting control of the missions from Spain and Portugal.

In 1627 Urban VIII founded the Urban College to be under the jurisdiction of the Propaganda (bull *Immortalis Dei Filius*, Aug. 1, 1627). The college was originally proposed by Bishop Vendville in 1578. In 1632 under the pontificate of Urban VIII, there emerged a collateral Congregazione dell'Economia to supervise the temporal affairs of the Congregation. This continued in existence until it was suppressed by Pius X's *Sapienti consilio* (Jun. 29, 1908).

The congregation remained practically unchanged for almost two centuries, but in 1862 Pius IX divided it into two sections, establishing within the Congregation for the Propagation of the Faith a Congregatio de Propaganda Fide pro Negotiis Ritus Orientalis. That latter congregation was made autonomous in 1917 by Benedict XV and renamed the Congregatio pro Ecclesia Orientalis.

Pius X's apostolic constitution *Sapienti consilio* (Jun. 29, 1908) substantially restricted the territory of the Congregation for the Propagation of the Faith and changed the juridical position of the mission countries with regard to the Roman Curia as a whole. It also attached to the congregation the Commission for the Union of Dissident Churches established by Leo XIII's motu proprio *Optatissime* (Mar. 19, 1895).

Benedict XV in his motu proprio *Dei providentis* (May 1, 1917) separated the Congregatio de Propaganda Fide pro Negotiis Ritus Orientalis from the Congregatio de Propaganda Fide and set it up as a new congregation of the Roman Curia under the name Congregatio pro Ecclesia Orientali, with complete autonomy for Oriental affairs. Paul VI's apostolic constitution *Regimini Ecclesiae Universae* (Aug. 15, 1967) changed the name to Congregatio pro Ecclesiis Orientalibus and decreed that there be a separate office for each rite of the Eastern church in communion with the Apostolic See.

Subject to the Congregation for the Propagation of the Faith are the four principal missionary associations: the Society for the Propagation of the Faith, the Society of St. Peter for the Training of a Native Clergy, the Missionary Union of the Clergy, and the Association of the Holy Childhood. The International Fides News Service, an agency for the dissemination of mission news, is also under its direction.

Paul VI's apostolic constitution *Regimini Ecclesiae Universae* (Aug. 15, 1967) changed the name of the congregation to Congregatio pro Gentium Evangelizatione, seu de Propaganda Fide. It also stated that the congregation was to have authority "in matters regarding all missions established to spread Christ's kingdom everywhere and, therefore, in the appointment and transfer of the required ministers, and the ecclesiastical boundaries; in proposing those who are to govern these areas; in making more effective provision for a native clergy, who should gradually assume a greater role and authority; and in directing and coordinating all missionary activity around the world, with regard to the missionaries themselves and the missionary contribution of the faithful." It also set up a supreme commission for the direction of the Pontifical Mission Aid Societies. John Paul II's apostolic constitution *Pastor bonus* (Jun. 28, 1988) redefined the functions of the congregation.

At first the authority of the Congregatio de Propaganda Fide was very broad, embracing all matters related to missionary activity. The word "missions" in this case encompasses a variety of responsibilities including conversion of non-Christian peoples, ministry to Catholics living in a predominantly Protestant or Orthodox areas, and dialogue among Christian denominations. This authority was exclusive for each and every mission territory, and it included all persons and cases, even those of the internal forum. In terms of ecclesiastical authority, it had not only administrative and legislative power but also judicial within its territory. As a result, the jurisdiction of the Propaganda from its earliest days was extensive. Its geographical domain included all of the Americas, Asia, Africa, Australia, the Protestant areas of northern Europe, and the Orthodox areas of

eastern Europe. These extensive powers were modified by Pius X's apostolic constitution *Sapienti consilio* (Jun. 29, 1908). This restricted the congregation in regard to territory, matters of faith, matrimonial cases, the discipline of the sacred rites, and religious as missionaries.

In general, the congregation has charge of the Catholic missions for the spread of the faith, and whatever is connected with and necessary for their management. It has ordinary administrative and executive but no longer judicial power.

Within the territories subject to it, the congregation takes the place, in most matters, of the various congregations of the Roman Curia. However, it may not handle matters pertaining to the Holy Office (in cases concerning faith), the Ceremonial Congregation, the Congregation for Extraordinary Ecclesiastical Affairs, the Congregation for the Oriental Church, and the Penitentiary (in the internal forum). Its jurisdiction is also limited by that of the Congregation of Religious in matters concerning religious as such. Today the jurisdiction of the congregation reaches into practically all those portions of the world where the hierarchy has not been regularly established. (See Annuario Pontificio under the following headings: Vicariati Apostolici, Prefetture Apostoliche, Missioni Sui Iuris, Amministrazioni Apostoliche.)

A NOTE ON THE ARCHIVES OF THE PROPAGANDA FIDE (APF)

The congregation maintains its own archives at its historic quarters in the Piazza di Spagna in Rome. The archives are divided into two sections, the historical archives for material prior to 1922 and the modern archives. The modern archives is exclusively in support of the ongoing work of the congregation and is not open for research use. In general the contents of the historical archives are open to research. However, a significant percentage of the holdings of the historical archives remain unprocessed and is thus not generally available for consultation.

The description of the records of the Propaganda that follows is divided into two sections. The first, in considerable detail, pertains to the processed material available for research. These series contain the most important records of the congregation and document its extensive involvement all over the world. The second, in summary form, lists unprocessed materials, which are essentially a variety of smaller collections of documents and registers. Because the material is considered unprocessed, the project staff had limited access to the materials described in the second section of documents even though they were created prior to 1922. Also please note that because of limited access to the stacks of the archives full information on the bulk (in linear meters) could not be obtained in a consistent way for each series in the archives of the Propaganda Fide.

References. For a good general overview of the history of Propaganda, see J. Metzler, ed., *Compendio di storia della Sacra Congregazione per l'evangelizzazione dei popoli o "De Propaganda Fide,"* 1622–1972 (Rome, 1973). The standard work that introduces the archives in English is N. Kowalsky and J. Metzler, *Inventory of the Historical Archives of the Congregation for the Evangelization of Peoples or "de Propaganda Fide,"* 3d enl. ed. (Rome, 1988). Throughout the description of the records of the Propaganda Fide, this work is cited as Kowalsky-Metzler. In addition see J. Metzler, "Indici dell'Archivio storico della S. C. de Propaganda Fide," *Euntes Docete* 21 (1968): 109–130. This article is cited as "Metzler indici."

The following works are also useful. J. Beckmann, *La Congregation de la Propagation de la Foi face a la politique internationale* (Schöneck-Beckenried, 1963). C. Costantini, "Ricerche d'archivio sull'istruzione 'de clero indigena:' emanata dalla S.C. de Propaganda Fide il 23 novembre 1845," in *Miscellanea Pietro Fumasoni-Biondi* (Rome, 1947), vol. 1, pp. 1–78. I. F. de Espinosa, *Crónica de los colegios de Propaganda Fide de la Nueva España,* new ed. (Washington, D.C., 1964). N. C. Fabri de Peiresc, *Correspondance de Peiresc avec plusieurs missionaires et religieux de l'ordre des Capucins, 1631–1637* (Paris, 1891). B. Jacqueline, "L'organisation interne du dicastère missionaire après 350 ans," in *Sacrae Congregationis de Propagande Fide Memoria Rerum: 350 anni a servizio delle missioni,* edited by J. Metzler (Rome, 1972), pp. 382–412 [this title was noted but not verified by project staff]. N. Kowalsky, *Inventario dell'Archivio storico della S. Congregazione de Propaganda Fide* (Schöneck-Beckenried, 1961). B. Millett, "The Archives of the Congregation de Propaganda Fide," *Proceedings of the Irish Catholic Historical Committee* (1956): 20–27. G. Nicolio, *Un inventaire des Archives de la Propagande, milieu du XVIIe siècle (fra Girolamo Nicolio, augustin, 14 avril 1662, son Journal historique des missions d'Afrique, d'Amerique et d'Asie),* edited by F. Combaluzier (Schöneck-Beckenried, 1947).

Users interested in documents in the Propaganda archives relating to North America should be aware of the following sources:

F. Kenneally, *United States Documents in the Propaganda Fide Archives: A Calendar* (Washington, D.C., 1966–). Entries are organized chronologically and contain a reference to specific series with a summary of the document in English, an original language note, and occasionally a reference to related entries in the calendar. There is a name index at the end of the volume. There is also a combined index volume that lists all proper names, dioceses, and religious orders appearing in vols. 1–7.

A. Debevec, *United States Documents in the Propaganda Fide Archives: A Calendar,* 2d ser. (Washington,

D.C., 1966–) [this title was noted but not verified by project staff]. The format is a continuation of Kenneally, above.

L. Codignola, *Guide des documents relatifs à l'Amérique du Nord française et anglaise dans les archives de la Sacrée Congrégation de la Propagande à Rome, 1622–1799* (Ottawa, 1990). This is the index to a set of microfiche or a printed volume also by Codignola entitled, *Vatican, Archives of the Sacred Congregation "de Propaganda Fide" 1622–1799* (Ottawa, 1990). This work is Finding Aid No. 1186, prepared for the Manuscript Division of the National Archives of Canada and the Research Centre for Religious History in Canada, Saint Paul University. The guide provides a very good introduction to the Propaganda and one of the best explanations of the internal processes that led to the creation of the major series. The guide then provides an alphabetical listing of proper names, geographic entities, religious orders, missionary societies, and limited subjects (e.g., Quakers, Puritans). The Roman and Arabic numerals next to these entries lead one to either the microfiche or the printed guide noted above, the Roman numerals signifying the supplied series number and the Arabic numeral signifying the supplied item number within that series. Individual entries list the series name, volume, year of volume, folio number(s), item number(s), the place, date of the letter, correspondents, a description of the letter, a summary in English, information about the file, and cross references. Because of the time period covered, the guide includes references to parts of the United States.

L. Codignola, *Calendar of Documents relating to Canada in the Archives of the Sacred Congregation "de Propaganda Fide" in Rome, 1800–1830* (Ottawa, 1993) [this title was noted but not verified by project staff]. This follows in the same format as the previously cited work.

L. Codignola, *Calendar of Documents relating to Canada in the Archives of the Sacred Congregation "de Propaganda Fide" in Rome, 1831–1846* (Ottawa, forthcoming) [this title was noted but not verified by project staff]. See above for a description of the format and the contents of the entries. This volume continues the series.

M. Benoit, *Inventaire des principales séries de documents intéressant le Canada, sous le pontificat de Léon XIII (1878–1903), dans les archives de la Sacrée Congrégation "De Propaganda Fide" a Rome* (4 volumes: I/IA - Index, Acta, and Scritture originali . . . congregazioni generali; IIB - SC, IIIA - SC, Nuovo serie; and IIIB - SC, Nuovo serie) [this title was noted but not verified by project staff]. Benoit's guide begins approximately where Codignola's ends. She provides access to documents in the *Acta,* the *Scritture originali riferite nei Congressi,* and the *Scritture riferite nei Congressi 1878–1903.* Volume 1 is an index to the other three volumes. The index lists proper names, religious communities, subjects (dispenses matrimoniales), and periodicals and refers researchers to a page number in one of the other volumes. At this point a researcher must peruse the page for the specific reference. Each page lists the series and volume number under consideration at the top of the page. Individual entries give the date of the document, the correspondents or a title, an occasional very brief summary in French, and the first folio number. As in the Codignola guide, there may be items pertaining to the United States indexed here, although the Kenneally guide would be the place to start.

G. Pizzorusso, *Inventaire des documents d'intérêt canadien dans les archives de la Congrégation de "Propaganda Fide," 1904–1914* (Rome, 1993). This is a continuation of the guides by Codignola and Benoit. Pizzorusso provides an introduction to each series treated in this volume (*Acta* and *Scritture riferite nei Congressi*), and to the relationship between the Propaganda Fide and Canada in its last years as a missionary territory. He then explains the organization and compilation of the series (which is organized according to rubrica numbers signifying a certain subject) and the volumes. There is an index of proper names, religious communities and some types of transactions (matrimonia, acta) in the back of the work. A header on each page indicates the series, the volume number, a rubrica number, and the year. Individual entries begin with the date and are followed by the correspondents, a brief summary in French, and the folio numbers. As in the other Canadian guides, some United States subjects are indexed.

RECORDS. Records of the congregation consist of the following series. This list is divided into two sections, Processed Records and Unprocessed Records.

Processed Records of the APF

3.1.6.1 Acta sacrae congregationis

[DATABASE ID:VATV20258-A]

Inclusive Dates: 1622–1982.

Bulk: 31 linear m. (346 vols.).

Organization: Chronological.

Scope: The *Acta* are the minutes of the monthly meetings of the Cardinals and the other members of the Congregation (congregazione generale), the reports (ristretti) of the cardinal ponente or of the secretary and the resolutions (riscritti). The series begins with volume 3. Numbers 1 and 2 were reserved for minutes of earlier congregations not yet acquired. When these records were recovered, they seem to have been arranged in various series and are now placed under number 21 of the *Miscellanee diverse.* Numbers 1 and 2 of the *Acta* are duplicates as are also volumes 5, 9, 11, and 40.

For the first decades, each volume of the *Acta* generally contains the minutes of two years, except volume 3 (1622–1625) and volume 18 (1648). From 1651 onward each year has one volume with, however, a few exceptions. Thus the years 1808–1814 have only one volume (the so-called diario or diary), and the same is true for the years 1914/15 and 1917/18. The years 1866, 1868, 1873, 1874, 1883, 1904, 1905 have two volumes each. After thirty-five years the editing of the minutes of the congregazioni generali was changed both in form and content. The first two secretaries, Ingoli (1622–1649) and Massari (1649–1657), composed the minutes in Latin. The minutes were entered in the register without any break between the individual meetings; often the minutes of a new year continued on the same page as those of the previous year. The date is entered at the beginning of each session along with the number of the current congregazione generale. In the margin there are notes on the substance of the matter or the person or object being discussed.

From May/June 1657, the minutes are transcribed in Italian. After 1657, a distinction is made between the report of the cardinal ponente (ristretto) and the list (sommario) of documents on which the report of the secretary is made at the beginning. Often the entire original text is transcribed in the sommario. The third element in the minutes is made up of the rescriptum or, as it is less often called, cecretum, which contains the decisions of the congregation itself.

References: Kowalsky-Metzler, pp. 21–26.

F. Kenneally, *United States Documents in the Propaganda Fide Archives: A Calendar* (Washington, D.C., 1966–). Entries are organized chronologically and contain a reference to specific series with a summary of the document in English, an original language note, and occasionally a reference to related entries in the calendar. There is a name index at the end of the volume. There is also a combined index volume that lists all proper names, dioceses, and religious orders appearing in vols. 1–7. Portions of volumes 5 and 6 contain a calendar of some documents from the *Acta* relating to the United States. The entries begin on page 195 of volume 5 and are organized chronologically, although the entries are interspersed with the entries from other APF series. Each entry contains the following information: series name, volume and folio numbers, date, congregation number and congregation item number, place, and author of the document. A summary of the letter follows with a note concerning the original language, and occasionally a reference to related entries in the calendar. The calendar is limited to certain volumes of the *Acta.* Other volumes dealing with European countries or other parts of the Americas might also contain pertinent entries concerning the United States, but are not included in this index. There is a name index at the end of each calendar volume. There is also a combined index for volumes 1–7 that indexes all proper names, dioceses, and religious orders.

A. Debevec, *United States Documents in the Propaganda Fide Archives: A Calendar,* 2d ser. (Washington, D.C., 1966–) [this title was noted but not verified by project staff]. The format is a continuation of Kenneally, above. Portions of volumes 8–11 contain a calendar of items in the *Acta.*

There are many works based on the *Acta.* A majority of these historical studies are focused on the history of a certain geographic area. A few contain notes of interest to those interested in nongeographic subject areas or geographic areas other than the one under consideration in a given study. A few of these studies are listed below to provide examples of this research:

L. Campeau, *Établissement à Québec, 1616–1634* (Rome,

1979). This work makes use of several Propaganda Fide series, particularly the *Acta*. Documents from the *Acta* are reprinted. The reprints include form, the volume number, the congregation number and date, the item and folio numbers. For each reprinted document there is an introduction that focuses on the background of the issues considered; the document is then summarized in French and then reprinted in full in the original language. There are some analytical notes.

B. Jacqueline, "Actes de la S.C. 'de Propaganda Fide' concernant la province de Normandie (1622–1658)," *Cahiers Leopold Delisle* 17, fasc. 1–2 (1968): 3–21. The volume can be used as an index to *Acta* materials concerning Normandy between 1622 and 1658. The entries include the date of the *congregatio*, a brief summary in French, the volume, folio, and item number. The acta is then reprinted in the original Latin. Finally, analytic and or bibliographic notes are given. These notes may include a history of persons involved, books concerning the person or event, and other books that have reprinted or used the document.

See G. Denzler, *Die Propagandakongregation in Rom und die Kirche in Deutschland im ersten Jahrzehnt nach dem Westfälischen Frieden: Mit Edition der Kongregationsprotokolle zu deutschen Angelegenheiten 1649–1657* (Paderborn, 1969). This work is in two sections: (1) a history of the region, and (2) reprints of documents from the *Acta* concerning Westfalia. Reprinted documents begin with the date of the congregation, a German summary, the volume and folio numbers, an introduction to those present at the congregation, and finally a reprint of the item with exact volume, folio, and item number listed. The reprints are in the original language and analytical footnotes provide contextual information. This work is continued by H. Tüchle, *Die Protokolle der Propagandakongregation zu deutschen Angelegenheiten 1657–1667 diasporasorge unter Alexander VII* (Paderborn, 1972). This work reprints items from the *Acta* concerning German affairs from 1657 to 1667. Entries provide the name of the addressee, the *Acta* volume, folio, and item numbers; a summary in German or Italian of the request and a summary in Latin of the rescript. The entries are analytical and the annotations provide biographical and historical notes. Publications that have reproduced all or part of the *Acta* item under consideration are also footnoted. This is a continuation of the work by Denzler and relates to other works by Tüchle. There is an index to names and places represented in the *Acta* covered by this work at the end of the volume. See also Tüchle's earlier work, *Acta S.C. de Propaganda Fide Germaniam spectantia: Die Protokolle der Propaganda-Kongregation zu deutschen Angelegenheiten 1622–1649* (Paderborn, 1962).

B. Jennings, "Acta S. Congregationis de Propaganda Fide, 1622–1650 (Irlanda)," *Archivium hibernicum* 22 (1959): 28–139. Jennings goes through the first twenty-eight years of the *Acta* and extracts all of the atti relating (broadly interpreted) to Irish affairs. The transcriptions are presented in *Acta* volume (i.e., chronological) order. General information about each volume is given, probably taken from the spine. The introduction to each volume is transcribed, then the date of the *congregatio*, the atti introduction (where held, cardinals in attendance, etc.), and the folio numbers are given. Each entry pertaining to Ireland includes the atti in the original Latin with folio and item numbers. There are few analytical notes.

H. Fenning, "A Guide to Eighteenth-Century Reports on Irish Dioceses in the Archives of Propaganda Fide," *Collectanea hibernica*, no. 11 (1968): 19–35. Fenning has identified several series in the Propaganda, including the *Acta*, in which the reports might be located. He calendars all the Irish diocesan reports that he located in these series in this article. Entries include the date, place, bishop, title (if any) of the report, a brief contents summary, and the series volume and folio numbers.

C. Giblin, *Irish Franciscan Mission to Scotland, 1619–1646: Documents from Roman Archives* (Dublin, 1964). Giblin reprints pertinent documents from the ASV and the APF. APF documents are from the *Acta* and the *Scritture originali riferite nelle congregazioni generali* (SOCG). Documents are reprinted in full in the original language and then translated into English. Current series, volume, and folio numbers are given. There are few annotations.

I. Kollmann, ed., *Acta Sacrae Congregationis de Propaganda Fide res gestas bohemicas illustrantia* (Prague, 1923–1955). This work provides reprints and summaries of documents concerning Bohemia in various series of the APF. Although *Acta* and *Lettere volgari* are the primary series used, reprints of documents from other Congregatio de Propaganda Fide series are also in these volumes.

L. Lemmens, *Hierarchia latina orientis, 1622–1922* (Rome, 1923–1924). In the first of two volumes, after a historical introduction, Lemmens reprints from the *Acta* the appointment letters for bishops in four areas: (1) Naxivan, (2) Smyrna-Asia Minor, (3) Constantinople, and (4) Cyprus-Paphos. The entries include the volume, folio numbers, the year, and an excerpt from the *Acta*. The volume and page numbers, however, are not always correct. Lemmens also refers to other series in the APF, to the Sec. Brev. (in the ASV), and to numerous secondary sources. The second volume has similar information on nine other areas: (1) Persia, (2) Baghdad, (3) Cairo-Memphis, and (4) Aleppo. These entries contain the same information as noted above. Information concerning appointments without excerpts from the *Acta* are given for (5) Egypt, (6) Jerusalem, (7) Aden-Arabia, (8) Nile Delta, and (9) Libya-Tripoli. There is also an index to titular sees and persons mentioned.

The following works are also helpful. Catholic Church, Congregatio de Propaganda Fide, *Collectanea constitutionum, decretorum, indultorum ac instructionum Sanctae Sedis: Ad usum operariorum apostolicorum Societatis Missionum ad Exteros*, ed. altera (Hong Kong, 1905). H. Fenning, "John Kent's Report on the State of the Irish Mission, 1742," *Archivium hibernicum* 28 (1966): 59–102. É. de Jonghe and T. Simar, *Archives congolaises* (Brussels, 1919). G. Nicolio, *Un inventaire des Archives de la Propaganda, milieu du XVIIe siècle (fra Girolamo Nicolio, augustin, 14 avril 1662, son Journal historique des missions d'Afrique, d'Amerique et d'Asie)*, edited by F. Combaluzier (Schöneck-Beckenried, 1947). G. Sorge, *Il "Padroado" regio e la S. Congregazione "de Propaganda Fide" nei secoli XIV–XVII* (Bologna, 1985). A. H. Velykyi, *Acta S.C. de Propaganda Fide Ecclesiam Catholicam Ucrainae et Bielarusjae spectantia* (Rome, 1953–1955). A. H. Velykyi, *S. Josaphat Hieromartyr: Documenta romana beatificationis et canonizationis* (Rome, 1952–). A. van den Wyngaert, G. Mensaert, and F. Margiotti, *Sinica Franciscana: Itinera et relationes Fratrum Minorum saeculi XIII et XIV* (Florence, 1929–).

Finding Aids: Most volumes of the *Acta* possess an internal index that is of greater or less detail according to the particular volume. For the first thirty-five years when the secretaries were first Ingoli and then Massari, the indices are no more than a repetition of the margin headings arranged alphabetically. Indeed the alphabetical order is observed only for the first letter of each word. In these early indices, there is a preponderance of geographical terms over the names of people or things.

In 1657 the old mixed index was divided into three parts: geographical (index locorum); personal (index personarum), which uses the word "person" in a very broad sense to include such terms as archbishop, college, and vicar; and finally the index of the congregazioni generali with indications as to the material discussed under each heading. After 1668 the three indices were reduced to one and in doing so the personal element was eliminated and the list of subject matter was greatly restricted. The basic element was a list of geographical names taken in the widest sense of the term. On the other hand the index not only enumerates facts under the heading of the country in question but it also gives a resume, however brief, of each matter raised. Besides these indices in each volume of the Acta, there are also general indices available to the researcher. The most important of these are: Indice Generale (1622–1829), 14 volumes; Indice delle Ponenze (1830–1903), 1 volume; Indice degli atti della S.C. per Ordine di Materie (1622–1908), 9 volumes.

L. Codignola, Guide des documents relatifs à l'Amérique du Nord française et anglaise dans les archives de la Sacrée Congrégation de la Propagande à Rome, 1622–1799 (Ottawa, 1990). This is the index to a set of microfiche or a printed volume also by Codignola entitled Vatican, Archives of the Sacred Congregation "de Propaganda Fide" 1622–1799 (Ottawa, 1990). This work is Finding Aid No. 1186, prepared for the Manuscript Division of the National Archives of Canada and the Research Centre for Religious History in Canada, Saint Paul University. The guide provides a very good introduction to the Propaganda and one of the best explanations of the internal processes that led to the creation of the major series. The guide then provides an alphabetical listing of proper names, geographic entities, religious orders, missionary societies, and limited subjects (e.g., Quakers, Puritans). The Roman and Arabic numerals next to these entries lead one to either the microfiche or the printed guide noted above, the Roman numerals signifying the supplied series number, and the Arabic numeral signifying the supplied item number within that series. Individual entries list the series name, volume, year of volume, folio number(s), item number(s), the place, date of the letter, correspondents, a description of the letter, a summary in English, information about the file, and cross-eferences. Because of the time period covered, the guide includes references to parts of the United States.

L. Codignola, Calendar of Documents relating to Canada in the Archives of the Sacred Congregation "de Propaganda Fide" in Rome, 1800–1830 (Ottawa, 1993) [this title was noted but not verified by project staff]. This follows in the same format as the previously cited work.

L. Codignola, Calendar of Documents relating to Canada in the Archives of the Sacred Congregation "de Propaganda Fide" in Rome, 1831–1846 (Ottawa, forthcoming) [this title was noted but not verified by project staff]. See above for a description of the format and the contents of the entries. This volume continues the series.

M. Benoit, Inventaire des principales séries de documents intéressant le Canada, sous le pontificat de Léon XIII (1878–1903), dans les archives de la Sacrée Congrégation "De Propaganda Fide" à Rome [this title was noted but not verified by project staff]. Benoit's guide begins approximately where Codignola's ends. She provides access to documents in the Acta and other series from 1878 to 1903. Volume 1 is an index to the other three volumes. The index lists proper names, religious communities, subjects (dispenses matrimoniales), and periodicals, and refers researchers to a page number in one of the other volumes. Once one reaches that page, one must read through each item until one finds the reference for the desired items. Each page lists the series and volume number under consideration at the top of the page. Individual entries give the date of the document, the correspondents or a title, an occasional very brief summary in French, and the first folio number. As in the Codignola guide, there may be items of United States interest indexed here, although the Kenneally guide would be the place to start.

Location: Archives of the Propaganda Fide.

3.1.6.2 Archivio della procura della congregazione nell'Estremo Oriente

[DATABASE ID: VATV20278-A]

Inclusive Dates: 1749–1873.

Bulk: 47 numbered boxes.

Scope: This series, now in the custody of the Archives of the Propaganda Fide, was transferred to Rome through the intervention of the first apostolic delegate in China, Archbishop Celso Costantini, acting on the orders of Cardinal Van Rossum, prefect of the Congregation for the Missions, during the second decade of the twentieth century.

The importance and value of this abundant documentation, especially the letters from the missionaries, is due to the position and duties of the procurator. According to the instructions of the Congregatio de Propaganda Fide (CPF), the papal legate, Patriarch Charles Thomas Maillard de Tournon, established in Canton a procurator for the missions in China in the year 1705. At first the duties of the procurator were mainly administrative and economic: administration of the delegate's ecclesiastical properties and those of the Propaganda. He had also to see that the subsidies reached the missions and to ensure the delivery of correspondence between Rome and the missionaries. As time went on, his duties and powers were greatly increased and the procurator became the trusted representative of the Propaganda for all the missions of the Far East. Often he had to transmit pontifical briefs and gifts to the emperor of China. He was also entrusted with special faculties concerning the Chinese priests in the Holy Family College in Naples. During the nineteenth century, he was given the task of preparing and convening a General Council for China and the "surrounding Kingdoms" (which, however, did not take place because the majority of apostolic vicars judged that the convening of such a council would not be opportune).

The procurator, as representative of the CPF, was involved in the longstanding controversy between the Roman Congregation and Portugal on the subject of the Missionary "Padroado" of that country. Often too, he suffered because of the persecutions in China. This explains why the procurator's office was frequently changed from Canton to Macao and back again, and eventually, to Hong Kong. From 1841 onward, the office of procurator was temporarily attached to that of the prefect and vicar apostolic of Hong Kong. With the establishment of the apostolic delegation in China in 1922 and the subsequent death of the then procurator in 1923, it no longer seemed necessary to maintain this office since the duties of the procurator were assumed by the apostolic delegate. In all there were twenty who held the office of either procurator, vice-procurator or procurator ad interim.

These archives contain the original letters of about 360 missionaries in China and the "surrounding Kingdoms" as well as the letters of many native clergy and the original letters of the Congregatio de Propaganda Fide itself and in some cases the minute letters of the procurator, his correspondence with various apostolic nunciatures, such as that of Paris, with bishops, agents, directors of the Missionary Societies in France, with the superiors of the "College for Chinese" in Naples, acta of the martyrs, and so forth. On the basis of these letters and accounts from the missionaries, the Procurator composed his "Memorie" (annual reports) for the Missionary Congregation in Rome. They are consequently a most valuable source for the history of the missions in China and in the "surrounding Kingdoms."

Reference: Kowalsky-Metzler, pp. 82–86.

Location: Archives of the Propaganda Fide.

3.1.6.3 Atti della Commissione per la revisione delle regole
[DATABASE ID: VATV20269-A]

Inclusive Dates: 1887–1908.

Bulk: 2 linear m. (26 items).

Organization: There are two unnumbered index volumes at the beginning titled "Regole Indice" and "Atti Commissione Revisione Regole-Indice." Volumes 1–17 are chronological. In addition there are about eleven miscellaneous volumes and buste at the end primarily containing rules and constitutions of different religious orders.

Scope: In 1887 the Congregation de Propaganda Fide established a special commission presided over by a cardinal for the revision of the rules of institutes dependent on the Propaganda. After publication of the constitution *Sapienti consilio* (1908), the commission ceased to exist. It was re-established in a new form in 1933. This series contains acta of the Commission for the Revision of Rules and copies of rules and constitutions.

Reference: Kowalsky-Metzler, p. 66.

Finding Aids: The two unnumbered index volumes at the beginning of the series provide limited access. The first is entitled "Regole Indice." The second, "Atti Commissione Revisione Regole-Indice"(1887–1908), is arranged geographically and lists the rubric number, provides a summary of the business, and gives the "posizione in archivio," that is, a year and a number. Neither of these indici is thoroughly effective for locating documents, but they do provide an indication of the range of business of the Commissione Revisione.

Location: Archives of the Propaganda Fide.

3.1.6.4 Brevi e bolle
[DATABASE ID: VATV20265-A]

Inclusive Dates: 1775–1952.

Bulk: 1 linear m. (13 vols.).

Scope: According to Kowalsky and Metzler, this series contains pontifical decisions concerning the territories of the Propaganda relating to such matters as the establishment of

ecclesiastical provinces and apostolic vicariates and appointment of bishops.

Reference: Kowalsky-Metzler, p. 62.

Finding Aids: The Propaganda Archives itself does not have a finding aid to this series. For useful citations to particular documents in the series, users should consult Kenneally; vol. 6 of the first series contains a calendar of documents in selected *Brevi* volumes. The entries are organized chronologically by volume of the *Brevi.*

A. Debevec, *United States Documents in the Propaganda Fide Archives: A Calendar,* 2d ser. (Washington, D.C., 1966–) [this title was noted but not verified by project staff]. Portions of volumes 8, 10, and 11 of Debevec contain a calendar of items in selected volumes of the *Brevi.*

Location: Archives of the Propaganda Fide.

3.1.6.5 Collezione d'istruzioni, circolari e decreti a stampa
[DATABASE ID: VATV20277-A]

Inclusive Dates: ca. 1650–1903.

Bulk: .3 linear m. (3 vols).

Organization: Volumes are marked I, IA, and II.

Scope: This is a collection of copies of each printed matter issued by the congregation. The series includes instructions, circular letters, and decrees of the congregation from the middle of the seventeenth century up to 1903. They are not arranged in chronological order, nor are the three volumes paginated, but the documents are numbered. These numbers should be given in citations.

Reference: Kowalsky-Metzler, p. 82.

Location: Archives of the Propaganda Fide.

3.1.6.6 Congregatio Particularis de rebus Sinarum et Indiarum Orientalium
[DATABASE ID: VATV20261-A]

Inclusive Dates: 1665–1856.

Bulk: 102 vols. and 3 miscelleanea.

Organization: This series has two subseries: Acta Congregationis Particularis super rebus Sinarum et Indiarum Orientalium (Acta CP), 1665–1856 (24 vols.); and Scritture Originali della Congregazione Particolare dell'Indie e Cina (original documents from the special commission on the Indies and China; SOCP), 1667–1856 (78 vols. and 3 miscellanea [duplicates]).

Scope: According to Kowalsky and Metzler, the permanent special commission for China and the East Indies was in existence from 1664 onward. In 1665 two special archive sections were formed for the documentation generated by the special commission meetings: the Atti, together with the minutes of the meetings, and the original documents to which the commission referred. The internal arrangement of these two sections is identical with that of the sections from the general meetings.

References: Kowalsky-Metzler, pp. 47–48. A. van den Wyngaert, G. Mensaert, and F. Margiotti, *Sinica Franciscana: Itinera et relationes Fratrum Minorum saeculi XIII et XIV* (Florence, 1929–).

Finding Aids: There are three volumes of indices arranged according to subject matter and three further volumes according to locality. They are very well made and therefore very useful, although a certain amount of patience and experience is necessary for their use because the page numbers of the volumes referred to are, today, different from what they were when the indices were made.

Location: Archives of the Propaganda Fide.

3.1.6.7 Congregazioni particolari (referred to as CP)
[DATABASE ID: VATV20260-A]

Inclusive Dates: 1622–1864.

Bulk: 14 linear m. (161 vols. plus 2 unnumbered vols.).

Organization: Subseries with volume numbers include: vols. 1–4, 24, de Status temporalis missionum e typographis; —vols. 11–13, circa le cose d'Hibernia d'Inghilterra; ; —vols. 14, 25, 91–92, 103, 114, 117, 120, de rebus Polonia et Ruthenorum; — vols. 17. Caldei Calendar Piedmonte, Olanda, Ruteni; —vols. 26, 86, di Scozia; —vols. 27 , 63, 71, Terra Santa e Cipro; —vol. 28, Stato Temporale/Visita del Seminario di S. Panacrazio; —vols. 33, 49, Sopra i collegi di Avignone; —vols. 35–47, Sopra le materie/Sulla cassa del Sale di Boemia; —vols. 50–62, Sopra le materie d i Olanda; —vols. 64–65, Armeni di Leopoldi; —vols. 75–82, 128–129, Greci melchiti; ; —vol. 83, Greci melchiti e maroniti; —vols. 94–95, 99, 113, 118, 135–136, 138–139, Maroniti; —vol. 84, Tibet; —vol. 107, Rezia; —vol. 121, Archipelago.

Scope: These are the records of commissions of cardinals established by the pope to deal with questions under the jurisdiction of the congregation about which there were special difficulties. Most were ad hoc commissions, but some had a longer life span or even became permanent.

For the period 1622–1668 the minutes of these special commissions are scattered among the minutes of the general meetings and the original documents referring to them are included without distinction in the collection of the first 417 volumes belonging to the *Scritture originali . . . congregazioni generali* (SOCG) or the first ten volumes of this series. These last mentioned concern especially the temporal state of the missions, the Propaganda polyglot printing press, a number of colleges including the Urbanian College of Propaganda Fide, and, scattered among them, a number of records from the period 1648–1668. Beginning with volume 11 the internal arrangement of each volume becomes more regular and is identical with the second series of the SOCG with, however, one exception: the minutes of the sessions are together with the original documents referred to in the special meetings. The order is chronological but it happens from time to time that documents concerning a certain country are all bound together.

References: Kowalsky-Metzler, pp. 40–46. C. Giblin, "A Congregatio Particularis on Ireland, at Propaganda Fide, May 1671." *Collectanea hibernica*, nos. 18–19 (1976–1977): 19–39. B. Jennings, "Ireland and the Propaganda Fide, 1672–6," *Archivium hibernicum* 17 (1955): 16–66; 18 (1956): 1–60. A. H. Velykyi, *Congregationes particulares Ecclesiam Catholicam Ucrainae et Bielarusjae spectantes* (Rome, 1956–1957). A. H. Velykyi, *Litterae nuntiorum apostolicorum historiam Ucrainae illustrantes (1550–1850)* (Rome, 1959–). See citations for the Congregatio de Propaganda Fide series *Acta sacrae congregationis*, many of which pertain to this series as well.

Finding Aids: There are three volumes of indices with lists according to locality and to subject matter. They are quite detailed and very well made but their value is diminished by the fact that the page numbers they indicate do not correspond to the present numbers. Although the old page numbers in the CP

are still generally legible, the order of pages has been somewhat mixed. Before being bound definitively, pages were rearranged and numbered several times so that today many pages have as many as five different numbers, thus compromising the usefulness of this index. See also the work of Luca Codignola and others cited in the introduction to the section on this congregation.

Location: Archives of the Propaganda Fide.

3.1.6.8 Congressi
[DATABASE ID: VATV10464-A]

Inclusive Dates: 1768–1851.

Bulk: .5 linear m. (7 vols.).

Organization: Volume titles are as follows: Congressi missioni, 1796; —Congressi missioni, 1816–1823; —Congressi missioni, 1827–1832; —Congressi missioni, 1827–1831; —Congressi economici, 1768–1801; —Congressi (missioni?), 1838–1841; —Congressi (missioni?), 1847–1851.

Location: Archives of the Propaganda Fide.

3.1.6.9 Decreta
[DATABASE ID: VATV10461-A]

Inclusive Dates: 1622 (copy)–1742.

Bulk: .5 linear m. (9 vols.).

Organization: Titles are as follows: Tom. I–V. "Decreta, resolutiones et instructiones Sacrarum Congregationum super Missionibus et Missionariis Apostolici Collecta jussu SSmi. D.N. PP. Benedicti XIV"; —Index to Tom. I–V; —Alcune lettere e costitutioni in stampa di Benedetto XIV; —Decreti utili, 1651–1701 (primarily copies); —Compendium excerptum e plurimis summorum pontificum constitutionibus sacrarumque Congregationis Sancti Officii e de Propaganda Fide, Decreti ac responsis circa causus in missionibus Sinarum, Turkin, Cocincinae, Siami, etc., 1828 (contains copies of material 1634–1816 and carte sciolte; there is an internal index).

Finding Aids: Vol. 6 in the series is an index to vols. I–V "Decreta, resolutiones et instructiones," and the like. The index is contemporary with the volumes it indexes and is a good guide for locating individual documents in the first five volumes. Volume, folio, and position numbers are given, although it is not indicated if an item is on the verso side of a folio, which can cause some confusion.

Location: Archives of the Propaganda Fide.

3.1.6.10 Decreti
[DATABASE ID: VATV20267-A]

Inclusive Dates: 1615–1831.

Bulk: 1 linear m. (14 vols.).

Organization: Volumes are unnumbered. Volumes 9–14 are not mentioned in Kowalsky and Metzler (1988) and are as follows: vol. 9, Minute di decreti, 1741–1767; —vol. 10, Minute di decreti, 1779–1789; —vol. 11, Minute di decreti, 1800–1809; —vol. 12, Decreta S. Congressus super Statu Economico, 1694–1768; —vol. 13, Decreti relativi a cose orientali dal 1675 [i.e., 1615] al 1831 (spine states "copie di vari decreti"); —vol. 14, "Decreta diversa ac decisiones quedam Sacrae Congregationis in rebus concernentibus Praxim Missionariorum," 1622–1671. [These volume numbers were supplied by project staff.]

Scope: According to Kowalsky and Metzler, the first volumes are from the time of the first secretary, Ingoli, who often added his own supplementary notes in the margin. In this series are found transcribed the decrees of the general meetings. It is only by way of exception that one may also find one or other decree of the weekly meetings. From 1820 onward the decrees were added at the end of the letters, and thus this series was continued by the *Lettere e decreti* (Letters and Decrees). Note that twelve volumes separated from this series are found in the series *Fondo di Vienna*.

References: Kowalsky-Metzler, p. 63. Catholic Church, Congregatio de Propaganda Fide, *Collectanea constitutionum, decretorum, indultorum ac instructionum Sanctae Sedis: Ad usum operariorum apostolicorum Societatis Missionum ad Exteros*, ed. altera (Hong Kong, 1905).

Finding Aids: There are no formal finding aids to this series. The works of Luca Codignola cited in the general introduction to the congregation can serve as a useful introduction.

Location: Archives of the Propaganda Fide.

3.1.6.11 Deputazioni e facoltà ordinarie

[DATABASE ID: VATV20435-A]

Inclusive Dates: 1722–1856.

Bulk: 6 vols.

Organization: The buste are organized chronologically. Within each busta, however, materials are arranged according to posizioni (geographic and subject designations).

Scope: This series forms a part of the *Regestum facultatum* series of the Propaganda Fide (described separately among the records of the Propaganda) and is a continuation of the Propaganda Fide series *Regestum facultatum et litterarum patentium*. As the *Regestum facultatum et litterarum patentium*, the *Deputazioni* series is versatile in the sense that it can be used as a crude index to faculties in both Propaganda Fide series *Acta* and *Udienze*. At the same time, it is itself a summary of the decrees of the faculties. The volumes are marked "Deputazioni e Facoltà ordinarie dall'Anno . . . al . . ." on the spine. There are busta numbers indicated. Two buste were examined, the first in the series (covering the years 1722–1738) and the last (covering the years 1817–1856). The volumes are organized in the same manner as the *Regestum facultatum et literarum patentium* series. An initial internal index contains posizioni that represent geographic and subject designations. The designations in the first busta are even carried over from the earlier series (e.g., America = 14; collegi = 8). In the actual volume, decrees granting faculties are reprinted in full. Later items in the regestum appear to be summarized and the volume tends to become a registro.

The final busta of the series boasts a title page reading "Registro delle deputazioni e facoltà ordinarie dall'Anno 1817 a tutto il 1856." This is followed by the "Avvertimento necessario," which explains the reason for changing the system (e.g., some of the older posizioni were no longer used much and others had become overused and needed to be broken down into several sections. This note also discussed changes in the forms of the faculties. Following the avvertimento is the "Indice delli Numeri," which reflects the new numbering system. This is followed by an extensive "Indice Generale de'Luoghi con le missioni e Provincie dalle quali dipendono." The "Indice Generale" lists countries and occasionally cities, noting the name of the mission and position number under which

faculties granted in the location would be filed. Individual items in the register are abbreviations of the decrees issued by the Congregation. The date of the Congregation is given, then the abbreviated decree. Locations are noted in the right margins and other notes (sometimes cross references to other faculties or decrees are provided in the left-hand margin).

Reference: Kowalsky-Metzler, pp. 60–61, 82. Kowalsky and Metzler link this series to the following Propaganda Fide series: *Udienza*, *Acta*, and the group of series that comprises the *Regestum facultatum*. Although the descriptions of this series vary on the pages indicated, these are the same series listed in two locations.

Location: Archives of the Propaganda Fide.

3.1.6.12 Facoltà straordinarie

[DATABASE ID: VATV20542-A]

Inclusive Dates: 1760–1850.

Bulk: 9 buste.

Organization: Chronological.

Scope: The spines of the buste indicate that these volumes contain the "Facultates Extraordinariae ab anno . . . usque ad. . . ." Two volumes were consulted by project staff; the first and the last. There are no busta numbers on the volumes. They can be requested by year, however. The first busta has no title page, the last one says "Facultates Extraordinariae ab anno 1847 ad." There are handwritten folio numbers in the upper right recto corner. Each item begins with the date of the audience in which the appointment was discussed and then provides a copy of the faculty. In some cases there is an Italian summary of the request prior to the faculty, which is always in Latin. A geographical designation is usually provided in the margins, but this is more or less precise (Irlanda vs. America Settentrionale, which can be anything in Canada or the United States).

Reference: Kowalsky-Metzler, pp. 61 and 82. Kowalsky and Metzler appear to refer to this series as two different things relating to two separate series. On page 61, they cite it as an internally compiled index to the *Udienze*; on page 82, they refer to this series as part of the *Regestum facultatum*.

Finding Aids: The following indices at the Propaganda Fide, the "Indice del Registro delle Udienze ossia Facoltà Straordinarie disposto per ordine di località dal 1760 al 1840" and the "Indice delle Facoltà Straordinarie dall'Anno 1841 a tutto il 1850 (2)" appear to provide an index to part of this series. The indices appear to be contemporary with the volumes and are organized geographically, with designations similar to those in the margins of the regular series. Entries are alphabetical by geographical designation, then chronological. In the earlier volume, the diocese is listed in the left margin with the type of transaction noted underneath it, a summary of the decree follows with the year and the folio number in the right margin. The later volume provides the diocese in the left margin, followed by a summary of the faculty, and a folio number. America Settrionale (which includes the United States) appears to be the only section with a subject note in the right hand margin with the page numbers. When a new year is starting, that too is noted in the right-hand margin. It does not appear to be easy to tie entries from the index to the actual volumes. Faculties can be described in different ways in the series and the index. Since the actual registers are in chronological order, they may be the best place to begin if a year is known. Metzler discusses this index in his article "Indici," p. 127.

F. Kenneally, *United States Documents in the Propaganda Fide Archives: A Calendar* (Washington, D.C., 1966–). Entries are organized chronologically and contain a reference to specific series with a summary of the document in English, an original language note, and occasionally a reference to related entries in the calendar. There is a name index at the end of the volume. There is also a combined index volume that lists all proper names, dioceses, and religious orders appearing in vols. 1–7. Volume 6 contains a calendar of documents in selected volumes of *Facoltà straordinarie*.

Location: Archives of the Propaganda Fide.

3.1.6.13 Fondo di Vienna

[DATABASE ID: VATV20272-A]

Inclusive Dates: 1566 and 1622–1809.

Bulk: 6.5 linear m. (74 vols.).

Organization: The *Fondo di Vienna* has eight subseries: I. Scritture originali riferite nelle congregazioni generali, 1636–1669, 20 vols. (vols. 1–20); these were separated from the Propaganda Fide series of the same name as the series title; —II. Scritture riferite nelle congregazioni particolari, 1657–1679, 4 vols. (vols. 21–24); —III. Scritture riferite nei congressi, 1675–1798, 14 vols. (vols. 25–38); —IV. Decreti della S.C. de Propaganda Fide, 1626–1797, 12 vols. (vols. 39–50); these were at one time part of the Propaganda Fide series *Decreti*; —V. Collectio cecretorum de sacris missionibus, 1622–1742, 5 vols. (vols. 50–55); —VI. Dubia et resolutiones diversarum congregationum: Officij, concilij et rituum, 1668–1807, 6 vols. (vols. 56–61); —VII. Registri dei brevi, 1701–1809, 9 vols. (vols. 62–70); —VIII. Varia, 1566–1809, 4 vols. (vol. 71, trial or proceedings between the Pontifical Agent and William Gonzaga, duke of Mantova, regarding the juspatronatus of the Church of Mantova, 1566; vol. 72, Miscellanea Irlanda-Cina, 1710–1770; vol. 73, Indice generale delle materie, ca. 1750–1790; vol. 74, Miscellanea).

Scope: According to Kowalsky and Metzler, the *Fondo di Vienna* consists of seventy-four volumes that were transferred to Vienna on the occasion of the restitution of the Propaganda Archives by the French government (1815). In 1925 the then Austrian ambassador and historian of the popes, Von Pastor, succeeded in having them restored to the Propaganda Archives. The volumes are mainly from the following Propaganda Fide series: *Scritture originali riferite nelle congregazioni generali* (original documents referred to in the general meetings), *Scritture riferite nei congressi* (documents referred to in the weekly meetings), and *Decreti* (decrees). Since the restitution took place when the other related series had already been numbered, it was considered opportune to keep them apart under the title as indicated above.

Reference: Kowalsky-Metzler, pp. 68–71.

Finding Aids: Fondo di Vienna, vol. 55, is an index to the Collectio decretorum de sacris missionibus (vols. 51–54) of the *Fondo di Vienna*. *Fondo di Vienna*, vol. 70, is a geographical index to the briefs in the Registri dei Brevi (vols. 62–69) of the *Fondo di Vienna*.

F. Kenneally, *United States Documents in the Propaganda Fide Archives: A Calendar* (Washington, D.C., 1966–). En-

tries are organized chronologically and contain a reference to specific series with a summary of the document in English, an original language note, and occasionally a reference to related entries in the calendar. There is a name index at the end of the volume. There is also a combined index volume that lists all proper names, dioceses, and religious orders appearing in vols. 1–7. Volumes 5 and 6 of the first series contain a calendar of documents in selected *Fondo di Vienna* volumes. The entries are organized chronologically, by volume of the *Fondo di Vienna*. The calendar is limited to certain volumes of the *Fondo di Vienna*.

B. Millett, "Calendar of Irish Material in Vols. 12 and 13 (ff. 1–200) of Fondo di Vienna in Propaganda Archives," *Collectanea hibernica*, no. 24 (1982): 45–80. Millett presents a good introduction to the *Fondo di Vienna* series before beginning the calendar of Irish materials in volumes 12 and 13. The materials are available on microfilm at the National Library of Ireland, Dublin (*Fondo di Vienna* 12 = positive #5532; *Fondo di Vienna* 13 = positive #5533). Information from the spine of the volume is transcribed. Each calendar entry is given in English and includes the folio numbers, any formal names of the document, the original language, its date, a summary, and the incipit. There are analytical footnotes and notations in the text that clarify phrases and provide biographical background. Supplied information is in brackets and unknown elements are indicated by question marks. Millett also notes if a document has been published or is related to other documents in this volume or in other APF series of which he is aware. The calendar of Irish materials in *Fondo di Vienna* 13 is continued in B. Millett, "Calendar of Volume 13 of the Fondo di Vienna in Propaganda Archives: Part 2, ff. 201–401," *Collectanea hibernica*, no. 25 (1983): 30–62.

L. Codignola, *Guide des documents relatifs à l'Amérique du Nord française et anglaise dans les archives de la Sacrée Congrégation de la Propagande à Rome, 1622–1799* (Ottawa, 1990). This is the index to a set of microfiche or a printed volume also by Codignola entitled *Vatican, Archives of the Sacred Congregation "de Propaganda Fide" 1622–1799* (Ottawa, 1990). This work is Finding Aid No. 1186, prepared for the Manuscript Division of the National Archives of Canada and the Research Centre for Religious History in Canada, Saint Paul University. The guide provides a very good introduction to the Propaganda and one of the best explanations of the internal processes that led to the creation of the major series. The guide then provides an alphabetical listing of proper names, geographic entities, religious orders, missionary societies, and limited subjects (e.g., Quakers, Puritans). The Roman and Arabic numerals next to these entries lead one to either the microfiche or the printed guide noted above, the Roman numerals signifying the supplied series number, and the Arabic numeral signifying the supplied item number within that series. Individual entries list the series name, volume, year of volume, folio number(s), item number(s), the place, date of the letter, correspondents, a description of the letter, a summary in English, information about the file, and cross references. Because of the time period covered, the guide includes references to parts of the United States.

L. Codignola, *Calendar of Documents relating to Canada in the Archives of the Sacred Congregation "de Propaganda Fide" in Rome, 1800–1830* (Ottawa, 1993) [this title was noted but not verified by project staff]. This follows in the same format as the previously cited work.

L. Codignola, *Calendar of Documents relating to Canada in the Archives of the Sacred Congregation "de Propaganda Fide" in Rome, 1831–1846* (Ottawa, forthcoming) [this title was noted but not verified by project staff]. See above for a description of the format and the contents of the entries. This volume continues the series.

Location: Archives of the Propaganda Fide.

3.1.6.14 Indie: Visite apostolici

[DATABASE ID: VATV10468-A]

Inclusive Dates: ca. 1865.

Bulk: .05 linear m.

Organization: One volume in two sections: Parte Prima, Visita dei Vicariati Apostolici delle Indie Orientali cominciata da Monsignor Clemente Bonnard, Vescovo di Drusipara e Vicario Apostolico di Pondichery e proseguita da Monsig. Stefano Ludovico Charbonneaux, Vescovo di Jassa e Vicario Apostolico di Mayssour; —Parte Seconda, Articoli della Visita dei Vicariati delle Indie Orientali tolti da alcuni scritti di Monsig. Claudio Depommier e di Monsig. Francesco Laouen già Assessore nella visita medesima, a supplemento delle relazione originali perdute.

Scope: These reports of visits present a detailed picture of the Catholic church in India in the late nineteenth century. A historical perspective on this region is also included in these works, particularly in the Parte Seconda.

Location: Archives of the Propaganda Fide.

3.1.6.15 Informazioni

[DATABASE ID: VATV20271-A]

Inclusive Dates: 1696–ca. 1730.

Bulk: 2 linear m. (17 vols.).

Organization: Subseries with titles or contents designations are: Pro missione sinensi (3 vols., marked lib. 118, 120, 134); —Pro missione Aethiopiae, Turchini, Cocincinae, et Siamensis, collectus anno 1701 (lib. 135); —Pro missionibus diversis (lib. 136); —Pro missione Sinense (3 vols., lib. 156, 157, 158); —Pro mission. Sinen. Acta Pekinen. (lib. 162); —Pro missione Sinen. (5 vols., lib. 163–167); —Informationes Pro Sacrae Congregationis de Propaganda Fide (3 vols., Tom. I, II, III).

Scope: According to Kowalsky and Metzler, the series has two parts. Part I includes volumes with the general title "Informationum liber pro Missione Sinensi." There are twelve volumes covering the period 1696 to 1713. One volume has the title "Informationum liber pro Missione Aethiopiae, Tunchini, Cocincinae et Siamesi, collectus anno 1701." Another volume is "Informationum liber Pro Missionibus diversis, collectus anno 1701." Part II, "Informationes pro S. Congregatione de Propaganda Fide," consists of three volumes containing information and notes on the temporal state of the Congregation de Propaganda Fide from the beginning of the eighteenth century. According to Kowalsky and Metzler, the volumes of the first part of this collection probably came from the archives of the Jesuits.

References: Kowalsky-Metzler, p. 67. See also the works of Luca Codignola cited in the introduction to the Archives of the Propaganda. A. van den Wyngaert, G. Mensaert, and F. Mar-

giotti, *Sinica Franciscana: Itinera et relationes Fratrum Minorum saeculi XIII et XIV* (Florence, 1929–).

Location: Archives of the Propaganda Fide.

3.1.6.16 Istruzioni

[DATABASE ID: VATV20266-A]

Inclusive Dates: 1623–1880.

Bulk: .5 linear m. (8 vols. or buste).

Scope: According to Kowalsky and Metzler, these are instructions and minute di istruzioni sent by the Propaganda to the nuncios, bishops, vicars apostolic, and other superiors of missions concerning various points of discipline. The Instructions show the guidelines provided by Propaganda for the activity of the missionaries and the missionary program of the congregation together with the methods employed for its implementation. The present series contains only seven volumes and one busta. The first two cover the period 1623 to 1648 and include Ingoli's tenure as secretary. Three further volumes are marked with the numbers 1, 2, and 3 and two more are marked B and C. These contain instructions from the second half of the eighteenth and the beginning of the nineteenth centuries. The fact that volume A is missing shows that there are lacunae in the series. The instructions for the rest of the nineteenth century are to be found among the following Propaganda Fide series: *Lettere* (letters), the *Scritture riferite nei congressi* (documents referred to in the weekly meetings), and the *Scritture originali riferite nelle congregazioni generali* (original documents referred to in the general meetings). There is also a more recent printed collection of instructions.

References: Kowalsky-Metzler, pp. 62–63. See also A. H. Velykyi, *Litterae S.C. de Propaganda Fide ecclesiam catholicam Ucrainae et Bielarusjae spectantes* (Rome, 1954–1957). This work contains reprints in the original language of entire letters concerning Ukraine and Belarus from the Instruzioni and other series in the APF. Entries include the volume and folio numbers, a Latin summary, and citations for other publications in which the item has been printed. There are minimal annotations. Each volume contains a name and subject index at the end. G. Sorge, *Il "Padroado" regio e la S. Congregazione "de Propaganda Fide" nei secoli XIV–XVII* (Bologna, 1985).

Location: Archives of the Propaganda Fide.

3.1.6.17 Lettere e decreti della Sacra Congregazione e biglietti di Monsignor Segretario

[DATABASE ID: VATV20268-A]

Inclusive Dates: 1622–1892.

Bulk: 27 linear m. (388 vols.).

Organization: Subseries with volume enumerations and contents designations are: vol. 1, 9, Lettere latine, 1622–1629; —vols. 2–8, 10–32, Lettere volgari, 1622–1657; —Lettere della Sacrae Congregationis, 1647–1657; —[Lettere, geographically arranged], 1658–1669; —Lettere di Monsignore Segretario; —vols. 69–109, 294–305, Lettere della Sacrae Congregationis e di Monsignore Segretario, 1680–1720, 1808–1819; —vols. 306–388, Lettere e Decreti della S. Cong. e Biglietti di Mons. Segretario, 1820–1892.

Scope: The letters of the Congregation refer to the execution of decisions taken either by the prefect alone, or by the general or particular meetings, or by the weekly meetings. The letters often explain the content and the spirit of the rescritto (decision) which is usually written in a very concise style. These letters are copies and therefore do not include the conventional formulae at the beginning and at the end but are limited to indicating merely the person to whom they are addressed and the date.

Occasionally in the first decades and regularly in later times, it was customary to refer in the margin to the person, country, or institute dealt with in the letter. The arrangement of the section entitled "Lettere" was neither constant nor uniform. Originally, there were Lettere latine (Latin letters), volume 1: 1622–1629, volume 9: 1630–1646; and Lettere volgari (in languages other than Latin), 1622–1657, volumes 2–8, 10–32. The latter series contains letters written in Italian and occasionally in French. From 1647 to 1657, there is no longer any distinction made in the organization of the series between languages. In 1658 the geographical division was introduced for the letters and maintained until 1669 (vols. 33–54). From 1670 until 1679 (vols. 55–68), two volumes were made each year: (1) register of letters from the Congregation; (2) letters written by the secretary. From 1680 to 1720 (vols. 69–109) the two volumes were bound into one: letters from the Congregation and from the secretary. For the period from 1721 to 1807 (vols. 110–293) the two sources were once again separated: (1) register of letters from the Congregation; (2) letters written by the secretary.

From time to time there are volumes devoted to a special question, that is, letters collected according to geographical criteria. From 1808 to 1819 the letters from the Congregation and the secretary were once again put together in one volume with the title "Lettere della Sacra Congregazione e Biglietti di Monsignor Segretario" (Letters from the Sacred Congregation and notes from the Secretary). During the period 1820–1892 the decrees were also included in the collection of letters and the whole series took on its definitive title *Lettere e decreti della Sacra Congregazione e biglietti di Monsignor Segretario* (LDB).

References: Kowalsky-Metzler, pp. 63–66. F. Kennelly, *United States Documents in the Propaganda Fide Archives: A Calendar* (Washington, D.C., 1966–). Entries are organized chronologically and contain a reference to specific series with a summary of the document in English, an original language note, and occasionally a reference to related entries in the calendar. There is a name index at the end of the volume. There is also a combined index volume that lists all proper names, dioceses, and religious orders appearing in vols. 1–7. In the first series, volumes 3–6, there is a calendar of particular documents taken from this series. They are organized chronologically by volume of the *Lettere e decreti*.

A. H. Velykyi, *Litterae S.C. de Propaganda Fide ecclesiam catholicam Ucrainae et Bielarusjae spectantes* (Rome, 1954–1957). See also references in the entry for the Congregatio de Propaganda Fide series *Acta sacrae congregationis*. Many of those sources also relate to this series.

Finding Aids: Most volumes are internally indexed through 1804. Sometimes, however, these indices are imperfect. In the volumes from 1814 to 1892 there is an Indice delle lettere della Sacra Congregazione e dei Biglietti di Monsignor Segretario per ordine di localita (Index of the Letters of the Sacred Congregation and of the Notes of the Secretary According to Locality). This index is forty volumes. From volume 13 onward the title is "Indice delle Lettere, Parte Occidentale" (Index of the Letters, Western Section). This index contains a short syn-

thesis of each letter, the name of the person to whom it is addressed, the year, and the page. The index has been very well made but unfortunately it does not always register the dates of the letters. In addition, there is one volume entitled "Indice delle Lettere 1750–1755" and it too is very well made. For the decrees included in this series of letters there are three volumes of indices (according to locality) from 1719 onward. See also the work of Luca Codignola cited in the introduction to this congregation.

Location: Archives of the Propaganda Fide.

3.1.6.18 Mandati
[DATABASE ID: VATV10462-A]
Inclusive Dates: 1845–1919.
Bulk: 24 linear m.
Organizaton: Chronological.
Location: Archives of the Propaganda Fide.

3.1.6.19 Mandati estinti
[DATABASE ID: VATV10463-A]
Inclusive Dates: 1870–1887.
Bulk: 1 linear m. (10 buste).
Organization: Chronological.
Location: Archives of the Propaganda Fide.

3.1.6.20 Minute delle udienze
[DATABASE ID: VATV20555-A]
Inclusive Dates: 1764–1803.
Bulk: 6 buste.
Organization: Chronological.
Scope: Buste are marked "Minute di Udienza dal . . . al . . ." on the spine. There are no volume numbers on the buste, but they can be requested by year. According to Kowalsky and Metzler, this is one of several internal indexes to the *Udienze* series compiled by the Propaganda Fide for its own use (p. 61). The title page says: "Udienze dell'anno dall'anno 1800 al 1803 Registrate." The volume begins with a stray minute from May 1800 but begins truly with a minute from July 1800. From July 1800 onward, each month is introduced with a dividing page noting the new month, sometimes this sheet indicates that "tutte registrate nel libro delle Udienze del 1802." The individual pages are not numbered. Each minute has a geographic designation in the upper left corner of the page. This is followed by an introductory phrase "Ex Aud. SS.mi habita," the date of the audience, and the minute. At times, the minute is written down the right side of the page. Under the geographic designation there are occasionally subject notes and there is always a large # symbol, which seems to indicate that the audience has been formally registered in another place. Unless there are some minutes that have not in fact been registered, this series appears to be a duplication of the Udienza series.
Reference: Kowalsky-Metzler, pp. 60–61.
Location: Archives of the Propaganda Fide.

3.1.6.21 Miscellanea
[DATABASE ID: VATV20273-A]
Inclusive Dates: [ca. 1476–1892].
Bulk: 7 linear m. (121 numbered volumes).
Organization: There are three major series: *Miscellanee varie*, 3.5 linear m. (51 vols.); —*Miscellanee generali*, 1 linear m. (35 vols.); —*Miscellanee diverse*, 2 linear m. (35 vols.).

There are these three series simply because the documents were once stored on three separate sets of shelves. Each of these series is described separately in the entries that follow this general description. The material is often cited as a whole but equally often is cited by reference to the separate parts.

Scope: According to Kowalsky and Metzler, this series is composed of volumes from a variety of sources. The contents are not in any particular order, but they contain a large number of documents that would be very difficult to classify. "There are, for example, the protocol minutes of sessions of the Congregation; reports of a variety of content and composition; a variety of papers gathered here either because it did not seem useful to arrange them in the Archives or because it could not be decided in which collection they belonged; papers which had belonged to private persons and which are sometimes of a literary nature; diaries and reports of journeys, etc." (p. 71).

Reference: Kowalski-Metzler, pp. 71–80.

Finding Aids: Users should consult Kowalsky and Metzler (pp. 71–80) for detailed description of the 121 volumes. See also the works of Luca Codignola.

Location: Archives of the Propaganda Fide.

3.1.6.22 Miscellanee diverse

[DATABASE ID: VATV30003-A]

Inclusive Dates: 1563–1902.

Bulk: 35 vols.

Scope: Kowalsky and Metzler indicate that this series is rich and diverse, holding a variety of types of materials from many countries. "There are, for example, the protocol minutes of sessions of the Congregation; reports of a variety of content and composition; a variety of papers gathered here either because it did not seem useful to arrange them in the Archives or because it could not be decided in which collection they belonged; papers which had belonged to private persons and which are sometimes of a literary nature; diaries and reports on journeys, etc." (p. 71).

Reference: Kowalsky-Metzler, pp. 71, 78–80.

Finding Aids: Kowalsky and Metzler provide a listing of all volumes in the series, which indicates the variety of documents in the series. The works of Luca Codignola are pertinent to this series.

Location: Archives of the Propaganda Fide.

3.1.6.23 Miscellanee generali

[DATABASE ID: VATV20538-A]

Inclusive Dates: 1572–1902.

Bulk: 35 vols.

Scope: According to Kowalsky and Metzler, this is a true miscellanea. "There are, for example, the protocol minutes of sessions of the Congregation; reports of a variety of content and composition; a variety of papers gathered here either because it did not seem useful to arrange then in the Archives or because it could not be decided in which collection they belonged; papers which had belonged to private persons and which are sometimes of a literary nature; diaries and reports on journeys, etc." (p. 71). There are also a surprising number of beatification and canonization materials in these volumes.

Reference: Kowalsky-Metzler, pp. 71, 75–77.

Finding Aids: The Kowalsky and Metzler guide provides a volume-by-volume listing of the entire series. See also the works of Luca Codignola, which are pertinent to this series.

Location: Archives of the Propaganda Fide.

3.1.6.24 Miscellanee varie

[DATABASE ID: VATV20560-A]

Inclusive Dates: 1489–1892.

Bulk: 51 vols.

Scope: According to Kowalsky and Metzler, this is a true miscellany. "There are, for example, the protocol of minutes of sessions of the Congregation; reports of a variety of content and composition; a variety of papers gathered here either because it did not seem useful to arrange them in the Archvies or because it could not be decided in which collection they belonged; papers which had belonged to private persons and which are sometimes of a literary nature; diaries and reports on journeys, etc." (p. 71). Note that *Miscellanee varie*, vol. 10, was formerly part of the *Fondo Albani* in Archivio Segreto Vaticano.

Reference: Kowalsky-Metzler, pp. 71–75.

Finding Aids: The Kowalsky and Metzler guide, pp. 71–75, provides a volume-by-volume listing of the entire series. I. Kollmann, ed., *Acta Sacrae Congregationis de Propaganda Fide res gestas bohemicas illustrantia* (Prague, 1923–1955). This work contains reprints and summaries of documents concerning Bohemia in various series of the APF. *Acta* and *Lettere volgari* are the primary series used, although reprints of documents from this and other Congregatio de Propaganda Fide series are also in these volumes.

F. Kenneally, *United States Documents in the Propaganda Fide Archives: A Calendar* (Washington, D.C., 1966–). Entries are organized chronologically and contain a reference to specific series with a summary of the document in English, an original language note, and occasionally a reference to related entries in the calendar. There is a name index at the end of the volume. There is also a combined index volume that lists all proper names, dioceses, and religious orders appearing in vols. 1–7. Volume 5 of the first series contains a calendar of documents in selected *Miscellanee varie* volumes.

L. Codignola, *Guide des documents relatifs à l'Amérique du Nord française et anglaise dans les archives de la Sacrée Congrégation de la Propagande à Rome, 1622–1799* (Ottawa, 1990). This is the index to a set of microfiche or a printed volume also by Codignola entitled *Vatican, Archives of the Sacred Congregation "de Propaganda Fide" 1622–1799* (Ottawa, 1990). This work is Finding Aid No. 1186, prepared for the Manuscript Division of the National Archives of Canada and the Research Centre for Religious History in Canada, Saint Paul University. The guide provides a very good introduction to the Propaganda and one of the best explanations of the internal processes that led to the creation of the major series. The guide then provides an alphabetical listing of proper names, geographic entities, religious orders, missionary societies, and limited subjects (e.g., Quakers, Puritans). The Roman and Arabic numerals next to these entries lead one to either the microfiche or the printed guide noted above, the Roman numerals signifying the supplied series number, and the Arabic numeral signifying the supplied item number within that series. Individual entries list the series name, volume, year of volume, folio number(s), item number(s), the place, date of the letter, correspondents, a description of the letter, a summary in English, information about the file, and cross references. Because of the time period covered, the guide includes references to parts of the United States.

L. Codignola, *Calendar of Documents relating to Canada in the Archives of the Sacred Congregation "de Propaganda*

Fide" in Rome, 1800–1830 (Ottawa, 1993) [this title was noted but not verified by project staff]. This follows in the same format as the previously cited work.

L. Codignola, *Calendar of Documents relating to Canada in the Archives of the Sacred Congregation "de Propaganda Fide" in Rome, 1831–1846* (Ottawa, forthcoming) [this title was noted but not verified by project staff]. See above for a description of the format and the contents of the entries. This volume continues the series.

Location: Archives of the Propaganda Fide.

3.1.6.25 Missioni

[DATABASE ID:VATV352-A]

Inclusive Dates: 1177(copy of document)–1927 (bulk 1750–1899).

Bulk: 12 linear m. (234 numbered volumes).

Organization: Roughly chronological. The Index personarum is alphabetical by diocese.

Scope: This is a rich series consisting of original and duplicate materials primarily produced or received by the Congregazione de Propaganda Fide that came to the ASV through a variety of means. (See Burns, 1973, below.) The series begins with a number of indices to personnel in dioceses, geographic locations, acts of the Propaganda Fide, and the like. After that, the series is a miscellany. The numbers in parentheses refer to designations in the indice 1087. Sample items include: a printed copy of the bull establishing the Propaganda Fide in 1622 (128/1); correspondence to the Propaganda Fide and the vicar general from the French colony in America, 1764–1769 (53); the memoirs of Cardinal Guiglielmo Massaja of Ethiopian missions, 1846–1870 (164–168); a Malayan volume on moral theology, and materials on the church in China, Tibet, Asia, India, and Europe, and elsewhere, as well as materials regarding different rites (Melchite, Maronite). There are also samples of materials addressing questions concerning religious orders including: Capuchins (75); the Redemptorists in Detroit, Michigan (162/3); and the Jesuits in Tibet (130). The series demonstrates the wide range of materials in the Propaganda Fide Archives and the range of business with which that Congregation was concerned. Researchers probably would not want to begin their work with this series but rather should consult it for supplemental information.

Note: Vols. 13, 23, 40, 41, 43, 54–55, 105, 111–112, and 146 are available on microfilm.

References: Pásztor (1970), pp. 206–208; Pásztor (1983), pp. 190–195; Boyle, p. 98. C. Burns. "A Calendar of Scottish Documents in the Missioni Collection of the Vatican Archives," *Innes Review* 24 (1973): 51–68. C. Burns. "Additions to the 'Fondo Mission' Handlist," *Innes Review* 33 (1982): 31–43. H. Fenning, "Documents of Irish Interest in the Fondo Missioni of the Vatican Archives," in *Miscellanea in onore di Monsignor Martino Giusti* (Vatican City, 1978), vol. 1, pp. 191–254. H. Hoberg, "Der Fonds Missioni des Vatikanisches Archivs." *Euntes Docete* 21 (1968): 91–107. J. Metzler, "The Vatican Archives and their Missionary Holdings," *Mission Studies* 7.1 (1990): 108–117.

Finding Aids: See H. Hoberg, "Der Fonds Missioni des Vatikanischen Archivs," *Euntes Docete* 21 (1968). Hoberg provides an introduction to the series and then lists the titles for volumes 1–163. Between this article and the one cited below, these provide better access to the series than ASV Indice 1087

because of the introductions to the series and the slightly amplified descriptive volume titles.

H. Hoberg, "Aggiunte recenti al Fondo 'Missioni' dell'Archivio vaticano," in *Ecclesiae Memoria: Miscellanea in onore del R. P. Josef Metzler OMI, prefetto dell'Archivio segreto vaticano*, edited by W. Henkel (Rome, 1991) [this title was noted but not verified by project staff]. Hoberg provides an introduction to additional items in the *Missioni* series that provides information on their provenance, content, and organization. He then gives an inventory of items 164–234. Entries include the volume number, the date, and a brief description of the contents.

ASV Indice 1087, compiled by H. Hoberg, gives a volume-by-volume description of the first 169 of the 234 volumes. The index gives inclusive dates and a brief subject annotation, thus demonstrating the variety of materials available. The indices to personnel and place in the *Missioni* series and the printed materials are easily accessed through the index, as exact titles of the items are listed. Index 1087 also points to larger groups of materials dealing with a certain subject. However, access is less consistent to the rich groups of original letters, which are simply noted as "Scritture riguardanti la Cina e altri paesi asiatici" or "Lettere varie pervenute alla Propaganda." These letters are liable to contain anything from lists of missionaries to a letter from parishioners in a Dublin parish stating that there was no riot on the appointment of a new priest at their church.

Location: Archivio Segreto Vaticano.

3.1.6.26 Regestum facultatum

[DATABASE ID: VATV20276-A]

Inclusive Dates: 1670–1895.

Bulk: 1.5 linear m. (19 vols.).

Scope: According to Kowalsky and Metzler, this is an index, partly in alphabetical order (according to countries), partly in chronological order, of the ordinary and extraordinary missionary faculties granted by the Propaganda Fide or by the Holy Office. The first nine volumes are practically an index of the two Propaganda Fide series: *Acta* (for the faculties), and the *Udienza*, with the full text of the rescriptum. The titles on the covers of the volumes are as follows: Regestum facultatum et litterarum patentium ab anno 1670 usque ad annum 1722 (3 vols.); this series is listed separately among the record series of the Propaganda; —Deputazioni e facoltà ordinarie dell'anno 1722 a tutto il 1856 (6 vols.); this series is listed separately among the records of the Propaganda; —Rescritti facoltà 1894–1895 (1 vol.); —Facultates extraordinariae ab anno 1760 usque ad 1850 (9 vols.).

Reference: Kowalsky-Metzler, pp. 60–61, 82. Although there are some discrepancies in the description of the *Regestum facultatum*, the *Deputazione e facoltà ordinarie*, and the *Facultates extraordinatiae* on pages 61 and 82, the series listed are the same.

Location: Archives of the Propaganda Fide.

3.1.6.27 Regestum facultatum et litterarum patentium

[DATABASE ID: VATV30009-A]

Inclusive Dates: 1670–1722.

Bulk: 3 buste.

Organization: The buste are chronological: vol. 1 (1670–1698), vol. 2 (1699–1707), vol. 3 (1708–1722). Within each busta, materials are arranged according to geographic region or by subject.

Scope: The *Regestum facultatum et litterarum patentium* stands alone as a source for ordinary and extraordinary faculties. At the same time, this series acts as an index to these faculties in both Propaganda series *Udienza* and *Acta*. The three buste marked "Regestum facultatum et litterarum ab anno . . . usque ad anno . . ." have busta numbers written lightly in pencil on the lower part of the spine of each busta. All three buste were examined in 1990 by the project staff. Each volume has an index toward the front of the volume. These indices are organized according to geographical designations with a few other subject headings (e.g., collegi); there are twenty-seven of these posizioni in total. The posizione numbers for geographic areas (e.g., America = 14) and subjects (e.g., collegi = 8) do not change between volumes. None of the volumes have folio numbers. Within each posizione, the summaries of the decreti are given chronologically. In the far left (verso) or far right (recto) margins, a more precise geographical designation is sometimes provided.

Reference: Kowalsky-Metzler, pp. 60–61, 82. Kowalsky and Metzler demonstrate the relationship of this series to the *Udienza* and the *Acta*, as well as the *Regestum facultatum*. Although the descriptions of this series vary on the pages indicated, the descriptions refer to the same series.

Location: Archives of the Propaganda Fide.

3.1.6.28 Scritture originali riferite nelle congregazioni generali (SOCG)

[DATABASE ID: VATV20259-A]

Inclusive Dates: 1622–1892.

Bulk: 90 linear m. (1044 volumes).

Organization: The records divide into two subseries. The first contains volumes 1–417 (30 linear m.), covering the period 1622–1668, and is arranged geographically. The second subseries contains volumes 418–1044 (60 linear m.), covering the years 1669–1892, and is arranged chronologically. The numbering of volumes occurred after the return of volumes from Paris. Thus, despite the continuous numbering system, many volumes have been lost.

Scope: This series consists of documents used as a basis for discussion in the congregazioni generali: letters and pro memoria from bishops, missionaries, and princes, dispatches from nuncios and delegates, the acta of synods, apostolic visitations, the opinions of consultors. Note that twenty volumes separated from this series are found in the Propaganda Fide series *Fondo di Vienna*.

References: Kowalsky-Metzler, pp. 26–40. There has been extensive scholarly work done out of this series. What follows is a discussion of several publications that serve as a very useful introduction to this complex series.

T. F. Casey, *The Sacred Congregation de Propaganda Fide and the Revision of the First Provincial Council of Baltimore (1829–1830)* (Rome, 1957). G. Sorge, *Il "Padroado" regio e la S. Congregazione "de Propaganda Fide" nei secoli XIV–XVII* (Bologna, 1985).

F. Kenneally, *United States Documents in the Propaganda Fide Archives: A Calendar* (Washington, D.C., 1966–). Entries are organized chronologically and contain a reference to specific series with a summary of the document in English, an original language note, and occasionally a reference to related

entries in the calendar. There is a name index at the end of the volume. There is also a combined index volume that lists all proper names, dioceses, and religious orders appearing in vols. 1–7. Volumes 5 and 6 of the first series contain a calendar of documents in the selected *SOCG* volumes. The entries are organized chronologically, by volume of the *SOCG*. The calendar is limited to certain volumes of the *SOCG*; other volumes dealing with European countries or other parts of the Americas might also contain pertinent entries concerning the United States that are not included in this index. There is a name index at the end of each volume. There is also a combined index for volumes 1–7 that indexes all proper names, dioceses, and religious orders.

A. Debevec, *United States Documents in the Propaganda Fide Archives: A Calendar*, 2d ser. (Washington, D.C., 1966–) [this title was noted but not verified by project staff]. Portions of volumes 8–11 contain a calendar of items in selected volumes of the *SOCG*. The format is a continuation of Kenneally.

H. Fenning, "The Dominicans and the Propaganda Fide, 1622–1668: A Catalogue of the First Series of the SOCG Volumes 1 to 30," *Archivum Fratrum Praedicatorum* 41 (1971): 241–323. This is an important article for anyone consulting the *SOCG*, volumes 1–30, also known as the *Lettere d'Italia*. Entries include the modern volume number and then the full title as it appears on the spine. This is followed by a paragraph that indicates the actual period during which all letters contained in the volume were written (which may not coincide with information provided on the spine) and a list of all countries mentioned in the volume, with the names of the more frequently mentioned countries written in italics. This analysis of the countries is more detailed than appears in any other published index and will help all scholars, not just those interested in Dominican history. This analysis by country is followed by a description of each document concerning Dominican history. The description includes: the definitive folio number, the place the document was written, date, the name and status of the writer and recipient, and an English contents summary. The date and number of the congregation are given (so one can also find the *Acta*) and the date of the response is noted (to trace down the *Lettere*).

H. Fenning, "A Guide to Eighteenth-Century Reports on Irish Dioceses in the Archives of Propaganda Fide," *Collectanea hibernica*, no. 11 (1968): 19–35. Fenning has identifed several series in the Propaganda, including the *SOCG*, in which the relatio status reports might be located. He calendars all the Irish diocesan reports that he located in these series in this article. Entries include the date, place, bishop, title (if any) of the report, a brief contents summary, and the series, volume, and folio numbers.

H. Fenning, "John Kent's Report on the State of the Irish Mission, 1742," *Archivium hibernicum* 28 (1966): 59–102. This is a reprint of six documents relating to Irish affairs between 1740 and 1758. The article provides a good introduction to the historiography and related documentation. Each of the edited documents is presented in full in the original language (Latin) with the date, the writer, and folio numbers provided. The Kent report and two of the other documents are in *CP* 88, the others are in the *SOCG*, the *Acta*, and the ASV *Nunziatura di Fiandra*. There are few analytical notes.

The extensive work of Benignus Millett on the documents in

this series serves as a very useful introduction in English to this vast series:

B. Millett, "Catalogue of Volume 294 of the Scritture Originali Riferite nelle Congregazione Generali in Propaganda Archives," *Collectanea hibernica*, no. 8 (1965): 7–37. Millett presents a brief introduction to the SOCG series. In the original volume there is an index at the end. Note that Millett makes reference to a microfilm copy in the National Library of Ireland in Dublin. This catalog is almost a calendar. The entries are organized by folio number. Each entry begins with a folio number(s), and includes: a summary in English, an original language note, and the date. There are analytical footnotes that note errors in the volume, clarify phrases, and provide historical background. Supplied information is in brackets; question marks are substituted for unknown elements. Millett also notes if the document has been published or is related to other documents in the volume or in other APF series.

B. Millett, "Catalogue of Irish Materials in Fourteen Volumes of the Scritture Originali Riferite nelle Congregazioni Generali in Propaganda Archives," *Collectanea hibernica*, no. 10 (1967): 7–59. This article calendars Irish materials in SOCG volumes 14, 73, 83, 89, 94, 97, 100–102, 105–106, 108, and 119. See the surrounding entries for information concerning the contents of calendar entries.

B. Millett, "Catalogue of Irish Material in Vols. 129–131 of the Scritture Originali Riferite nelle Congregazioni Generali in Propaganda Archives," *Collectanea hibernica*, no. 11 (1968): 7–18; and B. Millett, "Catalogue of Irish Material in Vols. 132–139 of the Scritture Originali Riferite nelle Congregazioni Generali in Propaganda Archives," *Collectanea hibernica*, no. 12 (1969): 7–44. Millett gives information about the volume: title, information on spine, pagination, indexing, and so forth. He then goes on to calendar just the materials of Irish interest. Information in the calendar includes: folio numbers, date(s), the correspondents, original language, a summary in English, and the incipit. If an indication of the date of the general meeting in which the matter was discussed is noted, Millett provides this information. There are few analytical footnotes.

Millett continued his work in similar format in the following publications. B. Millett, "Catalogue of Irish Material in Vols. 140–143 of the Scritture Originali Riferite nelle Congregazioni Generali in Propaganda Archives," *Collectanea hibernica*, no. 13 (1970): 21–60. B. Millett, "Catalogue of Irish Material in Vols. 370 and 371 of the Scritture Riferite Originali nelle Congregazioni Generali in Propaganda Archives," *Collectanea hibernica*, nos. 27–28 (1985–1986): 44–85. The article's title misidentifies the name of the series being calendared. It should read, "Scritture originali riferite nei Congressi."

P. Rabikauskas, *Relationes status dioecesium in magno ducatu Lithuanie* (Rome, 1971–1978). This work provides Latin transcriptions of documents from the Vatican Archives and the Propaganda Fide Archives with analytic biographical and bibliographical notes (particularly to other transcriptions) and notes of the volume and folio numbers, when appropriate. There is a note indicating if the document is an original or a copy and cross references to the ASV and APF archives when documents appear in both places. Transcribed documents from the SOCG can be found in this work.

A. H. Velykyi, *S. Josaphat Hieromartyr: Documenta romana beatificationis et canonizationis* (Rome, 1952–). There

are reprints of the beatification and canonization documents, some of which are from the Propaganda Fide Archives. Documents are presented in full in Latin with minimal explanatory footnotes. There is a brief beginning summary and a citation to the original Propaganda documents located in the SOCG and other series.

T. T. Halushchynskyi and A. H. Velykyi, *Epistolae metropolitarum, archiepiscoporum et episcoporum* (Rome, 1956–1980). These are reprints of letters dated 1613–1862 from different members of the Ukranian and Belarussian hierarchy. Documents are from the SOCG and the ASV Warsaw nunciature series, among other series in the ASV and the APF. Reprints contain a date, summary of the documents, series title, volume, and folio numbers. Each letter is reprinted in full in Latin. There are some analytical annotations.

C. Giblin, *Irish Franciscan Mission to Scotland, 1619–1646: Documents from Roman Archives* (Dublin, 1964). Giblin reprints pertinent documents from the ASV and the APF. APF documents are from the *Acta* and the SOCG. Documents are reprinted in full in the original language and then translated into English. Modern series, volume, and folio numbers are given. There are few annotations.

I. Kollmann, ed., *Acta Sacrae Congregationis de Propaganda Fide res gestas bohemicas illustratia* (Prague, 1923–1955). This work provides reprints and summaries of documents concerning Bohemia in various series of the APF. *Acta* and *Lettere volgari* are the primary series used, although reprints of documents from this and other Congregatio de Propaganda Fide series are also in these volumes.

L. Codignola, *Guide des documents relatifs à l'Amérique du Nord française et anglaise dans les archives de la Sacrée Congrégation de la Propagande à Rome, 1622–1799* (Ottawa, 1990). This is the index to a set of microfiche or a printed volume also by Codignola entitled *Vatican, Archives of the Sacred Congregation "de Propaganda Fide" 1622–1799* (Ottawa, 1990). This work is Finding Aid No. 1186, prepared for the Manuscript Division of the National Archives of Canada and the Research Centre for Religious History in Canada, Saint Paul University. The guide provides a very good introduction to the Propaganda and one of the best explanations of the internal processes that led to the creation of the major series. The guide then provides an alphabetical listing of proper names, geographic entities, religious orders, missionary societies, and limited subjects (e.g., Quakers, Puritans). The Roman and Arabic numerals next to these entries lead one to either the microfiche or the printed guide noted above, the Roman numerals signifying the supplied series number, and the Arabic numeral signifying the supplied item number within that series. Individual entries list the series name, volume, year of volume, folio number(s), item number(s), the place, date of the letter, correspondents, a description of the letter, a summary in English, information about the file, and cross references. Because of the time period covered, the guide includes references to parts of the United States.

L. Codignola, *Calendar of Documents relating to Canada in the Archives of the Sacred Congregation "de Propaganda Fide" in Rome, 1800–1830* (Ottawa, 1993) [this title was noted but not verified by project staff]. This follows in the same format as the previously cited work.

L. Codignola, *Calendar of Documents relating to Canada in the Archives of the Sacred Congregation "de Propaganda*

Fide" in Rome, 1831–1846 (Ottawa, forthcoming) [this title was noted but not verified by project staff]. See above for a description of the format and the contents of the entries. This volume continues the series.

M. Benoit, *Inventaire des principales séries de documents intéressant le Canada, sous le pontificat de Léon XIII (1878–1903), dans les archives de la Sacrée Congrégation "De Propaganda Fide" à Rome* [this title was noted but not verified by project staff]. Benoit's guide begins approximately where Codignola's ends. She provides access to documents in the SOCG and other series from 1878 to 1903. Volume 1 is an index to the other three volumes. The index lists proper names, religious communities, subjects (dispenses matrimoniales), and periodicals, and refers researchers to a page number in one of the other volumes. Once one reaches that page, one must read through each item until one finds the reference for the desired items. Each page lists the series and volume number under consideration at the top of the page. Individual entries give the date of the document, the correspondents or a title, an occasional very brief summary in French, and the first folio number. As in the Codignola guide, there may be items of United States interest indexed here, although the Kenneally guide would be the place to start.

G. Nicolio, *Un inventaire des Archives de la Propagande, milieu du XVIIe siècle (fra Girolamo Nicolio, augustin, 14 avril 1662, son Journal historique des missions d'Afrique, d'Amerique et d'Asie)*, edited by F. Combaluzier (Schöneck-Beckenried, 1947). A. van den Wyngaert, G. Mensaert, and F. Margiotti, *Sinica Franciscana: Itinera et relationes Fratrum Minorum saeculi XIII et XIV* (Florence, 1929–).

Note: Volumes 132–143, 370 and 371 are available on microfilm.

Finding Aids: There is no formal finding aid to this series. The researcher should refer to the Propaganda Fide series *Acta sacrae congregationis* as an index to the scritture originali (original documents) referred to in the congregazioni generali (general meetings). The Kowalsky and Metzler guide (pp. 29–39) provides a geographical listing of material in SOCG vols. 1–417. That section of the guide is not reproduced here. However, what follows is a list of the headings used in the index, which indicates the extraordinary range of material in this section of the general series that covers the early seventeenth century.

The geographical headings (including some subject titles and names) are: Africa, Albania, Aleppo, Alessio, Algeria, Alsazia, Amburgo, America, Anatolia, Anglia, Antivari (Jugoslavia), Arabi, Arcipelago (dell'Egeo), Arda (Africa Occid), Arequipa (Peru), Argentiera (Arcipelago), Armeni, Armeni di Asia, Armeni di Italia, Armeni di Polonia, Armenia, Asia, Atene, Austria, Avignone, Barbaria (Africa Sett.), Bastione de Francia (Africa Sett.), Batabia nuova (Indonesia), Beccioli (Bejapur, India), Belgio, Belgio o Fiandra (Jesuitissae), Benin (Africa Occid.), Berito (Vescovo di), Boemia, Bosnia, Brasile, Budua (Dalmazia), Bulgaria, Caldei, Canada, Candia, Cannonizzazione (de S. Giosafat), Cattaro (Dalmazia), Cause, Cefalonia, Ceylon, Cicladi (Arcipelago egeo), Cimarra (Illirico), Cina, Cirillo (Lucari, gia Patriarca de Constantinopoli), Colonia, Collegi, Commissario, Congo, Corcyra (Corgu), Constantinopoli, Constantinopoli (Crillo . . .), Creta, Crisopoli (Vescovo . . .), Dalmazia, Dania, Durazzo, Durazzo (Arcivescovo Greco), Ebrei, Egeo, Egitto, Eliopoli (Vesco-

vo . . .), Enos (Turchia europea), Etopia, Fiandra, Filippine, Firenze, Francescani, Francia, Frati (Illirico), Fallia, Gallipoli, Genova, Georgia, Germania, Gerusalemme, Gesuitesse, Gesuiti (in India), Giappone, Goa, Golconda (India), Grecia, Guinea, Holsatia (Holstein), Ibernia, Idalcan (India), Illirico, Indie, Inghilterra, Isole (del Mediterraneo), Istria, Italia, Italo-Greci, Lettere di lingua straniera (orentali), Levante, Littorale (Dalmazia), Lotaringia, Macao, Macedonia, Madagascar, Malabar, Malta, Marocco, Maroniti, Memoriali, Mesopotamiam Messina, Metellopoli (Vescovo . . .), Miconé (Arcipelago), Milano, Mingrelia (Caucaso), Missionari (Illirico), Missionari (Italia), Moldavia, Monti (di Pietà), Moravia, Morea (Peloponneso), Morlacchi (Adriatici), Moscovia, Munster, Mustachia (Illirico), Napoli, Naxia (Arcipelago), Nigrizia, Nona (Dalmazia), Norvegia, Ocrida (Illirico), Olanda, Ossero (Illirico), Oweri (Africa Occid.), Palatinato, Palestina, Pantelleria, Paronaxia, Paros (Cicladi), Patmo, Pegù (Birmania), Peloponneso, Perasto (Dalmazia), Persia, Pola, Polonia, Portogallo, Porto di S. Michele (Africa Sett.), Pulati in Albania, Rezia, Rodi, Roma, Romania, Russia, San Salvador, Santorino (Arcipelago), Sappa (Albania), Sardegna, Sassonia, Savoia, Scio (Arcipelago), Scozia, Seminario Romano, Scuttari, Serra Lione (Africa Occid.), Servia, Settentrione (di Europa), Sicilia, Sifanto (Arcipelago), Silesia, Siria, Smirne, Spagna, Stiria, Svezia, Svizzera, Tabarca (Africa Sett.), Tartaria (Crimea), Teatini (in India), Termia (Cicladi), Tine (Cicladi), Tipografia (di Propaganda), Torino, Transilvania, Tripoli, Tunisi, Ungheria, Vallachia, Venezia, Vescovi, Zante (Corfù), Zea (Cicladi), Zeilan.

Location: Archives of the Propaganda Fide.

3.1.6.29 Scritture riferite nei congressi (SC)

[DATABASE ID: VATV20263-A]
Inclusive Dates: 1424–1896.

Bulk: 131 linear m. (1451 vols.).

Scope: This series consists of documents discussed in weekly meetings, not the general meetings. For the most part, the materials pertain to the daily life of the missions. Early records are variously referred to as *Scritture riferite nei congressi* (documents referred to in the weekly meetings), *Scritture riferite nei congressi dell'Em.mo Prefetto* (documents referred to in the weekly meetings of the cardinal prefect), or *Scritture non riferite* (documents not referred to, i.e., in the general meetings).

These records are divided into two series. The first series contains the letters that reached the Propaganda from the mission lands and is arranged alphabetically by country or geographic area. The second series contains material that refers directly to the Congregation or to institutes dependent on it. The subseries in the second series are generally divided according to subject matter: Collegio Urbano, Printing Press, Visits and Colleges, and so forth, but this division is not followed throughout. The same may be said of the documents concerning each subject matter: they are generally arranged in chronological order but not always. Each volume has written on the cover the year or years to which the documents refer. Interesting addenda documents and undated items are bound in special volumes marked "Miscellanea" at the end of each subseries. These groups of miscellanea can contain anything from inventories of the stamperia or printing press from the eighteenth and nineteenth centuries to an undated relation of the Jesuits in Paraguay.

Important subseries in the second series include: *Cardinali, segretari, protonotari, consultori,* 1669–1892 (3 vols.); — *Collegi vari,* 1424–1892 (66 vols. and 12 miscellanea); — *Collegio urbano,* 1677–1892 (22 vols. and 11 miscellanea); —*Esami de'missionari,* 1724–1896 (4 vols.); —*Ministri,* 1623–1892 (11 vols. and 1 miscellanea)—*Missioni,* 1646–1892 (28 vols. and 22 miscellanea); —*Missioni: Giuramenti dei missionari,* 1844–1892 (3 vols.); —*Missioni: Opera apostolica,* 1859–1892 (1 vol.); —*Ospizi,* 1632–1892 (10 vols. and 1 miscellanea); —*Sacra congregazione,* 1622–1892 (2 vols.); — *Stamperia,* 1622–1892 (8 vols. and 6 miscellanea); —*Stato temporale,* 1622–1892 (47 vols. and 6 miscellanea); —*Visite e collegi,* 1622–1836 (45 vols.).

Each of these subseries is described separately as a series in the entries that follow this general description. The material is often cited as a whole but equally often is cited by reference to a particular subseries.

Fourteen volumes separated from this series are found in the Congregatio de Propaganda series *Fondo di Vienna.*

References: Kowalsky-Metzler, pp. 48–60. É. de Jonghe and T. Simar, *Archives congolaises* (Brussels, 1919). G. Nicolio, *Un inventaire des Archives de la Propagande, milieu du XVIIe siècle (fra Girolamo Nicolio, augustin, 14 avril 1662, son Journal historique des missions d'Afrique, d'Amerique et d'Asie),* edited by F. Combaluzier (Schöneck-Beckenried, 1947).

Finding Aids: Many works provide partial guides to materials in the SC. The guides are compiled to assist researchers interested in a certain geographic area find materials from that area. A few of these sources are listed below. If a researcher is looking for information on a specific subject, these guides might be of use if the researcher can identify persons, places, or events in a given country that are associated with that subject.

F. Kenneally, *United States Documents in the Propaganda Fide Archives: A Calendar* (Washington, D.C., 1966–). Volumes 1–3 and 7 of the first series contain a calendar of documents in the SC dated 1673–1865. The entries are organized according to SC volume, which Kenneally calls sections in volume 1. Each entry contains the following information: folio numbers (for the SC volume under consideration), correspondents, date of the missive and place, a summary of the letter, a language note, and occasionally a reference to related entries in the calendar.

The calendar is limited to certain volumes of the SC, others dealing with European countries or other parts of the Americas might also contain pertinent entries concerning the United States are not included in this index. There is a name index at the end of each calendar volume. There is also a combined index for volumes 1–7 that indexes all proper names, diocese, and religious orders.

A. Debevec, *United States Documents in the Propaganda Fide Archives: A Calendar,* 2d ser. (Washington, D.C., 1966–) [this title was noted but not verified by project staff]. Portions of volumes 8–11 contain a calendar of items in selected volumes of the SC. Debevec also uses the Kenneally's format, see above.

B. Millett, "Calendar of Volume 1 (1625–1668) of the Scritture Riferite nei Congressi, Irlanda, in Propaganda Archives," *Collectanea hibernica,* nos. 6–7 (1963–1964): 18–211. Millett presents a brief introduction to the congregation and a particularly good introduction to the volume in question, which appears to have been compiled around 1669. There is a microfilm copy of volume 1, ff. 156r–668r, at the National Library of

Ireland, Dublin (negative #5232, positive #5337). Millett is explicit concerning his methodology. He gives an extensive English language summary of all documents and a word-forword translation of others. No proper names have been omitted. Each entry consists of the folio numbers, the summary, a note on the original language of the document, and its date. There are analytical footnotes that note errors in the SC volume, clarify phrases, and provide biographical background. Supplied information is in brackets and unknown elements are indicated by question marks. Millett also notes if a document has been published or is related to other documents in this volume or in other APF series of which he is aware.

B. Millett, "Calendar of Volume 2 (1669–71) of the Scritture Riferite nei Congressi, Irlanda, in Propaganda Archives," *Collectanea hibernica,* no. 16 (1973): 7–47; no. 17 (1974–1975): 17–68. Millett presents a brief introduction to the congregation and a particularly good introduction to the volume in question, which appears to have been compiled between 1669 and 1671. There is a microfilm copy of volume 2 at the National Library of Ireland, Dublin (negative #5234, positive #5338). Millett is explicit concerning all of his methodology. He gives an extensive English language summary of all documents and a word-for-word translation of others. No proper names have been omitted. Each entry consists of the folio numbers, the summary, a note on the original language of the document, and its date. There are analytical footnotes that note errors in the SC volume, clarify phrases, and provide biographical background. Supplied information is in brackets and unknown elements are indicated by question marks. Millett also notes if a document has been published or is related to other documents in this volume or in other APF series of which he is aware.

B. Millett. "Calendar of Volume 3 (1672–5) of the Scritture Riferite nei Congressi, Irlanda, in Propaganda Archives," *Collectanea hibernica,* nos. 18–19 (1976–1977): 40–71; nos. 21–22 (1979–1980): 7–81. Millett uses the same methodology described above.

H. Fenning, "A Guide to Eighteenth-Century Reports on Irish Dioceses in the Archives of Propaganda Fide," *Collectanea hibernica,* no. 11 (1968): 19–35. Fenning has identified several series in the Propaganda, including the SC, in which the relatio status reports might be located. He calendars all the Irish diocesan reports that he located in these series in this article. Entries include the date, place, bishop, title (if any) of the report, a brief contents summary, and the series, volume, and folio numbers.

L. Codignola, *Guide des documents relatifs à l'Amérique du Nord française et anglaise dans les archives de la Sacrée Congrégation de la Propagande à Rome, 1622–1799* (Ottawa, 1990). This is the index to a set of microfiche or a printed volume also by Codignola entitled *Vatican, Archives of the Sacred Congregation "de Propaganda Fide" 1622–1799* (Ottawa, 1990). This work is Finding Aid No. 1186, prepared for the Manuscript Division of the National Archives of Canada and the Research Centre for Religious History in Canada, Saint Paul University. The guide provides a very good introduction to the Propaganda and one of the best explanations of the internal processes that led to the creation of the major series. The guide then provides an alphabetical listing of proper names, geographic entities, religious orders, missionary societies, and limited subjects (e.g., Quakers, Puritans). The Roman and Arabic numerals next to these entries lead one to either the microfiche or the printed guide noted above, the Roman numerals signifying the supplied series number, and the Arabic numeral signifying the supplied item number within that series. Individual entries list the series name, volume, year of volume, folio number(s), item number(s), the place, date of the letter, correspondents, a description of the letter, a summary in English, information about the file, and cross references. Because of the time period covered, the guide includes references to parts of the United States.

L. Codignola, *Calendar of Documents relating to Canada in the Archives of the Sacred Congregation "de Propaganda Fide" in Rome, 1800–1830* (Ottawa, 1993) [this title was noted but not verified by project staff]. This follows in the same format as the previously cited work.

L. Codignola, *Calendar of Documents relating to Canada in the Archives of the Sacred Congregation "de Propaganda Fide" in Rome, 1831–1846* (Ottawa, forthcoming) [this title was noted but not verified by project staff]. See above for a description of the format and the contents of the entries. This volume continues the series.

M. Benoit, *Inventaire des principales séries de documents intéressant le Canada, sous le pontificat de Léon XIII (1878–1903), dans les archives de la Sacrée Congrégation "De Propaganda Fide" à Rome* [this title was noted but not verified by project staff]. Benoit's guide begins approximately where Codignola's ends. She provides access to documents in the SC and other series from 1878 to 1903. Volume 1 is an index to the other three volumes. The index lists proper names, religious communities, subjects (dispenses matrimoniales), and periodicals and refers researchers to a page numer in one of the other volumes. Once one reaches that page, one must read through each item until one finds the reference for which one was searching. Each page lists the series and volume number under consideration at the top of the page. Individual entries give the date of the document, the correspondents or a title, an occasional very brief summary in French, and the first folio number. As in the Codignola guide, there may be items of U.S. interest indexed here, although the Kenneally guide would be the place to start.

G. Pizzorusso, *Inventaire des documents d'interet canadien dans les archives de la Congregation de "Propaganda Fide," 1904–1914* (Rome, 1993). This is a continuation of the guides by Codignola and Benoit. Pizzorusso provides an introduction to each series treated in this volume (*Acta* and *SC*), and to the relationship between the Propaganda Fide and Canada in its last years as a missionary territory. He then explains the organization and compilation of the series (which is organized according to rubrica numbers signifying a certain subject) and the volumes. There is an index of proper names, religious communities and some types of transactions (matrimonia, acts) in the back of the work. A header on each page indicates the series, the volume number, a rubrica number, and the year. Individual entries begin with the date and are followed by the correspondents, a brief summary in French, and the folio numbers. As in the other Canadian guides, some U.S. subjects are indexed.

A. van den Wyngaert, G. Mensaert, and F. Margiotti, *Sinica Franciscana: Itinera et relationes Fratrum Minorum saeculi XIII et XIV* (Florence, 1929–). Reprints or summaries of documents from a variety of series, including some at the Propaganda Fide such as the *Acta congregationum particularium super rebus Sinarum et Indiarum orientalium; Informationum libri; Lettere delle S. Cong; Miscellanea della Cina; Scritture originali delle congregazioni particolari (Indie orientali e Cina); Scritture originali riferite nelle congregazioni generali; Udienze; Missioni;* and *Scritture riferite nei congressi (Indie orientali e Cina)*.

I. Kollmann, ed., *Acta Sacrae Congregationis de Propaganda Fide res gestas bohemicas illustrantia* (Prague, 1923–1955). Reprints and summaries of documents concerning Bohemia in various series of the APF. *Acta* and *Lettere volgari* are the primary series used, although reprints of documents from this and other Congregatio de Propaganda Fide series are also in these volumes.

G. Pizzorusso, "Le 'Lettere di Stato': Una fonte documentaria dell'Archivio della Congregazione 'de Propaganda Fide' di particolari interesse canadese (1893–1908)," *Annali Accademici Canadesi* 5 (1989): 101–114. There is also a good bibliography. This is a good description of the kinds of information that can be found in the SC.

G. Spinelli, "Registro del volume I (1649–1713) della serie 'Congressi,' dell'Archivio storico della Sacra Congregazione 'de Propaganda Fide,' Roma." (Ph.D. diss., Università degli studi di Pisa, 1986–1987) [this title was noted but not verified by project staff]. This is a summary of volume 20 of the SC. There is a good introduction to the series and then each document is summarized. Each is assigned a number by the author, then the folio numbers are given. Other information includes the type of document, the original language, the correspondents, the date and place. An Italian summary follows. There are occasional cross-references to other documents in this volume.

Location: Archives of the Propaganda Fide.

3.1.6.30 Scritture riferite nei congressi: Cardinali, segretari, protonotari, consultori

[DATABASE ID: VATV30005-A]

Inclusive Dates: 1669–1892.

Bulk: 3 buste.

Organization: Chronological.

Scope: According to Kowalsky and Metzler, this series contains the so-called Biglietto di nomina (decree of appointment) of cardinals, secretaries, and protonotaries of the Congregation. The lists of prefects and secretaries were compiled mainly from the material in this section, which is mainly biographical. This series is part of the *Scritture riferite nei congressi.* However, the buste themselves have no indication of this. The spines of the buste indicate: "S. Cong.ne Card.li Segretari Consultori della med dal 1669 att. il 1830." There are busta numbers on the bottom part of the spine. As usual, items are sewn into the busta. The title page indicates "S. Cong. Card. Segretari, Consultory della medessima dal 1669 a tutto 1833." The date on the outside is correct. Folio numbers are written and stamped in the upper right-hand (recto) corner. They are, however, different numbers. Kowalsky and Metzler call these "biglietti di nomini." Busta 1 was examined. These biglietti are from cardinals and secretaries of the Propaganda Fide to the secretary of state. Items in this busta have a similar form, for example, "Essendosi degnata la San. di N. S. di surrogare . . . nel luogo che . . . occupatta nella A. Cong. di Propaganda Fide, se ne da' questo cenna a' Mons. Segretario . . . per sua notizia." The appointments are to many posts including that of consultori, segretario, protonotari, prefettura della Sacra Congregatio di Correzione di Libri della Chiesa Orientali, and componenti.

Reference: Kowalsky-Metzler, pp. 51–52.

Location: Archives of the Propaganda Fide.

3.1.6.31 Scritture riferite nei congressi: Collegi vari (referred to as CV)

[DATABASE ID: VATV20556-A]

Inclusive Dates: 1430–1892.

Bulk: 78 buste.

Organization: There are 66 buste in the regular subseries and 12 identified as Miscellanea collegi vari. The series is organized by specific college or seminary.

Scope: According to Kowalsky and Metzler, this series contains all materials on colleges dependent on the Propaganda except the Urban College. Four buste were examined from this subseries. These were the first two and the last two. On all of the busta spines there was an indication that they were from the "Scritture riferite nei congressi" with the contents (collegi) identified. This subseries does have volume numbers, that is, a C.V. with a busta number. Buste relating to one seminary can be scattered throughout the subseries. The buste are very fragile. Items are sewn into the spine and many are loose. Because these are materials that were sent to the Propaganda from different sources there is a variety of sizes, often much bigger or smaller than the busta. In general, the content designations and dates listed on the outside of the buste and in the Metzler guide are correct. There are some discrepancies, though. Folio numbers are stamped or written in the upper right-hand corner of the documents.

The contents of the buste are diverse. A brief description of the four buste viewed demonstrates the variety of materials that can be found. CV 1 relates to the North American College (Rome). This busta contains an added "avvertenza" that refers readers to information on the North American College in other Propaganda Fide series. Within this busta there are financial records (introito e esito) showing contributions from American bishops, an 1859 architectural drawing of the seminary, a pamphlet to Pius IX celebrating the opening of the North American College with an address by Bishop Bacon of Portland, and a list of students. There are also letters concerning seminary rules, relationes, notizie, apostolic letters, and memoriale. CV 2, Collegio Armen. e Rit.e di Leopoli, 1664–1780, contains much of the same, including a brief history, "Note di Archivio," of the inception of the college. The spine of CV 65 indicates that it is "Collegi di Spagne e di Protogallo e di quello di Ossieri in Sardegna dispentio dalla Spagna." Unlike the other buste, there are materials relating to eight separate seminaries in this busta, which are outlined in the Kowalsky and Metzler guide. Not mentioned in the guide are two letters at the end from the Abbé Duray concerning the Collegi Mélan (Piemonte). The same types of materials noted above are in CV 66, Coll. di Vilna e di Craslau nella diocese di Smolesko, 1502–1780.

The twelve miscellanea buste contain a variety of materials from apostolic visits to decreta (e.g., Originali del Messale Ruteno, Visitatio Apostolica Ecclesiae Parochialis s. Apollinaris, necnon Collegii Germanici Hungarici [1696]). The contents of these are also outlined in the Kowalsky and Metzler guide.

Reference: Kowalsky-Metzler, pp. 51, 54–58.

Finding Aids: Though not a formal finding aid, the Kowalsky and Metzler guide presents a busta-by-busta listing of materials in this subseries that is provided along with an introduction to the larger series.

Location: Archives of the Propaganda Fide.

3.1.6.32 Scritture riferite nei congressi: Collegio Urbano

[DATABASE ID: VATV30020-A]

Inclusive Dates: 1677–1892.

Bulk: 33 vols. (22 regular vols. and 11 miscellanea).

Scope: According to Kowalsky and Metzler, this series contains all the documentation concerning the foundation and the history of the Urbanian College and many documents concerning students, regulations, inventories, and the like. The registers of the students and of the oaths are kept in the archives of the college itself.

Reference: Kowalsky-Metzler, pp. 51, 54.

Location: Archives of the Propaganda Fide.

3.1.6.33 Scritture riferite nei congressi: Esami dei missionari

[DATABASE ID:VATV30017-A]

Inclusive Dates: 1724–1896.

Bulk: 4 vols.

Scope: According to Kowalsky and Metzler, this series consists of a register of the missionary examiners and examinees from 1742 to 1896, with the results of the examinations: optime, laudabiliter, bene, mediocriter, male.

Reference: Kowalsky-Metzler, pp. 51, 53.

Location: Archives of the Propaganda Fide.

3.1.6.34 Scritture riferite nei congressi: Ministri

[DATABASE ID: VATV30001-A]

Inclusive Dates: 1632–1892.

Bulk: 12 buste.

Organization: Buste 1–11, chronological. One additional busta, "Miscellanea Drach," ca. 1838–1885, is unorganized.

Scope: According to Kowalsky and Metzler, this series contains material concerning the officials of the Congregatio de Propaganda Fide. Three buste were examined from this series; the first and last from the regular series and the "Miscellanea Drach." "Scritture riferite nei Congressi—Ministri" and the dates are written on the outside of the eleven buste in the regular series. Inside the buste, items are sewn into the spine. There is a stamped and a written number in the upper right corner of each folio. These are one off from each other (e.g., 31 stamped and 32 written). Materials in the first busta ("Ministri dal 1623 att il 1730") are incoming requests, largely concerning financial matters. From notations on the back of the letters, many of the letters are written by agents of the Propaganda, passing along a request. There is no indication of the nature of the response. There are often summaries of the business on the back of the letter. In addition to the financial correspondence there are instruzione (requests for letters from missionaries to substantiate who they are), and other documents such as a letter from the architect, Giuseppe Paglia, asking for recognition. There are several copies of selected istruzioni (a minute and a bella copia). The second busta examined was "Ministri, 1877–1892." At the beginning of this busta are letters from priests seeking positions primarily in the Propaganda. Toward the end, the character changes and there are posizioni concerning ospizi (Ospizio Basiliani Greco Melchito), collegi (e.g., the English and Scottish Colleges in Rome), and the like. The final busta examined, "Miscellanea Drach," is an unorganized miscellany of materials. "Ministri" is written in pencil on the top of the spine of the busta. The materials in this busta are largely in French with a few in English. This busta appears to be more of a personal scrapbook than a file of official archival materials. The busta contains letters to Drach and his successor Ciccolini regarding offerings and announcements of publications. The correspondence intimates that Drach also assisted in research for French and American scholars. There are also some odd items: a thank-you resolution from the New York Geographical Society for a copy of a map by Verrazano, a United States passport for Bart Sullivan from 1873, and photos and other memorabilia of Drach.

Reference: Kowalsky-Metzler, pp. 51–52.
Location: Archives of the Propaganda Fide.

3.1.6.35 Scritture riferite nei congressi: Missioni

[DATABASE ID: VATV30002-A]
Inclusive Dates: 1646–1892.
Bulk: 50 buste.
Organization: Buste 1–28 constitute the regular subseries and are chronological. In addition there are twenty-two miscellaneous buste organized by subject.
Scope: According to Kowalsky and Metzler, this series concerns requests for admission by aspirant missionaries, information required concerning them, the approval and appointment of missionaries, the number of persons belonging to a specific mission, and so forth. Of considerable historical value in the nineteenth century are the papers and reports from the missionary cooperation societies, such as the Society for the Propagation of the Faith and the Society of the Holy Childhood. More than half of the section entitled "Miscellanea Missioni" is made up of various papers not registered at the moment of reception in the archives and subsequently arranged in more or less chronological order. The titles of these papers include: "Names of the Missionaries"; "Status of the Different Missions belonging to the Sacred Congregation, 1794–1804"; and "Documents Concerning the Execution of the Brief of Suppression of the Jesuit Fathers in the Missions." The regular subseries, buste 1–28, is clearly marked on the spine "Scritture riferite nei Congressi-Missioni dal . . . al. . . . " There is also a volume number on the spine (e.g., 1, 28). Like the *Scritture . . . congressi: Ministri* series, this series contains incoming correspondence to the Congregation from missionaries, missionary societies, and different missions. There is usually no indication of the official response of the Congregation. Busta 1 contains letters and other items from different sources that have been bound together and sewn into the busta. The contents include, lists of bishops and missionaries, juramenta, requests for missions, copies of decreta from other congregations, mandatorum, and faculties, among other requests. Busta 28 contains more modern looking statistical accounts of missionaries, letters from the Propaganda regarding the distribution of funds to missionaries. Items in this latter busta have been stamped with a protocollo number and presumably entered into a protocollo. The nature of the items in busta 28 differs somewhat from the initial busta. The busta contains an entire section on the missionary society, Ludovicio in Munich, and there is a great deal of correspondence about the Ca-

puchins. There is a note concerning the Eucharistic Congress in Constantinople and the usual amount of financial materials.

The Miscellanea volumes look different from the buste in the regular subseries. Kowalsky and Metzler indicate that these papers were not registered at the time of their reception into the archives and so they are attached as miscellanea here. They state that the miscellanea are primarily in three subject areas: the suppression of the Jesuits, the names of missionaries, and the status of different missions belonging to the Congregation, 1794–1804. The busta examined pertained to the suppression of the Jesuits. The spine indicates "Scritture-Riguardante l'esecuzione del Breve di soppressione de PP. Gesuiti di Missione 1774–Missioni Miscellan. Tom. 5." Folio numbers are both stamped and written in the upper right-hand corner of the recto side. The indication "tome 5" is in black and appears to have been added later. This is an interesting busta, again primarily composed of incoming correspondence from ex-Jesuits and officials in dioceses with ex-Jesuits. There are a number of professions to the pope by the ex-Jesuits. The countries most represented here are England, Ireland, and Scotland, although there are some letters from the Middle East (Syria), Belgium, and France. There is one letter from an American ex-Jesuit, Gerard Mattingly.

Reference: Kowalsky-Metzler, pp. 51–53.
Location: Archives of the Propaganda Fide.

3.1.6.36 Scritture riferite nei congressi: Missioni, giuramenti dei missionari

[DATABASE ID: VATV30019-A]
Inclusive Dates: 1844–1892.
Bulk: 3 vols.
Scope: According to Kowalsky and Metzler, this series includes the formulas of the prescribed oaths, signed by all the missionaries in the Far East, which have been collected in three volumes covering the period 1844–1892. Before the year 1844 these signed formulas are found in the different volumes of the SC, first series.
Reference: Kowalsky-Metzler, pp. 51, 53.
Location: Archives of the Propaganda Fide.

3.1.6.37 Scritture riferite nei congressi: Missioni, opera apostolica

[DATABASE ID: VATV30018-A]
Inclusive Dates: 1859–1892.
Bulk: 1 vol.
Scope: According to Kowalsky and Metzler, this series concerns activities of the so-called apostolic work for the outfitting of the missionaries. The purpose was to send to the missionaries sacred furnishings and vestments as well as items for personal use.
Reference: Kowalsky-Metzler, pp. 51, 53.
Location: Archives of the Propaganda Fide.

3.1.6.38 Scritture riferite nei congressi: Ospizi

[DATABASE ID: VATV20557-A]
Inclusive Dates: 1632–1892.
Bulk: 11 buste.
Organization: 10 buste in the regular series and 1 miscellaneous busta. Organized by name of hospice, materials in each busta are chronological.
Scope: According to Kowalsky and Metzler, this series con-

cerns hospices in Rome for pilgrims of the Eastern rites. These hospices often provided accommodation for ecclesiastical students who, although not having their own college, frequented the Roman schools. The contents of two buste were examined. These were the "Ospizio dei Ruteni Pascolo dal 1639–1800" and the "Ospizio di S. Stefano de Mori dal 1700–1849 (1891)." There is only a volume number on the second busta. The volume number reads "O. 10." The original ending date on the busta was 1849, but someone has written, at a later point, "1891" under this. These buste are made up of loose documents. The title page of busta 1 indicates that it contains the "Ospizio dei Ruteni nella chiesa dei SS. Sergio e Bacco dall anno 1639 all'anno 1800." The contents include correspondence from the hospice to the Congregatio de Propaganda Fide concerning finances, the erection of new chapels, and other business. The series also contains correspondence during the Roman Republic, which is addressed to both the Propaganda and the state. Busta 10, "Ospizio di S. Stefano de Mori dal 1700 all'anno 1849," contains information on the Copts in Egypt and Ethiopia as well as rules and regulations that the Propaganda expected the Ospizio to follow.

Reference: Kowalsky-Metzler, pp. 51, 58–59.

Finding Aids: Though there is no formal finding aid for this series, Kowalsky and Metzler provide a busta-by-busta listing of this subseries. Their information is primarily from the spines of the buste.

Location: Archives of the Propaganda Fide.

3.1.6.39 Scritture riferite nei congressi: Sacra congregazione
[DATABASE ID: VATV30016-A]

Inclusive Dates: 1622–1892.

Bulk: 2 vols.

Scope: According to Kowalsky and Metzler, this series contains various documents regarding the Congregation itself: foundation, history, internal regulations, and lists and biographical notes of cardinals and others.

Reference: Kowalsky-Metzler, pp. 51–52.

Location: Archives of the Propaganda Fide.

3.1.6.40 Scritture riferite nei congressi: Stamperia
[DATABASE ID: VATV30021-A]

Inclusive Dates: 1622–1892.

Bulk: 14 vols.

Organization: 8 regular vols. and 6 miscellanea.

Scope: According to Kowalsky and Metzler, this series documents the history of the Propaganda polyglot printing press which in 1908 was annexed to the Vatican press, which itself consequently became polyglot.

Reference: Kowalsky-Metzler, pp. 51, 54.

Location: Archives of the Propaganda Fide.

3.1.6.41 Scritture riferite nei congressi: Stato temporale
[DATABASE ID: VATV30004-A]

Inclusive Dates: 1622–1892.

Bulk: 53 vols.

Organization: The 47 volumes in the regular series are organized chronologically. There are also 6 volumes listed as miscellanea.

Scope: According to Kowalsky and Metzler, this series contains documents concerning goods and buildings in the possession of the Congregatio de Propaganda Fide. Two buste in the

regular series and all the miscellanea volumes were examined. The buste in the regular series are clearly marked "Scritture Riferite, Stato Temporale" on the spine. The inclusive dates of materials in the particular busta and the volume number are also on the spine. The first busta covers 1622–1639; the title page indicates "Stato Temporale dall'Anno 1622 all'Anno 1639 1." Folios are paginated with both stamped and written numbers, which are the same at the beginning, but diverge at folio 50. The busta contains mainly incoming correspondence, bulls, and instrumenta about the growing holdings to support the work of the Propaganda. These are organized chronologically. Many of the items relate to donations of property and monies. Toward the end, however, there are some requests for money. Over half of the first busta contains documents from 1639; the rest of the materials are primarily from the first few years. The records in the busta go to 1656 and there are two "lettere antichi" (Paul V, eleventh year; Paul I, fifth year). In busta 47, all items are stamped with a number. The contents deal with property owned by and financial matters of the Propaganda. Within this subject, items include inventories (f. 22), summaries of income and maintenance of properties, financial affairs, claims and requests. Finally, there are some letters from nuncios (Portugal, Spain, Vienna, and France) and the sentenze of a few court cases.

Five of the Miscellanea volumes of the *Stato temporale* were located and viewed (1990). The sixth volume could not be located. These volumes provide diverse sources of information. The first busta, "Palazzo Propaganda Fide," contains a variety of materials dating from 1847 to 1858. Folio numbers are stamped on the upper corners. The materials concern both the Palazzo Propaganda Fide and Collegio Urbaniano and relate to maintenance, renovations, and the purchase of new furnishings for the buildings. There is a very rich description of some of the rooms from 1855 (f. 108).

The second volume is marked "2" on the spine but otherwise contains no indications that it is part of this series. Page numbers are written in the upper corners. The title page contains the following information: "Inventario Generale della Stamperia della S. Congregazione de Propaganda Fide fatto nell'Anno 1795." This is followed by an indice from which researchers can see the organization of the volume (which is by location) and a fuller explanation of the contents which reads as follows: "Inventario generale della Stamperia della Sagra Congregazione de Propaganda Fide cioé degl'Utensili, Mobili, Caratteni, Madri, Punzoni, Intagli in Roma e in lengo e di futt'altro ch'eseste nella Medesima, come pure della Gettaria, Magazzini, Fagotteria, e Custodia de Libn' fatto per ordine dell' Emo. Rmo. Signor Cardinale Leonardo Antonelli Prefetto della Medesima nell'Anno 1795." The inventory lists books both published by and collected by the Stamperia.

Another miscellanea volume is also marked "Stato Temp., Stato Generali dei capitali, 1727, 2." Inside the volume is written: "Stato gen.le di tutti li Capitali et effetti attivi e passivi qualsivoglia sorte posti in Roma che fuori spettanti alla Sagra Congregazione de Propaganda Fide con le sue provenienze quali sono in essere a tutto d. tempo estrattosi dall'Archivio e dalla Computisteria di essa Sagra Congregazione. . . ." This is followed by a table of contents to the volume, "Indice del presente Stato gen.le." This volume could perhaps be used as a crude index to a few of the *Eredità* series in the APF (e.g., Gallio, S. Onofrio, Barnerini, D'Adda, and Ferrari).

Miscellanea 3 contains information dating between 1844 and 1854 on various properties around Rome belonging to the Propaganda: Casa V. dei Pontifici e Ripetta (ff. 1–161), Casa alle Tre Pile (ff. 162–280), Eredi Meda (ff. 281–312), Casa alla V. Frattina (ff. 313–349), Coniugi (eredità dei fratellli Angelo Gatti e Clementi Maria) (ff. 350–376), and Palazzo S. Congregazione (ff. 375–469). There are stamped folio numbers in this volume. The subjects range from the sale of properties in V. dei Pontifici e Ripetta and the Casa alle Tre Pile to eredità of the fratelli Coniugi to rental agreements with the shop owners in the Palazzo S. Congregazione.

The final Miscellanea volume that was examined does not contain a volume number. The spine indicates that it is "Decreta Super bono-Regimine & Statu Temporali S.C." An inside title page says "Collectanea Decretorum super bono regimine et Statu Temporali S. Cong.ne." The first section does contain decrees from the 1650s. This is followed by a second section: "Ricordi fatti da Sig. Card. Spinola." A final section appears to be a subject listing of decrees given to the Propaganda. Examples of the types of decrees are: "Alumni Collegi," "Bona e Effectus Sac. Congregationis," and "Dispensarius Collegi." These are followed by a summary of the decree in Latin and the date. Another copy of the ricordi by Spinola, now entitled "Ricordi fatti dal Sig.r Cardinal Spinola per il Rettore," appears in the section "Rector Collegi de Prop.a Fide."

Location: Archives of the Propaganda Fide.

3.1.6.42 Scritture riferite nei congressi: Visite e collegi

[DATABASE ID: VATV20558-A]

Inclusive Dates: 1622–1836.

Bulk: 45 buste.

Scope: According to Kowalsky and Metzler (pp. 59–60), "this section contains a collection of reports on visits done by order of the Propaganda in various missions and principally in colleges dependent on the Congregation. For the most part the documents belong to the first decades of the Congregation's history. The other visits may be found in other sections especially in the original documents referred to in the general meetings. The volumes are arranged in chronological order while the contents of each volume are arranged according to subject matter. Many volumes have an index."

Reference: Kowalsky-Metzler, pp. 51, 59–60.

Finding Aids: While there is no formal finding aid to this series, Kowalsky and Metzler provide a comprehensive listing of the information on the spines of the buste.

Location: Archives of the Propaganda Fide.

3.1.6.43 Sinodi diocesani

[DATABASE ID: VATV20270-A]

Inclusive Dates: 1700–1920.

Bulk: 2.5 linear m.

Organization: Buste 1–18 contain 142 numbered files. Subseries of buste 1–18 are: Sinodi diocesani; —Sinodi provinciali; —Sinodi plenari; —Sinodi regionali. Busta 19 and miscellanea include: Acta et decreta concilii provincialis Westmonasteriensis, quarti/originali, 1874; —Sinodo del Sutchuen, 1803; —Esame nel sinodo Sutcuens celebrato 1803 approvato nel 1822; —Sinodi melchiti: Acta, Gerusalemme, 1849; — Sinodo melchiti: Scritture originale, Gerusalemme, 1849; — Sinodo Armeno, 1851; —Sinodo maronita, 1856; —Sinodi

[miscellanea] (Stati Uniti, Cina, Indie, Japon), 1873–1908 (2 vols.).

Scope: This series is a collection of acta from diocesan, provincial, regional, plenary, and Eastern rite synods held in territories under the jurisdiction of the Congregation de Propaganda Fide from the beginning of the nineteenth century until the first decade of the twentieth century. The series contains much material for the countries that were removed from the jurisdiction of the Propaganda by the constitution *Sapienti consilio* in 1908. Of special interest are the two volumes of miscellanea, namely, "Esame nel Sinodo Sutcuens celebrato 1803, approvato nel 1822"(Examination of Szechwan Synod [China] held in 1803, approved in 1822), and the acta of the Szechwan Synod (1803).

Reference: Kowalsky-Metzler, pp. 66–67.

Finding Aids: The "Indice Sinodi" contained within the series is an excellent index to buste 1–18. Entries list the type of synod, the diocese, region, and so forth followed by a number and the year. The number is the essential piece of information to note. The busta containing that number should then be requested.

Location: Archives of the Propaganda Fide.

3.1.6.44 Udienze di Nostro Signore

[DATABASE ID: VATV20264-A]

Inclusive Dates: 1665–1900.

Bulk: 30.5 linear m. (254 vols.).

Scope: According to Kowalsky and Metzler, from 1622 to 1665 the congregazioni generali (general meetings) were often held in the presence of the pope, coram Sanctissimo. Beginning in 1666, this custom of holding general meetings ceased and the secretary was entrusted with the duty of referring to the pope on prearranged days the more important matters being discussed and of requesting the necessary faculties for matters that exceeded the jurisdiction of the cardinal prefect or the Congregation. The series thus begun is a collection of requests (brevi suppliche) to the pope.

The *Udienze* series contains matters of a rather personal and private nature: requests for favors, indulgences, privileges, matrimonial dispensations, and the like. At the beginning the matters dealt with in the audiences were written in the form of a register but later a separate leaf was used for each question and at the end of the page the secretary noted the decision given by the pope. From the third volume onward the original documents, letters, requests, and so forth on which the main document was based, were added to the document itself. Because the number of these original documents grew from year to year, the register was no longer kept (e.g., in volumes 10, 11, 12, 13, 21, 28) and the secretary noted the decision on the back of each original request. Since the number of questions dealt with was continually increasing a return was made to the system of registers that were then called Ricordi per Mons. Segretario (memoranda for the secretary). The system later developed into the so-called Foglio di Udienza (audience sheets). In some volumes the materials for each audience are prefaced by a list of the business (supplications) for that audience.

The audience sheets contain a variety of questions and are numbered in progressive order, beginning each year with the number one. The numbers are followed by the date of the audience itself and then in turn by the questions to be dealt with, each one having its particular ordinal number that refers to the original document.

Reference: Kowalsky-Metzler, pp. 60–62.

Finding Aids: The *Udienze* were of primary importance in the daily work of the Propaganda and some indices were compiled for its internal use. These include Regestrum facultatum et litterarum patentium, 1670–1722 (3 vols.); —Deputations and ordinary faculties, 1722–1856 (6 vols.); —Extraordinary faculties, 1760–1850 (9 vols.); —Register of Audiences, 1764–1832 (23 vols.); —Minutes of Audiences, 1746–1803 (6 vols.); —and Audiences, 1810–1848 (3 vols.). This last source—Audiences—contains the minutes of the letters sent by Propaganda to the persons concerned after the audiences. The first three series mentioned above also make up the *Regestrum facultatum* series of the Propaganda Fide and are described separately as a whole and each as a separate series.

A 28-volume general index exists for the period 1666–1897. There are also specialized indices such as Latin Audiences, 1846–1889 (2 vols.) and Oriental Audiences, 1666–1861 (2 vols.). The index to oriental audiences is volumes 10 and 11 and is an index to materie orientali found in a number of different series. See Metzler, "Indici," for further information on these indices.

F. Kenneally, *United States Documents in the Propaganda Fide Archives: A Calendar* (Washington, D.C., 1966–). Entries are organized chronologically and contain a reference to specific series with a summary of the document in English, an original language note, and occasionally a reference to related entries in the calendar. There is a name index at the end of the volume. There is also a combined index volume that lists all proper names, dioceses, and religious orders appearing in vols. 1–7. Volumes 5 and 6 of the first series contain a calendar of documents in selected *Udienze* volumes. The entries are organized chronologically, by volume of the *Udienza*.

A. Debevec, *United States Documents in the Propaganda Fide Archives: A Calendar,* 2d ser. (Washington, D.C., 1966–) [this title was noted but not verified by project staff]. Portions of volumes 8–11 contain a calendar of items in selected volumes of the *Udienze.* The format is a continuation of Kenneally.

L. Codignola, *Guide des documents relatifs à l'Amérique du Nord française et anglaise dans les archives de la Sacrée Congrégation de la Propagande à Rome, 1622–1799* (Ottawa, 1990). This is the index to a set of microfiche or a printed volume also by Codignola entitled *Vatican, Archives of the Sacred Congregation "de Propaganda Fide" 1622–1799* (Ottawa, 1990). This work is Finding Aid No. 1186, prepared for the Manuscript Division of the National Archives of Canada and the Research Centre for Religious History in Canada, Saint Paul University. The guide provides a very good introduction to the Propaganda and one of the best explanations of the internal processes that led to the creation of the major series. The guide then provides an alphabetical listing of proper names, geographic entities, religious orders, missionary societies, and limited subjects (e.g. Quakers, Puritans). The Roman and Arabic numerals next to these entries lead one to either the microfiche or the printed guide noted above, the Roman numerals signifying the supplied series number and the Arabic numeral signifying the supplied item number within that series. Individual entries list the series name, volume, year of volume, folio number(s), item number(s), the place, date of the letter, correspondents, a de-

scription of the letter, a summary in English, information about the file, and cross references. Because of the time period covered, the guide includes references to parts of the United States.

L. Codignola, *Calendar of Documents relating to Canada in the Archives of the Sacred Congregation "de Propaganda Fide" in Rome, 1800–1830* (Ottawa, 1993) [this title was noted but not verified by project staff]. This follows in the same format as the previously cited work.

L. Codignola, *Calendar of Documents relating to Canada in the Archives of the Sacred Congregation "de Propaganda Fide" in Rome, 1831–1846* (Ottawa, forthcoming) [this title was noted but not verified by project staff]. See above for a description of the format and the contents of the entries. This volume continues the series.

Unprocessed Records of the APF

3.1.6.45 Collegio Urbano
[DATABASE ID: VATV10496-A]
Inclusive Dates: Undetermined.
Bulk: 25 linear m.
Organization: Major subseries include: Giustificazione; —Guardaroba, 1750–1751; —Entrata e Uscita; —Registro di censi; —Recapiti; —Stato temporale-eredità; —Registro di mandati.
Reference: G. Pizzorusso, "Archives du Collège Urbain de Propaganda Fide," *Annali Accademici Canadesi* 7 (1991): 94–97. Pizzorusso identifies these as the series (in Pizzorusso's order) he finds best for locating Canadian students: VII. Registro, 1633– contains the names of the students, vol. 205 relates to Canada. V. Elenco, lacunae from the previous series, vols. 1–5 of Canadian interest. VIII. Giuramento, chronological, vols. 2–6 of interest to Canada. II. Liber Ordinationum, chronological, vols. 1–2 of Canadian interest. III. Liber Mortuorum, lists students who died while in residence at the college. IV. Diario, is the day book of the rector, which would list any students involved in principal events. XI. Storia and X. Lettere might be of use in reconstructing the lives of students. Pizzorusso indicates that there are archives for Collegio Urbano at both the College on the Janiculum and at the Propaganda Fide, but he does not mention which of the series listed are in which location.
Location: Archives of the Propaganda Fide.

3.1.6.46 Eredità
[DATABASE ID: VATV40069-A]
Inclusive dates: Undetermined.
Bulk: Undetermined.
Organization: Series include: Eredità Andreozzi; —Eredità Antonelli; —Eredità Arceri; —Eredità Arezzo; —Eredità Arrighi; —Eredità Balzani; —Eredità Barberini; —Eredità Bartolomei; —Eredità Beni-Rustici; —Eredità Borgia; —Eredità Caleppi; —Eredità Carafa; —Eredità Cibo; —Eredità Colonna; —Eredità Consalvi; —Eredità Costantini; —Eredità D'Adda; —Eredità Cardinal Della Somaglia; —Eredità Della Somaglia; —Eredità Derheam; —Eredità Dì Pietro; —Eredità Cavaliere Paolo Drach; —Eredità ex-religiosi; —Eredità Falcomari; —Eredità Fannotini-Biondi; —Eredità Ferrari; —Eredità Filonardi; —Eredità Galamina; —Eredità Gallio;

—Eredità Gotti; —Eredità Gottifredi; —Eredità Livizzai; —Eredità Paganelli; —Eredità S. Onofrio; —Eredità Santucci; —Eredità Sciarra; —Eredità Van Brosses; —Eredità Varese; —Eredità vari; —Eredità Villa Montalto in Frascati; —Eredità Vives; —Stato temporale eredità Duca di York; —Stato temporale, eredità Varese.

Note: The *Eredità* of the archives of the Propaganda Fide appear to be records of the congregation generated in the administration of the extensive property held by the Propaganda through particular bequests. One entry point into the *Eredità* may be fogli 124–126 in the Congregatio de Propaganda Fide series *Scritture riferite nei congressi: Stato temporale,* Miscellanea 2, "Stato temporale dei capitali, 1727."

In addition, project staff located in the archives of the Propaganda Fide two collections of family papers not designated as eredità. These are listed in the section "Individual and Family Papers" as *Filonardi Family* and *Parisiani.*

Location: Archives of the Propaganda Fide.

3.1.6.47 Unprocessed series
[DATABASE ID: VATV40068-A]

Inclusive dates: Undetermined.

Bulk: Undetermined.

Organization: Series include: Abbazie di Castelleone; —Abbazie di Rieti; —Abbazie di Subiaco; —Abbazie di Todi; —Azienda generale degli spogli; —Biglietti S. Offizio; —Brevi; —Cassa; —Causa Aliprandi; —Causa Calidori; —Causa Ciofi; —Causa diverse; —Causa Iacobini; —Causa Muccichelli; —Causa S. Congregatio de Propaganda Fide e Ignazio Brunacci; —Causa Ugolini; —Circolari [2 series with this name]; —Collectanea; —Collegi dei missioni; —Collegio maronito; —Collegio ruteni: rendiconto; —Collegio scozzese; —Collegio urbano; —Concilio Vaticano I; —Conti e rendiconti; —Diverse scatole; —Diversi [2 series with this name]; —Esattore; —Fascicoli diversi; —Filza: Giuramenti, spogli e filze; —Fondo Macao; —Giustificazioni; —Indice registri lettere; —Indulgenze; —Introitus exitus; —Istromenti; —Lettere [2 series with this name]; —Lettere de spogli; —Lettere de succollettore di spogli; —Libri vari; —Libro mastro del maggiorascato Barberini; —Liste de mensariato; —Locazioni; —Mandati estinte; —Memoriali con rescritti di N.S.; —Mensariato; —Miscellanea: Generale e diverse; —Monte Carafa; —Notificazioni; —Pergamene; —Polize di cambio; —Ponenza; —Posizioni diversi e fondi diversi; —Principe di Roviano; —Recapiti; —Registri; —Registri degl'indulgenze; —Registri di mandati; —Registri di spogli; —Registro d'ordini; —Registro delle udienze; —Registro di lettere di spogli; —Registrum litterarum apostolicarum brevium, chirographorum, patentium, deputationum ad Sacrarum Congregationum de Propaganda Fide spectam de mandato S.D.N. Gregorii Papae XV; —Rendiconti Collegio urbano; —Riferite originale; —Riparto; —Riporti; —Risoluzioni diversi; —Riti; —Rubricelle località; —Salda conti; —Spese; —Spese postali; —Spogli giustificazioni; —Stati affari passivi di ecclesiastiche beni; —Succollettore di spogli; —Vacanze dei vescovati, abbadie e cardinali; —Verbali [2 series with this name]; —Verbali dei congressi; —Voti.

Note: In general, material that is not listed in the Kowalsky-Metzler guide is considered by the Congregation of the Propaganda Fide to be unprocessed. Access to this material is thus problematic.

Location: Archives of the Propaganda Fide.

3.1.7 Congregatio de Propaganda Fide pro Negotiis Ritus Orientalis
[DATABASE ID: VATV009-A]

This congregation was established by Pius IX in 1862 when he divided the Congregatio de Propaganda Fide into two congregations, one for the Latin Rite and one for the Eastern (or oriental) rites. Though each used the title *congregation,* they were in essence two administrative divisions of the Propaganda Fide. In 1917 the section for oriental rites was made autonomous by Benedict XV and renamed the Congregatio pro Ecclesia Orientalis.

RECORDS. Records for this congregation are found with the listings for the records of the Congregation de Propaganda Fide.

3.1.8 Congregatio de Rebus Graecorum
[DATABASE ID: VATV139-A]

This congregation was established in 1573 by Gregory XIII to reform Basilian monasteries in Italy. Later its responsibilities were expanded to include other matters pertaining to Greek-rite Catholics and the maintenance and propagation of the faith among other Christians of the Middle East. In 1599 Clement VIII transformed this congregation into the Congregatio super Negotiis Sanctae Fidei et Religionis Catholicae. This is sometimes referred to as a cardinalitial commission, not a congregation. It has also been known as the Congregatio pro Reformatione Graecorum.

RECORDS. No records for this congregation were located.

3.1.9 Congregatio de Seminariis et Studiorum Universitatibus
[DATABASE ID: VATV022-A]

Benedict XV (1914–1922), having reviewed the history of seminaries, concluded that the task of overseeing them was too burdensome for the Consistorial Congregation. With his motu proprio *Seminaria clericorum* (Nov. 4, 1915), he instituted the Congregation of Seminaries, joined to it the Congregation of Studies, defined its functions, and gave it the new name of Congregatio de Seminariis et Studiorum Universitatibus. All seminaries were to depend on this congregation with the exception of those under the jurisdiction of the Congregation for the Oriental Church and of the Propaganda Fide. Those seminaries instituted for the formation of members of religious orders were also excluded. Three years later these basic regulations were included in the Code of Canon Law [canon 256 supplemented by canons 1376 and 1377].

Pius XI in his constitution *Deus scientiarum Dominus* (May 24, 1931) reserved to the congregation authority over all seminaries, without prejudice to the rights of the Congregation for the Propagation of the Faith or of the Congregation for the Oriental Church. The congregation was assigned supreme authority over all Catholic universities or faculties designated as pontifical. However, certain other universities and colleges under Catholic auspices were not subject to this congregation.

The constitution of Paul VI, *Regimini Ecclesiae Universae* (Aug. 15, 1967), changed the name of the congregation to Congregatio pro Institutione Catholica (Congregation for Catholic Education). This newly named congregation was given authority over everything that concerned the formation of the clergy and the education of clergy and laity, without prejudice to the authority of the Congregation for Religious and Secular Institutes over matters that concerned the formation of members of religious orders as such, or the authority of the Congregation for the Evangelization of Peoples in certain specific areas of the globe.

Pope John Paul II with the apostolic constitution *Pastor bonus* (Jun. 28, 1988) once again changed the name of the congregation. It is now known as the Congregation for Seminaries and Institutes of Study.

As under Pope Paul VI, the congregation carries on its work by means of three offices: (1) an office for all matters connected with the direction, discipline, and temporal administration of seminaries and with the education of diocesan clergy, religious, and members of secular institutes; (2) and office for the supervision of Catholic universities, faculties of study, and other institutions of higher learning dependent on the authority of the church, and for the encouragement of cooperation between Catholic institutions and the establishment of Catholic hospices and centers on campuses of non-Catholic institutions; and (3) an office for general questions concerning education and studies for Catholic schools below the college/university level, and for cooperation with conferences of bishops and civil authorities in educational matters.

The congregation also supervises the Pontifical Works for Priestly Vocations founded by Pius XII with his motu proprio *Cum Nobis* (Nov. 4, 1941). The *Statuto e le Norme* (Sept. 8, 1943) give the guidelines for its application.

RECORDS. No records for this congregation were located.

3.1.10 Congregatio Examinis Episcoporum

[DATABASE ID: VATV459-A]

The Council of Trent (session 22, Sept. 17, 1562) decreed that bishops have a specific background in theology and canon law. Gregory XIV (1590–1591), on becoming pope, immediately took action on this but died before he could officially establish a means to ensure this outcome.

His successor, Clement VIII (1592–1605), instituted, in 1592, the Congregatio Examinis Episcoporum based on the plans outlined by Gregory XIV in his constitution *Onus apostolicae servitutis* (May 15, 1591). This gave the congregation the authority for examining and declaring candidates qualified for the episcopal sees in Italy and the adjacent islands, as well as those candidates of royal nomination.

Urban VIII (decree, May 16, 1625) reinforced this authority and reaffirmed the usefulness of the examination, binding the examiners by oath not to reveal to anyone the content of the tests. The prohibition began to be disregarded from the time of Clement XIII (1758–1769); later, even the obligation of the examination was ignored and the congregation became inactive.

In 1903 Pius X restored the obligation of the examination but transferred the functions of the congregation to the Congregation of the Holy Office.

RECORDS. No records for this congregation were located.

3.1.11 Congregatio Extraordinaria Praeposita Negotiis Ecclesiasticis Orbis Catholici

[DATABASE ID: VATV417-A]

Pius VII established this congregation in 1814 (constitution of June 18, 1814) as a reorganization of the Congregatio pro Negotiis Ecclesiasticis Extraordinariis. In 1827 it was reorganized again and returned to its former name. The congregation was responsible for negotiations with civil governments over religious matters and for the appointment of bishops for episcopal sees outside of Italy and in missionary territory. See history for the Congregatio pro Negotiis Ecclesiasticis Extraordinariis.

RECORDS. No records for this congregation were located.

3.1.12 Congregatio Indulgentiis Sacrisque Reliquiis Praepositae

[DATABASE ID: VATV462-A]

In 1593 Clement VIII was planning to create an appropriate department to set guidelines for eliminating abuses in the handling of indulgences. As an immediate solution for the problem he appointed a special cardinalatial commission to counsel him in matters which concerned indulgences, calling it the Congregation of Indulgences. Paul V, who as a cardinal had been a member of the commission, specifically continued the congregation as part of his constitution *Romanus Pontifex* (May 23, 1606), but it gradually became inactive.

The commission was not formally established as a permanent congregation until many years later when Clement IX issued his motu proprio *In ipsis* (Jul. 6, 1669). However, sessions of the members of this permanent Congregatio Indulgentiis Reliquiisque had been

held as early as 1667 and decrees had already been issued (see *Decreta Authentica Sacrae Congregationis Indulgentiis Sacrisque Reliquiis Praepositae ab anno 1668
ad annum 1882* [Ratisbon, 1883]). The congregation
was given ordinary or official authority to resolve all
doubts and difficulties concerning indulgences and
relics, and to correct abuses. (Responsibility for relics
had been held by the Congregation of Sacred Rites.) It
was also within its authority to prevent the publication
of false indulgences, to authenticate relics recently discovered, and to be vigilant over the granting of indulgences and the distribution of relics. The pope reserved
to himself the solution of dogmatic problems.

Over a period of time successive pontiffs had conceded to the congregation even the faculty of granting
indulgences, formerly a function of the Secretary of
Briefs, so that by the middle of the eighteenth century
the congregation was granting the rescripts of concession, a function formally recognized by Benedict XIV
(1740–1758).

With his motu proprio *Fidelis domus Domini* (Jan. 2,
1855), Pius IX reconfirmed the original provisions of
Clement IX, and withdrew the privilege for the granting
of indulgences, which was again reserved to the secretary of briefs. Leo XIII, with his motu proprio *Christianae reipublicae* (Oct. 31, 1897), enforced the order of
his immediate predecessor and authorized the secretary
of briefs to make grants of indulgences. The motu proprio also redefined the functions of the Congregation of
Indulgences and Relics, confirming the fourteen faculties already held by the congregation, in addition to the
original concessions of Clement IX. Of these, two pertained to jurisdiction over relics, while the others referred exclusively to indulgences. These were listed in a
syllabus attached to the motu proprio.

In 1904 Pius X suppressed the congregation with the
motu proprio *Quae in Ecclesiae* (Jan. 28, 1904), transferring its functions to the Congregation of Rites. In the
curial reform of 1908 the Congregation of Rites retained
the authority over relics but all other functions transferred to it from the Congregation of Indulgences and
Relics were given to the Congregation of the Holy Office. Paul VI's apostolic constitution *Regimini Ecclesiae
universae* (Aug. 15, 1967) entrusted all that concerns
the granting and application of indulgences to the Penitentiary, "leaving intact the rights of the Congregation
for the Doctrine of the Faith to see to those things that
relate to dogmatic doctrine on indulgences."

In addition to the records listed below, series listed
with other agencies relate directly to this agency and
should be consulted. See Miscellaneous official series
Armarium XXXIX and Poenitentiaria Apostolica series
Summaria and [*Miscellaneous buste SF/455*].

Reference. A. Larraona, and S. Goyeneche, "De SS.
Congregationum, Tribunalium et Officiorum constitutione et interna ordinatione post const. 'Sapienti Con-

silio,'" in *Romana Curia a Beato Pio X, Sapienti Consilio reformata* (Rome, 1951) [this title was noted but not
verified by project staff].

RECORDS. Records of the congregation consist of the following series.

3.1.12.1 Brevia et decreta
[DATABASE ID: VATV10173-A]
Inclusive Dates: 1667–1860.
Bulk: .5 linear m. (6 buste).
Organization: Roughly chronological. Busta 1 contains
some materials from the 1840s and 1850s.
Scope: These are printed copies of briefs, decreta, indul-
gences, and the like that which may have originated in this
office.
References: Pásztor (1970), p. 177; Pásztor (1983), p. 182.
Finding Aids: ASV Indice 1116 (formerly Indice 62) gives a
very brief busta-by-busta listing with inclusive dates and papa-
cies noted.
Location: Archivio Segreto Vaticano.

3.1.12.2 Decreta
[DATABASE ID: VATV10176-A]
Inclusive Dates: 1710–1808.
Bulk: 3 linear m. (89 vols.).
Organization: Alphabetical.
Scope: This series is an alphabetical index to a portion of the
Congregatio Indulgentiis Sacrisque Reliquiis Praepositae series
Rescripta, 1712–1908, which is described in this section.
The final volume, "Index resolutionum," may be the vol-
ume referred to by Pásztor (see citation below) that does not
correspond to any series currently housed in the ASV; other-
wise it could possibly index part of the Congregatio Indulgentiis
Sacrisque Reliquiis Praepositae series *Resolutiones* also de-
scribed in this section. No verification on the relation of the
final volume of the *Decreta* series to the *Resolutiones* series was
made by the project staff.
References: Pásztor (1970), pp. 177–178; Pásztor (1983),
pp. 182–183.
Finding Aids: ASV Indice 1116 identifies this series as
"Rubricelle (Registri d'Archivio) Vaccette 88 [sic] 1710–1808."
Location: Archivio Segreto Vaticano.

3.1.12.3 Dubia extra congregationum generalem resoluta
[DATABASE ID: VATV10184-A]
Inclusive Dates: 1824–1908.
Bulk: .5 linear m. (4 buste).
Organization: Chronological.
Scope: These are supplications.
Location: Archivio Segreto Vaticano.

3.1.12.4 Fogli d'udienza
[DATABASE ID: VATV10174-A]
Inclusive Dates: 1803–1854.
Bulk: .5 linear m. (5 buste).
Organization: Chronological.
Scope: Inside each busta reads "Suppliche d'Indulgenze per
l'Udienza de" plus a date. The information is organized as
follows: diocese, church, person, other place, type of indul-
gence and what for.

References: Pásztor (1970), p. 177; Pásztor (1983), p. 182.

Finding Aids: ASV Indice 1116 (formerly Indice 62) provides a very brief busta-by-busta listing with the inclusive dates of each.

Location: Archivio Segreto Vaticano.

3.1.12.5 [Miscellanea SF/451–SF/452]

[DATABASE ID: VATV10175-A]

Inclusive Dates: 1668–1908.

Bulk: 3 linear m.

Organization: Series/items include (numerical designations supplied by project staff): 1. Decreta authentica: parte del manoscritto per il volume Decreta authentica S.C., etc. pubblicata nel volume Rescripta authentica, etc., 1882; —2. Rescripta authentica: Manoscritto del volume Rescripta authentica S.C. Indulg. Ss.que Reliquiis, 1668–1882; —3. Decreta authentica, 1668–1861; —4. Miscellanea 1, S.C. Indulgentiarum et SS. Reliquaiarum: Super adscriptione absentium sive Piis Unionibus sive Confraternitatibus, 1878 (printed); —5. Miscellanea 2, Suprema Sacra Congregazione del S. Offizio del rito detto assoluzione generale in uso nel terz'ordine di S. Francesco, relazione e voto con sommario di G.M. Granniello Barnabita, consultore, 1878 (printed); —6. Miscellanea 3, Differenza esistenti fra le facoltà della Segreteria de brevi e quelle della Segreteria delle indulgenza in fatto di concessioni d'indulgenze, etc., 19th cent.; —7. Miscellanea 4, Dubia extra Cong.nem. Generalem resoluta, 1824–1891; —8. Carte diverse, 1756–1864; —9. Manoscritto raccolta, 1877; —10. Manoscritto per il raccolta del 1898; —11. Resolutiones 4, [Misc. osservazioni and printed indulgences], 1736–1859; —12. Stampa e versioni della indulgenza ap.liche, [18—]; —13. Communicazio di altre segretarie, 1830–1906; —14. Concenia particolari, [18—]; —15. Carte diverse (primarily printed indulgences) [16—]–[18—]; —16. Carte diverse: Voti su parecchi dubbi non accompagnati da riposte ufficiale, 1821–1881; —17. Approva di versioni della raccolta, 1856–1864; —18. Relique, [18—]; —19. [Materials regarding the granting of indulgences throughout the world], [18—]–[19—], 4 buste; —20. Indice rescriptorum a motu proprio, 1855–ca. 1879; —21. Indice rescriptorum, 1892–1908; —22. Protocollo generale della Sac. Cong. delle Indulgenze S.S. Reliquie dall'anno 1868–1891; —23. Penitenzienia S. Offizio for Luigi Santoro, Giuseppe A. y Gercia, Ferdinando Antonelli, Ferdinando de Thomas de Bossierre, Giuseppe Espicea, Antonio Salvati and Generoso Petrucci.

Note: This is a true miscellany, located in the SF/451–SF/452 in the ASV. There is no official designation for this material in the ASV. The title was assigned by the project staff.

Indice rescriptorum a motu proprio, 1855–1879 (no. 20 above) and Indice rescriptorum, 1892–1908 (no. 21 above) can be used as indexes to segments of the Congregatio Indulgentiis Sacrisque Reliquiis Praepositae series *Rescripta*. Indice rescriptorum a motu proprio (no. 20) is referred to by Pásztor as "Porziuncola." Miscellanea 3, Differenza esistenti fra le facoltà della Segretaria de Brevi e quelle della Segreteria delle Indulgenza in fatto di concessioni d'indulgenze, etc. (no. 6), discusses functions of different officials in the office.

References: To Protocollo (no. 22)—Pásztor (1970), p. 177; Pásztor (1983), p. 182. To Indice rescriptorum a motu proprio (no. 20)—Pásztor (1970), p. 178; Pásztor (1983), p. 182.

Finding Aids: ASV Indice 1116 (formerly Indice 62) provides brief annotations for Carte Diverse and Miscellanea materials and brief listings for the Rescripta authentica and Decreta authentica. Identification numbers in this record do not correspond to those in the Indice and those in the indice are not always reflected on the actual items. No. 19 is referred to in Indice 1116 and by Pásztor as Porziuncola(?). Nos. 21 and 22 are referred to in Indice 1116 as Protocolli, 2 vols., 1868–1909.

Location: Archivio Segreto Vaticano.

3.1.12.6 Rescripta

[DATABASE ID: VATV10172-A]

Inclusive Dates: 1712–October 1908.

Bulk: 35 linear m.

Organization: Chronological.

Scope: These appear to be incoming written and printed requests as well as some bulls, perhaps granting the indults. Later buste have the request as well as notes toward the answer written on the request. They are arranged by date of audience. Some audiences are indexed.

References: Pásztor (1970), pp. 176–177; Pásztor (1983), p. 182. M. Merlini-Nolfi, *Rescripta authentica Sacrae Congregationis Indulgengiis SS.que Reliquiis praepositae ab a. 1668 ad a. 1882* (Regensburg, 1882) [this title was noted but not verified by project staff]. *Decreta authentica Sacrae Congregationis Indulgentiis Sacrisque Reliquiis Praepositae, ab anno 1668 ad annum 1882* (Regensburg, 1883). J. Schneider, *Rescripta authentica Sacrae Congregationis Indulgentiis Sacrisque Reliquiis Praepositae, necnon Summaria Indulgentiarum* (Regensburg, 1885).

Finding Aids: ASV Indice 1116 (formerly Indice 62) is a very brief busta by busta listing through 1907. Entries include the date of the volume, volume number for the year, and a series number if applicable.

The following items within records series of the congregation may be useful:

In Congregatio Indulgentiis Sacrisque Reliquiis Praepositae series *Decreta*, *1710–1808* (see description in this section) is an alphabetical index to the *Rescripta* for the years indicated.

In Congregatio Indulgentiis Sacrisque Reliquiis Praepositae series [*Miscellanea SF/451–SF/452*], see Indice rescriptorum a motu proprio, 1855–1879 (no. 20), which is a chronological index to the *Rescripta*. This indice is missing the entries for the years 1856–1866 and 1874–1878. In the same series, see Indice rescriptorum, 1892–1908 (no. 21), which may have some value as an index to segments of the *Rescripta*.

Location: Archivio Segreto Vaticano.

3.1.12.7 Resolutiones

[DATABASE ID: VATV10178-A]

Inclusive Dates: 1667–1963 (bulk 1710–1908).

Bulk: 2.5 linear m. (50 numbered buste and 2 unnumbered vols.).

Organization: Chronological. Unnumbered volumes at the end are out of chronological order. The first volume is "Resolutiones Sacrae Congregatione Indulgentiarum ab anno 1667 usque ab annum 1681." The second volume is "Resolutiones S. Congregationis Indul.tiarum Annorum 1849 et 1850, Caietae et Neapoli in Suburbano Portici, Fabius Cardinalis Asquinius Prefectus." Buste 49 and 50 are identified as "Archivum S. Poenitentiariae Apostolicae, Resolutiones."

Scope: This series appears to be a miscellany.

Reference: A. Prinzivalli, *Resolutiones, seu decreta authentica Sacrae Congregationis Indulgentiis Sacrisque Reliquiis praepositae ab anno 1668 ad annum 1861* (Rome, 1862).

Finding Aids: In the records of the Congregatio Indulgentiis Sacrisque Reliquiis Praepositae see the series *Decreta*, which is described elsewhere in this section. The final volume of the *Decreta* is identified as "Index resolutionum." This volume may possibly provide some access points to this series. However, this was not verified by the project staff.

Location: Archivio Segreto Vaticano.

3.1.12.8 Varia

[DATABASE ID: VATV10177-A]

Inclusive Dates: 1565–1907.

Bulk: 1 linear m. (23 vols. or buste).

Organization: Item numbers and titles are: 1. Dilata non expedire negative, ca. 1905–1907; —2. Documenti sulla questione fra Vienna ed Arles circa il corpo di S. Antonio, 1836–1856; —3. Liber tertii ordinis S.P. Francisci Assisensis, 1881–1882, 3 vols.; —4. Arciconfraternità di Nostra Signora del S. Cuore de Gesu, Bourges e Romana, 1878–1879; —5. Apostolato della Preghiera, 1879 and Relquie, 1880; —6. Regestr. [Harem?] Privil. Concess. Confraternitabus Congregationibus et Sodalitiis pro Missis, 1565–1788; —7. Posizione sulle varie vertenze incontrate dalla segreteria della S. Congregazione dell'Indulgenze e S.S. Reliquie colla Segreteria de brevi pontifici sotto i pontificati di Pio VIII . . . e Gregorio XVI . . . sono aggiunte le facoltà confermate di nuovo con rescritto dei 12 Feb. 1831 e con altra dichiarazione dei 18 N.bre 1833; —8. Epistolario di Monsignor segretario, 1877–1885; —9. Indice di decreti di approvazione amanti dalla S.C. delle Indulgenze e S.S. Reliquie per la facoltà di stampare e dare alla luce libri a sommarii d'Ind., 1867–1873; —10. [Monthly register of supplications], Nov. 1879–Nov. 1883; —11. Regolamento da osservarsi nella Segreteria della S. Congregazione delle Indulgenze circa le concessioni generali di Indulgenze/Registro delle concessioni generali, 1855–1890; —12. Registro delle concessioni, 1668–1864; [Misc. loose indices to bulls, constitutions, and decrees concerning the granting of indulgences, 1677–1760]; —13. De indulgentiis, manoscritto fatto per ordine dell' Emo. e Rmo. Sig Card. Rizzarri prefetto della S.C. delle Indulgenze per stamparsi e distribuirsi ai Padre del Concilio Vaticano; —14. Protocollo dei posizioni, 1855–1891; —15. Repertorio per la segreteria, 1816–1824; —16. Vota et annotationes Rvmi. D. Telesphori Galli [Consultor], 1818–1841; —17. [Register of indulgences], 1607–1864; —18. not identified: —19. Module di rescritti, ca. 1835; —20. Da rescritti alle posizioni, ca. 1884–1911; —Rescripta S.C. Indulgentiarum et SS. Reliquiarum, 1851.

References: Pásztor (1970), p. 177; Pásztor (1983), p. 182.

Finding Aids: ASV Indice 1116 (formerly Indice 62) provides a brief annotated listing of the first twenty volumes or buste in this series. Identification numbers correspond to those in this description.

Location: Archivio Segreto Vaticano.

3.1.13 Congregatio Iurisdictionis et Immunitatis Ecclesiasticae

[DATABASE ID: VATV785-A]

Instituted by Urban VIII in 1620 *vivae vocis oraculo*, this congregation was eventually united by Leo XIII (1878–1903) to the Congregation of the Council (1879). See the history for the Congregatio Concilii.

In addition to the records listed below, series listed with another agency relate directly to this agency and should be consulted. See Miscellaneous official series *Miscellaneorum armarium IX.*

References. Pásztor (1970), pp. 173–174; Boyle, p. 89.

RECORDS. Records of the congregation consist of the following series.

3.1.13.1 Acta

[DATABASE ID: VATV10251-A]

Inclusive Dates: 1573–1846.

Bulk: 91 linear m.

Organization: Chronological.

Location: Archivio Segreto Vaticano.

3.1.13.2 Liber decretorum

[DATABASE ID: VATV10250-A]

Inclusive Dates: 1628–1805, 1817–1845 (bulk 1628–1805).

Bulk: 3 linear m. (56 vols.).

Organization: Chronological. Note that there are some alternate titles on some spines: "Registrum decretorum et litterarum," "Indices decretorum," "Regestum decretorum."

Location: Archivio Segreto Vaticano.

3.1.13.3 Liber litterarum

[DATABASE ID: VATV10249-A]

Inclusive Dates: 1624–1856.

Bulk: 10 linear m. (116 vols.).

Organization: Chronological. Vols. 114–116 are out of chronological order as follows: 114. Tom. 1 (1657–1659); —115. Tom. 2 (1660–1663); —116. Tom. 3 (1663–1665). There are alternate titles on some volumes: "Regestum litterarum et decretorum," "Regestum litterarum."

Finding Aids: Most volumes are indexed.

Location: Archivio Segreto Vaticano.

3.1.13.4 [Miscellanea]

[DATABASE ID: VATV10252-A]

Inclusive Dates: 1634–1732.

Bulk: 3.5 linear m.

Organization: Subseries/items include: Lettere e documenti trasmessi; —Ristretti; —Posizioni; —Registro delle lettere scritte della Segretaria di Stato, a nunzi pontificii, a diversi archivescovi e vescovi; —Risoluzione e discorsi sopra la bolle di Gregorio XIV; —Atti; —Declarationes et brevia pontificia; —Brevia e decreta impressa; —Scritture; —Immunità per Savoia; —Repertorio delle circolari e facoltà; —Discorso sopra le controversie giurisdizionali di Sardegna; —Criminalità Parmen.; —Cause contro Francisco Dionisio Ubaldini, Conte da Peconani, 1695; —Viterbo, Malta, Acquapendente, Pesaro,

Osimo, Foligno, Veroli, Camerino, Macerata, Fermo, Spoleto, Bagnoregio, 1722–1784; —Reggio-Emilia, 1718–1779; —Ventimillien - Processus, 1752; —Parmen., 1671; —Processus in causa Joan. Bap. Ronchini; —Relazioni; —Cause (misc.); —Affari diplomatici; —Misc. stampate.

Note: This is a true miscellany with no official designation by the ASV. The title was assigned by the project staff.

Location: Archivio Segreto Vaticano.

3.1.14 Congregatio Lauretana

[DATABASE ID: VATV466-A]

The sanctuary of Loreto was a very popular destination for pilgrims in the late Middle Ages. According to tradition, the home of the Virgin Mary, when threatened by destruction by the Turks, was carried from Nazareth by angels and deposited (in 1291) on a hill at Tersatto in Dalmatia, where an alleged apparition of Mary and subsequent cures attested to the holiness of the house. Three years later it was transported in like manner across the Adriatic to a laurel grove (hence Loreto) near Recanati (the Marches), Italy, and from there removed in 1295 to its present site. Because of its popularity, the administration of the sanctuary ammassed substantial holdings. Located in the diocese of Recanati, the shrine was removed from the jurisdiction of that diocese in 1476. Sixtus IV, with his constitution *Ad ecclesiam* (Nov. 28, 1476), placed it, with all its vast possessions, directly under the jurisdiction of the Holy See. However, because of protests from the people of the area, he himself revoked this arrangement with the constitution *Romanus Pontifex* (Feb. 8, 1477). Julius II, with his constitution *In sublimia* (Oct. 21, 1507), reclaimed the jurisdiction and, in the course of time, nominated a governor, removable at will, under whose spiritual and temporal jurisdiction were placed not only the inhabitants of Loreto and all connected with the Holy House of Loreto, but also visitors and pilgrims during their stay in the Lauretan territory.

Other successive pontiffs accorded the sanctuary new privileges. Leo X (constitution *Ex supernae providentia*, Dec. 8, 1514) erected the collegiate church Ecclesia Sanctae Mariae de Laureto, confirming at the same time exemption from episcopal jurisdiction for pilgrims and those attached to the sanctuary. Clement VII extended the limits of the exemptions (brief *Cum nonnulli Romani Pontifices*, Apr. 17, 1525), which Paul III confirmed with the constitution *Ad sacram beati Petri sedem* (Feb. 18, 1536).

Sixtus V finally declared the Church of Loreto a cathedral (constitution *Pro excellenti praeminentia*, Mar. 17, 1586), and constituted its territory a diocese, stabilizing precisely the jurisdiction of the bishop and that of the cardinal protector, or apostolic commissary of the sanctuary.

In spite of the exact boundaries of authority fixed by Sixtus V between the two powers of authority set up for the administration of the Holy House and all that belonged to it, there were many conflicts regarding jurisdictions. These increased to such an extent that Paul V had to address the questions and set even more precisely the jurisdiction of the cardinal protector and that of the bishop of Loreto (constitution *Divina disponente clementia*, Jul. 14, 1620). Nevertheless, with the passage of time new conflicts arose between the authorities regarding the administration of the sanctuary.

Innocent XII, in order to find a solution, reserved to the Roman pontiff the governance of Loreto, suppressed the task assigned to the office of the cardinal protector, vacant at the time, and erected in its place (constitution *Sacrosancta Redemptionis*, Aug. 10, 1698) a special Congregatio Lauretana for which he provided a specific internal constitution with a chirograph (Oct. 1, 1698) directed to the cardinal secretary of state, naming him prefect.

According to this document the Congregatio Lauretana was responsible for the spiritual and temporal administration of the sanctuary delegated in the first place to the bishop of Loreto and in the second place to a prelate governor, resident of the place. It exercised a triple power: beneficent, administrative, and contentious, being empowered in this last case to deal with all controversies arising out of the administration of the possessions of the sanctuary and disciplinary or strictly judicial matters.

Although Innocent XII was concerned with limiting more precisely the functions of both the bishop and the governor, jurisdictional interference between the two authorities continued to such an extent that often the congregation had to intervene to settle differences. Benedict XIV with his constitution *Humilitatis nostrae* (Jan. 7, 1742) ordered that all the resolutions drawn up by the congregation be gathered together, ordered alphabetically, and published in Rome in 1743 as the *Synopsis lauretana*, commonly called the *Raccolta*.

The Congregatio Lauretana had extensive authority until the time of Pius VII (1800–1823) since it included jurisdiction not only over the Holy House of Loreto and its property but also over civil and criminal matters connected with the sanctuary. These powers were successively limited by Pius VII with the constitution *Post diuturnas* (Oct. 30, 1800) and with his motu proprio *Quando per ammirabile* (Jul. 6, 1816), which abolished privileges and withdrew from the Congregatio Lauretana all jurisdiction over contentious issues, transferring that juristiction to ordinary tribunals.

Leo XII (brief *Sacra aedes*, Jul. 24, 1827) appointed a prelate of the Roman Curia as apostolic commissary of the House of Loreto and with the brief *Laureti civitas* (Dec. 21, 1827) provided also for the reestablishment of the contentious power of the congregation. Gregory

XVI (Nov. 21, 1831) published regulations for the administration of justice in the city of Loreto, and issued legislation for four turni to deal with civil and criminal cases (Feb. 20, 1832).

After the Italian occupation of the Marches in 1860 when the Piedmontese annexed the province of Pisenum, the entire administration of the Holy House of Loreto passed to the civil authorities. Although the congregation retained the fiscal management as well as the spiritual supervision of the sanctuary, it was declared a national monument. The congregation lost, however, almost all of its functions and retained only those regarding charitable bequests.

The constitution of Pius X (*Sapienti consilio*, Jun. 29, 1908) did not abolish the Congregatio Lauretana but provided that the congregation would remain distinct from the others, although attached to the Congregation of the Council. The office of prefect, formerly held by the cardinal secretary of state, would now be held by the prefect of the Congregation of the Council. The constitution of Pius X did not define the powers of the Congregation of Loreto but they were already much diminished by events that had taken place in Italy in the previous fifty years. The functions, therefore, related primarily to the restorations of the basilica and supervision of the numerous pilgrimages to the shrine. The Congregation of the Council transacted the business of the Lauretan Congregation in all other matters of its authority according to the established rules of procedure.

The Congregatio Lauretana was quietly suppressed in 1917. The sanctuary was placed under pontifical administration on October 11, 1935. It was named a prelature nullius on June 24, 1965, and is now called a territorial prelature.

In addition to the records listed below, series listed with another agency relate directly to this agency and should be consulted. See Miscellaneous official series *Miscellaneorum armarium IX*.

RECORDS. Records of the congregation consist of the following series.

3.1.14.1 Fondo Lauretano
[DATABASE ID: VATV277-A]

Inclusive Dates: 1562–1908.

Bulk: 60 linear m. (654 numbered volumes and buste).

Organization: Subseries, volume or buste numbers, and contents are: Santa Casa e Congregazione lauretana, ca. 1400–1799, vols. 1–117; —Registri di lettere e risoluzioni della Congregazione lauretana, 1698–1839, vols. 118–164; —Positiones Sacrae Congregationis Lauretanae, 1739–1892, vols. 165–267; —Santa Casa di Loretto nella Marca. Giustificazione, 1701–1872, vols. 268–310; —Santa Casa di Loretto. Registri di istrumenti, 1690–1867, vols. 311–320; —Santa Casa di Loretto, Registri di entrata ed uscita, 1675–1828, vols. 321–344; —Santa Casa di Loretto, Registri di rincontri, 1671–1849, vols. 345–351; —Santa Casa di Loretto, Registri di mandati ed ordini, 1678–1856, vols. 352–362; —Santa Casa di Loretto, Re-

gistri di patenti, 1702–1840, vols. 363–367; —Santa Casa di Loretto, Bilancio annuali, 1746–1859, vols. 368–469; —Santa Casa di Loretto nella Marca, Libri mastri, 1671–1881, vols. 470–482; —Congregazione Lauretana, Cause civili e criminali, 1733–1859, vols. 483–512; —Congregazione economica della Santa Casa di Loretto, 1736–1894, vols. 513–515; —Congregazione Lauretana. Atti di visite, 1816–1836, vols. 516–520; —Santa Casa di Loretto. Preventivi, 1845–1861, vols. 521–536; —Congregazione Lauretana, Amministrazione di Roma, Bilancio, 1857–1868, vols. 537–543; —Congregazione Lauretana, Amministrazione di Roma, Incassi e pagamenti, 1857–1906, vols. 544–551; —Congregazione Lauretana, Amministrazione di Roma, Mandati, 1857–1870, vols. 552–565; —Santa Casa e Congregazione lauretana, Miscellanea, ca. 1500–1900, vols. 566–637; —Piante e carte topografiche, ca. 1700–1899, vols. 638–642; —Rubricelle, inventari, protocolli, 1639–1903, vols. 643–654.

Scope: The records in this fondo represent both the Casa and the Congregatio.

References: Fink, p. 118; Boyle, p. 89.

Finding Aids: ASV Indice 1150 provides a listing of individual buste or volumes for vols. 1–654. Inventory entries include volume or buste number, exact and complete titles, when available, inclusive dates, and occasional annotations. There is a brief introduction and orientation to the fondo. See also F. Grimaldi and A. Mordenti, eds., *Guida degli archivi lauretani* (Rome, 1985–1986). This work contains a published version of ASV Indice 1150 by Ottavio Cavalleri. Other than having an abbreviated introduction to the Fondo, the published inventory is essentially the same as the one found in the ASV Sala dei Indici. Within the series vol. 648 is an inventory to the Archivio of the Congregatio in the nineteenth century. It is interesting to see the former arrangement and to note what has been lost, but it does not give any insight into the current contents or arrangement of the fondo.

Location: Archivio Segreto Vaticano.

3.1.15 Congregatio Negotiis et Consultationibus Episcoporum et Regularium Praeposita
[DATABASE ID: VATV004-A]

This congregation is generally known simply as Bishops and Regulars. Its origin can be traced to the cardinalatial commission set up by Pius V (1566–1572) under the apostolic visitor, Bartolomeo di Porcia in 1570, to examine relations with the patriarch of Aquileia. The commission continued to function even after its initial task had been accomplished. Gregory XIII (1572–1585), recognizing the usefulness of these visits, used it for other purposes from 1573 to 1576, particularly for problems arising between bishops and religious. With the increase of bishops having recourse to the commission, however, it began in 1576 to function as a permanent organization under the name Congregatio super Consultationibus Episcoporum.

Sixtus V (constitution *Romanus Pontifex*, May 17, 1586) created a new department called Congregatio super Consultationibus Regularium charged with caring for the many problems that were arising among religious of both sexes. His *Immensa aeterni Dei* (Jan. 22, 1588) included this and the above organization among the new congregations formally established by this constitution in the reorganization of the Roman Curia.

When these two congregations were united is not well documented, but it has been verified that during the pontificate of Clement VIII, from 1593 onward, there are indications of a single combined congregation; from 1601 onward, there is concrete evidence of a single congregation under the name Congregatio Negotiis et Consultationibus Episcoporum et Regularium Praeposita. For the sake of brevity, however, the entire new name was not always used in the compilation of the official acts of a case.

Invested with ordinary and extraordinary faculties delegated from time to time by the various popes, the functions of the Congregatio Episcoporum et Regularium (as the congregation came to be commonly called) were vast. Along with all the affairs relative to bishops and religious, it accumulated jurisdiction parallel to that of the Congregation of the Council with the sole difference that it did not have power as did the other to resolve proposed doubts *authentice* (in a legally valid way).

In the course of time three other congregations, whose functions were closely related, were united to the Congregation of Bishops and Regulars. The Congregatio super Statu Regularium was established by Innocent X with the constitution *Inter cetera* (Dec. 17, 1649) for the reform of regulars in Italy, but suppressed by Innocent XII's constitution *Debitum pastoralis officii* (Aug. 4, 1698). Congregatio super Disciplina Regulari was instituted by Innocent XII (Aug. 4, 1698), for the reform of regulars throughout the world. The Congregatio super Statu Regularium Ordinum was established by Pius IX (Sept. 7, 1846). These last two were suppressed by Pius X's motu proprio *Sacrae Congregationi* (May 26, 1906). Their functions were assigned to the Congregation of Bishops and Regulars.

Pius VII (constitution *Post diuturnas*, Oct. 30, 1800) reserved exclusively to this congregation appeals in criminal cases from diocesan curias and mandated that all such cases should be transferred to the Congregatio Episcoporum et Regularium from the curia of the auditor general of the Apostolic Camera, whose tribunal had been of such importance at one time that it was sufficient to refer to it by initials only (A.C. = Auditor Camerae).

The name of this congregation indicated to a certain extent the scope of its functions. It was responsible for most matters relating to bishops and other prelates, to religious, and to relations between bishops and religious. It did not, however, treat matters of doctrine; nor was it allowed to handle formal interpretation of Tridentine decrees or to conduct marriage processes, both of which belonged to the Congregation of the Council. It did not concern itself with rites and ceremonies. But in all other ecclesiastical affairs it possessed jurisdiction to the extent that Urban VIII and later popes called it a universal congregation. Appeals of priests and laity against decisions of bishops also came to this congregation for judgment. Its authority was not legislative but primarily administrative and judicial.

With the publication of Pius X's constitution *Sapienti consilio* (Jun. 29, 1908), the Congregation of Bishops and Regulars as such ceased to exist on November 3, 1908. Those of its functions relating to bishops and the administration of dioceses were assigned to the Consistorial Congregation; those referring to religious were given to the new congregation called Congregatio Negotiis Religiosorum Sodalium Praeposita.

The records of this congregation are just beginning to be discovered by scholars operating outside the boundaries of traditional ecclesiastical and diocesan history. Its various subseries are promising for art history, musicology, women's history (women as patrons and participants in religious communities), education (seminaries, schools, and catechetical instruction) and literacy, the study of early modern and modern parish life, confraternities, popular piety, preaching, confession, resistance to reform, the history of new and old religious orders and their churches, their cults, holy images, and relics. Records also supply glimpses into ceremonial life, including references to marriage and funeral practices.

In general, more of the quotidian nature of clerical and monastic life emerges from the records of this congregation than from the holdings of the Congregation of the Council and the Rota, whose administrative and judicial responsibilities complement and sometimes intertwine with the business of the Congregation of Bishops and Regulars. When the nun who served her convent as baker dies, the other sisters write this congregation to ask if they can accept another baker as a nun because they cannot afford to buy bread from the outside. This is the congregation to which a bishop writes when a cathedral canon confesses to pawning a chalice. A request for permission to alienate monastery property in order to renovate or buy a new organ would come here.

Note that throughout most of the subseries for this congregation, the term *regolari* is used generically, like *mankind* to refer to male and female religious of every stripe. Likewise, particularly during the first hundred years of the *Positiones* series, there may be files pertaining to male orders in a busta or series labeled *monache* and business concerning nuns under the classification *regolari*. Material dealing with confraternities, hospitals, and pilgrim's hospices may also be found in several subseries.

Permissions for the construction of chapels and for the pursuit of other religious projects turn up in all sezioni of the positiones series. Religious images are mentioned or described in the context of chapels, cult practices, and public processions. Occasionally the petitions to the Congregation touch directly on subjects of interest to art historians, for example, a request by religious communities or ecclesiastical figures to make changes in the fabric of a church or monastery. Sometimes these requests are accompanied by supporting documentation, which may include architectural descriptions, cost estimates from architects and even plans. In a related vein, when a nun of S. Giovanni Battista in Bologna needed to meet periodically with an architect to discuss plans for construction of a new church and monastery, she petitioned for permission to leave her convent to do so, supporting her request with a presentation of her architectural project. A separate case refers to the nuns of another Bolognese convent who burned their medieval altarpiece, after replacing it with a "modern" one. When the outraged bishop requested discipline for this action from the Congregation of Bishops and Regulars, the nuns defended themselves by criticizing the style and condition of the old altarpiece and by pointing out how their new one conformed to the aesthetic prescriptions of Trent.

Note that some material from this congregation may be found in the Archivio della Congregazione per i Religiosi e gli Istituti Secolari. According to Pásztor (1970), pp. 344–345, this archive houses mostly nineteenth-century material (address: Piazza Pio XII 3, 00193 Rome). This archive was not examined by the project staff.

In addition to the records listed below, series listed with another agency relate directly to this agency and should be consulted. See Miscellaneous official series *Miscellaneorum armarium VIII.*

References. G. A. Bizzarri, *Collectanea in usum Secretariae Sacrae Congregationis Episcoporum et Regularium* (Rome, 1885). B. Katterbach, "Archivio Vaticano," in *Enciclopedia italiana* (Rome, 1929), vol. 4, pp. 88–90. G. L. Masetti Zannini, "Sisto V, I 'Vescovi e Regolari' e le Indie Occidentali," in *Sisto V: I. Roma e Lazio* [this title was noted but not verified by project staff]. N. del Re, *La curia romana: lineamenti storico-giuridici,* 3d ed. (Rome, 1970). A. M. Stickler, *Historia iuris canonici latini institutiones academicae,* vol. 1, *Historia fontium* (Turin, 1950).

RECORDS. Records of the congregation consist of the following series.

3.1.15.1 Appunti: Sezione VV MM RR secolo XIX
[DATABASE ID: VATV10397-A]
Inclusive Dates: ca. 1800–1899.
Bulk: .1 linear m. (1 busta).
Location: Archivio Segreto Vaticano.

3.1.15.2 [Canonizzazione]
[DATABASE ID: VATV10399-A]
Inclusive Dates: 1600–1650.
Bulk: .5 linear m. (5 buste).
Organization: Alphabetical (usually by first name). Materials are numbered 1–120.
Scope: The series begins with "Trattato sulla beatificazione e canonizzazione," written during the pontificate of Urban VIII, and is followed by files on persons being promoted for canonization. Ninety percent of the cases deal with men.
Note: This series does not have an offical ASV designation. The title was supplied by the project staff.
Location: Archivio Segreto Vaticano.

3.1.15.3 Carte appartenute a Mons. DeMontal
[DATABASE ID: VATV10383-A]
Inclusive Dates: ca. 1762–1880.
Bulk: .2 linear m. (1 box).
Location: Archivio Segreto Vaticano.

3.1.15.4 Cassa
[DATABASE ID: VATV10410-A]
Inclusive Dates: ca. 1850–1905.
Bulk: 5 linear m. (4 boxes).
Scope: This series contains "Onorario per gli Officiali nella Congregazione" and "Stato di Cassa" reports.
Location: Archivio Segreto Vaticano.

3.1.15.5 [Cause]
[DATABASE ID: VATV10411-A]
Inclusive Dates: 1600–1779.
Bulk: 17 linear m.
Organization: Chronological.
Note: The title for this series was supplied by the project staff. It has no official ASV designation.
Location: Archivio Segreto Vaticano.

3.1.15.6 Circolari
[DATABASE ID: VATV10385-A]
Inclusive Dates: 1682–1697, 1800–1850.
Bulk: 1 linear m. (9 boxes).
Organization: Boxes 1–8 contain materials dating between 1800 and 1850. Box 9 contains circolari from 1682, 1689, and 1697.
Scope: These are printed materials.
Location: Archivio Segreto Vaticano.

3.1.15.7 Collectanea
[DATABASE ID: VATV10370-A]
Inclusive Dates: 1573–1927.
Bulk: 2.5 linear m. (28 numbered volumes and 17 unnumbered buste).
Organization: Volumes, titles, and enumeration are: 1. Decreta, "Compendium monialium," 1545–1658; —2. Sommario o vero compendio di tutte le lettere e decreti della Sacra Congregazione degli Emmin. Cardinali sopra i Negotii de Vescovi e Regolari, 1573–1656; —3. Regularium index capitum (Breve compendio per ordine alphabetico di decreti della Sacra Congregazione de Regolari), 1578–1604 (Monache, f. 213v); —4. Summa . . . compendium litterarum et decretorum

Sacrae Congr. Emin. RR. S.R.E. Cardinalium Negotiis et Consultationibus Episcoporum et Regularium Praepositae, 1573–1656 (duplicate of vol. 2); —5. Risoluzioni, decreti, e grazie piu speciali della Sagra Congregazione di Vescovi e Regolari raccolte da me Canonico Giuseppe Mola Romano primo minutante della segretaria di detta congregazione, 1573–1742 (Vescovi, Tom. 1) (indexed); —6. Risoluzioni, decreti e grazie piu speciali della S. Congregazione di Vescovi e Regolari raccolte da me Giuseppe Mola Romano sacerdote e ministro della segretaria di detta S. Congregazione (de Regolari, Tom. I), 1610–1741 (indexed); —7. Resoluzioni, decreti e grazie piu speciali della Sagra Congregazione di Vescovi e Regolari raccolte da me Canonico Guiseppe Mola Romano primo minutante della segretaria di detta congregazione (Regolari, Tom. II), 1736–1743 (indexed); —8. Regularium: Breve compendio per ordine alfabetico di decreti della Sacra Congregazione de Regolari pertinenti a frati e fatti a tempo di Mons. Agocchi e nel principio di Mons. Cipsio; —8a. [Decreta], (Restituzione, dispensa matrimoniale, facoltà), 1615–1768; —9. Repertorium regularum, 1640–1762 (indexed); —10. Episcoporum: Collectio resolutionum et . . . decretorum, 1657–1700 (indexed); —11. Monialium: Collectio seu medulla resolutionum et omnium decretorum, 1657–1700 (indexed); —12. Regularium: Collectio seu medulla resolutionum et eunctorum decretorum, 1657–1700 (indexed); —13. Index causarum et scriptarum miscellanearum, 1708–1720 (indexed); —14. Circolari, decreti, encicliche, 1800–1849 (indexed); —15. Collectanea in usum secretariae Sacra Congregationis Episcoporum et Regularium, 1821–1852; —16. [Alphabetical reference book] compiled by Mons. Boccafogli, 1833–1850; —17. Collectanea, 1834–1843; —18. Collectanea, 1835–1843 (indexed); —19. Collectanea [alphabetical annotated index to types of business, religious orders, etc.], 1836–1867; —20. Collectanea [alphabetical annotated index to types of business, religious orders, etc.], 1868–1895; —21. Registro delle massime, disposizioni erisoluzioni emanate dalla Sagra Cong.ne di Vescovi e Regolari da servire di norma nel disbrigo degli affari attevato nel 1851 per ordine di Mons.Bizzarri (alphabetical); —22. not noted; —23. Repertorio di tutti l'[approvationi] di regole ed istituti, 1814–1901; —24. La Congregazione di Vescovi e Regolari, Memorie ed appunti, 1884 (compiled by Mons. Boccafogli, sotto-segretario, 11 April 1899); —25. [Minute de consultazioni], [18—]; Commisso pro Regularibus, 1869; —26. Facoltà e attribuzioni, 1819–1878 (includes material from the Cong. sulla Disciplina Regulari); —27. Miscellanea manoscritti I, [16—]–[18—] (includes decrees, bulls, orations, material concerning St. Andrew the Apostle); —28. Miscellanea manoscritti II, ca. 1750 (includes discourses and orations); —[29.] In Congregazione, 1652 (alphabetical index to ?); —[30.] Duplicate of vols. 2 and 4 above; —[31.] [Alphabetical annotated index to types of business and religious orders], 1585–1604; —[32.] Registro delle posizioni cui viene apposto il "Proponatur in plenario, etc.," 1906–1908; —[33.] [Title page lost, initial page reads "Index alfabeticus causarum et decretorum"], this is a printed copy of vol. 16 (Boccafogli) or Bizzarri (cf. below); —[34.] Vertenze: Registro delle posizioni cui viene apposto il "Proponatur in plenario etc.," 1905–1908; —[35.] Clero, 1905 [Alphabetical index with protocol numbers, register is not very full]; —[36.] Registro delle posizioni rimesse "pro voto" ai R.mi Consultori, 1906–1908 (includes

an "Elenco dei R.mi Consultori"); —[37.] Protocollo della S. C. dei Religiosi, 1921–[post-1922].

References: Pásztor (1970), pp. 160–161; Pásztor (1983), p. 177. G. A. Bizzarri, *Collectanea in usum Secretariae Sacrae Congregationis Episcoporum et Regularium* (Rome, 1885). This is a later published version of *Collectanea*, vol. 15, and a version of *Collectanea*, vol. [33] (cf. above for both listings).

Finding Aids: In the ASV soffittone (V/1) there is a one-drawer schedario entitled "Per titolo" that serves as a partial index to materials regarding religious orders (ca. fifteenth century-nineteenth century) in the *Collectanea* as well as a number of other indexed and unindexed series in the ASV. Entries are brief and indicate the religious order, a short reference to the business, the fondo, and current volume number. This is not an official ASV finding aid and must be used in consultation with ASV staff.

Location: Archivio Segreto Vaticano.

3.1.15.8 Collezione di rescritti: Ponenza
[DATABASE ID: VATV10447-A]
Inclusive Dates: ca. 1871–1882.
Bulk: .05 linear m. (3 vols.).
Organization: Three volumes are as follows: Ponenza Vescovi; —Ponenza Regolari; —Ponenza Monache.
Scope: These may be excerpts of ponenze, perhaps examples. Each volume is indexed internally by type of case (material). Particularly in the Vescovi, but also occasionally in the Regolari and Monache, the protocollo numbers cited can be traced in the *Protocolli* series.
Finding Aids: The Congregatio Episcoporum et Regularium record series *Protocolli*, described in this section, cannot be effectively used as an index to this series. The *Collezione di rescritti* contains a very selected number of cases and the *Protocolli* does not indicate exactly which few cases are in the *Collezione di rescritti*.
Location: Archivio Segreto Vaticano.

3.1.15.9 Consultazioni
[DATABASE ID: VATV10387-A]
Inclusive Dates: 1835–1907.
Bulk: 17 linear m. (73 buste).
Organization: Subseries are: 1–29. Consultazioni [originali]; —30–69 (organized alphabetically by diocese). Consultazioni duplicati; —70–71 (organized alphabetically by diocese). Consultazioni varie; —[72.] Consultazioni, 1839; —[73.] [Consultazioni], 1589–1895 (includes apostolic visits).
Scope: Material is primarily printed. Final buste contain seventeenth-century apostolic visits to churches and hospitals in Rome and outside.
References: Pásztor (1970), p. 159; Pásztor (1983), p. 177.
Finding Aids: In the ASV soffittone (V/1) there is a one-drawer index to the initial two subseries described above: Consultazioni [originali] and the Consultazioni duplicati. The index is entitled "Schedario per uso personale incaricato alla ricerche di pratiche che vengono richieste dai studiosi." This schedario is alphabetical by diocese. Entries indicate the diocese, date, a brief reference to the religious order involved, and sometimes the business, and the current volume number (e.g., A.144). This is not an official ASV finding aid and must be used in consultation with ASV staff.
Location: Archivio Segreto Vaticano.

3.1.15.10 Feudi del Piedmonte
[DATABASE ID: VATV10400-A]
Inclusive Dates: ca. 1733.
Bulk: .1 linear m. (1 busta).
Organization: Two items are included in the busta: "Savoia: Scritture degli avvocati, 1733" and "Informazione storica."
Reference: Fink, p. 134.
Location: Archivio Segreto Vaticano.

3.1.15.11 Istituti feminili
[DATABASE ID: VATV10379-A]
Inclusive Dates: ca. 1589–1870.
Bulk: 1 linear m. (6 buste).
Organization: Alphabetical according to religious order.
Scope: There is a 1589 document in the Benedictine material regarding houses in Napoli. There is also a visitation in this busta.
Reference: Pásztor (1970), pp. 157–158 (note).
Finding Aids: In the ASV soffittone (V/1) there is a one-drawer schedario entitled "Per titolo" that serves as a partial index to materials regarding religious orders (ca. fifteenth century-nineteenth century) in the Istituti Feminili, as well as a number of other indexed and unindexed series in the ASV. Entries are brief and indicate the religious order, a short reference to the business, the fondo, and current volume number. The Istituti Maschili and Istituti Feminili are sometimes referred to simply as "Istituti" and a researcher must determine if the citation refers to the Istituti Maschili or Feminili by the content of the schedario itself. This is not an official ASV finding aid and must be used in consultation with ASV staff.
Location: Archivio Segreto Vaticano.

3.1.15.12 Istituti maschili
[DATABASE ID: VATV10378-A]
Inclusive Dates: ca. 1584–1855.
Bulk: 1 linear m. (6 buste).
Organization: 4 buste numbers used but there are 6 buste numbered as follows: 1, 1a, 2, 3, 3a, 4. They are alphabetical according to religious order. Busta 1a is all Capuchins. Busta 3a is all Ordine della Penitenza.
Summary: The 1584 document is under "R."
References: Pásztor (1970), pp. 157–158 (note).
Finding Aids: In the ASV soffittone (V/1) there is a one-drawer schedario entitled "Per titolo" that serves as a partial index to materials regarding religious orders (ca. fifteenth century–nineteenth century) in the Istituti Maschili, as well as a number of other indexed and unindexed series in the ASV. Entries are brief and indicate the religious order, a short reference to the business, the fondo, and current volume number. The Istituti Maschili and Istituti Feminili are sometimes referred to simply as "Istituti," and a researcher must determine if the citation refers to the Istituti Maschili or Feminili by the content of the schedario itself.
Location: Archivio Segreto Vaticano.

3.1.15.13 Miscellanea II
[DATABASE ID: VATV10401-A]
Inclusive Dates: 1625–1658.
Bulk: .1 linear m. (1 busta).
Scope: Spine states: "Cause di beatificazione e canonizzazione del Venerabile Servo di Dio, Francesco di Sales,

Vescovo di Ginevra"; "Lettere varie: Re di Francia, Clero di Francia, Principi e Clero di Savoie, Monasteri."
Location: Archivio Segreto Vaticano.

3.1.15.14 [Miscellanea V/7]
[DATABASE ID: VATV357-A]
Inclusive Dates: 1596–1905.
Bulk: .5 linear m.
Organization: Buste that compose the collection include: Segreteria, ca. 1860; —Varia (Regolari), ca. 1800; —Pro monialibus, 1596; —Registro Archivio segreto, 1821–1882; —Alienazione, 1700–1865; —Notizie diverse (Regolari), 1699–1735; —Minute, 1801–1804; —In Congregazione (selected acta of meetings), 1631; —Regestrum secretum, May 1736, November 1742, November 1743, April 1745; —Minute (Religiosi), 1633, 1637, 1639, 1652; —Minute, 1800; —Varie ("Elenco di novelli istituti, confraternite ad altre pie unione"), 1851–1905; —Posizioni . . . Consultori (summaries), 1876–1905.
Note: The "Elenco di novelli istituti" may be the "Indice degl'Istituti novelli" that Pásztor cites as an index to the *Positiones* series of this congregation described in this section. This is a true miscellany with no official ASV designation. The title was assigned by the project staff with reference to its location in 1990.
Reference: Pásztor (1970), p. 158.
Location: Archivio Segreto Vaticano.

3.1.15.15 [Miscellanea V/23]
[DATABASE ID: VATV10446-A]
Inclusive Dates: ca. 1736–1896.
Bulk: 20 linear m.
Organization: The series includes: Segreteria, 1788–1797; —Segreteria-Contabilità; —Voti, ca. 1826; —Atti; —Dispense matrimoniali, ca. 1800; —Ricevute; —Regolari spedizione, 1736–1756; —[Rubric], 1852–1880 (contains a note that what this refers to could not be located).
Note: This is a true miscellany without an official designation by the ASV. The title was assigned by project staff and refers to its location in 1990.
Location: Archivio Ségreto Vaticano.

3.1.15.16 Oratori privati
[DATABASE ID: VATV10391-A]
Inclusive Dates: 1868–1905.
Bulk: 10 linear m.
Organization: Chronological.
Scope: These records are supplications for different types of indults, for example, including those for private oratories, to say Mass before dawn, and special privileges when a member of the family was ill. There are also a number of requests to extend an indult already given to include more people, an additional residence, and so forth.
Finding Aids: Each supplication is summarized for presentation and the decisions are written on the back, often referring to earlier indults for oratori privati. The protocol number on the back refers to the Episcoporum et Regularium series *Protocolli*, described elsewhere among the records of this congregation. The top number is the item number, the bottom number is the *Protocolli* subseries.

The *Protocolli* list these briefly as "Solite amplificazioni ad estensioni di Indulti" with a list of the dioceses involved. No personal names or religious orders are listed for the oratory privati in the *Protocolli*, so it is of limited use in indexing this series. After the oratory was approved a brief was listed. These briefs, as well as any former briefs referred to on the supplications can sometimes be traced in the indices for briefs generated by the Secretariatus Brevium known as Sec. Brev. The Sec. Brev. issued briefs for other congregations, including that of the Bishops and Regulars.

Location: Archivio Segreto Vaticano.

3.1.15.17 [Ordini Religiosi]

[DATABASE ID: VATV10445-A]

Inclusive Dates: 1593–1850.

Bulk: 20 linear m.

Note: These materials were in the process of reorganization in 1990. The title was assigned by the project staff.

Location: Archivio Segreto Vaticano.

3.1.15.18 Positiones

[DATABASE ID: VATV10374-A]

Inclusive Dates: 1573–1908.

Bulk: 517 linear m.

Organization: Two major subseries: Positiones: Vescovi e regolari, 1573–1625 (includes monache); —Positiones: Sezione vescovi, 1626–1908. Buste are organized by the date of the meetings. Within buste dated between 1573 and 1625, material is divided into two groups: Episcoporum and Regularium (which includes monache). The Episcoporum material is alphabetical by diocese, but not strictly alphabetical within each letter. The Regularium material is alphabetical by the name of the religious order.

Within buste dated 1626–1908, material is organized alphabetically by diocese.

According to Index 1104, prepared by Charles Burns, in buste generated before 1626, Vescovi, regolari, and monache are all together.

Scope: In this series, one finds a great amount of business concerning ecclesiastical administration, at its most bureaucratic level: benefices and other financial concerns, disputes between diocesan and/or civic officials regarding property or jurisdiction, impediments to the execution duties specified by Trent, puzzling irregularities encountered, punishments and excuses for episcopal nonresidency or failure to conduct visitations, diocesan building campaigns, and the educational projects. The bishop also appears in these sources in his ceremonial and sacramental roles. His dealings with confraternities, alms distribution, and testamentary bequests also emerge from the files of this series.

References: Boyle, p. 89; Pásztor (1970), p. 158; Pásztor (1983), p. 177.

Finding Aids: ASV Indice 1104(I), compiled by Charles Burns, provides a brief inventory of the entire series. Entries include the year and months of the meeting for which particular positiones can be found in the buste.

Location: Archivio Segreto Vaticano.

3.1.15.19 Positiones: Archivio segreto

[DATABASE ID: VATV10377-A]

Inclusive Dates: 1727–1908.

Bulk: 29 linear m.

Organization: Subseries are: Vescovi; —Regolari; —Monache. Buste are organized chronologically by date of meeting. Within each buste material is divided into the three subseries (Vescovi, Regolari, Monache). The Vescovi and Monache subseries are alphabetical by diocese. The Regolari is alphabetical by name of the religious order.

Charles Burns has a brief note in index 1104 (I) concerning the seclusion of certain more sensitive materials in this series.

References: Boyle, p. 89; Pásztor (1970), p. 160; Pásztor (1983), p. 178.

Finding Aids: ASV Indice 1104 (II) (formerly Indice 129) contains a busta-by-busta listing of this entire series. Entries indicate the inclusive dates, the subseries included in the busta (Vescovi, Monache, Regolari), and some annotations to buste that solely treat a diocese (e.g., Bergamo, Montpelier) or a religious order (e.g., Passionisti).

In the ASV soffittone (V/1) there is a one-drawer schedario entitled "Per titolo" that serves as a partial index to materials regarding religious orders (ca. fifteenth century-nineteenth century) in the *Positiones*: *Archivio segreto*, as well as a number of other indexed and unindexed collections. Entries are brief and indicate the religious order, a short reference to the business, the fondo, and the current volume number. This is not an official ASV index and must be used in consultation with ASV staff.

Location: Archivio Segreto Vaticano.

3.1.15.20 Positiones: Sezione monache

[DATABASE ID: VATV10376-A]

Inclusive Dates: 1626–1908.

Bulk: 330 linear m.

Organization: Buste are organized chronologically by the date of the meeting. Within each busta, materials are organized alphabetically according to diocese.

Scope: Most of the files in the buste of this series deal in one way or another with convent "irregularities," taking the Tridentine decrees as the rule. As a rule, the more routine an issue, the less detail one receives about it. Since women's were more highly regulated than male monasteries and a nun's life was less public, material concerning women's institutions generally centers on convent life. Aside from an instance of the occasional unwanted pregnancy, the rare clandestine flight, and the ubiquitous predatory confessor, the files of the *Sezione monache* contain comparatively less of what the modern mind classifies as crime or scandal than the Congregatio Negotiis et Consultationibus Episcoporum et Regularium Praeposita series *Sezione regularium*. Since, particularly in minor matters, the Congregation functioned as a gracious as well as a surveillant and restrictive organ, the *Positiones* often contain various sorts of dispensations and special permissions (e.g., for more than two sisters of the same family to make profession in the same monastery, for the acceptance of an illiterate woman as a nun). Dispensations of a more serious nature were handled by the Congregazione del Concilio.

According to Charles Burns in Indice 1104 (I), similar materials that predate this series can be located in the Bishops and Regulars series *Positiones*.

References: Boyle, p. 89; Pásztor (1970), p. 158; Pásztor (1983), p. 177. A. I. Bassani, "Le fonti dell'Archivio Segreto Vaticano per una storia ecclesiastica della repubblica e del regno d'Italia," in *Vita religiosa e cultura in Lombardia e nel*

Veneto nell'età napoleonica, edited by F. Agostino et al. (Rome, 1990), pp. 363–393.

Finding Aids: ASV Indice 1104 (I), compiled by Charles Burns, contains a brief inventory of this entire series. Entries include the inclusive dates of each busta (year and months).

Location: Archivio Segreto Vaticano.

3.1.15.21 Positiones: Sezione regolari

[DATABASE ID: VATV10375-A]

Inclusive Dates: 1626–1875.

Bulk: 317 linear m. (794 numbered buste).

Organization: The buste are organized chronologically by the date of the meeting. Within each busta, material is alphabetical according to the religious order.

Scope: Crime, imprisonment, and public impropriety, together with the perennial benefice issues and conflicts over jurisdictions, characterize a large percentage of the records dealing with the clergy. Conflicts between orders or between a religious order and another ecclesiastical entity or authority appear with relative frequency. Other frequent cases include the transfer of a monk (less frequently a nun) from one order to another, abandonment of religious life or apostasy, clerical education and advancement, disagreements between superiors and subordinates, and the dilemmas a priest or friar might encounter in the normal day-to-day execution of his duties as he understands them. Here, too, requests for permission to build, expand, or renovate ecclesiastical buildings occur regularly.

According to Charles Burns in Indice 1104 (I), before this series began, similar materials were placed in the Bishops and Regulars series *Positiones*.

References: Boyle, p. 89; Pásztor (1970), p. 158; Pásztor (1983), p. 177. A. I. Bassani, "Le fonti dell'Archivio Segreto Vaticano per una storia ecclesiastica della repubblica e del regno d'Italia," in *Vita religiosa e cultura in Lombardia e nel Veneto nell'età napoleonica*, edited by F. Agostino et al. (Rome, 1990), pp. 363–393.

Finding Aids: ASV Indice 1104 (I), compiled by Charles Burns, provides a brief inventory of the entire series. Entries include the year (or year and month) covered by each busta.

Location: Archivio Segreto Vaticano.

3.1.15.22 Processus

[DATABASE ID: VATV10381-A]

Inclusive Dates: ca. 1581–1807.

Bulk: 36 linear m.

Organization: The first half of the series is roughly in alphabetical order by diocese. The first volume, which is from Assisi, appears to be the earliest.

Location: Archivio Segreto Vaticano.

3.1.15.23 Prospetto delle parrocchie dello Stato

[DATABASE ID: VATV10442-A]

Inclusive Dates: 1842.

Bulk: .1 linear m. (1 vol.).

Organization: Alphabetical by city or town.

Scope: This volume actually covers parishes, convents, and monasteries. It is a directory "elenco," organized alphabetically by locality. Within the listing for each locality all Catholic parishes are itemized and the following information is provided: name, whether the parish is regolare (run by a religious

order) and the name of the order, or secolare (administered by diocesan priests), the locality (or section of the town), the delegation under whose jurisdiction the locality falls, and observations. This is followed by a list of the convents and monasteries in the town, providing the name of the convent, the religious order, the locality or section, the delegation, and observations.

Location: Archivio Segreto Vaticano.

3.1.15.24 Protocollo

[DATABASE ID: VATV10389-A]

Inclusive Dates: 1839–1908.

Bulk: 8 linear m. (90 vols.)

Organization: Vols. 1–89 are chronological. Vol. 90 is entitled "Protocollo segreto degli affari più rilevanti della Sagra Cong.e di Vescovi e Regolari, 1852–1865."

Scope: Protocollo entries may include: protocol number, name of diocese or religious order, postulant, object of business, date the item was consigned to a secretary, date of response (seeking information), date of remission (answer to letter by secretary seeking further information), resolution, rescript, agent, and cost. This series provides a good overview of business conducted and the variety of individuals making requests. It is difficult to use these successfully as indice to the Bishops and Regulars series *Regestum* and *Oratori privati*. Even though entries in the *Regestum* and documents in the *Oratori privati* contain protocol numbers. One can go from each fondo to the protocolli, but the protocolli are particularly useless for the *Oratori privati* because the *Oratori privati* are often lumped together and personal or family names are usually not indicated in the protocolli.

Note: This series is located in the Index Room of the ASV.

References: Boyle, p. 89; Pásztor (1970), p. 159; Pásztor (1983), p. 176.

Finding Aids: In the ASV soffittone (V/1) there is a one-drawer schedario entitled "Per titolo" that serves as a partial index to materials regarding religious orders (ca. fifteenth century-nineteenth century) in the *Protocollo*, as well as a number of other indexed and unindexed series in the ASV. Entries are brief and indicate the religious order, a short reference to the business, the fondo, and current volume number. This is not an official ASV finding aid and must be used in consultation with the ASV staff.

Location: Archivio Segreto Vaticano.

3.1.15.25 Regestum episcoporum

[DATABASE ID: VATV10372-A]

Inclusive Dates: 1573–1908.

Bulk: 18 linear m. (344 numbered volumes).

Organization: Chronological.

Scope: According to Hermann Hoberg in Indice 1102, vols. 1–29 (1587–1597) contain material concerning regolari and monache.

References: Boyle, p. 89; Pásztor (1970), p. 159; Pásztor (1983), p. 177.

Finding Aids: ASV Indice 1102 (formerly Indice 111), ff. 1–10, compiled by Hermann Hoberg, provides an inventory of the entire series. Indice 1102 briefly lists each volume, indicating the inclusive dates and occasional other annotations, such as information written on the spine or the existence of internal indices.

Pásztor indicates that the following volume can be used as

an index to this series: "Indice degl'Instituti novelli o delle Pie Società lodati od approvati per organo della S. Congregazione di Vescovi e Regolari." This volume may have been located in the *Miscellanea* V/7 listed among the series of the Episcoporum et Regularium in this guide and is entitled "Elenco di novelli Istituti, Confraternite ed altri pie unione, 1851–1905."

Location: Archivio Segreto Vaticano.

3.1.15.26 Regestum monialium

[DATABASE ID: VATV10371-A]

Inclusive Dates: 1646–1908.

Bulk: 15 linear m. (240 numbered volumes).

Organization: Chronological.

Scope: Title page of volume 1 states "Regestum litterarum et decretorum Sacrae Congregationis Negociis et Consultationibus Regularium Praepositae." According to Hermann Hoberg in indice 1102, earlier material concerning monache can be found in volumes 1–29 (1587–1597) of the *Regestum episcoporum* and 1–53 (1599–1645) of the *Regestum regularium*, both described among the records of this congregation.

References: Boyle, p. 89; Pásztor (1970), p. 159; Pásztor (1983), p. 177.

Finding Aids: ASV Indice 1102 (formerly Indice 111), ff. 20–24, compiled by Hermann Hoberg, briefly inventories the entire series. Indice 1102 proceeds volume by volume, indicating inclusive dates (generally according to years). Indice 1102 also provides some annotations such as the information written on the spines or the existence of internal indices.

Location: Archivio Segreto Vaticano.

3.1.15.27 Regestum regularium

[DATABASE ID: VATV10373-A]

Inclusive Dates: 1599–1908.

Bulk: 16 linear m. (307 numbered volumes).

Organization: Chronological.

Scope: According to Hermann Hoberg in Indice 1102, earlier material of this nature on regolari can be located in vols. 1–29 (1587–1597) of the *Regestum episcoporum*. Likewise, information on monache can be found in this series between the years 1599 and 1645 (vols. 1–53).

References: Boyle, p. 89; Pásztor (1970), p. 159; Pásztor (1983), p. 177.

Finding Aids: ASV Indice 1102 (formerly Indice 111), ff. 11–19, compiled by Hermann Hoberg, is an inventory of the entire series. The brief entries for each volume indicate inclusive dates and provide some annotations such as the existence of internal indices or information on the spine of the volume.

Location: Archivio Segreto Vaticano.

3.1.15.28 Regolari

[DATABASE ID: VATV10373-A]

Inclusive Dates: ca. 1717–1882.

Bulk: .1 linear m. (1 busta).

Location: Archivio Segreto Vaticano.

3.1.15.29 Relazioni

[DATABASE ID: VATV10443-A]

Inclusive Dates: 1826.

Bulk: 1 linear m. (15 vols.).

Organization: Subseries, volume numbers, and contents are: 1, 3–6, 11, Relazioni di regolari; —2, 9, Relazioni degli ordinari sulli regolari; —12–15, Duplicati (of vols. 1 and 2). Vols. 7 and 8 are missing. Vol. 2 is a published version of vols. 10 and 11. Duplicates of parts of vol. 2 appear in vols. 12–15.

Location: Archivio Segreto Vaticano.

3.1.15.30 Répertoires de la Congrégation des Évêques et des Réguliers (L84–L161)

[DATABASE ID: VATV40058-A]

Inclusive Dates: 1594–1810.

Bulk: about 9.5 linear m.

Organization: In 1900 the archivist Delaborde classified the registers into four series.

A. *Episcoporum*, Décisions des congregations 1411–1807; he assigned these registers to Archives Nationales boxes numbered L85–L109.

B. *Regularium*, Décisions des congregations 1594–1809; he assigned these registers to Archives Nationales boxes numbered L110–L140.

C. *Monialium*, Décisions des Congregations 1646–1809; he assigned these registers to Archives Nationales boxes numbered L141–L161.

D. *Divers*, 1641–1757; he assigned these registers to Archives Nationales boxes numbered L162–L163.

In the 1960 analytical inventory of these registers, Martin-Chabot presents a different schema for classification and identifies five separate classes of registers: Episcoporium; —Regularium; —Monialium; —Registres secrets; —Libri delle ponenze. This latter organization is confirmed in Favier, *Fonds* (vol. 1, pp. 311–312). However, his division and dates disagree with Martin-Chabot. In any case, the physical organization of the material as determined by Delaborde still stands.

Scope: These appear to be summary registers. They contain brief reports for each session, a summary of matters submitted (with an indication of diocese, which is usually Italian, or of the religious order making the request), and the decision taken.

References: Favier, *Fonds*, vol. 1, pp. 311–312; Favier, *Inventaires*, p. 100.

Finding Aids: Archives Nationales finding aid L/2 lists each box L85–L163 by carton number and provides inclusive dates for the documents in the carton.

Archives Nationales microfilm 246mi is the Martin-Chabot analytical inventory of these registers. Part IV provides a description of each volume with some indication of their contents.

Location: Archives Nationales de Paris.

3.1.15.31 Rescritti

[DATABASE ID: VATV10380-A]

Inclusive Dates: 1800–1907.

Bulk: 2 linear m. (19 boxes).

Location: Archivio Segreto Vaticano.

3.1.15.32 Rubricellae

[DATABASE ID: VATV10388-A]

Inclusive Dates: 1590–1608, 1815–1917.

Bulk: 14 linear m. (250 vols.).

Organization: Subseries, volume numbers, and contents descriptions are as follows: 1. Episcoporum, regularium et monialium, 1590–1593; —2–61. Episcoporum, 1594–1860;

—62–114. 1598–1865; —115–160. Monialium, 1814–1859; —161–166. Secretae, 1746–1865; —167–170. Criminalium, 1836–1880; —171–237. Rubricella del protocollo generale, 1839–1908; —238–250. Affari riservati, 1860–1917.

Scope: This series gives a good overview of the business represented in the various *Regestum* series in the Episcoporum et Regularium, but locating items from the *Rubricellae* in the *Regestum* is very difficult.

Note: This series is located in the Index Room of the ASV.

References: Pásztor (1970), p. 160; Pásztor (1983), p. 176; Boyle, p. 89.

Finding Aids: ASV Indice 1103 (formerly Indice 116), compiled by Hermann Hoberg, provides a brief inventory of each volume. Entries include the current volume number, the type(s) of material in the rubric (Episcoporum, Regularium, Monialium, etc.), and the inclusive dates.

Location: Archivio Segreto Vaticano.

3.1.15.33 Secolarizzazione
[DATABASE ID: VATV10396-A]
Inclusive Dates: ca. 1820–1833.
Bulk: .2 linear m. (1 busta).
Location: Archivio Segreto Vaticano.

3.1.15.34 Sezione monache: Carte del XIX secolo
[DATABASE ID: VATV10404-A]
Inclusive Dates: ca. 1800–1899.
Bulk: .5 linear m. (4 boxes).
Organization: Alphabetical by name of diocese.
Scope: These may be supplications regarding dowries.
Location: Archivio Segreto Vaticano.

3.1.15.35 Sezione monache: Protocollo
[DATABASE ID: VATV10405-A]
Inclusive Dates: ca. 1800–1899.
Bulk: .5 linear m. (4 boxes).
Organization: Organized by "serie" (Ia–XVI).
Scope: These are actual letters, not registers.
Location: Archivio Segreto Vaticano.

3.1.15.36 Sezione monache: Ripristinazione dei monasteri
[DATABASE ID: VATV10402-A]
Inclusive Dates: 1814–1822.
Bulk: 1.5 linear m. (8 buste).
Organization: Buste 1–6, A–Z (alphabetical by diocese); —Busta 7, A–Z (alphabetical by diocese); —Busta 8, Varie.
Scope: These records appear to contain supplications to repair monasteries and reports of finances.
Location: Archivio Segreto Vaticano.

3.1.15.37 Sezione regolari
[DATABASE ID: VATV10406-A]
Inclusive Dates: 1809–1850.
Bulk: 1 linear m. (7 boxes).
Organization: Boxes are as follows: 1. Sezione regolari and Sezione monache, 1809–1810; —2. Sezione monache, 1837–1838; —3–6. Sezione regolari, Napoli, 1849–1850; —7. Sezione monache, Napoli, 1849–1850.
Sezione regolari is alphabetical by religious order. Sezione monache is alphabetical by diocese.
Location: Archivio Segreto Vaticano.

3.1.15.38 Sezione regolari: Carte del XIX secolo
[DATABASE ID: VATV10407-A]
Inclusive Dates: ca. 1800–1899.
Bulk: 2 linear m. (20 boxes).
Organization: These are organized in subseries according to religious orders as follows: Agostiniani; —Agostiniani scalzi; —Alcantarini; —Antoniani; —Barnabiti; —Basiliani; —Benedettini; —Benefratelli; —Camaldolesi; —Canonici Regolari Lateranensi; —Cappuccini, 1800–1840 (2 boxes); —Carmelitani; —Carmelitani scalzi; —Certosini; —Chierici Reg. Min. d. Madre d. Dio; —Cassinesi; —Cisterciensi; —Domenicani; —Dottrina; —Gesuiti; —Girolamini; —Lazzaristi; —Liguorini; —Mercedari; —Minori; —Minori Riformati; —Minimi; —Ministri degli infermi; —Minimi (PP. Michele Pascucci e Luigi Conti) 1839–1842 (2 boxes); —Minori conventuali; —Minori osservanti; —Oblati d. Maria; —Olivetani; —Oratoriani; —Ordine d. Penitenza; —Ordine Teitonico; —Osservanti; —Osservanti riformati; —Passionisti; —Pii operari; —Premonstratensi; —Rosminiani; —Scuole cristiane; —Scuole pie; —Serviti; —Silvestrini; —Somaschi; —Sulpiziani; —Teatini; —Terz'ordine; —Trappisti; —Trappisti della Francia, 1830; —Trinitari; —Vallombrosani; —Verginiari; —Varie.
Location: Archivio Segreto Vaticano.

3.1.15.39 Sezione regolari: Protocollo
[DATABASE ID: VATV10408-A]
Inclusive Dates: 1800–1899.
Bulk: 2 linear m. (16 boxes).
Organization: These are organized by "serie" (I–XV).
Scope: As in *Sezione monache* these are actual letters.
Location: Archivio Segreto Vaticano.

3.1.15.40 Sezione vescovi
[DATABASE ID: VATV10403-A]
Inclusive Dates: ca. 1604–1782.
Bulk: .4 linear m. (2 buste).
Organization: Titles on spines of buste are: "Conquista di Buda; Lettere risposte dei Vescovi Diocesiani circa il giubileo, indulgenza plenaria, predicatori, esposizione del SS. Sacramento, suffragi per i soldati defunti, ecc . . . ed elemosine raccolte nelle cassette delle pubbliche chiese; Guerra contro il Turco, anni 1683, 1684, 1685, 1686"; —"Carte importante per firme ragguardevoli e documentazioni storiche" (ca. 1604–1782).
Scope: Contains information on religious orders. The Carmelites are prominent in the second busta.
Location: Archivio Segreto Vaticano.

3.1.15.41 Sezione vescovi: Carte smistate, secolo XIX
[DATABASE ID: VATV10409-A]
Inclusive Dates: ca. 1800–1899.
Bulk: 5 linear m. (30 buste).
Organization: Alphabetical by diocese.
Scope: This series appears to contain material also relating to regulars.
Reference: Pásztor (1970), p. 158 (note).
Location: Archivio Segreto Vaticano.

3.1.15.42 Sezione vescovi: Ordinandi

[DATABASE ID: VATV10384-A]

Inclusive Dates: 1863–1872.

Bulk: 1 linear m. (9 boxes).

Organization: Alphabetical by diocese.

Scope: A variety of requests from priests and bishops, including, for example, requests for more priests because the faithful are falling away, and a request from a sick priest needing to go to a more moderate climate. The series includes position papers and supporting documents.

Location: Archivio Segreto Vaticano.

3.1.15.43 Stampe

[DATABASE ID: VATV10384-A]

Inclusive Dates: 1700, 1800–1835 (bulk 1800–1835).

Bulk: 5 linear m.

Scope: The series includes: Processi; —S. Giubilio, 1826–1833, 1 busta.

Location: Archivio Segreto Vaticano.

3.1.15.44 Studi

[DATABASE ID: VATV10386-A]

Inclusive Dates: 1896–1908.

Bulk: .5 linear m. (7 vols. and 4 buste).

Scope: This series primarily concerns vocational training in religious orders.

Location: Archivio Segreto Vaticano.

3.1.15.45 Tasse del clero

[DATABASE ID: VATV10382-A]

Inclusive Dates: ca. 1814–1873.

Bulk: 4 linear m.

Location: Archivio Segreto Vaticano.

3.1.15.46 Varie

[DATABASE ID: VATV10448-A]

Inclusive Dates: 1573–1799.

Bulk: 36 linear m.

Organization: This series is primarily chronological with some additional breakdowns according to Episcoporum, Regularium, Monialium, or to specific religious orders.

Location: Archivio Segreto Vaticano.

3.1.15.47 Visite apostoliche

[DATABASE ID: VATV10090-A]

Inclusive Dates: 1525–1881.

Bulk: 2.5 linear m. (18 buste).

Organization: Buste are numbered 1–3, 10–13, 13a, 14–17, 17a, 18–22. They are alphabetical by town (not diocese) and then chronological by date of the visitation.

Note: Vol. 22 is available on microfilm.

Scope: The eighteen buste of this subseries of Bishops and Regulars represent only a fraction of the sum total of pastoral visits to Roman ecclesiastical institutions that reside in the ASV. The largest ASV collections of pastoral visits within Rome are found in the records of the Congregatio Visitationis Apostolicae and in Miscellaneous official series *Miscellaneorum armarium VII*. Although their physical state is more dishevelled and fragile than other similar collections, there is nothing distinctive in the scope or content of these visits, which distinguishes them from other groups of visits in the ASV and elsewhere. At the moment, one cannot say why these eighteen buste are isolated within the Bishops and Regulars series.

Apostolic Visits are pastoral visits made within the pope's episcopal see, Rome. Like pastoral visits carried out elsewhere they offer fascinating views into the ritual and material settings of monasteries, oratories, parish churches, and the churches of cardinals, bishops, and religious orders. As sources for the state of parishes and diocese, visits have much in common with the "relations ad limina" and the acts of local synods (see S. Congregatio Concilii). The contents of visits vary widely and depend greatly on how the cardinal or commissioner conducting the Visit approached his job. Some were rather dry bureaucrats, who have left us simply lists of the location and condition of doors, windows, and liturgical furnishings inside a church; from him we may also learn what the priest reported as his age, his income, or the number of students studying catechism with him. Others render their point of view in strong autobiographical tones, allowing us to see them as they shake a broken door, or traipse around a neighborhood interrogating residents in an effort to track down the parish priest. While some are mainly concerned with administrative or sacramental affairs, others display a keen concern for the physical setting, describing altarpieces, the condition and subject of frescoes, and details pertaining to all aspects of decoration and architecture. Music, musical instruments, and theatrical activities are important to some. Others emphasize economic matters. Finally, attitudes may range from the sternly disciplinary to the magnanimous and protective. Many visits combine to some degree various of the above features. The visitor's point of view can be as revealing as the observations conveyed by it. The varie section contains many visits within Rome.

References: Pásztor (1970), p. 159. S. Pagano, "Le visite apostoliche a Roma nei secoli XVI–XIX," *Ricerche per la storia religiosa di Roma* 4 (1980): 350–351. This article provides information on Roman monasteries represented in the collection as well as a list of all the possible series in which to locate visitation materials.

Finding Aids: A series of ASV prospetti indici in a folder entitled "Visite Apostoliche: Vescovi e Regolari e Concilio" is available at the desk in the main ASV reading room. These prospetti indici provide access to the collection through a number of means. One prospetto is a busta listing of Vescovi e Regolari, *Visite apostoliche* nos. 1–17, which indicates the current volume number, the location visited, and year of the visit. This prospetto also outlines the visits of the Congregatio super Statum Regularium that have been removed from this series and were (in 1994) in the process of reorganization. Two other prospetti indici also pertain to the Vescovi e Regolari, *Visite apostoliche*: Prospetto chronologico and Prospetto alfabetico. The chronological and alphabetical prospetti provide integrated lists of apostolic visits from Vescovi e Regolari, the Congregatio Concilii, and the Congregatio Visitationis Apostolicae. These prospetti indicate the year of the visit, the location, and the current volume number. Vescovi e Regolari, *Visite* are identified by VR and the current busta number. This is not an official ASV index and must be used in consultation with ASV staff.

In the ASV soffittone (V/1) there is a one-drawer schedario entitiled "Per titolo" that serves as a partial index to materials regarding religious orders (ca. fifteenth century–nineteenth century) in the *Visite apostoliche*, as well as a number of other indexed and unindexed series in the ASV. Entries are brief and indicate the religious order, a short reference to the business, the fondo, and current volume number. This is not an official ASV index and must be used in consultation with ASV staff.

Location: Archivio Segreto Vaticano.

3.1.16 Congregatio Negotiis Religiosorum Sodalium Praeposita
[DATABASE ID: VATV013-A]

The Congregation of Religious was established as the central office of the Holy See for the governance of the states of perfection (i.e., religious orders) of the Latin rite throughout the world. Religious of the various Eastern rites are governed by the Congregation for the Eastern Churches.

As early as 1582 a board of cardinals had been appointed to direct the affairs of religious. Sixtus V's motu proprio *Romanus Pontifex* (May 17, 1586) formally established the Congregatio super Consultationibus Regularium and his constitution *Immensa aeterni Dei* (Jan. 22, 1588) confirmed it as distinct from the Congregatio super Consultationibus Episcoporum et Aliorum Praelatorum. In 1601, under Clement VIII (1592–1605), these two congregations were combined under the name Congregatio Negotiis et Consultationibus Episcoporum et Regularium Praeposita and given extensive functions that were retained until the reorganization of Pius X in 1908.

Pius X's constitution *Sapienti consilio* (Jun. 29, 1908) abolished the Congregation of Bishops and Regulars and transferred functions regarding bishops to the Consistorial Congregation, and those referring to regulars to a new congregation called Congregatio Negotiis Religiosorum Sodalium Praeposita, which by common usage and because of the name on its seal continued to be referred to as the Congregation of Religious.

The congregation's jurisdiction was over persons as members of religious orders and communities. It thus had no territorial limits. As a general rule it handled everything pertaining directly and primarily to orders or their members: questions pertaining to their government, discipline, programs of studies, financial and property matters, as well as their rights and privileges. Exceptions to the norm were the express prescriptions of canon law granting exclusive jurisdiction to another congregation, for example, in matters concerning faith and morals, missionary activities in missionary territory, strictly liturgical matters, and indulgences.

Secular Third Orders are under the jurisdiction of this congregation only as "moral persons." Individual members of these Third Orders, as such, are not subject to the Congregation of Religious. With the issuance of Pius XII's apostolic constitution *Provida Mater Ecclesia* (Feb. 2, 1947) and his motu proprio *Primo feliciter*

elapso (Mar. 12, 1948) the congregation assumed jurisdiction over secular institutes.

Pius X's changes were incorporated into the Code of Canon Law (canon 251) and reconfirmed by Paul VI's constitution *Regimini Ecclesiae universae* (Aug. 15, 1967), which changed the title of the congregation to Congregatio pro Religiosis et Institutis Saecularibus. Pope John Paul II's apostolic constitution *Pastor bonus* (June 28, 1988) renamed it Congregatio pro Institutis Vitae Consecratae et Societatibus Vitae Apostolicae.

RECORDS. No records for this congregation could be located.

3.1.17 Congregatio Particularis super Promovendis ad Archiepiscopatus et Episcopatus
[DATABASE ID: VATV458-A]

According to Giovanni Cardinal De Luca, Innocent XI (1676–1689) established the Congregazione sopra l'Elezione dei Vescovi, assigning it the task of proposing names for vacant episcopal sees. These nominations were to be made only after the congregation had made a thorough examination of the merits and qualifications of the candidates. Over a period of time, however, the congregation became inactive and fell into disuse.

Benedict XIV, convinced of the great need for qualified men for the governance of the dioceses, reestablished the congregation with the constitution *Ad apostolicae servitutis* (Oct. 17, 1740) giving it the official name Congregatio Particularis super Promovendis ad Archiepiscopatus et Episcopatus. This reorganized congregation had the task of proposing for vacant episcopal sees individuals of moral integrity and sound theology, experienced in theological matters, and zealous for the salvation of souls. The cardinal prefect was charged with inquiring every two years of the ordinaries, seeking and discussing names of secular and religious clergy whom they judged worthy of being raised to the episcopacy. Because this needed to be done with great circumspection, Benedict XIV imposed on them the bond of secrecy of the Holy Office.

Notwithstanding the pontiff's great concern, this second office did not last long, perhaps because of the opposition of some cardinals and foreign ministers who were particularly interested in naming their own preferences. It remained for the auditor of the pope to gather the necessary information on ecclesiastics proposed for the vacancies.

The congregation was revitalized for the third time by Leo XIII who conferred on it, with the constitution *Immortalis memoriae* (Sept. 21, 1878), the same functions but limited the congregation to the appointment of bishops for the dioceses of Italy. The canonical process was conducted according to the directions contained in the constitution of Gregory XIV, *Onus apostolicae ser-*

vitutis (May 15, 1591), and in the instruction of Urban VIII (*Si processus*, 1627).

The congregation functioned until 1903, when Pius X, with the motu proprio *Romanis Pontificibus* (Dec. 17, 1903), merged it with the Congregation of the Holy Office, to which were referred all the matters relative to the selection and promotion of bishops.

RECORDS. No records for this congregation were located.

3.1.18 Congregatio pro Ecclesia Orientali
[DATABASE ID: VATV416-A]

Up until 1852 this congregation was confused with that of the Congregation for the Propagation of the Faith. Although the Congregation for the Oriental Church was not established until 1917, its origin lies in the sixteenth century. In 1573 Gregory XIII established a special congregation under the name of Congregatio de Rebus Graecorum and assigned to it the duty of maintaining and propagating the Catholic faith among Christians of the East.

Clement VIII (1592–1605) instituted the Congregatio super Negotiis Fidei et Religionis Catholicae to care for the propagation of the faith even in Latin regions and later added to it the promotion of the faith in pagan lands. This was, in fact, the forerunner of the Congregation for the Propagation of the Faith.

With the apostolic letter *Inscrutabili* (Jun. 22, 1622) Gregory XV established the Congregatio de Propaganda Fide to which he assigned the care of all the Catholic missions in the East as well as in the West. Within this congregation Urban VIII set up two commissions: a Congregatio super Dubiis Orientalium, and a Congregatio super Correctione Euchologii Graecorum (1636), which became in 1717, by order of Clement XI, a stable and distinct congregation called Congregatio super Correctione Librorum Orientalium.

Pius IX with his constitution *Romani Pontifices* (Jan. 6, 1862) instituted within the same Congregatio de Propaganda Fide a special congregation with the name Congregatio de Propaganda Fide pro Negotiis Ritus Orientalis presided over by the prefect of the Congregatio de Propaganda Fide, but with its own secretary, consultors, officials, and archives.

The curial reform of 1908 (*Sapienti consilio*, Jun. 29, 1908) left the congregation unchanged, but Benedict XV, with the motu proprio *Dei providentis* (May 1, 1917), created a new independent Congregatio pro Ecclesia Orientali, the prefecture of which he reserved to himself and his successors.

Reserved to this congregation are all the affairs regarding persons, discipline, and rites of the Eastern churches. Authority is personal in that it extends to all the faithful attached to an Eastern rite wherever they may be; it is also territorial in that it has authority in regions in which a hierarchy of the Eastern rite has been established. Excluded from its authority are matters properly the concern of the Congregation of the Holy Office and of the Congregation of Seminaries and Universities of Studies (Pius XI, *constitution Deus Scientiarum Dominus*, May 24, 1931, art. 4), as well as that for indulgences (*notificazione*, Jul. 21, 1935).

On June 20, 1925, Pius XI set up in this congregation a special Commission for Russia, which on April 6, 1930, was made independent. On December 21, 1934, it was annexed to the Congregation for Extraordinary Ecclesiastical Affairs with limited authority for the faithful of the Latin rite living in Russia.

In order to unify the program and work of the apostolate in all the countries of the East, Pius XI's motu proprio *Sancta Dei Ecclesia* (Mar. 25, 1938) conceded to the Congregation of the Oriental Church full and exclusive jurisdiction over all the faithful, the hierarchy, works, institutions, pious societies, whether these were of Latin or Eastern rite, in specifically stated regions. Pius XII's motu proprio *Cleri sanctitati* (Jun. 2, 1957) clearly states that "all matters of whatever nature having to do with persons or with the discipline of the Oriental rites, solely, or mixed with the Latin rite, come under the jurisdiction of the Congregation of the Oriental Church." In other words the congregation had nearly exclusive juristiction over all matters in areas where the Eastern rite prevailed.

Paul VI's apostolic constitution *Regimini Ecclesiae universae* (Aug. 15, 1967) changed the name to Congregatio pro Ecclesiis Orientalibus and decreed that it have a separate office for each rite of the Eastern Church in communion with the Apostolic See. The constitution also provided for special relations with the Secretariat for Christian Unity and the Secretariat for Non-Christians. The congregation includes the Pontifical Mission for Palestine and a special commission for the liturgy.

Reference. *La Sacra Congregazione per le Chiese orientali nel cinquantesimo della fondazione (1917–1967)* (Grottaferrata, 1969).

RECORDS. No records for this congregation were located.

3.1.19 Congregatio pro Erectione Ecclesiarum et Provisionibus Consistorialibus
[DATABASE ID: VATV136-A]

Among the congregations founded by the constitution *Immensa aeterni Dei* (Jan. 22, 1588), Sixtus V gave third place to the Congregatio pro Erectione Ecclesiarum et Provisionibus Consistorialibus. The congregation was charged with preparing the acts regarding decisions for the formal approval of the cardinals. The congregation also had authority to transact all business that related to the governance of dioceses not under the

Congregation of the Propagation of the Faith. Its name was changed twice almost immediately: first to Congregatio Rebus Consistorialibus Praeposita, and then more simply to Congregatio Consistorialis. See the history for the Congregatio Consistorialis.

RECORDS. No records for the congregation under this name were located. See "Congregatio Consistorialis."

3.1.20 Congregatio pro Indice Librorum Prohibitorum
[DATABASE ID: VATV461-A]

The origin of this congregation can be found in a special commission of conciliar fathers appointed by the Council of Trent in its eighteenth session (Feb. 26, 1562). The specific task of the commission was to provide for the compilation of a new index of forbidden books and to revise the list published by Paul IV in 1559. In fulfilling this task the commission also drew up guidelines for readers. Pius IV approved and published the rules and so-called Tridentine Index in 1564 (constitution *Dominici gregis*, Mar. 24, 1564).

With the constitution *In apostolicae* (Apr. 4, 1571), Pius V created the Congregation of the Index, whose chief duty it was to attend to the prohibition of books dangerous to Catholic doctrine. This was a turning point for the Congregation of the Roman and Universal Inquisition, which had difficulty in exercising vigilance over the many new works that were being published.

Gregory XIII confirmed the work of Pius V and gave the newly established congregation a more definite form (constitution *Ut pestiferarum opinionum*, Sept. 13, 1572). The constitution *Immensa aeterni Dei* (Jan. 22, 1588) of Sixtus V stabilized the congregation and extended its jurisdiction even to the person of the authors, but only as related to their works. The new index with which the congregation had been charged was printed in 1590 but did not receive adequate distribution because of the death of the pope.

By order of Clement VIII (1592–1605), the congregation set to work on a new catalog, to which Robert Bellarmine and Caesar Baronius contributed. The work was ready in 1596. Instructions for the procedures for the preparation of this catalog had been provided by Clement himself.

Benedict XIV (constitution *Sollicita ac provida*, Jul. 9, 1753) stabilized the work of the congregation and determined more clearly the procedures to be followed in condemning books. Leo XIII, in order to adapt the procedures and regulations to the times, published the constitution *Officiorum ac munerum* and some *Decreta generalia* (Jan. 25, 1897). All preceding decrees relative to the prohibition of books were abolished; the Decreta generalia were to be substituted for them. The Congregation of the Index was to be guided by these new

decrees except that in the censorship of books the constitution *Sollicita ac provida* of Benedict XIV would continue in force.

The last innovations relative to this congregation were introduced by Pius X with his constitution *Sapienti consilio* (Jun. 29, 1908). This document indicated a further right as well as duty assigned to the congregation: (1) to investigate whether writings deserving of condemnation were being circulated; and (2) to remind bishops of their obligation to call to the attention of the Holy See such writings.

Benedict XV with his motu proprio *Alloquentes* (Mar. 25, 1917) suppressed the Congregation of the Index and transferred its functions back to a simple section under the Congregation of the Holy Office. In addition to the records listed below, there are likely records of this congregation housed in the archives of the Holy Office. This archives, however, is not open for consultation.

RECORDS. Records of the congregation consist of the following series.

3.1.20.1 Index alphabetic: Generalis
[DATABASE ID: VATV10366-A]
Inclusive Dates: ca. 1690–1727.
Bulk: .5 linear m. (6 volumes).
Organization: Alphabetical by personal or corporate name, or primarily by type of case (e.g., ad notationes, apologia, etc.).
Location: Archivio Segreto Vaticano.

3.1.21 Congregatio pro Negotiis Ecclesiasticis Extraordinariis
[DATABASE ID: VATV019-A]

This congregation is commonly known as the Congregazione degli Affari Ecclesiastici Straordinari, or by the initials AA. EE. SS.

For two centuries after the curial reorganization of Sixtus V, the popes continued to treat in public consistory questions of exceptional importance and graver affairs of the church that involved relations with civil governments. They also delegated matters involving relations with civil governments to restricted extraordinary commissions of cardinals constituting so-called congregazioni di Stato, which lasted only for the time necessary to resolve a case.

At the end of the eighteenth century Pius VI (1775–1799) inaugurated a new process for the treatment of extraordinary ecclesiastical affairs. He instituted a permanent department that had, as its first somewhat delicate task, responsibility for the formation of policy to be assumed in confronting the events and ideas of the French Revolution, particularly the establishment of the republic and its repudiation of religion.

The document for the formation of this congregation is still missing but is known because of the precise reference to it in the constitution *Sollicitudo omnium ecclesiarum* (May 28, 1793) in which Pius VI states that the responses given by this congregation to the questions presented by the French clergy had been discussed previously by the Consilium Selectae Cardinalium Congregationis.

Instituted in 1793 or perhaps even before, the Congregatio super Negotiis Ecclesiasticis Regni Galliarum, as it was then called, continued to be occupied with the religious interests of France, while seeking at the same time to reestablish political rapport between France and the Holy See. It was, however, constrained to suspend all activity in 1798 because of the deportation of the pontiff.

Reactivated by Pius VII (1800–1823) with greater tasks and with the new name Congregatio Negotiorum Ecclesiasticorum Extraordinariorum, the congregation was charged with preparing the concordat with Napoleon though assisted in this work by a special commission called "la piccola congregazione."

In 1809 the activity of the congregation had a new and longer interruption. Pius VII was interned by Napoleon from 1809 to 1814 in Savona, Genoa, and Fontainebleau in virtual isolation. With the abdication of Napoleon, the pope was able to return to Rome on May 24, 1814. Among the pope's first acts, because of the critical condition in which religious affairs stood, was the restoration of this congregation with a much broader scope. A letter (Jul. 19, 1814) from Bartolomeo Pacca, then cardinal pro-secretary of State, to Francesco Luigi Fontana, general of the Barnabites, discussed the reconstitution of the congregation under the new name Congregatio Extraordinaria Praeposita Negotiis Ecclesiasticis Orbis Catholici. It was at Pacca's suggestion that the congregation's authority for the affairs of France was extended to all questions that arose with other nations. The renewed congregation was thus given a universal character similar to that of the other ecclesiastical offices.

In a letter of August 11, 1814, Cardinal Pacca advised all the members of the newly established congregation that the pope, to avoid possible indiscretions, had imposed the secrecy of the Holy Office on the membership of the congregation.

Tasks assigned to the renewed congregation, which had its first meeting on August 16, 1814, included the political/religious settlements of the church and the reestablishment of internal harmony within the Papal States. In other respects its responsibilities remained constant until the curial reform of Pius X in 1908.

The constitution *Sapienti consilio* (Jun. 29, 1908) changed the name to Congregatio pro Negotiis Ecclesiasticis Extraordinariis. It also transferred the congregation's jurisdiction over Russia and the states of South America to the Congregatio de Propaganda Fide. The constitution distinctly specified that the congregation was to concern itself "only with those matters which are submitted to its examination by the Supreme Pontiff through the Cardinal Secretary of State." The business of the congregation was generally to deal with civil laws, and to the pacts to be entered into between the Holy See and the different states.

A letter of Pius XI directed to Pietro Cardinal Gasparri under dated July 5, 1925, published under the form of a notificatio, declared explicitly that the Congregation of Extraordinary Ecclesiastical Affairs was a truly autonomous congregation but under the prefecture of the Cardinal Secretary of State. Its task was to establish and to divide dioceses and to appoint bishops in those cases in which it was necessary to take these matters up with civil governments, and to discuss matters that the pope might turn over to it through the cardinal secretary of state.

With the general reform of the Roman Curia by Paul VI (constitution *Regimini Ecclesiae universae*, Aug. 15, 1967) the name of the congregation was changed to Consilium pro Publicis Ecclesiae Negotiis. The document stated that although the Consilium must be closely related to the Secretariat of State it would henceforth be distinct and separate from it and would be presided over by a cardinal prefect. The office of prefect of the Council for the Public Affairs of the Church and that of the secretary of state would be held by the same person.

The document stated that it would be the task of the council "to handle all business that must be conducted with civil governments; to devote itself to those matters the pope submits for its examination, especially those having some connection with civil laws; to foster diplomatic relations with nations; and to take care of matters pertaining to nunciatures, internunciatures, and apostolic delegations, after conferring with the Secretariat of State." Together with the Secretariat of State it would also supervise in a special way the Commission for the Social Communications Media.

Pope John Paul II (apostolic constitution *Pastor bonus*, Jun. 28, 1988) renamed the Council for the Public Affairs of the Church the Section for Relations with States within the Secretariat of State so it is no longer a separate department. The section has the task of handling diplomatic and other relations with civil governments. Still attached to it, however, is the Pontifical Commission for Russia assigned to it by Pius XI with his motu proprio *Quam sollicita* (Dec. 21, 1934).

References. P. de Leturia, "El Archivio de la S. Congregación de Negocios Eclesiástios Extraordinarios y la encíclica de León XII sobre la revolución hispanoamericana," in *Miscellanea archivistica Angelo Mercati* (Vatican City, 1952), pp. 169–199.

RECORDS. This congregation, now known as the Sezione dei rapporti con gli Stati, maintains its own archives. Founded in 1814, the archives is therefore primarily a nineteenth-century collection of documents concerning a wide range of topics relating to the worldwide interests of the Holy See (address: Palazzo Apostolico, 00120 Vatican City).

In the nineteenth and early twentieth centuries, some records from the Secretariatus Status series *Fondo Moderno* were transferred to the holdings of this congregation. These are noted in the Protocolli registers of the *Fondo Moderno*, by the letters "AE," and are located in the Archives of the Congregazione degli Affari Ecclesiastici. To see these documents, contact the office of the secretary of state. See L. Pásztor, "La Congregazione degli affari ecclesiastici straordinari tra il 1814 e il 1850," *Archivum historiae pontificiae* 6 (1968): 191–318.

No records for this congregation were located in the Archivio Segreto Vaticano, but ASV series listed with the following agency relate directly to this agency and should be consulted. See Permanent Commissions, Pontificia Commissio pro Ecclesiae Legibus in Unum Redigendis series *Archivio della codificazione del diritto canonico: Codex juris canonici* (the commission was headed by the secretary of this congregation).

3.1.22 Congregatio pro Sacris Ritibus et Caeremoniis
[DATABASE ID: VATV134-A]

This congregation was established by Sixtus V in his constitution *Immensa aeterni Dei* (Jan. 22, 1588). According to some authors, it absorbed a cardinalatial commission formed by Gregory XIII, as early as 1572, to reform the ceremonies of the papal chapel. Although the moderation of the Latin liturgy "in all the churches of Rome and throughout the world" was the principal task of the new congregation, its activity mainly concerned the causes of saints, including relics. Duties also included the supervision of the reception of visitors to the Roman court.

Lack of documentation leaves it unclear just when the Congregation for Rites and Ceremonies was divided into two distinct and autonomous congregations, but some authorities state that it was probably about 1601. Clement VIII decreed that the Congregation of Ceremonies be a separate department, taking with it the functions for civil ceremonies and those for the papal chapel. See the history for each of these successor congregations, the Congregatio Ceremonialis and the Congregatio Sacrorum Rituum.

References. P. Burchi, *Catalogus processuum beatificationis et canonizationis qui in tabulariis et bibliothecis urbis asservantur* (Rome, 1965). Catholic Church, Congregazione per le Cause dei Santi, *Miscellanea in occasione del IV centenario della congregazione per le cause dei santi (1588–1988)* (Vatican City, 1988).

RECORDS. No records for this congregation were located. See information on successor congregations noted above.

3.1.23 Congregatio pro Universitate Studii Romani
[DATABASE ID: VATV023-A]

There were many ecclesiastical schools in the early centuries of Christianity as well as those that arose later in connection with cathedrals, monasteries, parish churches, and episcopal residences. Many of these latter were established in response to the decrees of the Council of Rome (Nov. 15, 826) and later confirmed by decree of Leo IV (Dec. 20, 853). This latter decree ordered, among other things, that all bishops should provide for the education of their priests, deacons, and subdeacons, suspending them from their respective ministries until such time as they could obtain a rich cultural background.

By the thirteenth century public universities (*studia generalia*) were flourishing. Even the young who were preparing for the priestly ministry could conveniently follow the study of philosophy and theology since these disciplines were then a part of the general culture of the times. To safeguard the interests of the church, the popes intervened directly, naming from time to time special commissions for vigilance over these studies.

Leo X issued the constitution *Dum suavissimos* (Nov. 5, 1513) in which he confirmed a letter of Boniface VIII (Jun. 6, 1303) instituting a Studium Urbis Generale (University of Rome). In this letter Boniface pointed out that Rome, the first of all the world's cities and the home of the Holy See, should be outstanding in promoting the liberal arts. Leo reaffirmed Boniface's institution and appointed a permanent commission of three cardinals as protectors of the studium. This was the first time in history that the Holy See had delegated authority in university matters.

Julius III (1550–1555) supported the University of Rome and appointed a commission of cardinals to look into its reorganization. This commission made several recommendations. Julius's bull *Dum attentae sollecitudinis* (Jan. 23, 1552), based on a plan of Leo X, implemented these changes and, with the successive brief *Pastoralis officii* (Mar. 27, 1552), increased the rights and duties of the cardinals and gave to the commission authority for the protection of studies throughout the entire territory of the Papal States.

Sixtus V retained this commission when he created the Roman Curia of 1588 (*Immensa aeterni Dei*, Jan. 22, 1588), elevating it to the rank of a genuine congregation and giving it the title of Congregatio pro Universitate Studii Romani. The specific task of this congregation was to oversee the University of Rome (later called the Sapienza) and to regulate its cultural and administrative functions. It was given faculties to procure the best masters of theology, of the liberal arts, and of law on the basis of experience, integrity, learning, and "elegantia litterarum." Soon after the congregation was given the task of managing the affairs of other Roman institutions dependent on the Holy See. The congregation was likewise entrusted with the supervision of all the Catholic universities in the world, with the special mandate of watching over the orthodoxy of the doctrine taught by their faculties.

The pope made special mention of Paris, Oxford, Bologna, and Salamanca as being under the protection of himself and his successors, even though at the time Oxford was "in the midst of schism and heresy, Paris was overrun with Gallicanism, and Salamanca and Bologna had lost their original prestige." At first the provisions of *Immensa* seemed to assure the future of the congregation, but a combination of circumstances soon reduced its jurisdiction to a mere nominal level. Before the formation of the congregation, Sixtus himself had given over the rectorship of the Roman Studium to the College of Consistorial Advocates (constitution *Sacri Apostolatus Ministerio*, Aug. 23, 1587). This concession eventually diminished the authority of the congregation to such an extent that, combined with other circumstances, the congregation itself was rarely mentioned in papal documents.

The Congregatio Studiorum vel Sapientiae, nevertheless, carried on nominally until the time of Clement X (1670–1676). By that time, as Cardinal de Luca testified in his history of the Roman Curia of 1673, the congregation was for all practical purposes dead.

RECORDS. No records for this congregation were located.

3.1.24 Congregatio Rebus Consistorialibus Praeposita
[DATABASE ID: VATV787-A]

Among the congregations founded by the constitution *Immensa aeterni Dei* (Jan. 22, 1588), Sixtus V gave third place to the Congregatio pro Erectione Ecclesiarum et Provisionibus Consistorialibus. The congregation was charged with preparing the acts regarding decisions for the formal approval of the cardinals in Consistory. A second task assigned to it was transacting all business that related to the governance of dioceses not under the Congregation of the Propagation of the Faith. Its name was changed twice almost immediately: first to Congregatio Rebus Consistorialibus Praeposita, and then more simply to Congregatio Consistorialis. See the history for the Congregatio Consistorialis.

RECORDS. No records were located for the congregation under this name. See "Congregatio Consistorialis."

3.1.25 Congregatio Reverendae Fabricae Sancti Petri
[DATABASE ID: VATV025-A]

This congregation is better known by its Italian name, the Fabbrica di San Pietro. On April 18, 1506, Pope Julius II laid the first stone of the great new basilica dedicated to St. Peter that was to replace the first basilica constructed by Constantine the Great. By the bull *Admonet nos suscepti* of December 12, 1523, Pope Clement VII formally established the Reverenda Fabbrica di San Pietro in the Vatican, an administrative entity to provide for the basilica's reconstruction and subsequent maintenance. Even though its central task of watching over the physical integrity of St. Peter's has not varied, the organizational structure and legal attributions of the Fabbrica have been successively modified over the centuries of its existence. Its initial form was that of a "college" or corporate body of sixty, drawn from among the ambassadors of Catholic states, but later it became a Sacred Congregation on similar lines to others of the model administration created by the Sixtus V in 1588. More recently it has become a Palatine Administration.

The origin of this congregation can be found in the commission set up by Julius II (constitution *Liquet omnibus*, Jan. 11, 1510) to supervise the reconstruction of the old Basilica of St. Peter. Clement VII (*Admonet nos suscepti*, Dec. 12, 1523) replaced the commission with a permanent college of sixty experts of international background, directly dependent on the Holy See, charged with providing for the building and administration of the basilica. Sixtus V (constitution *Cum ex debito*, Mar. 4, 1589) placed this college under the jurisdiction of the cardinal archpriest of the basilica.

In 1593 Clement VIII suppressed the college and replaced it with a special office called the Congregatio Reverendae Fabricae S. Petri with all the functions of the college to which were added responsibility for contributions, legacies, and offerings for the basilica; the handling of all civil and criminal cases related directly or indirectly to employees; and the granting of favors, privileges, and indults.

Benedict XIV (constitution *Quanta curarum*, Nov. 15, 1751) introduced considerable changes. He divided the congregation into two sections: the first or general section, with responsibility for handling contentious cases connected with the building; and the second or particular section, with complete control of the administration of the basilica.

The functions of this congregation remained unaltered even after the reforms of Pius VII (1816), Leo XII (1824), and Gregory XVI (1834), but were greatly limited under the pontificate of Pius IX. With an edict of Nov. 28, 1863, Pius IX withdrew all faculties relative to special tribunals and transferred them to the Congregation of the Council, leaving the general section without any province. He abolished the two sections and established a single congregation once again to which he gave authority for the administration and conservation of the basilica, and the administration of legacies and Mass stipends with authority to modify them according to circumstances.

With the general reform of Pius X (constitution *Sapienti consilio*, Jun. 29, 1908), all functions regarding legacies, Masses, and questions regarding them were transferred to the Congregation of the Council. The congregation known as "that of the Reverenda Fabrica

S. Petri" would now be limited, according to the constitution, "to the sole care of the domestic affairs of the Basilica of the Prince of the Apostles." Paul VI's constitution *Regimini Ecclesiae universae* (Aug. 15, 1967) stated that the "Reverend Fabric of St. Peter's will continue to care for the matters concerning the Basilica of the Prince of the Apostles, according to the prescriptions of the constitution *Sapienti consilio* (Jun. 29, 1908), and in cooperation with the chapter of the basilica." Although not yet suppressed as such, the Reverenda Fabrica S. Petri is no longer listed with the congregations of the Roman Curia but under the Palatine Administration.

The Studio del Mosaico, established under Sixtus V (1585–1590) and canonically erected by Benedict XIII (1724–1730) is also under the authority of the Congregation of the Fabbrica.

A NOTE ON THE ARCHIVES OF THE FABBRICA

The Fabbrica maintains its own archives administratively separate from the ASV. The archives are under the direction of the Fabbrica itself. The archives contain a wealth of information. The most obvious areas of strength relate to artistic and architectural history with very special reference to St. Peter's Basilica. However, the collection offers much to administrative, legal, economic, and social historians, particularly regarding the city of Rome and of the Papal States. There are detailed accounts of expenditures following relatively consistent procedures and working methods over a period of almost five centuries. There is also considerable documentation regarding the religious, social, and economic life of individual cities throughout Italy, as well as in Malta, Spain, and Portugal. Traces exist, through extracts of wills and other details of bequests, and of the histories of individual families.

There are the day-to-day records of the gradual demolition of Old St. Peter's and the construction and maintenance of the new. These records include registers, accounts, receipts, bills of authorization, and the like, covering expenditures for payments to the architects, artists, workmen, and materials for the basilica. This is complemented by other records of the dealings of the Fabbrica with its commissars in the various Italian dioceses and with nuncios in the Catholic courts. Record types include legal cases, disputes, probation of wills, and pious bequests concerning the Fabbrica, especially in the period when the Fabbrica itself operated a legal tribunal, from 1547 to 1863.

It should be noted that the General Archives of the Reverenda Fabbrica of St. Peter's should not be confused with the Archives of the Chapter (or Canons) of St. Peter's Basilica. The manuscripts and records belonging to the Canons of St. Peter's are on deposit in the Vatican Library. No part is to be found in the archives of the Fabbrica, even though, here and there, documents

in the Archives of the Fabbrica necessarily refer to the Chapter. The Canons of St. Peter's form a local administration for the Basilica and are not part of the central government of the Holy See. Similarly distinct from the Fabbrica archives are those of the Cappella Giulia (see series listings under "Capella Musicale Pontificia" in the agencies of the Papal Court).

The Fabbrica also operates a photograhpic bureau for itself as well as for researchers called the Archivio Fotografico. This office is separate from the General Archives and is administered independently.

Like many archives, the Fabbrica of St. Peter's has known varying fortunes. Beginning in 1960, the documentation was rescued, cleaned, reassembled, and provided with a summary inventory. On October 22, 1984, Pope John Paul II reopened the Archives in a newly restored, impressive and spacious location high in the structure of St. Peter's itself, adjacent to the upper reaches of the Chapel of St. Leo the Great. In two octagonal chambers, each with its elegant cupola, and in a long passageway surrounding the cupola of the Chapel of St. Leo, are housed a multiplicity of modern glass-fronted metal cabinets each about one meter wide and three meters in height, and containing more than eight hundred linear meters of bound volumes, boxes, folders, and packs.

The archives of the Holy See, and in particular the archives of the Fabbrica, are characterized by a notable continuity. The Sack of Rome of 1527 bore down on an as yet young Fabbrica. While records of the Fabbrica did indeed perish, these were reconstructed from surviving sources shortly afterwards. Exceptional, too, among the extant series of Vatican archival material, no known losses occurred by way of confiscation in the Napoleonic era, so that overall the series are, with rare exceptions, continuous and complete from early days until the present time.

In addition to the core Fabbrica archives, three archival fonds, autonomous to varying degrees, are represented among the archival holdings of the Fabbrica. First are records relating to the monte di pietà operated by the Fabbrica, a combination of pawnshop and savings bank for the poor designed to protect them from fraud, usury, and extortion. Second, there are extensive records of the Quarantotti bank, seized by the Fabbrica in 1765. Finally, the Fabbrica archives also houses the records of the Venerable Archconfraternity of the Blessed Sacrament, erected in St. Peter's Basilica in 1540. This office is described elswhere in this guide.

In the process of reassembling the archives of the Fabbrica, two distinct kinds of records series were created. In some cases the organic nature of a group of materials were clearly evident and, as a result, they were grouped together as a distinct series. In other cases, however, the links were less clear and documents were gathered in somewhat artificial groupings. As a result, the series of the archives are designated by location rather than by content. The documents of the archives are found in several groupings assigned series names and numbers reflective of an older location system. The series title then is the official name assigned under this system. The series designation (shown as subtitle) is sometimes the title of an identifiable series; in other cases it is a description of an artificial grouping of documents. The character of each series is indicated in the scope section of each entry.

Reference. M. Basso, *I privilegi e le consuetudini della Rev.da Fabbrica di San Pietro in Vaticano* (Rome, 1987–1988). This private publication is in two volumes. Volume one contains salient historical information on the history of the Fabbrica and its various functions; it has information on the administration of the congregation and on the types of documentation to be found in the archives. Volume two is a list of the series in the archives that may be of some additional use to the list that follows. The location information contained therein is no longer valid.

Finding Aids. Finding aids for each series are listed in the descriptions that follow. Researchers in the archives should also be aware of the existence of an extensive card index in the archives that was prepared by Father Cipriano Cipriani, a former archivist. The cards reflect a set of observations on important or interesting documents with citations to specific series, packs, and individual documents.

In addition to the records listed below, series listed with another agency relate directly to this agency and should be consulted. See Papal States Miscellaneous series *Testamenti segreti.*

RECORDS. Records of the congregation consist of the following series.

3.1.25.1 Primo piano serie 1: Carte sciolte riguardanti la costruzione della basilica, pagamenti fatti ai commissari, e atti giudiziari
[DATABASE ID: VATV20279-A]
Inclusive Dates: 1468–1782.
Bulk: 77 linear m. (606 vols.).
Organization: Subseries include: Artisti diverse; —Diversi conti degli operai della Rev.da Fabbrica; Liste e conti degli artisti; —Conti e scritture dei seguenti commissari; —Scritture diverse; Memoriali di mandati; Testamente; —Copiae diversorum jurium; —Jura diversa.
Scope: This is a collection of documents (a retrospective regrouping done in the seventeenth century) of miscellaneous material dealing with documents primarily from the sixteenth century that relate to the construction of the basilica, fundraising, exercising of privileges, bequests to the Fabbrica, and general work of the tribunal.

These documents pertain to the earliest work of the Fabbrica. Some predate formal structure of the congregation so the documentation is not systematic. Many of the earliest documents were generated by the College of the Fabbrica, an or-ganization that predates the founding of the sacred congregations.
Finding Aids: "R.F.S.P. Lista topografica dei pacchi e volumi" lists each packet in this series with titles and inclusive dates. "R.F.S.P. Lista cronologica dei pacchi e volumi" has integrated all series from Piano 1, Piano 2, and Piano 3 into a single chronological sequence. Primo piano: Indice generale delle diverse serie, pp. 1–100, contains individual listings for each of the 606 packets with inclusive dates and an indication of contents.
Location: Archivio della Reverenda Fabbrica di S. Pietro, Vatican City.

3.1.25.2 Primo piano serie 2: Memoriale o suppliche diverse dirette alla S. Congregazione della Fabbrica per ottenere la dispenza o l'allegerimento dell'esecuzione dei legati pii
[DATABASE ID: VATV20280-A]
Inclusive Dates: 1574–1690.
Bulk: 8 linear m. (78 vols.).
Organization: Subseries are: Memoriali diversi (vols. 1–70;); —Congregazioni (vols. 71–74); —Patenti (vols. 75–76); —Rubricella (vols. 77); —Bolli (vols. 78).
Scope: These are records of the tribunal of the Fabbrica and are for the most part juridical. They pertain to dispensations, mitigations, and obligations under various wills and bequests to make pious donations not necessarily to the Fabbrica. The tribunal was empowered to adjudicate bequests or cancel them as circumstances required. For example, suppose there was a building with a chapel built by bequest with instructions that Mass be said for a certain purpose in the chapel in perpetuity. Then for some reason someone wanted the building torn down. The courts of the Fabbrica would have jurisdiction to receive a petition cancelling the perpetual Mass requirement and perhaps substituting another.
Finding Aids: "R.F.S.P. Lista topografica dei pacchi e volumi" lists each packet in this series with titles and inclusive dates. "R.F.S.P. Lista cronologica dei pacchi e volumi" has integrated all series from Piano 1, Piano 2, and Piano 3 into a single chronological sequence. Primo piano: Indice generale delle diverse serie, pp. 101–105a, lists each volume with inclusive dates and an indication of content.
Location: Archivio della Reverenda Fabbrica di S. Pietro, Vatican City.

3.1.25.3 Primo piano serie 3: Carte sciolte contenenti memoriali, suppliche, dirette alla Sacra Congregazione della Rev. Fabbrica di S. Pietro per ottenere la dispensa o la reduzione circa l'esecuzione dei Legati Pii
[DATABASE ID: VATV20281-A]
Inclusive Dates: 1536–1886.
Bulk: 33 linear m. (258 volumes and packets).
Organization: Subseries include: "La giurisdizione e i privilegi," Lavori e memorie, Amministrazione, Impiegati, Operai, Artisti, Commissarie, Vertenze, "Causae et appellationes" della Rev. da Fabbrica di San Pietro; —Supliche e rescritti per composizioni e riduzioni dei Regni di Spagna, Portogallo, Napoli-Sardegna, Francia, Germania, Polonia, Svizzera, Dalmazia, Brasile, Peru; —Studio dei musaici: Raccolte diminute, di lettere e carte diverse; —Memorie varie intorno al culto ed alle sacre funzioni nella Basilica vaticana; —Privilegi e diritti di immunità della Basilica vaticana; —Indulgenze e memorie

intorno alle sacre reliquie circa l'Aula del Concilio Vaticano I; —Chiese athliate alla basilica, come SS. Michele e Magno in Borgo, S. Biagio della Pagnotta, S. Giovanni de' Spinelli, S. Macuto, S. Balbina, S. Maria del Pozzo, S. Tommaso in Formis, S. Giacomo della Lungara, S. Egidio in Borgo, S. Caterina della Ruota, S. Pellegrino, S. Leonardo, S. Giacomo Scossacavalli, S. Lazzaro, S. Stefano Maggiore detto dei Mori, S. Stefano Minore detto degli Ungari, SS. Cosma e Damiano divenuti poi S. Elisabetta; —Decreta et resolutiones congregationis; —R. Fabbricae S. Petri; —Vota; —Res indicatae tribunalis; —Lettere; —Registro di lettere; —Liber revatationum; —Bolle e brevi diversi; —Sententiae et appelationes; —Liber sententiarum; —Liber legatorum.

Scope: This series is particularly important for the early packets, which are a series of dossiers constituted to document particular practical aspects of the maintenance of the basilica. For example, the introduction of gas lighting, maintenance on the tombs, who is responsible for payment, and work on other churches from which the Fabbrica drew revenues. Letter packets contain juridical material regarding inheritances and bequests, and the functioning of particular commisariats.

Finding Aids: "R.F.S.P. Lista topografica dei pacchi e volumi" lists each packet in this series with titles and inclusive dates. "R.F.S.P. Lista cronologica dei pacchi e volumi" has integrated all series from Piano 1, Piano 2, and Piano 3 into a single chronological sequence. Primo piano: Indice generale della diverse serie, pp. 106–155, contains a summary of each volume with some dates indicated.

Location: Archivio della Reverenda Fabbrica di S. Pietro, Vatican City.

3.1.25.4 Primo piano serie 4: Vi sono raggruppati diversi carteggi trovati sparsi qua e la riguardanti la Rev.da Fabbrica di S. Pietro duranti i vari anni, ed altre carte che non La riguardano affatto

[DATABASE ID: VATV20282-A]
Inclusive Dates: 1514(?)–1859.
Bulk: 4 linear m. (33 vols.).
Organization: A miscellany.
Scope: This series is a group of miscellaneous documents gathered together. There are some account books, miscellaneous receipts, and reports among the documents.
Finding Aids: "R.F.S.P. Lista topografica dei pacchi e volumi" lists each packet in this series with titles and inclusive dates. "R.F.S.P. Lista cronologica dei pacchi e volumi" has integrated all series from Piano 1, Piano 2, and Piano 3 into a single chronological sequence. Primo piano: Indice generale delle diverse serie, pp. 155–160, contains a summary for each volume with inclusive dates.
Location: Archivio della Reverenda Fabbrica di S. Pietro, Vatican City.

3.1.25.5 Primo piano serie 5: Mandati pagati

[DATABASE ID: VATV20283-A]
Inclusive Dates: 1800–1879.
Bulk: 8 linear m. (75 vols.).
Organization: Chronological.
Scope: These are authorizations for payment (in a standard format).
Finding Aids: "R.F.S.P. Lista topografica dei pacchi e volumi" lists each packet in this series with titles and inclusive

dates. "R.F.S.P. Lista cronologica dei pacchi e volumi" has integrated all series from Piano 1, Piano 2, and Piano 3 into a single chronological sequence. Primo piano: Indice generale delle diverse serie, pp. 161–163, lists each volume with inclusive dates.
Location: Archivio della Reverenda Fabbrica di S. Pietro, Vatican City.

3.1.25.6 Primo piano serie 6: Protocollo della computisteria

[DATABASE ID: VATV20284-A]
Inclusive Dates: 1819–1830.
Bulk: 12 linear m. (28 vols.).
Organization: Chronological.
Scope: These are dossiers constituted for various accounting matters brought to the office of the computisteria. The series also contains more general kinds of correspondence relating to the financial aspects of the administration of the Fabbrica.
Finding Aids: "R.F.S.P. Lista topografica dei pacchi e volumi" lists each packet in this series with titles and inclusive dates. "R.F.S.P. Lista cronologica dei pacchi e volumi" has integrated all series from Piano 1, Piano 2, and Piano 3 into a single chronological sequence. Primo piano: Indice generale delle diverse serie, pp. 164–165, lists each volume 1–28 with specific dates and protocol numbers.
Location: Archivio della Reverenda Fabbrica di S. Pietro, Vatican City.

3.1.25.7 Primo piano serie 7: Filza dei mandati

[DATABASE ID: VATV20285-A]
Inclusive Dates: 1815–1922.
Bulk: 27 linear m. (216 vols.).
Organization: Chronological.
Scope: This series consists of dossiers put together that relate specifically to the mandati, that is, they are backup papers for expense authorization.
Finding Aids: "R.F.S.P. Lista topografica dei pacchi e volumi" lists each packet in this series with titles and inclusive dates. "R.F.S.P. Lista cronologica dei pacchi e volumi" has integrated all series from Piano 1, Piano 2, and Piano 3 into a single chronological sequence. Primo piano: Indice generale delle diverse serie, pp. 166–173, lists each volume by date and file number through 1910.
Location: Archivio della Reverenda Fabbrica di S. Pietro, Vatican City.

3.1.25.8 Primo piano serie 8: Serie armadi

[DATABASE ID: VATV20286-A]
Inclusive Dates: 1466–1922.
Bulk: 54 linear m. (749 packets).
Organization: Subseries include: Libri di conti; —Libri delle entrate e delle uscite; —Registri delle giornate degli Artisti; —Giornali dei materiali; —Mandati; —Libri dei denari dati a diversi Artisti; —Giornali dei materiali entrati e delle opere fatte; —Registri degli scalpellini, con le liste dei travertini; —Registri degli emolumenti camerali; —Registri del Sovrastante dei manuali; —Registri delle giornate degli scalpellini, dei viaggi dei carrettieri, delle giornate dei muratori che lavoravano alla Cupola; —Libro mastro dei debitori e creditori; —Inventari dei materiali vari; —Libri "mastri" del fattore dei manuali; —Libri delle munizioni (libro delle entrate e uscite); —"Liber resignationum Montis Fabricae"; —Libri del

"Riscontro del Banco del Baccelli"; —Libri dei conti del Regno di Napoli; —Rubricella dei commissari della Rev.da Fabbrica per il Regno di Napoli.

Scope: This is an important retrospective intercollation of various account and inventory books. The first account book starts at 1513. There are many separate accounts for particular projects. There are records of payments to particular workers. The series includes books by foremen as well as from central accounting offices. Essentially this series provides a financial history of the building and maintenance of the basilica, commissions for decoration of the basilica, or contracts for such work on other churches. This has been the most consulted series in the Fabbrica Archives.

Finding Aids: "R.F.S.P. Lista topografica dei pacchi e volumi" lists each packet in this series with titles and inclusive dates. "R.F.S.P. Lista cronologica dei pacchi e volumi" has integrated all series from Piano 1, Piano 2, and Piano 3 into a single chronological sequence. Primo piano: Indice generale delle diverse serie, pp. 174–212, lists each packet with inclusive dates and some indication of content.

Location: Archivio della Reverenda Fabbrica di S. Pietro, Vatican City.

3.1.25.9 Secundo piano, antecamera, serie 1: Citationes
[DATABASE ID: VATV20287-A]
Inclusive Dates: 1571–1827.
Bulk: 10 linear m. (189 packets).
Organization: Chronological.
Scope: These are materials relating to the tribunal of the Fabbrica.
Finding Aids: "R.F.S.P. Lista topografica dei pacchi e volumi" lists each packet in this series with titles and inclusive dates. "R.F.S.P. Lista cronologica dei pacchi e volumi" has integrated all series from Piano 1, Piano 2, and Piano 3 into a single chronological sequence.
Location: Archivio della Reverenda Fabbrica di S. Pietro, Vatican City.

3.1.25.10 Secundo piano, antecamera, serie 2: Citationes camerales
[DATABASE ID: VATV20302-A]
Inclusive Dates: 1540–1825.
Bulk: 1 linear m. (13 packets).
Organization: Chronological.
Scope: This small series is comprised of more materials relating to the tribunal of the Fabbrica.
Finding Aids: "R.F.S.P. Lista topografica dei pacchi e volumi" lists each packet in this series with titles and inclusive dates. "R.F.S.P. Lista cronologica dei pacchi e volumi" has integrated all series from Piano 1, Piano 2, and Piano 3 into a single chronological sequence.
Location: Archivio della Reverenda Fabbrica di S. Pietro, Vatican City.

3.1.25.11 Secundo piano, serie 1: Articuli, instrumenta, jura diversa, mandata procurae, memoria et commissiones, minutae, monitoria, processus, sententiae et appelationes, etc.
[DATABASE ID: VATV20288-A]
Inclusive Dates: 1570–1830.
Bulk: 17 linear m. (154 packets).
Organization: Subseries include: Articuli et interrogatoria,

1570–1740; —Instrumenta, 1570–1631; —Jura diversa, 1570–1830; —Jura diversa non producta, 1647–1681; —Mandata procurae, 1570–1825; —Memoralia et commissiones, 1570–1824; —Minutae, 1599–1825; —Monitoria et sequestra, 1586–1825; —Processus, 1610–1826; —Sententiae et appellationes, 1806–1827; —Jura diversa Monti Fabricae, 1642–1686; —Rassegne del Monte Fabbrica (Erezione e spedizione di Spagna); —Fideiussiones commissariorum S. Congregationis Rev. Fabricae S. Petri, 1680.

Scope: This series is a grouping of documents regarding court actions. The documents relate to the tribunal of the Fabbrica.
Finding Aids: "R.F.S.P. Lista topografica dei pacchi e volumi" lists each packet in this series with titles and inclusive dates. "R.F.S.P. Lista cronologica dei pacchi e volumi" has integrated all series from Piano 1, Piano 2, and Piano 3 into a single chronological sequence.
Location: Archivio della Reverenda Fabbrica di S. Pietro, Vatican City.

3.1.25.12 Secundo piano, serie 2: Broliardi et manualia
[DATABASE ID: VATV20289-A]
Inclusive Dates: 1570–1832.
Bulk: 28 linear m. (256 packets).
Organization: This series consists of two subseries chronologically arranged: Broliardus, 1570–1831; —Manuale 1636–1832.
Scope: These are daily registers of the chancellor of the tribunal that record court actions in progress. They comprise what is essentially a docket.
Finding Aids: "R.F.S.P. Lista topografica dei pacchi e volumi" lists each packet in this series with titles and inclusive dates. "R.F.S.P. Lista cronologica dei pacchi e volumi" has integrated all series from Piano 1, Piano 2, and Piano 3 into a single chronological sequence.
Location: Archivio della Reverenda Fabbrica di S. Pietro, Vatican City.

3.1.25.13 Secundo piano, serie 3: Folia et positiones diversae congregationum particularium et generalium
[DATABASE ID: VATV20290-A]
Inclusive Dates: 1639–1796.
Bulk: 9 linear m. (106 packets).
Organization: Subseries include: Folia et positiones diverse congregationum generalium; —Congregationes particulares; —Folia et positiones diversae.
Scope: These are dossiers constituted for presenting a matter to the general congregation of the Fabbrica.
Finding Aids: "R.F.S.P. Lista topografica dei pacchi e volumi" lists each packet in this series with titles and inclusive dates. "R.F.S.P. Lista cronologica dei pacchi e volumi" has integrated all series from Piano 1, Piano 2, and Piano 3 into a single chronological sequence.
Location: Archivio della Reverenda Fabbrica di S. Pietro, Vatican City.

3.1.25.14 Secundo piano, serie 4: Liste mestrue e giustificazioni
[DATABASE ID: VATV20291-A]
Inclusive Dates: 1660–1785.
Bulk: 11 linear m. (129 packets).
Organization: Chronological.

Scope: These are reports of the chief accountant of the Fabbrica regarding expenses taken under the name of the Fabbrica.

Finding Aids: "R.F.S.P. Lista topografica dei pacchi e volumi" lists each packet in this series with titles and inclusive dates. "R.F.S.P. Lista cronologica dei pacchi e volumi" has integrated all series from Piano 1, Piano 2, and Piano 3 into a single chronological sequence.

Location: Archivio della Reverenda Fabbrica di S. Pietro, Vatican City.

3.1.25.15 Secundo piano, serie 5: Liste bimestrali della Rev.da Fabbrica di San Pietro

[DATABASE ID: VATV20292-A]

Inclusive Dates: 1786–1811.

Bulk: 7 linear m. (69 packets).

Organization: Chronological.

Scope: These are reports of the chief accountant of the Fabbrica regarding expenses taken under the name of the Fabbrica. This series continues the chronological sequence of the series *Secundo piano, serie 4,* but on a bimonthly basis.

Finding Aids: "R.F.S.P. Lista topografica dei pacchi e volumi" lists each packet in this series with titles, inclusive dates, and protocol numbers. "R.F.S.P. Lista cronologica dei pacchi e volumi" has integrated all series from Piano 1, Piano 2, and Piano 3 into a single chronological sequence.

Location: Archivio della Reverenda Fabbrica di S. Pietro, Vatican City.

3.1.25.16 Secundo piano, serie 6: Filza di giustificazioni

[DATABASE ID: VATV20293-A]

Inclusive Dates: 1814–1829.

Bulk: 9 linear m. (65 packets).

Scope: These are reports of the chief accountant of the Fabbrica regarding expenses taken under the name of the Fabbrica. This series continues the chronological sequence of *Secundo piano, serie 5.*

Finding Aids: "R.F.S.P. Lista topografica dei pacchi e volumi" lists each packet in this series with titles, inclusive dates, and protocol numbers. "R.F.S.P. Lista cronologica dei pacchi e volumi" has integrated all series from Piano 1, Piano 2, and Piano 3 into a single chronological sequence.

Location: Archivio della Reverenda Fabbrica di S. Pietro, Vatican City.

3.1.25.17 Secundo piano, serie 7: Carteggio della "Segreteria della Rev.da Fabbrica"

[DATABASE ID: VATV20294-A]

Inclusive Dates: 1612–1858.

Bulk: 2 linear m. (13 packets).

Organization: By specific bequest.

Scope: This series contains legacies of various families among other items. The series generally pertains to inheritance or probate questions dealt with by the Fabbrica under its particular jurisdiction.

Finding Aids: "R.F.S.P. Lista topografica dei pacchi e volumi" lists each packet in this series with an indication of content. "R.F.S.P. Lista cronologica dei pacchi e volumi" has integrated all series from Piano 1, Piano 2, and Piano 3 into a single chronological sequence.

Location: Archivio della Reverenda Fabbrica di S. Pietro, Vatican City.

3.1.25.18 Secundo piano, serie 8: Cartelle delle ventiquattro commissarie

[DATABASE ID: VATV20295-A]

Inclusive Dates: 1589–1800.

Bulk: 4 linear m. (24 packets).

Organization: Records are grouped by the geographical location to which they refer.

Scope: This small series is comprised of miscellaneous material regarding territorial divisions in the Papal States.

Finding Aids: "R.F.S.P. Lista topografica dei pacchi e volumi" lists each packet in this series with an indication of content. "R.F.S.P. Lista cronologica dei pacchi e volumi" has integrated all series from Piano 1, Piano 2, and Piano 3 into a single chronological sequence.

Location: Archivio della Reverenda Fabbrica di S. Pietro, Vatican City.

3.1.25.19 Secundo piano, serie 9: Duplicata

[DATABASE ID: VATV20296-A]

Inclusive Dates: 1801–1818.

Bulk: 13 linear m. (62 packets).

Organization: Chronological.

Scope: These packets contain duplicates of petitions for mercy and for absolution of pious bequests and requests for commutations.

Finding Aids: "R.F.S.P. Lista topografica dei pacchi e volumi" lists each packet in this series with titles and inclusive dates. "R.F.S.P. Lista cronologica dei pacchi e volumi" has integrated all series from Piano 1, Piano 2, and Piano 3 into a single chronological sequence.

Location: Archivio della Reverenda Fabbrica di S. Pietro, Vatican City.

3.1.25.20 Secundo piano, serie 10: Miscellanea

[DATABASE ID: VATV20297-A]

Inclusive Dates: 1484–1952.

Bulk: 8 linear m. (34 packets).

Organization: This is a true miscellany.

Scope: This is a very miscellaneous grouping of material discovered over time regarding political, financial, and artistic activities of the Fabbrica.

Finding Aids: "R.F.S.P. Lista topografica dei pacchi e volumi" lists each packet in this series with titles and inclusive dates. "R.F.S.P. Lista cronologica dei pacchi e volumi" has integrated all series from Piano 1, Piano 2, and Piano 3 into a single chronological sequence.

Location: Archivio della Reverenda Fabbrica di S. Pietro, Vatican City.

3.1.25.21 Secundo piano, serie 11: Miscellanea serie "armadi"

[DATABASE ID: VATV20298-A]

Inclusive Dates: 1457–1873.

Bulk: 116 linear m. (555 packets).

Organization: This is a true miscellany.

Scope: A very miscellaneous collection of documents that includes material relating to inheritance questions, particularly the case of Cardinal Giraud, who left property to the Fabbrica. The Fabbrica decided to keep the property in operation. Thus some papers pertain to the administration of the estate. There is also material regarding payments for work on the mosaics, pious bequest cases, and material regarding particular projects.

Finding Aids: "R.F.S.P. Lista topografica dei pacchi e volumi" lists each packet in this series with titles and inclusive dates. "R.F.S.P. Lista cronologica dei pacchi e volumi" has integrated all series from Piano 1, Piano 2, and Piano 3 into a single chronological sequence. Within this series, packets 196–399 form a chronological series of letters to the Deputati della R.F.S.P. (1529–1750). There is an index of names that appear in those letters.

Location: Archivio della Reverenda Fabbrica di S. Pietro, Vatican City.

3.1.25.22 Terzo piano: Miscellanea
[DATABASE ID: VATV20300-A]
Inclusive Dates: ca. 1615–1880.
Bulk: 177 linear m.
Scope: This is a collection of a variety of small identifiable series in some cases, and miscellaneous groupings of documents in others. It is divided into sixty numbered groupings. The *Terzo piano* material falls into two distinct sections:

A. The bank of the Quarantotti. This bank was established in Rome during the seventeenth century. In 1765 the bank failed and was taken over by the Fabbrica. Its records were then incorporated into the archives. See Carla Sbrana, "Un ignorato fondo di storia economica romana: Il Fondo Quarantotti," in *Cahiers internationaux d'histoire économique et sociale* 1 (1972): 370–376.

The Basso guide (M. Basso, *I privilegi e le consuetudini della Rev.da Fabbrica di San Pietro in Vaticano*, Rome, 1987–1988) suggests the following subseries can be found though there are some discrepancies between the information in the guide and in the finding aid: Quarantotti copialettere, 1697–1765; —Entrate e uscita, 1681–1763; Saldaconti, 1697–1765; —Copie di conti partite e bancarie, 1708–1764; —Ricontro, 1697–1765; —Ricevute, 1710–1765; —Quaderni di cambi e contazioni, 1708–1765; —Giornale, 1687–1765; —Ricontri di cassa, 1715–1765; —Tratte e rimesse, 1697–1765; —Libri delle riscossioni, 1697–1772; —Debitori, 1680–1777; —Quaderni di lista, 1697–1765; —Libri delle spedizioni, 1630–1689; —Monti e vacabili, 1741–1765; —Estratti di Monte Fede e Novennale per la Rev.da Fabbrica, 1711–1763; —Rincontri e rincontri di Cedole, 1725–1766; Conti diversi, 1694–1849; —Libri mastri, 1697–1866; —Lettere e recapiti, 1697–1765.

B. Miscellaneous historical material. These include financial records of the Fabbrica and extensive material on particular pious bequests and testaments including that of Cardinal Giraud. Also included are: Groups of records pertaining to payments for work and to workers in the nineteenth century (20 and 21); —Material relating to the tribunal; —Opera Pia delle Scuole Cristiane (27); —The Studio del mosaico in the nineteenth century (29); —The cupola of St. Peter's Basilica (39); —Absolutiones et compositiones 1816–1863 (44); —Minute di lettere della Segreteria 1821–1858 (46); —Minute di lettere to various commissariats within the Papal States 1821–1869 (49); —Duplicata e rescripta 1819–1857 (51); —Registri delle suppliche 1820–1857 (54); —Registri correnti 1789–1885 (55); —Rubricelle alfabetiche 1820–1858 (56); —Rubricelle 1819–1830 (57); Registri dei mandati 1796–1819 (58); —Giornale del libro mastro 1819–1880 (59). Note also that the inclusive dates

for the various subseries of Piano 3 listed in the Basso guide differ slightly from those listed in the finding aid. The dates listed in this description were taken from the finding aid.

Finding Aids: "R.F.S.P. Lista topografica dei pacchi e volumi" lists each packet in this series with titles and inclusive dates. "R.F.S.P. Lista cronologica dei pacchi e volumi" has integrated all series from Piano 1, Piano 2, and Piano 3 into a single chronological sequence.

Location: Archivio della Reverenda Fabbrica di S. Pietro, Vatican City.

3.1.25.23 Ottagono
[DATABASE ID: VATV20360-A]
Inclusive Dates: [14—]–[19—].
Bulk: About 600 packets.
Organization: The Ottagono material divides into two main sections: 1. the general administration of the Fabbrica (eight subseries) and 2. the mosaic studio (three subseries).
Scope: Material from the mosaic studio relates to specific works of art and decoration. The records pertain to works done primarily in the eighteenth and nineteenth centuries and include secular works as well as works intended for churches and religious institutions. Also of particular interest are documents relating to the interaction between the Fabbrica of St. Peter's and the civil authorities of the city of Rome after 1870 regarding services to the maintenance of St. Peter's Square. Among the variety of documents are extensive personnel files.
Finding Aids: See "R.F.S.P. Lista topografica delle posizioni dell'Ex-Piano Ottagoni." This lista contains a list of each packet in the eight subseries of section 1 and a list of each packet in the three subseries of section 2. See "R.F.S.P. Liste cronologiche delle positioni dell'Ex-Piano Ottagoni." This list integrates the dossiers from the packets in section 1 into a single chronological list. This list also integrates the dossiers from the packets in section 2 into a single and separate chronological list. There is a series of related indexes to the second section of this series (Studio del mosaico) that groups material by date, indexes works by motif, and provides names of workers and artists.
Location: Archivio della Reverenda Fabbrica di S. Pietro, Vatican City.

3.1.25.24 [Atti]
[DATABASE ID: VATV10189-A]
Inclusive Dates: 1858–1908.
Bulk: 28 linear m. (158 buste).
Organization: Chronological. The *Atti* are given protocol numbers; each year begins with no. 1.
Note: This series does not have an official ASV designation. The title was assigned by the project staff.
Reference: Pásztor (1970), pp. 171–173.
Location: Archivio Segreto Vaticano.

3.1.25.25 [Miscellanea SF/447]
[DATABASE ID: VATV10190-A]
Inclusive Dates: 1814–1908.
Bulk: 2 linear m.
Organization: Series/items include: Carte Sospese, 1858–1859, 1 busta; —Cappellanie e consolidato, 1859, 1 busta; —Amministrazione generale e commissarie, 1859–1860, 1 busta; —Miscellaneous correspondence, 1860–1906, 8 buste; —

Fabbrica di San Pietro e Capitolo, 1814–1839, 1 busta; —
Positiones, 1836–1852, 1 busta (printed); —Posizioni, 1891–
1908, 1 busta.
  Note: This is a true miscellany without official designation
by the ASV. The title was assigned by the project staff with
reference to its location in the ASV in 1990.
  Location: Archivio Segreto Vaticano.

3.1.25.26 Notai della fabbrica di S. Pietro
  [DATABASE ID: VATV20378-A]
  Inclusive Dates: 1571–1881.
  Bulk: 377 vols. and 1 repertorio.
  Scope: Sixteenth century, 4 vols. —Seventeenth century, 67
vols. —Eighteenth century, 254 vols. —Nineteenth century,
52 vols.
  Reference: D'Angiolini p. 1217.
  Finding Aids: Printed list of notai.
  Location: Archivio di Stato di Roma.

3.1.25.27 Registro generale delle suppliche
  [DATABASE ID: VATV10192-A]
  Inclusive Dates: 1859–1908.
  Bulk: 1.5 linear m. (50 vols.).
  Organization: Chronological.
  Scope: Entries include: protocol number, date of presentation, name of petitioner, parish, and name of representative,
accenno of petition, examination of the petition, date of transmission of the supplication for information, name of subject of
the petition, date of return of additional information, date of
decision, type of decree or rescript, date of rescript, and placement of case in archives. Most columns are blank for most
entries.
  Reference: Pásztor (1970), p. 173.
  Location: Archivio Segreto Vaticano.

3.1.25.28 Rubricella alfabetica
  [DATABASE ID: VATV10191-A]
  Inclusive Dates: 1859–1908.
  Bulk: 1 linear m. (50 vols.).
  Organization: Chronological by year and then alphabetical
according to name, organization, or office within each
year.
  Scope: Entries include: name of petitioner or representative,
page in the register of supplications, and protocol number of
the petition.
  Reference: Pásztor (1970), p. 173.
  Location: Archivio Segreto Vaticano.

3.1.26 Congregatio Romanae et Universalis Inquisitionis
  [DATABASE ID: VATV002-A]

The Congregation of the Holy Office was, until 1908,
called the Congregatio Romanae et Universalis Inquisitionis seu Sancti Officii. The primary function of this
congregation was to assist the pope in his task of preserv-
ing the integrity of the church doctrine on faith and
morals, although the manner of operation has varied
over the centuries.

The earliest traces of the church's concern for preserv-
ing this integrity can be found in Lucius III's constitution *Ad abolendam* (Nov. 4, 1184), which obliged all
bishops to visit twice a year, either personally or by
appropriate delegate, various dioceses to investigate any
teaching or practices that seemed to endanger Christian
faith or morals. Successive measures taken by Innocent
III (1198–1216) led to the appointment in 1231 by
Gregory IX of the inquisitores haereticae pravitatis with
a mandate to systematically search out heresy and heretics.

The office of inquisitors was entrusted by Gregory IX
to Dominicans, to whom Innocent IV, with his constitution *Quia tunc* (Mar. 18, 1254), added Franciscans.
These men were sent into various countries throughout
Europe vested with apostolic authority to exercise inquisitorial jurisdiction concurrently with the local
bishops. Even in Rome, as in other dioceses, a tribunal
of the Inquisition was initially set up and presided over
by the pope himself. The various inquisitors, however,
were never coordinated to form an organized papal department.

It was only with Paul III (constitution *Licet ab initio*,
Jul. 21, 1542) that a permanent Roman commission of
cardinals and tribunal of inquisition was set up with
power to defend and maintain the integrity of the faith
and to examine and proscribe errors and false teaching.
The commission's task was to proceed against all apos-
tates, heretics, and their accomplices and followers
even without the intervention of the ordinaries. They
were to examine doctrine as well as to try persons. Thus
the extent of their jurisdiction was considerably enlarged.

The inquisitors general could name fiscal promoters,
notaries, and delegates in countries or in single dioceses. But neither the cardinal inquisitors nor their delegates could receive recantations nor remit punishment
because these faculties were reserved to the pope. Cardinals could appeal cases decided by their delegates and in
such cases absolve kings from censure and from ecclesiastical penalties. No one was exempt from the jurisdiction of the inquisitors, but a sentence against cardinals
or major prelates had to be pronounced by the pope in
consistory (motu proprio *Saepius inter arcanas*, Oct. 31,
1562).

Although the examination and proscription of books
that endangered the faith and morals of Christians had
been assigned to the inquisitors general by Paul III
(confirmed by Pius IV in his motu proprio *Cum inter
crimina*, Aug. 27, 1564), this function was later transferred to the Congregatio pro Indice Librorum Prohibi-
torum founded by Pius V in March 1571.

Paul IV increased the number of cardinal inquisitors
first in 1556 and again in 1557. In 1558 he officially
changed the tribunal to a congregation and with the
constitution *Pastoralis officii munus* (Oct. 14, 1562)

strengthened and increased its powers and stabilized its functions.

Sixtus V (constitution *Immensa aeterni Dei*, Jan. 22, 1588) formally confirmed it as a congregation, further defined its work, and ranked it first in the Roman Curia. He also renamed the congregation the Congregatio Sanctae Inquisitionis Haereticae Pravitatis. Later the name became Congregatio pro Romanae et Universalis Inquisitionis seu Sancti Officii, which eventually became more commonly known as the Congregatio Sancti Officii. Benedict XIV, in the constitution *Sollicita ac provida* (Jul. 9, 1753), called it the Congregation of the Universal Roman Inquisition. Later it had the official name of Suprema Congregatio Sanctae Romanae et Universalis Inquisitionis.

With the motu proprio *Romanis Pontificibus* (Dec. 17, 1903), Pius X transferred the responsibilities of the Congregatio Examinis Episcoporum and the Congregatio Particularis super Promovendis ad Archiepiscopatus et Episcopatus to the Congregatio Sancti Officii. The curial reform of Pius X (constitution *Sapienti consilio*, Jun. 29, 1908) introduced new modifications. This document officially renamed the congregation the Congregatio Sancti Officii, suppressed the Congregation of Indulgences, and transferred its functions to that of the Holy Office. See the entry for the Congregatio Sancti Officii in this section for the history after 1908.

The archives of the Holy Office suffered significant losses in the process of their return from Paris. The only significant historical records of the Congregation that are consultable are those that fell into private hands in the early nineteenth century and were subsequently donated to the library at Trinity College, Dublin. Those series are listed in this section.

In addition to the records listed below, series listed with another agency relate directly to this agency and should be consulted. See Miscellaneous official series *Miscellaneorum armarium X*.

References. L. Amabile, *Il Santo Officio della Inquisizione in Napoli: Narrazione con molti documenti inediti* (Città Di Castello, 1892). F. Bock, "Studien zum politischen Inquisitionsprozess Johanns XXII," *Quellen und Forschungen aus italienischen Archiven und Bibliotheken* 26 (1935–1936): 21–142; 27 (1936–1937): 109–134. L. Fumi, "L'Inquisizione romana e lo Stato di Milano: Saggio di ricerche nell'Archivio di Stato," *Archivio storico lombardo* ser. 4, vol. 37, no. 13 (1910) [this title was noted but not verified by project staff]. P. F. Grendler, *The Roman Inquisition and the Venetian Press, 1540–1605* (Princeton, 1977). A. Mercati, *Il sommario del processo di Giordano Bruno: Con appendice di documenti sull'eresia e l'Inquisizione a Modena nel secolo XVI* (Vatican City, 1942).

RECORDS. Records of the congregation consist of the following series.

3.1.26.1 [Archivio Storico]
[DATABASE ID: VATV263-A]
Inclusive Dates: Not Known.
Bulk: Boyle estimated about 7,000 vols.
Scope: This is the historical archives of the Congregation for the Holy Office. Leonard Boyle notes the existence of this archives. It is not open for research and its holdings are not generally known. Presumably any extant records of the Inquisition (aside from those located at Trinity College, Dublin) are located in this archives along with any extant records relating to the Index of Forbidden Books.
Reference: Boyle, p. 85.
Location: Palazzo del S. Uffizio, Piazza S. Offizio, 11, Rome, Italy.

3.1.26.2 Casa (Pia) del S. Offizio
[DATABASE ID: VATV40003-A]
Inclusive Dates: [16—]–[19—].
Bulk: 108 buste and 1 vol.
Note: This series was cited in Natalini et al., p. 269, but not seen by project staff in 1990.
Location: Archivio Segreto Vaticano.

3.1.26.3 Denunciations, examinations, etc.
[DATABASE ID: VATV40062-A]
Inclusive Dates: 1565–1789.
Bulk: 2.2 linear meters (36 vols.).
Organization: This series is not in any particular order; however, the arrangement is fixed by the numbers assigned to the volumes by the library at Trinity College. They are TCD 1243–TCD 1277. There is one additional volume of fragments numbered TCD 1277a. Note that it is generally agreed that TCD 1232 from the Holy Office series *Sentences* belongs with this series.
Scope: This series consists of thirty-five volumes of progress reports on litigation before provincial tribunals of the inquisition in Italy. It is, therefore, more a collection of miscellaneous papers and documents bound together reflecting the results of preliminary inquiries. These were then sent to the Holy Office in Rome for its information or decision. There is one trial in the first volume of the series that dates to 1565. However, the rest of the volumes contain documentation from 1625 to 1789. John Tedeschi in his article "A 'Queer Story': The Inquisitorial Manuscripts," in *Treasures of the Library, Trinity College Dublin*, edited by P. Fox (Dublin, 1986), p. 70, is struck by the clear interest in the uniformity of procedure that led to measures that "assigned to Rome the final disposition of all but the most ordinary cases. By the end of the century, for example, interrogations under torture, hedged in by many restrictions and precautions even in earlier periods, rarely were conducted without the prior authorization of the central tribunal." This generally was not given until the cardinal inquisitor had sufficient information to render such a decision. Hence these documents were compiled in the regions of Italy for this purpose.
Reference: Boyle, pp. 85–86.
Finding Aids: Marvin L. Colker, *Trinity College Library Dublin: Descriptive Catalogue of the Mediaeval and Renaissance Latin Manuscripts* (Aldershot, 1991), vol. 2, pp. 1226–1238, provides a listing of each volume with some indication of its contents.
T. K. Abbott, *A Catalogue of the Manuscripts in the Library*

of Trinity College Dublin (Dublin, 1900), pp. 261–284, provides a more detailed list of each volume in the series including inclusive dates, place of origin of the documents, and a general sense of the contents of the volumes. Note that TCD 1255, for example, contains only three cases; so the documentation can be substantial. In the manuscripts reading room of the library at Trinity College there is an annotated copy of the Abbott guide. However, it has little additional information for this series.

Note: Copies of these volumes are available on microfilm.

Location: Trinity College Library, Dublin, Ireland.

3.1.26.4 Giustificazione

[DATABASE ID: VATV10365-A]

Inclusive Dates: 1830–1884.

Bulk: 9 linear m.

Organization: Subseries include: Giustificazioni, 1830–1855, 7 linear m. (Chronological); —Libro mastro, 1868–1884, 1 vol.; —[Miscellanea], 1 linear m.

Note: Full title on giustificazioni is "Ven. Pia Casa de S. Offizio Filza delle giustificazione del Libro mastro dell anno. . . ."

Reference: Fink, p. 139.

Location: Archivio Segreto Vaticano.

3.1.26.5 Recapiti

[DATABASE ID: VATV10364-A]

Inclusive Dates: 1739–1778.

Bulk: 10 linear m.

Organization: Chronological.

Location: Archivio Segreto Vaticano.

3.1.26.6 Sentences

[DATABASE ID: VATV264-A]

Inclusive Dates: 1564–1659.

Bulk: 1.1 meters (19 vols.).

Organization: These volumes are organized in chronological order and are housed in the library of Trinity College, Dublin. The volumes are cataloged as TCD 1224–TCD 1242. Note that it is generally agreed that TCD 1232 properly belongs with the Holy Office series *Denunciations.*

Scope: This series consists of nineteen volumes of sentences, with accompanying abjurations, issued by the Supreme Congregation of the Holy Office in Rome or by provincial Italian tribunals under its jurisdiction between 1564 and 1659. John Tedeschi, "A 'Queer Story': The Inquisitorial Manuscripts," in *Treasures of the Library, Trinity College Dublin,* edited by P. Fox (Dublin, 1986), pp. 67–74, notes that "only four volumes in this series deal with the sixteenth century, spanning the years 1564–8 and 1580–2 and containing roughly five hundred sentences." He continues: "Sentences do more than declare a defendant's guilt or innocence; they summarize in detail the charges against him and sometimes even his responses to them. They frequently run to many pages and consequently are often satisfactory substitutes for the records of the complete trials, which, for the most part, perished in Paris."

Marvin L. Colker, *Trinity College Library Dublin: Descriptive Catalogue of the Mediaeval and Renaissance Latin Manuscripts* (Aldershot, 1991), introduces the series and notes that most of the sentences and abjurations deal with "heresy, but some deal with other charges, e.g. sodomy or bigamy." The heresy sentences and abjurations reproduce such assertions of

the accused as: the pope has no spiritual authority, the saints do not intercede, there is no purgatory, that meat may be eaten on any day, that clergy may marry, and that the eucharist is not the true body and blood.

References: Boyle, pp. 85–86. C. Corvisieri, "Compendio dei processi del Santo Uffizio di Roma (da Paolo III a Paolo IV)," *Archivio della Società romana di storia patria* 3 (1879): 261–290, 449–471.

Finding Aids: M. L. Colker, *Trinity College Library Dublin: Descriptive Catalogue of the Mediaeval and Renaissance Latin Manuscripts* (Aldershot, 1991), vol. 2, pp. 1226–1238, provides a brief chronological list of each volume in the series. He notes where each volume has a list of contents or an alphabetical index in the beginning of the volume (in item TCD 1233 this appears at the end).

T. K. Abbott, *A Catalogue of the Manuscripts in the Library of Trinity College Dublin* (Dublin, 1900), pp. 243–261, contains a much more detailed description of each volume providing a select listing of specific cases by name and dates. It is not clear by what criteria Abbott selected the particular cases listed.

In the reading room of the Manuscripts Division at the Trinity College Library there is an annotated copy of Abbott that for some volumes in the series provides added citations to individual cases.

Also in the reading room there is a typscript volume prepared by Josiah Gilbert Smyly, "A calendar of part of the Roman Inquisition Papers" (no date). Smyly provides a very detailed calendar including a general desc.iption of each case found in four of the volumes of this series (TCD 1225–TCD 1228). For TCD 1226 he provides an index by Italian city; for TCD 1228 he provides an index by charge (blasphemy, Calvinism, etc.) and by country.

Note: These volumes are available on microfilm.

Location: Trinity College Library, Dublin, Ireland.

3.1.27 Congregatio Sacrorum Rituum

[DATABASE ID: VATV017-A]

This congregation was established by Sixtus V as the Congregatio pro Sacris Ritibus et Caeremoniis (constitution *Immensa aeterni Dei,* Jan. 22, 1588). According to some authors, it absorbed a cardinalatial commission formed by Gregory XIII, as early as 1572, to reform the ceremonies of the papal chapel. Although the principal task of the new congregation was to attend to the moderation of the Latin liturgy "in all the churches of Rome and throughout the world," the bulk of its work was devoted to the causes of saints, including relics.

Lack of documentation leaves it unclear just when the Congregation for Rites and Ceremonies was divided into two distinct and autonomous congregations, but some authorities state that it was probably about 1601. Clement VIII decreed that the Congregation of Ceremonies be a separate department, taking with it the functions for civil ceremonies and those for the papal chapel.

With the foundation of the Congregatio de Propaganda Fide by Gregory XV in 1622, all liturgical questions concerning the Eastern church were transferred to this congregation and remained there until the establishment of the Congregation for the Oriental Church in 1917. Clement IX (motu proprio *In ipsis pontificatus*, Jul. 6, 1669) transferred all matters relevant to the veneration and preservation of relics to the newly instituted Congregatio Indulgentiis Sacrisque Reliquiis Praepositae. With the suppression of this congregation in 1904 its duties were transferred back to the Congregation of Rites (motu proprio *Quae in Ecclesiae*, Jan. 28, 1904).

Although the original scope of the Congregation of Rites was restricted to issues regarding liturgy and to the process of canonization, its faculties were gradually extended. Liturgical matters were still the exclusive perogative of the congregation. However, the congregation came to possess other functions mostly in conjunction with the Congregation of Bishops and Regulars and the Congregation of the Council. On September 3, 1903, Pius X (*Acta Sanctae Sedis* 36: 412–413) published a list of 142 responsibilities assigned to the Congregation of Rites. Many of these were later transferred to the Congregation of the Sacraments.

In the course of time three commissions were set up to assist the congregation in its work. Leo XIII added two commissions: (1) the Liturgical Commission (1891), to codify past decrees and to advise the congregation on liturgical questions; and (2) the Historico-Liturgical Commission (1902), to settle historical questions, with special reference to the eventual reform of liturgical books. In 1904 Pius X added a third commission for sacred music and chant.

With the curial reform of Pius X (constitution *Sapientia consilio*, Jun. 29, 1908), the Congregation of Rites was restricted in its authority to matters directly related to the rites and ceremonies of the Latin church; this included not only the Roman liturgy but also the non-Roman rites of the West. The document enumerated the congregation's specific duties: to exercise vigilance that the rites and ceremonies be carefully observed in the celebration of Mass and the divine office, in the administration of the sacraments, and in all that pertains to the worship of the Latin church; to concede suitable dispensations; to grant insignia and privileges that pertain to "sacred rites"; and to handle all questions of beatification and canonization, including relics, as before.

Authority for indulgences, which had been transferred to the congregation along with authority for relics just four years before (1904), was now given to the Congregation of the Holy Office. Questions of precedence and of the discipline of the sacraments, as distinct from the rite of the sacraments, were transferred respectively to the Congregation of the Council and the Congregation of Religious.

With the motu proprio *Quanta semper cura* (Jan. 16, 1914), Pius X suppressed the three commissions attached to the Congregation of Rites and set up two sections within the congregation itself, one for beatification and canonization and one for rites.

Pius XI's motu proprio *Già da qualche tempo* (Feb. 6, 1930) added a historical section for research necessary for the beatification and canonization processes and for the revision of liturgical books. In 1948 Pius XII established a Pontifical Commission for the General Restoration of the Liturgy and attached it to the congregation. During the Second Vatican Council, however, a consilium separate from the Congregation of Rites was set up and called the Consilium for the Implementation of the Constitution on the Sacred Liturgy. This consilium was entrusted with the reform of all the liturgical books of the Roman rite (motu proprio *Sacram liturgiam*, Jan. 25, 1964).

In 1949 the Congregation of Rites annexed a college of doctors for the scientific study of alleged miracles. Paul VI's apostolic constitution (*Regimini Ecclesiae universae*, Aug. 15, 1967) established the Congregation for the Discipline of the Sacraments to moderate the discipline of the seven sacraments in areas not touched by the Congregation for the Doctrine of the Faith; the functions of the Congregation of Rites remained intact, but the congregation was divided into two sections: liturgical, handling the rites and ceremonies for the preparation, administration, and reception of the sacraments; and judicial, for the processes of beatification and canonization causes, including those of the Eastern rites, and for sacred relics. Both sections would have available to them the historico-hagiographical office set up in 1930 by Pius XI. The Roman Rota would have authority for cases of marriage nullity.

Just two years later (constitution *Sacra Rituum Congregatio*, May 8, 1969), Paul VI suppressed the Congregation of Rites as it had been functioning and replaced it with two new congregations, one for each of the sections: a Congregation for Divine Worship and a Congregation for the Causes of Saints.

The Congregatio pro Causis Sanctorum maintains its own archive, which includes records of the Congregation of Rites. The archive is located in Piazza Pio XII 10, 00193 Rome. Though small in comparison to the ASV, it does have holdings from the sixteenth through the twentieth centuries. This archive was not consulted by the project staff.

References. Pásztor (1970), pp. 339–344. Catholic Church, Congregazione pro Causis Sanctorum, *Miscellanea in occasione del IV centenario della congregazione per le cause dei santi (1588–1988)* (Vatican City, 1988). F. Antonelli, "L'archivio della S. Congregazione dei Riti," in *Il libro e le biblioteche: Atti del primo Congresso bibliografico francescano internazionale, 20–27 febbraio 1949* (Rome, 1950), vol. 2, pp. 61–76. F. Antonelli, "L'archivio della S. Congregazione dei Riti," in *Relazioni del X Congresso internazionale di scienze stori-*

che, International Congress of Historical Sciences (Florence, 1955), vol. 7, pp. 99–100. F. Antonelli, "S. C. dei Riti," in *Enciclopedia cattolica* (Vatican City, 1950), vol. 4, cols. 330–333. A. P. Frutaz, *La sezione storica della Sacra Congregazione dei Riti: Origini e metodo di lavoro,* 2d ed. (Vatican City, 1964). P. Galavotti, ed., *Index ac Status Causarum* (Vatican City, 1988). F. R. McManus, *The Congregation of Sacred Rites* (Washington, D.C., 1954). Note also that the decrees of the congregation have been published, generally under the title *Decreta Authentica Congregationis Sacrorum Rituum.*

RECORDS. Records of the congregation consist of the following series.

3.1.27.1 Processus
[DATABASE ID: VATV271-A]
Inclusive Dates: 1610?–1985.
Bulk: 484 linear m.
Organization: This is a vast series consisting of 7,483 numbered volumes. (Some numbers may comprise more than one volume.) Volumes 7016–7030, regarding Pius X, are still held in the Congregatio pro Causis Sanctorum.
Note: A number of the published volumes of processi are available on the primo piano of the ASV Sala degl'Indici. Since 1990 there have been several accessions of additional material from the congregation. These are not reflected in the bulk figure above but are noted in the finding aids listed below.
Note: Vols. 1–3, 323, 326, 330, 332, 335, 337, 338, 401, 411–413, 698, 1570, 1573, 1574, 1803, 1882, 1883, 1923, 1959, 1960, 2016, 2092, 2174, 2265, 2269, 2277, 2658, 2714, 2717, 2878–2839, 2840, 2863, 2864, 2925, 3072–3076, 3127, 3290–3300bis, 3725, 3879, 4137, 4165, 6866 (part), and 6877 are available on microfilm.
References: Boyle, p. 87; Fink, pp. 120–121; Pásztor (1970), pp. 170–171; Natalini et al., p. 270. L. Wahrmund, *Quellen zur Geschichte des römisch-kanonischen Prozesses im Mittelalter* (Innsbruck, 1905–).
Finding Aids: ASV Indice 1147, compiled by P. Yvon Beaudoin, O.M.I., in 1982, is divided into three sections. The first part (pp. 1–228) is organized alphabetically by the name of the person canonized. This list of canonization processi between 1588 and 1982 (vols. 1–7030) itemizes and dates the final documents generated by each process; provides brief information on the subject; and gives the diocese, and often the languages and a physical description of the material (foliation, etc.). The second section (p. 229) lists processi apparently concerning two visions of the Virgin Mary in Ancona in the seventeenth century. The final section (pp. 231–261) is a brief numerical inventory of vols. 1–7030. Although this index lists canonization processes after 1922, these are not consultable.
ASV Indice 1147a is an index to material transferred from the congregation to the ASV between 1982 and 1994. It contains an alphabetical index similar to ASV Indice 1147 and covers volume numbers 7018–9732.
ASV Indice 1174 provides a brief introduction to the processi and lists the different types of processi (levels of canonization and beatification) granted by the Riti.

ASV Indice 1047 contains the same information as sections one and three of ASV Indice 1147, although in a more abbreviated form. Indice 1047 does provide two separate concordances to the former organization of the Riti *Processus.* The first, on p. 114, shows the relationship between the former alphanumeric volume identifications and the current volume numbers. The second (p. 136) translates the former volume numbers (of only the numbered volumes) into the current volume numbers. At the end of the indice there is also a list of processi (and other documents concerning the canonization process) that are in the Bibliothèque Nationale in Paris.
Location: Archivio Segreto Vaticano.

3.1.27.2 Processuum authenticorum beatificationis et canonizationis
[DATABASE ID: VATV10536-A]
Inclusive Dates: ca. 1600–1900.
Bulk: 35 linear m. (7,666 volumes).
Organization: Alphabetical.
Scope: This is a series of primarily unique printed volumes issued in the process of determining eligibility for beatification and/or canonization. The series contains volumes concerning individuals such as Ignatius Loyola, Martin de Porres, and Stanislas Kostka. The volumes were brought to Paris by Napoleon.
Finding Aids: See A. de Bourmont, "Fonds des canonisations," *Analecta Bollandiana* 5 (1886): 147–161. C. de Clercq, "Le fonds dit de canonisations à la Bibliothèque Nationale de Paris," *Revue de droit canonique* 4 (1954): 76–90. W. Schamoni, *Inventarium Processuum Beatificationis et Canonizationis Bibliothecae Nationalis Parisiensis Provenientium ex Archivis S. Rituum Congregationis Typis Mandatorum inter Annos 1662–1809* (Hildesheim, 1983). This also includes a list of which processes are published and publication data.
Location: Bibliothèque Nationale, Paris.

3.1.28 Congregatio Sancti Officii
[DATABASE ID: VATV001-A]

The Congregation of the Holy Office was, until 1908, called the Congregatio Romanae et Universalis Inquisitionis seu Sancti Officii. See the entry for that congregation in this section for the history prior to 1908. The curial reform of Pius X (constitution *Sapienti consilio,* Jun. 29, 1908), officially renamed the congregation the Congregatio Sancti Officii, suppressed the Congregation of Indulgences, and transferred its functions to that of the Holy Office. All questions relative to the precepts of the church were placed under the jurisdiction of the Congregation of the Council. Responsibility for the election of bishops for places outside the jurisdiction of the Propaganda Fide was transferred to the Consistorial Congregation. Responsibility for the dispensation from religious vows was transferred to the Congregation for the Affairs of Religious. The pope withdrew all authority with regard to the substantial form of the celebration of mixed marriages, stating that the decree *Ne temere* (article 11) would remain in force. The Congregation of the

Holy Office, however, would continue to have authority over questions concerning the Pauline Privilege, disparity of worship, and mixed religion. In former times the Holy Office even dealt with causes of canonization; this was assigned exclusively to the Congregation of Rites.

Benedict XV with his motu proprio *Alloquentes* (Mar. 25, 1917) transferred to the Apostolic Penitentiary authority for the granting and use of indulgences, leaving only doctrinal questions under the Congregation of the Holy Office. The Congregation of the Index was also suppressed and its functions transferred back to a simple section under the Congregation of the Holy Office.

Paul VI (apostolic letter *Integrae servandae*, Dec. 7, 1965) began his reorganization of the Curia with this congregation to which he gave the new name of Congregatio pro Doctrina Fidei with authority for all questions touching on a doctrine of faith and morals or questions relating to faith. The document decrees the change in name and function in twelve statements. The orientation of the entire decree is to promote doctrine rather than to condemn error.

Attached to the congregation are the Pontifical Biblical Commission (instituted by Leo XIII, Oct. 30, 1902; restructured by Paul VI, Jun. 27, 1971) and the Theological Commission (instituted by Paul VI, Apr. 11, 1969).

RECORDS. No records for this congregation were located. This congregation does maintain its own archive, which is not consultable. See the entry for the Congregatio Romanae et Universalis Inquisitionis.

3.1.29 Congregatio Studiorum
[DATABASE ID: VATV024-A]

After the restoration of the Papal States in 1814, Pius VII appointed a commission of cardinals to organize all the courses of study in the papal territory (motu proprio *Quando per ammirabile disposizione*, Jul. 6, 1816), and drew up a plan for the "reorganization of the public administration and the tribunals of the papal regions." The pontiff's death in 1823, however, prevented the proposed reorganization from being carried out.

During the following year Leo XII put the reorganization into effect (constitution *Quod divina sapientia*, Aug. 28, 1824). The constitution provided that a Congregatio Studiorum would have authority over all the public and private, lay and ecclesiastical schools both in Rome and throughout the Papal States, and that all universities within the papal territory were to be subject to this congregation. In 1841 Gregory XVI conferred increased powers on the congregation. With Pius IX's motu proprio *Quando coi due* (Dec. 29, 1847), the congregation was transformed into what was, in effect, a new juridical body, a "ministero dell'istruzione pubblica" for the Papal States.

Unique among the ministries, it was returned to being a congregation after the restoration of 1849. The prefect of studies was never made a part of the Council of Ministers.

With the motu proprio *L'uniformità di regime* (Dec. 28, 1852), Pius IX made some minor changes including a reduction of the power of the College of Consistorial Advocates, which still held the rectorship of the congregation; the pope himself was henceforth to nominate the rector. The Congregation of Studies retained these powers until the Papal States were dissolved on September 20, 1870. With the loss of temporal power, the congregation ceased to exist civilly. A State Minister of Public Instruction took over the function of the congregation and confiscated its archives. Over the protest of the cardinal prefect, the new state forced the congregation to have nothing further to do with public instruction or with the University of Rome. Nevertheless the congregation carried on, though its activity was greatly diminished.

After 1870 the Congregation of Studies began to assert influence over all the Catholic universities in the world that depended on the authority of the church, including those administered by the members of religious societies.

Shortly before he died (in 1878), Pius IX decreed that henceforth the conferral of academic degrees would belong exclusively to the authority of the Congregation of Studies. Leo XIII (1878–1903) also entrusted to it the direction of a number of Roman institutions.

Meanwhile the seminaries were being brought more and more under the control of the Holy See. They had never been subject to the Congregation of Studies but had been originally under the authority of the Congregation of the Council and then under the jurisdiction of the Congregation of Bishops and Regulars.

On June 29, 1908, Pius X issued his constitution *Sapienti consilio* revising the whole schema of the Roman Curia and assigning distinct tasks to each congregation. The Congregation of Studies was given authority over universities and faculties dependent on the church, including those that were administered by religious. It was to approve new institutions, to grant the faculties to confer degrees, and to confer them itself, if it wished, on men of outstanding knowledge, as well as to confer honorary degrees on persons of unusual merit. Seminaries were entrusted to the Consistorial Congregation, in which a special office was established to care specifically for them.

The Congregatio Studiorum was superseded in 1915 by the Congregatio de Seminariis et Studiorum Universitatibus, established by Benedict XV (motu proprio *Seminaria clericorum*, Nov. 4, 1915).

RECORDS. Records of the congregation consist of the following series.

3.1.29.1 Congregazione degli studi
[DATABASE ID: VATV20138-A]

Inclusive Dates: 1763–1870 (bulk 1815–1870).

Bulk: 471 buste, 80 registri and 1 protocollo.

References: D'Angiolini, pp. 1160–1161; Lodolini (1960), pp. 138–139.

Finding Aids: Inventory, 1904.

Location: Archivio di Stato di Roma.

3.1.29.2 Università
[DATABASE ID: VATV10312-A]

Inclusive Dates: 1815–1870.

Bulk: 33 linear m.

Organization: Subseries include: Concorsi, 1825–1847, 1851–1852; —Anni scolastici, admissione, e premiazioni, 1836–1840; —Università, 1825–1870; —[Supplications] a S. Cong. degli Stud., 1832–1870; —Stampati; —Miscellanea; —Elenco generale dei medici e chirurgi matricolati dello Stato Ecclesiastico, 2 vols.; —Rubricella, 1830; —Elenco generale degli esercenti le arti salutari minori nello Stato Ecclesiastico, 2 vols.; —Statuti; —Elenco generale di tutti gli autorizzati all'esercizio degli inferiori rami delle Arti salutari dall'Anno 1815–1824, 2 vols.; —Registri delle pagelle d'ammissione alle scuole dell'Università di Roma, 1832–1852, 2 vols.; —[Financial records].

Note: The description of the subseries does not include materials in buste located (in 1990) in the ASV on SF/318.

Location: Archivio Segreto Vaticano.

3.1.30 Congregatio super Consultationibus Episcoporum et Aliorum Praelatorum
[DATABASE ID: VATV015-A]

The origin of this congregation can be traced to the Cardinalatial Commission set up by Pius V (1566–1572) under the apostolic visitor, Bartolomeo di Porcia in 1570, to examine relations with the patriarch of Aquileia. The commission continued to function even after its initial task had been accomplished. Gregory XIII (1572–1585), recognizing the usefulness of these visits, used them for other purposes from 1573 to 1576, particularly for problems arising between bishops and religious. However, as bishops increasingly brought issues to the commission, it began in 1576 to function as a permanent organization under the name Congregatio super Consultationibus Episcoporum.

Sixtus V, in his constitution *Immensa aeterni Dei* (Jan. 22, 1588), included this among the new congregations formally established in this reorganization of the Roman Curia.

In the 1590s this congregation was united with the Congregatio super Consultationibus Regularium to form the Congregatio Negotiis et Consultationibus Episcoporum et Regularium Praeposita, although when the congregations were united is not well documented. See the history for the Congregatio Negotiis et Consultationibus Episcoporum et Regularium Praeposita.

RECORDS. No records for this congregation were located.

3.1.31 Congregatio super Consultationibus Regularium
[DATABASE ID: VATV014-A]

Sixtus V (constitution *Romanus Pontifex*, May 17, 1586) created a new department called Congregatio super Consultationibus Regularium charged with caring for the many problems that were arising among religious of both sexes. His constitution *Immensa aeterni Dei* (Jan. 22, 1588) included this organization among the new congregations formally established by this reorganization of the Roman Curia.

In the 1590s this congregation was united with the Congregatio super Consultationibus Episcoporum to form the Congregatio Negotiis et Consultationibus Episcoporum et Regularium Praeposita, although when they were united is not well documented. See the history for the Congretatio Negotiis et Consultationibus Episcoporum et Regularium Praeposita.

RECORDS. No records for this agency were located.

3.1.32 Congregatio super Correctione Librorum Orientalium
[DATABASE ID: VATV141-A]

This congregation traces its origin to the ancient Congregatio super Correctione Euchologii Graecorum established in 1636 within the Congregazione di Propaganda Fide by Urban VIII. Philip IV of Spain, having been informed that a euchologion (a book of liturgies, prayers, and occasional rites) containing many errors had been published by Greek schismatics, worked with the Holy See to provide a corrected version for the use of the Greek Uniates of Calabria and Sicily. In spite of Urban's interest and support, much time was spent by the experts assigned to the task without concrete results.

At a meeting of the Congregation of the Propagation of the Faith held on January 23, 1645, shortly after Urban's death, it was reported that the members of the congregation formed to provide these corrections had met in eighty-two sessions. Innocent X attended this meeting but since the corrections of the euchologion were not yet finished a new edition could not be published. In 1717 Clement XI established a new office independent of the Congregation for the Propagation of the Faith to carry on the revision and to include all the Eastern liturgical books in their work. With succeeding popes, although the revision was never completely abandoned, the completion of the work was delayed by other business.

When Benedict XIV (1740–1758) was elected pope one of his first concerns was the revision of the Eastern liturgical books, particularly the euchologion of the Greeks. He immediately ordered that the transactions of the congregations that met during the pontificate of Urban VIII and his successors be collected and put in order; he assigned qualified cardinals and consultors to continue the work, which they did for the next ten years. With this strong stimulus from Benedict XIV, the revision of the euchologion was finally published in 1754 by the press of the Congregation for the Propagation of the Faith based on the model of the critical Parisian edition of 1647 edited by the noted Dominican liturgist, Jacques Goar (1601–1653). On March 1, 1756, Benedict sent his encyclical epistle *Ex quo primum* to the bishops of the Greek rite to inform them that the Greek euchologion had been completed after "a lengthy scrutiny of every detail and most careful correction." The letter also gives a brief history of the new edition and explains in detail certain admonitions placed at the beginning of the revised text.

With its principal task fulfilled the Congregation for the Correction of the Eastern Liturgical Books continued its activity with revisions of various liturgical works and such individual tasks as were assigned it, such as the examination of the acts of the Greek-Melchite Synod held in 1806. The congregation ceased to function in 1862 when Pius IX gave the task of revision of all the religious books of the Eastern churches to the new Congregatio de Propaganda Fide pro Negotiis Ritus Orientalis, which he instituted with the constitution *Romani Pontifices* (Jan. 6, 1862), charging it above all to provide for the spiritual needs of Catholics of the Eastern rites.

RECORDS. Records of the congregation consist of the following series.

3.1.32.1 Congregatio super Correctione Librorum Ecclesiae Orientalis (CLO)

[DATABASE ID: VATV20262-A]

Inclusive Dates: 1724–1840.

Bulk: 1 linear m. (13 vols.).

Organization: Volume titles are as follows: 1. Miscellanea de Congregationii sulla correzione de Libri Orientali, vol. 1; — 2. Animadversiones in libros Eccles. Oriental. Pars. I, 1724–1734; —3. Rescripta, tom. III, 1730–1734; —4. Acta, 1730–1734; —5. Acta, 1733–1744; —6. Rescripta, tom. IIII, 1734–1744; —7. Animadversiones in libros Eccles. Oriental. Pars. II, 1734–1744; —8. Rescripta Congregationis Particularibus, 1744–1750; —9. Animadversiones in libros Eccles. Oriental., 1752–1754; —10. Animadversiones in libros Eccles, Oriental., 1766–1819; —11. Cong. . . . libri Orientali condanna dal Sinodo di Karafe di Greci Melchiti, 1834; —12. Originale e copie del messale Arabo de Greci-Melchiti, 1840; —13. Indice congregazioni per la correzione dei libri Orientali.

References: Kowalsky-Metzler, p. 48. O. Raquez, "La Congrégation pour la correction des livres de l'Église orientale (1719–1862)," in *Sacrae Congregationis de Propaganda Fide Memoria Rerum: 350 anni a servizio delle missioni*, edited by J. Metzler (Rome, 1973), vol. 2, pp. 514–534.

Finding Aids: Volume 13 is an "Indice congregazioni per la correzione dei libri Orientali," which is an effective aid in locating materials. This index first presents a summary of the contents of the first twelve volumes and then provides a quasi calendar or detailed summary of each document in volumes 1, 2, 4, 5, and 7–10. These are not presented in the numerical order they are found today, but exact titles are given as listed above. At the end of the "Indice congregazioni" is another indice that approachs these volumes through the different types of "materie" (i.e., business or subject) contained therein.

Location: Archives of the Propaganda Fide.

3.1.33 Congregatio super Disciplina Regulari

[DATABASE ID: VATV138-A]

Innocent XII (1691–1700) had established a cardinalatial commission to evaluate the requests for new foundations of religious houses and the reconstitution of some of those suppressed as well as to make a study of all questions relative to the normal functioning of religious life. He then proceeded to raise the commission to the status of a permanent congregation with the name Congregatio super Disciplina Regulari (constitution *Debitum pastoralis officii*, Aug. 4, 1698).

The new congregation, which replaced the suppressed Congregatio super Statu Regularium, was charged with regulating the internal discipline of religious houses throughout the world with all that concerned the acceptance of candidates, investiture services, behavior of young professed, nullity of vows, transfers and eventual dismissals of religious, and requests for secularization.

Pius VI (constitution *Singulari providentia*, Jan. 5, 1790) defined more precisely the limits of the functions of the congregation in order to settle questions of juridical interference between this Congregation and the Congregation for Bishops and Regulars. Gregory XVI, in 1833, made some effort to settle the question of jurisdiction between the two congregations, but the functions of the Congregation for Regular Discipline declined rapidly.

Pius IX, with a decree of September 7, 1846, proceeded to reorganize the responsibilities of this congregation, dividing them between the Congregation on Regular Discipline and a newly established Congregation on the State of Regular Orders. His encyclical letter *Ubi primum arcanum* (Jun. 17, 1847), sent to the superiors of the various religious orders, stated the reasons for his action.

This congregation carried on its activity until the first years of the twentieth century. Then Pius X (motu proprio *Sacrae Congregationi*, May 26, 1906) suppressed it and transferred its functions to the Congregation of Bishops and Regulars, which was itself suppressed in the curial reform of 1908.

RECORDS. Records of the congregation consist of the following series.

3.1.33.1 Amministrazione
[DATABASE ID: VATV10422-A]
Inclusive Dates: 1845–1864.
Bulk: .25 linear m.
Scope: These brief registers list the protocol number, the agent, and the cost of the service.
Location: Archivio Segreto Vaticano.

3.1.33.2 Audientiae
[DATABASE ID: VATV10415-A]
Inclusive Dates: 1773–1877.
Bulk: 1 linear m. (8 nos.).
Reference: Pásztor (1970), p. 167. Pásztor describes this material differently though it appears to be the *Audientiae.*
Location: Archivio Segreto Vaticano.

3.1.33.3 Capuccini
[DATABASE ID: VATV10429-A]
Inclusive Dates: ca. 1782–1792.
Bulk: .2 linear m. (1 vol.).
Scope: The spine states: "Capuccin. Positio provinciarum S. Iosephi a Leonissa et B. Laurentii a Brindasio."
Location: Archivio Segreto Vaticano.

3.1.33.4 Carte del '800
[DATABASE ID: VATV10427-A]
Inclusive Dates: ca. 1800–1899.
Bulk: .5 linear m. (4 scatole).
Location: Archivio Segreto Vaticano.

3.1.33.5 Decreta
[DATABASE ID: VATV10390-A]
Inclusive Dates: 1656–1906.
Bulk: 88 linear m. (592 numbered buste).
Organization: Two subseries: Nos. 1–51. Congregatio super Statu Regularium; —Nos. 52–592. Congregatio super Disciplina Regularium.
Vols. 1–591 are chronological. Vol. 592 contains material from 1880, 1886, 1890, 1895, 1896, 1898–1905. Vols. 1 and 3 were missing in 1990.
Reference: Pásztor (1970), p. 167.
Finding Aids: ASV Indice 1105 (formerly Indice 113), compiled by Hermann Hoberg, contains a volume-by-volume inventory of the entire series. Entries include the current volume number, inclusive dates, and a few general annotations on busta contents (e.g., which religious orders are represented in selected buste). Most volumes are indexed internally according to religious orders.
E. Boaga, *La soppressione innocenziana dei piccoli conventi in Italia* (Rome, 1971). Boaga provides a historical introduction to the Congregatio super Statu Regularium and volumes 1–23 of the *Decreta* series. Boaga also publishes an inventory of Giovanni Bissaiga (Sept. 24, 1678) now identified as ASV *Miscellaneorum Armarium* VII, n. 116, par. 8. Bissaiga briefly lists volumes 1–23 of the *Decreta* series as CSR 53–76.
Location: Archivio Segreto Vaticano.

3.1.33.6 [Ordini religiosi]
[DATABASE ID: VATV10423-A]
Inclusive Dates: ca. 1695–1800.
Bulk: 3 linear m. (30 scatole).

Organization: Subseries are: Agostiniani; —Agostiniani Scalzi; —Agostiniani di Lombardia; —Barnabiti; —Basiliani; —Benedettini; —Camaldolesi; —Canonici Lateranensi; —Cappuccini; —Celestini; —Certosini; —Carmelitani, carte del '700; —Carmelitani, Prov. S. Alberto in Sicilia; —Carmelitani di Mantova; —Carmelitani scalzi; —Cassinensi; —Cistercienci; —Conventuali; —Domenicani, 1698–1800; —Dottrinari; —Francescani; —Gesuiti; —Girolamitani (Pisa); —Minimi, 1695–1799; —Mercedari; —Montevergini; —Olivetani; —Osservanti, 1695–1799; —Osservanti riformati, 1695–1799; —Serviti '700; —Terz'ordini; —Trinitarii.
Note: This series does not have an official ASV designation. The title was assigned by the project staff.
Location: Archivio Segreto Vaticano.

3.1.33.7 [Ordini religiosi: Nuovo serie]
[DATABASE ID: VATV10441-A]
Inclusive Dates: 1764–1860.
Bulk: 1 linear m.
Organization: 10 scatole. Subseries are: Agostiniani; —Agostiniani scalzi; —Basiliani; —Carmelitani; —Carmelitani scalzi; —Chierici regolari minori; —Conventuali; —Domenicani; —Minimi; —Minori; —Osservanti; —Penitenza; —Regolari (Belgio); —Regolari (Sicilia); —Religioni diverse; —Riformati; —Ritiri; —Serviti; —Scuole pie; —Teatini; —Terz'ordini.
Note: This series has no official ASV designation. The title was assigned by the project staff.
Finding Aids: Many of the scatole contain internal indices.
Location: Archivio Segreto Vaticano.

3.1.33.8 Pendenze
[DATABASE ID: VATV10431-A]
Inclusive Dates: 1834–1872.
Bulk: .5 linear m.
Organization: 7 boxes. The series utilizes numbers 1–15999, but few of the numbers are actually represented in this series.
Reference: Pásztor (1970), p. 167 (note). This series could be a larger version of the "Registro delle suppliche rimesse pro informazione et voto tanto agli ordinari che ai priori generali delle religiosi," 1837–1857 (1 vol.), which Pásztor mentions. He notes that the series numbered 9,586 in 1970. The reference is curious.
Location: Archivio Segreto Vaticano.

3.1.33.9 [Posizione]
[DATABASE ID: VATV10430-A]
Inclusive Dates: 1833–1838.
Bulk: 1 linear m. (9 scatole).
Organization: Files numbered 1–64.
Note: This series does not have an official ASV designation. The title was assigned by the project staff.
Summary: These appear to be fuller case files than the *Pendenze.*
Location: Archivio Segreto Vaticano.

3.1.33.10 Registri
[DATABASE ID: VATV10416-A]
Inclusive Dates: 1653–1834 (bulk 1653–1809).
Bulk: 1 linear m. (23 vols.).

Organization: Subseries are: 1–2. Congregatio super Statu Regularium; —3–23. Congregatio super Disciplina Regularium.

Scope: Volume 1 (Congregatio super Statu Regularium) states "Registro di lettere scritte di ordine della Sagra Congregazione sopra lo Stato di Regolari a diversi Vescovi per la restituzione alle religioni de Conventi suppressi eb altri emergenti concernanti l'istruzione della costituzione della . . . Innocenza."

Reference: Pásztor (1970), p. 167.

Finding Aids: Volumes contain internal alphabetical indices by religious order.

Location: Archivio Segreto Vaticano.

3.1.33.11 [Registri]
[DATABASE ID: VATV10428-A]

Inclusive Dates: 1872–1882, 1884–1906.

Bulk: .25 linear m. (6 vols.).

Organization: Chronological, volumes cover the following dates: 1. 1872–1873; —2. 1874–1882; —3. 1884–1889; —4. 1890–1896; —5. 1896–1900; —6. 1900–1906.

Scope: The title page of the initial volume, 1872–1873 states "Registro delle petizioni e corrispondenze," whereas the title page of the second volume states "Alfabetico registro degli atti e decreti della S. Congregazione sulla Disciplina Regulare concernanti ordini o communità regolari giusta il no. del registro generale dove si annotano tutte le petizioni presentate alla S.C. dal 1 gennaio 1874 in poi fino al. . . ." All the registers, however, follow the same format and provide the same information: number, oratore, object of business, date, informazione, agent, and result.

This series does not have an official ASV designation. The title was supplied by the project staff.

Location: Archivio Segreto Vaticano.

3.1.33.12 Rescritti
[DATABASE ID: VATV10424-A]

Inclusive Dates: 1653–1900.

Bulk: .1 linear m. (1 scatola).

Reference: Pásztor (1970) p. 167.

Location: Archivio Segreto Vaticano.

3.1.33.13 Risposte
[DATABASE ID: VATV10425-A]

Inclusive Dates: ca. 1699–1713.

Bulk: 1 linear m. (10 scatole).

Organization: Box labels for nine volumes are as follows: Agostiniani (including Agostiniani di Lombardia); —Agostiniani Scalzi; —Lettere B–C; —Carmelitani; —Domenicani; —Lettere F–G; —Lettere M–R; —Lettere S–T–V; —Lettere d. trasmissione.

Location: Archivio Segreto Vaticano.

3.1.33.14 Rubricellae
[DATABASE ID: VATV10417-A]

Inclusive Dates: 1698–1910.

Bulk: 3 linear m. (101 vols.).

Organization: Subseries are: 1–96. Rubricellae, 1698–1910; —97–101. Rubricellae segreto "Materiae segreta," 1802–1810.

Volumes are arranged chronologically. Within each volume, the order proceeds chronologically, meeting by meeting.

Religious orders are listed alphabetically under the date of each meeting.

Scope: Entries include the date of the meeting, the religious order concerned, and a summary of the business. The summaries become increasingly brief in the Rubricellae in the nineteenth century, but not in the Rubricellae segreti.

Reference: Pásztor (1970), p. 167.

Location: Archivio Segreto Vaticano.

3.1.33.15 Segreteria
[DATABASE ID: VATV10426-A]

Inclusive Dates: ca. 1700–1876.

Bulk: 1 linear m. (8 boxes).

Organization: Box titles are as follows: 1. Carte varie; —2. Carte varie d.700; —3–4. Appunti-Minute; —5. Foglietti vari; —6. Appunti Mons. DeVico; —7–8. Segreteria (includes Carte G.A. Bizzarri, Carte sciolte for Registra series, and [carte] Card. Denhoff).

Location: Archivio Segreto Vaticano.

3.1.34 Congregatio super Negotiis Extraordinariis Regni Galliarum
[DATABASE ID: VATV020-A]

This congregation was established in 1793 by Pius VI as a special congregation of state. Its activity was suspended in 1799 when the pope was taken captive, but was reconstituted by Pius VII shortly after his election in 1800. In 1805 the congregation was reorganized and renamed Congregatio pro Negotiis Ecclesiasticis Extraordinariis by Pius VII. See the history for the Congregatio pro Negotiis Ecclesiasticis Extraordinariis.

RECORDS. No records for this congregation were located.

3.1.35 Congregatio super Negotiis Sanctae Fidei et Religionis Catholicae
[DATABASE ID: VATV140-A]

Clement VIII established this congregation on August 11, 1599, to replace the Congregatio de Rebus Graecorum. In addition to the responsibility of the former congregation for Greek-rite Catholics and the preservation of the faith of other Christians in the Middle East was added responsibility for the promotion of the Catholic faith in Latin regions, and later also in pagan lands. By 1600 it was referred to as Propaganda Fide. In 1622 Gregory XV replaced it with the Congregatio de Propaganda Fide. The Congregatio super Negotiis Sanctae Fidei et Religionis Catholicae is sometimes referred to as a cardinalatial commission, not a congregation. See the history for the Congregatio de Propaganda Fide.

RECORDS. No records for this congregation were located. See the entry for the Congregatio de Propaganda Fide.

3.1.36 Congregatio super Residentia Episcoporum
[DATABASE ID: VATV147-A]

Because of the neglect of the law of residency by many bishops, the Council of Trent (6th session, Jan. 13,1547) issued a decree of reform. Reviewed by Gregory XIII (1572–1585) and Clement VIII (1592–1605), the Tridentine legislation was updated by Urban VIII and included in his constitution *Sancta synodus Tridentina* (Dec. 12, 1634). Two years later (1636), as Benedict XIV testifies (*constitution Ad universae christianae*, Sept. 3, 1746), Urban established the Congregatio super Residentia Episcoporum.

The congregation was vested with judicial and legislative powers, with authority for treating all questions relative to the obligation of residency of bishops and every other ecclesiastic in possession of a benefice; fixing the terms of their absence from their respective sees; prohibiting their absence except in urgent cases; and renewing the sanctions fixed by the Council of Trent.

Benedict XIV, in his constitution *Ad Universae Christianae* (1746), reorganized the structure of the congregation and expanded its duties. Clement XIII (1759) and Leo XII (1824) also took a particular interest in this congregation. With the curial reform of 1908, Pius X suppressed the Congregation on the Residency of Bishops and transferred its functions to the Consistorial Congregation.

RECORDS. Records of the congregation consist of the following series.

3.1.36.1 Regesta Residentiae Episcoporum
[DATABASE ID: VATV10253-A]
Inclusive Dates: 1625–1650.
Bulk: .5 linear m.
Scope: It is not clear if this series contains six or seven volumes. On the spine of a volume at the end of the Concilii material, a note in blue pencil says "Resid. Epp.orum 1631–165(4?)," which could be a seventh volume of this series. Pásztor acknowledges the volume but places it with the Concilio noting the interconnectedness in the Curia Romana. Because Pásztor's dates contradict the survey by the project staff, it is not entirely clear that this is the same volume. These are more like supplication letters for benefici.

There are five volumes immediately after this series that may relate to this same Congregatio. These volumes are several alphabetical lists of dioceses that seem to act as compiled directories to pensions, canon, and the like in dioceses between 1609 and 1791. These may be the five volumes Pásztor cites as indexes.
Reference: Pásztor (1970), p. 155.
Finding Aids: Regestum Parvum Decretorum S.C. super Residentia Episcoporum, 1708–1843 (5 vols.) is cited by Pásztor as an alphabetical index to dioceses in this series. Although it is a research aid to the Congregatio super Residentia, the ASV series is composed of buste dating between 1625 and 1650 and therefore predates the Regestum Parvum Decretorum of the Congregatio super Residentia, which is still housed in the Archives of the Congregatio per il Clero (Piazza Pio XII, 3, 00193 Rome).
Location: Archivio Segreto Vaticano.

3.1.37 Congregatio super Revisione Synodorum Provincialium
[DATABASE ID: VATV149-A]

This congregation was established by Pius IX (*viva vocis oraculo*, Jun. 3, 1849) for the revision of acts of provincial councils. It was subordinate to the Congregatio Concilii and was abolished in 1908 by Pius X, with its powers assumed by the Congregatio Concilii. It can be found also under the alternate name Congregatio pro Revisione Consiliorum Provincialium.

RECORDS. No records for this congregation were located.

3.1.38 Congregatio super Statu Ecclesiarum
[DATABASE ID: VATV150-A]

Benedict XIV established this congregation in 1740 with the constitution *Decet Romanum Pontificem* (Nov. 23, 1740). The congregation received and examined reports of bishops on the staate of their churches. Pius X transferred its functions to the Consistorial Congregation (constitution *Romanis Pontificibus*, Dec. 17, 1903). See the history for the Congregatio Consistorialis and for the Congregatio Concilii.

RECORDS. No records for this congregation were located.

3.1.39 Congregatio super Statu Regularium
[DATABASE ID: VATV465-A]

This congregation was established by Innocent X with the constitution *Inter cetera* (Dec. 17, 1649) for the reform of religious in Italy. Its task was to examine various aspects of life within each religious house. It was given the faculty of taking opportune measures to eliminate problems and abuses.

The congegation was confirmed and reorganized by Clement IX (constitution *Iniuncti*, Apr. 11, 1668). It was suppressed by Innocent XII (constitution *Debitum pastoralis officii*, Aug. 4, 1698) who at the same time replaced it with the new Congregatio super Disciplina Regulari.

In addition to the records listed below, series listed with other agencies relate directly to this agency and should be consulted. See Congregatio super Disciplina Regulari series *Decreta and Registri*, Segreteria dei brevi series *Cassa: Scatole* and *Indici: Diocesi*, and Miscellaneous official series *Miscellaneorum armarium VIII*.

RECORDS. Records of the congregation consist of the following series.

3.1.39.1 Relationes
[DATABASE ID: VATV10413-A]
Inclusive Dates: ca. 1640–1650.
Bulk: 2.5 linear m. (27 vols.).
Organization: Volumes utilize numbers 1 through 48 but volumes 1–5, 9, 11, 17–19, 21–22, 28–29, 32, 36, 38, 40–41,

44, and 47 are missing. The series is alphabetical by religious order.

Subseries are: Agostiniani; —Agostiniani scalzi; —Barnabiti; —B. Pietro di Pisa; —Camoldolesi; —Canonici regolari; —Capuccini; —Carmelitani di Mantova, Scalzi; —Cassinensi; —Cisterciensi; —Conventuali; —Crociferi; —Domenicani; —Fratebenefratelli; —S. Girolamo di Fiesole; —Mercedarii; —Mercedarii scalzi; —Minimi; —Ministri degli infermi; —Montevergine; —Olivetani; —Osservanti; —Riformati osservanti; —Servi; —Silvestrini; —Somaschi; —Teatini; —Valle Ombrosa.

Scope: The *Relationes* provide a good picture of monastic life during the mid-seventeenth century. Many religious houses in different orders are described, sometimes with elaborate histories that regularly go back to the fifteenth century and occasionally begin in the thirteenth century.

Finding Aids: E. Boaga, *La soppressione innocenziana dei piccoli conventi in Italia* (Rome, 1971). This work provides a general historical introduction to this series and reproduces a seventeenth-century (Sept. 24, 1678) inventory by Giovanni Bissaiga, which still serves as the only index to the *Relationes*. The volume numbers listed in the reproduced Bissaiga index are still valid and missing volumes are indicated. The current volume number of the Bissaiga inventory is *Misc. Arm. VII*, n. 116, par. 8.

Location: Archivio Segreto Vaticano.

3.1.39.2 Varia

[DATABASE ID: VATV10414-A]
Inclusive Dates: 1653–1689.
Bulk: 1.5 linear m. (14 boxes or buste).
Organization: Materials are divided into seventeen numerical divisions. Subseries divisions include: 1–2. Lettere de vescovi (A–L and L–V); —9–10. Registri di lettere, 1655–1661, 1661–1667; —11. Scripturae divers. al ordinum a lett A–C; —12. Scripturae divers. pro PP. Minor Convent. S. Francisci; —13. Scripturae divers. PP. Minor Observant. et Observat. Reformi.; —14. Scripturae PP. Divers. Ord. D–V; —15. Scripturae divers. per dioceses dispositae A; —16. Scripturae divers. per dioceses dispositae B–M; —17. Scripture divers. per dioceses dispositae N–Z.
Note: Vols. 1 and 2 are available on microfilm.
Finding Aids: E. Boaga, *La soppressione innocenziana dei piccoli conventi in Italia* (Rome, 1971). This work provides a general historical introduction related to this series and reproduces a seventeenth-century (Sept. 24, 1678) inventory by Giovanni Bissaiga, which briefly lists *Varia* volumes currently identified as 1 and 2 (CSR 109 and 110). The current volume number of the Bissaiga inventory is *Misc. Arm. VII*, n. 116, par. 8.
Location: Archivio Segreto Vaticano.

3.1.40 Congregatio super Statu Regularium Ordinum

[DATABASE ID: VATV137-A]

Pius IX, with a decree of September 7, 1846, divided the duties of the Congregation on Regular Discipline (Congregatio super Disciplina Regulari) between that congregation and a new Congregatio super Statu Regu-

larium Ordinum. His encyclical letter *Ubi primum arcanum* (Jun. 17, 1847), sent to the superiors of the various religious orders, stated the reasons for his action. The new congregation was responsible for preparation of rules for novices and regulations for community life in keeping with modern circumstances.

The congregation was suppressed as an independent congregation by Pius X's motu proprio *Sacrae Congregationi* (May 26, 1906). It was combined with the Congregation for Bishops and Regulars. See the history for the Congregatio Negotiis et Consultationibus Episcoporum et Regularium Praeposita.

RECORDS. Records of the congregation consist of the following series.

3.1.40.1 Consultazioni

[DATABASE ID: VATV10420-A]
Inclusive Dates: 1847–1866.
Bulk: .5 linear m. (6 boxes).
Organization: Organized in positioni, I–XIV.
Scope: This series contains information both historical and contemporary concerning monasteries in the mid-nineteenth century.
Reference: Pásztor (1970), pp. 168–169.
Location: Archivio Segreto Vaticano.

3.1.40.2 Dispense dei decreti

[DATABASE ID: VATV10433-A]
Inclusive Dates: ca. 1848–1861.
Bulk: .2 linear m. (2 boxes).
Organization: Organized according to "posizioni" 1–45, which apparently stand for religious orders as the files are alphabetical by religious order. Not all religious orders or posizioni numbers are represented.
Reference: Pásztor (1970), p. 169.
Location: Archivio Segreto Vaticano.

3.1.40.3 Miscellanea I

[DATABASE ID: VATV10432-A]
Inclusive Dates: ca. 1848–1867.
Bulk: .5 linear m. (4 boxes).
Organization: Organized according to numbers 1–563 with an appendice (numbers 511–558).
Scope: These are various supplications with minute of responses on verso from members of diverse religious orders.
Reference: Pásztor (1970), pp. 168–169.
Finding Aids: In the soffittone (V/1) there is a volume entitled "Rubric, 1866–1902 (22); Speciale Super Statum Reg." that serves as an alphabetical index to religious orders in *Miscellanea I*. Entries are arranged alphabetically by religious order. Each entry indicates the volume number (posizione number within the *Miscellanea I*), a brief note concerning the business and occasionally references to related material in the *Miscellanea I*.
Location: Archivio Segreto Vaticano.

3.1.40.4 Miscellanea II

[DATABASE ID: VATV10436-A]
Inclusive Dates: 1826–1900.
Bulk: 1 linear m. (9 boxes).
Organization: Subseries are: Agostiniani; —Alcantarini; —

Basiliani; —Barnabiti; —Benedettini; —Benefratelli; —Ca-maldolesi; —Canonici regolari; —Capuccini; —Carmelitani calzati; —Carmelitani scalzi; —Cassinesi; —Celliti; —Certo-sini; —Chierici regolari minori; —Cistercenci; —Cong. S. Cuore; —Ordini S. Croce; —Conventuali; —Domenicane; —Domenicani; —Dottrinari; —Gerosalimitani; —Girolamini; —Liguorini; —Mercedari; —Minimi; —Ministri degli infermi; —Cong. di missioni; —Oblati di Maria; —Olivetani; —Oratoriani; —Osservanti; —Osservanti recolletti; —Osser-vanti minori riformati; —Passionisti; —Padre d. Penitenza; —Premonstratensi; —"Regolari"; —Salvatoriani; —Scuole di Carita; —Scuole pie; —Serviti; —Silvestrini; —Somaschi; —Teatini; —Terz'ordini; —Trappisti; —Trinitari scalzi; —Val-lombrosani.

Reference: Pásztor (1970), pp. 168–169.
Location: Archivio Segreto Vaticano.

3.1.40.5 Novizi ammessi
[DATABASE ID: VATV10434-A]
Inclusive Dates: 1848–1867.
Bulk: .2 linear m. (2 boxes).
Organization: Chronological.
Scope: This series contains information regarding novices from many religious orders and includes lists of novices from the orders.
Location: Archivio Segreto Vaticano.

3.1.40.6 Progetti di riforma
[DATABASE ID: VATV10435-A]
Inclusive Dates: ca. 1848–1854.
Bulk: .1 linear m. (1 box).
Organization: Two small subseries: Studi; —Suppliche.
Reference: Pásztor (1970), pp. 168–169.
Location: Archivio Segreto Vaticano.

3.1.40.7 Relazioni
[DATABASE ID: VATV10419-A]
Inclusive Dates: 1847–1852.
Bulk: 1.5 linear m. (13 boxes and 1 busta).
Organization: Three subseries: Vescovi, 1847–1852, nos. 10–101, 5.5 boxes; —Nunzi, 1847, 1 folder; —Superiori, 1847–1852, nos. 1–60, 7 boxes and 1 busta; The Nunzi sub-series includes materials from: Florence, Lucerne, Bogotá, Paris, Munich, Turin, and Vienna. The Superiori is organized alphabetically by religious order.
Note: Vols. 14, 16, 24, 30, 31, 37, 39, 42, 43, 45, and 48 are available on microfilm.
Reference: Pásztor (1970), pp. 168–169.
Location: Archivio Segreto Vaticano.

3.1.40.8 Segreteria, 1840–1847
[DATABASE ID: VATV10421-A]
Bulk: .2 linear m. (2 boxes).
Scope: Both boxes contain primarily decreti. However, box 2 contains solely a register of "Decretum," 1846–1847.
Reference: Pásztor (1970), pp. 168–169.
Location: Archivio Segreto Vaticano.

3.1.41 Congregatio Visitationis Apostolicae
[DATABASE ID: VATV468-A]

In order to understand the significance of this institu-tion, it is necessary to recall the specific duty that every bishop had to visit his own diocese personally or to send a delegate. The visit was supposed to assure the bishop of the exact observance of ecclesiastical discipline (Council of Terragon, 1234). Nicholas V (1452) realizing that these visits were losing their character and usefulness, required periodic visitations to make them more effective. The need was also emphasized in the reforms of the Council of Trent (sess. 24, cap. 3, de reform., Nov. 11, 1563).

It is stated in the life of Gregory XIII that he wished to visit all the dioceses of Christianity, especially those in Italy. For this purpose the pontiff established (1572) a special commission of cardinals to study the difficulties that might stand in the way. The actual institution of the Congregazione della Sagra Visita Apostolica di Roma e Suo Distretto was, however, due to the zeal of Clement VIII. With the constitution *Speculatores domus Israel* (Jun. 8, 1592) he established a special congregation of cardinals to implement and maintain this work.

Only in 1624 under the pontificate of Urban VIII (1623–1644) did this office assume the name Congre-gatio Visitationis Apostolicae with the task of visiting the churches, convents, and other holy places of Rome. The congregation, according to De Luca, was not "re-ally papal for the entire Catholic Church, or for some provinces, but especially for the bishops of Rome" since the cardinal members would carry out by papal delega-tion the pastoral visitation of the Roman diocese. This duty belonged to the pope, as bishop of Rome, but mak-ing the visitations himself would have interfered with his greater obligation of universal governance.

The duties of the congregation were clearly defined by Alexander VII with his brief *Quoniam in prosequendo* (Jan. 16, 1656) and extended almost immediately with another brief, *Cum in pastorali visitatione* (Jan. 22, 1656). Then with two successive briefs of the same date he assigned to the congregation two new officials with specific functions as secretary (*Rerum quae nobis*) and as chancellor (*De singulari tua fide*). These and three other documents within the same month and another two months later (*Alias nos nonnullos*, Mar. 13, 1656) were issued rapidly because of the controversies arising in regard to the visitations. Most of these changes were those of personnel.

More important innovations were introduced by In-nocent XII in 1693. Besides extending greatly the au-thority of the congregation, he added to it civil, crimi-nal, and mixed cases, and ordered that no one subject to a visitation could evade it because of exemption or privi-lege (*Quoniam in prosequendo*, and *Cum in pastorali visitatione*, Jan. 16, 1693).

On September 1, 1818, Pius VII decreed that for some questions, such as the reduction of masses, the handling of pious legacies or any eventual modification of them, the authority of the Congregazione della Visita would be merged with that of the Congregazione della Reverenda Fabbrica di S. Pietro.

The Congregatio Visitationis Apostolicae ceased to function in 1908. The *Normae Peculiares* published on September 29, 1908, three months after the publication of the constitution *Sapienti consilio* and appended to it, appointed a new commission of the same name to take the place of the congregation with all its rights and functions. The function of this commission included making an annual visitation to the churches of Rome, inquiring into the fulfillment of the endowed masses and other pious foundations, and examining the financial condition of the churches and institutions of the city. The functions of this commission, limited as they were to the city of Rome, are altogether distinct from those of the Consistorial Congregation, which has the function of directing apostolic visitations in other parts of the Catholic world.

Like the documents concerning pastoral visits carried out elsewhere, the documents generated by this congregation offer fascinating views into the ritual and material life of monasteries, oratories, parish churches, and the churches of cardinals, bishops, and religious orders. As sources for the state of parishes and diocese, visits have much in common with the "relations ad limina" and the acts of local synods (see S. Congregatio Concilii). The contents of visits vary widely and depend greatly on how the cardinal or commissioner conducting the visit approached his job. Some were rather dry bureaucrats, who have left us simply lists of the location and condition of doors, windows, and liturgical furnishings inside a church; from him we may also learn what the priest reported as his age, his income, or the number of students studying catechism with him. Others render their point of view in strong autobiographical tones, allowing us to see them as they shake a broken door, or traipse around a neighborhood interrogating residents in an effort to track down the parish priest. While some are mainly concerned with administrative or sacramental affairs, others display a keen concern for the physical setting, describing altarpieces, the condition and subject of frescoes, and details pertaining to all aspects of decoration and architecture. Music, musical instruments, and theatrical activities are important to some. Others emphasize economic matters. Finally, attitudes may range from the sternly disciplinary to the magnanimous and protective. Many visits combine to some degree various of the above features. The visitor's point of view can be as revealing as the observations conveyed by it.

In addition to the records listed below, series listed with another agency relate directly to this agency and should be consulted. See Miscellaneous official series *Miscellaneorum armarium VII.*

RECORDS. Records of the congregation consist of the following series.

3.1.41.1 Visite apostoliche
[DATABASE ID: VATV281-A]
Inclusive Dates: 1564–1918.
Bulk: 45 linear m. (339 numbered vols.).
Organization: Subseries include (numbers supplied by project staff): 1. Atti e decreti, 1564–1918; —2. Suppliche (Petitiones cum rescriptis), 1800–1866; —3. Acta tabellionum; —4. Testamenti olografi, 1738–1836; —5. Fogli di udienza, 1802–1913; —6. Indice alfabetico delle S. Visite di Urbano VIII, Alessandro VII e Clement XI, 1624, 1659, e 1700; —7. Indice alfabetico delle S. Visite di Leone XII, 1824–1825; —8. Indici delle tabelle, 1853–1865. The Suppliche (Petitiones cum rescriptis) are chronological. The fogli d'udienza are chronological.
Scope: These are reports of visits to parishes, chapels, hospitals, oratorios, religious houses, conservatori, and the like. Benefactors are often listed in the Tabellae subseries. Books from which information was taken during a visit are also listed. The Tabellae subseries appears to deal exclusively with Roman pious institutions.
Reference: Fink, p. 144.
Finding Aids: ASV Indice 1145, prepared by Sergio Pagano, is the most modern index to the collection. The index calendars all visits in the Acta and then calendars only visits in Rome or provides a summary for the remaining volumes. The index omits the Suppliche (Petitiones cum rescriptis) volumes (numbers 151–192), which are calendared in Indice 1117, and only briefly mentions the Acta Tabellionum (volumes 193–249). Entries include the volume number, title, inclusive dates, and a list of visits. If the visits are numbered, this is also noted.

S. Pagano, "Le visite apostoliche a Roma nei secoli XVI–XIX," *Ricerche per la storia religiosa di Roma* 4 (1980): 317–464. This work duplicates information found in Indice 1045 but has a number of added features, including an introduction, a comprehensive index to all churches, confraternities, visitors, and so forth (so that in one place all the visits to certain Roman churches can be located) and a thorough list of all the possible locations to look for visitations.

Volume 9 of the collection "Indice delle S. Visite di Urbano VIII, Alessandro VII e Clemente XI" indexes the previous volumes 2–7 alphabetically by geographic location and visitor. ASV Indice 1117 lists all of the subseries, provides a busta-by-busta listing for the Fogli d'udienza and the Suppliche (Petitiones cum rescriptis), and then calendars the forty buste of the Suppliche (Petitiones cum rescriptis) and the one busta of the Petitiones Sanctissimo Relatae. Index entries include the busta number, the packet number, the item number within the packet, name of the petitioner (often given as "Priore e Religiosi di . . ."), and the town.

ASV Indice 1144 provides an index to visits to Roman parishes around the years 1700 and 1825. The format is: parish, tabella, visite del 1700, visite del 1825, miscellanea. Parishes are organized alphabetically. The tabella column refers to and indexes the tabellae onerum missarum, buste 278–325. The visite del 1700 column refers to visits around the year 1700 and is an old index to the miscellanea 1700 buste 97–130. This section of index 1144 is out of date and Indice 1145 should be used to access this section of the series. The visite del 1825 column refers to visits around 1825 and indexes the miscellanea 1825, buste 131–150. The miscellanea column indexes the subseries by that name, buste 56–96. This index is most effectively used in conjunction with indice 1145.

A series of ASV prospetti indici in a folder entitled "Visite Apostoliche: Vescovi e Regolari e Concilio" are available on request at the desk in the main ASV reading room. These prospetti indici include numerical indices (brief busta by busta listings) of the Vescovi e Regolari, *Visite apostoliche* 1–17, and the Congregatio Concilio (which has been superseded by ASV Indice 1154). Two other prospetti indici, however, pertain more directly to the Cong. Visitationis Apostolicae: Prospetto cronologico and Prospetto alfabetico. These chronological and alphabetical prospetti provide integrated lists of apostolic visits from the Cong. Visitationis Apostolicae series *Visite apostoliche* (this series); the Cong. Vescovi e Regolari series *Visite apostoliche*; and the Cong. Concilio series *Visite apostoliche*. Cong. Visitationis Apostolicae *Visite apostolicae* items are identified in the prospetti with an "A," a roman numeral, and an arabic numeral (eg. A VIII, 2). These prospetti are not official finding aids of the ASV and thus must be used in consultation with ASV staff.

Location: Archivio Segreto Vaticano.

3.1.41.2 Visite ospedale Roma
[DATABASE ID: VATV10170-A]

Inclusive Dates: 1714–1830 (bulk 1800–1830).

Bulk: 2 linear m. (84 numbered buste and vols.).

Finding Aids: ASV Indice 1078 provides a good introduction and calendars the entire collection. Entries include the volume or busta number, the pagination, inclusive dates, and a description of each item.

S. Pagano, "Le visite apostoliche a Roma nei secoli XVI–XIX," *Ricerche per la storia religiosa di Roma* 4 (1980): 317–464, provides a useful introduction to the Congregation and visitations. This article also contains an index at the end which assists in locating all materials in a variety of ASV series that contain information on visits to hospitals in Rome.

Location: Archivio Segreto Vaticano.

3.1.42 Congregazione degli spogli
[DATABASE ID: VATV867-A]

This was a cameral congregation established to regulate the succession of benefices of deceased ecclesiastics and of cardinals elected pope. (See "Camera Apostolica.")

RECORDS. Records of the congregation consist of the following series.

3.1.42.1 Congregazione degli spogli
[DATABASE ID: VATV20030-A]

Inclusive Dates: 1685–1773.

Bulk: 196 vols. and registri.

Reference: D'Angiolini, pp. 1092–1093.

Finding Aids: Old partial inventory; summary inventory.

Location: Archivio di Stato di Roma.

3.1.43 Congregazione sopra l'Elezione dei Vescovi
[DATABASE ID: VATV788-A]

According to Giovanni Cardinal De Luca, Innocent XI (1676–1689) established this office, assigning it the task of proposing names for vacant episcopal sees. These nominations were to be made only after the congregation had made a thorough examination of the merits and qualifications of the candidates. Over a period of time, however, the congregation became inactive and fell into disuse.

Benedict XIV, convinced of the great need for qualified men for the governance of the dioceses, reestablished the congregation with the constitution *Ad apostolicae servitutis* (Oct. 17, 1740), giving it the official name Congregatio Particularis super Promovendis ad Archiepiscopatus et Episcopatus. See the history for the Congregatio Particularis super Promovendis ad Archiepiscopatus et Episcopatus.

RECORDS. No records for this congregation were located.

3.2
OFFICES

3.2.1 Abbreviatores Apostolici de Curia
[DATABASE ID: VATV143-A]

Within the Apostolic Datary there existed a specialized office for the dispatch of certain bulls composed by the cardinal pro-datarius, by the abbreviatore di curia, by a substitute, or by a secret writer (per viam secretam). The dispatch of these bulls was called *per viam de curia*.

The term *via de Curia* refers to a method of expedition or handling of pontifical letters, which were prepared according to the form of bulls. The redaction or preparation of bulls (per viam de Curia) was entrusted to the abbreviator of the Curia, whose responsibilities were purely executive and who received his instructions from various departments at whose command the bull was to be sent. In the modern period, the abbreviator was under the authority of the pro-datario. The term *per viam de Curia* generally indicates bulls issued in the interest of various departments of the Roman Curia, or of the pope. These bulls principally concerned issues of dogma, condemnation of doctrinal error, censorship of institutions, undertakings or sects; ratification of agreements, ratification of canonizations of saints, ratification of major excommunications, interdicts and absolutions. These bulls also deal with disciplinary rules, particularly pertaining to episcopacies, dioceses, and nations—dispositions or decisions regarding ecclesiastical discipline, suspension from office or benefice, general decisions or constitutions regarding important ecclesiastical affairs and also civil affairs.

Those bulls dispatched from this office of the abbreviatori di Curia pertained to papal laws and constitutions, concerned such actions as the canonizations of saints and other motu proprio matters of the pope (such as the bull promulgating a Holy Year).

Bulls regarding relatives of the pope or others receiving very special favors were also prepared in this office. In order to avoid drawing attention to the beneficiaries, these particular bulls were given to a scrittore, who was called a scrittore segreto. After the customary seal of the Apostolic Chancery was affixed, the bulls were subscribed by the abbreviatore di Curia, by the cardinal pro-datarius, and by the secretary of briefs, and then registered in the Secretariat.

The office of abbreviator originated some time during the Middle Ages, but gained great power and importance during the period of the popes' residence at Avignon (1309–1378), when the number of benefices conferred through the Curia greatly increased. With the development of the Datary in the early fifteenth century and the Secretariat of Briefs in 1502, the work of the abbreviators declined and their numbers were reduced.

The constitution *Sapienti consilio* (Jun. 29, 1908) of Pius X suppressed the abbreviatores. Their responsibility for signing apostolic bulls was transferred to the college of apostolic protonotaries.

References. H. Bresslau, *Handbuch der Urkundenlehre für Deutschland und Italien* (Berlin, 1958–1968). Giuseppe Dell'Aquila-Visconti, *Del prelato abbreviatore de Curia sinossi istorica e catalogo cronologico dal 1382 al 1870* (Rome, 1870). G. G. Ciampini, *Abbreviatoris de Curia Compendiaria Notitia* (Rome, 1696). G. G. Ciampini, *De Abbreviatorum de parco maiori, sive Assistentium S.R.E. vicecancellario in litterarum apostolicarum expeditionibus antiquo statu, illorumve in collegium erectione, munere, dignitate, praerogativis ac privilegiis dissertatio historica* (Rome, 1691). E. Fournier, "Abréviateurs," in *Dictionnaire de droit canonique,* edited by R. Naz (Paris, 1935), vol. 1, pp. 98–106. T. Frenz, "Abbreviator," in *Lexikon des Mittelalters* (Munich, 1980), vol. 1, pp. 16–17. T. Frenz, "Die 'computi' in der Serie der Brevia Lateranensia im Vatikanischen Archiv," *Quellen und Forschungen aus italienischen Archiven und Bibliotheken* 55–56 (1976): 251–275. W. von Hofmann, *Forschungen zur Geschichte der kurialen Behörden vom Schisma bis zur Reformation* (Rome, 1914). B. Katterbach, "Archivio Vaticano," in *Enciclopedia italiana* (Rome, 1929), vol. 4, pp. 88–90. B. Schwarz, "Die Abbreviatoren unter Eugen IV: Päpstliches Reservationsrecht, Konkordatspolitik, und kuriale Aemterorganisation," *Quellen und Forschungen aus italienischen Archiven und Bibliotheken* 60 (1980): 200–274. B. Schwarz, "Abbreviature Officium est Assistere Vicecancellario in Expeditione Litterarum Apostolicarum: Zur Entwicklung des Abbreviatorenamtes vom Grossen

Schisma bis zur Gründung des Vakabilistenkollegs der Abbreviatoren durch Pius II," in *Römische Kurie, kirchliche Finanzen, vatikanisches Archiv: Studien zu Ehren von Hermann Hoberg* (Rome, 1979), pp. 789–823. B. Schwarz, "Ämterkäuflichkeit eine Institution des Absolutismus und ihre mittelalterlichen Wurzeln," in *Staat und Gesellschaft in Mittelalter und Früher Neuzeit: Gedenkschrift für Joachim Leuschner* (Göttingen, 1983), pp. 176–196. B. Schwarz, "Der Corrector litterarum apostolicarum: Entwicklung des Korrektorenamtes in der päpstlichen Kanzlei von Innozenz III. bis Martin V.," *Quellen und Forschungen aus italienischen Archiven und Bibliotheken* 54 (1974): 122–191. B. Schwarz, *Die Organisation kurialer Schreiberkollegien von ihrer Entstehung bis zur Mitte des 15. Jahrhunderts* (Tübingen, 1972).

RECORDS. Records of the office consist of the following series. (Note that the records for the abbreviatores apostolici de curia consist of personal registers [minutes of bullae and motu proprios]. At the ASV they form one consecutively numbered series described in ASV Index 1061. Because they are in reality four distinct groups, each of the groups is described in this guide as a separate series.)

3.2.1.1 Appendix positionum
[DATABASE ID: VATV10100-A]
Inclusive Dates: 1744–1809, 1814–1870.
Bulk: .5 linear m. (6 vols.).
Organization: Vols. are numbered 32–37 and are chronological.
References: Pásztor (1970), p. 60; Boyle, p. 55; Fink, pp. 72–73.
Location: Archivio Segreto Vaticano.

3.2.1.2 Miscellanea manuscritti e constitutionum
[DATABASE ID: VATV10087-A]
Inclusive Dates: 1737–1752.
Bulk: .25 m. (3 vols.).
Organization: Subseries include: Miscellanea MSS, 2 vols. (vol. 1, 3); —Miscellanea constitutionum, 1 vol. (vol. 4). Vol. 2 was missing in 1990.
Scope: This series contains written and printed versions of documents, including epistole, istruzioni, encyclicals, and constitutions. Earlier volumes are arranged by case number within a given year; this case number can be used to refer to items in the other abbreviatore series.
References: Pásztor (1970), p. 60; Boyle, p. 55; Fink, pp. 72–73.
Finding Aids: ASV Indice 1061 gives the exact title of each volume and lists the documents in each volume.
Location: Archivio Segreto Vaticano.

3.2.1.3 Registrum bullarum et motu proprio (Registrum autographum litterarum apostolicum)
[DATABASE ID: VATV10098-A]
Inclusive Dates: 1735–1809, 1814–1906.
Bulk: 1.5 linear m. (16 vols. and one small packet).
Organization: Volumes are numbered 5–21. They are chronological, except for vol. 21 (1860s).

Scope: These may be formal archival copies of the abbreviator. In any case they are mostly formal written copies, although earlier volumes do contain printed copies and drafts of bulls and motu proprios. This material is directly related to the other abbreviatore series: *Miscellanea, Registrum privatum*, and *Appendix positionum*.

References: Boyle, p. 55; Pásztor (1970), p. 59; Fink, pp. 72–73.

Finding Aids: ASV Indice 1061 gives the full title of each volume and calendars documents, noting which materials are printed, in each volume through vol. 17. It does not list the last packet. Note that there is a variant title on later volumes (as noted in Pásztor): *Registrum autographum litterarum apostolicum*.

Location: Archivio Segreto Vaticano.

3.2.1.4 Registrum privatum litterarum apostolicarum per viam de curia expeditarum

[DATABASE ID: VATV10099-A]

Inclusive Dates: 1735–1809, 1814–1908.

Bulk: 1.5 linear m. (10 vols.).

Organization: Volumes are numbered 22–31 and are chronological.

Scope: The series begins with primarily printed documents drafted by the abbreviator. Later in the series it becomes less formal and contains mostly written drafts. Numbers on cases relate to, or are copies of, materials in other Abbreviatores Apostolici de Curia series including *Registrum bullarum, Miscellanea*, and *Appendix positionum*. The first volume (vol. 22) is particularly interesting because it contains an 1857 copy of a 1735 document discussing the functions of the abbreviator as well as information on how different processes in various curial offices work (e.g., canonization and legal protocols), which would be important for the abbreviator to understand in order to fulfill his office. There is an index at the beginning of vol. 22 only.

References: Boyle, p. 55; Pásztor (1970), pp. 59–60; Fink, pp. 72–73.

Location: Archivio Segreto Vaticano.

3.2.2 Audientia Litterarum Contradictarum

[DATABASE ID: VATV037-A]

This Audientia is an old institution of the Roman Curia, and originally belonged to the Apostolic Chancery. It flourished from the thirteenth century to the sixteenth century, when it was replaced by the creation of the Signatura Gratiae et Iustitiae.

The function of this Audientia was to hear cases referred to the pope, and to hear judicial or administrative cases involving indults, privileges, or dispensations. Letters of justice were published by being read in this Audientia, and they could be protested here.

The head of the Audientia, the auditor contradictarum, was, after the thirteenth century, one of the ordinary judges of the Roman Curia. However, he was at the same time a functionary of the Apostolic Chancery. His task was to regulate and systematize the dispatch of papal letters. He also worked to ensure the more technical and precise expression of canon law, distinguishing between what was appropriate to judicial functions and to administrative functions.

The apostolic rescripts fell into two large categories of affairs: litterae de gratia and litterae de iustitia. The essential difference between the two categories was that the former had to be approved and signed by the pope while the others were dispatched by the vice-chancellor or a notary of the chancery.

References. G. Barraclough, "Audientia litterarum contradictarum," in *Dictionnaire de droit canonique*, edited by R. Naz (Paris, 1935), vol. 1, pp. 1387–1399. P. Herde, *Audientia litterarum contradictarum: Untersuchungen über die päpstlichen Justizbriefe und die päpstliche Delegationsgerichtsbarkeit vom 13. bis zum Beginn des 16. Jahrhunderts* (Tübingen, 1970). P. Herde, *Beiträge zum päpstlichen Kanzlei- und Urkundenwesen im dreizehnten Jahrhundert* (Kallmünz, 1967). P. Herde, "Ein Formelbuch Gerhards von Parma mit Urkunden des Auditor Litterarum Contradictarum aus dem Jahre 1277," *Archiv für Diplomatik, Schriftengeschichte, Siegel- und Wappenkunde* 13 (1967): 225–312. P. Herde, "Papal Formularies for Letters of Justice (13th–16th Centuries): Their Development and Significance for Medieval Canon Law," in *Proceedings of the Second International Congress of Medieval Canon Law*, edited by S. Kuttner and J. J. Ryan (Vatican City, 1965), pp. 321–346. P. Herde, "Zur Audientia litterarum contradictarum und zur 'Reskripttechnik,'" *Archivalische Zeitschrift* 69 (1973): 54–90. J. E. Sayers, "Canterbury Proctors at the Court of the Audientia Litterarum Contradictarum," *Traditio* 22 (1966): 311–345. J. Teige, *Beiträge zur Geschichte der Audientia litterarum contradictarum* (Prague, 1897).

RECORDS. No records of this office were located in the ASV. Boyle (pp. 67–68) notes that there is a link between this office and the Dataria Apostolica series *Registra contradictarum*.

3.2.3 Camera Apostolica

[DATABASE ID: VATV034-A]

The Apostolic Camera, one of the oldest of the offices of the Roman Curia, was originally responsible for the administration of all the revenue and temporal holdings of the Holy See. Although the term *camera* appeared for the first time in Benedict VIII's constitution *Quoties illa a Nobis* (May 24, 1017), some authors state it was the continuation of an office that had existed and been known for a long time as Palatium or Fiscus under the direction of the archdeacon who remained at the head of the Camera domini papae until the suppression of the position in 1073 by Gregory VII. In the twelfth century the head of this administration was called the camerarius or chamberlain and the office absorbed the functions of the vestiarius (who took care of the sacred vessels and treasures of the church), the arcarius (who administered papal finances from at least 599), and the sacellarius (who took care of expenses from about 700).

In the thirteenth century the chamberlain was a cardinal, but when the *servitia communia*, a tax for the appointment of bishops and abbots, began to be shared by the cardinals and the pope, two chief fiscal officials were needed. The College of Cardinals was served by a cardinal-camerarius, while the fourteenth-century popes appointed a succession of archbishops to the office of camerarius apostolicus. This powerful officer was in effect a minister of finance and prime minister. The Camera Apostolica under the direction of several talented chamberlains developed efficient methods of administration and record-keeping that were imitated by other European monarchies. The various registers of the Camera from the Avignon period are very rich, recording the fiscal activity of the department and its regional agents the collectors, and also the judicial work of the auditor of the Camera and of the chamberlain himself. By virtue of a generous commission, *Apostolicae Camerae*, granted by Innocent VI (6 December 1361) and repeated by his successors, a chamberlain had absolute, final, summary jurisdiction in any cause that he considered to involve the interest of the Camera.

The chamberlain's subordinates in the fourteenth-century Camera, the auditor, the treasurer, and some six clerks, constituted an informal cameral council. Eugene IV fixed the number of clerici Camerae at seven (constitution *Inter cetera gravia*, Jul. 11, 1438) and gave them the statutes of a college (*In eminenti*, Jul. 6, 1444). Pius V raised their number to twelve (*Romanus Pontifex*, Mar. 7, 1571); Gregory XIII reduced it to eight; Sixtus V increased it to ten, then twelve. From Leo XIII on, there were nine. From this college of chierici developed the posts of vice-camerlengo (later also governor of Rome); auditor general (with functions chiefly judiciary); and treasurer general (charged with all financial activities of the papacy).

The auditor's office attained such importance that to refer to it one had only to use the initials A.C. (Auditor Camerae). This office remained unaltered even after the reform of Pius IV in 1562 and of Clement VIII in 1596. For a short time, nevertheless, in the middle of the sixteenth century, the office of auditor was suppressed by Paul IV who substituted for it a new position of regent (constitution *Si ex praecepto*, 1558), with the same powers and faculties of the camerlengo and the vice-camerlengo. The position of regent lasted but a short time; it was suppressed by Pius IV (constitution *Romano Pontifex*, Apr. 14, 1561). At the same time the office of auditor general was reinstated with all its former powers (constitution *Ad examiae devotionis*, May 1, 1561).

For a certain time, under Benedict XIV (1740–1758), the general treasurer took to himself the task of supervising all the pontifical customs (tolls), the fortress of the Castel Sant'Angelo, and the general commissary of the sea. Later these tasks were withdrawn and the authority of the office was confined to economic matters.

Leo X in his constitution *Etsi pro cunctarum* (Jun. 28, 1514) clarified the functions of the camerarius, now commonly called camerlengo, in civil and penal matters. Shortly thereafter the Camera assumed responsibility for public security. More was added in the second half of the fifteenth century. These latter assignments were subsumed in the title *governor of Rome*. This title reflected a general set of responsiblities that had been true in practice from the beginning but had never been formally established. Sixtus V issued procedural norms for the office in *Sublimi beati* (Dec. 1, 1587).

By the seventeenth century the Camera had become less a ministry of finance for the broad interests of the Holy See and more a ministry of public works and general administration for Rome and the Papal States. It was in charge of the papal army, public works, agriculture, mining, archaeological excavations, food provisions for cities, and supervision of the police force.

Pius VII, at first with his constitution *Post diuturnas* (Sept. 30, 1800), which reorganized the administrative structure of the Papal States, then with two motu proprios (Jul. 6, 1816 and Nov. 22, 1817), restricted the various functions of the Camera. This began the gradual decline in the power of the department once so central to the Holy See. Its functions were further limited by Gregory XVI's *Regolamento legislativo e giudiziario e negli affari civili* (Nov. 10, 1834). With his motu proprio of June 12, 1847, Pius IX set up the Consiglio dei ministri and called on the camerlengo to take overall responsibility for commerce, fine arts, industry, and agriculture. But by February 1848 the pope, because of political pressure, had to return full authority to the ministers of these areas.

With the pope's loss of temporal power over the Papal States in 1870 whatever remained of the administrative authority of the the Camera over those territories was lost. For the camerlengo, there remained only the functions to be exercised during the Sede Vacante (the period between the death of one pope and the election of another). Gregory X with his constitution *Ubi periculum* (Jul. 7, 1274) had decreed that the chamberlain should not leave his office during the Sede Vacante. This decree was confirmed later by Clement V (constitution *Ne Romani*, 1311) and again by Pius IV (constitution *In elegendis*, Oct. 9, 1562).

After the dissolution of the Papal States, Pius IX entrusted the administration of all remaining temporal holdings and goods of the Holy See to the prefect of the Apostolic Palace (chirograph, Dec. 18, 1876). In 1878, so that the chierici of the Camera would not remain inactive because of the changed territorial conditions of the Holy See, Leo XIII decreed that their college would form the first section of prelates attached to the Congregation of the Council charged with the revision of the quinquennial reports on the general state of the dioceses that the residential bishops had to submit to the Holy See.

Pius X's 1908 curial reform defined the status of the Apostolic Camera. As long as the pope lives, the title and functions of the office are mainly honorary. The situation changes considerably during the vacancy of the Holy See. As stated in the constitution *Sapienti consilio* (Jun. 29, 1908), the cardinal camerlengo was to be governed by the constitution *Vacante Sede Apostolica* (Dec. 25, 1904). This constitution specified that when the pope dies the interim administration of the Holy See is entrusted to the cardinal camerlengo. Among his duties in this capacity are: to proceed immediately to take possession of the apostolic palace of the Vatican (and also, by deputies, of the Lateran and Castel Gandolfo), to ascertain officially the death of the pope, to attend the examination of the body, to make a juridical verification of the death, to seal the private apartments of the deceased pope, to inform the cardinal vicar of Rome, and to cooperate with the dean of the College of Cardinals in assembling and directing the conclave.

The constitution also states that the cardinal camerlengo will be assisted in the fulfillment of his duties by the senior cardinal of each order (bishops, priests, and deacons), and that he should obtain the approval of the College of Cardinals on questions of business. As soon as the new pope is elected, the cardinal camerlengo loses all authority and reverts to the purely honorary status of his office.

This document was replaced by Pius XII's *Vacantis Apostolicae Sedis* (Dec. 8, 1945) which was in turn amended by John XXIII's *Summi Pontificis electio* (Sept. 5, 1962). This constitution clarified the rights and functions of the cardinal camerlengo (nos. 13–15). Paul VI confirmed these functions with his constitution *Romano Pontifici eligendo* (Oct. 1, 1975).

The property and revenues of the Holy See are now no longer administered by the Apostolic Camera but by two separate bodies: the Prefecture of the Economic Affairs of the Holy See, a financial office that coordinates and supervises the administration of the temporal holdings of the Holy See; and the Administration of the Patrimony of the Apostolic See, which handles the estate of the Apostolic See under the direction of papal delegates acting with ordinary or extraordinary authorization. These small offices, both established by Paul VI (Aug. 15, 1967), work in close cooperation with one another and with the Institute for Works of Religion (the Vatican Bank).

The past glories of the Apostolic Camera are reflected in the honorary rank given its college of prelati chierici.

Among the offices formerly subordinate to the Camera were the Amministrazione dei sali e tabacchi, Commissariato generale, Congregazione camerale, Congregazione degli spogli, Congregazione dei diffalchi, Depositeria generale, and Procuratore del fisco.

Probably more than any other department, the Apostolic Camera for most of its history served both the spiritual and temporal interests of the Holy See. Many of the offices listed in this guide in the section "Papal States" were dependent on the Camera. Ruggiero argues persuasively that the Camera was in essence an office of the Papal States primarily concerned with civil affairs. However, because it was officially a part of the Curia, it is listed in this guide in this section. (See also Boyle, pp. 41–42.)

In addition to the records listed below, the series listed with other agencies relate directly to this agency after 1400 and should be consulted. See College of Cardinals series *Camerlengato sede vacante*; Dataria Apostolica series *Consensus*; Secretariatus Status series *Registri "Bullarum" (già Coadiutorie e commende)*, *Registri I*, and *Registri II*; Miscellaneous official series *Bandi sciolti*, *Instrumenta miscellanea*, and *Miscellaneorum armarium XI*; and Camerlengato series *Camerlengo*.

References. Maria Grazia Pastura Ruggiero, *La Reverenda Camera Apostolica e i suoi archivi (secoli XV–XVIII)* (Rome, 1987). Guglielmo Felici, *La Reverenda Camera Apostolica: Studio storico-giuridico* (Rome, 1940). M. Michaud, "Chambre apostolique," in *Dictionnaire de droit canonique*, edited by R. Naz (Paris, 1942), vol. 3, pp. 388–431. W. E. Lunt, *Papal Revenues in the Middle Ages* (New York, 1934). J. E. Weakland, "Administration and Fiscal Centralization under Pope John XXII (1316–1334)," *Catholic Historical Review* 54 (1968): 39–54, 285–310. C. Samaran and G. Mollat, *La fiscalité pontificale en France au XIVe siècle: Période d'Avignon et du Grand Schisme d'Occident* (Paris, 1905).

L. M. Bååth, ed., "Acta cameralia," vol. 1 of *Acta pontificum Suecia: Auspiciis archivi regni Sueciae* (Stockholm, 1829). L. M. Bååth, "L'inventaire de la Chambre apostolique de 1440," in *Miscellanea archivistica Angelo Mercati* (Vatican City, 1952), pp. 135–157. C. Bauer, "Studi per la storia della finanze papali durante il pontificato di Sisto IV," *Archivio della Società romana di storia patria* 50 (1927): 319–400. W. M. Brady, *The Episcopal Succession in England, Scotland and Ireland, A.D. 1400–1875: With Appointments to Monasteries and Extracts from Consistorial Acts Taken from mss. in Public and Private Libraries in Rome, Florence, Bologna, Ravenna and Paris* (Rome, 1876–1877). P. Cherubini, *Mandati della Reverenda Camera Apostolica (1418–1802)* (Rome, 1988). P. Gasnault, "Notes et documents sur la Chambre Apostolique a l'époque d'Urbain V," *Mélanges d'archéologie e d'histoire* 70 (1958): 367–394. E. Göller, "Inventarium instrumentorum Camerae apostolicae aus der Zeit Urbans V," *Römische Quartalschrift für christliche Altertumskunde und für Kirchengeschichte* 23 (1909): 65–109. E. Göller, "Untersuchungen über das Inventar des Finanzarchivs der Renaissancepäpste," in *Miscellanea Francesco Ehrle*

(Rome, 1924), vol. 5, pp. 229–250. J. Goñi Gaztambide, "El fiscalismo pontificio en España en tiempo di Juan XXII," *Anthologica annua* 14 (1966): 65–99. A. Gottlob, *Aus der Camera apostolica des 15. Jahrhunderts: Ein Beitrag zur Geschichte des päpstlichen Finanzwesens und des endenden Mittelalters* (Innsbruck, 1889). B. Guillemain, *Les recettes et les depenses de la Chambre apostolique pour la quatrieme annee du pontificat de Clement V (1308–1309): Introitus et exitus 75* (Rome, 1978).

A. Lodolini, *L'archivio di Stato di Roma: Epitome d'una guida degli archivi dell'amministrazione dello Stato Pontificio* (Rome, 1960). A. Lodolini, *L'archivio di Stato in Roma e l'archivio del Regno d'Italia: Indice generale storico descrittivo de analitico, con il concorso dei funzionari* (Rome, 1932). J. de Loye, *Les archives de la Chambre apostolique au XIVe siècle*, part 1, *Inventaire* (Paris, 1899). W. E. Lunt, *Accounts rendered by Papal Collectors in England, 1317–1378* (Philadelphia, 1968). W. E. Lunt, *Financial Relations of the Papacy with England* (Cambridge, Mass., 1939–1962). G. Mollat, "Contribution à l'histoire de la Chambre apostolique au XIVe siècle," *Revue d'histoire ecclésiastique* 45 (1950): 82–94. M. Monaco, *La situazione della reverenda Camera Apostolica nell'anno 1525: Ricerche d'archivio: Un contributo alla storia delle finanze pontificie* (Rome, 1960). M. D. O'Sullivan, "Italian Merchant Bankers and the Collection of Papal Revenue in Ireland in the 13th Century," *Galway Archeological Association Journal* 22 (1946–47): 132–163 [this title was noted but not verified by project staff]. P. Partner, "The 'Budget' of the Roman Church in the Renaissance Period," in *Italian Renaissance Studies: A Tribute to the Late Cecilia M. Ady*, edited by E. F. Jacob (London, 1960), 256–278. P. Partner, "Camera Papae: Problems of Papal Finance in the late Middle Ages," *Journal of Ecclesiastical History* 4 (1953): 55–68. P. Partner, "Papal Financial Policy in the Renaissance and Counter-Reformation," *Past and Present*, no. 88 (1980): 17–62. P. Partner, *Renaissance Rome, 1500–1559: A Portrait of a Society* (Berkeley, 1976). E. Pásztor, "I registri camerali di lettere pontificie del secolo XIII," *Archivum historiae pontificiae* 11 (1973): 7–83. J. Ptasnik, *Acta Camerae Apostolicae, 1207–1344* (Kraków, 1913). J. Ptasnik, *Acta Camerae Apostolicae, 1344–1374* (Kraków, 1913).

A. Ramacciotti, *Gli archivi della Reverenda Camera Apostolica, con inventario analitico-descrittivo dei registri camerali conservati nell'Archivio di Stato di Roma nel Fondo Camerale Primo* (Rome, 1961). Y. Renouard, "Intérêt et importance des Archives Vaticanes pour l'histoire économique du Moyen Age, spécialement du XIVe siècle," in *Miscellanea archivistica Angelo Mercati* (Vatican City, 1952), pp. 21–41. L. Sandri, "Note sui registri delle 'Rationes decimarum' dell'Archivio di Stato di Roma," in *Mélanges Eugène Tisserant* (Vatican

City, 1964), vo. 5, pp. 338–359. J. Trenchs Odena, "La Cámara Apostolica y sus documentos," *Boletín de la Sociedad Castellonense de Cultura* 58 (1982): 629–652. D. Williman, *Calendar of the Letters of Arnaud Aubert, Cameraris Apostolicus, 1361–1371* (Toronto, 1992). D. Williman, "The Camerary and the Schism," in *Genèse et débuts du Grand Schisme d'Occident* (Paris, 1980), pp. 65–71. D. Williman. "Letters of Etienne Cambarou, Camerarius Apostolicus (1347–1361)," *Archivum Historiae Pontificiae* 15 (1977): 195–215. D. Williman, *The Right of Spoil of the Popes of Avignon 1316–1415* (Philadelphia, 1988). D. Williman, "Summary Justice in the Avignonese Camera," in *Proceedings of the Sixth International Congress of Medieval Canon Law*, edited by S. Kuttner and K. Pennington (Vatican City, 1985), pp. 437–449.

RECORDS. Records of the office consist of the following series.

3.2.3.1 Amministrazione camerale del patrimonio ex gesuitico
[DATABASE ID: VATV20021-A]
Inclusive Dates: 1578–1869 (bulk 1773–1814).
Bulk: 204 buste, registri, and vols.
Reference: D'Angiolini, p. 1088.
Finding Aids: Inventory, 1977.
Location: Archivio di Stato di Roma.

3.2.3.2 Annatae
[DATABASE ID: VATV058-A]
Inclusive Dates: 1413–1797.
Bulk: 7 linear m. (136 numbered vols.).
Organization: Chronological.
Scope: These are a record of taxes levied by the Holy See on minor reserved benefices. There are some summary financial volumes in the series. Note that there are two variant spine titles: Diverso and Quietantie Annatatarum (Secretaria et Cancelleria).
Note: This series was transferred from the Archivio di Stato di Roma in 1919 as part of the Fondo dell'Archivio di Stato di Roma.
References: Fink, p. 55; Boyle, p. 46; Pásztor (1970), pp. 40–41. F. Baix and A. Uyttebrouck, eds., "La Chambre apostolique et les "Libri annatarum" de Martin V (1417–1431)," vol. 14 of *Analecta vaticano-belgica: Documents relatifs aux anciens diocèses de Cambrai, Liège, Thérouanne et Tournai* (Rome, 1942–1960), pp. xxviii–cdxlviii. E. Brouette, ed., "Les 'Libri annatarum' pour les pontificats d'Eugène IV à Alexander VI," vol. 4, "Pontificats d'Innocent VIII et d'Alexander VI, 1484–1503," vol. 24 of *Analecta vaticano-belgica: Documents relatifs aux anciens diocèses de Cambrai, Liège, Thérouanne et Tournai* (Rome, 1963). M. A. Costello, "Obligationes pro annatis diocesis Dublinensis, 1421–1520," *Archivium hibernicum* 2 (1913): 1–72 (this and the following works by Costello include selected transcriptions of medieval entries for Irish dioceses). M. A. Costello and D. Buckley, eds., "Obligationes pro annatis diocesis Cloynensis, 1413–1526," *Archivium hibernicum* 24 (1961): 1–30. M. A. Costello and T. J. Clohosey, eds., "Obligationes pro annatis diocesis Ossoriensis, 1413–

1531," *Archivium hibernicum* 20 (1957): 1–37. M. A. Costello and A. Coleman, eds., "Ulster," vol. 1 of *De Annatis Hiberniae: A Calendar of the First Fruits' Fees Levied on Papal Appointments to Benefices in Ireland A.D. 1400 to 1535* . . . (Dundalk, 1909). M. A. Costello and P. K. Egan, eds., "Obligationes pro annatis diocesis Clonfertensis, 1420–1531," *Archivium hibernicum* 21 (1958): 52–74. M. A. Costello and D. F. Gleeson, eds., "Obligationes pro annatis diocesis Laoniensis, 1421–1535," *Archivium hibernicum* 10 (1943): 1–103. M. A. Costello and G. Mac Niocaill, eds., "Obligationes pro annatis diocesis Elphinensis, 1426–1548," *Archivium hibernicum* 22 (1959): 1–27. M. A. Costello and M. Moloney, eds., "Obligationes pro annatis diocesis Limiricensis, 1421–1519," *Archivium hibernicum* 10 (1943): 104–162. M. A. Costello and J. O'Connell, eds., "Obligationes pro annatis diocesis Ardfertensis, 1421–1517," *Archivium hibernicum* 21 (1958): 1–51. M. A. Costello and J. F. O'Doherty, eds., "Obligationes pro annatis provinciae Tuamensis, 1413–1548," *Archivium hibernicum* 26 (1963): 56–117. M. A. Costello and P. Power, eds., "Obligationes pro annatis diocesis Lismorensis, 1426–1529," *Archivium hibernicum* 12 (1946): 15–61. M. A. Costello, ed., "Obligationes pro annatis diocesis Waterfordensis, 1421–1507," *Archivium hibernicum* 12 (1946): 1–14. M. A. Costello and J. Ranson, eds., "Obligationes pro annatis diocesis Fernensis, 1413–1524," *Archivium hibernicum* 18 (1955): 1–15. M. A. Costello, L. Ryan, and W. Skehan, eds., "Obligationes pro annatis diocesis Cassellensis, 1433–1534," *Archivium hibernicum* 28 (1966): 1–32. M. A. Costello, ed., "Obligationes pro annatis diocesis Imelacensis, 1429–1444," *Archivium hibernicum* 28 (1966): 33–44.

J. Haller et al., eds., *Repertorium Germanicum: Regesten aus den päpstlichen Archiven zur Geschichte des Deutschen Reichs und seiner Territorien im XIV. und XV. Jahrhundert: Pontifikat Eugens IV. (1431–1447)* (Berlin, 1897) calendars items concerning Germany in this series.

Finding Aids: ASV Index 1043 (3 volumes) gives (1) a listing of volumes and years covered and (2) an alphabetical list of dioceses with the volume number and pages on which each diocese appears. Volume 3 has three appendices: references(?), names of persons, and names of selected places and subjects. This alphabetical listing of dioceses gives one large list, preferable to the Camera Apostolica series *Annatae indice*, which breaks the list down into several chronological subdivisions. However, both should be checked to achieve the greatest degree of accuracy.

The Camera Apostolica series *Annatae indice* provides an annotated alphabetical index to this series that is broken down by years.

ASV Indice 1112 (former Indice 41), p. 14, provides a volume-by-volume listing with inclusive dates and the current ASV and former Archivio di Stato di Roma numbers. The final unnumbered pages of this index reiterate much of this information in tabular form, listing the current and former name and volume numbers.

Location: Archivio Segreto Vaticano.

3.2.3.3 Annatae et quindenni
[DATABASE ID: VATV059-A]
Inclusive Dates: 1742–1797.
Bulk: 1.5 linear m. (19 vols.).
Organization: Chronological by year and month.

Scope: These records are lists of benefice payments by year/month/day with a monthly summary financial accounting.

Note: The records were transferred from the Archivio di Stato di Roma in 1919 as part of the Fondo dell'Archivio di Stato di Roma.

References: Fink, p. 55; Boyle, p. 46; Pásztor (1970), pp. 41–42. B. Katterbach, "Archivio Vaticano," in *Enciclopedia italiana* (Rome, 1929), vol. 4, pp. 88–90.

Finding Aids: ASV Indice 1112 (former Indice 41) (p. 17) provides a volume-by-volume listing with their inclusive dates and their current ASV and former Archivio di Stato di Roma numbers. The final unnumbered pages of this index reiterate some of this information in a table listing current and former names and numbers for volumes in the series.

Location: Archivio Segreto Vaticano.

3.2.3.4 Annatae indice
[DATABASE ID: VATV10011-A]
Inclusive Dates: 1600–1797.
Bulk: 1 linear m. (10 vols.).
Organization: Subseries are: 1. 1600–1700 (vol. 1–6); —2. 1701–1758 (vol. 7); —3. 1759–1772 (vol. 8); —4. 1773–1786 (vol. 9); —5. 1787–1797 (vol. 10). Alphabetical.
Scope: This series is an annotated index to the Camera Apostolica series *Annatae*, described above. It should be used in conjunction with ASV Index 1043 to get the best results from the *Annatae*.
Reference: Pásztor (1970), p. 41.
Location: Archivio Segreto Vaticano.

3.2.3.5 Appendice camerale (Camerale I)
[DATABASE ID: VATV20015-A]
Inclusive Dates: 1434–1744.
Bulk: 228 registri.
Organization: Annona, 1588–1590, 1593–1596, 1598–1604, 1622, and 1686–1690 (8 registri and 2 rubriche); —Camera urbis, 1443–1446, 1459–1464, 1472–1486, 1492, 1548, 1685–1697, and 1718–1721 (13 registri and 2 librimastro); —Conti a parte, 1579, 1582, 1590–1610, 1619–1621, 1623–1627, 1631–1700, and 1706–1743 (50 registri and 4 libri-mastro); —Spogli, 1550–1554, 1577–1581, 1593–1597, 1606–1615, 1627–1633, 1639–1641, 1644–1730, and 1737 (44 registri, 14 libri-mastro, and 1 rubrica); —Stato di Castro e Ronciglione, 1644, 1649–1652, 1660–1671, and 1743–1744 (8 registri and 2 libri-mastro); —Terra di San Felice, 1728–1730 and 1735–1743 (2 registri); —Tesorerie provinciali, 1437–1735 (52 registri and 6 libri-mastro); —Varia, 1434–1435, 1447–1454, 1487–1499, 1515–1529, 1532–1540, 1554–1555, 1564–1565, 1600–1609, and 1622 (19 registri and 1 rubrica).
References: D'Angiolini, pp. 1063–1064; Lodolini (1960), pp. 68–72.
Finding Aids: List, 1962.
Location: Archivio di Stato di Roma.

3.2.3.6 Armarium XXIX: Diversa cameralia
[DATABASE ID: VATV048-A]
Inclusive Dates: 1389–1555.
Bulk: 10 linear m. (161 vols.).
Organization: Volumes are numbered 1–161. This series is continued in *Armarium XXX*.

Volume titles include: 1. Urbani VI et Bonifac. IX diversor.

regestrum ab an. 1389 ad 1391 (indexed); —2. Gregorii XII, nota Cameralis seu manuale ab ann. 1407–1412; —3. To. 23 Martin V et Eug. IV manuale ab ann. 1414–1423 [i.e., 1432]; —25. Nicolai V. Capla. cum capitaneis zecchae, et diversarum salariaers. ann., [1440–1458] [Spine: Eug. IV, Nic. V, Calis. 3].

Scope: This collection is largely the administrative correspondence of the Camera and is sometimes known as the *Libri diversorum negotiorum cameralium.* As would be expected, the series contains mandates from the camerarius to his subordinates, and letters from him or them to the collectors and fiscal agents of the papal states and elsewhere. There are besides, however, many entries of quittances of bishops on ad limina visits, and copies of dispensations in which the camera had a particular interest, like prorogations; there are testimonials and notes on salaries.

Note: Vols. 2, 13, 50, 77, and 78 are available on microfilm.

References: Fink, pp. 51–52; Boyle, pp. 43–44; Pásztor (1970), pp. 43–44; Pásztor (1983), pp. 106–107. The scope note above was taken directly from MacFarlane, p. 42.

L. Bauwens, "Analytisch Inventaris der Diversa Cameralia van het Vaticaans Archief (1500–1549)," *Bulletin de l'Institut historique Belge de Rome* 28 (1953): 31–50. U. Berlière, *Inventaire analytique des Diversa Cameralia des Archives Vaticanes (1389–1500) au point de vue des anciens diocèses de Cambrai, Liège, Thérouanne et Tournai* (Rome, 1906). A. I. Cameron, *The Apostolic Camera and Scottish Benefices, 1418–1488* (Edinburgh, 1934). A. Clergeac, *La curie et les bénéficiers consistoriaux: Étude sur les communs et menus services, 1300–1600* (Paris, 1911). E. von Ottenthal, *Regulae cancellariae apostolicae: Die päpstlichen Kanzleiregeln von Johannes XXII. bis Nikolaus V* (Innsbruck, 1888). P. Partner, *The Pope's Men: The Papal Civil Service in the Renaissance* (Oxford, 1990). A. E. Planchart, "The Early Career of Guillaume Du Fay," *Journal of the American Musicological Society* 46 (1993): 341–368.

J. Haller et al., eds., *Repertorium Germanicum: Regesten aus den päpstlichen Archiven zur Geschichte des deutschen Reichs und seiner Territorien im XIV. und XV. Jahrhundert: Pontifikat Eugens IV. (1431–1447)* (Berlin, 1897) calendars items concerning Germany in this series.

Finding Aids: ASV Indice 1170, "Arm. XXIX–XXX, Camera Apostolica, Diversa Cameralia voll. 1–251, Inventario Sommario," by Francesca Di Giovanni and Giuseppina Roselli, is divided into two sections. The first section is entitled "Prospetto dei volumi"; the second, "Indice dei nomi." The Prospetto dei volumi (pp. 1–14) lists the volume numbers, the pope(s), the type of transaction (e.g., diversorum cameralium, notarum cameralium, manuale, capitolorum militarium), dates, and an occasional liber number. The Indice dei nomi is more accurately called an index to the papacy; it is organized by the pope's name and gives the volume number and the type(s) of transactions. Indice 1170 provides quick access to volumes in a given papacy and a certain type of transaction.

ASV Indice 133, ff. 130r–136v, briefly lists summary titles of each volume. The index (compiled by Petrus De Pretis after 1741) is basically informative but often fails to note copies. The index also uses terms such as *regestrum* and *brevia* too inclusively and does not clearly note items that do not fit the basic thematic focus of each armarium, or which items are clearly from other offices.

A chronological calendar on index cards for the entire series is contained in twenty-eight drawers (bins). It was prepared by P. Sella and is located in the ASV Sala d'Indici.

ASV Indice 288 provides complete or partial contents for the following volumes in this armarium: 63–69, 73–74, 76–98, 100–104, 106–108, 110, 112, 115–116, 118, 121–122, 124, 131–132, 134–135, 140–141, 146. These rubrics proceed page by page for each volume and list.

ASV Indice 264 (p. 143) gives contents of *Arm. XXIX,* vol. 2.

ASV Indice 271 (p. 86) gives contents of *Arm. XXIX,* vol. 6.

ASV Indice 114 by Felice Contelori provides extracts of various *Diversa cameralia* volumes in *Armarium XXIX* (cf. pp. 276, 420, 542–611, passim).

ASV Indice 124, "Primo Sbozzo di Inventario di tutti i libri che sono nell'Archivio Segreto Vaticano," by Giovanni Bissaiga (1672), provides more descriptive and accurate volume titles for some armaria volumes. The following is a list of volumes in *Arm. XXIX,* which are listed in this index; also provided are citations, in parentheses, for Indice 124. *Arm. XXIX,* vol. 1 (f. 185v, no. 1980); vol. 2 (f. 253, no. 2751); vol. 3 (f. 185v, no. 1994); vols. 4–9 (f. 186, nos. 1981–1986); vol. 11 (f. 186, no. 1987); vol. 12 (f. 186v, no. 1989); vol. 13 (f. 186v, no. 1988); vol. 14 (parts 1 & 2) (f. 186v, nos. 1990 and 1991); vols. 15–22 (f. 186v, nos. 1993–2000); vol. 23 (f. 187v, no. 2007); vol. 24 (parts 1 & 2) (f. 187–187v, nos. 2001–2002); vol. 25 (f. 187v, no. 2006); vol. 26 (f. 187v, no. 2003); vol. 28 (f. 188, no. 2008); vols. 29–30 (f. 188, nos. 2010–2011); vols. 32–36 and 39–42 (part 1) (f. 188v, nos. 2013–2020); vol. 37 (f. 189, no. 2026); vol 38 (f. 189, no. 2021); vol. 42 (part 2) (f. 188, no. 2009); vol. 43 (f. 189, no. 2022); vol. 44 (f. 189, no. 2027); vols. 45–51 (f. 189v, nos. 2028–2034). The titles in Indice 124 are usually provided in a footnote in ASV Indice 133, so researchers can see exactly how generic the titles in ASV Indice 133 are.

ASV Indice 124 (continued): *Arm. XXIX,* vols. 52–57 (f. 190, nos. 2035–2040); vols. 58 and 59 (f. 190v, nos. 2043 and 2042); vol. 60 (f. 190, no. 2041); vols. 61 (parts 1 & 2) and 62 (f. 190v, nos. 2044–2046); vols. 63–66 (f. 191, nos. 2047–2053); vol. 70 (f. 191v, no. 2057); vols. 71–72 (f. 191v, nos. 2055 and 2054); vols. 73–75 (f. 191v, no. 2058–2060); vols. 76–78 (f. 192, nos. 2061–2063); vol. 79 (f. 192, no. 2067); vol. 80 (f. 192, no. 2065); vol. 81 (f. 192v, no. 2069); vol. 82 (f. 209v, no. 2266); vols. 83–84 (f. 192, nos. 2064 and 2066); vol. 85 (f. 192v, no. 2070); vol. 86 (f. 192v, no. 2071); vol. 87 (f. 192v, no. 2068); vol. 88 (f. 192v, no. 2072); vol. 89 (f. 193, no. 2078); vols. 90–91 (f. 192v, nos. 2073–2074); vols. 92–96 (f. 193, nos. 2076, 2078–2081); vol. 97 (f. 193v, no. 2083); vol. 98 (f. 193v, no. 2082); vol. 99 (f. 193v, no. 2084); vol. 100 (f. 194v, no. 2098); vol. 101 (f. 196, no. 2117); vol. 102 (f. 198, no. 2140); vol. 103 (f. 194, no. 2095); vol. 104 (f. 193v, no. 2086); vol. 105 (f. 197, no. 2127); vol. 106 (f. 196, no. 2119); vol. 107 (f. 193v, no. 2085); vol. 108 (f. 194v, no. 2099); vol. 109 (f. 198, no. 2139); vol. 110 (f. 195, no. 2103); vol. 111 (f. 196v, no. 2121); vol. 112 (f. 196v, no. 2124); vol. 113 (f. 194v, no. 2100); vol. 115 (f. 195, 2104); vol. 116 (f. 193v, n. 2087); vol. 117 (f. 194, no. 2094); vol. 118 (f. 194v, no. 2096).

ASV Indice 124 (continued): *Arm. XXIX,* vol. 120 (f. 195, no. 2105); vol. 121 (f. 193v, no. 2088); vol. 122 (f. 196, no. 2118); vol. 123 (f. 194v, no. 2097); vol. 124 (f. 194, no. 2092); vol. 126 (f. 195, no. 2107); vol. 127 (f. 194v, no. 2101); vol. 128 (f. 196, no. 2120); vol. 129 (f. 196v, no. 2122); vols. 130–132 (f. 195v, nos. 2108–2110); vol. 133 (f. 198, no. 2138); vols. 134–135 (f. 195v, nos. 2112–2113); vol. 136 (f. 195, no. 2102); vol. 137 (f. 197, no. 2126); vol. 138 (f. 195v, no. 2114); vol. 139 (f. 194, no. 2091); vols 140–141 (f. 196, nos. 2115–2116); vol. 142 (f. 197, no. 2128); vols. 144 (f. f197v, no. 2136); vol. 145 (f. 197, no. 2129); vol. 146 (f. 194, no. 2089); vol. 147 (f. 197, no. 2130); vol. 148 (f. 194, no. 2090); vol. 149 (f. 197v, no. 2137); vol. 151 (f. 197, no. 2131); vol. 152 (f. 196v, no. 2123); vol. 153 (f. 197v, no. 2132); vol. 154 (f. 196v, no. 2125); volumes 156–157 (f. 197v, nos. 2133–2134); vol. 159 (197v, no. 2135); vol. 161 (f. 198, no. 2144).

Location: Archivio Segreto Vaticano.

3.2.3.7 Armarium XXX: Diversa cameralia

[DATABASE ID: VATV049-A]

Inclusive Dates: 1550–1578.

Bulk: 90 vols.

Organization: This series is a continuation of *Armarium XXIX*, volumes numbered 162–251.

Scope: This collection is largely the administrative correspondence of the papal Camera and is sometimes known as the *Libri diversorum negotiorum cameralium.* As would be expected, the series contains mandates from the camerarius to his subordinates, and letters from him or them to the collectors and fiscal agents of the papal states and elsewhere. There are besides, however, many entries of quittances of bishops on ad limina visits, and copies of dispensations in which the camera had a particular interest, like prorogations; there are testimonials and notes on salaries.

References: Fink, pp. 51–52; Boyle, p. 44; Pásztor (1970), p. 43–44; Pásztor (1983), pp. 106–107. The scope note above is taken directly from MacFarlane, p. 42.

U. Berlière, *Inventaire analytique des Diversa Cameralia des Archives Vaticanes (1389–1500) au point de vue des anciens diocèses de Cambrai, Liège, Thérouanne et Tournai* (Rome, 1906). A. I. Cameron, *The Apostolic Camera and Scottish Benefices, 1418–1488* (Edinburgh, 1934). A. Clergeac, *La curie et les Bénéficiers consistoriaux: Étude sur les communs et menus services, 1300–1600* (Paris, 1911). E. von Ottenthal, *Regulae cancellariae apostolicae: Die päpstlichen Kanzleiregeln von Johannes XXII. bis Nikolaus V* (Innsbruck, 1888). P. Partner, *The Pope's Men: The Papal Civil Service in the Renaissance* (Oxford, 1990). A. E. Planchart, "The Early Career of Guillaume Du Fay," *Journal of the American Musicological Society* 46 (1993): 341–368.

J. Haller et al., eds., *Repertorium Germanicum: Regesten aus den päpstlichen Archiven zur Geschichte des Deutschen Reichs und seiner Territorien im XIV. und XV. Jahrhundert: Pontifikat Eugens IV. (1431–1447)* (Berlin, 1897) calendars items concerning Germany in this series.

Finding Aids: ASV Indice 1170, "Arm. XXIX–XXX, Camera Apostolica, Diversa Cameralia voll. 1–251, Inventario Sommario," by Francesca Di Giovanni and Giuseppina Roselli, is divided into two sections. The first section is entitled "Prospetto dei volumi"; the second, "Indice dei nomi." The Prospetto dei volumi (pp. 1–14) lists the volume numbers, the pope(s), the type of transaction (e.g., diversorum cameralium, notarum cameralium, manuale, capitolorum militarium),

dates, and an occasional liber number. The Indice dei nomi is more accurately called an index to the papacy, it is organized by the pope's name and gives the volume number and the type(s) of transactions. Indice 1170 provides quick access to volumes in a given papacy and a certain type of transaction.

ASV Indice 133, ff. 137r–141v, briefly lists summary titles of each volume. The index (compiled by Petrus De Pretis after 1741) is basically informative but often fails to note copies. The index also uses terms such as *regestrum* and *brevia* too inclusively and does not clearly note items that do not fit the basic thematic focus of each armarium, or which items are clearly from other offices.

In the ASV Sala d'Indici there is a chronological calendar to the *Diversa cameralia* in twenty-eight drawers (bins).

ASV Indice 288 provides contents of *Arm. XXX*, vol. 170, 178, and 191.

ASV Indice 114 by Felice Contelori provides excerpts from selected volumes throughout this series. Some of the pages where references to the *Diversa cameralia* are included are: pp. 276, 420, 542–611, passim.

ASV Indice 124, "Primo Sbozzo di Inventario di tutti i libri che sono nell'Archivio Segreto Vaticano," by Giovanni Bissaiga (1672), provides more descriptive and accurate volume titles for some armaria volumes. Many of the volumes in *Armaria XXX* are listed in this index on the following folios: 198r–205v, and 212r.

Location: Archivio Segreto Vaticano.

3.2.3.8 Armarium XXXI

[DATABASE ID: VATV370-A]

Inclusive Dates: 872–1605.

Bulk: 85 vols.

Scope: This armarium contains fifteenth–sixteenth-century cameral copies consisting of extracts from Chancery records dating between the twelfth and sixteenth centuries. It is arranged chronologically by pontificates, but with gaps and additions, and appears to have been little explored, though some of its volumes are of considerable interest. *Arm. XXXI*, vol. 1, is copied in Vatican Register 2 (ff. 1–83v).

References: Fink, p. 31; Boyle, p. 38; MacFarlane, p. 35.

Finding Aids: ASV Indice 213, "Indice di libri de Msgr. Ciampini alcune de quale sono stati comprati da Il. Sg.le. Clemente XI e posti nell'studi . . . e fuori sono stati segnali con la lett. 'C' e posti in diversi luoghi secundo le materie nelle quali trattavano," includes *Arm. XXXI*, vols. 27, 74, and 82 in this donation, which took place between 1700 and 1721. The description of these volumes in Indice 213 is fuller than the description in ASV Indice 133.

ASV Indice 133, ff. 196r–198v, briefly lists summary titles of each volume. The index (compiled by Petrus De Pretis after 1741) is basically informative but often fails to note copies. The index also uses terms such as *regestrum* and *brevia* too inclusively and does not clearly note items that do not fit the basic thematic focus of each armarium, or which items are clearly from other offices.

ASV Indice 110, "Index librorum 112 Diversorum scripturarum confecta Rmo. Dmo. Felice Contelori et unitorum per me Joannen Bissaigham & fuit compactus an 1694," [olim Arm 58, n. 41] indexes *Arm. XXXI*, vol. 46 (beginning on f. 151.) Entries note the dioceses in the margins and proceed folio by folio listing the following elements: place, type of business (e.g., venditio), recipient, summary of the document, date, cost (occasionally), and folio number. Although this does provide descriptive detail concerning the contents of the volume, it should not be assumed to be a complete index.

ASV Indice 124, "Primo Sbozzo di Inventario di tutti i libri che sono nell'Archivio Segreto Vaticano," by Giovanni Bissaiga (1672), provides more descriptive and accurate volume titles for some armarium volumes, such as Armarium 31, vols. 9 (f. 246, no. 2681), 36 (f. 253, no. 2750), and 55 (f. 246, no. 2680). Additional volume titles are listed on folios 237v–238r, 240r, 242v–247r, 248v, 251r, 253r, and 257r. The exact titles listed in Indice 124 are sometimes provided in a footnote in ASV Indice 133, so researchers can see exactly how generic the titles in ASV Indice 133 are.

ASV Indice 731 lists documents (it seems on a selected basis) found in *Arm. XXXI*, vol. 29. ASV Indice 1100 indicates which *Sec. Brev.* registers (series name and volume number) as well as which other series are indexed in ASV Indice 731–885.

Reference: D. Mansilla, *La documentación pontificia hasta Innozencio III, 965–1216* (Rome, 1955).

Location: Archivio Segreto Vaticano.

3.2.3.9 Armarium XXXII

[DATABASE ID: VATV371-A]
Inclusive Dates: [12—]–[15—].
Bulk: 62 vols.
Scope: This armarium contains fifteenth–sixteenth-century extracts from chancery records dating between the twelfth and sixteenth centuries. It is a diverse collection of letters and bulls, often without dates, and is of uncertain value.

References: Fink, p. 31; Boyle, p. 38; MacFarlane, p. 35. F. Gasparolo, ed., "Costituzione dell'Archivio Vaticano e suo primo indice sotto il pontificato di Paolo V: Manoscritto inedito de Michele Lonigo," *Studi e documenti di storia e diritto* 8 (1887): 44–48.

Finding Aids: ASV Indice 133 briefly lists summary titles of each volume. The index (compiled by Petrus De Pretis after 1741) is basically informative but often fails to note copies. The index also uses terms such as *regestrum* and *brevia* too inclusively and does not clearly note items that do not fit the basic thematic focus of each armarium, or which items are clearly from other offices. Therefore, volume titles are often incorrect. The more recent typed footnotes are also incorrect at times.

ASV Indice 110, "Index librorum 112 Diversorum scripturarum confecta Rmo. Dmo. Felice Contelori et unitorum per me Joannen Bissaigham & fuit compactus an 1694," [olim *Arm. LVIII*, n. 41] indexes *Arm. XXXII*, vol. 11 (ff. 337–346 and 351–355) in ASV Indice 110 (f. 176 and ff. 193–201v, respectively). Entries note the dioceses in the margins and proceed folio by folio listing the following elements: place, type of business (e.g., venditio), recipient, summary of the document, date, cost (occasionally), and folio number. Although this does provide descriptive detail concerning the contents of the volume, it should not be assumed to be a complete index.

ASV Indice 124, "Primo Sbozzo di Inventario di tutti i libri che sono nell'Archivio Segreto Vaticano," by Giovanni Bissaiga (1672), provides more descriptive and accurate volume titles for some armarium volumes. Select *Arm. XXXII* volume titles are listed on folios 240r, 242r, 246v, 247rv, 248r, 249r, 278v, 377v, and 378r. The exact titles listed in Indice 124 are sometimes provided in a footnote in ASV Indice 133, so re-

searchers can see exactly how generic title descriptions in Indice 133 are.

ASV Indice 213, "Indice di libri de Msgr. Ciampini alcune de quale sonostati comprati da Il. Sg.le. Clemente XI e posti nell'studi . . . e fuori sono stati segnali con la lett. 'C' e posti in diversi luoghi secundo le materie nelle quali trattavano," includes *Arm. XXXII*, vol. 50, in this donation, which took place between 1700 and 1721. The description of vol. 50 in Indice 213 is fuller than the description in ASV Indice 133.

Location: Archivio Segreto Vaticano.

3.2.3.10 Armarium XXXIII: Quindennia

[DATABASE ID: VATV050-A]
Inclusive Dates: 1419–1766.
Bulk: 90 vols.
Scope: This series was begun by the Camera clerks early in the fifteenth century, and now comprises ninety volumes. They may have begun as libri quindenniorum, but they soon began to include quittances for bishops' obligations, taxes on the papal states, tenths, the census and other dues of the Camera. Those who consult it, however, will find very useful information relating to the religious corporations then paying it. Boyle notes that quindennia are "taxes paid every fifteen years on benefices annexed to religious corporations." The volumes also contain records of other taxes, tenths, and quittances of census.

Note: Vols. 9 and 12 are available on microfilm.

References: Boyle, p. 44; Fink, pp. 31, 54; MacFarlane, p. 42–43. B. Katterbach, "Archivio Vaticano," in *Enciclopedia italiana* (Rome, 1929), vol. 4, pp. 88–90.

Finding Aids: ASV Indice 133, ff. 151r–154v, briefly lists summary titles of each volume. The index (compiled by Petrus De Pretis after 1741) is basically informative but often fails to note copies. The index also uses terms such as *regestrum* and *brevia* too inclusively and does not clearly note items that do not fit the basic thematic focus of each Armarium, or which items are clearly from other offices. Therefore, the volume titles presented in this index are often inexact.

ASV Indice 124, "Primo Sbozzo di Inventario di tutti i libri che sono nell'Archivio Segreto Vaticano," by Giovanni Bissaiga (1672), provides more descriptive and accurate volume titles for some armarium volumes, such as Armarium 33, volume 36 (f. 251v, no. 2731). Additional volume titles are listed on pages 189r, 235rv, 237r, 239rv, 241v, 250v, 251v–252r, and 253r. The exact titles listed in Indice 124 are sometimes provided in a footnote in ASV Indice 133, so researchers can see exactly how generic the titles in ASV Indice 133 are.

Location: Archivio Segreto Vaticano.

3.2.3.11 Armarium XXXIV: Instrumenta cameralia

[DATABASE ID: VATV051-A]
Inclusive Dates: 1313–1826.
Bulk: 57 vols.
Scope: The vague title of this series conceals valuable cameral information of a wide range. The volumes contain obligations of papal collectors, details of salaries and contracts within the papal states, quittances of bishops, procurations, libel suits, and much other miscellaneous fiscal material besides copies of the instruments of possession and of other land transactions that give the general heading to the series. Most, but not all, entries relate to Italy.

References: Fink, p. 31; Boyle, pp. 44–45. The scope note above was taken directly from MacFarlane, p. 43.

Finding Aids: ASV Indice 133, ff. 155r–157r, briefly lists summary titles of each volume. The index (compiled by Petrus De Pretis after 1741) is basically informative but often fails to note copies. The index also uses terms such as *regestrum* and *brevia* too inclusively and does not clearly note items that do not fit the basic thematic focus of each armarium, or which items are clearly from other offices. Therefore, the volume titles listed in ASV Indice 113 are often inexact.

ASV Indice 264, "Rubricellae Bullar. a Clemente VI usque ad Martinum quintum" (ff. 147–156), provides contents for *Arm. XXXIV*, vol. 4.

Ottoboni Lat. n. 3395 (ff. 124–131v) provides contents for *Arm. XXXIV*, vol. 4. This manuscript is located in the Vatican Library.

ASV Indice 288 provides contents for vol. 24A beginning on f. 118.

ASV Indice 114 provides excerpts from selected volumes in *Arm. XXXIV*, including vols. 11, 15, 16, 18, 20–23, 25, 27–30, 33–34, 37, 49–44, and 51. The excerpts, on pp. 612–619v, are not presented in alphabetical order.

ASV Indice 124, "Primo Sbozzo di Inventario di tutti i libri che sono nell'Archivio Segreto Vaticano," by Giovanni Bissaiga (1672), provides more descriptive and accurate volume titles for some armarium volumes, such as Armarium 34, volumes 19 (f. 251v, no. 2735) and 24A (f. 193, no. 2075) and additional volume titles on folios 207v–211v, 251v, 252r, 279rv, 305v, 377v, and 378r. The exact titles listed in Indice 124 are sometimes provided in a footnote in ASV Indice 133, so researchers can see exactly how generic the titles in ASV Indice 133 are.

Location: Archivio Segreto Vaticano.

3.2.3.12 Armarium XXXV

[DATABASE ID: VATV372-A]

Inclusive Dates: [11—]–[15—].

Bulk: 152 vols.

Scope: *Arm. XXXV* contains 152 volumes of documents relating to the fiefs and temporal rights of the Holy See, classified chronologically by their countries. These are copies of registers, volumes of privileges (esp. vol. 3–12). Vol. 34 is "Liber capitolorum inter diversos principes—Nicolas V, Clement VII, Leo X."

References: Fink, p. 31; Boyle, p. 38; MacFarlane, p. 35. F. Gasparolo, ed., "Costituzione dell'Archivio Vaticano e suo primo indice sotto il pontificato di Paolo V: Manoscritto inedito de Michele Lonigo," *Studi e documenti di storia e diritto* 8 (1887): 36–38. A. Mercati, "Schedario Garampi, Registri Vaticani, Registri Lateranensi, Rationes Camerae, Inventario del Fondo Concistoriale," vol. 1 of *Sussidi per la consultazione dell'Archivio Vaticano* (Rome, 1926), p. 39.

Finding Aids: ASV Indice 133, ff. 159r–165r, briefly lists summary titles of each volume. The index (compiled by Petrus De Pretis after 1741) is basically informative but often fails to note copies. The index also uses terms such as *regestrum* and *brevia* too inclusively and does not clearly note items that do not fit the basic thematic focus of each armarium, or which items are clearly from other offices. Therefore, the volume titles presented in this index are not exact. Some of the recent typed footnotes in this index are also inaccurate, the references below are correct.

ASV Indice 124, "Primo Sbozzo di Inventario di tutti i libri

che sono nell'Archivio Segreto Vaticano," by Giovanni Bissaiga (1672), provides more descriptive and accurate volume titles for some armarium volumes. Select Armarium 35 volumes are listed on folios 231r–234v, 236r–237v, 238v–241r, 254v–256r, 292v, 304v, 306r, 310r, and 311rv. The titles from Indice 124 are sometimes provided in a footnote in ASV Indice 133, so researchers can see exactly how generic the titles in ASV Indice 133 are.

ASV Indice 114 by Felice Contelori provides excerpts from *Arm. XXXV*, vol. 41, beginning on f. 54.

ASV Indice 71, Rubricelle di varii Papi da Gregorio X a Giulio II [olim *Arm. L* 40A](ff. 20–38, 52–60, and 63–74), is a table of contents to volumes 3–5. Entries proceed folio by folio and give the type of document, a summary of the business, and the folios.

ASV Indice 2, "Indici di diverse materie fragmenta, Tom. 2," is a number of different indexes that have been bound together at some point. ASV Indice 2, ff. 82–127v, "Index librorum trium privilegiorum sanctae Romanae ecclesie collectorum ab Urbano de Flisco . . . anno 1734," provides contents for Armarium 35, volumes 3–5. Place names are in the margins and the entries note the type of document or person, summarize the business, the date, and the folio. This indice appears to go through the volumes document by document, but full comprehensiveness cannot be determined at this point. ASV Indice 2, f. 536, "Tabula huius Libri," also contains contents to *Arm. XXXV*, vol. 4, which lists the type of business, a summary of the document, and the date.

ASV Indice 110, "Index librorum 112 Diversorum scripturarum confecta Rmo. Dmo. Felice Contelori et unitorum per me Joannen Bissaigham & fuit compactus an 1694" [olim Arm 58, n. 41], provides access to *Arm. XXXV*, vols. 3 (ASV Indice 110, ff. 216–226v), 5 (ff. 227–238v), 14 (ff. 240–252v), 16 (285–286v), 17 (ff. 287–289v), and 25 (ff. 290–290v) on the pages indicated. Entries for volumes 3–5 and 14 note the dioceses in the margins and proceed folio by folio, listing the following elements: place, type of business (e.g., venditio), recipient, summary of the document, date, cost (occasionally), and folio number. Although this does provide descriptive detail concerning the contents of the volume, it should not be assumed to be a complete index. The entries for volumes 16, 17, and 25 are very abbreviated and are more like modern indices. These indices are organized alphabetically according to place and give a sketchy summary and sometimes a folio number.

Location: Archivio Segreto Vaticano.

3.2.3.13 Armarium XXXVI: Informationes camerales

[DATABASE ID: VATV052-A]

Inclusive Dates: 1335–1700.

Bulk: 50 vols.

Scope: Vols. 10–25 of *Arm. XXXVI* are the informationes of Francisco de Rubeis, a fiscal advocate to the Holy See between 1644 and 1673.

References: Fink, p. 31; Boyle, p. 45; Pásztor (1970), pp. 14–15; MacFarlane, p. 43. A. Mercati, "Schedario Garampi, Registri Vaticani, Registri Lateranensi, Rationes Camerae, Inventario del Fondo Concistoriale," vol. 1 of *Sussidi per la consultazione dell'Archivio Vaticano*, (Rome, 1926), p. 25.

Finding Aids: ASV Indice 133, ff. 167r–168r, briefly lists summary titles of each volume. The index (compiled by Petrus De Pretis after 1741) is basically informative but often fails to note copies. The index also uses terms such as *regestrum* and *brevia* too inclusively and does not clearly note items that do not fit the basic thematic focus of each Armarium, or which items are clearly from other offices. Therefore, the volume titles are often not very precise. Also, the recent typed footnotes are sometimes incorrect.

ASV Indice 137, "Index iurum sanctae et apostol. Rom. Eccle. euisq. rev. cam. in civitatibus terris aliisq. sibi subiectis locis in Secretiori Vaticano Charthophylacio asseruatorum Iulio Monterentio et Fel.e Contilor.o olim eiusden Camerae Commissarrio Generalibus accurantibus Pars Prima Complectens, Civites, Terras, alias, loca &c. MDCCXXXIV," indexes Arm. XXXVI, vols. 1–9 and 38, and *Arm. XXXVII*, vols. 1–19, 27, and 40. This index is organized as one large alphabetical list of personal names, places, "diplomatic" type of business. Each entry is accompanied by a tome number and a folio. Once a volume number is listed it is often not repeated until the volume number for an entry changes. How it was determined that the entry applies to *Arm. XXXVI or XXXVII* for volumes 1–9 is not clear.

ASV Indice 138, "Indice generale delle scritture di Monsigr. de Rossi fatte per servitio della Rev. Camera dall'anno 1644 fino al 1673 le quali si conservano in Archivio Vaticano in 16 volumi, ne quali si principia dal 1673 andando in dietro. Quali Indice per maggior regola si e fatto con ordine retrogrado" [olim *Arm. XXXVI*, tom. 48], indexes *Arm. XXXVI*, vols. 10–25. The index is organized chronologically by year and then by folio. The entries proceed folio by folio, giving the type of business or place ("discorso," "Polonia") and then the folio number of the document. Each year is also given a section number and there is a typed concordance at the beginning of the index tying section numbers to precise armaria volumes.

ASV Indice 2, "Indici di diverse materie fragmenta, Tom. 2," contains, beginning on f. 395, the "Index materiarum cameralium," an alphabetical index by place (Ancona), type of business (altare), and some personal names in *Arm. XXXVI*, vols. 1–9.

ASV Indice 2, "Indici di diverse materie, Tom. 2," contains the "Index Tomi secundi sub littera B, R.P.D. Petri Francisci de Rubeis," on ff. 451–463v. This lists the contents of *Arm. XXXVI*, vol. 11. Entries include the names of persons involved, a summary of the document, and the folio number. The type of business is often in the margins. *Arm. XXXVI*, vol. 12, is given the same treatment in this index on ff. 466–479v, "Tom. III de Rubeis."

ASV Indice 110, "Index librorum 112 Diversorum scripturarum confecta Rmo. Dmo. Felice Contelori et unitorum per me Joannen Bissaigham & fuit compactus an 1694," [olim *Arm. LVIII*, n. 41] provides a sketchy index for *Arm. XXXVI*, vols. 1–9 on ASV Indice 110, ff. 260r–281v. The entries for this armarium are more abbreviated than the entries to the volumes from other amarii in this index. Entries are alphabetical by place and give a sketchy summary of the business and sometimes a folio number.

ASV Indice 124, "Primo Sbozzo di Inventario di tutti i libri che sono nell'Archivio Segreto Vaticano," by Giovanni Bissaiga (1672), provides more descriptive and accurate volume titles for some armarium volumes. Select volumes in *Arm. XXXVI* are listed on folios 388rv. The exact titles listed in Indice 124 are sometimes provided in a footnote in ASV Indice

133, so researchers can see exactly how generic the titles in ASV Indice 133 are.

Location: Archivio Segreto Vaticano.

3.2.3.14 Armarium XXXVII: Informationes camerales
[DATABASE ID: VATV053-A]

Inclusive Dates: ca. 1500–1700.

Bulk: 43 vols.

Scope: Vols. 1–27 of *Arm. XXXVII* are the informationes of Contelori, a commissioner-general of the papal Camera.

References: Boyle, p. 45; Fink, p. 32; MacFarlane, p. 43.

Finding Aids: ASV Indice 133, ff. 137 and 168r–169r, briefly lists summary titles of each volume. The index (compiled by Petrus De Pretis after 1741) is basically informative but often fails to note copies. The index also uses terms such as *regestrum* and *brevia* too inclusively and does not clearly note items that do not fit the basic thematic focus of each armarium, or which items are clearly from other offices. Therefore, the volume titles presented in this index are not exact. Some of the recent typed footnotes in this index are also incorrect.

ASV Indice 110, "Index librorum 112 Diversorum scripturarum confecta Rmo. Dmo. Felice Contelori et unitorum per me Joannen Bissaigham & fuit compactus an 1694" [olim Arm 58, n. 41], indexes *Arm. XXXVII*, vols. 27 (on f. 164) and 40 (on folio 129). Entries note the dioceses in the margins and proceed folio by folio, listing the following elements: place, type of business (e.g., venditio), recipient, summary of the document, date, cost (occasionally), and folio number. Although this does provide descriptive detail concerning the contents of the volume, it should not be assumed to be a complete index.

ASV Indice 137, "Index iurum sanctae et apostol. Rom. Eccle. euisq. rev. cam. in civitatibus terris aliisq. sibi subiectis locis in Secretiori Vaticano Charthophylacio asseruatorum Iulio Monterentio et Fel.e Contelori olim eiusden Camerae Commissarrio Generalibus accurantibus Pars Prima Complectens, Civites, Terras, alias, loca & c. MDCCXXXIV," indexes *Arm. XXXVI*, vols. 1–9 and 38 and *Arm. XXXVII*, vols. 1–19, 27, and 40 (according to Indice 133 and Indice 137 itself). Exactly which volumes are indexed is noted variously as *Arm. XXXVII*, vols. 1–9, 27, and 40; or 1–11, 27, and 40; or 1–27 and 40. This index is organized as one large alphabetical list of personal names, places, and "diplomatic" type of business. Each entry is accompanied by a volume number and a folio. Once a volume number is listed it is often not repeated until the volume number for an entry changes. How one determines if the entry applies to *Arm. XXXVI or XXXVII* for volumes 1–9 is not clear.

ASV Indice 126, "Indice de Libri di Mons. Contelori segnati as tergo A . . . V con l'Indice di Diverse Bolle Stampate," provides page by page contents of selected documents in vols. 1–19 and summarizes the contents of others in *Arm. XXXVII*, vols. 1–19. The index appears to be organized in a series of sections that correspond to volumes lettered A through V. Each letter appears to correspond to an individual volume. Entries proceed document by document (with some gaps) giving the place or type of business, and the folio number.

ASV Indice 124, "Primo Sbozzo di Inventario di tutti i libri che sono nell'Archivio Segreto Vaticano," by Giovanni Bissaiga (1672), provides more descriptive and accurate volume titles for some armarium volumes. Select volumes of *Arm.*

XXXVII are listed in this index on folios 242v and 389rv. The exact titles listed in Indice 124 are sometimes provided in a footnote in ASV Indice 133, so researchers can see exactly how generic the titles in ASV Indice 133 are.

Location: Archivio Segreto Vaticano.

3.2.3.15 Armaria L–LI

[DATABASE ID: VATV373-A]
Inclusive Dates: 872–1590.
Bulk: 77 vols.
Scope: These are rubricellae of papal registers; fifty of the volumes are now located in the index room and are called ASV Indici 240–289. See list of indici in the appendices.
References: Boyle, p. 39. F. Gasparolo, ed., "Costituzione dell'Archivio Vaticano e suo primo indice sotto il pontificato di Paolo V: Manoscritto inedito de Michele Lonigo," *Studi e documenti di storia e diritto* 8 (1887): 48. A. Mercati, "Schedario Garampi, Registri Vaticani, Registri Lateranensi, Rationes Camerae, Inventario del Fondo Concistoriale," vol. 1 of *Sussidi per la consultazione dell'Archivio Vaticano,* (Rome, 1926), pp. 52–54.
Finding Aids: ASV Indice 133/II briefly lists summary titles of each volume. The index, compiled by Petrus De Pretis sometime shortly after 1741, is basically informative but often fails to note copies. The index also uses terms such as *regestrum* and *brevia* too inclusively and does not clearly note items that do not fit the basic thematic focus of each armarium, or which items are clearly from other offices.
Location: Archivio Segreto Vaticano.

3.2.3.16 Assegne di bestiame alla dogana del Patrimonio e di Marittima e Campagna e Entrata della fida di Roma

[DATABASE ID: VATV20004-A]
Inclusive Dates: 1721–1738.
Bulk: 72 registri.
Reference: D'Angiolini, p. 1083.
Finding Aids: List, 1970.
Location: Archivio di Stato di Roma.

3.2.3.17 Bandi

[DATABASE ID: VATV20020-A]
Inclusive Dates: [14—]–1870.
Bulk: 585 buste.
Organization: Collezione I, [14—]–1870, 292 buste; —Collezione II, [14—]–1870, 222 buste; —Collezione III, [15—]–1870, 61 buste; —Appendice, undated, 10 buste.
Reference: D'Angiolini, p. 1088.
Finding Aids: Partial inventory and partial list; there is also a printed abstract of some bandi of the fifteenth and sixteenth centuries.
Location: Archivio di Stato di Roma.

3.2.3.18 Bullarum distributiones

[DATABASE ID: VATV062-A]
Inclusive Dates: 1478–1560.
Bulk: 5 linear m.
Organization: 14 vols., chronological by year and month.
Scope: These are monthly records of payments for expedition of bulls.
Note: These records were transferred from the Archivio di Stato di Roma in 1919 as part of the Fondo dell'Archivio di Stato di Roma. They were formerly identified in the Archivio di Stato di Roma as a part of the series *Registri dei pagamenti in bullaria.*
References: Fink, p. 55; Boyle, p. 47; Pásztor (1970), pp. 38–39.
Finding Aids: ASV Indice 1112 (former Indice 41), pp. 23 verso and 24, provides an individual listing of some volumes in this series, inclusive dates, and their current ASV and former Archivio di Stato numbers. The final unnumbered pages of this index reiterate some of this information in tables listing current and former names and numbers for the series.
Location: Archivio Segreto Vaticano.

3.2.3.19 Bullarum registra: Registri dei pagamenti in bullarae

[DATABASE ID: VATV063-A]
Inclusive Dates: 1643–1679.
Bulk: .2 linear m. (4 vols.).
Organization: Chronological by year and then month.
Note: These payment registers were transferred from the Archivio di Stato di Roma in 1919 as part of the Fondo dell'Archivio di Stato di Roma. They were formerly included as part of the series *Registri dei pagamenti in bullaria* in the Archivio di Stato di Roma.
References: Fink, p. 56; Boyle, p. 47 (series title cited as *Registra Bullarum*); Pásztor (1970), p. 38.
Finding Aids: ASV Indice 1112 (former Indice 41), pp. 23–24, provides an individual listing of some volumes in this series with inclusive dates and their current ASV and former Archivio di Stato di Roma numbers. The final unnumbered pages of this index reiterate some of this information in a table listing current and former names and numbers for volumes in the series.
Location: Archivio Segreto Vaticano.

3.2.3.20 Bullarum relaxationes: Registri dei pagamenti in bullaria

[DATABASE ID: VATV064-A]
Inclusive Dates: 1691–1798.
Bulk: .3 linear m. (6 vols.).
Organization: Chronological by year and month.
Scope: These are accounts dealing with payments for bulls.
Note: The series was transferred from the Archivio di Stato di Roma in 1919 as part of the Fondo dell'Archivio di Stato di Roma. The series was formerly included as part of the series *Registri dei pagamenti in bullaria* in the Archivio di Stato di Roma. There is a variant title on the spine, *Rubricellae Bullarum.*
References: Fink, p. 56; Boyle, p. 47; Pásztor (1970), p. 38.
Finding Aids: ASV Indice 1112 (former Indice 41) (pp. 23–24) provides an individual listing of some volumes, their inclusive dates, and their current ASV and former Archivio di Stato numbers. The final unnumbered pages of this index reiterate some of this information in a table listing current and former names and numbers for volumes in the series.
Location: Archivio Segreto Vaticano.

3.2.3.21 Camera urbis

[DATABASE ID: VATV20005-A]
Inclusive Dates: 1416–1743.
Bulk: 390 registri.
References: D'Angiolini, p. 1081; Lodolini (1960), p. 75.

Finding Aids: Inventory, 1932 (not completely reliable).
Location: Archivio di Stato di Roma.

3.2.3.22 Collectoriae

[DATABASE ID: VATV046-A]

Inclusive Dates: 1274–1447.

Bulk: 24 linear m.

Organization: 504 numbered volumes, in no consistent sequence, though the volumes are often identified with particular collectoriae. These were fiscal regions, each the responsibility of one collector or fiscal nuncio, and might be smaller than an ecclesiastical province (e.g., Bourges and Limoges) or as large as several kingdoms (e.g., Poland and Hungary). The *Fondo camerale* comprises this series, *Introitus et exitus*, and *Obligationes et solutiones*.

Scope: MacFarlane and Boyle emphasize the importance of this series, which consists mainly of the reports and accounts submitted to the Camera by the collectors appointed throughout western Christendom to gather various taxes and other debts claimed by the pope. Those taxes included the census, an annual tribute from exempt monasteries; annates, the assessed income of minor benefices for the first year of their tenure, when this was reserved to the pope; tenths, an income tax on benefices levied for particular purposes such as a Crusade; other emergency subsidies, for example, the thirtieths and subsidia caritativa; spoils, the money, movables and debts receivable belonging to deceased clerics, if these were reserved by the pope; the reserved income of vacant benefices; Peter's Pence. The collectors were commissioned with great executive and judicial powers, including excommunication and summary justice; their reports consequently give a valuable insight into the economic and social condition of their collectories. Their cash accounts, scrupulously drafted and audited in the Camera, reveal the ongoing business of papal finance.

Various records kept in the Camera itself were bound and stored with *Collectoriae* reports and became part of this series, for example some registers of letters of the camerarii and some dossiers of papal letters bearing on the functions of the Camera. A very large number of unbound documents that once accompanied *Collectoriae* material are now found in *Instrumenta miscellanea*.

Both this series and the *Introitus et exitus* include information on the administration of the papal states, instructions to local fiscal officials within them, and other valuable local information, and are thus a rich source for the social history of central Italy during the fourteenth and fifteenth centuries.

See Boyle, pp. 165–168, for an extensive discussion on the use of this series.

Note: Vols. 1, 24, 41, 54, 106, 111, 113, 133, 179, 191, 211, 244, 260, 279, 357, 381, 401, 404, 414, 419, 431A, 434, 436, 446–447, 459, 464–466, 486, and 492A are available on microfilm.

References: Fink, pp. 50–51; Boyle, pp. 43 and 165–168; MacFarlane, p. 41. U. Berlière, "Les collectories pontificales dans les anciens diocèses de Cambrai, Thérouanne et Tournai au XIVe siècle," vol. 10 of *Analecta vaticano-belgica: Documents relatifs aux anciens diocèses de Cambrai, Liège, Thérouanne et Tournai* (Rome, 1929). J. P. Kirsch, *Die päpstlichen Kollektorien in Deutschland während des XIV. Jahrhunderts* (Paderborn, 1894). W. E. Lunt, *Accounts rendered by Papal Collectors in England, 1317–1378* (Philadelphia,

1968). Y. Renouard, *Les relations des Papes d'Avignon et des compagnies commerciales et bancaires de 1316 à 1378* (Paris, 1941). C. Samaran and G. Mollat, *La fiscalité pontificale en France au XIVe siècle: Période d'Avignon et du Grand Schisme d'Occident* (Paris, 1905). D. Williman, "Letters of Etienne Cambarou, Camerarius Apostolicus (1347–1361)," *Archivum Historiae Pontificiae* 15 (1977): 195–215.

Finding Aids: ASV Indice 1036, part II, provides an individual volume listing to the series and a list of volumes in the Cancellaria Apostolica series *Registra Avenionensia* that include material astray from it. Entries include: volume number, inclusive dates, the exact spine title or a titular contents summary often with the type of transaction and geographic area. It is, however, difficult to distinguish an exact title from the summary. Some entries also include very brief annotations. Entries identify the participant and the business correctly but can sometimes be slightly misleading regarding their exact relationship. At the end of Indice 1036 there is an index to persons, churches, and dioceses. An important note on the reliability of the index appears on page 233. The index, though not complete, can be of assistance in locating geographic areas.

Also useful is Joseph de Loye, *Les archives de la Chambre apostolique au XIVe siècle*, part 1, *Inventaire* (Paris, 1899). In this work de Loye provides a more analytic index to all the volumes in this series. Entries include: old and new volume numbers, inclusive dates, exact title on the spine or a titular summary of material in the volume (although the exact title is not signaled in any way), and occasionally an excerpted example of the type of entry in a register. This book has a good introduction and appendices that index the series by materials (papal administration: manualia, inventaria, thesauri, Avignon papacy) and geography (provincial administration and collectors). There are also two tables in the back to Cameral letters and to the old and new enumeration of the *Collectoriae*.

ASV Indice 124, "Primo Sbozzo di Inventario di tutti i libri che sono nell'Archivio Segreto Vaticano," by Giovanni Bissaiga (1672), provides more descriptive and accurate volume titles for select volumes of some series. A few *Collectoriae* volumes are listed on folio 231v.

Location: Archivio Segreto Vaticano.

3.2.3.23 Collezione delle assegne

[DATABASE ID: VATV20055-A]

Inclusive Dates: 1744, 1764, 1793–1798, 1801, and 1811.

Bulk: 222 buste and vols.

Organization: Assegne sui beni e rendite di particolari, Roma e agro romano, 1744, 1764 and 1793–1797, 88 buste and vols.; —Assegne in Roma e nello Stato pontificio, 1796–1797, 55 buste; —Contribuzioni alle armate francesi, 1797, 26 buste; —Assegne dei beni e rendite per la perequazione dell'erario, 1797, 17 buste; —Argenti, ori e gioie dati alla zecca e beni dati per essi, 1796–1798, 6 buste; —Assegne dei censi e canoni in Roma e fuori, 1801, 3 buste; —Assegne dei beni venduti e affittati dal governo repubblicano, 1801, 14 buste; —Assegne delle enfiteusi dei beni gia camerali e religiosi, 1811, 13 buste.

Reference: D'Angiolini, pp. 1125–1126.

Finding Aids: Summary inventory.

Location: Archivio di Stato di Roma.

3.2.3.24 Congregazione super executione mandatorum contra barones

[DATABASE ID: VATV20051-A]
Inclusive Dates: 1674–1796.
Bulk: 20 vols.
Reference: D'Angiolini, p. 1121.
Finding Aids: List.
Location: Archivio di Stato di Roma.

3.2.3.25 Decretorum: Congregatione Quindenniorum

[DATABASE ID: VATV10007-A]
Inclusive Dates: 1690–1790 (bulk 1690–1720).
Bulk: 3 linear m.
Organization: Chronological.
Scope: These are incoming letters regarding quindenni payments. These are also identified as records of the Succollettore generale della cancelleria. There is a variant spine title, *Congregationi Particolari: Materie Trattare nelle Congregazioni Particolari dei Quindenniorum.*
Reference: Pásztor (1970), p. 68.
Finding Aids: At the beginning of each volume there is an annotated index to dioceses and types of payments.
Location: Archivio Segreto Vaticano.

3.2.3.26 Divisioni

[DATABASE ID: VATV10006-A]
Inclusive Dates: 1691–1854.
Bulk: 6 linear m. (109 vols.).
Organization: Chronological by year and month.
Scope: This series contains listings for payments of quindennia, quietationes, ristretti d'ordini, and mandati di divisioni. There are no records between 1809 and 1828. These records are also identified as records of the Succollettore generale della cancelleria. There is a variant subtitle that appears on some volumes: *delle Annate, Pensioni, e Quindenni.* Each volume begins with a rubricelle de quindenni.
Reference: Pásztor (1970), p. 69.
Location: Archivio Segreto Vaticano.

3.2.3.27 Entrata et uscita de quindenni

[DATABASE ID: VATV10008-A]
Inclusive Dates: 1691–1802.
Bulk: 1.5 linear m.
Organization: Chronological by year and month.
Scope: These records are a chronological accounting of payments. The diocese appears in the margins and then a brief note on the church or monastery which paid forms the text. These records are also identified as records of the Succollettore generale della cancelleria.
Reference: Pásztor (1970), p. 70.
Location: Archivio Segreto Vaticano.

3.2.3.28 Fondo camerale

[DATABASE ID: VATV044-A]
Inclusive Dates: 1274–1564.
Bulk: 48 linear m. (1,160 vols.).
Organization: Three series: *Obligationes et solutiones,* 1295–1555, 5 linear m. or 91 numbered volumes; —*Collectoriae,* 1274–1447, 19 linear m. or 504 numbered volumes; —*Introitus et exitus,* 1279–1564. 24 linear m. or 565 numbered volumes.

Note: Each of these series is described separately in the list of records for this office. However, the fondo is often cited as a unit.
References: Fink, pp. 49–52; Boyle, pp. 41–43 and 154–172; Pásztor (1970), pp. 29–31; Pásztor (1983), pp. 103–108. F. Gasparolo, ed., "Costituzione dell'Archivio Vaticano e suo primo indice sotto il pontificato di Paolo V: Manoscritto inedito de Michele Lonigo," *Studi e documenti di storia e diritto* 8 (1887): 48–50. A. Mercati, "Schedario Garampi, Registri Vaticani, Registri Lateranensi, Rationes Camerae, Inventario del Fondo Concistoriale," vol. 1 of *Sussidi per la consultazione dell'Archivio Vaticano* (Rome, 1926), pp. 193–201. This volume provides a concordance between the former Rationes Camerae arrangement and the current organization of the three series.
Finding Aids: Indice 1036 provides basic access to volumes in these series and a list of volumes of the Camera Apostolica series *Registra Avenionensia* that contain material astray from them. There is an important note concerning inaccuracies in the indice on page 286.
Location: Archivio Segreto Vaticano.

3.2.3.29 Fondo dell'Archivio di Stato di Roma

[DATABASE ID: VATV054-A]
Inclusive Dates: 1408–1869.
Bulk: 166 linear m.
Organization: This fondo comprises several series all of which are listed separately in this guide (numerical designations were supplied by project staff). Series, which are all part of the Camera Apostolica unless otherwise noted, are: 1. *Resignationes,* 1457–1594; —2. *Rubricelle resignationes,* 1523–1555; —3. (Dataria Apostolica) *Consensus,* 1536–1908; —4. (Dataria Apostolica) *Consensus rubricelle,* 1548–1591; —5. Annatae, 1421–1797; —6. *Annatae et quindennia,* 1742–1850; —7. *Formatarum libri,* 1425–1524; —8. *Obligationes communes,* 1408–1798; —9. *Obligationes particulares,* 1419–1482; —10. *Taxae,* 1426–1815; —11. *Servitia minuta,* 1416–1455; —12. *Bullarum distributiones,* 1478–1560; —13. *Liber computorum,* 1527–1679; —14. *Bullarum relaxationes,* 1691–1798; —15. *Bullarum registra,* 1643–1679; —16. *Rubricellae,* 1342–1579; —17. (Secretariatus Status) *Registri "Bullarum" già Coadiutorie e Commende,* 1787–1894; —18. (Secretariatus Status) *Registri I,* 1800–1809; —19. (Secretariatus Status) *Registri II,* 1814–1829.
Scope: The fondo is an artificial collection of materials whose common denominator is that they were transferred together from the Archivio di Stato di Roma in 1919. Each of the series listed is described separately among the records of the agencies that generated the record series. Materials were formerly in the custody of the Archivio di Stato di Roma.
References: Fink, pp. 54–57; Boyle, pp. 45–48; Pásztor (1970), pp. 33–43. E. Göller, "Die neue Bestände der Camera Apostolica im päpstlichen Geheimarchiv," *Römische Quartalschrift für christliche Altertumskunde und für Kirchengeschichte* 30 (1922): 38–53. A. Lodolini, *L'archivio di Stato di Roma: Epitome d'una guida degli archivi dell'amministrazione dello Stato Pontificio* (Rome, 1960).
Finding Aids: ASV Indice 1112 (formerly Indice 41) cross references the old Archivio di Stato di Roma names and reference numbers with the current ASV designations. ASV Indice 1036 provides access to the following series: *Obligationes com-*

munes and *Obligationes particulares*. ASV Indice 1043 provides access to the series *Annatae*. ASV Indice 1151 provides access to the Secretariatus Status series *Registri bullarum (già Coadiutore e Commende)*.

Location: Archivio Segreto Vaticano.

3.2.3.30 Formatarum libri

[DATABASE ID: VATV065-A]

Inclusive Dates: 1425–1524.

Bulk: 1 linear m.

Organization: 14 vols., chronological.

Scope: This series gives lists of ordinations of bishops, priests, and so forth, and of litterae dimissoriales and payments for dispensations.

Note: The series was transferred from the Archivio di Stato di Roma in 1919 as part of the Fondo dell'Archivio di Stato di Roma. The series was formerly identified in the Archivio di Stato di Roma as *Formatari*.

References: Fink, p. 55; Boyle, p. 47. G. Pellicia, *La preparazione 'ed ammissione dei chierici ai santi ordini nella Roma del sec. XVI* (Rome, 1946). L. Schmitz, "Die Libri Formatarum Camerae Apostolicae," *Römische Quartalschrift für christliche Altertumskunde und für Kirchengeschichte* 8 (1894): 451–472.

Finding Aids: ASV Indice 1112 (former Indice 41) provides an individual listing of volumes in the series including inclusive dates and their current ASV and former Archivio di Stato di Roma numbers. The final unnumbered pages of this index reiterate some of this information in tabular form, listing the current and former names and numbers.

Location: Archivio Segreto Vaticano.

3.2.3.31 Introitus et exitus

[DATABASE ID: VATV047-A]

Inclusive Dates: 1279–1564.

Bulk: 19 linear m.

Organization: 565 numbered volumes. Volumes 1–562 are chronological although within some individual volumes receipts and expenses are categorized by type. Volume numbers 563, 564, and 565 are out of place chronologically and cover the following years: 563 (1316), 564 (1319), 565 (1331). The *Fondo camerale* comprises this series, *Collectoriae*, and *Obligationes et solutiones*.

Scope: These are the cumulative form of the monthly income and expenditure reports by the papal treasurer. Some volumes from this series have wandered to the Cancelleria Apostolica series *Registra Avenionensia*, and some unbound *Introitus et exitus* material is in the Miscellaneous official series *Instrumenta miscellanea*.

MacFarlane notes that these are a precious source of information on the financial workings of the Curia itself, as well as being particularly useful for the exact dating of personal visits to the Holy See by clergy of all kinds, in order to pay their annates, common services, the census and the like. Procurators are also named. On the expense side they are also full of interesting information recounting the expenditure of each of the departments of the papal household, military expenses, building costs, payments for works of art, and so on.

Boyle adds that this series is a rich source for the economic or the social historian. To a local historian, however, the value of these ledgers often lies in the fact that they confirm if they do not add to information found in the Camera Apostolica series *Obligationes et solutiones* or *Collectoriae*. See Boyle, pp 168–172, for an extensive presentation on the use of this series.

Note: Vols. 4–7, 18, 35, 37, 53, 59, 67, 80, 130, 146, 150, 159, 164, 171, 172, 177, 185, 190, 206, 209, 215, 216, 220, 227, 234, 242, 247, 281, 288–289, 293, 295–296, 300, 301, 305, 311, 312, 320–323, 325, 327, 331–332, 336, 340, 343, 340, 344, 350, 351, 359, 361, 363, 365–367, 369–371, and 374–375 are available on microfilm.

References: Boyle, pp. 43 and 168–172; Fink, p. 49; MacFarlane, pp. 40–41. J. Favier, "'Introitus et Exitus' sous Clément VII et Benoît XIII: Problèmes de diplomatique et d'interpretation," *Bullettino dell'Archivio paleografico italiano*, n.s. 2–3, pt. 1 (1956–1957): 285–294. J. P. Kirsch, *Die Rückkehr der Päpste Urban V. und Gregor XI. von Avignon nach Rom: Auszüge aus den Kameralregistern des Vatikanischen Archivs* (Paderborn, 1898). P. Partner, *The Pope's Men: The Papal Civil Service in the Renaissance* (Oxford, 1990).

Income entries for the period covering 1316–1378 in the IE and in related sources are published in the Einnahmen volumes and expenditure entries are printed in the Ausgaben volumes of the *Vatikanische Quellen zur Geschichte des päpstlichen Hof- und Finanzverwaltung 1316–1378* (Paderborn, 1910–). An individual listing of volumes follows: vol. 1, E. Göller, ed., *Die Einnahmen der apostolischen Kammer unter Johann XXII* (Paderborn, 1910); vol. 2, K. H. Schäfer, ed., *Die Ausgaben der apostolischen Kammer unter Johann XXII., nebst den Jahresbilanzen von 1316–1375* (Paderborn, 1911); vol. 3, K. H. Schäfer, ed., *Die Ausgaben der apostolischen Kammer unter Benedikt XII., Klemens VI. und Innocenz VI. (1335–1362)* (Paderborn, 1914); vol. 4, E. Göller, ed., *Die Einnahmen der apostolischen Kammer unter Benedikt XII* (Paderborn, 1920); vol. 5, L. Mohler, ed., *Die Einnahmen der apostolischen Kammer unter Klemens VI* (Paderborn, 1931); vol. 6, K. H. Schäfer, ed., *Die Ausgaben der apostolischen Kammer unter den Päpsten Urban V. und Gregor XI. (1362–1378), nebst Nachträgen und einem Glossar für alle drei Ausgabenbände* (Paderborn, 1937); vol. 7, H. Hoberg, ed., *Die Einnahmen der apostolischen Kammer unter Innocenz VI. Die Einnahmenregister des päpstlichen Thesaurars* (Paderborn, 1955).

J. Haller et al., eds., *Repertorium Germanicum: Regesten aus den päpstlichen Archiven zur Geschichte des Deutschen Reichs und seiner Territorien im XIV. und XV. Jahrhundert: Pontifikat Eugens IV. (1431–1447)* (Berlin, 1897), calendars items concerning Germany in this series.

Finding Aids: ASV Index 1036, part I, provides a volume by volume series listing. Entries include: the former and current volume numbers, inclusive dates, the exact spine title or brief contents summary (although one cannot tell which is which), and sometimes a note on a particularly interesting item in the volume. Additional important information concerning the accuracy of this listing is on page 286 of Index 1036. Entries generally identify the participants and the business correctly, but the relationship referred to in Indice 1036 can sometimes be misleading. An alphabetical index to important churches, selected persons, and dioceses that are cited in Indice 1036 appears on p. 233.

Also useful is Joseph de Loye, *Les archives de la Chambre apostolique au XIVe siècle*, part 1, *Inventaire* (Paris, 1899). In this work, de Loye provides a more analytical index for the first

380 volumes. Entries include: volume number, inclusive dates, the exact spine title or a brief titular contents summary (although again it is difficult to tell which is which). In addition there are excerpts, sometimes fairly substantial, of actual entries. There are also indices at the end of the book to entries for papal administration (Camera in Avignon, Manualia, Inventaria Thesauri); provincial administration organized by geographic area; and collections, again organized by geographic area. De Loye lists *Registra Avenionensia* volumes that contain *Introitus et exitus* materials.

ASV Indice 194 (fols. 7–9) provides a concordance between the former and current volume numbers. The "numero vecchio" is found in many older historical studies and in the Schedario Garampi.

ASV Indice 114 (pp. 49–53v, 73–76), by Felice Contelori, provides curious excerpts of selected volumes in this series.

ASV Indice 124, "Primo Sbozzo di Inventario di tutti i libri che sono nell'Archivio Segreto Vaticano," by Giovanni Bissaiga (1672), provides more descriptive and accurate volume titles for select volumes of some series. A few *Introitus et exitus* volumes are listed on folios 216r–230v, 235rv, and 251v.

Location: Archivio Segreto Vaticano.

3.2.3.32 Liber provincialis e Liber iuramentorum
[DATABASE ID: VATV20008-A]
Inclusive Dates: 1467.
Bulk: 1 vol. (136 carte).
Reference: D'Angiolini, pp. 1080–1081.
Location: Archivio di Stato di Roma.

3.2.3.33 Liber quindenniorum indicationum
[DATABASE ID: VATV10005-A]
Inclusive Dates: 1588–1873.
Bulk: 1.5 linear m.
Organization: Organized by subcollector and then within each subseries by year and month.
Scope: These are subcollectors' records that form a diary of payments with descriptive notes. The records are also identified as records of Succollettore generale della cancelleria.
Reference: Pásztor (1970), p. 69.
Location: Archivio Segreto Vaticano.

3.2.3.34 Liber taxarum ecclesiarum et monasterium omnium
[DATABASE ID: VATV20007-A
Inclusive Dates: [15—].
Bulk: 1 vol.
Reference: D'Angiolini, p. 1081.
Location: Archivio di Stato di Roma.

3.2.3.35 Libri computorum
[DATABASE ID: VATV061-A]
Inclusive Dates: 1527–1679.
Bulk: 1 linear m. (10 numbered vols.).
Organization: Chronological by year then month.
Scope: These are monthly accounts and summaries of financial transactions organized by type (e.g., brevia expedita, brevia redempta, etc.).
Note: The records were transferred from the Archivio di Stato di Roma in 1919 as part of the Fondo dell'Archivio di Stato di Roma. The series was formerly identified as part of the Archivio di Stato di Roma series *Tasse di Segretaria*. Pásztor

(cf. below) states that Camera Apostolica, *Sec. Cam.* 215 and 217, are now Camera Apostolica, *Comput.* 5 and 8, respectively. He may be referring to volumes in this series.
References: Fink, p. 56; Boyle, p. 47; Pásztor (1970), p. 33.
Finding Aids: ASV Indice 1112 (former Indice 41) (p. 20) provides an individual listing of some volumes in the series with inclusive dates and their current and former Archivio di Stato di Roma numbers.
Location: Archivio Segreto Vaticano.

3.2.3.36 Luoghi di monte
[DATABASE ID: VATV20003-A]
Inclusive Dates: 1532–1824.
Bulk: 3,768 vols. and buste.
References: D'Angiolini, pp. 1083–1084; Lodolini (1960), pp. 80–83.
Finding Aids: Inventory.
Location: Archivio di Stato di Roma.

3.2.3.37 Miscellanea camerale per luoghi (Camerale III)
[DATABASE ID: VATV20016-A]
Inclusive Dates: [14—]–[18—].
Bulk: 2,510 buste.
Organization: Ascoli, [14—]–1821, 23 buste; —Avignone e Contado Venassino, 1639–1819, 26 buste; —Benevento, 1484–1807, 17 buste; —Bologna, 1613–1822, 40 buste; —Città di Castello, 1430–1832, 16 buste; — Conca, [17—], 3 buste; —Ferrara, 1400–1859, 86 buste; —Narni, 1466–1859, 4 buste; —Nettuno ed Anzio, 1544–1870, 60 buste; —Rieti, 1425–1870, 6 buste; —Roma, 1498–1870, 384 buste; —Senigallia, 1459–1842, 18 buste; —Tolfa, 1463–1870, 73 buste.
References: D'Angiolini, pp. 1077–1079; Lodolini (1960), p. 75.
Finding Aids: Summary inventory, 1911–1912; partial inventories.
Location: Archivio di Stato di Roma.

3.2.3.38 Miscellanea camerale per materia (Camerale II)
[DATABASE ID: VATV20017-A]
Inclusive Dates: [14—]–1870 (bulk [15—]–1870).
Bulk: 2,261 buste and registri.
Orgainzation: Accademie, 1718–1868, 4 buste; —Acque, 1682–1853, 17 buste; —Agricoltura, 1626–1847, 8 buste and 1 registro; —Agro romano, 1526–1855 (bulk [17—]–1855), 28 buste; —Annona, 1435, 1468–1469 and 1524–1857, 128 buste; —Antichita e belle arti, 1538–1830, 32 buste; —Appalti, 1709, 1792 and 1794, 5 buste; —Appannaggio del principe Beauharnais, 1815–1860, 8 buste; —Archivio della camera apostolica, 1553–[16—] and 1747–1868, 6 buste; —Arti e mestieri, [15—]–[18—], 45 buste; —Banca romana, 1834–1867, 2 buste; —Beni camerali, 197 buste; —Birri, 1596–1816, 3 buste;—Bollo e registro, 1741–1816, 6 buste; —Calcografia camerale, 1732–1870, 16 buste; —Camera dei tributi, 1593–1870, 86 buste; —Camerlengato e Tesorierato, 1534–1868, 36 buste; —Cancellerie e Segreterie di Stato, 1566–1816, 12 buste; —Carceri, 1600–1870, 21 buste; —Carte da giuoco, 1768–1890, 8 buste; —Cartiere, 1775, 1787, 1794, and 1800–1860, 9 buste; —Catasto, 1730–1869, 10 buste; —Cerimoniali ecclesiastici, di corte e civili, 1617–1843, 2 buste; —Collegio dei cardinali, 1671–1826, 1 busta; —Commercio e industria,

1587–1870, 23 buste; —Computisteria generale, 1677–1845, 12 buste; —Comunità, 1737–1850, 4 buste; —Conclavi e possessi, 1590–1846, 33 buste; —Confini, 1745–1778, 4 buste; —Congregazioni monastiche, 1434, 1507, and 1585–1817, 23 buste; —Consolati, 1717, 1753, and 1764–1807, 5 buste and 1 registro; —Conti delle entrate e delle uscite o stato generale del bilancio, 1587–1807 and 1815, 16 buste; —Cursori apostolici e camerali, 1742–1866, 7 buste; —Dataria e vacabili, 1478 and 1523–1867, 13 buste; —Dativa reale, 1801–1867, 28 buste; —Debito pubblico, 1719, 1798, 1806, 1810–1814, and 1816–1870, 18 buste; —Decime, 1510–1717, 3 buste; —Depositeria generale, 1713, 1742–1825, 1847, and 1866, 4 buste; —Dogane, 1481–1863, 314 buste; —Ebrei, 1428, 1524, and 1634–1870, 23 buste; —Erario sanziore in Castel Sant' Angelo, 1556–1859, 6 buste; —Gabelle, [15—]–[18—], 26 buste; —Grascia, 1575–1834, 32 buste; —Ipoteche ed intavolazioni, 1801–1853, 4 buste; —Lavori pubblici, 1798, 1800, and 1815–1866, 13 buste and 1 rubrica; —Lotti, 1550–1590 and 1676–1862, 57 buste; —Luoghi di monte, 1560–1850, 41 buste; —Macinato, [15—]–1870, 80 buste and rubriche; —Molini, [15—]–[18—], 36 buste; —Neve e ghiaccio, 1608–1841, 15 buste; —Nobiltà e feudi, undated, 277 fascicoli in 45 buste; —Notariato, 1551–1853, 58 buste; —Nunziature, 1560–1866, 9 buste; —Paludi pontine, 1501–1866, 143 buste; —Patrimonio gesuitico, 1754–1834, 14 buste; —Pesi e misure, [16—]–1841, 5 buste; —Popolazione, 1629–1870, 12 buste; —Poste, 1531–1862, 74 buste; —Sali, tabacchi, acquavite e polveri, 1432–1864, 210 buste; —Sanità, 1547–1854, 25 buste; —Spogli e vacabili, 1539–1854, 2 buste; —Stamperia camerale, 1574–1877, 29 buste; —Strade, 1674–1870, 10 buste; —Terremoti, 1747–1832, 4 buste; —Tevere, 1547–1869, 12 buste; —Vetriolo, 1602–1852, 23 buste; —Zecca, 1525–1870, 52 buste.

References: D'Angiolini, pp. 1064–1077; Lodolini (1960), pp. 73–74.

Finding Aids: Summary inventory and partial inventories.

Location: Archivio di Stato di Roma.

3.2.3.39 Miscellanea di congregazioni diverse
[DATABASE ID: VATV20052-A]

Inclusive Dates: 1686–1698, 1704–1706, 1723, 1814, 1816–1817, and 1829–1830 (with documents from 1532).

Bulk: 3 vols., 4 fascicoli, and 1 mazzo.

Organization: Subseries include Congregazione dei quindenni, 1696–1698, 1 vol.; —Congregazioni particolari, 1686–1697 and 1723, 1 fascicolo; —Pragmatica per Roma, 1694, 1 mazzo (Congregazione particolare sopra la moderazione del lusso, e spese eccessive dell'alma citta di Roma); —Congregatio super Visitatione ac Reformatione Officiorum et Archiviorum Notariorum Urbis, 1704–1706, 1 fascicolo; —Governo provvisorio di Roma, 1814, 1 vol.; —Commissione di Stato, 1814, 1 fascicolo; —Congregazione governativa, 1816–1817, 1 fascicolo;—Congregazione di Stato, 1829–1830, 1 vol.

References: D'Angiolini, pp. 1121–1122; Lodolini (1960), pp. 91, 95.

Finding Aids: List (non rispondente).

Location: Archivio di Stato di Roma.

3.2.3.40 Miscellanea paesi stranieri
[DATABASE ID: VATV20014-A]

Inclusive Dates: [14—]–[17—].

Bulk: 29 buste.

Organization: Subseries include Francia e altri paesi di lingua francese fra cui il Belgio; —Germania; —Polonia e Russia; —Portogallo; —Spagna; —Inghilterra; —Ungheria e Transilvania; —Bulgaria; —Grecia ed Albania; —Turchia, Armenia, Levante ed altri paesi; —Cina e Giappone; —Goa e Indie orientali; —Messico e Indie occidentali; —Angola, Congo ed Ethiopia.

Reference: D'Angiolini, p. 1079.

Finding Aids: Inventory, 1910, with annotations, 1942.

Location: Archivio di Stato di Roma.

3.2.3.41 [Miscellanea, SF/97]
[DATABASE ID: VATV10010-A]

Inclusive Dates: 1575–1822.

Bulk: 2 linear m.

Scope: Items include (numerical designation supplied by project staff): 1. Regestrum mandatorum ecclesiarum et monasteriorum reductorum, 1757–1777; —2. Quindenniorum taxata et illorum solutionum, 1700–1789; —3. Annatara dei deputati, 1589; —4. Annatate diverse (e quindennia), libro del Collegio dei chiese di camera, 1642–1651, 2 vols.; —5. Quindennia taxata, et illorum solutionum, 1636–1758; —6. Liber receptorum collectoris, 1575–1591, 3 vols.; —7. Annate e quindennia, 1584–1591; —8. Quindennia maturanda, 1577–1591; —9. Rubricella, 1606–1609; —10. Libri di ricevute della cancelleria, 1576–1593; —11. Institucione del Collegio de cancelleria (de urbe), supliche di cancelleria per resignatione dell'ufficio, 1576–1597; —12. Quietantiarum cancellariorum, 1590; —13. Annata et quindennia, [16—]–[17—]; —14. Rubricella dei debitori dei quindenni, [15—], 2 vols.; —15. Debitori d'annate antiche, 1611–1688; —16. Spoglio delle chiese, monasteri, e pensioni che hanno pagati l'annate, 1600–1672; —17. Rata della collectoria spettante al Collegio dell'archivio sopra li quindenni, 1804–1822.

Note: This is a true miscellany of material that has no official ASV designation. The title was assigned by the project staff based on its location in 1990.

Location: Archivio Segreto Vaticano.

3.2.3.42 Notai segretari e cancellieri della Camera apostolica
[DATABASE ID: VATV20034-A]

Inclusive Dates: 1519–1871.

Bulk: 2,148 vols., 13 rubricelle, and 12 repertorii.

Scope: Sixteenth century, 210 vols.; —Seventeenth century, 886 vols.; —Eighteenth century, 667 vols.; —Nineteenth century, 385 vols.

References: D'Angiolini, pp. 1094–1095; Lodolini (1960), pp. 59–60.

Finding Aids: Summary inventories, printed list of notai.

Location: Archivio di Stato di Roma.

3.2.3.43 Obligationes communes
[DATABASE ID: VATV055-A]

Inclusive Dates: 1408–1798.

Bulk: 2.5 linear m. (31 numbered vols.).

Organization: The series is roughly in chronological order.

Note: This series was transferred from the Archivio di Stato di Roma in 1919 as part of the Fondo dell'Archivio di Stato di Roma. It was formerly identified in the Archivio di Stato di Roma as *Obbligazioni per servizi comuni*.

References: Fink, p. 56; Boyle, p. 45; Pásztor (1970), p. 39;

Pásztor (1983), p. 104. W. M. Brady, *The Episcopal Succession in England, Scotland and Ireland, A.D. 1400–1875: With Appointments to Monasteries and Extracts from Consistorial Acts Taken from mss. in Public and Private Libraries in Rome, Florence, Bologna, Ravenna and Paris* (Rome, 1876–1877).

Finding Aids: ASV Index 1036, part V, lists individual volumes and years covered and some additional annotations such as full title in each volume, an example of an entry, etc. There is an index to churches, persons, and dioceses listed in this index on page 233.

ASV Indice 1112 (formerly Indice 41), p. 18, provides an individual listing of volumes in the series and their current ASV and former Archivio di Stato di Roma numbers. The final unnumbered pages of this index reiterate much of this information in a table listing the current and former names and numbers of volumes in the series.

Location: Archivio Segreto Vaticano.

3.2.3.44 Obligationes et solutiones

[DATABASE ID: VATV045-A]

Inclusive Dates: 1295–1678.

Bulk: 5 linear m. (91 numbered vols.).

Organization: The series is roughly in chronological order. Each volume is chronological by type of transaction. Volumes at the end of the series are greatly out of chronological order. The *Fondo camerale* comprises this series, *Introitus et exitus*, and *Collectoriae*.

Scope: In these registers were copied formal bonds of debt to the Camera that were drawn up when the debtor recognized or confessed a debt and obligated himself (together with his heirs and his church) to pay it within certain set terms. As payments on an obligation were made these solutiones were recognized in instruments called quittantia, and likewise registered in this series. The debts could be for loans, spoils, the income of a vacant church, or for any settlement (compositio) reached in the court of the auditor of the Camera or of the chamberlain. Most frequently, however, and long after the inauguration of this registry system in the fourteenth century, the obligationes were for the servitia, taxes on major benefices (bishoprics and abbeys), which had to be settled by a new appointee before he could receive his bulls of appointment; usually he would make an obligatio for them.

There were two groups of servitia: servitia communia which were equally divided between the College of Cardinals and the Camera; and servitia minuta, which went to officials in the curia (vice-chancellor, camerarius, clerks, etc.) and in the College of Cardinals.

Boyle points out that the solutiones in the *Obligationes et solutiones* registers parallel the introitus of the *Introitus et exitus*, and both are needed to show the whole story of an appointment. The *Obligationes et solutiones* also overlap with the Camera Apostolica series *Taxae* but again the *Obligationes et solutiones* provide more informative and inclusive information. Various subtitles of the volumes, which are fully listed in Index 1036, include: Servitorium Communium, Provisionum, Obligationum Sacro Collegio, Divisionum, and Registrum Litterarum Camerarii Apostolici.

According to MacFarlane, these registers contain much more material than their title suggests. For example, they name the cardinals living at the time of the appointments, since each had a share in the services; they record the recent deaths of

cardinals, giving exact dates; they sometimes record current disputes over consistorial benefices; they note ad limina visits, and list other payments like annates and the census. In short, they are a mine of limited but precise information on cardinals, archbishops, bishops, abbots and their procurators, and as such the series has been carefully inventoried and widely used.

Note: Vols. 1–2 are available on microfilm.

References: Fink, p. 51; Boyle, pp. 43 and 157–164; Pásztor (1970), p. 40; Pásztor (1983), p. 105; MacFarlane, pp. 41–42. U. Berlière, *Inventaire analytique des Libri obligationum et solutionum des Archives Vaticanes au point de vue des anciens diocèses de Cambrai, Liège, Thérouanne et Tournai* (Rome, 1904). E. Göller, "Untersuchungen über das Inventar des Finanzarchivs der Renaissancepäpste," in *Miscellanea Francesco Ehrle* (Rome, 1924), vol. 5, pp. 229–250. H. Hoberg, *Taxae pro communibus servitiis, ex libris obligationum ab anno 1295 usque ad annum 1455 confectis* (Vatican City, 1949), is a listing of obligations for servitia communia (1295–1455).

Payments (solutiones) for both common and minute services (1316–1378) in the *Obligationes et solutiones* are published along with related sources (such as the *Introitus et exitus*) in the Einnahmen volumes of the *Vatikanische Quellen zur Geschichte des päpstlichen Hof- und Finanzverwaltung 1316–1378* (Paderborn, 1910–): vol. 1, E. Göller, ed., *Die Einnahmen der apostolischen Kammer unter Johann XXII* (Paderborn, 1910); vol. 4, E. Göller, ed., *Die Einnahmen der apostolischen Kammer unter Benedikt XII* (Paderborn, 1920); vol. 5, L. Mohler, ed., *Die Einnahmen der apostolischen Kammer unter Klemens VI* (Paderborn, 1931); vol. 7, H. Hoberg, ed., *Die Einnahmen der apostolischen Kammer unter Innocenz VI. Die Einnahmenregister des päpstlichen Thesaurars* (Paderborn, 1955).

J. Haller et al., eds., *Repertorium Germanicum: Regesten aus den päpstlichen Archiven zur Geschichte des Deutschen Reichs und seiner Territorien im XIV. und XV. Jahrhundert: Pontifikat Eugens IV. (1431–1447)* (Berlin, 1897), calendars items concerning Germany in this series.

Finding Aids: ASV Index 1036, part IV, provides a volume by volume listing of the series. Entries include old and new volume numbers, inclusive dates, exact title or titular contents summary (it is not always clear what is an exact title), and sometimes a brief annotation of a typical entry or item of interest. Entries generally identify the participants and the business correctly, but the exact relationship between these two elements can sometimes be misleading. A list of selected people, important churches, and dioceses that appear in the index is on page 233.

Also useful are the following two publications: Joseph de Loye, *Les archives de la Chambre apostolique au XIVe siècle*, part 1, *Inventaire* (Paris, 1899). In this work, de Loye provides an annotated index to the first sixty volumes in the series. Entries include: old and new volume numbers, inclusive dates, exact spine title or a brief contents summary (it is difficult to determine which is which from the book), and sometimes an entry is excerpted to demonstrate form. The book has a good introduction as well as geographic and textual indices. Paul Maria Baumgarten, *Untersuchungen und Urkunden über die Camera Collegii Cardinalium für die Zeit von 1295 bis 1437* (Leipzig, 1898), pp. iii–xxviii, provides a volume-by-volume listing of the initial eighty-eight registers in this series. The inventory includes former and current volume numbers, the relationship of individual volumes to the Camera Apostolica series *Introitus et exitus* and *Collectoriae*, and a brief title listing.

ASV Indice 124, "Primo Sbozzo di Inventario di tutti i libri che sono nell'Archivio Segreto Vaticano," by Giovanni Bissaiga (1672), provides more descriptive and accurate volume titles for select volumes of some series. A few *Obligationes et solutiones* volumes are listed on folios 208r, 212r–214v, and 216rv.

Location: Archivio Segreto Vaticano.

3.2.3.45 Obligationes particulares
[DATABASE ID: VATV056-A]
Inclusive Dates: 1419–1482.
Bulk: 6 vols.
Scope: This small series, noted in Boyle, was not located in 1990. From Indice 1036 it looks as if these are now the Camera Apostolica series *Sec. Cam.* and *Taxae*, both listed individually among the records of the Camera Apostolica. *Obligationes particulares* no. 7, "Expensae bullarum," no. 8, "Compositiones Datariae," and no. 9, "Compositiones Datariae," are now identified as *Taxae* nos. 35, 36, and 37, according to ASV Indici 1112 and 1036.
Reference: Boyle, p. 45. J. Haller et al., eds., *Repertorium Germanicum: Regesten aus den päpstlichen Archiven zur Geschichte des Deutschen Reichs und seiner Territorien im XIV. und XV. Jahrhundert: Pontifikat Eugens IV. (1431–1447)* (Berlin, 1897), calendars items concerning Germany in this series.
Finding Aids: ASV Indice 1112, "Archivio Vaticano—Fondo camerale venuto dall'Archivio di Stato nel 1919," (f. 19), provides a brief volume listing of the "Regestrum obligationum particularium debitorum ratione visatationum." The entries note the former and new volume numbers, the inclusive dates of each volume, and the former Archivio di Stato volume numbers. The index also notes that three former *Obligationes particulares* volumes, nos. 7–9, are now *Taxae* nos. 35–37.

ASV Indice 1036, "Inventari dell'Archivi Camerale, compitato da Mgr. Pieto Guidi vice perfetto dall'Archivio Vaticano," provides more descriptive entries for each of the Obligationes particulares volumes than ASV Indice 1112. Entries provide information on the current volume number, foliation, dorsal notes, internal title(s), and inclusive dates.

Location: Archivio Segreto Vaticano.

3.2.3.46 Registres financiers (L24–L52)
[DATABASE ID VATV40056-A]
Dates: 1434–1784.
Bulk: 3.5 linear m.
Organization: These registers were first classified by H. Delaborde into four subseries. Subseries A, Registres 1434–1593, consists of forty-two volumes divided among twelve archival boxes designated L24–L36. Subseries B, Registres 1540–1784, consists of twenty-four volumes divided among ten archival boxes designated L37–L46. Subseries C, Registres 1444–1515, consists of nine volumes divided among four archival boxes designated L47–L50. Subseries D, Registres 144–1484, consists of five volumes divided among two archival boxes designated L51 and L52.

Delaborde's arrangement was reexamined by E. Martin-Chabot in 1960. He examined the substance of the registers and determined that among the four series are the following:

A. from the Camera Apostolica:

1a. Obligationes Communium Camere
1b. Obligationes Communium Colegii Cardinalium
2. Obligationes Annatarum
3. Obligationes particulares
4a. Quittantiae annatarum
4b. Quittantiae annatarum quindennsorum et cessationum pensionum
5. Payments made "in Cancellaria"
6. Consensus et resignationes

B. from the Camera Urbis:

1. Mandats cameraux de Boniface 1x
2. Sale e facatico
3. Imposition du sel
4. Taxe sur le vin
5. Taxe sur le bétail
6. Tracta grani et salis patrimonii
7. Compte du trésorier du patrimoine
8. Douanne romaine de Ripa et Ripetta

In the finding aid listed below Martin-Chabot presents the reorganization of the four series of Delaborde according to his schema.

There seems to be some disagreement as to the precise designations of Martin-Chabot. In *Les Archives Nationales: L'État général des fonds*, prepared under the direction of Jean Favier, there is a list that suggests the presence of the kinds of material identified by Martin-Chabot, but not an exact duplication of his classification. The Favier guide also notes that these registers are badly deteriorated.

Scope: These are all financial registers.
Reference: Favier, *Fonds*, vol. 1, p. 311; Favier, *Inventaires*, p. 100.
Finding Aids: Archives Nationales finding aid L/2 provides a simple list of the volumes that are contained in each of the archival boxes L24–L52 and are divided according to Delaborde's classification.

The extensive analytic inventory of this material prepared by E. Martin-Chabot is available (with permission) on microfilm (246mi). In the introduction to his work Martin-Chabot presents a history of the transfer of the material to Paris and its return to Rome. He also presents his particular classification of each register. In parts II and III of his inventory he then describes each volume of the financial registers in considerable detail, noting particular entries of note.

Location: Archives Nationales, Paris

3.2.3.47 Registri camerali conservati dai notai, segretari e cancellieri della Camera apostolica (Camerale I)
[DATABASE ID: VATV20010-A]
Inclusive Dates: 1396–1870.
Bulk: 952 registri.
Organization: Signaturarum Sanctissimi libri, 1570–1870, 153 registri; —Regesti di chirografi, 1520–1758, 10 registri; —Diversorum del camerlengo, 1467–1839, 348 registri; —Diversorum del tesoriere, 1590–1784, 109 registri; —Mandati, 1418–1802, 166 registri; —Mandati apostolici in materia beneficiale o Expectativarum libri, 1486–1536, 13 registri; —Diversorum, [15–], 1632–1675, and 1825–1846, 6 buste; —Quietanze per comuni o minuti servizi, 1396–1511, 31 registri; —Ufficiali camerali, 1417–1710, 17 registri; —Collegio dei

segretari apostolici, 1528–1631, 8 registri; —Tasse di segreteria, 1513–1517 and 1654–1668, 2 registri; —Libri decretorum, 1508–1850, 32 registri; —Decreta, 1559–1707, 46 registri.

References: D'Angiolini, pp. 1053–1056; Lodolini (1960), pp. 68–72.

Finding Aids: List and partial inventories.

Location: Archivio di Stato di Roma.

3.2.3.48 Registri camerali conservati in computisteria (Camerale I)

[DATABASE ID: VATV20011-A]

Inclusive Dates: 1387–1840.

Bulk: 2,418 registri, vols., buste, and fascicoli.

Organization: This series divides as follows: Chirografi pontifici A, 1581–1797, 1800–1809, and 1814–1816, 61 registri; —Chirografi pontifici B, 1474–1779, 23 registri; —Chirografi pontifici C, 1552–1840, 42 vols.; —Regesti di mandati camerali, 1596–1743, 101 registri; —Spese del maggiordomo, 1459–1460, 1538, 1576–1743, and 1745–1816, 117 registri, and 51 fascicoli; —Spese minute di palazzo o del cubiculario, 1433–1435, 1454–1537, 1552, and 1562–1566, 29 registri; —Fabbriche, 1437–1475 and 1536–1753, 56 registri; —Depositeria della crociata, 1463–1490, 5 registri; —Collettorie, 1387–1715, 542 registri and fascicoli in 89 buste; —Entrata e uscita delle decime, 1501–1718, 48 registri; —Biblioteca vaticana, 1475–1481 and 1623, 4 registri; —Inventari, 1518–1578, 26 registri; —Viaggi di pontefici, 1543, 1547, 1598, and 1653, 5 registri and carte sciolte in 1 busta; —Viaggi di sovrani, 1536, 1593–1594, 1597, 1630–1632, and 1656–1657, 2 buste; —Regalie camerali, 1670–1744, 10 registri and 8 quinterni; —Tasse di malefici, 1479–1480, 1505–1613, and 1663–1686, 31 registri in 5 buste; —Depositeria del concilio di Trento, 1545–1549 and 1561–1564, 4 registri; —Depositeria generale, entrata e uscita A, 1539–1743, 147 registri; —Depositeria generale, entrata e uscita B, 1428–1473 and 1521–1743, 269 registri; —Giustificazioni di tesoreria, 1431–1744, 696 buste; —Computisteria, 1486–1744, 76 registri.

References: D'Angiolini, p. 1056–1063; Lodolini (1960), pp. 68–72.

Finding Aids: List and partial inventories.

Location: Archivio di Stato di Roma.

3.2.3.49 Resignationes

[DATABASE ID: VATV067-A]

Inclusive Dates: 1457–1594.

Bulk: 15 linear m.

Organization: 295 vols., chronological.

Scope: These records are conditions for resignations of benefices as well as notarial instruments presented at the Curia to certify that benefices really were vacant.

Note: Related consensus material is located in the Datary. These records were transferred from the Archivio di Stato di Roma in 1919 as part of the Fondo dell'Archivio di Stato di Roma. They were formerly identified in the Archivio di Stato di Roma as *Consensi e Rassegne (collez. A).*

References: Fink, p. 56; Boyle, p. 47 (series identified as *Resignationes et Consensus A*); Pásztor (1970), pp. 42–43. J. Haller et al., eds., *Repertorium Germanicum: Regesten aus den päpstlichen Archiven zur Geschichte des deutschen Reichs und seiner Territorien im XIV. und XV. Jahrhundert: Pon-*

tifikat Eugens IV. (1431–1447) (Berlin, 1897), calendars items concerning Germany in this series.

Finding Aids: ASV Indice 1112 (former Indice 41) lists each volume, the inclusive dates, and the former Archivio di Stato di Roma title and volume numbers along side the current ASV title and volume numbers.

ASV Indice 1044 gives an alphabetical listing of dioceses in the series with the volume and page numbers on which the diocese appears. Indice 1044 also has three appendices: (1) a list of pontificates and the volumes that fall chronologically within each papacy (other volumes that contain material for each papacy are also noted); (2) a chronological list of volumes, noting any differences between the years on the cover and the years included in each volume; and (3) a concordance between the current ASV and former Archivio di Stato volume numbers.

The Camera Apostolica series *Rubricellae resignationes* listed below forms an index to this series for the years 1523–1555.

Location: Archivio Segreto Vaticano.

3.2.3.50 Rubricellae

[DATABASE ID: VATV066-A]

Inclusive Dates: 1342–1809, 1814–1829 (bulk 1549–1800).

Bulk: 1.5 linear m. (38 vols.).

Organization: Chronological. Vols. 1–31, 1342–1829; vols. 32–38, [15—]–1579. Individual registers are alphabetical.

Scope: This series is generally identified as indices to Miscellaneous official series *Bullarium generale* and *Registra Vaticana* (RV). *Rubricellae* vols. 1–8 and 32–36 index portions of the RV series as follows: Rub. 1–8 indexes RV of Clement VI–Julius III (with only a few penciled annotations of current RV numbers); Rub. 32 indexes Alexander VI (RV 879–883); Rub. 33 indexes Julius II (RV 985–987); Rub. 34 indexes Clement VII (RV 1442–1452); Rub. 35 indexes Julius III (RV 1796–1802), Paul IV (RV 1853–1854), Pius IV (RV 1918–1922), Pius V (RV 2002–2003); Rub. 36 indexes Paul IV (RV 1853–1854), Pius IV (RV 1918–1922), Pius V (RV 2002). Current guides present these as indexes to RV registers of bulls sent "per viam camerae." They briefly note bulls that have been traced to 1,037 registers, primarily of the RV series, but also to four registers of the *Sec. Cam.* and sixtythree registers of the *Registra bullarum.* About nine hundred of the 1,037 registers, indexed by the *Rubricellae*, are known to be lost. Therefore, the *Rubricellae* citations are the only record we have of the contents of those registers (cf. Pásztor [1970] and Giusti below). Although the *Rubricellae* are often presented as indices to the RV series, their original limited scope ("per viam camerae" bulls) and the losses suffered by the RV series have rendered most of the *Rubricellae* of little functional use as indexes.

For researchers interested in the RV, indices in the ASV Sala d'Indici are generally a better starting point. The value of the *Rubricellae* today is more historical, supplying brief indications of some existing and many lost bulls. Some *Rubricellae* are contemporary, others postdate the registers they index by several centuries.

Note: These records were transferred from the Archivio di Stato di Roma in 1919 as part of the Fondo dell'Archivio di Stato di Roma. They were formerly identified in the Archivio di Stato di Roma as part of the series *Registri dei pagamenti in Bullaria.* Note that volume 37 was formerly ASV Indice 683 and volume 38 was formerly ASV Indice 684. There is a variant title on the spine, *Rubricellae Bullarum*.

References: Boyle, p. 47; Fink, p. 56; Pásztor (1970), p. 38; Pásztor (1983), pp. 107–108. M. Giusti, *Studi sui registri di bolle papali* (Vatican City, 1968), pp. 86–90.

Finding Aids: ASV Indice 1112 (formerly Indice 41), page 17 verso, provides a listing of selected volumes in this series. Entries include the former Archivio di Stato di Roma and current ASV volume numbers and inclusive dates. The final unnumbered pages of this index reiterate this information and give the former Archivio di Stato di Roma name as well as volume numbers for the series.

Location: Archivio Segreto Vaticano.

3.2.3.51 Rubricellae resignationes

[DATABASE ID: VATV069A]
Inclusive Dates: 1523–1555.
Bulk: 1 linear m. (14 vols.).
Organization: Two subseries: Rubricellae resignationes (vols. 1–13); —Rubricellae consensus (vol. 14). Alphabetical.
Scope: These volumes index the Camera Apostolica series *Resignationes*. The volumes list dioceses.
Note: The series was transferred from the Archivio di Stato di Roma in 1919 as part of the Fondo dell'Archivio di Stato di Roma. The records were formerly identified in the Archivio di Stato di Roma as *Consensi e Rassegne* (A) *Rubrica*. *Rubr. resig.* 7 was formerly identified as Camera Apostolica, *Sec. Cam.* 211.
References: Fink, pp. 56–57; Pásztor (1970), pp. 42–43; Boyle, pp. 47–48 (identified as *Rubricellae. A. Resignationum*).
Finding Aids: ASV Indice 1112 (former Indice 41) provides a partial listing of volumes, inclusive dates, their former Archivio di Stato di Roma titles and volume numbers, and their current ASV titles and volume numbers (p. 13 verso and section 3 in the back of the index).
Location: Archivio Segreto Vaticano.

3.2.3.52 S. Casa di Loreto e Collegio degli orefici e argentieri di Roma

[DATABASE ID: VATV20031-A]
Inclusive Dates: 1672–1692.
Bulk: 13 vols.
Reference: D'Angiolini, p. 1093.
Finding Aids: Summary inventory, 1971.
Location: Archivio di Stato di Roma.

3.2.3.53 Secretarius Camerae: Indulgentiarum (abbreviated as Sec. Cam.)

[DATABASE ID: VATV10004-A]
Inclusive Dates: 1481–1725.
Bulk: 19 linear m. (222 numbered vols.).
Organization: Chronological with the following exceptions: Vols. 221 (1435–1436, with a copy of a 1421 document) and 222 (1470–1472).
Scope: This series is a very mixed collection of indulgences and other Datary material. Though both the Secretariat and Camera are frequently involved, MacFarlane suggests that the series is probably best considered as a part of the Datary. Boyle puts *Secretarius Camerae* with the Datary (see p. 54). Pásztor puts it with the Camera. Vols. 65, 74, 78–83, 108–112, 115–

124, 146–149, 154–156, 163, and 166 form the Secretaria Apostolica series *Diversorum*.
Several *Secretarius Camerae* volumes are now parts of other series. *Sec. Cam.* 211 is now Camera Apostolica, *Rubricelle resignationes* 7; *Sec. Cam.* 213 is now Camera Apostolica, *Taxae* 23; *Sec. Cam.* 215 and 217 are now, respectively, Camera Apostolica, *Computorum* 5 and 7. There is a variant title on select spines: "Matrimonialia."
References: Fink, pp. 52–54; Boyle, p. 54; Macfarlane, p. 39; Pásztor (1970), pp. 33–35; Pásztor (1983), pp. 105–107. M. Giusti, "I registri Vaticani e la loro continuazione," *La Bibliofilia* (Florence) 60 (1958): 130–140. M. Giusti, *Studi sui registri di bolle papali* (Vatican City, 1968).
Finding Aids: ASV Index 1048 lists the exact title of each volume, inclusive volume dates, and brief content notes for the series.
Location: Archivio Segreto Vaticano.

3.2.3.54 Servitia minuta

[DATABASE ID: VATV057-A]
Inclusive Dates: 1416–1455.
Bulk: .15 linear m. (3 numbered vols.).
Organization: Chronological.
Note: These volumes were transferred from the Archivio di Stato di Roma in 1919 as part of the Fondo dell'Archivio di Stato di Roma. These records were formerly indentified as part of the Archivio di Stato di Roma series *Tasse di Segretaria*.
References: Fink, p. 56; Boyle, p. 46. J. Haller, "Die Verteilung der Servitia Minuta und die Obligation der Prälaten im 13. und 14. Jahrhundert," *Quellen und Forschungen aus italienischen Archiven und Bibliotheken* 1 (1898): 281–295. H. Hoberg, "Die Servitientaxen der Bistümer im 14. Jahrhundert," *Quellen und Forschungen aus Italienischen Archiven und Bibliotheken* 33 (1944): 101–135.
Finding Aids: ASV Indice 1112 (former Indice 41) provides an individual listing of some volumes in the series with inclusive dates and their current ASV and former Archivio di Stato di Roma numbers.
Location: Archivio Segreto Vaticano.

3.2.3.55 Taxae

[DATABASE ID: VATV060-A]
Inclusive Dates: 1426–1815 (bulk 1426–1599).
Bulk: 2 linear m. (38 numbered vols.).
Organization: Vols. 1–30 are chronological. Individual volumes within that group are also chronologically organized. Vols. 31–38 overlap and fill in the chronological series established by vols. 1–30. Each individual volume of the second group is also organized chronologically.
Scope: This series contains notes regarding the sum of money promised for common service upon election to a see, abbey, and so forth. For more inclusive information about the obligations that comprise the fees, the individuals involved, the diocese or abbey in question, and the like, see Camera Apostolica series *Obligationes et solutiones*. The series breaks during the Napoleonic period, 1809–1814.
Note: These records were transferred from the Archivio di Stato di Roma in 1919 as part of the Fondo dell'Archivio di Stato di Roma.
Taxae 31 is formerly Indice 684 though it is not clear to what it served as an index. *Taxae* 23 was formerly identified as Ca-

mera Apostolica, *Sec. Cam.* 213. Vols. 35, 36, and 37 were formerly identified as *Obligationes particulares* 7, 8, and 9; see ASV Index 1036. Within the series there are some variant spine titles: "Rubricellae Bullarum," "Expeditiones Bullarum," "Indulgentia," "Perpetu," and "Diverse."

This series was formerly identified in the Archivio di Stato di Roma as part of the series *Tasse di Segreteria* and as part of the series *Registri giornali dei pagamenti delle bolle esguiti in Bullaria*.

References: Fink, p. 56; Boyle, pp. 47 and 157–164; Pásztor (1970), pp. 38–39. E. Göller, "Der Liber Taxarum der päpstlichen Kammer: Eine Studie über seine Entstehung und Anlage," *Quellen und Forschungen aus italienischen Archiven und Bibliotheken* 8 (1905): 113–173, 305–343. E. Göller, "Die neue Bestände der Camera Apostolica im päpstlichen Geheimarchiv," *Römische Quartalschrift für christliche Altertumskunde und für Kirchengeschichte* 30 (1922): 38–53. E. Göller, "Untersuchungen über das Inventar des Finanzarchivs der Renaissancepäpste," in *Miscellanea Francesco Ehrle* (Rome, 1924), vol. 5, pp. 229–250.

J. Haller et al., eds., *Repertorium Germanicum: Regesten aus den päpstlichen Archiven zur Geschichte des Deutschen Reichs und seiner Territorien im XIV. und XV. Jahrhundert: Pontifikat Eugens IV. (1431–1447)* (Berlin, 1897), calendars items concerning Germany in this series.

Finding Aids: ASV Indice 1112 (former Indice 41), p. 20, provides an individual listing of volumes in the series, inclusive dates, and their current ASV and former Archivio di Stato di Roma numbers. Page 23 provides a listing of some volumes in their old Archivio di Stato series. The final unnumbered pages of this index reiterate this information in tabular form, listing current and former names and numbers of the series.

ASV Indice 1036 (ff. 230–231) provides descriptive titles and some contents annotations for three *Taxae* volumes (vols. 35–37) that were formerly identified as *Obligationes particulares*, vols. 7, 8, and 9.

Location: Archivio Segreto Vaticano.

3.2.3.56 Tesoriere provinciali

[DATABASE ID: VATV20006–A]

Inclusive Dates: 1397–1816 (bulk 1397–1799).

Bulk: 7,157 registri and filze and 2 fascicoli.

Organization: This series is divided as follows: Ascoli, 1426–1427, 1449–1454, 1456–1457, 1459–1460, 1462–1470, 1477, 1519, 1526–1535, 1538–1541, 1545–1557, 1559–1576, 1581–1590, 1592–1612, 1615, 1617–1619, and 1624–1795, 308 registri and filze; —Avignone e Contado Venassino, 1562, 1565, 1573–1603, 1611–1614, 1616, 1618–1621, 1623–1662, 1677–1681, 1691–1695, 1725–1740, 1744–1768, and 1774–1794, 260 registri and filze and 2 fascicoli; —Benevento, 1469–1472, 1477–1481, 1483–1487, 1520–1524, 1571–1572, 1588–1619, 1621–1646, 1651, 1653–1767, 1774–1793, 1796–1797, and 1802, 188 registri and filze; —Bologna, tesoreria e pagatorato della soldatesca, 1432, 1468–1469, 1477–1486, 1542, 1553–1555, 1561–1594, and 1596–1796, 418 registri and filze; —Camerino, 1539–1540, 1545–1546, 1549, 1555–1590, 1600–1796, and 1801–1808, 359 registri and filze; —Campagna, Marittima, Lazio e Sabina, 1427–1428, 1449–1451, 1453–1454, 1456–1457, 1459–1460, 1463–1474, 1478–1480, 1482–1488, 1514–1516, 1532–1540, 1542–1809, and 1814–1816, 539 registri e filze; —Città di Castello, 1430–

1431, 1435–1438, 1444–1446, 1449–1458, 1460–1466, 1470–1471, 1474–1477, 1485–1493, 1566–1567, 1569–1585, 1643–1644, and 1716–1724, 52 registri and filze; —Fermo, 1397, 1454–1455, 1537–1545, 1566–1572, 1576–1579, 1702–1794, 1797, and 1806–1808, 124 registri and filze; —Ferrara, tesoreria e pagatorato della soldatesca, 1548–1549, 1552, 1554–1556, 1558, and 1597–1796, 1,132 registri and filze; —Marca, 1422–1433, 1447–1458, 1462–1463, 1466–1471, 1478–1481, 1484–1502, 1505–1507, 1510–1797, and 1806, 733 registri and filze; —Patrimonio, 1420–1422, 1424–1425, 1429–1435, 1439, 1441–1477, 1479–1490, 1492–1504, 1511–1525, and 1530–1816, 691 registri and filze; —Romagna, 1465–1466, 1468–1491, 1494–1495, and 1511–1795, 563 registri and filze; —Spoleto, 1514–1516, 1545–1546, 1550, 1556–1562, 1567–1798, 1800–1809, and 1814–1816, 325 registri and filze; —Umbria e Perugia, 1424–1427, 1429–1431, 1433–1439, 1442–1503, 1506–1507, 1511–1520, 1525–1528, 1531–1798, 1801–1802, 1807–1809, and 1816, 740 registri and filze; —Urbino, 1519–1523 and 1617–1816, 725 filze and registri.

Reference: D'Angiolini, pp. 1081–1083.

Finding Aids: Inventory, 1956, with index to names of persons; partial printed inventory.

Location: Archivio di Stato di Roma.

3.2.4 Camera Secreta

[DATABASE ID: VATV036–A]

The Camera Secreta was the office of the pope's private staff of secretaries. Established by Martin V (1417–1431) to handle secret and political correspondence, the Camera Secreta was a stage in the development of the Secretaria Apostolica and the Secretariatus Status. See the agency histories for those offices for more information.

RECORDS. No records for this office were located.

3.2.5 Camerlengato

[DATABASE ID: VATV778–A]

The chief officer of the Camera Apostolica was known as the camerarius or camerlengo ("chamberlain"). This official appears in the mid-twelfth century as successor to the archdeacon of Rome (suppressed by Gregory VII, 1073–1085) who was responsible for the administration of the property of the diocese of Rome.

The camerarius then served as administrator of the property of the Holy See and fiscal administrator of the Papal States. His chief duties included collection of taxae, or dues paid by bishops and abbots for delivery of bulls of appointment to dioceses and abbacies; registry of oblations or gifts of the faithful; supervision of the civil coinage (moneta); and civil and criminal jurisdiction over officials of the Curia. The duties of the office increased under the Avignon popes.

In the sixteenth century the camerlengo became one of highest officers of the Papal States, and remained so until a new administration was instituted in the early nineteenth century. The camerlengo administered finance, public works, and commerce of the Papal States.

The duties of the camerlengo were redefined by Benedict XIV in 1742. In 1800 his duties were expanded by Pius VII to include health (also the responsibility of the Sacra Consulta), food supply, public instruction, fine arts, archeology, museums, mines, agriculture, commerce, and other areas. The civil and criminal jurisdiction of the camerlengo was limited in 1828, and at the same time the Congregazione di revisione was established independent of the camerlengo to review the budget. In 1847, with the establishment of the Consiglio dei ministri, the camerlengo became a member of the Consiglio, while his position as chief minister passed to the secretary of state. Later in 1847, in another reform, most of the office's duties passed to the ministers of commercio, belle arti, industria e agricoltura, lavori pubblici, finanze, and interno. [The latter four ministries are described separately in the section "Papal States."] During periods of papal vacancy (known as sede vacante) the camerlengo had several crucial functions including charge of the conclave.

Most of the records of this officer are found in the series under Camera Apostolica; only a few series of eighteenth- and nineteenth-century records wandered from the archival holdings of the Camera.

RECORDS. Records of the office consist of the following series.

3.2.5.1 Camerlengato
[DATABASE ID: VATV20173-A]
Inclusive Dates: 1816–1854.
Bulk: 1,006 buste.
References: D'Angiolini, pp. 1180–1181; Lodolini (1960), pp. 167–173.
Finding Aids: There is an inventory of the individual titles with indexes to names, places, and subjects, and a partial printed inventory.
Location: Archivio di Stato di Roma.

3.2.5.2 Camerlengo
[DATABASE ID: VATV10368-A]
Inclusive Dates: 1838–1857.
Bulk: 2 linear m. (10 buste).
Organization: Subseries are Censi, canoni, camerali (4 buste); —Preventivi consuntivi (1 buste); —Incarti processuali per titolo di spicilegio, 1838–1848 (2 buste); —Disposizioni generali, 1846 (1 busta); —Miscellanea (2 buste).
Location: Archivio Segreto Vaticano.

3.2.5.3 Carteggio del camerlengo
[DATABASE ID: VATV20009-A]
Inclusive Dates: 1766–1807.
Bulk: 51 registri and mazzi.
Reference: D'Angiolini, p. 1080.
Finding Aids: Inventory, 1983.
Location: Archivio di Stato di Roma.

3.2.5.4 Uditore del camerlengo
[DATABASE ID: VATV20240-A]
Inclusive Dates: 1818–1831.
Bulk: 8 registri and 6 buste.
Reference: D'Angiolini, p. 1200.
Finding Aids: Inventory, 1970.
Location: Archivio di Stato di Roma.

3.2.6 Cancellaria Apostolica
[DATABASE ID: VATV032-A]
The origin of this office goes back to the fourth century when notaries were appointed to draw up papal documents. These notaries of the Roman church were headed by the primicerius, who was in turn aided by a secundicerius. The notaries, in their capacity as scriniarii, also supervised the archives. Up until the eighth century documentation concerning this office is limited.

Gregory the Great, following the example of the Roman emperors of the East, gathered the notarii of the church into a school (schola notariorum) presided over by the primicerius notariorum and assisted by the secundicerius (letter of March 598). The primicerius, in his office as head of the palatine judges (iudices palatini), was the most influential official in the papal administration. By the end of the eighth century the duties of primicerius had been united to those of the bibliothecarius (librarian) and the latter title was used for nearly a century.

In the middle of the tenth century a great change took place in the general direction of the office. The term *cancellarius* was substituted for *primicerius*, first appearing in a document of Pope Formosus (Nov. 894). [See P. Jaffé, *Regesta pontificum romanorum ab condita ecclesia ad annum post Christum natum MCXCVIII* (Leipzig, 1885–1888), vol. 1, pp. 435 and 438, n. 3499.] The last authentic papal document from the primicerius is a bull of Benedict VII (Dec. 30, 982) [Jaffé, vol. 1, p. 483].

Shortly after this an entirely new title appeared in the Curia, that of archicancellarius. In 1051 Leo IX conferred this title on Hermann, archbishop of Cologne, who already served Holy Roman Emperor Henry III as arch-chancellor for the affairs of Italy. This title disappeared under Gregory VII (1073–1085) and that of bibliothecarius et cancellarius, by now common in all documents, continued to be used. By the time of Lucius II (1144) that of cancellarius prevailed. Notarii also began gradually to replace scriniarii so that from the pontificate of Honorius II (1124–1130) onward, the latter title disappears.

Innocent III (1198–1216) was the first to establish a consistent archival policy and to regularize the care of records. The series of Vatican Registers begins with his pontificate. In 1227 Honorius III entrusted the chancellorship to persons not of cardinalatial rank and the title of the head of the Chancery was changed to vice-chancellor. This title was kept even when, under John XXII (1325), the supervision of the office was placed in the hands of a cardinal.

Toward the end of the fourteenth century the substitute, who had already begun to function in the absence of the vice-chancellor, was given the title of regens (regent) or locumtenens cancellariae. The task of this office was defined by Gregory XI who in 1377 conferred the title for the first time on Bartolomeo Prignano, archbishop of Bari (the future Urban VI), giving him the duties of Cardinal Pierre de Monteruc, vice-chancellor, who had refused to follow Gregory XI from Avignon to Rome.

As the Chancery became busier, specialized sub-departments developed at various times: abbreviatores to prepare the notae, brevia, or minutae that conveyed the essential data of a letter; scriptores or grossatores to write out the beautiful final copies; registratores to keep the Chancery's own copies in its registra; and bullatores to affix the pope's lead seal to the finished letters. Nicholas III (1278) drew up the oldest surviving regulations for the Chancery; John XXII gave it a complete set of norms (constitution *Ratio iuris*, Nov. 16, 1331); Benedict XII (1335) confirmed these; Nicholas V (Mar. 7, 1447) expanded them; Paul V (1605–1621) added to them. But the Regulae Cancellariae ceased to be effective with the death of each pope who had given or confirmed them. From 1730 onward, however, the Regulae, then totaling seventy-two, carried over from one papacy to another.

The Regulae applied specifically to four classes of letters: (1) Litterae Expeditoriae (rules for formal dispatch), (2) Reservatoriae (benefices), (3) Iudiciariae (rules defining procedures to be followed), and (4) Revocatoriae (those letters that annulled the faculties accorded by the preceding popes). To these were added the rules that determined the rights and duties of the vice-chancellor.

The notaries of the Chancery, who assumed the title protonotarii in the middle of the fifteenth century, attended to the preparation of the papal letters, assisted by abbreviatores and grossatores or scrittori. Suppressed for a short time by Paul II (constitution *Illa quorum*, Dec. 3, 1464), the abbreviatores were reestablished by Sixtus IV who, with his constitution *Divina aeterna Dei* (Jan. 11, 1478), fixed their number at seventy-two, divided into three categories but forming one college.

Until the fifteenth century the Apostolic Chancery was the only office of dispatch of papal documents. Martin V (1417–1431) separated the Dataria Apostolica from the Cancellaria. In the course of the fifteenth century the Datary took on a greater share of the work previously done solely by the Cancellaria. During this time Datary responsibilities expanded far beyond those of dating and countersigning pontifical letters to include

grants of favor. When the use of briefs became generalized, Alexander VI (1502) separated a secretary of briefs with responsibility for letters of nondiplomatic and nonspiritual content. This office occasionally provided the means for dispatching such letters under the lead seal. In the late sixteenth century many of the duties of the Consistory were assigned to the newly established Roman congregations. This development in turn contributed to the ultimate diminution of the functions of the Apostolic Chancery. There remained for this office, then, only the execution of favors that were to be dispatched in solemn form by way of a bull or letters apostolic sub plumbo.

With the exception of minor innovations as were introduced by Innocent XI (constitution *Decet Romanum Pontificem*, Jun. 28, 1689) and by Clement XII (1730–1740) at the end of his pontificate, the office remained practically unchanged up to the beginning of the nineteenth century. The collection of taxes for letters of appointment to vacant benefices, called vacabili, were transferred from the Chancery to a Collegio dei Vacabili by Pius VII. Leo XIII decreed the complete suppression of the vacabili (motu proprio *La cura*, Jul. 4, 1898) and confirmed it with a chirograph of June 11, 1901. He also ordered a commission of cardinals to prepare a plan for reorganization of the Chancery itself. This was approved in audiences of February 5 and July 30, 1901.

Pius X's constitution *Sapienti consilio* (Jun. 29, 1908) stated that the sole purpose of the Cancellaria was to seal and dispatch the apostolic letters concerning the provision of consistorial benefices; the institution of new ecclesiastical provinces, dioceses, and chapters; and the proclamation of canonized saints, doctors of the church, and jubilee years. These letters or bulls were to be sent only on order of the Congregatio Consistorialis or the pope. The manner of forwarding the letters was to be *per viam Cancellariae*, according to rules given separately; the former methods, known as *per viam secretam*, *de Camera*, and *de Curia*, were then suppressed. The abbreviatores were suppressed and their office of signing apostolic bulls was transferred to the College of Apostolic Protonotaries. Pius X also provided for the revision of the Regole della Cancellaria (motu proprio *In Romanae Curiae*, Dec. 8, 1910) but these rules were later abrogated by the norms of the 1917 Code of Canon Law.

Paul VI reconfirmed the above functions with his constitution *Regimini Ecclesiae universae* (Aug. 15, 1967). It stated that the Apostolic Chancery was to be so arranged that it would be one single office for sending apostolic letters, presided over by a cardinal chancellor with the help of a regent. Its function was to dispatch decrees, apostolic constitutions, and apostolic letters in the form of bulls or briefs of major importance, as established by law or as entrusted to it by the pope or by departments of the Roman Curia. The chancellor was to preserve with the utmost care the lead seal and the fisherman's ring. The document also made provision for the Secretariat of State to include an office for issuing in Latin the apostolic letters, epistles, and other documents committed to it by the pope.

In the motu proprio *Quo aptius* (Feb. 27, 1973), Paul VI dissolved the Apostolic Chancery as a separate curial office and transferred its functions to the Secretariat of State.

In addition to the records listed below, series listed with another agency relate directly to this agency and should be consulted. See Miscellaneous official series *Armarium LIII*, *Armarium LIV*, *Bullarium generale*, and Family collections series *Bullarum Benedicti XIII*.

References. B. Barbiche, "Le personnel de la chancellerie pontificale au XIII et XIV siecles," in *Prosopographie et genèse de l'état moderne*, edited by F. Autrand (Paris, 1986), pp. 117–130. B. Barbiche, "Les 'scriptores' de la chancellerie apostolique sous le pontificat de Boniface VIII (1295–1305)," *Bibliothèque de l'École des Chartes* 128 (1970): 114–187. G. Barraclough, "Corrector litterarum apostolicarum," in *Dictionnaire de droit canonique*, edited by R. Naz (Paris, 1942), vol. 3, pp. 681–689. G. Barraclough, "The English Royal Chancery and the Papal Chancery in the Reign of Henry III," *Mitteilungen des Instituts für österreichische Geschichtsforschung* 62 (1954): 365–378. P. M. Baumgarten, "Die transsumierende Tätigkeit der apostolischen Kanzlei," *Römische Quartalschrift für christliche Altertumskunde und für Kirchengeschichte* 28 (1914): 215–219. P. M. Baumgarten, "Über einige päpstliche Kanzleibeamte des XIII. und XIV. Jahrhunderts," In *Kirchengeschichtliche Festgabe Anton de Waal* (Freiburg, 1913), pp. 37–102. F. Bock, "Die Geheimschrift in der Kanzlei Johanns XXII: Eine diplomatische Studie," *Römische Quartalschrift für christliche Altertumskunde und für Kirchengeschichte* 42 (1934): 279–303. P. Ciprotti, "Cancelleria apostolica," in *Enciclopedia del diritto* (Varese, 1959), vol. 5, pp. 1070–1071. H. Diener, "Rubrizellen zu Kanzleiregistern Johanns XXIII. und Martins V," *Quellen und Forschungen aus italienischen Archiven und Bibliotheken* 39 (1959): 117–172. G. Erler, *Der Liber Cancellariae Apostolicae vom Jahre 1380 und der Stilus palatii abbreviatus* (Leipzig, 1888). T. Frenz, *Die Kanzlei der Päpste der Hochrenaissance (1471–1527)* (Tübingen, 1986). E. Göller, "Die Kommentatoren der päpstlichen Kanzleiregeln vom Ende des 15. bis zum Beginn des 17. Jahrhunderts," *Archiv für katholisches Kirchenrecht* 85 (1905): 441–460; 86 (1906): 20–34, 259–265. R. von Heckel, "Beiträge zur Kenntnis des Geschäftsgangs in der päpstlichen Kanzlei im 13. Jahrhundert," in *Festschrift Albert Brackmann*, edited by L. Santifaller (Weimar, 1931), pp. 434–460. R. von Heckel, "Eine Kanzleianweisung über die schriftmassige Ausstattung der Papsturkunden aus dem 13. Jahrhundert in Durantis Speculum iudiciale," in *Festschrift für Georg Leidinger zum 60. Gerburtztag an 30. Dezember 1930* (Munich, 1930), pp. 109–118. R. von Heckel, "Studien über die Kanzleiordnung Innozenz' III," *Historisches Jahrbuch* 57 (1937): 258–289. L. Jackowski, "Die päpstlichen Kanzleiregeln und ihre Bedeutung fur Deutschland," *Archiv für katholisches Kirchenrecht* 90 (1910): 3–47, 197–235, 432–463. M. Jansen, "Zur päpstlichen Urkunden- und Taxwesen um die Wende des 14. und 15. Jahrhunderts," in *Festgabe Karl Theodor von Heigel zur Vollendung seines sechzigsten Lebensjahres gewidmet* (Munich, 1903), pp. 146–159. J. P. Kirsch, "Ein Formelbuch der päpstlichen Kanzlei aus der Mitte des 14. Jahrhunderts," *Historisches Jahrbuch* 14 (1893): 814–820. H. Leclercq, "Chancellerie apostolique," in *Dictionnaire d'archéologie chrétienne et de liturgie* (Paris, 1907), vol. 3, pp. 175–207. R. C. Logoz, *Clément VII (Robert de Genève): Sa chancellerie et le clergé romand au début du grand schisme (1378–1394)* (Lausanne, 1974). M. Monaco, "Le finanze pontificie al tempo di Clemente VII," *Studi romani* 6 (1958): 278–296. H. Nélis, "L'application en Belgique de la règle de chancellerie apostolique: 'De idiomate beneficiatorum' aux XIVe et XVe siècles," *Bulletin de l'Institut historique Belge de Rome* 2 (1922): 129–141. G. F. Nüske, "Untersuchungen über das Personal der päpstlichen Kanzlei 1254–1304," *Archiv für Diplomatik, Schriftengeschichte, Siegel- und Wappenkunde* 20 (1974): 39–240; 21 (1975): 249–431. T. Nyberg, "Der Geschäftsgang bei der Ausfertigung der Grünungsdokumente des Birgittenkloster Altomünster durch die römischen Kurie," *Archivum Historiae Pontificiae* 9 (1971): 209–248. E. von Ottenthal, *Regulae Cancellariae Apostolicae: Die päpstlichen Kanzleiregeln von Johannes XXII. bis Nikolaus V.* (Innsbruck, 1888). G. Palmieri, ed., *Viaggio in Germania, Baviera, Svizzera, Olanda, e Francia compiuto negli anni 1761–1763: Diario del Cardinal Giuseppe Garampi* (Rome, 1889). H. Paulus, *Practica Cancellariae Apostolicae cum stylo et formis in Romana Curia usitatis* (Lyons, 1549). W. M. Peitz, *Regestum dni. Innocentii tertii pp. super negotio Romani Imperii (Reg. Vat. 6)* (Rome, 1927). V. Petra, *Commentaria ad constitutiones apostolicas, seu bullas singulas summorum pontificum in Bullario Romano contentas, secundum collectionem Cherubini* (Venice, 1729). J. von Pflugk-Harttung, "Die Schreiber der päpstlichen Kanzlei bis auf Innocenz II (1130)," *Römische Quartalschrift für christliche Altertumskunde und für Kirchengeschichte* 1 (1887): 212–230. E. Pitz, *Papstreskript und Kaiserreskript im Mittelalter* (Tübingen, 1971). P. Rabikauskas, "Cancellaria apostolica (In eius memoriam: Saec. XI– die 31 martii 1973)," *Periodica de re morali, canonica, liturgica* 63 (1974): 243–273. P. Rabikauskas, *Die römische Kuriale in der päpstlichen Kanzlei* (Rome, 1958). G. B. Riganti, *Commentaria in regulas, consti-*

tutiones et ordinationes Cancellariae Apostolicae (Rome, 1744–1747).

RECORDS. Records of the office consist of the following series.

3.2.6.1 Abbreviatori e giudicatura

[DATABASE ID: VATV10085-A]

Inclusive Dates: 1820–1869.

Bulk: .5 linear m.

Organization: These records are chronological by year and month. Within each month they are organized by type of benefice, dispensation, proviste, and so forth. There are some variant subtitles within the series: Introito e riparto delle giudicatura e revisione delle bolle Apostolici Cassiere; and Lista dei fruttato degli offici di Abbreviatore di Maggiore e Minor Presidenza.

Location: Archivio Segreto Vaticano.

3.2.6.2 Archivio segreto

[DATABASE ID: VATV10132-A]

Inclusive Dates: ca. 1854–1923.

Bulk: 1 linear m. (11 buste and 1 vol.).

Organization: Buste/volumes are entitled: 1. Vacabili private; —2. Vacabili (Notizie storico, giuridiche, enti morale ecclesiastici, monasteri, enti morali civili); —3. Cassa della Cancelleria apostolica (movimento e quitanze, nomine vescovile; suppliche, grazie); —4. Regole di Cancelleria; —5. Corrispondenza; —6. Card. Vice Cancelleria (Sommista di S.R.E.); —7. Giuramenti (Formule); —8. Giuramenti dei sostituti della Cancelleria apostolica; —9. Piombo e piombatore; —10. Scrittori apostolici; —13. Decretali—Costituzioni; —Archivio segreto della cancelleria (Protocollo), ca. 1854–[post-1922]. Note that the buste are numbered 1–10 and 13.

Scope: This is an internal reference collection of the Chancery.

Finding Aids: The "Archivio Segreto della Cancelleria, Protocollo," found within this series serves as an index to buste 1–10. The Protocollo contains a brief but descriptive listing of the major documents in each of these buste.

Location: Archivio Segreto Vaticano.

3.2.6.3 Lateran registers

[DATABASE ID: VATV40061-A]

Inclusive Dates: 1389–1787.

Bulk: .8 linear m. (13 vols.).

Organization: This record series, though thirteen volumes, is organized under one manuscript number (TCD 1223) at Trinity College, Dublin. The series is arranged chronologically.

Scope: These are registers of letters and bulls separated from the Cancellaria Apostolica series *Registra Lateranensia*. The contents date from the papacies of Boniface IX, Eugenius IV, Pius II, Innnocent VIII, Alexander VI, Clement VII, Paul IV, Pius IV, Benedict XIV, and Pius VI. The last volume in the series contains fragments from Clement XIII.

Notes: These registers were originally part of the Cancellaria Apostolica series *Registra Lateranensia* described below. These volumes are available on microfilm.

References: Boyle, pp. 145–148. J. Haller et al., eds., *Repertorium Germanicum: Regesten aus den päpstlichen Archiven zur Geschichte des Deutschen Reichs und seiner Territorien im XIV. und XV. Jahrhundert: Pontifikat Eugens IV. (1431–1447)* (Berlin, 1897), and its continuation, *Repertorium Germanicum: Verzeichnis der in den päpstlichen Registern und Kameralakten vorkommenden Personen, Kirchen und Orte des Deutschen Reiches, seiner Diözesen und Territorien, vom Beginn des Schismas bis zur Reformation* (Berlin, 1916–), calendar items concerning Germany in this series.

Finding Aids: Marvin L. Colker, *Trinity College Library Dublin: Descriptive Catalogue of the Mediaeval and Renaissance Latin Manuscripts* (Aldershot, 1991), vol. 2, pp. 1226–1238, gives a brief listing of each volume in this series. T. K. Abbott, *A Catalogue of the Manuscripts in the Library of Trinity College Dublin* (Dublin, 1900), pp. 241–243, lists of each volume with inclusive dates and some indication of its contents. There is a similar but more extensive listing in Boyle.

In the reading room of the Manuscripts Department at Trinity College Library there is an annotated copy of Abbott that has a few additional bibliographic notes for this series. Also in the reading room there is a typescript calendar of the first volume in this series (TCD 1223/1). This detailed calendar was done by H. J. Lawlor in 1923. At the end of the calendar, Lawlor provides an index to names and places.

Location: Trinity College Library, Dublin, Ireland.

3.2.6.4 [Miscellanea SF/183–SF/184]

[DATABASE ID: VATV10128-A]

Inclusive Dates: 1870–1959.

Bulk: 2 linear m.

Organization: Volumes/buste include: Regestum omnium actorum concilii oecumenici vaticani, 1870; —Regolamenti Cancelleria apostolica, 1904, 1915, [post-1922], 2 buste (includes Costituzioni); —Protocolli, 1909–[post-1922], 6 vols. and 2 unidentified protocolli; —Formulae Apostolicae Datariae pro matrimonialibus dispensationibus, 1901; —Atti diversi, 1 busta (includes Regulae Datariae, 1902); —Formule di giuramenti, [18—]–[19—]; —Schema di bolla apostolica per la nomina di un cardinale; —[6 volumes/buste post-1922].

Note: This is a true miscellany with no official ASV designation. The title was assigned by the project staff and reflects the location of the material in 1990.

Location: Archivio Segreto Vaticano.

3.2.6.5 Regesta litterarum apostolicarum

[DATABASE ID: VATV10129-A]

Inclusive Dates: 1901–1963.

Bulk: 16 linear m. (111 boxes, 4 pacchi, and 1 vol.).

Organization: These are chronological by year of decision. Subseries are Beneficialia and Consistorialia.

Scope: This series contains records dealing with election to sees and transfer of benefices, as is noted in the subtitles Expeditarum and Beneficialia on selected volumes. Each case is grouped together with a copy of the outgoing correspondence and internal notes regarding payments. Cases are numbered and have protocol numbers from both the Cancellaria and the Sacra Congregatio Consistorialis.

Location: Archivio Segreto Vaticano.

3.2.6.6 Registra Avenionensia (cited as RA)
[DATABASE ID: VATV178-A]
Inclusive Dates: 1316–1418.

Bulk: 49 linear m. (349 numbered vols. and 4 appendices).

Organization: The volumes are in chronological order. The appendices are out of the primary chronological order. The appendices are identified by roman numerals I–IV, as follows: I. Johannes XXII; —II. Benedictus XII; —III. Clemens VII, Urbanus V, Gregorius IX; —IV. Clemens VI (1345).

Scope: These registers are so named because they remained in Avignon until 1783, when they were sent to the Vatican Archives. The Avignon registers chiefly contain the minutes or drafts of bulls and letters sent out by the papal chancery at Avignon between 1316 and 1418. The Avignon registers contain a considerable amount of cameral material that was bound into the volumes for its preservation.

See Boyle, pp. 114–131, for an extensive discussion on the nature of these registers. Boyle notes that "although the term 'register' usually means a file-copy of an incoming or outgoing letter, it is more elastic in the case of the Avignon Registers. Basically the entries in the RA are drafts rather than copies of letters, yet the Chancery clearly looked on these drafts as registered copies." In many cases the RA draft was later copied into the more formal Vatican Registers. However, for a number of reasons explicated by Boyle, the texts in the RV do not always agree with the text in the RA.

Note: Vols. 173–184, 187 are available on microfilm.

References: Boyle, pp. 49, 114–131; MacFarlane, pp. 36–37; Fink, pp. 37–39.

G. Mollat, *La collation des bénéfices ecclésiastiques sous les papes d'Avignon (1305–1378)* (Paris, 1921). *Le fonctionnement administratif de la papauté d'Avignon: Aux origines de l'état moderne* (Rome, 1990). F. Bock, "Einführung in das Registerwesen des Avignonesischen Papsttums," *Quellen und Forschungen aus italienischen Archiven und Bibliotheken* 31 (1941): 1–107.

G. Barraclough, "Minutes of Papal Letters (1316–1317)," in *Miscellanea archivistica Angelo Mercati* (Vatican City, 1952), pp. 109–127. L. Carolus Barre, "Le cardinal de Dormans chancelier de France, principal conseiller de Charles V, d'après son testament et les archives du Vatican," *Mélanges d'archéologie et d'histoire* 52 (1935): 315–365. F. Bock, "Über Registrierung von Sekretbriefen (Studien zu den Sekretregistern Benedikts XII)," *Quellen und Forschungen aus italienischen Archiven und Bibliotheken* 29 (1938–1939): 41–88. F. Bock, "Über Registrierung von Sekretbriefen (Studien zu den Sekretregistern Johanns XXII)," *Quellen und Forschungen aus italienischen Archiven und Bibliotheken* 28 (1937–1938): 147–234. H. Denifle, "Die päpstlichen Registerbände des 13. Jahrhunderts und das Inventar derselben vom J. 1339," *Archiv für Literatur- und Kirchengeschichte des Mittelalters* 2 (1886): 1–105. K. Eubel, "Der Registerband des Gegenpapstes Nikolaus V," *Archivalische Zeitschrift* 4 (1893): 123–212. G. Lang, "Stephanus de Fonte und Symon de Vares: Zwei Supplikenregistratoren unter Innozenz VI," *Quellen und Forschungen aus italienischen Archiven und Bibliotheken* 33 (1944): 259–268. M. Laurent, *Le culte de S. Louis d'Anjou a Marseille au XIVe siècle: Les documents de Louis Antoine de Ruffi suivis d'un choix de lettres de cét érudit* (Rome, 1954). T. D. Leccisotti and C. Taberelli, *Le carte dell'archivio di S. Pietro di Perugia*

(Milan, 1956). E. Leonard, *Histoire de Jeanne Ire, reine de Naples, comtesse de Provence (1343–1382)* (Monaco, 1932–1936). J. de Loye, *Les archives de la Chambre apostolique au XIVe siècle*, pt. 1, *Inventaire* (Paris, 1899). A. Mercati, "Il 'Bullarium generale' dell'Archivio Segreto Vaticano," in *Sussidi per la consultazione dell'Archivio Vaticano* (Vatican City, 1947), vol. 3, pp. v–xiv, 1–58. G. Mollat, "La juridiction d'un prieuré au XIVe siècle," *Revue d'histoire ecclésiastique* 52 (1957): 491–498. G. Mollat, *Les papes d'Avignon, 1305–1378*, 10th ed. (Paris, 1964). G. Mollat, "A propos du droit de dépouille," *Revue d'histoire ecclésiastique* 29 (1933): 316–343.

Boyle, pp. 114–127, makes a compelling argument for using the calendars of the French School as a finding aid for the Avignon Registers. The calendars use the RA as a primary source and cross reference the RV as appropriate. A complete list of the second and third series of these calendars follows:

Bibliothèque des Écoles françaises d'Athènes et de Rome, 2d ser., *Registres des papes du XIIIe siècle*:

Gregory IX (1227–1241): L. Auvray, *Les registres de Grégoire IX: Recueil des bulles de ce pape publiées ou analysées d'après les manuscrits originaux au Vatican* (Paris, 1896–1955) [2d ser., vol. 9].

Innocent IV (1243–1254): É. Berger, ed., *Les registres d'Innocent IV: Publiées ou analysés d'après les manuscrits originaux du Vatican et de la Bibliothèque nationale* (Paris, 1884–1920) [2d ser., vol. 1].

Alexander IV (1254–1261): C. B. de la Roncière et al., *Les registres d'Alexandre IV: Recueil des bulles de ce pape, publiées ou analysées d'après les manuscrits originaux des Archives du Vatican* (Paris, 1902–1959) [2d ser., vol. 15].

Urban IV (1261–1264): L. Dorez and J. Guiraud, *Les registres d'Urbain IV (1261–1264): Recueil des bulles de ce pape publiées ou analysées d'après les manuscrits originaux du Vatican* (Paris, 1899–1929) [2. sér., vol. 13].

Clement IV (1265–1268): E. Jordan, *Les registres de Clément IV (1265–1268): Recueil des bulles de ce pape publiées ou analysées d'après les manuscrits originaux des Archives du Vatican* (Paris, 1893–1945) [2d ser., vol. 11].

Gregory X (1271–1276): J. Guiraud, *Les Registres de Grégoire X (1272–1276): Recueil des bulles de ce pape publiées ou analysées d'après les manuscrits originaux des Archives du Vatican* (Paris, 1892–) [2d ser., vol. 12]. J. Guiraud and E. Cadier, *Les registres de Grégoire X (1272–1276) et de Jean XXI (1276–1277): Recueil des bulles de ces papes: Tables publiées ou analysées d'après le manuscrit des Archives du Vatican* (Paris, 1960) [2d ser., vol. 12].

John XXI (1276–1277): [See J. Guiraud and E. Cadier above under Gregory X.]

Nicholas III (1277–1280): J. Gay and S. Vitte, *Les registres de Nicolas III (1277–1280): Recueil des bulles de ce pape, publiées ou analysées d'après les manuscrits originaux du Vatican* (Paris, 1898–1938) [2d ser., vol. 14].

Martin IV (1281–1285): F. Olivier-Martin, *Les registres de Martin IV (1281–1285): Recueil des bulles de ce pape publiées ou analysées d'après les manuscrits originaux des Archives du Vatican* (Paris, 1901–1935) [2d ser., vol. 16].

Honorius IV (1285–1287): M. Prou, *Les registres d'Honorius IV: Publiées d'après le manuscrit des Archives du Vatican* (Paris, 1888) [2d ser., vol. 7].

Nicholas IV (1288–1292): E. Langlois, *Les registres de Nicolas IV: Recueil des bulles de ce pape publiées ou analysées d'après le manuscrit original des Archives du Vatican* (Paris, 1886–1905) [2d ser., vol. 5].

Boniface VIII (1294–1303): G. A. L. Digard et al., *Les Registres de Boniface VIII: Recueil des bulles de ce pape publiées ou analysées d'après les manuscrits originaux des Archives du Vatican* (Paris, 1884–1939) [2d ser., vol. 4].

Benedict XI (1303–1304): C. A. Grandjean, *Le registre de Benoît XI: Recueil des bulles de ce pape publiées ou analysées d'après le manuscrit original des Archives du Vatican* (Paris, 1883–) [2d ser., vol. 2].

Bibliothèque des Écoles françaises d'Athènes et de Rome, 3d ser., *Registres et lettres des papes du XIVe siècle*:

Clement V (1305–1314): Benedictines of Monte Cassino, ed., *Regestum Clementis Papae V: Ex Vaticanis archetypis sanctissimi domini nostri Leonis XIII pontificis maximi iussu et munificenta nunc primum editum* (Rome, 1885–1888). This calendar is indexed by Y. Lanhers et al., *Tables des registres de Clément V, publiés par les Bénédictins* (Paris, 1948–1957) [3d ser.].

John XXII (1316–1334): A. Coulon and S. Clémencet, eds., *Lettres secrètes et curiales du pape Jean XXII 1316–1334 relatives à la France* (Paris, 1900–) [3e ser., vol. 1]. G. Mollat, *Lettres communes Jean XXII (1316–1334): Analysées d'après les registres dits d'Avignon et du Vatican* (Paris, 1904–1947) [3d ser., vol. 1 bis].

Benedict XII (1334–1342): G. Daumet, ed., *Lettres closes, patentes et curiales [du pape Benoît XII] se rapportant à la France: Publiées ou analysées d'après les registres du Vatican* (Rome, 1899–1920) [3d ser., vol. 2]. J. M. Vidal, *Benoît XII (1334–1342): Lettres communes analysées d'après les registres dits d'Avignon et du Vatican* (Paris, 1903–1911) [3d ser., vol. 2 bis]. J. M. Vidal and G. Mollat, *Benoît XII (1334–1342): Lettres closes et patentes intéressant les pays autres que la France* (Paris, 1913–) [3d ser., vol. 2 bis].

Clement VI (1342–1352): E. Déprez, *Clément VI (1342–1352): Lettres closes, patentes et curiales se rapportant à la France* (Paris, 1910–1961) [3d ser., vol. 3]. E. Déprez and G. Mollat, *Lettres closes, patentes et curiales intéressant les pays autres que la France [Clément VI]* (Paris, 1960–1961) [3d ser., vol. 3].

Innocent VI (1352–1362): E. Déprez, *Innocent VI: Lettres closes, patentes et curiales se rapportant à la France: publiées ou analysées d'après les registres du Vatican* (Rome, 1909–) [3d ser., vol. 4]. P. Gasnault and M. H. Laurent, *Lettres secrètes et curiales [Innocent VI]: Publiées ou analysées d'après les registres des Archives vaticanes* (Paris, 1959–) [3d ser., vol. 4].

Urban V (1362–1370): P. Lecacheux and G. Mollat, eds., *Lettres secrètes et curiales du pape Urbain V (1362–1370) se rapportant à la France: Publ. ou analysées d'après les registres du Vatican [puis] d'Avignon et du Vatican* (Paris, 1902–1955) [3d ser., vol. 5]. H. Dubrulle, *Les registres d'Urbain V (1362–1363): Recueil des bulles de ce pape publiées ou analysées d'après les manuscrits originaux du Vatican* (Paris, 1926) [3d ser.]. M. H. Laurent, P. Gasnault, and M. Hayez, *Lettres communes analysées d'après les registres dits d'Avignon et du Vatican [Urbain V]* (Paris, 1954–) [3d ser., vol. 5 bis].

Gregory XI (1370–1378): L. Mirot and H. Jassemin, eds., *Lettres secrètes et curiales du pape Grégoire XI [1370–1378] relatives à la France: Extraites des registres du Vatican* (Paris, 1935–1957) [3d ser., vol. 7]. G. Mollat, *Lettres secrètes et curiales du pape Grégoire XI (1370–1378) intéressant les pays autres que la France: Publiées ou analysées d'apres les registres du Vatican* (Paris, 1962–1965) [3d ser.] A. M. Hayez, ed., *Gregoire XI, 1370–1378: Lettres Communies Analysées d'apres les registres dits d'Avignon et du Vatican* (Rome, 1992–) [3d ser., vol. 6 bis].

Finding Aids: ASV Indice 1101 is a tabular prospectus to the entire series. If a researcher already has a pontifical year or a former volume number, this skeletal index will provide the current volume number. Indice 1101 proceeds volume by volume, listing the current volume number, pontificate, pontifical year, volume number within a pontifical year, tome number, selected notes, and the current volume number. While this is the most comprehensive index of the series, other indexes have more descriptive details.

ASV Indici 642–669, "Indice dell'Archivio Apostolico di Avignone," known as the "Martin Index" (1711), compiled in Avignon, calendars the RA volumes from Clement V to Clement VII (of Avignon), tome 1–4, that is, RA 205–208. The RA volumes of Gregory XI are omitted. Early volumes of ASV Indici 642–669 are prefaced with internal indexes. The calendar's entries give the folio number, diocese, category of business (e.g., gratia, indultum, decretum, dispensatio, provisio, mandatum, confirmatio, collatio, aggregatio, inhibitio, etc.), recipient, and the object of the business, and infrequently a date. The Martin Index indicates the pontificate, the pontifical year, and liber number. Researchers must refer to Indice 1101 for the current RA volume number.

ASV Indici 557–641, "Index Bullarum," compiled in Avignon by Montroy between 1718 and 1732, provide alphabetical access to RA volumes. These indices are incomplete for the pontificate of Clement VII (of Avignon) (approx. RA 209–244) and the first half of Benedict XIII (of Avignon) (approx. to RA 293 or RA 294). Indici 557–641 are selective, and do not calendar every item. The Montroy indices are alphabetical (first letter only) by dioceses, with some names of countries as well. References are given according to pontificate, pontifical year, and liber number, so researchers must consult Indice 1101 for the current volume numbers.

ASV Indice 1036 (pp. 148v–189r) includes a list of cameral materials found in RA vols. 1–349. Entries include: RA volume number, inclusive dates of the cameral materials in the RA volume, brief description of material (including type of business, e.g., manuale, instrumentum, introitus et exitus, processus, inventarium, solutiones, etc.), and RA folio numbers. On page 233, there is an alphabetical list of dioceses, regions, provinces, types of business, and so froth, and references to the pages on which they can be located in Indice 1036. The best overview of the cameral materials in the RA can be gained by using ASV Indice 1036, the old indice numbered 34, and DeLoye (cf. below) in tandem.

ASV Indice 34 (old number), by Dr. P. Sella, is available at the desk in the main ASV reading room. This index also lists the same cameral materials located in the RA as Indice 1036; however, Indice 34 provides different, complementary information. This is not an official ASV finding aid and must be used in consultation with ASV staff.

Joseph de Loye, *Les archives de la Chambre apostolique au XIVe siècle*, pt. 1, *Inventaire* (Paris, 1899), pp. vii–x, 197–269, provides a more selective list of the cameral materials in the RA; however, some of these are more fully described than in ASV Indice 1036 and 34 (old number). DeLoye also includes several tables of materials that indicate where, for example, stray *Introitus et exitus* can be located in different series. He also indexes some of the dioceses cited in various cameral series. DeLoye gives the former papal-year-tome numbers, although the copy in the ASV Sala d'Indice has annotations of the current RA volume numbers.

ASV Indice 260 contains contemporary tables of contents and fragments of contents for the following RA vols.: 21, 43, 117, 136, 182, 197, 201, and 202.

Most volumes of RA have contemporary indices, as noted by Boyle, p. 127.

Instrumenta Miscellanea 6646, "Rubricae litterarum Gregorii PP. XI," provides partial lists of bulls of the papacy of Gregory XI (1377–1378). The citations are given according to category, for example, litterae de vacantibus, litterae de canonicatu, litterae de beneficiis, litterae tabellionatus officii, and so forth, and refer to the following RA registers and folios: RA 202 (ff. 501–513), RA 203 (ff. 136–153), RA 204 (ff. 19–34, 215–217, 221, 222–239, 367–369, 370).

See also J. Lenzenweger, "Konkordanzen," in *Acta Pataviensia Austriaca*, vol. 1, *Klemens VI (1342–1352)* (Vienna, 1974), pp. 43–176. This article is a concordance between Registra Vaticana volumes 147–213E and Registra Avenionensia volumes 56–120A. Lenzenweger lists the type of business, and then the RV and RA volume and folio(s), and any other identifying information (e.g., number).

Location: Archivio Segreto Vaticano.

3.2.6.7 Registra Lateranensia (cited as RL)

[DATABASE ID: VATV180-A]

Inclusive Dates: 1389–1892.

Bulk: 174 linear m. (2467 numbered vols. and 13 drawers of index cards).

Organization: The registers proceed pontificate by pontificate with the exception of nos. 2461–2467. Within each pontificate, however, there can be numerous registers containing business for a given year. In each register documents are grouped according to type of business. RL 2461–2467 form a parallel series of selected "Miscellanea Litterarum Apostolicarum" (1559–1758). Some RL volumes, especially of popes named Pius and Paul, are misattributed.

The chronology of this series is also disturbed by earlier materials (including some of parchment), bound into the register volumes where reference was made to them.

Scope: These paper registers are so called because they were kept in the Lateran Palace after their return to Rome in 1817 and were only transferred to the Vatican in 1892. They contain copies of the letters issued from the Roman Chancery in the Schism (parallel to the *Registra Avenionensia*, which continued at Avignon), then, from the mid-fifteenth century, from the new office of the Datary. The official designation of this series, *Regesta bullarum datariae apostolicae*, applies to the registered letters generated after the establishment of the Datary. The bulls, granting ecclesiastical favors of every kind in foro externo, were registered according to the actual date of their expedition rather than the date of their being signed by the

pope or his vice-chancellor. Many volumes of the series were lost when it was removed to Paris (1810–1817).

Boyle, pp 132–148, provides an extensive analysis of these registers. He argues that the registers consist of common letters sent through the Chancery. As such he suggests that though they are Datary by their custodial provenance, they are in fact Chancery in origin.

The *Registra Lateranensia* record routine letters prepared in reply to "petitions for benefices, dispensations of various kinds, indulgences, graces, and the like" (L. E. Boyle, Introduction, *Calendar of Entries in the Papal Registers Relating to Great Britain and Ireland: Calendar of Papal Letters*, vol. XV [1484–1492], edited by M. J. Haren, Dublin, 1978, p. xv). Approved petitions were registered in the Dataria Apostolica series *Registra supplicationum*. If a supplicant wanted a papal letter communicating the grant of favor, additional fees and steps were required. The *Registra Lateranensia* contain those approved supplications, which were not only recorded in the *Registra supplicationum* but were followed up with a formal letter. From the late fifteenth century onward, letters in the shorter form of briefs increasingly communicated routine favors and graces and were registered in a different series, Dataria Apostolica series *Brevia Lateranensia*, whose scope and content are closely related to the *Registra Lateranensia*.

The contents of the *Registra Lateranensia* fall into three main categories of business: beneficiary, judicial, and dispensatory or spiritual. As in the *Registra supplicationum*, the vast majority of letters registered here relate to beneficiary activity. Since a great variety of individuals held and received income from benefices in the medieval and early modern period, papal grants relating to benefices have been used to glean information about the careers not only of high ecclesiastical figures but also of muscians, literary figures, professors of theology and law, scholars, and members of the households of cardinals and popes. Judical business includes: requests to obtain commision of cases to judge delegates in matters pertaining to ecclesiastical jurisdiction, grants or confirmations of legal privileges, confirmations of the terms of wills or foundation documents (altars, chapels, monasteries), the extension of papal protection, licenses, and requests for papal intervention, pardons, and exemptions. For example, in 1492 Alexander IV commissioned two canons to settle a dispute between the "masters of works" in charge of London Bridge and a parish rector, both of whom claimed rights to the alms offered to a recently placed image of the Virgin on the bridge (RL 918 f. 210r–v). In 1399, Margaret the Duchess of Norfolk sought confirmation of her will from Boniface XIII (RL 52, ff. 113v–114r). Ecclesiastical officials were also commisioned to settle conflicts relating to marriage, divorce, annulment, dowries, and inheritence. The third general category for grants of favor comprehends and responds to a wide range of requests for dispensations, absolutions, indults, and indulgences, some of which are discussed below.

The most common sorts of dispensations found in the RL series are for illegitimacy, which impedes a cleric from office. Clerics also sought dispensations in order to hold multiple benefices. Monks and priests received dispensations to remove canonical disqualification resulting from their involvement with events, even judicial processes, that have resulted in death and bloodshed. Confessors to noble households, court musicians, clerical tutors, and students at universities sought dispensations for absentee enjoyment of their benefices. Clerics and lay persons might seek absolution for homicide and other violent crimes. Dispensations for consanguinity as an impediment to marriage was a very frequent lay petition. Laypersons also petitioned for indults that allowed them to have portable altars, to have their own priests celebrate private masses, to elect their own confessors, to say divine office in their households, and to otherwise exert control over their own expressions of piety. Noble laypersons also petitioned indulgences for their relics and altars, though most petitions for indulgences to attract visitors and alms come from churches and confraternities. The lay patronage of churches, religious houses, chapel, oratories, and altars received frequently backing from *RL* letters. For example, in the mid-fifteenth century, Nicholas V gave a confraternity of Spanish artisans in Rome, associated with the hospital of St. Thomas, permission to erect a hospital for poor artisans (see ASV Indice 556, f. 172v). Finally, religious communities are well represented in the *RL* volumes, where there is evidence of hermits, tertiaries, beguines, hospitals, leprosaria, and confraternities receiving support and papal assistance, along with members of the traditional religious orders. *RL* 10, fols. 248–255r contains the canonization proclamation, issued in the second year of Boniface IX's pontificate, for Brigit of Sweden.

Dataria Apostolica series *Registra supplicationum* is the source of choice for successful petitions to the papacy. However, the *RL* volumes have the advantage of being more comprehensively indexed. They are also included in the *Schedario Garampi*.

Notes: For related material, see also Registra Lateranensia [fragment], Urban VI, anno IX (1386–1387), Biblioteca Apostolica Vaticana (Ottob. lat. 1443). Additional registers are located at Trinity College in Dublin, Ireland. See Cancelleria Apostolica series *Lateran Registers* for a more detailed description. There is also a Rubricella in the Biblioteca Vallicelliana in Rome. ASV *Fondo Santini*, volume XIII (pp. 14–16), contains a list of items referring to Oxford from a lost *RL* volume of Eugene IV.

References: Fink, pp. 39–42; Boyle, pp. 51, 132–148; Pásztor (1970), pp. 25–27; Pásztor (1983), p. 102; MacFarlane, p. 38.

M. Giusti, "Note sui registri Lateranensi," in *Mélanges Eugène Tisserant* (Vatican City, 1964), vol. 4, pp. 229–249. H. Diener, "Rubrizellen zu Kanzleiregistern Johanns XXIII. und Martins V," *Quellen und Forschungen aus italienischen Archiven und Bibliotheken* 39 (1959): 117–172. H. Diener, "Die grossen Registerserien im Vatikanischen Archiv (1378–1523): Hinweise und Hilfsmittel zu ihrer Benutzung und Auswertung," *Quellen und Forschungen aus italienischen Archiven und Bibliotheken* 51 (1972): 305–368. M. Giusti, *Studi sui registri di bolle papali* (Vatican City, 1968). A. Mercati, "Schedario Garampi, Registri Vaticani, Registri Lateranensi, Rationes Camerae, Inventario del Fondo Concistoriale," vol. 1 of *Sussidi per la consultazione dell'Archivio Vaticano* (Rome, 1926). A. E. Planchart, "The Early Career of Guillaume Du Fay," *Journal of the American Musicological Society* 46 (1993): 341–368. A. L. Tautu, ed., *Acta Urbani P.P. VI (1378–1379), Bonifacii P.P. IX (1389–1404), Innocentii P.P. VII (1404–1406), et Gregorii P.P. XII (1406–1415) e registris vaticanis ed lateranensibus aliisque fontibus* (Rome, 1970).

The *RL* has also been calendared in several different projects. The series *Calendar of Entries in the Papal Registers Relating to Great Britain and Ireland: Calendar of Papal Letters*, edited by W. H. Bliss, C. Johnson, and J. A. Twemlow (London, 1893–1955), calendars selected volumes of the *RL* (1389–1484) pertaining to the British Isles as follows. The latter volumes (XV and XVI) provide excellent general descriptions for all users of this series of the diplomatic processes used to dispatch these letters and how these registers relate to others in the Vatican Archives. These calendars also have subject, place, and personal name indices:

Boniface IX (1389–1404): Vol. 4, *RL* 1–43; Vol. 5, *RL* 44–118.
Innocent VII (1404–1406): Vol 6, *RL* 119–127.
Gregory XII (1406–1415): Vol. 6, *RL* 128–135.
Alexander V (of Pisa, 1409–1410): Vol. 6, *RL* 136–138.
John XXIII (of Pisa, 1410–1415): Vol. 6, *RL* 139–185.
Council of Constance (1415): Vol. 6, *RL* 186.
Martin V (1417–1431): Vol. 7, *RL* 187–276; Vol. 8, *RL* 277–301.
Eugene IV (1431–1447): Vol. 8, *RL* 302–358; vol. 9: *RL* 359–431.
Nicholas V (1447–1455): Vol. 10, *RL* 432–497.
Calixtus III (1455–1458): Vol. 11: *RL* 498–534.
Pius II (1458–1464): Vol. 12, *RL* 535–599.
Paul II (1464–1471): Vol. 12, *RL* 600–712.
Sixtus IV (1471–1484): Vol. 13, part 1, *RL* 713–757; vol. 13, part 2, *RL* 758–838.
Innocent VIII (1484–1492): Vol. 14, *RL* 838–840; vol. 15, *RL* 841–924, 929.
Alexander VI (1492–1498): vol. 16, part 1, *RL* 924–1026, 2463.

J. Haller et al., eds., *Repertorium Germanicum: Regesten aus den päpstlichen Archiven zur Geschichte des deutschen Reichs und seiner Territorien im XIV. und XV. Jahrhundert: Pontifikat Eugens IV. (1431–1447)* (Berlin, 1897), and its continuation, *Repertorium Germanicum: Verzeichnis der in den päpstlichen Registern und Kameralakten vorkommenden Personen, Kirchen und Orte des deutschen Reiches, seiner Diözesen und Territorien, vom Beginn des Schismas bis zur Reformation* (Berlin, 1916–), calendar items concerning Germany in this series.

Finding Aids: There are two types of finding aids to this series. The first type generally presents an inventory or contents list of the registers and provides basic information: volume number, inclusive dates, and general title summary of the type of business. These inventories are useful if you already have a reference (either an old or current volume number). Reference to the contents of the *RL* can also be found in the *Schedario Garampi* (see Separate Collections, Individual and Family Papers series *Schedario Garampi*). The inventories of this first type are Gualdo (see below) and four ASV Indici: 1039, 1040, 705, and 319A. The second type of finding aid can be characterized as more descriptive and subject/geographic oriented. These indexes are useful if you are looking for information on a specific diocese, religious order, or perhaps even a person. The indexes of this second type are: BAV Vat. Lat. 6952 and ASV Indici numbers 1, 320–324, 325–430, and 690. The latter group of indices provides information on the contents of many *RL* volumes that are no longer extant. Additionally there are thirteen drawers of index cards to entries between 1455 and 1479. All of the above mentioned indexes are discussed in greater detail below.

See in particular Germano Gualdo, *Sussidi per la consultazione dell'Archivio Vaticano*, new ed. (Vatican City, 1989), vol. 1, pp. 245–313. Gualdo's work is invaluable in providing access to the *RL*. In addition to introducing the collection and providing a strong bibliography, Gualdo is essential to tying the various indexes and such that have been done over the years with the current organization of the collection. He does this through a table demonstrating the correspondence between each papacy and ASV Indici 320–430 and has constructed the most useful concordance between *Schedario Garampi* reference numbers and the current volume numbers. Gualdo's notes to the registers of each pope are also indispensible in locating misattributions (particularly for papacies of popes named Pius and Paul) or misfiled items.

At the end of the collection there is a "Schede" composed of thirteen drawers of index cards. This is a chronological presentation of *RL* 534A–796 (1455–1479). Each card provides information on the date of registration, the diocese, recipient, business, and date of request(?), in addition to the register and page number on which the entire letter can be located. These are dense and a researcher may prefer to call up the actual volumes for a given year.

ASV Indici 1039 and 1040, by M. H. Laurent, O.P., cover the entire series vols. 1–2467 (1389–1903). This index proceeds numerically according to the current volume number, listing the papacy, the inclusive dates in the volume, the pontifical year of the volume, the old volume number, the type of business found in the register, and the number of pages. Indici 1039 and 1040 also provide Garampi's reference number "Gar = ." The Garampi number, however, frequently presents a pontifical year that is different from the actual year. With a reference from Garampi, it is easier to proceed directly to the concordance in Gualdo to locate the correct, current volume number. The advantage of these indici over Gualdo is that they list the type of business being conducted, albeit briefly.

ASV Indice 705, "Inventarium Regestorum Lateranensium seu de Dataria in Tabularium Vaticanum jussu Leonis XIII," was done ca. 1900 by Pietro Wenzel. This indice has been superseded by Gualdo and/or ASV Indici 1039 and 1040, but may be useful in reconciling some old citations, such as those from earlier volumes of Hierarchia Catholica. This index, organized by pontificate, lists the former and current volume numbers, the type of business conducted (using the identical terminology employed in Indici 1039, 1040, and 1041), and the pontifical year. *Schedario Garampi* references are usually noted (in red ink).

ASV Indice 319A, "Concordata numeri Rubricellarum [= *Schedario Garampi*] Regestorum Lateranensium seu verterio cum novo numero," covers the pontificates of Boniface IX—Pius VII (1389–1823) and was completed in 1903. The Num (anno) and Rub (Liber) refer to the *Schedario Garampi* references that come after the AB + Name of Pope (or A.U.E. instead of AB in the case of Clement VII) in the *Schedario Garampi*. This has also been superseded by Gualdo.

In the Vatican Library (BAV) Vat. Lat. 6952, pp. 97r–362r, is a "Summarium of the Registra Lateranensia from Boniface IX to Martin V (1389–1431)," done by A. Raynaldi in 1618. This calendar provides summaries of selected bulls within these registers. Raynaldi's criteria for selection are not explicit, but

since his work predates the loss of many Lateran Registers he can offer information derived from registers no longer extant. ASV Indice 320 is a fair copy of Raynaldi's "Summarium" for the papacy of Boniface IX. A table of the parallel entries between the autograph (BAV Vat. Lat. 6952) and the fair copy (ASV Indice 320) can be found in Boyle, pp. 137–142. After locating a desired volume, researchers must proceed to Gualdo's concordance or ASV Indice 705 to locate the current volume number.

ASV Indici 320–324 also provide selected summaries of bulls in the *RL*. These indices have a history of their own for which Boyle and Gualdo provide a good beginning, even if they are not always in accord. Indice 320, "Summarium quarundam Bullarum Pontificatus Bonifatii noni," is a fair copy of the entries for Boniface IX, probably commissioned by Raynaldi (ca. 1618), of Raynaldi's "Summarium" (see above BAV Vat. Lat. 6952). Indice 320 includes Raynaldi's index to cardinals and Roman churches. Indici 321, by Contelori, reproduces pages 97–362 of Raynaldi's "Summarium," in other words, the main body of the text, without the indexes. G. B. Confalonieri compiled 322, 323, and 324A (ca. 1618) directly from the *RL*. These indices cover Gregory XII (1407–1408), Alexander V (of Pisa, 1409–1410), and John XXIII (of Pisa, 1410–1415). 324A provides summaries of the *RL* of John XXIII and is an index to 322 and 323. Index 324 appears to be yet another fair copy of Raynaldi's "Summarium" for Innocent VII (1404–1406) and John XXIII (of Pisa, 1410–1415). These indici do not usually note the current ASV volume number or the fact that the register is now missing. If the current volume number is missing, Gualdo's concordance or ASV Indice 705 will give it.

ASV Indici 325–430 proceed more or less chronologically and cover the pontificates of Calixtus III (1455) through Pius VI (1799). They provide various types of indices and occasionally summaries of the *RL* between those years. Most of these indices were constructed prior to the great losses in this series and therefore some insight into lost registers can be gleaned from these volumes. Generally, these indices follow the actual registers page by page, listing diocese, person, and occasionally the type of business transacted. These indexes would be chiefly useful for researchers seeking information on a specific locale, person, or function.

ASV Indice 690, "Indice di Brevi (sic. Bolle) Pontifici relativi a ordini religiose dei Regestra Lateranensia da Martino V a Paolo IV" (1417–1621), by Gaetano Marini, was also completed prior to the significant losses in the series. This roughly drafted index, organized by congregation or order, lists pontifical year, volume, and page number.

ASV Indice 1, pp. 692–720, provides a list of volumes from Boniface IX (1389) to John XXIII (of Pisa, 1415). Since it was done before the significant losses in the series it does not reflect the current state of the series or the current volume numbers. The listings are brief: original volume number, a brief summary title, and what appears to be a former volume number. This index is a curiosity and not particularly useful.

ASV Indice 685 is a compilation of the lost bulls of Calixtus III (1455–1458) derived from ASV Indici 325 and 326. It was done by E. Ranuzzi in 1918.

ASV Indice 112 by Contelori provides a summary of the Lateran Registers of Martin V (1417–1431) on pp. 276–345.

Location: Archivio Segreto Vaticano.

3.2.6.8 Registra Vaticana (cited as RV, sometimes as Reg. Vat.)

[DATABASE ID: VATV362-A]

Inclusive Dates: 872 (copy ca. 1070)–1605 (bulk 1198–1572).

Bulk: 98 linear m.

Organization: 2,042 numbered volumes.

Scope: The series *Registra Vaticana* is so called because it was already housed in the Vatican palace (in the Bibliotheca Secreta) when it became part of the original Archives under Paul VI. The RV volumes fill Armaria I–XXVIII in the ASV. These are copies of papal bulls and letters, and so this is one of the largest series in the Archives, numbering 2,042 volumes, of which twenty-one are duplicates. RV 1 was written at Montecassino and contains letters of John VIII (872). RV 2 contains letters and notitiae of Gregory VII (1073–1085) and RV 3 is a later copy. RV 4 begins the continuous series with letters of Innocent III (1198–1216).

Through the thireenth and fourteenth centuries papal letters were generated in several ways. The process that led from a supplication to a common letter of grace was carried out within the Chancery. Later, in the course of the fifteenth century, the expedition of grants of favor was increasingly the work of the specialized and separate Datary. "Curial" letters began with privileged petitions from cardinals and curial officials, but often ended in common letters. "Close," "secret," and "cameral" letters were prepared by papal secretaries or by notaries of the Camera. But all papal letters were physically prepared and sealed in the Chancery, and then they were registered in these parchment Chancery volumes. Boyle, pp. 103–113, provides an excellent introduction to the origins and use of RV and explains the relation of this series to other medieval holdings of the ASV. He cautions that the RV text of a letter was normally taken, in the fourteenth century, from the *Registra Avenionensia* copy rather than directly from the original letter itself, and also that many extant original papal letters were never registered, so that the registers cannot be assumed to contain a complete record of any papal business.

In 1389 the paper *Registra Lateranensia* began in the Roman Curia, to fulfill the first-record purpose of the *Registra Avenionensia*. Common letters were registered in RL, while the secret and cameral letters were recorded in parchment volumes, which should now be in RV. Later volumes of the RV series mostly contain letters originating in the Camera and Secretariat.

Note: "There are some RV volumes (e.g. RV 214–218, 242–244, 251, 262, 272–281, 288–290, 300–309, 321–322) in the present arrangement which really belong to the paper Registra Avenionensia series, while there are some others (e.g. RV 318, 357–358) which have the characteristics of Registra Lateranensia" (Boyle, p. 107).

Register 27 of the Poenitentiaria Apostolica series *Registra matrimonialium et diversorum* properly belongs between RV 670 and 671. See the series entry there.

According to ASV Indice 213, "Indice di libri de Msgr. Ciampini alcune de quale sono stati comprati da Il. Sg.le. Clemente XI e posti nell'studi . . . e fuori sono stati segnali con la lett. 'C' e posti in diversi luoghi secundo le materie nelle quali trattavano," RV 2018 was included in a donation that took place between 1700 and 1721.

Note: Vols. 1–1297, 1300, 1343, 1411, 1413, 1441, 1624,

1746, 1906, 1926, 1935–2016, 2018, and 2020 are available on microfilm.

Note: Registers of Gregory XIII (1572–1585) and Urban VIII (1623–1644) are found in the Archives Nationales de France, Paris. See Miscellaneous official series *Registres de copies de bulles* (L53–L84) for a description.

References: Fink, pp. 34–37; Pásztor (1970), p. 38; Boyle, pp. 103–113; MacFarlane, pp. 33–34. There is a particularly large bibliography relating to the *Registra Vaticana*. What follows is a selection from the most important and relevant. It is divided into three sections: (1) Calendars, (2) Studies of particular portions of the RV, and (3) Studies not limited to particular volumes.

1. Several series of published calendars and editions provide access, indexing, and sometimes full transcriptions from RV:

E. L. E. Caspar, "Registrum Iohannis VIII papae," in *Epistolae karolini aevi* (Berlin, 1928), vol. 5, pp. 1–272. E. L. E. Caspar, ed., *Das Register Gregors VII* (Berlin, 1920–23). O. Hageneder and A. Haidacher, eds., *Die Register Innocenz III.* (Graz, 1964–). F. Kempf, ed., *Regestum Innocentii III papae super negotio Romani Imperii* (Rome, 1947).

W. H. Bliss, C. Johnson, and J. A. Twemlow, eds., *Calendar of Entries in the Papal Registers Relating to Great Britain and Ireland: Calendar of Papal Letters* (London, 1893–1955), uses the RV as its major resource and calendars letters with pertinence to the British Isles from Innocent III (1198) through Innocent VIII (1492). The British calendar contains subject, person, and place indexes. It covers RV 4–771 as follows:

Innocent III (1198–1216): Vol. 1, RV 4–8
Honorius III (1216–1227): Vol. 1, RV 9–13
Gregory IX (1227–1241): Vol. 1, RV 14–20
Innocent IV (1243–1254): Vol. 1, RV 21–23
Alexander IV (1254–1261): Vol. 1, RV 24–25A
Urban IV (1261–1264): Vol. 1, RV 26–29
Clement IV (1265–1268): Vol. 1, RV 30–35
Gregory X (1271–1276): Vol. 1, RV 36–37
John XXI (1276–1277): Vol. 1, RV 38
Nicholas III (1277–1280): Vol. 1, RV 39l
Martin IV (1281–1285): Vol. 1, RV 41–42
Honorius IV (1285–1287): Vol. 1, RV 43
Nicholas IV (1288–1292): Vol. 1, RV 44–46
Boniface VIII (1294–1303): Vol. 1, RV 47–50
Benedict XI (1303–1304): Vol. 1, RV 51
Clement V (1305–1314): Vol. 2, RV 52–61
John XXII (1316–1334): Vol. 2, RV 63–117
Nicholas V (1328–1330): Vol. 2, RV 118
Benedict XII (1334–1342): Vol. 2, RV 119–136
Clement VI (1342–1352): Vol. 3, RV 137–213
Innocent VI (1352–1362): Vol. 3, RV 219–244K
Urban V (1362–1370): Vol. 4, RV 245–250, 252–261
Gregory XI (1370–1378): Vol. 4, RV 263–271, 274–287
Clement VII (of Avignon, 1378–1394): Vol. 4, RV 291–299
Urban VI (1378–1389): Vol. 4, RV 310–312
Boniface IX (1389–1404): Vol. 4, RV 312–320; vol. 5, RV 347
Innocent VII (1404–1406): Vol 6, RV 333–334

Gregory XII (1406–1415): Vol. 6, RV 335–338
Alexander V (of Pisa, 1409–1410): Vol. 6, RV 339
John XXIII (of Pisa, 1410–1415): Vol. 6, RV 340–346
Martin V (1417–1431): Vol. 7, RV 348–350, 352–359
Eugene IV (1431–1447): Vol. 8, RV 359–384
Nicholas V (1447–1455): Vol. 10, RV 380–435
Calixtus III (1455–1458): Vol. 11: RV 436–467, 502
Pius II (1458–1464): Vol. 11, RV 468–523
Paul II (1464–1471): Vol. 12, RV 519, 524–545
Sixtus IV (1471–1484): Vol. 13, RV 546–681
Innocent VIII (1484–1492): Vol. 14, RV 682–771

J. Haller et al., eds., *Repertorium Germanicum: Regesten aus den päpstlichen Archiven zur Geschichte des Deutschen Reichs und seiner Territorien im XIV. und XV. Jahrhundert: Pontifikat Eugens IV. (1431–1447)* (Berlin, 1897), and its continuation, *Repertorium Germanicum: Verzeichnis der in den päpstlichen Registern und Kameralakten vorkommenden Personen, Kirchen und Orte des Deutschen Reiches, seiner Diözesen und Territorien, vom Beginn des Schismas bis zur Reformation* (Berlin, 1916–), calendar items concerning Germany in this series:

Clement VII (of Avignon, 1378–1394): Vol. 1
Urban VI (1378–1389): Vol. 2
Boniface IX (1389–1404): Vol. 2
Innocent VII (1404–1406): Vol 2
Gregory XII (1406–1415): Vol. 2
Alexander V (of Pisa, 1409–1410): Vol. 3
John XXIII (of Pisa, 1410–1415): Vol. 3
Council of Constance (1415): Vol. 3
Martin V (1417–1431): Vol. 4
Eugene IV (1431–1447): Vol. 1 (Haller)
Nicholas V (1447–1455): Vol. 6
Calixtus III (1455–1458): Vol. 7
Pius II (1458–1464): Vol. 8

A. L. Tautu edited select calendars of papal letters concerning the Oriental Church, mostly from *RV*, in the series *Pontificia commissio ad redigendum codicem iuris canonici orientalis, fontes*, ser. 3 (Rome, 1943–1971):

Honorius III (1216–1227), Gregory IX (1227–1241): A. L. Tautu, ed., *Acta Honorii III (1216–1227) et Gregorii IX (1227–1241) e registris Vaticanis aliisque fontibus* (Rome, 1950).

Urban IV (1261–1264), Clement IV (1265–1268), and Gregory X (1271–1276): A. L. Tautu, *Acta Urbani IV, Clementis IV, Gregorii X (1261–1276) e registris Vaticanis aliisque fontibus* Vatican City, 1953).

Innocent V (1276) through Benedict XI (1303–1304): A. L. Tautu and F. M. Delorme, eds., *Acta romanorum pontificum ab Innocentio V ad Benedictum XI (1276–1304) e regestis Vaticanis aliisque fontibus* (Vatican City, 1954).

Clement V (1305–1314): F. M. Delorme and A. L. Tautu, eds., *Acta Clementis pp. V (1305–1314) e registris Vaticanis aliisque fontibus* (Vatican City, 1955).

John XXII (1316–1334): A. L. Tautu, ed., *Acta Ioannis XXII (1317–1334) e registribus Vaticanis aliisque fontibus* (Vatican City, 1952).

Benedict XII (1334–1342): A. L. Tautu, ed., *Acta Benedicti XII, 1334–1342, e regestis Vaticanis aliisque fontibus* (Vatican City, 1958).

Clement VI (1342–1252): A. L. Tautu, ed., *Acta Clementis VI*

(*1342–1352*) *e regestis Vaticanis aliisque fontibus* (Vatican City, 1960).

Innocent VI (1352–1362): A. L. Tautu, ed., *Acta Innocentii pp. VI (1352–1362) e regestis Vaticanis aliisque fontibus* (Vatican City, 1961).

Urban V (1362–1370): A. L. Tautu, ed., *Acta Urbani PP. V (1362–1370) e regestis Vaticanis aliisque fontibus* (Vatican City, 1964).

Gregory XI (1370–1378): A. L. Tautu, ed., *Acta Gregorii P.P. XI (1370–1378) e regestis Vaticanis aliisque fontibus* (Vatican City, 1966).

Urban VI (1378–1379), Boniface IX (1389–1404), Innocent VII (1404–1406), and Gregory XII (1406–1415): A. L. Tautu, ed., *Acta Urbani P.P. VI (1378–1379), Bonifacii P.P. IX (1389–1404), Innocentii P.P. VII (1404–1406), et Gregorii P.P. XII (1406–1415) e regestris vaticanis ed lateranensibus aliisque fontibus* (Rome, 1970).

Clement VII (1378–1394) and Benedict XIII (1394–1417) of Avignon, Alexander V (1409–1410) and John XXIII (1410–1415) of Pisa: A. L. Tautu, ed., *Acta pseudopontificum Clementis VII (1378–1394), Benedicti XIII (1394–1417), Alexandri V (1409–1410), et Johannis XXIII (1406–1415) e registis Avenionensibus, Vaticanis, Lateranensibus et supplicationum* (Rome, 1971).

Bibliothèque des Écoles françaises d'Athènes et de Rome. 2d ser., *Registres des papes du XIIIe siècle* is cited as BEFAR 2. These calendars depend almost exclusively on *RV*:

Gregory IX (1227–1241): L. Auvray, *Les Registres de Grégoire IX: Recueil des bulles de ce pape publiées ou analysées d'après les manuscrits originaux au Vatican* (Paris, 1896–1955) [2d ser., vol. 9].

Innocent IV (1243–1254): É. Berger, ed., *Les registres d'Innocent IV: Publiées ou analysés d'après les manuscrits originaux du Vatican et de la Bibliothèque nationale* (Paris, 1884–1920) [2d ser., vol. 1].

Alexander IV (1254–1261): C. B. de la Roncière et al., *Les registres d'Alexandre IV: Recueil des bulles de ce Pape, publiées ou analysées d'après les manuscrits originaux des Archives du Vatican* (Paris, 1902–1959) [2d ser., vol. 15].

Urban IV (1261–1264): L. Dorez and J. Guiraud, *Les registres d'Urbain IV (1261–1264): Recueil des bulles de ce pape publiées ou analysées d'après les manuscrits originaux du Vatican* (Paris, 1899–1929) [2d ser., vol. 13].

Clement IV (1265–1268): E. Jordan, *Les registres de Clément IV (1265–1268): Recueil des bulles de ce Pape publiées ou analysées d'après les manuscrits originaux des Archives du Vatican* (Paris, 1893–1945) [2d ser., vol. 11].

Gregory X (1271–1276): J. Guiraud, *Les Registres de Grégoire X (1272–1276): Recueil des bulles de ce pape publiées ou analysées d'après les manuscrits originaux des Archives du Vatican* (Paris, 1892–) [2d ser., vol. 12]. J. Guiraud and E. Cadier, *Les registres de Grégoire X (1272–1276) et de Jean XXI (1276–1277): Recueil des bulles de ce papes: tables publiées ou analysées d'après le manuscrit des Archives du Vatican* (Paris, 1960) [2d ser., vol. 12].

John XXI (1276–1277): [See J. Guiraud and E. Cadier above under Gregory X].

Nicholas III (1277–1280): J. Gay and S. Vitte, *Les registres de Nicolas III (1277–1280): Recueil des bulles de ce pape, pu-*

bliées ou analysées d'après les manuscrits originaux du Vatican (Paris, 1898–1938) [2d ser., vol. 14].

Martin IV (1281–1285): F. Olivier-Martin, *Les registres de Martin IV (1281–1285): Recueil des bulles de ce pape publiées ou analysées d'après les manuscrits originaux des Archives du Vatican* (Paris, 1901–1935) [2d ser., vol. 16].

Honorius IV (1285–1287): M. Prou, *Les registres d'Honorius IV: Publiées d'après le manuscrit des Archives du Vatican* (Paris, 1888) [2d ser., vol. 7].

Nicholas IV (1288–1292): E. Langlois, *Les registres de Nicolas IV: Recueil des bulles de ce pape publiées ou analysées d'après le manuscrit original des Archives du Vatican* (Paris, 1886–1905) [2d ser., vol. 5].

Boniface VIII (1294–1303): G. A. L. Digard et al., *Les Registres de Boniface VIII: Recueil des bulles de ce pape publiées ou analysées d'après les manuscrits originaux des Archives du Vatican* (Paris, 1884–1939) [2d ser., vol. 4].

Benedict XI (1303–1304): C. A. Grandjean, *Le registre de Benoît XI: Recueil des bulles de ce pape publiées ou analysées d'après le manuscrit original des Archives du Vatican* (Paris, 1883–) [2d ser., vol. 2].

Bibliothèque des Écoles françaises d'Athènes et de Rome, 3d ser., *Registres et lettres des papes du XIVe siècle* is cited as BEFAR 3. These calendars depend primarily on RA, but they also cite the fair copies of the letters in RV:

Clement V (1305–1314): Benedictines of Monte Cassino, eds., *Regestum Clementis Papae V: Ex Vaticanis archetypis sanctissimi domini nostri Leonis XIII pontificis maximi iussu et munificenta nunc primum editum* (Rome, 1885–1888). This calendar is indexed by Y. Lanhers et al., *Tables des registres de Clément V, publiés par les Bénédictins* (Paris, 1948–1957) [3d ser.].

John XXII (1316–1334): A. Coulon and S. Clémencet, eds., *Lettres secrètes et curiales du pape Jean XXII 1316–1334 relatives à la France* (Paris, 1900–) [3d ser., vol. 1]. G. Mollat, *Lettres communes Jean XXII (1316–1334): Analysées d'après les registres dits d'Avignon et du Vatican* (Paris, 1904–1947) [3d ser., vol. 1 bis].

Benedict XII (1334–1342): G. Daumet, ed., *Lettres closes, patentes et curiales [du pape Benoît XII] se rapportant à la France: Publiées ou analysées d'après les registres du Vatican* (Rome, 1899–1920) [3d ser., vol. 2]. J. M. Vidal, *Benoît XII (1334–1342): Lettres communes analysées d'après les registres dits d'Avignon et du Vatican* (Paris, 1903–1911) [3d ser., vol. 2 bis]. J. M. Vidal and G. Mollat, *Benoît XII (1334–1342): Lettres closes et patentes intéressant les pays autres que la France* (Paris, 1913–1950) [3d ser., vol. 2 bis].

Clement VI (1342–1352): E. Déprez, *Clément VI (1342–1352): Lettres closes, patentes et curiales se rapportant à la France* (Paris, 1910–1961) [3d ser., vol. 3]. E. Déprez and G. Mollat, *Lettres closes, patentes et curiales intéressant les pays autres que la France [Clément VI]* (Paris, 1960–1961) [3d ser., vol. 3].

Innocent VI (1352–1362): E. Déprez, *Innocent VI: Lettres closes, patentes et curiales se rapportant à la France: publiées ou analysées d'après les registres du Vatican* (Rome, 1909–) [3d ser., vol. 4]. P. Gasnault and M. H. Laurent, *Lettres secrètes et curiales [Innocent VI]: Publiées ou analysées d'après les registres des Archives vaticanes* (Paris, 1959–) [3d ser., vol. 4].

Urban V (1362–1370): P. Lecacheux and G. Mollat, eds., *Lettres secrètes et curiales du pape Urbain V (1362–1370) se rapportant à la France: Publ. ou analysées d'apres les registres du Vatican [puis] d'Avignon et du Vatican* (Paris, 1902–1955) [3d ser., vol. 5]. H. Dubrulle, *Les registres d'Urbain V (1362–1363): Recueil des bulles de ce pape publiées ou analysées d'après les manuscrits originaux du Vatican* (Paris, 1926) [3d ser.]. M. H. Laurent, P. Gasnault, and M. Hayez, *Lettres communes analysées d'après les registres dits d'Avignon et du Vatican [Urbain V]* (Paris, 1954–) [3d ser., vol. 5 bis].

Gregory XI (1370–1378): L. Mirot and H. Jassemin, eds., *Lettres secrètes et curiales du pape Grégoire XI [1370–1378] relatives à la France: Extraites des registres du Vatican* (Paris, 1935–1957) [3d ser., vol. 7]. G. Mollat, *Lettres secrètes et curiales du pape Grégoire XI (1370–1378) intéressant les pays autres que la France: Publiées ou analysées d'apres les registres du Vatican* (Paris, 1962–1965) [3d ser.]. A. M. Hayez, ed., *Gregoire XI, 1370–1378: Lettres communes analysées d'apres les registres dits d'Avignon et du Vatican* (Rome, 1992–) [3d ser., vol. 6 bis].

2. Studies of particular portions of the *Registra Vaticana* include:

RV 1 (John VIII, 872–882): E. L. E. Caspar, ed., "Fragmenta registri Iohannis VIII papae," and "Johannis VIII papae epistolae dubiae," in *Epistolae karolini aevi* (Berlin, 1928), vol. 5, pp. 273–312 and 330–333. E. L. E. Caspar and G. Laehr, "Johannis VIII papae epistolae passim collectae," In *Epistolae karolini aevi* (Berlin, 1928), vol. 5, pp. 313–329. P. Heigl, "Zum Register Johanns VIII," *Mitteilungen des Instituts für österreichische Geschichtsforschung* 32 (1911): 618–622. G. Levi, "Il tomo I dei Regesti Vaticani (lettere di Giovanni VIII)," *Archivio della Società romana di storia patria* 4 (1881): 161–194. D. Lohrmann, *Das Register Papst Johannes VIII. (872–883): Neue Studien zur Abschrift Reg. Vat. 1, zum verlorenen Originalregister und zum Diktat der Briefe* (Tübingen, 1968). H. Steinacker, "Das Register Papst Johanns VIII," in *Homenatge a Antoni Rubió i Lluch: Miscellania d'estudis literaris, històrics i lingüistics* (Barcelona, 1936), vol. 1, pp. 479–505.

RV 2–3 (Gregory VII, 1073–1085): O. Blaul, *Studien zum Register Gregors VII (Teildruck)* (Strasbourg, 1911). F. Bock, "Annotationes zum Register Gregors VII," *Studi Gregoriani per la storia di Gregorio VII e della riforma gregoriana* 1 (1947): 281–306. B. Borino, "Note Gregoriane per la storia di Gregorio VII e della Riforma Gregoriana: Può il Reg. Vat. 2 (Registro di Gregorio VII) essere il registro della cancelleria?" *Studi Gregoriani per la storia di Gregorio VII e della riforma gregoriana* 5 (1956): 391–402; 6 (1959–1961): 363–389. A. Brackmann, *Papsturkunden* (Leipzig, 1914). E. L. E. Caspar, "Studien zum Register Gregors VII," *Neues Archiv der Gesellschaft für ältere deutsche Geschichtskunde* 38 (1913): 145–226. H. Hoffmann, "Zum Register und zu den Briefen Papst Gregors VII," *Deutsches Archiv für Erforschung des Mittelalters* 32 (1976): 86–130. H. W. Klewitz, "Das 'Privilegienregister' Gregors VII," *Archiv für Urkundenforschung* 16 (1939): 413–424. R. Morghen, "Ricerche sulla formazione del registro di Gregorio VII," *Bullettino dell'Istituto storico italiano per il medio evo e Archivio muratoriano* 73 (1961): 1–40. A. Murray, *Pope Gregory VII and his Letters* (New York,

1966). L. Santifaller et al., *Quellen und Forschungen zum Urkunden- und Kanzleiwesen Papst Gregors VII.* (Vatican City, 1957–). R. Schieffer, "Tomus Gregorii papae: Bemerkungen zur Diskussion um das Register Gregors VII," *Archiv für Diplomatik, Schriftengeschichte, Siegel- und Wappenkunde* 17 (1971): 169–184.

RV 4–7a, 8 (Innocent III, 1198–1216): F. Bock, "Studien zu den Originalregistern Innocenz III (Reg. Vat. 4–7A)," *Archivalische Zeitschrift* 50–51 (1955): 329–364. L. E. Boyle, "Review of O. Hageneder and A. Haidacher, eds., Die Register Innocenz' III., I, Band 1, Pontifikatsjahr 1198–1199: Texte, Graz-Cologne, 1964," *Speculum* 42 (1967): 153–162. C. R. Cheney and M. Cheney, *The Letters of Pope Innocent III (1198–1216) Concerning England and Wales: A Calendar with an Appendix of Texts* (Oxford, 1967). C. R. Cheney and W. H. Semple, *Selected Letters of Pope Innocent III Concerning England (1198–1216)* (London, 1953). L. V. Delisle, "Lettres inédites d'Innocent III," *Bibliothèque de l'École des Chartes* 34 (1873): 397–419. L. V. Delisle, "Les registres d'Innocent III," *Bibliothèque de l'École des Chartes* 46 (1885): 84–94. P. J. Dunning, "The Letters of Innocent III as a Source for Irish History," *Proceedings of the Irish Catholic Historical Committee* (1958): 1–10. P. J. Dunning, "The Letters of Innocent III to Ireland," *Traditio* 18 (1962): 229–253. H. Feigl, "Die Registrierung der Privilegien unter Papst Innocenz III," *Mitteilungen des Instituts für österreichische Geschichtsforschung* 68 (1960): 114–127. H. Feigl, "Die Überlieferung der Register Papst Innocenz III," *Mitteilungen des Instituts für österreichische Geschichtsforschung* 65 (1957): 242–295. O. Hageneder, "Die äusseren Merkmale der Originalregister Innocenz III," *Mitteilungen des Instituts für österreichische Geschichtsforschung* 65 (1957): 296–339. O. Hageneder, "Quellenkritisches zu den Originalregistern Innocenz III," *Mitteilungen des Instituts für österreichische Geschichtsforschung* 68 (1960): 128–239. O. Hageneder, "Über 'Expeditionsbündel' in Registrum Vaticanum 4," *Römische historische Mitteilungen* 12 (1970): 111–124. A. Haidacher, "Beiträge zur Kenntnis der verlorenen Registerbände Innocenz' III," *Römische historische Mitteilungen* 4 (1960–61): 36–62. T. T. Halushchynskyi, *Acta Innocentii pp. III (1198–1216) e registris Vaticanis aliisque eruit* (Vatican City, 1944). K. Hampe, "Aus verlorenen Registerbänden der Päpste Innocenz III. und Innocenz IV.," *Mitteilungen des Instituts für österreichische Geschichtsforschung* 23 (1902): 545–567; 24 (1903): 198–237. R. von Heckel, "Untersuchungen zu den Registern Innocenz' III," *Historisches Jahrbuch* 40 (1920): 1–43. R. von Heckel, "Die Verordnung Innocenz' III. über die absolute Ordination und die Forma 'Cum secundum apostolum'," *Historisches Jahrbuch* 55 (1935): 277–304. F. Kempf, *Papsttum und Kaisertum bei Innocenz III: die geistigen und rechtlichen Grundlagen seiner Thronstreitpolitik* (Rome, 1954). F. Kempf, *Die Register Innocenz III: Eine paläographisch-diplomatische Untersuchung* (Rome, 1945) (RV 6). F. Kempf, "Zu den Originalregistern Innocenz III," *Quellen und Forschungen aus italienischen Archiven und Bibliotheken* 36 (1956): 86–137. M. Laufs, *Politik und Recht bei Innonzenz III: Kaiserprivilegien, Thronstreitregister und Egerer Goldbulle in der Reichs- und Rekuperationspolitik Papst Inozenz' III* (Cologne, 1980). V. Pace, "Cultura dell'Europa medievale nella Roma di Innocenzo III: Le illustrazioni marginali del Registro Vaticano 4," *Römisches Jahrbuch für Kunstgeschichte* 22 (1985): 45–61.

E. Pásztor, "Studi e problemi relativi ai registri di Innocenzo III," *Annali della Scuola speciale per Archivisti e Bibliotecari dell'Università di Roma* 2 (1962): 289–304. K. Peball, "Zu den kanonistischen Randziechnen im Register Papst Innozenz III," *Römische historische Mitteilungen* 1 (1956–1957): 77–105. W. M. Peitz, *Regestum dni. Innocentii tertii pp. super negotio Romani Imperii* (Reg. Vat. 6) (Rome, 1927). L. Santifaller, ed., "Studien und Vorarbeiten zur Edition der Register Papst Innozenz III," *Mitteilungen des Instituts für österreichische Geschichtsforschung* 65 (1957): 237–241. G. Tangl, *Das Register Innocenz' III. über die Reichsfrage 1198–1209* (Leipzig, 1923). G. Tangl, *Studien zum Register Innozenz' III.* (Weimar, 1929). G. Tangl. "Ein verschollenes Originalregister Innozenz' III.," *Quellen und Forschungen aus italienischen Archiven und Bibliotheken* 26 (1935–1936): 1–20; 27 (1936–1937): 264–267. H. Tillmann, "Zum Regestum super negotio Romani imperii Innocenz' III.," *Quellen und Forschungen aus italienischen Archiven und Bibliotheken* 23 (1931–1932): 53–79.

RV 9–13 (Honorius III, 1216–1227): F. Bock, "Originale und Registereintrage zur Zeit Honorius III," *Bullettino dell'Archivio paleografico italiano*, n.s., 2–3, pt. 1 (1956–1957): 99–116.

RV 21–23 (Innocent IV, 1243–1254): P. Abate, "Lettere 'secretae' d'Innocenzo IV e altri documenti in una raccolta inedita del secolo XIII (Regesto)," *Miscellanea Franciscana* 55 (1955): 317–324. F. Bock, "Studien zu den Registern Innocenz IV," *Archivalische Zeitschrift* 52 (1956): 11–48. C. Mooney, "Letters of Pope Innocent IV Relating to Ireland," *Collectanea hibernica*, no. 2 (1959): 1–12. P. Sambin, *Lettere inedite di Innocenzo IV* (Padua, 1961).

RV 42 (Martin IV, 1281–1285): E. Pásztor, "Il Registro Vaticano 42," *Annali della Scuola speciale per Archivisti e Bibliotecari dell'Università di Roma* 10 (1970): 25–103.

RV 63–117 (John XXII, 1316–1334): G. Barraclough, "Minutes of Papal Letters (1316–1317)," in *Miscellanea archivistica Angelo Mercati* (Vatican City, 1952), pp. 109–127.

RV 137–218 (Clement VI, 1342–1352): J. Lenzenweger, "Konkordanzen," in *Acta Pataviensia Austriaca*, vol. 1, *Klemens VI (1342–1352)* (Vienna, 1974), pp. 43–176. This article is a concordance between *Registra Vaticana* volumes 147–213E and *Registra Avenionensia* volumes 56–120A. Lenzenweger lists the type of business, and then the RV and RA volume and folio(s), and any other identifying information (e.g., number).

3. The following studies provide information about the *Registra Vaticana*, not limited to particular volumes:

F. Arndt and M. Tangl, *Schrifttafeln zur Erlernung der lateinischen Palaeographie*. 4. erweiterte Aufl. (Berlin, 1904–1929). G. Battelli, "'Membra disiecta' di registri pontifici dei secoli XIII e XIV," in *Mélanges Eugène Tisserant* (Vatican City, 1964), vol. 4, pp. 1–34. H. Denifle, "Die päpstlichen Registerbände des 13. Jahrhunderts und das Inventar derselben vom J. 1339," *Archiv für Literatur- und Kirchengeschichte des Mittelalters* 2 (1886): 1–105. H. Diener, "Die grossen Registerserien im Vatikanischen Archiv (1378–1523): Hinweise und Hilfsmittel zu ihrer Benutzung und Auswertung," *Quellen und Forschungen aus italienischen Archiven und Bibliotheken* 51 (1972): 305–368. F. Gasparolo, ed., "Costituzione dell'Archivio Vaticano e suo primo indice sotto il pontificato di Paolo V: Manoscritto inedito de Michele Lonigo," *Studi e documenti di storia e diritto* 8 (1887): 36–39. M. Giusti, *Inventario dei Registri vaticani* (Vatican City, 1981). M. Giusti, "I registri vaticani e la loro continuazione," *La Bibliofilia (Florence)* 60 (1958): 130–140. M. Giusti, "I registri vaticani e le loro provenienze," in *Miscellanea archivistica Angelo Mercati* (Vatican City, 1952), pp. 383–459. M. Giusti; *Studi sui registri di bolle papali* (Vatican City, 1968), pp. 86–90. E. Göller, "Mitteilungen und Untersuchungen über das päpstliche Register- und Kanzleiwesen im 14. Jahrhundert, besonders unter Johann XXII. und Benedikt XII," *Quellen und Forschungen aus italienischen Archiven und Bibliotheken* 6 (1903): 272–315; 7 (1904): 42–90. G. Gualdo, *Sussidi per la consultazione dell'Archivio Vaticano*, new ed. (Vatican City, 1989). O. Hageneder, "Die päpstlichen Register des 13. und 14. Jahrhunderts," *Annali della Scuola speciale per archivisti e bibliotecari dell'Università di Roma* 12 (1972): 45–76. F. J. Hernáez, *Colección de bulas, breves y otros documentos relativos a la Iglesia de América y Filipinas, dipuesta, anotada e ilustrada* (Brussels, 1879). J. C. Heywood, *Documenta selecta e tabulario secreto vaticano quae romanorum pontificum erga Americae populos curam ac studia . . . testantur phototypia descripta* (Rome, 1893). P. Partner, *The Pope's Men: The Papal Civil Service in the Renaissance* (Oxford, 1990). L. Santifaller, *Beiträge zur Geschichte der Beschreibstoffe im Mittelalter, mit besonderer Berücksichtigung der päpstlichen Kanzlei* (Graz, 1953).

Finding Aids: ASV Indice 2, "Indice di diverse materie, Tom. 2," contains a table of contents to RV 24, beginning on f. 342. The entries include a summary of the business and the folio number.

ASV Indice 71, "Rubricelle di varii Papi da Gregorio X a Giulio II" [olim Arm. 50, vol. 40A], contains a number of summaries for the RV. Note that not all of these are contained in Gualdo's chronological list of indices (pp. 146–155) for the RV. A Renaissance selection of documents concerning the seige of the Holy Land (i.e., Crusades), which may be found in the registers of Gregory X and Innocent III, is located on pages 1r–16v. Another Rennaissance summary, "In isto volumine sunt duo libri duorum annorum Innocentii Pape tercii sui pontificatus videlicet octavi et nonii" (pp. 75r–84v), summarizes RV 7. "Indici di diversi Registri di Bolle che sono stati ricopati e posti ne suoi luoghi" lists contents to Calixtus III (105r–150r), RV 436 and 465, and Pius II (p. 151r–178v), RV 470 and 515. The contents for RV 465 is particularly interesting because it lists professional title and/or diocese. A volume listing of RV 682–768, 772–866, and 886–925 begins on f. 179. "Materie perpetue Innocencii octavi et alia" (pp. 181r–196r) lists notices of various types of graces granted culled from RV of Innocent VIII (now RV 682–768). The volume contains similar listings for Alexander VI (pp. 201r–216r), RV 772–866; Pius III (p. 216), RV 885; and Julius II (pp. 221r–227r), RV 886–925. A list of the contents of RV 1700 begins on f. 231. Two contents lists, "Desiderius Filippi Decanus Ecclesie Tullen." (pp. 231r–246r) and Rubricellae (pp. 247r–256r), cover the papacies of Paul III (RV 1700) and Clement VII (RV 1453) together, as a single volume. Individual indices are in the actual volumes. "Supplementum ad rubricellam Julii II: Rubricella libri XLIII Bullarum D. Julii Papae II. an. 1.2.3.4.5.9." (pp. 265r–304v) corresponds to RV 928.

ASV Indice 114 by Felice Contelori first gives an inventory of selected volumes concerning the pontificate of Innocent VIII, eleven of which have been signalled as RV volumes.

Selected summaries of bulls from various RV volumes, between Innocent VIII and Pius V, appear throughout this index according to undeterminable criteria. The index reads like footnotes without a text. Although offering tantalizing details of papal history, Contelori often leaves the reader without a specific reference to any ASV volume. Students of the period (1484–1572) will find a wealth of untraceable and unverifiable historical information in this index.

ASV Indice 124, "Primo Sbozzo di Inventario di tutti i libri che sono nell'Archivio Segreto Vaticano" [di Giovanni Bissaiga de 1672] (olim Arm. 56, t. 54), contains a listing of some RV volumes on folios 10r–13v, 15r–16v, 174rv, 187r–209v, 234v, 240r, 249v–250v, 252v, and 364r.

ASV Indice 240, "Repertorium Bullarum Joannis 8 et Gregorii VII," by Michael Leonicus (1614), under the direction of Cardinal Scipio Borghese, librarian, contains an index to RV 1 and 2 and is alphabetical by city (diocese).

ASV Indice 242 and 243 index geographic and personal names in RV 4, 5, 7, 7A, and 8. Indice 242, "Index prosographicus et geographicus in Epistolas Innocentii PP. III," is by Garampi. Indice 243 is a more selective later version of the same.

ASV Indici 244–252 is a set of are alphabetical indici primarily to family names, episcopal sees, and religious orders in RV 9–50 (i.e., 1216–1303). The final volume, indice 252, "Indice delle chiese e persone particolari . . . ," is an alphabetical index of the preceding Indici 244–251.

ASV Indice 253 is a select calendar of Innocent II (RV 4, 7), Honorius III (RV 10, 11), and Gregory IX (RV 14, 16, 17, 18, 19, 20).

ASV Indice 254, a compilation from the Camera Apostolica from the thirteenth century, covers extant and lost registers of Innocent III, Honorius III, Gregory IX, Innocent IV, Alexander IV, Urban IV, and Clement IV. This index gives indications of the financial arrangements (largely taxation) between the papacy and monasteries and churches throughout Christendom from the RV.

ASV Indice 255, "Repertorium Bullarum Honorii III," by Michael Leonicus in 1614 (under the auspices of Paul V and Scipio Borghese), provides access to RV 9–13 by diocese and baptismal name. Note that Liber I is RV 9, II is RV 10, III is RV 11, IV is RV 12, and V is RV 13.

ASV Indice 256, "Index Bullarum Gregorii IX," is a partial index, excluding, for example collations to benefices, to the bulls of Gregory IX appearing in RV 14–20.

ASV Indice 257, "Rubricellarum Liber: Urbani IIII (RV 28–29), Clementis IIII (RV 30, 32), Nicolai III (RV 40), Martini IIII (RV 41), Nicolai IIII (RV 45), Bonifatii VIII (47–50), Clementis V (RV 53, 61)," proceeds chronologically, page by page, functioning as a table of contents to selected RV volumes of some popes. Entries are succinct and informative, giving the recipient and business.

ASV Indice 258 and 259, "Repertorium Bullarum Alexandri 4" and "Repertorium Bullarum Gregorii X et Joannis XXI," respectively, were compiled by Michael Leonicus under the patronage of Paul V and Scipio Borghese. Indice 258 indexes RV 24 (in Liber I) and RV 25 (in Liber 2). Indice 259 indexes RV 38 (Gregory X, pp. 4r–46r) and RV 39 (John XXI, pp. 48r–67v). These indici function as Indice 255 above, providing access by diocese and baptismal name.

ASV Indice 260, "Fragmenta Rubricellarum seu Indicum

Bullarum Scriptorum et Beneficiorum collatorum," is a miscellaneous collection of fragmentary contents listings. According to a handwritten preface by A. Mercati, the contemporary listings relate to certain RV volumes of the following popes: Clement VII, Gregory XI, John XXII (RV 77, pp. 47–61; RV 104, pp. 121–135; RV 106, pp. 278–307), Clement VI (RV 156, 153, pp. 65–66), Innocent VI, Benedict XII, Urban V, Urban IV. Some listings of Indice 260 also pertain to the Avignon Registers.

ASV Indice 261, "Rubricellarum liber Joannis XXII" relates to four RV of John XXII: RV 110 (pp. 2r–47v), RV 113 (pp. 48–132), RV 116 (pp. 134–202), and RV 117 (pp. 204–269). Following the order of registration of each letter, this index then lists the recipient and business. Recipients are largely royalty, ruling nobility, and ecclesiastical authorities.

ASV Indice 264, "Rubricellae Bullarum a Clemente VI usque ad Martinum quintum," contains no rubricellae for RV volumes of Urban V or Gregory XI. This indice relates to the following RV: Clement VI (RV 242), Innocent VI (RV 242), Boniface IX (RV 313, 315, 316, 319, 320), Innocent VII (RV 333, 334), Gregory XII (RV 335–338), John XXIII (of Pisa; RV 343, 345, 346), Martin V (RV 352, 356). BAV Ottob. Lat. 3395 is a companion volume to this index. This index provides the recipient's name, a brief description of the business, and the page number.

ASV Indice 265, "Rubricae registri litterarum apostolicarum secretarum tam patentium quam clausarum sanctissimi patris et domini nostri domini Innocentii papae VI quae per eius cameram transiverunt" (p. 2), and "Rubricae regestri litterarum secretarum et commissionum sanctissimi in Christo patris et domini nostri domini Urbani PP. V" (p. 194), indexes six RV volumes of Innocent VI (RV 235–240) and six RV volumes of Urban V (RV 245–250) and provides the name of the recipient, a brief summary of business, and the page number.

ASV Indice 266, "Gregorii . . . Rubricae litterarum secretarum missarum per reverendissimos patres dominos sanctae romanae ecclesiae Cardinales Apostolica sede vacante per obitum felicis recordationis domini Urbani papae quinti," relates to seven RV volumes of Gregory XI (RV 263, 264, 266, 267, and 269–271) and provides the name of the recipient, a summary of the business, the page number, and the registering secretary.

ASV Indice 268, "Index diversarum bullarum et privilegiorum et aliorum iurium pro sancta Romana Ecclesia," contains notes from a number of RV volumes of Innocent III to Pius IV. Indice 268 resembles more jottings (primarily concerning Rome, heads of state, and the Jews) toward a history of the papacy than an index. This is not the most expedient index for gaining access to the records.

ASV Indice 269, "Rubricae tertii libri litterarum apostolicarum de curia domini Martini Papae V" (p. 1), and also for Eugene IV (pp. 29, 69, 89, 113), are rubrics that correspond respectively with RV volumes of Martin V (RV 353) and Eugene IV (RV 365, 374–376), providing the recipient's name, brief business note, and folio number.

ASV Indice 270 [Rubrica] corresponds to Nicholas V (RV 385–402) and provides the diocese, recipient, business, and folio. This is a contemporary index, a copy of which is found in Indice 271 (pp. 198–301). Within Indice 270, the rubrica do not follow the numerical order of the RV.

ASV Indice 271 consists of partial and fragmentary indexes relating to RV volumes of Innocent III (RV 5, 7, 8), Honorius III (RV 9–13), Gregory IX (RV 14–16, 18–20), Innocent IV (RV 21–23), Alexander IV (RV 24–25), Urban IV (28–29), Clement IV (RV 32), Gregory X (37), John XXI (RV 38), Nicolas III (RV 39–40), Martin IV (41), Honorius IV (RV 43), Nicholas IV (RV 44–46), Boniface VIII (RV 47–50), John XXII (RV 109), Benedict XII (RV 130–136), Clement VI (RV 137–141, frag.), and Nicholas V (RV 385–402). Since all the volumes mentioned above have more complete lists of contents, this indice appears to be redundant and difficult to use.

ASV Indice 272, "Rubricelle librorum S.d.n. Pii papae II lit terarum apostolicarum . . . ," relates to thirteen RV volumes from Pius II (RV 498–499, 501–511) and gives diocese or genre of letter, recipient, and folio number.

ASV Indice 273, "Rubricella seu index bullarum Pauli PP. II," corresponds to twenty-one RV volumes of Paul II (RV 524–540, 542–545). This index (pp. 2r–14v) signals the contents of RV 545 and 544, which contain letters to offices and office holders (e.g., treasurers, protonotaries, auditors of the rota, acolytes, secretaries, chaplains, governors, chamberlains, jailers) connected with the political, administrative, and household affairs of the pope. The index to RV 540 is presented by type of business and the indexes to RV 524–539 are presented in the more traditional manner by diocese. All list the recipient, business, and folio number. Note that the indexes to RV volumes are not presented in the numerical order of the RV volumes.

ASV Indice 274–278, "Rubricelle libri," correspond to the following RV volumes and papacies: Indice 274 for Sixtus IV (RV 551–652, 654), Indice 275 for Innocent VIII (RV 698–714, 720–738, 740–768), Indice 276 for Alexander VI (RV 772–866), Indice 277 for Pio III (RV 885) and Julius II (RV 885 folio 2v., 886–888, 890–927, 929, 936, 939–944, 951–983), and Indice 278 for Leo X (RV 991–1192, 1213–1214).

ASV Indice 274–278 are contemporary indexes that list the diocese, recipient, a brief phrase indicating content, and folio number. Index 274 presents particularly consistent details that make it a valuable research instrument and provides more information than Indici 275–278.

ASV Indice 279, "Leonis X. Bullae Secretae," provides an alphabetical listing of dioceses for each of the RV of Leo X (RV 1193–1204). This indice does not contain all the bulls in the registers, but only those identified as "bullae per cameram secretam." The index lists diocese, recipient, summary of business, date, and folio number.

ASV Indice 280 is a selective index of some bulls of Leo X in RV 1193–1204. Indice 279, above, covers the same RV in another manner, although neither is comprehensive.

ASV Indice 281–282 are contemporary indexes to the RV. Indice 281 covers Adrian VI (RV 1215–1236) and Clement VII (RV 1238–1434). Indice 282 covers Paul III (RV 1454–1695). Both indices proceed volume by volume, listing diocese, recipient, a brief summation of the business, and folio number. Indice 1037 is an alphabetical index by diocese to Indice 282. ASV Indice 1037, "Indice alfabetico per diocese dell'indice 282 Paolo III" (1534–1549), RV 1454–1684, is derived from Indice 282, not from the actual RV, and it does not cover all the RV of Paul III. Entries include diocese and names of persons. Indice 1037 also includes page numbers in Indice 282 on which these names appear.

ASV Indice 283 provides a table of contents to Julius III (RV 1724–1782) and to Julius III's bulls in RV 1790, which is largely devoted to Marcellus II. ASV Indice 1038 is an index to dioceses listed in Indice 283 in RV 1724–1782.

ASV Indice 284 is an alphabetical listing of recipients in Paul IV (RV 1805–1849). Each RV is treated individually under each letter of the alphabet. Most of the bulls indexed appear to concern church offices. Entries include name, business, and folio number.

ASV Indice 285 is an alphabetical index to Pius IV (RV 1855–1917) and is organized according to the same principle as Indice 284, above. This index, however, does not list the business and lists solely name and folio number.

ASV Indice 286 to Pius V (RV 1935–2000) is a very selective, alphabetical index to dioceses. Entries include diocese, name, folio numbers, and occasionally business.

ASV Indice 287 provides alphabetical access to various bulls from 1471 to 1572: Sixtus IV (RV 660–667), Innocent VIII (RV 682–690), Alexander VI (RV 879–883), Julius II (RV 985–988), Leo X (RV 1205–1208), Adrian VI (RV 1237), Clement VII (RV 1442–1452, 1453 in index to 1700), Paul III (RV 1700–1720), Julius III (RV 1796–1802), Paul IV (RV 1853–1854), Pius IV (RV 1918–1922), Pius V (RV 2002, 2003). The index proceeds papacy by papacy, creating an alphabetical index for each letter, for each pope. The introduction to the index acts as a concordance between RV citations in this index and current volume numbers. Note that the index to RV 1700 indexes RV 1453 and RV 1700, together as one volume. A note in the index cites ASV Indice 71 as more complete for RV 1453 and 1700, and there are individual indexes at the beginning of both RV 1453 and RV 1700.

ASV Indice 288 provides access to Paul III (RV 1693–1698), Julius III (RV 1791–1795), Paul IV (RV 1850–1852), Pius IV (RV 1923–1934), Pius V (RV 2004–2017). This index also contains indices to Diversa Cameralia volumes in Armaria XXIX, XXX, and XXXIV; and the Fondo Concistoriale, Acta misc. 60. The pontificate of Paul III receives special attention. Indexes to volumes in four different series are included and Michelangelo's presence is noted by volume and page. Entries include diocese, recipient, brief summary of business, and folio number.

Indice 1037 is an alphabetical index by diocese to Indice 282. ASV Indice 1037, "Indice alfabetico per diocese dell'indice 282 Paolo III" (1534–1549), RV 1454–1684, is derived from Indice 282, not from the actual RV, and it does not cover all the RV of Paul III. Entries include diocese and names of persons. Indice 1037 also includes page numbers in Indice 282 on which these names appear.

ASV Indice 1038 is an alphabetical index to dioceses that appear in ASV Indice 283 (q.v.). The indexer did not use the actual RV to compile this volume.

RV 8A contains indexes to Innocent III (RV 5, 6, 7A). A note on the title page informs researchers that these fourteenth-century indexes were originally found in the RV of Innocent VI.

Camera Apostolica series Rubricellae, nos. 1–8 and 32–36, index portions of the RV series as follows: Rub. 1–8 for RV of Clement VI–Julius III (with only a few penciled annotations to extant RV); Rub. 32 for Alexander VI (RV 879–883); Rub. 33 for Julius II (RV 985–987); Rub. 34 for Clement VII (RV 1442–1452); Rub. 35 for Julius III (RV 1796–1802), Paul IV (RV

1853–1854), Pius IV (RV 1918–1922), and Pius V (RV 2002–2003); and Rub. 36 for Paul IV (RV 1853–1854), Pius IV (RV 1918–1922), and Pius V (RV 2002). Current guides present these as indexes to registers of bulls sent "per viam camerae." They briefly note bulls that have been traced to 1,037 registers, primarily of the RV series, but also to four registers of Sec. Cam. and sixty-three of the Registra bullarum. About 900 of the 1,037 registers indexed by the Rubricellae are known to be lost. Therefore, the Rubricellae citations are the only record we have of those RV and the bulls therein contained (cf. Pásztor, 1970, and Giusti below). Although the Rubricellae are often presented as indices to the RV series, their original limited scope ("per viam camerae" bulls) and the losses suffered by the RV series have rendered most of the Rubricellae of little functional use as indexes. Their value today is more historical, supplying brief indications of some existing and many lost bulls. For researchers, indices in the ASV Sala d'Indici generally offer a better starting point. Some Rubricellae are contemporary, others may postdate the RV volumes that they index by several centuries.

Armarium XXXV, vol. 34 (pp. 97–115v), provides indexes to Innocent VIII (RV 691–693), Alexander VI (RV 868), Julius II (RV 984), and Leo X (RV 1193, 1195, 1199–1201, 1203); although not in strict numerical order. While most of these volumes receive adequate treatment by Indice (cf. above) in the Sala d'Indici, the indexes to RV 691–693, RV 868, and RV 984 are unique.

Several Registra Avenionensia (RA) provide partial access to the RV as follows: RA 242 (ff. 513–518v) for Innocent III (RV 7, pp. 30r–134v); RA 268 (pp. 533–544) for Clement IV (RV 32, pp. 1–55); and RA 200 (p. 544) for Gregory XI (RV 287, 289). According to current guides, RA 242 has been identified as pertaining to RV 7 of Innocent III and lists recipient and business but does not provide any specific folio number citations. The index in RA 268, identified by Dr. Javier Serra Estelles, is a fascicle inserted in this RA volume of Clement VII (of Avignon). Despite the poor condition of the fascicle, specific RV page numbers are often legible. RA 200 (ff. 544–565r for RV 289 and ff. 566–577v for RV 287) provides partial lists of bulls of Gregory XI. The citations to bulls are grouped by category, for example, litterae de vacantibus, litterae de canonicatu, litterae de beneficiis, litterae de tabellionatus officiis, and so forth. No folio numbers are cited. More complete indexes do exist in the ASV Sala d'Indice, and researchers should consider requesting the actual RV volumes, rather than the partial indices in the RA.

Camera Apostolica series Collectoriae 350 and 351 cover John XXII (RV 109–117).

Miscellaneous official series Instrumenta miscellanea 6646 (pergamene), "Rubricae litterarum Gregorii PP. XI," is a partial list of bulls that have been traced to the pontificate of Gregory XI (1377–1378) and can be found in RV 287 (pp. 129r–131r, 202–229). The citations are grouped according to category, for example, litterae de provisionibus, litterae de vacantibus, litterae de canonicatu, litterae de beneficiis, litterae de tabellionatus officio, and so forth. This small fascicle is contemporary with the pontificate of Gregory XI. No folio members are cited in this index and researchers should consider simply requesting RV 287.

Datary series Registra supplicationum (Rubricelle no. 1) was formerly considered to be an index to the RV. At this time, however, it has been removed from the Sala d'Indici and replaced with its original series, to serve as a table of contents to the Supplications.

Location: Archivio Segreto Vaticano.

3.2.6.9 Regulae ordinationes et constitutiones cancellariae apostolicae

[DATABASE ID: VATV10069-A]

Inclusive Dates: 1758–1823.

Bulk: .15 linear m. (11 vols.).

Scope: These are essentially handbooks of the Cancellaria that contain descriptions of functions, and the like.

Location: Archivio Segreto Vaticano.

3.2.7 Dataria Apostolica

[DATABASE ID: VATV033-A]

As early as the fourteenth century, the precise date on which the pope granted a particular favor was often a matter of crucial importance. The dating of the supplication, which could be also antedated, signaled the moment from which the grant of the grace had juridical validity. This became important if the same benefice was granted to two persons, because the earliest dated concession generally carried priority. There were other instances where a date might be important, for example, if a cleric was ineligible for particular promotions until a certain age, or if the grant of a benefice might be made before or after the day on which its quarterly incomes were due.

In the fourteenth and the fifteenth centuries, an official of the Chancery was responsible for dating supplications received. Up until 1406, this person was simply called "he who dates, or will date." Under the pontificate of Martin V (1417–1431) the duty of assigning a date to all pontifical letters granting favors was completely separated from the Apostolic Chancery and assigned to an autonomous officer. This is evident from the uninterrupted series of datarii beginning with Giovanni de Feys, called *supplicacionum apostolicarum datarius*, in a document as early as September 1, 1418, in which is recorded for the first time the term *Dataria* for his office.

Although the original function of the datarius and his staff was simply to date approved petitions, especially those requesting nonconsistorial (or minor) benefices, indulgences, and dispensations, the responsibilities and functions of this office grew dramatically in the course of the fifteenth century. The formally established curial department that emerged at the end of the fifteenth century quickly gained major stature, largely owing to the booming practice of selling curial offices. Some would argue that it came to function as a second treasury, supplementing the Apostolic Camera and serving more directly than the older treasury the financial needs of the pope.

The Datary's ability to generate money was the mo-

mentum behind its growth as an office. One observes frequently in the history of the curia how certain offices and officers sought to expand their areas of responsibility, creating new bureaucratic mechanisms (often with a fiscal dimension) and coopting business from other departments. Likewise, the nature and consistency of office records could change in response to talented leadership or expediency. The Datary of the fifteenth through the eighteenth centuries offers a dramatic example of bureaucratic metamorphosis. "At the beginning of the fifteenth century the datarius had been an obscure minor official responsible for dating petitions; at its close he had become one of the main papal officers, and his bureau had assumed key importance in papal finance" (Partner, *The Pope's Men*, pp. 21–22).

From the early fifteenth century Datary officials increasingly handled and received compositions or fees for grants of favor: principally minor or nonconsistorial benefices, certain indulgences, and certain dispensations from canon law, particularly in the area of sacerdotal, monastic, and matrimonial law. Although the Chancery and the Secretaria Apostolica continued to administer grants of favor, in the sixteenth century the Datary became the main office through which the pope exercised his gracious jurisdiction in the external forum, that is, in this case the routine concession of requests regarding benefices, legal intervention, confirmation of rights and privileges, indults, dispensations, and indulgences. In addition, the Datary administered venal or salable offices. With the resources deriving from grants of favor and sale of offices, the Datary functioned increasingly as a private treasury for the popes. From these funds the popes met ordinary and extraordinary expenses, such as pensions, gifts, alms, building projects, patronage interests, and household and military expenses.

So important was the sale of offices to the growth of the Datary that more must be said regarding this form of income. What follows owes a heavy debt to Barbara Hallman's *Italian Cardinals*, pp. 129–163. Hallman notes four developments in the administration of church finances in the late fifteenth and early sixteenth centuries that significantly shaped the functioning of the Datary and hence the production, nature, and contents of its documents. To a lesser degree, the Apostolic Camera, some of whose fiscal power and functions the Datary usurped, underwent parallel transformations. These four developments were: (1) a dramatic rise and routinization of the sale of curial offices (also referred to as venal offices or saleable offices), beginning with the pontificate of Sixtus IV, 1471–1484; (2) the separation of the Dataria from the Camera Apostolica as a distinct treasury under Sixtus IV; (3) the invention, beginning with Leo X, of a new category of venal offices, the Honorary Knighthoods or cavalierati; and (4) the institution by Clement VII in 1526 of the Monte della Fede, which offered the public an opportunity to invest in shares (luoghi) of the church, creating a sort of investment bank.

Venal offices functioned as lucrative sources of income both for the popes and for those who invested in them. Examples of salable offices were camerlengo, abbreviator, writer of briefs, secretary, cameral clerk, consistorial advocate, treasurer, and shield-bearer. The honorary knighthoods included: Cavalieri or Knights of St. Peter (1520), Knights of Loreto (1545), Knights of St. George and Knights of the Lily (1546), and Cavalieri Pii (1560).

Venal offices had to be purchased with gold and those requiring actual labor, such as abbreviator, writer of briefs, or secretary, were much more expensive than the honorary knighthoods. Clerks of the Camera Apostolica paid 10,000 scuti for the office in 1514, with the price rising dramatically every decade. The highest offices of the church were very expensive. For example, Francesco Armellini paid 50,000 ducats to Leo X for the position of camerlengo in 1521. The same office went for 70,000 ducats in 1554.

Investments in venal offices by curial servants created opportunities for other Italians to participate in investment. Office titleholders could share the office with others at a fixed price for a fixed annual return. In this way, vested interest in venal offices spread far beyond the titleholders themselves to clergy, nuns, laymen, bankers, citizens, or anyone with money to invest. The system was versatile and capacious: it was possible to buy an office for a person under age, to hold plural offices, and to obtain dispensations to possess curial offices and sacred offices simultaneously. Relatives often assumed positions vacated when an officeholder became a cardinal. Women also could gain control of vacated offices or positions. For example, in August 1547, the Datary paid 150 gold scuti to Madonna Bernadina Capodisserro for the full value of half of the offices left vacant by the death of her nephew or grandson, Giulio Mignanelli.

Venal offices were not only lucrative, they also could offer a means of advancement in the church hierarchy. By the strategic ascent of their members through the papal bureaucracy, Italian dynasties, like the Borghese family, could rise to prominence and achieve noble status (Wolfgang Reinhard, *Papstfinanz und Nepotismus unter Paul V (1605–1621)* [Stuttgart, 1974]).

The Datary was responsible to the pope alone, and funds from this office were directly at his disposal. The Datary thus had the characteristics of a "secret treasury," or private purse for the pope. Cameral funds were also at the disposition of popes, but those transactions were public in nature, and more complicated in procedure. The head of the Apostolica Camera, the camerarius, or in vernacular Italian, camerlengo, had a certain independence from the pope as well. His appointment did not cease with the death of the reigning pope, as did that of the datarius. "Unlike gifts or grants of money from the Camera Apostolica, few people were involved in administering grants of money from the Datary. The pope simply ordered the Datary to pay moneys directly to the recipient or to his or her agent. Disbursements from the Apostolic Camera were not so simple" (Hallman, *Italian Cardinals*, p. 148). The important difference between the two departments meant that the popes of the sixteenth century gained a new freedom to support their families and friends with funds from their private treasury, the Datary.

As the private treasury of the pope, the Datary functioned in the sixteenth century as a source for monthly pensions for cardinals, and helped support members of curial households and extended family members, especially female, of popes and cardinals. In fact, most papal pensioners in the sixteenth and seventeenth centuries were women. Male pensioners were usually children. Pensions could be ordinary or extraordinary (i.e., issued for particular needs or purposes). Occasionally pensions continued after the death of the benefactor or beneficiary. However, the use of the datarial funds varied from pontificate to pontificate, and from year to year.

Survival of a handful of introitus et exitus (income and expenditure) volumes that have been identified as Datary in origin allows a glimpse into the full range of papal expenditure from Datary funds. Seven volumes, once missing, came to light during the prefecture of Father F. Ehrle and were acquired by him for the Vatican Library manuscript collection, where they now may be found cataloged as Vat. Lat. 10599–10605 (these volumes are listed below as *Libri introitus et exitus Datariae*). These volumes yield information regarding papal patronage, financial arrangements, and creditors and debtors of every sort.

During this period there were specific documents that affirmed changes in the structure and function of the datary. Pius IV (1560–1565) expanded the functions of the office; Sixtus V (brief *Decet Romanum Pontificem*, Apr. 5, 1588, and constitution *Immensa aeterni Dei*, Jan. 22, 1588) clarified the functions of the Datary and gave it broader authority in matters relating to matrimonial dispensation. Throughout this period the office acquired such importance that it was called oculus papae (eye of the pope) or organum mentis et vocis papae (mind and voice of the pope).

From the middle of the seventeenth century, the office was usually entrusted to a cardinal with the title of pro-datarius. Under him there were three major officials: the sub-datarius, the officialis per obitum (for vacancies through death), and the officialis per concessionem (in charge of dispensations or concessions). In addition the pro-datarius had a considerable staff of minor officials.

The importance of the Datary gradually diminished

from the end of the eighteenth century, as a result of the lessening of ecclesiastical benefices reserved to the Holy See and the abolition of venal offices. Benedict XIV was the first to restrict the tasks of the Apostolic Datary. With his constitution *Gravissimum Ecclesiae universae* (Nov. 26, 1745), he removed from the office many duties unnecessary or unrelated to its main purpose.

Leo XIII, by statute of 1897, regulated petitions for dispensations, and on February 6, 1901, approved a new Regolamento drawn up at his request by a special commission of cardinals. This reorganization divided the business of the Datary into three sections, each with its own head or prefect: a section for conferring benefices, a section for matrimonial dispensations, and an administrative section. These modifications aimed at a simplification of procedure and a greater expedition and regularity of business. In accordance with article 2 of the Regolamento there were added to the office a secretary and a theological consultant.

The curial reform of Pius X (constitution *Sapienti consilio*, Jun. 29, 1908) brought about more rigorous restrictions on the Datary. The office lost its autonomy and was reunited to the Apostolic Chancery; its faculty of granting dispensations from matrimonial impediments and irregularities was withdrawn and divided between the newly erected Congregation of the Sacraments and the Congregation of the Holy Office. Likewise, every power of conceding graces and special favors was withdrawn.

The document stated that in the future the special function of the Dataria would be to investigate the fitness of those who aspired to nonconsistorial benefices reserved to the Apostolic See; to draw up and forward the apostolic letters conferring these benefices; to dispense from the requisite conditions for conferring of these benefices; and to look after the pensions and charges that the pope shall have imposed for the conferring of them. The document also stated that henceforth "the office is under the charge of a cardinal of the Holy Roman Church, who would henceforth have the title of datarius," rather than pro-datarius. The cardinal datary was named the first of the palatine cardinals. Pius X also established that, in the case of a legitimate impediment of the cardinal datary, the bulls would be signed by the cardinal secretary of state and countersigned by the first of the officials present in the office.

Paul VI's constitution *Regimini Ecclesiae universae* (Aug. 15, 1967) indicated that "there would be one single office for sending apostolic letters." The Dataria Apostolica ceased to exist on January 1, 1968.

Note: In the list below, several series have no finding aids. Moreover, there is a substantial amount of material that has been grouped together in several listings titled miscellaneous. These are in essence unprocessed records. This all indicates that much work remains to be done to bring the records of the Datary up to the level of organization of other major sections of the ASV.

In addition to the records listed below, series listed with other agencies relate directly to this agency and should be consulted. See Miscellaneous official series *Armarium LIII*, Abbreviatores apostolici de curia series *Abbreviatore apostolica de curia*, Camera Apostolica series *Secretarius camerae: Indulgentiarum*, and Segreteria dei memoriali series, *Segreteria dei memoriali e Dataria apostolica*.

References. Fink, pp. 72–73. M. M. Bullard, *Filippo Strozzi and the Medici: Favor and Finance in Sixteenth-Century Florence and Rome* (Cambridge, 1980). L. Célier, *Les dataires du XVe siècle et les origines de la Daterie apostolique* (Paris, 1910). J. Delumeau, *Vie économique et sociale de Rome dans la seconde moitié du XVIe siècle* (Paris, 1957–1959). P. Fedele, "L'Uffiziolo di Madonna rilegato da Benvenuto Cellini," *Mélanges d'archéologie ed d'histoire* 29 (1909): 329–339. K. Frey, "Studien zu Michelagniolo Buonarroti und zur Kunst seiner Zeit [Part 3]," *Jahrbuch der königlich preuszischen Kunstsammlungen* 30 (1909): Beiheft 103–180, esp. pp. 137–167. B. M. Hallman, *Italian Cardinals, Reform, and the Church as Property* (Berkeley, 1985). H. Gross, *Rome in the Age of Enlightenment: The Post-Tridentine Syndrome and the Ancien Regime* (Cambridge, 1990). W. von Hofmann, *Forschungen zur Geschichte der kurialen Behörden vom Schisma bis zur Reformation* (Rome, 1914). F. Litva, "L'attività finanziaria della Dataria durante il periodo tridentino," *Archivum historiae pontificiae* 5 (1967): 79–174. A. Menzer, "Die Jahresmerkmale in den Datierung der Papsturkunden bis zum Ausgang des 11. Jahrhunderts," *Römische Quartalschrift für christliche Altertumskunde und für Kirchengeschichte* 40 (1932): 27–103. P. Partner, "Papal Financial Policy in the Renaissance and Counter-Reformation." *Past and Present*, no. 88 (1980): 17–62. A. Schulte, *Die Fugger im Rom, 1495–1523* (Leipzig, 1904).

RECORDS. Records of the office consist of the following series.

3.2.7.1 Archivio dello scrittore segreto

[DATABASE ID: VATV189-A]

Inclusive Dates: 1734–1897.

Bulk: 3 linear m. (49 numbered vols.).

Organization: There are five chronological subseries: 1. Bullarum per viam secretam (vols. 1–26) and Canones et provisiones per viam secretam (vol. 27), 1734–1853; —2. Constitutiones et bullarum per viam secretam, 1734–1853, vols. 28–41; —3. Fructatus officii scriptoris, 1781–1878, vols. 42–43; —4. Liber officiorum et decretorum D.D. . . . Minori grazie, 1771–1813, vols. 44–45; —5. [Miscellaneous] Leo XIII, 1878–1897, vol. 46; —Bolle segreto (Gregory XVI-Pius IX), 1843–1849, vol. 47; —Bolle segreto (Pius IX), 1846–1878, vol. 48; —Bolle segreto (Leo XII, Gregory XVI, Pius IX, and Leo XIII), 1823–1897, vol. 49.

References: Boyle, p. 55; Pásztor (1970), pp. 62–63. A. Marquis, "Le collège des correcteurs et scripteurs d'archives: Contribution à l'étude des charges vénales de la Curie Romaine," in *Römische Kurie, kirchliche Finanzen, vatikanisches Archiv: Studien zu Ehren von Hermann Hoberg* (Rome, 1979), pp. 459–471. V. Petra, *Commentaria ad constitutiones apostolicas, seu Bullas singulas summorum pontificum in bullario romano contentas, secundum collectionem Cherubini* (Venice, 1729).

Finding Aids: ASV Indice 1058 provides a calendar of documents with brief annotations for vols. 1–45. Entries for the latter part of this section are less descriptive. Packets 46–49 are described briefly.

Location: Archivio Segreto Vaticano.

3.2.7.2 Benefici/parrocchie
[DATABASE ID: VATV10547-A]
Inclusive Dates: 1929–1967.
Bulk: 4 linear m.
Location: Archivio Segreto Vaticano.

3.2.7.3 Benefici, suppliche, minute, lettere
[DATABASE ID: VATV10072-A]
Inclusive Dates: 1700–1966.
Bulk: 37 linear m.
Organization: Two series. Earlier materials (1700–1897) are alphabetical by diocese within each year; —later records (1898–) are organized by case number, but this is not a strictly numerical organization. Organization is by case number and the chronological date when a certain case was settled.

Nonspedite cases for each year are in a separate bundle at the end of each year.

Scope: These records appear to be petitions.

Finding Aids: Dataria Apostolica series *Rubricella*, 1898–1938, listed among the records of the Datary, provides an index to part of the series. The *Rubricella* is very difficult to use because it provides case summaries by the case number assigned as the case entered the Datary. However, case materials are filed according to their settlement date.

Location: Archivio Segreto Vaticano.

3.2.7.4 [Bersani collection]
[DATABASE ID: VATV10142-A]
Inclusive Dates: ca. 1817–1899 (bulk 1846–1899).
Bulk: 1.5 linear m.
Organization: Five subseries: Collectio minutarum, 1846–1893, 15 vols.; —Minutae: Supplicationum et bullarum a Jacobo Bersani collectae, [18—], 6 vols.; —Repertorium rerum notabilium collectarium a Jacobo Bersani, ca. 1895–1899, 5 vols.; —Motu proprio, Pio VII, 1817, 1 vol.; —Bersani collection: Fogli dell'indice del vecchio notabilia e minute.

The subseries entitled "Repertorium rerum notabilium . . . " is divided as follows: vols. 1–3, alphabetical (A–Z), 1895–1899; vol. 4 (A–Z); vol. 5 index to subseries by type of document, for example, dignitatis.

Subseries 1 has some indexes at the end of individual volumes to type of documents issued and dioceses.

References: K. A. Fink, "Untersuchungen über die päpstlichen Breven des 15. Jahrhunderts," *Römische Quartalschrift für christliche Altertumskunde und für Kirchengeschichte* 43 (1935): 55–86. A. Petrucci, "Note di diplomatica

pontificia: I, Un privilegio solenne di Innocenzo III; II, I capitoli di Innocenzo VIII per Perugia; III, L'origine dei brevi pontifici e gli antichi eruditi," *Archivió della Società romana di storia patria* 89 (1966): 47–85.

Location: Archivio Segreto Vaticano.

3.2.7.5 Brevia Lateranensia
[DATABASE ID: VATV10056-A]
Inclusive Dates: 1490–1809, 1814–1908.
Bulk: 286 linear m.
Organization: Chronological. *Brev. Lat.* 883, "Indulti ed altre grazie del 1807, 1808, 1809," contains brief notes concerning supplications received and a few drafts of supplications. This material is out of chronological order, though, and relates to vols. 282, 292, 327, 333, 345, 356, and 693. Vol. 882, "Minutae Brevium April–Maia–Juini 1807 Pius VII," changes from bound vols. to loose sheafs in paper bundles.

Scope: In the Datary, special registers of briefs (the Lateranensia) began in 1490, while registers containing minutes of Briefs in forma gratiosa came into being about 1523. The early volumes of the *Brevia Lateranensia* are valuable because they include the original supplications as well as the text of the outgoing brief. After 1520, the registers mostly cease to record the content of the supplications and simply note the fact that an original signed petition reached the Datary.

This series is principally composed of registers and of minutes of common briefs that were prepared until 1678 in the Secretaria Apostolica and after that in the Datary. The designation *Lateranensia* derives from the place (i.e., the Lateran Palace) where these registers were kept until 1904, when they were deposited in the ASV. The briefs contain concessions of ordinary graces, most of which are dispensations pertaining to priestly ordination and matrimonial dispensation. However, the project staff found, particularly for the early decades of this series, a much greater variety of graces. In addition to the briefs directed to supplicants (brevia extensa), one finds in this series many commissiones or assignments of tasks, pertaining to judicial matters (like the ones cited by Boyle). In this case the brief consists simply of a few lines in which the business or the object of the petition is entrusted by the pope to someone else who is usually a high-ranking or highly qualified official (e.g., a bishop nuncio). These kinds of delegations of authority carry a special formula, "Mittimus vobis supplicationem presentibus introclusam . . . volumusque et vobis committimus ac mandamus quatenus . . . ad illius executionem procedatis. . . ." The briefs are registered in the volumes according to their date of expedition. The minute or abbreviated versions of brevia extensa contained in the registers, especially for the period 1523 to 1599, are found in another Dataria Apostolica series, *Minutae brevium in forma gratiosa*. Some minutes preceding 1523 are in the Secretaria Apostolica series *Armarium XL*, vol. 1.

There is a close relationship between the two Dataria Apostolica series *Brevia Lateranensia* and *Registra supplicationum*. In the *Brev. Lat.* registers, at the end of each brief, there is a reference to the *Registra supplicationum* in which the relevant supplication has been transcribed. For more on the relationship between the *Reg. suppl.*, the *Brev. Lat.*, and the *Minutae brevium in forma gratiosa*, see Pásztor (1970), pp. 54–56 and Boyle, p. 150.

In the *Brev. lat.* series one finds registration, with varying levels of detail, of papal consent to a wide range of requests for graces of favor. The scope and content of this series is similar to that of the the *Registra Lateranensia*, with the difference being that the Brevia were shorter replies to petitions. Volume 2, from 1493, is suggestive of the subjects and recipients typically addressed in the early volumes of this series. There are many concessions relating to religious life: a priest seeks permission to go without censure to study law at the university of Paris; a hospital director obtains permission on behalf of tertiaries living in a hermitage to formally receive into their community a new member; an Augustinian friar who entered the order as a child and has abandoned it to serve as a chaplain of the archbishop of Florence wants absolution from penalties and censures he may have incurred; impoverished religious women in Pamplona receive permission to have lay patrons and laborers within their monastery precinct; a cleric who has been condemned to exile asks that his sentence be commuted "to fasts or other pious works"; numerous religious men and women seek to change orders or to return to secular life. Members of royal and aristocratic houses petition favors for themselves or others: Frederick and Sigismund, electors of Brandenburg, seek license for their mother and wives, with their entourage, to visit their sister, a nun of St. Clare, in her monastery; a countess receives permission to eat meat and eggs during Lent; a noble couple may have a Dominican friar as part of their household; a family in Genoa may receive medical treatment from a Jewish doctor along with Christian ones. The *Brev. lat.* registers also record various sorts of legal interventions: pardons for homicide and other acts of violence; rulings concerning debtors and thieves. We find grants of protection and priviledge for Jews, as well as relaxations from censures. In response to a petition a cardinal is charged with reforming the canons of Santa Maria Rotonda, in the Pantheon in Rome. Indulgences for fundraising purposes also appear in these pages, for example, an indulgence is granted to those making feast day offerings to the Cathedral of Florence in order to raise money for "the enlarging of the structure" and "extension of the nave." Other groups or individuals receive permission to reuse parts of existing ecclesiatical structures in building or renovation projects.

Material relating to marriages may also be found here. The unnumbered bundle after 883 contains a variety of business "suppressio," "Indulgentiae," "Facultates," and so forth. Vol. 541 is an in-house record of briefs/graces processed, giving name, diocese, and price, for years 1709, 1718, 1719, 1726, 1729–1742. Some volumes have "Commissiones" on spine. The series is chronological and seems to be only matrimonialia beginning with the nineteenth century. For example, already in 1806 (vol. 877) documents seem to be largely dispensations for consanguinity.

Arm. XXXI, vol. 12 is an early volume of the *Brev. Lat.* series from the pontificate of Paul II (1470,1471). There is a relatively high frequency of letters in this volume, as in other early volumes of this series pertaining to the administration of the Papal States, judicial intervention, and lay piety.

References: Boyle, p. 56, 150; Fink, pp. 68–70; Pásztor (1970), pp. 54–56. K. A. Fink, "Zu den Brevia Lateranensia des Vatikanischen Archivs," *Quellen und Forschungen aus italienischen Archiven und Bibliotheken* 32 (1942): 260–266. K. A. Fink. "Untersuchungen über die päpstlichen Breven des 15. Jahrhunderts," *Römische Quartalschrift für christliche Altertumskunde und für Kirchengeschichte* 43 (1935): 55–86.

T. Frenz, "Die 'computi' in der Serie der Brevia Lateranensia im Vatikanischen Archiv," *Quellen und Forschungen aus italienischen Archiven und Bibliotheken* 55–56 (1976): 251–275. A. Petrucci, "Note di diplomatica pontificia: I, Un privilegio solenne di Innocenzo III; II, I capitoli di Innocenzo VIII per Perugia; III, L'origine dei brevi pontifici e gli antichi eruditi," *Archivio della Società romana di storia patria* 89 (1966): 47–85.

Finding Aids: ASV Indice 195A provides an inventory of vols. 1–852 with inclusive dates, and the relevant papacy. It notes which volumes contain brevia per extensum, that is, briefs that contain a summary of the supplication.

ASV Indice 1041 provides a brief introduction to the series, particularly the different methods of locating items (by registratione, speditione, etc.). The index also lists vols. 1–883 with their exact titles, and a brief synopsis of content (brevi communi, commissioni, etc.). The inside cover of Indice 1041 also points to the *Brevia Lateranensia* volumes that can be used as indices to parts of the series, such as vol. 81, and to the occasional "Registri delle Tasse" scattered throughout the series.

Selected *Brevia Lateranensia* volumes entitled "Registri delle Tasse" can also be used as indices to the series. These are: vol. 541 (1709, 1717–1719, 1726, 1729–1742); vol. 647 (1742–1748); vol. 658 (1746–1748); vol. 666 (1749–1751); vol. 675 (1752–1757); vol. 691 (1758–1762); vol. 709 (1763–1764); vol. 717 (1765–1766); vol. 734 (1769–1771); vol. 748 (1772–June 1773); vol. 754 (July–December 1773); vol. 760 (January–September 1774); vol. 766 (March 1775–December 1776); vol. 774 (1777–1779); vol. 785 (1780–1782); vol. 796 (1783–April 1787); vol. 819 (May 1787–1790); vol. 823 (1791–1794); vol. 835A (1795–1796); vol. 848 (April–October 1799); and vol. 852 (April 1800–1803).

Brevia Lateranensia vol. 81 indexes the Brevia and the Commissiones between November 1569 and May 1575.

Location: Archivio Segreto Vaticano.

3.2.7.6 Brogliardo di suppliche
[DATABASE ID: VATV10060-A]
Inclusive Dates: 1695–1810.
Bulk: 1 linear m.
Organization: Chronological.
Scope: These are ledgers recording supplications to the Datary.
Reference: Boyle, p. 56.
Location: Archivio Segreto Vaticano.

3.2.7.7 Broliardus decretorum
[DATABASE ID: VATV10028-A]
Inclusive Dates: 1701–1750.
Bulk: .5 linear m.
Organization: Chronological.
Scope: These are ledgers listing datary decisions after credential review of seekers of benefices. It is not clear whether this series relates to Boyle's "Broliardus supplicationum" (p. 56).
Location: Archivio Segreto Vaticano.

3.2.7.8 [Canonizzazione]
[DATABASE ID: VATV10071-A]
Inclusive Dates: 1814–1838.
Bulk: 2 linear m.
Organization: Subseries are: Relazione informativa, 1832; —Istromenti, cessioni, prouve; —Giustificazioni, 1814–1893;

—Repertorio del protocollo; —Registro di mandati, 1796–1857; —Entrata ed uscita, 1796–1836; —Bilancio, 1796–1811; —Saldaconti, 1808–1821; —Riparto annuale, 1821–1838; —Registro delle esigenze de cinque santi: Francesco Caracciolo, Benedetto da San Fratello, Coletta Boilet, Giacinta Marescotti, Angela Merici, 1832–1857; —Stato dei creditori; —Protocollo, 1801–1845.

Scope: These appear to be mainly financial records concerning canonization processes. The title of the series was assigned by project staff. It may be considered a miscellany by the ASV.

Location: Archivio Segreto Vaticano.

3.2.7.9 Cavalieri: Lista del fruttato dei signori cavalieri . . . per il mese . . .

[DATABASE ID: VATV10078-A]

Inclusive Dates: 1818–1870.

Bulk: 1 linear m.

Organization: Chronological within series. Series are: Cavalieri Laurentani, 1820–1870; —Cavalieri San Paolo, 1822–1870; —Cavalieri Giglio, 1854–1870; —Cavalieri Pio, 1818–1866; —Cavalieri San Pietro, 1822–1866. A variant title use for this series is *Cavalieri: Lista dei signori cavalieri*.

Scope: These are records relating to the honorary knighthoods sold by the papacy.

Location: Archivio Segreto Vaticano.

3.2.7.10 Compositiones

[DATABASE ID: VATV10009-A]

Inclusive Dates: 1815–1891.

Bulk: 1 linear m.

Organization: Chronological.

Scope: These appear to be payments of fees for benefices.

Location: Archivio Segreto Vaticano.

3.2.7.11 Computa officiorum

[DATABASE ID: VATV10039-A]

Inclusive Dates: 1680–1774.

Bulk: 1 linear m.

Organization: Chronological.

Scope: This series is a full listing of the variety of payments that had to be made upon assumption of an office including payments for consensus, charity, componende, registro, master of registri, expeditione, and so forth. The registers also indicate the type of appointment. This series complements other Datary series including *Decretorum, Decretorum cum consensus, Minute di decreti, Nomini,* and *Consensuum* by illustrating the costs of the positions sought after in those records. Taken as a whole, these series form a remarkable and relatively unexplored source for social history.

Location: Archivio Segreto Vaticano.

3.2.7.12 Consensus

[DATABASE ID: VATV10076-A]

Inclusive Dates: 1528–1908.

Bulk: 32 linear m. (270 vols.).

Organization: Two subseries: 1. Consensus; —2. Rubricelle, by diocese (vol. 1, 1548–1566; vol. 2, 1564–1591). Boyle places this series with *Resignationes* in cameral materials. Earlier volumes have "Sec. Cam" written on the outside. Later volumes, ca. 1692, have "Sec." and "Can. Dat. Apost." on the

outside. There appear to have been many secretaries working simultaneously and therefore the series does not proceed in chronological order. Certain periods have frequent marginal annotations. Many volumes have rubricellae in them, and the rubricellae from other volumes seem to have been pulled out to form subseries 2 of this series.

Scope: This series contains documents from various agencies and of varying provenance. They are documents connected with the process of establishing a candidate's right to a desired benefice. The documents also can establish that the benefice is in no way encumbered by possession by another, unconfirmed vacancy, or previous agreements concerning control of the benefice and its income. Pásztor indicates that consensus were a kind of certificate of title required of candidates in the process of assuming a benefice or by benefice-holders in the process of resigning, ceding, or exchanging their benefice.

The series *Consensus* consists in part of registers in which the consensus are recorded, and in part, of original documents that are the original acts drawn up to record the consensus. Sometimes they are corroborated by other legal documents that can also be found with them. The series developed in the Camera until the mid-seventeenth century, and then it was maintained by the Datary.

Entries include: diocese, type of beneficial business (e.g., translatio, permutatio, pensiones, cessio, resignatio, cassatio, concordia, etc.), persons involved, evidence produced to substantiate the request (often a paraphrase of a notarial act), and often a record of supplication(s) made in an effort to gain the request. Entries are signed and dated, for example, "Missa XIX Aprilis C. Dat." The series needs an index by diocese.

This series was transferred from the Archivio di Stato di Roma in 1919 as part of the Fondo dell'Archivio di Stato di Roma. This series was formerly identified in the Archivio di Stato di Roma as "Consensi e Rassegne (collez. B)." Series 1 is identified by Boyle as "Resignationes and Consensus. B." Series 2 is identified by Boyle as "Rubricellae. B. Consensuum."

References: Fink, p. 57; Boyle, pp. 47–48; Pásztor (1970), pp. 50–51.

Finding Aids: Series 2: Rubricellae provides an index to selected portions of subseries 1. This Rubricellae appears to be taken out of selected volumes of the Consensus subseries and is primarily organized by secretary. Most of the indices in this series identify both secretary and chronological span, a few give only the chronological span. It can be difficult to match one of the Rubricellae booklets bound together in this series with a Consensus volume because there were often several secretaries working simultaneously and in order to identify the Consensus volume to which a given Rubricella corresponds a researcher must designate not only the year, but also the secretary. Added confusion occurs because the quinterni (notebooks) of several secretaries can be bound together in a single Consensus volume. Many of the Consensus volumes have names of the secretary(s) on the spine. This is vital in matching Rubricellae with the Consensus volumes they index. It is very difficult to match Consensus volumes to Rubricellae which indicate solely the chronological span covered.

Some volumes from the 1530s in Series 1 have indices at the beginning or end. These indices are organized alphabetically by name or diocese. The indices can be difficult to use because tomes are often bound together and retain their individual pagi nation. Also, indices to tomes now bound together can be hidden in the middle of the books.

Location: Archivio Segreto Vaticano.

3.2.7.13 Consensuum

[DATABASE ID: VATV10031-A]
Inclusive Dates: 1587–1837.
Bulk: 4 linear m.
Organization: Chronological.

Scope: These are notes concerning the filling of (primarily) vacancies in lay offices (military, household officers, etc.). The series outlines how the offices were procured (largely who were the sponsors) and provides biographical information on the applicants, especially in the later volumes. A few volumes have indices. This series is similar in scope and content to other Datary series including *Decretorum*, *Decretorum cum consensus*, *Nomini*, and *Minute di decreti*. A complementary Datary series is *Computa officiorum*, which outlines all of the payments that had to be made upon assuming an office.

Location: Archivio Segreto Vaticano.

3.2.7.14 Cubiculari e scudieri

[DATABASE ID: VATV10139-A]
Inclusive Dates: 1820–1870.
Bulk: .3 linear m.
Organization: Chronological.

Scope: These registers list person, reason for payment, amount, day, and signature.

Location: Archivio Segreto Vaticano.

3.2.7.15 Decretorum

[DATABASE ID: VATV10030-A]
Inclusive Dates: 1650-1805.
Bulk: 3 linear m.
Organization: Chronological.

Scope: This series deals with the filling of vacant positions and promotions (lay soldiers, secretaries, etc.) primarily within the papal palace and household. The series is very descriptive and outlines how the applicants were chosen. This appears to be through the process of patronage, with some indication of who knew whom. The documents provide elaborate genealogies of the applicants. Similar Datary series include *Decretorum cum Consensus*, *Minute di Decreti*, *Consensuum*, and *Nomini*. A complementary Datary series is *Computa officiorum*, which outlines all the payments that an imcumbent had to make upon assuming an office.

Location: Archivio Segreto Vaticano.

3.2.7.16 Decretorum cum Consensus

[DATABASE ID: VATV10029-A]
Inclusive Dates: 1760–1809.
Bulk: 1 linear m.
Organization: Chronological.

Scope: A descriptive listing of vacant positions (lay soldiers, etc.) with details concerning the historical circumstances surrounding the acquisition of the office. Often biographical information on the applicant is included. Applicants appear to be primarily Roman. Dataria Apostolica series with similar scope and content include *Decretorum*, *Minute di decreti*, *Nomini*, and *Consensuum*. A complemcntary Datary series that outlines

the variety of payments that had to be made upon assuming an office is *Computa officiorum*.

Location: Archivio Segreto Vaticano.

3.2.7.17 Dispense matrimoniali

[DATABASE ID: VATV10042-A]
Inclusive Dates: 1829–1878.
Bulk: .05 linear m. (1 vol.).
Organization: Chronological.

Scope: These are documents relating to dispensations (tassari, formulari, suppliche).

Location: Archivio Segreto Vaticano.

3.2.7.18 Elemosinarum

[DATABASE ID: VATV10034-A]
Inclusive Dates: 1801–1821.
Bulk: 1 linear m.
Organization: Chronological.

Scope: This series begins in January 1801, the first year of the pontificate of Pius VII, and records alms either received in the hand of the recipient in person or attested with the recipient's signature. "I received from [person's name] 6 scudi as from the list on this day [name of recipient]." The money passed through the pro-datarius, though his role in distributing alms is not clear. Many women are recipients, either in person or through representatives. Payments may be for goods and services, returns of dowries to monasteries and convents, and so on. Many entries deal with ecclesiastical institutions in Rome. Series breaks during the Napoleonic period (1809–1815).

Reference: Boyle, p. 56.
Location: Archivio Segreto Vaticano.

3.2.7.19 Entrata ed uscita delle mezze annate, pensioni e quindenni

[DATABASE ID: VATV10037-A]
Inclusive Dates: 1800–1845.
Bulk: 2 linear m.
Organization: Chronological by type of transaction.
Location: Archivio Segreto Vaticano.

3.2.7.20 Expeditiones

[DATABASE ID: VATV10041-A]
Inclusive Dates: 1620–1799.
Bulk: 18 linear m. (64 vols.).
Organization: Chronological by year, month, day.

Scope: This is a part of a series that began earlier. It contains summaries of bulls and briefs responding to supplications. The series consists of indexes in which information relative to the concession of graces are briefly registered. Information is organized by kind of business, which appears also to have dictated specific handling procedures within the datary. Boyle notes that part of this series was lost during the relocation of the archives to Paris. See also Dataria Apostolica series *Per obitum* and *Brevia Lateranensia* as well as the Lateran Registers for complementary information. Boyle also notes that there are three additional packets (1878–1896). These were not located in 1990 by the project staff.

References: Boyle, p. 55; Fink, pp. 71–72; Pásztor (1970), p. 56.

Finding Aids: ASV Indice 1113 (formerly Indice 45) provides a brief introduction for select series and two inventories of the volume numbers and the years covered. The second inventory lists the current volume numbers and notes missing volumes. The origin of this index is not clear. It is very difficult to use and appears to bear little resemblance to the current order of Datary material. this indice has, since 1990, been withdrawn.

Location: Archivio Segreto Vaticano.

3.2.7.21 Giannizzeri: Lista del fruttato dei vacabili solicitationi apostolici

[DATABASE ID: VATV10140-A]
Inclusive Dates: 1820–1870.
Bulk: .3 linear m.
Organization: Chronological.
Scope: This register notes name, money to, amount, and signature.
Location: Archivio Segreto Vaticano.

3.2.7.22 [Index to matrimonial dispensations]

[DATABASE ID: VATV10080-A]
Inclusive Dates: 1801, 1806–1808, 1814–1874.
Bulk: 1.5 linear m.
Organization: Chronological by year and month, then organized by name and diocese in order of receipt.
Note: These volumes have no official ASV designation. The title was supplied by the project staff.
Location: Archivio Segreto Vaticano.

3.2.7.23 Lauretanorum

[DATABASE ID: VATV10084-A]
Inclusive Dates: 1832–1897.
Bulk: .5 linear m. (10 vols.).
Organization: Chronological, then according to diocese.
Scope: This series relates to the honorary knighthood of Loreto, established in the sixteenth century.
Location: Archivio Segreto Vaticano.

3.2.7.24 Liber edictorum chirographorum et aliorum notabilium datariae apostolicae

[DATABASE ID: VATV10063-A]
Inclusive Dates: 1655–1964.
Bulk: .5 linear m. (4 vols.).
Organization: Chronological.
Scope: This small series consists of four volumes of miscellaneous information pertaining to administration of datary. Volume 4 is entitled "Votum datariae" and lists appointments to the Datary and outlines the functions of different datarial offices.
Location: Archivio Segreto Vaticano.

3.2.7.25 Liber provisionum

[DATABASE ID: VATV10016-A]
Inclusive Dates: 1771–1808, 1814–1898.
Bulk: 2 linear m.
Organization: Chronological by year and alphabetical by diocese within each year.
Scope: This series deals primarily with the filling of vacancies in parishes and canonries, although there are some entries concerning bishops and prefects. Each entry includes: diocese, dignity, mode of conferral (e.g., per obitum), previous office holder, proposed candidate, a brief description of the candi-

date, any dispensation accompanying the grant of office. Entries become more detailed regarding age and training in later volumes. There is a break during the Napoleonic period (1808–1814).
References: Boyle, p. 56; Pásztor (1970), pp. 53–54.
Location: Archivio Segreto Vaticano.

3.2.7.26 Liber quietantiorum quindenniorum taxatorum

[DATABASE ID: VATV10035-A]
Inclusive Dates: 1701–1853.
Bulk: .5 linear m. (7 vols.).
Organization: Chronological.
Scope: This is an index of payments of taxes known as quindennia (taxes paid every fifteen years on benefices).
Reference: Boyle, pp. 44, 56; Pásztor (1970), p. 42. [Pásztor puts this with the cameral materials.]
Location: Archivio Segreto Vaticano.

3.2.7.27 Libri introitus et exitus Datariae

[DATABASE ID: VATV40072-A]
Inclusive Dates: 1531–1555.
Bulk: 7 vols.
Organization: This series is found in the Vatican Library and is organized under seven Vat. Lat. numbers, 10599–10605. The first six volumes form a continuous chronological series 1531–1550. The seventh volume contains entries for 1554–1555.
Scope: These volumes yield information regarding papal patronage, financial arrangements, and creditors and debtors of every sort. They contain payments to artists, for example, Michelangelo and Cellini.
Finding aids: M. Vattasso and E. Carusi, *Codices vaticani latini: Codices 10301–10700* (Rome, 1920), pp. 317–318, provides a brief description of each volume.
Location: Biblioteca Apostolica Vaticana.

3.2.7.28 Libro delle decreti della congregatione

[DATABASE ID: VATV10070-A]
Inclusive Dates: 1715–1804.
Bulk: .05 linear m. (1 vol.).
Location: Archivio Segreto Vaticano.

3.2.7.29 Mandati di pagamento

[DATABASE ID: VATV191-A]
Inclusive Dates: [15—]–[18—].
Bulk: 48 vols.
References: Fink, p. 74; Boyle, p. 56.
Note: This series was not located by the project staff in 1990.
Location: Archivio Segreto Vaticano.

3.2.7.30 Matrimoniali

[DATABASE ID: VATV10001-A]
Inclusive Dates: 1904–1908.
Bulk: 28 linear m.
Organization: Two subseries: Matrimoniali per breve grazie; —Matrimoniali per bolle. Each subseries is chronological by year and month and alphabetical within each month.
Scope: These are copies (primarily form letters) of bulls and briefs from the Sezione Matrimoniale of the Dataria Apostolica. All are dated by the tassatore.
Location: Archivio Segreto Vaticano.

3.2.7.31 Matrimoniali [buste]

[DATABASE ID: VATV10209-A]

Inclusive Dates: 1885–1908.

Bulk: 250 linear m.

Organization: This series is chronological, each year is alphabetical.

Scope: This series consists of requests for dispensations relative to impediments to marriage. The Matrimoniali [registers] of the Datary (description follows) cannot be used effectively as an index to this series.

Location: Archivio Segreto Vaticano.

3.2.7.32 Matrimoniali [registri]

[DATABASE ID: VATV10208-A]

Inclusive Dates: 1862–1908.

Bulk: 11 linear m.

Organization: The series is chronological, each register is alphabetical by diocese.

Scope: These registers contain brief entries that include diocese, name of petitioners and degree of consanguinity, date of presentation (and acceptance?) and agent, and a presenter. Although the same names can be located in the Dataria Apostolica series *Matrimoniali* [buste], it is very difficult to do so. These registers therefore cannot be easily used as an index to the buste.

Location: Archivio Segreto Vaticano.

3.2.7.33 Matrimonialium

[DATABASE ID: VATV10081-A]

Inclusive Dates: 1808, 1815–1899.

Bulk: 6 linear m.

Organization: Chronological.

Scope: Day by day records of marital dispensations granted for consanguinity. Entries note diocese, names of the couple, degree of consanguinity, and oblation (offering).

Finding Aids: The Dataria Apostolica series [*Rubricella matrimonialium*] is a partial index to this series.

Reference: Boyle, p. 56.

Location: Archivio Segreto Vaticano.

3.2.7.34 Matrimonialium in primo et segundo

[DATABASE ID: VATV10079-A]

Inclusive Dates: 1815–1898.

Bulk: 2 linear m.

Organization: Chronological by year and month.

Scope: These are records of favorable decisions regarding marital dispensations for consanguity, occasionally with payments indicated. Entries are somewhat formulaic: diocese, pro dispensatione matrimoniale in [degree] probatis et honestis familiis [name of husband and wife]. Entries become increasingly brief as the series progresses.

Reference: Boyle, p. 56.

Location: Archivio Segreto Vaticano.

3.2.7.35 Minutae brevium in forma gratiosa

[DATABASE ID: VATV182-A]

Inclusive Dates: 1523–1599.

Bulk: 28 linear m. (465 bundles or 30,059 items).

Organization: Chronological.

Scope: These are dated minutes (460 bundles: 29,770 items) and undated minutes (5 bundles: 289 items). Minutes include

date of the expedition of the brief, also the volume and folio where the brief has been registered. These are useful as summaries of supplications and briefs (*Brevia Lateranensia*), and to provide information where registers have been lost or destroyed. The files include rough drafts of responses to supplications.

References: Fink, p. 70; Boyle, pp. 53–54.

Finding Aids: ASV Indice 1042 provides limited access to the *Minutae brevium*. This indice begins with a brief summary inventory of the series, listing the inclusive numbers and dates of the brevi in each pacco. This inventory then provides an alphabetical list mostly of dioceses but also of a few personal names, institutions, and religious orders (ordinis . . .). Papal States (Patrimonii S. Petri) are also listed. On pages 124v–125 there is a list of brevi inserted. The origin of this list is unclear and its completeness uncertain. In some cases it provides dates, which the compiler of this index may not have been able to treat in the main section of Indice 1042.

Location: Archivio Segreto Vaticano.

3.2.7.36 Minute de brevi e suppliche

[DATABASE ID: VATV10057-A]

Inclusive Dates: 1810–1860.

Bulk: .5 linear m.

Scope: These are rough drafts, done by the abbreviators, of outgoing briefs granting requests primarily to bishops for the transfer of sees. There are a few supplications with the accompanying papal responses.

Location: Archivio Segreto Vaticano.

3.2.7.37 Minute di decreti

[DATABASE ID: VATV10025-A]

Inclusive Dates: 1731–1854.

Bulk: 1 linear m.

Organization: Chronological.

Scope: These are "promotions sent out by the judge and chancellor" that deal with the filling of lay positions. The series provides a thorough description of the position and goes into detail concerning how it was filled. This series is similar in scope and content to other Datary series including *Decretorum*, *Decretorum cum consensus*, *Consensuum*, and *Nomini*. The Datary series *Computa officiorum* complements these series by outlining all the payments that had to be made upon assuming an office.

Location: Archivio Segreto Vaticano.

3.2.7.38 [Miscellanea SF/110]

[DATABASE ID: VATV10043-A]

Inclusive Dates: 1819–1960 (bulk 1819–1920).

Bulk: 8 linear m.

Organization: The miscellany includes the following (numerical designations assigned by project staff): 1. Minute, [18—] (correspondence re: benefices, per obitum, etc); —2. Segretaria, dimande de benefice, [ca. 1890–1910]; —3. Documenti varie per la storia della Dataria, [18—]; —4. Cassa pensioni sui benefici, 1900–1910; —5. Causae; —6. Riforma della Dataria: documenti varii, pratica consegna d'archivio, 1896–1899; —7. Fabbricati moduli matrimoniali; —8. Repertorio pratico di formule, 1819; —9. Inventario degli oggetti esistenti nei vari offici del dicastero pontificio della Dataria apostolica, 1861; —10. Repertorio delle formule e delle clausole, 1897–

1907; —11. Verbale dei congresso, 1897–1907; —12. Protocollo/Moduli, [18—]; —13. Dignitates, [18—]; —14. Quietani Benedettini, 1914–[post-1922]; —15. [1 series/item post-1922]; —16. Carte private vescovi di Spoleto, Assisi, Todi; —17. Riserve di pensioni; —18. Registro di casse, 1908–[post-1922]; —19. Tassario; —20. Rescritta per pensione sui benefici; —21. Stato attivo e passivo dei benefici della diocesi Aretina, 1890; —22. Cataloghi archivio delle carte lasciate dal defunto amministratore Luigi Aloisi; —23. Concorso per gli scrittore; —24. Camera degli spogli.

Scope: These are primarily financial records although some records may be useful for a study of the operations and history of the Datary. These latter items include appointments for working in the Segretaria (e.g., no. 2, cf. above), handbooks and formularies explaining how to execute the various functions of the office (e.g., no. 8 and 12, cf. above), and inventories of documents and objects (e.g., no. 6, 22, 23, cf. above). Item 3 (cf. above) contains the following designation on the spine: "Sancti Deodati seu sinarum beatificazione e canonizzazione." The contents are Datary history materials and do not contain any reference to the canonization process.

Finding Aids: ASV Indice 1113 (formerly Indice 45), section I, represents an attempt to catalog miscellaneous items in the Datary. The title listings may correspond to items in this series. The origins of this index are unclear. The entries seem to bear little resemblence to any current order in the records of the Datary. This indice has, since 1990, been withdrawn.

Note: This is a true miscellany of material essentially unprocessed. The title was supplied by the project staff based on the location of the material in the ASV in 1990.

Location: Archivio Segreto Vaticano.

3.2.7.39 [Miscellanea SF/111]
[DATABASE ID: VATV10050-A]
Inclusive Dates: 1859–1948.
Bulk: 4 linear m.
Organization: The miscellany includes the following (numerical designations assigned by project staff): 1. Officio del cassiere, 1913–[post-1922]; —2. Posizione dei capitolati delli diverse articoli della nuova fabbrica (Palazzo della Dataria), 1859; —3. Administrazione: documenti vari, 1893–1908; —4. Pergamenus; —5. Secretaria: Decreti, documenti varii/Riforma della Dataria, 1897–1899; —6. Libretti delle ricevute postali: Raccomandate; —7. Foglie di udienza, 1859–1897; —8. Lettere dispense matrimoniali, ca. 1908.

Finding Aids: ASV Indice 1113 (formerly Indice 45) section I, may list some of the titles in this record. The origins of this index are unclear. The index appears to bear little resemblance to the current order of Datary material. This indice has, since 1990, been withdrawn.

Note: This series is a true miscellany of material, essentially unprocessed. The title was supplied by the project staff based on the location of the material in the ASV in 1990.

Location: Archivio Segreto Vaticano.

3.2.7.40 [Miscellanea SF/112]
[DATABASE ID: VATV10052-A]
Inclusive Dates: 1700–1874.
Bulk: 3 linear m.
Organization: The miscellany includes the following (numerical designations assigned by project staff): 1. Posizione

riguardante il velporto[?] di Velletri e il archipretura di San Pietro, 1788; —2. Stato di vacabili creati del antico governo pontificio, liquidati in esecuzione del decreto imperiale dei 2 Febbraio 1811; —3. Litterae testimoniales, 1700–1768; —4. Archivio privato, 1851; —5. Eminentissimo vescovo di Osimo, ca. 1840; —6. Protocollo, 1863–1874; —7. Vertenza tra la Dataria e Filipino Schiaro e Angelini e Capocci; —8. Notabilia Gallicarum; —9. Cedule et controcedule, 1733.

Finding Aid: ASV Indice 1113 (formerly ASV Indice 45), section I, may list the titles of some series/items in this record. The origins of this index are unclear. The organization of the index seems to bear little resemblance to the current order of Datary material. This indice has, since 1990, been withdrawn.

Note: This is a true miscellany of material, essentially unprocessed. The title was supplied by the project staff based on the location in the ASV in 1990.

Location: Archivio Segreto Vaticano.

3.2.7.41 [Miscellanea SF/130 and SF/151]
[DATABASE ID: VATV10045-A]
Inclusive Dates: 1736–1907.
Bulk: 10 linear m.
Organization: The miscellany includes the following (numerical designations assigned by project staff): 1. Filza dell'introito delli capitali del compenso, 1842–1897; —2. Conto del fruttato de capitali de compenso, 1824–1878; —3. Giustificazioni delle spese, 1776–1790, e pagamenti, 1768–1897; —4. Gente del compenso e de conti degl'artisti (delle Palazzo Madama), 1790–1818; —5. Rincontro con il cassiere delle componde, 1736–1825; —6. Registro degl'ordini al cassiere della Dataria, 1814–1821; —7. Bollettari dei mandati, 1878–1897; —8. Introiti delle compende e compenso, 1875–1896; —9. Componende filza delle giustificazione, 1886–1897; —10. Componende filza degl'introiti, 1814–1879; —11. Componende e compenso discarichi mensili di cassa, 1870–1897; —12. Resconti di cassa, 1898–1905; —13. Giustificazioni di cassa, 1898–1905; —14. Mandati lettere, 1898–1906; —15. Assegnamenti mensuali, 1814–1822; —16. Conto di cassa, 1825–1878; —17. Stati mensili di cassa, 1839–1897; —18. Rescritti, 1814–1865.

Scope: These are primarily financial records from the Compenso. Numerous series break in 1897 when there was a major reorganization of the Datary.

Finding Aids: ASV Indice 1113 (formerly Indice 45), section I, lists the titles of items that may appear in this record. The origins of this index are unclear. The organization of the index bears little resemblance to the current order of Datary material. This indice has, since 1990, been withdrawn.

Note: This is a true miscellany of material, essentially unprocessed. The title was supplied by the project staff based on the location in the ASV in 1990.

Location: Archivio Segreto Vaticano.

3.2.7.42 [Miscellanea SF/139]
[DATABASE ID: VATV10047-A]
Inclusive Dates: 1701–1895.
Bulk: 2 linear m.
Organization: The miscellany includes the following (numerical designations assigned by project staff): 1. Beneficiorum collat. lista, 1759–1800; —2. Receptorum, 1861–1879, 1895;

—3. Beneficiorum, 1600–1700; —4. Alternativarum, 1701–1724; —5. Pro compo, 1775–1784; —6. Accomodatorum, 1738–1777; —7. Catasto de Terreni, e case mensali, ed enfiteutiche dell'abbadia di Chiaravalle detta in Castagnola. Nullius et formato per ordine, e commandamento dell eminentia reverendisimo signore le il signore le cardinale Alessandro Falconieri, 1731.

Finding Aids: ASV Indice 1113 (formerly Indice 45), section I, may list some titles appearing in this record. The origins of this index are unclear. The order of the information in the index bears little resemblance to the current order of Datary material. This indice has, since 1990, been withdrawn.

Note: This is a true miscellany of material, essentially unprocessed. The title was supplied by the project staff based on location in the ASV in 1990.

Location: Archivio Segreto Vaticano.

3.2.7.43 [Miscellanea SF/140]
[DATABASE ID: VATV10051-A]

Inclusive Dates: 1621–1863.

Bulk: 1 linear m.

Organization: The miscellany includes the following (numerical designations assigned by project staff): 1. Liber mandatorum, 1696–1701; —2. Registrum mandatorum, 1735–1756; —3. Giustificationes per li quindenni, 1705–1789; —4. Liber provisiones, 1740–1810; —5. Copie di lettere di cambio, 1712–1741, 3 vols.; —6. Pensionati diversi sul canone, 1842–1863; —7. Rubricella delle dispense matrimoniale, 1802; —8. [Provisiones]; —9. Status pensionum Hispaniarum, Portugalliae et Sardinia, 1651, (1113/no. 48); —10. Pensioni Portogallo, Sardegna, Spagna, 1777–1789, 2 vols.; —11. Pensiones a reverendissimus cardinalibus indultarius ed episcopis, 1680–1764; —12. Liber pensionum Italiae, 1731–1739, (1113/no. 50); —13. Registrum mandatorum taxae, 1721–1740, 2 vols.; —14. Index beneficio Hispaniarum, Portugallo, et Sardinia, (1113/no. 51); —15. Fruttato in compensa, 1740–1758; —16. Benefici, provisiones, 1621–1800, 6 vols.; —17. Rassegne di Spagne: benefici, 1748–1758, (1113/no. 107).

Finding Aids: ASV Indice 1113 (formerly Indice 45), section I, lists some of the series/items found in this record by title. If a match has been found in the organization section above, an indication has been made following the item in parentheses that gives the index number followed by the number assigned to an item by the index (1113/no.). The origins of this index are unclear. The order of information in the index bears little resemblance to the current order of Datary material. This indice has, since 1990, been withdrawn.

Note: This is a true miscellany of material, essentially unprocessed. The title was supplied by the project staff based on the location in the ASV in 1990.

Location: Archivio Segreto Vaticano.

3.2.7.44 [Miscellanea SF/141]
[DATABASE ID: VATV10046-A]

Inclusive Dates: ca. 1500–1901.

Bulk: 7 linear m.

Organization: The miscellany includes the following (numerical designations assigned by project staff): 1. Fruttado delle dispense matrimoniale, 1500–1800; —2. Liber taxarum, 1690–1782, 3 vols. (1113/nos. 9–11); —3. Taxa coadjutoriarum (canonicatus, decanatus, sacristra, priotus, etc.) Index,

1611–1672, 1816–1901, 2 vols. (vol. 1, 1611–1672; vol. 2 1816–1901); —4. Obligationum: Rubricella to liber 1, 1688–1793, 3 vols. (1113/nos. 19–21); —5. Compenso ex. matrimoniales, 1856–1878; —6. Registro di depositi chiesi fanno al Banco di Santo Spirito e Sagra monte di pietà, 1796–1797; —7. Registro degli ordinatratti dalla Dataria Apostolica sopra depositi al Sagre monte di pietà, 1823–1877; —8. Registro al Banco di Santo Spirito, 1821–1877; —9. Libretti dei depositi pagamenti presso il banco del Sagra monte di pietà, 1823–1870; —10. Repertorio de mandati spediti: Sagra monte della pietà a Roma, 1827–1873; —11. Registro de chirographi, 1675–1814; —12. [Registri taxa matrimoniale, fruttado], 1838–1855; —13. Rescriti, 1809–1810; —14. Regestrum rescriptorum, 1768–1804; —15. Sanctissimus Annuit, 1817–1897; —16. Depositi al Sagra monte di pietà, 1821–1827; —17. [Conto delle somme provenien partitario], 1878–1887; —18. Rescribendarius, 1712–1824; —19. Rollo della famiglia di Signore (figlio) di D. Giacomati; —20. Patenti, 1716–1730; —21. Liber mastro, 1796–1811; —22. Liber dell'entrata e uscita, 1806–1809, 1814–1819; —23. Suppressio, 1770–1790.

Scope: These are primarily financial records for payments received by the Datary for various transactions.

Finding Aids: ASV Indice 1113 (formerly Indice 45), section I, lists the titles of some items/series in this record. If a match has been found in the organization section above, an indication has been made following the listing for the item that gives the index number followed by the reference number for the item assigned in the index (1113/no.). The origins of this index are unclear. The organization of the information in the index bears little resemblance to the current order of Datary material. This indice has, since 1990, been withdrawn.

Note: This is a true miscellany. The title was supplied by the project staff based on the location in the ASV in 1990.

Location: Archivio Segreto Vaticano.

3.2.7.45 [Miscellanea SF/142]
[DATABASE ID: VATV10048-A]

Inclusive Dates: ca. 1400–1879.

Bulk: 2 linear m.

Organization: The miscellany includes the following (numerical designations assigned by project staff): 1. Ragioni di Santa Sede contro Torino, 1732, 4 vols., printed; —2. Mandati, benefici, bullarium, [14—]–[15—]; —3. Miscellania dataria, 1740–1748; —4. Index ecclesiarum et monasterium et eorum taxa, 1750; —5. Formula suppliche; —6. Matrimonialium dispensarum, 1700–1770; —7. Regulae cancelleria, 1773; —8. Congregatione particulari: Sabaudien privilegiorum, 1698, printed; —9. Thesaurus resolutionum: Sacra Congregatione Concilii, 1879; —10. Emphyte licentia a prima erectione adhuc et prius; —11. Pensionis; —12. Absolutiones/dispensationes; —13. Dismissiones: Cessio; —14. Prorogationes, subrogationes; —15. Indultum; —16. Pro electo; —17. Dignitates; —18. Canonicatus; —19. Juxta decretum; —20. Parociae; —21. Simplicia commende titulus cardinale; —22. Resignationes; —23. Gratae speciales; —24. Coadjutorum pensiones; —25. Varia; —26. Matrimoniales; —27. Distincta ed esatta tariffa; —28. Libreria della Dataria, 1790, (1113/no. 114); —29. Liber ecclesiarum et monasterium cum eorum taxa, ca. 1640.

Finding Aids: ASV Indice 1113 (formerly ASV Indice 45), section I, lists some titles in this record. If a match has been

found in the organizartion section above, the index number
and the reference number assigned in the index to the item
follows the listing in this record (1113/no.). The origins of this
index are unclear. The organization of information in the index bears little resemblance to the current order of Datary material. This indice has, since 1990, been withdrawn.

Note: This is a true miscellany of material, essentially unprocessed. The title was supplied by the project staff based on
location in the ASV in 1990.

Location: Archivio Segreto Vaticano.

3.2.7.46 [Miscellanea SF/144]
[DATABASE ID: VATV10049-A]
Inclusive Dates: 1535–1863.
Bulk: 4 linear m.
Organization: Series/items include: 1. Liber admissionum
resignationum, 1535–1700; —2. Offitorum, ca. 1600–1799;
—3. Commissionum de sussidi, clargili dalla Dataria; —4.
Compende, 1830–1863; —5. Distribuzione, 1834–1835; —6.
Conti di pigione, 1892–1896; —7. Divisione minutorum ser-
vitiorum, 1750–1863, 10 vols.
Finding Aids: ASV Indice 1113 (formerly ASV Indice 45),
section 1, may provide a title listing for selected items in this
record. The origins of this index are unclear. The organization
of the index bears little resemblance to the current order of the
Datary material. This indice has, since 1990, been withdrawn.
Note: This series is a true miscellany of material, essentially
unprocessed. The title was supplied by the project staff based
on location of the material in the ASV in 1990.
Location: Archivio Vaticano Segreto.

3.2.7.47 [Miscellanea SF/169]
[DATABASE ID: VATV10077-A]
Inclusive Dates: 1587–1900.
Bulk: 5 linear m.
Organization: The miscellany includes the following (nu-
merical designations assigned by project staff): 1. Vacabili; —2.
Manuali citazionum coram emo. et rev. dno. cardinale pro
dataria, 1816–1834; —3. Stanza diverse agli atti; —4. Spedizione delle materie beneficiale Roma ed estero, 1881; —5.
[Account books], 1690–1740; —6. Formularium ad usum substituti Datarie Apostolice pro efformandis rogatibus, [18—]; —
7. Liber actorum Joannis Finalis (?), cancelliere substituti,
1587; —8. Registro del fruttado dei vacabili, 1846–1887; —9.
Registro dell'ordini e mandati...vacabili, 1751–1770; —10.
Receptarium, 1796–1810; —11. Cavalieri di San Pietro, 1814;
—12. Cavalieri del Giglio, 1814; —13. Cavalieri Laurentani,
1814; —14. Scrittore apostolici; —15. Collegio: Custode de
registri di bolle, [17—]; —16. Liber degli offizi vacabili, 1753;
—17. Vacanze d'offici, 1743; —18. Entrata e uscita, 1801–
1805, 1814–1819; —19. Scriptores; —20. Ricevute de ministri
delle dogana de causallie rollo de Medesimi, [17—]; —21.
Liber taxarum cancellariae: registrum brevium, 1664–1687; —
22. Libro de tasse; —23. Receptorum, 1758, 1767–1768; —24.
Minute schedalurum: Motus propris, 1726–1795; —25. Carte
resguardanii: Scrittori principi de maggiore grazia, 1870–1900.
Finding Aids: ASV Indice 1113 (formerly Indice 45) may list
some of the titles found in this record. The origins of this index
are unclear. The organization of the index bears little resemblance to the current order of the Datary material. This indice
has, since 1990, been withdrawn.

Note: This is a true miscellany of material, essentially unprocessed. The title was supplied by the project staff based on
the location of the material in the ASV in 1990.

Location: Archivio Segreto Vaticano.

3.2.7.48 [Miscellanea SF/171–SF/172]
[DATABASE ID: VATV10044-A]
Inclusive Dates: ca. 1600–1900.
Bulk: 10 linear m.
Organization: The miscellany includes the following (numerical designations assigned by project staff): 1. Relatum,
1825, 1829; —2. Fiat ut petitur, 1746, 1859–1869, 2 vols.; —
3. Lista di fiat, 1776–1869, 2 vols.; —4. Memoriali supplicationi; —5. Supplicationi liste, [17—], 8 vols.; —6. Supplicationi, 1851–1859; —7. Minute di suppliche e bolle pontificio
Pio IX, 1846–1878; —8. [not noted]; —9. Benefici, memoriali,
suppliche, 1700–1899; —10. Red taxae/memoriali supplicationi, 1762–1807, 3 vols.; —11. Benefice domande, 1750–
1808; —12. Benefici fede ed attesti, [17—], 2 vols.; —13. Pensioni liste; —14. Lista di tasse benefici, 1776; —15. Benefici,
provisione, pensioni, 1773–1794; —16. Benefici, memoriali,
supplicationi, 1770–1794; —17. Benefici varia, [17—]; —18.
Benefici, proviste, 1824–1879; —19. Benefici prorogativi,
1767–1783; —20. Benefici, per obitum, attestatione, et speciale, 1713–1792; —21. Benefici concorrenza al canonicato di
Santa Maria in Trastevere, 1891; —22. Resignationi, suppliche, attesti, 1640–1778; —23. Pozitione, [17—]–[18—]; —
24. Canonicatus vacantes in Tivoli, 1838–1867; —25. Petitae
dispensatione in extr. circ.
Scope: These are primarily incoming supplications of all
types.
Finding Aids: ASV Indice 1113 (formerly Indice 45), section I, may list the titles of some items found in this record.
The origins of this index are unclear. The organization of the
index bears little resemblance to the current order of the Datary
material. This indice has, since 1990, been withdrawn.
Note: This is a true miscellany of material, essentially unprocessed. The title was supplied by the project staff based on
location of the material in the ASV in 1990.
Location: Archivio Segreto Vaticano.

3.2.7.49 [Miscellanea SF/173, SF/174, SF/175]
[DATABASE ID: VATV10053-A]
Inclusive Dates: 1520–1900.
Bulk: 7 linear m.
Organization: The miscellany includes the following (numerical designations assigned by project staff): 1. Vacabilia,
1750–1899; —2. Computum expensarum, 1815; —3. Memo-
rali suppliche; —4. Riassunto dello stato prodotto brevi, 1895;
—5. Computista, 1890–1900; —6. Vari scritti, ca. 1600–1699;
—7. Exempla taxarum; —8. Instructivi et responsa; —9. Instructivi brevi, 1800–1850; —10. Formulae, 1901; —11. De-
duzione: abbati di Farfa, 1811–1828; —12. Archivio dell'ad-
ministratore; —13. Miscellanae, 1720–1729; —14. Varia
juria, 1520–1814; —15. Procure, ca. 1800–1899.
Finding Aids: ASV Indice 1113 (formerly ASV Indice 45),
section 1, may provide a title listing of some series/items in this
record. The origins of this index are unclear. The organization
of the index bears little resemblance to the order of the Datary
material. This indice has, since 1990, been withdrawn.
Note: This is a true miscellany of material, essentially un-

processed. The title was supplied by the project staff based on the location of the material in the ASV in 1990.

Location: Archivio Vaticano Segreto.

3.2.7.50 [Miscellanea SF/180]
[DATABASE ID: VATV10054-A]
Inclusive Dates: 1620–1902.
Bulk: 1 linear m.
Organization: The miscellany includes the following (numerical designations assigned by project staff): 1. Pratica della Dataria: Tomus prior, 1700–1710, vol. 1; —2. Pratica della Cancelleria, 1700–1717, vol. 2; —3. Rubricella broliardi, 1640; —4. San Panacrazio: Merce, oglio, carne, legname, e carbone, ca. 1700–1799; —5. Debitori del carbone, 1790; —6. Liber expeditionum: D. Matth. Trincia, secretarius, 1807; —7. Romagna: Tabelle entrata/uscita, 1620–1622; —8. Praxis, 1902; —9. San Giovanni: Pesce e cascio; —10. Contado di molise; —11. Saldaconti della tassa delle strade corriere e provinciali, 1814; —12. [Receipts], ca. 1900.
Finding Aids: ASV Indice 1113 (formerly Indice 45), section I, may list some of the titles found in this record. The origins of this index are unclear. The organization of the index bears little resemblance to the current order of the Datary material. This indice has, since 1990, been withdrawn.
Note: This is a true miscellany of material, essentially unprocessed. The title was supplied by the project staff based on the location of the material in the ASV in 1990.
Location: Archivio Vaticano Segreto.

3.2.7.51 [Miscellanea SF/181]
[DATABASE ID: VATV10137-A]
Inclusive Dates: ca.1850–1899.
Bulk: 1 linear m.
Organization: The miscellany includes the following (numerical designations assigned by project staff): 1. Notaro di Cancelleria (Sostituto del sommista): note de pagamenti alla Dataria et alla Reverenda Cancellaria Apostolica; —2. Apostolici Abbreviatoria (Cavalieri San Pietro, San Paolo), 1899; —3. Procura scrittoria: Cubiculari, scudieri, ripa, annona, Laurentani, brevi, 1899.
Note: This is a true miscellany of material, essentially unprocessed. The title was supplied by the project staff based on the location of the material in the ASV in 1990.
Location: Archivio Segreto Vaticano.

3.2.7.52 [Miscellanea SF/356–SF/357]
[DATABASE ID: VATV10210–A]
Inclusive Dates: 1844–1906.
Bulk: 3 linear m.
Organization: This miscellany includes: Dataria Apostolica, Sezione delle matrimoniali, nota dei pagamenti eseguiti in cassa, 1908, 1 vol.; —Controllo dell'esaziene giornaliera, 1882, 1 vol.; —Nota dei diritti di scrittura delle bolle and Diritti di Cancelleria pagati nella cassa Dataria, 1902–1906, 1 vol.; —Tassario delle dispense matrimoniale: tariffe delle dispense di breve, di bolla di maggior grazia, di bolla di minor grazia, di breve, e di breve e di bolla, [18—]–[19—], 6 vols.; —Registro particolari riservato, no. 2, 1844–1847, 1 vol.; —Matrimoniali transmissis, 1878–1879; —Dispense matrimoniali spedite con tasse nel (mese) and miscellaneous supplications for matrimonial dispensations, 1876–1898, 5 bundles; —

Matrimoniali di udienza rimesse in Dataria sospese o negate, 1880–1906, 7 buste; —Transmissis, 1879–1906, 3 buste;—Facoltà dei particolari, ca. 1888–1889, 2 buste; —Miscellaneous matrimonial supplications, 1.5 linear m.
Note: This is a true miscellany of material, essentially unprocessed. The title was supplied by the project staff based on the location of the material in the ASV in 1990.
Location: Archivio Segreto Vaticano.

3.2.7.53 Missis
[DATABASE ID: VATV10024-A]
Inclusive Dates: 1717–1809.
Bulk: 1 linear m.
Organization: Chronological.
Scope: This is a list (by diocese and name of person) of filled vacancies with the type of vacancy indicated (per obitum, etc.).
Reference: Pásztor (1970), p. 51 (cited as *De Missis*).
Finding Aids: ASV Indice 1113 (formerly Indice 45) provides a title listing for this series (1113/no. 132). This indice has, since 1990, been withdrawn.
Location: Archivio Segreto Vaticano.

3.2.7.54 Nomini
[DATABASE ID: VATV10026-A]
Inclusive Dates: 1844–1888.
Bulk: 2 linear m.
Organization: Chronological.
Scope: These records are resignations "ad favorem" and applications for lay positions. The files include some biographical information on applicants. Datary series with similar scope and content include *Decretorum*, *Decretorum cum consensus*, *Minute di decreti*, and *Consensuum*. The Datary series *Computa officiorum* provides complementary information outlining the variety of payments that had to be made upon assuming an office.
Location: Archivio Segreto Vaticano.

3.2.7.55 Notabilia datariae
[DATABASE ID: VATV10141-A]
Inclusive Dates: [1—]–1773.
Bulk: 1 linear m. (20 vols. and 3 index vols.).
Summary: There are a few indexes at the beginning or end of individual volumes.
Finding Aids: Index volumes I, II, and III provide access to parts of the series by the type of document issued, for example, motu proprio, commende, spolium, and so forth. Volume 2 also indexes the dioceses and regna that the example documents concern.
Location: Archivio Segreto Vaticano.

3.2.7.56 Notabilia datariae apostolicae
[DATABASE ID: VATV10064-A]
Inclusive Dates: ca.1925–1964.
Bulk: .25 linear m. (6 vols.).
Location: Archivio Segreto Vaticano.

3.2.7.57 Officio del cassiere
[DATABASE ID: VATV10542-A]
Inclusive Dates: 1859–1930.
Bulk: 6 linear m.
Organization: Three subseries [2 subseries post-1922]. The

subseries with pre–1922 material is subdivided as follows: 1. Segreteria: Palazzo del Dataria ampliando e restauri/Posizione dei capitolati della diverse artisti della nuova fabbrica, 1859; — 2. Progetto di riforma Via Nazionale e Palazzo di Trevi, 1874; —3. Saldaconti generale, 1859–1892.

Scope: This is a collection of receipts and ledger payments. Among other items, several documents relate to a variety of renovation projects involving the Palazzo della Dataria, the Casa Annessa, and others.

Location: Archivio Segreto Vaticano.

3.2.7.58 Officiorum vacabilium
[DATABASE ID: VATV187-A]
Inclusive Dates: 1522–1809.
Bulk: about 160 vols.
Scope: MacFarlane notes that this series consists of material relating to offices that could be sold. He also cites an inventory, compiled by Guidi (not seen by project staff).
References: Boyle, p. 55; Fink, p. 72; MacFarlane, p. 39.
Note: This series was not located in 1990.
Location: Archivio Segreto Vaticano.

3.2.7.59 Pensioni
[DATABASE ID: VATV10018-A]
Inclusive Dates: 1576–1854.
Bulk: 1 linear m.
Organization: These documents are chronological by year and alphabetical within each year.
Scope: These are records of promotions to offices listing diocese, office, Roman numeral, deceased person, and other categories of information that were not determined by project staff. This shelf also has Datary formularies that are not necessarily considered part of the *Pensioni* series.
Reference: Boyle, p. 56.
Location: Archivio Segreto Vaticano.

3.2.7.60 Pensioni sulle prebende
[DATABASE ID: VATV10032-A]
Inclusive Dates: 1890–1910.
Bulk: .16 linear m. (2 vols.).
Organization: Chronological.
Scope: These are payment records.
Location: Archivio Segreto Vaticano.

3.2.7.61 Per obitum
[DATABASE ID: VATV190-A]
Inclusive Dates: 1587–1899.
Bulk: 20 linear m. (275 numbered vols.).
Organization: Materials are organized in three ways: (1) chronological, (2) chronological and then alphabetical by diocese, and (3) alphabetical by diocese and then chronological within each diocesan listing. Vol. 2 was missing in 1990.
Scope: These are registers of collations to vacant benefices compiled by an official who bore the title *per obitum*. However, the collations concern more than benefices vacant because of the death of the holder. The per obitum position also handled benefices vacant for other reasons, for example, dismissal and vacancy due to incompetency, murder, abandonment, abuse, illness, assumption of another position. The registers of this series present the provisions in alphabetical order by diocese.
Donnelly (cf. below) states that the importance of this series

is that it provides the only record for some of the priests listed, and on occasion, a researcher can trace the succession in benefices through this series when other records fail. This series is continued by the Dataria Apostolica series *Summaria provisionum*, 1900–1916.
References: Fink, p. 74; Boyle, p. 55; Pásztor (1970), p. 51. A. Donnelly, "The Per Obitum Volumes in the Archivio Vaticano," *Archivium hibernicum* 1 (1912): 28–38.
Location: Archivio Segreto Vaticano.

3.2.7.62 Porzionari di ripa e presidenti d'annona
[DATABASE ID: VATV10138-A]
Inclusive Dates: 1822–1870.
Bulk: .3 linear m.
Organization: Chronological.
Summary: These are financial registers. There is another title on the spine, "Ripa ad annona: lista del fruttato dei porzionari di ripa e presidenti di annona."
Location: Archivio Segreto Vaticano.

3.2.7.63 Posizioni, nomine e correspondenza
[DATABASE ID: VATV10020-A]
Inclusive Dates: 1844–1895.
Bulk: 5 linear m.
Organization: Chronological.
Location: Archivio Segreto Vaticano.

3.2.7.64 Processus datariae
[DATABASE ID: VATV183-A]
Inclusive Dates: 1622–1897.
Bulk: 21 linear m. (258 numbered vols.).
Organization: Chronological.
Scope: The title of this series is somewhat misleading since its registers and file bundles contain the material reviewed in the process evaluating the candidacy of persons seeking promotion to consistorial benefices. The Datary began to conserve these "application files" only from 1754, at which date the Datary acquired the curial office of Notaries, which had been established in 1621 for the preparation of processi canonici in Rome. According to Pásztor, Rome was usually the site of processus or investigations into the suitable candidacy of bishops who would serve in the dioceses of the Italian peninsula, Sicily, Sardinia, and adjacent territories. Other candidacies commonly reviewed in Rome included those seeking sees subject to the free disposal of the pope and those that for some reason could not be handled in the country of appointment. Many processus of this series are ones that had to be redone because of some sort of procedural error or omission. As Boyle notes, these represent the originals of informative processes held in the Roman curia in the post-Tridentine period. Notarial copies of the candidates' qualifications without corroborating documentation are in the Congregatio Consistorialis series *Processus consistoriales*. For copies of processus outside the Curia, the originals are in the *Processus consistoriales*. There are usually rough alphabetical indices to dioceses at the beginning of each volume.
References: Fink, pp. 70–71; Boyle, p. 54; Pásztor (1970), pp. 64–65; MacFarlane, p. 39. L. Jadin, "Procès d'information pour la nomination des évêques et abbés des Pays-Bas, de Liège et de Franche-Comté d'après les archives de la Daterie, 1631–1775," *Bulletin de l'Institut historique Belge de Rome* 11

(1931): 347–389. R. Ritzler, "Die archivalischen Quellen der 'Hierarchia catholica,'" in *Miscellanea archivistica Angelo Mercati* (Vatican City, 1952), pp. 51–74. R. Ritzler, "Bischöfliche Informativprozesse im Archiv der Datarie," *Römische Quartalschrift für christliche Altertumskunde und für Kirchengeschichte* 50 (1955): 95–101. R. Ritzler, "Procesos informativos de los obispos de España y sus dominios en el Archivo Vaticano," *Anthologica annua* 4 (1956): 465–498. C. Giblin, "The Processus Datariae and the Appointment of Irish Bishops in the Seventeenth Century," in *Father Luke Wadding Commemorative Volume* (Dublin, 1957), pp. 508–616.

Finding Aids: ASV Indice 1046 provides an alphabetical list of dioceses with the years in which entries appear, volume numbers, and folios of the *Processus.* Dioceses are in Latin and the listing is not always strictly alphabetical.

Location: Archivio Vaticano Segreto.

3.2.7.65 Protocollo

[DATABASE ID: VATV10543-A]
Inclusive Dates: 1939–1962.
Bulk: 1 linear m.
Location: Archivio Segreto Vaticano.

3.2.7.66 Provisiones abbatarum et beneficiorum

[DATABASE ID: VATV10013-A]
Inclusive Dates: 1730–1750.
Bulk: .2 linear m. (5 vols.).
Organization: Alphabetical by diocese and chronological within each diocesan listing.
Location: Archivio Segreto Vaticano.

3.2.7.67 Registra contradictarum

[DATABASE ID: VATV10061-A]
Inclusive Dates: 1575–1790.
Bulk: 6 linear m. (198 numbered volumes).
Organization: Chronological.
Scope: MacFarlane notes that in early days the Registrum Bullarum per officium contradictarum audientiae was the proper concern of the Chancery. Later, the function passed into the Datary and then the Secretariat. In fact, Boyle lists this series as part of the Secretariat of Contradicted Letters (Audientia Litterarum Contradictarum). These 198 volumes of registers contain summaries of certain bulls and are only a fragment of the original collection.
References: Fink, p. 80; Boyle, pp. 67–68. The scope note above was taken directly from MacFarlane, p. 86.
Finding Aids: ASV Indice 1113 (formerly Indice 45) provides a brief introduction to the series and a numerical listing of volumes and years covered (pp. 21–26). This indice has, since 1990, been withdrawn.

Volume 198 in this series (Rubricella) provides an alphabetical index of dioceses in the series.

Location: Archivio Segreto Vaticano.

3.2.7.68 Registra supplicationum (cited as RS)

[DATABASE ID: VATV179-A]
Inclusive Dates: 1342–1899.
Bulk: 512 linear m. (7,363 numbered vols.).
Organization: Chronological.
Scope: This is one of the largest, best known, and most

consulted series in the ASV. Boyle notes that a "supplication, as a diplomatic term, is a petition addressed to a sovereign to obtain a grace." These supplications primarily concern benefices, requests for graces, and matrimonial business. Evidence suggests that registration of supplications began in the pontificate of Benedict XII. Initially, the official registering of supplications did not belong to any particular curial organ but was an official responsibility of the Apostolic Palace serving under the oversight of the camerarius. Under Sixtus V, the registrar of supplications, for a brief time, functioned as part of the Chancery. But under Innocent VIII, he served under the Datary. The vice-chancellor signed the supplication (per consensum), from the pontificate of Innocent VII (though not in the year 1484). After this time, the supplications were signed by the pope, or by a referendarius ("per fiat"—by order of the pope). Grants in answer to supplications were registered in the *Brev. Lat.* series if they were briefs, or in the *Reg. Lat.* series if they were bulls. The supplication registers are very important and concern all aspects of ecclesiastical life and religious practice in various countries. Next to every supplication in the register, there is an initial of the diocese to which the supplicant belonged or where the object of the request was located, and this can help research in this very poorly indexed series. The office of registrar of supplications was suppressed by Leo XIII in 1900.

From the twelfth century, formal petitions were the normal way of seeking concessions from popes for a broad range of graces, favors, and interventions. Acquisition of benefices, dispensations from canon law, indults for special privileges and exemptions, confirmations of rights, and indulgences for the enhancement of cult or the promotion of building projects outline the broad categories into which most petitions fall. Long before the series of *Registra supplicationum* began, petitions to the pope had to be presented in legally proper language and had assumed an official character. Marked with the approval of the pope, the vice-chancellor, or an authorized referendary, the supplication document itself bore legal value. From 1342 there are registers that reproduce the text of successful petitions.

Many successful supplicants were willing to pay additional fees to have papal letters drafted that embodied the text of their petition. Even though the supplication itself had already been registered, these letters communicating the grant of favor were also registered (in the *Registra Avenionensia* for the Avignon period; then in the *Registra Lateranensia*, and from the end of the fifteenth century also in the *Brevia Lateranensia* series). As a historical source, the *Registra supplicationum* are the series of choice for a number of reasons. The registered supplications often contain contextual information that would not have been reproduced in the written replies registered in the *Registra Avenionensia*, *Registra Lateranensia*, or the *Brevia Lateranensia*. Moreover, as W. H. Bliss explains, the rules of the Chancery excluded from bulls "mention of any person not the object of the grace at whose instance the petition was granted, except in the case of kings, queens, cardinals, and, under certain circumstances, bishops and abbots" (*Calendar of Entries in the Papal Registers Relating to Great Britian and Ireland: Petitions to the Pope*, vol. 1, *1342–1419* [London, 1896], p. v). Finally, as noted above, letters communicating the grant were not always requested by supplicants. However, the *Registra supplicationum* have suffered great losses, so the *Registra Avenionensia*, *Registra Lateranensia*, and the *Brevia Lateranensia* can supply information about supplications no longer extant. Moreover, these registers of letters have been better indexed and are served by better finding aids than the *Registra supplicationum*. Unfortunately, Garampi did not use the *Registra supplicationum* in his great indexes. Finally, it should be noted that the RV series contains replies to supplications for which some technical defect or irregularity excluded processing through normal channels. A cooperative project involving several French institutes and the Archives departmentales du Vaucluse in Avignon is presently producing a comprehensive index (in electronic and printed form) of supplications for the pontificate of Urban V (see B. Guillemain, "Une operation en cours: Le traitement informatique des suppliques d'Urbain V," in P. Vian, *L'Archivio Segreto Vaticano e le ricerche storiche: Città del Vaticano, 4–5 giugno 1981* [Rome, 1983], pp. 193–203).

The vast majority of supplications are connected in some way with acquiring, receiving promise of, holding or exchanging ecclesiastical office or benefice, but many aspects of lay and religious life are reflected in this collection. The records here of beneficiae activity have yielded information about the careers not only of high ecclesiastical figures but also of muscians, literary figures, professors of theology and law, scholars, and members of the households of cardinals and popes. After beneficial business, dispensation for illegitimacy is the major theme of clerical supplications (with abbots and abbesses frequently requesting the same.) As with the *Registra Lateranensia* the judical business reflected in this series includes: requests to obtain referral of cases to judges delegate in matters pertaining to ecclesiastical jurisdiction, grants or confirmations of legal privileges, confirmations of the terms of wills or foundation documents (altars, chapels, monasteries), the extension of papal protection, licenses, requests for papal intervention, and pardons and exemptions. Indults, indulgences, and marital dispensations are the object of most lay requests.

Notes: The principal part of the series, the registers from Martin V to Pius VII, became part of the ASV in 1892. These were not used by Garampi in his index. Vols. 43–46, 61–81, and 175 are available on microfilm.

References: Fink, pp. 42–45; Boyle, pp. 51, 149–153; Pásztor (1970), pp. 52–53.

Good starting points for orientation to the Supplication Registers are Boyle, 149–153; L. Boyle's introduction to *Calendar of Entries in the Papal Registers Relating to Great Britain and Ireland*, vol. 15 (1484–1492), edited by M. J. Haren (Dublin, 1978), in which he describes the complex process that yielded sucessful petitions and letters of grace; and the introductions to E. R. Lindsay and A. I. Cameron's *Calendar of Scottish Supplications to Rome*, cited among the references for Scotland below.

G. Barraclough, "Formulare für Suppliken aus der ersten Hälfte des 13. Jahrhunderts," *Archiv für katholisches Kirchenrecht* 115 (1935): 435–463. F. Bartoloni, "Suppliche pontificie dei secoli XIII e XIV," *Bullettino dell'Istituto storico italiano per il medio evo e Archivio muratoriano* 67 (1955): 1–187. A. I. Cameron, ed., *Calendar of Scottish Supplications to Rome, 1423–1428* (Edinburgh, 1956). H. Dubrulle, *Suppliques du pontificat de Martin V. (1417–1431)* (Dunkirk, 1922). G. Erler, "Ein Band des Supplikenregisters Bonifactius' IX, in dem königlichen Bibliothek zu Eichstatt," *Historisches Jahrbuch* 8 (1887): 487–495. A. Fierens, ed., "Suppliques

d'Urbain V (1362–1370): Textes et analyses," vol. 7 of *Analecta vaticano-belgica: Documents relatifs aux anciens diocèses de Cambrai, Liège, Thérouanne et Tournai* (Rome, 1914). T. Frenz, "Randbemerkungen zu den Supplikenregistern Calixts III," *Quellen und Forschungen aus italienischen Archiven und Bibliotheken* 55–56 (1976): 410–420. P. Gasnault, "Une supplique originale de l'Abbaye de Cluny approuvée par Martin V," *Revue Mabillon* 51 (1961): 325–328. P. Gasnault, "Trois lettres secrètes sur papier de Clément VII (Robert de Genève) et une supplique originale signée par ce pape," in *Palaeographica, diplomatica et archivistica: Studi in onore di Guilio Battelli* (Rome, 1979), vol. 2, pp. 337–351. T. Gasparrini Leporace, "Una supplica originale per 'fiat' del papa Giovanni XXII," *Bullettino dell'Istituto storico italiano per il medio evo e Archivio muratoriano* 75 (1963): 247–257. A.-M. Hayez et al., "De la supplique à la lettre: Le parcours des grâces en Cour de Rome sous Urbain V (1362–1366)" in *Le fonctionnement administratif de la papauté d'Avignon: Aux origines de l'état moderne* (Rome, 1990), pp. 171–205. W. von Hofmann, *Forschungen zur Geschichte der kurialen Behörden vom Schisma bis zur Reformation* (Rome, 1914). H. Kallfelz, "Fragmente eines Suppliken-Rotulus aus der 2. Hälfte des 14. Jahrhunderts im Archiv der Marktgemeinde Burgstadt am Main," *Wurzburger Dio zesangeschichtsblätter* 42 (1980): 159–174. B. Katterbach, *Inventario dei registri delle suppliche* (Vatican City, 1932). B. Katterbach, "Päpstliche Suppliken mit der Klausel der sola Signatura," *Römische Quartalschrift für christliche Altertumskunde und für Kirchengeschichte* 31 (1923): 185–196. B. Katterbach, *Referendarii utriusque signaturae a Martino V ad Clementem IX et praelati Signaturae supplicationum a Martino V ad Leonem XIII* (Rome, 1931). P. F. Kehr, "Bemerkungen zu den päpstlichen Supplikenregistern des 14. Jahrhunderts," *Mitteilungen des Instituts für Österreichische Geschichtsforschung* 8 (1887): 84–102. L. Kern, "Une supplique adressée au pape Paul III (1534–1549) par un groupe de Valaisans," in *Études d'histoire ecclésiastique et de diplomatique* (Lausanne, 1973), pp. 171 ff. G. Lang, "Stephanus de Fonte und Symon de Vares: Zwei Supplikenregistratoren unter Innozenz VI," *Quellen und Forschungen aus italienischen Archiven und Bibliotheken* 33 (1944): 259–268. G. P. Marchal, "Supplikenregister als codicologisches Problem: Die Supplikenregister des Basler Konzils," *Basler Zeitschrift für Geschichte und Altertumskunde* 74 (1974): 201–235. E. van Móe, "Suppliques originales adressées a Jean XII, Clément VI et Innocent VI," *Bibliothèque de l'École des Chartes* 92 (1931): 253–276. G. Muzzioli, *Rotulo originale di suppliche per "fiat" di Benedetto XIII antipapa* (Rome, 1947) [this title was noted but not verified by project staff]. E. Pitz, *Supplikensignatur und Briefexpedition an der römischen Kurie im Pontifikat Papst Callixts III*. (Tübingen, 1972). E. Planchart, "The Early Career of Guillaume Du Fay," *Journal of the American Musicological Society* 46 (1993): 341–368.

There are several published series that calendar documents in the RS. Each takes a geographic focus. Supplications mentioning multiple geographic areas are often duplicated in the different series. These series are listed below:

Belgium. *Analecta vaticano-belgica: Recueil des documents concernants les anciens diocèses de Cambrai, Liège, Thérouanne et Tournai.* Rome: Institut Historique Belge de Rome, first series. (Brussels and Rome, 1906–):

John XXII (1316–1334): A. Fayen, ed., "Lettres de Jean XXII (1316–1334): Textes et analyses, Part 1 (1316–1324)" (Rome, 1908), vol. 2; and "Lettres de Jean XXII (1316–1334): Textes et analyses, Part 2, (1325–1334)" (Rome, 1909 and 1912), vol. 3.

Benedict XII (1334–1342): A. Fierens, ed., "Lettres de Benoît XII (1334–1342): Textes et analyses" (Rome, 1910), vol. 4.

Clement VI (1342–1352): U. Berlière, ed., "Suppliques de Clément VI (1342–1352): Textes et analyses" (Rome, 1906), vol. 1. P. Van Isacker and U. Berlière, eds., "Lettres de Clement VI (1342–1352)" (Rome, 1924), vol. 6.

Innocent VI (1352–1362): U. Berlière, ed., "Suppliques d'Innocent VI (1352–1362): Textes et analyses" (Rome, 1911), vol. 5. G. Despy, ed., "Lettres d'Innocent VI (1352–1362): Textes e analyses" (Brussels, 1953), vol. 17.

Urban V (1362–1370): A. Fierens, ed., "Suppliques d'Urbain V (1362–1370): Textes et analyses" (Rome, 1914), vol. 7. A. Fierens and C. Tihon, "Lettres d'Urbain V (1362–1370): Textes et Analyses, Part 1 (1362–1366)" (Brussels, 1928), vol. 9. C. Tihon, "Lettres d'Urbain V: Textes et Analyses, Part 2 (1366–1370)" (Brussels, 1932), vol. 15.

Gregory XI (1370–1378): C. Tihon, ed., "Lettres de Grégoire XI (1371–1378), Part 1" (Brussels, 1958), vol. 11; "Lettres de Grégoire XI (1371–1378), Part 2" (Brussels, 1961), vol. 20; "Lettres de Grégoire XI (1371–1378), Part 3" (Brussels, 1964), vol. 25; and "Lettres de Grégoire XI (1371–1378), Part 4" (Brussels, 1975), vol. 28.

Urban VI (1378–1389): M. Gastout, "Suppliques et lettres d'Urbain VI (1378–1389) et de Boniface IX (cinq premières années, 1389–1394)," vol. 7 of Documents relatifs au Grand Schisme, which is vol. 29 of Analecta vaticano-belgica . . . (Brussels, 1976).

Clement VII (of Avignon, 1378–1394): K. Hanquet, ed., "Suppliques de Clément VII (1378–1379)," vol. 1 of Documents relatifs au Grand Schisme, which is vol. 8 of Analecta vaticano-elgica . . . (Rome, 1924). K. Hanquet and U. Berlière, eds. "Lettres de Clément VII (1378–1379)." vol. 2 of Documents relatifs au Grand Schisme, which is vol. 12 of Analecta vaticano-belgica . . . (Rome, 1930). H. Nélis, "Suppliques et lettres de Clement VII (1379–1394)" vol. 3 of Documents relatifs au Grand Schisme, which is vol. 13 of Analecta vaticano-belgica . . . (Brussels, 1934).

Benedict XIII (of Avignon, 1394–1423): P. Briegleb and A. Laret-Kayser, "Suppliques de Benoît XIII (1394–1422)," vol. 6 of Documents relatifs au Grand Schisme, which is vols. 26–27 of Analecta vaticano-belgica . . . (Brussels, 1973). J. Paye-Bourgeois, ed., "Lettres de Benoît XIII (1394–1422), Part 1 (1394–1395)," vol. 4 of Documents relatifs au Grand Schisme, which is vol. 31 of Analecta vaticano-belgica . . . (Brussels, 1983). M. Tits-Dieuaide, ed., "Lettres de Benoît XIII (1394–1422), Part 2 (1395–1422)," vol. 5 of Documents relatifs au Grand Schisme, which is vol. 19 of Analecta vaticano-belgica . . . (Brussels, 1960).

Innocent VII (1404–1406): M. Maillard-Luypaert, "Lettres d'Innocent VII (1404–1406)," vol. 8 of Documents relatifs au Grand Schisme, which is vol. 32 of Analecta vaticano-belgica . . . (Brussels, 1987).

Gregory XII (1406–1415): M. Soenen, "Lettres de Gregoire XII, 1406–1415," vol. 9 of Documents relatifs au Grand

Schisme, which is vol. 30 of Analecta vaticano-belgica . . . (Brussels, 1976). U. Berlière, ed., "Les collectories pontificales dans les anciens diocèses de Cambrai, Thérouanne et Tournai au XIVe siècle" (Rome, 1929), vol. 10.

Germany. J. Haller et al., eds., Repertorium Germanicum: Regesten aus den päpstlichen Archiven zur Geschichte des deutschen Reichs und seiner Territorien im XIV. und XV. Jahrhundert: Pontifikat Eugens IV. (1431–1447) (Berlin, 1897), and its continuation, Repertorium Germanicum: Verzeichnis der in den päpstlichen Registern und Kameralakten vorkommenden Personen, Kirchen und Orte des deutschen Reiches, seiner Diözesen und Territorien, vom Beginn des Schismas bis zur Reformation (Berlin, 1916–).

Great Britain. W. H. Bliss, ed., Calendar of Entries in the Papal Registers Relating to Great Britain and Ireland: Calendar of Petitions to the Pope, A.D. 1342–1419 (London, 1896).

Hungary. B. Arpád, Regesta supplicationum: Avignoni korszak [1342–1394] (Budapest, 1916–1918) [this title was noted but not verified by project staff].

Italy. T. Gasparrini Leporace, Le suppliche di Clemente VI (Rome, 1948–).

Netherlands. R. R. Post, Supplieken gericht aan de pausen Clemens VI, Innocentius VI en Urbanus V, 1342–1366 (Utrecht, 1936–1937).

Pomerania. A. Motzki, Urkunden zur Caminer Bistumsgeschichte, auf Grund der Avignonesischen Supplikenregister (Stettin, 1913).

Scotland. E. R. Lindsay and A. I. Cameron, eds., Calendar of Scottish Supplications to Rome, 1418–1422 (Edinburgh, 1934). A. Cameron (Dunlop), ed., Calendar of Scottish Supplications to Rome, 1423–1428 (Edinburgh, 1956).

Finding Aids: See Bruno Katterbach, Inventario dei registri delle suppliche (Vatican City, 1932). Katterbach provides an introduction and volume-by-volume listing of the entire series with old and new numbers, pagination, inclusive dates, and a brief note on the volume, that is, title variations or additions such as de fiat, de vac, manca gia sotto . . . , pagination changes, conservation notes, and so forth.

ASV Indice 195, "Inventarium Supplicationum Datariae Apostolicae a Clemente PP. VI ad Pium Papam VII," prepared in 1900, conforms initially to old diplomatic principles, identifying RS vols. 1–407 by the mode in which the supplications contained therein were approved (e.g., fiat, concessum, etc.); date; and place. Beginning with Nicholas V (vol. 408) this indice gives only the former and current volume numbers. This has been superseded by Katterbach, noted above.

The Dataria Apostolica series Registrorum supplicationum rubricelle was assembled by Bruno Katterbach in the early nineteenth century to serve as indexes, of a sort, to the Registra supplicationum (RS). Vols. 3–35 of that series contain rubricelle extracted from the actual RS of popes Pius VII to Leo XIII, and thus the series proceeds with consistency only for the period 1800–1899. These later rubricelle (vols. 3–35) are primarily concerned with matrimonial supplications. The earlier volumes do not function easily as indices to the supplications. Vol. 1 is a late fourteenth-century table of contents of the Registra supplicationum of Clement VII (of Avignon, 1378–1390) proceeding year by year, volume by volume. Vol. 1A (not listed in Katterbach), like vol. 1, is also a contemporary index for Clement VII. Vol. 1A bears the title "Rotulus Beneficiatorum sub Clem. VII 1378" and was formerly included in the Camera Apostolica series *Collectoriae*, vol. 293. The volume contains lists of benefice holders. How this functions as an index is not clear. Vol. 2 is a 1633 inventory by Felice Contelori. It presents the number of then existing RS volumes within each pontifical year from Martin V to Urban VIII but provides no descriptions or volume numbers that will aid researchers in using the collection today. For a clear overview of this series, see Katterbach (pp. 335–339), above.

ASV Indice 431, "Rubricelle del libro primo del pontificato di Nostro Signore PP. Pio Settimo dell'anno VIII," is an alphabetical index to RS vol. 6968. Entries are organized by diocese and list the first name(s) of the supplicant(s) and folio number.

ASV Indice 432, "Rubricelle [beneficiorum] annorum 1806, 1807, 1808 scilicet annorum septimi et octavi Pii Pape Septimi," is an index to the benefices in RS vols. 6965–6969. Entries are organized by diocese. They list the name of the supplicant for the benefice and the type of benefice (e.g., obit., prov., resig., etc.) and folio number.

ASV Indice 433, "Rubricelle secretorum . . . Pii PP. VII lib. sexto," indexes RS vol. 7010. Entries are organized by diocese and list the first name(s) of the supplicant(s) and folio number.

ASV Indice 434, "Rubricelle [beneficiorum] anni 1803 anni quarti Pii PP. VII" indexes benefices in RS vols. 6956–6958. Entries are organized by diocese. They list the name of the supplicant for the benefice and the type of benefice (e.g., obit., resig., etc.) and folio number.

ASV Indice 435, "Liber secundus anni XV Ssmi. Dni. Nri. Pii PP. VII," and [Liber terzo] index RS vols. 6945–6948. Entries are organized by diocese and list the first name(s) of the supplicant(s) and folio number.

ASV Indice 436, "Rubricelle [beneficiorum] 1806 anni primi Dni. Nri. Pii PP. VII," indexes benefices in RS vols. 6945–6948. Entries are organized by diocese. They list the name of the supplicant for the benefice and the type of benefice (e.g., obit., resig., etc.) and folio number.

Also useful is *Relève alphabetique des noms de personnes et de lieux: Contenus dans les registres de suppliques d'Urbain V* (Rome, 1991–) [this title was noted but not verified by project staff]. There are eight volumes covering RS 36–46 (1362–1366) as of June 1994. This book is part of an ongoing project to provide better access to the supplications. This series begins with RS 36 (November/December 1362). Each Relève tends to treat one or two RS volumes. The personal and place names appear in one alphabetical list. A typical entry reads, "Nic Jacobide canonic. et preb. eccl. Roskilden. (assecut.) 1362/12/19 SO36O1729 fol. 172v." (e.g., name or place, type of supplication or a note on the status of the person, date (year/month/day), a control number that includes the RS volume number, and folio number. The "Regles d'Utilisation" are sporadic, first appearing in volume 3.
Location: Archivio Segreto Vaticano.

3.2.7.69 [Registri di benefici]
[DATABASE ID: VATV10014-A]
Inclusive Dates: ca. 1828–1902.
Bulk: .5 linear m. (10 vols.).
Organization: Eight unnumbered volumes A–Z, and two unnumbered appendix volumes A–Z. The volumes are alphabetical by diocese and then each diocese is divided into three categories: canonicatus, parochiales, and simplicia.

Scope: These are very brief notices concerning benefices noting officeholders and sometimes the income (fructus) from the benefice.
Note: This series does not have an official ASV designation. The title was supplied by the project staff.
Location: Archivio Segreto Vaticano.

3.2.7.70 Registro degl'ordini
[DATABASE ID: VATV10040-A]
Inclusive Dates: 1689–1796.
Bulk: 1 linear m.
Organization: Chronological.
Scope: These are provisori concerning the Banco di Santo Spirito and Sacro Monte di Pietà. In the records the bank in question states that it will pay money liberated through vacancies and resignations to someone, primarily on the occasion of vacating the office.
Location: Archivio Segreto Vaticano.

3.2.7.71 Registro dell'esecuzioni e possessi
[DATABASE ID: VATV10019-A]
Inclusive Dates: 1725–1806.
Bulk: .15 linear m. (3 vols.).
Organization: Chronological.
Scope: These documents may relate to vacancies.
Location: Archivio Segreto Vaticano.

3.2.7.72 Registro delle dispense di maggiore e minore grazia spedite per bolla e stampa
[DATABASE ID: VATV10207-A]
Inclusive Dates: 1901–1908.
Bulk: 1.5 linear m. (16 vols.).
Organization: The series is chronological; each volume is alphabetical by supplicant.
Scope: Register entries include number, diocese, type of grace, name of supplicants, date of presentation, date of response, date of bolla o stampa, expediter, cost, and observations (usually blank).
Location: Archivio Segreto Vaticano.

3.2.7.73 Registro delle spedizione
[DATABASE ID: VATV10544-A]
Inclusive Dates: 1939–1966.
Bulk: 1 linear m.
Location: Archivio Segreto Vaticano.

3.2.7.74 Registro di supplichi: Lista de maestri, chierici, rubricelle, registratori, porzioni di registro di suppliche
[DATABASE ID: VATV10135-A]
Inclusive Dates: 1818–1861.
Bulk: .3 linear m.
Organization: Chronological.
Scope: These registers record supplicant, reason for supplication, cost, date, and note of payment. There are monthly fiscal summaries at the end of each month.
Location: Archivio Segreto Vaticano.

3.2.7.75 Registrorum supplicationum rubricelle
[DATABASE ID: VATV10075-A]
Inclusive Dates: 1378–1899 (bulk 1800–1899).
Bulk: 5 linear m. (35 numbered vols.).
Organization: Chronological.

Scope: This series of rubricelle was assembled by Bruno Katterbach in the early nineteenth century to serve as indexes, of a sort, to the *Registra supplicationum* (RS). Vols. 3–35 contain rubricelle extracted from the actual *RS* of Popes Pius VII to Leo XIII and thus, the series proceeds with consistency only for the period 1800–1899. These later rubricelle (3–35) are primarily concerned with matrimonial supplications. The earlier volumes do not function easily as indices to the supplications. Vol. 1 is a late fourteenth-entury table of contents of the *Registra supplicationum* of Clement VII (of Avignon, 1378–1390) proceeding year by year, volume by volume. Vol. 1A (not listed in Katterbach), like vol. 1, is also a contemporary index for Clement VII. Vol. 1A bears the title "Rotulus Beneficiatorum sub Clem. VII 1378" and was formerly included in the Camera Apostolica series *Collectoriae*, vol. 293. The volume contains lists of benefice holders. How this fuctions as an index is not clear. Vol. 2 is a 1633 inventory by Felice Contelori. It presents the number of then existing *RS* volumes within each pontifical year from Martin V to Urban VIII but provides no descriptions or volume numbers that will aid researchers in using the collection today. For a clear overview of this series, see Katterbach, as noted below.

Finding Aids: See Bruno Katterbach, *Inventario dei registri delle suppliche* (Vatican City, 1932), p. 7 footnote and pp. 333–339. Katterbach inventories the series volume by volume (except for 1A, which was added later). Entries, beginning with vol. 3 (e.g. 1800), note to which *RS* volumes each *Registrorum supplicationum rubricelle* corresponds. These Rubricelle are not as useful as indexes to the *RS* as Katterbach's published Inventari.

ASV Indice 124, "Primo Sbozzo di Inventario di tutti i libri che sono nell'Archivio Segreto Vaticano," by Giovanni Bissaiga (1672), provides more descriptive and accurate volume titles for select volumes in some series including the *RS Rub.* on folio 238r.

Location: Archivio Segreto Vaticano.

3.2.7.76 Resignationes

[DATABASE ID: VATV10017-A]

Inclusive Dates: 1709–1800.

Bulk: 5 linear m.

Organization: Chronological by year and alphabetical within each year.

Reference: Boyle, p. 56.

Location: Archivio Segreto Vaticano.

3.2.7.77 Rubricella

[DATABASE ID: VATV10073-A]

Inclusive Dates: 1898–1938.

Bulk: 3 linear m.

Organization: Subseries: Alphabetical index by diocese with names and list of protocol numbers, 1898–[post-1922]; —Alphabetical index by diocese with selected case numbers and a case summary, 1917–[post-1922]; —Case summaries by number and year in which they were received, 1898–[post-1922].

Scope: This series forms an index to the Dataria Apostolica series *Benefici, suppliche, minute, lettere*, 1700–1966. This series is described among the records of the Datary. These rubricellae are difficult to use because cases are filed as they were settled, and not in any precise numberical order.

Location: Archivio Segreto Vaticano.

3.2.7.78 [Rubricella matrimonialium]

[DATABASE ID: VATV10082-A]

Inclusive Dates: 1856–1900.

Bulk: 1 linear m.

Scope: This is a partial index to the Datary series *Matrimonialium*.

Note: This series does not have an official ASV designation. The title was supplied by the project staff.

Location: Archivio Segreto Vaticano.

3.2.7.79 Rubricelle per protocolli

[DATABASE ID: VATV10545-A]

Inclusive Dates: 1939–1962.

Bulk: 1 linear m.

Location: Archivio Segreto Vaticano.

3.2.7.80 Ruolo degli assegni

[DATABASE ID: VATV10036-A]

Inclusive Dates: 1821–1876.

Bulk: 2 linear m.

Organization: Chronological by year and month.

Finding Aids: ASV Indice 1113, no. 174, lists the title of this series. This indice has, since 1990, been withdrawn.

Location: Archivio Segreto Vaticano.

3.2.7.81 Statum officiorum vacabilium

[DATABASE ID: VATV10027-A]

Inclusive Dates: 1644–1764.

Bulk: 1 linear m.

Organization: 6 vols., alphabetical by name of office or by the first name of the solicitor.

Scope: The series gives descriptive accounts of who filled vacant offices, brief histories of the office, who was replaced, whether this was a promotion from another office, and how much the person was paid. Vol. 1 provides a list (first and last names and native place) of apostolic solicitors (iannizzerorum), clerks, registrars, and writers of bulls.

Location: Archivio Segreto Vaticano.

3.2.7.82 Summaria provisionum

[DATABASE ID: VATV10012-A]

Inclusive Dates: 1900–1916.

Bulk: .5 linear m.

Organization: The series is chronological and each volume is arranged alphabetically by diocese.

Location: Archivio Segreto Vaticano.

3.2.7.83 Supplicationes originales

[DATABASE ID: VATV10059-A]

Inclusive Dates: 1480–1898.

Bulk: 92 linear m.

Organization: Subseries (types of supplications) include: Pro diversis gratis concessum, 1480–1806; —Indulgentarum/Concessium et fiat, 1703–1751; —Matrimonium hispanorum: matrimoniales, beneficiales, 1815–1898; —Supplicationes, 1800–1806; —Beneficiales, 1728–1810; —Supplicationes per vacatibus, 1670–1682.

Scope: These are requests concerning different matters, particularly marital dispensations and vacant sees. According to Pásztor, the supplications in this series come from every part of the Catholic world and pertain to every kind of grace. He notes

that they provide important information concerning the ecclesiastical and religious life of various countries. He also notes
that they are drawn up according to the stylus curiae. On the
back of the original supplications, one finds information regarding the volume of the supplication registers in which that
supplication was transcribed. Often, however, the original supplication is the only document of a grace, because so many
volumes of registers have been lost.

Pásztor is useful for a sample of supplications from early
modern South and Central America. Pásztor has noted a supplication from Mariana Ferdandez de Loiasa, who asks to
entrust her legal suit concerning her inheritance to an ecclesiastical tribunal (Aug. 13, 1668) and a supplication from a
secular cleric from Lima who wants to be ordained "extra-
tempora" (Sept. 10, 1668). More generally Pásztor's selection
includes: concessions of indulgences for the establishment
of confraternities, dispensations for illegitimacy for clerics
seeking the priesthood or the master of theology degree, a request for an extension of long-term rent arrangement and other
requests for intervention in financial matters, enfiteusi, a
dispensation for Jewish origins from a supplicant seeking
the priesthood who was born a Jew (1668) in San Salvador in
the Indies, and numerous supplications for indulgences presented by Latin-American confraternities in the eighteenth
century.

The series appears to begin with Alexander VI at SF/148,
where project staff found mazze bound with ribbon and paper.
On the paper was written "Supplicationes pro diversis gratiis"
and then Fiat A or Beneficiales. Range 148–149 goes from
Alexander VI to Pius VII (1804), but material is only organized
by type and bound in clear new paper through Alexander VII
(1659). Range 132 has similar eighteenth-century material
bound by type, and Range 172 has similar eighteenth-century
material organized by type and unorganized. There is much
more than noted by Boyle, et al.
References: Fink, p. 74; Boyle, p. 56; Pásztor (1970),
pp. 49–50.
Location: Archivio Segreto Vaticano.

3.2.7.84 [Supplications]
[DATABASE ID: VATV10055-A]
Inclusive Dates: 1672–1897.
Bulk: 22 linear m.
Organization: Chronological.
Scope: These are incoming materials concerning supplica-
tions already approved by another curial office (e.g., requests
for vacant offices, recommendations for action, etc.). Some-
times the entire case file is included.
Reference: Boyle, p. 56.
Note: This series does not have an official ASV designation.
The title was supplied by project staff.
Location: Archivio Segreto Vaticano.

3.2.7.85 Taxae brevium
[DATABASE ID: VATV10038-A]
Inclusive Dates: 1818–1850.
Bulk: .5 linear m. (3 vols.).
Organization: Chronological.
Scope: These are daily entries of taxes collected for briefs
regarding supplications and benefices.
Location: Archivio Segreto Vaticano.

3.2.7.86 Titoli cardinale e palli
[DATABASE ID: VATV10022-A]
Inclusive Dates: 1852–1921.
Bulk: .1 linear m. (1 vol.).
Organization: There are two subseries: Titoli (1852–1916);
—Palli (1861–1921). Each series is chronological.
Scope: These are records of payments.
Location: Archivio Segreto Vaticano.

3.2.7.87 [Vacabili]
[DATABASE ID: VATV10015-A]
Inclusive Dates: 1800–1897.
Bulk: 24 linear m.
Organization: The series is chronological. Individual vol-
umes are alphabetical by diocese.
Scope: This series contains correspondence to the pro-
datarius from bishops regarding obtaining or holding eccle-
siastical offices. The series also includes supplications asking
for testimonials that a person has a certain faculty, that is, to
give sacraments, to teach a subject, to preach, and so forth.
The series breaks during the Napoleonic period 1808–1814.
Reference: Boyle, p. 56.
Note: This series has no official ASV designation. The title
was supplied by the project staff. This may be the same series
that Boyle calls *Attestationes episcoporum*.
Location: Archivio Segreto Vaticano.

3.2.7.88 Vacabilia
[DATABASE ID: VATV10546-A]
Inclusive Dates: 1939–1963.
Bulk: 14 linear m.
Location: Archivio Segreto Vaticano.

3.2.7.89 Varie
[DATABASE ID: VATV10023-A]
Inclusive Dates: 1737–1897.
Bulk: .05 linear m.
Organization: This small series contains three subseries: 1.
Monasteriorum et confraternatis; —2. Contention; —3. De
ordinibus. Each is chronological.
Location: Archivio Segreto Vaticano.

3.2.7.90 Vescovati: Provviste, elenchi, clausole, tasse
[DATABASE ID: VATV10033-A]
Inclusive Dates: 1697–1921, (bulk 1830–1921).
Bulk: .5 linear m. (7 vols.).
Organization: Volume 1 is an index, "Stati della chiesa
(1697–1882)." The series is chronological, grouped by peti-
tion.
Scope: Each petition usually has a printed cover sheet
"Propositio" to the Consistory and a handwritten draft of the
response.
Location: Archivio Segreto Vaticano.

3.2.8 Deputazione dei conservatori di Roma
[DATABASE ID: VATV669-A]

Leo XII, recognizing the need for the general reform
of all the houses of religious women in Rome, formally
established a Deputazione per Conservatori di Roma
with his motu proprio *I gloriosi Nostri* (Nov. 14, 1826).

This document ordered a special commission or deputation in the form of a visitation as part of an examination of the actual state of the convents. It also called for an investigation to gather the necessary information regarding abuses that had been identified, to find ways of enriching the spirit of the institutions, and to assist the houses in organizing themselves more efficiently.

The deputation having been carried out to his satisfaction, Leo XII (*Inter praeclara*, Aug. 28, 1829) then drew up regulations to insure the reform of the institutions. Article 1 of the document states: "All the convents of Rome will from now on be exclusively regulated, directed, and administered by a cardinal president, by 4 assessors, and a secretary." Cardinal Ludovico Micara was named president of the special department in charge.

The deputation was dissolved with the apostolic letter of August 28, 1829, and the religious houses under their new regulations were returned to their original state.

RECORDS. Records of the office consist of the following series.

3.2.8.1 Deputazione per i conservatori di Roma

[DATABASE ID: VATV20211-A]
Inclusive Dates: 1826–1829.
Bulk: 15 buste and 4 registri.
References: D'Angiolini, p. 1195; Lodolini (1960), p. 95.
Finding Aid: Inventory, 1978.
Location: Archivio di Stato di Roma.

3.2.9 Notarius Arcanarum Sancti Patris Vulgo Cifrarum Secretarius

[DATABASE ID: VATV144-A]

This office was originally the depository for messages in code. In 1814 Carlo Mauri was named substitute secretary of state and absorbed, along with his other responsibilities, the tasks of the segretario della cifra. See the agency history for the Secretariatus Status (alternate English name: secretary of the cipher).

RECORDS. No records for this agency were located.

3.2.10 Secretaria Apostolica

[DATABASE ID: VATV038-A]

The origin of the Secretaria Apostolica (the Apostolic Secretariat for official correspondence in Latin) and the Camera Secreta (the private staff of the pope) go back to the pontificate of Martin V (1417–1431). They were established because of the pope's need to have, independently of the Apostolic Chancery, more frequent, rapid, and secret relations with the outside world.

The Secretaria Apostolica, whose powers were formally defined by Innocent VIII in his constitution *Non debet reprehensibile* (Dec. 31, 1487), was composed of twenty-four apostolic secretaries, one of whom was the secretarius domesticus, so called because he resided in the papal palace in order to be constantly available. He also supervised and coordinated the work of the other secretaries. His principal duty, however, was the transaction of any secret business the pope might assign to him. As a result, he came to possess and exercise great influence in the government of the church as interpreter and executor of the directives of the Holy See.

With the emergence of the cardinal nephew system under Leo X (1513–1521) the direction of the affairs of state ceased to be entrusted to the secretarius domesticus who was subordinated to the cardinal nephew. In fact, from the pontificate of Paul III (1534–1549) to the late seventeenth century, there were few pontificates in which the cardinal nephew did not hold the real power.

By the end of the sixteenth century the new Secretariats of State, Briefs, Letters to Princes, and Latin Letters had assumed most of the duties of the Secretaria Apostolica. Innocent XI suppressed the latter and its college of apostolic secretaries with his constitution *Romanus Pontifex* (Apr. 1, 1678).

In addition to the records listed below, series listed with other agencies relate directly to this agency and should be consulted. See Miscellaneous official series *Armarium XXXIX* and Camera Apostolica series *Secretarius camerae: Indulgentiarum*.

Reference. L. Pásztor, "L'histoire de la curie romaine, problème d'histoire de l'Église," *Revue d'histoire ecclésiastique* 64 (1969): 353–366.

RECORDS. Records of the office consist of the following series.

3.2.10.1 Armaria XL–XLI: Minutae brevium

[DATABASE ID: VATV197-A]
Inclusive Dates: 1478–1554.
Bulk: 129 vol.
Scope: The functions of this office were taken over in part in 1560 by the Secretariat of Briefs. This series is continued by Secretaria Brevium series *Armaria XLII–XLIII: Minutae brevium*. MacFarlane notes that these minutes are the diplomatic counterpart of the minutes of the Dataria Apostolica series *Brevia Lateranensia*, but whereas the *Brevia Lateranensia* deal with material of a purely ecclesiastical nature, such as appeals from decisions of diocesan officials, this series is frequently political in content. As minutes, they are drafts of briefs with corrections, and occasionally they contain added remarks of the pope or his Secretariat officials.
Note: Arm. XLI, vol. 31, is available on microfilm.
References: Fink, pp. 75–76; Boyle, p. 64; MacFarlane, pp. 84–85. Reprints of selected letters appear in J. Lestocquoy, ed., *Correspondance du nonce en France: Prospero Santa Croce (1552–1554)* (Rome, 1972).
Finding Aids: ASV Indice 133 (180r–182r, 183r–185r, 290–316) briefly lists summary titles of each volume. The index (compiled by Petrus De Pretis after 1741) is basically informative but often fails to note copies. The index also uses terms such as *regestrum* and *brevia* too inclusively and does not clearly note items that do not fit the basic thematic focus of

each armarium, or which items are clearly from other offices. The indice appears to list the titles of volumes, but these are not always accurate. There are also some inaccuracies in the more recent typed footnotes which refer to ASV Indici by their former volume numbers.

ASV Indice 124, "Primo Sbozzo di Inventario di tutti i libri che sono nell'Archivio Segreto Vaticano," by Giovanni Bissaiga (1672), provides more descriptive and accurate volume titles for some armarium volumes. Select volumes in *Armarium XL* are listed on folios 259v–315v. *Armarium XLI* volume titles are listed on folios 264v–268v, 276r–277. The titles from Indice 124 are sometimes provided in a footnote in ASV Indice 133, so researchers can see exactly how generic the titles in ASV Indice 133 are.

ASV Indici 290–314, "Index Brevium," provide access to the minutae brevium in *Armaria XL* to *XLIII*. The volumes appear to date from the early sixteenth century. Most of the volumes have a later typed concordance at the beginning of the volume stating the year of the brief, the internal tome or section number, and the current armarium and volume number. The indexes are arranged chronologically. Within each year, the materials are organized alphabetically by the Latin name of the diocese. Entries are brief and list the diocese, name of the person or organization, the type of response, and the old volume/folio number.

ASV Indice 290, "Clem. VII Index Brev. ab anno 1523 ad 1528, Tom. 1," covers *Armarium XL*, volumes 5–17 (1523–1527).

ASV Indice 291, "Clem. VII Index Brev. ab anno 1528 ad 1530, Tom. II," covers *Armarium XL*, volumes 18–31 (1528–1530).

ASV Indice 292, "Clem. VII Index Brev. ab anno 1531 ad 1534, Tom. III," covers *Armarium XL*, volumes 32–48.

ASV Indice 293, "Clem. VII Expeditiones Secreti Brev.," has not been tied to any particular volumes in the Minutae brevium. It is part of this series of volumes and presumably does index some part of *Armarium XL*.

ASV Indice 294, "Index Brev. Clement VII ab an 1526 ad 1536," has also not been tied to any particular section of the Minutae brevium. It is part of this series of indexes; however, it does organize the material differently, according to the type of business or request.

ASV Indici 295–297, "Paul III Index Brev. a Littera A usque ad E, Tom. I," "a Littera F usque ad O," and "a Littera P usque ad Z," are a series of three volumes that cover *Armarium XL*, volumes 49–53, and *Armarium XLI*, volumes 1–46.

ASV Indice 298, "Index Brev. Matrim. 1534–1550," serves as an index to one type of business in *Armarium XLI*, volumes 51–54.

ASV Indice 299, "Rubricella Brevium Indulgentiarum ab an: 1535 (sic 1534) ad 1566," covers the papacies of Julius III, Paul IV, Pius IV, and Pius V and indexes minutae brevium dealing with indulgences in *Armarium XLI*, volumes 47–49, and in *Armarium XLII*, volumes 2–3.

ASV Indice 300–304, "Paul III, Brevium Summar. Ind, 1534–1537," "1538–1541," "1542–1545," and "1546–1549," have not been tied to any specific section of the *Armaria XL–XLIII* that has minutae brevium. The entries in these volumes are fuller than those in the plain indexes and since these were created prior to some losses in the collection, they may provide some evidence for actions.

ASV Indice 304, "Index Brevium Paul III," provides access to all or part of *Armarium XL*, volume 49. This index, which is very difficult to read in some of the sections, indicates the name of the person, sometimes lists the type of business, and then a folio and brevia number.

ASV Indice 304A, "Index," provides access to *Armarium XLI*, volumes 5–8. This index is not one of the regular series. It is arranged chronologically. Within each year, entries are alphabetical by either person (architecti) or in later years, diocese, and then person (prioratus, electus). A tome and an item number are then listed.

ASV Indice 305, "Index Brevium . . . Julii ac suarum Epistolarum Brevia Indulgentiarum et Dispensationum Matrimonialium . . . ," provides access to *Armarium XLI*, volumes 55–72.

Location: Archivio Segreto Vaticano.

3.2.10.2 Armaria XLIV–XLV: Brevia ad principes et alios viros

[DATABASE ID: VATV199-A]

Inclusive Dates: 1513–1730.

Bulk: 102 vols.

Scope: MacFarlane notes that this series should not be confused with *Brevia seu epistolae ad principes* (identified in this guide as Secretariatus Epistolae ad Principes et Optimates series [*Registri*] *Viros et alios*). They are briefs sent not only to princes, but to archbishops and the greater abbots.

References: Fink, pp. 75–76; Boyle, pp. 64–65; MacFarlane, p. 85. L. Nanni, ed., *Epistolae ad principes*, vol. 1, *Leo X–Pius IV (1513–1565)*; vol. 2, *S. Pius V–Gregorius XIII (1566–1585)* (Vatican City, 1992–1994). Nanni presents summaries of letters to princes. The two primary collections that the book draws from are records of the Secretariatus Epistolae ad Principes and these armaria. There is an introduction, then the summary begins. Entries include the date, summary of the document, location (series, volume, and foglio numbers). There is a name/place index at the end of each volume.

Reprints of selected documents appear in the following works. B. Barbiche, ed., *Correspondance du nonce en France, Innocenzo del Bufalo, évêque de Camerino, 1601–1604* (Rome, 1964). H. E. Bell, *The Proposed Continuation of the Calendars of Roman State Papers Relating to English Affairs* (1939) [this title was noted but not verified by project staff]. P. Blet, ed., *Girolamo Ragazzoni évêque de Bergame, nonce en France: Correspondance de sa nonciature, 1583–1586* (Rome, 1962). J. Fraikin, *Nonciatures de Clément VII*, vol. 1, *Depuis la bataille de Pavie jusqu'au rappel d'Acciaiuoli, 25 févier 1525–juin 1527* (Paris, 1906). F. M. Jones, "Papal Briefs to Father Mansoni, Papal Nuncio to Ireland," *Archivium hibernicum* 17 (1953): 51–68. A. O. Meyer, "Die Prager Nuntiatur des Giovanni Stefano Ferreri und die Wiener Nuntiatur des Giacomo Serra (1603–1606)," vol. 3 of *Nuntiaturberichte aus Deutschland nebst ergänzenden Actenstücken. Vierte Abteilung, siebzehntes Jahrhundert* (Berlin, 1913). J. M. Rigg, ed., *Calendar of State Papers Relating to English Affairs, Preserved Principally at Rome in the Vatican Archives and Library* (London, 1916–1926). R. Toupin, ed., *Correspondance du nonce en France, Giovanni Battista Castelli (1581–1583)* (Rome, 1967).

Finding Aids: ASV Indice 133, ff. 196r–198v and 200r–201v, briefly lists summary titles of each volume in Armarium XLIV and XLV. The index (compiled by Petrus De Pretis after

1741) is basically informative but often fails to note copies. The index also uses terms such as *regestrum* and *brevia* too inclusively and does not clearly note items that do not fit the basic thematic focus of each armarium, or which items are clearly from other offices. Therefore, the volume titles presented in this index are not exact. Some of the recent typed footnotes in this index are also inaccurate, but the references below are correct.

ASV Indice 124, "Primo Sbozzo di Inventario di tutti i libri che sono nell'Archivio Segreto Vaticano," by Giovanni Bissaiga (1672), provides more descriptive and accurate volume titles for some armarium volumes. Select Armarium XLIV volumes are listed on folios 264v–268v and 276r–277v. Volume titles for Armarium XLV are listed on folios 268v–270v. The titles from ASV Indice 124 are sometimes provided in a footnote in ASV Indice 133, so researchers can see exactly how generic the titles in ASV Indice 133 are.

Location: Archivio Segreto Vaticano.

3.2.10.3 Diversorum

[DATABASE ID: VATV185-A]

Inclusive Dates: 1572–1676.

Bulk: about 30 vols.

Organization: This series is now integrated with the volumes of the Camera Apostolica series *Secretariatus camerae*. Volume numbers are as follows: 65, 74, 78–83, 108–112, 115–124, 146–149, 154–156, 163, and 166. According to Boyle, the volumes passed to the Camera when the Apostolic Secretariat was supressed in 1678.

Reference: Boyle, p. 55. L. E. Halkin, *Les sources de l'histoire de la Belgique aux Archives et à la Bibliothèque Vaticanes: État des collections et répertoire bibliographique* (Brussels, 1951).

Finding Aid: ASV Indice 1048 is an index to the Secretariatus Camerae and lists these volumes.

Location: Archivio Segreto Vaticano.

3.2.11 Secretaria Brevium

[DATABASE ID: VATV039-A]

Up to the fifteenth century the Apostolic Chancery was the only office for the expedition of every kind of papal document. When the use of the brief became more generalized, however, in 1502, Alexander VI (1492–1503) set up a distinct department with responsibility for letters of nondiplomatic and spiritual content. This office also occasionally provided the means for dispatching letters sub plumbo. The Secretariat of Briefs, as it was called, was formally established by Innocent XI with the constitution *Romanus Pontifex* (Apr. 1, 1678). At the same time the pope created and separated from the Secretariat of Briefs a Secretariat of Briefs to Princes.

The Secretariat of Briefs had the exclusive authority to expedite briefs that by common law or by special order of the pope were required for certain matters. Benedict XIV (constitution *Gravissimum Ecclesiae*, Nov. 26, 1745) enumerated a list of favors and privileges that

this secretariat could confer either exclusively or in concurrence with the Dataria.

In the granting of indulgences, there existed the custom of having the petitions considered and decided by the Congregation of Indulgences and Relics (Clement IX, motu proprio *In ipsis pontificatus*, Jul. 6, 1669) while having the expedition of the decrees handled by the secretary of briefs. Later on indulgences were issued either through rescript of the congregation, through briefs by the Secretariat of Briefs, or through a memorial of the Secretariat of Memorials. This unrestricted practice of granting indulgences resulted in abuses. For this reason Pius IX (motu proprio, Jan. 2, 1855) withdrew from the Congregation of Indulgences and Relics the faculty of granting indulgences. As this decree, however, was soon ignored, Leo XIII found it necessary to reconfirm (motu proprio *Christianae reipublicae*, Oct. 31, 1897) the explicit motu proprio of Clement IX and to forbid the congregation the practice of the granting of indulgences. Pius X in 1908 transferred the responsibility for decisions regarding indulgences to the Congregation of the Holy Office when he suppressed the Secretariat of Briefs as a separate office of the Roman Curia and made it a section or department of the Secretariat of State.

Paul VI (motu proprio *Quo aptius*, Feb. 27, 1973) dissolved the Apostolic Chancery as a separate curial department and transferred its functions to the Secretariat of State's third section under the direction of the Chancery of Apostolic Letters.

John Paul II's constitution *Pastor bonus* (Jun. 28, 1988) reduced the sections within the Secretariat to two: (1) General Affairs, which is charged with, among other things, the preparation of drafts of documents entrusted to it by the pope; and (2) Relations with States (formerly the Council for Public Affairs of the Church, a separate body).

References. L. E. Halkin, *Les sources de l'histoire de la Belgique aux Archives et à la Bibliothèque Vaticanes: État des collections et répertoire bibliographique* (Brussels, 1951). L. Pásztor, "L'histoire de la curie romaine, problème d'histoire de l'Église," *Revue d'histoire ecclésiastique* 64 (1969): 353-366.

RECORDS. Records of the office consist of the following series.

3.2.11.1 Altare privilegiatum ad tempus

[DATABASE ID: VATV205-]

Inclusive Dates: 1771–1908.

Bulk: 12 linear m. (187 vols.).

Organization: Chronological.

References: Fink, p.77; Pásztor (1970), p. 119; Pásztor (1983), p. 152; Boyle, p. 66.

Finding Aids: ASV Indici 1098 (formerly Indice 35), 1099, and 127, "Inventario-prospetto della serie 'Sec. Brev.,'" by Mons. Pietro Guidi and Mons. Carlo Natalini, list volumes in the *Altare privilegiatum ad tempus* and the following other Secretariat of Briefs (abbreviated as Sec. Brev.) series: *Sec. Brev.* (a records series generated by the office of the Sec. Brev.), *Indulgentiae ad tempus, Indulgentiae perpetuae, Indulta personalia,* and *Altare privilegiatum perpetuum.* Indice 1098 covers the *Altare priv. ad tempus* vols. 1–90 (1771–1846). Indice 1099 covers *Altare priv. ad tempus* vols. 91–149 (1846–1878). Indice 127 (old number) is available at the desk in the main ASV reading room. The indice is not a formal finding aid and must be used in consultation with the archives staff. Indice 127 covers *Altare priv. ad tempus* vols. 150–187 (1878–1908). All of these indici give the following information for each volume: current number, inclusive dates, and business, as stated on the spine. These indici are of use to researchers tracing all volumes from a given year or papacy or looking for a current volume number.

ASV Indice 1100 is an introduction to ASV Indici 731–885, of which 740–885 are the primary analytical indici for the series *Sec. Brev.* as well as its related series, such as *Altare ad tempus.* Indice 1100 refers to Indici 740–885 using their former volume numbers, that is, numbers 10–150. However, the former numbering is still visible on the spines of Indici 740–885. Indice 1100 provides an overall view of Indici 740–885, which allows researchers to easily note their uneven chronological progression and the different categories of business indexed.

ASV Indici 740–885 employ a number of different indexing methods, including rubrics that provide page-by-page summaries of documents in selected *Altare privilegiatum ad tempus* volumes and classified subject-based indici (e.g., de Camera Apostolica, de Monialibus, de Ordinibus Militaribus, etc.). These indici, which cover the years 1554–1872, also provide access to selected items in the registers in the following Sec. Brev. series: *Sec. Brev., Indulgentiae ad tempus, Indulgentiae perpetuae, Indulta personalia,* and *Altare privilegiatum perpetuum.*

The registers do not appear in strict numerical order in the indici, but rather in a rough chronological order. Therefore, there are several steps to follow in order to determine if an *Altare priv. ad tempus* volume is included in these indici. First, armed with a date, one can proceed to Indice 1100, which provides a list of Indici 731–885, and learn which of Indici 731–885 cover the period and type of business sought. One can then select from Indici 740–885 the volumes containing rubrics or subject indici to registers whose chronological span encompasses one's desired dates. Entries in these indici extract the following information from some *Altare privilegiatum ad tempus* registers, the name of the diocese, recipient, nature of the business, and folio number. Note that *Altare privilegiatum ad tempus* material is also found in the Sec. Brev. series *Sec. Brev.* (in the subseries Diversorum). For a complete list of *Altare privilegiatum ad tempus,* consult Indici 1098, 1099, and 127 (cf. above).

Chronological coverage of ASV Indici 740–885 for *Altare privilegiatum ad tempus* series (old vol. numbers are still visible on spines) is as follows: vol. 31 (1578–1867).

When using ASV Indice 740–885 the following caveats apply. (1) Indice 740, entitled on the spine "Cedul. Consi. Martin V–Clement VIII," is actually a liber taxarum, organized alphabetically by diocese. This volume covers several centuries and is not useful as an index to this series. (2) Most of the rubrics in Indici 740–885 bear later annotations to current

volume numbers. In the indexes to earlier volumes (1554–1723), references in the rubrics without these modern annotations could not be traced and presumably correspond to lost volumes. In later volumes, after 1723, items in both the rubrics and the classified indexes without annotations could often be located in volumes covering the month cited in the indici. However, the part ("pars prima," etc.) and the page numbers are usually incorrect. (3) Pásztor (1983) refers to these indici as "Liber Sussidiario." He also notes that the titles on these indici are not precise, for example, cedole concistoriale can be located in the indici entitled "Bullarum." (4) After 1872, the indici described below (nomi, diocesi, registro di cassa) provide the best access.

The second floor of the ASV Sala d'Indici houses three more sets of indici to the *Altare ad tempus.* These are "Nomi" (1834–1926); "Diocesi" (1869–1922); and "Registro di Cassa della Segreteria de Breve" (1845–1897). After 1878, these indici provide the only means of access to the following Sec. Brev. series: *Sec. Brev., Indulgentiae ad tempus, Indulgentiae perpetuae, Indulta personalia, Altare privilegiatum ad tempus,* and *Altare privilegiatum perpetuum.* These sets of indici are straightforward. Desired information can be approached by name (personal or corporate), diocese, or date. Each of these sets gives a different protocol number, date, name, diocese, agent or referring congregation, and business (in some order). The essential pieces of information to note from all these registers are the dates and the type of business (e.g., appointment of an archbishop, altare priv., indulg.). From here, researchers should proceed to Indici 1098, 1099, and 127, to locate the current volume numbers.

Note: This series is continued by the Secretariatus Status series *Brevi apostolici.*

Location: Archivio Segreto Vaticano.

3.2.11.2 Altare privilegiatum perpetuum

[DATABASE ID: VATV206-A]

Inclusive Dates: 1579–1908.

Bulk: 13 linear m. (210 vols.).

Organization: Chronological.

References: Fink, p. 77; Pásztor (1970), p. 119; Pásztor (1983), p. 152; Boyle, p. 66.

Finding Aids: ASV Indici 1098 (formerly Indice 35), 1099, and 127, "Inventario-prospetto della serie 'Sec. Brev.,'" by Mons. Pietro Guidi and Mons. Carlo Natalini, list volumes in the *Altare privilegiatum perpetuum* and the following other Secretariat of Briefs (abbreviated as Sec. Brev.) series: *Sec. Brev.* (a record series generated by the office of Sec. Brev.), *Indulgentiae ad tempus, Indulgentiae perpetuae, Indulta personalia,* and *Altare privilegiatum ad tempus.* Indice 1098 covers *Altare priv. perpetuum* vols. 1–136 (1579–1846). Indice 1099 covers *Altare priv. perpetuum* vols. 137–184 (1846–1878). Indice 127 (old number) is available at the desk in the main ASV reading room. The indice is not a formal finding aid and must be used in consultation with the archives staff. Indice 127 covers *Altare priv. perpetuum* vols. 185–210 (1878–1908). All of these indici give the following information for each volume: current number, inclusive dates, and business, as noted on the spine. These indici are of use to researchers tracing all volumes from a given year or papacy or looking for a current volume number.

ASV Indice 1100 is an introduction to ASV Indici 731–885,

of which 740–885 are the primary analytical indici for the series *Sec. Brev.* and its related series, such as *Altare priviligiatum perpetuum*. Indice 1100 refers to Indici 740–885 using their former volume numbers, that is, numbers 10–150. However, the former numbering is still visible on the spines of Indici 740–885. Indice 1100 provides an overall view of Indici 740–885 and researchers can easily note their uneven chronological progression and the different categories of business indexed.

ASV Indici 740–885 employ a number of different indexing methods, including rubrics that provide page-by-page summaries of documents in selected *Altare privilegiatum perpetuum* volumes and classified subject-based indici (e.g., de Camera Apostolica, de Monialibus, de Ordinibus Militaribus, etc.). These indici, which cover the years 1554–1872, also provide access to selected material in the registers of the following *Sec. Brev* series: *Sec. Brev., Indulgentiae ad tempus, Indulgentiae perpetuae, Indulta personalia,* and *Altare privilegiatum ad tempus.*

The registers do not appear in strict numerical order in the indici, but rather in a rough chronological order. Therefore, there are several steps to follow in order to determine if an *Altare priv. ad tempus* volume is included in these indici. First, armed with a date, one can proceed to Indice 1100, which provides a list of Indici 731–885 and learn which of Indici 731–885 cover the period and type of business sought. One can then select from Indici 740–885, the volumes containing rubrics or subject indici to registers whose chronological span encompasses one's desired dates. Entries in these indici extract from some *Altare privilegiatum perpetuum* registers the following information: the name of the diocese, recipient, nature of the business, and folio number. Note that *Altare privilegiatum perpetuum* material is also found in the Sec. Brev. series *Sec. Brev.* (in the subseries Diversorum). For a complete list of *Altare privilegiatum perpetuum* volumes, consult Indici 1098, 1099, and 127 (cf. above).

Chronological coverage of Indici 740–885 for the *Altare privilegiatum perpetuum* series (old vol. numbers are still visible on spines) is as follows: vol. 123 (1758–1787), vol. 130 (1788–1803).

When using ASV Indici 740–885 the following caveats apply. (1) Indice 740, entitled on the spine "Cedul. Conci. Martin V–Clement VIII," is actually a liber taxarum, organized alphabetically by diocese. This volume covers several centuries and is not useful as an index to this series. (2) Most of the rubrics in Indici 740–885 bear later annotations to current volume numbers. In the indexes to earlier volumes (1554–1723), references in the rubrics without these modern annotations could not be traced and presumably correspond to lost volumes. In later volumes, after 1723, items in both the rubrics and the classified indexes without annotations could often be located in volumes covering the month cited in the indici. However, the part ("pars prima," etc.) and the page numbers are usually incorrect. (3) Pásztor (1983) refers to these indici as "Liber Sussidiario." He also notes that the titles on these indici are not precise, for example, cedole concistoriale can be located in indici entitled "Bullarum." (4) After 1872, the indici described below (nomi, diocesi, registro di cassa), provide the best access.

The second floor of the ASV Sala d'Indici houses three more sets of indici to the *Altare perpetuum*. These are "Nomi" (1834–1926); "Diocesi" (1869–1922); and "Registro di Cassa

della Segreteria de Breve" (1845–1897). After 1878, these indici provide the only means of access to the following Sec. Brev. series: *Sec. Brev., Indulgentiae ad Tempus, Indulgentiae perpetuae, Indulta personalia, Altare privilegiatum ad tempus,* and *Altare privilegiatum perpetuum.* These sets of indici are straightforward. Desired information can be approached by name (personal or corporate), diocese, or date. Each of these sets gives a protocol number, date, name, diocese, agent or referring congregation, and business (in some order). The essential pieces of information to note from all these registers are the dates and the type of business (e.g., appointment of an archbishop, altare priv., indulg.). Researchers should then proceed to Indici 1098, 1099, and 127, (cf. above) to locate the current volume numbers.

Note: This series is continued by the Secretariatus Status series *Brevi apostolici.*

Location: Archivio Segreto Vaticano.

3.2.11.3 Armarium XXXVIII

[DATABASE ID: VATV200-A]
Inclusive Dates: 1508–1734.
Bulk: 30 vols.
Scope: Boyle notes that this armarium consists of letters of nondiplomatic and spiritual content primarily in the period 1502–1560. He describes this series as "Original Secretariat of Briefs."

References: Fink, p. 32; Boyle, p. 66.

Finding Aids: ASV Indice 133, ff. 174r–175r, briefly lists summary titles of each volume. The index (compiled by Petrus De Pretis after 1741) is basically informative but often fails to note copies. The index also uses terms such as *regestrum* and *brevia* too inclusively and does not clearly note items that do not fit the basic thematic focus of each armarium, or which items are clearly from other offices. The volume appears to list the titles of volumes, but these are not always accurate.

ASV Blocchetti 3 has two sections, the second of which is not noted at the beginning of the blocchetti. These two parts are "Schede dei Brevi Originali, Cartella A. I. nn. 1–192 (a. 1503–1734)" and "Schede dei Brevi Originali, Cartella B. II. nn. 193–311 (a. 1741–1836)."

ASV Indice 317, "Index Brevium Urbani Pape VIII per alphabeticum Diocesium ac Materiarum Ordinem dispostus in quo nomina Indultandorum atque argumenta materiarum plene expressa sunt studio ac labore Philippi Antonii Ronconis Tabularii Secreti Aplici. Vaticani Prefecti," provides access to *Armarium XXXVIII*, volumes 10 to 16A, *Armarium XLII*, volumes 58–63; and *Armarium XLIII*, volumes 1–10. The volumes date from the early sixteenth century and a later typed concordance is at the beginning of the volume stating the year of the brief, the internal tome or section number, and the current armarium and volume number. The index is arranged chronologically. Within each year, the materials are organized alphabetically by the Latin name of the diocese. Entries are brief and list the diocese, recipient, the type of response, and the old volume/folio number.

Location: Archivio Segreto Vaticano.

3.2.11.4 Armaria XLII–XLIII: Minutae brevium

[DATABASE ID: VATV198-A]
Inclusive Dates: 1555–1656.
Bulk: 95 vols.

Scope: Following a reorganization in 1560, some of the functions of the Apostolic Secretariat were taken over by the Secretariat of Briefs. This material reflects both offices and continues the Secretaria Apostolica series *Armaria XL–XLI: Minutae brevium.* MacFarlane notes that these minutes are the diplomatic counterpart of the minutes of the Dataria Apostolica series *Brevia Lateranensia,* but whereas the *Brevia Lateranensia* deal with material of a purely ecclesiastical nature, such as appeals from decisions of diocesan officials, this series is frequently political in content. As minutes, they are drafts of briefs with corrections, and occasionally they contain added remarks of the pope or his Secretariat officials. The records consist of corrected drafts of briefs.

References: Fink, pp. 75–76; Boyle, p. 64; MacFarlane, pp. 84–85. H. E. Bell, *The Proposed Continuation of the Calendars of Roman State Papers Relating to English Affairs* (1939) [this title was noted but not verified by project staff]. J. M. Rigg, ed., *Calendar of State Papers Relating to English Affairs, Preserved Principally at Rome in the Vatican Archives and Library* (London, 1916–1926).

Finding Aids: ASV Indice 133, ff. 187r–194r and 290r–316, briefly lists summary titles of each volume. The index (compiled by Petrus De Pretis after 1741) is basically informative but often fails to note copies. The index also uses terms such as *regestrum* and *brevia* too inclusively and does not clearly note items that do not fit the basic thematic focus of each armarium, or which items are clearly from other offices. The volume appears to list the titles of volumes, but these are not always accurate. There are also some inaccuracies in the footnotes, particularly concerning ASV indici that have changed number.

ASV Indici 290–314, "Index Brevium," provide access to the minutae brevium in *Armaria XL* to *XLIII.* The volumes appear to date from the early sixteenth century. Most of the volumes have a later typed concordance at the beginning of the volume stating the year of the brief, the internal tome or section number, and the current armarium and volume number. The indexes are arranged chronologically. Within each year, the materials are organized alphabetically by the Latin name of the diocese. Entries are brief and list the diocese, name of the person or organization, the type of response, and the old volume/folio number.

ASV Indice 299, "Rubricella Brevium Indulgentiarum ab an: 1535 (i.e. 1534) ad 1566," covers the papacies of Julius III, Paul IV, Pius IV, and Pius V, and indexes minutae brevium dealing with indulgences in *Armarium XLI,* volumes 47–49 and in *Armarium XLII,* volumes 2–3.

ASV Indice 307, "Index Brevium Pauli PP. IV, 13 Maii 1555 usque ad 18 Augusti 1559," indexes *Armarium XLII,* volumes 6–12.

ASV Indice 309, "Index Brevium Pio PP. IV ab an: 1559–1565," covers *Armarium XLII,* volumes 13–23.

ASV Indice 311, "Pii 1566–1572," covers *Armarium XLII,* volumes 25–27.

ASV Indice 313, "Gregorii XIII 1572–1585," covers *Armarium XLII,* volumes 28–46.

ASV Indice 314, "Index Brevium . . . Sixti PP. V existentium in Archivio Secreto Vaticano ab anno 1585 ad 1590 creatus fuit Pontifex die 24 Aprilii 1585 . . . die 27 Augusti 1590," covers *Armarium XLII,* volume 47.

ASV Indice 316, "Index Brevium Leonis Papa XI et Pauli V per alphabeticum diocesium ac materiarum ordinem dispositus in quo nomina Indultaniorum atque argumenta materiarum expressa sunta studio ac labore Philippi Antonis Ronconis Tabularis Secretior Aplici. Vaticani Prefect," provides access to *Armarium XLII,* volumes 52–57.

ASV Indice 317, "Index Brevium Urbani Pape VIII per alphabeticum diocesium ac materiarum ordinem dispositus in quo nomina Indultandorum atque argumenta materiarum expressa sunta studio ac labore Philippi Antonii Ronconis Tabularii Secretior Aplici. Vaticani Prefect," provides access to *Armarium XLII,* volumes 58–63; *Armarium XLIII,* volumes 1–10; and *Armarium XXXVIII,* volumes 10–16A.

Location: Archivio Segreto Vaticano.

3.2.11.5 Brevi originali

[DATABASE ID: VATV10221-A]

Inclusive Dates: 1647–1913.

Bulk: 2.5 linear m. (52 vols.).

Organization: Chronological.

Scope: These appear to be actual presentation copies of selected briefs on parchment.

Reference: Pásztor (1983), p. 152.

Location: Archivio Segreto Vaticano.

3.2.11.6 Cassa: Scatole

[DATABASE ID: VATV10068-A]

Inclusive Dates: 1824–1927.

Bulk: 13 linear m.

Organization: Chronological.

Location: Archivio Segreto Vaticano.

3.2.11.7 Cassa: Volumi

[DATABASE ID: VATV10232-A]

Inclusive Dates: 1898–1908.

Bulk: .5 linear m. (14 vols.).

Organization: Chronological.

Scope: These registers list date of brief, agent, postulant, diocese, object, and amount of tax.

Reference: Pásztor (1983), p. 149. Pásztor identifies this series as part of the "Libri di Cassa" along with the Secreteria Brevium series *Liber brevium: Exactorum* (1585–1843) and *Registro di cassa* (1845–1897).

Location: Archivio Segreto Vaticano.

3.2.11.8 Doti

[DATABASE ID: VATV10223-A]

Inclusive Dates: 1836–1888.

Bulk: 13 linear m.

Organization: Chronological.

Scope: The labels on the boxes that comprise this series indicate that they contain "Attestati di dote concessa." Some boxes are identified as Dotazione.

Location: Archivio Segreto Vaticano.

3.2.11.9 Esercizi

[DATABASE ID: VATV10225-A]

Inclusive Dates: 1845–1896.

Bulk: 3 linear m.

Organization: Chronological. Subseries are: Giubilazione; —Gratificazione; —Doti; —Officiali dei Brevi.

Location: Archivio Segreto Vaticano.

3.2.11.10 Giubilazione

[DATABASE ID: VATV10224-A]
Inclusive Dates: 1870–1905.
Bulk: 3 linear m.
Organization: Chronological.
Location: Archivio Segreto Vaticano.

3.2.11.11 Indici: Diocesi

[DATABASE ID: VATV10220-A]
Inclusive Dates: 1869–1928.
Bulk: 3.5 linear m. (60 vols.).
Organization: Chronological by year and then alphabetical within each year.
Scope: These indici, located on the second floor of the ASV Sala d'Indici and in the stacks, provide access to the later volumes in the following Secretaria Brevium series: *Sec. Brev., Indulgentiae ad tempus, Indulgentiae perpetuae, Indulta personalia, Altare privilegiatum ad tempus,* and *Altare privilegiatum perpetuum*; and their continuation in the Secretariatus Status series *Brevi apostolici.*

Entries are alphabetical primarily by diocese, but also include religious corporations, institutions, cities, and territories in the alphabetical list. Entries include the number, date of audience, agent, postulant, object of business, rescript date and who issued the rescript (e.g., Propaganda), and selected observations. To retrieve the actual brief the dates are the important pieces of information to note.

Reference: Pásztor (1983), pp. 150–151.
Location: Archivio Segreto Vaticano.

3.2.11.12 Indici: Nomi

[DATABASE ID: VATV10219-A]
Inclusive Dates: 1834–1967.
Bulk: 2.5 linear m. (90 vols)
Organization: Alphabetical.
Scope: These indexes are located in the ASV Sala d'Indici on the second floor. They provide access to later volumes in the Secretaria Brevium series: *Sec. Brev., Indulta personalia, Indulgentiae ad tempus, Indulgentiae perpetuae, Altare privilegiatum ad tempus,* and *Altare privilegiatum perpetuum.* These indices proceed alphabetically, listing number, name, diocese, audience date, business, agent or referring papal office (e.g., Propaganda). The index is alphabetical by name, but names are derived from a number of categories including: personal names, offices (archbishop, bishop), institutions (seminaries, churches), and titles (prefect, vicar). In order to use these volumes as indexes to other series, the date is the important piece of information to note.

References: Fink, p. 77; Pásztor (1983), p. 150.
Location: Archivio Segreto Vaticano.l

3.2.11.13 Indulgentiae ad tempus

[DATABASE ID: VATV202-A]
Inclusive Dates: 1625–1908.
Bulk: 43 linear m. (578 vols.).
Organization: Chronological.
References: Fink, p. 77; Pásztor (1970), p. 118; Pásztor (1983), p. 151; Boyle, p. 66.
Finding Aids: ASV Indici 1098 (formerly Indice 35), 1099, and 127, "Inventario-prospetto della serie 'Sec. Brev.,'" by Mons. Pietro Guidi and Mons. Carlo Natalini, list volumes in

the *Indulgentiae ad tempus* series and the following other Secretaria Brevium (abbreviated as Sec. Brev.) series: *Sec. Brev.* (a records series generated by the office of the Sec. Brev.), *Indulgentiae perpetuae, Indulta personalia, Altare privilegiatum ad tempus,* and *Altare privilegiatum perpetuum.* Indice 1098 covers *Indulgentiae ad tempus* vols. 1–142 (1625–1846). Indice 1099 covers *Indulgentiae ad Tempus* vols. 143–357 (1846–1878). Indice 127 (old number) is available at the desk in the main ASV reading room. The indice is not a finding aid and must be used in consultation with the archives staff. Indice 127 covers *Indulg. ad tempus* vols. 358–578 (1878–1908). All of these indici give the following information for each volume: current number, inclusive dates, and business, as stated on the spine. These indici are of use to researchers tracing all volumes from a given year or papacy or looking for a current volume number.

ASV Indice 1100 is an introduction to ASV Indici 731–885, of which 740–885 are the primary analytical indexes for the series *Sec. Brev.* and its related series, such as *Indulgentiae ad tempus.* Indice 1100 refers to Indici 740–885 using their former volume numbers, that is, numbers 10–150. However, the former numbering is still visible on the spines of Indici 740–885. Indice 1100 provides an overall view of Indici 740–885, which allows a researcher to easily note their uneven chronological progression and the different categories of business indexed.

ASV Indici 740–885 employ a number of different indexing methods, including rubrics that provide page-by-page summaries of documents in selected *Indulgentiae ad tempus* volumes, and classified subject-based indici (e.g., de Camera Apostolica, de Monialibus, de Ordinibus Militaribus, etc.). These indici, which cover the years 1554–1872, also provide access to selected material from the registers in the following Sec. Brev. series: *Sec. Brev., Indulgentiae Perpetuae, Indulta personalia, Altare privilegiatum ad tempus,* and *Altare privilegiatum perpetuum.*

Registers do not appear in strict numerical order in the indici, but rather in a rough chronological order. Therefore, there are several steps to follow in order to determine if an *Indulgentiae ad tempus* volume has a rubric in these indici. First, armed with a date, one can proceed to Indice 1100, which provides a list of Indici 731–885, and learn which of Indici 731–885 cover the period and type of business sought. One can then select from Indici 740–885 the volumes containing rubrics or subject indici to registers whose chronological span encompasses one's desired dates. Entries in these indici extract from some Indulgentiae registers the following information: the name of the diocese, recipient, nature of the business, and the folio number, . Note that *Indulgentiae ad tempus* material is also found in the Sec. Brev. series *Sec. Brev.* (in the subseries Diversorum). For a complete list of *Indulgentiae ad tempus* volumes consult Indici 1098–1099 and 127 (old number, cf. above).

Chronological coverage of Indici 740–885 for *Indulgentiae ad tempus* series (old vol. numbers are still visible on spines) is as follows: vol. 117 (1763–1799), vol. 119 (1764–1788), vol. 122 (1788–1799).

When using ASV Indici 740–885 the following caveats apply: (1) Indice 740, entitled on the spine, "Cedul. Conci. Martin V–Clement VIII," is actually a liber taxarum, organized alphabetically by diocese. This volume covers several centuries and is not useful as an index to this series. (2) Most of the rubrics in Indici 740–885 bear later annotations to current volume numbers. In the indexes to earlier volumes (1554–1723), references in the rubrics without these modern annotations could not be traced and presumably correspond to lost volumes. In later volumes, after 1723, items in both the rubrics and the classified indexes without annotations could often be located in volumes covering the month cited in the indice. However, the part ("pars prima," etc.) and the page numbers are usually incorrect. (3) Pásztor (1983) refers to these indici as "Liber Sussidiario." He also notes that the titles on these indici are not precise, for example, cedole concistoriale can be located in indici entitled "Bullarum." (4) After 1872, the indici described below (nomi, diocesi, registro di cassa), provide the best access.

The second floor of the ASV Sala d'Indici houses three more sets of indici to the *Indulgentiae ad tempus*. These are "Nomi" (1834–1926); "Diocesi" (1869–1922); and "Registro di Cassa della Segreteria de Breve" (1845–1897). After 1872, these indici provide the best means of access to the following Sec. Brev. series: *Sec. Brev., Indulgentiae ad tempus, Indulgentiae perpetuae, Indulta personalia, Altare privilegiatum ad tempus,* and *Altare privilegiatum perpetuum.* These sets of indici are straightforward to use. Desired information can be approached by name (personal or corporate), diocese, or date. Each of these sets gives a protocol number, date, name, diocese, agent or referring congregation, and business (in some order). The essential pieces of information to note from all these registers are the dates and the type of business (e.g., appointment of an archbishop, altare priv., indulg.). After consulting these indici, researchers must proceed to Indici 1098, 1099, and 127 (cf. above) to locate the current volume numbers.

Note: This series is continued by the Secretariatus Status series *Brevi apostolici.*

Location: Archivio Segreto Vaticano.

3.2.11.14 Indulgentiae perpetuae

[DATABASE ID: VATV203-A]
Inclusive Dates: 1580–1909.
Bulk: 23 linear m. (325 vols.).
Organization: Chronological.
References: Fink, p. 77; Pásztor (1970), p. 118; Pásztor (1983), p. 151; Boyle, p. 66.
Finding Aids: ASV Indici 1098 (formerly Indice 35), 1099, and 127, "Inventario-prospetto della serie 'Sec. Brev.,'" by Mons. Pietro Guidi and Mons. Carlo Natalini, list volumes in the *Indulgentiae perpetuae* and the following other Secretariat of Briefs series: *Sec. Brev.* (a record series generated by the office of the Sec. Brev.), *Indulgentiae ad tempus, Indulta personalia, Altare privilegiatum ad tempus,* and *Altare privilegiatum perpetuum.* Indice 1098 covers *Indulgentiae perpetuae* vols. 1–195 (1580–1846). Indice 1099 covers *Indulgentiae perpetuae* vols. 196–357 (1846–1878). Indice 127 (old number) is available at the desk in the main ASV reading room. The indice is not a formal finding aid and must be used in consultation with the archives staff. Indice 127 covers *Indulgentiae perpetuae* vols. 358–578 (1878–1908). All of these indici give the following information for each volume: current number, inclusive dates, and business, as stated on the spine. These indici are of use to researchers tracing all volumes from a given year or papacy or looking for a current volume number.

ASV Indice 1100 is an introduction to ASV Indici 731–885,

of which 740–885 are the primary analytical indexes for the series *Sec. Brev.* and its related series, such as *Indulgentiae perpetuae.* Indice 1100 refers to Indici 740–885 using their former volume numbers, that is, numbers 10–150. However, the former numbering is still visible on the spines of Indici 740–885. Indice 1100 provides an overall view of Indici 740–885, which allows a researcher to easily note their uneven chronological progression and the different catagories of business indexed.

ASV Indici 740–885 employ a number of different indexing methods, including rubrics that provide page-by-page summaries of documents in selected *Indulgentiae perpetuae* volumes and classified subject-based indici (e.g., de Camera Apostolica, de Monialibus, de Ordinibus Militaribus, etc.). These indici, which cover the years 1554–1872, also provide access to selected material from the registers in the following Secretaria Brevium series: *Sec. Brev., Indulgentiae ad tempus, Indulta personalia, Altare privilegiatum ad tempus,* and *Altare privilegiatum perpetuum.*

Registers do not appear in strict numerical order in the indici, but rather in a rough chronological order. Therefore, there are several steps to follow in order to determine if an Indulgentiae perpetuae volume is included in these indici. First, armed with a date, one can proceed to Indice 1100, which provides a list of Indici 731–885, and learn which of Indici 731–885 cover the period and type of business sought. One can then select from Indici 740–885 the volumes containing rubrics or subject indici to registers whose chronological span encompasses one's desired dates. Entries in these indici extract from some *Indulgentiae* registers the folowing information: the name of the diocese, recipient, nature of the business, and the folio number. Note that *Indulgentiae perpetuae* material is also found in the Sec. Brev. series *Sec. Brev.* (in the subseries Diversorum). For a complete list of *Indulgentiae perpetuae* volumes consult Indici 1098–1099 and 127 (old number, cf. above).

Chronological coverage of Indici 740–885 for *Indulgentiae perpetuae series* (old vol. numbers are still visible on spines) is as follows: vol. 27 (1605–1610), vol. 28 (1605–1623), vol. 61 (1724–1769), vol. 116 (1769–1787), vol. 118 (1769–1803), vol. 120 (1788–1792), vol. 121 (1793–1798), vol. 131 (1800–1803), vol. 139 (1824–1830), and senza numero (1831–1839).

When using ASV Indici 740–885 the following caveats apply: (1) Indice 740, entitled on the spine, "Cedul. Consi. Martin V–Clement VIII," is actually a liber taxarum, organized alphabetically by diocese. This volume covers several centuries and is not useful as an index to this series. (2) Most of the rubrics in Indici 740–885 bear later annotations to current volume numbers. In the indexes to earlier volumes (1554–1723), references in the rubrics without these modern annotations could not be traced and presumably correspond to lost volumes. In later volumes, after 1723, items in both the rubrics and the classified indexes without annotations could often be located in volumes covering the month cited in the indice. However, the part ("pars prima," etc.) and the page numbers are usually incorrect. (3) Pásztor (1983) refers to these indici as "Liber Sussidiario." He also notes that the titles on these indici are not precise, for example, cedole concistoriale can be located in the indici entitled "Bullarum." (4) After 1872, the indici described below (nomi, diocesi, registro di cassa), provide the best access.

The second floor of the ASV Sala d'Indici houses three more sets of indici to the *Indulgentiae perpetuae*. These are "Nomi" (1834–1926); "Diocesi" (1869–1922); and "Registro di Cassa della Segreteria de Breve" (1845–1897). After 1878, these indici provide the only means of access to the following Sec. Brev. series: *Sec. Brev.*, *Indulgentiae ad tempus*, *Indulgentiae perpetuae*, *Indulta personalia*, *Altare privilegiatum ad tempus*, and *Altare privilegiatum perpetuum*. These sets of indici are straightforward to use. Desired information can be approached by name (personal or corporate), diocese, or date. Each of these sets gives a different protocol number, date, name, diocese, agent or referring congregation, and business (in some order). The essential pieces of information to note from all these registers are the dates and the type of business (e.g., appointment of an archbishop, altare priv., indulg.). From here, researchers should proceed to Indici 1098, 1099, and 127 to locate the current volume numbers.

Note: This series is continued by the Secretariatus Status series *Brevi apostolici*.

Location: Archivio Segreto Vaticano.

3.2.11.15 Indulta personalia

[DATABASE ID: VATV204-A]
Inclusive Dates: 1824–1908.
Bulk: 17 linear m. (236 vols.).
Organization: Chronological.
References: Fink, p. 77; Pásztor (1970), p. 119; Pásztor (1983), p. 151; Boyle, p. 66.
Finding Aids: ASV Indici 1098 (formerly Indice 35), 1099, and 127, "Inventario-prospetto della serie 'Sec. Brev.,'" by Mons. Pietro Guidi and Mons. Carlo Natalini, list volumes in the *Indulta personalia* and other Secretaria Brevium (abbreviated as Sec. Brev.) series: *Sec. Brev.*(a records series of the office of the Sec. Brev.), *Indulgentiae ad tempus*, *Indulgentiae perpetuae*, *Altare privilegiatum ad tempus*, and *Altare privilegiatum perpetuum*. Indice 1098 covers *Indulta personalia* vols. 1–23 (1824–1846). Indice 1099 covers *Indulta personalia* vols. 24–145 (1846–1878). Indice 127 (old number) is available at the desk in the main ASV reading room. The indice is not a formal finding aid and must be used in consultation with the archives staff. Indice 127 covers *Indulta personalia* vols. 146–236 (1878–1908). All of these indici give the following information for each volume: current number, inclusive dates, and business, as stated on the spine. These indici are of use to researchers tracing all volumes from a given year or papacy or looking for a current volume number.

ASV Indice 1100 is an introduction to ASV Indici 731–885, of which 740–885 are the primary analytical indexes for the series *Sec. Brev.* as well as its related series, such as *Indulta personalia*. Indice 1100 refers to Indici 740–885 using their former volume numbers, that is, numbers 10–150. However, the former numbering is still visible on the spines of Indici 740–885. Indice 1100 provides an overall view of Indici 740–885, which allows a researcher to easily note their uneven chronological progression and different categories of business indexed in 740–885.

ASV Indici 740–885 employ a number of different indexing methods, including rubrics that provide page-by-page summaries of documents in selected *Indulta personalia* volumes and classified subject-based indici (e.g., de Camera Apostolica, de Monialibus, de Ordinibus Militaribus, etc.). These indici, which cover the years 1554–1872, also provide access to selected material in the registers in the following Sec. Brev. series: *Sec. Brev.*, *Indulgentiae ad tempus*, *Indulgentiae perpetuae*, *Altare privilegiatum ad tempus*, and *Altare privilegiatum perpetuum*.

Registers do not appear in strict numerical order in the indici, but rather in a rough chronological order. Therefore, there are several steps to follow in order to determine if an *Indulta personalia* volume is included in these indici. First, armed with a date, one can proceed to Indice 1100, which provides a list of Indici 731–885, and learn which of Indici 731–885 cover the period and type of business sought. One can then select from Indici 740–885 the volumes containing rubrics or subject indici to registers whose chronological span encompasses one's desired dates. Entries in these indici extract the following information from some *Indulta* registers: the name of the diocese, recipient, nature of the business, and the folio number. Note that *Indulta personalia* material is also found in the Sec. Brev. series *Sec. Brev.* (in the subseries Diversorum). For a complete list of *Indulta personalia* volumes, consult Indici 1098, 1099, and 127 (cf. above).

When using ASV Indici 740–885 the following caveats apply: (1) Indice 740, entitled on the spine, "Cedul. Consi. Martin V–Clement VIII," is actually a liber taxarum, organized alphabetically by diocese. This volume covers several centuries and is not useful as an index to this series. (2) Most of the rubrics in Indici 740–885 bear later annotations to current volume numbers. In the indexes to earlier volumes (1554–1723), references in the rubrics without these modern annotations could not be traced and presumably correspond to lost volumes. In later volumes, after 1723, items in both the rubrics and the classified indexes without annotations could often be located in volumes covering the month cited in the indici. However, the part ("pars prima," etc.) and the page numbers are usually incorrect. (3) Pásztor (1983) refers to these indici as "Liber Sussidiario." He also notes that the titles on these indici are not precise, for example, cedole concistoriale can be located in indici entitled "Bullarum." (4) After 1872, the indici described below (nomi, diocesi, registro di cassa), provide the best access.

The second floor of the ASV Sala d'Indici houses three more sets of indici to the *Indulta personalia*. These are "Nomi" (1834–1926); "Diocesi" (1869–1922); and "Registro di Cassa della Segreteria de Breve" (1845–1897). After 1878, these indici provide the only means of access to the following Sec. Brev. series: *Sec. Brev.*, *Indulgentiae ad tempus*, *Indulgentiae perpetuae*, *Indulta personalia*, *Altare privilegiatum ad tempus*, and *Altare privilegiatum perpetuum*. These sets of indici are straightforward to use. Desired information can be approached by name (personal or corporate), diocese, or date. Each of these sets gives a protocol number, date, name, diocese, agent or referring congregation, and business (in some order). The essential pieces of information to note from all these registers are the dates and the type of business (e.g., appointment of an archbishop, altare priv., indulg.). From here, researchers should proceed to Indici 1098, 1099, and 127, to locate the current volume numbers.

Note: This series is continued by the Secretariatus Status series *Brevi apostolici*.

Location: Archivio Segreto Vaticano.

3.2.11.16 Liber brevium: Exactorum incipiens a principio
[DATABASE ID: VATV10217-A]
Inclusive Dates: 1586–1843.
Bulk: 5 linear m. (79 vols.).
Organization: Chronological.
Scope: These registers list month and year, page number, business (facultas, dispensatio, privilegio, electio, etc.), recipient, and cost.
References: Pásztor (1983), p. 149. Pásztor identifies this series as "Libri di Cassa," along with the Secretaria Brevium series *Registro di cassa* (1845–1897) and *Cassa: Volumi* (1898–1908).
Location: Archivio Segreto Vaticano.

3.2.11.17 [Miscellanea SF/269]
[DATABASE ID: VATV10228-A]
Inclusive Dates: 1319 (copy)–1922.
Bulk: 2 linear m. (16 boxes).
Organization: Titles include: Ricerche d'archivio, 1319(copy)–1922; —Formulari per minute di brevi, [17—]–1908; —Oratori privati, Indulgenze, tasse, [17—]–1908; —Dignita ecclesiastica (minute norme), ca. 1850–1905; —Misc. stampate, ca. 1755–1900.
Note: This series does not have an official ASV designation. The title was supplied by the project staff based on the location of the material in the ASV in 1990.
Location: Archivio Segreto Vaticano.

3.2.11.18 [Miscellanea, financial records]
[DATABASE ID: VATV532-A]
Inclusive Dates: 1790–1852.
Bulk: 15 linear m.
Organization: The series includes: Entrata ed uscita della Segreteria dei brevi, 1790–1852, 18 buste; —Ruoli degli officiali della Segreteria dei brevi, 1814–1816, 1 vol.; —Uscita di cassa della Segreteria dei brevi, 1814–1823, 5 buste; —Uscita di cassa della Segreteria dei brevi concernante sovrani, benigni, rescritti e pensioni di diverse impiegati, 1814, 1 busta; —Uscita di cassa concernante conti e sovrani . . . 1816–1820; —Memoriali de' poveri delle parrocchie per la somministrazione di scudo, 1814, 1816, 2 buste; —Rolli ed assegnamente quietanzati, 1822, 1 busta; —Filza di giustificazione, 1775–1791, 5 buste; —Proviste, misc., 1865–1870, 1.5 linear m.; —Registro di cassa per le bolle, 1744–1805, 1 vol. (formerly *Sec. Brev.* 82); —Stato delle doti giacenti conferite dalla Segreteria di brevi a tutto l'anno 1869, 1 vol.; —[Doti, natale e pasqua], 1870–1893, 1 vol.; —Doti, 1870–1908, 2 vols.; —Introito di cassa, 1843–1882, 3 vols.; —Registro di cassa, 1883–1891, 9 vols.; —Libertà eguaglianza . . . Entrata ed uscita de brevi, 1798–1801, 1 vol.; —[correspondence register?], 1845–1868, 1 vol.; —Conto de sopraranzi degli esercizi e ritenuta delle giub., 1845–1854, 1 vol.; —Tassa: Registro di cassa, 1852–1881, 1 vol.; —Registro degli esercizi, 1869–1877, 1 vol.; —Giornale delle tasse esercizi giubilarioni doti, 1878–1891. 1 vol.; —Cassa esercizi, 1891–1904, 13 vols.; —Cassa S. Santità, 1878–1908, 14 vols.; —Esercizi-Conto tassa, 1878–1904, 1 vol.; —Giornale dalle cassa esercizi: Giubilizione e doti, 1869–1877, 1 vol.; —Fondo di riserva, 1875–1896, 2 vols.; —Gratificazioni, 1880–1904, 1 vol.; —Giubilazioni, 1878–1904, 2 vols.; —Conto giubilazioni e pensioni, 1869–1877, 1

vol.; —Doti conferite da natale, 1869–1870, 1877; —Rubrica: Registro di scritture del Comm. Belli, 1897–1903, 1 vol.; —Informazioni, 1833–1854, 2 vols.; —Recueil des privileges et des indulgences à l'usage des filles de la charité (printed) Paris, 1860, 1 vol.; —Registro degli advertatur, 1836–1858.
Note: This series does not have an official ASV designation. The title was supplied by the project staff.
Location: Archivio Segreto Vaticano.

3.2.11.19 Registro degli esercizi per i brevi d'indulgenza
[DATABASE ID: VATV10222-A]
Inclusive Dates: 1845–1904.
Bulk: 2.5 linear m.
Organization: Chronological.
Scope: These registers contain the following format: number, date, diocese-city-religious order, name of postulant, type of grace, and cost.
Location: Archivio Segreto Vaticano.

3.2.11.20 Registro della corrispondenza epistolare della Segreteria dei Brevi
[DATABASE ID: VATV531-A]
Inclusive Dates: 1892–1908.
Bulk: .06 linear m. (2 vols.).
Organization: Alphabetical.
Scope: These volumes could possibly be used to access later materials in the Sec. Brev. although numerous other indici are available in the ASV Sala d'Indici. This register presents the number, postulant, diocese, request, date of the letter of request, the object of the letter, the date of the reply, observations, and the agent.
Location: Archivio Segreto Vaticano.

3.2.11.21 Registro di cassa della Segreteria dei Brevi
[DATABASE ID: VATV10218-A]
Inclusive Dates: 1845–1897.
Bulk: 2 linear m. (53 vols.).
Organization: Chronological by date of brief.
Scope: These financial records are located in the ASV Sala d'Indici and can be used as indexes to later volumes in the Secretaria Brevium series: Sec. Brev., *Indulta personalia, Altare privilegiatum ad tempus, Altare privilegiatum perpetuum, Indulgentiae ad tempus,* and *Indulgentiae perpetuae.* The registers list the numerical order of the brief, date of brief, agent, postulant, diocese, and object of the transaction. To use these registers as an index, the date is the vital piece of information to record.
References: Pásztor (1983), p. 149. Pásztor identifies this series as "Libri di Cassa" along with the Secretaria Brevium series *Liber brevium: Exactorum* (1586–1843) and *Cassa: Volumi* (1898–1908).
Location: Archivio Segreto Vaticano.

3.2.11.22 Rescritti
[DATABASE ID: VATV10226-A]
Inclusive Dates: 1823–1898.
Bulk: 8 linear m. (60 boxes)
Organization: Chronological.
References: Pásztor (1983), p. 152.
Location: Archivio Segreto Vaticano.

3.2.11.23 Secretaria brevium (often referred to as Sec. Brev.)

[DATABASE ID: VATV201-A]

Inclusive Dates: 1554–1908 (bulk 1561–1907).

Bulk: 500 linear m. (6218 numbered vols.).

Organization: Primarily chronological, proceeding pontificate by pontificate. Individual volumes within each pontificate are not in strict chronological order. The volumes of the five subseries are intermingled. Volumes in the subseries 2–5, listed below, are usually grouped among the final volumes of each pontificate.

Subseries include: 1. Brevium, 1554–1908; —2. Bullarium, 1572–1907; —3. Cedulae concistoriales, 1561–1907; —4. Diversorum, 1566–1907; —5. Matrimoniorum, 1566–1907.

Sec. Brev. 21 is now part of the Secretariatus Epistolae ad Principes et Optimates series [*Registri*] *Viros et Alios.*

Scope: MacFarlane notes that as the main collection of briefs of the Secretariat (brevia secreta), these have filed with them many of the documents that relate to the briefs themselves. Thus original supplications or copies of supplications, drafts of briefs and original briefs are also included with the main body of entries. Although some briefs are quasi-political in content, the majority are devoted to purely ecclesiastical matters and are comparable to the Dataria Apostolica series *Brevia Lateranensia.*

It also appears that the Secretariat of Briefs (also abbreviated as Sec. Brev.) provided services to certain offices (e.g., briefs issued by the Propaganda Fide went through Sec. Brev.), so it may be possible to augment one's knowledge of mission territories through this office (i.e., United States, Central and South America, Asia, Africa). The cedole concistoriali are related to the conferring of concistorial benefices. According to Pásztor (1973, p. 210) there are two types of cedole and there is also a controcedole concistoriale. The relationship between the two types of cedole and the controcedole of the vicecancelleria is an unsolved question. It appears from Pásztor (p. 14) that the controcedole, which served as the basis for bulls conferring consistorial benefices, are less informative than the cedole, which communicate the consistorial decision to confer the benefice. ASV Indice 753, "Index Brevium Greg. XIII," notes that there are many permissions for liturgical and quasi liturgical acts (e.g., nuns can pray the rosary instead of the office, a marchionessa can hear Mass at home and can have an indulgence for a chapel in her house). ASV Index 763, "Indulgentiarum," notes many permissions given to confraternities, religious orders, and oratories; after the name of the recipient some index entries specify "indulgentia"; others do not specify anything.

For additional information on the scope of this series, see the note by Guidi at beginning of ASV Indice 1098. Note in particular the miscellaneous contents of *Sec. Brev.*: briefs, minutes, original supplications, and so forth.

Many sixteenth-century letters from this series have been published by Father Josef Metzler in *America pontificia primi saeculi evangelizationis 1493–1592: Documente pontificia ex registris et minutis praesertim in Archivio Secreto Vaticano existentibus* (Vatican City, 1991). These include: annulments of licenses to return from American provinces obtained by false pretext; licenses to bishops to ordain priests with no benefice or income; requests to bishops to protect native converts from soldiers; indulgences to support Jesuit efforts; declaration that Dominicans do not need episcopal license to establish founda-

tions in the Americas; confirmations of donations to religious; exhortations to spread the faith; dispensations from the impediment of consanguinity for native converts (Incas); authorization for an investigation into a bishop's alleged concubinage and simony; license for burying poor persons in the church of a confraternity; prohibition against secular legal intervention; absolution for a native Mexican who married after professing religious vows; license for a Dominican friar to leave Mexico in order to carry out the work of evangelization in the Philippines and China; licenses for trade with infidels; and approval of the transformation of a failing religious house into a hospice for the poor in Panama.

The same general categories of business are also found in the *Sec. Brev.* for Europe, for example, licenses, dispensations, absolutions, indulgences, and confirmations relating to religious foundations, chapels, and churches.

References: Fink, pp. 76–78; Pásztor (1970), pp. 115–118; Pásztor (1983), pp. 147–151; Boyle, p. 66; MacFarlane, p. 85. Lajos Pásztor, "Le cedole concistoriali," *Archivum historiae pontificiae* 11 (1973): 209–268. B. Barbiche, ed., *Correspondance du nonce en France, Innocenzo del Bufalo, évêque de Camerino, 1601–1604* (Rome, 1964).

Finding Aids: ASV Indici 1098 (formerly Indice 35), and 1099 "Inventario-prospetto della serie 'Sec. Brev.,'" by Mons. Pietro Guidi and Mons. Carlo Natalini, are partial lists of volumes in the following Sec. Brev. series: *Sec. Brev., Indulgentiae ad tempus, Indulgentiae perpetuae, Indulta personalia, Altare privilegiatum ad tempus,* and *Altare privilegiatum perpetuum.* Indice 1098 covers *Sec. Brev.* vols. 1–5094 (1554–1846) and also contains separate compilations of all Cedulae Concistoriales and Bullarium volumes, as well as a table and concordanze to the former and current ennumeration of selected volumes. Indice 1099 covers *Sec. Brev.* vols. 5075–5737 (1831–1878). Both indici give the following information for each volume: current number, inclusive dates, pontifical year/volume, and business, as stated on the spine. These indici are of use to researchers who want to know all the volumes of a given year or papacy, or who are following up older citations which only list the pontifical year and volume.

ASV Indice 127 (old number), "Prospetto dei registri," is available at the desk in the main ASV reading room. The indice is not a formal finding aid and must be used in consultation with the archives staff. This prospectus covers *Sec. Brev.* vols. 5738–6218 (1879–1908) in the same manner as ASV Indici 1098 and 1099 (cf. above) and is primarily useful for locating current volume numbers. Note that *Sec. Brev.* volumes from the papacies of Leo X (pp. 1–25) and Pius X (pp. 25–28) are listed separately in Indice 127.

ASV Indice 315, "Index Brevm. Sixti, 1585 & 1586," provides some access to *Sec. Brev.* vols. 113–122. The entries are chronological by month. Within each month, the entries are alphabetical by type of business (absolutio, licentia, etc.). Information listed includes a concise summary of the brief, the recipient, and a folio number. This indice contains a number of alphabetical subject indexes (e.g., absolutio, indultum, suspensio) to selected *Sec. Brev.* documents covering 1585 and 1586. The only index in Indice 315 that is attributed in the actual volume is the one on page 58, which corresponds to *Sec. Brev.* 122. Pásztor (cf. above) states that pp. 1–40v of this indice correspond to *Sec. Brev.* 113–119, pp. 42–55 correspond to *Sec. Brev.* 113–119, and pp. 42–55 correspond to *Sec. Brev.* 120.

ASV Indice 1100 is an introduction to ASV Indice 731–885, of which 740–885 are the primary analytical indexes for the *Sec. Brev.* series. Indice 1100 refers to Indici 740–885 using their former volume numbers, that is, 10–150. However, the former numbering is still visible on the spines of Indici 740–885. Indice 1100 provides an overall view of Indici 740–885, which allows a researcher to easily note their uneven chronological progression and the different indexing methods as well as the various categories of business indexed in 740–885.

ASV Indici 740–885 employ a number of different indexing methods, including rubrics that provide page-by-page summaries of documents in selected *Sec. Brev.* volumes (including the major subseries Diversorum, Matrimonialiorum, Bullarum, and Brevium) and classified subject-based indici (e.g., de Camera Apostolica, de Monialibus, de Ordinibus Militaribus, etc.). These indici, which cover the years 1554–1872, also provide access to selected volumes of other series of the Secretaria Brevium: *Indulgentiae perpetuae, Indulta personalia, Altare privilegiatum ad tempus,* and *Altare privilegiatum perpetuum. Sec. Brev.* registers do not appear in strict numerical order in the indici, but rather in a rough chronological order. Therefore, there are several steps to follow in order to determine if a *Sec. Brev.* volume has a rubric in these indici. First, armed with a date, one can proceed to Indice 1100, which provides a list of Indici 731–885 and learn which of Indici 731–885 cover the period sought. One can then select from Indici 740–885 the volumes containing rubrics or subject indici to *Sec. Brev.* registers whose chronological span encompasses one's desired dates.

Entries in ASV Indici 740–885 extract the name of the diocese, recipient, nature of the business, folio number, from most *Sec. Brev.* registers. However, not all volumes are indexed here. For a complete list of *Sec. Brev.* volumes consult Indici 1098–1099 and 127 (old number, cf. above).

When using ASV Indici 740–885 the following caveats apply: (1) Indice 740, entitled on the spine, "Cedul. Consi. Martin V–Clement VIII," is actually a liber taxarum, organized alphabetically by diocese. This volume covers several centuries and is not useful as an index to the *Sec. Brev.* series. (2) Most of the rubrics in the earlier volumes (roughly to 1723) of Indici 740–885 bear later annotations to current *Sec. Brev.* volume numbers. References in the rubrics without these modern annotations could not be traced and presumably correspond to lost volumes. (3) The rubrics and classified indici from approximately 1723–1872 in Indici 740–885 rarely have annotations to the current volume numbers and therefore must be used in tandem with ASV Indici 1098, 1099, and 127 (old number). Citations to parts of volumes and page numbers in these latter indici are not reliable, although the desired item can usually be located somewhere in the *Sec. Brev.* volumes covering the month given in the indici. (4) Pásztor (1983) refers to these indici as "Liber Sussidiario." He also notes that the titles on these indice are not precise, for example, cedole concistoriale can be located in indice entitled "Bullarum." (5) After 1872, the indices described below (nomi, diocesi, registro di cassa), provide the best access to *Sec. Brev.* volumes, although Indici 1098, 1099, and 127 must still be consulted to locate.

ASV Indice 904, entitled on the spine "Curia Romana: Ricerche d'Archivio," is a subject-based index to materials on the Curia, papal offices, national colleges, and the like that can be located in *Sec. Brev.* registers between the dates of about 1550 and 1900. This index is itself an archival volume, as it lists office holders and the dates they held offices and indexes many bulls erecting congregations and offices. Later annotations for the current volume numbers have usually been annotated in Indice 904. If the citation simply gives a year and a liber number, researchers must consult Indice 1098, 1099, and 127 (old number, cf. above), to locate the current volume number. Before proceeding to Indici 1098, 1099, or 127, researchers should carefully note the type of document sought (e.g., bull, cedole), in order to select the appropriate *Sec. Brev.* series or subseries in which an item has been filed.

ASV Indici 905–909, entitled "Vescovadi—Recerche d'Archivio" on the spine, is an alphabetical listing (primarily according to diocese) of the appointment of bishops, apostolic vicars, and the like, between the years of about 1564 and 1774, which can be found in the *Sec. Brev.* series as well as its related subseries Cedulae, Bullarium, and so forth. Later annotations have usually been made to inform researchers of the current volume numbers of volumes cited in these indici. If only a year and liber number are given, researchers must consult ASV Indici 1098, 1099, and 127 (cf. above) to locate the current volume numbers. Before proceeding to Indici 1098, 1099, and 127, researchers should carefully note the type of document (e.g., bull, cedole, etc.), so that the appropriate *Sec. Brev.* series or subseries in which an item has been filed can be selected.

ASV Indici 898–903 index briefs concerning entrants into honorary papal military orders as follows: Indice 898 for Ordine di S. Gregorio Magno (1831–1868); Indici 899–901 for Cavalieri dello Speron d'Oro (1814–1867) [because Indice 901 is an index to Indici 899 and 900, the numbers listed refer to the "numero di ordine" and not to page numbers]; Indici 902–903 for Equestre Ordine Piano Adlegendo (1847–1868). Indice 903 is an index to Indice 902; in this case the numbers listed refer to page numbers. These indici should not be considered complete; indice 899 states "non credo sia completo."

This same information is indexed in Indici 740–885 under the category "de Ordinis Militaribus." Indici 898–903 do not list current volume numbers. It is prudent to recheck data from Indici 898–903 in Indici 740–885, and then proceed to Indici 1098, 1099, and 127 for the current volume numbers.

The second floor of the ASV Sala d'Indici houses three more sets of indici to the *Sec. Brev.* These are "Nomi" (1834–1926); "Diocesi" (1869–1922); and "Registro di Cassa della Segreteria de Breve" (1845–1897). These indici are described in this guide as separate series among the records of the Secretary of Briefs. After 1872, these indici provide the best means of access to the *Sec. Brev.* series, as well as the related series *Indulgentiae ad tempus, Indulgentiae perpetuae, Indulta personalia, Altare privilegiatum ad tempus,* and *Altare privilegiatum perpetuum.* These sets of indici are straightforward to use. Desired information can be approached by name (personal or corporate), diocese, or date. Each of these sets gives a protocol number, date, name, diocese, agent or referring congregation, and business. The essential pieces of information to note from all these registers are the dates and the type of business (e.g., appointment of an archbishop, altare priv., indulg.). Researchers should then proceed to Indici 1098, 1099, and 127 (old number, cf. above), to locate the current volume number of the volume that covers the appropriate time period and type of business. For *Sec. Brev.* registers between 1834 and 1878, researchers can also use Indici 740–885.

ASV Indice 114 (ff. 647v–649v), by Felice Contelori, provides a very sketchy recounting and selected extracts by type of business (erectio, confirmatio) from *Sec. Brev.* volumes between numbers 75 and 105.

Note: This series is continued by the Secretariatus Status series *Brevi apostolici.*

Location: Archivio Segreto Vaticano.

3.2.11.24 Specchio generale dell'Archivio delle indulgenze esistente nella Segreteria dei brevi
[DATABASE ID: VATV10233-A]

Inclusive Dates: 1574–1830.

Bulk: .05 linear m. (1 vol.).

Organization: Chronological.

Scope: This appears to be an inventory of volumes (dating from 1574 to 1830) concerning different types of indulgences existing in the office of the Segreteria dei Brevi in the latter nineteenth century.

Location: Archivio Segreto Vaticano.

3.2.11.25 Udienze
[DATABASE ID: VATV10227-A]

Inclusive Dates: 1852–1901.

Bulk: 1.5 linear m. (10 boxes).

Organization: Chronological.

Note: This series is cited as *Segreteria dei Brevi. Udienze.*

Location: Archivio Segreto Vaticano.

3.2.12 Secretariatus Epistolae ad Principes et Optimates
[DATABASE ID: VATV040-A]

It is difficult to trace the actual origin of this secretariat but it had its roots in the Secretaria Apostolica or College of Secretaries formally established by Innocent VIII (constitution *Non debet reprehensibile*, Dec. 31, 1487). One of these secretaries was always expressly charged with drawing up letters intended for princes, sovereigns, or persons of rank. It appears certain, however, that the office must have constituted a special section of the Segreteria Domestica of the popes from which it came, in time, to be separated, receiving finally an almost autonomous form through the constitution of Innocent XI (*Romanus Pontifex*, Apr. 1, 1678). On the other hand, even at the beginning of the second half of the sixteenth century a distinction had been made between the briefs to princes prepared in this department and the Latin letters compiled by the Secretariatus Litterae Latinae. We know this clearly from information noted by Giovanni Cargo (Oct. 26, 1574).

Besides the dispatch of official correspondence (letters in the form of briefs to princes) written in solemn form and in Latin between the Holy See and the sovereigns and foreign heads of state, this secretariat was responsible for the credentials for new papal representatives and the replies to the credentials presented by new diplomats credited to the Holy See.

It was also charged with the direct correspondence with members of reigning families as well as those letters which it is customary to send on special occasions or for particular events (ascent to the throne of sovereigns, sending of legates, of nuncios, and apostolic internuncios, baptism of princes, etc.). The secretariat also took care of those letters that the pope judged best handled without the intervention of diplomatic agents, especially in affairs of a political/religious nature. Prepared by the Secretariat of Briefs to Princes, all of these documents were sent, after papal approval, to the Secretariat of State for dispatch.

In addition to its ordinary functions, very often this office was also charged with preparing the addresses that the pope had to give in the consistories, the encyclicals directed to all the bishops of the world or to a great number of them, apostolic letters, some apostolic constitutions and motu proprios, and homilies for the canonization of saints.

Pius X (constitution *Sapienti consilio*, Jun. 29, 1908) joined the Secretariat of Briefs to Princes and the Secretariat of Latin Letters to form an office with dual responsibilities; but their functions continued as before. The Secretariat of Briefs to Princes originally had the faculty to grant matrimonial dispensations to heads of state and members of the royal families. With the curial reform of 1908, however, Pius X took the function of granting these dispensations to all the faithful without distinction and assigned it to the newly established Congregation for the Discipline of the Sacraments and to the Congregation of the Holy Office. Moreover, the third section of the Secretariat of State, which had been charged with the editing and the dispatch of apostolic briefs, absorbed all those functions which had been assigned to the Secretariat of Briefs to Princes by Benedict XIV (constitution *Gravissimum Ecclesiae*, Nov. 26, 1745). With these changes the secretariat lost almost all of its earlier importance.

The secretariat was presided over by a secretary of briefs to princes who was required by the nature of his task to be a proficient Latinist. To him was assigned also the task of announcing in Latin the solemn proclamation of new saints during the ceremonies of canonization and the *Oratio de eligendo Summo Pontifice* immediately after the celebration of the Mass of the Holy Spirit just before the opening of a conclave.

Paul VI's constitution *Regimini Ecclesiae universae* (Aug. 15, 1967) stated that the Apostolic Chancery was to be so arranged that there would be one single office for sending apostolic letters. He also noted that the Secretariat for Briefs to Princes and the Secretariat for Latin Letters were "to continue their function" until some other provision could be made. All documents are now handled in an office under the Secretariat of State.

Note that epistolae were used for routine letters in Latin, unlike the brevia (of the series *Brevia ad principes et alios viros*), which was used for special occasions.

References. A. Bacci, "Segreteria dei brevi ai principi," in *Enciclopedia cattolica* (Vatican City, 1953), vol. 11, pp. 247–248. A. Kraus, "Das päpstliche Staatssekretariat im Jahre 1623: Eine Denkschrift des ausscheidenden Sostituto an den neuernannten Staatssekretär," *Römische Quartalschrift für christliche Altertumskunde und für Kirchengeschichte* 52 (1957): 93–122. A. Kraus, *Das päpstliche Staatssekretariat unter Urban VIII., 1623–1644* (Rome, 1964). A. Kraus, "Zur Geschichte des päpstlichen Staatssekretariats: Quellenlage und Methode," *Jahresbericht der Görres-Gesellschaft* (1957): 5–16. J. Motsch, ed., *Balduin von Luxemburg, Erzbischof von Trier, Kurfürst des Reiches 1285–1354: Festschrift aus Anlass des 700. Geburtsjahres* (Mainz, 1985). L. Nanni, ed., *Epistolae ad principes* (Vatican City, 1992–1994). L. Pásztor, "L'histoire de la curie romaine, problème d'histoire de l'Église," *Revue d'histoire ecclésiastique* 64 (1969): 353–366. L. Pásztor, "Per la storia degli Archivi della Curia Romana nell'epoca moderna: Gli archivi delle Segreterie dei Brevi ai Principi e delle Lettere Latine," in *Römische Kurie, kirchliche Finanzen, vatikanisches Archiv: Studien zu Ehren von Hermann Hoberg* (Rome, 1979), pp. 659–686. P. Richard, "Origine et développement de la secrétairerie de l'État apostolique, 1417–1823," *Revue d'histoire ecclésiastique* 11 (1910): 56–72, 505–529, 728–754. A. Serafini, "Le origini della pontificia Segretaria di Stato e la 'Sapienti consilio' del Pio X," *Apollinaris* 25 (1952): 165–239. R. Toupin, ed., *Correspondance du nonce en France, Giovanni Battista Castelli (1581–1583)* (Rome, 1967).

RECORDS. Records of the office consist of the following series.

3.2.12.1 Posizioni e minute
[DATABASE ID: VATV10092-A]
Inclusive Dates: 1609–1969 (bulk 1823–1969).
Bulk: 22 linear m. (216 numbered vols.).
Organization: Vols. 1–213 are chronological by year; within each year the material is divided into (a) Posizioni-cardinali and (b) Registrate-carte relative a lettere registrate nel registri. Vols. 214–216 cover the following years: vol. 214 (1609–1798), vol. 215 (1846–1861), vol. 216 (1862–1869).

Note the existence of vol. 2A, "Schediasmata autographa epistolarum. S.Pii V ann. I–III," which is listed in Indice 1069 before the full list of volumes. This volume is located in the Sala Cimelli and a photocopy is available behind the desk in the ASV.
Scope: These are incoming requests to the pope. This series interrelates with the responses in Secretariatus Epistolae ad Principes et Optimates series [*Registri*] *Viros et alios* and in the Secretariatus Litterae Latinae series *Epistolae Latine*, subseries Posizioni e minute. It is important to check all three of these series if a survey of all the possible types of requests is desired.

Note: Vols. 54–57, 137 are available on microfilm.
References: Boyle, p. 67, Pásztor (1970), pp. 121–122, Pásztor (1983), pp. 153–155, Natalini et al., p. 271. (All authors before Natalini identify this series as *Epistolae* [or *Epistulae*] *ad Principes*.)
Finding Aids: ASV Indice 1146 provides a good introduction to the organization and contents of the Epistolae ad Principes series [*Registri*] *Viros et alios* and *Posizioni e minute*. The index also lists each volume, inclusive dates of each, and pontificate. The Secretariatus Epistolae ad Principes et Optimates series [*Registri*] *Viros et alios*, vol. 296, lists the former arrangement of this series when it was combined with the Secretariatus Litterae Latinae series *Epistolae Latinae*, subseries Posizioni e minute.
Location: Archivio Segreto Vaticano.

3.2.12.2 [Registri] Viros et alios
[DATABASE ID: VATV10093-A]
Inclusive Dates: 1560–1809, 1814–1969 (bulk 1560–1915).
Bulk: 17 linear m. (297 numbered vols. and one unnumbered appendix).
Organization: These are chronological with case numbers that relate to the Secretariatus Epistolae ad Principes et Optimates series *Posizioni e minute*. Recipients are often listed in upper left corner.

Alphabetical indices usually are at the beginning of each year. The indices relate to the type of request followed by the diocese (e.g., Abbati Campidonensi or Archiepiscopo Salisburgensi). These indexes begin in the seventeenth century. Note that since individual years are often bound together, indices may be located throughout a volume. Vols. 1–294 are letters (1560–1915). Vol. 295 is incomplete (1915–1920). Vol. 296 contains two indices: 1. "Catalogo dell'archivio pontificio dei Brevi ad Principes e delle Lettere Latine dall'anno 1823" is an index to the former combined arrangement of Secretariatus Litterae Latinae records: *Epistolae Latinae* series, Posizioni e minute subseries; and the Secretariatus Epistolae ad Principes et Optimates series *Posizioni e minute*. 2. "Indice ad Att (a Epistolae ad Principes)."

Vol. 297 "Segretaria di Stato di Sua Santità (1915–[post-1922]): Registro della spedizione delle lettere pontificie (Brevi ai Principes e Lettere Latine)," is an appendix divided into four sections: 1. Lettere di augurio, 1886–1889; —2. Elenco degli atti piu importante di Leone XIII (a Epistolae ad Principes); —[sections 3 and 4, post-1922].
Scope: This series consists of registers of briefs, minutes, and letters, not only to princes but to cardinals, bishops, and papal nuncios, and is therefore of considerable value for the post-Reformation diplomatic history of the papacy.

These are letters originating at the invitation of the pope. Some materials are printed items including some encyclicals. Selected requests that stimulated these responses can be found by matching the case numbers with those in the Epistolae ad Principes series *Posizioni e minute*. This series interrelates with the responses in the Secretariatus Epistolae ad Principes et Optimates series *Posizioni e minute* and in the Secretariatus Litterae Latinae series *Epistolae Latinae*, subseries Posizioni e minute. It is important to check all three of these series if a survey of all the possible types of requests is desired. Alternative titles found on different spines of volumes in the series include: Minute, Lettere Latine, Minute e documenti, Minute di lettere pontificie con posizioni relative, Pontificis maximi litterae ad principes viros et alios, Brevi ad principes. Pásztor (1983, p.148), states that Sec. Brev. vol. 21 should be a part of this series. Since the publication of Pásztor's work, the volume has been transferred to this series. Also note that the Camera Apostolica series Armarium XXXV, vol. 34, is letters of princes.

The series is quite distinct from the Secretaria Apostolica series Armaria XLIV–XLV: Brevia ad principes et alios viros, with which it is often confused, since it bears the same general heading.

References: Fink, p. 79, Boyle, p. 67, Pásztor (1970), pp. 121–122, Pásztor (1983), pp. 153–155, Natalini et al., p. 271, MacFarlane, p. 85. (All authors before Natalini identify this series as Epistolae [or Epistulae] ad Principes.)

Finding Aids: ASV Indice 1069 provides an inventory giving the inclusive years covered by each volume, the exact title of each volume, and the name of the secretary responsible for each volume. At the beginning of this index, materials from the Epistolae ad Principes series Viros et alios that are part of the Archivio Rospigliosi in the ASV are listed briefly. At the end, volumes are listed according to pontificate and more details are given on the insertions in the volume.

ASV Indice 1128 to the Archivio Rospigliosi provides more information on the Epistolae ad Principes, Viros et alios materials briefly listed at the beginning of ASV Indice 1069. In addition to inclusive dates and exact title, Indice 1128 notes whether a volume is an original, its completeness, and its physical condition.

Location: Archivio Segreto Vaticano.

3.2.13 Secretariatus Litterae Latinae
[DATABASE ID: VATV041-A]

This secretariat, along with the Secretariat of Briefs to Princes, had its roots in the Secretaria Apostolica or College of Secretaries formally established by Innocent VIII (constitution Non debet reprehensibile, Dec. 31, 1487). The Secretaria Apostolica was composed of twenty-four secretaries and it was from this group that the Secretaries of Latin Letters came. With the passing of time the Secretaria Epistolarum Latinarum became a separate office We know this from information noted by Giovanni Cargo (Oct. 26, 1574).

Collaterally with the Secretariat of State, the Secretariat of Latin Letters had the task of handling in the Latin language the correspondence of lesser solemnity sent by the pope to persons of high position (cardinals, patriarchs, archbishops, bishops, religious superiors, rectors of Catholic universities, and other notable persons both ecclesiastical and lay) that did not come within the ordinary function of the Secretariat of State nor of the Secretariat of Briefs to Princes, nor of any other office. The pope could, however, use this secretariat for solemn documents if he wished (CIC 1917: canon 264). The Secretariat of Latin Letters, like that of Briefs to Princes, depended directly on the pope, who transmitted his orders either personally or through his cardinal secretary of state.

Pius X (constitution Sapienti consilio, Jun. 29, 1908) joined the Secretariat of Briefs to Princes and the Secretariat of Latin Letters to form an office with dual responsibilities, but their functions continued as before. In fact, although they were united in the 1917 Code of Canon Law (canon 264), they continued to be considered distinct by the Annuario Pontificio. The office of Latin letters was directed by a secretary. The College of Cardinals usually assigned to him the pronouncing of the Oratio de Pontifice Defuncto in the Vatican Basilica on the third day of the solemn funeral rites for a pope.

With Paul VI's constitution Regimini Ecclesiae universae (Aug. 15, 1967) the Secretariat of Latin Letters was made a part, as anticipated, of the Secretariat of State, from which it was able to separate itself for a short time as an automonous office. It was officially suppressed when Paul VI decreed that all documents were to be handled in an office under the Secretariat of State (motu proprio Quo aptius, Feb. 27, 1973).

References. H. Dessart, L. E. Halkin, and J. Hoyoux, "Inventaire analytique de documents relatifs à l'histoire du diocèse de Liège sous le régime des nonces de Cologne," vols. 2–6 of Analecta vaticano-belgica, ser. 2, section B, Nonciature de Cologne (Brussels, 1957–1962). A. Kraus, "Das päpstliche Staatssekretariat im Jahre 1623: Eine Denkschrift des ausscheidenden Sostituto an den neuernannten Staatssekretär," Römische Quartalschrift für christliche Altertumskunde und für Kirchengeschichte 52 (1957): 93–122. L. Pásztor, "Per la storia degli Archivi della Curia Romana nell'epoca moderna: Gli archivi delle Segreterie dei Brevi ai Principi e delle Lettere Latine," in Römische Kurie, kirchliche Finanzen, vatikanisches Archiv: Studien zu Ehren von Hermann Hoberg (Rome, 1979), pp. 659–686. A. Perugini, "Segreteria delle lettere latine," in Enciclopedia cattolica (Vatican City, 1953), vol. 11, p. 248.

RECORDS. Records of the office consist of the following series.

3.2.13.1 Epistolae Latinae
[DATABASE ID: VATV10094-A]
Inclusive Dates: 1823–1958.

Bulk: 23 linear m. (174 numbered vols.).

Organization: There are two subseries: [Registri], 1823–1890, 52 numbered volumes and one packet; —Posizioni e minute, 1823–1958, 22 vols.

Scope: Registri (subseries 1) is solely the response to the requests found in Posizioni e minute (subseries 2). The two subseries are linked by case numbers. Some Registri volumes also have indices, some of these are identified by Pásztor as "Index alphabeticus Litterarum Latinarum" (1839–1842). This series is interrelated with the Epistolae ad Principes series Posizioni e minute (with which it was once interfiled) and [Registri] Viros et alios. In order to locate the full range of papal responses to requests, all three series should be checked.

References: Fink, pp. 79–80; Pásztor (1970), pp. 126–127;

Pásztor (1983), pp. 158–160; Boyle, p. 68; Natalini et al., p. 271.

Finding Aids: ASV Indice 1148 provides an excellent introduction to the organization of the series, the way in which this correspondence was treated, and the archivists' organizational notes. The indice then gives a volume by volume inventory with inclusive dates, whether the volume is indexed, and the full title of each volume.

Vol. 296 in the Secretariatus Epistolae ad Principes et Optimates series [*Registri*] *Viros et alios* is a catalog of this series in its former arrangement, when it was intermingled with the Epistolae ad Principes series *Posizioni e minute.*

Many of the Registri volumes contain contemporary indices. Pásztor (see below) identifies these for the years 1839–1842 as "Index alphabeticus Litterarum Latinarum."

Pásztor also cites a series of "Index epistularum" for the years 1825–1838, 1840, and 1843. These are also found in the actual Registri volumes.

This series is referred to by Boyle, Pásztor, and others, as *Litterae latine.*

Location: Archivio Segreto Vaticano.

3.2.14 Secretariatus Status (often referred to as SS)
[DATABASE ID: VATV035-A]

The need of the sovereign pontiff for more frequent, prompt, and secret correspondence gave rise to new offices outside the Apostolic Chancery. Among these, in the time of Martin V (1417–1431), were the Camera Secreta, including a number of secretaries, and the Secretaria Apostolica for official correspondence in Latin.

For a time there was no limit to the number of these secretaries a pope could appoint. However, Callistus III (constitution *Decet Romanum Pontificem*, May 7, 1456) restricted the number to six. As a result they came to be called secretarii numerarii. Sixtus IV (1471–1484) called the chief of these Episcopus ac Superior Officio Secretariatus. Innocent VIII (constitution *Non debet reprehensibile*, Dec. 31, 1487) defined the functions of the Secretaria Apostolica and extended the number of secretaries to twenty-four, one of whom was known as the secretarius domesticus, because he lived in the pope's residence. To the Secretaria Apostolica can be traced the Chancery of Briefs, the Secretariat of Briefs to Princes and the Secretariat of Latin Letters.

The office of secretarius intimus (private secretary) was entrusted by Leo X (1513–1521) to Pietro Ardighello, an assistant to Cardinal Giulio de' Medici (the future Clement VII [1523–1534] and a cousin of Leo X), who took over the direction of foreign affairs dealing with all correspondence in the vernacular, especially with the apostolic nuncios who were entrusted by that time with diplomatic missions of a permanent character. The correspondence was carried on in the name but no longer under the signature of the pope. So began what has evolved into the modern Secretariat of State.

The office was subsequently directed by the cardinal nephew acting in his capacity as the prime minister of the pope, and thus gradually developed as an office of considerable power and influence, especially during the period of the Council of Trent (1545–1563).

The secretarius intimus, who was also known as the secretary of the pope, or major secretary (secretarius papae/maior) was nearly always invested with episcopal rank. In order to ensure for themselves a greater freedom of action and protection from the pressure of the other cardinals, the popes began to entrust their secretarial work to a prelate chosen from among their own relations and known as the cardinalis-nepos (cardinal nephew). Only at the beginning of the pontificate of Innocent X (1644) was this high office entrusted to a person already a cardinal and not a member of the family of the pope. The appointment of Giangiacomo Panciroli to this office (perhaps the first time the title secretary of state was used on official stationery) together with the later suppression of the Collegio dei Segreteri Apostolici by Innocent XI (constitution *Romanus Pontifex*, Apr. 1, 1678) were the first signs of the organization of the Secretariat of State in the modern sense of the term.

Later, Innocent XII (constitution *Romanum decet Pontificem*, Jun. 22, 1692) ordered the complete abolition of nepotism and the consequent elimination of the office of cardinal nephew, which had been extended to include the general superintendence of the Papal States. As a result of this action the office of the Secretariat of State became a reality with a cardinal at the head with the affirmed title of secretary of state. This office would centralize the direction of all political affairs, both internal and external, of the Holy See.

The direction assumed by the Secretariat of State by the end of the seventeenth century was maintained unchanged throughout the eighteenth and remained substantially the same even after the restoration of the Papal States in 1814. However, some restructuring occurred as when (Aug. 3, 1814) Carlo Mauri was named sostituto and absorbed, along with his other responsibilities, the tasks of the segretario della cifra. Pius IX later (1847) established the segretario della cifra.

Gregory XVI, finding it a burden for one secretary to handle both internal and external affairs, directed a chirograph (Feb. 20, 1833) to the cardinal secretary of state instituting a Segreteria per gli Affari di Stato Interni. The new secretariat was defined as "the organ of communication for the various ministers and dicasteries of the State of all the orders relative to internal affairs." This change was of short duration. Pius IX (Aug. 1, 1846) suppressed the new office and, though retaining the two divisions of the secretariat, reunited the two offices once again under one person. Pius IX's motu proprio of December 29, 1847, named the cardinal secretary of state president of the Consiglio dei Ministri and ministro degli affari esteri. This last task was relinquished when the Ministero degli Affari Esteri was transferred to lay hands.

With the loss of the territories of the Papal States and the concurrent curtailment of the temporal power of the pope in 1870, the power and range of activities of the office of the Secretariat of State inevitably declined. The office adjusted itself quickly to the change of direction, but was not freed from some confusion until Pius X gave it a new form.

Pius X (constitution *Sapienti consilio*, Jun. 29, 1908) divided the Secretariat of State into three sections. This form was incorporated into the 1917 Code of Canon Law (canon 263). The three sections were: (1) extraordinary ecclesiastical affairs, presided over by the secretary of the Congregation for Extraordinary Ecclesiastical Affairs, who handled questions related to civil laws and concordats concluded between the Holy See and civil governments; (2) ordinary affairs under the direction of the sostituto (substitute) who directed correspondence with the nuncios and legates, prepared the nomination of members of the Roman Curia approved by the pope, replied to messages of loyalty and congratulation sent to the pope, expedited the bestowal of pontifical honors and distinctions on clerics and lay persons, had the custody and use of the cipher reserved for secret messages, and handled the appointments to the papal diplomatic corps; and (3) dispatches, documents, or briefs related to the business of the Secretariat of State, under the direction of the chancellor for apostolic briefs, who compiled and transcribed the final drafts of papal briefs. The document stipulated that the cardinal secretary of state be the "supreme moderator" of the Secretariat of State, namely, of the three sections.

Formerly the cardinal secretary of state was only a member of the Congregation for Extraordinary Ecclesiastical Affairs, leaving the senior cardinal present with more weight in the discussions than the secretary. In July 1925 Pius XI changed this. In a letter to Cardinal Pietro Gasparri he gave the cardinal secretary of state the title of prefect of the Congregation for Extraordinary Ecclesiastical Affairs.

Pius XII initiated a still broader development of the Secretariat of State, but dispensed altogether with a cardinal secretary of state during the last fourteen years of his pontificate (1944–1958), serving as his own secretary of state and leaving the heads of the first two of the three sections of the secretariat jointly in charge. John XXIII (motu proprio *Boni Pastoris*, Feb. 22, 1959) ordered that the Pontifical Commission for Motion Pictures, Radio, and Television be joined to the Secretariat of State as an office of the Holy See.

Paul VI (motu proprio *In fructibus*, Apr. 2, 1964) extended the scope of the Pontifical Commission for Motion Pictures, Radio, and Television to include the press; changed its name to the Pontifical Commission for the Media of Social Communications; and defined its functions, including that of assisting the bishops in developing the pastoral use of these media. In his reorganization of the Roman Curia on August 15, 1967 (constitution *Regimini Ecclesiae universae*), based on the recommendations of the Roberti Commission, the Secretariat of State was assigned a coordinating role among the congregations. The pope also defined as the major role of the secretariat that of assisting the pope in his care of the universal church. The Congregation for Extraordinary Ecclesiastical Affairs was replaced by the Council for the Public Affairs of the Church to deal with civil governments, including the supervision of papal legates. The cardinal prefect of the Council for the Public Affairs of the Church and the papal secretary of state were required to be the same person. The Secretariat of State and the Council for the Public Affairs of the Church were to supervise jointly the Pontifical Commission for the Media of Social Communications.

Quo aptius (motu proprio, Feb. 27, 1973) dissolved the Apostolic Chancery as a separate curial department and transferred its functions to the Secretariat of State's third section under the direction of the Chancery of Apostolic Letters. The Secretariat exercises supervision over the government of the Vatican City State and the publication of the Acta Apostolicae Sedis and the Annuario Pontificio (official yearbook). The General Statistics Office for the Church is also subordinate to it. It has the power to grant diplomatic and service passports issued under the name of the cardinal secretary of state, and identification cards for all the officers of the Curia.

Pope John Paul II in the apostolic constitution *Pastor bonus* (Jun. 28, 1988) ordered modifications of the Curia based on the broad outline of Paul VI's reorganization. The Secretariat of State now has two sections: (1) General Affairs, which assists the pope in expediting the daily business of the Holy See; coordinates curial operations; prepares drafts of documents entrusted to it by the pope; has supervisory duties over the Acta Apostolicae Sedis and the Annuario Pontificio, the Vatican Press Office, and the Central Statistics Office; and (2) Relations with States (formerly the Council for the Public Affairs of the Church, a separate body), which handles diplomatic and other relations with civil governments. The Pontifical Commission for Russia is also attached to the secretariat. A special group of fifteen cardinals offers advice to the Secretariat of State on financial matters related to the Vatican. The cardinal secretary of state is one of the palatine cardinals.

The Congregatio pro Negotiis Ecclesiasticis Extraordinariis has been associated with the Secretariat of State. See the agency history for that congregation for more information.

The records of the Secretariat of State constitute the largest section of the ASV. Taken as a whole the records amount to 4,900 linear meters.

In addition to the records listed below, series listed

with other agencies relate directly to this agency and should be consulted. See Miscellaneous official series *Miscellaneorum armarium I*, *Miscellaneorum armarium II*, and *Miscellaneorum armarium III*; Secretaria Brevium series *Brevi originali*; Congregazione di Vigilanza (Papal States) series [*Archivio*]; and Consiglio Centrale di Censura (Papal States) series *Consiglio centrale di censura* (1849–1878).

References. J. Gelmi, *La Segreteria di Stato sotto Benedetto XIV* (Trent, 1975). L. Hammermayer, "Grundlinien der Entwicklung des päpstlichen Staatssekretariats von Paul V. bis Innozenz X., 1605–1655," *Römische Quartalschrift für christliche Altertumskunde und für Kirchengeschichte* 55 (1960): 157–202. A. Kraus, "Die Aufgaben eines Sekretärs zur Zeit Urbans VIII (1623)," *Römische Quartalschrift für christliche Altertumskunde und für Kirchengeschichte* 53 (1958): 89–92. A. Kraus, "Das päpstliche Staatssekretariat im Jahre 1623: Eine Denkschrift des ausscheidenden Sostituto an den neuernannten Staatssekretär," *Römische Quartalschrift für christliche Altertumskunde und für Kirchengeschichte* 52 (1957): 93–122. A. Kraus, *Das päpstliche Staatssekretariat unter Urban VIII., 1623–1644* (Rome, 1964). A. Kraus, "Secretarius und Sekretariat: Der Ursprung der Institution des Staatssekretariats und ihr Einfluss auf die Entwicklung moderner Regierungsformen in Europa," *Römische Quartalschrift für christliche Altertumskunde und für Kirchengeschichte* 55 (1960): 43–84. R. Naz, "Secretaire d'État," and "Secretairie d'État," in *Dictionnaire de droit canonique*, edited by R. Naz (Paris, 1960–1961), vol. 7, pp. 899–900 and 901–904. L. Pásztor, "L'Archivio della Segretaria di Stato tra il 1833 e il 1847," *Annali della Scuola speciale per archivisti e bibliotecari dell'Università di Roma* 10 (1970): 104–148. L. Pásztor, "La classificazione delle carte della Segreteria di Stato tra il 1833 e il 1847," in *Miscellanea in memoria di Giorgio Cencetti* (Turin, 1973), pp. 639–663. L. Pásztor, "L'histoire de la curie romaine, problème d'histoire de l'Église," *Revue d'histoire ecclésiastique* 64 (1969): 353–366. L. Pásztor, "Per la storia della Segreteria di Stato nell'Ottocento: La riforma del 1816," in *Mélanges Eugène Tisserant* (Vatican City, 1964), vol. 5, pp. 209–272. L. Pásztor, "La Segretaria di Stato di Pio IX durante il triennio 1848–1850," *Annali della Fondazione italiana per la storia amministrativa* 3 (1966): 308–365. P. Richard, "Origine et développement de la secrétairerie de l'État apostolique, 1417–1823," *Revue d'histoire ecclésiastique* 11 (1910): 56–72, 505–529, 728–754. G. Schreiber, "Das päpstliche Staatssekretariat," *Historisches Jahrbuch* 79 (1960): 175–198. J. Semmler, "Beiträge zum Aufbau des päpstlichen Staatssekretariats unter Paul V (1605–1621)," *Römische Quartalschrift für christliche Altertumskunde und für Kirchengeschichte* 54 (1959): 40–80. This article is continued by J. Semmler, *Das päpstliche Staatssekretariat in den*

Pontifikaten Pauls V. und Gregors XV., 1605–1623 (Rome, 1969). A. Serafini, "Le origini della pontificia Segretaria di Stato e la 'Sapienti consilio' del Pio X," *Apollinaris* 25 (1952): 165–239. W. van der Steen and K. Meerts, *Belgie in het Vaticaans Archief: Staatssecretariaat (rubriek 256), 1878–1903: Regestenlijst* (Louvain, 1989).

RECORDS. Records of the office consist of the following series.

3.2.14.1 Affari ecclesiastici
[DATABASE ID: VATV40009-A]
Inclusive Dates: 1797–1832.
Bulk: 120 buste.
Note: This series was cited in Natalini et al., p. 273, but not seen by project staff in 1990.
Location: Archivio Segreto Vaticano.

3.2.14.2 Aiuti per terremotati
[DATABASE ID: VATV10480-A]
Inclusive Dates: 1908–1915.
Bulk: 1 linear m. (8 buste and 1 box of index cards).
Location: Archivio Segreto Vaticano.

3.2.14.3 Anno Santo 1925
[DATABASE ID: VATV10548-A]
Inclusive Dates: 1924–1927.
Bulk: 25 linear m. (179 numbered buste and unnumbered miscellaneous items).
References: Fink, p. 126; Natalini et al., p. 265.
Location: Archivio Segreto Vaticano.

3.2.14.4 Anno Santo 1934
[DATABASE ID: VATV10549-A]
Inclusive Dates: 1933–1934.
Bulk: .25 linear m. (1 box).
Location: Archivio Segreto Vaticano.

3.2.14.5 Anno Santo 1950
[DATABASE ID: VATV10550-A]
Inclusive Dates: 1949–1951.
Bulk: 16 linear m. (112 numbered buste and some unnumbered miscellaneous items).
Reference: Natalini et al., p. 265.
Location: Archivio Segreto Vaticano.

3.2.14.6 Anno Santo 1975
[DATABASE ID: VATV40010-A]
Inclusive Dates: 1974–1976.
Bulk: 362 buste and fascicoli.
Note: This series was cited in Natalini et al., p. 265, but not seen by project staff in 1990.
Location: Archivio Segreto Vaticano.

3.2.14.7 Archivio degli commissioni soccorse
[DATABASE ID: VATV10503-A]
Inclusive Dates: [ca. 1949–ca. 1952].
Bulk: 16 linear m.
Location: Archivio Segreto Vaticano.

3.2.14.8 Archivio delle nunziature

[DATABASE ID: VATV164-A]

Inclusive Dates: ca. 1500–[19—].

Bulk: about 1,775 linear m.

Scope: The records generated by each delegation, internunciature, and nunciature constitute a substantial amount of material collectively known as the Archivio delle nunziature. Inactive records generated by a nunciature at its particular foreign location are required to be deposited in the ASV. These records constitute the Archivio delle nunziature. Because of the vast quantity of these records, they are described in a separate section in this guide. Note also that the Secretary of State office in the Vatican generates files on nunciatures as well. Nunciature material generated by the central office of the secretary is described within this section of this guide, under titles beginning *Nunziatura di. . . .*

3.2.14.9 Archivio di Mons. Antonio Riberi

[DATABASE ID: VATV10504-A]

Inclusive Dates: [ca. 1935–ca. 1940].

Bulk: 2 linear m.

Location: Archivio Segreto Vaticano.

3.2.14.10 Armarium XLVI

[DATABASE ID: VATV366-A]

Inclusive Dates: Not determined.

Bulk: 62 vols.

Summary: Boyle notes that these are copies of papal letters to the dukes of Ferrara (mostly fifteenth–sixteenth-century copies).

References: Fink, p. 32; Boyle, p. 39.

Finding Aids: ASV Indice 133 briefly lists summary titles of each volume. The index (compiled by Petrus De Pretis after 1741) is basically informative but often fails to note copies. The index also uses terms such as *regestrum* and *brevia* too inclusively and does not clearly note items that do not fit the basic thematic focus of each armarium, or which items are clearly from other offices.

ASV Indice 124, "Primo Sbozzo di Inventario di tutti i libri che sono nell'Archivio Segreto Vaticano," by Giovanni Bissaiga (1672), provides more descriptive and accurate volume titles for some armarium volumes. Select volume titles from *Armarium XLVI* are listed on folios 254r, 328r, 330r–332r, 333v–334r, and 335v–377v, and 378r. The exact titles listed in Indice 124 are sometimes provided in a footnote in ASV Indice 133, so researchers can see exactly how generic the titles in ASV Indice 133 can be.

Location: Archivio Segreto Vaticano.

3.2.14.11 Armarium XLVII

[DATABASE ID: VATV367-A]

Inclusive Dates: Not determined.

Bulk: 30 vols.

Scope: This is the Barrofaldi collection of documents concerning Ferrara.

Note: This collection has been transferred to the Vatican Library (Vat. Lat. 12576–12605).

References: Fink, p. 32; Boyle, p. 39.

Finding Aids: ASV Indice 133 briefly lists summary titles of each volume. The index (compiled by Petrus De Pretis after 1741) is basically informative but often fails to note copies. The index also uses terms such as *regestrum* and *brevia* too inclu-

sively and does not clearly note items that do not fit the basic thematic focus of each armarium, or which items are clearly from other offices.

Location: Biblioteca Apostolica Vaticana.

3.2.14.12 Armarium XLVIII

[DATABASE ID: VATV368-A]

Inclusive Dates: Not determined.

Bulk: 54 vols.

Scope: Boyle notes that these are largely copies of materials relating to Ferrara, Modena, Comacchio, and Reggio nell'Emilia.

References: Boyle, p. 39; Fink, p. 32.

Finding Aids: ASV Indice 133, briefly lists summary titles of each volume. The index (compiled by Petrus De Pretis after 1741) is basically informative but often fails to note copies. The index also uses terms such as *regestrum* and *brevia* too inclusively and does not clearly note items that do not fit the basic thematic focus of each armarium, or which items are clearly from other offices. Therefore, the volume titles presented in Indice 133 are not exact. There are also some inaccuracies in the more recently typed and written footnotes.

ASV Indice 124, "Primo Sbozzo di Inventario di tutti i libri che sono nell'Archivio Segreto Vaticano," by Giovanni Bissaiga (1672), provides more descriptive and accurate volume titles for some armarium volumes. Select volumes in *Armarium XLVIII* are listed on folios 283r, 329rv, 332v, 333r, and 335r. The exact titles listed in Indice 124 are sometimes provided in a footnote in ASV Indice 133, so researchers can see exactly how generic the titles in ASV Indice 133 are.

Location: Archivio Segreto Vaticano.

3.2.14.13 Armarium XLIX

[DATABASE ID: VATV369-A]

Inclusive Dates: Not determined

Bulk: 52 vols.

Scope: Boyle simply notes that this is material relating to various Italian cities.

Note: Vol. 47 is available on microfilm.

References: Fink, p. 32; Boyle, p. 39.

Finding Aids: ASV Indice 133 briefly lists summary titles of each volume. The index (compiled by Petrus De Pretis after 1741) is basically informative but often fails to note copies. The index also uses terms such as *regestrum* and *brevia* too inclusively and does not clearly note items that do not fit the basic thematic focus of each armarium, or which items are clearly from other offices.

ASV Indice 124, "Primo Sbozzo di Inventario di tutti i libri che sono nell'Archivio Segreto Vaticano," by Giovanni Bissaiga (1672), provides more descriptive and accurate volume titles for some armarium volumes. Select *Armarium XLIX* volumes are listed on folios 234r, 241r, 280v–281v, 305v, 306v, 327v, 337v, 363v, and 365v. The titles of these volumes are sometimes provided in a footnote in ASV Indice 133, so researchers can see just how generic the titles in ASV Indice 133 are.

Location: Archivio Segreto Vaticano.

3.2.14.14 Armarium LX

[DATABASE ID: VATV363-A]

Inclusive Dates: Not determined.

Bulk: 52 vols.

Scope: Boyle notes that these records are mainly copies relating to the dukedom of Urbino.

Note: According to Boyle, the records probably came to the ASV from Castel S. Angelo in 1614.

Note: Vols. 21 and 30 are available on microfilm.

References: Fink, p. 33; Boyle, p. 40.

Finding Aids: ASV Indice 133 briefly lists summary titles of each volume. The index (compiled by Petrus De Pretis after 1741) is basically informative but often fails to note copies. The index also uses terms such as *regestrum* and *brevia* too inclusively and does not clearly note items that do not fit the basic thematic focus of each armarium, or which items are clearly from other offices. Therefore, the titles presented in this index are not exact. There are also some inaccuracies in the later typed footnotes.

ASV Indice 124, "Primo Sbozzo di Inventario di tutti i libri che sono nell'Archivio Segreto Vaticano," by Giovanni Bissaiga (1672), provides more descriptive and accurate volume titles for some armarium volumes, such as *Armarium LX*, volumes 1–22 on folios 242r, 279v, 282rv, 327rv, 330r, 335r, and 337r. The exact titles listed in Indice 124 are sometimes provided in a footnote in ASV Indice 133, so researchers can see exactly how generic the titles in ASV Indice 133 are.

Location: Archivio Segreto Vaticano.

3.2.14.15 Armarium LXI

[DATABASE ID: VATV364-A]

Inclusive Dates: Not determined.

Bulk: 64 vols.

Scope: MacFarlane notes that the contents of *Armarium LXI* refer to the duchies of Parma and Piacenza. They are of interest for the history of the papal states and the temporal relations of the papacy with the duchies concerned, as also for the history of the late medieval German empire. Boyle notes that these records are mainly copies.

References: Fink, p. 33; Boyle, p. 40; MacFarlane, p. 35.

Finding Aids: ASV Indice 1158 lists all volumes in *Armarium LXI*. ASV Indice 133 briefly lists summary titles of each volume. The index (compiled by Petrus De Pretis after 1741) is basically informative but often fails to note copies. The index also uses terms such as *regestrum* and *brevia* too inclusively and does not clearly note items that do not fit the basic thematic focus of each armarium, or which items are clearly from other offices. Therefore, the volume titles presented are not very precise. There are also some inaccuracies in the more recently typed footnotes.

ASV Indice 124, "Primo Sbozzo di Inventario di tutti i libri che sono nell'Archivio Segreto Vaticano," by Giovanni Bissaiga (1672), provides more descriptive and accurate volume titles for some armarium volumes, such as *Armarium LXI*, volumes 1–22. What follows is a list of the current *Arm. LXI* volume numbers with the ASV Indice 124 folio and item number in parentheses vol. 1 (f. 324, n. 1); vol. 2 (f. 324, n. 2); vol. 3 (f. 324. no. 3); vol. 4 (f. 324, no. 4); vol. 5 (f. 324v, no. 5); vol. 6 (f. 324v, no. 6); vol. 7 (f. 325v, no. 7); vol. 8 (f. 325v, no. 8); vol. 9 (f. 325, no. 9); vol. 10 (f. 325, no. 10); vol. 11 (f. 325, no. 11); vol. 12 (f. 325, no. 12); vol. 13 (f. 325v, no. 13); vol. 14 (f. 325v, no. 14); vol. 15 (f. 326, no. 17); vol. 19 (f. 326, no. 18); vol. 20 (f. 326, no. 19); vol. 21 (f. 326, no. 20); vol. 22 (f. 326, vol. 21); vol. 23 (f. 326v, no. 22); vol. 24 (f. 326v, no. 23); vol. 26 (f. 326v, no. 24); vol. 28

(f. 327, no. 27); vol. 31 (f. 335, no. 105). The exact titles listed in Indice 124 are sometimes provided in a footnote in ASV Indice 133, so researchers can see exactly how generic the titles in ASV Indice 133 are.

Location: Archivio Segreto Vaticano.

3.2.14.16 Armaria LXII–LXIII

[DATABASE ID: VATV365-A]

Inclusive Dates: 1537–1588.

Bulk: 154 vols.

Scope: These two armaria contain documents relating to Council of Trent. They are mostly chancery copies of the Acta and the diaries and letters of cardinals, bishops, and other delegates

Notes: According to Boyle, the records came to the ASV from Castel S. Angelo in 1630. Vols. 45–48 and 85–86 are located in the Vatican Library. Vol. 36 is available on microfilm.

References: Fink, pp. 33–34; Boyle, p. 40; MacFarlane, p. 36.

Finding Aids: ASV Indice 133 briefly lists summary titles of each volume. The index (compiled by Petrus De Pretis after 1741) is basically informative but often fails to note copies. The index also uses terms such as *regestrum* and *brevia* too inclusively and does not clearly note items that do not fit the basic thematic focus of each armarium, or which items are clearly from other offices.

ASV Indice 114 (p. 620) by Felice Contelori provides selected excerpts from *Armarium LXII*.

ASV Indice 124, "Primo Sbozzo di Inventario di tutti i libri che sono nell'Archivio Segreto Vaticano" by Giovanni Bissaiga (1672), provides more descriptive and accurate volume titles for some armarium volumes. Select volumes from *Armaria LXII–LXIII* are listed on folios 251r and 380r. The exact titles listed in Indice 124 are sometimes provided in a footnote in ASV Indice 133, so researchers can see exactly how generic the titles in ASV Indice 133 are.

Location: Archivio Segreto Vaticano.

3.2.14.17 Armarium LXIV

[DATABASE ID: VATV151-A]

Inclusive Dates: ca. 1520–1630.

Bulk: 34 vols.

Scope: Boyle notes that these are nunciature reports relating to various European countries; vols. 1–27 concern Germany; vol. 28 concerns England, Ireland, and Scotland; and vols. 29–34 concern Poland, Portugal, Spain, France and Savoy.

Note: Vols. 13 and 20 are available on microfilm.

References: Fink, p. 34; Boyle, p. 70; Pásztor (1970), pp. 18–19; Pásztor (1983), pp. 97–99.

Finding Aids: ASV Indice 213, "Indice di libri de Msgr. Ciampini alcune de quale sono stati comprati da Il. Sg.le. Clemente XI e posti nell'studi . . . e fuori sono stati segnali con la lett. 'C' e posti in diversi luoghi secundo le materie nelle quali trattavano," includes *Armarium LXIV*, vols. 32 and 44, in this donation, which took place between 1700 and 1721. The description of these volumes in Indice 213 is fuller than the description in ASV Indice 133.

ASV Indice 133, ff. 196r–198v, briefly lists summary titles of each volume. The index (compiled by Petrus De Pretis after 1741) is basically informative but often fails to note copies. The index also uses terms such as *regestrum* and *brevia* too inclusively and does not clearly note items that do not fit the basic thematic focus of each armarium, or which items are clearly from other offices. Therefore, the volume titles presented in Indice 133 are not exact. There are also some inacuracies in the more recently typed and written footnotes.

ASV Indice 124, "Primo Sbozzo di Inventario di tutti i libri che sono nell'Archivio Segreto Vaticano," by Giovanni Bissaiga (1672), provides more descriptive and accurate volume titles for some armarium volumes. Select volumes in *Armarium LXIV* are listed on folios 304v, 351v–353r, and 355r–358v. The exact titles listed in Indice 124 are sometimes provided in footnotes in Indice 133, so researchers can see the difference in the titles.

ASV Indici 731 and 736–739 contain selected lists of documents in various parts of *Armarium LXIV* as follows: Ind. 731 for vol. 1; Ind. 736 for vol. 5; Ind. 737 for vol. 9; Ind. 738 for vols. 2, 4, 7, 10, 11; Ind. 739 for vols. 4, 10, 11.

ASV Indice 1100 indicates which *Sec. Brev.* registers (series name and volume number) as well as which other series are indexed in ASV Indice 731–885. Information regarding *Armarium LXIV* is summarized in the previous paragraph.

Location: Archivio Segreto Vaticano.

3.2.14.18 Autografi di SS. Pio X
[DATABASE ID: VATV10519-A]
Inclusive Dates: 1903–1913.
Bulk: .2 linear m.
Location: Archivio Segreto Vaticano.

3.2.14.19 Avvisi
[DATABASE ID: VATV165-A]
Inclusive Dates: 1559–1889 (bulk 1605–1710).
Bulk: 10 linear m. (160 numbered vols. and buste).
Organization: There are several chronological and one alphabetical subseries within the *Avvisi* and each of these is broken down geographically. A few volumes do not form any specific chronological subseries but are still organized geographically.

The printed materials (notizie) are primarily concentrated in the final twenty buste. These subseries are roughly as follows: vols. 1–76 (1605–1709); —vols. 77–118 (1625–1676); —vols. 120–122, 124 (1600–1700); —vols. 123 (1768); —vols. 128–137 (alphabetical, 1605–1696); —vols. 138–139 (1701–1835); —vols. 140–159 (1565–1889) stampati; —vol. 160, misc. mss. (1605–1714). Note that because of the overlapping chronological subseries Indice 1026 is essential for locating materials. For example information on Venezia in 1657 is in at least three buste: 27, 105, and 136.

Other subseries include: Colonia, 1601–1697 (also notizie); —Fiandra, 1563–1746 (also notizie); —Firenze, 1651–1696 and 1784–93; —Francia, 1562–1793 (also notizie); —Malta, 1667–1672; —Napoli, 1618–1704; —Polonia, 1607–1697, 1770; —Portogallo, 1587–1697 (also notizie); —Spagna, 1587–1719 (also notizie); —Svizzera, 1620–1696; —Venezia, 1605–1698, 1791 (also notizie); —Vienna, Praga, Germania, 1563–1709 (also notizie); —Ancona, 1669–1684, 1738 (notizie only); —Belgrado, 1668; —Bologna, 1654–1673 (notizie only); —Dalmazia, 1647–1668; —Ferrara, 1702–1706 (notizie only);

—Foligno, 1687–1696, 1704, 1738 (notizie only); —Forli, 1706, 1738 (notizie only); —Genova, 1628–1697, 1797 (also notizie); —Inghilterra, 1622–1697, 1707, 1719 (also notizie); —Levante, 1565–1672, 1722–1793; —Macerata, 1658–1673 (also notizie); —Mantova, 1628–1706 (also notizie); —Milano, 1622–1697, 1733–1734 (also notizie); —Modena, 1628; —Olanda, 1630–1709, 1717, 1740 (also notizie); —Parma, Piacenze, 1628, 1663, 1733–34; —Pavia, 1658;—Pesaro, 1738–1739 (notizie only); —Ravenna, 1737–1738 (notizie only); —Rimini, 1738, 1739 (notizie only);—Roma, 1595–1697, 1703, 1768 (also notizie); —Spoleto, 1683, 1692 (also notizie); —Svizia, 1646–1647.

Avvisi vol. 119 is now *Archivio della Nunziatura Apostolica di Francia* vol. 179A.

For related material see also the SS. *Interni-Esteri* and SS. *Esteri*, as well as in the archivi of the nunciatures mentioned in the organizational note above.

References: Pásztor (1970), p. 91; Pásztor (1983), p. 131; Boyle, p. 78. A. H. Velykyi, *Litterae nuntiorum apostolicorum historiam Ucrainae illustrantes (1550–1850)* (Rome, 1959–). R. Ancel. "Etude critique sur quelque recueils d'Avvisi," *Mélanges d'archéologie et d'histoire* 28 (1908): 115–139. B. Neveu, ed., *Correspondance du nonce en France, Angelo Ranuzzi 1683–1689* (Rome, 1973). K. Repgen. "Zur Diplomatik der Nuntiaturberichte: Dienstvorschrift für das Abfassen von Avvisi aus dem Jahre 1639," *Römische Quartalschrift für christliche Altertumskunde und für Kirchengeschichte* 49 (1954): 123–126.

Finding Aids: ASV Indice 1026 (pp. 87–109, 221–257) contains a detailed volume-by-volume index that is essential for locating materials among the multiple chronological and then geographical divisions (see organizational note above). This index lists the former and current volume numbers, the inclusive dates within the volume or busta, the geographic area/diocese concerned with the dates covered, a note as to whether the material is manuscript or printed, and the page numbers for the manuscript materials. If a researcher is looking for materials from a specific geographic area, the "Schedario cronologico del gruppo Avvisi" (pp. 221–257) is the best place to begin. This section is organized into two alphabetical divisions that list geographic area or diocese. Each diocese or other area is then broken down more or less chronologically, so one can see which volumes include specific years and/or overlap. It is also noted if the volume contains *Avvisi* manuscripts or printed material.

ASV Indice 194 (f. 5–6v) contains a very brief listing of vols. 1–125 and the year(s) covered.

Location: Archivio Segreto Vaticano.

3.2.14.20 Benedizioni
[DATABASE ID: VATV10479-A]
Inclusive Dates: 1911–1914.
Bulk: 1 linear m. (12 buste).
Location: Archivio Segreto Vaticano.

3.2.14.21 Beneficenza pontificia
[DATABASE ID: VATV10514-A]
Inclusive Dates: 1937–1964.
Bulk: Extent not available.
Location: Archivio Segreto Vaticano.

3.2.14.22 Beneficenza pontificia
[DATABASE ID: VATV10513-A]
Inclusive Dates: 1940–1965.
Bulk: 141.5 linear m.
Reference: Natalini et al., p. 273.
Location: Archivio Segreto Vaticano.

3.2.14.23 Beneficenza pontificia: Giovanni XXIII
[DATABASE ID: VATV10511-A]
Inclusive Dates: [1950s]–[1960s].
Bulk: 1 linear m.
Location: Archivio Segreto Vaticano.

3.2.14.24 Beneficenza pontificia: Reparto
[DATABASE ID: VATV10517-A]
Inclusive Dates: 1944–1947.
Bulk: Extent not available.
Location: Archivio Segreto Vaticano.

3.2.14.25 Beneficenza pontificia: Reparto
[DATABASE ID: VATV10524-A]
Inclusive Dates: 1945–1965.
Bulk: 187 linear m.
Location: Archivio Segreto Vaticano.

3.2.14.26 Beneficenza pontificia: Reparto diocese estere
[DATABASE ID: VATV10525-A]
Inclusive Dates: [ca. 1940–1960].
Bulk: 4 linear m.
Location: Archivio Segreto Vaticano.

3.2.14.27 Beneficenza pontificia: Schedario nomi, Paolo VI
[DATABASE ID: VATV10510-A]
Inclusive Dates: [196–?]–[197–?].
Bulk: .1 linear m.
Location: Archivio Segreto Vaticano.

3.2.14.28 Beneficenza pontificia: Schedario nomi, Pio XII
[DATABASE ID: VATV10512-A]
Inclusive Dates: [193–?]–[195–?].
Bulk: 5 linear m.
Location: Archivio Segreto Vaticano.

3.2.14.29 Biglietti
[DATABASE ID: VATV40011-A]
Inclusive Dates: 1817–1819.
Bulk: 11 vols.
Note: This series was cited in Natalini et al., p. 273, but not seen by project staff in 1990.
Location: Archivio Segreto Vaticano.

3.2.14.30 Biglietti epoca napoleonica
[DATABASE ID: VATV172-A]
Inclusive Dates: 1800–1809.
Bulk: 24.3 linear m. (130 vols.).
Organization: Subseries include the following (numerical description supplied by project staff): 1. Tesoriere generale, 1800–1809, vols. 1–15; —2. Congr. militare, 1800–1808, vols. 16–35; —3. Governatore di Roma, 1800–1809, vols. 36–51 (note: vols. 42–48, Protocolli 2–281, 1803–1809); —4. Prelati in carica, 1800–1809, vols. 52–93a (includes misc. fiscale,

1800–1808; Camera, 1801–1809; Congr. economica, 1801–1803; Sacra Rota, 1800–1809; Signatura, 1800–1805; Propaganda Fide, 1800–1808; Brevi a principi, 1802; Congr. Ceremon., 1807; Cong. Concilio, 1802–1806; Cong. Consist., 1802; Cong. Dicpl. Regol., 1803; Beni enfiteusi, 1802–1806; Congr. Lauretana, 1802–1805; Maggiordomato, 1806; Cong. Vesc. e Reg., 1807; Viceregenti, 1802–1807; Indulgenza, 1801–1805; Riti, 1802–1805; S.O., 1800–1807; Penitenzeria, 1809; Camerlengato, 1801–1807; Grescia, 1800–1805; Archivi acque, 1801–1809 ; Deput. annonaria, 1800–1809; Buon governo, 1800–1809. vol. 56–61 ; S. Consulta, 1800–1809, vols. 63–79; Udit SSmo, 1800–1808, vols. 89–90); —5. Prelati semplici, 1800–1809, vols. 94–99; —6. Biglietti cardinali, 1800–1809, vols. 100–103 (includes also two additional vol. of letters, 1800–1809, added to the series); —7. Biglietti principi, 1800–1809, vols. 104–110; —8. Biglietti comuni, 1800–1808 [note that the inventory lists Biglietti 1800–1802 (da riordinare)].
References: Boyle, p. 78; Natalini et al., p. 274.
Finding Aids: ASV Indice 1125 provides a listing of each volume in the series with an indication of subseries and inclusive dates.
Location: Archivio Segreto Vaticano.

3.2.14.31 Brevi apostolici
[DATABASE ID: VATV167-A]
Inclusive Dates: 1908–1968.
Bulk: 46 linear m.
Organization: Chronological. Subseries are: Diversorum; —Indulgentiae ad tempus; —Indulgentiae perpetuae; —Indulta personalia; —Secreta.
References: Boyle, p. 78; Natalini et al., p. 274.
Finding Aids: The second floor of the ASV Sala d'Indici houses three sets of indici to the *Brevi Apostolici* as well as to its predecessor series *Sec. Brev.* from the office of the Secretaria Brevium. These three indici are "Nomi" (1834–1926); "Diocesi" (1869–1922); and "Registro di Cassa della Segreteria de Breve" (1845–1897). These sets of indici are straightforward to use. Desired information can be located by searching for personal or corporate names (religious orders, organizations). Each of these sets gives a protocol number, date, name, diocese, agent or referring congregation, and business (in various orders). The essential items of information to note from all these registers are the dates and the type of business (e.g., appointment of an archbishop, altare priv., indulg.). Researchers should then request *Brevi Apostolici* registers by the date (year and month) and type (Brevia, Indulgentiae ad tempus, Indulgentiae perpetuae, Indulta personalia, etc.).
Note: This series continues the Secretaria Brevium series *Altare privilegiatum ad tempus, Altare privilegiatum perpetuum, Indulgentiae ad tempus, Indulgentiae perpetuae, Indulta personalia,* and *Secretaria brevium.*
Location: Archivio Segreto Vaticano.

3.2.14.32 Cancelleria dei brevi apostolici: Miscellanea
[DATABASE ID: VATV10231-A]
Inclusive Dates: 1848–1956.
Bulk: 2 linear m.
Organization: Subseries/items include: [1 vol. post-1922]; —Registro ricerche, 1916–[post-1922], 3 vols.; —[Alphabetical index to correspondence], 1908–1913, 1 vol.; —Brevi

consegnati, 1911–[post-1922], 7 vols.; —[5 vols. post-1922]; —
Assegni annui e mensili, ca. 1848–1900, 8 boxes (numbered 1–
462); —Pio X atti consistoriali, 1848–1870, 1 box; —Timbre
d'ufficio; —Brevi spedite all'estero con sospensione di tassa,
1916–[post-1922], 3 vols.; —[1 vol. post-1922]; —Notula dei
brevi spedite per la S. Congregazione di Propaganda Fide,
1910–[post-1922], 1 vol.; —[1 vol. post-1922]; —[Alphabetical
indexes], undated, 3 vols.

Location: Archivio Segreto Vaticano.

3.2.14.33 Carte varie

[DATABASE ID: VATV515-A]
Inclusive Dates: 1745–1833.
Bulk: 1 linear m. (25 buste).

Organization: Buste 1–7 contain Posizioni 18–135. Subseries are: buste 1–7, Nomine e corrispondenza varia, 1745–
1833; —busta 8, del Card. Consalvi come Segretario dei Brevi,
1817–1823; —buste 9–23, Biglietti particolari a vari impiegati
della Segreteria di Stato, 1814–1833; —busta 24, Lettere e
biglietti e minutanti Segr. Stato, 1815–1824; —busta 25, Miscellanea.

Scope: This relatively small series is a very miscellaneous collection of Secretary of State correspondence with other congregations and offices of the Papal States. There may be a connection
between this series and the Secretariatus Status series *Varia*,
which contains 17 buste, possibly the 17 missing posizioni.

Finding Aids: An index to the *Carte varie* is available behind
the desk in the main ASV reading room. This index provides
very detailed access to other congregations and papal offices
and officers in the first 7 buste. For buste 8–25 there is a cursory
busta listing. There is no indication of where Posizioni 1–17
are located. This is not an official ASV index and must be used
in consultation with the ASV staff.

Location: Archivio Segreto Vaticano.

3.2.14.34 Carte varie: Benedizioni

[DATABASE ID: VATV10489-A]
Inclusive Dates: 1914–1921.
Bulk: 1 linear m. (8 buste).
Location: Archivio Segreto Vaticano.

3.2.14.35 Cassa

[DATABASE ID: VATV10230-A]
Inclusive Dates: 1908–1949.
1 linear m.

Organization: Chronological. There are two subseries: 1.
[Cassa] 1908–[post-1922] (21 vols.); —2. Cancelleria dei Brevi
Apostolici, 1909–[post-1922] (12 vols.).

Location: Archivio Segreto Vaticano.

3.2.14.36 Collegi

[DATABASE ID: VATV10481-A]
Inclusive Dates: 1909–1913.
Bulk: .3 linear m. (3 buste).
Location: Archivio Segreto Vaticano.

3.2.14.37 Commissariato straordinario delle quattro legazione

[DATABASE ID: VATV317-A]
Inclusive Dates: 1832–1839.
Bulk: 25 linear m. (279 numbered buste and 18 unnum-
bered boxes, volumes and buste).

Organization: Subseries breakdown and volume enumeration is as follows: vols. 1–44, Registri di protocollo; —vols. 45–
176, Posizioni (probably sent to other offices) primarily dealing with the Papal States; —vol. 179, Protocollo riservatissimo,
1832–1833; —vols. 180–187, Prospetti e stati relativi agli impiegati delle quattro legazioni; —vols. 188–190, Registro e stati
dei compromessi politici e dei volontari pontifici sospetti o
prossati;—vols. 191–193, Stati delle cause criminale; —vols.
194–197, Visite alle carceri; —vols. 198–212, Bollettini e rapporti politici; —vol. 213, Miscellanea; —vol. 214, Commissione per le quattro legazioni e per la delegazione di Pesaro e
Urbino, 1826–1828; —vols. 215–232, Ispettorato generale dei
volontari pontifici delle quattro legazioni. Informazioni set-
timanali; —vol. 233, Ispettorato generale: Recapiti distribu-
zioni armi cappotti e muniglie; —vols. 234–258, Ispettorato
generale. Corrispondenza ordinaria; —vols. 259–269, Ispettorato generale. Corrispondenza riservata; —vols. 270–272,
Ispettorato generale, Recapiti relativi a disposizioni di massima
ed appendice; —vol. 273, Ispettorato generale. Recapiti relativi
alle due notificazioni di segreteria di Stato, 18 luglio 1834; —
vol. 274, Ispettorato generale. Recapiti relativi all'ultima
girata di Romagna; —vols. 275–278, Ispettorato generale,
Posizioni relative a nomine ed a rinnuzie d'uffiziali; —vol.
279, Ispettorato generale, Posizioni relative ad onorificenze e
premi ai volontari.

Unnumbered boxes, etc.: Segretario di Stato per l'interno,
15 boxes, etc.; —Vice commissariato delle quattro legazioni e
Ispettorato generale, 2 boxes; —Faziosi cospiratori, 1839, 1
vol.

Note: See the agency history for "Papal States: Local Administration" for information about the use of legations in the
Papal States.

References: Fink, p. 131; Boyle, p. 96.

Finding Aids: ASV Indice 1118 includes a good introduction to the series as well as an explanation of the use of the 44
Protocollo volumes. The index also lists the topic/area and
inclusive dates covered in each volume, and sometimes each
fascicolo.

Location: Archivio Segreto Vaticano.

3.2.14.38 Commissioni soccorse

[DATABASE ID: VATV10505-A]
Inclusive Dates: [ca. 1935–1952].
Bulk: 70.5 linear m.

Organization: Three series: *Archivio di Mons. Antonio
Riberi*, [ca. 1935–ca. 1940]; —*Guerra*, [ca. 1938–ca. 1939]; —
[*Archivio degli commissioni soccorse*], [ca. 1949–ca. 1952].

Note: Each of these series is described as a separate series in
the list of records for this office.

Location: Archivio Segreto Vaticano.

3.2.14.39 Confini

[DATABASE ID: VATV496-A]
Inclusive Dates: ca. 1700–1852.
Bulk: 15 linear m. (59 numbered buste and 2 unnumbered
packets).
Organization: Geographical.
Finding Aids: ASV Indice 686 (formerly Indice 107), part 2,
pp. 25–27, lists each busta with the geographic area it covers,

and occasionally provides an annotation concerning the nature of the materials in the buste. This part 2 is a later addition to the primary index in Indice 686, which is an 1839 index to the Archivio Segreto della Congregazione de Confini.

Location: Archivio Segreto Vaticano.

3.2.14.40 Croci "Pro Ecclesia" e Medaglie benemeriti

[DATABASE ID: VATV10515-A]
Inclusive Dates: 1936–1958.
Bulk: 5 linear m.
Location: Archivio Segreto Vaticano.

3.2.14.41 Delegazione di Ancona

[DATABASE ID: VATV40012-A]
Inclusive Dates: [16—]–[18—].
Bulk: 265 buste.
Note: This series was cited in Natalini et al., p. 274, but not seen by project staff in 1990.
Location: Archivio Segreto Vaticano.

3.2.14.42 Delegazione di Macerata

[DATABASE ID: VATV40013-A]
Inclusive Dates: [18—]–[18—].
Bulk: 42 buste.
Note: This series was cited in Natalini et al., p. 274, but not seen by project staff in 1990.
Location: Archivio Segreto Vaticano.

3.2.14.43 Delegazione di Perugia

[DATABASE ID: VATV40014-A]
Inclusive Dates: [18—]–[18—].
Bulk: 98 buste.
Note: This series was cited in Natalini et al., p. 274, but not seen by project staff in 1990.
Location: Archivio Segreto Vaticano.

3.2.14.44 Delegazioni (Legazioni)

[DATABASE ID: VATV40015-A]
Inclusive Dates: [16—]–[18—].
Bulk: 720 buste.
Note: This series was cited in Natalini et al., p. 274, but not seen by project staff in 1990.
Location: Archivio Segreto Vaticano.

3.2.14.45 Domanda di autografi pontifici

[DATABASE ID: VATV10516-A]
Inclusive Dates: 1939–1956.
Bulk: 3 linear m.
Location: Archivio Segreto Vaticano.

3.2.14.46 Domande

[DATABASE ID: VATV10484-A]
Inclusive Dates: 1910–1921.
Bulk: .2 linear m. (2 buste).
Location: Archivio Segreto Vaticano.

3.2.14.47 Doni

[DATABASE ID: VATV10488-A]
Inclusive Dates: 1904–1919.

Bulk: 1 linear m. (9 buste).
Location: Archivio Segreto Vaticano.

3.2.14.48 Doni arredamenti sacri

[DATABASE ID: VATV10487-A]
Inclusive Dates: 1908–1921.
Bulk: 2 linear m. (17 buste).
Location: Archivio Segreto Vaticano.

3.2.14.49 Emigrati della rivoluzione francese

[DATABASE ID: VATV171-A]
Inclusive Dates: 1708–1805 (bulk 1792–1797).
Bulk: 5.5 linear m. (52 numbered vols. and buste).
Organization: Principal subseries include: Lettere degli arcivescovi e vescovi dello Stato Pontificio all'Emo Segretario di Stato, 1792–1797 (also includes a variety of series of lettere di vescovi, nunzi, governatori, lettere di particolari); —Lettere e memorie di diversi (particolari, emigrati, etc) a mons. Lorenze Caleppi, 1792–1797; —Biglietti di cardinale, prelati, (emigrati) ed altri a mons. Caleppi, 1792–1792; —Istituzione generale per l'ospitalità degli emigrati francesi, "Progetto generale della ospitalità, cui si aggiungono della medesima ospitalità ed inoltre il corrispondente carteggio dell'em.mo sig. zie e degl'ordini a mons. Caleppi," 1792–1802; —Minute di lettere e biglietti scritti dall'Em.mo Segretario di Stato (e da mons. Caleppi) a cardinali, legati, nunzi, vescovi, prelati, etc.; —Minute di lettere e biglietti scritte e recevute dai prelati presidenti, 1792–1803; —Biglietti, riscontri, passaporti ed attestati degli emigrati francesi, 1793–1802; —Circolari stampate e viglietti di accompagno per gli emigrati francesi, 1792–1797; —Vescovi francesi, 1792–1797; —Monache francesi, 1795–1805; —Memorie diverse, 1792–1801; —Suppliche diverse degli emigrati francesi, 1803; —Cataloghi degli emigrati francesi situati nello Stato Pontificio, 1793–1794; —Cassa de sussidi, offerte e somministrazioni, 1793–1804; —Carte di eredità degli emigrati francesi (spogli) 1708–1802; —Carte informi, 1792–1799; —Biglietti di mons. Caleppi all'abate Venditti, 1792–1796; —Biglietti e carte relative a passa porti, 1792–1795; —Manoscritti di L. Tournefort, Les admirations du curé de Villes sur Basilique de Saint Pierre, 1792 e Le pontifical ou la cérémonie solemnelle de la messe papale, le saint jour de Noel, 1792; —Elenchi di emigrati e circolari relative si medesimi, 1792–1793; —Particolari; —Miscellaneous histories/papers, "La doctrine de l'Eglise Romaine," "Defence en faveur de Jean François Gutel, prétre français prévenu d'emigration."
Scope: This series relates primarily to emigrant priests and religious as a result of events in France at the end of the eighteenth century. Note that the old segnatura to volume 50 lists it as an index. It is a list of émigrés and cannot be used as an index to the series.
References: Fink, p. 134; Boyle, p. 78. A. Theiner, *Documents inédits relatifs aux affaires religieuses de la France 1790 a 1800* (Paris, 1857–1858).
Finding Aids: ASV Indice 1026 (pp. 135–140) briefly lists each volume. Entries include: the old and new volume number, title on the spine of the volume, inclusive dates, pagination, size, and notes of markings on the volume or alphabetical organization, if applicable.

Paola Carucci and Raffaele Santoro, eds., "Le fonti archivistiche," vol. 1 of *La Rivoluzione Francese* (1787–1799): *Repertorio delle fonti archivistiche e delle fonti a stampa conservate in Italia e nella Città del Vaticano* (Rome, 1991). This work identifies series in the ASV that pertain to the French Revolution. Materials from the following series are mentioned: *Francia*, SS. *Particolari*, *Emigrati della rivoluzione francese* (vols. 1–50), *Epoca napoleonica: Francia and Italia*, *Legazione di Avignone*, and *Fondo Garampi*. Entries list the volume number, identify the total number of folios in a volume, provide the formal or a supplied title, summarize the materials in the volume, and note the inclusive dates. At times, individual documents are identified and described. Because every volume of this collection is mentioned, this section of the work (pp. 244–250) acts as a published index to this series. The information in ASV Indice 1026 is only slightly more detailed and descriptive.

Location: Archivio Segreto Vaticano.

3.2.14.50 Epoca napoleonica: Baviera

[DATABASE ID: VATV10540-A]

Inclusive Dates: 1786–1815.

Bulk: 1.5 linear m. (buste numbered 1–8).

Scope: This series contains a variety of material regarding church affairs in Munich during the Napoleonic period.

Finding Aids: ASV Indice 1135 provides inclusive dates for each volume and summarizes the contents.

Reference: A. I. Bassani, "Le fonti dell'Archivio Segreto Vaticano per una storia ecclesiastica della repubblica e del regno d'Italia," in *Vita religiosa e cultura in Lombardia e nel Veneto nell'età napoleonica*, edited by F. Agostino et al. (Rome, 1990), pp. 363–393.

Location: Archivio Segreto Vaticano.

3.2.14.51 Epoca napoleonica: Cardinali e governo

[DATABASE ID: VATV40016-A]

Inclusive Dates: 1800–1809.

Bulk: 12 buste.

Note: This series was cited in Natalini et al., p. 274, but not seen by project staff in 1990. However, this may be a subseries of Secretariatus Status series *Registri I*.

Reference: A. I. Bassani, "Le fonti dell'Archivio Segreto Vaticano per una storia ecclesiastica della repubblica e del regno d'Italia," in *Vita religiosa e cultura in Lombardia e nel Veneto nell'età napoleonica*, edited by F. Agostino et al.(Rome, 1990), pp. 363–393.

Location: Archivio Segreto Vaticano.

3.2.14.52 Epoca napoleonica: Francia

[DATABASE ID: VATV10539-A]

Inclusive Dates: 1798–1815.

Bulk: 3.5 linear m. (buste numbered 1–27).

Scope: This series covers church relations with France during the Napoleonic regime, 1798–1815, including correspondence with Talleyrand and a report to him regarding religious affairs in France. The material also covers the concordats with Napoleon concerning bishops.

References: E. Audard, "L'histoire religieuse de la Révolution française aux Archives Vaticanes," *Revue d'histoire de l'Église de France* 4 (1913): 516–535, 625–639. A. I. Bassani, "Le fonti dell'Archivio Segreto Vaticano per una storia eccle-

siastica della repubblica e del regno d'Italia," in *Vita religiosa e cultura in Lombardia e nel Veneto nell'età napoleonica*, edited by F. Agostino et al. (Rome, 1990), pp. 363–393. J. Leflon and A. Latreille, "Répertoire des fonds napoléoniens aux Archives Vaticanes," *Revue historique* 203 (1950): 59–63.

Finding Aids: ASV Indici 1135 lists each buste, its inclusive dates, and summarizes selected contents. In order to get a sense of what is not summarized, see the Carucci/Santoro work cited below.

Chanoine Leflon and Andre Latreille, "Répertoire des fonds napoléoniens aux Archives Vaticanes," *Revue historique* 203 (1950): 59–63. This article is virtually a word-for-word publication of ASV Indice 1135. The primary difference is that the article does not list the final busta, XXVII, which apparently arrived in the ASV after 1950.

Paola Carucci and Raffaele Santoro, eds., "Le fonti archivistiche," vol. 1 of *La Rivoluzione Francese* (1787–1799): *Repertorio delle fonti archivistiche e delle fonti a stampa conservate in Italia e nella Città del Vaticano* (Rome, 1991). This work identifies the series in the ASV that pertain to the French Revolution. Materials from the following series are mentioned: *Francia* (vols. 458B, 463, 463A, 529C, 529D, and mazzo 529 E.II, vols. 570A, 571–575, 578–583, 585, 596, mazzo 639, vol. 640, mazzi 645, 658, cart. 659 and insupplemento Francia cart. 9, 18, mazzo 38, 50, and 55), SS. *Particolari* (vols. 272–281), *Emigrati della rivoluzione francese* (vols. 1–50), *Epoca napoleonica: Francia* (b. 1, 4, 9, 11, 15, 17–25) and *Epoca napoleonica: Italia* (b. 10, 22, and 25), *Legazione di Avignone* (vols. 145–150, 199, 215–218, 222–224, 226–231, 245, 254, 335–339, and mazzi 376, 378, 381), and *Fondo Garampi* (b. 95, 154, 159, 179, 214,and 264). Entries list the volume number, identify the total number of folios in a volume, provide the formal or a supplied title, summarize the materials in the volume, and note the inclusive dates. Because of the different emphasis of ASV Indice 1135 and this guide, the analytical entries listed in each source are different. One cannot get a complete sense of the series without looking at both these sources.

Location: Archivio Segreto Vaticano.

3.2.14.53 Epoca napoleonica: Governatori

[DATABASE ID: VATV40017-A]

Inclusive Dates: 1800–1809.

Bulk: 12 buste.

Note: This series was cited in Natalini et al., p. 274, but not seen by project staff in 1990. However, this may be a subseries of Secretariatus Status series *Registri I*.

Reference: A. I. Bassani, "Le fonti dell'Archivio Segreto Vaticano per una storia ecclesiastica della repubblica e del regno d'Italia," in *Vita religiosa e cultura in Lombardia e nel Veneto nell'età napoleonica*, edited by F. Agostino et al. (Rome, 1990), pp. 363–393.

Location: Archivio Segreto Vaticano.

3.2.14.54 Epoca napoleonica: Italia

[DATABASE ID: VATV10527-A]

Inclusive Dates: 1782–1815 (bulk 1798–1815).

Bulk: 5.5 linear m. (27 buste).

Organization: Numbered 1–27.

Scope: This series is composed of material regarding church affairs during the Napoleonic occupation of Rome. It includes information on apostolic delegations. Several files relate to the invasion of Rome and its implications for specific jurisdictions. There is some data on suppression of monasteries and clerical administrative matters.

Reference: A. I. Bassani, "Le fonti dell'Archivio Segreto Vaticano per una storia ecclesiastica della repubblica e del regno d'Italia," in *Vita religiosa e cultura in Lombardia e nel Veneto nell'età napoleonica,* edited by F. Agostino et al. (Rome, 1990), pp. 363–393.

Finding Aids: Paola Carucci and Raffaele Santoro, eds., "Le fonti archivistiche," vol. 1 of *La Rivoluzione Francese (1787–1799): Repertorio delle fonti archivistiche e delle fonti a stampa conservate in Italia e nella Città del Vaticano* (Rome, 1991). This work identifies the series in the ASV that pertain to the French Revolution. Materials from the following series are mentioned: *Francia* (vols. 458B, 463, 463A, 529C, 529D, and mazzo 529 E.II, vols. 570A, 571–575, 578–583, 585, 596, mazzo 639, vol. 640, mazzi 645, 658, cart. 659 and insupplemento Francia cart. 9, 18, mazzo 38, 50, and 55), SS. *Particolari* (vols. 272–281), *Emigrati della rivoluzione francese* (vols. 1–50), *Epoca napoleonica: Francia* (b. 1, 4, 9, 11, 15, 17–25) and *Epoca napoleonica: Italia* (b. 10, 22, and 25), *Legazione di Avignone* (vols. 145–150, 199, 215–218, 222–224, 226–231, 245, 254, 335–339, and mazzi 376, 378, 381), and *Fondo Garampi* (b. 95, 154, 159, 179, 214, and 264). Entries list the volume number, identify the total number of folios in a volume, provide the formal or a supplied title, summarize the materials in the volume, and note the inclusive dates. Due to the varying emphasis of ASV Indice 1135 and this guide, the analytical entries in each describe different items. One gets a very different sense of the collection from these two works.

ASV Indice 1135 lists the contents of each busta, in French, with a brief summary and inclusive dates. This is followed by an Italian section that lists selected volumes in greater detail.

Location: Archivio Segreto Vaticano.

3.2.14.55 Epoca napoleonica: Vescovi e governo

[DATABASE ID: VATV40019-A]

Inclusive Dates: 1800–1809.

Bulk: 50 buste.

Note: This series was cited in Natalini et al., p. 274, but not seen by project staff in 1990. However, this may be a subseries of Secretariatus Status series *Registri I.*

Reference: A. I. Bassani, "Le fonti dell'Archivio Segreto Vaticano per una storia ecclesiastica della repubblica e del regno d'Italia," in *Vita religiosa e cultura in Lombardia e nel Veneto nell'età napoleonica,* edited by F. Agostino et al. (Rome, 1990), pp. 363–393.

Location: Archivio Segreto Vaticano.

3.2.14.56 Esteri

[DATABASE ID: VATV494-A]

Inclusive Dates: 1815–1850 (bulk 1815–1845).

Bulk: 237.7 linear m. (666 fasc.).

Scope: This series forms one of the four component parts of the Secretariatus Status series *Fondo Moderno.* It continues in part the Secretariatus Status series *Interni-Esteri,* 1814–1822. The series is then continued by the Secretariatus Status series *Esteri,* 1846–1922.

This particular series consists of correspondence and other

files of the Secretariatus Status with representatives outside the Papal States. Though the files include scattered papers after 1845, the series contains documents primarily from the years 1815–1845. These files are arranged by rubric number, then within each rubric, chronologically.

Finding Aids: There are two means of locating documents in the Secretary of State series *Esteri,* 1815–1850. One method is directly through the rubric numbers; the other possibility is through the *Rubricelle* and *Protocolli* registers. Note that the rubric numbers, a subject-based system of classification, and the *Rubricelle,* registers of correspondence, are two completely different elements and are not interchangeable. The approach through rubric numbers is described in the next several paragraphs, along with a description of the uses of all the ASV Indici that provide information on these Secretary of State series. For information about using the *Rubricelle* and *Protocolli,* see the general description for the *Fondo Moderno.* In addition each of these two series is described separately among the records of the Secretary of State.

One method of locating documents in *Esteri,* 1815–1850, is directly through the rubric filing system employed by the Secretary of State. Under the rubric system, Roman Congregations, Papal States offices, countries, major subjects, and so forth are assigned a rubric number. The rubric numbers (which changed periodically) for the period before 1850 are explained in several published essays by L. Pásztor available in the Index Room of the Vatican Archives including: (1) "L'Archivio della Segretaria di Stato tra il 1833 e il 1847," *Annali della Scuola speciale per archivisti e bibliotecari dell'Università di Roma* 10 (1970): 104–148, which contains a detailed discussion of each rubric including a listing of each year that a rubric number was used; (2) "L'archivio della Segreteria di Stato di Pio IX durante il triennio 1848–1850," *Annali della Scuola speciale per archivisti e bibliotecari dell'Università di Roma* 21–22 (1981–1982): 54–148, which includes a listing of rubric numbers as well as individual fascicoli; and (3) "La classificazione delle carte della Segreteria di Stato tra il 1833 e il 1847," in *Miscellanea in memoria di Giorgio Cencetti* (Turin, 1973), pp. 639–663, which provides further information. In the ASV Sala d'Indici, ASV Indice 1110 provides an annotated list of rubrics and a one-sheet summarization of the rubric number system (both before and after 1847 when it was altered). After 1851, the Indici 1089-I, 1089-II, and 1089-III provide the clearest outline of the rubrics.

There are a number of caveats in approaching the component parts of the *Fondo Moderno* through the rubric numbers. First, few documents contain only one subject. For example, if a researcher is concerned with seminaries or universities in Cuba in the early twentieth century, a researcher should request the materials classified under the rubric numbers dealing with seminaries, universities, and Cuba (i.e., 18, 43, and 251, respectively). If an issue lasted over a period of years, the number of possible buste or fascicoli needed to research a subject thoroughly can become quite high. Another problem with simply requesting rubrics dealing with certain topics for certain years, is that the designated year on the busta or fascicolo does not necessarily mean that all the documents in that busta are from that year. Earlier materials usually of a supporting nature are often attached to documents dated and filed with the particular year of a specific busta.

ASV Indici 1031, 1032, and 1033, assist researchers who

prefer to approach, respectively, the *Interni*, *Esteri*, and *Interni-Esteri* series through rubric numbers. Indici 1031, 1032, and 1033, are chronologically arranged listings (subdivided by year and then according to rubric numbers, buste, and fascicoli). Indici 1031, 1032, and 1033, also indicate any subseries in the rubrics (e.g., in Indice 1033, Rubric 27 breaks down by city: Ferrara, Forli, Ravenna, etc.), which can help to clarify the nature of the subject matter classified under a rubric number. Not all rubric numbers are represented in each year and the yearly designation for a rubric number does not mean that all materials in the busta are from that year. Earlier materials are often contained in the fascicoli requested. After identifying material desired in Indici 1032, (for the Esteri, 1815–1850), copy down the year, the rubric, and the buste numbers to request materials.

Location: Archivio Segreto Vaticano.

3.2.14.57 Esteri
[DATABASE ID: VATV495-A]
Inclusive Dates: 1846–1922.
Bulk: 517 linear m.
Scope: This series is a continuation of the SS. *Esteri* series for 1815–1846 and forms a part of the Secretariatus Status (SS.) series *Fondo Moderno*. This later *Esteri* series is arranged by year, then by rubric number. It is then further divided by fascicule and then protocol number.
Finding Aids: There are two means of locating documents in the Secretary of State series *Esteri*, 1846–1922. One method is directly through the rubric numbers; the other possibility is through the *Rubricelle* and *Protocolli* registers. Note that the rubric numbers, a subject based system of classification, and the *Rubricelle*, registers of correspondence, are two completely different elements and are not interchangeable. The approach through rubric numbers is described in the next several paragraphs, along with a description of the uses of all the ASV Indici that provide information on this Secretary of State series. For information about the *Rubricelle* and *Protocolli*, see the general description for the SS. series *Fondo Moderno*. In addition, each is described as a separate series of the Secretariatus Status.

One method of locating documents in *Esteri*, 1846–1922, is directly through the rubric filing system employed by the Secretary of State. Under the rubric system, Roman Congregations, Papal States offices, countries, major subjects, and so forth are assigned a rubric number. The rubric numbers (which changed periodically) for the period before 1850 are explained in several published essays by L. Pásztor available in the Index Room of the Vatican Archives including: (1) "L'Archivio della Segretaria di Stato tra il 1833 e il 1847," *Annali della Scuola speciale per archivisti e bibliotecari dell'Università di Roma* 10 (1970): 104–148, which contains a detailed discussion of each rubric including a listing of each year that a rubric number was used; (2) "L'archivio della Segreteria di Stato di Pio IX durante il triennio 1848–1850," *Annali della Scuola speciale per archivisti e bibliotecari dell'Università di Roma* 21–22 (1981–1982): 54–148, which includes a listing of rubric numbers as well as individual fascicoli; and (3) "La classificazione delle carte della Segreteria di Stato tra il 1833 e il 1847," in *Miscellanea in memoria di Giorgio Cencetti* (Turin, 1973), pp. 639–663, which provides further information. In the ASV Sala d'Indici, ASV Indice 1110 provides a much annotated list of rubrics

and one-sheet summarization of the rubric number system (both before and after 1847 when it was altered). After 1851, the Indici 1089-I, 1089-II, and 1089-III provide the clearest outline of the rubrics.

There are a number of caveats in approaching the *Fondo Moderno* through the rubric numbers. First, few documents contain only one subject. For example, if a researcher is concerned with seminaries or universities in Cuba in the early twentieth century, a researcher should request the materials classified under the rubric numbers dealing with seminaries, universities, and Cuba (i.e., 18, 43, and 251, respectively). If an issue lasted over a period of years, the number of possible buste or fascicoli needed to research a subject thoroughly can become quite high. Another problem with simply requesting rubrics dealing with certain topics for certain years, is that the designated year on the busta or fascicolo does not necessarily mean that all the documents in that busta are from that year. Earlier materials were often attached to documents dated and filed under the particular date of the buste in the series.

ASV Indici 1031, 1032, and 1033, assist researchers who prefer to approach, respectively, *Esteri* series material through rubric numbers. Indici 1031, 1032, and 1033, are chronologically arranged listings (subdivided by year and then according to rubric numbers, buste, and fascicoli). Indici 1031, 1032, and 1033, also indicate any subseries in the rubrics (e.g., in Indice 1033, Rubric 27 breaks down by city: Ferrara, Forli, Ravenna, etc.), which can help to clarify the nature of the subject matter classfied under a rubric number. Not all rubric numbers are represented in each year and the yearly designation for a rubric number does not mean that all materials in the busta are from that year. Earlier materials are often contained in fascicoli requested. After identifying material desired in Indici 1032 (*Esteri*, 1815–1850), copy down the year, the rubric, and the buste numbers to request materials.

ASV Indici 1089-I, 1089-II, and 1089-III provide an outline of the rubrics for material dated after 1850. They are arranged similarly to ASV indici 1031–1033. Not all rubric numbers are represented for each year and the yearly designation for a rubric does not indicate that only materials from that year are represented in the file(s).

Location: Archivio Segreto Vaticano.

3.2.14.58 Firme questione romana
[DATABASE ID: VATV10522-A]
Inclusive Dates: 1887–1888.
Bulk: 2 linear m.
Subseries include: Roma; —Emilia; —Romagna e Piedmonte; —Napoletana; —Veneta; —Lombardia.
Location: Archivio Segreto Vaticano.

3.2.14.59 Fondo Moderno
[DATABASE ID: VATV173-A]
Inclusive Dates: 1814–1922.
Bulk: 1,111 linear m.
Organization: This vast fondo is organized into four series: *Interni-Esteri*, 1814–1822, 194.4 linear m.; —*Interni*, 1822–1833, 162 linear m.; —*Esteri*, 1815–1850, 238 linear m.; —*Esteri*, 1846–1922, 517 linear m.

With the defeat of Napoleon and the resetablishment of the Holy See in Rome, the secretary of state's office reorganized its method of filing incoming correspondence. Cardinal Consalvi undertook to arrange files into broad subject categories called rubrics. In most cases, rubrics were further divided into bundles of documents (called buste or fascicoli) and then finally by protocol (or assigned numbers that refer to individual documents). At first the arrangement included a distinction between correspondence within the Papal States (interni) and with other countries (esteri). This distinction was phased out in 1833 when all documents were folded into a more comprehensive *Esteri* series.

Each of the four series that constitute the *Fondo Moderno* is described separately in this section of this guide. It is important to understand the Fondo as a complete entity as well as to learn the individual characteristics of the four component series.

Scope: This series consists of office files for the office of Secretariatus Status, including incoming correspondence and drafts of responses. Within the *Fondo Moderno* are records that are a continuation of earlier series, such as nunciature records formerly kept separate, but after 1814 were folded together into a single office file.

References: Boyle, p. 79; Fink, pp. 105–113; Pásztor (1970), pp. 98–111.

The collected works of Pásztor form the most complete introduction to the nature of this complex series. See: Lajos Pásztor, "Per la storia della Segreteria di Stato nell'Ottocento: La riforma del 1816," in *Mélanges Eugène Tisserant* (Vatican City, 1964), vol. 5, pp. 209–272. Lajos Pásztor, "L'Archivio della Segreteria di Stato tra il 1833 e il 1847," *Annali della Scuola speciale per archivisti e bibliotecari dell'Università di Roma* 10 (1970): 104–148. Lajos Pásztor, "La classificazione delle carte della Segreteria di Stato tra il 1833 e il 1847," in *Miscellanea in memoria di Giorgio Cencetti* (Turin, 1973), pp. 639–663. Lajos Pásztor, "La Segreteria di Stato di Gregorio XVI, 1833–1846," *Archivum Historiae Pontificiae* 15 (1977): 295–332. Lajos Pásztor, "La Segretaria di Stato di Pio IX durante il triennio 1848–1850," *Annali della Fondazione italiana per la storia amministrativa* 3 (1966): 308–365.

Finding Aids: There are two means of locating documents in the Secretary of State, *Fondo Moderno* series (*Interni-Esteri,* 1814–1822; *Interni,* 1822–1833; *Esteri,* 1815–1850; and *Esteri,* 1846–1922). One method is directly through the rubric numbers; the other possibility is through the *Rubricelle* and *Protocolli* registers. Note that the rubric numbers form a subject-based system of classification. The *Rubricelle*, on the other hand, are registers of correspondence. The rubric numbers and the Rubricelle are two completely different elements and are not interchangeable. Each approach is described in the next several paragraphs, along with a description of the uses of all the ASV Indici that provide information on these series.

One method of locating documents in the *Fondo Moderno* is directly through the rubric filing system employed by the Secretary of State. Under the rubric system, Roman Congregations, Papal States offices, countries, major subjects, and so forth are assigned a rubric number. The rubric numbers (which are changed periodically) for the period before 1850 are explained in several published essays by L. Pásztor available in the Index Room of the Vatican Archives including: (1) "L'Archivio della Segretaria di Stato tra il 1833 e il 1847," *Annali della Scuola speciale per archivisti e bibliotecari dell'Università di Roma* 10 (1970): 104–148, which contains a detailed discussion of each rubric including a listing of each year that a rubric number was used; (2) "L'archivio della Segretaria di Stato di

Pio IX durante il triennio 1848–1850," *Annali della Scuola speciale per archivisti e bibliotecari dell'Università di Roma* 21–22 (1981–1982): 54–148, which includes a listing of rubric numbers as well as individual fascicoli; and (3) "La classificazione delle carte della Segreteria di Stato tra il 1833 e il 1847," in *Miscellanea in memoria di Giorgio Cencetti* (Turin, 1973), pp. 639–663, which provides further information. In the ASV Sala d'Indici, ASV Indici 1110 provides a much annotated list of rubric numbers and a one-sheet summarization of the rubric number system (both before and after 1847 when it was altered). After 1851, the ASV Indici 1089-I, 1089-II, and 1089-III provide the clearest outline of the rubrics.

There are a number of caveats in approaching the *Fondo Moderno* through the rubric numbers. First, few documents contain only one subject. For example, if a researcher is concerned with seminaries or universities in Cuba in the early twentieth century, a researcher should request the materials classified under the rubric numbers dealing with seminaries, universities, and Cuba (i.e., 18, 43, and 251, respectively). Using this approach, if an issue lasted over a period of years, the number of possible buste or fascicoli needed to research a subject thoroughly can become quite high. Another problem with simply requesting rubrics dealing with certain topics for certain years is that the designated year on the busta or fascicolo does not necessarily mean that all the documents in that busta are from that year. Earlier documents or items, usually of a supporting nature, are often attached to documents dated and filed with the particular year of a specific busta.

ASV Indici 1031, 1032, and 1033 assist researchers who prefer to approach, respectively, the *Interni, Esteri,* and *Interni-Esteri* series through rubric numbers. Indici 1031, 1032, and 1033 are chronologically arranged listings (subdivided by year and then according to rubric numbers, buste, and fascicoli). Indici 1031, 1032, and 1033, also indicate any subseries in the rubrics (e.g., in Indice 1033, Rubric 27 breaks down by city: Ferrara, Forli, Ravenna, etc.), which can help to clarify the nature of the subject matter classified under a particular rubric number. Not all rubric numbers are represented in each year and the yearly designation for a rubric number does not mean that all materials in the busta are from that year. Earlier materials are often contained in the fascicoli requested. After identifying material desired in Indici 1031 and 1032 (*Interni,* 1822–1833, and *Esteri,* 1815–1850, respectively) copy down the year, the rubric, and the buste numbers to request materials. To request rubric numbers from Indice 1033 (*Interni-Esteri,* 1814–1822), note the year, the rubric, and the fascicoli numbers.

ASV Indici 1089-I, 1089-II, and 1089-III are the key indici to the Esteri, 1851–1922. Indice 1089-I covers the years 1851–1877, 1089-II covers the years 1878–1913, and 1089-III covers the years 1914–1922. All three indici are arranged similarly to ASV Indice 1031, 1032, and 1033. Thus, entries indicate rubric numbers, any subdivisions of a rubric (e.g., in Indice 1089-III [1916], Rubric 251, "America Rappresentati Pontifici," breaks down according to delegations [e.g., Chile Internunzio, Cuba e Portorico delegato, Haiti delegato, etc.]), buste, and fascicoli numbers. To request materials, the rubric number, year, and fascicoli numbers are the essential pieces of information to note. Not all rubric numbers are represented each year and the yearly designation for a rubric does not indicate that only materials from that year are represented in the file(s).

The SS. *Rubricelle*, 1816–1922, and SS. *Protocolli*, 1816–1922 (located in the ASV Sala degli Indici) lead to specific documents in the *Fondo Moderno* series. Researchers should begin with the *Rubricelle*, which provide a yearly alphabetical listing of correspondents. In the late nineteenth century broad subject or geographical categories (e.g., breve, congressi, concistoriale) were added as access points in the *Rubricelle*. A few of the larger subjects, such as "Nunziature" and "Vescovi," were respectively subdivided again by specific nunciatures and alphabetically. Each entry provides a one-line description of the business, correspondent, and the (usually five-digit) protocol number in the right-hand column. Some mid-nineteenth-century *Rubricelle* also list the corresponding rubric number. Note that the rubric numbers are related to, but serve an entirely different function than, the rubricelle. From the *Rubricelle*, researchers who have both the protocol and rubric numbers can proceed directly to ASV Indici 1031, 1032, 1033, or to ASV Indici 1089-I, 1089-II, or 1089-III, to get the rest of the information necessary to request an item. Researchers desiring more information on the contents of a document, related items, or the rubric number should proceed to the *Protocolli*.

From the Rubricelle proceed to the *Protocolli*, which provide rubric numbers and contain a concise but amplified listing of individual items. Researchers should note the year and protocol number in the *Rubricelle* and proceed to the *Protocolli* registers covering the year and protocol number desired. The *Protocolli* registers are organized numerically according to protocol number. Entries indicate the place, date, and correspondent, the object of business, the person assigned to deal with the request, and the date. They also note briefly the response or "risoluzione," and an "Archivio" or rubric number. The rubric number is written largely in the "Archivio" column. Numbers written in smaller print sometimes appear above or below the rubric number. These numbers refer to the protocol numbers of related documents, either before (above) or after (below) a given item. When a desired item is located, the rubric number and the year of the protocollo volume should be noted and the appropriate Indici 1031, 1032, 1033, or 1089-I, 1089-II, or 1089-III, should be consulted to get the rest of the information necessary to request an item. Items that have not been assigned a rubric number cannot be retrieved. Documents followed by the letters "AE," are in the Archives of the Congregazione degli Affari Ecclesiastici, outside the ASV. To see these documents, contact the office of the secretary of state. See Pásztor (1970), pp. 305–328.

Location: Archivio Segreto Vaticano.

3.2.14.60 Guerra

[DATABASE ID: VATV487-A]

Inclusive Dates: 1914–1918.

Bulk: 32 linear m.

Organization: Records organized into eighteen subseries: A. Santa Sede. Questioni generali; —B. Iniziative-proposte-interventi del S. Padre; —C. Per la pace; —D. Stati belligeranti; —E. Stati neutrali: Italia; —F. Territori urvasi: Questioni politiche e religiose; —G. Gerarchia ecclesiastica, episcopati delle varie nazioni; —H. Prigionieri di guerra (gruppi)-Assistensa religiosa e morale; —I. Prigionieri di guerra (individui): Assistensa religiosa e morale; —J. not listed; —K. Popolasioni civili: Assistensa religiosa e morale; —L. Individui civili: Assistensa religiosa e morale; —M. Esercite e soldati combattenti:

Assistensa religiosa e morale; —N. Sussidi in danaro; —O. Soccorsi materiale e morali: Diuti ad opere e comitati di beneficensa; —P. Facoltà in materia religiosa; —Q. Croce Rossa; —R. Esenzioni militari e de requisisioni: Passaporti e passaggi di frontiera; —S. Libri e pubblicazioni varie.

Scope: These records are communications of the Secretariatus Status office (including some drafts of communications), documenting the concerns and activities of the Vatican during World War I. The researcher should note that the *Guerra* series is separate from the large general series of Sec. Status correspondence files. See SS. *Fondo Moderno* and SS. *Esteri*. For comprehensive coverage of the war years, the researcher should thus also consult the Esteri series, first beginning with the appropriate *Protocolli* and *Rubricellae* index volumes.

Finding Aids: There are several unnumbered indici to this series in the Vatican Archives index room. The major index is a 33-volume compilation of photocopies of the cover sheets that accompany each file folder in the *Guerra* series. This index is arranged by a letter code (A–S) that represents a subdivision within the Rubrica 244 (or the World War I classification). To lead the researchers to these subject areas, there is an index that describes each of the divisions, subdivisions, and so forth. To further narrow the search, there is also an index that translates the subject areas into a specific fascicolo (bundle) and if needed into Protocol (item within folder).

Location: Archivio Segreto Vaticano.

3.2.14.61 Guerra

[DATABASE ID: VATV10506-A]

Inclusive Dates: [ca. 1938–ca. 1939].

Bulk: 52.5 linear m.

Location: Archivio Segreto Vaticano.

3.2.14.62 Inquisizione di Malta

[DATABASE ID: VATV441-A]

Inclusive Dates: 1432–1797 (bulk 1572–1797).

Bulk: 13.2 linear m.

Organization: 186 numbered volumes. Principal subseries include: Lett. orig. gran maestri al Papa ed alla Segreteria (1572–1584, 1588–1599); —Lett. orig. inquisitore alla Segreteria (1610–1613, 1645–1651, 1653–1796); —Min. Segreteria al gran maestri, cavalieri, e vescovo (1572–1585); —Reg. lett. Segreteria all'inquisitore (1623–1651 with gaps, 1655–1792); —Min. lett. Segreteria all'inquisitore (1667–1785 with gaps); —Privilegi accordati all'Isola di Malta (1432–1596); —Descrizione dei beni del Priorata de Roma (1602–1603); —Amministrazione dei beni de Gesuiti in Malta (1768–1771).

Vols. 124, 124a, 124b were acquired by the ASV in 1910. Vol. 106 was acquired by Benedict XIII from the Libreria Ottoboniana.

References: Boyle, p. 76; Fink, pp. 84–86. Paolo Piccolomini, "Corrispondenza tra la corte di Roma e L'Inquisizione di Malta durante la guerra di Candia (1645–1669)," *Archivio storico italiano*, 5th ser., 41 (1908): 45–127; 45 (1910): 303–355; 46 (1910): 3–52; 49 (1912): 34–80, 322–354. The series of articles by Piccolomini summarizes selected letters in this series and provides an introduction to the series. B. Barbiche, ed., *Correspondance du nonce en France, Innocenzo del Bufalo, évêque de Camerino, 1601–1604* (Rome, 1964), reprints letters from the nuncio in this series.

Finding Aids: A. Bonnici, "Il fondo 'Malta' della Segreteria di Stato nell'Archivio Segreto Vaticano," *Melita Historica* 4 (1992): 375–411 [this title was noted but not verified by project staff]. Bonnici provides a good introduction to the series with some bibliographic references and references to other collections that contain materials concerning the Inquisition in Malta. He then proceeds with volume-by-volume (which he refers to as Ms. or manuscript) descriptions of the contents. Bonnici lists the volume (Ms.) number and then outlines what can be found on certain folios within the volume. The descriptive information usually lists type of material, correspondents, inclusive dates, folio numbers, the former and current volume number, and the size. A typical entry reads, "18A: ff. 166 (scr166) V.S.: Niente Mis. mm. 285x198 Registro di lettere, cifre, e fogli a colonna dell'Inquisitore G. Casanate alla Segreteria, Curia Romana, Nunzi, ed a Diversi dal 1 novembre al 7 giugno 1663 (ff. 3–166). This article provides more detail and descriptive information than either of the ASV Indice 1024–I or 1024–II described below.

ASV Indice 1024–I (ff. 39–55) lists vols. 1–186. Entries proceed volume by volume and include brief descriptions of the contents (lettere, cifre, minute), inclusive dates, the inquisitor involved, a physical description of the volume, the presence of an internal index, and the former and current volume number.

ASV Indice 1024–II provides a chronological list of vols. 1–186 of SS. *Inquisizione di Malta* between foli 245–251. It provides briefer descriptions of the contents than ASV Indice 1024–I.

ASV Indice 134, by De Pretis (1731), provides a more succinct listing of vols. 1–168, beginning on fol. 136. The listing for SS. *Inquisizione di Malta* in Indice 134 contains many later annotations and additions.

Pompeo Falcone, "La nunziatura di Malta dell'Archivio Segreto della S. Sede," *Archivio storico di Malta* 5 (1934): 172–267, serves a number of purposes. First, it provides a historical introduction and a bibliography of works that have used SS. *Malta* and refers to selected other ASV fondi concerning Malta. Second, Falcone's article reprints a slightly amplified version of the Malta section from the De Pretis ASV Indice 134 (olim vol. 1–168). Entries briefly indicate the type of volume (registro di lettere, cifre, etc.) and inclusive dates. To ensure accuracy in requesting volumes, all volume numbers should be double-checked in ASV Indice 1024. Third, Falcone has compiled four appendices that give researchers a more detailed look at the documentation concerning Malta in the ASV. Appendice I, "Elenco dei documenti contenuti in Malta, 1," provides the date, correspondent, a brief or occasionally an even more detailed summary of the document (minute), and folio number. Appendice II, "Documenti contenuti in Malta, 1," reprints selected documents from *Malta*, 1 and cites the folio number(s). Appendice III, "Scritture cauate di Cancelleria et di Castellania per ser. di Monsig. Illmo. Gran M.ro La Cassiera," lists these documents, which are found in *Malta*, 103. Appendice IV, "Documenti vari," reprints letters and briefs from *Malta*, 124; *Armarium XLII*; and *Archivum Arcis Armaria I–XVIII*, no. 2341.

Location: Archivio Segreto Vaticano.

3.2.14.63 Interni
[DATABASE ID: VATV493-A]
Inclusive Dates: 1822–1833.

Bulk: 162 linear m. (1,005 fasc.).

Scope: This series forms a part of the Secretariatus Status (SS.) series *Fondo Moderno* and continues in part Secretariatus Status series *Interni-Esteri*, 1814–1822. The series contains correspondence and other files of the Secretariatus Status relating to representatives within the Papal States. Except for the first year, 1822, which begins with rubric 165, the files are arranged chronologically, then by rubric number. Each rubric is further divided into fascicles, and then by individual protocol numbers.

Note: Vols. 1822, 1823, 1833 (not complete for any year) are available on microfilm.

Finding Aids: There are two means of locating documents in the series *Interni*, 1822–1833. One method is directly through the rubric numbers; the other possibility is through the *Rubricelle* and *Protocolli* registers. Note that the rubric numbers, a subject-based system of classification, and the Rubricelle, registers of correspondence, are two completely different elements and are not interchangeable. The first approach is described in the next several paragraphs, along with a description of the uses of all the ASV Indici that provide information on this Secretariatus Status series. For information about using the *Rubricelle* and *Protocolli*, see the general description for the SS. *Fondo Moderno*. These are also described as individual series of the Secretariatus Status.

One method of locating documents in the *Interni*, 1822–1833, series is directly through the rubric filing system employed by the secretary of state. Under the rubric system, Roman Congregations, Papal States offices, countries, major subjects, and so forth are assigned a rubric number. The rubric numbers (which changed periodically) for the period before 1850 are explained in several published essays by L. Pásztor available in the Index Room of the Vatican Archives including: (1) "L'Archivio della Segretaria di Stato tra il 1833 e il 1847," *Annali della Scuola speciale per archivisti e bibliotecari dell'Università di Roma* 10 (1970): 104–148, which contains a detailed discussion of each rubric including a listing of each year that a rubric number was used; (2) "L'archivio della Segreteria di Stato di Pio IX durante il triennio 1848–1850," *Annali della Scuola speciale per archivisti e bibliotecari dell'Università di Roma* 21–22 (1981–1982): 54–148, which includes a listing of rubric numbers as well as individual fascicoli; and (3) "La classificazione delle carte della Segreteria di Stato tra il 1833 e il 1847," in *Miscellanea in memoria di Giorgio Cencetti* (Turin, 1973), pp. 639–663, which provides further information. In the ASV Sala d'Indici, ASV Indice 1110 provides an annotated list of rubrics and a one-sheet summarization of the rubric number system (both before and after 1847 when it was altered).

There are a number of caveats in approaching the various series of the *Fondo Moderno* through the rubric numbers. First, few documents contain only one subject. For example, if a researcher is concerned with seminaries or universities in Cuba in the early twentieth century, a researcher should request the materials classified under the rubric numbers dealing with seminaries, universities, and Cuba (i.e., 18, 43, and 251, respectively). If an issue lasted over a period of years, the number of possible buste or fascicoli needed to research a subject thoroughly can become quite high. Another problem with simply requesting rubrics dealing with certain topics for certain years is that the designated year on the busta or fascicolo does not necessarily mean that all the documents in that busta are from that year. Earlier materials are often attached to particular documents dated and accordingly placed in a specific busta.

ASV Indici 1031, 1032, and 1033 assist researchers who prefer to approach the *Interni* series through rubric numbers. Indici 1031, 1032, and 1033 are chronologically arranged listings (subdivided by year and then according to rubric numbers, buste, and fascicoli). Indici 1031, 1032, and 1033 also indicate any subseries in the rubrics (e.g., in Indice 1033, Rubric 27 breaks down by city: Ferrara, Forli, Ravenna, etc.), which can help to clarify the nature of the subject matter classified under a rubric number. Not all rubric numbers are represented in each year and the yearly designation for a rubric number does not mean that all materials in the busta are from that year. Earlier materials are often contained in fascicoli requested. After identifying material desired in Indici 1031 (for *Interni*, 1822–1833) copy down the year, the rubric, and the buste numbers to request materials.

Location: Archivio Segreto Vaticano.

3.2.14.64 Interni-Esteri

[DATABASE ID: VATV492-A]

Inclusive Dates: 1814–1822.

Bulk: 194.4 linear m.

Scope: This series contains correspondence and other files of the Secretariatus Status (SS.) with representatives in the Papal States (interni) and other countries (esteri). The files are arranged chronologically, then by rubric (or subject) number. The sequence is continued (or supplemented) by the SS. series *Interni*, 1822–1833, *Esteri*, 1815–1850, and *Esteri*, 1846–1922. Together these series form the *Fondo Moderno* of the Secretariatus Status.

Note: Vol. A: 1802, rub. 125, fasc. 1–4, 7; 1814/1815, rub. 125, 283; 1816; 1819; and 1822 (not complete for any year) are available on microfilm.

Finding Aids: There are two means of locating documents in the series *Interni-Esteri*, 1814–1822. One method is directly through the rubric numbers; the other possibility is through the *Rubricelle* and *Protocolli* registers. Note that the rubric numbers, a subject-based system of classification, and the *Rubricelle*, registers of correspondence, are two completely different elements and are not interchangeable. The first approach is described in the next several paragraphs, along with a description of the uses of all the ASV Indici that provide information on these Secretariatus Status series. For information about using the *Rubricelle* and *Protocolli*, see the general description for the SS. *Fondo Moderno*. Each of this series is also listed separately as record series of the office of the Secretariatus Status.

One method of locating documents in the *Interni-Esteri*, 1814–1822, is directly through the rubric filing system employed by the Secretary of State. Under the rubric system, Roman Congregations, Papal States offices, countries, major subjects, and so forth are assigned a rubric number. The rubric numbers (which changed periodically) for the period before 1850 are explained in several published essays by L. Pásztor available in the Index Room of the Vatican Archives including: (1) "L'Archivio della Segretaria di Stato tra il 1833 e il 1847,"

Annali della Scuola speciale per archivisti e bibliotecari dell'Università di Roma 10 (1970): 104–148, which contains a detailed discussion of each rubric including a listing of each year that a rubric number was used; (2) "L'archivio della Segreteria di Stato di Pio IX durante il triennio 1848–1850," *Annali della Scuola speciale per archivisti e bibliotecari dell'Università di Roma* 21–22 (1981–1982): 54–148, which includes a listing of rubric numbers as well as individual fascicoli; and (3) "La classificazione delle carte della Segreteria di Stato tra il 1833 e il 1847," in *Miscellanea in memoria di Giorgio Cencetti* (Turin, 1973), pp. 639–663, which provides further information. In the ASV Sala d'Indici, ASV Indice 1110 provides an annotated list of rubrics and a one-sheet summarization of the rubric number system (both before and after 1847 when it was altered).

There are a number of caveats in approaching the *Fondo Moderno* through the rubric numbers. First, few documents contain only one subject. For example, if a researcher is concerned with seminaries or universities in Cuba in the early twentieth century, a researcher should request the materials classified under the rubric numbers dealing with seminaries, universities, and Cuba (i.e., 18, 43, and 251, respectively). If an issue lasted over a period of years, the number of possible buste or fascicoli needed to research a subject thoroughly can become quite high. Another problem with simply requesting rubrics dealing with certain topics for certain years is that the designated year on the busta or fascicolo does not necessarily mean that all the documents in that busta are from that year. Earlier materials are often attached to documents dated and accordingly located in a particular busta.

ASV Indici 1031, 1032, and 1033 assist researchers who prefer to approach the *Interni-Esteri* series through rubric numbers. Indici 1031, 1032, and 1033, are chronologically arranged listings (subdivided by year and then according to rubric numbers, buste, and fascicoli). Indici 1031, 1032, and 1033 also indicate any subseries in the rubrics (e.g., in Indice 1033, Rubric 27 breaks down by city: Ferrara, Forli, Ravenna, etc.), which can help to clarify the nature of the subject matter classified under a rubric number. Not all rubric numbers are represented in each year and the yearly designation for a rubric number does not mean that all materials in the busta are from that year. Earlier materials are often contained in fascicoli requested. To request rubric numbers from Indice 1033 (for *Interni-Esteri*, 1814–1822), note the year, the rubric, and the fascicoli numbers.

Location: Archivio Segreto Vaticano.

3.2.14.65 Legazione di Avignone

[DATABASE ID: VATV452-A]

Inclusive Dates: 1231–1792 (bulk 1561–1792).

Bulk: 29.9 linear m. (381 numbered vols. and 2 pacchi).

Note: Vol. 169 was acquired by the ASV between 1761 and 1763 and was formerly part of a Diversorum series; for more detailed provenance information see Pásztor, below.

References: Lajos Pásztor, "Per la storia dell'Archivio Segreto Vaticano nei secoli XVII–XVIII," *Archivio della Società romana di storia patria* 91 (1968): 157–249. Pásztor discusses the provenance of volume 169 in this series and its interrelationship with other series in the ASV and the Biblioteca Apostolica Vaticana. A brief description of volume 169 can be extracted from this article. P. Hurtubise and R. Toupin, *Correspondance du nonce en France, Antonio Maria Salviati 1572–1578* (Rome, 1975).

Finding Aids: ASV Indice 1023 (pp. 1–36) covers vols. 1–381. Indice 1023 proceeds volume by volume providing a brief contents summary, inclusive dates, and a concordance between the former and current volume numbers. A chronological index to this series begins on page 155.

ASV Indice 134, compiled by P. De Pretis in 1731, contains a listing of the first 340 volumes of this series (pp. 120–126). Annotations to volumes added to the series after De Pretis and to the current volume numbers are visible throughout Indice 134.

See Paola Carucci and Raffaele Santoro, eds., "Le fonti archivistiche," vol. 1 of *La Rivoluzione Francese (1787–1799): Repertorio delle fonti archivistiche e delle fonti a stampa conservate in Italia e nella Città del Vaticano* (Rome, 1991). This work identifies series in the ASV that pertain to the French Revolution. Materials listed from *Legazione di Avignone* are vols. 145–150, 199, 215–218, 222–224, 226–231, 245, 254, and 335–339, and mazzi 376, 378, and 381. Entries list the volume number, identify the total number of folios in a volume, provide the formal or a supplied title, summarize the materials in the volume concerning the French Revolution, and note the inclusive dates. At times, individual items are identified and described.

Location: Archivio Segreto Vaticano.

3.2.14.66 Legazione di Bologna
[DATABASE ID: VATV453-A]

Inclusive Dates: 1450–1796 (bulk 1543–1796).

Bulk: 30 linear m. (402 numbered vols.).

Note: Vols. 36, 38, 40, 45a, 56, 290, and 291 were acquired by the ASV between 1761 and 1763. For detailed provenance information see Pásztor's article cited below. Vols. 398–402 were transferred from the Propaganda Fide Archives. They were formerly identified as *Fondo Consalvi 20–24*.

References: Boyle, p. 77. Lajos Pásztor, "Governo di Bologna nel secolo XVIII nei fondi dell'Archivio segreto vaticano," in *Famiglie senatorie e istituzioni cittadine a Bologna nel settecento: Atti del I Colloquio, Bologna, 2–3 febbraio 1980* (Bologna, 1980), pp. 173–177. Lajos Pásztor, "Per la storia dell'Archivio Segreto Vaticano nei secoli XVII–XVIII," *Archivio della Società romana di storia patria* 91 (1968): 157–249. Pásztor discusses the provenance of seven volumes now in this series and their interrelationships with other series in the ASV and the Biblioteca Apostolica Vaticana. A brief listing of the seven volumes noted above can also be extracted from this article.

Finding Aids: ASV Indice 1023 (p. 472 bis) covers volumes 1–402. Indice 1023 proceeds volume by volume providing a brief contents summary, inclusive dates, and a concordance between the former and current volume numbers. More detailed contents information is provided for 397–402 on sheets inserted after p. 472. A chronological index to this series begins on p. 175.

ASV Indice 134, compiled by P. De Pretis in 1731, contains a listing of the first 390 volumes of this series (pp. 142–149). Annotations to volumes added to the series after De Pretis and to the current volume numbers are visible throughout Indice 134.

Location: Archivio Segreto Vaticano.

3.2.14.67 Legazione di Ferrara
[DATABASE ID: VATV454-A]

Inclusive Dates: 1597–1797.

Bulk: 28 linear m. (409 numbered vols. and 2 pacchi).

Reference: Boyle, p. 77.

Finding Aids: ASV Indice 1023 (pp. 77–105) covers vols. 1–409. Indice 1023 proceeds volume by volume providing a brief contents summary, inclusive dates, and a concordance between the former and current volume numbers. The foliation and physical dimensions are often included. A chronological index to this series begins on page 193.

ASV Indice 134, compiled by P. De Pretis in 1731, contains a listing of the first 326 volumes of this series (pp. 150–155). Annotations to volumes added to the series after De Pretis and to the current volume numbers are visible throughout Indice 134.

Location: Archivio Segreto Vaticano.

3.2.14.68 Legazione di Romagna
[DATABASE ID: VATV455-A]

Inclusive Dates: 1524–1797 (bulk 1643–1797).

Bulk: 11 linear m. (197 numbered vols. and 2 pacchi).

Finding Aids: ASV Indice 1023 (ff. 110–124), compiled by Mons. P. Savio, covers vols. 1–197. Indice 1023 proceeds volume by volume providing a brief contents summary, inclusive dates, and a concordance between the former and current volume numbers. The foliation and physical dimensions are often included. A chronological index to this series begins on p. 211.

ASV Indice 134, compiled by P. De Pretis in 1731, contains a brief listing of the first 152 volumes of this series (pp. 156–159v). Annotations to volumes added to the series after De Pretis and to the current volume numbers are noted throughout Indice 134.

Location: Archivio Segreto Vaticano.

3.2.14.69 Legazione di Urbino
[DATABASE ID: VATV456-A]

Inclusive Dates: 1624–1798.

Bulk: 13 linear m. (233 numbered vols., 2 pacchi, also 1 linear m. misc.).

Reference: Boyle, p. 77.

Finding Aids: ASV Indice 1023 (pp. 130–143) covers vols. 1–233. Indice 1023 proceeds volume by volume providing a brief contents summary, inclusive dates, and a concordance between the former and current volume numbers. The foliation and physical dimensions are often included. A chronological index to this series begins on p. 224.

ASV Indice 134, compiled by P. De Pretis in 1731, contains a partial and brief listing of vols. 1–132 (pp. 160–155). Later annotations to the current volume numbers are visible.

Location: Archivio Segreto Vaticano.

3.2.14.70 Legazione di Velletri
[DATABASE ID: VATV499-A]

Inclusive Dates: 1830–1848.

Bulk: 4.5 linear m. (67 numbered buste).

Organization: Buste 1–59 are arranged chronologically. Buste 60–67 are as follows: 60. Lettere e carte diverse della legazione, 1831–1839; —61–62. Suppliche, ca. 1835; —63. Vertenze civili, 1831, 1835; —64. Cause criminali del governo, 1830–1832; —65. Cause criminali, Curia vescovile di Velletri, 1832–1836; —66. Ristretti di processi criminali, 1838–1840; —67. Vertenze motivate, 1830–1834.

Scope: This series consists of correspondence with the Governatura Prefectus of Ostia and Velletri.

Reference: Fink, p. 137.

Location: Archivio Segreto Vaticano.

3.2.14.71 Lettere di cardinali

[DATABASE ID: VATV153-A]

Inclusive Dates: 1523–1803.

Bulk: 14.5 linear m. (215 numbered vols.).

Organization: Vols. 1–15, miscellaneous letters, 1523–1649; —Vols. 16–91B, unbroken chronology, 1649–1739; —Vols. 92–118, not indexed in ASV 1013, listed by volume in 1071, small series include letters of the bishop of Milan, 1572–1658, Cardinal le Monti, 1635–1643, general chronology, 1657–1669, 1701–1712; —Vol. 119, indexed miscellaneous letters, 1598–1600; —Vols. 120–134, not indexed, listed in 1071, miscellaneous series, 1554–1730, broken chronology;—Vol. 134a, indexed, miscellaneous, 1610–1614; —Vol. 159–172, indexed, general chronology, 1740–1790 (no letters for 1749–1755); —Vols. 173–191, not indexed, listed in 1071, miscellaneous series, 1730–1803 (Vol. 190, 1607–1688).

Note: Vols. 7, 99, 133a, 133b, and 133c were acquired by the ASV in 1761 and 1763; for detailed provenance information see Pásztor's 1968 article cited below.

References: Fink, pp. 95–96; Boyle, p. 73; Pásztor (1970), p. 94; Pásztor (1983), p. 132. Lajos Pásztor, "Per la storia dell'Archivio Segreto Vaticano nei secoli XVII–XVIII," *Archivio della Società romana di storia patria* 91 (1968): 157–249. Pásztor discusses the provenance of five volumes now in this series and their interrelationships with other series in the ASV and the Biblioteca Apostolica Vaticana. Brief listings for these five volumes can be extracted from this article. A. I. Bassani, "Le fonti dell'Archivio Segreto Vaticano per una storia ecclesiastica della repubblica e del regno d'Italia," in *Vita religiosa e cultura in Lombardia e nel Veneto nell'età napoleonica,* edited by F. Agostino et al. (Rome, 1990), pp. 363–393.

Reprints of selected documents can be found in the following works. B. Barbiche, ed., *Correspondance du nonce en France, Innocenzo del Bufalo, évêque de Camerino, 1601–1604* (Rome, 1964). P. Blet, ed., *Girolamo Ragazzoni évêque de Bergame, nonce en France: Correspondance de sa nonciature, 1583–1586* (Rome, 1962). R. Toupin, ed., *Correspondance du nonce en France, Giovanni Battista Castelli (1581–1583)* (Rome, 1967).

Finding Aids: ASV Indici 1013–1014 provide detailed access to vols. 1–5, 8–9, 12–91b, 119, 134a, and 159–172 of the *Lettere di cardinali.* Indice 1013 proceeds numerically (volume by volume, page by page), indicating the writer, recipient, diocese, date, and folio. Indice 1014 is an alphabetical inventory of the same volumes. Entries include the name of the author (a cardinal), the recipient (usually a cardinal or the pope), diocese, date, volume, and folio.

ASV Indice 134, compiled by De Pretis in 1731, contains a brief listing of vols. 1–189 (pp. 164–168v). The current volume number, inclusive dates, and some volumes located after De Pretis' index are noted in later annotations.

ASV Indice 1071 contains a typed copy of De Pretis (pp. olim 175v–177v or nuovi numeri 166v–168v) including

later annotations in De Pretis. The list then continues by indicating the titles of volumes added to the series after De Pretis, in total covering *Lettere di cardinali* vols. 92–215.

ASV Indice 124, "Primo Sbozzo di Inventario di tutti i libri che sono nell'Archivio Segreto Vaticano," by Giovanni Bissaiga in 1672, provides more descriptive and accurate volume titles for some series in the ASV. *Lettere di cardinale* volumes are listed on folios 280r and 307r.

Location: Archivio Segreto Vaticano.

3.2.14.72 Lettere di particolari

[DATABASE ID: VATV156-A]

Inclusive Dates: 1518 (1519)–1809.

Bulk: 37.4 linear m.

Organization: about 421 vols. or buste.

Note: Vols. 152–154 were acquired by the ASV in 1761 and 1763. Detailed provenance information is available in the 1968 Pásztor article cited below. *Lettere di particolari* vols. 314 and 315 are now identified as part of the series SS. *Registri I,* vols. 53 and 55, respectively.

References: Fink, p. 96; Boyle, p. 73; Pásztor (1970), p. 95; Pásztor (1983), p. 133. Lajos Pásztor, "Per la storia dell'Archivio Segreto Vaticano nei secoli XVII–XVIII," *Archivio della Società romana di storia patria* 91 (1968): 157–249. Pásztor discusses the provenance of three volumes now in this series and their interrelationships with other series in the ASV and the Biblioteca Apostolica Vaticana. A brief listing of vols. 152–154 can also be extracted from this article. A. I. Bassani, "Le fonti dell'Archivio Segreto Vaticano per una storia ecclesiastica della repubblica e del regno d'Italia," in *Vita religiosa e cultura in Lombardia e nel Veneto nell'età napoleonica,* edited by F. Agostino et al. (Rome, 1990), pp. 363–393.

Finding Aids: ASV Indici 1019–1021 provide the most detailed access to vols. 1–347 of the *Lettere di particolari.* Indice 1019 covers vols. 1–91; Indice 1020 covers vols. 92–150, 214–282, and 312–313; and Indice 1021 covers vols. 314–347. Indici 1019–1021 proceed volume by volume, letter by letter, and indicate the names of the correspondents and the place and date of the letter. Indici 1019 and 1020 indicate the folio. Indice 1021 also contains the only, albeit brief, listing of vols. 314–421, beginning on p. 223.

ASV Indice 134, compiled by De Pretis in 1731, contains a brief listing of vols. 1–315 (pp. 186–192). The current volume number, inclusive dates, and some volumes located after De Pretis's index are noted in later annotations.

ASV Indice 1071 contains a typed copy of De Pretis (pp. olim 198v–177v or nuovi numeri 189v–192), including the later annotations to De Pretis. Indice 1071 therefore provides a brief list of *Lettere di particolari* vols. 152–311.

Paola Carucci and Raffaele Santoro, eds., "Le fonti archivistiche," vol. 1 of *La Rivoluzione Francese (1787–1799): Repertorio delle fonti archivistiche e delle fonti a stampa conservate in Italia e nella Città del Vaticano* (Rome, 1991). This work identifies series in the ASV that pertain to the French Revolution. Materials from the following series are mentioned: *Francia,* SS. *Particolari* (vols. 272–281), *Emigrati della rivoluzione francese, Epoca napoleonica: Francia* and *Epoca napoleonica: Italia, Legazione di Avignone,* and *Fondo Garampi.* Entries list the volume number, identify the total number of folios in a volume, provide the formal or a supplied title, summarize the materials in the volume, and note the inclusive dates. At times, individual items are identified and described.

Location: Archivio Segreto Vaticano.

3.2.14.73 Lettere di principi
[DATABASE ID: VATV155-A]
Inclusive Dates: 1515–1815 (bulk 1515–1801).
Bulk: 28 linear m. (299 numbered vols.).
Organization: Chronological. Principal series and volume enumeration: Vols. 1–146A. Lettere diverse di principi, ecc., 1515–1740 (original copies of incoming correspondence in roughly chronological order); —vols. 207A–267. Lettere di principi, 1598–1801 (original copies of incoming correspondence in roughly chronological order, overlaps but does not duplicate the previous series); —vols. 146B–179, 278–279, Registro di lettere scritte a diversi principi, 1541–1721 (copies of outgoing correspondence in roughly chronological order); —vols. 181–207, 280, Minute di lettere a diversi, 1575–1740 (drafts of outgoing correspondence in roughly chronological order, overlaps but does not duplicate the previous series).
Scope: This series consists of correspondence between the pope, secretary of state, and other curial officials, and rulers, members of royal families, and some cardinals.
Note: Vols. 147, 149–199, 168–171, 180, 181, 183, 185, 186, 188, and 191 were acquired by the ASV in 1761 and 1763. For detailed provenance information see Pásztor's 1968 article cited below.
References: Fink, p. 96; Boyle, p. 73; Pásztor (1970), pp. 91–93; Pásztor (1983), pp. 131–132. Lajos Pásztor, "Per la storia dell'Archivio Segreto Vaticano nei secoli XVII–XVIII," *Archivio della Società romana di storia patria* 91 (1968): 157–249. Pásztor discusses the provenance of thirty volumes now in this series and their interrelationships with other series in the ASV and the Biblioteca Apostolica Vaticana. A brief listing for each of these thirty volumes can be extracted from this article.
B. Barbiche, ed., *Correspondance du nonce en France, Innocenzo del Bufalo, évêque de Camerino, 1601–1604* (Rome, 1964). P. Blet, ed., *Girolamo Ragazzoni évêque de Bergame, nonce en France: Correspondance de sa nonciature, 1583–1586* (Rome, 1962). J. Lestocquoy, ed., *Correspondance des nonces en France: Dandino, Della Torre et Trivultio, 1546–1551 avec des documents relatifs a la rupture des relations diplomatiques, 1551–1552* (Rome, 1966). J. Lestocquoy, ed., *Correspondance des nonces en France: Lenzi et Gualterio, Légation du Cardinal Trivultio (1557–1561)* (Rome, 1977). A. L. Martin, ed., *Correspondance du nonce en France, Fabio Mirto Frangipani 1568–1572 et 1586–1587, Nonce extraordinaire en 1574, 1575–1576 et 1578* (Rome, 1984).
Finding Aids: ASV Indici 1017–1018 calendar SS. *Lettere di principi* vols. 1–125 and 126–146A, respectively (i.e., the first two series described above). Entries proceed page by page, volume by volume, and include the names of writer and recipient, the place and date of the letter, and the current pages in a specific volume where the letter can be located (e.g., Enrico II a Guilio III, S. Germain 17 Nov 1556, fol. 160–161).
ASV Indice 1071 is a typed copy of De Pretis (ASV Indice 134, olim. ff. 191–193, nuovi ff. 182–184v), including the later annotations to De Pretis. This index lists the volume titles of series three and four (vols. 146B–207, 229, 278–280, described above), providing current volume numbers, inclusive dates, and titles, as found on the spines.

ASV Indice 134, compiled by De Pretis in 1731 (ff. 187–194), provides a listing of the titles found on the spines of vols. 1–278 in this series. Entries list type of document (i.e., lettere, minute) and inclusive dates, and bear some later annotations.
Location: Archivio Segreto Vaticano.

3.2.14.74 Lettere di soldati
[DATABASE ID: VATV157-A]
Inclusive Dates: 1572–1755.
Bulk: 6.3 linear m. (about 88 vols.).
Scope: This series contains correspondence. The general range could not be determined.
References: Fink, p. 97; Boyle, p. 73.
Finding Aids: ASV Indice 134, compiled by De Pretis in 1731, contains a later insertion and brief listing of volume titles for vols. 1–79 (ff. 194–196v). The current volume number, the general type of documents (i.e., corrispondenza, dispacci, minute), and inclusive dates are noted.
ASV Indice 1022 covers vols. 1–88 in this series. Entries for vols. 1–60 proceed volume by volume listing the current volume number and inclusive dates of the volume and then calendar each letter in the volume (writer, recipient, place, and date) and folio. After vol. 61, each volume is summarized.
Location: Archivio Segreto Vaticano.

3.2.14.75 Lettere di vescovi e prelati
[DATABASE ID: VATV154-A]
Inclusive Dates: 1505–1797.
Bulk: 32 linear m. (385 numbered vols.).
Organization: Organized in part into eight subseries: I. [Early series], 1505–1664; —II. Registro di lettere a vescovi (variously designated), 1606–1797; —III. Lettere dei vescovi interrotta (variously designated), 1645–1791; —IV. [Miscellaneous], 1644–1730; —V. Registro di lettere di Monsig. Menatti Vescovo di Lodi, 1669–1673; —VI. Lettere dei vescovi a Benedetto XIV . . . , 1742–1758; —VII. Minute di Segretariato di Stato a prelati, 1741–1757; —VIII. Lettere del Card. Pentucci ol Card. Or Chinto Orch. di Milano, 1701–1712.
Scope: This series consists of various letters and minute of various bishops and prelates with the SS. office; it also contains registers of correspondence.
Note: Volumes 8, 9, 17, 18, 166a, 169a, 169b, 169c, and 169d were acquired by the ASV in 1761 and 1763; for detailed provenance information see Pásztor's 1968 article cited below.
References: Fink, p. 96; Boyle, p. 73; Pásztor (1970), pp. 94–95; Pásztor (1983), pp. 132–133. G. Bourgin, *La France et Rome de 1788 à 1797: Regestes des dépêches du cardinal secrétaire d'état tirées du fonds des "Vescovi" des archives secrètes du Vatican* (Paris, 1909). A. Clergeac, "Inventaire analytique et chronologique de la Série des Archives du Vatican, dite 'Lettere di Vescovi'," *Annales de St.-Louis-des-Français* 10 (1906): 215–268, 319–375, 419–470.
Lajos Pásztor, "Per la storia dell'Archivio Segreto Vaticano nei secoli XVII–XVIII," *Archivio della Società romana di storia patria* 91 (1968): 157–249. Pásztor discusses the provenance of nine volumes now in this series and their interrelationships with other series in the ASV and the Biblioteca Apostolica Vaticana. A brief listing of these nine volumes can also be extracted from this article. A. I. Bassani, "Le fonti dell'Archivio Segreto Vaticano per una storia ecclesiastica della repubblica e

del regno d'Italia," in *Vita religiosa e cultura in Lombardia e nel Veneto nell'età napoleonica*, edited by F. Agostino et al. (Rome, 1990), pp. 363–393.

Finding Aids: ASV Indici 1015 and 1016 provide the most detailed access to part of the *Lettere di vescovi e prelati*. Indice 1015 covers vols. 1–27, 29–166, and 231–322a. Entries proceed volume by volume, page by page, and indicate the correspondents, the place and date of the letter, and folio number. Indice 1016 is an alphabetical index to the volumes covered in Indice 1015. Entries proceed alphabetically by diocese and include the names of the correspondents, the place and date of the letter, the volume number, and folio.

ASV Indice 134, compiled by De Pretis in 1731, contains a brief listing of vols. 1–374 (ff. 170–177v). The current volume number, inclusive dates, and some volumes located after De Pretis's index are noted in later annotations.

ASV Indice 1071 contains a typed copy of De Pretis (ff. olim 183v–184v, 186–186v, or nuovi numeri 175–177v), including the later annotations in De Pretis. The list then continues by indicating the titles of volumes added to the series after De Pretis, in total covering Vescovi e prelati vols. 166a–385.

Location: Archivio Segreto Vaticano.

3.2.14.76 Lettere diverse
[DATABASE ID: VATV10437-A]
Inclusive Dates: 1587–1782.
Bulk: 121 pacchi.
Location: Archivio Segreto Vaticano.

3.2.14.77 Libri di corrispondenza
[DATABASE ID: VATV514-A]
Inclusive Dates: 1644–1823.
Bulk: 1.5 linear m. (60 vols.).
Organization: Primarily chronological.

Scope: This series consists, for the most part, of lists of dispatches to nunciatures and legations. There is very little indication of the contents of these missives.

Note: Vols. 1 and 3–11 were acquired by the ASV in 1761–1763; see Pásztor, below. Spine titles include: "Dispacchi a nunziature e legazione," "Registro generale delle corrispondenze," "Registro delle posizione," and "Registro delle carte trasmettono."

Reference: Lajos Pásztor, "Per la storia dell'Archivio Segreto Vaticano nei secoli XVII–XVIII," *Archivio della Società romana di storia patria* 91 (1968): 157–249. Pásztor discusses the provenance of this series and its interrelationship with other series in the ASV and the Biblioteca Apostolica Vaticana. A partial listing of volumes can also be extracted from this article.

Location: Archivio Segreto Vaticano.

3.2.14.78 Libri rationum
[DATABASE ID: VATV10229-A]
Inclusive Dates: 1908–1941.
Bulk: 1 linear m. (22 vols.).
Organization: Chronological. Two subseries include: Conto di Cassa della Segreteria dei Brevi and Cancelleria dei Brevi Apostolici.

Scope: The initial few months of this series were created by the Segreteria dei Brevi. The first volume includes "Ruolo degli officiali della Segreteria dei Brevi per il mese. . . ."

Location: Archivio Segreto Vaticano.

3.2.14.79 Memoriali e biglietti
[DATABASE ID: VATV174-A]
Inclusive Dates: 1578–1798.
Bulk: 32 linear m. (327 numbered vols. and buste and 22 unnumbered buste).

Organization: Includes following subseries and volume enumeration: 1. Memoriali diversi, 1578–1673 (includes: Memoriali orig. di diversi al pontifice ed alla segreteria, 1647–1654, vols. 1–16; Memoriali orig. al pontifice ed alla segreteria, 1654–1676, vols. 17–20; Misc. memoriali, 1677–1692, vol. 71A); —2. Memoriali e biglietti, 1653–1740, vols. 21–75, 122–127, 129–154; —3. Biglietti autografi del Cardinale Torrigiani, 1761–1769, vol. 128; —4. Viglietti e memoriali comunale, 1740–1791, vols. 76–121; —5. Minute di biglietti della segreteria, 1723–1798, vols. 156–266; —6. Registro de viglietti (della segreteria), 1716–1794, vols. 267–286, 289; —7. Viglietti/Biglietti di mons. governatore di Roma, 1741–1792, vols. 294–302; —8. Viglietti/Biglietti a mons. governatore di Roma, 1741–1782, vols. 303–305; —9. Viglietti de mons. commissario del mare (alla segreteria), 1775–1784 (1779–1780 missing), vols. 306–312.

In addition there are the following volumes: vol. 313. Indice di biglietti della segreteria e di lettere della medesima a particolari e prelati, 1788–1794; —vol. 314. Rubricella della carte trasmesse dalla Segreteria di Stato alle congregazioni ed uffici di Roma, 1794–1795; —vol. 315. Ristretto dei dispacci, viglietti diversi, passaporti e patenti, 1758; —vol. 316. Memoriali e viglietti della posta pontificia, 1774–1775; —vol. 317. Registro dei viglietti che si scrivono alla Segreteria di Stato a mons. Liberati sottodatario, 1683–1688.

References: Pásztor (1970), p. 96; Pásztor (1983), p. 133; Boyle, p. 79. R. Toupin, ed., *Correspondance du nonce en France, Giovanni Battista Castelli (1581–1583)* (Rome, 1967).

Finding Aids: ASV Indice 1026 (pp. 115–128, 263–272), compiled by Mons. P. Savio, lists volumes 1–317. Entries indicate the former and current volume numbers and provide a brief descriptive indication of type of business, inclusive dates, pagination, and some additional annotations. Pages 263–272 provide a simpler list of volumes 1–314, giving inclusive dates, abbreviated titles, and the current volume number.

ASV Indice 134 compiled by De Pretis in 1731 contains a very brief listing of part of this series on folii 206–208. No volume numbers are given.

Location: Archivio Segreto Vaticano.

3.2.14.80 Messe
[DATABASE ID: VATV10490-A]
Inclusive Dates: 1904–1921.
Bulk: 6 linear m. (47 buste).
Location: Archivio Segreto Vaticano.

3.2.14.81 Ministri esteri
[DATABASE ID: VATV488-A]
Inclusive Dates: 1800–1809.
Bulk: 4.5 linear m. (102 fasc.).
Organization: Three subseries: Francia; —Portogallo; —Spagna.

References: Pásztor (1970), p. 90; Pásztor (1983), p. 130.

Finding Aids: The SS. *Rubricelle* and *Protocolli* can also be used as indices to this series. For further information on their use, see the general description for the Secretariatus Status series *Fondo Moderno*.

Location: Archivio Segreto Vaticano.

3.2.14.82 [Miscellanea]

[DATABASE ID: VATV10526-A]

Inclusive Dates: 1831–1836, 1915–1968.

Bulk: 14 linear m.

Organization: Subseries include: [4 subseries post-1922]; —Fondo Carlo Costantini, 1915–1918; —[6 subseries post-1922]; —Legislazioni libanese; —[1 subseries post-1922]; —S.C. Concistoriale; —[2 subseries post-1922]; —Curzione Gregorio XVI, 1831–1836; —[1 subseries post-1922].

Note: This series is a true miscellany and has no official ASV designation.

Location: Archivio Segreto Vaticano.

3.2.14.83 Miscellanea Leo XIII

[DATABASE ID: VATV10473-A]

Inclusive Dates: [18—]–[19—].

Bulk: 5.5 linear m.

Organization: Subseries are: Questione Romana, Curia Romana, Stati Esteri, and Miscellanea.

Location: Archivio Segreto Vaticano.

3.2.14.84 Miscellanea Pio X

[DATABASE ID: VATV10477-A]

Inclusive Dates: 1903–1914.

Bulk: .5 linear m. (6 buste).

Location: Archivio Segreto Vaticano.

3.2.14.85 Missione della Santa Sede all'UNESCO

[DATABASE ID: VATV40021-A]

Inclusive Dates: 1950–1960.

Bulk: 26 buste.

Note: This series was cited in Natalini et al., p. 274, but not seen by project staff in 1990.

Location: Archivio Segreto Vaticano.

3.2.14.86 Morte di pontefici e conclavi

[DATABASE ID: VATV40022-A]

Inclusive Dates: 1878–1922.

Bulk: 29 buste.

Organization: Subseries include: Pio IX; —Leone XIII; —Pio X; —Benedetto XV.

Note: This series was cited in Natalini et al., p. 274. Project staff have identified three of the subseries as Secretariatus Status *Spogli di Leone XIII*, *Spogli di SS. Pio X*, and *Spogli SS. Benedetto XV* but have not identified the Pio IX subseries, which apparently consists of two buste.

Location: Archivio Segreto Vaticano.

3.2.14.87 Nunzi

[DATABASE ID: VATV489-A]

Inclusive Dates: 1800–1810.

Bulk: 2.7 linear m. (51 fasc.).

Note: This series could not be consulted in July 1990.

References: Pásztor (1970), p. 89; Pásztor (1983), pp. 129–130.

Finding Aids: Pásztor identifies the SS. *Rubricelle* and *Protocolli* as indices to this series. For further information on the

use of the *Rubricelle* and *Protocolli*, consult the general description for the Secretariatus Status series *Fondo Moderno*.

Location: Archivio Segreto Vaticano.

3.2.14.88 Nunziatura di Baviera

[DATABASE ID: VATV432-A]

Inclusive Dates: 1786–1808.

Bulk: 7.2 linear m. (77 numbered vols. and 2 unnumbered pacchi).

References: Boyle, p. 76; Fink, pp. 85, 91–92. J. Schlecht and T. J. Scherg, eds., *Bavarica aus dem Vatikan, 1461–1491* (Munich, 1932).

Finding Aids: ASV Indice 134, compiled by De Pretis in 1731, contains a later insertion and brief listing of volume titles for vols. 1–49 (ff. 92v–93v). The current volume number, the general type of documents (correspondenza, dispacci, minute), and inclusive dates are noted.

ASV Indice 1071 (ff. 3–5) contains a typed copy of the insertion in De Pretis (ff. olim 101v–102v or nuovi numeri 92v–93v). Between folios 5 and 6 there is a 1965 insertion by Josef Steinruck that provides more detailed information on vols. 13–46.

Location: Archivio Segreto Vaticano,

3.2.14.89 Nunziatura de Colonia

[DATABASE ID: VATV433-A]

Inclusive Dates: 1573–1799.

Bulk: 26.2 linear m. (339 numbered vols.).

Note: Vols. 34 and 216a were acquired by the ASV between 1761 and 1763. For detailed provenance information, see the Pásztor article cited below.

Note: Vol. 174t is available on microfilm.

References: Boyle. p. 76; Fink, pp. 85, 90–91. W. Reinhard, "Katholische Reform und Gegenreformation in der Kölner Nuntiatur 1584–1621: Aufgaben und erste Ergebnisse eines Editionsunternehmens der Görres-Gesellschaft (Nuntiaturberichte aus Deutschland. Die Kölner Nuntiatur I–V," *Römische Quartalschrift für christliche Altertumskunde und für Kirchengeschichte* 66 (1971): 8–65.

Lajos Pásztor, "Per la storia dell'Archivio Segreto Vaticano nei secoli XVII–XVIII," *Archivio della Società romana di storia patria* 91 (1968): 157–249. Pásztor discusses the provenance of two volumes now in this series and their interrelationship with other series in the ASV and the Biblioteca Apostolica Vaticana. A partial listing of volumes can also be extracted from this article.

Leo Just, "Die Quellen zur Geschichte der kölner Nuntiatur in Archiv und Bibliothek des Vatikans," *Quellen und Forschungen aus italienischen Archiven und Bibliotheken* 29 (1938–39): 249–296.

Leon E. Halkin, *Les Archives des nonciatures* (Brussels, 1968). While this is the best place to begin a study of Belgian sources in the ASV in the modern period, Halkin notes the importance of records in the nunciatures outside Belgium and provides a list of all the published volumes concerning each one. He then provides an in-depth look at Flanders, Cologne, and Brussels. Halkin proceeds nuncio by nuncio and lists publications and the status of future publications of materials from their nunciatures. He sometimes lists the primary collections where materials from the nunciatures can be found. Although the *Nunz. Colonia* series is listed, it is always one among several series which should be consulted in both the ASV and the BAV.

Michael F. Feldkamp, *Studien und Texte zur Geschichte der kölner Nuntiatur* (Vatican City, 1993–1995), vol. 1, "Die Kölner Nuntiatur und ihr Archiv: Eine behördengeschichtliche und quellenkundliche Untersuchung"; vol. 2, "Dokumente und Materialien über Jurisdiktion, Nuntiatursprengel, Haushalt, Zerimoniell und Verwaltung der kölner Nuntiatur (1584–1794)"; vol. 3, "Inventar des Fonds 'Archivio della Nunziatura di Colonia' im Vatikanischen Archiv." Feldkamp concentrates on the *Archivio della Nunziatura di Colonia*.

Nuntiaturberichte aus Deutschland nebst ergänzenden Actenstücken, Die Kölner Nuntiatur (Paderborn, 1969–) and *Analecta vaticano-belgica* are the two major sources where reprints and summaries of records concerning the Cologne nunciature can be found. Although the volumes vary in applying the selection methods, one is sure to find a lengthy introduction with footnotes and bibliography. The entries include the correspondents, the series and volume number citing where the original document can be found, a German summary of the business, and the reprint or summary. Earlier volumes in the series are more likely to have a reprint. Documents come from ASV *Nunz. Colonia* as well as other series. Volumes are indexed by person, place, and subject. A list of volumes follows:

Vol. 1: S. Ehses and A. Meister, *Bonomi in Köln, Santorio in der Schweiz, die Strassbuger Wirren*, originally published as vol. 1 of *Nuntiaturberichte aus Deutschland nebst ergänzenden Actenstücken, 1585 (1584)–(1592). Erste Abteilung* (Paderborn, 1895), reprinted 1969 as vol. 1 of this series. Vol. 2: S. Ehses, *Ottavio Mirto Frangipani in Köln, 1587–1590*, originally published as vol. 2 of *Nuntiaturberichte aus Deutschland nebst ergänzenden Actenstücken, 1585 (1584)–(1592). Erste Abteilung* (Paderborn, 1899), reprinted 1969 as vol. 2 of this series. Vol. 4: K. Wittstadt, *Nuntius Atilio Amalteo (1606 September–1607 September)* (Munich, 1975), is a particularly useful volume because it prints a few documents as examples. Vol. 5: W. Reinhard, *Nuntius Antonio Albergati (1610 Mai–1614 Mai)* (Munich, 1972–). Vol. 6: L. Jaitner, *Nuntius Pietro Francesco Montoro (1621 Juli–1624 Oktober)* (Munich, 1977). Vol. 7: J. Wijnhoven, *Nuntius Pier Luigi Carafa (1624 Juni–1627 August)* (Paderborn, 1980).

Analecta vaticano-belgica, ser. 2, section B, *Nonciature de Cologne*, (Brussels, 1956–). This is a series of reprints and/or summaries of selected items regarding the nunciature of Cologne from the SS. *Nunz. Colonia* and other related series and collections. At a minimum, each new nunciature is introduced with a history and bibliography of the period, a note concerning the sources, and the rationale or method used in the compilation or selection. Each entry includes: the correspondents' names, place and date, a French language summary, the citation (volume number) to a specific series, and the reprint in the original language. There are minimal analytical footnotes and bibliographic references in the actual reprints or summaries. There are indexes to persons, places, and limited topics at the end of each volume. A list of volumes follows:

Vol. 1: W. Brulez, *Correspondence de Martino Alfieri (1634–1639)* (Brussels, 1956). Vols. 2–6: H. Dessart, L. E. Halkin, and J. Hoyoux, *Inventaire analytique de documents relatifs à l'histoire du diocèse de Liège sous le régime des nonces de Cologne* (Brussels, 1957–1991). Vol. 7: F. Donnay, *Inventaire analytique de documents relatifs à l'histoire du diocèse de Liège sous le régime des nonces de Cologne: Giuseppe-Maria Sanfelice (1652–1659)* (Brussels, 1991). Vol. 8: P. Derkenne and P. Gemis, *Inventaire analytique de documents relatifs à l'histoire du diocèse de Liège sous le régime des nonces de Cologne: Marco Galli (1659–1666)* (Brussels, 1993).

F. Diaz, *Francesco Buonvisi: Nunziatura a Colonia* (Rome, 1959), provides a good introduction to the nunciature and notes the sources, such as *Nunz. Colonia* vols. 44, 45, 46, 47, 220, 220A and the Archivio Buonvisi in the Archivio di Stato di Lucca.

Finding Aids: ASV Indice 1027 (ff. 116–157) lists vols. 1–339. Entries proceed volume by volume and contain a brief description of contents, inclusive dates, the former and current volume number, and selected additional notes. Indice 1027 also provides a chronological index to SS. *Nunz. Colonia* between foli 224 and 239.

ASV Indice 134, compiled by De Pretis in 1731, provides a more succinct listing of vols. 1–298, beginning on fol. 85. The listing for SS. *Nunz. Colonia* in Indice 134 contains many later annotations and additions.

Location: Archivio Segreto Vaticano.

3.2.14.90 Nunziatura di Corsica
[DATABASE ID: VATV434-A]

Inclusive Dates: 1655–1801 (bulk 1746–1770).

Bulk: 1 linear m. (11 vols.).

Organization: Subseries include: Misc. letters, register cifre, and minute (1746–1770), 7 vols.; —Miscellanea (1655–1801), 4 vols.

References: Boyle, p. 76; Fink, pp. 85–86.

Finding Aids: P. Pecchiai, "Le carte del fondo 'Corsica' nell'Archivio vaticano," *Archivio storico di Corsica* 9, no. 4 (1933): 3–7. This article provides the most detailed inventory of vols. 1–10. Pecchiai proceeds packet by packet, describing the nature of the contents, providing some itemized examples of the material, and/or exact volume titles. This article also briefly introduces the series and gives some bibliographic data and cross-references to other materials in the ASV.

ASV Indice 1024-I (ff. 33–34) lists vols. 1–11 of SS. *Nunz. Corsica*. Entries proceed volume by volume and contain a brief description of contents, inclusive dates, and the former and current volume number. ASV Indice 1024-II provides a chronological index to this series on folio 239–240.

ASV Indice 134, compiled by De Pretis in 1731, contains a later addition that briefly lists vols. 1–10 of the SS. *Nunz. Corsica* series on folio 67.

Location: Archivio Segreto Vaticano.

3.2.14.91 Nunziatura di Fiandra
[DATABASE ID: VATV435-A]

Inclusive Dates: 1553–1795.

Bulk: 18.9 linear m. (209 numbered vols. and 2 pacchi).

Notes: Vols. 48 and 53 were acquired by the ASV in 1761–1763. They were formerly part of a Diversorum series. For additional information on the provenance see the 1968 Pásztor article cited below. Vol. 61 is available on microfilm.

References: Boyle, p. 76; Fink, pp. 85, 86–87; Pásztor (1970), pp. 81–82; Pásztor (1983), pp. 124–125. Lajos Pásztor, "Per la storia dell'Archivio Segreto Vaticano nei secoli XVII–XVIII," *Archivio della Società romana di storia patria* 91 (1968): 157–249. Pásztor discusses the provenance of two volumes now in this series and their interrelationships with other series in the ASV and the Biblioteca Apostolica Vaticana.

A. Cauchie, "De la création d'une école belge à Rome," in *Compte rendu des travaux du dixième congrès tenu à Tournai du 5 au 8 août 1895*, of the Congrès de la Fédération archéologique et historique de Belgique (Tournai, 1896), pp. 739–802. A. Cauchie and R. Maere, *Recueil des instructions générales aux nonces de Flandre (1596–1635)* (Brussels, 1904). H. J. Elias, "La nonciature de Guido Bentivoglio, archevêque de Rhodes, à Bruxelles (1607–1615)," *Bulletin de l'Institut historique Belge de Rome* 8 (1928): 273–281. L. E. Halkin, *Les sources de l'histoire de la Belgique aux Archives et à la Bibliothèque Vaticanes: État des collections et répertoire bibliographique* (Brussels, 1951). J. Lestocquoy, ed., *Correspondance du nonce en France: Prospero Santa Croce (1552–1554)* (Rome, 1972). F. Santy, *Belgie in het Vaticaans Archief: Nuntiatuur te Brussel 1875–1904: Regestenlijst* (Louvain, 1989).

Leon E. Halkin, *Les Archives des nonciatures* (Brussels, 1968), is the best place to begin a study of Belgian sources in the ASV in the modern period. Halkin notes the importance of records in the nunciatures outside Belgium and provides a list of all the published volumes concerning each one. He then provides an in-depth look at the nunciatures of Flanders, Cologne, and Brussels. Halkin proceeds nuncio by nuncio and lists publications and the status of future publications of materials from their nunciatures. He sometimes lists the primary collections where materials from the nunciature can be found. Although the *Nunz. Fiandra* series is listed, it is always one among several series that should be consulted in both the ASV and the BAV.

Analecta vaticano-belgica, ser. 2, section A, *Nonciature de Flandre*. This series reprints selected documents in the *Nunziatura di Fiandra* series. Individual volumes in this series are: Vols. 1–3: L. van der Essen and A. Louant, *Correspondance d'Ottavio Mirto Frangipani, premier nonce de Flandre (1596–1606)* (Rome, 1924–1942). Vol. 4: L. van Meerbeeck, *Correspondance des nonces Gesualdo, Morra, Sanseverino, avec la Secrétairerie d'Etat pontificale, 1615–1621* (Brussels, 1937). Vols. 5–6: B. de Meester, *Correspondance du nonce Giovanni-Francesco Guidi di Bagno (1621–1627)* (Brussels, 1938). Vol. 10: W. Brulez, *Correspondance de Richard Pauli-Stravius (1634–1642)* (Brussels, 1955). Vol. 11: L. van Meerbeeck, *Correspondance du Nonce Fabio de Lagonissa, archevêque de Conza, 1627–1634* (Brussels, 1966). Vol. 12: J. Thielens, *La correspondance de Vincenzo Santini internonce aux Pays-Bas, 1713–1721* (Brussels, 1969). Vol. 13: L. van Meerbeeck, *Correspondance du nonce Decio Carafa, archevêque de Damas (1606–1607)* (Brussels, 1979). Vol. 14: L. Demoulin, *Correspondance de Vincenzo Montalto, administrateur de la nonciature de Flandre* (Brussels, 1985). Vol. 15: H. Lambert, *Correspondance d'Andrea Mangelli internonce aux Pay-bas (1652–1655)* (Brussels, 1993).

Finding Aids: ASV Indice 1026 (ff. 5–27) briefly describes vols. 1–209. Entries proceed volume by volume and indicate the type of material (e.g., lettere, minute, posizioni), inclusive dates, and sometimes the correspondent(s).

ASV Indice 134, compiled by De Pretis in 1731, provides a more succinct listing of vols. 1–194, beginning on fol. 128. Indice 134 also contains later annotations and additions.

Location: Archivio Segreto Vaticano.

3.2.14.92 Nunziatura di Firenze

[DATABASE ID: VATV436-A]

Inclusive Dates: 1532–1809 (bulk 1570–1809).

Bulk: 19 linear m. (272 numbered vols. and 5 pacchi).

Organization: Principal series include: Lett. orig. nunzio alla segreteria (1570–1809); —Reg. cifre nunzio alla segreteria (1623–1643); —Decifrata nunziatura alla segreteria (1588–1806 with many gaps); —Lett. orig. e confid. nunzio alla segreteria (1740–1756); —Min. di lett. segreteria al nunzio (1572–1807 with gaps); —Reg. lett. segreteria al nunzio (1605–1802 with gaps); —Reg. cifre segreteria al nunzio (1623–1768 with gaps); —Min. e biglietti del ministro de Toscana in Roma alla segreteria (1758–1805).

Note: Vols. 46, 51, and 256 were acquired by the ASV between 1761 and 1763 and were formerly part of a Diversorum series. For more detailed provenance information see the article by Pásztor cited below.

References: Boyle, p. 76; Fink, pp. 85–86. Lajos Pásztor, "Per la storia dell'Archivio Segreto Vaticano nei secoli XVII–XVIII," *Archivio della Società romana di storia patria* 91 (1968): 157–249. Pásztor discusses the provenance of three volumes from this series and their interrelationship with other series in the ASV and the Biblioteca Apostolica Vaticana. A brief listing of the three volumes noted above can also be extracted from this article.

Reprints of selected documents from several nunciatures can be found in the following works. A. L. Martin, ed., *Correspondance du nonce en France, Fabio Mirto Frangipani 1568–1572 et 1586–1587, Nonce extraordinaire en 1574, 1575–1576 et 1578* (Rome, 1984). P. Hurtubise and R. Toupin, *Correspondance du nonce en France, Antonio Maria Salviati 1572–1578* (Rome, 1975).

Finding Aids: ASV Indice 1024 I (ff. 1–25) lists vols. 1–272. Entries proceed volume by volume and indicate the current and former volume number, inclusive dates, correspondent(s), and a brief description of contents. ASV Indice 1024 II (ff. 223–233) provides a chronological listing of vols. 1–271.

ASV Indice 134, compiled by De Pretis in 1731, provides a more succinct listing of vols. 1–194, beginning on fol. 104. Indice 134 contains many later annotations and additions.

Location: Archivio Segreto Vaticano.

3.2.14.93 Nunziatura di Francia

[DATABASE ID: VATV437-A]

Inclusive Dates: 1527–1826.

Bulk: 66 linear m. (727 numbered vols.).

Organization: Six subseries: I. Lett. orig. nunzio alla segreteria 1527–1808, includes letters, registers, letters in code, letters deciphered, other misc. correspondence; —II. Lettere segreteria al nunzio 1535–1808, includes registers, registers in code, letters deciphered, (Spada), misc. letters; —III. Biglietti ambasciatore di Francia alla segreteria 1741–1809 (8 vols.); —IV. Reg. biglietti segreteria all'ambasciatore di Francia 1758–1809 (8 vols.); —V. Misc. material including Lettere diverse, Istruzioni diverse, Relazione sulle rendite della Francia, Relazione della morte di Montesquieu 1755, Controversia della regalia 1677–1689, Misc. carte. Material covers 1520–1796; —VI. Includes Carte diverse, Stampe diverse, 1288–1826 with the bulk between 1530–1796, about 50 vols.

Volumes are numbered 1–672 and I–LV. Vols. 1a, 25, 105, 114, 116, 118, 286, 297, 299, and 310 were acquired by the

ASV in 1761 and 1763. For detailed provenance information see Pásztor's article cited below.

References: Boyle, p. 76; Fink, pp. 84, 86; Pásztor (1970), pp. 82–84; Pásztor (1983), pp. 125–126. Lajos Pásztor, "Per la storia dell'Archivio Segreto Vaticano nei secoli XVII–XVIII," *Archivio della Società romana di storia patria* 91 (1968): 157–249. Pásztor discusses the provenance of ten volumes now in this series and their interrelationships with other series in the ASV and the Biblioteca Apostolica Vaticana. A brief listing of the ten volumes noted above can also be extracted from this article.

R. Ancel, *Nonciatures de France: Nonciatures de Paul IV avec le derniere annee de Jules III et Marcel II* (Paris, 1909–1911). J. Fraikin, *Nonciatures de Clément VII*, vol. 1, *Depuis la bataille de Pavie jusqu'au rappel d'Acciaiuoli, 25 févier 1525–juin 1527* (Paris, 1906). L. de Stefani, *La nunziatura di Francia del Cardinale Guido Bentivoglio: Lettere a Scipione Borghese* (Florence, 1863–1870).

J. Lestocquoy, ed., *Correspondance des nonces en France: Carpi et Ferrerio 1535–1540, et legations de Carpi et de Farnese* (Rome, 1961). Reprints of documents from the nunciatures are very much alike. This is the first volume in the *Acta Nuntiaturae Gallicae* series and it sets the tone for the entire run. The complete series is listed below. There is a good introduction to the persons, period, and the nunciature with footnotes and a bibliography. There is little information concerning the methodology behind the document selection process, other than an indication that political documents have been selected. However, there is information about the series from which the documents have been extracted. Entries contain the names of the correspondents, the place and date, the collection(s) in which the document has been located (series name, volume, and folio), and finally the reprinted or summarized document in the original language(s). A minimal number of footnotes accompany the text of the documents. Later volumes may also have a French language summary of the document with the reprint. Each volume is indexed by name, place, and some subjects. Lestocquoy's work demonstrates the interconnection of various series that can be used to reconstruct the history of a nunciature. This volume draws documents from ASV series *Archivum Arcis* and SS. *Principi*, as well as collections in other repositories.

Vol. 2: P. Blet, ed., *Girolamo Ragazzoni évêque de Bergame, nonce en France: Correspondance de sa nonciature, 1583–1586* (Rome, 1962). Vol. 3: J. Lestocquoy, *Correspondance des nonces en France, Capodiferro, Dandino et Guidicione, 1541–1546: Légations des cardinaux Farnèse et Sadolet et missions d'Ardinghello, de Grimani et de Hieronimo da Correggio* (Rome, 1963). Vol. 4: B. Barbiche, ed., *Correspondance du nonce en France, Innocenzo del Bufalo, évêque de Camerino, 1601–1604* (Rome, 1964). Vol. 5: P. Blet, ed., *Correspondance du nonce en France Ranuccio Scotti, 1639–1641* (Rome, 1965). Vol. 6: J. Lestocquoy, ed., *Correspondance des nonces en France: Dandino, Della Torre et Trivultio, 1546–1551 avec des documents relatifs a la rupture des relations diplomatiques, 1551–1552* (Rome, 1966). Vol. 7: R. Toupin, ed., *Correspondance du nonce en France, Giovanni Battista Castelli (1581–1583)* (Rome, 1967). Vol. 8: I. Cloulas, ed., *Correspondance du nonce en France, Anselmo Dandino (1578–1581)* (Rome, 1970). Vol. 9: J. Lestocquoy, ed., *Correspondance du nonce en France: Prospero Santa Croce (1552–1554)* (Rome,

1972). Vols. 10–11: B. Neveu, ed., *Correspondance du nonce en France, Angelo Ranuzzi 1683–1689* (Rome, 1973). Vols. 12–13: P. Hurtubise and R. Toupin, *Correspondance du nonce en France, Antonio Maria Salviati 1572–1578* (Rome, 1975). Vol. 14: J. Lestocquoy, ed., *Correspondance des nonces en France: Lenzi et Gualterio, Légation du Cardinal Trivultio (1557–1561)* (Rome, 1977). Vol. 15: S. de Dainville-Barbiche, ed., *Correspondance du nonce en France, Fabrizio Spada, 1674–1675* (Rome, 1982). Vol. 16: A. L. Martin, ed., *Correspondance du nonce en France, Fabio Mirto Frangipani 1568–1572 et 1586–1587, Nonce extraordinaire en 1574, 1575–1576 et 1578* (Rome, 1984).

Finding Aids: ASV Indice 1025 (ff. 1–70) is a volume by volume listing of vols. 1–672 and I–LV. Entries indicate the current and former volume number, the type of material (e.g., lettere, minute), the inclusive dates, and selected other information. ASV Indice 1025 also contains a chronological listing of volumes on pages 159–170.

ASV Indice 134, compiled by De Pretis in 1731, provides a more succinct listing of vols. 1–615, beginning on fol. 15. Indice 134 also contains later annotations and additions.

Paola Carucci and Raffaele Santoro, eds., *Le fonti archivistiche*, vol. 1 of *La Rivoluzione Francese (1787–1799): Repertorio delle fonti archivistiche e delle fonti a stampa conservate in Italia e nella Città del Vaticano* (Rome, 1991). This work identifies series in the ASV that pertain to the French Revolution. The following series from the *Francia* series are mentioned: vols. 458B, 463, 463A, 529C, 529D, and mazzo 529 E.II, volumes 570A, 571–575, 578–583, 585, 596, mazzo 639, volume 640, mazzi 645, 658, cart. 659 and in supplemento Francia cart. 9, 18, mazzo 38, 50, and 55. Entries list the volume number, identify the total number of folios in a volume, provide the formal or a supplied title, summarize the materials in the volume, and note the inclusive dates. At times, individual items are identified and described.

Location: Archivio Segreto Vaticano

3.2.14.94 Nunziatura di Genova
[DATABASE ID: VATV438-A]

Inclusive Dates: 1463–1809 (bulk 1572–1809).

Bulk: 2 linear m. (21 numbered vols.).

References: Boyle, p. 76; Fink, pp. 85–86.

Finding Aids: ASV Indice 1024-I (ff. 31–32) lists vols. 1–21. Entries proceed volume by volume and include brief descriptions of the contents (e.g., lettere, cifre, minute), inclusive dates, the nuncio involved, a physical description of the volume, the presence of an internal index, and the former and current volume number. ASV Indice 1024-II provides a chronological list of vols. 1–21 of this series on folio 239.

ASV Indice 134, compiled by De Pretis in 1731, provides a more succinct listing of vols. 1–10 on fol. 67. The listing for this series in Indice 134 contains later annotations and additions.

Location: Archivio Segreto Vaticano.

3.2.14.95 Nunziatura di Germania
[DATABASE ID: VATV439-A]

Inclusive Dates: 1515–1809, with some additions to 1816.

Bulk: 63.8 linear m. (797 numbered vols.).

Organization: This series falls into two distinct groupings. See the scope note below.

1. The principal subseries of Secretariatus Status office files: Minute di lettere della segreteria al nunzio, 1578–1809 (duplicate copies or drafts of outgoing correspondence); —Registro lettere della segreteria al nunzio, 1515, 1591–1809 (duplicate copies of outgoing correpondence); —Lettere originale del nunzio alla segreteria, 1571–1801 (original copies of incoming correspondence); —Lettere originale e cifre del nunzio alla segreteria, 1551–1699 (original copies of incoming correspondence).

2. Principal office files regarding the nunciature for the Holy Roman Empire: Registro lettere e cifre del nunzio alla segreteria, 1587–1764 (duplicate copies of outgoing correspondence); —Registro cifre del nunzio alla segreteria, 1623–1788 (duplicate copies of outgoing correspondence); —Minute di lettere e cifre del nunzio alla segreteria, 1570–1784 (duplicate copies or drafts of outgoing correspondence); —Lettere originale della segreteria all nunzio, 1659, 1703–1772 (original copies of incoming correspondence); —Lettere originale e cifre della segreteria all nunzio, 1658–1764 (original copies of incoming correspondence).

All these subseries are in rough chronological order, but the volume numbering of the entire group of records has been jumbled, so volumes are not numbered by subseries. Note that volumes are missing from all of these subseries so chronological coverage is incomplete. There are a large number of other, smaller subseries, both within these two sections and from other sources.

Scope: These are files brought together by the Secretariatus Status concerning Germany, the Holy Roman Empire, the Austrian court, and Austrian possessions in Italy. The records are made up of two major sections: office files of the Secretariatus Status and office files of the nunciature for the Holy Roman Empire. (For the period 1524–1560 separate nuncios were appointed for the empire and for Germany. These files seem to relate to the nuncio for Germany for that period.) Also included in these records are files relating to or produced by other papal officers concerned with the empire, including nuncios and legates in Graz, Salzburg, Frankfurt, Buda, Prague, and Cologne (but most records relating to the nuncio to Cologne are found under the name Nunziatura di Colonia); special legates; and others. (Note that records relating to the nuncio to Bavaria are found under the name Nunziatura di Baviera.) These records also contain scattered volumes relating in part to several non-German nuncios.

Note: Vols. 1, 3, 4, 27, 30, 49a, 54, 110, 153, 155, 156, 164, 166, 168, 168a, 170, 172, 216, 302, and 454a were acquired by the ASV in 1761 and 1763. For detailed provenance information, see the Pásztor article cited below.

References: Boyle, p. 76; Fink, pp. 84, 90. H. Jedin, "Nuntiaturberichte und Durchführung des Konzils von Trient: Hinweise und Fragen," *Quellen und Forschungen aus Italienischen Archiven und Bibliotheken* 53 (1973): 180–213. This volume of *Quellen and Forschungen* contains a number of articles that discuss how these records can be used for specific research topics.

The series *Nuntiaturberichte aus Deutschland nebst ergänzenden Actenstücken* is a multivolume, multiseries work reprinting selected documents from SS. *Germania.* The work is organized in four main series, and one additional series from a different publisher, covering 1533–1559 (Erste Abteilung), 1560–1572 (Zweite Abteilung), 1572–1585 (Dritte Abteilung), and 1603–1630 (Vierte Abteilung). The fifth series (including two subseries called Erste and Zweite Abteilungen) covers 1585–1592. A volume listing by series follows.

Nuntiaturberichte aus Deutschland nebst ergänzenden Actenstücken. Erste Abteilung, 1533–1559: vol. 1, W. Friedensburg, *Nuntiaturen des Vergerio, 1533–1536* (Gotha, 1892); vol. 2, W. Friedensburg, *Nuntiatur des Morone, 1536–1538* (Gotha, 1892); vols. 3–4, W. Friedensburg, *Legation Aleanders, 1538–1539* (Gotha, 1893); vol. 5, L. Cardauns, *Nuntiaturen Morones und Poggios, Legationen Farneses und Cervinis, 1539–1540* (Berlin, 1909); vol. 6, L. Cardauns, *Gesandtschaft Campegios, Nuntiaturen Morones und Poggios 1540–1541* (Berlin, 1910); vol. 7, L. Cardauns, *Berichte vom Regensburger und Speierer Reichstag, 1541–1542, Nuntiaturen Verallos und Poggios, Sendungen Farneses und Sfondratos, 1541–1544* (Berlin, 1912); vols. 8–9, W. Friedensburg, *Nuntiatur des Verallo* (Gotha, 1898–1899); vol. 10, W. Friedensburg, *Legation des Kardinals Sfondrato, 1547–1548* (Berlin, 1910); vol. 11, W. Friedensburg, *Nuntiaturen des Bischofs Pietro Bertano von Fano, 1548–1549* (Berlin, 1910); vol. 12, G. Kupke, *Nuntiaturen des Pietro Bertano und Pietro Camaiani, 1550–1552* (Berlin, 1901); vol. 13, H. Lutz, *Nuntiaturen des Pietro Camaiani und Achille de Grassi, Legation des Girolamo Dandino (1552–1553)* (Tübingen, 1959); vol. 14, H. Lutz, *Nuntiatur des Girolamo Muzzarelli, Sendung des Antonio Agustin, Legation des Scipione Rebiba (1554–1556)* (Tübingen, 1971); vol. 15, H. Lutz, *Friedenslegation des Reginald Pole zu Kaiser Karl V. und König Heinrich II (1553–1556)* (Tübingen, 1981); vol. 16, H. Goetz, *Nuntiatur des Girolamo Martinengo (1550–1554)* (Tübingen, 1965); vol. 17, H. Goetz, *Nuntiatur Delfinos, Legation Morones, Sendung Lippomanos (1554–1556)* (Tübingen, 1970); Ergänzungsband 1, G. Müller, *Legation Lorenzo Campeggios, 1530–1531, und Nuntiatur Girolamo Aleandros, 1531* (Tübingen, 1963); Ergänzungsband 2, G. Müller, *Legation Lorenzo Campeggios, 1532, und Nuntiatur Girolamo Aleandros, 1532* (Tübingen, 1969).

Nuntiaturberichte aus Deutschland nebst ergänzenden Actenstücken. Zweite Abteilung, 1560–1572: vol. 1, S. Steinherz, *Die Nuntien Hosius und Delfino, 1560–1561* (Vienna, 1897); vol. 2, A. Wandruszka, *Nuntius Commendone 1560 (Dezember)–1562 (März)* (Graz, 1953); vols. 3–4, S. Steinherz, *Nuntius Delfino 1562–1565* (Vienna, 1903–1914); vol. 5, I. P. Dengel, *Nuntius Biglia 1565–1566 (Juni): Commendone als Legat auf dem Reichstag zu Augsburg 1566* (Vienna, 1926); vol. 6, I. P. Dengel, *Nuntius Biglia 1566–1569: Commendone als Legat 1568–1569* (Vienna, 1939); vol. 7, I. P. Dengel and H. Kramer, *Nuntius Biglia 1570 (Jänner) bis 1571 (April)* (Graz, 1952); vol. 8, J. Rainer, *Nuntius G. Delfino und Kardinallegat G.F. Commendone, 1571–1572* (Graz, 1967).

Nuntiaturberichte aus Deutschland nebst ergänzenden Actenstücken. Dritte Abteilung, 1572–1585: vol. 1, J. Hansen, *Der Kampf um Köln, 1576–1584* (Berlin, 1892); vol. 2, J. Hansen, *Der Reichstag zu Regensburg 1576: Der Pacificationstag zu Köln 1579: Der Reichstag zu Augsburg 1582* (Berlin, 1894); vols. 3–5, K. Schellhass, *Die süddeutsche Nuntiatur des Grafen Bartholomäus von Portia* (Berlin, 1896–1909); vol. 6, H. Goetz, *Nuntiatur Giovanni Delfinos, 1572–1573* (Tübingen, 1982); vol. 7, A. Bues, *Nuntiatur Giovanni Dolfins, 1573–1574* (Tübingen, 1990).

Nuntiaturberichte aus Deutschland nebst ergänzenden Ac- tenstücken. Vierte Abteilung, siebzehntes Jahrhundert: vols. 1– 2, H. Kiewning, *Nuntiatur des Pallotto, 1628–1630* (Berlin, 1895–1897); vol. 3, A. O. Meyer, *Die prager Nuntiatur des Giovanni Stefano Ferreri und die wiener Nuntiatur des Gia- como Serra (1603–1606)* (Berlin, 1913).

Nuntiaturberichte aus Deutschland nebst ergänzenden Actenstücken, 1585 (1584)–(1592). Erste Abteilung: vol. 1, S. Ehses and A. Meister, *Bonomi in Köln, Santorio in der Schweiz, die strassburger Wirren* (Paderborn, 1895); vol. 2, S. Ehses, *Ottavio Mirto Frangipani in Köln, 1587–1590* (Paderborn, 1899).

Nuntiaturberichte aus Deutschland nebst ergänzenden Ac- tenstücken, 1585 (1584)–(1592). Zweite Abteilung, Die Nun- tiatur am Kaiserhofe: Erste Hälfte, R. Reichenberger, *Ger- manico Malaspina und Filippo Sega (Giovanni Andrea Caligari in Graz)* (Paderborn, 1905); vol. 2, J. Schweizer, *An- tonio Puteo in Prag, 1587–1589* (Paderborn, 1912), vol. 3, J. Schweizer, *Die Nuntien in Prag: Alfonso Visconte 1589– 1591, Camillo Caetano 1591–1592,* (Paderborn, 1919).

Other titles relating to this series include the following works. I. P. Dengel, *Die politische und kirchliche Tätigkeit des Monsignor Josef Garampi in Deutschland, 1761–1763: Ge- heime Sendung zum geplanten Friedenskongress in Augsburg und Visitation des Reichsstiftes Salem* (Rome, 1905). F. Ditt- rich, *Nuntiaturberichte Giovanni Morones vom deutschen Königshofe, 1539, 1540* (Paderborn, 1892). A. Ellemunter, *Antonio Eugenio Visconti und die Anfänge des Josephinismus: Eine Untersuchung über das theresianische Staatskirchentum unter besonderer Beruchsichtigung der Nuntiaturberichte, 1767–1774.* (Graz, 1963). H. Goetz, "Die Nuntiaturberichte des 16. Jahrhunderts als Komplementärquelle zur Geschichts- schreibung," *Quellen und Forschungen aus italienischen Ar- chiven und Bibliotheken* 53 (1973): 214–226. M. Linhartová, *Epistulae et Acta Antonii Caetani, 1607–1611* (Prague, 1932– 1940) [concerns the Czech Republic and Slovakia]. G. Lutz, "Glaubwürdigkeit und Gehalt von Nuntiaturberichten," *Quel- len und Forschungen aus italienischen Archiven und Biblio- theken* 53 (1973): 227–275. H. Lutz, "Die Bedeutung der Nun- tiaturberichte für die europäische Geschichtsforschung und Geschichtsschreibung," *Quellen und Forschungen aus italie- nischen Archiven und Bibliotheken* 53 (1973): 152–167. H. Lutz, "Nuntiaturberichte aus Deutschland: Vergangenheit und Zukunft einer 'klassischen' Editionsreihe," *Quellen und Forschungen aus italienischen Archiven und Bibliotheken* 45 (1965): 274–324. J. Rainer, ed., *Nuntiatur des Germanico Malaspina, Sendung des Antonio Possevino 1580–1582* (Vienna, 1973) [concerns Austria]. W. E. Schwarz, *Die Nuntiatur-Korrespondenz Kaspar Groppers nebst verwandten Aktenstücken, 1573–1576* (Paderborn, 1898). S. Weiss and J. Rainer, *Nuntiatur des Germanico Malaspina und des Gio- vanni Andrea Caligari 1582–1587* (Vienna, 1981).

N. Mosconi, *La Nunziatura di Praga di Cesare Speciano, 1592–1598: Nelle carte inedite vaticane e ambrosiane* (Brescia, 1966–). Volume 2 reprints documents from SS. *Nunz. Ger- mania* 15 and Separate Collections, Individual and Family Papers series *Fondo Borghese,* tome 109, volume 4. There is a good biography of Speciano in volume 1 and an introduction to his diplomatic work and the times.

Lajos Pásztor, "Per la storia dell'Archivio Segreto Vaticano nei secoli XVII–XVIII," *Archivio della Società romana di storia*

patria 91 (1968): 157–249. Pásztor discusses the provenance of twenty-one volumes now in this series and their interrelation- ships with other series in the ASV and the Biblioteca Apostolica Vaticana. A brief listing of the volumes noted above can be extracted from this article.

Finding Aids: ASV Indice 1027 (ff. 1–113) lists vols. 1–797. Entries proceed volume by volume and contain brief descrip- tions of contents, inclusive dates, the former and current vol- ume number, and selected additional notes. Indice 1027 also provides a chronological index to SS. *Germania* between ff. 161 and 222.

ASV Indice 134, compiled by De Pretis in 1731, provides a more succinct listing of vols. 1–351, beginning on fol. 1. The listing for SS. *Germania* in Indice 134 is continued in Indice 135. It contains many later annotations and additions.

Location: Archivio Segreto Vaticano.

3.2.14.96 Nunziatura di Inghilterra
[DATABASE ID: VATV440-A]
Inclusive Dates: 1544–1856.
Bulk: 2 linear m. (32 numbered volumes, 5 pacchi, and 6 loose fascicoli).
Note: Vols. 11–12, and 14–15 are available on microfilm.
References: Boyle, p. 76; Fink, p. 85.
Finding Aids: ASV Indice 134, compiled by De Pretis in 1731, contains a brief listing of volume titles for vols. 1–31 (ff. 65–66). The current volume number, inclusive dates, and some volumes located after De Pretis's index are noted in later annotations.

ASV Indice 1071 contains a typed copy of De Pretis (pp. olim 71–72 or nuovi numeri 65–66), including the later annotations to De Pretis.

Location: Archivio Segreto Vaticano.

3.2.14.97 Nunziatura di Napoli
[DATABASE ID: VATV442-A]
Inclusive Dates: 1191–1808 (bulk 1560–1808).
Bulk: 53.5 linear m. (646 numbered volumes and 5 pacchi).
Note: Vols. 39a, 47, 50, 56, 60, 61, 61c, 74, 74a, and 325– 326 were acquired by the ASV in 1761–1763; for more detailed provenance information, see Pásztor article below.
Note: Vols. 20, 492–493 are available on microfilm.
References: Boyle, p. 76; Fink, pp. 85–86; Lajos Pásztor, "Per la storia dell'Archivio Segreto Vaticano nei secoli XVII– XVIII," *Archivio della Società romana di storia patria* 91 (1968): 157–249. Pásztor discusses the provenance of several volumes now part of this series and their interrelationship with other series in the ASV and the Biblioteca Apostolica Vaticana. A brief listing of the volumes indicated above can also be ex- tracted from this article.

P. Villani, D. Veneruso, and M. Bettoni, *Nunziature di Napoli* (Rome, 1962–). This is a series of three volumes re- printing documents from SS. *Napoli.* The organization and format of the three volumes are very similar. The volumes reprint "important" documents concerning Naples from ASV collections. The first volume reprints items from SS. *Napoli* volumes 1–5 and 321, dating from 26 Luglio 1570 to 24 Mag- gio 1577. Volume 2 covers the period 24 Maggio 1577 to 26 Giugno 1587, SS. *Napoli* vols. 5–10 and *Francia* 286. Volume 3 covers the period 11 Luglio 1587 to 21 Sett. 1591, SS. *Napoli* vols. 5–10, SS. *Francia* 286, and *Epistolae ad Principes* 151.

Each volume provides an introduction to the period and the series under consideration and an "Indice Sommario" of the documents reprinted containing the item number supplied by the compiler, the place and date of the document, correspondents, subject, and page number in the book. The actual documents are reprinted after these introductory materials. The reprints provide the names of the correspondents, the volume and folio numbers from SS. *Napoli*, and then the document. Sometimes a note, such as "minute" is added, so the assumption seems to be that unless this is noted, the item is the actual letter. The volumes have analytical footnotes and end with indexes to persons and places that are cited in the volume.

Finding Aids: ASV Indice 1024–I (ff. 61–120) lists vols. 1–646. Entries proceed volume by volume and include brief descriptions of the contents (e.g., lettere, cifre, minute), inclusive dates, the nuncio involved, a physical description of the volume, the presence of an internal index, and the former and current volume numbers. ASV Indice 1024–II provides a chronological list of vols. 1–646 of SS. *Napoli* on ff. 257–276.

ASV Indice 134, compiled by De Pretis in 1731, provides a more succinct listing of vols. 1–411, beginning on fol. 77. The listing for SS. *Napoli* in Indice 134 contains many later annotations and additions.

Location: Archivio Segreto Vaticano.

3.2.14.98 Nunziatura di Polonia

[DATABASE ID: VATV444-A]

Inclusive Dates: ca. 1100–1810.

Bulk: 31 linear m. (396 numbered volumes and 1 unnumbered pacco).

Organization: Subseries are: 1. Lettere e cifre del nunzio alla Segreteria di Stato, 1561–1806; —2. Lettere e cifre della Segreteria di Stato al nunzio, 1560–1804; —3. Biglietti e carteggi ministri, 1564–1804; —4. Lettere dell'episcopato al pontifice ed alla Segreteria di Stato, 1563–1829; —5. Lettere d'affari al nunzio, 1561–1797; —6. Lettere diverse (principi, titolati e particolari al pontifice ed alla Segreteria di Stato e varie), secolo XIII–XVIII bolle e breve diversi, 1541–1814; —7. Scritti informativi, secolo XII–XVII notizie sui legati e nunzi di Polonia, 1525–1832; —8. Affari, 1543–1809; —9. Carte e stampe diverse, 1559–1834.

Note: Vols. 29, 30, 153, 162, 174, and 179 were acquired by the ASV between 1761–1763 and were formerly considered part of a Diversorum series; see Pásztor below.

Note: Vols. 5b, 7–9, 13, 14, 38, 39, 41, 47, 137, and 138 are available on microfilm.

References: Boyle, p. 77; Fink, p. 84.

H. D. Wojtyska, ed., *Acta Nuntiaturae Polonae* (Rome, 1990–). This series is currently in production and reprints documents from a wide range of ASV and BAV series. This is a good place to start a study of materials in the ASV that concern Poland because the introduction demonstrates the interconnectedness of many series. Entries note the type of document, the correspondents, and the date, and then reprint the document. There are notes as to where the document (as well as any minute or other version of the document) can be found, and if the document has been published. There are analytical footnotes and bibliographic notes as well as a person/place index at the end of each volume.

Lajos Pásztor, "Per la storia dell'Archivio Segreto Vaticano nei secoli XVII–XVIII," *Archivio della Società romana di storia patria* 91 (1968): 157–249. Pásztor discusses the provenance of several volumes now in this series and their interrelationships with other series in the ASV and the Biblioteca Apostolica Vaticana.

F. Diaz and N. Carranza, *Francesco Buonvisi: Nunziatura a Varsavia* (Rome, 1965), vol. 1, "3 gennaio 1673–2 giugno 1674"; vol. 2, "6 giugno 1674–28 agosto 1675." This is part of a series that reprints significant documents regarding the papal nunciatures. The format of the volumes is similar. The first volume for each nunciature has a good introduction to the history of the nunciature, the provenance, and the contents of the records. This is in much greater depth than any of the ASV indici for the nunciature materials. The introduction also indicates the series from which documents are reprinted. In the case of Varsavia, the documents reprinted come not only from ASV SS. *Polonia*, but also from the Archivio di Stato di Lucca (*Archivio Buonvisi*). These reprints act as a good introduction to the series and as a partial index to contents. The actual reprints note the date, correspondents, and the original volume and folio numbers. The document is then reprinted. There are also analytical footnotes and bibliographic notes.

Finding Aids: See P. Savio, *De Actis Nuntiaturae Poloniae quae partem Archivi Secretariatus Status constituunt* (Vatican City, 1947), which describes vols. 1–396 and appendici I–XXIV (1–4). Entries proceed volume by volume indicating the type of material (e.g., lettere, cifre, minute, etc.), the nuncio involved, inclusive dates, a physical description of each volume, and the former and current volume numbers. This is followed by four chronological schede beginning on p. 79. These are divided by type of material titled as follows: 1. Lettere e cifre del nunzio alla Segreteria di Stato, 1561–1806; 2. Lettere e cifre della Segreteria di Stato al nunzio, 1560–1804; 3. Biglietti e Carteggi Ministri, 1564–1804; 4. Lettere dell'episcopato al pontifice ed alla Segreteria di Stato, 1563–1829; 5. Lettere d'affari al nunzio, 1561–1797; 6. Lettere diverse (Principi, titolati e particolari pontifice ed alla Segreteria di Stato e varie), secolo XIII–XVIII bolle e breve diversi, 1541–1814; 7. Scritti informativi, secolo XII–XVII notizie sui legati e nunzi di Polonia, 1525–1832; 8. Affari, 1543–1809; 9. Carte e stampe diverse, 1559–1834. The chronological schede refer back to the volume number in which the item can be found.

ASV Indice 134, compiled by De Pretis in 1731, provides a more succinct listing of vols. 1–360, beginning on fol. 45. The listing for SS. *Polonia* in Indice 134 contains later additions and annotations.

Location: Archivio Segreto Vaticano,

3.2.14.99 Nunziatura di Polonia-Russia

[DATABASE ID: VATV445-A]

Inclusive Dates: 1793–1806.

Bulk: 3.8 linear m. (24 numbered volumes and 2 unnumbered pacchi).

References: Boyle, p. 77; Fink, p. 84.

Finding Aids: See M. J. Rouet de Journal, *Nonciatures de Russie d'après les documents authentiques* (Rome, 1922–). These volumes reprint significant documents from this and other ASV series. After a lengthy introduction, documents are reprinted. Entries include the names of the correspondents, the place, date, a summary of the document in French, the location of the document (Arch. Vat. = SS. *Polonie-Russia*), and the reprint of the document in the original language. There are analytical footnotes and bibliographic notes throughout the work and a name/place index at the end of each volume.

Location: Archivio Segreto Vaticano.

3.2.14.100 Nunziatura di Portogallo

[DATABASE ID: VATV446-A]

Inclusive Dates: 1142–1851 (bulk 1568–1809).

Bulk: 16.9 linear m. (245 numbered vols.).

Note: Vols. 151–152 and 236 were acquired by the ASV in 1761–1763; see 1968 Pásztor article cited below.

References: Boyle, p. 77; Fink, pp. 84, 86; Pásztor (1970), p. 84; Pásztor (1983), pp. 126–127.

Lajos Pásztor. "Per la storia dell'Archivio Segreto Vaticano nei secoli XVII–XVIII," *Archivio della Società romana di storia patria* 91 (1968): 157–249. Pásztor discusses the provenance of several volumes now in this series and their interrelationships with other series in the ASV and the Biblioteca Apostolica Vaticana. A brief description of vols. 151–152 and 236 can be extracted from this article.

C. M. de Witte, ed., *La correspondance des premiers nonces permanents au Portugal, 1532–1553* (Lisbon, 1980–1986). This work reprints documents concerning the nunciature for Portugal from many collections, primarily outside the ASV. In volume 1, the chapter on the documents is very good for orienting researchers interested in Portugal during this period to all the archives with nunciature papers. In addition to the ASV SS. *Portogallo,* the other ASV collections used include Archivum Arcis, *Armaria I–XVIII,* no. 6534; SS. *Lettere di principi;* and the *Carte Farnesiane.*

Finding Aids: ASV Indice 1025 (ff. 77–98), compiled by Mons. Savio, lists vols. 1–245. Entries proceed volume by volume and include brief descriptions of the contents (e.g., bullae, lettere, cifre, minute), inclusive dates, the nuncio involved, a physical description of the volume, the presence of an internal index, and the former and current volume numbers. ASV Indice 1025 also provides a chronological list of vols. 1–245 of SS. *Portogallo* between foli 195 and 204.

ASV Indice 134, compiled by De Pretis in 1731, provides a more succinct listing of vols. 1–204, beginning on fol. 55. The listing for SS. *Portogallo* in Indice 134 contains later additions and annotations.

Location: Archivio Segreto Vaticano.

3.2.14.101 Nunziatura di Savoia

[DATABASE ID: VATV447-A]

Inclusive Dates: 1560–1803.

Bulk: 27.6 linear m. (349 numbered vols.).

Note: Vol. 86 was acquired between 1761 and 1763 and was formerly part of a *Diversorum* series; see Pásztor below.

References: Boyle, p. 77; Fink, pp. 85–86. A. L. Martin, ed., *Correspondance du nonce en France, Fabio Mirto Frangipani 1568–1572 et 1586–1587, Nonce extraordinaire en 1574, 1575–1576 et 1578* (Rome, 1984).

Lajos Pásztor, "Per la storia dell'Archivio Segreto Vaticano nei secoli XVII–XVIII," *Archivio della Società romana di storia patria* 91 (1968): 157–249. Pásztor discusses the provenance of vol. 86 of this series and its interrelationship with other series in the ASV and the Biblioteca Apostolica Vaticana.

F. Fonzi, *Nunziature di Savoia* (Rome, 1960). This work is part of a series that reprints significant documents regarding the papal nunciatures. The format of the volumes is similar. The

first volume for each nunciature has a good introduction to both the history of the nunciature, the provenance, and the contents of the records. This is in much greater depth than any of the ASV Indici for the nunciature materials. The introduction also indicates the series from which documents are reprinted. In the case of Savoia, the documents reprinted come not only from ASV SS. *Savoia,* but also from other ASV series: SS. *Polonia,* SS. *Spagna,* SS. *Firenze,* SS. *Francia, Fondo Pio,* and *Archivio Boncompagne* as well as from series at other archives: BAV (Barb. Lat.); Biblioteca Ambrosiana; Archivio di Stato di Torino. These reprints act as a good introduction to the series and as a partial index to contents. The actual reprints note the date, correspondents, and the original volume and folio numbers. The document is then reprinted. There are also analytical footnotes and bibliographic notes.

Finding Aids: ASV Indice 1024-I (ff. 125–155) lists vols. 1–349. Entries proceed volume by volume and include brief descriptions of the contents (e.g., lettere, cifre, minute), inclusive dates, the nuncio involved, a physical description of the volume, the presence of an internal index, and the former and current volume numbers. ASV Indice 1024-II provides a chronological list of vols. 1–349 of SS. *Savoia* on ff. 281–292.

ASV Indice 134, compiled by De Pretis in 1731, provides a more succinct listing of vols. 1–281, beginning on fol. 112. The listing for SS. *Savoia* in Indice 134 contains many later annotations and additions.

Location: Archivio Segreto Vaticano.

3.2.14.102 Nunziatura di Spagna

[DATABASE ID: VATV448-A]

Inclusive Dates: 1471–1818 (bulk 1524–1808).

Bulk: 38.4 linear m.

Note: 469 numbered volumes and appendici numbered I–XXIII). Vols. 61, 128, and 242 were acquired by the ASV in 1761 and 1763. For detailed provenance information, see the 1968 Pásztor article cited below.

Note: Vols. 13, 19, and 32–35 are available on microfilm.

References: Boyle, p. 77; Fink, pp. 84, 86; Pásztor (1970), p. 85; Pásztor (1983), pp. 127–128. R. de Hinojosa y Naveros, *Los despachos de la diplomacia pontificia en España: Memoria de una missión oficial en el Archivo Secreto de la Santa Sede* (Madrid, 1896). A. L. Martin, ed., *Correspondance du nonce en France, Fabio Mirto Frangipani 1568–1572 et 1586–1587, Nonce extraordinaire en 1574, 1575–1576 et 1578* (Rome, 1984).

Lajos Pásztor, "Per la storia dell'Archivio Segreto Vaticano nei secoli XVII–XVIII," *Archivio della Società romana di storia patria* 91 (1968): 157–249. Pásztor discusses the provenance of three volumes (61, 128, 1nd 242) now in this series and their interrelationships with other series in the ASV and the Biblioteca Apostolica Vaticana. A brief listing of vol. 61, 128 and 242 can also be extracted from this article.

N. Mosconi, *La Nunziatura di Spagna di Cesare Speciano, 1586–1588: Su documenti inediti dell'Archivio segreto vaticano,* 2d ed. (Brescia, 1961).

Finding Aids: ASV Indice 1025 (ff. 103–150), compiled by Mons. Savio, lists vols. 1–469 and appendici I–XXIII. Entries proceed volume by volume and include brief descriptions of the contents (e.g., bullae, lettere, cifre, minute), inclusive dates, the nuncio involved, a physical description of the volume, the presence of an internal index, and the former and current volume numbers. ASV Indice 1025 also provides a chronological list of vols. 1–469 and the appendici of SS. *Spagna* between ff. 209 and 227.

ASV Indice 134, compiled by De Pretis in 1731, provides a more succinct listing of vols. 1–428, beginning on fol. 33. The listing for SS. *Spagna* in Indice 134 contains later additions and annotations.

J. Olarra Garmendia and M. L. Larramendi de Olarra, *Indices de la correspondencia entre la Nunciatura en Espana y la Santa Sede durante el reinado de Felipe II* (Madrid, 1948–1949). This is a calendar of documents concerning relations between Spain and the Holy See from 1248 to 1598. It includes materials primarily from the SS. *Spagna*, but other series are represented. Although Olarra states that this consists of summaries, the entries are brief and are in the style of a calendar. However, this itemized calendar far surpasses the ASV Indici 1025 and 134 to the series. The entries in this work are in chronological order. The year is posted and each item from that year is then listed. Entries include an item number (supplied by the authors), the date, place, correspondents or type of business (e.g., nota concistoriale), the summary of the document in Spanish, volume and folio numbers. This is continued in a work of the same authors: *Correspondencia entre la Nunciatura en Espana y la Santa Sede: Reinado de Felipe III (1598–1621)* (Rome, 1960–1967). The volumes cover the following years: vol. 1, 1598–1621; vol. 2, 1602–1605; vol. 3, 1606–1609; vol. 4, 1610–1612; vol. 5, 1613–1614; vol. 6, 1615–1617; vol. 7, 1618–1621. This calendar provides an itemized description of documents in the SS. *Spagna*. Entries include the date and place, correspondents, a summary in Spanish, and volume and folio numbers where the document can be found.

Location: Archivio Segreto Vaticano.

3.2.14.103 Nunziatura di Svizzera
[DATABASE ID: VATV449-A]
Inclusive Dates: 1532–1815.
Bulk: 24.5 linear m. (305 numbered volumes, additions numbered I–XXII, and misc. pacchi).
Note: Vols. 1 and 46 were acquired by the ASV in 1761 and 1763. For detailed provenance information, see the Pásztor article cited below.
References: Boyle, p. 77; Fink, pp. 85, 91. Lajos Pásztor, "Per la storia dell'Archivio Segreto Vaticano nei secoli XVII–XVIII," *Archivio della Società romana di storia patria* 91 (1968): 157–249. Pásztor discusses the provenance of two volumes now in this series and their interrelationships with other series in the ASV and the Biblioteca Apostolica Vaticana. A brief listing of vols. 1 and 46 can also be extracted from this article.
Finding Aids: ASV Indice 1028, compiled by Mons. Paolo Krieg, calendars and/or provides a detailed synopsis of the contents of vols. 1–305 and additions I–XXII. Entries indicate the type of document (e.g., lettere, cifre, inventorio), whether the material is a copy, inclusive dates, correspondents, a physical description of the volume, the presence of an internal index, the former and current volume numbers, and folio number of the document.
ASV Indice 134, compiled by De Pretis in 1731, provides a more succinct listing of vols. 1–301, beginning on fol. 95. The listing for SS. Svizzera in Indice 134 contains many later annotations and additions.
Location: Archivio Segreto Vaticano.

3.2.14.104 Nunziatura di Venezia
[DATABASE ID: VATV450-A]
Inclusive Dates: 1524–1807.
Bulk: 35 linear m. (422 numbered vols.).
Note: Vols. 64, 94, 98, 98a, 135, 181, 272, 273, and 279 were acquired by the ASV in 1761–1763 and were formerly part of a *Diversorum* series. For more detailed provenance information, see the Pásztor article cited below.
Note: Vols. 32 and 134 are available on microfilm. *Dispacci del Nunzio a Venezia alla Segreteria di Stato* in ASV, unpublished correspondence of the nuncio in Venice, is available on microfilm at the Fondazione Girogio Cini, Venice.
References: Boyle, p. 77; Fink, pp. 85–86. A. I. Bassani, "Le fonti dell'Archivio Segreto Vaticano per una storia ecclesiastica della repubblica e del regno d'Italia," in *Vita religiosa e cultura in Lombardia e nel Veneto nell'età napoleonica*, edited by F. Agostino et al. (Rome, 1990), pp. 363–393.
Lajos Pásztor, "Per la storia dell'Archivio Segreto Vaticano nei secoli XVII–XVIII," *Archivio della Società romana di storia patria* 91 (1968): 157–249. Pásztor discusses the provenance of several volumes now in this series and their interrelationships with other series in the ASV and the Biblioteca Apostolica Vaticana. A brief listing of volumes noted above can also be extracted from this article.
Finding Aids: ASV Indice 1024-I (ff. 161–204) lists vols. 1–422. Entries proceed volume by volume and include brief descriptions of the contents (e.g., lettere, cifre, minute), inclusive dates, the nuncio involved, a physical description of the volume, the presence of an internal index, and the former and current volume numbers. ASV Indice 1024-II provides a chronological list of vols. 1–422 of SS. *Venezia* between ff. 297 and 313.
ASV Indice 134, compiled by De Pretis in 1731, provides a more succinct listing of vols. 1–360, beginning on fol. 69. The listing for SS. *Venezia* in Indice 134 contains many later annotations and additions.
Location: Archivio Segreto Vaticano.

3.2.14.105 Nunziature diverse
[DATABASE ID: VATV451-A]
Inclusive Dates: 1462–1807.
Bulk: about 30 linear meters (313 vols.).
Note: Vols. 31, 34, 100, 102–103, 144, 195bis, 199–201, 207–229, 230–236, and 247 were acquired by the ASV in 1761–1763; see the 1968 Pásztor article cited below.
Scope: This is a well-known miscellany of the records of the Secretariatus Status. It contains materials relating to the following nunciatures: Colonia (1605–1686), Fiandra (1605–1686), Firenze (1607–1684), Francia (1521–1689), Germania (1591–1686, 1703–1807), Inghilterra (1553–1686), Malta (1678–1681), Napoli (1605–1714), Nimega (1676–1679), Polonia (1563–1685 and 1705), Portogallo (1560–1561, 1611–1614, 1676–1684), Savoia (1605–1685), Spagna (1560–1686), Svizzera (1605–1686), and Venezia (1596–1686). There is also information on Legazioni (1607–1686) and records of istruzioni, lettere varie, relazioni, testi, atti politici, and affari.
Note: Vol. 249 is available on microfilm.
References: Boyle, p. 77; Fink, pp. 86–89; Pásztor (1970), pp. 86–87; Pásztor (1983), pp. 128–129. B. Neveu, ed., *Correspondance du nonce en France, Angelo Ranuzzi 1683–1689* (Rome, 1973).

Lajos Pásztor, "Per la storia dell'Archivio Segreto Vaticano nei secoli XVII–XVIII," *Archivio della Società romana di storia patria* 91 (1968): 157–249. Pásztor discusses the provenance of numerous volumes now in this series and their interrelationships with other series in the ASV and the Biblioteca Apostolica Vaticana. A partial listing of volumes in this series can also be extracted from this article.

Finding Aids: Indice 1026 (beginning on p. 45) is a detailed inventory of volumes in the *Nunziature diverse.* Entries indicate volume titles, inclusive dates, major correspondents, type of business at hand (relazioni, istruzioni, etc.). Indice 1026 (beginning on page 170) contains a series of chronological indices to the records from each of the different nunciatures represented in this series as well as chronological indexes to a few of the different types of documents found in the *Nunziature diverse* (istruzioni, relazioni, lettere varie, etc.).

Location: Archivio Segreto Vaticano.

3.2.14.106 Nunziature e legazioni
[DATABASE ID: VATV163-A]
Inclusive Dates: 1187–1851.
Bulk: about 590 linear m. (about 7,700 vols.).
Scope: This is a vast collection of correspondence received by the Secretariat of State from the various nunciatures and legations. It is divided into subgroups for each of the geographical units. Each of the subgroups is described separately among the records of the Secretariatus Status. Look under "I" for the *Inquisizione di Malta*, "L" for legations (legazioni), and "N" for nunciatures (nunziature). This material should be used in conjunction with the Secretariatus Status series *Archivio delle nunziature*, which is described in general among the records of the Secretariatus Status but whose component parts form a separate section in this guide.

References: Boyle, pp. 76–77; Fink, pp. 82–92.

For bibliographies of works relating to the records of the nunciatures, see L. E. Halkin, *Les Archives des nonciatures* (Brussels, 1968); and J. Rainer, "Nuntiaturberichte: Forschungsstand und Forschungsprobleme," *Innsbrucker historische Studien* 9 (1986): 69–90.

Finding Aids: ASV Indice 134, 1023–1028, and 1071 are all pertinent to these materials. Consult individual listings for details on the use of these finding aids.

Location: Archivio Segreto Vaticano,

3.2.14.107 Nunziature per le Paci
[DATABASE ID: VATV443-A]
Inclusive Dates: 1628–1716.
Bulk: 6 linear m. (71 numbered volumes and 1 box).
Note: Vols. 1–3, 5–13, 30–42, 46–59, and 63–67 were acquired by the ASV in 1761–1763. For more detailed provenance information see Pásztor's 1968 article cited below.
Note: Vol. 46 is available on microfilm.
References: Boyle, p. 76; Fink, pp. 85, 86–87; Pásztor (1970), p. 88; Pásztor (1983), p. 129.

Lajos Pásztor, "Per la storia dell'Archivio Segreto Vaticano nei secoli XVII–XVIII," *Archivio della Società romana di storia patria* 91 (1968): 157–249. Pásztor discusses the provenance of forty-three volumes now in this series and their interrelationships with other series in the ASV and the Biblioteca Apostolica Vaticana. A brief listing of the volumes noted above can also be extracted from this article.

Finding Aids: ASV Indice 1026 (ff. 33–39), compiled by Petrus Savio, lists vols. 1–71. Entries proceed volume by volume and indicate the type of material (e.g., lettere, minute, posizioni), inclusive dates, the nuncio involved, a physical description of the volume, and the former and current volume numbers. Beginning on page 161, there is a chronological presentation of vols. 1–71 of SS. *Paci.*

ASV Indice 134, compiled by De Pretis in 1731, provides a more succinct listing of vols. 1–60, beginning on fol. 94. Much of this listing in Indice 134 is later annotations and additions.

Location: Archivio Segreto Vaticano.

3.2.14.108 Omaggi/oboli
[DATABASE ID: VATV10520-A]
Inclusive Dates: 1881.
Bulk: 3 linear m. (27 pacchi).
Location: Archivio Segreto Vaticano.

3.2.14.109 Onorificenze e decorazioni
[DATABASE ID: VATV10509-A]
Inclusive Dates: 1936–1956.
Bulk: .5 linear m.
Location: Archivio Segreto Vaticano.

3.2.14.110 Onorificenze e decorazioni
[DATABASE ID: VATV10523-A]
Inclusive Dates: 1947–1978.
Bulk: 48 linear m.
Note: According to *L'Attività della Santa Sede* (1991), during May and June 1991, 35 linear m. or 265 cassette concerning "pratiche di conferimento di onorificenze pontificie, 1958–1978" were transferred to the ASV.
Location: Archivio Segreto Vaticano.

3.2.14.111 Onorificenze e decorazioni: Camerieri segreti soprannumero e prelati domestici
[DATABASE ID: VATV10507-A]
Inclusive Dates: 1929–1958.
Bulk: Extent not available.
Location: Archivio Segreto Vaticano.

3.2.14.112 Particolari Pio X
[DATABASE ID: VATV10518-A]
Inclusive Dates: 1904–1914.
Bulk: 15.5 linear m.
Organization: Buste are numbered 1–135. Subseries include: Riposte, 1904–1906; —Correspondenze, 1907–1914.
Location: Archivio Segreto Vaticano.

3.2.14.113 Pio IX
[DATABASE ID: VATV10475-A]
Inclusive Dates: 1846–1878.
Bulk: 5 linear m. (45 buste).
Location: Archivio Segreto Vaticano.

3.2.14.114 Primi communioni
[DATABASE ID: VATV10485-A]
Inclusive Dates: 1910–1921.
Bulk: .5 linear m. (2 buste).
Location: Archivio Segreto Vaticano.

3.2.14.115 Protocolli

[DATABASE ID: VATV176-A]

Inclusive Dates: 1816–1922.

Bulk: 25 linear m. (472 vols.).

Scope: The *Protocolli* were originally generated by the Secretariat of State to keep track of its own correspondence. Today, the *Protocolli* are one link in the chain that researchers use to retrieve documents from the Secretariatus Status series *Fondo Moderno*. That series is composed of the following four parts: *Interni-Esteri*, 1814–1822; *Interni*, 1822–1833; *Esteri*, 1815–1850; and *Esteri*, 1846–1922. Each of these is listed separately among the records series of the Secretariatus Status. The following is an explanation of the entire system. This explanation is repeated in this guide as it relates to each of the four series mentioned above. It also appears in the general record for the *Fondo Moderno*. There is also a specific description for the Secretariatus Status series *Rubricelle*, another important link in this chain.

Scope: The *Protocolli* are used in conjunction with the *Rubricelle* to locate individual documents in the archives of the Secretariat of State. Both these series are located in the Sala degli Indici in the ASV. Researchers should first turn to the *Rubricelle*. The *Rubricelle* series is chronological, although the volumes for each year are alphabetical, primarily by personal or corporate names. In the late nineteenth century broad subject or geographical categories (e.g., breve, congressi, consistoriale) were added as access points in the *Rubricelle*. A few of the larger subjects, such as "Nunziature" and "Vescovi," were respectively subdivided again by specific nunciatures and alphabetically. Each entry provides a one-line description of the business, correspondent, and the (usually five-digit) protocol number, in the right-hand column. Some mid-nineteenth-century *Rubricelle* also list the corresponding rubric number. Note that the rubric numbers are related to, but serve an entirely different function than, the *Rubricelle*. From the *Rubricelle*, researchers who have both the protocol and rubric numbers can proceed directly to ASV Indici 1031, 1032, 1033 or to ASV Indici 1089-I, 1089-II, or 1089-III, described below, to get the rest of the information necessary to request an item. Researchers desiring more information on the contents of a document, related items, or the rubric number should proceed to the *Protocolli*.

The *Protocolli* provide rubric numbers and contain a concise but amplified listing of individual items. Researchers should note the year and protocol number in the *Rubricelle* and proceed to the *Protocolli* registers covering the year and protocol number desired. The *Protocolli* registers are organized numerically according to protocol number. Entries indicate the place, date, and correspondent; the object of business; the person assigned to deal with the request; the date; a brief note of the response or "risoluzione"; and an "Archivio" or rubric number. The rubric number is written largely in the "Archivio" column. Numbers written in smaller print sometimes appear above or below the rubric number. These numbers refer to the protocol numbers of related documents, either before (above) or after (below) a given item. When a desired item is located, the rubric number and the year of the protocollo volume should be noted and the appropriate Indici 1031, 1032, 1033 or 1089-I, 1089-II, or 1089-III should be consulted to get the rest of the information necessary to request an item. Specific items that have not been assigned a rubric number cannot be retrieved. Documents followed by the letters "AE" are in the archives of the Congregazione degli Affari Ecclesiastici, outside the ASV. To see these documents, contact the secretary of state archives.

ASV Indici 1031, 1032, and 1033 correspond respectively to the following three series: *Interni*, 1822–1833; *Esteri*, 1815–1850; and *Interni-Esteri*, 1814–1822. These indici are arranged chronologically by year and then numerically by rubric number. Researchers with a year in mind and a rubric number can turn to these indici for the correct busta or fascicolo number to request a desired item. Indici 1031, 1032, and 1033 are chronologically arranged listings (subdivided by year and then according to rubric numbers, buste, and fascicoli). Indici 1031, 1032, and 1033, also indicate any subseries in the rubrics (e.g., in Indice 1033, Rubric 27 breaks down by city: Ferrara, Forli, Ravenna, etc.), which can help to clarify the subject matter classified under a rubric number. Not all rubric numbers are represented in each year and the year designation for a rubric number does not mean that all materials in the busta are from that year. Earlier materials are often contained in a fascicolo. After identifying material desired in Indici 1031 and 1032 (*Interni*, 1822–1833, and *Esteri*, 1815–1850, respectively), copy down the year, the rubric, and the buste numbers to request materials. To request rubric numbers from Indice 1033 (*Interni-Esteri*, 1814–1822), note the year, the rubric, and the fascicoli numbers.

ASV Indici 1089-I, 1089-II, and 1089-III are the key indici to the *Esteri*, 1851–1922. Indice 1089-I covers the years 1851–1877, 1089-II covers the years 1878–1913, and 1089-III covers the years 1914–1922. All three indici are arranged similarly to ASV Indice 1031, 1032, and 1033. Thus, entries indicate rubric numbers, any subdivisions of a rubric (e.g., in Indice 1089-III (1916), rubric 251, "America Rappresentanti Pontifici," breaks down according to delegations (Chile Internunzio, Cuba e Portorico delegato, Haiti delegato, etc.), busta, and fascicolo numbers. To request materials, the rubric number, year, and fascicoli numbers are the essential pieces of information to note. Not all rubric numbers are represented each year and the year designation for a rubric does not indicate that only materials from that year are represented in the file. Earlier materials are often contained in fascicoli requested.

Reference: Boyle, p. 79. For information on the contents of one specific rubric (256) concerning Belgium, see W. van der Steen and K. Meerts, *Belgie in het Vaticaans Archief: Staatssecretariaat (rubriek 256), 1878–1903: Regestenlijst* (Louvain, 1989).

Finding Aids: ASV Indice 1034, by Giuseppe Gullotte (part II), contains a "Prontuario per la consultazione dei Protocolli dell'Archivio della Segreteria di Stato, 1816–1851." Indice 1034 provides two lists of the *Protocolli* registers between 1816 and 1851. The initial inventory is chronological and indicates the year(s), inclusive dates of the registers, and the range of protocol numbers. The second listing proceeds volume by volume, giving the inclusive dates and protocol numbers in each protocollo register. *Protocolli* containing special material are also noted (e.g., suppliche, Alta Polizia).

Location: Archivio Segreto Vaticano.

3.2.14.116 Registri I

[DATABASE ID: VATV512-A]

Inclusive Dates: 1800–1809.

Bulk: 3 linear m. (71 vols.).

Organization: Subseries include: 1. Diversi,; —2. Vescovi,; —3. Presidi,; —4. Prelati,; —5. Governatori,; —6. Lettere a particolari,; —7. Cardinali.

Scope: These are registers of outgoing correspondence.

Note: This series was transferred from the Archivio di Stato di Roma in 1919 where it had been identified as *Biglietti, dispacci e lettere.* Registri I, vols. 53 and 55, were formerly part of the Secretariatus Status series *Lettere di particolari* (numbered vols. 314 and 315, respectively).

References: Pásztor (1970), pp. 97–98; Pásztor (1983), p. 134; Boyle, p. 78 (cited as *Biglietti, dispacci e lettere*).

Finding Aids: ASV Indice 1112 (formerly Indice 41), pp. 20v–23r, provides a listing of the old Archivio di Stato and the current ASV names of the series. There are few accurate volume numbers in the sections dealing with *Registri I* in this index.

Location: Archivio Segreto Vaticano.

3.2.14.117 Registri II

[DATABASE ID: VATV513-A]

Inclusive Dates: 1814–1829.

Bulk: 3 linear m.

Organization: 134 volumes. Subseries with current buste designations include: 1. Registro di lettere credenziali spedite ai sovrani, loro famiglia e respettivi ministri dalla Segreteria di Stato nell'inviarsi i nunzi alle loro corte, 1814–1815; —2. Lettere del cardinale Consalvi, 1814; —3. Lettere inviate in cifra ai rappresentanti della Santa Sede all'estero, 1814–1818; —4. Circolari ai nunzi, 1818; —5, 7–8. Nunziatura a Firenze, 1814–1820; —6. Mons. Arezzo, arcivescovo di Seleucia, delegato apostolico presso la corte di Toscana, 1815; —9–11. Nunziatura a Lisbona, 1814–1819; —12. Nunzio a Rio de Janeiro, 1816–1819; —13–14. Nunziatura a Lucerna, 1814–1820; —15–16. Nunziatura a Madrid, 1814–1820; —17. Nunziatura a Monaco, 1820; —18. Missioni d'Olanda in Munster, 1814–1815; —19–20. Cardinale Caracciolo a Napoli, 1815–1819; —21. Mons. A. Giustiniani a Napoli, 1920; —22. Nunziatura a Parigi, 1820; —23. Nunziatura a Torino, 1815–1820; —24–26. Nunziatura a Vienna, 1814–1820; —27–29. Rappresentanti diplomatici a Roma-Austria, 1814–1820; —30–31. idem. Baviera; —32. idem. Francia; —33. idem. Hannover; —34. idem. Lucca; —35. idem. Modena;—36–38. idem. Napoli; —39. idem. Paesi Bassi; —40. idem. Portogallo; —41. idem. Prussia; —42. idem. Russia; —43. idem. Sacro Ordine Gerosolomitano; —44. idem. Sardegna; —45. idem. Sassonia; —46. idem. Spagna; —47. idem. Toscana; —48. idem. Wuertemberg; —49–50. Ministri esteri fuori di Roma, 1815–1817; —51–54. Consoli pontifici in generale, 1814–1820; —55–56. Commissione pontificia a Milano, 1816; —57–58. Consolato a Milano, 1817–1820; —59. Consoli esteri, Francia, 1815–1816; —60. idem. Napoli, 1815–1819; —61. idem. Prussia, 1816–1819; —62. idem. Sardegna, 1815–1817;—63 and 96. Delegati e legati; —Generale, 1814–1819; —64 and 97. idem. Circolari a legati, etc., 1815–1819; —65–66. idem. Ancona, 1815–1817; —67. idem. Ascoli, 1816–1817; —68. idem. Benevento, 1815–1817; —69–70. idem. Bologna, 1815–1817; —71–72. idem. Camerino, 1815–1817; —73–74. idem. Civitavecchia, 1815–1817; —75–76. idem. Fermo, 1815–1817; —77–78. idem. Ferrara, 1815–1817; —79–80. idem. Forli, 1815–1817; —81–82. idem. Frosinone, 1815–1817; —83–85. idem. Macerata, 1815–1817; 86–87. idem. Perugia, 1815–

1817; —88–89. idem. Pesaro, 1815–1817; —90. idem. Ravenna, 1816–1817; —91. idem. Rieti, 1816–1817; —92–93. idem. Spoleto, 1815–1817; —94–95. idem. Viterbo, 1815–1817; —98–101. Governatori, 1814–1817; —102. Gonfalonieri, 1817; —103–117. Lettere di Sua Santità (alli sovrani, principi, particolari, cardinali, vescovi, etc), 1814–1818; —118–134. Biglietti—Promozione alla sacra porpora di Mgr. Talleyrand Perigord, Mgr. de la Luzerna, Mgr. Bousset, 1814; —119–121. idem. Cardinali, 1814–1817; —122. idem. Sacra Consulta, 1814–1816; —123–124. idem. Congregazione militare, 1815–1816; —125–126. idem. Governatore di Roma, 1814–1817; —127–128. idem. Tesoriere generale, 1814–1817; —129–130. idem. Prelati, 1814–1817;—131–132. idem. Particolari e nobili, 1814–1817; —133–134. Biglietti di nomine e destinazioni, 1814–1829.

Scope: These are registers of outgoing letters.

Note: The series was transferred from the Archivio di Stato di Roma in 1919 as part of the Fondo dell'Archivio di Stato di Roma. At the Archivio di Stato di Roma the series had three titles: *Biglietti, dispacci e lettere*; *Registri di lettere*; and *Registri delle posizione.*

References: Pásztor (1970), pp. 97–98; Pásztor (1983), p. 134; Boyle, p. 78 (cited as *Biglietti, dispacci e lettere*).

Finding Aids: A detailed listing of each busta by Lajos Pásztor is available at the desk in the main ASV reading room. This index, a large part of which has been reproduced in the organizational note above, provides a busta-by-busta listing, inclusive dates, the current and some former Archivio di Stato di Roma volume numbers, and some explanatory notes of interest to users of this series. This index is not a formal finding aid and must be used in consultation with the archives staff.

ASV Indice 1112 (formerly Indice 41), pp. 20v–23r, provides a listing of the old Archivio di Stato and the current ASV names of the series. There are few accurate numerical designations in this index.

Location: Archivio Segreto Vaticano.

3.2.14.118 Registri "Bullarum" (già Coadiutorie e commende)

[DATABASE ID: VATV169-A]

Inclusive Dates: 1787–1894.

Bulk: 6 linear m. (64 vols.).

Organization: Chronological.

Scope: This series contains material regarding local churches as well as information on ecclesiastical careers. Through the records it is possible to trace the careers of many high ranking officials (offices, quality, character, etc.) or information regarding benefices. Spine titles read "Bullae" and the name of the pope.

Note: This series was transferred from the Archivio di Stato di Roma in 1919.

References: Boyle, p. 78; Pásztor (1970), pp. 36–37; Pásztor (1983), p. 107.

Finding Aids: ASV Indice 1151 provides a good introduction to the provenance and history of this series and introduces its contents. The index continues with an item by item calendar, listing the page, destination or person, diocese, and date.

ASV Indice 1112, p. 24v, gives a volume-by-volume listing of the series but has been supplanted by Indice 1151.

Pásztor (cf. above) cites two additional indices that may aid in locating materials in this series: 1. Camera Apostolica,

Rubricellae 28–31, in which the rubricellae are arranged alphabetically by diocese; 2. "Index Registrorum Bullarum, 1870–1901," a chronological index to bulls that indicates the name, type of bull, and the tax. [The latter was not located by project staff in 1990.]

Location: Archivio Segreto Vaticano.

3.2.14.119 Risposte varie
[DATABASE ID: VATV10491-A]
Inclusive Dates: 1914–1921.
Bulk: 2 linear m. (12 buste).
Location: Archivio Segreto Vaticano.

3.2.14.120 Rubricelle
[DATABASE ID: VATV175-A]
Inclusive Dates: 1816–1922.
Bulk: 30 linear m. (663 vols.).
Organization: Chronological. Vol. 1a is "Norme per la spedizioni delle lettere di nomina." Vols. 1, 22, 43, 62, 72, and 115 are rubricelle to the Secretariatus Status series *Suppliche* and do not correspond to the *Protocolli.*

Scope: The *Rubricelle* were created to serve the office of the Secretariatus Status as functional indexes to documents and files. Today they serve to aid researchers who are interested in locating specific documents in the Secretariatus Status (SS.) series *Fondo Moderno.* This large series is divided into four subseries: *Interni-Esteri,* 1814–1822; *Interni,* 1822–1833; *Esteri,* 1815–1850; *Esteri,* 1846–1922. There are several methods for the retrieval of documents in the *Fondo Moderno* and its component parts (each of which is described separately among the records of the Secretariatus Status). These methods are described in the general series description for the Secretariatus Status series *Fondo Moderno* and are repeated in this guide as appropriate to series description for each of the four SS. series that form the *Fondo Moderno.*

The *Rubricelle* are organized chronologically. Documents are treated individually in the *Rubricelle.* The *Rubricelle* index documents alphabetically, primarily by personal or corporate names. In the late nineteenth century broad subject or geographical categories (e.g., breve, congressi, concistoriale) were added as access points in the *Rubricelle.* A few of the larger subjects, such as "Nunziature" and "Vescovi," were respectively subdivided again by specific nunciatures and alphabetically. Each entry provides a one-line description of the business, correspondent, and the (usually five-digit) protocol number, in the right-hand column. Some mid-nineteenth-century *Rubricelle* also list the corresponding rubric number. Note that the rubric numbers are related to, but serve an entirely different function than, the *Rubricelle.* From the *Rubricelle,* researchers who have both the protocol and rubric numbers can proceed directly to ASV Indici 1031, 1032, 1033, or to ASV Indici 1089-I, 1089-II, or 1089-III, described below, to get the rest of the information necessary to request an item. Researchers desiring more information on the contents of a document, related items, or the rubric number should proceed to the *Protocolli.*

The *Protocolli* (also located in the Sala degli Indici) are used in conjunction with the *Rubricelle.* The *Protocolli* provide rubric numbers and contain a concise but amplified listing of individual items, compared to the *Rubricelle.* Researchers should note the year and protocol number in the *Rubricelle* and proceed to the *Protocolli* registers covering the year and proto-

col number desired. The *Protocolli* registers are organized numerically according to protocol number. Entries indicate the place, date, and correspondent; the object of business, the person assigned to deal with the request; the date; a brief note of the response or "risoluzione"; and an "Archivio" or rubric number. The rubric number is written largely in the "Archivio" column. Numbers written in smaller print sometimes appear above or below the rubric number. These numbers refer to the protocol numbers of related documents, either before (above) or after (below) a given item.

When a desired item is located the rubric number and the year of the protocollo volume should be noted and the appropriate Indici 1031, 1032, 1033, or 1089-I, 1089-II, or 1089-III should be consulted to get the rest of the information necessary to request an item. Specific items that have not been assigned a rubric number cannot be retrieved. Documents followed by the letters "AE," are in the Archives of the Congregazione degli Affari Ecclesiastici, outside the ASV. To see these documents one should contact the secretary of state archives.

ASV Indici 1031, 1032, and 1033 correspond respectively to the following three series: *Interni,* 1822–1833; *Esteri,* 1815–1850; and *Interni-Esteri,* 1814–1822. These indici are organized chronologically by year. Within each year the listings are organized numerically by rubric number. Researchers with a year in mind and a rubric number can turn to these indici for the correct busta or fascicolo number to request a desired item. Indici 1031, 1032, and 1033 are chronologically arranged listings (subdivided by year and then according to rubric numbers, buste, and fascicoli). Indici 1031, 1032, and 1033 also indicate any subseries in the rubrics (e.g., in Indice 1033, Rubric 27 breaks down by city: Ferrara, Forli, Ravenna, etc.), which can help to clarify the nature (subject matter classfied under) of a rubric number. Not all rubric numbers are represented in each year and the year designation for a rubric number does not mean that all materials in the busta are from that year. Earlier materials are often contained in a particular fascicolo.

After identifying material desired in Indici 1031 and 1032 (*Interni,* 1822–1833, and *Esteri,* 1815–1850, respectively), copy down the year, the rubric, and the busta numbers to request materials. To request rubric numbers from Indice 1033 (*Interni-Esteri,* 1814–1822), note the year, the rubric, and the fascicolo numbers.

ASV Indici 1089-I, 1089-II, and 1089-III are the key indici to the *Esteri,* 1851–1922. Indice 1089-I covers the years 1851–1877; 1089-II covers the years 1878–1913; and 1089-III covers the years 1914–1922. All three indici are arranged similarly to ASV Indice 1031, 1032, and 1033. Thus, entries indicate rubric numbers, any subdivisions of a rubric (e.g., in Indice 1089-III (1916), Rubric 251, "America Rappresentanti Pontifici," breaks down according to delegations (Chile Internunzio, Cuba e Portorico delegato, Haiti delegato, etc.), buste, and fascicoli numbers. To request materials, the rubric number, year, and fascicoli numbers are the essential pieces of information to note. Again, not all rubric numbers are represented each year and the year designation for a rubric does not indicate that only materials from that year are represented in the file(s). Earlier materials are often contained in a particular fascicolo.

Reference: Boyle, p. 79.

Finding Aids: ASV Indice 1034, compiled by G. Gullotta, provides a brief listing of the *Rubricelle* between the years 1816 and 1860. First, a summary of the number of *Rubricelle* for each year is given, and then the *Rubricelle* are listed individually with an indication of inclusive dates and the alphabetical letters or types of materials included in each volume.

ASV Indice 1035, "Prontuario per la consultazione delle Rubricelle dell'Archivio della Segreteria di Stato, 1816–1860," by G. Gullotta (1949), provides alphabetical, subject, and largely geographical access to the *Rubricelle* for those years. Entries are primarily geographical, but some access to papal agencies (e.g., Armi, Buon Governo) is included.

Location: Archivio Segreto Vaticano.

3.2.14.121 Rubriche
[DATABASE ID: VATV10476-A]
Inclusive Dates: 1903–1915.
Bulk: .2 linear m.
Location: Archivio Segreto Vaticano.

3.2.14.122 Ruolo pagamenti
[DATABASE ID: VATV10508-A]
Inclusive Dates: 1884–1957.
Bulk: 2 linear m.
Organization: Subseries includes: Mandati spese, 1884–1920.
Location: Archivio Segreto Vaticano.

3.2.14.123 Seminari
[DATABASE ID: VATV10483-A]
Inclusive Dates: 1910–1921.
1 linear m. (7 buste).
Location: Archivio Segreto Vaticano.

3.2.4.124 Soccorsi concessi dal S. Padre
[DATABASE ID: VATV10521-A]
Inclusive Dates: 1872–1873.
Bulk: .5 linear m.
Location: Archivio Segreto Vaticano.

3.2.14.125 Spogli di Leone XIII
[DATABASE ID: VATV10472-A]
Inclusive Dates: 1878–1903.
Bulk: 4.5 linear m. (17 buste).
Location: Archivio Segreto Vaticano.

3.2.14.126 Spogli di SS. Pio X
[DATABASE ID: VATV10471-A]
Inclusive Dates: 1903–1914.
Bulk: 1.5 linear m. (5 buste).
Location: Archivio Segreto Vaticano.

3.2.14.127 Spogli SS. Benedetto XV
[DATABASE ID: VATV10470-A]
Inclusive Dates: 1914–1922.
Bulk: .5 linear m. (5 buste).
Location: Archivio Segreto Vaticano.

3.2.14.128 Stampe Pio IX
[DATABASE ID: VATV10474-A]
Inclusive Dates: [18—].
Bulk: 1 linear m. (10 buste).
Location: Archivio Segreto Vaticano.

3.2.14.129 Suppliche
[DATABASE ID: VATV10482-A]
Inclusive Dates: 1909–1921.
Bulk: .5 linear m.
Location: Archivio Segreto Vaticano.

3.2.14.130 Sussidi
[DATABASE ID: VATV10478-A]
Inclusive Dates: 1904–1921.
Bulk: 4 linear m. (40 numbered buste).
Location: Archivio Segreto Vaticano.

3.2.14.131 Varia
[DATABASE ID: VATV10450-A]
Inclusive Dates: 1567–1832.
Bulk: 1 linear m.
Organization: 17 buste. Buste are as follows: 1. Lettere al Card. Scipione Rebiba, 1567; Carte riguardanti il S. Officio; —2. Carte diverse, [15—]; —3. Lettere di Antonio Carnazzani al Card. Farnese, 1601–1620; Vertenze fra Francescani recolletti, i Francescani, e Osservanti riguardante le missioni di Goa, 1620; —4. Carte di Giovanni Domenico Gibellini, maestro di casa del Principe Savelli, 1650–1660; —5. Cancelleria apostolica, S.C. Concistoriale, S.C. Confini, S.C. Immunità e Propaganda, 1600; —6. Anno 1600; —7. S.C. Particolare causa Arboren-Plureruim, 1729; —8. Cartier C. Argentinenois Monache Benedictinum in Monastero D. Ettonis, 1738; —9. Lettere di Francesco Pace a un Cardinale, 1717–1722; Lettere di Giovanni Batt. Frontoni, 1721–1725; S.C. Economica, 1747–1748; Proposit. eccl., 1599–1757; Carte del Cav. Giuseppe Lanze, 1763–1786; Eredità Podiani; Lettere di Francesco Piransi, 1784–1797; —10. Carte diverse, [17—]; —11. Carte Mazio Rafaelle, 1792–1815; Segr. Lettere latine, Carte Alertz, 1825–1858; —12. Carte Lattansi, 1830–1854; —13. Suppliche a Leone XII, Gregorio XVI, Pio IX; —14. Carte diverse, 1801–1829; —15. Carte diverse, 1832–1876; —16. Carte diverse, [17—]; —17. Carte diverse, [17—].
Scope: This may be part of one series with the Secretariatus Status series *Carte varie*. The *Carte varie* begins with "posizione" 18.
Location: Archivio Segreto Vaticano.

3.2.14.132 Vicario castense, militari
[DATABASE ID: VATV10486-A]
Inclusive Dates: 1916–1921.
1 linear m. (7 buste).
Location: Archivio Segreto Vaticano.

3.2.14.133 Visita apostolica in Messico
[DATABASE ID: VATV10091-A]
Inclusive Dates: 1886–1900 (bulk 1896–1900).
Bulk: 1.5 linear m. (19 boxes)
Organization: Arranged by case or by chronology. There are some miscellaneous newspaper articles at the end.
Scope: These are the records of Archbishop Nicola Averardi who became the apostolic delegate to Mexico in 1895 and apostolic visitor to all of Mexico in 1896. He presumably gave these records to the Secretariat of State. The records provide a good picture of the Catholic Church in Mexico at the end of the nineteenth century.

Reference: Pásztor (1970), pp. 198–200.

Finding Aids: ASV Indice 1139 provides a box and sometimes file listing of contents with inclusive dates.

Location: Archivio Segreto Vaticano.

3.2.15 Secretarius Intimus
[DATABASE ID: VATV043-A]

The office of the secretarius intimus was a stage in the development of the Secretariatus Status.

The work of secretarius intimus (private secretary) was entrusted by Leo X (1513–1521) to Pietro Ardighello, an assistant to Cardinal Giulio de' Medici (the future Clement VII [1523–1534] and a cousin of Leo X), who took over the direction of foreign affairs dealing with all correspondence in the vernacular, especially with the apostolic nuncios who were entrusted by that time with diplomatic missions of a permanent character. The correspondence was carried on in the name but no longer under the signature of the pope. The Secretariatus Status began in this way. This office was subsequently directed by the cardinal-nephew acting as the prime minister of the pope. It gradually developed into a more powerful office, especially during the period of the Council of Trent (1545–1563).

The secretarius intimus, who was also known as the secretary of the pope, or major secretary (secretarius papae/maior) was nearly always invested with episcopal rank. In order to ensure for themselves a greater freedom of action and protection from the pressure of the other cardinals, the popes began to entrust their secretarial work to a prelate chosen from among their own relations and known as the cardinalis-nepos (cardinal-nephew). Only at the beginning of the pontificate of Innocent X (1644) was this high office entrusted to a person already a cardinal and not a member of the family of the pope. The appointment of Giangiacomo Panciroli to this office (and perhaps the first time the title was used on official stationery) together with the later suppression of the Collegio dei Segreteri Apostolici by Innocent XI (constitution *Romanus Pontifex*, Apr. 1, 1678) were the first signs of the organization of the Secretariat of State in the modern sense of the term.

RECORDS. No records for this office were located. It is likely that records generated by the Secretariatus Intimus were considered by the officeholder to be personal papers and were thus removed at the conclusion of the term of service.

3.2.16 Segreteria dei memoriali
[DATABASE ID: VATV464-A]

Little information could be found on the history of this agency. It was abolished sometime before 1912.

Reference: A. Serafini, "Le origini della pontificia

Segretaria di Stato e la 'Sapienti consilio' del Pio X," *Apollinaris* 25 (1952): 165–239.

RECORDS. Records of the office consist of the following series.

3.2.16.1 Memoriali: Registro di suppliche presentate alla Santità di Nostra Signor . . .
[DATABASE ID: VATV210-A]
Inclusive Dates: 1814–1897.
Bulk: 70 linear m. (260 buste)
Organization: Chronological.
Scope: A few of the earlier buste contain indexes to the supplicants by name and then the actual supplications. Later buste have only the supplications. Some supplications have notations written on them, occasionally these refer to a specific audience.
References: Boyle, p. 68; Pásztor (1970), pp. 122–124; Pásztor (1983), pp. 156–158.
Finding Aids: ASV Indice 1065 briefly mentions the existence of these packets.
Location: Archivio Segreto Vaticano.

3.2.16.2 Registro de memoriali
[DATABASE ID: VATV209-A]
Inclusive Dates: 1636–1804.
Bulk: 23 linear m. (296 volumes).
Organization: Subseries include (numerical designations added by project staff): 1. Registro de memoriali, passim; —2. Registro di mem.li dati in audentia publica, 1605–1725, vols. 37–60; —3. Diversi ristretti di mem.li, 1725–1733, vols. 61–74; —4. Informazioni originali sopra diversi memoriali riferiti alla Santità . . . ; —5. Sunti e suppl. originali. These records are organized chronologically, then geographically, and then by type of supplicant (vescovi, prelati, monache). Many volumes are indexed by surname, religious order, and/or town.
Scope: Through vol. 74 (1733), volumes are registers of requests with a note as to where they were sent (the Congregation of Bishops and Regulars was a major recipient). After vol. 74, the actual supplications are retained. Responses may be written on the supplications; some may have a note by a secretary on them. Marginal notes in the first seventy-four registers may state if the supplication was accepted or not.
References: Fink, p. 80; Pásztor (1970), pp. 122–124; Pásztor (1983), pp. 156–157; Boyle, p. 68.
Finding Aids: ASV Indice 1065 gives a volume-by-volume listing of the first 292 volumes and summarizes numbers 293–296. Entries include: volume number, inclusive dates, sometimes pagination, exact title and variations, annotations regarding the type of information one is likely to find, the organization, and so forth.
Location: Archivio Segreto Vaticano.

3.2.16.3 Segreteria dei memoriali e Dataria apostolica
[DATABASE ID: VATV20022-A]
Inclusive Dates: 1784–1797 and 1753–1856.
Bulk: 69 filze, 11 mazzi, and 1 registro.
Reference: D'Angiolini, pp. 1088–1089.
Finding Aids: Inventory, 1979.
Location: Archivio di Stato di Roma.

3.2.16.4 [Suppliche]

[DATABASE ID: VATV10167-A]

Inclusive Dates: ca. 1815–1890.

Bulk: 11 linear m. (59 buste).

Organization: Subseries include: [Suppliche]; —Carte diverse; —Facoltà; —Lettere relazioni; —Lettere; —Lettere quittanze.

This series is unorganized. Subseries titles are written in pencil on the outside of the buste. Many are stamped with the office's stamp and numbered. The stamp reads primarily "Segreteria dei Memoriali," "Sezione Civile," or "Secr. Sup. Lib." The series is not in chronological, alphabetical, or numerical order.

Note: There is no official ASV designation for this series. The title was supplied by the project staff.

Location: Archivio Segreto Vaticano.

3.3
TRIBUNALS

3.3.1 Poenitentiaria Apostolica

[DATABASE ID: VATV026-A]

The Apostolic Penitentiary has jurisdiction for the sacramental and nonsacramental internal forum (i.e., matters affecting the private spiritual good of individuals); issues decisions on questions of conscience; grants absolutions, dispensations, commutations, sanations and condonations; and has charge of nondoctrinal matters pertaining to indulgences.

It is one of the three tribunals of the Holy See. Some find traces of it, or at least the idea for it, in the works of the *presbyteri poenitentium* instituted in the time of Pope Cornelius (251–253) for the absolution of the lapsi (those Christians who during the imperial persecutions had renounced the faith in order to escape torture and then later repented and sought to be reunited to the ecclesiastical community).

Some authorities, however, trace its history back to the seventh century during the brief pontificate of Benedict II (684–685). At that time cardinal penitentiaries were charged with representing the pope before all the faithful who were invited to Rome by their individual bishops for the resolution and absolution from the gravest questions of conscience. The most ancient record of a cardinal functioning in this way is found in a document of 1193 where Johannes de Sancto Paulo is mentioned as the first cardinal who heard confessions in the name of the pope. A penitentiary (a cardinal whose duty it was to absolve from sin and censures) was first designated by Honorius III (1216–1227).

The first mention of the term *penitentiary* occurs in a rescript of November 24, 1256, with which Cardinal Ugo da San Caro, the famous exegete and Dominican theologian, is mentioned as the first to bear the title *poenitentiarius summus* or *sedis apostolicae poeniten-*

tiarius generalis. From the beginning of the fourteenth century, this function was fulfilled by one of the cardinals under the title *poenitentiarium maior.*

Toward the end of the twelfth century a special group was formed to handle cases of conscience. This group became a permanent institution in the first half of the thirteenth century as is evident in the records of Innocent IV in 1248 and in those of his successor, Alexander IV (1254–1261).

Little is known of the Penitentiary during the thirteenth century; it is only at the beginning of the following century that there are any authentic records. Clement V, with his constitution *Dignum est* (Sept. 2, 1311), entrusted to his penitentiary, Cardinal Berengario Fredol, the task of reorganizing the tribunal. It was also Clement V who, in a council held at Vienne, France (1311–1312), established that the faculties for the forum of conscience of the Penitentiary would continue during a vacancy of the Holy See.

The constitution of Benedict XII (*In agro dominico*, Apr. 8, 1338) is the first document to define precisely the structure and function of this tribunal. He also established that the cardinal penitentiary would be assisted by a canonist and specified details governing personnel. He decreed that the Penitentiary would not be limited to the internal forum but would provide also for numerous favors relative to the external forum (i.e., matters affecting the public welfare of the church and its members).

By the end of the fourteenth century a reform of the tribunal had become imperative. The Council of Constance (1414–1418) moved to reorganize the functions and personnel of the tribunal, but its actions had little effect. As a result, Martin V, in 1415, had to intervene and, shortly after, Eugene IV did likewise with his constitution *In apostolicae dignitatis* (Oct. 14, 1438).

Since the popes, over a period of time, had conceded new faculties to the tribunal, the Penitentiary had acquired extended jurisdiction for handling cases in the external forum. These were recognized and confirmed by Sixtus IV (constitution *Quoniam nonnulli*, May 9, 1484) although he strove to control the extension.

In the sixteenth century Paul III instituted a commission to review the situation, but there was such strong opposition from the Penitentiary itself that it was not until the time of Julius III that the dispute could finally be settled (constitution *Rationi congruit*, Feb. 22, 1550). The first effort to limit what was perceived to be excessive power of this tribunal was exerted by Pius IV when he reorganized the various Roman tribunals (constitution *In sublimi*, May 4, 1562) and greatly reduced the cardinal penitentiaries' powers in the external forum. Their authority to continue in office during the sede vacante was revoked, and severe penalties were set for violations.

The reform of the Penitentiary, initiated by Pius IV, was successively carried on by Pius V, who attempted to reform the entire Roman Curia. With a series of three constitutions, *In omnibus rebus, Ut bonus,* and *In earum rerum,* all bearing the date of May 18, 1569, Pius V totally transformed the Penitentiary. He had decreed the temporary suppression of the tribunal (Apr. 23, 1569), but then reestablished it (May 18, 1569) radically reformed. He reduced to an absolute minimum the faculties of the cardinal penitentiary in the external forum and created the offices of theologian and canonist. He also gave the Penitentiary a new task: to settle controversies and questions of conscience "authentice."

In spite of the restrictive dispositions of Pius V, the Penitentiary began to reacquire from time to time many of its lost faculties, obtained by the penitentiaries in great part vivae vocis oraculo, through which they obtained some faculties of other offices. With time, therefore, another revision of their faculties became necessary.

Urban VIII made a first attempt to restore the discipline imposed by Pius V with his brief of September 17, 1634; Innocent XII soon after, with the constitution *Romanus Pontifex* (Sept. 3, 1692), tried again to categorize the functions proper to the Apostolic Penitentiary. A further reorganization of faculties and procedures took place under Benedict XIV. With his constitution *Pastor bonus* (Apr. 13, 1744) Benedict, a former canonist of the Penitentiary, described clearly the complexity of the functions belonging to this tribunal.

In spite of the complete reorganization of the Penitentiary effected by Benedict XIV in 1744, the tribunal continued to lack a true and proper office of secretary. This office was not established until the beginning of the following century through the work of Cardinal Leonardo Antonelli who attempted to discipline the work of the Penitentiary with appropriate norms, issued on September 21, 1805, substituted soon after by the new Regolamento made public on April 1, 1818, by Antonelli's successor, Cardinal Michele Di Pietro.

Between the time of Benedict XIV and Pius X the tribunal began to acquire, especially during the period of the French Revolution, some lost faculties of the external forum. These were again withdrawn by Pius X, who transferred them (constitution *Sapienti consilio,* Jun. 29, 1908) to the newly instituted Congregation for the Discipline of the Sacraments. This restricted the jurisdiction of the Penitentiary once again to the internal forum. A further change by Benedict XV (motu proprio *Alloquentes,* Mar. 25, 1917) separated the Office of Indulgences from the Congregation of the Holy Office and placed it under the Penitentiary.

Pius XI's constitution *Quae divinitus Nobis* (Mar. 25, 1935) defined the functions again and clarified the authority of the tribunal. Paul VI's constitution *Regimini Ecclesiae universae* (Aug. 15, 1967) confirmed the functions of the tribunal noting the "all that concerns the granting of indulgences is entrusted to the Penitentiary,

leaving intact the rights of the Congregation for the Doctrine of the Faith to see to those things that relate to dogmatic doctrine on indulgences."

A decree of the Penitentiary (Mar. 20, 1935) noted that in the future only the Penitentiary can directly grant faculties to bless articles of devotion and to annex to them the Apostolic indulgences, to give the papal benediction at the close of sermons, or to grant the indulgence of a personal privileged altar.

Paul VI's motu proprio *Pastorale munus* (Nov. 30, 1963) extended to all bishops the following privileges: to bless articles of devotion with the sign of the cross only, to annex all the indulgences usually conceded by the Holy See, and to bless crucifixes for the purpose of enabling persons impeded from making the Way of the Cross to gain the indulgences annexed to it.

In addition to the records listed below, series listed with other agencies relate directly to this agency and should be consulted. See Miscellaneous official series *Armarium XXXIX* and Congregatio Indulgentiis Sacrisque Reliquiis Praeposita series *Resolutiones.*

References. A. Battistella, *Il S. Officio e la riforma religiosa in Friuli: Appunti storici documentati* (Udine, 1895). P. Lecacheux, "Un formulaire de la Pénitencerie Apostolique au temps du cardinal Albornoz (1357–1358)," *Mélanges d'archéologie et d'histoire* 18 (1898): 37–49. K. Eubel, "Der Registerband des Cardinal Grosspönitentiars Bentevenga," *Archiv für katholisches Kirchenrecht* 64 (1890): 3–69. K. A. Fink, "Das Archiv der Sacra Poenitentiaria Apostolica," *Zeitschrift für Kirchengeschichte* 83 (1972): 88–92. L. P. Gachard, "Les archives du Vatican," *Bulletin de la Commission royale d'histoire de Belgique* 1 (1874): 211–386. E. Göller, "Das alte Archiv der päpstlichen Pönitentiarie," in *Kirchengeschichtliche Festgabe Anton de Waal* (Freiburg, 1913), pp. 1–19. E. Göller, "Hadrian VI. und der Aemterkauf an der päpstlichen Kurie," in *Abhandlungen aus dem Gebiete der mittleren und neueren Geschichte und ihrer Hilfswissenschaften: Eine Festgabe zum siebzigsten Geburtstag Geh. Rat Prof. Dr. Heinrich Finke* (Münster, 1925), pp. 375–407. E. Göller, *Die päpstliche Pönitentiarie von ihren Ursprung bis zu ihrer Umgestaltung unter Pius V* (Rome, 1907–1911). E. Göller, "Zur Geschichte der päpstlichen Poenitentiarie unter Clemens VI," *Römische Quartalschrift für christliche Altertumskunde und für Kirchengeschichte* 17 (1903): 413–417. L. Gomes, *Commentaria R.P.D. Ludovici Gomes . . . in regulas cancellariae iudiciales quae usu quotidiano in curia & torgo saepe versantur* (Paris, 1543). C. H. Haskins, "The Sources for the History of the Papal Penitentiary," *American Journal of Theology* 9 (1905): 421–450. A. Larraona and S. Goyeneche, "De SS. Congregationum, Tribunalium et Officiorum constitutione et interna ordinatione post const. 'Sapienti Consilio,'" in *Romana Curia a Beato Pio X, Sapienti*

Consilio reformata (Rome, 1951) [this title was noted but not verified by project staff]. H. C. Lea, *A Formulary of the Papal Penitentiary in the Thirteenth Century* (Philadelphia, 1892). H. C. Lea, *The Inquisition in the Spanish Dependencies: Sicily, Naples, Sardinia, Milan, the Canaries, Mexico, Peru, New Granada* (London, 1908). T. Majic, "Die apostolische Pönitentiarie im 14. Jahrhundert," *Römische Quartalschrift für christliche Altertumskunde und für Kirchengeschichte* 50 (1955): 129–177. G. C. Menis, ed., *1000 processi dell'Inquisizione in Friuli (1551–1647)*, 2d ed. (Udine, 1985). S. Miccio, "Vita di Don Pietro di Toledo, Marchese di Villafranca," *Archivio storico italiano* 9 (1846): 1–144. P. Paschini, *Venezia e l'Inquisizione romana da Giulio III a Pio IV* (Padua, 1959). V. Petra, *Commentaria ad constitutiones apostolicas, seu Bullas singulas summorum pontificum in bullario romano contentas, secundum collectionem Cherubini* (Venice, 1729). B. S. Pullan, *The Jews of Europe and the Inquisition of Venice, 1550–1670* (Oxford, 1983). A. Santosuosso, "Religious Orthodoxy, Dissent and Suppression in Venice in the 1540s," *Church History* 42 (1973): 476–485. G. Sforza, "Riflessi della Controriforma nella Repubblica di Venezia," *Archivio storico italiano* 93.1 (1935): 5–34, 189–216; 93.2 (1935): 25–52, 173–186. J. Trenchs Odena, "La Penitenciaria Apostolica: documentos y registros," *Boletín de la Sociedad Castellonense de Cultura* 58 (1982): 653–692.

RECORDS. Records of the tribunal consist of the following series.

3.3.1.1 Concessioni generali
[DATABASE ID: VATV10183-A]
Inclusive Dates: ca. 1700–1967.
Bulk: 1 linear m. (16 buste).
Organization: Buste 2–16 are chronological. Busta 1 is entitled "Antiche concessioni generali, divise per materia." Busta 2 contains references to indulgences granted in 1264, but actually spans ca. 1700–1933.
Summary: These are grants of indulgences with notes to existing grants. They are mainly rescripts and notes toward rescripts.
Finding Aids: Busta 1 contains lists of indulgences, apparently by type from ca. 1735 to 1886.
Location: Archivio Segreto Vaticano.

3.3.1.2 [Miscellanea S/F 445]
[DATABASE ID: VATV10186-A]
Inclusive Dates: 1743–1960 (bulk 1900–1940).
Bulk: .25 linear m. (5 vols.).
Organization: Volumes are: Registro delle materie, 1898–[post-1922]; —1 vol. [post-1922]; —Sommari primarii arciconfraternite—arcisodalizi oppure indulgenze perpetua ad assoc., 1743–[post-1922]; —(Congregationis Indulgentiis et Sacrisque Reliquiis) Concessiones generales, 1856–1872; —Facoltà comunicabili, [18—?].
Note: This series does not have an official ASV designation.

It was located in S/F 445 in 1990. The title was supplied by the project staff.
Location: Archivio Segreto Vaticano.

3.3.1.3 [Miscellanea SF/455]
[DATABASE ID: VATV10185-A]
Inclusive Dates: 1741–1966.
Bulk: 1 linear m.
Organization: This miscellany includes: 1 busta [post-1922]; —Biglietti di nomine pontificia (Segretario di Stato) 1741–1907; —5 buste [post-1922]; —Memorie riguardanti l'officio della Segreteria delle indulgenze, 1896–[post-1922]; —Recognitiones, ca. 1910–1917 (3 buste); —1 busta [post-1922]; —Decreti (2A), 1911–[post-1922]; —(Congregatione indulgentiarum et SS. Reliquiarum) Approvazioni di libri, 1862–1908; —2 buste [post-1922]; —Oracoli, 1829–[post-1922].
Note: This series does not have an official ASV designation. The title, which reflects the location of the series in 1990, was supplied by project staff.
Location: Archivio Segreto Vaticano.

3.3.1.4 [Register of Indulgences Alphabetically by Diocese]
[DATABASE ID: VATV10182-A]
Inclusive Dates: 1909–1968.
Bulk: .3 linear m. (6 vols.).
Organization: Alphabetical (chronological within each letter).
Scope: These registers provide access to two Poenitentiaria Apostolica series: [*Rescripta*] and *Summaria*. Entries include: protocol number, diocese, type of indulgence, date of presentation, agent, and the date and type of rescript. A related Poenitentiaria series is the [*Register of Indulgences by Protocol Number*].
Note: This series does not have an official ASV designation. The title was supplied by project staff.
Location: Archivio Segreto Vaticano.

3.3.1.5 [Register of Indulgences by Protocol Number]
[DATABASE ID: VATV10179-A]
Inclusive Dates: 1910–1964.
Bulk: .5 linear m. (32 vols.).
Organization: Organized by year and then by protocol numbers within each year.
Scope: Entries in these registers include indulgence number, diocese, type of indulgence, agent, date of presentation, date of rescript, and date of consignment. These registers relate to the following two Poenitentiaria Apostolica series: [*Rescripta*] and *Summaria*. For an index register organized chronologically by year and then alphabetically by diocese see the Poenitentiaria Apostolica series [*Register of Indulgences Alphabetically by Diocese*].
Note: This series does not have an official ASV designation. The title was supplied by project staff.
Location: Archivio Segreto Vaticano.

3.3.1.6 Registra matrimonialium et diversorum
[DATABASE ID: VATV10235-A]
Inclusive Dates: ca. 1410–1411, 1438–1890.
Bulk: 100 linear m. (746 numbered vols.).
Organization: Chronological. Subseries are: Bolle (1569–1890); —Suppliche (1410–1411, 1438–1585).
Scope: This series includes two distinct but related subseries:

registers of supplications (suppliche) granted, and registers of bulls (bolle) produced by the office of the Penitentiary from about 1410 to 1890. From 1410 to 1569 the series consists solely of supplications. The bulls commence in 1569 with the reform of the Penitentiary by Pius V. The two series dovetail for a period of sixteen years until the registers of supplications end in the first year of the pontificate of Sixtus V (1585). Register 27 of the supplications was not produced by the Penitentiary, but by the papal secretaries Leonardo Grifo and Andrea da Trebisonda and properly belong between Registra Vaticana 670 and 671 (cf. Tamburini below, where the index to this volume is published). Register 162 contains letters and approved supplications by Poenitentiarius Maior Carlo Borromeo.

The bulls primarily concern matrimonial dispensations. They were prepared in the office of minor graces of the Penitentiary, but they were sent through the Chancery. These records were transferred from the Penitenzieria Apostolica (Via della Conciliazione 34, Rome, Italy) in 1980.

References: Pásztor (1970), p. 351.

F. Tamburini, "Il primo registro di suppliche dell'Archivio della Sacra Penitenzieria Apostolica (1410–1411)," *Rivista di storia della chiesa in Italia* 23 (1969): 384–427. This article dates, analyzes, and publishes two examples from the initial register in this series. Tamburini then describes the structure of the Penitentiary, its functionaries, and the process of approval and registration of supplications. This article serves as a good orientation to the series.

E. Göller, *Die päpstliche Pönitentiarie von ihren Ursprung bis zu ihrer Umgestaltung unter Pius V.* (Rome, 1907–11); this is the classic monographic study. C. H. Haskins, "The Sources for the History of the Papal Penitentiary," *American Journal of Theology* 9 (1905): 421–450. H. C. Lea, *A Formulary of the Papal Penitentiary in the Thirteenth Century* (Philadelphia, 1892). F. Tamburini, "Un registro di bolle di Sisto IV nell'Archivio della Penitenzieria Apostolica," In *Palaeographica, Diplomatica et Archivistica: Studi in onore di Giulio Battelli* (Rome, 1979), vol. 2, pp. 375–405; this article discusses register 27. F. Tamburini, "L'Archivio delle Penitenzieria Apostolica e il primo registro delle suppliche (1410–1411)" (Ph.D. diss., Pontifical Lateran University, 1969).

Finding Aids: There are two Prospetti to this series available on request at the desk in the main ASV reading room. These Prospetti provide a brief volume listing, including the current number, subseries (bolle or suppliche), and pontificate(s). The dates in these prospetti, which were taken from the spines or guard pages, may be approximate. The prospetti also contain a listing of other Poenitentiaria Apostolica series. These are not official ASV finding aids and must be used in consultation with the ASV staff.

Location: Archivio Segreto Vaticano.

3.3.1.7 Registri

[DATABASE ID: VATV10234-A]
Inclusive Dates: 1540–1774.
Bulk: 2 linear m. (15 vols.).
Organization: Chronological.
Scope: The ASV staff consider these *Registri* as a part of the Poenitentiaria Apostolica series *Registra matrimonialium et diversorum.*
Location: Archivio Segreto Vaticano.

3.3.1.8 [Rescripta]

[DATABASE ID: VATV10181-A]
November 1908–1966.
Bulk: 13 linear m.
Organization: Chronological.
Summary: These records are from the Poenitentiaria Apostolica, Sectio de Indulgentiis. They are a continuation of the Congregatio Indulgentiis Sacrisque Reliquiis Praepositae series *Rescripta.* The bulk of this material is post-1922.
Finding Aids: These records are indexed numerically by protocol number and alphabetically by diocese in two series described among the records of the Poenitentiaria Apostolica: [*Register of Indulgences by Protocol Number*] and [*Register of Indulgences Alphabetically by Diocese*], respectively.
Note: This series has no official ASV designation. The title was supplied by the project staff.

Special permission from the Apostolic Penitentiary is required to consult these records. No photocopying or microfilming is permitted.

Location: Archivio Segreto Vaticano.

3.3.1.9 Summaria

[DATABASE ID: VATV10180-A]
Inclusive Dates: 1740–1964.
Bulk: 1 linear m. (10 buste).
Organization: Chronological.
Scope: After 1910 there are case numbers that relate to the Poenitentiaria Apostolica series [*Register of Indulgences by Protocol Number*], which is organized by these numbers. Prior to about 1908 these are the records of the Congregatio Indulgentiis Sacrisque Reliquiis Praepositae.
Finding Aids: The Poenitentiaria Apostolica series that this project has titled *Register of Indulgences by Protocol Number*, 1910–1964, is an index to this series. The Poenitentiaria Apostolica series that this project has titled *Register of Indulgences Alphabetically by Diocese*, 1909–1968, may also provide some indexing for this series.
Location: Archivio Segreto Vaticano.

3.3.1.10 Taxe: Pergamene

[DATABASE ID: VATV10236-A]
Inclusive Dates: Unknown.
Bulk: 1 vol.
Scope: These taxes are grouped by type.
Location: Archivio Segreto Vaticano.

3.3.2 Rota Romana

[DATABASE ID: VATV030-A]

From the earliest days of the church, judicial problems and reserved cases were referred to Rome for solution. By the end of the twelfth century this continual and ever-increasing flood of requests became too burdensome for the Consistory of Cardinals. The popes, therefore, began to refer cases to members of the papal household who were called cappellani papae. This group, which was dependent on the Apostolic Chancery, seems to be the antecedent, if not the origin, of the Roman Rota. Because the cappellani "heard" the cases they began to be called auditores (auditors), the title still given to judges of the Rota.

At first the auditors merely heard the cases, gathered the evidence, submitted their opinions, and then referred them to the pope for decision. Pope Innocent III (1198–1216) was the first to give the auditors the power, in certain cases, to render decisions themselves, although he still reserved confirmation of the decision to himself. His successors extended this concession. After Gregory X (1271–1276), the popes rarely intervened in judicial cases. During the pontificate of Nicholas IV (1288–1292), five auditors handled the cases. A half-century later, however, the number had increased to twenty-one, but there was not yet any diversity of function.

These auditors constituted a college called Auditores Causarum Sacri Palatii Apostolici. Nicholas appointed some of them to take charge of civil suits for the Papal States; Clement V (1305–1314) established an independent court for ecclesiastical cases. These two were later merged into one.

John XXII (constitution *Ratio iuris*, Nov. 16, 1331) stabilized the group as an organization and gave them, as an ordinary power of their office, the faculty of rendering decisions. With the constitutions *Ad regimen* (Jan. 10, 1335) and *Cum sint accepimus* (Oct. 1, 1335), Benedict XII located the tribunal in the papal palace at Avignon separating the members from the other cappellani. The tribunal continued to acquire ever greater functions not only by the actual extension of its powers but also by virtue of the expert opinions of its judgments. Because of this reputation it began to assume also the position of counselor of the pope.

Martin V (constitution *In apostolicae dignitatis*, Sept. 1, 1418) imposed the obligation of an oath on the auditors; listed the qualities expected of them; decreed that their decisions should conform with canonical and civil legislation; stated auditors were to be financially independent; and specified norms for exercising office in the tribunal. The official name *Rota* had appeared for the first time in 1337 in the decision of the auditor Tommaso Fastolf (or Fastoli), but Martin V was the first to use the term in an official document (constitution *Romani Pontificis*, Feb. 1424). With the constitution *Statuimus* (Apr. 7, 1421) and the above-mentioned *Romani Pontificis*, Martin called for new procedural rules and determined precisely the duties and rights of the notaries.

Later on, the Rota was distinguished by the addition of *Sacra* to its title, indicating it as a tribunal of the pope, and *Romana* to differentiate it from all the other rotal institutes. Under the pontificate of Sixtus IV the number of auditors was fixed at twelve (constitution *Romani Pontificis*, May 14, 1472). This number remained constant until the suspension of the tribunal in 1870, when all its authority over civil cases was withdrawn.

Under Innocent VIII (constitution *Finem litibus*, Jan. 10, 1488), authority for treating civil cases was given to Rota members. Innocent also prescribed the order and form of rotary judgments to obtain greater expediency in the handling of cases.

Clement VII (constitution *Convenit aequitati*, Aug. 15, 1525) gave greater privileges to Rota members. These were later confirmed by Paul III (constitution *Romani Pontificis*, Aug. 17, 1537). Pius IV (constitution *In throno iustitiae*, Dec. 27, 1561) extended the authority of the Rota to the entire Catholic world in order to answer once and for all those who questioned the broad function of the Rota. Pius IV's constitution *Dudum siquidem* (Jul. 27, 1562) decreed that the Rota could omit some of its formalities and make judgments in a more summary way provided that the cases would not prejudice decisions or harm others.

To reaffirm the importance of the Rota in the face of the increasing development of the Roman Congregations, Paul V extended its authority to benefices and marriage cases as well as to the processes for beatifications and canonizations (constitution *Universi agri dominici*, Mar. 1, 1612).

Benedict XIV (constitution *Iustitiae et pacis*, Oct. 9 1746) redefined the Rota's jurisdiction listing the cases falling within its authority: beatifications and canonizations; nullity of religious profession and dispensation from Holy Orders; contentious civil, ecclesiastical, and lay cases; benefices and marriage cases arising from the lower tribunals for which the Rota came to assume almost the nature of a tribune of appeal.

In 1814, after almost twenty years of absolute inactivity caused by the political problems of the Papal States, the Roman Rota was reactivited by Pius VII. With an edict of 1821 he also assigned to it the faculty of treating in appeal commercial cases of the Papal States. This function was modified, however, by Gregory XVI's *Regolamento legislativo e giudiziario par gli affari civili* issued in the form of a motu proprio (*Elevati appena*, Nov. 10, 1834).

After the dissolution of the Papal States in 1870, the Rota ceased to function (suppression ordered by rotal decision, Oct. 27, 1870, n. 5975). Their cases were transferred to the various Roman Congregations deemed most appropriate to specific functions. Leo XIII returned limited authority to the Rota in 1878 and gave it two specific tasks: (1) that of judging on the legality of the ordinary and apostolic processes on the virtues and validity of the Servants of God (Oct. 23, 1878); and (2) that of examining and resolving the doubts of "non cult and of reputation in kind of the Servants of God" (Dec. 19, 1895).

Pius X's *Sapienti consilio* (Jun. 29, 1908) called for a complete reorganization of the entire Roman Curia. The *Lex propria* accompanying the reorganization laid down certain judicial rules of a general nature for the

Tribunal of the Roman Rota, restoring it to its former dignity and prestige. However, even though it appeared that the Rota had reassumed all of its ancient appearance, this document designated the beginning of new life for the tribunal. These regulations were approved on an experimental basis by Pius X on September 7, 1909, and given final approval on August 2, 1910. The 1917 Code of Canon Law confirmed these regulations in substance.

The organization of the roman Rota is now actually directed by the *Normae Sacrae Romanae Rotae* of the tribunal issued on September 1, 1934, under the pontificate of Pius XI. This document, containing 185 articles, aimed to unify all previous legislation relative to the Roman Rota, supplanting the regulations approved by Pius X on August 2, 1910.

Paul VI's *Regimini Ecclesiae Universae* (Aug. 15, 1967) states that the Roman Rota was to be governed by its own rules but noted that the authority of the Rota over cases of marriage nullity was also to be extended to cases involving a Catholic and a non-Catholic party, or involving two non-Catholic parties, whether one or both of the baptized parties belong to the Latin rite or to an Eastern rite. Doctrinal questions touching on faith, however, were to be left to the Congregation for the Doctrine of the Faith. Some new norms were approved by John Paul II in 1982 and again in 1987.

Today the Roman Rota is no longer a supreme tribunal but is subordinate to the Apostolic Signatura and is, in effect, a tribunal of appeal. However, it is also the tribunal of first instance in cases that are reserved to the Holy See or that the pope has reserved for himself by means of a special rescript of the Apostolic Signature (1917 Code: can. 1603, no. 2). It is still regulated by the *Normae Sacrae Romanae Rotae* approved by Pius XI on June 22, 1934. Since it is a tribunal of the Holy See, the Roman Rota has no territorial limits in its authority. Even though most of the decisions it has rendered have been in matrimonial cases, it can and does hear all types of ecclesiastical cases, even criminal ones. Some cases, however, are withdrawn from its authority by law.

Since 1929 the Rota has also served as a court of appeals for the state of Vatican City.

The Rota also conducts a Rota Studium, founded in 1909 to train advocates, clerical and lay, for the Rota; the courses may also be followed by other clerical students. Pius XII reorganized the studium to meet contemporary needs with his decree *Nihil antiquius* (Jun. 8, 1945).

References. The archivist Hermann Hoberg devoted a major portion of his life's work to the records of the Rota. His collected bibliography constitutes an excellent introduction to the history of the tribunal and of the records it generated. See H. Hoberg, "Die 'Admissiones' des Archivs der Rota," *Archivalische Zeitschrift* 50–51 (1955): 391–408. H. Hoberg, "Das älteste Inventar der liturgischen Geräte und Paraments des Rotakollegs (1430)," *Quellen und Forschungen aus Italienischen Archiven und Bibliotheken* 35 (1955): 275–281. H. Hoberg, "Die ältesten Informativprozesse über die Qualifikation neuernannter Rotarichter (1492–1547)," in *Reformata Reformanda: Festgabe für Hubert Jedin zum 17 Juni 1965*, edited by E. Iserloh and K. Repgen (Münster, 1965), pp. 129–141. H. Hoberg, "Der Amtsantritt des Rotarichters Antonio Albergati (1649)," *Römische Quartalschrift für christliche Altertumskunde und für Kirchengeschichte* 49 (1954): 112–122. H. Hoberg, "Die Amtsdaten der Rotarichter in den Protokollbüchern der Rotanotare von 1464 bis 1566," *Römische Quartalschrift für christliche Altertumskunde und für Kirchengeschichte* 48 (1953): 43–78. H. Hoberg, "Die Antrittsdaten der Rotarichter von 1566 bis 1675," *Römische Quartalschrift für christliche Altertumskunde und für Kirchengeschichte* 48 (1953): 211–224. H. Hoberg, "Die diarien der Rotarichter," *Römische Quartalschrift für christliche Altertumskunde und für Kirchengeschichte* 50 (1955): 44–68. H. Hoberg, "Der Informationsprozess über die Qualifikation des Rotarichters Antonio Corsetti (1500)," in *Mélanges Eugène Tisserant* (Vatican City, 1964), vol. 4, pp. 389–406. H. Hoberg, "Der Informativprozess des Rotarichters Dominikus Jacobazzi (1492)," *Römische Quartalschrift für christliche Altertumskunde und für Kirchengeschichte* 51 (1956): 228–235. H. Hoberg, *Inventario dell'Archivio della Sacra Romana Rota (sec. XIV–XIX)* (Vatican City, 1994). H. Hoberg, "Passauer Prozesse in den ältesten im Vatikanischen Archiv erhaltenen Protokollbüchern der Rotanotare (1464–1482)," in *Ecclesia Peregrinans: Josef Lenzenweger zum 70 Geburtstag*, edited by K. Amon et al. (Vienna, 1986), pp. 153–158. H. Hoberg, "Die Protokollbücher der Rotanotare von 1464–1517," *Zeitschrift der Savigny-Stiftung für Rechtsgeschichte. Kanonistische Abteilung* 39 (1953): 177–227. H. Hoberg, "Register von Rotaprozessen des 14. Jahrhundert im Vatikanischen Archiv," *Römische Quartalschrift für christliche Altertumskunde und für Kirchengeschichte* 51 (1956): 54–69. H. Hoberg, "Die Tätigkeit der Rota am Vorabend der Glaubensspaltung," in *Miscellanea in onore di Monsignor Martino Giusti* (Vatican City, 1978), vol. 2, pp. 1–32.

The following works are also useful: E. Cerchiari, *Capellani Papae et Apostolicae Sedis Auditores causarum sacri palatii apostolici seu Sacra Romana Rota, ab origine ad diem usque 20 Septembris 1870: Relatio historica-iuridica SSMO D.N. Benedicto Papae XV dicata . . .* (Rome, 1919–1921). D. S. Chambers, *Cardinal Bainbridge in the Court of Rome, 1509 to 1514* (Oxford, 1965). C. Lefebvre, "La S. Congrégation du Concile et le Tribunal de la S. Rote Romaine à la fin du XVI siècle," in *La sacra Congregazione del Concilio: Quarto centenario della fondazione (1564–1964), studi e ricerche* (Vatican City, 1964), pp. 163–177. Ch. Lefebvre, "Rote romaine," in *Dictionnaire de droit canonique*, edited by R. Naz (Paris, 1960–1961), vol. 7, pp. 741–771. F. E. Schneider, *Die römische Rota: Nach geltendem Recht auf geschichtlicher Grundlage* (Paderborn, 1914–). F. E. Schneider, "Über den Ursprung und die Bedeutung des Namens Rota als Bezeichnung für den obersten päpstlichen Gerichtshof," *Römische Quartalschrift für christliche Altertumskunde und für Kirchengeschichte* 41 (1933): 29–43. F. E. Schneider, "Zur Entstehungsgeschichte der römischen Rota als Kollegialgericht," in *Kirchengeschichtliche Festgabe Anton de Waal* (Freiburg, 1913), pp. 20–36. A. M. Stickler, *Historia iuris canonici latini: Institutiones academicae*, vol. 1, *Historia fontium* (Turin, 1950).

RECORDS. Records of the tribunal consist of the following series.

3.3.2.1 Appendix
[DATABASE ID: VATV10299-A]
Inclusive Dates: 1585(copy)–1909 (bulk 1615–1909).
Bulk: 4.5 linear m. (43 numbered buste).
Scope: The 1585 copy of a bull is in busta 41. These records may include decisions by other congregations kept by the Rota for reference. Busta 33 is original Pentienzieria suppliche (1802–1809).
Reference: Pásztor (1970), p. 183.
Finding Aids: ASV Indice 1138 (pp. 18–23), by Hermann Hoberg, contains a brief contents listing for each busta in the series. Entries identify the creating office (if possible), the type of document (entrate ed uscita, broliardus, statuti, bulla, etc.), the inclusive dates, and other annotations (stampati, relegati, etc.). This index has been published; see H. Hoberg, *Inventario dell'Archivio della Sacra Romana Rota (sec. XIV–XIX)* (Vatican City, 1994). Hoberg provides an introduction to all Rota records in the ASV with an extensive bibliography.
Location: Archivio Segreto Vaticano.

3.3.2.2 Cause
[DATABASE ID: VATV10247-A]
Inclusive Dates: 1909–1955.
Bulk: 325 linear m. (1468 buste).
Organization: Chronological by year, then by diocese within each year.
Scope: These records primarily concern marriage nullifications from dioceses around the world.
Location: Archivio Segreto Vaticano.

3.3.2.3 Commissiones
[DATABASE ID: VATV285-A]
Inclusive Dates: 1480–1792.
Bulk: 7.5 linear m. (44 numbered buste and 2 loose files).
Organization: Nos. 1–42 are chronological, 1480–1792, by date the commission was given to an uditore. No. 43 contains material dated 1628–1645. No. 44 contains material dated 1632–1634. Loose folders include commissiones from about 1860 and 1551/1557, respectively.
Scope: The indice only lists buste in the regular series run

and not miscellaneous buste and volumes at the end of the series.
References: Pásztor (1970), p. 181; Boyle, p. 92.
Finding Aids: ASV Indice 1109 (pp. 2–6), by Hermann Hoberg, introduces the collection and provides a brief inventory of the forty-four numbered buste. Entries indicate the current volume number and inclusive dates for each busta.

H. Hoberg, *Inventario dell'Archivio della Sacra Romana Rota (sec. XIV–XIX)* (Vatican City, 1994). After providing an introduction to all Rota records in the ASV with an extensive bibliography, Hoberg publishes an inventory of the volumes in the series. Entries are briefer than those in ASV Indice 1109 but still provide the current volume number and the inclusive dates. The volume provides individual introductions to the series and some bibliographic references (pp. 185–186).
Location: Archivio Segreto Vaticano.

3.3.2.4 Decisiones
[DATABASE ID: VATV10306-A]
Inclusive Dates: 1511–1870.
Bulk: 45 linear m. (496 numbered buste).
Organization: Nos. 1–491 are roughly chronological by date of ultimate decision. See ASV index 1095 for inclusive dates for nos. 492–496. Subseries include: Decisiones; —Libri particulares (nos. 1–4, 6–9, 12); —Positiones (nos. 10–11); —Memoriali (no. 23); —Repertorium (nos. 450–452); —Index decisiones (nos. 448–449 and 453–472).
Scope: In the *Decisiones* series one primarily finds the conclusions of the Tribunal that have been prepared by the legal representative (uditore ponente) in charge of the case and that will be sent to the litigating parties. In addition, this series includes nine "Libri particulares," the collected notes and personal reflections of individual auditores concerning cases brought before the Rota (e.g., nos. 1–4, 6–9, 12). These notes were also commonly called decisiones. Vols. 10 and 11 contain positiones from 1551 with very brief notes regarding the conclusions of the Rota. Many volumes have internal indexes by diocese.
References: Pásztor (1970), p. 181. A. Fliniaux, "Contribution à l'histoire des sources de droit canonique: Les anciennes collections des Decisiones Rotae," *Revue historique de droit français et étranger*, 4th ser., 4 (1925): 61–93, 382–410. W. Ullmann, "A Decision of the Rota Romana on the Benefit of Clergy in England," in *Collectanea Stephan Kuttner* (Bologna, 1967), vol. 3, pp. 457–489.
Finding Aids: ASV Indice 1095, compiled by Hermann Hoberg, provides an introduction and a brief listing of volumes of *Decisiones*. Entries indicate the current volume number, the name of the uditore(s), inclusive dates, and occasionally title, volume, or subseries information. This index has been published; see H. Hoberg, *Inventario dell'Archivio della Sacra Romana Rota (sec. XIV–XIX)* (Vatican City, 1994). After providing an introduction to all Rota records in the ASV with an extensive bibliography, Hoberg publishes ASV Indice 1095.

Within this series, the subseries Repertorium and Index decisiones (primarily seventeenth–eighteenth centuries) are organized alphabetically by juridical designation for a decision (or part of a decision). These indices direct users to a decision number and section within a given year. Decisions in the ASV are not organized by this number, but chronologically according to the date of the final decision which would make these difficult to use without a concordance.

Location: Archivio Segreto Vaticano.

3.3.2.5 Diaria

[DATABASE ID: VATV283-A]

Inclusive Dates: 1566–1870.

Bulk: 12 linear m. (188 numbered vols.).

Organization: Three subseries: Diaria privata, 1566–1870, vols. 1–157; —Diaria camerariorum, 1688–1893, vols. 158–184A; —Diaria decanorum, 1590–1886, vols. 185–188.

References: Pásztor (1970), pp. 181–182; Boyle, p. 92. H. Hoberg, "Die diarien der Rotarichter," *Römische Quartalschrift für christliche Altertumskunde und für Kirchengeschichte* 50 (1955): 44–68.

Finding Aids: ASV Indice 1073, compiled by Hermann Hoberg, provides a detailed inventory of each volume in the Diaria series. Entries proceed volume by volume; give a physical description of the volume; and indicate the inclusive dates, the author(s) of the diary or from whose diary the information has been excerpted, notations on the spine, and occasionally, contents notes. Indice 1073 (pp. 53–57) contains an alphabetical list of "Nomina Auditorum" followed by the volume numbers that contain their diaries or excerpts from their diaries. See H. Hoberg, *Inventario dell'Archivio della Sacra Romana Rota (sec. XIV–XIX)* (Vatican City, 1994). After providing an introduction to all Rota records in the ASV with an extensive bibliography, Hoberg publishes an inventory of the volumes in this series. Entries are briefer than those in ASV Indice 1073 but still provide the current volume number, inclusive dates, the names of the "auditores," and some contents notes (e.g., fol. 344': "Concordat cum originali asservato in tabulario domus Pamphilii. C. Elephantutius, S.R. auditorum sollegi camerarius"). The volume provides individual introductions to the series and some bibliographic references.

Location: Archivio Segreto Vaticano.

3.3.2.6 Frammenti

[DATABASE ID: VATV10307-A]

Inclusive Dates: [14—]–1864.

Bulk: .5 linear m. (8 buste).

Organization: Subseries are: Frammenti stampati; —Frammenti di manoscritti.

Scope: Contains pergamene.

Location: Archivio Segreto Vaticano.

3.3.2.7 Informationes

[DATABASE ID: VATV10303-A]

Inclusive Dates: 1626–1669.

Bulk: 3 linear m. (25 numbered vols.).

Organization: Chronological.

Scope: Each volume has an internal index organized alphabetically by diocese. An indication of the dispute, for example, "jurisdictionis," or the name of the litigant or accused (a parish, monastery, etc.) is also usually given in this internal index.

References: Pásztor (1970), p. 182. H. Hoberg, "Der Informationsprozess über die Qualifikation des Rotarichters Antonio Corsetti (1500)," in *Mélanges Eugène Tisserant* (Vatican City, 1964), vol. 4, pp. 389–406.

Finding Aids: ASV Indice 1109 (pp. 7–10), by Hermann Hoberg, introduces and gives a brief inventory of the Informa-

tiones series. Entries include the current volume number and the inclusive dates of each volume. This is published in H. Hoberg, *Inventario dell'Archivio della Sacra Romana Rota (sec. XIV–XIX)* (Vatican City, 1994). After providing an introduction to all Rota records in the ASV with an extensive bibliography, Hoberg publishes ASV Indice 1109 (pp. 7–10).

Location: Archivio Segreto Vaticano.

3.3.2.8 Iura diversa

[DATABASE ID: VATV10298-A]

Inclusive Dates: 1512–1882.

Bulk: 156 linear m. (636 numbered buste).

Organization: Nos. 1–594 are chronological, 1600–1802; nos. 595–614 are chronological, 1512–1599. No. 615 is sixteenth century. Nos. 616–630 are chronological, 1600–1878. No. 631 contains architectural plans and maps, seventeenth-nineteenth century. Nos. 632–635 are chronological, 1515–1882. No. 636 is not dated.

Scope: The series *Iura diversa* is composed of original documents and copies of documents presented by the lawyers and proctors of the litigants. The documents are organized in buste more or less according to the dates of their presentation. The dates (year, month[s]) in which the documents were presented are marked on the outside of the buste. Sometimes these buste also contain documents from other months and even other years. Buste 615–636 contain documents taken from unorganized files. According to Lodolini (1932), an additional 239 volumes of the *Iura diversa* entitled "Iura diverse et cedulae privatae" (1802–1869) are available at the Archivio di Stato di Roma. This material is listed in this guide as a part of the Rota Romana series *Tribunale della rota.*

References: Pásztor (1970), p. 182; Lodolini (1932), p. 141.

Finding Aids: ASV Indice 1097, by Hermann Hoberg, contains a brief introduction and inventory of the entire *Iura diversa* series. The dates in the inventory are those that appear on the outside of the buste, and may not incorporate all the materials therein (cf. scope note above). Indice 1097 proceeds busta by busta and indicates the current volume number and the inclusive dates (year and month[s]). This index is published in H. Hoberg, *Inventario dell'Archivio della Sacra Romana Rota (sec. XIV–XIX)* (Vatican City, 1994). After providing an introduction to all Rota records in the ASV with an extensive bibliography, Hoberg publishes ASV Indice 1097.

Location: Archivio Segreto Vaticano.

3.3.2.9 Manualia actorum et citationum

[DATABASE ID: VATV282-A]

Inclusive Dates: 1464–1800.

Bulk: 113 linear m. (1043 numbered vols.).

Organization: Chronological.

Scope: These are case files relating in part to prebends, deaneries, chaplaincies, the census, fruits of benefices, dowries, goods, and marriages.

References: Boyle, pp. 91–92; Fink, pp. 122–124; Pásztor (1970), pp. 182–183. N. Hilling, *Die römische Rota und das Bistum Hildesheim am Ausgange des Mittelalters (1464–1513): Hildesheimische Prozessakten aus dem Archiv der Rota zum Rom* (Münster, 1908). H. Hoberg, "Die "Admissiones" des Archivs der Rota," *Archivalische Zeitschrift* 50–51 (1955): 391–408. H. Hoberg, "Die Protokollbücher der Rotanotare von

1464–1517," *Zeitschrift der Savigny-Stiftung für Rechtsge-schichte. Kanonistische Abteilung* 39 (1953): 177–227.

Finding Aids: ASV Indice 1057, by Hermann Hoberg, contains four sections that elucidate the series for researchers. The initial section (pp. iii–iv) is a brief introduction to the series. The second section, and focal point of Indice 1057 (pp. 1–642), is an analytical index to the entire *Manualia* series. The analytical section of Indice 1057 is a descriptive volume-by-volume inventory. Entries include the current volume number, inclusive dates, the identity of the uditore (writer of the volume, if known), the exact title on the spine, and occasionally selected other annotations such as an example of an interesting entry or type of document (e.g., cedulae, minutae, nota) in the busta or an indication of which pages contain entries from each year covered in the busta. The third section of Indice 1057 is entitled "Nomina Auditorum" and begins on page 651. This section is an alphabetical list of the auditore identified in the series with their corresponding volume numbers. The final section of Indice 1057, "Conspectus," is a brief listing of the entire series indicating the current volume number, the inclusive dates, and the auditore responsible for the busta.

H. Hoberg, *Inventario dell'Archivio della Sacra Romana Rota (sec. XIV–XIX)* (Vatican City, 1994). After providing an introduction to all Rota records in the ASV with an extensive bibliography, Hoberg publishes an inventory of the volumes in the series. Entries are briefer than those in ASV Indice 1057 but still provide the current volume number, inclusive dates, and the names of the auditores. The volume provides individual introductions to the series and some bibliographic references.

Location: Archivio Segreto Vaticano.

3.3.2.10 Miscellanea

[DATABASE ID: VATV10300-A]

Inclusive Dates: 1317–1922 (bulk 1650–1850).

Bulk: 10 linear m. (160 numbered buste).

Scope: The 1317 document is in no. 8. There is more Rota material here than in the *Appendix* series. There is also other material such as in no. 59, where there is an inventory of Palazzo Pontificio, 1741, and information on the Rota uditori. In no. 37 there is the "Acta visitationis officiorum rotalium." In no. 8 there is a Regulae Cancellarie (pp. 17–23).

References: Pásztor (1970), p. 183; Boyle, p. 92.

E. Cerchiari, *Capellani Papae et Apostolicae Sedis Auditores causarum sacri palatii apostolici seu Sacra Romana Rota, ab origine ad diem usque 20 Septembris 1870: Relatio historica-iuridica SSMO D.N. Benedicto Papae XV dicata . . .* (Rome, 1919–1921). In vol. 3 (pp. viii–xxxv), Cerchiari highlights the contents and diversity in *Miscellanea* nos. 2–4, 6–10, 12, and 148.

Finding Aids: ASV Indice 1138 (pp. 1–16) provides a brief description of each busta in the series. Entries indicate the types of documents that can be found (e.g., bolle, constitutiones, cause, inventori, testamenti), inclusive dates, and a note as to other papal or civil offices involved. ASV Indice 1138 (ff. 1–12) has been published in H. Hoberg, *Inventario dell'Archivio della Sacra Romana Rota (sec. XIV–XIX)* (Vatican City, 1994). After providing an introduction to all Rota records in the ASV along with an extensive bibliography, Hoberg publishes an inventory of all the volumes in this series (1–160). Entries

include the current volume number, inclusive dates, physical description notes (e.g., pergamene, rileg.), a transcription of information on the spine, and a general description of the contents at the volume level. This is an exact reprint of the information provided in ASV Indice 1138 noted above.

ASV Indice 1108, by Herman Hoberg, calendars the contents of *Miscellanea* nos. 1–28. Hoberg proceeds page by page, item by item and indicates the folio, a date (if identifiable), the title or type of document, and other annotations such as whether the item has been published or if the item is an original or a copy. Later entries give briefer descriptions and may summarize groups of documents. From this index one notes the many small items that are lost in the general descriptions given in Indice 1138.

Location: Archivio Segreto Vaticano.

3.3.2.11 Miscellanea

[DATABASE ID: VATV287-A]

Inclusive Dates: 1395–1889.

Bulk: 28 vols.

Reference: Boyle, p. 92.

Note: This series was not located by project staff in 1990.

Location: Archivio Segreto Vaticano.

3.3.2.12 Miscellanea giudiziaria di curie vescovili

[DATABASE ID: VATV20247-A]

Inclusive Dates: 1781–1871 (bulk 1814–1871).

Bulk: 593 fascicoli.

Reference: D'Angiolini, p. 1202.

Finding Aids: List, 1970.

Location: Archivio di Stato di Roma.

3.3.2.13 Notai del tribunale della rota

[DATABASE ID: VATV20062-A]

Inclusive Dates: 1568–1870.

Bulk: 85 vols.

Scope: Sixteenth century, 1 vol.; —Seventeenth century, 33 vols.; —Eighteenth century, 36 vols.; —Nineteenth century, 15 vols.

References: D'Angiolini, pp. 1128–1129; Lodolini (1960), p. 59.

Finding Aids: There are old alphabetical indexes and an old chronological list. In addition there is an inventory, prepared in 1980 and a printed list of notai.

Location: Archivio di Stato di Roma.

3.3.2.14 Peritiae

[DATABASE ID: VATV10305-A]

Inclusive Dates: 1644–1863 (bulk 1670–1863).

Bulk: 8 linear m. (28 numbered vols. and one unnumbered folder).

Organization: Vols. 1–26, chronological; —vol. 27, "Tavola lettere ABCD unite ai rilievi emessi dall'Ingegnere Paolo Cavi e dal Perito Agronomo controverso tra il Lago Caprolace e la Selva Marittima di Terracina".; —the unnumbered folder, 1644–1645, includes "Confino de le Monache di S. Sisto (Rome)."

Scope: None of the indexes note the unnumbered folder at the end of the series.

Reference: Pásztor (1970), p. 183.

Finding Aids: ASV Indice 1109 (pp. 11–14), by Hermann

Hoberg, introduces and provides a brief inventory of the *Peritiae* series, nos. 1–27. Entries include the current segnature and the inclusive dates of each volume. This index has been published in H. Hoberg, *Inventario dell'Archivio della Sacra Romana Rota (sec. XIV–XIX)* (Vatican City, 1994). After providing an introduction to all Rota records in the ASV along with an extensive bibliography, Hoberg publishes ASV Indice 1109 (pp. 11–14), described above.

Location: Archivio Segreto Vaticano.

3.3.2.15 Positiones

[DATABASE ID: VATV284-A]

Inclusive Dates: 1627–1870.

Bulk: 760 linear m. (3,837 numbered buste and 6 unnumbered volumes that are appendices).

Organization: Chronological. Within each busta materials are organized alphabetically according to diocese. Nos. 3818–3837 and the appendices are not in chronological order and span the years 1639–1870.

References: Pásztor (1970), pp. 183–184; Boyle, p. 92.

Finding Aids: The indices only list buste in the regular series run and not miscellaneous items located at the end of the series. ASV Indici 1072, compiled by Hermann Hoberg, provides access to *Positiones* nos. 1–268. Indice 1072 begins with a brief introduction to the series and then proceeds busta by busta, page by page, listing each case (positioni) in the busta. Entries include: diocese, business (dotis, nullitatis professionis, beneficii, etc.), date, and folio number(s). On page 266, Hoberg has constructed an alphabetical list of "ponentes," entitled "Index Auditorum" in *Positiones* 1–268.

ASV Indice 1092, also by Hermann Hoberg (1968), provides a brief but expanded introduction (compared to Indice 1072) to the *Positiones*. Indice 1092 proceeds volume by volume or busta by busta. For approximately the first 228 buste, the ponenti are the major identifying feature. The inventory lists the the name of the "ponente" (uditore) and the year(s) covered. The cases of each ponente or uditore listed in Indice 1092 are usually organized alphabetically by diocese. After approximately busta 228, buste are organized by year and then alphabetically by diocese. Sometimes the name of the uditore or ponenti is provided with the name of the first and sometimes last diocese represented in the buste; sometimes only diocesan names or the uditore's name is identified. This inventory is published exactly in H. Hoberg, *Inventario dell'Archivio della Sacra Romana Rota (sec. XIV–XIX)* (Vatican City, 1994). After providing an introduction to all Rota records in the ASV along with an extensive bibliography, Hoberg publishes an inventory of all the volumes (1–3837) in this series. Entries are exactly like those in ASV Indice 1092. This work provides individual introductions to the series and some bibliographic references.

ASV Indice 701, "Protocollo delle cause ventilate in Sacra Rota dal 1800 a tutto il mese di Settembre 1870," is an alphabetical index to litigants in the Positiones (1801–September 1870). Entries list the litigants (pro and con), the diocese, the uditore, and the date (year, day, month). Indice 701 provides excellent access to cases during this period. Researchers should copy all the information concerning the case(s) in question and then refer to Indice 1092 to locate the current volume number for the Positiones busta which covers the year(s), uditore(s), and diocese(s) sought.

Location: Archivio Segreto Vaticano.

3.3.2.16 Processus actorum

[DATABASE ID: VATV286-A]

Inclusive Dates: 1497–1800.

Bulk: 65 linear m. (1,080 numbered buste).

Organization: Nos. 1–1063 are chronological, 1500–1800. Nos. 1064–1080 cover the years 1497–1862 but are not organized in a strictly chronological fashion.

Scope: The *Processus actorum* series contains the records of cases presented on behalf of both parties, that is, "in partibus." These cases were those following the normal procedure. The cover of each register indicates the title of the case, the name of the representative (uditore ponente) presenting the case for the parties, and the date of the hearing. Sometimes the names of other successive legal representatives (uditore ponente) and other dates pertinent to the case appear on the cover. The registers are grouped in buste that proceed according to the date of their presentation. There are a few items from other Rota series, for example, *Iura diversa* and *Processus in admissione auditorum*. (The 1497 document is in no. 1067, which is not listed in any of the indici.) The indices only list items in the regular series run, not miscellaneous buste and volumes at the end of the series.

References: Boyle, p. 92; Pásztor (1970), p. 184. H. Hoberg, "Register von Rotaprozessen des 14. Jahrhundert im Vatikanischen Archiv," *Römische Quartalschrift für christliche Altertumskunde und für Kirchengeschichte* 51 (1956): 54–69.

Finding Aids: ASV Indice 1094, by Hermann Hoberg, is a brief introduction and prospectus to *Processus actorum* nos. 1–1061. The current volume number for each of buste 1–1061 is listed followed by its inclusive year(s) and usually month(s). Note that *Processus actorum* no. 1061 no longer covers the years 1601–1618, but covers the *Processus actorum* for January–March 1800.

ASV Indice 1106, by Hermann Hoberg, provides a slightly longer introduction to the series and more detailed information about *Processus actorum* nos. 1–100. Entries for buste 1–100 indicate the inclusive dates (i.e., registration dates), the diocese or papal office concerned in each processus, and the nature of the business (e.g., iuris visitandi, hereditatis, exequutionis bullarum, beneficii, census, decimarum, etc.). In Indice 1106, Hoberg indicates both the dates signaled on the spine and the actual dates of the material in each busta. He also states that a few documents properly belonging to other Rota series, for example, *Iura Diversa* and *Processus in admissionum auditorum*, have found their way into the *Processus actorum* and that these are noted in Indice 1106.

H. Hoberg, *Inventario dell'Archivio della Sacra Romana Rota (sec. XIV–XIX)* (Vatican City, 1994). After providing an introduction to all Rota records in the ASV with an extensive bibliography, Hoberg publishes an inventory of the volumes in this series. Entries are briefer than those in ASV Indice 1106 and 1094 but still provide the current volume number and inclusive dates (year and months). The volume provides individual introductions to the series and some bibliographic references.

Location: Archivio Segreto Vaticano.

3.3.2.17 Processus in admissione auditorum

[DATABASE ID: VATV10304-A]

Inclusive Dates: 1492–1908.

Bulk: 2 linear m. (12 numbered buste).

Organization: Chronological. Note that no. 12, which is not listed in the finding aids, contains materials from 1816 and 1851–1906.

References: Pásztor (1970), p. 181. H. Hoberg, "Die "Admissiones" des Archivs der Rota," *Archivalische Zeitschrift* 50–51 (1955): 391–408.

Finding Aids: ASV Indice 1109 (pp. 33–43), by Hermann Hoberg, introduces the *Processus in admissione auditorum* series and provides a detailed description of buste 1–11. Entries for each busta include a physical description of each busta (e.g., current segnatura, missing pages, titles/identification given on the spine and internally) and then list numbers within the busta, the date (year, month, day) and the name of the "eletto" for each admissione in the busta. This indice has been published in H. Hoberg, *Inventario dell'Archivio della Sacra Romana Rota (sec. XIV–XIX)* (Vatican City, 1994). After providing an introduction to all Rota records in the ASV with an extensive bibliography, Hoberg publishes ASV Indice 1109 (pp. 33–43) described above.

Location: Archivio Segreto Vaticano.

3.3.2.18 Sententiae
[DATABASE ID: VATV10302-A]

Inclusive Dates: 1474–1890 (bulk 1531–1803).

Bulk: 7 linear m. (42 numbered buste and 1 unnumbered busta).

Organization: Nos. 1–42 are chronological by the date the sentence was promulgated. The unnumbered final busta contains copies of sentences and minutes of sentences from 1572–1576, 1774, and 1890. Note that this final busta is not mentioned in any of the finding aids.

Reference: Pásztor (1970), p. 184.

Finding Aids: ASV Indice 1109 (pp. 30–32), by Hermann Hoberg, provides a short introduction and a brief inventory of buste 1–42 of the *Sententiae*. Entries indicate the current volume number and inclusive dates of each busta. This index has been published in H. Hoberg, *Inventario dell'Archivio della Sacra Romana Rota (sec. XIV–XIX)* (Vatican City, 1994). After providing an introduction to all Rota records in the ASV with an extensive bibliography, Hoberg publishes ASV Indice 1109 (pp. 30–32).

Location: Archivio Segreto Vaticano.

3.3.2.19 Tribunale della rota
[DATABASE ID: VATV20061-A]

Inclusive Dates: 1492–1809 and 1814–1870.

Bulk: 1,602 buste, 813 vols., 57 registri, and 1 fascicolo.

References: D'Angiolini, pp. 1128, 1201–1202; Lodolini (1960), pp. 111–112.

Finding Aids: Inventory; list of duplicates, 1970.

Location: Archivio di Stato di Roma.

3.3.2.20 Vota
[DATABASE ID: VATV10301-A]

Inclusive Dates: 1626–1870.

Bulk: 48 linear m. (274 numbered buste).

Organization: Organized by the name of the uditore in roughly chronological order.

Reference: Pásztor (1970), p. 184.

Finding Aids: ASV Indice 1109 (pp. 15–28), by Hermann Hoberg, includes a brief introduction and inventory for the *Vota.* Entries indicate the current volume number, name of the uditore, inclusive dates, and usually an indication of the alphabetical range of dioceses which may be included in each busta. This inventory has been published in H. Hoberg, *Inventario dell'Archivio della Sacra Romana Rota (sec. XIV–XIX)* (Vatican City, 1994). After providing an introduction to all Rota records in the ASV with an extensive bibliography, Hoberg publishes ASV Indice 1109 (pp. 15–28).

Location: Archivio Segreto Vaticano.

3.3.3 Signatura Apostolica
[DATABASE ID: VATV027-A]

In the mid-thirteenth century the popes used the services of referendarii apostolici (official reporters) to prepare petitions for the signature (signatura) of the pope, or his delegate, or to refer questions involving favors or matters of justice to the cardinal or chaplain auditors. With the passage of time and the increase in requests, the number of referendarii increased considerably.

Eugene IV (1431–1447) made the Signatura a permanent office and gave to the referendarii the faculty of signing certain supplications, but always in the presence of the pope. This led to a gradual division of the Signatura into two distinct but parallel bodies: the Signatura Gratiae, competent in administrative matters, and the Signatura Iustitiae, competent in judicial matters. For lack of documentation it is difficult to say just when this division took place. Some authorities hold that it was with Innocent VIII's constitution *Officii nostri debitum* (Jan. 25, 1491). Others attribute it to Alexander VI (1492–1503) who, some say, did it in order to define the functions of the office more clearly. By the time of Julius II (1503–1513), however, the division of the two Signatures had been completed, each had its own prefect, and the Signatura Iustitiae had become a genuine tribunal.

In his curial reorganization (constitution *Sapienti consilio* and *Lex propria*, Jun. 29, 1908), Pius X formally suppressed the Signatura Gratiae and the Signatura Iustitiae as originally established and restored the latter as a new body, called the Signatura Apostolica, to be the supreme tribunal of the Holy See. Its province is confined to questions relating to auditors of the Rota and to the sentences pronounced by them. This revised Signatura is a genuine tribunal with jurisdiction in four kinds of cases: (1) accusations of suspicions against an auditor of the Rota; (2) accusations of violation of secrecy by an auditor of the Rota; (3) appeals against a sentence of the Rota; and (4) petitions for the nullification of a decision of the Rota that has already passed into a res iudicata. It has other duties related to the juridical organization of the Vatican City State, and from certain concordats. The *Lex propria* was more clearly defined by the *Regulae servandae* approved by Benedict XV on March 6, 1912, to which that pope also added an appendix on November 3, 1915.

Benedict XV reestablished the college of votanti and that of the referendaries as consultative organs of the tribunal (chirograph *Attentis expositis*, Jun. 28, 1915). The faculties and privileges of the voting prelates and of the referendary prelates were determined by Pius XI's constitution *Ad incrementum*, August 15, 1934.

Paul VI's *Regimini Ecclesiae universae* (Aug. 15, 1967) changed the name to Supremum Tribunal Signaturae Apostolicae and divided the tribunal into two sections: (1) strictly judicial affairs—to oversee the administration of justice in the lower tribunals, resolve disputes over judicial authority, erect regional and interregional tribunals, hear cases involving accusations of nullity against rotal proceedings, try cases assigned to it by the pope, and enjoy the rights recognized by various concordats; and (2) service as an administrative court—to resolve conflicts of authority among Roman offices, deal with questions about the exercise of administrative jurisdiction in the church, and examine administrative questions referred to it by the pope or the congregations. The Signatura is governed by its own proper law.

RECORDS. See the entries "Signatura Gratiae" and "Signatura Iustitiae" below.

3.3.4 Signatura Gratiae
[DATABASE ID: VATV028-A]

In the mid-thirteenth century the popes used the services of referendarii apostolici (official reporters) to prepare petitions for the signature (signatura) of the pope, or his delegate, or to refer questions involving favors or matters of justice to the cardinal or chaplain auditors. With the passage of time and the increase in requests the number of referendarii increased considerably.

Eugene IV (1431–1447) made the Signatura a permanent office and gave to the referendarii the faculty of signing certain supplications, but always in the presence of the pope. This led to a gradual division of the Signatura into two distinct but parallel bodies: the Signatura Gratiae, competent in administrative matters, and the Signatura Iustitiae, competent in judicial matters. For lack of documentation it is difficult to say just when this division took place. Some authorities hold that it was with Innocent VIII's constitution *Officii nostri debitum* (Jan. 25, 1491). Others attribute it to Alexander VI (1492–1503) who, some say, did it in order to define the functions of the office more clearly. By the time of Julius II (1503–1513), however, the division of the two Signatures had been completed and each had its own prefect.

Paul III (constitution *Debita consideratione*, Jul. 30, 1540) gave numerous privileges to the referendaries. Sixtus V (constitution *Quemadmodum*, Sept. 22, 1586) established detailed regulations for both offices.

Sixtus V, in his reorganization of the Roman Curia

(constitution *Immensa aeterni Dei*, Jun. 29, 1588), gave second place to the reordered Signatura Gratiae under the name of Congregatio Signatura Gratiae (also referred to as the Congregation of Favors and Commissions). Alexander VII confirmed the regulations established by Sixtus V in 1586 (constitution *Inter ceteras*, Jun. 14, 1659) and combined a select group of referendaries of both Signatures into a single college (Jul. 13, 1659). These were called voting referendaries; the others remained as supernumerary referendaries. The Signatura Gratiae was held in the presence of the pope and was therefore also called the Signatura Sanctissimi (of the Holy Father). The members voted on the matters under consideration but the vote was merely consultative. The pope reserved to himself the decision in each case. Over time, the Signatura Gratiae gradually declined in importance, mainly because of the evolution of the office of the Datary and the broadening function of the Rota and Apostolic Camera.

Because of numerous disputes and controversies over the functions of the Signatura Gratiae, Benedict XIV made an effort to clarify the various jurisdictions (constitution *Romanae Curiae*, Dec. 21, 1744) and definitively determined the jurisdictions with his constitution *Iustitiae et pacis* (Oct. 9, 1746).

Pius VII made some changes in the tribunal (motu proprio *Quando per ammirabile*, Jul. 6, 1816) but died (1823) before he could carry out his plans. Leo XII with his motu proprio *Quam plurima et gravissima* (Apr. 11, 1826) broadened the faculties of the Signatura, but they were actually used only in the civil forum for the Papal States.

Although it was not formally abolished, there is no mention of the Signatura Gratiae after 1847. In 1899 Leo XIII abolished the office of the registry of supplications.

In his curial reorganization (constitution *Sapienti consilio* and *Lex propria*, Jun. 29, 1908), Pius X formally suppressed the Signatura Gratiae and the Signatura Iustitiae as originally established and restored the latter as a new body, the Signatura Apostolica, to be the supreme tribunal of the Holy See.

References. K. A. Fink, "Zur Geschichte des päpstlichen Referendariats," *Analecta sacra tarraconensia* 10 (1934): 75–100. B. Katterbach, "Referendarii utriusque signaturae a Martino V ad Clementem IX et praelati signaturae supplicationum a Martino V ad Leonem XIII," vol. 2 of *Sussidi per la consultazione dell'Archivio Vaticano* (Vatican City, 1931). A. M. Stickler, *Historia iuris canonici latini institutiones academicae*, vol. 1, *Historia fontium* (Turin, 1950).

RECORDS. No records for this agency were located in the ASV, but series listed with another agency relate directly to this agency and should be consulted. See Signatura Iustitiae series *Tribunale della segnatura di grazia e di giustizia*.

3.3.5 Signatura Iustitiae
[DATABASE ID: VATV029-A]

In the mid-thirteenth century the popes used the services of referendarii apostolici (official reporters) to prepare petitions for the signature (signatura) of the pope, or his delegate, or to refer questions involving favors or matters of justice to the cardinal or chaplain auditors. With the passage of time and the increase in requests the number of referendarii increased considerably.

Eugene IV (1431–1447) made the Signatura a permanent office and gave to the referendarii the faculty of signing certain supplications, but always in the presence of the pope. This led to a gradual division of the Signatura into two distinct but parallel bodies: the Signatura Gratiae, competent in administrative matters, and the Signatura Iustitiae, competent in judicial matters. For lack of documentation it is difficult to say just when this division took place. Some authorities hold that it was with Innocent VIII's constitution *Officii nostri debitum* (Jan. 25, 1491). Others attribute it to Alexander VI (1492–1503) who, some say, did it in order to define the functions of the office more clearly. By the time of Julius II (1503–1513), however, the division of the two Signatures had been completed, each had its own prefect, and the Signatura Iustitiae had become a genuine tribunal.

Paul III (constitution *Debita consideratione*, Jul. 30, 1540) gave numerous privileges to the referendaries. Pius IV (constitution *Cum nuper*, Jul. 1, 1562) reformed the Signature of Justice. Sixtus V (constitution *Quemadmodum*, Sept. 22, 1586) established for both offices detailed regulations.

Alexander VII confirmed the regulations established by Sixtus V in 1586 (constitution *Inter ceteras*, Jun. 14, 1659) and combined a select group of referendaries of both Signatures into a single college (Jul. 13, 1659). These were called voting referendaries; the others remained as supernumerary referendaries. The Signatura Iustitiae was a true tribunal: the voters of this Signature were present at it and their vote was definitive not consultative. While the Signatura Gratiae gradually declined in importance, the Signatura Iustitiae remained active as a tribunal and served as the prototype for the present Signatura Apostolica.

Leo XII, with his motu proprio *Quam plurima et gravissima* (Apr. 11, 1826), broadened the faculties of the Signatura, but they were actually used only in the civil forum for the Papal States. In 1834 Gregory XVI reorganized the Signatura Iustitiae once again.

In his curial reorganization (constitution *Sapienti consilio* and *Lex propria*, Jun. 29, 1908), Pius X formally suppressed the Signatura Gratiae and the Signatura Iustitiae as originally established and restored the latter as a new body, the Signatura Apostolica, to be the supreme tribunal of the Holy See.

Reference. B. Katterbach, "Referendarii utriusque signaturae a Martino V ad Clementem IX et praelati signaturae supplicationum a Martino V ad Leonem XIII," vol. 2 of *Sussidi per la consultazione dell'Archivio Vaticano*, (Vatican City, 1931).

RECORDS. Records of the tribunal consist of the following series.

3.3.5.1 Notai del tribunale della segnatura
[DATABASE ID: VATV20058-A]
Inclusive Dates: 1630–1870.
Bulk: 42 vols. and 1 rubricella.
Scope: Seventeenth century, 14 vols.; —Eighteenth century, 8 vols.; —Nineteenth century, 20 vols.
References: D'Angiolini, p. 1127; Lodolini (1960), p. 59.
Finding Aids: There are some lists, an inventory prepared in 1980, indexes of notai, and a printed list of notai.
Location: Archivio di Stato di Roma.

3.3.5.2 Notai del tribunale della segnatura
[DATABASE ID: VATV20249-A]
Inclusive Dates: 1831–1870.
Bulk: 23 vols.
Reference: D'Angiolini, p. 1202.
Finding Aids: Inventory, 1974, with alphabetical index of addressees of chirografi.
Location: Archivio di Stato di Roma.

3.3.5.3 Positiones
[DATABASE ID: VATV289-A]
Inclusive Dates: 1679–1700.
Bulk: 25 linear m. (148 vols.).
Organization: These are chronological by the order in which cases were considered and decided. Cases are numbered within each month.
Scope: The case write-ups often refer to earlier dates. A few volumes have monthly summaries that provide a minimal index to cases. However, these summaries list the month, diocese, and an abbreviation of the action under consideration only.
References: Fink, p. 124; Boyle, pp. 93–94.
Location: Archivio Segreto Vaticano.

3.3.5.4 Tribunale
[DATABASE ID: VATV10143-A]
Inclusive Dates: ca. 1832–1893.
Bulk: 2 linear m. (15 vols.).
Organization: Four subseries are: Tribunale, 1832–1868, 12 vols.; —Questioni e competenza e altri affari, 1868–1870, 1 vol.; —Giuramenti e processi dei referenderi, 1872–1893, 1 vol; —Carte varie, 1825–1870, 1 vol.
All series are roughly chronological.
Reference: Boyle, pp. 93–94.
Location: Archivio Segreto Vaticano.

3.3.5.5 Tribunale della segnatura di grazia e di giustizia
[DATABASE ID: VATV20057-A]
Inclusive Dates: 1614–1809 and 1814–1870.
Bulk: 259 vols., 434 buste, 17 registri, 19 protocolli, and 1 rubrica.
References: D'Angiolini, pp. 1126–1127, 1202; Lodolini (1960), p. 116.
Finding Aids: Inventories.
Location: Archivio di Stato di Roma.

PART 4

Apostolic Nunciatures, Internunciatures, and Delegations

THE HOLY SEE IS BOTH HEAD OF THE WORLDWIDE ROMAN CATHOLIC church and head of the sovereign state of the Vatican City. As such, the Holy See has maintained diplomatic relations reflecting in various degrees this dual responsibility with most countries of the world. The title of the specific post is an indication of the status of relations between the Holy See and a particular country. Papal diplomatic legates can be assigned two functions: internal, concerned with relations between the pope and local churches and subordinate ecclesiastical authorities; and external, concerned with relations with civil governments.

Internal legation began as early as the fourth century. From the fifth to the eighth centuries external legation began with apocrisiaries or responsales sent to the Byzantine Empire, first sent by Leo I (440–461). From the fourth century to the eleventh century residential archbishops were appointed *legati nati*, with an ecclesiastical role. *Legati missi* appeared in the ninth century (or later) as special envoys sent from Rome. Beginning in the eleventh century the most important legations were entrusted to cardinals, with the title *legati a latere*.

In the thirteenth century, *nuntii et collectores iurium, redituum et omnium bonorum Camerae Apostolicae* collected alms and tithes and otherwise raised funds for the pope. Their duties also included diplomatic functions. Modern permanent nunciatures began with Alexander VI's legates to Spain in 1492 and Venice in 1500. Nuncios are equivalent to ambassadors, representing the Holy See to the civil authorities in the countries to which they are accredited. They also have a religious mission, representing the church before the civil government as well as to local prelates.

The title *internuncio* was used in the seventeenth and eighteenth centuries to identify a representative sent to a nunciature where for some reason a nuncio could not be sent. Beginning with the establishment of the internunciature for the Netherlands in 1829, the term referred to a permanent legation lower in rank than a nunciature. In the 1960s, all remaining internunciatures were raised to nunciatures, and the rank was eliminated.

As a result of an administrative order of the secretary of state of May 8, 1916, apostolic delegates have been strictly internal legates, not accredited to a civil government. They represent the pope to the local church in the area to which they are sent. Before 1916, delegates sometimes had diplomatic status, especially in Latin America where they were titled *apostolic delegate and envoy extraordinary*. The first modern apostolic delegate was sent to Syria in 1761.

Lower-ranking titles used by the diplomatic corps of the Holy See include *chargé d'affaires* and *regent*, both used by an agent in charge of a nunciature or internunciature in the absence of the nuncio or internuncio. The titles *legate* and *delegate* were also used in the local administration of the Papal States. See the section "Papal States: Local Administrations."

For a complete list of nuncios see Henry Biaudet, *Les nonciatures apostoliques permanentes jusqu'en 1648* (Helsinki, 1910); Liisi Karttunen, *Les nonciatures apostoliques permanentes de 1650 à 1800* (Helsinki, 1912); *Repertorium der diplomatischen Vertreter aller Länder seit dem Westfalischen Frieden (1648) [to 1815]* (Oldenburg, 1936–1965); Giuseppe de Marchi, *Le nunziature apostoliche dal 1800 al 1956* (Rome, 1957).

For bibliographies citing reprints of selected records of European nunciatures, see Leon-E. Halkin, *Les archives des nonciatures* (Brussels, 1968); and Johann Rainer, "Nuntiaturberichte: Forschungsstand und Forschungsprobleme," *Innsbrucker Historische Studien* 9 (1986): 69–90.

A NOTE ON THE ARCHIVES

It is a policy of the Holy See that all inactive records generated by a diplomatic post, whatever the rank, be deposited with the Archivio Segreto Vaticano. As a result a user can reconstruct both sides of the interchange between the Secretary of State at the Vatican and the diplomatic representatives in the particular posts. The records described in this section were all generated in the country named. In this guide, see the Secretarius Status records that are listed in the section "Roman Curia." Of particular relevance are the series of records generated by the secretary of state relating to particular countries for the period prior to 1809, and the Secretariatus Status series *Esteri* for the period after 1815.

It is important to note that the structure of the Vatican diplomatic corps has shifted over time. Users of records described in this section should note the histories of specific posts so as to identify predecessor and successor posts. In many cases jurisdictions were consolidated and/or subdivided, especially in Latin America, Central America, Africa, and Asia. As a result, documents for particular countries can be found in several places other than the nunciatures for those countries.

In some cases, records for a specific nunciature were not located in the Archivio Segreto Vaticano. For material prior to 1922 that was not located, the project staff has the highest degree of confidence that the records indeed are not in the ASV. For material after 1922, records not located may indeed be under the control of the archives but maintained in a secured area that is under the joint jurisdiction of the Secretariat of State and the ASV. In any case, of course, records dated after 1922 are not currently available for consultation in the ASV.

It is important to cite all the material described in this section as the archives of the particular post housed in the ASV. For example, for the collection of the nunciature for Brazil: Apostolic Nunciature for Brazil, Archivio della Nunziatura Apostolica in Brazil deposited in the ASV.

References. L. E. Halkin, "Les Archives des nonciatures: Rapport au comité directeur de l'Institut historique Belge de Rome," *Bulletin de l'Institut historique Belge de Rome* 33 (1961): 649–700. P. Richard, "Origines des nonciatures permanentes: La représentation pontificale au XVe siècle (1450–1513)," *Revue d'histoire ecclésiastique* 7 (1906): 52–70, 317–338.

4.1 Albania, Apostolic Delegation in
[DATABASE ID: VATV578-A]

Established in 1920, dependent on the Congregation Propaganda Fide, the apostolic delegation in Albania was abolished in 1945.

RECORDS. Records of the delegation consist of the following series.

4.1.1 Archivio della Delegazione Apostolica di Albania
[DATABASE ID: VATV10498-A]
Inclusive Dates: 1921–1936.
Bulk: .5 linear m.
Organization: Two principal subseries: Gossi, 1921–1926; and 1 series [post-1922].
Location: Archivio Segreto Vaticano.

4.2 Antilles, Apostolic Delegation in
[DATABASE ID: VATV565-A]

Established in 1925 from a reorganization of the apostolic delegation in Cuba and Puerto Rico, the apostolic delegation for the Antilles was located in Havana. The delegation's jurisdiction was extended to all the Greater and Lesser Antilles, British Honduras, Bermuda, and the Bahamas. The envoy also held the office of apostolic delegate to Mexico. Haiti and the Dominican Republic were removed from the office's responsibility in 1930 when a nuncio was appointed to those countries. In 1935 Cuba was also removed from the office's responsibility when that nuncio was established. The office was abolished in 1938 and the remaining territory was divided: Jamaica and British Honduras were given to the nunciature for Cuba, Barbados and the Venezuelan islands to Venezuela, Bermuda to Canada, the Bahamas to the United States, and Puerto Rico and all other islands to the nunciature for Haiti and the Dominican Republic. A new apostolic delegation in the Antilles was established in 1975, with responsibility for the West Indies except Cuba, Haiti, the Dominican Republic, and Puerto Rico and responsibility also for the Bahamas, Belize, Bermuda, French Guiana, Guyana, Jamaica, and Suriname.

RECORDS. Records of the delegation consist of the following series.

4.2.1 Archivio della Delegazione Apostolica delle Antille
[DATABASE ID: VATV070-A]
Inclusive Dates: 1907–1937.
Bulk: .5 linear m. (5 boxes and 3 bundles)
Organization: Fascios are numbered 1–16.
Scope: The series dates from 1907, prior to the establishment of the delegation (in 1925). It primarily concerns Puerto Rico and the earliest materials deal with claims to property and financial reparations by the Catholic Church in Puerto Rico in American courts as a result of the Spanish-American War as well as earlier seizures of property by the Spanish. ("Questione dei beni della Chiesa in Portorico.") Records also provide some information on the Catholic Church in Cuba during the years prior to 1922. Additional archival materials of this delegation can be located in the series for the Dominican Republic, *Archivio della Nunziatura nella Repubblica Dominicana*. Records can also be located in the archives of other Latin American nunciatures (especially Cuba and Brazil); the series for Spain, *Archivio della Nunziatura di Spagna*; as well as in the Secretariatus Status series *Esteri*.
Location: Archivio Segreto Vaticano.

4.2.2 Archivio della Nunziatura in Portorico
[DATABASE ID: VATV40002-A
Inclusive Dates: 1925–1942.
Bulk: 10 buste.
Note: This series was cited in Natalini et al., p. 266, but not seen by project staff in 1990.
Location: Archivio Segreto Vaticano.

4.3 Arabia, Apostolic Delegation in
[DATABASE ID: VATV587-A]

The apostolic delegation in Egypt and Arabia was established in 1839 to represent the Holy See to churches in those areas. In 1947 the mission to Egypt became a separate internunciature and the delegation in Arabia was separated. From 1947 to 1949 the office was filled by a regent. In 1950 the mission was attached to the apostolic delegation in Iraq, and in 1969 to the apostolic delegation in the Region of the Red Sea.

RECORDS. No records for this delegation were located in the ASV.

4.4 Argentina, Apostolic Nunciature for
[DATABASE ID: VATV400-A]

Before 1877 the interests of the Holy See were represented in Argentina by papal representatives in Brazil (1829–1836, 1840–1849, 1851–1857, and 1864–1877) and Colombia (1836–1840). The first apostolic delegate to Argentina, Paraguay, and Uruguay served from 1849 to 1851. From 1857 to 1864 an apostolic delegate was appointed to Argentina, Bolivia, Buenos Aires (independent 1852–1860), Chile, Paraguay, and Uruguay. The office was permanently established in 1877 as apostolic delegate and envoy extraordinary to Argentina, Paraguay, and Uruguay. Relations were severed from 1884 to 1900. In 1900 relations were reestablished with the posting of an internunciature for Argentina united with the apostolic delegation in Paraguay and Uruguay (although relations were not resumed with Paraguay until 1919 and with Uruguay until 1939). In 1916 the internunciature for Argentina was raised to a nunciature. In 1939 the missions to Paraguay and Uruguay were separated from the jurisdiction of the nuncio for Argentina.

Reference. For a complete list of nuncios (through 1956) see Giuseppe de Marchi, *Le nunziature apostoliche dal 1800 al 1956* (Rome, 1957).

RECORDS. Records of the nunciature consist of the following series.

4.4.1 Archivio della Nunziatura in Argentina
[DATABASE ID: VATV530-A]
Inclusive Dates: 1900–1953.
Bulk: 24 linear m. (194 buste and 12 volumes)
Organization: Subseries include: Gobierno; —Diocesis (Cuestiones economicas, Obispo-Clero, Varias, Facultades, Oratorios, Dispensas); —Obispos (Procesos canonicos, Candidature vescovili); —Religiosos; —Religiosas; —Emigracion; —Terrirorios nacionales; —Accion Catolica; —Anticlericalismo; —Varias; —Internunziatura; —Protocolli.
Scope: This series covers the period of the apostolic internunciature for Argentina, Paraguay, and Uruguay and the apostolic nunciature for Argentina. The records demonstrate the growth and changes in the Catholic Church in Argentina as well as a careful monitoring of the political situation throughout South America. In particular, the protocolli registers, described below, relate to the entire region covered by the internunciature: Argentina, Paraguay, and Uruguay. Additional materials concerning Argentinian religious and political affairs can be located in the archives of other South American nunciatures, particularly Brazil, Ecuador, and Chile, as well as the Secretariatus Status series *Esteri*.
Finding Aids: ASV Indice 1159 provides detailed access to the archives of the first three nuncios (1900–1922). This indice generally lists the title of each file folder and calendars selected sections of the series (Diocesis, Religiosos).

This series contains a number of internal indices that are found among the miscellaneous volumes at the end of the series. These are: Indice (nomi), 1922; —Nunziatura Apostolica del Paraguay (Protocollo), 1917–[post-1922]; —Registro no. 1, da 1 al 396 incl con segreto papale, 1900–1904; —Actas, 1904–1906 (registro no. 2); —Internunziatura Apostolica di Mons. Achille Locatelli, Protocollo Arrivi, 29 Abrile 1907–3 Giugno 1916; —Internunziatura Apostolica di Mons. Achille Locatelli, Protocollo Spedizioni, 29 Abrile 1907–3 Giugno 1916; —Protocollo, 1916–1922 (Arrivi e spedizioni). These items listed on page 137 of ASV Index 1159 are now located in the ASV.
Reference: Natalini et al., p. 266.
Location: Archivio Segreto Vaticano.

4.5 Australia, New Zealand, and Oceania, Apostolic Delegation in
[DATABASE ID: VATV583-A]

The apostolic delegation in Australasia was established in 1914, with responsibility for representing the Holy See to churches in Australia, Tasmania, and New Zealand. It was located in Sydney, Australia, and was dependent on the Congregation Propaganda Fide. Responsibility for all the Pacific islands, including the Dutch East Indies, was added in 1919. In 1921 responsibility for the Marshall, Mariana, and Caroline Islands

was transferred to the apostolic delegation in Japan. Also in 1921, Hawaii was transferred to the United States delegation. In 1947 Indonesia was made a separate apostolic delegation and the remainder of the delegation in Australia was renamed apostolic delegation in Australia, New Zealand, and Oceania. In 1968 it was split into two delegations, in Australia and Papua New Guinea and in New Zealand and the Pacific Islands.

RECORDS. Records of the delegation consist of the following series.

4.5.1 Archivio della Delegazione Apostolica d' Australasia
[DATABASE ID: VATV503-A]
Inclusive Dates: 1915–1945.
Bulk: 17 linear m. (202 buste and 15 vols.)
Organization: Subseries are: Delegazione Apostolica (includes Relazioni con autori civili); —Australasia; —Diocesi; —Liste episcopali; —Seminari; —Instituti religiosi; —Societe cattoliche; —Affari matrimoniali; —Diverse; —Aborigene; —Oceania Insulare; —Assistenza tempo guerra; —Protocolli.

Volumes at end of series include: Protocolli (1915–[post-1922]) 13 vols.; —Erezione Delegazione Apostolica (1914) 1 vol.; —Tasse SS. Messe, 1 vol.
Scope: Additional material concerning the Catholic Church in Australasia can be located in other series including the Secretariatus Status series *Esteri*.
Finding Aids: Protocolli (1915–[post-1922]) are very detailed with good summaries of correspondence. All protocolli indicate the subseries and location of the actual material indexed. These volumes are internal to the series and are available only by request.
Reference: Natalini et al., p. 266.
Location: Archivio Segreto Vaticano.

4.6 Austria, Apostolic Nunciature for
[DATABASE ID: VATV228-A]

The nuncio for the Holy Roman Empire became the nuncio for Austria with the abolition of the empire in 1806. (For earlier relations, see the agency history for the nunciature to the Holy Roman Empire.) From 1824 to 1827, the office was held by an internuncio. The nunciature was closed in 1938, after the German occupation. Relations were reestablished in 1946 after Austrian independence was restored. Until 1951 the office was held by an internuncio.

References. For a complete list of nuncios (through 1956) see *Repertorium der diplomatischen Vertreter aller Länder seit dem Westfälischen Frieden* (1648) [to 1815] (Oldenburg, 1936–1965); Giuseppe de Marchi, *Le nunziature apostoliche dal 1800 al 1956* (Rome, 1957).

Other useful publications include: L. Lukács, *The Vatican and Hungary, 1846–1878: Reports and Correspondence on Hungary of the Apostolic Nuncios in Vienna* (Budapest, 1981); J. Rainer, "Bartholomäus Portia als Nuntius bei Erzherzog Ferdinand II. von Tirol 1573/74," in *Neue Beitrage zur geschichtlichen*

Landeskunde Tirols: Festschrift für Univ. Prof. Dr. Franz Huter anlässlich der Vollendung des 70. Lebensjahres, edited by E. Troger and G. Zwanowitz (Innsbruck, 1969), vol. 2, pp. 347–360; J. Rainer, ed., *Nuntiatur des Germanico Malaspina, Sendung des Antonio Possevino 1580–1582* (Vienna, 1973); S. Weiss and J. Rainer, *Nuntiatur des Germanico Malaspina und des Giovanni Andrea Caligari 1582–1587* (Vienna, 1981); R. Reichenberger, "Germanico Malaspina und Filippo Sega (Giovanni Andrea Caligari in Graz)," *Erste Hälfte* of *Nuntiaturberichte aus Deutschland nebst ergänzenden Actenstücken, 1585 (1584)–(1592). Zweite Abteilung, Die Nuntiatur am Kaiserhofe* (Paderborn, 1905).

RECORDS. Records of the nunciature consist of the following series.

4.6.1 Archivio della Nunziatura di Austria

[DATABASE ID: VATV431-A]

Inclusive Dates: 1587–1938.

Bulk: 124 linear meters.

Organization: Principal series: Archivio della Nunziatura di Vienna, 1607–1889 (641 vols.); —Agliardi nunzio, 1893–1895; —Taliani nunzio, 1896–1903; —Granito Pignatelli di Belmonte nunzio, 1904–1910; —Bavona nunzio, 1911; —Rossi incaricato d'affari, 1911; —Scapinelli nunzio, 1912–1915; —Valfre' di Bonzo nunzio, 1916–1919; —Oggetto, ca. 1919–1920; —Marchetti Selvaggiani nunzio, 1920–1921; —Sibilia nunzio, 1922–1935; —Punzolo, ca. 1920s; —Cicognani nunzio, 1936; —Miscellanea, ca. 1600–1824 (includes Dispensazioni Matrimoniali, Examina, Petitiones, Negotia Epist., Brevi, Bolle costitutiones, Negotiae Regulari, Misc.) Negotia varia alienationem bonorum ecclesiasticorum concernentia (Alienazioni), 1614–1710 (position numbers 1–19); —Controversiarum inter ecclesiastics ipsos et seculares ex ortarum, 1612–1782 (position numbers 1–221); —Causarum omnium beneficialium in archivio huius Apostolica Nuntiatura existentium (Cause beneficiali), 1633–1780 (position numbers 1–40); —Negotia diversa Immunitatem Ecclesiasticam spectantia (Immunitates), 1653–1712 (position numbers 1–88); —Causarum omnium civilium (Cause civili), 1602–1781 (position numbers 1–162); —Causarum omnium criminalium in Archivio huius S. Apostolicae nuntiatura existentium (Cause criminali), 1607–1788 (position numbers 1–197); —Causarum omnium de matrimonia in Archivio S. Apostolicae Nuntiatura Viennensis existentium (Causae matrimoniale), 1614–1797 (position numbers 1–459); —Dispense matrimoniali, 1621–1803 (10 meters.); —Regularium, 1607–1782 (152 position numbers); —Negotia varia Nuntiis per acta ab anno 1615–1745 (Negotia varia); —Negotia regulari, 1614–1666, 1800–1821; —Examina, 1635–1753; —Bolle costitutiones, 1792–1803; —Brevi, 1721–1731; —Petitiones varie, 1601–1795; —Processi canonici, 1587–1866 (numbered 1–982); —Miscellanea di catalogare; —Cassa del sale di Boemia; —Miscellanea (numerata); —Lettere diversi; —Epistolae e negotia, 1670–1738; —Estratti delle stampe; —Protocolli.

Note: Volumes 75–77, 80, 415, 424bis, 425, 570, 587, 595, and 640 of the *Archivio della Nunziatura di Vienna* are available on microfilm.

References: Boyle, p. 78; Fink, pp. 93–94. Andreas Cornaro et al., *Der Schriftverkehr zwischen dem päpstlichen Staatssekretariat und dem Nuntius am Kaiserhof Antonio Eugenio Visconti, 1764–1774* (Vienna, 1970), is an index to selected documents concerning political events in Austria during this period. Entries give the place and date, the correspondents and/or the type of business, the first few words of the document, and the series, volume, and folio numbers of the place(s) where the document can be found in various forms. There is an index to names, places, and subjects at the end.

Finding Aids: ASV Indici 1055–I, 1055–II, 1055–III, 1055–IV, and 1055A, are a five-volume series of indici that provide access to the *Archivio della Nunziatura di Austria.* Indice 1055–I covers the years 1607–1890 (vols. 1–641). It provides the volume number, a contents note, a transcription of information from the spine of the volume, and other descriptive notes (e.g., "leg. scritture in perg. con scrittura del sec. XIII"). Indice 1055–II, "Processi canonici dei vescovati e delle abbazie," is a geographic listing by diocese of one type of transaction (e.g., processi) ca. 1600–ca. 1900 in the Processi Canonici subseries. Indice 1055–III, "Indice dei processi dei vescovi e degli abbati," presents the processi transactions chronologically (1582–1879). Indice 1055–IV, "Inventarium . . . in Archivio hujus Apostolicae Nuntiaturae existentium," provides chronological indexes to different types of business (e.g., Controversiarum inter Ecclesiasticos ipsos et saeculares exortarum, Causarum omnium civilium, Dispense matrimoniali, Cause beneficiali, and Negotia Varia, etc.). Indice 1055A, "Archivio Nunziatura di Vienna, vols. 483–549 (1874–1880), Inventario," by Sr. Ines Bassani and Mons. Aldo Martini, provides the volume number, total number of pages, information from the spine, and a description of the contents of each volume of the Jacobini nunciature.

Walter Wagner provides an expanded description of vols. 1–201 and a brief listing of volumes 202–252 (1607–1792) in "Die Bestände des Archivio della Nunziatura Vienna bis 1792," *Römische historische Mitteilungen* 2 (1957–1958): 82–203 (ASV Stampate XX B 35 [10]). The detailed description of vols. 1–201 surpasses ASV Indice 1055. Entries note the existence of internal indici, dates, types of business occasionally doing an analysis of items, and transcribe information on the spine. For volumes 202–252, only indici and spinal information are noted by Wagner. A chronological index ends the article.

Within the series *Archivio della Nunziatura di Vienna,* vol. 549 is a protocol register and index to selected volumes between vols. 483 and 549 (1874–1879). Bassani and Martini, cited above, indicate that this index is a good place to begin if one is interested in the nunciature of Jacobini.

Location: Archivio Segreto Vaticano.

4.7 Avignon, France, Legation for

[DATABASE ID: VATV590-A]

No history was prepared for this agency.

RECORDS. No records of this legation were located in the ASV, but series listed with the Secretariatus Status relate directly to Avignon and should be consulted. See Secretariatus Status series *Legazione di Avignone.*

4.8 Bavaria, Apostolic Nunciature for
[DATABASE ID: VATV240-A]

In 1784 the Elector of Bavaria requested the appointment of a nuncio with responsibility for all his possessions, including the Palatinate and territory along the Rhine, which had been divided among the jurisdictions of the nuncios to the Holy Roman Empire, Cologne, and Switzerland. The first nuncio took office in 1786. From 1800 to 1817 no nuncio was appointed. The office was filled from 1800 to 1808 by a minister (not resident) and an auditor. The nuncio to Cologne also served as minister and special nuncio for Bavaria, until 1805. A special nuncio was appointed in 1806 to negotiate a concordat. The office was filled by an internuncio in 1838–1841 and 1847–1851. From 1920 to 1925 the nuncio to Bavaria also served as nuncio to Germany. The office was abolished in 1934, when the German states lost their autonomy.

Reference. For a complete list of nuncios see Liisi Karttunen, *Les nonciatures apostoliques permanentes de 1650 à 1800* (Helsinki, 1912); *Repertorium der diplomatischen Vertreter aller Länder seit dem Westfälischen Frieden (1648) [to 1815]* (Oldenburg, 1936–65); Giuseppe de Marchi, *Le nunziature apostoliche dal 1800 al 1956* (Rome, 1957).

RECORDS. Records of the nunciature consist of the following series.

4.8.1 Archivio della Nunziatura di Baviera
[DATABASE ID: VATV425-A]
Inclusive Dates: 1818–1934.
Bulk: 47.5 linear m. (435 numbered volumes and boxes)
Organization: Principal series: Archivio della Nunziatura di Monaco (v. 1–241); —Fruehwirth nunzio, 1907–1915; —Aversa nunzio, 1916; —Pacelli nunzio, 1917–[post-1922]; —1 series [post-1922]; —Protocolli 1–37, 1786–1898; —Protocolli (13 vols.), 1902–[post-1922]; —Schedario "Nomi" (6 boxes), ca. 1920–[post-1922].
Note: Protocollo e Indice, vols. 15–19, are available on microfilm.
References: Boyle, p. 78; Fink, p. 93; Pásztor (1983), pp. 247–248; Natalini et al., p. 266.
Finding Aids: Indice 1096 includes list of volume titles and brief descriptions of contents for vols. 1–139 (1818–1877). ASV Indice 1096 also provides brief descriptions of volumes 1–19 (1786–ca. 1800) of the protocols and registers of letters. (Vols. 20–37 are not so described.)
Egon Johannes Greipl, "Die Bestände des Archivs der Münchner Nuntiatur in der Zeit von 1877 bis 1904." *Römische Quartalschrift für christliche Altertumskunde und Kirchengeschichte* 78 (1983): 192–269, provides an introduction to the series and a detailed description of vols. 140–201 and their respective protocolli and indici (vols. 20, 21, 29, and 34).
There are two series of protocol registers in this series. The numbered series (1–37) is partially indexed above (see entry for ASV Indice 1096). The other series is composed of thirteen volumes covering the years 1902–[post-1922]. The nature of

the Protocolli as indici to the Archivio della Nunziatura di Baviera could not be determined.
A six-box schedario "Nomi" (ca. 1920–[post-1922]) also forms part of this *Archivio della Nunziatura di Baviera*. The accuracy of this as a finding aid is not known.
Location: Archivio Segreto Vaticano.

4.9 Belgium, Apostolic Nunciature for
[DATABASE ID: VATV238-A]

As part of the kingdom of the Netherlands, Belgium was the responsibility of the internuncio to the Netherlands appointed in 1829. A separate internuncio was appointed to Belgium in 1831, after that country's independence. The mission was raised to a nunciature in 1841. Relations were severed from 1880 to 1885 during a liberal government. From 1911 to 1918, the nuncio also served as interim manager of the internunciature for the Netherlands and from 1918 to 1921 as the internuncio to the Netherlands. From 1917 to 1955, the nuncio also served as internuncio to Luxembourg, and beginning in 1955 as nuncio to Luxembourg.

Reference. For a complete list of nuncios (through 1956) see Giuseppe de Marchi, *Le nunziature apostoliche dal 1800 al 1956* (Rome, 1957).

RECORDS. Records of the nunciature consist of the following series.

4.9.1 Archivio della Nunziatura di Belgio
[DATABASE ID: VATV418-A]
Inclusive Dates: [ca. 1830?]–1958.
Bulk: 43 linear m.
Organization: Principal series: Archivio della Nunziatura di Bruxelles (buste 1–76); —Vico nunzio; —Tacci nunzio; —Locatelli nunzio; —Nicotra nunzio; —Micara nunzio, 1923–1938; —Cartelle di lettere (151 boxes).
Note: Busta 63, fasc. 29, and busta 102 are available on microfilm.
References: Fink, p. 92; Boyle, p. 78; Pásztor (1970), pp. 246–248; Pásztor (1983), p. 210. Leon E. Halkin, *Les Archives des nonciatures* (Brussels, 1968), is the best place to begin a study of Belgian sources in the ASV in the modern period. Halkin notes the importance of records in the nunciatures outside of Belgium and provides a list of all the published volumes concerning each one. He then provides an in-depth look at Flanders, Cologne, and Brussels. Halkin proceeds nuncio by nuncio and lists publications and the status of future publications of materials from their nunciatures. He sometimes lists the primary collections where materials from the nunciature can be found. Although the Archivio della Nunziatura di Bruxelles series is listed, it is always one among several series that should be consulted in both the ASV and the BAV. Henri Dessart, Leon E. Halkin, and Jean Hoyoux, *Inventaire analytique de documents relatifs à l'histoire du diocèse de Liège sous le régime des nonces de Cologne* (Brussels, 1957–) is also helpful.
The following publications contain reprints of selected documents from this series: A. Simon, "Documents relatifs a la nonciature de Bruxelles (1834–1838)," vol. 2 of *Analecta*

vaticano-belgica, ser. 2, section C, *Nonciature de Bruxelles* (Brussels, 1958); A. Simon, "Correspondance du nonce Fornari (1838–1843)," vol. 1 of *Analecta vaticano-belgica*, ser. 2, section C, *Nonciature de Bruxelles* (Brussels, 1956); A. Simon, "Lettres de Pecci (1834–1846)," vol. 3 of *Analecta vaticano-belgica*, ser. 2, section C, *Nonciature de Bruxelles* (Brussels, 1959); A. Simon, "Instructions aux nonces de Bruxelles, 1835–1889," vol. 4 of *Analecta vaticano-belgica*, ser. 2, section C, *Nonciature de Bruxelles* (Brussels, 1961).

Finding Aids: ASV Indice 1082 briefly describes buste 1–43 (1835–1874). It provides the former and current segnature for the busta, titolo, and posizione numbers. Indice 1082 also gives a sezione number and brief description of the contents of the sezione. A typical entry reads: "Busta 1, Posizioni 1 Carte Pontificia Segretario di Stato . . . Sez. 5 Segreteria di Stato-Cambiamento dell'Emo. Segretario di Stato-Circolari e bolletani diversi." This indice is in poor condition and has been published by A. Simon (see below).

A. Simon, "Archives de la nonciature a Bruxelles (Rome)," *Cahiers* (*Centre Interuniversitaire d'Histoire Contemporaine*) 3 (1957): 23–36, is a published version of ASV Indice 1082. This article contains an extra index to the inventory that expedites access to buste 1–43. Simon's article is identified in the ASV Sala degli Indici as "stampate ASV XX B 31."

Filip Santy, *Belgie in het Vaticaans Archief: Nuntiatuur te Brussel 1875–1904: Regestenlijst* (Louvain, 1989), provides an inventory of buste 44–76 of the nunciature. He first lists the busta number, then the posizioni in each busta and a brief description of the contents. In general, these descriptions are one to three lines long; dates, correspondents or actors are listed, if appropriate. At the end of the volume there are five indici. The first lists subjects including: political movements, the social situation, economics, ecclesiastical matters (religious orders, Roman congregations, etc.), and education. The second index is according to personal name, and the third to organizations and institutions. The fourth index lists periodicals. The fifth is a geographic index. Santy's work is also known as Institut Historique Belge de Rome, *Analecta vaticano-belgica VIII*, ser. 2, section C, *Nonciature de Bruxelles*.

ASV Indice 1162 describes the contents of buste 77–131 (1904–1922). It lists the busta number, the name of the nuncio, the posizione number, and a brief description of the materials within each posizione (e.g., "Archivio di S.E. Mons. Antonio Vico, Titolo V. Affari religiosi d'indole generale o politico religiosi, sez. III. Corrispondenza colla Segretaria di Stato, Rubrica I Nota officiali e circolari - Protesta dall Santa Sede pelviaggio di Loubet a Roma . . . "). The entries for later nuncios are generally more sparse.

Location: Archivio Segreto Vaticano.

4.10 Bolivia, Apostolic Nunciature for
[DATABASE ID: VATVA401-A]

Before 1877 the interests of the Holy See were represented in Bolivia by papal representatives in Brazil (1829–1836, 1840–1857, and 1864–1877), Colombia (1836–1840), and Argentina (1857–1864). An apostolic delegate and envoy extraordinary to Peru, Ecuador, Bolivia, and Chile was established in 1877, with its residence in Lima. Relations were severed with Chile be-

ginning in 1882 and with Ecuador beginning in 1901. The mission to Bolivia was separated from the mission to Peru and raised to an internunciature in 1916. Later, in 1925, it was raised to a nunciature.

Reference. For a complete list of nuncios (through 1956) see Giuseppe de Marchi, *Le nunziature apostoliche dal 1800 al 1956* (Rome, 1957).

RECORDS. Records of the nunciature consist of the following series.

4.10.1 Archivio della Nunziatura in Bolivia
[DATABASE ID: VATV529-A]
Inclusive Dates: 1864–1970.
Bulk: 21 linear m. (392 fascios and about 50 unnumbered buste).
Organization: Materials are organized chronologically by nuncio. Subseries within the records for each nuncio include: Diocesi; —Religiosi; —Santa Sede; —Delegazione Apostolica; —Governo; —Questioni politico-religiose; —Clero; —Dispense, Alienationes, Oratorii privati, Secularizzazioni, Facoltà; —Corpo diplomatico; —Seminarii; —Protocolli.

Subseries of special interest are: Guerra con Cile; —Problemo Indio; —Assemblea Nazione di protesta contro persecuzione religiosa in Messico; —Conflitto con l'Italia circa l'Azione Cattolica; —Azione Cattolica; —Visite Apostoliche.

Scope: This series incorporates the records of the apostolic internunciature and the nunciature in Bolivia from 1864 to 1970. Materials dealing with the internunciature are organized and available for consultation. These deal primarily with religious and political concerns in Bolivia, although there are a number of records concerning religious issues in Argentina and political questions in Chile. Additional materials concerning Bolivian affairs can be found in the archives of other South American nunciatures, especially the *Archivio della Nunziatura Apostolica in Peru*, particularly in the early letterbooks, "Copia Lettere," and Protocolli volumes beginning in 1877; the *Archivio della Nunziatura Apostolica in Portogallo*; as well as in the Secretariatus Status series *Esteri*.

Finding Aids: ASV Indice 1160 by C. Lopez (1980) covers the 392 numbered fascios (1864–1932). This index generally provides file folder access to the collection and occasionally itemizes the contents of a fascio. This index, however, does not list the Protocollo registers at the end of the series.

The Protocollo registers at the end of the collection can also be used to assist in accessing the collection or to see the variety of business with which the nunciature was concerned. The initial register covers 1917–1919.

Fascio 176 (92) is an Indici Summario to the archive of the nuncio Mons. Rodolfo Caroli; however, ASV Indice 1160 provides a more detailed account of these materials.

Reference: Natalini et al., p. 266.
Location: Archivio Segreto Vaticano.

4.11 Brazil, Apostolic Nunciature for
[DATABASE ID: VATV241-A]

From 1808 to 1820 the nuncio to Portugal resided in Brazil with the Portuguese court. In 1829 a nuncio was appointed to Brazil who also acted as apostolic delegate to all of Latin America. From 1832 to 1840 the office was held by a chargé d'affaires. In 1836 the office of apostolic delegate to Latin America was transferred to the papal representative in Colombia. From 1840 to 1847 and 1856 to 1901 the title of the papal representative in Brazil was internuncio and envoy extraordinary. From 1848 to 1856 and beginning in 1901 a nuncio once again represented the Holy See in Brazil. Between 1840 and 1877 the envoy in Brazil also represented the affairs of the Holy See in Argentina, Paraguay, and Uruguay (1840–1849, 1851–1857, and 1864–1877), and in Bolivia and Chile (1840–1857 and 1864–1877).

References. For a complete list of nuncios (through 1956) see Giuseppe de Marchi, *Le nunziature apostoliche dal 1800 al 1956* (Rome, 1957). The following publications are also useful: W. J. Coleman, *The First Apostolic Delegation in Rio de Janeiro and Its Influence in Spanish America: A Study in Papal Policy, 1830–1840* (Washington, D.C., 1950); E. Lodolini, "Il consolato pontificio in Brasile (1831–1846) e il consolato brasiliano nello Stato Pontificio (1847–1857)," *Rassegna storica del Risorgimento* 68 (1981): 303–324.

RECORDS. Records of the nunciature consist of the following series.

4.11.1 Archivio della Nunziatura Apostolica in Brasile
[DATABASE ID: VATV539-A]

Inclusive Dates: ca. 1750–1964 (bulk 1808–1946).

Bulk: 50 linear m. (291 buste and 82 numbered volumes [91 actual volumes]).

Organization: There are two major groups of records: Nuncios and Repubbliche Spagnole. Within these sections the following subseries can be detected: Diocesi; —Religiosi; —Governo; —Segretaria di Stato; —Dispense-Facoltà; —Tribunal Arbitral Brasileiro-Boliviano; —Collegio-Seminario; —Corpo diplomatico; —Affari generali politico-religiosa; —Breve e rescritti (1808–1894); —Lettere segreteria (1829–1897); —Lettere vescovi (1830–1844); —Lettere governo (1833–1848); —Lettere missionari (1829–1846); —Lettere repubbliche (1830–1885); —Originale riunite, A. Conti (1892–1895); —Candidate vescovile (1918); —Protocolli (1863–1946).

Scope: This series is divided into two sections: Nuncios (to Brazil) and Repubbliche Spagnole. Records of the nuncios document all aspects of religious life in Brazil since the eighteenth century. These materials also demonstrate the relationship between Brazil and Portugal and Spain throughout the nineteenth century. The Repubbliche Spagnole section provides insight into the development of the Catholic Church in Argentina, Paraguay, and Uruguay, although information on the Catholic Church in these countries is also available in the records of the nuncios. Furthermore, materials regarding developments in the church in Colombia, Bolivia, Peru, Venezuela, Cuba, and Puerto Rico, are scattered throughout this series. Special attention should be paid to the subseries of Breve e rescritti, Lettere segretaria, Lettere missionari, and so forth, and Protocolli. These are not noted in ASV Indice 1153. (For information on this indice see below.) The Breve and Lettere

registers are original copybooks of correspondence and documents that may not be duplicated in other parts of the series.

Additional information on Brazilian religious and political questions can also be found in the Secretariatus Status series *Esteri*, and in the series *Archivio della Nunziatura Apostolica in Lisbona (Portogallo)* and *Archivio dello Studio Belli*. Information on Brazil appears, albeit infrequently, in the records of other South American nunciatures.

Finding Aids: ASV Indice 1153 by C. Lopez provides detailed access to each fascio (file folder) in the first 165 boxes of the series. At times, individual documents in each fascio are also listed. The index is dense and must be read through carefully to extract the most possible information. It should be noted that the Protocolli registers and various types of copybooks listed below are not included in this indice.

Fascio 69 contains several contemporary indices (1830s) to the archival records at that time. While these do provide an overview of the business of the nunciature in the early nineteenth century, it could not be determined if these indices were currently functional.

The Protocolli registers, which date from 1863 to 1946, may also provide some access to sections of this series. These are not listed in Indice 1153.

Location: Archivio Segreto Vaticano.

4.12 British East and West Africa, Apostolic Delegation in
[DATABASE ID: VATV570-A]

The delegation in British East and West Africa was dependent on the Congregation Propaganda Fide. Located in Mombasa, Kenya, it was established in 1930 as the apostolic delegation in Africa, with responsibility for representing the Holy See to churches in British possessions of Africa, except in southern Africa. (Until 1935 the apostolic delegation in Bloemfontein, South Africa, was also called the apostolic delegation in Africa, with responsibility for British possessions in southern Africa.) In 1947 it was renamed apostolic delegation in British East and West Africa with responsibility for representing the Holy See to churches in British Togoland, Gambia, Gold Coast, Kenya, Mauritius, Nigeria, Nyasaland, Rhodesia (North and South), Seychelles, Sierra Leone, Somaliland, Sudan, Tanganyika, Uganda, and Zanzibar. Abolished in 1960 when the apostolic delegations in Africa were reorganized to meet the needs of the newly independent countries, the delegate moved his residence to Nairobi and became apostolic delegate for East Africa.

RECORDS. Records of the delegation consist of the following series.

4.12.1 Archivio della Delegazione Apostolica in Mombasa
[DATABASE ID: VATV519-A]

Inclusive Dates: 1929–1934.

Bulk: .1 linear m. (1 box).

Location: Archivio Segreto Vaticano.

4.12.2 Archivio della Delegazione Apostolica in Nigeria

[DATABASE ID: VATV517-A]
Inclusive Dates: 1927–1940.
Bulk: .3 linear m.
Location: Archivio Segreto Vaticano.

4.13 Buda, Hungary, Legation for

[DATABASE ID: VATV592-A]

No history was prepared for this agency.

RECORDS. No records of this legation were located in the ASV, but series listed with the Secretariatus Status relate directly to Buda and should be consulted. See Secretariatus Status series *Nunziatura di Germania.* For records in the later period 1917–1938, see the series for Hungary, *Archivio della Nunziatura d'Ungheria.*

4.14 Bulgaria, Apostolic Delegation in

[DATABASE ID: VATV579-A]

The apostolic delegation in Bulgaria was established in 1931 and was dependent on the Congregation for the Oriental Church. From 1946 to 1948 the office was represented by a charge of regency. In 1948 the office was abolished.

RECORDS. Records of the delegation consist of the following series.

4.14.1 Archivio della Delegazione Apostolica in Bulgaria

[DATABASE ID: VATV485-A]
Inclusive Dates: ca. 1920–1939.
Bulk: 5.5 linear m.
Organization: Principal series: Roncalli del. apost., 1920s; —1 series [post-1922].
Reference: Natalini et al., p. 265.
Location: Archivio Segreto Vaticano.

4.15 Burundi, Apostolic Nunciature for

[DATABASE ID: VATV558-A]

The apostolic nunciature for Burundi was established in 1963. Previously this area had been the responsibility of the apostolic delegation in the Congo and Ruanda-Urundi. The nuncio to Zaire also serves as the nuncio to Burundi.

RECORDS. No records for this nunciature were located in the ASV.

4.16 Canada, Apostolic Nunciature for

[DATABASE ID: VATV563-A]

An apostolic delegation in Canada was established in 1899, dependent on the Consistorial Congregation. Responsibility for Newfoundland was added in 1900 (name changed to apostolic delegation in Canada and Newfoundland). Responsibility for Bermuda was transferred

in 1938 from the apostolic delegation in the Antilles. When Newfoundland joined Canada in 1949, its name was dropped from the title of the mission. The delegation was raised to a nunciature in 1969. In 1975 responsibility for Bermuda was transferred to the new apostolic delegation in the Antilles.

Reference. M. Sanfilippo, *Inventaire des documents d'interêt canadien dans l'Archivio segreto vaticano sous le pontificat de Leon XIII, 1878–1903: Délégation apostolique du Canada, Délégation apostolique des Etats units, epistolae ad principes et epistolae latinae, et autres series mineures* (Rome, 1987).

RECORDS. Records of the delegation consist of the following series.

4.16.1 Archivio della Delegazione Apostolica del Canada

[DATABASE ID: VATV538-A]
Inclusive Dates: 1899–1959.
Bulk: 103 linear m. (775 boxes and 30 volumes)
Organization: Protocollo, 1899–1959; —Indici sommari dei protocolli, 1899–1953; —Diocesi; —Affari civili; —Affari generali (includes Acadiana); —Concilio plenario canadese; —Scuole bilingui; —Immigranti; —Delegazione apostolica; —Ruteni; —Società (later called Azione Cattolica); —Università; —Religiose; —Religiosi; 14a. [post 1922 series]; — Congressi; —Missioni; —Correspondence with other Vatican offices; —Governatore (Canadian); —Comunismo in Canada; —Comunismo e persecuzione religiosa (Poland, Hungary, Yugoslavia, Albania, Bulgaria, Czechoslovakia, China, Romania, Ukraine, Russia); —Prigionieri di Guerra (World War II); —Assistenza alle vittime della guerra (World War II); —Istituzioni e questioni scolastici.

Note that materials for the first three delegates appear to be filed together.

Scope: This series, transferred from the delegation in Canada, provides information on the major religious and social concerns in Canada in the early twentieth century. Although there is a distinct subseries for dioceses, a researcher should examine other subseries such as Religiosi, Ruteni, and so forth, to ascertain all activities of concern to the apostolic delegate within a diocese. The groups of miscellaneous or documenti vari also contain information that could have been filed in the appropriate subseries, but a careful reading of Indice 1163, described below, will lead a researcher to these items. The Sanfilippo article, "Fonti Vaticane," provides a good introduction to the series.

References: Natalini et al., p. 266. Matteo Sanfilippo, "Fonti Vaticane per la storia canadese: La delegazione apostolica in Canada, 1899–1910," *Annali accademici canadesi* 3–4 (1988): 63–79, provides the best overview of the series and a good bibliography of sources for the study of relations between the Holy See and Canada. Matteo Sanfilippo, "La Santa Sede, il Canada e la delegazione apostolica ad Ottawa," *Annali accademici canadesi* 2 (1986): 112–119, is a good introduction to the interplay between the Canadian political and social situation in the late nineteenth and early twentieth century and the apostolic delegations of that time. Matteo Sanfilippo, "Monsignor Pisani e il Canada," *Annali accademici canadesi* 6 (1990): 61–75. Giovanni Pizzorusso, "Donato Sbarretti, delegato apostolico a Ottawa e la difficile organizzazione del Concilio plenario canadese (1909)," *Annali accademici canadesi* 6 (1990): 77–88. Giovanni Pizzorusso, "Un diplomat du Vatican en Amerique: Donato Sbarretti a Washington, le Havane et Ottawa (1893–1910)," *Annali accademici canadesi* 9 (1993): 5–33.

Finding Aids: ASV Indice 1163 provides a comprehensive introduction and inventory of materials in this series that are open to researchers (scatole 1–191, 1899–1921). The inventory, completed in 1989 by Claudio De Dominicis, gives a brief history of the delegation (nunciature since 1969). The index then proceeds scatola by scatola listing the title of each fascio (i.e., file folder) with its inclusive dates. The index provides the researcher with a reliable overview of topics covered in the series.

Location: Archivio Segreto Vaticano.

4.17 Central America, Apostolic Internunciature for

[DATABASE ID: VATV564-A]

The apostolic internunciature for Central America was established in 1922 from the apostolic delegates and envoys extraordinary to Costa Rica, Honduras, and Nicaragua and the apostolic delegates to Guatemala and El Salvador. Panama was added to its jurisdiction in 1923. In 1933 the mission was reorganized and the internuncio became nuncio to Costa Rica, Nicaragua, and Panama. A separate nuncio was appointed to Honduras, El Salvador, and Guatemala.

Reference. For a complete list of nuncios (through 1956) see Giuseppe de Marchi, *Le nunziature apostoliche dal 1800 al 1956* (Rome, 1957).

RECORDS. Records of the internunciature consist of the following series.

4.17.1 Archivio della Nunziatura in America Centrale

[DATABASE ID: VATV534-A]
Inclusive Dates: 1908–1933.
Bulk: 3.5 linear m. (35 boxes)
Organization: The series is divided into two sections: 1908–1922 and [post-1922]. The first section is roughly broken down into the following five subseries: Apostolic Delegate; —Correspondence with the Santa Sede; —Dioceses; —Correspondence with governments; —Diplomatic Corps.

Scope: This series includes the records of the predecessor offices of the apostolic internunciature for Central America. These records include materials from the apostolic delegate and envoy extraordinary to Costa Rica, Honduras, and Nicaragua from 1908 to 1917; records from the period during which this area was the internunciature for Costa Rica, Honduras, and Nicaragua; and records dating from 1920 to 1922, when Guatemala and El Salvador were added to its jurisdiction. The records document both religious and political concerns of the Catholic Church in this region. Additional materials on these countries can be located in the Secretariatus Status series *Esteri.*

Finding Aids: ASV Indici 1156 and 1157 provide a detailed listing of materials in the entire series. These indici either give summaries of each fascio (i.e., file folder) or calendar the letters in each folder, listing the content or correspondent.

Reference: Natalini et al., p. 265.
Location: Archivio Segreto Vaticano.

4.18 Chile, Apostolic Nunciature for

[DATABASE ID: VATV249-A]

The apostolic nunciature for Chile was represented by an apostolic vicar who served from 1823 to 1825. This vicar is sometimes referred to as a nuncio but was not part of a permanent mission. Before 1877 the interests of the Holy See were represented in Chile by papal representatives in Brazil (1829–1836, 1840–1857, and 1864–1877), in Colombia (1836–1840), and in Argentina (1857–1864). An apostolic delegate and envoy extraordinary to Peru, Ecuador, Bolivia, and Chile was established in 1877 with its residence in Lima. In 1882 a separate apostolic delegate and envoy extraordinary was appointed to Chile. That same year relations were severed. Relations were reestablished in 1902 and an apostolic delegate and envoy extraordinary appointed. The mission was raised to an internunciature in 1908 and to a nunciature in 1916.

Reference. For a complete list of nuncios (through 1956) see Giuseppe de Marchi, *Le nunziature apostoliche dal 1800 al 1956* (Rome, 1957).

RECORDS. Records of the nunciature consist of the following series.

4.18.1 Archivio della Nunziatura Apostolica in Chile

[DATABASE ID: VATV528-A]
Inclusive Dates: 1877–1953.
Bulk: 30 linear m. (472 fascios and 32 volumes).
Organization: The series is organized chronologically by nuncios and then systematized under the following subseries: Santo Padre; —Segretaria di Stato; —Sacre Congregazioni Romane; —Nunzio Apostolico; —Amministrazione; —Corrispondenza; —Presidente repubblica; —Parti politici; —Ministri esteri; —Corpo diplomatico; —Diocesi; —Religiosi/e; —Attività cattolica; —Emigrazione; —Immigrazione; —Protocolli; (1917–[post-1922]).

Scope: This series documents religious and political affairs in Chile since 1877, when the first apostolic delegate was appointed. Although relations were officially halted between 1882 and 1902, some materials concerning the church in Chile remain from this period. However, records are sparse until 1916, when the nunciature was established. Additional information on Chile can be located in the records of other South American nunciatures, particularly Bolivia, and in the Secretariatus Status series *Esteri.*

Finding Aids: ASV Indice "Nunziatura Apostolica in Cile" by Sr. Lucina Bianchini, FSP, contains an "Inventario Sommario" (1877–1953) and an "Inventario Analitico" (1877–1918). The analytic section provides excellent access to the series. This indice is available at the circulation desk in the main reading room. The indice is not a formal finding aid and may be used only in consultation with the archives staff.

Protocolli registers at the end of the series covering the years 1917, 1920–1922, [and post-1922] are useful in locating materials within this collection as well as capsulizing the different issues to which the nuncios responded.

Reference: Natalini et al., p. 266.

Location: Archivio Segreto Vaticano.

4.19 China, Apostolic Nunciature for
[DATABASE ID: VATV378-A]

An apostolic delegation in China was established in 1922; the delegation was dependent on the Congregation Propaganda Fide. In 1923 its jurisdiction was extended to Macao. The office was raised to an internunciature in 1946 and to a nunciature in 1966. The office was located in Beijing (Peking) until 1947, then in Nanjing (Nanking) from 1948 to 1951, in Hong Kong in 1952, and in Taipei beginning in 1953. Before 1949 Taiwan was the responsibility of the apostolic delegation in Japan. The internunciature represented the Holy See to the nationalist government of China; after 1949 the internunciature represented the Holy See to Taiwan.

Reference. For a complete list of nuncios (through 1956) see Giuseppe de Marchi, *Le nunziature apostoliche dal 1800 al 1956* (Rome, 1957).

RECORDS. Records of the nunciature consist of the following series.

4.19.1 Archivio dell'Internunziatura in Cina
[DATABASE ID: VATV511-A]

Inclusive Dates: 1923–1948.

Bulk: 30 linear m.

Organization: 158 boxes and undetermined buste.

Reference: Natalini et al., p. 265.

Location: Archivio Segreto Vaticano.

4.20 Cologne, Apostolic Nunciature for
[DATABASE ID: VATV237-A]

During the reign of Gregory XIII (1572–1585) the duties of the nuncio to the Holy Roman Empire were expanded to include overseeing the implementation of the decrees of the Council of Trent in the empire. Several new nunciatures were established to assist in carrying out this task. The nunciature for Cologne was established in 1573, with responsibility for dioceses in the northwestern part of the empire, particularly in the Rhineland. The nunciature was vacant from 1578 to 1584. In 1584 its responsibility was expanded to include Flanders, Strasbourg, and Basel. Flanders was detached from its responsibility in 1595 and made a separate nunciature. From 1794, when the city was seized by the French, the nuncio did not reside in Cologne. For periods of time after 1794 the nuncio was also responsible for Bavaria. The nunciature was abolished in 1805.

In addition to the records listed below, series listed

with other agencies relate directly to this agency and should be consulted. See Secretariatus Status series *Nunziatura de Colonia, Nunziatura di Germania*, and *Nunziature diverse.*

References. For a complete list of nuncios see Henry Biaudet, *Les nonciatures apostoliques permanentes jusqu'en 1648* (Helsinki, 1910); Liisi Karttunen, *Les nonciatures apostoliques permanentes de 1650 à 1800* (Helsinki, 1912); *Repertorium der diplomatischen Vertreter aller Länder seit dem Westfälischen Frieden (1648)* [to 1815] (Oldenburg, 1936–1965).

RECORDS. Records of the nunciature consist of the following series.

4.20.1 Archivio della Nunziatura di Colonia
[DATABASE ID: VATV419-A]

Inclusive Dates: 1450–1796.

Bulk: 24 linear m.

Organization: 318 numbered buste and 2 unnumbered buste.

Scope: The series includes registers of letters from the nuncios to the secretary of state as well as from the secretary of state to the nuncios, materials concerning controversies over ecclesiastical benefices, and "Informazioni della curia romana."

Note: Vols. 255 and 297 are available on microfilm.

References: Boyle, p. 78, Fink, p. 92, Michael F. Feldkamp, *Studien und Texte zur Geschichte der Kölner Nuntiatur*, vol. 1, "Die Kölner Nuntiatur und ihr Archiv: Eine behördengeschichtliche und quellenkundliche Untersuchung"; vol. 2, Dokumente und Materialien über Jurisdiktion, Nuntiatursprengel, Haushalt, Zerimoniell und Verwaltung der Kölner Nuntiatur (1584–1794)"; vol. 3, "Inventar des Fonds 'Archivio della Nunziatura di Colonia' im vatikanischen Archiv" (Vatican City, 1993–1995). The third volume contains a detailed inventory of the series and includes an extensive index of names, places, and subjects.

Finding Aid: ASV Indice 1083 includes a listing of busta titles, inclusive dates of each busta, and brief contents notes.

Location: Archivio Segreto Vaticano.

4.21 Colombia, Apostolic Nunciature for
[DATABASE ID: VATV402-A]

Relations were established in 1835 as an internunciature. From 1836 to 1840 this office also served as apostolic delegate to all of South America except Brazil. The office was held by a chargé d'affaires from 1842 to 1850. In 1853 diplomatic relations were severed as a result of the separation of church and state by a liberal government. The envoy remained in Colombia with the title apostolic delegate until 1861, when he was expelled. After the election of a conservative government, relations were reestablished in 1882 with the appointment of an apostolic delegate and envoy extraordinary. In 1917 the mission was raised to a nunciature. Until 1861 Colombia was called New Granada. In 1923 responsibility for the affairs of the Holy See in Panama (until 1903 part of Colombia) was transferred to the internunciature for Central America.

Reference. For a complete list of nuncios (through 1956) see Giuseppe de Marchi, *Le nunziature apostoliche dal 1800 al 1956* (Rome, 1957).

RECORDS. No records for this nunciature were located in the ASV.

4.22 Corsica, Apostolic Nunciature for
[DATABASE ID: VATV593-A]

No history has been found for the nunciature for Corsica. A permanent nunciature was never established there. The island was ruled by Genoa until 1768, when it became a dependency of France. In 1789 Corsica was incorporated into the French state.

RECORDS. No records of this nunciature were located in the ASV, but series listed with the Secretariatus Status relate directly to Corsica and should be consulted. See Secretariatus Status series *Nunziatura di Corsica*.

4.23 Costa Rica, Apostolic Nunciature for
[DATABASE ID: VATV403-A]

A nuncio for Costa Rica was appointed in 1882 and an apostolic delegate and envoy extraordinary in 1885, but neither was admitted by the Costa Rican government. In 1908 an apostolic delegate and envoy extraordinary to Costa Rica, Honduras, and Nicaragua was appointed. In 1917 the mission was raised to an internunciature. Guatemala and El Salvador were added to its jurisdiction in 1920. In 1922 it was reorganized to an internunciature for Central America. In 1933 the internunciature for Central America was abolished and the envoy became the nuncio to Costa Rica, Nicaragua, and Panama. In 1948 Nicaragua was separated from the jurisdiction of the nuncio to Costa Rica and Panama. Beginning in 1953 a chargé d'affaires represented the nuncio in Costa Rica, and in 1955 a separate nuncio was named to that country.

Reference. For a complete list of nuncios (through 1956) see Giuseppe de Marchi, *Le nunziature apostoliche dal 1800 al 1956* (Rome, 1957).

RECORDS. Records of the nunciature consist of the following series.

4.23.1 Archivio della Nunziatura Apostolica in Costarica
[DATABASE ID: VATV527-A]
Inclusive Dates: ca. 1937–1957.
Bulk: 3 linear m.
Organization: 24 buste and 4 vols.
Reference: Natalini et al., p. 266.
Location: Archivio Segreto Vaticano.

4.23.2 Archivio della Nunziatura in Costarica, Nicaragua, e Panama
[DATABASE ID: VATV181-A]
Inclusive Dates: 1932–1940.

Bulk: 4 linear m.
Reference: Natalini et al., p. 266.
Location: Archivio Segreto Vaticano.

4.24 Cuba, Apostolic Nunciature for
[DATABASE ID: VATV407-A]

An apostolic delegate to Cuba and Puerto Rico (residing in Havana) was appointed in 1906. In 1925 the office was reorganized as an apostolic delegation in the Antilles. In 1935 the mission to Cuba was raised to a nunciature, with the additional responsibility as apostolic delegate to the Antilles. In 1938 the apostolic delegation was abolished, and the nunciature for Cuba became responsible for relations with churches in Jamaica and British Honduras. (This responsibility was transferred to the nunciature for Haiti in 1968.) Beginning in 1962, in reaction to the revolution in Cuba, the office of nuncio to Cuba was vacated. A new nuncio was appointed in 1975.

Reference. For a complete list of nuncios (through 1956) see Giuseppe de Marchi, *Le nunziature apostoliche dal 1800 al 1956* (Rome, 1957).

RECORDS. Records of the nunciature consist of the following series.

4.24.1 Archivio della Nunziatura Apostolica in Cuba e Portorico
[DATABASE ID: VATV526-A]
Inclusive Dates: 1906–1939.
Bulk: 2.5 linear m. (26 buste or 90 fascios)
Organization: Materials are organized according to nuncio and within each nuncio the following subseries: Santo Padre; —Segretaria di Stato; —Sacre Congregazione Romane; —Diocesi; —Parocchie e Clero; —Seminari; —Religiosi/e; —Dispense.
Scope: This series concentrates on relations of the Catholic church in Cuba in the early part of the twentieth century. The records also include several longer studies that provide information on the history of the seminary and dioceses in Cuba. Of special interest to researchers in Catholicism in the United States, this series does demonstrate some of the assistance given to the Catholic church in Cuba by the Archdiocese of New York. Material regarding Puerto Rico is evident throughout the pre-1922 portion of the series. There is also a scattering of items concerning Mexico. Additional material can be located in the archives of other Central and South American nunciatures (particularly Brazil), the archives of the nunciature in Spain, and in the Secretariatus Status series *Esteri*.
Reference: Natalini et al., p. 266.
Location: Archivio Segreto Vaticano.

4.25 Czechoslovakia, Apostolic Nunciature for
[DATABASE ID: VATV377-A]

Relations with Czechoslovakia were established in 1919 with a chargé d'affaires in Prague. The mission was established as a nunciature in 1920. In 1939, following the partition of Czechoslovakia, the nuncio transferred his residence to Bratislava where he became the envoy to Slovakia. Relations were reestablished in 1945 with the reconstitution of the Czechoslovak government. The office was represented by a chargé d'affaires. The nuncio returned to the country in 1946 but left in 1948. A chargé d'affaires remained until 1950 when he was expelled. Relations were restored in 1990.

Reference. For a complete list of nuncios see Giuseppe de Marchi, *Le nunziature apostoliche dal 1800 al 1956* (Rome, 1957).

RECORDS. Records of the nunciature consist of the following series.

4.25.1 Archivio della Nunziatura di Cecoslovacchia
[DATABASE ID: VATV540-A]
Inclusive Dates: 1919–ca. 1939 and 1945–1950.
Bulk: 7.5 linear m.
Organization: Four subseries: Materials dated between 1919 and 1923; and 3 subseries [post-1922].
Finding Aids: Contains Protocolli registers.
Reference: Natalini et al., p. 266.
Location: Archivio Segreto Vaticano.

4.26 Dominican Republic, Apostolic Nunciature for
[DATABASE ID: VATV408-A]

Established in 1874 as apostolic delegation in Santo Domingo, Haiti, and Venezuela, the post was held by an apostolic delegate and envoy extraordinary in 1881. Vacant because of political instability beginning in 1902, relations resumed with Santo Domingo in 1930 as part of the nunciature for Haiti and Santo Domingo (called Dominican Republic beginning 1936). Beginning in 1938 the nunciature was also responsible for relations with churches in Puerto Rico and most smaller islands of the West Indies. The office was held by a chargé d'affaires from 1942 to 1946. Separate nuncios to Haiti and the Dominican Republic were appointed in 1953, with the nunciature for Haiti assuming responsibility for Puerto Rico and the other West Indies islands. Beginning in 1968 the nuncio to the Dominican Republic also served as the apostolic delegate for Puerto Rico.

Reference. For a complete list of nuncios (through 1956) see Giuseppe de Marchi, *Le nunziature apostoliche dal 1800 al 1956* (Rome, 1957).

RECORDS. Records of the nunciature consist of the following series.

4.26.1 Archivio della Nunziatura Apostolica nella Repubblica Dominicana
[DATABASE ID: VATV533-A]
Inclusive Dates: 1875–1953.
Bulk: 5 linear m.

Organization: Fascios numbered 1–14, plus 53 boxes, plus 5 volumes; generally chronological.
Scope: These records date from prior to the formal establishment of relations between the Holy See and the Dominican Republic (then identified as San Domingo). The materials document both political life in the country and the Catholic church in the area. Although the office of nuncio was vacant between 1903 and 1930, various reports of the political and ecclesiastical situation in the country are included in this series.
Reference: Natalini et al., p. 267.
Finding Aids: There are four internal protocol registers in the five final volumes of the series. These may assist in providing access to the series. They cover the years 1884–1891 [and post-1922]. The 1884–1891 Protocollo is interesting because it also has transcriptions of the letters in the same volume and covers both San Domingo and Venezuela.
See also the series for Haiti, *Archivio della Nunziatura in Haiti*. Fascio 32 (appendice), page 6 (col. 3 or 5), gives an old inventory of materials in the archives of this delegation for the years 1892–1898 when Mons. Giulio Tonti was delegate. The "Indice generale dell'Archivio della Delegazione Apostolica della Repubblica Domenicana in ordine di posizioni" is still a valid representation of the organization and contents of the archivio for those years.
Location: Archivio Segreto Vaticano.

4.27 East Africa, Apostolic Delegation in
[DATABASE ID: VATV556-A]

The apostolic delegation in East Africa was established in 1960 after the reorganization of African apostolic delegations that was designed to meet the needs of the newly independent countries. The delegation was dependent on the Congregation Propaganda Fide. Located in Nairobi, Kenya, the delegation was responsible for representing the Holy See to churches in French Somaliland, Kenya, Northern Rhodesia, Nyasaland, Seychelles, Sudan, Tanganyika, Uganda, and Zanzibar. Countries were removed from the mission's responsibility as separate nuncios were named: Kenya and Zambia in 1965, Malawi in 1966, and Tanzania and Uganda in 1967. The apostolic delegation was abolished in 1969 and responsibility for French Territory of the Afars and the Issas, Seychelles, and Sudan were transferred to other apostolic delegations.

RECORDS. No records could be located in the ASV for this delegation.

4.28 East Indies, Apostolic Delegation in
[DATABASE ID: VATV584-A]

The apostolic delegation in the East Indies, established in 1884, was dependent on the Congregation Propaganda Fide. It was located in Bangalore, India, and was responsible for relations with churches in India, Ceylon, and Malaya. In 1920 its jurisdiction was extended to Burma and in 1923 to Goa. In 1948 it was replaced by the internunciature for India.

RECORDS. Records of the delegation consist of the following series.

4.28.1 Archivio della Delegazione Apostolica d'India
[DATABASE ID: VATV508-A]

Inclusive Dates: 1857–1942 (bulk 1891–1942).

Bulk: 35 linear m. (796 fascio numbers and 24 volumes)

Organization: Two major series that overlap chronologically: series I, 396 fascios, 1887–[post-1922]; series II, 400 fascios, 1857–[post-1922].

Series II subseries include Santo Padre; —Segretario di Stato; —Propaganda Fide; —Congregazioni; —Diocesi; —Religiosi/e; —Burma.

Miscellaneous volumes at end are Archivio, 1887–1891 (1 vol.); —Protocolli, 1917–1920 (1 vol.), 1922–[post-1922] (1 vol.); [1 post-1922 subseries]; —Lettere spedite, 1920 (1 vol.); 1921–1922 (1 vol.); —Dispacci ricevute, 1892–1904 (1 vol.); —[1 post-1922 subseries]; —"Ark of Hope" Minute Book, HMS Ranger, 1880–1882 (1 vol.).

Finding Aids: The following registers of correspondence exist in the volumes at the end of the collection; however, it could not be determined to which series these pertain: Archivio, 1887–1891 (1 vol.); Protocolli, 1917–1920 (1 vol.), 1922–[post-1922] (1 vol.), [1 post-1922 subseries]; Lettere spedite, 1920 (1 vol.), 1921–1922 (1 vol.); and Dispacci ricevuti, 1892–1904 (1 vol.).

Reference: Natalini et al., p. 265.

Location: Archivio Segreto Vaticano.

4.29 Ecuador, Apostolic Nunciature for
[DATABASE ID: VATV411-A]

Before 1861 the interests of the Holy See in Ecuador were represented by papal representatives in Brazil (1829–1836) and Colombia (1836–1861). An apostolic delegate to Ecuador was appointed in 1861. (He was also responsible for papal interests in Peru.) In 1877 an apostolic delegate and envoy extraordinary to Peru, Ecuador, Bolivia, and Chile, was appointed with residence in Lima. Relations were severed with Chile beginning in 1882. Relations with Ecuador were broken in 1901 after the inauguration of an anticlerical government, but the envoy in Lima retained the title of apostolic delegate to Ecuador. Relations were reestablished with Ecuador in 1937, when it became a separate nunciature.

Reference. For a complete list of nuncios (through 1956) see Giuseppe de Marchi, *Le nunziature apostoliche dal 1800 al 1956* (Rome, 1957).

RECORDS. Records of the nunciature consist of the following series.

4.29.1 Archivio della Nunziatura Apostolica in Equatore
[DATABASE ID: VATV525-A]

Inclusive Dates: 1861–1954.

Bulk: 18 linear m. (168 boxes or 373 fascicles and 6 volumes)

Organization: Records are divided by delegate or nuncio and then according to the following subseries (posizioni): Santa Sede; —Governo-Politico; —Diocesi; —Religiosi/e; —Seminari.

Scope: The *Archivio della Nunziatura Apostolica in Equatore* contains one of the strongest collections from a South American nunciature in the nineteenth century. Approximately half of the present collection concerns the Catholic church in Ecuador in the latter part of that century. This series documents the Catholic church as well as church and state relations in Ecuador. During the period when relations were severed between the Holy See and Ecuador (1902–1937), the Holy See's interests in Ecuador were monitored by the nuncio in Peru. Records from this period are sparse but are extant both in the normal order of fascios and in the six miscellaneous volumes at the end of this collection. Records concerning Ecuador can also be located in the archives of other South American nunciatures, particularly in the Copia lettere (letterbooks) and Protocolli of the *Archivio della Nunziatura in Peru*, the *Archivio della Nunziatura Apostolica in Portogallo*, as well as in the Secretariatus Status series *Esteri*.

Finding Aids: ASV Indice "Nunziatura Apostolica in Equatore" is available at the circulation desk in the main reading room. The indice is not a formal finding aid and may be used only in consultation with the archives staff. This index, by Sr. Lucina Bianchini, FSP, contains an "Inventario Sommario" covering the years 1861–1925. The index does provide an overall view of the collection, although it does not reflect the density and strength of the nineteenth-century sections of this series.

See also the Protocolli registers in the *Archivio della Nunziatura in Peru*, which contain entries for correspondence of the apostolic delegate and extraordinary visitor to Ecuador during the period when papal representation to these two countries was headquartered in Lima, Peru (1877–1881).

Reference: Natalini et al., p. 266.

Location: Archivio Segreto Vaticano.

4.30 Egypt, Apostolic Nunciature for
[DATABASE ID: VATV379-A]

The apostolic nunciature for Egypt was established as an internunciature in 1947. Formerly Egypt had been the responsibility of the apostolic delegation in Egypt and Arabia, located in Cairo. From 1958 to 1971 the office was known as the internunciature (later nunciature) for the United Arab Republic. The office was raised to a nunciature in 1966.

Reference. For a complete list of nuncios (through 1956) see Giuseppe de Marchi, *Le nunziature apostoliche dal 1800 al 1956* (Rome, 1957).

RECORDS. Records for this nunciature could not be located in the ASV.

4.31 Egypt and Arabia, Apostolic Delegation in
[DATABASE ID: VATV586-A]

The apostolic delegation in Egypt and Arabia, located in Cairo, was established in 1839 to represent the Holy

See to churches in those areas. In the twentieth century it was dependent on the Congregation for the Oriental Church. Responsibility for Eritrea and Abyssinia (Ethiopia) was added in 1928. In 1929 responsibility for churches in Palestine, Transjordan, and Cyprus was transferred from the apostolic delegation for Syria to the apostolic delegation in Egypt and Arabia; responsibility for Eritrea and Ethiopia was transferred to the apostolic delegation in Italian East Africa in 1937. In 1947 this office's responsibility was divided among the internunciature for Egypt, apostolic delegation in Arabia, and apostolic delegation in Jerusalem and Palestine.

RECORDS. Records of the delegation consist of the following series.

4.31.1 Archivio della Delegazione Apostolica per l'Egitto e l'Arabia
[DATABASE ID: VATV518-A]
Inclusive Dates: 1874–1942.
Bulk: 12 linear m.
Organization: Volumes at end of series include: Letterbook, 1896–1904, 1 vol.; —Protocolli, 1904–[post-1922], 5 vol.; —Corrispondenza con la congregazione de la Propaganda Fide, 1889–1896, 1 vol.; —Stato delle parrocchie, 1922, 1 vol.; —Miscellaneous financial records, [18—]–[19—].
Scope: This series contains approximately 1 linear meter of material dating prior to 1922. The best place to begin research is in the volumes at the end of the series. The Letterbook (which may be a protocollo, 1896–1904) and the first two volumes of the Protocolli (1904–1911 and 1911–1922) provide full copies of letters (perhaps selected) from the late nineteenth and early twentieth centuries. Additional material on the Catholic Church in Egypt and the Middle East can be located in the Secretariatus Status series *Esteri.*
Finding Aids: The early protocol volumes (1904–1911 and 1911–1922) are actually letterbooks and can serve as a guide to the correspondence in this period.
Reference: Natalini et al., p. 266.
Location: Archivio Segreto Vaticano.

4.32 El Salvador, Apostolic Nunciature for
[DATABASE ID: VATV406-A]

In 1920 the internuncio to Costa Rica, Honduras, and Nicaragua became in addition the apostolic delegate to El Salvador. In 1922 the office was reorganized as the internunciature for Central America. In 1933 the internunciature was reorganized and raised to two nunciatures. A new nuncio was appointed for Honduras and El Salvador (who also served as apostolic delegate to Guatemala). In 1936 the mission to Guatemala was raised to a nunciature and the nuncio served all three countries. In 1938 a separate nuncio was appointed for Honduras, leaving one nuncio serving El Salvador and Guatemala.
Reference. For a complete list of nuncios (through 1956) see Giuseppe de Marchi, *Le nunziature apostoliche dal 1800 al 1956* (Rome, 1957).

RECORDS. Records of the nunciature consist of the following series.

4.32.1 Nunziatura Apostolica in Honduras, Salvador, e Guatemala
[DATABASE ID: VATV186-A]
Inclusive Dates: 1933–1941.
Bulk: 3 linear m.
Location: Archivio Segreto Vaticano.

4.33 England, Apostolic Nunciature for
[DATABASE ID: VATV242-A]

A permanent nunciature was never established, although various papal emissaries were sent at different times. For example, a cardinal legate was sent by Leo X in 1518 and a nuncio by Adrian VI in 1523. A legate sent by Julius III in 1553 remained in England until the death of Queen Mary in 1558. Nuncios were sent to Ireland in 1561 and to Scotland in 1566. During the reign of James II (1685–1688) a minister apostolic was named nuncio, but his office was ended with the accession of William III. For relations after 1707, see the agency history for the nuncio to Great Britain.
References. For a complete list of nuncios see Henry Biaudet, *Les nonciatures apostoliques permanentes jusqu'en 1648* (Helsinki, 1910); *Repertorium der diplomatischen Vertreter aller Länder seit dem Westfälischen Frieden (1648)* [to 1815] (Oldenburg, 1936–1965).

RECORDS. No records of this nunciature could be found in the ASV, but series listed with the Secretariatus Status relate directly to England and should be consulted. See Secretariatus Status series *Nunziatura di Inghilterra* and *Nunziature diverse* and *Archivio della Nunziatura apostolica in Londra.*

4.34 Estonia, Apostolic Nunciature for
[DATABASE ID: VATV380-A]

An apostolic delegation in Estonia, Latvia, and Lithuania was established in 1922. Diplomatic relations with Estonia were established in 1933 when the chargé d'affaires in Lithuania became also the chargé for Estonia. The mission was raised to a nunciature in 1935, with the chargé being promoted to nuncio while also becoming nuncio to Latvia and remaining chargé in Lithuania. Relations were severed in 1940 when Estonia was annexed by the Soviet Union.
Reference. For a complete list of nuncios see Giuseppe de Marchi, *Le nunziature apostoliche dal 1800 al 1956* (Rome, 1957).
[DATABASE ID: VATV541-A]

RECORDS. Records of the nunciature consist of the following series.

4.34.1 Archivio della Nunziatura d'Estonia
Inclusive Dates: 1933–1940.
Bulk: 1 linear m. (7 vols.).
Location: Archivio Segreto Vaticano.

4.35 Ethiopia, Apostolic Nunciature for
[DATABASE ID: VATV554-A]

From 1937 to 1945 the apostolic delegation in Italian
East Africa had responsibility for this area. In 1947 a
special envoy was named to Ethiopia. In 1956 the envoy
became an apostolic delegate, dependent on the Congregation for the Oriental Church. In 1957 the mission
was raised to an internunciature and in 1970 to a nunciature.

RECORDS. No records for this nunciature could be located in
the ASV.

4.36 Flanders, Apostolic Nunciature for
[DATABASE ID: VATV235-A]

The nunciature for Flanders was established by
Clement VIII in 1595; it had responsibility for representing the Holy See in the Spanish (later Austrian)
Netherlands. Clement VIII detached this area from the
responsibility of the nunciature for Cologne. (A nuncio
who took office in 1594 is not considered part of the
permanent nunciature.) The office was filled by an internuncio from 1634 to 1725. The nuncio was expelled
from Brussels in 1787, and the Holy Roman emperor
requested that the office be abolished. The nuncio returned to Brussels in 1790 when relations with the emperor had improved. The last nuncio left the office
about 1795, and the office was abolished. The nunciature for Belgium, established in 1831, had responsibility
for this same region.

References. For a complete list of nuncios see Henry
Biaudet, *Les nonciatures apostoliques permanentes
jusqu'en 1648* (Helsinki, 1910); Liisi Karttunen, *Les
nonciatures apostoliques permanentes de 1650 à 1800*
(Helsinki, 1912); *Repertorium der diplomatischen Vertreter aller Länder seit dem Westfälischen Frieden (1648)
[to 1815]* (Oldenburg, 1936–1965).

RECORDS. No records of this nunciature could be located in
the ASV, but series listed with the Secretariatus Status relate
directly to Flanders and should be consulted. See Secretariatus
Status series *Nunziatura di Fiandra* and *Nunziature diverse.*

4.37 France, Apostolic Nunciature for
[DATABASE ID: VATV226-A]

A permanent nunciature was established in 1514 by
Leo X, following earlier legations. Conflict between the
popes and Louis XIV left the post vacant or filled on an
interim basis for most of the period from 1671 to 1690.

The nuncio left France in 1791 after anticlerical legislation was passed. The office was then abolished. Several
special envoys were sent to France during the revolutionary and Napoleonic eras, including a legate a latere
who served from 1801 to 1810. The permanent nunciature was reestablished by Pius VII in 1817. The office
was held by a nuncio, except during the period of Louis
Philippe, when it was held by a chargé d'affaires (1831–
1836); the nuncio was promoted to an internuncio and
envoy extraordinary (1836–1842). Relations were severed during the period 1904–1921.

In addition to the records listed below, series listed
with other agencies relate directly to this agency and
should be consulted. See Secretariatus Status series
Nunziatura di Francia and *Nunziature diverse.*

References. For a complete list of nuncios (through
1956) see Henry Biaudet, *Les nonciatures apostoliques
permanentes jusqu'en 1648* (Helsinki, 1910); Liisi Karttunen, *Les nonciatures apostoliques permanentes de
1650 à 1800* (Helsinki, 1912); *Repertorium der diplomatischen Vertreter aller Länder seit dem Westfälischen
Frieden (1648) [to 1815]* (Oldenburg, 1936–1965); Giuseppe de Marchi, *Le nunziature apostoliche dal 1800 al
1956* (Rome, 1957). Also useful are the following:
P. Richard, "La légation Aldobrandini et le traité de
Lyon (septembre 1600–mars 1601): La diplomatie pontificale, ses agents au temps de Clément VIII," *Revue
d'histoire et de littérature religieuses* 7 (1902): 481–509,
8 (1903): 25–48, 133–151; P. Richard, "Origines de la
nonciature de France: Débuts de la représentation permanent sous Léon X (1513–1521)," *Revue des questions
historiques* 80 (1906): 112–180; P. Richard, "Origines
de la nonciature de France: Nonces résidants avant
Léon X (1456–1511)," *Revue des questions historiques*
78 (1905): 103–147.

RECORDS. Records of the nunciature consist of the following
series.

4.37.1 Archivio della Nunziatura in Francia
[DATABASE ID: VATV427-A]
Inclusive Dates: 1818–1959.
Bulk: 85 linear m.
Organization: Principal subseries: Macchi nunzio, 1818–
1825 (8 vols.); —Lambruschini nunzio, 1826–1831; —Gari-
baldi nunzio, 1831–1842, 1850–1853; —Fornari nunzio,
1842–1850; —Sacconi nunzio, 1853–1861; —Chigi nunzio,
1861–1973; —Meglia nunzio, 1874–1879; —Czacki nunzio,
1879–1887; —Siciliano di Rende nunzio, 1882–1887; —
Rotelli nunzio, 1887–1891; —Ferrata nunzio, 1891–1896; —
Clari nunzio, 1896–1899; —Lorenzelli nunzio, 1899–1904;
—Cerretti nunzio, 1921–1926; —Maglione nunzio, 1926–
1936; —Valeri nunzio, 1936–1943; —1945–1959.

Vols. 1–8 were formerly part of the Carte Macchi, which
was acquired by the ASV in 1919.

L'Attività della Santa Sede, 1992 states that 15 casse containing materials dating from 1945–1959 were transferred to
the ASV on February 15, 1992.

References: Boyle, p. 78; Fink, p. 93; Pásztor (1970), p. 301; Pásztor (1983), pp. 248–249; Natalini et al., p. 266.

Finding Aids: Indice 1086 includes a list of volume titles and inclusive dates for vols. 1–82 (1819–1850). See also Ottavio Cavalleri, *Le Carte Macchi dell'Archivio segreto vaticano: Inventario* (Vatican City, 1979). This book (pp. 121–126) calendars the first eight volumes of this series "Rapporti inviati alla Segreteria di Stato da Mons. Vincenzo Macchi, Nunzio Apostolico in Francia" (1818–1827).

Location: Archivio Segreto Vaticano.

4.38 Frankfurt am Main, Germany, Legation for
[DATABASE ID: VATV596-A]

No history was prepared for this agency.

RECORDS. No records of this legation could be located in the ASV, but series listed with the Secretariatus Status relate directly to Frankfurt am Main and should be consulted. See Secretariatus Status series *Nunziatura di Germania.*

4.39 French Africa, Apostolic Delegation in
[DATABASE ID: VATV562-A]

The apostolic delegation in French Africa was established in 1948 and originally named apostolic delegation for Dakar, dependent on the Congregation Propaganda Fide and located in Dakar, French West Africa. The delegation was responsible for representing the Holy See to churches in French West Africa, French Equatorial Africa, Cameroon, Madagascar, Reunion, French Morocco, French Somaliland, and French Togoland. In 1960 the apostolic delegations in Africa were reorganized to meet the needs of the newly independent countries. The apostolic delegation was renamed apostolic delegation in West Africa and continued in Dakar.

RECORDS. No records of this legation could be located in the ASV, but series listed with the West Africa apostolic delegation relate directly to French Africa and should be consulted. See the series for West Africa, *Archivio della Delegazione Apostolica per l'Africa Occidentale.*

4.40 Genoa, Apostolic Nunciature for
[DATABASE ID: VATV243-A]

No history of this nunciature has been found. A permanent nunciature was never established. Genoa was an independent state, although under the influence of France, Milan, Spain, and Austria, at various times, until 1797. In 1797 it was transformed under French pressure into the Ligurian Republic, and was annexed to France in 1805. In 1814 Genoa was united with the Kingdom of Sardinia.

RECORDS. No records of this nunciature could be found in the ASV, but series listed with the Secretariatus Status relate

directly to Genoa and should be consulted. See Secretariatus Status series *Nunziatura di Genova.*

4.41 Germany, Apostolic Nunciature for
[DATABASE ID: VATV231-A]

The apostolic nunciature for Germany was established by Clement VII in 1524 to represent the pope specifically in Germany during the period when the nuncio to the Holy Roman Empire under Charles V was concerned with affairs in Spain. However, the office was not filled continuously, being vacant in 1527–1529, 1532–1533, 1545–1548, 1556–1558, and 1558–1560. The office was abolished in 1560. The nunciature for Germany was reestablished in 1920. From 1920 to 1925, the nuncio to Bavaria also served as nuncio to Germany. From 1925 to 1934, the nuncio to Germany also held the title of nuncio to Prussia. In 1946 the nunciature moved from Berlin to the western zone of Germany. The office was filled by an apostolic visitor (1946–1949) and a regent (1949–1951) before a new nuncio was appointed.

In addition to the records listed below, series listed with another agency relate directly to this agency and should be consulted. See Secretariatus Status series *Nunziature diverse.*

References. For a complete list of nuncios (through 1956) see Henry Biaudet, *Les nonciatures apostoliques permanentes jusqu'en 1648* (Helsinki, 1910); Giuseppe de Marchi, *Le nunziature apostoliche dal 1800 al 1956* (Rome, 1957).

RECORDS. Records of the nunciature consist of the following series.

4.41.1 Archivio della Nunziatura di Germania
[DATABASE ID: VATV542-A]
Inclusive Dates: 1920–1959.
Bulk: 26.5 linear m.
Organization: Subseries according to nuncio: Pacelli, 1920–post-1922; —Orsenigo, post-1922; —Muench, post-1922; —Protocolli.
Reference: Natalini et al., p. 266.
Location: Archivio Segreto Vaticano.

4.42 Great Britain, Apostolic Nunciature for
[DATABASE ID: VATV569-A]

An apostolic delegation in Great Britain was established in 1938; it was also responsible for Gibraltar and Malta. (Malta was removed from its jurisdiction in 1965 when a nuncio was appointed to that country.) The delegation was dependent on the Consistorial Congregation. In 1982 the mission was raised to a nunciature. For earlier relations (before 1707) see the agency history for the nunciature for England.

RECORDS. Records of the nunciature consist of the following series.

4.42.1 Archivio della Nunziatura apostolica in Londra
[DATABASE ID: VATV30013-A]
Inclusive Dates: 1939–1973.
Bulk: 48 linear m. (16 casse).
References: Natalini et al., p. 266; L'Attivita dell Santa Sede (1990).
Location: Archivio Segreto Vaticano.

4.43 Greece, Apostolic Nunciature for
[DATABASE ID: VATV580-A]

The apostolic delegation in Greece was established in 1834. In the twentieth century the delegation was dependent on the Congregation for the Oriental Church. From 1945 to 1950 the office was represented by an auditor, then a chargé; after 1950 the office was empty. Diplomatic relations were reestablished in 1980 with the appointment of a nuncio.

RECORDS. Records of the delegation consist of the following series.

4.43.1 Archivio della Delegazione Apostolica in Grecia
[DATABASE ID: VATV486-A]

Inclusive Dates: [ca. 1940–1950].
Bulk: 3 linear m. (36 buste).
Reference: Natalini et al., p. 266.
Location: Archivio Segreto Vaticano.

4.44 Guatemala, Apostolic Nunciature for
[DATABASE ID: VATV566-A]

In 1920 the internuncio to Costa Rica, Honduras, and Nicaragua took on the additional responsibiliity as the apostolic delegate to Guatemala. In 1922 the office was reorganized as the internunciature for Central America. Relations with Guatemala were unclear from 1922 until 1932, when the internuncio to Central America also became the apostolic delegate to Guatemala. In 1933 the internunciature was reorganized and raised to two nunciatures. A new nuncio was appointed for Honduras and El Salvador (who also served as apostolic delegate to Guatemala). In 1936 the mission to Guatemala was raised to a nunciature and the nuncio served all three countries. In 1938 a separate nuncio was appointed to Honduras.

Reference. For a complete list of nuncios (through 1956) see Giuseppe de Marchi, *Le nunziature apostoliche dal 1800 al 1956* (Rome, 1957).

RECORDS. No records of this nunciature could be found in the ASV, but series listed with the El Salvador nunciature relate directly to Guatemala and should be consulted. See the series for El Salvador, *Nunziatura Apostolica in Honduras, Salvador, e Guatemala.*

4.45 Haiti, Apostolic Nunciature for
[DATABASE ID: VATV409-A]

Relations with Haiti were first established in 1874 through an apostolic delegation in Santo Domingo, Haiti, and Venezuela. In 1881 the post was held by an apostolic delegate and envoy extraordinary. It was vacant because of political instability beginning in 1902. Relations resumed with Haiti in 1915 with the reappointment of an apostolic delegate and envoy extraordinary. In 1916 the mission was raised to an internunciature. From 1920 to 1927 the office was held by a regent. From 1927 to 1930 an internuncio was appointed who also served as apostolic delegate to the Antilles. In 1930 relations were resumed with Santo Domingo (called Dominican Republic beginning in 1936), and the mission to Haiti and Santo Domingo was raised to a nunciature. Beginning in 1938, the nunciature was responsible for relations with churches in Puerto Rico and most of the smaller West Indian islands. The office was held by a chargé d'affaires from 1942 to 1946. Separate nuncios to Haiti and the Dominican Republic were appointed in 1953, with the nunciature to Haiti keeping responsibility for Puerto Rico and the smaller islands. Beginning in 1968 the nunciature also became responsible for affairs in Jamaica, Martinique, and Trinidad, and responsibility for Puerto Rico was transferred to the nunciature for the Dominican Republic. Beginning in 1975 the nuncio served as apostolic delegate for the Antilles and took responsibility for the various West Indian islands.

Reference. For a complete list of nuncios (through 1956) see Giuseppe de Marchi, *Le nunziature apostoliche dal 1800 al 1956* (Rome, 1957).

RECORDS. Records of the nunciature consist of the following series.

4.45.1 Archivio della Nunziatura Apostolica in Haiti
[DATABASE ID: VATV524-A]
Inclusive Dates: 1874–1902, 1916–1942.
Bulk: 5 linear m. (113 fascios in 51 boxes and 8 buste)
Organization: Records are principally divided according to nuncios: Cocchia; —di Milia; —Tonti; —Cherubini; —Benedetti; —[3 series post-1922]. Within each nuncio's records the following subseries (posizioni) can be found: Istruzioni e facoltà di delegato o nuncio; —Segretaria di Stato e Santa Sede; —Religiosi/e; —Diocesi; —Governo; —Formazione; del clero indigene haitiano.
Scope: This series documents religious and political life in Haiti, as well as in the neighboring Carribean islands, particularly San Domingo, Puerto Rico, and Guadalupe and Martinique.
Finding Aids: Fascio 32 (appendice) within the collection itself contains an "Indice generale dell'Archivio della Delegazione Apostolica della Repubblica di Haiti in ordine di posizioni," 1892–1898. The index is located on page 11, 12, or 13, depending on how one interprets the numbering. It is not

the first item in this busta. This index represents the current organization of the first boxes in the collection.

Reference: Natalini et al., p. 266.
Location: Archivio Segreto Vaticano.

4.46 Holy Roman Empire, Apostolic Nunciature for
[DATABASE ID: VATV227-A]

The apostolic nunciature for the Holy Roman Empire was established in 1513 by Leo X. During the reign of Emperor Charles V (1519–1558) the affairs of the nuncios to Spain and the empire became intermingled and a separate nuncio was appointed to Germany. For most of the period 1522–1544 the nuncio to Spain also served as nuncio to the empire. Diplomatic relations were severed between 1556 and 1560. During the reign of Gregory XIII (1572–1585) the duties of the nuncio to the Holy Roman Empire were expanded to include overseeing the implementation of the decrees of the Council of Trent in the empire. New nunciatures for Cologne, Graz (Styria), Salzburg (South Germany), and Switzerland were established to assist in carrying out this task. In 1784 a nuncio was appointed with responsibility for the possessions of the elector of Bavaria, which had been divided among the jurisdictions of the nuncios to Cologne, Switzerland, and the empire. With the abolition of the empire in 1806, the nuncio to the empire became the nuncio to Austria. For relations after that date, see the agency history for the nunciature for Austria.

References. For a complete list of nuncios see Henry Biaudet, *Les nonciatures apostoliques permanentes jusqu'en 1648* (Helsinki, 1910); Liisi Karttunen, *Les nonciatures apostoliques permanentes de 1650 à 1800* (Helsinki, 1912); *Repertorium der diplomatischen Vertreter aller Länder seit dem Westfälischen Frieden (1648)* [to 1815] (Oldenburg, 1936–1965).

RECORDS. For records of this nunciature see the series for Austria, *Archivio della Nunziatura di Austria.* In addition, series listed with other agencies relate directly to this agency and should be consulted. See Secretariatus Status series *Nunziatura di Germania* and *Nunziature diverse.*

4.47 Honduras, Apostolic Nunciature for
[DATABASE ID: VATV404-A]

In 1908 an apostolic delegate and envoy extraordinary to Costa Rica, Honduras, and Nicaragua was appointed. In 1917 the office was raised to an internunciature. Guatemala and El Salvador were added to its jurisdiction in 1920. In 1922 it was reorganized into an internunciature for Central America. In 1933 the internunciature was reorganized and raised to two nunciatures. A new nuncio was appointed for Honduras and El Salvador. In 1936 the apostolic delegation in Guatemala,

also the responsibility of this nuncio, was raised to a nunciature, with the nuncio serving all three countries. In 1938 a separate nuncio was appointed for Honduras. In 1948 Nicaragua was added to the jurisdiction of this office.

Reference. For a complete list of nuncios (through 1956) see Giuseppe de Marchi, *Le nunziature apostoliche dal 1800 al 1956* (Rome, 1957).

RECORDS. No records of this nunciature could be found in the ASV, but series listed with the El Salvador nunciature relate directly to Honduras and should be consulted. See the series for El Salvador, *Nunziatura Apostolica in Honduras, Salvador, e Guatemala.*

4.48 Hungary, Apostolic Nunciature for
[DATABASE ID: VATV399-A]

The apostolic nunciature for Hungary was established in 1920. Relations were severed in 1945 and reestablished in 1990.

Reference. For a complete list of nuncios see Giuseppe de Marchi, *Le nunziature apostoliche dal 1800 al 1956* (Rome, 1957).

RECORDS. Records of the nunciature consist of the following series.

4.48.1 Archivio della Nunziatura d'Ungheria
[DATABASE ID: VATV543-A]
Inclusive Dates: 1917–1938.
Bulk: 6 linear m. (58 buste, 2 protocol registers, and one miscellaneous packet).
Organization: Principal subseries: Schioppa nunzio, 1920–[post-1922] (13 buste); —[2 series post-1922]; —Protocolli registers, vol. 1 1920–[post-1922], vol. 2 [post-1922]; —[Miscellaneous packet], ca. 1917–1920.
Reference: Natalini et al. p. 267.
Location: Archivio Segreto Vaticano.

4.49 India, Apostolic Nunciature for
[DATABASE ID: VATV383-A]

The apostolic nunciature for India was established in 1948 as an internunciature. Formerly, India had been the responsibility of the apostolic delegate for the East Indies. In 1957 responsibility for churches in the Malay Peninsula was transferred to the apostolic delegation in Thailand. The office was raised to a nunciature in 1967.

Reference. For a complete list of nuncios (through 1956) see Giuseppe de Marchi, *Le nunziature apostoliche dal 1800 al 1956* (Rome, 1957).

RECORDS. No records for this nunciature could be located in the ASV, but see the series *Archivio della Delegazione Apostolica d'India* described in the records of the apostolic delegation in the East Indies.

4.50 Indochina, Apostolic Delegation in
[DATABASE ID: VATV577-A]

The apostolic delegation in Indochina was established in 1925, dependent on the Congregation Propaganda Fide. In 1964 it was renamed apostolic delegation in Vietnam and Cambodia. Responsibility for Laos was transferred at that time to the apostolic delegation in Thailand. The office was located in Hue until 1951, in Hanoi from 1951 to 1956(?), and thereafter in Saigon.

RECORDS. For records of this delegation see the series for Vietnam and Cambodia, *Archivio della Delegazione Apostolica nel Vietnam.*

4.51 Indonesia, Apostolic Nunciature for
[DATABASE ID: VATV384-A]

An apostolic delegation in the Indonesian Archipelago was established in 1947, dependent on the Congregation Propaganda Fide. The area had formerly been under the jurisdiction of the apostolic delegation in Australasia. In 1950 the delegation was raised to an internunciature, and in 1965 to a nunciature. Thailand was under the jurisdiction of the apostolic delegation and internunciature in Indonesia until 1957, when an apostolic delegation for Thailand was established.

Reference. For a complete list of nuncios (through 1956) see Giuseppe de Marchi, *Le nunziature apostoliche dal 1800 al 1956* (Rome, 1957).

RECORDS. Records of the internunciature consist of the following series.

4.51.1 Archivio dell'Internunziatura d'Indonesia-Thailand
[DATABASE ID: VATV509-A]
Inclusive Dates: [1900s].
Bulk: 170 buste.
Note: This series was noted on a stack guide, but not physically located in October 1987 or in March 1990.
Location: Archivio Segreto Vaticano.

4.52 Iran, Apostolic Nunciature for
[DATABASE ID: VATV385-A]

The apostolic delegation in Persia was established in 1874, dependent on the Congregation for the Oriental Church. It became known as the apostolic delegation in Iran when the name of the country was changed in 1935. The office was held by a regent from 1946 to 1948. The mission was raised to an internunciature in 1953 and to a nunciature in 1966.

Reference. For a complete list of nuncios (through 1956) see Giuseppe de Marchi, *Le nunziature apostoliche dal 1800 al 1956* (Rome, 1957).

RECORDS. Records of the nunciature consist of the following series.

4.52.1 Archivio della Nunziatura Apostolica in Iran
[DATABASE ID: VATV505-A]
Inclusive Dates: 1910–1983 (bulk 1921–1975).
Bulk: 26 linear m. (358 fascio nos. plus 2 unnumbered boxes)
Organization: Chronological by nuncio.
Finding Aids: There is an indice behind the reference desk. The indice is not a formal finding aid and must be used in consultation with the archives staff.
Reference: Natalini et al., p. 266.
Location: Archivio Segreto Vaticano.

4.53 Iraq, Apostolic Nunciature for
[DATABASE ID: VATV588-A]

The apostolic delegation in Mesopotamia, Kurdistan, and Armenia Minor (located in Baghdad) was established in 1834 to represent the Holy See to churches in those areas. In 1938 the name was changed to apostolic delegation in Iraq. From 1950 to 1969, the office was also responsible for the apostolic delegation in Arabia. In 1966 the office was raised to a nunciature.

RECORDS. No specific records series for this nunciature were located in the ASV.

4.54 Ireland, Apostolic Nunciature for
[DATABASE ID: VATV386-A]

The nunciature for Ireland was established in 1929.
Reference. For a complete list of nuncios (through 1956) see Giuseppe de Marchi, *Le nunziature apostoliche dal 1800 al 1956* (Rome, 1957).

RECORDS. Records of the nunciature consist of the following series.

4.54.1 Archivio della Nunziatura d'Irlanda
[DATABASE ID: VATV544-A]
Inclusive Dates: 1929–1948.
Bulk: 1.5 linear m.
Reference: Natalini et al., p. 266.
Location: Archivio Segreto Vaticano.

4.55 Italian East Africa, Apostolic Delegation in
[DATABASE ID: VATV555-A]

The apostolic delegation in Italian East Africa was established in 1937, dependent on the Congregation for the Oriental Church. Eritrea and Ethiopia had previously been under the jurisdiction of the apostolic delegation in Egypt and Arabia. The delegation was abolished in 1945.

RECORDS. No records for this delegation could be found in the ASV.

4.56 Italy, Apostolic Nunciature for

[DATABASE ID: VATV387-A]

In September 1860 all the lands of the Papal States, with the exception of Rome and its environs, were annexed to the new Kingdom of Italy. Ten years later Rome itself was occupied and incorporated into the Italian state, formally unified and established in October 1870. His forces defeated and his temporal power declared at an end, Pius IX refused to recognize the new reality of a unified Italian state. For fifty-nine years the Holy See had no formal relations with Italy. In 1922, representatives from the Italian state and from the Holy See began formal discussions that culminated in the Lateran Treaty (Feb. 11, 1929). Signed by Pius XI and then prime minister of Italy, Benito Mussolini, the treaty established the Vatican City as an independent and neutral state. The Holy See recognized Italy as a country with Rome as its capital. Under the terms of the treaty, the Italian state would indemnify the Holy See for the loss of the Papal States and Catholicism would be established in Italy as the official religion. As a result of the agreement a nunciature was established in Rome in 1929.

References. For a complete list of nuncios (through 1956) see Giuseppe de Marchi, *Le nunziature apostoliche dal 1800 al 1956* (Rome, 1957). Also useful is N. Raponi, "Recenti edizioni di Nunziature pontificie e le 'Nunziature d'Italia.'" *Rassegna degli Archivi di Stato* 25 (1965): 245–266.

RECORDS. Records of the nunciature consist of the following series.

4.56.1 Archivio della Nunziatura d'Italia

[DATABASE ID: VATV545-A]
Inclusive Dates: 1929–1969.
Bulk: 29 linear meters.
Reference: Natalini et al., p. 266.
Location: Archivio Segreto Vaticano.

4.57 Japan, Apostolic Nunciature for

[DATABASE ID: VATV382-A]

An apostolic delegation in Japan, with responsibility also for churches in Korea and Taiwan, was established in 1919, dependent on the Congregation Propaganda Fide. In 1921 responsibility for churches in the Caroline, Marshall, and Mariana Islands was transferred from the apostolic delegation in Australasia. In 1946 that responsibility was transferred to the apostolic delegation in the United States. The delegation's responsibility for representing the Holy See to churches in Korea and Taiwan (both ruled by Japan before World War II) ended in 1949. In 1952 the office was raised to an internunciature and in 1966 to a nunciature.

Reference. For a complete list of nuncios (through 1956) see Giuseppe de Marchi, *Le nunziature apostoliche dal 1800 al 1956* (Rome, 1957).

RECORDS. Records of the delegation consist of the following series.

4.57.1 Archivio della Delegazione Apostolica in Giappone

[DATABASE ID: VATV10259-A]
Inclusive Dates: 1939.
Bulk: .1 linear m. (1 box).
Reference: Natalini et al., p. 266.
Location: Archivio Vaticano Segreto.

4.58 Jerusalem and Palestine, Apostolic Delegation in

[DATABASE ID: VATV581-A]

The apostolic delegation for Palestine, Transjordan, and Cyprus was separated from the jurisdiction of the apostolic delegation in Egypt and Arabia in 1947, but not formally established until 1948, dependent on the Congregation for the Oriental Church. Its official name was later changed to apostolic delegation in Jerusalem and Palestine. The apostolic delegation represented the Holy See to churches in Palestine, Jordan, and Cyprus. The office was represented by a regent in 1947 and 1948. Responsibility for Israel was added in 1963. Cyprus was removed from the jurisdiction of the apostolic delegation in 1973 when a separate nuncio was appointed to that country.

RECORDS. No records of this delegation were found in the ASV.

4.59 Korea, Apostolic Nunciature for

[DATABASE ID: VATV576-A]

An apostolic delegation in Korea was established in 1949, dependent on the Congregation Propaganda Fide. Previously, Korea was the responsibility of the apostolic delegation in Japan. In 1963 the office was raised to an internunciature and in 1966 to a nunciature. The office represents the Holy See to the Republic of Korea (South Korea).

RECORDS. No records for this nunciature were found in the ASV.

4.60 Latvia, Apostolic Nunciature for

[DATABASE ID: VATV389-A]

An apostolic delegation in Estonia, Latvia, and Lithuania was established in 1922. In 1925 an internunciature for Latvia was established, but no internuncio was named until 1926. The office was raised to a nunciature in 1928. In 1935 the chargé d'affaires in Lithuania also became nuncio to Latvia and Estonia.

Relations were severed in 1940 when Latvia was annexed by the Soviet Union.

Reference. For a complete list of nuncios see Giuseppe de Marchi, *Le nunziature apostoliche dal 1800 al 1956* (Rome, 1957).

RECORDS. Records of the nunciature consist of the following series.

4.60.1 Archivio della Nunziatura Apostolica di Lettonia
[DATABASE ID: VATV546-A]
Inclusive Dates: 1926–1940.
Bulk: 2 linear m.
Reference: Natalini et al. p. 266.
Location: Archivio Segreto Vaticano.

4.61 Lebanon, Apostolic Nunciature for
[DATABASE ID: VATV390-A]

The apostolic nunciature for Lebanon was established in 1947. Previously, Lebanon was the responsibility of the apostolic delegation in Syria, which had been located in Beirut.

Reference. For a complete list of nuncios (through 1956) see Giuseppe de Marchi, *Le nunziature apostoliche dal 1800 al 1956* (Rome, 1957).

RECORDS. No records for this nunciature could be located in the ASV, but see the series *Archivio della Nunziatura Apostolica in Libano* described in the records of the apostolic nunciature for Syria.

4.62 Liberia, Apostolic Nunciature for
[DATABASE ID: VATV391-A]

The Holy See established a post in Liberia in 1927 as a chargé d'affaires. This office was raised to an internunciature in 1951 and to a nunciature in 1966. In 1970 the nuncio took on additional responsibility as the apostolic delegate for Ghana and Sierra Leone. Previously the apostolic delegation in West Central Africa was responsible for Ghana and Sierra Leone. In 1976 a nunciature for Ghana was established.

Reference. For a complete list of nuncios (through 1956) see Giuseppe de Marchi, *Le nunziature apostoliche dal 1800 al 1956* (Rome, 1957).

RECORDS. No records for this nunciature could be located in the ASV.

4.63 Lithuania, Apostolic Nunciature for
[DATABASE ID: VATV392-A]

An apostolic delegation in Estonia, Latvia, and Lithuania was established in 1922. In 1927 an internunciature for Lithuania was established. The internuncio to the Netherlands also served as internuncio to Lithuania in 1927 and 1928. The office was raised to a

nunciature in 1928. The nuncio was expelled in 1931 (although he kept his title until 1933) and the mission was represented by a chargé d'affaires. In 1935 the chargé d'affaires also became the nuncio to Latvia and Estonia. In 1940 a new nuncio was appointed, but relations were severed the same year when Lithuania was annexed by the Soviet Union.

Reference. For a complete list of nuncios see Giuseppe de Marchi, *Le nunziature apostoliche dal 1800 al 1956* (Rome, 1957).

RECORDS. Records of the nunciature consist of the following series.

4.63.1 Archivio della Nunziatura Apostolica di Lituania
[DATABASE ID: VATV547-A]
Inclusive Dates: 1927–1940.
Bulk: 6 linear m.
Reference: Natalini et al., p. 266.
Location: Archivio Segreto Vaticano.

4.64 Luxembourg, Apostolic Nunciature for
[DATABASE ID: VATV393-A]

Until 1890 Luxembourg was ruled by the king of the Netherlands and was under the jurisdiction of the internuncio to that country. In 1891 an internunciature for Luxembourg was established, with the office filled by the internuncio to the Netherlands. The internuncio was recalled to Rome in 1899 over papal displeasure at being excluded from the Hague Peace Conference. A chargé d'affaires held the office until 1910. In 1917 relations were reestablished with Luxembourg when the nuncio to Belgium also became the internuncio to Luxembourg (and in 1918 the internuncio to the Netherlands). In 1921 a separate internuncio to the Netherlands was appointed, but the nuncio to Belgium remained also the internuncio to Luxembourg. In 1955 the mission to Luxembourg was raised to a nunciature but was still united with the nunciature for Belgium.

Reference. For a complete list of nuncios (through 1956) see Giuseppe de Marchi, *Le nunziature apostoliche dal 1800 al 1956* (Rome, 1957).

RECORDS. No specific record series from this nunciature were located in the ASV.

4.65 Madagascar, Apostolic Nunciature for
[DATABASE ID: VATV574-A]

An apostolic delegation was established in 1960 with responsibility for representing the Holy See to churches in Madagascar, Mauritius, and Réunion. Previously these areas had been under the apostolic delegations for French Africa (Madagascar and Réunion) and British East and West Africa (Mauritius). The delegation was raised to a nunciature in 1967.

RECORDS. No specific records series from this nunciature were found in the ASV.

4.66 Malta, Apostolic Nunciature for
[DATABASE ID: VATV244-A]

Before the twentieth century there was no permanent nunciature for Malta. An inquisitor, perhaps with diplomatic rank, was accredited to the Knights of St. John, who had been granted the island of Malta by Emperor Charles V in 1530. Special nuncios were sometimes sent to Malta. For example, nuncios were sent by Gregory XIII in 1576 and 1581 to reform the order. The knights were expelled from Malta by the French in 1798. In the twentieth century, churches in Malta were the responsibility of the apostolic delegation in Great Britain until 1965, when the nunciature for Malta was established.

RECORDS. No records of this nunciature were found in the ASV, but series listed with the Secretariatus Status relate directly to Malta and should be consulted. See Secretariatus Status series *Inquisizione di Malta* and *Nunziature diverse.*

4.67 Mesopotamia, Kurdistan, and Armenia Minor, Apostolic Delegation in
[DATABASE ID: VATV589-A]

The apostolic delegation in Mesopotamia, Kurdistan, and Armenia Minor (located in Baghdad) was established in 1834 to represent the Holy See to churches in those areas. In the twentieth century it was dependent on the Congregation for the Oriental Church. In 1938 the name was changed to apostolic delegation in Iraq.

RECORDS. No records for this delegation could be found in the ASV.

4.68 Mexico, Apostolic Delegation in
[DATABASE ID: VATV410-A]

An apostolic delegate was first sent to Mexico in 1851. He was expelled in 1861. A nunciature was established during the reign of Maximilian in 1864–1865, but was abolished when he was overthrown. Other delegates, visitors, and chargés d'affaires were sent to Mexico in 1896–1899, 1902, and since 1904, with some vacancies caused by expulsions in 1923, 1925, and 1926–1929. Beginning in 1951 a permanent apostolic delegation was established. See also the agency history for the apostolic delegation in the Antilles.

Reference. For a complete list of delegates (through 1956) see Giuseppe de Marchi, *Le Nunziature apostoliche dal 1800 al 1956* (Rome, 1957).

RECORDS. Records of the delegation consist of the following series.

4.68.1 Archivio della Nunziatura Apostolica in Messico
[DATABASE ID: VATV536-A]
Inclusive Dates: 1904–1937.
Bulk: 7 linear m. (93 boxes and 1 busta)
Organization: Materials are organized into series by delegate or nuncio as follows: 1. Mons. Domenico Serafini, 1904–1905 (3 boxes); —2. Mons. Giuseppe Ridolfi, 1905–1911 (18.5 boxes); —3. Mons. Tommaso Boggiani, 1912–1914 (7.5 boxes); —4. Mons. Giovanni Bonzano, 1915–1921 (5 boxes); —5. Mons. Ernesto Filippi, 1921–[post-1922] (11 boxes); —[4 series post-1922].

The following subseries are repeated in most of the nuncios' records: 1. Diocesi (alphabetical); —2. Instituti religiosi; —3. Santa Sede and correspondence with various offices in the Vatican; —4. Liste episcopali, 1915–1921; —5. Partito cattolico nazionale messicano, 1912–1913; —6. Nuova costituzione; —7. Persecuzione contro la chiesa, 1915–1921; —8. Santa Sede y Delegacion Apostolica de Estados Unidos, 1915–1921.

Scope: This series documents all aspects of religious life in Mexico in the early twentieth century. Particularly problematic areas for the church such as the relationship between church and state and religious persecution are represented in this series. This series continues and is related to the Secretariatus Status series *Visita Apostolica in Messico* (1896–1900).

Finding Aid: ASV Indice 1155 provides a detailed description of boxes 1–34 (1904–1921). Most entries calendar each item in each fascio (file), giving the subject and or person involved.

Location: Archivio Segreto Vaticano.

4.69 Naples, Apostolic Nunciature for
[DATABASE ID: VATV230-A]

Office of collector in Naples was raised to a nunciature by Paul IV in 1555. From 1779 to 1822 the office was vacant, filled on an interim basis but not accredited to the government of the country. The office was abolished in 1860 when the country was annexed by Sardinia.

In addition to the records listed below, series listed with other agencies relate directly to this agency and should be consulted. See Secretariatus Status series *Nunziatura di Napoli* and *Nunziature diverse.*

References. For a complete list of nuncios see Henry Biaudet, *Les nonciatures apostoliques permanentes jusqu'en 1648* (Helsinki, 1910); Liisi Karttunen, *Les nonciatures apostoliques permanentes de 1650 à 1800* (Helsinki, 1912); *Repertorium der diplomatischen Vertreter aller Länder seit dem Westfälischen Frieden* (1648) [to 1815] (Oldenburg, 1936–1965); Giuseppe de Marchi, *Le nunziature apostoliche dal 1800 al 1956* (Rome, 1957).

RECORDS. Records of the nunciature consist of the following series.

4.69.1 Archivio della Nunziatura di Napoli

[DATABASE ID: VATV426-A]

Inclusive Dates: 1818–1860.

Bulk: 28 linear m. (413 numbered vols. and one busta)

References: Boyle, p. 78; Fink, p. 93.

Finding Aids: ASV Indice 1085 lists vols. 1–410. Entries for each volume include the inclusive dates and a descriptive title. The unnumbered busta is also described. Within the series itself there is a protocol register about 1825–1850 that is organized by diocese. The effectiveness of this as an index to the *Archivio della Nunziatura di Napoli* was not determined.

Location: Archivio Segreto Vaticano.

4.69.2 Transazioni

[DATABASE ID: VATV20465-A]

Inclusive Dates: [1—]–[18—?].

Bulk: 32 scatole.

Note: This series is among the unprocessed series of the archives of the Propaganda Fide and thus may not be available for consultation. See entry for Propaganda Fide in the section "Roman Curia: Congregations."

Location: Archives of the Propaganda Fide.

4.70 Netherlands, Apostolic Nunciature for

[DATABASE ID: VATV246-A]

From 1814 to 1828 a chargé d'affaires was appointed to the Netherlands and Westphalia, although he was rejected by the Netherlands. An internunciature for the Netherlands was established in 1829. This office also had responsibility for Belgium and Luxembourg, which at that time were a part of the kingdom of the Netherlands. A separate internuncio to Belgium was appointed in 1831, after that country became independent. From 1831 to 1848 the office was represented by a chargé d'affaires. In 1891, after Luxembourg was separated from the Netherlands, the internuncio became in addition the internuncio to Luxembourg. Relations were severed in 1899 over papal displeasure at being excluded from the Hague Peace Conference. A chargé d'affaires held the office until 1910. From 1911 to 1918 the internunciature was managed on an interim basis by the nuncio to Belgium, who in 1918 became also the internuncio to the Netherlands and Luxembourg. In 1921 a separate internuncio was appointed to the Netherlands. In 1927 and 1928 the internuncio also served as internuncio to Lithuania. In 1967 the mission was raised to a nunciature.

Reference. For a complete list of nuncios (through 1956) see Giuseppe de Marchi, *Le nunziature apostoliche dal 1800 al 1956* (Rome, 1957).

RECORDS. Records of the internunciature consist of the following series.

4.70.1 Archivio della Nunziatura di Olanda

[DATABASE ID: VATV421-A]

Inclusive Dates: 1802–1938.

Bulk: 7 linear meters.

Organization: Principal series: Archivio della Nunziatura di L'Aia (29 buste), 1802–1899; —Tacci nunzio, 1911–1918; —Locatelli nunzio, 1916–1918; —Nicotra nunzio, 1918–1921; —Vincentini nunzio, 1921–1922; —Orsenigo nunzio; —Schioppa nunzio, 1925–1935; —Protocolli, 1830–1938.

References: Boyle, p. 78; Pásztor (1970), p. 244–246; Natalini et al., p. 266. The following is also useful: J. P. de Valk, "Inventaris van Romeinse Archivalia Betreffende het Verenigd Koninkrijk der Nederlanden 1813–1831," vols. 9–10 of *Analecta vaticano-belgica*, ser. 2, section C, *Nonciature de Bruxelles* (Brussels, 1991), pp. 5–6, 63. This is the place to begin an investigation of the Netherlands in the ASV. See also J. P. de Valk, *Lettres de Francesco Capaccini: Agent diplomatique et internonce du Saint-Siege au Royaume Uni del Pays Bas, 1828–1831*, (Brussels, 1983). J. P. de Valk, "Het Archief van de Haagse Nuntiatuur, 1802–1879," *Jaarboek van het Katholiek Documentatie Centrum* (Overdruk, 1977) [this is bound in the rear of ASV Indice 1081].

Finding Aids: ASV Indice 1081 briefly describes the contents of buste 1–22 (1802–1879). ASV Indice 1082 briefly describes the contents of buste 23–29 (1879–1899).

Location: Archivio Segreto Vaticano.

4.71 Nicaragua, Apostolic Nunciature for

[DATABASE ID: VATV567-A]

In 1908 an apostolic delegate and envoy extraordinary to Costa Rica, Honduras, and Nicaragua was appointed. In 1917 the office was raised to an internunciature. Guatemala and El Salvador were added to its jurisdiction in 1920. In 1922 the office was reorganized into the internunciature for Central America. In 1933 the internunciature was reorganized and raised to two nunciatures. The envoy to Central America became the nuncio to Costa Rica, Nicaragua, and Panama. In 1948 Nicaragua was transferred from the jurisdiction of the nuncio to Costa Rica, while Panama was transferred to the jurisdiction of the nuncio to Honduras.

Reference. For a complete list of nuncios (through 1956) see Giuseppe de Marchi, *Le nunziature apostoliche dal 1800 al 1956* (Rome, 1957).

RECORDS. No records of this nunciature were found in the ASV, but series listed with the Costa Rica nunciature relate directly to Nicaragua and should be consulted. See the series for the apostolic nunciature for Costa Rica, *Archivio della Nunziatura in Costarica, Nicaragua, e Panama.*

4.72 Nigeria, Apostolic Nunciature for

[DATABASE ID: VATV553-A]

The nunciature for Nigeria was established in 1973 as an apostolic delegation. Before that the apostolic delegation in West Central Africa, with responsibility for several countries in the region, was located in Nigeria. In 1976 the mission was raised to a nunciature.

RECORDS. No records for this nunciature were found in the ASV, but see the series titled *Archivio della Delegazione Apo-*

stolica in Nigeria described in the records of the apostolic delegation to British East and West Africa.

4.73 Pakistan, Apostolic Nunciature for
[DATABASE ID: VATV394-A]

The apostolic delegation in Pakistan was established in 1950. In 1951 the office was raised to an internunciature. The office was held by a chargé d'affaires from 1951 to 1958. The post was raised to a nunciature in 1965.

Reference. For a complete list of nuncios (through 1956) see Giuseppe de Marchi, *Le nunziature apostoliche dal 1800 al 1956* (Rome, 1957).

RECORDS. No records for this nunciature could be found in the ASV.

4.74 Panama, Apostolic Nunciature for
[DATABASE ID: VATV405-A]

Before 1923 Panama was under the jurisdiction of the nunciature for Colombia. In 1923 Panama was transferred to the jurisdiction of the internunciature for Central America. In 1933 the internunciature was reorganized and raised to two nunciatures, and the envoy became the nuncio to Costa Rica, Nicaragua, and Panama. In 1948 Nicaragua was separated from the jurisdiction of the group. In 1955 a separate nuncio was appointed for Costa Rica.

Reference. For a complete list of nuncios (through 1956) see Giuseppe de Marchi, *Le nunziature apostoliche dal 1800 al 1956* (Rome, 1957).

RECORDS. No records for this nunciature could be found in the ASV, but series listed with the Costa Rica nunciature relate directly to Panama and should be consulted. See the series for the apostolic nunciature for Costa Rica, *Archivio della Nunziatura in Costarica, Nicaragua, e Panama.*

4.75 Paraguay, Apostolic Nunciature for
[DATABASE ID: VATV412-A]

Before 1877 the interests of the Holy See were represented in Paraguay by papal representatives in Brazil (1829–1836, 1840–1849, 1851–1857, and 1864–1877) and Colombia (1836–1840). The first apostolic delegate to Argentina, Paraguay, and Uruguay served from 1849 to 1851. From 1857 to 1864 an apostolic delegate was appointed to Argentina, Bolivia, Buenos Aires, Chile, Paraguay, and Uruguay. The post was established permanently in 1877 as apostolic delegate and envoy extraordinary to Argentina, Paraguay, and Uruguay. Relations were severed with Argentina in 1884, which also ended relations with Paraguay. Relations were reestablished with Argentina in 1900 as an internunciature, which also held the title of apostolic delegation in Para-

guay and Uruguay, although relations with Paraguay were not restored until 1919 and with Uruguay not until 1939. The mission to Paraguay was raised to a nunciature in 1920 and was united with the nunciature to Argentina. In 1939 responsibility for Paraguay was removed from the nunciature for Argentina and a nuncio to Paraguay and Uruguay was appointed. Beginning in 1941 a separate nuncio to Paraguay was appointed. This office was held by a chargé d'affaires from 1941 to 1946.

Reference. For a complete list of nuncios (through 1956) see Giuseppe de Marchi, *Le nunziature apostoliche dal 1800 al 1956* (Rome, 1957).

RECORDS. No records for this specific nunciature could be found in the ASV. See Argentina.

4.76 Peru, Apostolic Nunciature for
[DATABASE ID: VATV414-A]

Before 1877 the interests of the Holy See in Peru were represented by papal representatives in Brazil (1829–1836), Colombia (1836–1861), and Ecuador (1861–1877). In 1877 an apostolic delegate and envoy extraordinary to Peru, Ecuador, Bolivia, and Chile was appointed. Relations were severed with Chile beginning in 1882 and with Ecuador beginning in 1901. The missions to Peru and Bolivia were separated and the mission to Peru raised to an internunciature in 1916. In 1917 the mission was raised to a nunciature.

Reference. For a complete list of nuncios (through 1956) see Giuseppe de Marchi, *Le nunziature apostoliche dal 1800 al 1956* (Rome, 1957).

RECORDS. Records of the nunciature consist of the following series.

4.76.1 Archivio della Nunziatura di Peru
[DATABASE ID: VATV548-A]
Inclusive Dates: 1851–1958.
Bulk: 40 linear m. (735 numbered fascios)
Organization: 264 boxes, 53 vols., and Carte geografiche. Materials are principally divided according to nuncio, although there is a subseries of miscellaneous records from all nuncios (1869–[post-1922]), Carte geografiche (1900–[post-1922]), and bound volumes (1877–[post-1922]), largely protocolli and letterbooks. Within the tenure of each nuncio the following subseries (posizioni) are generally apparent: Istruzioni-Presentazione credenziali; —Santa Sede; —Facoltà; —Diocesi; —Religiosi/e; —Visitas Apostolicas; —Seminari.

Volumes at the end of the series that are not included in the index include: Copia lettere, 1877–1882 (6 vols. covering Peru, Ecuador, Bolivia); —Protocolli, 1878–[post-1922] (26 vols., early volumes cover Peru, Ecuador, Bolivia); —Indice del'Archivio, Bavona, 1901–1907 (Peru, Bolivia, Equador); —Gestation Mons. Dolci, 1907–1910 (Ecuador and Peru); —Indice (incomplete) (Ecuador, Bolivia, Peru), ca. 1900; —Rapporti spediti al Segretaria di Stato, 1869–1875; —Assemblea Episcopal, 1915 and 1917; —Libro de la Visita Apostolica del Monastero de Santa Catalina de Lima, 1877–

1879 (copies of letters); —Informa sobre las missiones de infides en la Peru, 1911; —Appunti sulle legislazione peruana in materia politico-religiosa da tenersi presente nelle trative per un concordato, 1891.

There is also a subseries of five miscellaneous boxes before the bound volumes. These are not included in the index. Box 5 contains materials dating from 1869–[post-1922] including: Communicazioni con Roma relativi al Concilio Vaticano; —Usurpazioni di Roma, Proteste, 1870–1871; —Santa Sede e il 20 Sett., 1871–1921; —Santa Sede e Sua relazioni diplomatici.

Scope: The *Archivio della Nunziatura Apostolica in Peru* documents the development of the Catholic church in Peru since the mid-nineteenth century and the relations between the Catholic church and the Peruvian governments over the years. The archivio also contains more materials concerning other South American countries, particularly Ecuador and Bolivia in the nineteenth century and early twentieth century, than are apparent from the index. Information on Ecuador and Bolivia is found in the regular series, in the miscellaneous series, the Carte geografiche, and in the protocolli and letterbooks at the end. Additional information on Peru can be found in the archives of other South American nunciatures, particularly Chile and Brazil; the archives of the nunciature for Portugal; and in the Secretariatus Status series *Esteri.*

Finding Aids: ASV Indice 1152 gives a general description of the initial 100 fascios (1862–1921). At times, the contents of a fascio are itemized. The index does not include all materials, however, that date prior to 1921. Information from the Carte geografiche, miscellaneous boxes, protocolli, and letterbook volumes listed above do not appear in this index.

Location: Archivio Segreto Vaticano.

4.77 Philippines, Apostolic Nunciature for
[DATABASE ID: VATV381-A]

An apostolic delegation was established in 1902, dependent on the Consistorial Congregation. In 1951 the post was raised to a nunciature.

Reference. For a complete list of nuncios (through 1956) see Giuseppe de Marchi, *Le nunziature apostoliche dal 1800 al 1956* (Rome, 1957).

RECORDS. Records of the nunciature consist of the following series.

4.77.1 Archivio della Nunziatura Apostolica nelle Filippine
[DATABASE ID: VATV510-A]
Inclusive Dates: 1937–1959.
Bulk: 22 linear m.
Reference: Natalini et al., p. 266.
Location: Archivio Segreto Vaticano.

4.78 Poland, Apostolic Nunciature for
[DATABASE ID: VATV232-A]

The apostolic nunciature for Poland was established in 1555 by Julius III, following earlier legations. From 1705 to 1760, the nuncio sometimes resided in Dresden and served also as nuncio to Saxony. In 1783–1784 and

1797–1799 the nuncio also served as nuncio to Russia, with responsibility for the areas annexed by Russia from Poland. From 1803 to 1806 a new nuncio to Russia was appointed. The nuncio was expelled from Russia in 1804, residing thereafter in Dresden. The nunciature for Poland was abolished in 1797 after the abolition of the Polish state. The nunciature was reestablished in 1919. (The nuncio had previously been apostolic delegate for Poland, appointed in 1918.) In 1925 the Free City of Danzig was added to the jurisdiction of the nunciature for Poland. Beginning in 1939 the nuncio resided in London with the Polish government in exile. From 1947 to 1949 the Holy See was represented in Poland by a chargé d'affaires in Warsaw. The office was abolished in 1949. Partial relations were reestablished in 1975, when a special nuncio was appointed. Full relations were restored in 1989.

In addition to the records listed below, series listed with other agencies relate directly to this agency and should be consulted. See Secretariatus Status series *Nunziatura di Polonia, Nunziatura di Polonia-Russia,* and *Nunziature diverse.*

References. For a complete list of nuncios (through 1956) see Henry Biaudet, *Les nonciatures apostoliques permanentes jusqu'en 1648* (Helsinki, 1910); Liisi Karttunen, *Les nonciatures apostoliques permanentes de 1650 à 1800* (Helsinki, 1912); *Repertorium der diplomatischen Vertreter aller Länder seit dem Westfalischen Frieden (1648) [to 1815]* (Oldenburg, 1936–65); Giuseppe de Marchi, *Le nunziature apostoliche dal 1800 al 1956* (Rome, 1957). Also useful is the work by W. Meysztowicz, *Repertorium bibliographicum pro rebus polonicis Archivi secreti vaticani* (Vatican City, 1943).

RECORDS. Records of the nunciature consist of the following series.

4.78.1 Archivio della Nunziatura Apostolica di Polonia
[DATABASE ID:VATV429-A]
Inclusive Dates: 1587–1818 and 1915–1939.
Bulk: 31 linear m.
Organization: Principal subseries: Archivio della Nunziatura di Varsavia (189 buste), 1587–1818; —Occupazione tedesca in Polonia anni 1915–1918; —Processi dei vescovi; —Ratti nunzio (8 boxes), 1919–1921; —Lauri nunzio (30 buste), 1921–[post-1922]; —[2 series post-1922].
Note: Vols. 44, 58, 166, 190–196, 198–200, and 205 are available on microfilm.
References: Boyle, p. 78; Fink, p. 93. Henryk Damian Woytyska, *Acta Nuntiaturae Polonae* (Rome, 1990–). This series is currently in production and reprints documents from a wide range of ASV and BAV series. This is a good place to start a study of materials in the ASV that concern Poland because the introduction demonstrates the interconnectedness of many series. Entries note the type of document, the correspondents, the date, and then reprint the document. There are notes as to where the document (as well as any minute or other version of

the document) can be found and if the document has been published. There are analytical and bibliographical footnotes and a name/place index at the end of each volume. Also useful is Atanasii Velykyi, *Litterae nuntiorum apostolicorum historiam Ucrainae illustrantes, 1550–1850* (Rome, 1959–).

Finding Aids: Valerianus Meysztowicz, *De Archivo Nuntiaturae Varsaviensis quod nunc in Archivo secreto vaticano Servatur* (Vatican City, 1944), provides a brief description of the series, biographies of the nuncios from 1754 to 1796, and describes volume titles, dates, and contents for vols. 1–189 (1587–1818) [also identified as ASV Indice XX B 33 (1–3)]. Meysztowicz also provides information concerning several other contemporary, internal indexes in the series. This was also published by the Archivio Segreto Vaticano in 1944.

ASV Indici 190–191, "Index rerum praecipue ecclesiasticarum Regni Poloniae," is a copy of *Archivio della Nunziatura di Varsavia* nos. 2–5 (which were formerly identified as ASV Indici 186–189). This index is organized according to subject (e.g., abbat., austriaci, festa, Leopolien Colleg. Pontifi., synodus). Entries are chronological within each subject area and list the year, type of business or document and a summary of the business, the date of the document, a page and sometimes a tome number. Since no modern segnature are listed, these probably do not function well as indici. However, they do demonstrate the range of activities in which a nunciature was involved.

Ottavio Cavalleri, *L'Archivio di Mons. Achille Ratti Visitatore Apostolico e Nunzio a Varsavia (1918–1921): Inventario* (Vatican City, 1990) is a detailed description of the Ratti materials. This section of the *Archivio della Nunziatura Apostolica di Polonia* is divided into eleven titoli: I. Nunzio, Nunziatura e personale di Nunziatura; II. Corrispondenze diplomatiche, affari diplomatici e politici; III. Episcopato polacco, questione agraria, dotazione di clero e concordato; IV. Affari delle diocesi; V. Organizzazioni cattolica, universita, beneficenza; VI. Ordini e famiglie religiose; VII. Galizia orientale, rito e Chiese orientale; VIII. Facoltà e dispense; IX. Messe, obbligazioni, onorari, tasse e rendiconti; X. Alta Silesia, Prussia orientale ed occidentale; XI. Visità "extra Polonium." There are good introductions to the history of the nunciature and this part of the series by Josef Metzler and Germano Gualdo. The entries are organized by titolo. At the beginning of each new titolo: the inclusive dates are given, the first box number, and the total number of folios. Within each box, a general description of a group of fascicoli is provided and then more detailed descriptions of the contents of significant fascicoli within each group are given. The level of description in this index is very good. At the end of this published work there are two appendices. Appendix I contains two items: (a) is a reprint of the istruzioni per Mons. Achille Ratti, visitatore apostolico in Polonia for *Archivio della Nunziatura Apostolica di Polonia* 191, ff. 1116–1134, originale; and (b) is the relazione finale sulla missione di Mons. Ratti in Polonia from Polonia 527 (Segretario di Stato, prot. no. 23790, a. 1921), originale and ASV *Archivio della Nunziatura di Varsavia* 193, ff. 426–498, copia conforme. Appendix II contains an article by Cavellari entitled "La missione di Mons. Achille Ratti nei paesi baltici (1918–1921)" and various documents regarding the nunciature. There is an index at the end of the volume that lists personal names, places, and religious orders.

ASV Indice 227, "Inventarium omnium et singulorum privilegiorum, litterarum, diplomatum et monumentorum quaecumque in Archivio Regni in Avce. Cracov. continentur per Commissarios a Sac. Reg. Maiestate et Republica ad revidendum et connotandum omnes scripturas in eodem Archivio existentes deputato confectum Anno Domini MDCLXXXII, et repositum in Archivio Molis Hadrianae die 20 Martii 1713 Dominico Rivera," formerly ASV Indici 102, can no longer be used as an effective index to this series. However, it is a collection of reprinted and regested bulls, briefs, and letters important to the history of Poland.

Location: Archivio Segreto Vaticano.

4.79 Portugal, Apostolic Nunciature for
[DATABASE ID: VATV229-A]

The nunciature for Portugal was established in 1513 by Leo X. The office was vacant from 1563 to 1578, in consideration of cardinal legate Henry of Portugal. The duties of the nunciature were handled by a collector for this period. The nunciature was suppressed during the period Portugal was united with Spain, 1580–1670, but its duties were handled by a collector who remained in Lisbon. Relations were severed from 1760 to 1769 after the nuncio was expelled in a dispute over the Jesuits. From 1808 to 1820 the nuncio resided in Brazil with the Portuguese court, while an internuncio remained in Portugal. A new nuncio arrived in Portugal in 1822. Relations with the nuncio were severed, 1833–1844. The office was held by an internuncio, 1844–1855. In 1915 the nuncio was recalled to Rome as a result of a revolution, with a secretary remaining in Lisbon to represent the Holy See. A new nuncio was appointed in 1918.

In addition to the records listed below, series listed with other agencies relate directly to this agency and should be consulted. See Secretariatus Status series *Nunziatura di Portogallo* and *Nunziature diverse*.

References. For a complete list of nuncios (through 1956) see Henry Biaudet, *Les nonciatures apostoliques permanentes jusqu'en 1648* (Helsinki, 1910); Liisi Karttunen, *Les nonciatures apostoliques permanentes de 1650 à 1800* (Helsinki, 1912); *Repertorium der diplomatischen Vertreter aller Länder seit dem Westfalischen Frieden (1648) [to 1815]* (Oldenburg, 1936–1965); Giuseppe de Marchi, *Le nunziature apostoliche dal 1800 al 1956* (Rome, 1957). Also useful is the work by M. F. de Barros e Sousa, Visconde de Santarem, L. A. Rebello da Silva, and J. J. da Silva Mendes Leal, "Relaçoes politicas e diplomaticas entre Portugal e la Curia de Roma," secçao 17, vols. 9–13 of *Quadro elementar das relaçoes politicas e diplomaticas de Portugal com as diversas potencias do mundo* (Lisbon, 1864–1876).

RECORDS. Records of the nunciature consist of the following series.

4.79.1 Archivio della Nunziatura di Portogallo
[DATABASE ID: VATV422-A]
Inclusive Dates: 1580–1940.
Bulk: 90 linear m. (587 numbered buste and boxes, plus libri sussidiari [29 vols. and miscellaneous registers]).
Organization: Principal subseries: Archivio della Nunziatura di Lisbona, 1580–1910 (vols. 1–380); —Libri sussidiari (29 vols.) to subseries 1; —Tonti nuncio, 1906–1917 (vols. 414–587); —Locatelli nunzio, 1918–1922; —[3 series post-1922]; —Regista, 1605–[post-1922] (362 vols.); —Libri sussidiari (29 vols.).
Scope: Additional information on Portugal can be located in the Secretariatus Status series *Esteri*, the *Archivio dello Studio Belli*, and a number of the records of nunciatures in the former Portuguese colonies, particularly Brazil.
References: Boyle, p. 78; Fink, p. 92; Pásztor (1970), pp. 248–268; Pásztor (1983), pp. 211–232; Natalini et al., p. 266.
Finding Aids: ASV Indice 1161 (I) and 1161 (II) describe vols. 1–380 (1580–1910). These indici provide both an "Inventario Sommario" that gives general information on each busta or box and an "Inventario Analitico" that presents more detailed information on each busta or box. At the end of Indice 1161 (II) there is a volume by volume list of each of the "Libri sussidiari." ASV Indice 1161 (III) provides a brief listing for buste 381–413, which cover the years 1906–1917.
Location: Archivio Segreto Vaticano.

4.80 Prague, Czechoslovakia, Legation in
[DATABASE ID: VATV597-A]

No history was prepared for this agency.

RECORDS. No records of this legation were located in the ASV, but series listed with the Secretariatus Status relate directly to Prague and should be consulted. See Secretariatus Status series *Nunziatura di Germania*.

4.81 Prussia, Apostolic Nunciature for
[DATABASE ID: VATV395-A]

Relations between the Holy See and Prussia were established in 1925 as a result of the accreditation of an ambassador of Germany to the Holy See who had the added title of representative of Prussia. The office was held by the nuncio to Germany. The title was abolished in 1934 with the elimination of the autonomy of the German states.
Reference. For a complete list of nuncios (through 1956) see Giuseppe de Marchi, *Le nunziature apostoliche dal 1800 al 1956* (Rome, 1957).

RECORDS. No specific records series relating to this nunciature were located in the ASV.

4.82 Romania, Apostolic Nunciature for
[DATABASE ID: VATV396-A]

An apostolic nunciature for Romania was established in 1920. The office was represented by a regent from 1947 until 1950; the regent was expelled in 1950. Relations were reestablished in 1990.
Reference. For a complete list of nuncios see Giuseppe de Marchi, *Le nunziature apostoliche dal 1800 al 1956* (Rome, 1957).

RECORDS. Records of the nunciature consist of the following series.

4.82.1 Archivio della Nunziatura di Romania
[DATABASE ID: VATV549-A]
Inclusive Dates: 1920–1951.
Bulk: 10.5 linear m.
Organization: Principal subseries: Marmaggi nunzio, 1920–1922; —[5 subseries post-1922].
Reference: Natalini et al. p. 266.
Location: Archivio Segreto Vaticano.

4.83 Rwanda, Apostolic Nunciature for
[DATABASE ID: VATV559-A]

The nunciature for Rwanda was established in 1964. This area had previously been the responsibility of the apostolic delegation in the Congo and Rwanda. The nuncio to Zaire also serves as the nuncio to Rwanda.

RECORDS. See records for the nunciature for Zaire.

4.84 Sardinia, Apostolic Nunciature for
[DATABASE ID: VATV234-A]

The nunciature for Sardinia was established in Turin as the nunciature for Savoy in 1560 by Pius IV. Beginning in 1701, no nuncio was appointed. Affairs were conducted during this period by interim agents and "pontifical ministers." In 1718 Savoy became part of the kingdom of Sardinia. The mission was closed in 1798 when Turin was occupied by the French. Until 1817 the office was filled first by a custodian, later by an agent. In 1817 the agent was promoted to chargé d'affaires. A nuncio was appointed in 1839. After 1851 no nuncio was named. The office was filled by an auditor from 1852 to 1856, then diplomatic relations were ended. The office was also called nunciature for Turin.

In addition to the records listed below, series listed with other agencies relate directly to this agency and should be consulted. See Secretariatus Status series *Nunziatura di Savoia* and *Nunziature diverse*.
References. For a complete list of nuncios see Henry Biaudet, *Les nonciatures apostoliques permanentes jusqu'en 1648* (Helsinki, 1910); Liisi Karttunen, *Les nonciatures apostoliques permanentes de 1650 à 1800* (Helsinki, 1912); *Repertorium der diplomatischen Vertreter aller Länder seit dem Westfälischen Frieden (1648) [to 1815]* (Oldenburg, 1936–1965); Giuseppe de Marchi, *Le nunziature apostoliche dal 1800 al 1956* (Rome, 1957).

RECORDS. Records of the nunciature consist of the following series.

4.84.1 Archivio della Nunziatura di Torino
[DATABASE ID: VATV428-A]
Inclusive Dates: 1561–1879.
Bulk: 51 linear m.
Organization: The series divides into two subseries: 1. a numbered series, vols. 1–253, including one unnumbered packet, 1561–1865 (17 linear m.); —2. miscellaneous buste, ca. 1600–1825 (34 linear m.).
References: Boyle, p. 78; Fink, p. 93.
Finding Aid: ASV Indice 1141 includes list of titles and inclusive dates for vols. 1–253.
Location: Archivio Segreto Vaticano.

4.85 Scandinavia, Apostolic Delegation in
[DATABASE ID: VATV568-A]

The delegation in Scandinavia was established in 1960 with responsibility for representing the Holy See to churches in Denmark, Finland, Iceland, Norway, and Sweden. Separate nuncios were appointed to Finland in 1966 and Iceland in 1976. In 1982 nuncios were appointed to Denmark, Norway, and Sweden and the apostolic delegation was abolished.

RECORDS. No records for this delegation were located in the ASV.

4.86 Senegal, Apostolic Nunciature for
[DATABASE ID: VATV572-A]

An internunciature for Senegal was established in 1961. The country was previously the responsibility of the apostolic delegation in West Africa. The office was raised to a nunciature in 1966.

RECORDS. No records for this nunciature were located in the ASV.

4.87 Slovakia, Apostolic Nunciature for
[DATABASE ID: VATV398-A]

After the partition of Czechoslovakia in 1939, the nuncio moved his residence to Bratislava to continue his mission in Slovakia. He left the country soon thereafter, after he had difficulty being accredited to the new government. From 1940 to 1945 the office was represented by a chargé d'affaires. The office was closed in 1945 with the reconstitution of Czechoslovakia.
Reference. For a complete list of nuncios see Giuseppe de Marchi, *Le nunziature apostoliche dal 1800 al 1956* (Rome, 1957).

RECORDS. No records for this nunciature were located in the ASV.

4.88 South Africa, Apostolic Delegation in
[DATABASE ID: VATV561-A]

The apostolic delegation in South Africa was dependent on the Congregation Propaganda Fide and located in Bloemfontein, later in Pretoria, South Africa. Established in 1922 as apostolic delegation in Africa, the delegation had responsibility for representing the Holy See to churches in British possessions in Africa. In 1930 a new apostolic delegation was established in Mombasa, Kenya, which also took the name apostolic delegation in Africa. Until 1935 both offices were known by the same name. The original delegation was renamed apostolic delegation in South Africa in 1935, with responsibility for representing the Holy See to churches in Basutoland, Bechuanaland, South West Africa, South Africa, and Swaziland. In 1960 responsibility for Southern Rhodesia was added. Countries were removed from the responsibility of the mission when separate nuncios were appointed, that is, Lesotho in 1967 and Zimbabwe in 1981.

RECORDS. Records of the delegation consist of the following series.

4.88.1 Archivio della Delegazione Apostolica per l'Africa Meridionale
[DATABASE ID: VATV520-A]
Inclusive Dates: 1921–1945.
Bulk: 3.5 linear m.
Scope: Earlier materials concerning the Catholic church in southern Africa can be found in other ASV series, such as the Secretariatus Status series *Esteri*. For a partial listing of references to this area in different ASV series consult Lajos Pásztor, *Guida delle fonti per la storia dell'Africa a Sud del Sahara negli Archivi della Santa Sede e negli Archivi ecclesiastici d'Italia* (Zug, 1983).
Reference: Natalini et al., p. 265.
Location: Archivio Segreto Vaticano.

4.89 South Germany, Apostolic Nunciature for
[DATABASE ID: VATV239-A]

During the reign of Gregory XIII (1572–1585), the duties of the nuncio to the Holy Roman Empire were expanded to include overseeing the implementation of the decrees of the Council of Trent in the empire. Several new nunciatures were established to assist in carrying out this task. The nunciature for South Germany, in Salzburg, was established in 1573, with responsibility for Salzburg, Tyrol, Bavaria, and Styria. In 1580 a permanent nunciature for Styria was established. The office of nuncio to South Germany was not filled after 1583.
Reference. For a complete list of nuncios see Henry Biaudet, *Les nonciatures apostoliques permanentes jusqu'en 1648* (Helsinki, 1910).

RECORDS. No records for this nunciature were located in the ASV, but series listed with the Secretariatus Status relate directly to South Germany and should be consulted. See Secretariatus Status series *Nunziatura di Germania*.

4.90 Spain, Apostolic Nunciature for
[DATABASE ID: VATV223-A]

Sources differ as to when the office of the papal representatives in Spain became a permanent nunciature, with the dates 1484, 1492, and 1506 being mentioned. During the reign of Emperor Charles V (1519–1558) the affairs of the nuncios to Spain and to the Holy Roman Empire were intermingled. For most of the period from 1522 to 1544 the nuncio to Spain also served as nuncio to the empire. During the period from 1709 to 1720, which corresponded to the latter part of the War of the Spanish Succession and afterward, the office was often vacant (1713–1716 and 1718–1720), or held on an interim basis (1709, 1713, and 1716–1717). The office in Madrid was closed in 1709, and until 1713 the nuncio resided in Barcelona. From 1808 to 1813 the nuncio resided in Cadiz with the Spanish government, while the country was occupied by Napoleon's forces. In 1813 the nuncio was expelled for his opposition to the suppression of the Spanish Inquisition. The nuncio returned to Spain in 1814 with the return of King Ferdinand VII. Relations were severed from 1835 to 1848 over the secularization of monastic lands. The office was held by a chargé d'affaires from 1853 to 1857 and from 1869 to 1875 because of political instability and revolution. No nuncio served from 1936 to 1938, only a chargé d'affaires representing the Holy See to the nationalist forces.

In addition to the records listed below, series listed with other agencies relate directly to this agency and should be consulted. See Secretariatus Status series *Nunziatura di Spagna* and *Nunziature diverse*.

References. For a complete list of nuncios (through 1956) see Henry Biaudet, *Les nonciatures apostoliques permanentes jusqu'en 1648* (Helsinki, 1910); Liisi Karttunen, *Les nonciatures apostoliques permanentes de 1650 à 1800* (Helsinki, 1912); *Repertorium der diplomatischen Vertreter aller Länder seit dem Westfälischen Frieden (1648)* [to 1815] (Oldenburg, 1936–65); Giuseppe de Marchi, *Le nunziature apostoliche dal 1800 al 1956* (Rome, 1957). Also useful is the work ed. by L. Serrano, *Correspondencia diplomatica entre España y la Santa Sede durante el pontificado di S. Pio V* (Madrid, 1914).

RECORDS. Records of the nunciature consist of the following series.

4.90.1 Archivio della Nunziatura di Spagna
[DATABASE ID:VATV424-A]
Inclusive Dates: 1623–1951.
Bulk: 270 linear m.

Organization: Principal subseries: Archivio della Nunziatura di Madrid, 1623–1912, 709 vols. and buste;—Ragonesi nunzio, 1912–1920, 66 buste; —Tedeschini nunzi o, 1921–[post-1922], 192 buste; —[1 series post-1922];—Libri sussidia ri, 1794–[post-1951], 37 vols.; —Libri protocolli, 1913–[post-1922]; —[Miscellaneous index volumes, ca. 1700–1800 and 1921–[post-1922].

Note: Archivio della Nunziatura di Madrid, vols. 257 and 277 are available on microfilm.

References: Boyle, p. 78; Fink, p. 92; Pásztor (1970), pp. 268–300; Pásztor (1983), pp. 232–247; Natalini et al., p. 266. R. Ritzler, "Procesos informativos de los obispos de España y sus dominios en el Archivo Vaticano," *Anthologica annua* 4 (1956): 465–498. Vicente Cárcel Ortí, "La correspondance diplomatique des nonces apostoliques dans l'Espagne du XIXe siècle," *Revue d'histoire diplomatique* 96 (1982): 320–334, is an excellent introduction to the Spanish nunciature materials dating from the nineteenth century. Cárcel Ortí focuses on three primary areas for research: the Secretariatus Status, the *Archivio della Nunziatura di Spagna*, and the archive of the Congregatio pro Negotiis Ecclesiasticis Extraordinariis. Cárcel Ortí notes that the original reports, dispatches, and so forth are in the archives of the Secretariatus Status or the Congregatio pro Negotiis Ecclesiasticis Extraordinariis and the minutes are in the *Archivio della Nunziatura di Spagna*. He also notes that the nunciature materials he cites are largely diplomatic, although the materials in the fonds are more diverse. He provides one example of a religious nature, but a researcher can also find ample materials concerning social history. Cárcel Ortí ends with a discussion of his editions of dispatches and a brief description of his own methods. He does not tie in his work with editions of documents from earlier periods.

Franco Diaz de Cerio Ruiz, *Regesto de la correspondencia de los obispos de España en el siglo XIX con los nuncios, segun el Fondo de la Nunciatura de Madrid en el Archivo Vaticano (1791–1903)* (Vatican City, 1984), vol. 1, *Albarra-Cuenca;* vol. 2, *Gerona-Oviedo;* vol. 3, *Palencia-Zaragoza*. This series reprints solely nunciature correspondence between the bishops and the nuncios. After an introduction to the correspondence, the actual reprints begin. Entries list the series, the bishop, the year, the type of business or correspondents, date of the document, a subject (sometimes), and then the caja. Some entries also include some or all of the following other identification numbers: titolo, rubrica, sezioni, and numero. In the copy of this volume housed in the bibliography room of the ASV, folio numbers have been written in pencil. There are minimal analytical footnotes. There is an index to persons and some places at the end of each volume.

Vicente Cárcel Ortí, *Correspondencia diplomatica del Nuncio Tiberi (1827–1834)* (Pamplona, 1976), provides a good introduction to the nunciature and then reprints selected documents of a political nature. Although only a small portion of materials are from the *Archivio della Nunziatura di Spagna*, this work demonstrates the interconnectedness of various ASV fondi. Entries include the names of the correspondents, a brief (1–2 lines) Spanish recapitulation, the series, volume, and sometimes folio numbers, and the reprint itself. There are analytical footnotes with cross references, clarifications, and bibliography. The volume ends with a personal name/place index.

Finding Aids: ASV Indici 1090, 1090a, and 1090b list volume titles, inclusive dates, and contents for vols. 1–777 (original

Archivio series and Ragonesi series). ASV Indice 1090a covers vol. 1–639b (1623–1899), and Indice 1090b covers vols. 640–777 (1899–1921). Indice 1090a also lists vols. 1–37 of the Libri Sussidiari beginning on page 55 in the second section. These indici were changed slightly between 1990 and 1994. Indice 1090a is now an amalgam of the old 1090, which is now bound into the front of 1090a. Indice 1090a provides a sparse listing of the contents of the series. Entries for volumes 1–300 list only the volume number, year, and the briefest of titles for the volume. The entries for volumes 301–639b give the scatola number and the titoli, rubric, and sezioni numbers with a brief description. ASV Indice 1090b provides more description and gives researchers a better idea of the contents of the buste. The index lists the scatola number, followed by the titoli, rubric, and sezioni numbers, with descriptive information concerning the contents of the buste. For a much more detailed description of scatole 1–639B (1664–1899), see the indici listed below by Marques and Cárcel Ortí. These published indici provide a much more detailed description of the materials and are the best place to begin to understand and access the contents of this series.

José María Marqués, *Indices del Archivo de la Nunciatura de Madrid* (Rome, 1976–1985). The first volume provides detailed contents information for the first 102 volumes of the series (1664–1754). The entries give a general note concerning the contents of a volume and then give a more detailed description of the contents of each fascicolo within the volume. Volume 2 provides the same detailed information for volumes 103–228 of the series (1754–1803). In addition, at the end of this volume is an index to persons, places, subjects, and some types of materials (e.g., bulla), which appear in both volumes.

For the period between 1803 and 1899 (scatola or caja 229–639B), the indici by Cárcel Ortí are the best place to start. They are more detailed than the official ASV Indice and provide introductory, bibliographic, biographical, and descriptive notes, on the collection. Furthermore, these indici analyze the collection at much greater depth than the ASV Indice for this period. Whereas the ASV Indice lists the scatola number, titolo, rubric, and perhaps sezione designation, the Cárcel Ortí indici also give the fascicolo titles and the titles of the numbers within the fascicoli. When appropriate, this is followed by the scatola or caja numbers that the article covers in brackets [e.g., 229–235, 304, for this article] and finally the stampate number for locating the references in the ASV Sala degl'Indici [e.g., ASV XXX B 34 (1) for this article].

Vicente Cárcel Ortí, "El archivo de Pietro Gravina, Nuncio en Espana (1803–1817)," *Escritos del Vedat* 9 (1979): 303–320 [229–235, 304] ASV XXX B 34 (1).

Vicente Cárcel Ortí, "El archivo del nuncio en España, Giacomo Giustiniani (1817–1827)," *Escritos del Vedat* 6 (1976): 265–300.

Vicente Cárcel Ortí, ed., *Correspondencia diplomatica del Nuncio Amat (1833–1840)* (Pamplona, 1982).

Vicente Cárcel Ortí, "Los despachos de la Nunciatura de Madrid (1847–1857)," *Archivum Historiae Pontificiae* 13 (1975): 311–400. [305–325] ASV XX B 34 (3).

Vicente Cárcel Ortí, "Los despachos de la Nunziatura de Madrid," *Archivum Historiae Pontificiae* 14 (1976): 265–356. [326–352] ASV XX B 34 (4).

Vicente Cárcel Ortí, "El archivo del nuncio Barili (1857–1868)," *Archivum Historiae Pontificiae* 17 (1979): 289–355. ASV XX B 34 (5).

Vicente Cárcel Ortí, "El archivo de la Nunciatura de Madrid desde 1868 hasta 1875," *Archivum Historiae Pontificiae* 15 (1977): 363–376. [462–470] ASV XX B 34 (6).

Vicente Cárcel Ortí, "El archivo del nuncio Simeoni y del encargado de negocios Rampolla (1875–1877)," *Scriptorium Victoriense* 26 (1979): 338–352. [471–473] ASV XX B 34 (7).

Vicente Cárcel Ortí, "El archivo del nuncio Simeoni y del encargado de negocios Rampolla (1875–1877)," *Scriptorium Victoriense* 27 (1980): 102–110. [473–476] ASV XX B 34 (8).

Vicente Cárcel Ortí, "El archivo del nuncio Simeoni y del encargado de negocios Rampolla (1875–1877)," *Scriptorium Victoriense* 27 (1980): 199–233. [476–487] ASV XX B 34 (9).

Vicente Cárcel Ortí, "El archivo de los nuncios de León XIII en España. I, Nunciatura del Cattani (1877–1879)," *Italica* 16 (1982): 237–264. [488–503] ASV XX 34 B (10).

Vicente Cárcel Ortí, "El archivo de los nuncios del León XIII en España. II, Nunciatura de Bianchi (1879–1883)," *Italica* 17 (1984): 231–262. [504–518] ASV XX B 34 (11).

Vicente Cárcel Ortí, "El archivo del nuncio Mariano Rampolla (1833–1887)," *Hispania sacra* 39 (1987): 747–788. [519–551] ASV XX B 34 (12).

Vicente Cárcel Ortí, "El archivo del nuncio Angelo di Pietro (1887–1893)," *Hispania sacra* 41 (1989): 183–226. [552–584] ASV XX B 34 (13).

Vicente Cárcel Ortí, "El archivo del nuncio Serafino Cretoni (1893–1896)," *Hispania sacra* 42 (1990): 537–572. [585–615] ASV XX B 34 (14).

Vicente Cárcel Ortí, "El archivo del nuncio Giuseppe Francia-Nava di Bontife (1896–1899)," *Hispania sacra* 44 (1992): 459–485. [616–639B] ASV XX B 34 (15).

Franco Diaz de Cerio Ruiz, *Indice-catalogo del Fondo de la Nunciatura de Madrid en el Archivo Vaticano (1794–1899)* (Rome, 1993), vol. 1, 1794–1899 (196–303); vol. 2, 1847–1874 (305–470); vol. 3, 1875–1899 (471–639B). Díaz's inventories are also more complete than ASV Indice 1090A. Díaz begins slightly before Cárcel Ortí, that is, he begins in 1794 with box 196, whereas Cárcel Ortí begins in 1803 with box 229. They also both contain current segnature for requesting materials. In general, researchers should try to use this work along with the Cárcel Ortí work; each tends to describe the *Archivio della Nunziatura di Spagna* in slightly different terms, which may provide researchers with slightly varying ideas on the contents: In general, Díaz gives deeper contents descriptions for the fascicoli. However, Cárcel Ortí provides an introduction to each nunciature, its records, and a biography of the nuncio. Cárcel Ortí's work is in Spanish and tends to give more detailed "titoli" descriptions. Díaz's book lists sezioni, titoli, rubrica, and fascicoli in Italian and any contents descriptions in Spanish. In some cases (probably since Díaz is later) additional items that were not present or had not been organized are noted by Díaz, which were not noted by Cárcel Ortí. Entries in the three Díaz volumes provide the volume or box (caja) number. When describing a volume, the contents of each volume are presented page by page. Boxes are broken down into sezioni, titoli, and rubrica. The titles of all these are provided in Italian and then contents descriptions of each rubrica are given in Spanish. This gives the researcher very detailed access to the series. At the beginning of each volume is a list of all the ASV *Archivio della Nunziatura di Spagna* volumes or boxes described in the book.

At the end of each volume, is a personal name, place, and subject index, for that volume.

Location: Archivio Segreto Vaticano.

4.90.2 Collectoriali

[DATABASE ID: VATV20464-A]

Inclusive Dates: Unknown.

Bulk: 14 scatole.

Scope: This series is also referred to as *Giustificazioni.* See the introduction to the archives of the Propaganda Fide in the section "Roman Curia."

Location: Archives of the Propaganda Fide.

4.91 Styria, Apostolic Nunciature for

[DATABASE ID: VATV236-A]

During the reign of Gregory XIII (1572–1585), the duties of the nuncio to the Holy Roman Empire were expanded to include overseeing the implementation of the decrees of the Council of Trent in the empire. Several new nunciatures were established to assist in carrying out this task. The nunciature for Styria, in Graz, was established in 1580. The office was vacant from 1586 to 1592. It was abolished in 1622.

Reference. For a complete list of nuncios see Henry Biaudet, *Les nonciatures apostoliques permanentes jusqu'en 1648* (Helsinki, 1910).

RECORDS. No records series for this nunciature were found in the ASV, but series listed with the Secretariatus Status relate directly to Styria and should be consulted. See Secretariatus Status series *Nunziatura di Germania.*

4.92 Switzerland, Apostolic Nunciature for

[DATABASE ID: VATV225-A]

The nunciature for Switzerland, also known as the nunciature for Lucerne, was established by Julius II in 1510, although the nuncio was not permanently in residence in Switzerland. During the reign of Gregory XIII (1572–1585), the duties of the nuncio to the Holy Roman Empire were expanded to include overseeing the implementation of the decrees of the Council of Trent in the empire. Several new nunciatures were established to assist in carrying out this task. The nunciature for Lucerne was made permanent in 1579, and the nuncio began to reside in Switzerland. The office was vacant from 1581 to 1586. Until 1786, the nuncio was also responsible for representing the Holy See in parts of Bavaria. The nuncio was expelled by the French in 1798 but was able to return in 1802. From 1823 to 1827 the office was held by a chargé d'affaires. From 1848 to 1868, no nuncio was named because of the passage of anticlerical legislation. The office was held by a chargé during that period. In 1874 relations were severed after a religious controversy. Relations were reestablished in 1920.

In addition to the records listed below, series listed

with other agencies relate directly to this agency and should be consulted. See Secretariatus Status series *Nunziatura di Svizzera* and *Nunziature diverse.*

References. For a complete list of nuncios (through 1956) see Henry Biaudet, *Les nonciatures apostoliques permanentes jusqu'en 1648* (Helsinki, 1910); Liisi Karttunen, *Les nonciatures apostoliques permanentes de 1650 à 1800* (Helsinki, 1912); *Repertorium der diplomatischen Vertreter aller Länder seit dem Westfälischen Frieden (1648) [to 1815]* (Oldenburg, 1936–65); Giuseppe de Marchi, *Le nunziature apostoliche dal 1800 al 1956* (Rome, 1957).

RECORDS. Records of the nunciature consist of the following series.

4.92.1 Archivio della Nunziatura di Svizzera

[DATABASE ID: VATV423-A]

Inclusive Dates: 1617–1952.

Bulk: 51 linear m.

Organization: Principal subseries: Archivio della Nunziatura di Lucerna (451 volumes and buste), 1617–1872; — Maglione nunzio, 1920–[post-1922]; —[2 series post-1922].

References: Boyle, p. 78; Fink, pp. 92–94.

Finding Aids: ASV Indice 1070 provides a brief descriptive listing of buste 1–340 and vols. 341–451. The post-1922 material is not described.

Location: Archivio Segreto Vaticano.

4.93 Syria, Apostolic Nunciature for

[DATABASE ID: VATV397-A]

The apostolic delegation in Syria was established in 1762. In the twentieth century it was dependent on the Congregation for the Oriental Church. It was located initially in Aleppo, then in Beirut until 1947, then in Damascus. In 1929, Palestine, Transjordan, and Cyprus were transferred from the jurisdiction of the apostolic delegation in Syria to the apostolic delegation in Egypt and Arabia. The office was vacant from 1948 to 1951, then held by a chargé d'affaires until 1953, when it was raised to an internunciature. From 1958 to 1961, while Syria was part of the United Arab Republic, the office was closed. In 1966 the mission was raised to a nunciature.

Reference. For a complete list of nuncios (through 1956) see Giuseppe de Marchi, *Le nunziature apostoliche dal 1800 al 1956* (Rome, 1957).

RECORDS. Records of the nunciature consist of the following series.

4.93.1 Archivio della Nunziatura Apostolica in Libano

[DATABASE ID VATV507-A]

Inclusive Dates: 1834–1947.

Bulk: 30 linear m.

Organization: Major subseries include: Corrispondenza con la S.C. Propaganda Fide e Chiese Orientale, 1834–[post-

1922] (71 vols.); —Corrispondenza ufficiale, 1834–[post-1922] (287 items); —[1 series post-1922].

Corrispondenza ufficiale includes the following divisions: Copie de lettres; —S.C. Orientale; —Propaganda Fide; —Stampate da Roma; —Corrispondenza in Arabo; —Corrispondenza con secolari; —Corrispondenza con ecclesiastici; —Corrispondenza con diocesi, delegati, etc.; —Ristretti religiosi; —Corrispondenza parochiale; —Documenti in arabo; —Greci; —Siri; —Armeni; —Maroniti; —Visità apostolica; —Padre Francescani; —Padre Capuccini; —Padre Gesuiti; —Padre Carmeliti; —Cause matrimoniali; —Opere della Propagenda Fide; —Statistica; —Ristretti di giornali; —Processi beatificazioni; —Prediche.

Archivio LePretre subseries includes: Facoltà; —Interventi; —Acattolici; —Seminari; —Passaggio di Riti; —Onorificenze; —Sussidi; —Santa Sede; —Conferenze episcopali; —Latini; —Corriere; —Emigranti; —Matrimonialia; —Statuto personale; —Rappresentatanze pontificie; —Situazione politico-religiosa; —Ricorsi; —Messe; —Statistiche; —Delegazione apostolica; —Vicario apostolico; —WAKS; —Legati; —Siria; —Armeni; —Caldei; —Melchiti; —Maroniti; —Varia.

Reference: Natalini et al., p. 266.
Location: Archivio Segreto Vaticano.

4.93.2 Archivio della Nunziatura di Siria
[DATABASE ID: VATV882-A]
Inclusive Dates: 1953–1969.
Bulk: 7 linear m.
Reference: Natalini et al., p. 267.
Location: Archivio Segreto Vaticano.

4.94 Thailand, Laos, and Malay Peninsula, Apostolic Delegation in
[DATABASE ID: VATV575-A]

An apostolic delegation in Thailand was established in 1957, separated from the jurisdiction of the internunciature for Indonesia. Later that year, responsibility for the Malay Peninsula transferred from the internunciature for India, and the office was renamed apostolic delegation in Thailand and the Malay Peninsula. The office was vacant until 1962. The apostolic delegation was dependent on the Congregation Propaganda Fide. In 1964, when it took responsibility for affairs in Laos from the apostolic delegation in Indochina, it was renamed apostolic delegation in Thailand, Laos, and the Malay Peninsula. In 1967 the name was changed to Thailand, Laos, Malaysia, and Singapore. In 1969 the mission to Thailand was raised to a nunciature and the mission to Laos, Malaysia, and Singapore remained an apostolic delegation with its seat in Bangkok.

RECORDS. No records for this nunciature were found in the ASV.

4.95 Turkey, Apostolic Nunciature for
[DATABASE ID: VATV585-A]

An apostolic delegation was established in Constantinople in 1868, dependent on the Congregation for the Oriental Church. It was responsible for relations between the Holy See and churches in parts of the Ottoman Empire, and later in Turkey. The name was changed from apostolic delegation in Constantinople to apostolic delegation in Turkey in 1931. In 1960 the apostolic delegation was raised to an internunciature, and in 1966 to a nunciature.

RECORDS. Records of the delegation consist of the following series.

4.95.1 Archivio della Delegazione Apostolica in Turchia
[DATABASE ID: VATV506-A]
Inclusive Dates: 1765–1953 (bulk 1821–1953).
Bulk: 30 linear m. (196 numbered boxes, 100 volumes, and 3 unnumbered boxes)
Organization: Subseries, organized by delegate, are listed by box number as follows: Boxes 1–2, Coressi; —3–6, Hillereau; —7, Borgomanero; —8, Mussabini; —9–20, Brunoni; —21–25, Pluym; —26–28, Grasselli; —28 bis–32, Vanutelli; —33–42, Rotelli; —43–67, Bonetti; —68–71, Tacci; —72–88, Sardi; —89–104, Dolci; —Unnumbered box after 104 and 105–196 [post-1922].

Volumes at the end of the series include: Protocolli (20th century); —Account books, 1830–1920; —Mass books (20th century); —Information on Catholic Cemeteries (Feri-Keui).
Scope: This series provides a rich source of information on the role and development of the Catholic church in Turkey, from the early nineteenth century when Constantinople was established as an apostolic vicariate. Materials from box 3 on deal with the developments, issues, and activities, of the Catholic church in Turkey. Boxes 1 and 2 hold some unexpected items, including a list of members of the Confraternity of Santa Anna, 1741–1774 (2 vols); the diary of trips between Vienna and Constantinople and Vienna and Rome in 1828, and recollections of the Venetian Revolution of 1797.
Reference: Natalini et al., p. 267.
Location: Archivio Segreto Vaticano.

4.96 Tuscany, Apostolic Nunciature for
[DATABASE ID: VATV233-A]

The nunciature for Tuscany was established by Paul IV in 1560. Relations were severed from 1643 to 1645. During the period of the Kingdom of Etruria (1801–1807), the nuncio remained in Florence. From 1806 to 1809, the office was held by a vice-auditor and chargé d'affaires. The vice-auditor was imprisoned when Florence was annexed by France in 1809. In 1814, released from prison, he revived the nunciature as auditor and served until 1830. The office was held by a chargé d'affaires from 1833 to 1856, and an internuncio (who also served as internuncio to Modena) from 1856 to 1859. The office was abolished in 1859 with Italian unification. The post is also called nuncio to Florence.

In addition to the records listed below, series listed with other agencies relate directly to this agency and should be consulted. See Secretariatus Status series *Nunziatura di Firenze* and *Nunziature diverse.*

References. For a complete list of nuncios see Henry Biaudet, *Les nonciatures apostoliques permanentes jusqu'en 1648* (Helsinki, 1910); Liisi Karttunen, *Les nonciatures apostoliques permanentes de 1650 à 1800* (Helsinki, 1912); *Repertorium der diplomatischen Vertreter aller Länder seit dem Westfalischen Frieden* (1648) [to 1815] (Oldenburg, 1936–1965); Giuseppe de Marchi, *Le nunziature apostoliche dal 1800 al 1956* (Rome, 1957).

RECORDS. Records of the nunciature consist of the following series.

4.96.1   Archivio della Nunziatura di Firenze

[DATABASE ID: VATV420-A]

Inclusive Dates: 1590–1859 (bulk 1700–1859).

Bulk: 23 linear m.

Organization: 427 volume numbers (in some cases more than one volume uses the same number) and 3 unnumbered buste. Subseries include: Lettere di collettori al nunzio; —Lettere di negozi camerali; —Registri di lettere del nunzio; —Posizione diverse; —Fabbrica; —Cause; —Lettere a [Pietro] Valentini, 1813–1826.

Note: Vol. 191 is available on microfilm.

References: Boyle, p. 78; Fink, p. 92.

Finding Aids: ASV Indice 1084 provides a list of volume titles with the inclusive dates of each volume.

Location: Archivio Segreto Vaticano.

4.97   United States, Apostolic Nunciature for

[DATABASE ID: VATV250-A]

An apostolic delegation in the United States was established in 1893, equivalent in rank to a nunciature of the first class. The delegation was dependent on the Consistorial Congregation. Hawaii was transferred from the jurisdiction of the apostolic delegation in Australasia in 1921; the Bahamas were transferred from the apostolic delegation in the Antilles in 1938; and the Caroline, Marshall, and Mariana Islands were transferred from the apostolic delegation in Japan in 1946. Beginning in 1968 the apostolic delegation was responsible for affairs of churches in the U.S. Virgin Islands. In 1975 the Bahamas were transferred to the jurisdiction of the new apostolic delegation in the Antilles. Full diplomatic relations established in 1984 and a nuncio appointed.

4.97.1   Archivio della Delegazione Apostolica degli Stati Uniti d'America

[DATABASE ID: VATV537-A]

Inclusive Dates: 1887–1976 (bulk 1892–1939).

Bulk: 81 linear m.

Organization: 931 scatole or 15,000 fascicoli. Subseries are: I. Delegazione Apostolica, 1892–1970; —II. Stati Uniti-USA, 1892–1970; —III. Nazioni Unite (ONU), 1961–1976; —IV.

Liste episcopali, 1893–1953; —V. Affari esteri, 1893–1939; —VI. Canada, 1889–1906; —VII. Isole Filippine, 1899–1942; —VIIIa. Messico, 1925–1935; —VIIIb. Delegazione Apostolica, Messico, ca. 1935; —IX. Diocesi, 1893–1934; —X. Diverse, 1893–1940; —XI. Varie, 1922–1939; —XII. Società segrete, 189?–1928; —XIII. Società, 1891–1940; —XIV. Società cattolica, 1905–1939; —XV. Greci orientali, 1909–1939; —XVI. Stravaganti, 1893–1920; —XVII. Università Cattolica, 1887–1939; —XVIII. Ruteni, 1892–1939; —XIX. Istituti religiosi, 1895–1952; —XX. Finanze, 1895–1952; —XXI. Collegio Giuseppino (Pontificium Collegium Josephinum de Propaganda Fide), 1891–1939; —XXII. Documenti aggiunti, 1892–1943.

Subseries IX, Diocesi, is alphabetical by diocese, except for box 1, which deals with Alaska.

Scope: Records in this series date primarily from the establishment of the apostolic delegation in the United States in 1893. The largest subseries is IX, Diocesi, which includes formal business transacted between the ordinary of each diocese and the apostolic delegate, as well as information regarding each diocese collected by the apostolic delegate through newspapers, publications, and unsolicited letters from priests and lay people. It should not be assumed, however, that all the information on a diocese is filed in the Diocesi subseries. Subjects covered in other subseries (e.g., IV, Liste episcopali) that also concern specific dioceses may be filed under the other subseries. Subseries I, Delegazione Apostolica, contains a miscellany of materials including talks by the apostolic delegate, invitations, and both private and official correspondence. Subseries II, Stati Uniti-USA, also presents a miscellany of correspondence concerning such varied issues as scholastic training and formation of priests, Italian immigration, and changes in the diocesan boundaries. Subseries III, Nazioni Uniti (ONU), contains primarily printed news and resolutions of that organization. Subseries IV, Liste episcopali, are episcopal nominations. Subseries V, Affari esteri, reflects the delegates' involvement in various foreign affairs, largely in Mexico, Central and South America, and Cuba. This subseries also contains letters from people representing different ethnic background in the United States asking the delegate to comment about events in their native countries. Subseries VI, Canada, primarily concerns priests who emigrated to the United States. Subseries VII, Isole Filippine, concerns Filipino Catholics after the Spanish American War, as well as printed material regarding Cuba and Puerto Rico. Subseries VIIIa, Messico, deals largely with religious persecution, and VIIIb covers priests who emigrated or were ordained in the United States and some social issues or disputes over church property. Subseries IX has been mentioned. Subseries X, XI, and XXII, titled Diverse, Varie, and Documenti aggiunti, respectively, are justly titled and contain additional miscellaneous diocesan information. Subseries XII, XIII, and XIV, titled Società segrete, Società, and Società cattolica, respectively, contain information on both diocesan and national organizations. It is possible to find the same organization in more than one of these series. Subseries XV, Greci orientali, contains information as to the acceptance of Eastern Rite parishes in U.S. dioceses and cases involving Eastern Rite priests and lay people. Subseries XVI, Stravaganti, regards cases involving priests without dioceses in the United States and Canada. Subseries XVII, Università Cattolica, concerns that institution, as subseries XXI, Collegio Giuseppino, regards the Pontificium Collegium Josephinum de Propaganda Fide in Cincinnati, Ohio. Subseries XVII, Ruteni, deals with the establishment of a diocese for Byzantine Rite Russians in the United States. There is much information on the relationship between Greek and Latin rite priests and bishops, and Greek and other Eastern Rite Catholics in general. Suberies XIX, Istituti religiosi, concerns the variety of issues faced by religious orders, particularly regarding their sponsorship of educational institutions. Subseries XX, Finanze, covers a variety of economic issues from the support of the apostolic delegate and to the financing of the "colored" missions.

Note: Fasc. 26A–D, 160B 1–2 are available on microfilm.

References: Natalini et al., p. 265. Giovanni Pizzorusso, "Un diplomat du Vatican en Amerique: Donato Sbarretti a Washington, le Havane et Ottawa (1893–1910)," *Annali accademici canadesi* 9 (1993): 5–33.

Finding Aid: ASV Indice 1168, "Inventario dell'Archivio della Nunziatura (gia' Delegazione) Apostolica degli Stati Uniti d'America, 1893–1921," vol. 1 (sez. I–IX Duluth), by Claudio Dominicis (1991), is the only inventory to this series. This indice provides a brief introduction to the series which includes the names of the delegates, nunzi, and other personnel in the delegation (uditore, segretario, consigliere). This is followed by a box listing of materials in the following subseries: I, II, IV, V, VI, VII, IX (Alaska-Duluth). The indice is dense, but a patient and careful reading of all the sections currently available can yield much information.

Location: Archivio Segreto Vaticano.

4.98 Uruguay, Apostolic Nunciature for

[DATABASE ID: VATV413-A]

Before 1877 the interests of the Holy See were represented in Uruguay by papal representatives in Brazil (1829–1836, 1840–1849, 1851–1857, and 1864–1877), and Colombia (1836–1840). The first apostolic delegate to Argentina, Paraguay, and Uruguay served from 1849 to 1851. From 1857 to 1864 an apostolic delegate was appointed to Argentina, Bolivia, Buenos Aires, Chile, Paraguay, and Uruguay. In 1877 an apostolic delegate and envoy extraordinary to Argentina, Paraguay, and Uruguay was appointed. Relations were severed in 1884. An internuncio to Argentina and apostolic delegate to Paraguay and Uruguay was named in 1900, although relations with Uruguay were not reestablished until 1939. (The mission to Argentina was raised to a nunciature in 1916; the mission to Paraguay was raised to nunciature in 1920.) In 1939 the mission to Paraguay and Uruguay was separated from the nunciature for Argentina, and the Uruguay mission was reestablished as a nunciature. In 1941 Paraguay was removed from the responsibility of the nuncio to Uruguay.

Reference. For a complete list of nuncios (through 1956) see Giuseppe de Marchi, *Le nunziature apostoliche dal 1800 al 1956* (Rome, 1957).

RECORDS. Records of the nunciature consist of the following series.

4.98.1 Archivio della Nunziatura Apostolica in Uruguay

[DATABASE ID: VATV523-A]

Inclusive Dates: 1900–1960.

Bulk: 14 linear m.

Organization: The series comprises 38 fascicles and is divided into sections according to nuncio. Within the records of each nuncio the following subseries are generally found: Santo Padre; —Segreteria di Stato; —Nunziatura Apostolica; —Amministrazione; —Governo; —Corpo diplomatico; —Curia Romana; —Provincia Ecclestica dell'Uruguay; —Seminari; —Religiosi/e; —Stampa cattolica; —Scuola cattolica; —Associazioni cattoliche (inc. Azione Cattolica); —Questioni esteri e internazionali; —Varie; —Pontificie Opera missionari; —Gerarchia Ecclesiastica Latino Americana; —Provvista delle diocesi; —Candidati vescovili.

Scope: The records series begins in 1900, although formal diplomatic relations did not begin until 1939. The early records of the apostolic delegates, who primarily resided in Buenos Aires, document anticlericism and religious presecution as well as a close monitoring of the political situation within the country. The records do not have any major gaps. Additional records regarding Uruguay can be located in the archives of other South American nunciatures, particularly Argentina and Brazil, and the Secretariatus Status series *Esteri*.

Reference: Natalini et al., p. 267.

Finding Aids: ASV Indice "Nunziatura Apostolica in Uruguay, 1900–1939," by Sr. Lucina Bianchini, FSP, is available at the circulation desk in the main reading room. The indice is not a formal finding aid and must be used in consultation with the archives staff. The indice presents a brief introduction to the series and then an "Inventario Sommario" and an "Inventario Analitico." The "Inventario Analitico" is very detailed and calendars items in the initial 16 fascios (1900–1922). See also: Argentina, the protocolli in the Archivio della Nunziatura Apostolica in Argentina. The early Protocolli registers in this series cover Uruguay and Paraguay, in addition to Argentina, reflecting the nature of the internunciature.

Location: Archivio Segreto Vaticano.

4.99 Venezuela, Apostolic Nunciature for

[DATABASE ID: VATV415-A]

The post in Venezuela was established in 1874 as an apostolic delegation in Santo Domingo, Haiti, and Venezuela. In 1881 it was held by an apostolic delegate and envoy extraordinary, and then in 1902 became vacant because of political instability. In 1909 a separate apostolic delegate and envoy extraordinary was appointed to Venezuela. The post was raised to a nunciature in 1920. In 1938 the delegate to Venezuela took on responsibility for Barbados; the responsibility was transferred from the jurisdiction of the apostolic delegation in the Antilles. Barbados was transferred to the new apostolic delegation in the Antilles in 1975.

Reference. For a complete list of nuncios (through 1956) see Giuseppe de Marchi, *Le nunziature apostoliche dal 1800 al 1956* (Rome, 1957).

RECORDS. Records of the nunciature consist of the following series.

4.99.1 Archivio della Nunziatura Apostolica in Venezuela
[DATABASE ID: VATV522-A]

Inclusive Dates: 1872–1903 and 1910–1940.

Bulk: 8 linear m. (72 buste or 218 fascicles and 5 volumes).

Organization: Materials are divided according to nuncio. Within the records of each nuncio the following general sub-series often exist: Santo Padre; —Governo; —Segretario di Stato/Curia Romana; —Nunziatura apostolica; —Diocesi; —Apostolato missionario e religioso; —Seminario e clero; —Situazione politico-religiosa; —Protocolli (1913–[post-1922]).

Scope: This series documents religious life in Venezuela as well as the relationship between the Catholic Church and the Venezuelan government, as demonstrated by materials concerning papal mediation of boundary disputes between Venezuela and British Guiana. There are no records for the period beween 1903 and 1909 when political strife and religious persecution disrupted relations. Additional information on the church in Venezuela can be located in the archives of other South American nunciatures, particularly Brazil; the achives of the nunciature in Portugal; and in the Secretariatus Status series *Esteri*.

Reference: Natalini et al., p. 267.

Finding Aids: ASV Indice "Nunziatura Apostolica in Venezuela," by Sr. Lucina Bianchini, FSP, is available at the circulation desk in the main reading room. (The indice is not a formal finding aid and must be used in consultation with the archives staff.) This index briefly introduces the series, covers the archivio from 1872–1939, and contains both an "Inventario Sommario" (1872–1926) and an "Inventario Analitico" (1872–1922, fascio 66). The analytic inventory generally calendars items in each fascio and provides a good overall view of the collection. This largely replaces the internal indici mentioned below. The Protocolli registers are not listed in the index.

"Indice generale dell'Archivio della Delegazione Apostolica della Repubblica di Venezuela in ordine di posizioni, 1893–1899" (with inserts for 1909–1910) is found within the series itself.

Protocolli registers (4 vols. 1913–1915, 1915–[post-1922], and 2 vols. post-1922.) may be of use in locating items within the collection or in ascertaining the scope of business conducted by the nunciature. These are not listed in the index.

Location: Archivio Segreto Vaticano.

4.100 Venice, Apostolic Nunciature for
[DATABASE ID: VATV224-A]

The nunciature for Venice was established in 1500 by Alexander VI and abolished in 1797 with the occupation of Venice by Austria. The post was vacant for two brief periods 1505–1509 and 1528–1532.

The *Archivio della Cancelleria della Nunziatura Veneta* is one of the most complex in the Archivio Segreto Vaticano. It includes material dated between 1226 and 1853. However, there are many parchment documents (pergamene) that may be as early as the year 900. Its total bulk measures 156 linear meters. These records are particularly well known not only for the documents pertaining to the functioning of a nunciature of obvious importance, but also for the collections of documents from monasteries suppressed in the Veneto region and in Tuscany which at various points in time were deposited with the nuncio in Venice.

This series is divided into seven separate series: *Fondo Veneto I*, pergamene (or parchment documents), ca. 900–1800; —*Fondo Veneto II: Monasteri soppressi*, 1300–1853; —*Monasteri soppressi*, 1513–1800; —*Archivio della Nunziatura di Venezia I*, 1658–1795; —*Archivio della Nunziatura di Venezia II*, ca. 1500–1800; —*Fondo Toscano*, 1164–1751; —*[Buste numerate 1–229]*, 1550–ca. 1800. Each of these series is described separately.

In December 1853, a large group of materials arrived in the ASV. These had been requested by the Pope in September of that year and were the contents of the Archivio della Cancelleria della Nunziatura Veneta, which had been inactive since the 1600s. When the collection arrived in 1853, there was a division between the paper and the pergamene. Later, the materials in each of these categories were broken down into *Archivio della Nunziatura di Venezia* and *Monasteri soppressi*, and *Fondo Toscano*. There are now two paper collections of *Archivio della Nunziatura*: *Archivio della Nunziatura di Venezia I* is diplomatic, especially between the secretary of state and the nuncio; *Archivio della Nunziatura di Venezia II* is the background materials developed in the nunciature office. *Fondo Veneto I* is the pergamene; it primarily concerns suppressed monasteries, but the first two blochetti cover pergamene materials that come from the nunciature. *Fondo Veneto II* is the paper materials from the suppressed monasteries (with a bit from the nunciature). *Fondo Toscano* now stands on its own and pertains to monasteries suppressed in the region of Tuscany.

In addition to the records listed below, series listed with other agencies relate directly to this agency and should be consulted. See Secretariatus Status series *Nunziatura di Venezia* and *Nunziature diverse*.

References. For a complete list of nuncios see Henry Biaudet, *Les nonciatures apostoliques permanentes jusqu'en 1648* (Helsinki, 1910); Liisi Karttunen, *Les nonciatures apostoliques permanentes de 1650 à 1800* (Helsinki, 1912); *Repertorium der diplomatischen Vertreter aller Länder seit dem Westfalischen Frieden* (1648) [to 1815] (Oldenburg, 1936–1965).

Boyle, p. 61; Fink, pp. 94, 149–150. The following publications are also useful: A. Stella and A. Bolognetti, ed. *Chiesa e Stato nelle relazione dei nunzi pontifici a Venezia: Ricerche sul giurisdizionalismo veneziano dal XVI al XVIII secolo* (Vatican City, 1964); Pio Cenci, "L'archivio della cancellaria della Nunziatura Veneta," in *Miscellanea Francesco Ehrle* (Rome, 1924), vol. 5, pp. 273–330; F. Gaeta et al., ed., *Nunziature di Venezia* (Rome, 1958–).

RECORDS. Records of the nunciature consist of the following series.

4.100.1 Fondo Veneto I
[DATABASE ID: VATV30015-A]
Inclusive Dates: ca. 900–1799.
Bulk: 16,820 items.
Organization: Items are numbered 1–16820. The order of the convents, canonici, religious orders, and places, etc., is as follows: Nunziatura; —S. Giorgio (Alga); —S. Maria (Orto); —S. Michele (Mirano); —S. Pietro (Oliveto); —S. Pietro (Monte); —S. Brigida; —S. Agostino; —SS. Fermo e Rustico; —S. Rocco; —S. Giovanni di Baldaria; —S. Giovanni Decollato; —S. Maria (Avancia); —S. Giacomo di Monselice; —S. Angelo (Monte); —S. Pietro (Castelco); —S. Giorgio in Braida; —Gesuati; —S. Maria Elis.ta e Buon Gesu; —S. Girolamo (Vincenza); —S. Girolamo (Treviso); —SS. Corpo di Cristo (Brescia); —S. Spirito (Padova); —S. Maria della Grazia (Venezia); —S. Maria della Grazia (Brescia); —S. Maria della Grazia (Vincenza); —S. Girolamo (Padova); —Brescia; —Padova; —Venezia; —Verona; —Vincenza; —Treviso; —Varia; —Appendice.
Note: Fondo Toscano is numbered within this series using nos. 15863–16712; but forms a separate series listed below. Pergamene nos. 1962–3919, 7412, 9702, and 13459–15626 are available on microfilm.
References: Boyle, p. 61; Fink, pp. 94, 149–150. Pio Cenci, "L'archivio della cancellaria della Nunziatura Veneta," in *Miscellanea Francesco Ehrle* (Rome, 1924), vol. 5, pp. 273–330.
Finding Aids: ASV Blochetti III, *Fondo Veneto I,* is 62 vols. of blochetti (essentially a card index bound into 62 volumes). Items are arranged according to religious house, geographic area, subject, etc. The calendar entries proceed item by item and include date and place, the dimensions, a regest of the document, a physical description of each item (material, seals, etc.), and its current segnatura.
Location: Archivio Segreto Vaticano.

4.100.2 Fondo Veneto II: Monasteri soppressi
[DATABASE ID: VATV10501-A]
Inclusive Dates: [ca. 1300–ca. 1700] (bulk 1450–1650).
Bulk: 36 linear m. (912 volume numbers [in some cases there may be more than one volume per number] and 22 buste).
Organization: The series is organized according to religious congregations and then by the individual religious houses. Within each religious house materials are broken down into categories that include: Processi, Istrumenti e carte, Carte e fascicolo ammistrazione.
Finding Aids: ASV Indice 1114 provides a detailed description of the entire series. The index proceeds volume by volume, first identifying the nunciature materials and then treating each suppressed congregation and the religious houses attached to them. Typical entries include the inclusive dates, the volume number, the type of business included in the volume (e.g., "Chartularium 1528–1548 Instrumentum livelli ecclesiae S. Maria in Avancio"), and a physical description of the volume. Researchers should note that additional materials added to the series between 1979 and 1981 from many different religious houses of the suppressed congregations are briefly described out of order on p. 98 of this index.
Location: Archivio Segreto Vaticano. *

4.100.3 Archivio della Nunziatura di Venezia I
[DATABASE ID: VATV430-A]
Inclusive Dates: 1226–1795 (bulk 1735–1795).
Bulk: 4 linear m.
Organization: The series comprises 95 volumes. Vol. 95 was moved to *Archivio della Nunziatura di Venezia II* sometime between 1990 and 1994.
References: Boyle, p. 78; Fink, pp. 85–86.
Finding Aids: ASV Indice 1024–I (fol. 209–215v) lists vols. 1–94. Entries proceed volume by volume and include brief descriptions of the contents (lettere, cifre, minute), inclusive dates, the nuncio involved, a physical description of the volume, the presence of an internal index, and the former and current segnature. ASV Indice 1024–II provides a chronological list of vols. 1–94 of the *Archivio della Nunziatura di Venezia I* between foli 317–319.
Location: Archivio Segreto Vaticano.

4.100.4 Archivio della Nunziatura di Venezia II
[DATABASE ID: VATV550-A]
Inclusive Dates: 1476–ca. 1800 (bulk 1550–1750).
Bulk: 96 linear m. (about 2450 vols. and 40 pacchi)
Organization: Principal subseries: Processi, 1550–1799 (position numbers 1–1840, 27 linear m.); —Allegati, ca. 1550–1800 (position numbers 1841–2417, 50 linear m.); —Lettere suppl. decreti., ca. 1700s (1 linear m.); —Segue pacchi, 40 buste.
Vol. 95 of *Archivio della Nunziatura di Venezia I* was transferred to this series sometime between 1990 and 1994.
Finding Aids: ASV Indice 72*, "Minuta de l'Inventario dell'Archivio della Cancelleria della Nunziatura Veneta dal 1500 al 1899," compiled in the early twentieth century by Mons. Pio Cenci, is available at the ASV reference desk. This inventory provides an outline of the contents of volumes 1–1840. This is a very rough draft. A reorganization and new inventory of *Archivio della Nunziatura di Venezia II* has been done by Giuseppina Roselli (1994).
Location: Archivio Segreto Vaticano.

4.100.5 Monasteri soppressi
[DATABASE ID: VATV10500-A]
Inclusive Dates: 1513–1800.
Bulk: 4.5 linear m.
Organization: This series is divided into three sections: Buste numbered 1–22; —Schedario (.8 linear m.); —[Miscellanea] (.3 linear m.).
Finding Aid: ASV Indice 1114 provides brief contents notes for the 22 numbered buste in this series.
Location: Archivio Segreto Vaticano.

4.100.6 [Buste numerate 1–229]
[DATABASE ID: VATV10502-A]
Inclusive Dates: 1550–ca. 1800.
Bulk: 20 linear m. (229 numbered buste)
Finding Aids: ASV Indice 1024 I lists buste 1–95. A descriptive title and inclusive dates are also indicated. ASV Indice

1024 II provides a chronological listing of buste between the dates 1658 and 1782.

Note: This series does not have an official ASV designation. The title was assigned by the project staff.

Location: Archivio Segreto Vaticano.

4.100.7 Fondo Toscano

[DATABASE ID: VATV345-A]
Inclusive Dates: 1164–1751.
Bulk: 849 items.
Organization: Subseries are: S. Francesco, Siena, 1181–1751, 449 items; —S. Agostino, S. Geminiano, 1164–1749, 162 items; —S. Caterina, S. Geminiano, 1345–1704, 37 items; —S. Francesco, S. Geminiano, 1262–1615, 63 items; —S. Girolamo, S. Geminiano, 1340–1502, 26 items (includes material from S. Marie de Capriglio); —S. Francesco, S. Miniato, 1298–1519, 31 items; —S. Francesco, Colle val d'Elsa, 1279–1735, 35 items; —S. Giacomo, S. Miniato, 1345–1469, 48 items.

Note that items are numbered consecutively within the *Fondo Veneto I* numbering system, beginning with no. 15863 and ending with no. 16712.

References: Boyle, p. 98. Pio Cenci, "L'archivio della cancellaria della Nunziatura Veneta," in *Miscellanea Francesco Ehrle* (Rome, 1924), vol. 5, pp. 310–313, provides a general overview on the different groups represented in the *Fondo Toscana.*

Finding Aids: ASV Blocchetti Indice III, "Fondo Veneto 63–65 or Fondo Toscano 63–65," calendars the entire *Fondo Toscana.* See finding aids description in the entry for *Fondo Veneto I.* Entries indicate the date and place of origin of each document and provide a summary or regest of the item. Physical information (dimensions, seals, etc.) is also often included.

Location: Archivio Segreto Vaticano.

4.101 Vietnam and Cambodia, Apostolic Delegation in

[DATABASE ID: VATV582-A]

In 1964 the apostolic delegation in Indochina was renamed apostolic delegation in Vietnam and Cambodia, and its responsibility was limited to churches in South Vietnam and Cambodia. The delegation was closed in 1976. It was dependent on the Congregation Propaganda Fide.

RECORDS. Records of the delegation consist of the following series.

4.101.1 Archivio della Delegazione Apostolica nel Vietnam

[DATABASE ID: VATV504-A]
Inclusive Dates: 1923–1972.
Bulk: 37 linear m.
Reference: Natalini et al., p. 265.
Location: Archivio Segreto Vaticano.

4.102 West Africa, Apostolic Delegation in

[DATABASE ID: VATV573-A]

The delegation in West Africa was established in 1960 as the successor to the apostolic delegation in French Africa, after the apostolic delegations in Africa were reorganized to meet the needs of the newly independent countries. The delegation was dependent on the Congregation Propaganda Fide and located in Dakar, Senegal. It was responsible for representing the Holy See to churches in Dahomey, Gambia, Ghana, Guinea, Ivory Coast, Mauritania, Niger, Senegal, Sierra Leone, Soudan (Mali), Togo, and Upper Volta. Countries were removed from its responsibility as nuncios were appointed or they became the responsibility of other apostolic delegations: Senegal in 1961; Ghana and Sierra Leone in 1965; Ivory Coast in 1972; Dahomey, Gambia, and Niger in 1971. The office was renamed apostolic delegation in Mali and Mauritania in 1973 and separate nuncios or apostolic delegates were appointed for the remaining countries.

RECORDS. Records of the delegation consist of the following series.

4.102.1 Archivio della Delegazione Apostolica per l'Africa Occidentale

[DATABASE ID: VATV521-A]
Inclusive Dates: 1950–1965.
Bulk: 15 linear m.
Reference: Natalini et al., p. 265.
Location: Archivio Segreto Vaticano.

4.103 West Central Africa, Apostolic Delegation in

[DATABASE ID: VATV557-A]

The delegation in West Central Africa was established in 1960 when apostolic delegations in Africa were reorganized to meet the needs of newly independent countries. Located in Lagos, Nigeria, the delegation was responsible for representing the Holy See to churches in Cameroon, Chad, Gabon, Middle Congo, Nigeria, and Oubangi Chari. The mission was reorganized in 1965 and responsibility for Cameroon, Central African Republic, Chad, Congo (Brazzaville), and Gabon were transferred to a new apostolic delegation in Central Africa; responsibility for Ghana and Sierra Leone were added from the apostolic delegation in West Africa. In 1970 the apostolic delegation in Ghana and Sierra Leone was transferred to the responsibility of the nunciature for Liberia, leaving only Nigeria as the responsibility of the apostolic delegation in West Central Africa. In 1973 the apostolic delegation was renamed apostolic delegation in Nigeria.

RECORDS. Records of the delegation consist of the following series.

4.103.1 Archivio della Delegazione Apostolica in Africa Centrale
[DATABASE ID: VATV40001-A]
Inclusive Dates: 1930–1946.
Bulk: 1 busta.
Reference: Natalini et al., p. 265. According to Natalini, this series includes material relating to Ivory Coast, Togo, Sierra Leone, Gambia, Nigeria, and Cameroon.
Location: Archivio Segreto Vaticano.

4.104 Yugoslavia, Apostolic Nunciature for
[DATABASE ID: VATV388-A]

The nunciature for Yugoslavia was established in 1920. Between 1941 and 1946 the nuncio was absent from Yugoslavia because of wartime conditions but kept his title. Beginning in 1946 the mission was represented by a regent (1946–1950) and a chargé d'affaires (1950–1952). Relations were severed in 1952 when the chargé was expelled. Relations were reestablished in 1966 with the appointment of an apostolic delegate and envoy. In 1970 a new nuncio was appointed.

Reference. For a complete list of nuncios (through 1956) see Giuseppe de Marchi, *Le nunziature apostoliche dal 1800 al 1956* (Rome, 1957).

RECORDS. Records of the nunciature consist of the following series.

4.104.1 Archivio della Nunziatura d'Jugoslavia
[DATABASE ID: VATV551-A]
Inclusive Dates: 1919–1936.
Bulk: 3 linear m.
Reference: Natalini et al., p. 266.
Location: Archivio Segreto Vaticano.

4.105 Zaire, Apostolic Nunciature for
[DATABASE ID: VATV560-A]

An apostolic delegation in the Belgian Congo was established in 1930. In 1947 responsibility for Ruanda-Urundi was added. In 1960 the Congo became independent, and the apostolic delegation continued under that name. (Rwanda and Burundi became independent in 1962.) The missions to the three countries were raised to nunciatures in 1963, with the nuncio to the Congo also serving as nuncio to Rwanda and Burundi. (The Rwanda nunciature was established in 1964.) The Congo was renamed Zaire in 1971.

RECORDS. Records for the delegation consist of the following series.

4.105.1 Archivio della Delegazione Apostolica in Zaire
[DATABASE ID: VATV516-A]
Inclusive Dates: 1930–1954.
Bulk: 22 linear m. (189 boxes containing 470 fascios).
Reference: Natalini et al., p. 267.
Location: Archivio Segreto Vaticano.

PART 5

Papal States

THE PAPAL STATES, ALSO KNOWN AS THE STATES OF THE CHURCH, took shape as a region under the civil control of the papal court during the Middle Ages. The pope's authority over the territory rose and fell with the political fortunes of the various powers interested in Italy, but in the sixteenth century the boundaries of the state became more or less fixed. The state occupied an irregularly shaped area of central Italy, from the Po River in the region of Ferrara through Emilia and Romagna in the north, through the Marches and Umbria in the center, to the patrimony of St. Peter around Rome and Campagna-Marittima in the south, extending as far as Terracina. Pontecorvo and Benevento in southern Italy, and Avignon and the county of Venaissin in France, were noncontiguous areas of the state.

The power of the central government of the Papal States grew in the thirteenth and fourteenth centuries, assuming powers formerly held by local communes, feudal lordships, and tyrants. From the early fourteenth century onward, the Apostolic Camera was responsible for financial control of the state, as well as of the Apostolic See in general.

During the sixteenth century the government of the Papal States evolved into an absolute monarchy, administered by the camerlengo and the secretary of state. In this period a structure of offices grew within the Camera with responsibility for various governmental functions. At the same time, two congregations of cardinals, Buon governo, with responsibility for economic affairs, and Sacra Consulta, with responsibility for administrative and judicial affairs, shared jurisdiction for major parts of the government. A major characteristic of the government of the Papal States was the great diffusion of judicial authority. Most of the offices within the Camera served as tribunals as well as administrative offices, and many other officials had judicial competence, with the title of a tribunal attached to their office along with their chief title. The camerlengo, for instance, was also in charge of the Tribunale criminale del camerlengo and was a member of the Tribunale della Camera apostolica and the Tribunale della piena camera.

The government of the Papal States went through a severe crisis and several reforms during the French revolutionary period that led to a series of reorganizations and reforms in the nineteenth century ending only with the extinction of the state in 1870. A major result of the reforms was to remove the government of the state from the Camera and congregations and make the secretary of state the chief minister of the state, with ultimately a series of ministries under his authority.

In 1798 the pope's authority was overthrown and a republic proclaimed in Rome, comprising all the Papal States less Pesaro and the four legations in the north, which were annexed by the Cisalpine Republic. The republic was in turn overthrown in 1799, and the following year Pius VII entered Rome and instituted a reformed government, but with no significant changes. In 1809 the pope was deposed by the French, the Marches were annexed by the Kingdom of Italy, and the remaining area of the Papal States was annexed by France. The old agencies of government were abolished and a French administration was instituted.

The pope's rule over the Papal States was restored in 1814, and the government was reestablished with few changes. After an insurrection in the north in 1831, Gregory XVI reformed the government, reorganizing the large numbers of tribunals, creating the Segretaria per gli affari di Stato interni to administer the state, and increasing the power of the tesoriere generale to oversee the financial affairs of the state.

The reign of Pius IX (1846–1878) saw a complex series of reforms and reorganizations. In 1846 the Segretaria per gli affari di Stato interni was combined with the secretary of state, who assumed responsibility for administration of the state. In June 1847 a consiglio dei ministri was established, with the secretary of state as president, to unite the major offices of state. In December of the same year the consiglio was reformed, and all the major offices of state were abolished and replaced with ministries. Also in 1847 a consultative assembly was established, the Consulta di Stato. In 1848 the assembly was replaced with a constitutional assembly, the Consiglio di Stato.

In November 1848 the Pope fled Rome, and a few months later a republic was proclaimed. When he was restored to rule in 1850, Pius IX abandoned the constitutional government of 1848, and ruled through the secretary of state and the Consiglio dei ministri, along with a consultative Consiglio di Stato.

In 1860 all the territory of the Papal States except the Patrimony of St. Peter (the region around Rome) was annexed to the Kingdom of Sardinia (later renamed Kingdom of Italy). The Patrimony was annexed by Italy in 1870, ending the pope's rule over the Papal States.

Individual offices within the government of the Papal States have separate agency histories in the sections that follow. Please note that in 1870 with the annexation of the Patrimony of St. Peter to the newly formed Italian state, a decision was made to transfer records of the Holy See that pertained to the administration of civil affairs in the Papal States to a repository under the control of the state. Therefore most, but not all, the records listed in this section can be found in the Archivio di Stato di Roma. The records of the Archivio di Stato di Roma were not inventoried by the project staff. The project relied on information in the section titled "Archivio di Stato di Roma," by Edvige Aleandri Barletta and Carla Lodolini Tupputi, in *Guida generale degli Archivi di Stato Italiani*, edited by Piero D'Angiolini and Claudio Pavone (Rome, 1986); and *L'Archivio di Stato di Roma: Epitome di una guida degli archivi dell'amministrazione centrale dello Stato Pontificio*, by Armando Lodolini (Rome, 1960). Researchers should note that these guides describe the size of record series in terms of volumes, boxes, or other containers, not in linear meters, and so are not strictly comparable to descriptions of records in the Archivio Segreto Vaticano and select other repositories where the project staff was able to secure linear measurements.

It is important to note that probably more than any other office, the Apostolic Camera for most of its history served both the spiritual and temporal interests of the Holy See. Many of the offices listed among the adminstrative divisions of the Papal States, described in this section, were dependent on the Camera. In this guide the Camera is listed among the offices of the Roman Curia of which it was officially a part. However, researchers interested in the administrative history of the Papal States should become familiar with that particular record series.

Note also that several record groups were found for agencies for which histories could not be located. These are placed at the end of the section and are so noted.

5.1 GENERAL ADMINISTRATION

5.1.1 Alto consiglio
[DATABASE ID: VATV816-A]

This agency was established in the 1848 constitution of the Papal States, replacing in part the Consulta di Stato.

RECORDS. No records for this agency could be located, but series listed with another agency relate directly to this agency and should be consulted. See Papal States miscellaneous series *Miscellanea del periodo costituzionale*.

5.1.2 Amministrazione dei beni camerali
[DATABASE ID: VATV659-A]

This agency was active in the nineteenth century.

RECORDS. No records for this agency could be located.

5.1.3 Amministrazione dei boschi e delle foreste
[DATABASE ID: VATV730-A]

Established in 1827 to assure Rome of sufficient fuel wood, this agency was dependent on the tesoriere generale. The administration was located in Civitavecchia, but was responsible for forests in all the Papal States.

RECORDS. Records of the agency consist of the following series.

5.1.3.1 Amministrazione dei boschi e delle foreste camerali
[DATABASE ID: VATV20153-A]
Inclusive Dates: 1814–1858 (bulk 1827–1858).
Bulk: 34 buste and 1 registro.
References: D'Angiolini, p. 1174; Lodolini (1960), p. 198.
Finding Aid: Summary inventory.
Location: Archivio di Stato di Roma.

5.1.4 Amministrazione dei sali e tabacchi
[DATABASE ID: VATV850-A]

A cameral administration, also known as Regia pontificia dei sali e tabacchi, this agency was responsible for production of salt and tobacco.

RECORDS. Records of the agency consist of the following series.

5.1.4.1 Amministrazione dei sali e tabacchi
[DATABASE ID: VATV20152-A]
Inclusive Dates: 1821–1870 (bulk 1836–1870).
Bulk: 97 buste; 386 rubrice, protocolli, and registri.
References: D'Angiolini, p. 1174; Lodolini (1960), p. 196.
Finding Aid: Summary inventory, 1970.
Location: Archivio di Stato di Roma.

5.1.5 Amministrazione della deviazione dell'Aniene
[DATABASE ID: VATV774-A]

This agency is related to diversion of the Aniene River at Tivoli. In 1847 its responsibility was taken over by the Prefettura generale delle acque e strade.

RECORDS. Records of the agency consist of the following series.

5.1.5.1 Amministrazione della deviazione dell'Aniene
[DATABASE ID: VATV20180-A]
Inclusive Dates: 1831–1848.
Bulk: 21 buste and 1 registro.
References: D'Angiolini, p. 1187; Lodolini (1960), p. 153.
Finding Aids: Summary inventory; partial index, 1880.
Location: Archivio di Stato di Roma.

5.1.5.2 Commissione consultiva per la deviazione dell'Aniene
[DATABASE ID: VATV20179-A]
Inclusive Dates: 1826–1828.
Bulk: 6 buste and 7 registri.
References: D'Angiolini, p. 1187; Lodolini (1960), p. 153.
Finding Aid: Summary inventory.
Location: Archivio di Stato di Roma.

5.1.6 Amministrazione delle saline di Cervia e di Comacchio
[DATABASE ID: VATV725-A]

This agency was dependent on the Direzione generale delle dogane. It was active in the first half of the nineteenth century.

RECORDS. Records of the agency consist of the following series.

5.1.6.1 Amministrazione delle saline di Cervia e di Comacchio
[DATABASE ID: VATV20147-A]
Inclusive Dates: 1815–1857.
Bulk: 127 buste.
References: D'Angiolini, p. 1172; Lodolini (1960), p. 197.
Finding Aid: Summary inventory.
Location: Archivio di Stato di Roma.

5.1.7 Auditor Camerae
[DATABASE ID: VATV715-A]

In the thirteenth century the office of Auditor Camerae was established and given responsibility for administrative work relating to justice, including personnel and discipline, and for handling of judicial cases. The uditore was the chief judge in all cases concerning the financial administration of the curia. The auditor general's office attained such importance that to refer to it one had only to use the initials A.C. (Auditor Camerae). This office remained unaltered even after the reform of

Pius IV in 1562 and of Clement VIII in 1596. Nevertheless, for a short time in the middle of the fifteenth century the office of auditor was suppressed by Paul IV, who substituted for it a new position of Regent (constitution *Si ex praecepto*, 1558) with the same powers and faculties of the camerlengo and the vice-camerlengo. This position lasted but a short time; it was suppressed by Pius IV (constitution *Romano Pontifex*, Apr. 14, 1561) and the office of auditor general was reinstated along with all its former powers (constitution *Ad examiae devotionis*, May 1, 1561).

In 1800 responsibility for appeals of criminal cases from diocesan curias was transferred from the uditore to the Congregation of Bishops and Regulars. In 1847 the uditore became a member of the Consiglio dei ministri. Later that year the uditore was transformed into the Ministero di grazia e giustizia and ceased its judicial function.

RECORDS. Records of the agency consist of the following series.

5.1.7.1 Uditorato generale della Camera apostolica
[DATABASE ID: VATV20135-A]
Inclusive Dates: 1818–1847.
Bulk: 15 buste, 13 protocolli, and 2 rubricelle.
References: D'Angiolini, p. 1159; Lodolini (1960), p. 207.
Finding Aid: Summary inventory.
Location: Archivio di Stato di Roma.

5.1.8 Avvocato del fisco
[DATABASE ID: VATV789-A]

This was an office of the Camera Apostolica.

RECORDS. No records for this agency could be located.

5.1.9 Avvocato e procuratore dei poveri
[DATABASE ID: VATV790-A]

This was an office of the Camera Apostolica.

RECORDS. No records for this agency could be located.

5.1.10 Camera Apostolica
[DATABASE ID: VATV034-A]

Probably more than any other office, the Apostolic Camera for most of its history served both the spiritual and temporal interests of the Holy See. Many of the offices listed among the agencies of the Papal States were dependent on the Camera. In this guide the Camera and its records are listed in the section "Roman Curia: Offices." Anyone interested in the financial history of the Papal States should, however, become familiar with cameral records.

5.1.11 Camera di commercio di Roma
[DATABASE ID: VATV892-A]

This agency was established in 1831 by the Secretariatus Status.

RECORDS. Records of the agency consist of the following series.

5.1.11.1 Camera di commercio di Roma
[DATABASE ID: VATV20375-A]
Inclusive Dates: 1831–1871.
Bulk: 42 buste.
Reference: D'Angiolini, p. 1223.
Finding Aid: Inventory, 1962.
Location: Archivio di Stato di Roma.

5.1.12 Cancelleria delle carceri nuove
[DATABASE ID: VATV666-A]

This agency was active in the nineteenth century.

RECORDS. Records of the agency consist of the following series.

5.1.12.1 Carceri nuove
[DATABASE ID: VATV20204-A]
Inclusive Dates: 1811–1870 (bulk 1835–1870).
Bulk: 104 buste; 198 registri and protocolli.
References: D'Angiolini, pp. 1193–1194; Lodolini (1960), p. 123.
Finding Aid: Summary inventory, 1970.
Location: Archivio di Stato di Roma.

5.1.13 Carabinieri pontifici
[DATABASE ID: VATV124-A]

The carabinieri were established in 1816 for police duty and the enforcement of justice. Their authority was partly police and partly military, and they were dependent on the Direzione generale di polizia. They were formed into two regiments, located in Rome and Bologna. In 1848 the bersaglieri were merged into the carabinieri. After siding with the republican government in 1848, the carabinieri were suppressed when the pope's authority was restored in 1849. They were replaced by the gendarmeria.

RECORDS. No records for this agency could be located.

5.1.14 Cavalieri di guardia de N. S.
[DATABASE ID: VATV112-A]

The Cavaliere di guardia was disbanded in 1798 when the French occupied Rome. It was succeeded by the Pontifical Noble Guard.

RECORDS. No records for this agency could be located.

5.1.15 Chierici di camera
[DATABASE ID: VATV603-A]

The camerlengo, chief officer of the Camera Apostolica, was assisted in his many duties by various collaborators called *chierici* (*clerici*) *camerae*. Eugene IV organized them into a college and gave them their first statutes (*In eminenti*, Jul. 6, 1444). They varied in number throughout the centuries. Eugene IV set the number at seven (constitution *Inter cetera gravia*, Jul. 11, 1438). Pius V raised it to twelve (*Romanus Pontifex*, Mar. 7, 1571); Gregory XIII (1572–1585) reduced it to eight; Sixtus V (1585–1590) increased it to ten, then twelve. From Leo XIII (1878–1903) on, there were nine. From the chierici developed the posts of vice-camerlengo (later also governor of Rome); auditor general (with functions chiefly judiciary); and treasurer general (charged with all financial activities of the papacy). Several special assignments, branching off from the office of the camerlengo, subsequently developed into independent offices.

Until 1870 the chierici managed the property and income of the Holy See, and officiated as a court in disputes affecting the papal exchequer. In 1828, four chierici were appointed to a commission to examine the accounts of the Camera. Pius IX, after the installation of ministerial government in 1847, assigned each clerk the presidency of a section of the Ministry of Finance. During periods of papal vacancy (sede vacante) the clerks took possession of the apostolic palaces, made an inventory, and managed the internal or domestic administration until the new pope took power.

With the pope's loss of temporal power in 1870 every remaining competence exercised by the Camera during the papal administration was lost; there remained only the function to be exercised during the sede vacante. In 1878, so that the chierici of the Camera would not remain inactive because of the changed territorial conditions of the Holy See, Leo XIII decreed that their college would form the first section of prelates attached to the Congregation of the Council charged with the revision of the quinquennial reports on the general state of the dioceses that the residential bishops had to submit to the Holy See.

The principal chierici (all of which have separate agency histories) are: prefetto dell'annona, presidente della grascia, presidente delle strade, commissario (intendente) delle armi, presidente delle dogane, prefetto di Castel Sant'Angelo, prefetto degli archivi, commissario del mare, presidente della zecca, presidente delle ripe, presidente degli acquedotti, and presidente delle carceri. The chierici together formed the Tribunale della Camera. For the most important questions all joined together in the Tribunale della piena camera.

RECORDS. No records specific to this group as a whole could be located. See various agencies as indicated in the history for related material.

5.1.16 Collegio dei notai capitolini
[DATABASE ID: VATV897-A]

This college was established by Julius II in 1507. In 1586 Sixtus V reorganized the office and fixed the number of notaries at thirty. The college was under the jurisdiction of the Camera Apostolica but notaries were nominated by the conservatori. The notaries acted as cancellieri of the Tribunale del senatore. The college was abolished in 1847 and the notaries placed under the jurisdiction of the Ministero dell'interno.

In addition to the records listed below, series listed with another agency relate directly to this agency and should be consulted. See Papal States miscellaneous series *Testamenti segreti*.

RECORDS. Records of the agency consist of the following series.

5.1.16.1 Collegio dei notai capitolini
[DATABASE ID: VATV20380-A]
Inclusive Dates: 1588–1833.
Bulk: 13 registri.
Organization: Subseries are: Entrata e uscita, 1588–1638; —Verbali della Congregazione dei notai capitolini, 1667–1749 and 1814–1833; —Verbali della Congregazione dei sindaci, 1687–1730; —Depositario A. Bardi, 1642–1644 and 1667–1682.
Reference: D'Angiolini, p. 1216.
Finding Aid: Inventory.
Location: Archivio di Stato di Roma.

5.1.16.2 Miscellanea dei notai capitolini
[DATABASE ID: VATV20382-A]
Inclusive Dates: 1223–1833 (bulk 1347–1638).
Bulk: 1,939 vols. and 1 rubricella.
Organization: [Prima parte], 1223–1628 (bulk 1347–1628). 1,920 vols.; —[Seconda parte], 1588–1833. 19 vols. and 1 rubricella.
Scope: [Prima parte]: Fourteenth century, 10 vols.; —Fifteenth century, 175 vols.; —Fifteenth–Seventeenth century, 15 vols.; —Sixteenth century, 1,632 vols.; —Sixteenth–Seventeenth century, 12 vols.; —Seventeenth century, 76 vols.
References: D'Angiolini, p. 1212; Lodolini (1960), p. 60.
Finding Aids: [Prima parte]: Printed list of notai; alphabetical index by notaio; chronological list; old inventories; index of some protocolli.
Location: Archivio di Stato di Roma.

5.1.16.3 Notai capitolini
[DATABASE ID: VATV20381-A]
Inclusive Dates: 1477–1899.
Bulk: 23,466 vols., 298 repertorii, 9 buste, and 2 fascicoli.
Organization: Ufficio 1, 1538–1899: 1,168 vols. istrumenti, 32 vols. testamenti, 7 repertorii and 1 rubricella; —Ufficio 2, 1568–1884: 885 vols. and 1 repertorio; —Ufficio 3,

1477–1855: 753 vols. istrumenti, 5 vols. testamenti, 13 vols. protesti, 16 repertorii, and 6 rubricelle; —Ufficio 4, 1522–1878: 837 vols. istrumenti, 12 vols. testamenti, 13 vols. protesti, 10 repertorii, 5 rubricelle and 9 buste; —Ufficio 5, 1586–1898: 636 vols. and 10 repertorii; —Ufficio 6, 1562–1884: 882 vols. istrumenti, 2 vols. testamenti, 8 repertorii and 5 rubricelle; —Ufficio 7, 1578–1847: 561 vols. and 1 rubricella; —Ufficio 8, 1585–1866: 783 vols. istrumenti, 13 vols. testamenti, 10 repertorii, and 1 rubricella; —Ufficio 9, 1553–1884: 864 vols., 16 repertorii, and 5 rubricelle; —Ufficio 10, 1560–1875: 537 vols. istrumenti and 4 vols. testamenti; —Ufficio 11, 1576–1875: 541 vols. istrumenti, 7 vols. testamenti, and 3 repertorii; —Ufficio 12, 1544–1854: 450 vols, 6 repertorii, 1 rubricella, and 1 vol. protesti; —Ufficio 13, 1510–1879: 980 vols. istrumenti, 9 vols. testamenti, 6 vols. protesti, 6 rubricelle, and 13 repertorii; —Ufficio 14, 1550–1888: 681 vols. istrumenti, 41 vols. testamenti, 24 vols. protesti, and 14 repertorii; —Ufficio 15, 1577–1877: 688 vols. istrumenti, 23 vols. testamenti, and 24 vols. protesti.

Ufficio 16, 1511–1897: 679 vols. istrumenti, 36 vols. testamenti, 7 vols. protesti, and 24 repertorii; —Ufficio 17, 1567–1866: 866 vols. istrumenti, 30 vols. testamenti, 5 repertorii, and 1 fascicolo; —Ufficio 18, 1548–1898:. 757 vols. istrumenti, 23 vols. testamenti, 2 repertorii, and 1 rubricella; —Ufficio 19, 1576–1884: 785 vols., 13 vols. protesti, 52 repertorii, and 2 rubricelle; —Ufficio 20, 1570–1888: 692 vols. istrumenti, 2 vols. testamenti, 10 repertorii, and 3 rubricelle; —Ufficio 21, 1563–1876: 904 vols. istrumenti, 18 vols. testamenti, 6 vols. protesti, and 5 repertorii; —Ufficio 22, 1565–1887: 757 vols. istrumenti, 16 vols. testamenti, 2 vols. protesti, 10 repertorii, and 3 rubricelle; —Ufficio 23, 1560–1888: 759 vols. istrumenti, 3 vols. testamenti, 1 perizia, 2 sommari, 24 repertorii, 22 rubricelle, and 1 fascicolo; —Ufficio 24, 1579–1891: 763 vols., 3 vols. protesti, 19 repertorii, and 1 rubricella; —Ufficio 25, 1578–1867: 679 vols. istrumenti, 12 vols. testamenti, and 1 repertorio; —Ufficio 26, 1568–1856: 1,120 vols. istrumenti, 23 vols. testamenti, 3 repertorii, and 1 vol. protesti; —Ufficio 27, 1573–1884: 678 vols. istrumenti, 33 vols. testamenti, 6 repertorii, and 2 rubricelle; —Ufficio 28, 1545–1896: 906 vols. istrumenti, 16 vols. testamenti, 17 vols. protesti, 4 rubricelle, and 11 repertorii; —Ufficio 29, 1571–1885: 638 vols., 1 repertorio, and 1 rubricella; —Ufficio 30, 1579–1875: 747 vols. istrumenti, 8 vols. testamenti, 2 vols. protesti, 6 repertorii, and 2 rubricelle.

Scope: Ufficio 1: Sixteenth century, 49 vols. istrumenti and 1 vol. testamenti; —Seventeenth century, respectively 505 and 15; —Eighteenth century, 400 and 11; —Nineteenth century, 214 and 5.

Ufficio 2: Sixteenth century, 7 vols.; —Seventeenth century, 455 vols.; —Eighteenth century, 290 vols. and 1 vol. testamenti; —Nineteenth century, 132 vols.

Ufficio 3: Fifteenth century, 5 vols. istrumenti; —Sixteenth century, 62 vol. istrumenti and 1 vol. testamenti; —Seventeenth century, 230 vols. istrumenti and 1 vol. testamenti; —Eighteenth century, 235 vols. istrumenti and 3 vols. testamenti; —Nineteenth century, 221 vols. istrumenti and 13 vol. protesti.

Ufficio 4: Sixteenth century, 57 vols. istrumenti and 2 vol. testamenti; —Seventeenth century, respectively 284 and 9; —Eighteenth century, respectively 241 and 1; —Nineteenth century, 255 vols. istrumenti and 13 vols. protesti.

Ufficio 5: Sixteenth century, 13 vols.; —Seventeenth century, 252 vols.; —Eighteenth century, 201 vols.; —Nineteenth century, 170 vol.

Ufficio 6: Sixteenth century, 43 vols.; —Seventeenth century, 331 vols. istrumenti and 2 vols. testamenti; —Eighteenth century, 299 vols. istrumenti; —Nineteenth century, 208 vols. istrumenti and 1 vols. protesti.

Ufficio 7: Sixteenth century, 31 vols.; —Seventeenth century, 255 vols.; —Eighteenth century, 208 vols.; —Nineteenth century, 67 vols.

Ufficio 8: Sixteenth century, 29 vols.; —Seventeenth century, 316 vols. istrumenti and 5 vols. testamenti; —Eighteenth century, 275 vols. istrumenti and 8 vols. testamenti; —Nineteenth century, 163 vols.

Ufficio 9: Sixteenth century, 44 vols.; —Seventeenth century, 275 vols.; —Eighteenth century, 287 vols.; —Nineteenth century, 255 vols. and 3 broliardi.

Ufficio 10: Sixteenth century, 32 vols.; —Seventeenth century, 202 vols.; —Eighteenth century, 172 vols. and 4 vols. testamenti; —Nineteenth century, 131 vols.

Ufficio 11: Sixteenth century, 21 vols.; —Seventeenth century, 230 vols. istrumenti and 3 vols. testamenti; —Eighteenth century, 195 vols. istrumenti and 4 vols. testamenti; —Nineteenth century, 95 vols.

Ufficio 12: Sixteenth century, 31 vols.; —Seventeenth century, 154 vols.; —Eighteenth century, 191 vols.; —Nineteenth century, 74 vols. and 1 vol. protesti.

Ufficio 13 Sixteenth century, 83 vols.; —Seventeenth century, 368 vols. and 5 vols. testamenti; —Eighteenth century, 335 vols. and 4 vols. testamenti; —Nineteenth century, 194 vols. istrumenti and 6 vols. protesti.

Ufficio 14: Sixteenth century, 54 vols.; —Seventeenth century, 203 vols. and 8 vols. testamenti; —Eighteenth century, 206 vols. and 22 vols. testamenti; —Nineteenth century, 218 vols., 11 vols. testamenti and 24 vols. protesti.

Ufficio 15: Sixteenth century, 12 vols.; —Seventeenth century, 275 vols. istrumenti and 13 vols. testamenti; —Eighteenth century, 260 vols. istrumenti and 18 vols. testamenti; —Nineteenth century, 141 vols. and 3 vols. testamenti.

Ufficio 16: Sixteenth century, 12 vols.; —Seventeenth century, 244 vols. and 13 vols. testamenti; —Eighteenth century, 223 vols. and 21 vols. testamenti; —Nineteenth century, 200 vols. and 2 vols. testamenti.

Ufficio 17: Sixteenth century, 48 vols. and 1 vol. testamenti; —Seventeenth century, 389 vols. and 24 vols. testamenti; —Eighteenth century, 294 vols. istrumenti and 5 vols. testamenti; —Nineteenth century, 135 vols.

Ufficio 18: Sixteenth century, 36 vols. istrumenti and 1 vol. testamenti; —Seventeenth century, 287 vols. and 10 vols. testamenti; —Eighteenth century 302 vols. and 12 vols. testamenti; —Nineteenth century, 132 vols.

Ufficio 19: Sixteenth century, 33 vols.; —Seventeenth century, 224 vols.; —Eighteenth century, 269 vols.; —Nineteenth century, 259 vols.

Ufficio 20: Sixteenth century, 18 vols. and 1 vol. testamenti; —Seventeenth century, 209 vols. and 1 vol. testamenti; —Eighteenth century, 252 vols.; —Nineteenth century, 213 vols.

Ufficio 21: Sixteenth century, 46 vols. istrumenti and 2 vols. testamenti; —Seventeenth century, 277 vols. and 8 vols.

testamenti; —Eighteenth century, 307 vols. and 7 vols. testamenti; —Nineteenth century, 274 vols. and 1 vol. testamenti.

Ufficio 22: Sixteenth century, 45 vols.; —Seventeenth century, 318 vols. and 12 vols. testamenti; —Eighteenth century, 235 vols. and 3 vols. testamenti; —Nineteenth century, 159 vols. and 2 vols. protesti.

Ufficio 23: Sixteenth century, 39 vols. istrumenti and 1 vol. testamenti; —Seventeenth century, 181 vols. and 1 vol. testamenti; —Eighteenth century, 269 vols. and 1 vol. testamenti; —Nineteenth century, 270 vols., 1 perizia, and 2 sommari.

Ufficio 24: Sixteenth century, 26 vols.; —Seventeenth century, 204 vols.; —Eighteenth century, 223 vols.; —Nineteenth century, 310 vols. testamenti.

Ufficio 25: Sixteenth century, 47 vols.; —Seventeenth century, 337 vols. and 10 vols. testamenti; —Eighteenth century, 202 vols. and 2 vols. testamenti; —Nineteenth century, 93 vols.

Ufficio 26: Sixteenth century, 34 vols.; —Seventeenth century, 506 vols. and 14 vols. testamenti; —Eighteenth century, 389 vols. and 8 vols. testamenti; —Nineteenth century, 191 vols., 1 vol. testamenti and 1 vol. protesti.

Ufficio 27: Sixteenth century, 62 vols. and 6 vols. testamenti; —Seventeenth century, 233 vols. and 17 vols. testamenti; —Eighteenth century, 218 vols. and 10 vols. testamenti; —Nineteenth century, 165 vols.

Ufficio 28: Sixteenth century, 108 vols.; —Seventeenth century, 330 vols. and 15 vols. testamenti; —Eighteenth century, 248 vols. and 1 vol. testamenti; —Nineteenth century, 220 vol.

Ufficio 29: Sixteenth century, 23 vols.; —Seventeenth century, 180 vols.; —Eighteenth century, 276 vols.; —Nineteenth century, 159 vols.

Ufficio 30: Sixteenth century, 44 vols. and 2 vols. testamenti; —Seventeenth century, 236 vols. and 5 vols. testamenti; —Eighteenth century, 235 vols. and 1 vol. testamenti; —Nineteenth century, 232 vols. and 2 vols. protesti.

References: D'Angiolini, pp. 1213–1216; Lodolini (1960), pp. 60–61.

Finding Aids: Printed list of notai; separate inventories of single offices.

Location: Archivio di Stato di Roma.

5.1.17 Commissariato delle armi
[DATABASE ID: VATV792-A]

This agency was established circa 1634 with responsibility for the Papal States militia. The commissario was a chierico di camera. In 1797 it was united with the Commissariato della mare to form the Congregazione militare.

In addition to the records listed below, series listed with another agency relate directly to this agency and should be consulted. See Papal States, Presidenza delle armi series *Soldatesche e galere.*

RECORDS. Records of the agency consist of the following series.

5.1.17.1 Registro di lettere e Lettere di negozio militare di . . .
[DATABASE ID: VATV316-A]
Inclusive Dates: 1643–1749.
Bulk: 85 linear m. (984 vol. nos.).
Organization: Two subseries: Registro di lettere; —Lettere di negozio militare di. . . . The series are intermixed but roughly chronological. Lettere are arranged by location (Ferrara, Civitavecchia, etc.) then chronologically. Registro is arranged chronologically.
Scope: Incoming letters (Lettere di . . .) and outgoing correspondence (Registro). Some of the Registro volumes are indexed by city, with a note concerning the correspondent. This is followed by a number that leads the researcher to both a page number in the Registro and in the Lettere volume that treats the particular city and year. These indices are not complete. Otherwise, locating a letter and a response is difficult.
Note: Volumes in this series were originally interspersed with the Tesoriere generale series [*Archivio*].
References: Fink, p. 131; Boyle, p. 56.
Finding Aids: ASV Indice 195A lists the volumes with their former arrangement and numbers, provides the full title and inclusive dates of each, noting which volumes are now part of the Tesoriere generale series [*Archivio*]. There is also a loose sheet of paper in the front of this volume that lists Registro, Lettere, and Tesoriere generale volumes with their old and new numbers and series designations.

ASV Indice 223, "Inventario delle materie dell'Archivio Camerale-Diversorum," is an old index to this series that does not provide the current segnature. It does, however, provide more detailed contents descriptions.
Location: Archivio Segreto Vaticano.

5.1.17.2 [Miscellanea SF/507]
[DATABASE ID: VATV10127-A]
Inclusive Dates: 1691–1792.
Bulk: .2 linear m.
Scope: Items included are: 1. Decisione contro le pretensioni del Castellano della Rocca di Fano, 1669–1730; —2. Registro soldati giubilati dell'infrascritti presidi doppo i novi piani formati in virtù di motu proprio di Nostro Signor Papa Clemente XIV dalli 21 Maggio 1770; —3. Compendio di regolamenti militari da osservanda per la guardia giornaliera nella piazza di Civitavecchia, 1770; —4. Misc., 1691–1692; —5. Rubricella delle patenti, 1741–1751; —6. Misc., 1792; —7. Ristretto de viveri somministrati e denari pagati dall'annona di Roma per le regie armate Austriaca e Napolitana, 1744–1745; —8. Account book, [16—].
Note: This collection does not have an official ASV designation. The title was assigned by the project staff based on the location of the material in 1990.
Location: Archivio Segreto Vaticano.

5.1.18 Commissariato delle mare
[DATABASE ID: VATV791-A]

This agency was responsible for galleys, soldiers, maritime fortresses, towers, and Castel Sant'Angelo. The commissario was a chierico di camera. At the end of the eighteenth century it was united with the Commissariato delle armi to form the Congregazione militare.

RECORDS. No records for this agency could be located, but series listed with another agency relate directly to this agency and should be consulted. See Papal States, Presidenza delle armi series *Soldatesche e galere*.

5.1.19 Commissariato generale
[DATABASE ID: VATV605-A]

The origins of this office are uncertain. It may have been established during the fifteenth century. It was a subordinate office of the Camera Apostolica and was concerned with the finances of the church and the Papal States.

RECORDS. Records of the agency consist of the following series.

5.1.19.1 Commissariato generale della Camera apostolica
[DATABASE ID: VATV20105-A]
Inclusive Dates: 1801–1818.
Bulk: 20 buste.
Ristretti fiscali della sacra consulta, 1801–1818, 16 buste; —Allegationes advocati pauperum, 1801–1804, 4 buste.
Reference: D'Angiolini, p. 1143.
Finding Aid: Summary inventory, 1977.
Location: Archivio di Stato di Roma.

5.1.19.2 Commissario generale della Camera apostolica
[DATABASE ID: VATV20019-A]
Inclusive Dates: 1582–1870.
Bulk: 940 vols. and 25 registri.
Organization: Informationes diversorum, 1582–1605, 10 vols.; —Informationes de Rubeis, 1642–1672, 36 vols.; —Informationes de Rubeis, 1661–1682, 23 vols.;—Instrumenta cameralia, 1602–1869, 368 vols. and 12 vols. of old indexes; —Collectio prima: diversorum cameralium, 1612–1679, 6 vols.; —Collectio secunda: diversorum cameralium, 1726–1766, 28 vols.; —Collectio de Cavaleriis et Rubini, 1737–1756, 31 vols.; —Collectio Campilli, 1737–1756, 38 vols.; —Collectio Buferli, 1773–1779, 6 vols.; —Collectio Nicolai, 1806–1809, 12 vols.; —Collectio Gasparri, 1814–1829, 73 vols.; —Collectio Perfetti, 1823–1829, 65 vols.; —Collectio Gasparri Fabricius, 1829–1832, 23 vols.; —Collectio Vannini, 1832–1855, 76 vols. and 8 registri; —Collectio Pagnoncelli, 1855–1861, 30 vols. and 5 registri; —Collectio Vassalli, 1861–1870, 6 vols. and 12 registri; —Collectio Benetti, 1830–1853, 40 vols.; —Collectio Bartoli, 1831–1853, 18 vols.; —Collectio Vasselli, 1831–1870, 44 vols.; —Collectio Giansanti, 1853, 5 vols.
References: D'Angiolini, pp. 1086–1087; Lodolini (1960), pp. 76–78.
Finding Aids: There are some old inventories for this series; a partial summary inventory was prepared in 1977.
Location: Archivio di Stato di Roma.

5.1.19.3 Congregazioni particolari deputate
[DATABASE ID: VATV20018-A]
Inclusive Dates: 1545 and 1672–1767.

Bulk: 103 buste.
References: D'Angiolini, pp. 1087–1088; Lodolini (1960), pp. 85–88.
Finding Aids: There is an inventory, by file, with alphabetical index by names and subjects; another alphabetical index, less complete and including an obsolete numeration scheme, is combined with the inventories for the series *Commissario generale della Camera apostolica*.
Location: Archivio di Stato di Roma.

5.1.20 Commissariato generale delle ferrovie
[DATABASE ID: VATV713-A]

Established in 1858 to supervise railroads in the Papal States, this agency was suppressed in 1861. It was dependent on the Ministero dei lavori pubblici, which took responsibility for railroads after the commissariato's suppression.

RECORDS. Records of the agency consist of the following series.

5.1.20.1 Commissariato generale delle ferrovie
[DATABASE ID: VATV20181-A]
Inclusive Dates: 1856–1871.
Bulk: 63 buste.
References: D'Angiolini, p. 1187; Lodolini (1960), pp. 206–207.
Finding Aid: Printed inventory.
Location: Archivio di Stato di Roma.

5.1.21 Commissione consultiva per il miglioramento della finanza pubblica
[DATABASE ID: VATV20154-A]

Established in 1819, this agency had responsibility for state contracts, estimates of agencies and provinces, and reform proposals.

RECORDS. Records of the agency consist of the following series.

5.1.21.1 Commissione consultiva per il miglioramento della finanza pubblica
[DATABASE ID: VATV20154-A]
Inclusive Dates: 1815–1822.
Bulk: 25 buste.
References: D'Angiolini, p. 1174; Lodolini (1960), p. 182.
Finding Aids: Summary inventory.
Location: Archivio di Stato di Roma.

5.1.22 Commissione dei crediti camerali arretrati
[DATABASE ID: VATV656-A]

This commission was established in 1833 by the tesoriere generale.

RECORDS. Records of the commission consist of the following series.

5.1.22.1 Commissione dei crediti camerali arretrati
[DATABASE ID: VATV20156-A]
Inclusive Dates: 1833.
Bulk: 19 buste and 3 vols.
References: D'Angiolini, p. 1175; Lodolini (1960), p. 182.
Finding Aid: Summary inventory.
Location: Archivio di Stato di Roma.

5.1.23 Commissione delle recupere
[DATABASE ID: VATV779-A]

This commission was established in 1849 by the prefect of police of Rome (Direzione generale di polizia).

RECORDS. No records for this commission could be located.

5.1.24 Commissione deputata per il recupero dei beni e diritti ecclesiastici in Faenza
[DATABASE ID: VATV883-A]

This commission was established in 1827 to recover cameral property.

RECORDS. Records of the commission consist of the following series.

5.1.24.1 Commissione deputata per il recupero dei beni e diritti ecclesiastici in Faenza
[DATABASE ID: VATV20170-A]
Inclusive Dates: [18—].
Bulk: 4 buste.
Reference: D'Angiolini, p. 1180.
Location: Archivio di Stato di Roma.

5.1.25 Commissione di liquidazione dei crediti a tutto giugno 1849
[DATABASE ID: VATV703-A]

This commission was established in 1849 by the Ministero delle finanze to liquidate debts incurred by the Roman republic of 1849 and by the previous papal administration, as well as to indemnify for war damage and requisitions.

RECORDS. Records of the commission consist of the following series.

5.1.25.1 Commissione di liquidazione dei crediti a tutto giugno 1849
[DATABASE ID: VATV20161-A]
Inclusive Dates: 1849.
Bulk: 103 buste and 7 registri.
References: D'Angiolini, p. 1177; Lodolini (1960), p. 214.
Finding Aid: Summary inventory.
Location: Archivio di Stato di Roma.

5.1.26 Commissione di revisione dei conti consuntivi anteriori al 1850
[DATABASE ID: VATV839-A]

This commission was established in 1854 by the secretary of state to examine the final accounts for the years prior to the establishment of the Consulta di Stato per le finanze.

RECORDS. Records of the commission consist of the following series.

5.1.26.1 Commissione di revisione dei conti consuntivi anteriori al 1850
[DATABASE ID: VATV20163-A]
Inclusive Dates: 1861–1870.
Bulk: 13 buste and 3 vols.
Reference: D'Angiolini, p. 1177.
Finding Aid: List.
Location: Archivio di Stato di Roma.

5.1.27 Commissione di revisione dei crediti verso la Francia
[DATABASE ID: VATV649-A]

This commission was established in 1819 by the secretary of state, parallel to the Commissione pontificia di liquidazione dei crediti insinuati in tempo utile contro la Francia. The commission was reestablished in 1825.

RECORDS. Records of the commission consist of the following series.

5.1.27.1 Commissione di revisione dei crediti verso la Francia
[DATABASE ID: VATV20167-A]
Inclusive Dates: 1819–1843 and some earlier.
Bulk: 4 buste.
References: D'Angiolini, p. 1179; Lodolini (1960), p. 189.
Finding Aids: Inventory, 1963.
Location: Archivio di Stato di Roma.

5.1.28 Commissione governativa di Stato
[DATABASE ID: VATV702-A]

This commission was established by Pius IX in 1849 to reorganize the state after his return to power.

RECORDS. Records of the commission consist of the following series.

5.1.28.1 Miscellanea della commissione governativa di Stato
[DATABASE ID: VATV20193-A]
Inclusive Dates: 1849–1850.
Bulk: 1 busta.
References: D'Angiolini, pp. 1191–1192; Lodolini (1960), pp. 213–214.
Finding Aid: Inventory.
Location: Archivio di Stato di Roma.

5.1.29 Commissione mista pel brigantaggio
[DATABASE ID: VATV694-A]

This commission was established in 1867 by the Ministero dell'interno.

RECORDS. No records for this commission could be located.

5.1.30 Commissione per i codici legislativi
[DATABASE ID: VATV668-A]

Commissions to reform the laws were established in 1816 and again in 1823.

RECORDS. Records of the commission consist of the following series.

5.1.30.1 Miscellanea per la riforma dei codici
[DATABASE ID: VATV20137-A]
Inclusive Dates: 1800–1858.
Bulk: 9 buste.
Reference: D'Angiolini, p. 1160.
Finding Aid: Inventory.
Location: Archivio di Stato di Roma.

5.1.31 Commissione per la conservazione delle chiese di Roma
[DATABASE ID: VATV667-A]

This commission was active in the nineteenth century.

RECORDS. Records of the commission consist of the following series.

5.1.31.1 Commissione per la conservazione delle chiese di Roma
[DATABASE ID: VATV20115-A]
Inclusive Dates: 1810–1821.
Bulk: 13 buste and 7 registri.
References: D'Angiolini, p. 1147; Lodolini (1932), p. 138; Lodolini (1960), p. 95.
Finding Aid: Inventory.
Location: Archivio di Stato di Roma.

5.1.32 Commissione per la liquidazione dei crediti dello Stato Pontificio verso la Francia
[DATABASE ID: VATV648-A]

This commission was established in 1815 in Paris to liquidate claims against France arising from war contributions, supplies, forced loans, and pensions. It ceased operation in 1818 and was succeeded by the Commissione pontificia di liquidazione dei crediti insinuati in tempo utile contro la Francia and the Commissione di revisione dei crediti verso la Francia.

RECORDS. Records of the commission consist of the following series.

5.1.32.1 Commissione francese per la liquidazione dei crediti dello Stato Pontificio verso la Francia
[DATABASE ID: VATV20165-A]
Inclusive Dates: 1816–1818.
Bulk: 16 buste.
References: D'Angiolini, p. 1178; Lodolini (1960), p. 189.
Finding Aid: Inventory, 1963.
Location: Archivio di Stato di Roma.

5.1.33 Commissione per la revisione dei contratti non compiuti sotto il Regno italico
[DATABASE ID: VATV842-A]

This commission for the review of the unfulfilled contracts under the Italian reign was established by a dispatch of the secretary of state dated July 15, 1820.

RECORDS. Records of the commission consist of the following series.

5.1.33.1 Commissione per la revisione dei contratti non compiuti sotto il Regno italico
[DATABASE ID: VATV20168-A]
Inclusive Dates: 1820–1830.
Bulk: 4 buste.
Reference: D'Angiolini, p. 1179.
Finding Aid: Inventory, 1978.
Location: Archivio di Stato di Roma.

5.1.34 Commissione pontificia di liquidazione dei crediti insinuati in tempo utile contro la Francia
[DATABASE ID: VATV841-A]

This commission was established in 1819 to continue the work of the French commission relating to claims arising from the French regime in the Papal States. Its work ceased in 1825. The Commissione di revisione dei crediti verso la Francia had parallel responsiblity.

RECORDS. Records of the commission consist of the following series.

5.1.34.1 Commissione pontificia di liquidazione dei crediti insinuati in tempo utile contro la Francia
[DATABASE ID: VATV20166-A]
Inclusive Dates: 1819–1825.
Bulk: 20 buste and 2 registri.
Reference: D'Angiolini, pp. 1178–1179.
Finding Aid: Inventory with name index, 1977.
Location: Archivio di Stato di Roma.

5.1.35 Commissione speciale per la repressione del brigantaggio
[DATABASE ID: VATV759-A]

This commission functioned in Rome from 1814 to 1826. Another office with the same name was located in Frosinone.

RECORDS. Records of the commission consist of the following series.

5.1.35.1 Commissione speciale per la repressione del brigantaggio

[DATABASE ID: VATV20257-A]

Inclusive Dates: 1821–1826.

Bulk: 15 buste.

References: D'Angiolini, p. 1204; Lodolini (1960), p. 96.

Finding Aid: Inventory, 1959.

Location: Archivio di Stato di Roma.

5.1.36 Computisteria generale

[DATABASE ID: VATV652-A]

This office was established in 1743 by Benedict XIV to replace the three officers of the computisteria established by Sixtus V. It was responsible for bookkeeping and financial administration of the Papal States. Its responsibility had formerly been held by the Congregazione dei conti and Congregazione dei residui. In 1828, responsibility for customs was transferred to the Direzione generale delle dogane. By orders of 1832 and 1836, most of its duties were transferred to the Tesorierato generale, the Controllo generale, and the Direzione generale del debito pubblico.

RECORDS. Records of the agency consist of the following series.

5.1.36.1 Computisteria generale della Camera apostolica

[DATABASE ID: VATV20002-A]

Inclusive Dates: 1744–1865.

Bulk: 3,503 filze, vols., registri and buste.

Organization: Mandati, registri di mandati, entrata e uscita, saldaconti e giustificazioni, 1744–1851, 1,186 filze, 544 registri and 1 busta; —Dogane ai confini, poi divol. IX, 1786–1832, 26 registri and 304 filze; —Dogane generali, poi divol. III, 1744–1829, 322 filze and 192 registri; —Soldatesche e galere, Congregazione militare, 1744–1816 and 1804–1849, 553 filze and 72 registri; —Libri mastri, 1744–1809 and 1814–1865, 290 registri and 2 buste; —Repertori di istrumenti camerali detti "synopsis," [17—]–[18—], 11 vols.

References: D'Angiolini, pp. 1084–1086; Lodolini (1960), pp. 177–180.

Finding Aids: Inventory, 1937, and partial printed inventory, 1974.

Location: Archivio di Stato di Roma.

5.1.36.2 Computisteria generale della Camera apolstolica

[DATABASE ID: VATV20140-A]

Inclusive Dates: 1772–1870 (bulk 1814–1870).

Bulk: 10,381 buste, mazzi, vol. and registri.

Organization: Bilanci, 1816–1870, 553 buste; —Divisione I: Beni camerali, 1814–1844 (bulk 1816–1836), 521 buste and 153 registri; —Divisione II: Tassa fondiaria: dativa reale, 1816–1836, 225 buste and 227 registri; —Divisione III: Dazi indiretti, regalie, privative, opifici camerali, 1816–1831, 499 buste and registri; —Divisione IV: Milizia, sanità, lavori pubblici e privative e proventi diversi, 1815–1844 (bulk 1815–1836), 428 buste and 71 registri.

Divisione V: Beni ecclesiastici e comunitativi, 1814–1825, 237 buste and 105 registri; —Divisione VI: Spese ordinarie e straordinarie, 1816–1835, 2,827 buste and 210 registri; —Divisione VII: Debito pubblico, 1816–1835, 487 buste and 64 registri; —Divisione VIII: Soldatesche, marina e forniture di truppe estere e sanità, 1814–1833, 1,196 buste, mazzi and vols. and 85 registri; —Divisione IX: Dogane e dazi di consumo, 1816–1832 39 buste, mazzi and registri; —Divisione XI: Arretrati, 1816–1835, 220 vols. and buste and 18 registri; —Divisione V e XI: Scritture riunite. Sezione arretrati, 1814–1836, 687 buste; —Personale, [18—], 47 buste; —Affari generali, 1843–1870, 38 buste; —Atti per luoghi, 1835–1870, 172 buste; —Mandati, Bollettari, 1836–1870, 314 mazzi; —Giustificazioni dei mandati tratti, 1835–1870, 650 buste; —Giustificazioni del libro mastro, 1835–1870, 67 mazzi.

Archivio. Posizioni, denominato anche Archivio dell'archivista, [17—]–[18—], 124 buste; —Polizia. Giustificazioni, 1832–1846, 39 pacchi (attribution uncertain); —Affrancazioni, 1832–1833 and 1848, 31 pacchi.

References: D'Angiolini, pp. 1163–1165; Lodolini (1960), pp. 177–180.

Finding Aids: Inventories, most of them partial, for most of the series.

Location: Archivio di Stato di Roma.

5.1.36.3 Miscellanea degli archivi finanziari

[DATABASE ID: VATV20172-A]

Inclusive Dates: [18—].

Bulk: 2,783 registri and buste.

Reference: D'Angiolini, p. 1180.

Location: Archivio di Stato di Roma.

5.1.37 Congregatio pro Classe Paranda et Servanda ad Status Ecclesiastici Defensionem

[DATABASE ID: VATV833-A]

This congregation was established in 1588 by Sixtus V to organize a fleet of galleys to control piracy. Its functions were later taken over by the Commissariato delle mare.

RECORDS. No records for this congregation were located.

5.1.38 Congregatio pro Consultationibus Negociorum Status Ecclesiastici

[DATABASE ID: VATV672-A]

This office was established by Paul IV and confirmed by Sixtus V in 1588. The congregation, commonly known as the Sacra Consulta, presided over the administrative and judicial affairs of the Papal States. Its jurisdiction was parallel to that of the Congregazione del buon governo, which was responsible for economic affairs. The prefect of the Sacra Consulta was the secretary of state. The competence of the Sacra Consulta was vast, including civil and criminal actions, appeals against feudatories and governors, election of magistrates, and public health. Local officials referred important matters to the Sacra Consulta. Its judicial responsibilities grew to become its principal activity, and it became known as the Tribunale della Sacra consulta.

The Sacra Consulta was abolished during the French regime (1809–1814). Beginning in 1833 its responsibility was shared with the Segretaria per gli affari di stato interni. In 1847 responsibility for prisons was transferred from the Tesorierato generale. The Sacra Consulta is not the same as the Consulta di stato, a consultative assembly established in 1847.

In addition to the records listed below, series listed with other agencies relate directly to this agency and should be consulted. See Miscellaneous official series *Miscellaneorum armarium IX* and Papal States miscellaneous series *Miscellanea del periodo costituzionale* and *Miscellanea di carte politiche e riservate*.

RECORDS. Records of the agency consist of the following series.

5.1.38.1 Causae criminales
[DATABASE ID: VATV275-A]
Inclusive Dates: 1592 (copy)–1846 (bulk 1820–1846).
Bulk: 11.5 linear m. (172 vol. plus index cards).
Organization: Subseries include: Allegazioni criminali, 1820–1846, 127 vols.; —Miscellanie; —Allegazioni criminali, Miscellanea; —Allegazioni criminale, Polizia; —Allegazioni criminale, riservate; —Voti e difese criminale.
References: Fink, pp. 116–117; Boyle, p. 89.
Finding Aids: There are index cards to 145 volumes in this collection. These cards are arranged by volume and calendar cases, according to the numerical order of pages in each volume.
Location: Archivio Segreto Vaticano.

5.1.38.2 Congregazione della Sacra consulta
[DATABASE ID: VATV20035-A]
Inclusive Dates: 1633–1854.
Bulk: 7 vols. and registri, and 17 buste.
Organization: Voti, 1717–1719, 2 vols.; —Corrispondenza, 1633–1711, 4 vols.; —Rubrica, 1733, 1 vols.; —Segreteria, 1814–1842, 1854, 17 buste.
References: D'Angiolini, pp. 1097–1098, 1152; Lodolini (1960), p. 114.
Location: Archivio di Stato di Roma.

5.1.38.3 [Miscellanea SF/467–SF/469]
[DATABASE ID: VATV10254-A]
Inclusive Dates: ca. 1820–1856.
Bulk: 30 linear m.
Organization: Subseries include: Lettere, ca. 1840, 1 linear m., 13 vols.; —Camerlengato, ca. 1835; —Politici, ca. 1830; —Ristretti, ca. 1835; —Cause; —Processi; —Cause criminale del Tribunale del Governo, ca. 1820–1827, 1 linear m., 8 vols., with index cards; —Cause criminale di diversi Tribunale di Roma, ca. 1820; —Cause criminale del Tribunale della Sacra Consulta, 1820–1840, 37 vols., 3 linear m.; —[Acta of the Consulta], ca. 1850–1856; —Protocolli, ca. 1820–1850.
Note: This is not a recognized series in the ASV, rather it is a true miscellany. Title was assigned by the project staff based on the location of the material in 1990.
Location: Archivio Segreto Vaticano.

5.1.38.4 Tribunale della Sacra consulta
[DATABASE ID: VATV20251-A]
Inclusive Dates: 1804–1870 (bulk 1816–1870).
Bulk: 810 buste, 42 registri, 36 protocolli, and 6 rubriche.
References: D'Angiolini, pp. 1202–1203; Lodolini (1960), p. 115.
Finding Aid: Inventory, 1937.
Location: Archivio di Stato di Roma.

5.1.39 Congregatio pro Status Ecclesiastici Gravamibus Sublevandis
[DATABASE ID: VATV834-A]

Sixtus V established this congregation in 1588 to examine questions of tribute imposed by cameral employees and to serve as a court of appeals for cases decided by magistrates of the Papal States.

RECORDS. No records for this office could be located.

5.1.40 Congregatio pro Typographia Vaticana
[DATABASE ID: VATV835-A]

Established in 1588 by Sixtus V, this congregation was to oversee the official Vatican press. The press was concerned with publication of religious books.

RECORDS. No records for this office could be located.

5.1.41 Congregatio pro Ubertate Annonae Status Ecclesiastici
[DATABASE ID: VATV832-A]

This congregation was established in 1588 by Sixtus V to prevent famine in the Papal States. It had a short existence but was continued by other agencies with similar names.

RECORDS. No records for this congregation could be located.

5.1.42 Congregatio Sublevaminis
[DATABASE ID: VATV758-A]

This congregation was established in 1701 by Clement XI to promote agriculture and the public economy in general in the Papal States. After three years of activity the congregation remained inactive until it was suppressed in 1715.

RECORDS. Records of the congregation consist of the following series.

5.1.42.1 Congregazione del sollievo
[DATABASE ID: VATV20045-A]
Inclusive Dates: 1611–1706 (bulk 1701–1706).
Bulk: 2 buste.
References: D'Angiolini, p. 1110; Lodolini (1960), p. 94.
Finding Aid: Summary inventory (non più rispondente).
Location: Archivio di Stato di Roma.

5.1.43 Congregatio super Baronibus
[DATABASE ID: VATV869-A]

Established in 1596 by Clement VIII, this congregation was given authority to guard the interests of creditors with regard to loans made to barons.

RECORDS. Records of the congregation consist of the following series.

5.1.43.1 Congregazione dei baroni (o dei monti e baroni)
[DATABASE ID: VATV20050-A]
Inclusive Dates: [15—]–1830 (bulk [16—]–1830).
Bulk: 34 vols.
Reference: D'Angiolini, pp. 1120–1121.
Finding Aid: Partial inventory of the first 25 volumes, with index of names and places.
Location: Archivio di Stato di Roma.

5.1.44 Congregatio super Negotiis Avenionis
[DATABASE ID: VATV873-A]

This congregation was established in 1763 by Innocent XII with responsibility for the government of the province of Avignon. Clement XIV in 1774 reduced its powers and transformed it to a presidenza. It was suppressed in 1797 when Avignon was annexed by France.

In addition to the records listed below, series listed with another agency relate directly to this agency and should be consulted. See Miscellaneous official series *Miscellaneorum armarium VIII.*

RECORDS. Records of the congregation consist of the following series.

5.1.44.1 [Archivio]
[DATABASE ID: VATV276-A]
Inclusive Dates: 1657–1790.
Bulk: 24 linear m.
Organization: 319 numbered buste and volumes and approximately 13 unnumbered buste. Subseries include: Registri [di lettere] per la segreta d'Avignone, 1693–1768, vols. 1–4, 6, 77, 222, Indexed; —Registri di patente, 1717–1785, vols. 5, 58, 223; —Carte diverse del tesoriere camerale, 1776–1787, vol. 7;—Sommaire de toutes les conclusions et deliberations prises par les trois états du pays du comte Venaissin depuis l'an 1400 auprès al'année 1700 inclusivemens aux inventaires des les papiers livres et documents existants dans les archives des trois états, vol. 8; —Scritture diverse e risolutiones, 1693–1703, vols. 11–18; —Posizioni, 1704–1768, vols. 19–76; —Minute registrate, 1758–1785, vols. 78–100; —[List of some of the following miscellaneous buste with the incorrect numbers].

vol. 101; —[Miscellaneous subjects, letters, etc.]. vols. 102–319.
Reference: Fink, p. 118.
Finding Aids: See Fernand Benoît, "Les archives de la Sacrée Congrégation d'Avignon au Vatican (1693–1790)." *Mémoires de l'Académie de Vaucluse* 23 (1923): 1–28. This article provides a good introduction to this series and is an inventory list of volumes 1–221 (of a total 351 volumes) of the Congregatio super Negotiis Avenionis. The entries give the volume number, a brief description of the contents or business that is derived from the information on the spine of the volumes, and the inclusive dates of the volumes.
Location: Archivio Segreto Vaticano.

5.1.45 Congregatio super Reformatione Tribunalium Romanae Curiae
[DATABASE ID: VATV871-A]

This congregation was established in 1608 by Paul V to reform the judiciary of the Papal States.

RECORDS. No records for this congregation could be located.

5.1.46 Congregatio super Viis, Pontibus, et Aquis Curandis
[DATABASE ID: VATV607-A]

This congregation was established in 1588 by Sixtus V and reorganized in 1590. It was responsible for maintaining and constructing roads and bridges, as well as work on rivers, reclamation of marshes, preservation of aqueducts, and ruling on water concessions for mills. These duties were previously the responsibility of the Camera. The Tribunale delle strade paralleled its responsibilities, as did the Prefettura generale di acque e strade (established in 1833), and the Ministero dei lavori pubblici (established in 1848).

RECORDS. Records of the congregation consist of the following series.

5.1.46.1 Congregazione super viis, pontibus et fontibus
[DATABASE ID: VATV20036-A]
Inclusive Dates: 1594–1690 and 1708–1710.
Bulk: 3 registri.
References: D'Angiolini, pp. 1098–1100; Lodolini (1960), pp. 152–153.
Finding Aid: Summary inventory.
Location: Archivio di Stato di Roma.

5.1.47 Congregatio Super Visitatione ac Reformatione Officiorum et Archiviorum Notariorum Urbis
[DATABASE ID: VATV753-A]

This office was established in 1704.

RECORDS. No records for this office could be located, but series listed with another agency relate directly to this agency and should be consulted. See Camera Apostolica series *Miscellanea di congregazioni diverse.*

5.1.48 Congregazione ad referendum
[DATABASE ID: VATV840-A]

This congregation was established in 1816 to determine the indemnity due purchasers of church property sold during the French regime.

RECORDS. Records of the congregation consist of the following series.

5.1.48.1 Congregazione ad referendum
[DATABASE ID: VATV20164-A]
Inclusive Dates: 1816–1831.
Bulk: 4 buste.
References: D'Angiolini, p. 1178.
Finding Aid: Inventory, 1952.
Location: Archivio di Stato di Roma.

5.1.49 Congregazione camerale
[DATABASE ID: VATV606-A]

This congregation was a tribunal of the Camera. Its origins are unknown. The Congregazione camerale decided actions relating the cameral contracts, autonomous cameral administrations, and immunity from taxes. In 1669 its competence was distinguished from that of the Congregazione per la revisione dei conti. In 1743 its composition was stabilized. It was suppressed in 1800 and its responsibilities were taken over by the Tribunale della Camera apostolica.

RECORDS. Records of the congregation consist of the following series.

5.1.49.1 Congregazione camerale
[DATABASE ID: VATV20025-A]
Inclusive Dates: 1692–1766.
Bulk: 98 vols.
References: D'Angiolini, p. 1091; Lodolini (1960), pp. 78–79.
Finding Aids: Old index of posizione of the cases; index of cases, 1743–1765.
Location: Archivio di Stato di Roma.

5.1.49.2 Congregazione camerale per la revisione generale dei titoli relativi a privilegi ed esenzioni
[DATABASE ID: VATV20026-A]
Inclusive Dates: 1749–1755.
Bulk: 8 vols.
Reference: D'Angiolini, p. 1091.
Finding Aid: Inventory.
Location: Archivio di Stato di Roma.

5.1.50 Congregazione camerale pel contenzioso amministrativo
[DATABASE ID: VATV838-A]

This congregation was established in 1835 to judge administrative disputes. The congregation was headed by the tesoriere generale. Beginning in 1847 it was headed by the uditore del camerlengato. The office was abolished in 1870.

RECORDS. Records of the congregation consist of the following series.

5.1.50.1 Congregazione camerale pel contenzioso amministrativo
[DATABASE ID: VATV20157-A]
Inclusive Dates: 1835–1848.
Bulk: 9 buste, 1 vol., 1 registro and 1 protocollo.
References: D'Angiolini, p. 1175; Lodolini (1960), p. 118.
Location: Archivio di Stato di Roma.

5.1.51 Congregazione civile dell'A. C.
[DATABASE ID: VATV682-A]

This congregation was active in the nineteenth century.

RECORDS. No records for this congregation could be located.

5.1.52 Congregazione criminale
[DATABASE ID: VATV885-A]

This congregation examined the most serious cases to come before the Tribunale criminale del governatore (to 1809), the Tribunale del governo di Roma (1814–1847), and the Tribunale criminale di Roma (1847–1870).

RECORDS. Records of the congregation consist of the following series.

5.1.52.1 Congregazione criminale
[DATABASE ID: VATV20074-A]
Inclusive Dates: 1657–1809 and 1814–1871.
Bulk: 43 registri and 4 vols.
Reference: D'Angiolini, pp. 1134, 1198.
Finding Aids: Inventories.
Location: Archivio di Stato di Roma.

5.1.53 Congregazione dei confini
[DATABASE ID: VATV830-A]

This congregation was established in 1627 by Urban VIII to protect the territorial integrity of the Papal States and to prevent the alienation of castles and land as well as to prevent the entry of contagious diseases. After a brief existence, its duties were transferred. The Secretariat of State took on responsibility for the physical defense of the state. The Sacra Consulta took responsibility for health and sanitation.

In addition to the records listed below, series listed with other agencies relate directly to this agency and should be consulted. See Miscellaneous official series *Miscellaneorum armarium* and *Piante e carte geografiche*.

RECORDS. Records of the congregation consist of the following series.

5.1.53.1 [Archivio]
[DATABASE ID: VATV10205-A]
Inclusive Dates: 1628–1791.
Bulk: 7 linear m. (92 buste numbers).
Organization: Series include: 1–7, 14a, Romagna, 1726–1789; —8–11a, 84, 85, Bologna, 1784–1791; —12, 57–61, 66, 69, Ferrara, 1757–1786; —13–18, Urbino, 1768–1789; —19–36, Umbria, 1778–1788; —38–40, Posizione/Dispute; —41–48, 85, Campagna (43–46 also Marittima); —50–52, Marca, 1746–1784; —53–55, 76, 78, 79, Scritture riguardanti la controversia dei Confini con Venezia; —76, Lettere della Congregazione, 1628–1700; —80, Relatio Jurium Sedis Apostolicae in Civitatem; —86, Sicilia.
Note: The title of this series, *Archivio*, was supplied by project staff. It is not officially designated by the ASV.
Reference: Boyle, p. 89.
Finding Aids: ASV Indice 686 (formerly Indice 107) is an 1839 index entitled "Inventario e Descrizione dell'Archivio Segreto della S. Congregazione de Confini." This inventory remains useful to current researchers. The inventory provides an introduction to the series, and then lists each busta or volume with a complete title, inclusive dates, and occasional annotations.
Location: Archivio Segreto Vaticano.

5.1.53.2 [Territori e comunità pontifici]
[DATABASE ID: VATV10206-A]
Inclusive Dates: 1830.
Bulk: .5 linear m. (6 vols.).
Organization: Volumes are: 1. Vicariato di Radicofani nei territorj pontificj di Proceno, Trevimano, Allerona, Fabbro, Salci, e Atta della Pieve : Confinazione territoriale fra lo stato pontificio; —2. Vicariato Toscano di Arcidosso nella communità pontificia di Proceno; —3. Contro visita del vicariato di Manciano nella communita pontificie di Montalto, Canino, Ischia; —4. Vicariato Toscano di Pitigliano nella communità pontificia d'Ischia, Farnese, Valentano, Latera, Onano, e Proceno; —5. Vicariato Toscano di Orbetello nella communità pontificia di Montalto; —6. Vicariato dell'Abbadia San Salvatore nel territorio pontificio di Proceno.
Note: The title of this series was given by project staff. It does not have an official ASV designation.
Reference: Boyle, p. 89.
Location: Archivio Segreto Vaticano.

5.1.54 Congregazione dei diffalchi
[DATABASE ID: VATV752-A]

This congregation was established by Pius VI in 1779 to grant benefits to farmers of the Campagna after a drought. This was a cameral congregation.

RECORDS. Records of the congregation consist of the following series.

5.1.54.1 Congregazione dei diffalchi
[DATABASE ID: VATV20028-A]
Inclusive Dates: 1780–1781.
Bulk: 74 fascicoli and 2 vols.
References: D'Angiolini, p. 1092; Lodolini (1960), pp. 90–91.
Finding Aid: Inventory, 1973, with list of cases and parties and index of names and places.
Location: Archivio di Stato di Roma.

5.1.55 Congregazione dei residui
[DATABASE ID: VATV617-A]

This congregation was established by Clement XII in 1735 and confirmed by Benedict XIV in 1746. This cameral congregation regulated the administration of the treasury and resolved disputes relating to the budget. Previously, its functions had in part been performed by the three computisti. It was inactive from 1800 to 1809 and abolished during the French regime from 1809 to 1814. It was reestablished in 1814 and its responsibility increased, becoming similar to a court of accounts. In 1832 it was abolished and replaced by the Consiglio fiscale.

RECORDS. Records of the congregation consist of the following series.

5.1.55.1 Congregazione dei residui
[DATABASE ID: VATV20029-A]
Inclusive Dates: 1695–1837 (bulk 1735–1837).
Bulk: 115 buste.
References: D'Angiolini, p. 1092; Lodolini (1960), pp. 143–144.
Finding Aids: Summary inventory; rubricella delle posizioni of debtors for the years 1822–1831; rubricella of transfers of wealth and cameral rents from 1822 to 1831.
Location: Archivio di Stato di Roma.

5.1.56 Congregazione del buon governo
[DATABASE ID: VATV615-A]

This congregation was established in 1592 by Clement VIII to regulate economic activity and public administration in the Papal States. Its responsibilities paralleled those of the Sacra Consulta, which was responsible for administrative and judicial affairs. The congregation was given extensive authority over many aspects of public life, including control over the budget, apportionment of taxes, liquidation of public debts, the census, local elections, and criminal and civil actions. It was reformed many times, by Paul V, Clement XII, Benedict XIV, Clement XIII, and Pius VII. In 1800 responsibility for roads was transferred in large part from the Presidenza delle strade. The congregation's importance diminished in the early nineteenth century. In 1831 Gregory XVI took away its jurisdiction over the communes and left it only a judicial role, as an appellate tribunal. The congregation was suppressed in 1847 by Pius IX and its responsibilities transferred to the Ministero dell'interno.

RECORDS. Records of the congregation consist of the following series.

5.1.56.1 Buon governo
[DATABASE ID: VATV10194-A]

Inclusive Dates: 1660–1910 (bulk 1671–1866).

Bulk: 10 linear m.

Organization: 73 numbered buste or volumes, plus four unnumbered buste, volumes, and boxes. Series/items include: vols. 1–29, Positiones, 1671–1698; —vols. 30 and 65, Elenchi delle questioni trattate nelle congregazioni particolari del 1808, 1784; —vol. 31, Controversia con la Consulta su la giurisdizione nelle cause di fraudi delle gabelle, sulla facoltà dei subdelegati, 1748–1762; —vols. 37–40, Raccolta delle circolari, 1814–1834; —vols. 48–49, Tabelle di entrate e uscite di comuni, tesoriere ecc. dello Stato Pontificio, 1649–1662; —vols. 50–51, Spese straordinarie di diverse comunità, 1670–1684; —vol. 66. Titolario-Indice de' Governi. Formulario e Memorie al uso della Segretaria della Sacra Congregazione del Buon governo, [17—]; —vol. 67, Protocollo de' Biglietti della Segreteria di Stato e di altri Dicasteri, 1795–1847; —vols. 68–70, Rubricella dei decreti della Congregazione, 1817–1825; —vol. 71, Manuale notarile di controversie, 1822–1830; —vol. 72, Carte riguardanti i danni causati dal passaggio dell' "Armate Alemanna"; —vol 73, Contabilita e carteggio relativo alla costruzione di strade e ponte, 1781–1783.

Unnumbered buste are: 1. Miscellaneous letters, 1714–1791 and Lettere scritte alla Sacra Congregazione del Buon Governo alla Sacra Consulta: Cardinali, Prelati, ed altri; —2. Index to letters, ca. 1744, of Congregazione del Buon Governo or the Congregatio Consulta; —3. Protocollo delle domande di ricerche presentate all'Archivio della S. Congregazione del Buon Governo, 1872–1910 and Domande de ricerche; —4. Domande di ricerche, 1860–1907 and Memoria per l'Emo., e Rmo. Sig. Card.: Segretario di Stato rapporto a vari Luoghi o controversi con Domini Esteri o poteri Indipendenti, 1786.

Finding Aids: ASV Indice 1076 by Hermann Hoberg provides a brief introduction to the fondo and a listing of each busta or volume from 1 to 73. The index does not include the unnumbered buste. The inventory includes inclusive dates and descriptive titles.

One of the final unnumbered volumes purports to be an index to either this congregation or to the S. Cong. Consulta (Causa Criminale?). It is very difficult to read.

Location: Archivio Segreto Vaticano.

5.1.56.2 Congregazione del buon governo
[DATABASE ID: VATV20047-A]

Inclusive Dates: 1582–1870 (bulk 1582–1847).

Bulk: 13,124 buste, registri, and volumes.

Organization: This vast series divides as follows: I. Affari generali, memorie e massime, 1582–1870. 107 buste, filze, registri and volumi; —II. Miscellanea in ordine alfabetico per località, (Atti per luoghi), 1601–1855 (bulk 1630–1847), 5,625

buste; —III. Repubblica romana, impero napoleonico, regno d'Italia, amministrazioni provvisorie, 1798–1814, 235 buste and registri; —IV. Visite economiche e relazioni sullo stato delle comunità, 1655–1830, 997 registri and vols.; —V. Lettere, 1605–1847, 399 buste, registri, and vols.; —VI. Catasti, 1678–1841, 143 buste and vols.; —VIIa. Amministrazioni particolari, 1627–1853; 376 buste, filze, registri, and vols. —VIIb. Stati di beni delle comunità, 1821–1828, 555 quinternoni; —VIIc. Vendite dei beni ed estinzione del debito delle comunità, 1784–1847, 534 buste, registri, and vols.; —VIII. Atti giudiziari, 1611–1866, 82 buste and vols.; —IX. Congregazione fermana, 1740–1761, e Stato di Fermo, 1731–1767, 50 buste, registri, vacchette, and vols.; —X. Strade e acque, 1616–1857, 326 buste, filze, registri, and vols.; —XI. Conti e tasse diverse, 1588–1854, 444 buste, filze, registri, and vols.; —XII. Bilanci comunali e conti economici, 1600–1837, 1,802 buste, filze, registri, and vols.; —XIII. Registri e vacchette, 1634–1849, 752 registri, volumi and vacchette; —XIV. Collezione di piante, mappe e disegni, 272 piante. Fondo antico dell'Archivio di Stato di Roma: A. Cause, decisioni, 1664–1865, 19 buste and vols. (785 fascicoli); —B. Atti giudiziari, 1586–1831, 247 buste; —C. Broliardi, sentenze, manuali di udienze, 1636–1831, 159 vols.

References: D'Angiolini, pp. 1111–1119; Lodolini (1960), pp. 130–135.

Finding Aids: There is a general printed inventory for the entire series. In addition there are particular inventories for single subseries.

Location: Archivio di Stato di Roma.

5.1.57 Congregazione del censo
[DATABASE ID: VATV829-A]

From the early fourteenth century the Apostolic Camera was both the financial and juridical bureau for the Papal States as well as for the church itself. Moreover, its financial policy and that of the Papal States were always closely related. During the second half of the fifteenth century, however, a great change occurred in ecclesiastical finance. Income from total ecclesiastical sources of revenue amounted to only a third of what it had been in the fourteenth century, but that from the Papal States was increasing dramatically. There are records of taxes imposed by Paul III (1543), Paul V (1605), and Innocent XI (1676). Clement XI (1708) also attempted to make his authority more effective in the provinces in this way.

Throughout these pontificates legislation in this area was exercised by the Congregazione del Buon Governo. Taxes were based on fixed income or declaration of proprietorship confirmed by oath. A general tax could not be imposed for the entire Papal States because each community had the faculty of imposing its own tax independently of one another.

The need then to bring some sort of order out of this confusion induced Pius VI (1775–1799) to design an economic/financial reform movement. Pius VI had been minister of finance under Clement XIII (1758–

1769). By an edict dated December 15, 1777, he ordered through Antonio Cardinal Casali, prefect of the Congregazione degli Sgravi e del Buon Governo, a general tax of the entire territory of the Papal States. The implementation of this so-called Catasto Piano was entrusted to the prefect of the Annona. With successive compilations, norms for the appraisal of lands were stabilized. These were based for a second time on the old and hurried method of the *assegne* (fixed income or allowance) but fully controlled by the Papal States. In spite of the best intentions of the pope, however, this plan also failed.

Pius VII (1800–1823) assumed a territory reduced in size and economically less viable than before. He appointed four commissions to reorganize the government and administration of the Papal States and to draw up a new plan (*Post diuturnas*, Oct. 10, 1800). On March 19, 1801 he issued an edict abolishing the manner and kinds of taxes then in effect. From 1809 to 1813 the Italian governor included the Papal States, occupied by the French for the second time, in the general measurements of land and making of maps. Pius VII utilized this work when he reentered Rome in 1814 and again took up the plan initiated by Pius VI.

The new pontifical tax, ordered by the motu proprio *Quando per ammirabile* (July 6, 1816), applied to the entire Papal States including Benevento and Pontocorvo lands formerly seized by Naples. The motu proprio also established an appropriate department called the Congregazione dei Catasti with the competency of establishing taxes that were lacking and adding to and perfecting those already in existence. The precarious system of *assegne* was completely abandoned and replaced by a general tax based on proportion and analytic evaluation of capital in the various parts of the Papal States.

For the execution of the work of this congregation a technical office was set up which functioned as a coordinating center for taxes. This office was suppressed after the death in 1838 of Luigi Marini, its first director.

With the Regolamento of February 22, 1817, the Congregazione dei Catasti stabilized detailed norms for appraisal and for the measurement of land and preparation of maps. In the motu proprio *Manifestammo già* (Mar. 3, 1819), Pius VII stated that the new tax had been ordered "to correct the innumerable errors in the earlier appraisals for tax purposes."

In the first years the president of the Congregazione dei Catasti was Cesare Guerrieri Gonzaga, the treasurer general of the Apostolic Camera; then from 1819, when Guerrieri Gonzaga was elevated to the cardinalate, the president of the congregation was a cardinal and assumed the title *presidente del censo*. The director general of the catasti was named *direttore generale del censo*; this general directorship continued until 1845.

Both the Congregazione dei Catasti and the presidency of the censo continued to exist, united at first under the same president. In 1822 several cardinals were added to the seven prelates who composed the congregation, the congregational treasurer and the general soliciter of finance being included among the latter. Under this structure the congregation, which had been reorganized and given more power, assumed the new title of Congregazione Generale del Censo. On August 11, 1823, an instruction was issued for the inspectors and *periti* (experts) who would be compiling the new estimates for the rural farms of the ecclesiastical state.

Gregory XVI (1831–1846) carried on the plan of Pius VII and supported the work of distributive justice in the new tax arrangement, but first gave time for the complaints of property owners of each province to be placed before a commission for examination and study. To obtain common satisfaction the Congregazione del Censo ordered that all such claims were to be submitted by 1833. In 1835, claims of property owners having been dealt with, it was possible to proceed to the publication of the new papal tax that was known as the Catasto Piano-Gregoriano. It became effective on November 1, 1835.

After the restoration of Pius IX in 1849 the Congregazione del Censo was composed of nine cardinals and the presidency was held by a cardinal who was not even a member of the congregation. At the time of the dissolution of the Papal States, the congregation was composed of ten cardinals, a secretary, the treasurer-general of the Camera, the minister of the interior, the financial general advocate, and the commissioner of the Apostolic Camera. The general direction of the censo was headed by a cardinal member of the congregation assisted by a secretary general and various officials attached to the topographical section and to the Chancery. After the dissolution of the Papal States in 1870 the Congregazione del Censo ceased to exist.

RECORDS. Records of the agency consist of the following series.

5.1.57.1 Presidenza generale del censo

[DATABASE ID: VATV20139-A]

Inclusive Dates: 1800–1875 (bulk 1816–1870).

Bulk: 2,749 buste, mazzi, registri, and vols.; 11,723 mappe and broliardi; 48 pacchi; and about 1,000 other items.

Organization: This series includes the following subseries: Atti della presidenza classificati secondo il titolario, 1816–1870, 1,733 buste, mazzi, and registri; —Affari speciali, catasti, biblioteca e stampati, 1816–1870, 354 buste, mazzi, and registri; —Giunta di revisione del nuovo estimo, 1800–1875 (bulk 1819–1870), 414 buste, mazzi, and registri; —Giunta di revisione. Graduazioni di Roma e Comarca, 1850–1856, 35 buste; —Catasto urbano di Roma, [18—], 54 buste; —Catasto gregoriano, mappe e broliardi, 1808–1859 (bulk 1816–1859), 11,723 mappe and broliardi and 48 pacchi di lucidi.

References: D'Angiolini, pp. 1161–1163; Lodolini (1960), pp. 125–130.

Finding Aids: Inventories of buste, mazzi, and volumi, 1925, 1927, 1930. Card index of maps and surveys, 1980.
Location: Archivio di Stato di Roma.

5.1.58 Congregazione del commercio e porto franco di Ancona
[DATABASE ID: VATV771-A]

This congregation is also known as the Congregazione anconetana, which was established in 1734 by Clement XII to control the free port of Ancona.

RECORDS. No records for this congregation could be located.

5.1.59 Congregazione dell'abbondanza
[DATABASE ID: VATV872-A]

This congregation was established in 1611 by Paul V to provide food supplies for the Papal States and for Rome in particular. Its responsibilities were parallel to those of the Congregazione dell'annona.

RECORDS. No records for this congregation could be located.

5.1.60 Congregazione della visita alle carceri
[DATABASE ID: VATV887-A]

This congregation was related to the Tribunale del governatore (to 1809), the Tribunale del governo di Roma (1814–1847), and the Tribunale criminale di Roma (1847–1870).

RECORDS. Records of the congregation consist of the following series.

5.1.60.1 Congregazione della visita alle carceri
[DATABASE ID: VATV20075-A]
Inclusive Dates: 1567–1807 and 1814–1870.
Bulk: 138 registri and 9 busta.
Reference: D'Angiolini, pp. 1134, 1198 (where it is named "Congregazione di lettura delle liste dei carcerati").
Finding Aids: Inventories.
Location: Archivio di Stato di Roma.

5.1.61 Congregazione delle acque
[DATABASE ID: VATV608-A]

This congregation was established in 1621 by Paul V, for the regulation of water flow, especially the Po and Tiber Rivers. Later its responsibility was expanded to include supervision of the Roman aqueducts. Note that it is also known as Presidenza delle acque. In 1833 it was replaced by the Prefettura generale di acque e strade.

RECORDS. Records of the congregation of the following series.

5.1.61.1 Congregazione delle acque
[DATABASE ID: VATV20038-A]
Inclusive Dates: [14—]–1833 (bulk 1619–1833).
Bulk: 300 buste (192 containing registri, 21 vols., and several fascicoli) and 32 registri.
Reference: D'Angiolini, p. 1102.
Finding Aids: Summary inventory of buste; old index of chirografi, deputazioni, editti, inibizioni, informazioni, istrumenti, istruzioni, patenti, piante, profili e disegni, possessi, relazioni (con richiami non piu attuali).
Location: Archivio di Stato di Roma.

5.1.62 Congregazione deputata per gli affari di governo
[DATABASE ID: VATV852-A]

This congregation was established in 1800 upon the restoration of papal authority in the Papal States. It briefly served as a provisional government.

RECORDS. No records for this congregation could be located.

5.1.63 Congregazione deputata per il nuovo piano di riforma dell'antico sistema di governo
[DATABASE ID: VATV851-A]

This congregation was established in 1800, after the restoration of papal authority in the Papal States, to study the reorganization of its public administration. It was divided into three departments: civil, criminal (for the reform of the tribunals), and economic (for the reform of public finance).

RECORDS. Records of the congregation consist of the following series.

5.1.63.1 Congregazione deputata per il nuovo piano di riforma dell'antico sistema di governo
[DATABASE ID: VATV20102-A]
Inclusive Dates: 1800.
Bulk: 1 busta.
Reference: D'Angiolini, p. 1142.
Finding Aid: Inventory, 1978.
Location: Archivio di Stato di Roma.

5.1.64 Congregazione deputata per il ripristino dei monasteri nelle province di seconda recupera
[DATABASE ID: VATV757-A]

This congregation was established after the restoration of 1814 to restore property to the clergy of the Marches.

RECORDS. Records of the congregation consist of the following series.

5.1.64.1 Congregazione deputata per il ripristino dei monasteri nelle province di seconda recupera
> [DATABASE ID: VATV20171-A]
> *Inclusive Dates:* 1817–1825.
> *Bulk:* 3 buste.
> *References:* D'Angiolini, p. 1180; Lodolini (1960), p. 94.
> *Finding Aid:* Inventory, 1951.
> *Location:* Archivio di Stato di Roma.

5.1.65 Congregazione deputata per la revisione dei conti degli appaltatori ed amministratori camerali
> [DATABASE ID: VATV886-A]

Established in 1804, this congregation, as its name implies, was related to reform of cameral administration and contracting.

RECORDS. Records of the congregation consist of the following series.

5.1.65.1 Congregazione deputata per la revisione dei conti degli appaltatori ed amministratori camerali
> [DATABASE ID: VATV20104-A]
> *Inclusive Dates:* 1804–1808.
> *Bulk:* 3 vols.
> *Reference:* D'Angiolini, p. 1143.
> *Finding Aid:* Index of cases, in alphabetical order by names of parties and of places, 1952.
> *Location:* Archivio di Stato di Roma.

5.1.66 Congregazione deputata per la revisione delle enfiteusi e dei beni alienati
> [DATABASE ID: VATV639-A]

This congregation was established in 1800 to examine the situation of ecclesiastical, state, and commune property alienated by the Roman republic of 1799. The congregation also examined the emphyteusis (land grants) of 1797.

RECORDS. Records of the congregation consist of the following series.

5.1.66.1 Congregazione deputata per la revisione delle enfiteusi e dei beni alienati
> [DATABASE ID: VATV20103-A]
> *Inclusive Dates:* 1800–1809.
> *Bulk:* 19 buste.
> *References:* D'Angiolini, p. 1143; Lodolini (1960), p. 187.
> *Finding Aids:* Summary inventory.
> *Location:* Archivio di Stato di Roma.

5.1.67 Congregazione deputata per le cause del Marchese Alessandro Pallavicini di Parma
> [DATABASE ID: VATV756-A]

This congregation was established in 1826 by Leo XII to resolve a dispute over the ownership of Castel Sant'Angelo di Madama, in the diocese of Tivoli.

RECORDS. Records of the congregation consist of the following series.

5.1.67.1 Congregazione deputata per le cause del marchese Alessandro Pallavicini di Parma
> [DATABASE ID: VATV20169-A]
> *Inclusive Dates:* 1827–1830.
> *Bulk:* 2 buste.
> *References:* D'Angiolini, pp. 1179–1980; Lodolini (1960), p. 94.
> *Finding Aid:* Index of cases, 1951.
> *Location:* Archivio di Stato di Roma.

5.1.68 Congregazione di revisione dei conti consuntivi arretrati anteriori al 1848
> [DATABASE ID: VATV658-A]

This congregation was established in 1848 from a proposal of the Consulta di Stato to revise the final accounts of the years 1835–1847. Previously this had been the responsibility of the Congregazione di revisione dei conti e degli affari di pubblica amminiatrazione. The congregation ceased operation in 1852/53.

RECORDS. Records of the congregation consist of the following series.

5.1.68.1 Congregazione di revisione dei conti consuntivi arretrati anteriori al 1848
> [DATABASE ID: VATV20160-A]
> *Inclusive Dates:* 1846–1853 (bulk 1848–1853).
> *Bulk:* 6 buste.
> *References:* D'Angiolini, p. 1177; Lodolini (1960), pp. 88–89.
> *Finding Aid:* Inventory with index, 1950.
> *Location:* Archivio di Stato di Roma.

5.1.69 Congregazione di revisione dei conti e degli affari di pubblica amministrazione
> [DATABASE ID: VATV657-A]

Leo XII established this congregation in 1828 to revise the budget of the Camera and other state agencies and to propose improvements in the system of public finance. The congregation also had a contentious jurisdiction. It was composed of four of the chierici di camera. The congregation's duties were formerly the responsibility of the Tribunale della piena camera per la revisione dei conti. Responsibility for audit was transferred in 1835 to the Controllo generale. In 1847 the congregation was abolished. The major part of its responsibility was absorbed by the Consulta di Stato, while its contentious jurisdiction was transferred to the Tribunale della Camera, and responsibility for revision of the budget was transferred to the Congregazione di revisione dei conti consuntivi arretrati anteriori al 1848.

RECORDS. Records of the congregation consist of the following series.

5.1.69.1 Congregazione di revisione dei conti e degli affari di pubblica amministrazione
[DATABASE ID: VATV20158-A]

Inclusive Dates: 1828–1847.

Bulk: 164 buste and 30 vols.

Reference: D'Angiolini, pp. 1175–1176.

Finding Aids: There is a summary inventory and a partial inventory.

Location: Archivio di Stato di Roma.

5.1.70 Congregazione di Stato
[DATABASE ID: VATV671-A]

This congregation was established in 1829.

RECORDS. No records were located for this congregation but series listed with another agency relate directly to this agency and should be consulted. See Camera Apostolica series *Miscellanea di congregazioni diverse.*

5.1.71 Congregazione di vigilanza
[DATABASE ID: VATV755-A]

Leo XII established this congregation in 1826 to watch over public employees in the Papal States and investigate their activities. It had a short existence.

RECORDS. Records of the congregation consist of the following series.

5.1.71.1 [Archivio]
[DATABASE ID: VATV170-A]

Inclusive Dates: 1826–1829.

Bulk: 13 linear m.

Organization: The series is divided into 48 casella numbered groupings and 5 unnumbered boxes. Each casella number represents a different subject; however, casella numbers do not exactly correspond with the boxes, that is, some caselle take up whole boxes and others are filed together in one box. Casella numbers are as follows: 1. Providenze generale; —2–4. Camerlengato; —5. Tribunale della segnatura; —6. Buon governo; —7. Direzione del censo; —8. Tribunale dell'apostolica camera; —9. Tribunale del governo e cronaca di Roma; —10. Direzione generale di polizia; —11. Tesorierato generale; —12. Stati criminale and S. consulta; —13–14. Palazzi, ospizio apostolico; —16. Presidenza delle strade; —17. Acque e ripa; —18. Grascia; —19. Presidenza della zecca; —20. Prefettura dell'annona; —21. Prefettura degli archivi; —22. Congregazione economica; —23. Congregazione delle acque; —24. Senatore di Roma; —25. Conservatori di Roma; —26. Comando generale civico; —27. Congregazione militare; —28. Legazioni di Bologna; —29. Ibid. Ferrara; —30. Ibid. Forlì; —31–32. Delegazione di Urbino e Pesaro; —33. Ibid. Macerata e Camerino; —34. Ibid. Ascoli e Fermo (includes "Carte originali delle questioni Marini); —35. Delegazione di Rieti e Spoleto; —36. Ibid. Civitavecchia e Viterbo; —37. Ibid. Ancona; —38. Ibid. Perugia (including posizioni cancellieri); —39. Ibid. Frosinone; —40. Ibid. Benevento; —41–42. Commissione speciale di Romagna settari; —43–45. Risoluzioni della congregazione; —46–47. Istanze per impieghi; —48. Relazioni a sua santita.

Unnumbered boxes are divided as follows: Miscellaneous (2 boxes); —Suppliche (2 boxes organized alphabetically); —Sommario e relazione della consultazione (1 box).

References: Fink, p. 119; Boyle, p.78.

Finding Aids: ASV Indici 886 and 887 are protocolli to this series. Running from May 1826 to October 1829, protocollo entries list the progressive number of each item; its provenance, date, and another number; the object of the letter; date and summary of the response; and "Archivio" numbers, which correspond to the casella numbers listed above. Occasionally, in the "Archivio" section there is another, generally smaller, number written above or below the archivio/casella number. This number refers to the progressive number of a related item in the series.

This congregation should be cited as SS. Congregazione di Vigilanza. This series does not have an ASV designated title. Project staff assigned the title *Archivio* to distinguish it from the series described below. It is identified by Boyle as "Commissione di vigilanza."

Location: Archivio Segreto Vaticano.

5.1.71.2 Congregazione di vigilanza
[DATABASE ID: VATV20129-A]

Inclusive Dates: 1826–1830.

Bulk: 6 buste.

References: D'Angiolini, p. 1152; Lodolini (1960), pp. 91–93.

Finding Aids: Inventory, 1962; there is also a printed inventory.

Location: Archivio di Stato di Roma.

5.1.72 Congregazione economica
[DATABASE ID: VATV616-A]

Several congregations with this name existed in different periods. The first was established by Clement XI in 1708 to study a system of taxation to support the papal army. The second was established by Benedict XIV in 1746 to direct and administer the treasury of the Papal States and to improve the functioning of the state's economic offices in Rome and other cities. The third was established in 1800 by Pius VII. In 1815, by action of the secretary of state, a congregation with this name was established a fourth time, with increased powers; it was given control over the Tesoreria and the Buon governo. In addition it had responsibility for commerce, industry, taxes, and customs.

RECORDS. Records of the congregation consist of the following series.

5.1.72.1 [Archivio]
[DATABASE ID: VATV278-A]

Inclusive Dates: 1463–1830 (bulk 1815–1830).

Bulk: 20 linear m.

Organization: There are 98 numbered buste. Buste 1–68 are chronological by date of meeting.

Scope: The initial 68 buste are organized around the date of what perhaps was an actual meeting when the congregation discussed a certain issue. Materials in these packets can therefore be radically different from the date of the meeting, as in some cases (e.g. busta 41) materials from much earlier (1463) was gathered to inform the congregation on a current decision. Materials often contain notes of past decisions.

References: Fink, pp. 118–119; Boyle, p. 89.

Finding Aids: ASV Blocchetti Indice 11 provides a very detailed inventory of each busta. This index includes the busta title, inclusive dates, and a detailed list of contents. Although inclusive dates are always listed, the corresponding items are not always calendared. Even though the index is very comprehensive and appears to be a calendar, it is not entirely complete. It is safe to assume that contents are summarized.

Note: The title to this series was supplied by the project staff. It has no designated title in the ASV.

Location: Archivio Segreto Vaticano.

5.1.72.2 Congregazioni economiche
[DATABASE ID: VATV20048-A]

Inclusive Dates: 1708–1722, 1746–1748, 1800–1808, and 1815–1835.

Bulk: 152 buste, vols., and registri.

Organization: Congregazione economica, 1708–1722, 65 buste, vols., and registri; —Congregazione economica, 1746–1748, 1 vol.; —Congregazione economica, 1800–1808, 60 buste, vols., and registri; —Congregazione economica, 1815–1835, 18 buste, vols., and registri; —Commissione mista per la liquidazione dei debiti comunitativi nelle province di prima recupera, 1820–1825, 1 busta and 3 vols.; —Commissione deputata per la dimissione dei debiti comunitativi nelle province di prima recupera, 1826–1835, 2 buste and 2 registri.

References: D'Angiolini, pp. 1119–1120; Lodolini (1960), pp. 135–138.

Finding Aid: Inventory, 1978.

Location: Archivio di Stato di Roma.

5.1.72.3 Luoghi pii
[DATABASE ID: VATV10124-A]

Inclusive Dates: ca. 1500–1824 (bulk 1790–1803).

Bulk: 2 linear m.

Organization: 36 numbered volumes and 1 unnumbered formulary. Vols. 1–34 are alphabetical.

Scope: In general this series contains materials resulting from a census done by the congregation to determine the financial state of pious societies. There is information on the material, spiritual, economic, and political state of dioceses and hospitals (see vol. 21) in Italy. Information concerning Rome can be found in vol. 36. There are also some records of transactions with Monte di Pietà.

Finding Aids: ASV Indice 1142 by Sergio Pagano provides a good introduction to the series and then gives detailed information of the contents. The index is divided into columns giving the packet number, pagination, and then inclusive dates for the major divisions of the packet. Many documents and/or reports receive brief annotations. There is a separate index by diocese at the end of the indice.

Location: Archivio Segreto Vaticano.

5.1.72.4 [Miscellanea SF/439 1/2]
[DATABASE ID: VATV10193-A]

Inclusive Dates: 1815–1830.

Bulk: 6 linear m.

Scope: This series contains miscellaneous correspondence and reports from delegates throughout the Papal States (some organized by locality). It includes positions, rubrics, and so forth.

Note: This series has no official ASV designation. The title was supplied by the project staff based on the location of the material in 1990.

Location: Archivio Segreto Vaticano.

5.1.72.5 Servitù di Pascolo
[DATABASE ID: VATV10188-A]

Inclusive Dates: ca. 1790–1823.

Bulk: 1 linear m. (6 numbered buste and one unnumbered bundle)

Organization: Subseries are: Busta 1, Studi e Memorie, 1801–1823; —Busta 2, Corneto, 1801–1823; —Busta 3, Liberazione, 1790–1822; —Buste 4 and 5, Discarichi della comunita; —Busta 6 and bundle, Miscellanea.

Scope: Printed materials as well as written.

Location: Archivio Segreto Vaticano.

5.1.73 Congregazione governativa delle province dello Stato pontificio
[DATABASE ID: VATV874-A]

This congregation was established in 1816 by Pius VII. The congregation had a consultative function in the administration of the delegations of the Papal States. In 1831 a deliberative responsibility for the budget of the Papal States was added to its functions, but in 1850 it was returned to a consultative role only.

RECORDS. No records for this congregation were located, but series listed with another agency relate directly to this agency and should be consulted. See Camera Apostolica series *Miscellanea di congregazioni diverse.*

5.1.74 Congregazione militare
[DATABASE ID: VATV793-A]

Pius VII established this congregation in 1797 from the combination of the Commissariato della mare and the Commissariato delle armi. In 1800 the congregation was made dependent on the secretary of state. After being abolished by the Roman republic and later by the French, the congregation was reestablished in 1801 and 1815, respectively. In 1828 Gregory XVI transformed it into the Presidenza delle armi.

In addition to the records listed below, series listed with another agency relate directly to this agency and should be consulted. See Papal States, Presidenza delle armi series *Soldatesche e galere.*

RECORDS. Records of the congregation consist of the following series.

5.1.74.1 Congregazione militare
[DATABASE ID: VATV20185-A]
Inclusive Dates: 1823–1828.
Bulk: 169 buste.
Reference: D'Angiolini, pp. 1188–1189.
Finding Aid: Summary inventory.
Location: Archivio di Stato di Roma.

5.1.75 Congregazione per la revisione dei conti
[DATABASE ID: VATV772-A]

This cameral congregation was established by Pius IV (1559–1565) to revise the budgets of provincial treasurers, collectors, and contractors. It was reorganized by Paul V in 1605. It was suppressed in 1800 and its responsibilities transferred to the Tribunale della Camera apostolica.

RECORDS. Records of the congregation consist of the following series.

5.1.75.1 Congregazione per la revisione dei conti
[DATABASE ID: VATV20027-A]
Inclusive Dates: 1671–1795.
Bulk: 96 vols.
References: D'Angiolini, pp. 1091–1092; Lodolini (1960), pp. 140–142.
Finding Aids: There is an inventory of the first 56 volumes and a separate inventory with index for the other 40 volumes.
Location: Archivio di Stato di Roma.

5.1.76 Congregazione per la riedificazione della basilica di S. Paolo
[DATABASE ID: VATV670-A]

Leo XII established this congregation in 1825 to oversee the reconstruction of the Basilica of St. Paul Outside the Walls, which had been destroyed by fire in 1823. The office was also called a commission.

RECORDS. Records of the congregation consist of the following series.

5.1.76.1 Commissione per la riedificazione della basilica di S. Paolo
[DATABASE ID: VATV20210-A]
Inclusive Dates: 1825–1880 (bulk 1825–1870).
Bulk: 229 buste, 15 vols., 84 registri, 23 rubrice, and 1 protocollo.
References: D'Angiolini, p. 1195; Lodolini (1960), p. 95.
Finding Aids: A summary inventory prepared in 1934 is not reliable. A new list was prepared in 1972.
Location: Archivio di Stato di Roma.

5.1.77 Congregazione speciale di sanità
[DATABASE ID: VATV677-A]

Gregory XVI established this congregation in 1834 for the study and reform of health legislation and regulations governing the health professions. It may also have been known as Ramo sanità.

In addition to the records listed below, series listed with another agency relate directly to this agency and should be consulted. See Papal States miscellaneous series *Miscellanea del periodo costituzionale.*

RECORDS. Records of the congregation consist of the following series.

5.1.77.1 Congregazione speciale di sanità
[DATABASE ID: VATV20184-A]
Inclusive Dates: 1800–1870.
Bulk: 792 buste, vols., and registri.
References: D'Angiolini, p. 1188; Lodolini (1960), pp. 115–116.
Finding Aids: There is a summary inventory and indexes of pharmacies and pharmacists and of maps of tree-cutting concessions.
Location: Archivio di Stato di Roma.

5.1.78 Conservatores Almae Urbis
[DATABASE ID: VATV902-A]

The conservatori were representatives of the noble families of Rome, who watched over aqueducts, antiquities, statues, and the city walls. They punished merchants for cheating on weights and prices and granted the rights of Roman citizenship. As a tribunal, they had civil and criminal jurisdiction. See also the entry in this section for the Tribunale dei conservatori.

RECORDS. Records of the agency consist of the following series.

5.1.78.1 Conservatori
[DATABASE ID: VATV10125-A]
Inclusive Dates: 1726–1854 (bulk 1800–1828).
Bulk: 1 linear m. (There are 13 numbered volumes and 1 unnumbered volume.)
Organization: They divide into fourteen series: 1. Divina providenza a Ripetta, 1726–1828; —2. Pio, 1827; —3. Santa Enfermia, 1809–1827; —4. Mendicanti, 1810–1827; Conservatorio di S. Pasquale, 1810–1827; Conservatorio dei Pericolanti, 1810–1814; Depositi di Mendicità, 1815; —5. Conservatorio di Santa Caterina della Rosa, 1815; Conservatorio Borromeo, 1811–1817; —6. Santa Maria del Refugio, 1811–1815; —7. Conservatorio di San Vito e Modesto, 1811–1812; Conservatorio delle Zoccolette, 1814–1820; San Paolo primo eremita, 1827; Ospizio Ponte Sisto 1835–1854; Pia Casa d'Industria, 1827–1828; —8. Commissione dei Conservatori, 1810–1812; —9. Amministrazioni dei Conservatori, 1810–1813; —10. Commissioni dei Conservatori, 1811–1814; —11. Amministrazione dei Conservatori, 1810–1814; —12. Amministrazione dei Conservatori di Terracina, 1817–1827; —13. Carte Diverse delle deputazione permanente dei Conservatori di Roma, 1825–1829; Conservatorio Trinitonie, 1827; Conservatorio delle Zoccolette, 1814–1820; —14. Carte varie, 1771–1794.
Finding Aid: A prospectus to the Conservatori series is avail-

able behind the main desk in the ASV reading room. The prospectus is located in a file designated as Luoghi Pii. The prospectus, which is largely reproduced in the organizational note above, provides busta number, location, and dates for the first thirteen items in the series.

Location: Archivio Segreto Vaticano.

5.1.79 Consiglio centrale di censura
[DATABASE ID: VATV248-A]

This office was established in the mid-nineteenth century. The records extant from the office indicate that it had rather broad jurisdiction. However, no precise history of the office could be found.

RECORDS. Records of the agency consist of the following series.

5.1.79.1 [Archivio]
[DATABASE ID: VATV10198-A]
Inclusive Dates: 1849–1851.
Bulk: 14 linear m. (48 buste)
Organization: Subseries include: 1. Verbali e risoluzioni durante la Commissione governativa; —2–5. Correspondence and the like with other offices, for example, Interno ministero, Grazia e giustizia ministero, Commercio e lavori pubblici ministero, Finanze ministero; —6–26. [Correspondence, etc. concerning towns within the Papal States], (organized alphabetically by town); —27–42. Censura di grazia, Lettere (alphabetical); —43–45. Censura di grazia, Rapporti diversi; —46–48. Censura.
Finding Aid: ASV Indice 1120 lists each busta briefly with the inclusive dates and its exterior title.
Note: This series has no official ASV designation. The title of the series, *Archivio*, was supplied by project staff.
Location: Archivio Segreto Vaticano.

5.1.79.2 Consiglio dei ministri: Posizioni d'affari e decisioni
[DATABASE ID: VATV10204-A]
Inclusive Dates: 1850–1873.
Bulk: .3 linear m. (2 buste).
Organization: Chronological.
Scope: These appear to be complete positions. Some have elaborate biographies, and there are diverse issues discussed such as conservation of forests, police, and so forth.
Finding Aid: ASV Indice 1120 briefly lists these buste.
Location: Archivio Segreto Vaticano.

5.1.79.3 Protocollo degli atti della Segreteria
[DATABASE ID: VATV10202-A]
Inclusive Dates: 1849–1853.
Bulk: .3 linear m. (3 vols.).
Organization: Chronological.
Scope: Entries are recorded under "iniziativa" (date, provenienza, oggetto) or "evasiva" (date, risoluzione, collocazione, osservazioni).
Location: Archivio Segreto Vaticano.

5.1.79.4 Sussidi concessi agli impiegati e militari dimessi o in riposo
[DATABASE ID: VATV10203-A]
Inclusive Dates: 1871–1878.
Bulk: 1 linear m. (9 buste).
Organization: Chronological.
Finding Aid: ASV Indice 1120 briefly lists each busta and its inclusive dates.
Location: Archivio Segreto Vaticano.

5.1.80 Consiglio d'arte
[DATABASE ID: VATV664-A]

This office was established in 1817 as a consultative organ of the Presidenza delle strade, which in 1833 became the Prefettura generale delle acque e strade and in 1847 the Ministero dei lavori pubblici. It had responsibility for inspection of street work.

RECORDS. Records of the agency consist of the following series.

5.1.80.1 Consiglio d'arte
[DATABASE ID: VATV20177-A]
Inclusive Dates: 1815–1870.
Bulk: 134 buste and 73 registri.
Reference: D'Angiolini, p. 1186.
Finding Aid: Summary inventory.
Location: Archivio di Stato di Roma.

5.1.81 Consiglio dei deputati
[DATABASE ID: VATV815-A]

This office was established in the 1848 constitution of the Papal States, replacing in part the Consulta di Stato.

RECORDS. No records for this office were located, but series listed with another agency relate directly to this agency and should be consulted. See Papal States miscellaneous series *Miscellanea del periodo costituzionale.*

5.1.82 Consiglio dei ministri
[DATABASE ID: VATV794-A]

This office was established in June 1847 as a result of a reform of the Papal States government. It included the segretario di stato as president, the camerlengo, the prefetto delle acque e strade, the uditore di camera, the governatore di Roma, the tesoriere generale, and the presidente delle armi. In December 1847 it was expanded to nine departments: Estero (headed by the segretario di stato, who also served as president of the council); Armi; Commercio, belle arti, industria, e agricoltura; Finanze; Grazia e giustizia; Interno; Instruzione pubblica; Lavori pubblica; and Polizia. Each ministry has a separate agency history.

In addition to the records listed below, series listed with another agency relate directly to this agency and should be consulted. See Papal States miscellaneous series *Miscellanea del periodo costituzionale*.

RECORDS. Records of the office consist of the following series.

5.1.82.1 [Archivio]
[DATABASE ID: VATV10286-A]
Inclusive Dates: 1847–1865.
Bulk: 1.5 linear m.
Organization: Subseries/items include: Verbali [Rubricelle], 1847–1865, 11 vols.; —Miscellanea, 3 buste; —Presidenza, 1 busta.
Note: The ASV has no designation for this series. The title was supplied by project staff.
Location: Archivio Segreto Vaticano.

5.1.83 Consiglio di finanza
[DATABASE ID: VATV847-A]

This office was established in 1832 to assist the tesoriere generale. In 1832 the Cassa di ammortizzazione and Consiglio di liquidazione del debito pubblico were transferred to this council from the Direzione generale del debito pubblico.

RECORDS. No records for this office were located.

5.1.84 Consiglio di guerra pontificio
[DATABASE ID: VATV708-A]

This office was active in the nineteenth century.

RECORDS. No records for this office were located.

5.1.85 Consiglio di Stato (1848–1849)
[DATABASE ID: VATV699-A]

This office was established in 1848, replacing in part the Consulta di Stato. It was suppressed by the Roman republic of 1849. This was the first body with this name, known as the Costituzionale.

RECORDS. Records of the office consist of the following series.

5.1.85.1 Consiglio di Stato
[DATABASE ID: VATV20190-A]
Inclusive Dates: 1848–1849.
Bulk: 4 buste, 1 registro, and 1 protocollo.
Reference: D'Angiolini, pp. 1190–1191.
Finding Aid: Inventory.
Location: Archivio di Stato di Roma.

5.1.86 Consiglio di Stato (1850–1870)
[DATABASE ID: VATV735-A]

This office was established by the secretary of state in 1850. This is the second body with this name. It had consultative and contentious jurisdiction.

In addition to the records listed below, series listed with another agency relate directly to this agency and should be consulted. See Papal States, Direzione generale di polizia series *Direzione generale di polizia*.

RECORDS. Records of the offfice consist of the following series.

5.1.86.1 Consiglio di Stato
[DATABASE ID: VATV20194-A]
Inclusive Dates: 1851–1870.
Bulk: 73 buste, 8 vols., and 2 protocolli.
References: D'Angiolini, p. 1192; Lodolini (1960), p. 207.
Finding Aids: Summary inventory accompanied by rubricelle of the posizioni.
Location: Archivio di Stato di Roma

5.1.86.2 [Miscellanea SF/473–SF/475]
[DATABASE ID: VATV10284-A]
Inclusive Dates: ca. 1818–1870.
Bulk: 15 linear m.
Organization: Subseries/items include: Congressi dei signori presidenti, 1860–1869; —Protocolli; —Passaporti; —Posizioni; —Codice penale; —Codice di procedura civile; —Miscellanea giuridica; —Opinamenti e pareri; —Politica; —Legislativa; —Leggi e regolamenti di altri stati; —Contenzioso amministrativo.
Note: This title was supplied by the project staff. There is no official ASV designation for this material.
Location: Archivio Segreto Vaticano.

5.1.86.3 Processi
[DATABASE ID: VATV10255-A]
Inclusive Dates: ca. 1842–1860.
Bulk: 5 linear m.
Organization: Cases numbered 1–1037.
Location: Archivio Segreto Vaticano.

5.1.87 Consiglio fiscale
[DATABASE ID: VATV731-A]

This office was established in 1832, to replace the Congregazione dei residui. The council assisted the tesoriere generale, with responsibility for examining questions related to the financial administration of the Camera. In 1850 its jurisdiction was extended to all the ministries. It was also known as the Ufficio generale fiscale.

RECORDS. Records of the office consist of the following series.

5.1.87.1 Consiglio fiscale denominato anche Ufficio generale fiscale
[DATABASE ID: VATV20155-A]
Inclusive Dates: 1832–1870.
Bulk: 45 buste, 8 registri, 53 vols., and 5 rubrice.
References: D'Angiolini, pp. 1174–1175; Lodolini (1960), p. 198.
Finding Aids: Partial summary inventory.
Location: Archivio di Stato di Roma.

5.1.88 Consulta di Stato
[DATABASE ID: VATV828-A]

This was a consultative assembly of state established in 1847 by Pius IX. It was replaced in 1848 by the Alto consiglio, Consiglio dei deputati, and Consiglio di stato. This is not the same as the Sacra Consulta established in 1588.

RECORDS. Records of the agency consist of the following series.

5.1.88.1 Consulta di Stato
[DATABASE ID: VATV20189-A]
Inclusive Dates: 1847–1848.
Bulk: 6 buste.
Reference: D'Angiolini, p. 1190.
Finding Aid: Inventory, 1952.
Location: Archivio di Stato di Roma.

5.1.89 Consulta di Stato per le finanze
[DATABASE ID: VATV722-A]

This office was established in 1849 to examine and revise budgets of state and give opinions on financial matters.

RECORDS. Records of the office consist of the following series.

5.1.89.1 Consulta di Stato per le finanze
[DATABASE ID: VATV20162-A]
Inclusive Dates: 1850–1870.
Bulk: 109 buste and 56 vols.
References: D'Angiolini, p. 1177; Lodolini (1960), pp. 194–195.
Finding Aid: Inventory.
Location: Archivio di Stato di Roma.

5.1.90 Controllo generale
[DATABASE ID: VATV721-A]

This office was established in 1835 to conduct audits. Its responsibilities had formerly been performed by the Computisteria generale and the Congregazione di revisione. In 1847 its responsibility was extended to include all income and expenses of the Papal States. It was initially dependent on the tesoriere generale. From 1848 to 1870 it was an independent agency.

RECORDS. Records of the office consist of the following series.

5.1.90.1 Controllo generale denominato anche Ufficio del controllo o Controlleria generale
[DATABASE ID: VATV20159-A]
Inclusive Dates: 1835–1870.
Bulk: 15 buste and 7 protocolli.
References: D'Angiolini, p. 1176; Lodolini (1960), pp. 193–194.

Finding Aid: Printed inventory.
Location: Archivio di Stato di Roma.

5.1.91 Corpo degli ingegneri di acque e strade
[DATABASE ID: VATV714-A]

This office was established in 1817 to supervise and inspect public works.

RECORDS. Records of the office consist of the following series.

5.1.91.1 Corpo degli ingegneri di acque e strade
[DATABASE ID: VATV20178-A]
Inclusive Dates: 1817–1870.
Bulk: 89 buste.
References: D'Angiolini, pp. 1186–1187; Lodolini (1960), p. 207.
Finding Aid: Summary inventory.
Location: Archivio di Stato di Roma.

5.1.92 Delegazione speciale dei telegrafi
[DATABASE ID: VATV719-A]

This office was active in the nineteenth century.

RECORDS. No records for this office were located.

5.1.93 Depositeria generale
[DATABASE ID: VATV653-A]

The depositeria was a subordinate office of the Camera Apostolica. It served as a cashier's office, and received all revenues.

RECORDS. Records of the agency consist of the following series.

5.1.93.1 Depositeria generale della Camera apostolica
[DATABASE ID: VATV20141-A]
Inclusive Dates: 1816–1870.
Bulk: 2,097 buste, mazzi and registri.
References: D'Angiolini, p. 1165; Lodolini (1960), pp. 180–181.
Finding Aids: Summary inventory; there are also indexes to some of the series.
Location: Archivio di Stato di Roma.

5.1.94 Depositeria urbana
[DATABASE ID: VATV620-A]

This office was established in 1629 by Urban VIII to regulate mortgages, provide for the security of lenders, and guard debtors from injury. It also served as bank of deposit for judicial pledges. The depositeria was suppressed in 1855, and its functions taken over by the Monte di pietà.

RECORDS. Records of the office consist of the following series.

5.1.94.1 [Archivio]

[DATABASE ID: VATV10367-A]
Inclusive Dates: ca. 1842–1850.
Bulk: 2 linear m.
Organization: There are 20 buste with documents arranged alphabetically by papal land holdings. Only the following alphabetical letters are represented: A, C, F, G, L–P, R, S, T, V, Z. The final volume is entitled *Stampati.*
Scope: This is for the most part correspondence between the Presidenza della comarca and the camerlengo.
Note: The title for this series was supplied by the project staff. There is no specific ASV designation for this material.
Location: Archivio Segreto Vaticano.

5.1.94.2 Depositeria urbana

[DATABASE ID: VATV20033-A]
Inclusive Dates: 1630–1874.
Bulk: 243 buste and 45 registri.
Organization: Esecuzioni e depositi, 1816–1871, 46 buste; —Subaste e delibere, 1814–1871, 36 buste; —Editti, 1649–1801, 13 buste; —Delibere, 1630–1803, 9 buste; —Vendite e delibere di beni stabili, 1800–1873, 53 buste; —Avvisi di vendite, 1856–1868, 4 buste; —Vendite d'ufficio: verbali, 1853–1871, 1 busta; —Mandati di consegna, 1814–1871, 72 buste; —Entrata e uscita e giustificazioni di cassa, 1792–1858 and 1871–1874, 8 buste; —Personale, 1784–1819, 1 busta; —Registri generali e rubricelle, 1820–1872, 45 registri.
References: D'Angiolini, p. 1094; Lodolini (1960), pp. 181–182.
Finding Aid: Inventory.
Location: Archivio di Stato di Roma.

5.1.95 Deputazione dell'annona e grascia

[DATABASE ID: VATV776-A]

About 1828 this deputazione was formed by uniting the former Deputazione dell'annona and Deputazione della grascia. Its authority was parallel to that of the Presidenza dell'annona e grascia. It was responsible for supplies of grain, meat, oil, and other provisions. Its responsibility ended about 1847.

RECORDS. No records for this office could be located, but series listed with another agency relate directly to this agency and should be consulted. See Papal States, Presidenza dell'annona e grascia series *Presidenze e Deputazioni dell'annona e della grascia.*

5.1.96 Direzione dei telegrafi

[DATABASE ID: VATV718-A]

This office was established in the 1850s, dependent on the Ministero del commercio, belle arti, industria, agricoltura, e lavori pubblici.

RECORDS. Records of the office consist of the following series.

5.1.96.1 Direzione dei telegrafi

[DATABASE ID: VATV20182-A]
Inclusive Dates: 1853–1870.
Bulk: 26 buste and 3 registri.
References: D'Angiolini, p. 1187; Lodolini (1960), p. 208.
Finding Aid: Inventory.
Location: Archivio di Stato di Roma.

5.1.97 Direzione generale degli archivi

[DATABASE ID: VATV845-A]

This office was established in 1848 from the Presidenza degli archivi as a dependency of the Ministero dell'interno. Responsibility for the supervision of the notarial profession was added at that time. The office was abolished in 1870.

RECORDS. Records of the office consist of the following series.

5.1.97.1 Presidenza poi Direzione generale degli archivi

[DATABASE ID: VATV20131-A]
Inclusive Dates: 1822–1871.
Bulk: 390 buste and 112 vol.
References: D'Angiolini, pp. 1154–1155; Lodolini (1960), pp. 62–64.
Finding Aid: Summary inventory. There is also an asphabetical index of notai.
Location: Archivio di Stato di Roma.

5.1.98 Direzione generale dei dazi diretti e proprietà camerali

[DATABASE ID: VATV848-A]

This office was established in 1832 as a dependency of the tesoriere generale. As the name implies, the direzione was responsible for taxes and cameral property. In 1848 it became a dependency of the Ministero delle finanze. In 1850 responsibility for taxes was transferred to the Direzione generale delle dogane, and this agency was renamed Direzione generale delle proprietà camerali.

RECORDS. See Papal States, Direzione generale delle proprietà camerali series *Direzione generale dei dazi diretti e delle proprietà camerali poi Direzione generale delle proprietà camerali.*

5.1.99 Direzione generale del bollo e registro

[DATABASE ID: VATV727-A]

This office was established in 1816 as the Amministratione del bollo e registro, and was subordinate to the tesoriere generale. It served as a registry office. The administration was reorganized in 1827. In 1832 it became a direzione generale of the tesoriere generale with responsibility for mortgages transferred from the Presidenza degli archivi. In 1848 the office became a direzione generale of the Ministero delle finanze. A later name of the office was *Direzione generale del bollo, registro, ipoteche, e tasse riunite.*

RECORDS. Records of the office consist of the following series.

5.1.99.1 Amministrazione poi Direzione generale del bollo, registro, ipoteche, e tasse riunite

[DATABASE ID: VATV20149-A]
Inclusive Dates: 1801–1881 (bulk 1816–1870).
Bulk: 757 buste and 281 registri.
References: D'Angiolini, p. 1172; Lodolini (1960), p. 197.
Finding Aids: There is a summary inventory of buste and a list of registri.
Location: Archivio di Stato di Roma.

5.1.99.2 Conservatoria delle ipoteche

[DATABASE ID: VATV20208-A]
Inclusive Dates: 1809–1918.
Bulk: 237 buste and 1,616 registri.
Reference: D'Angiolini, p. 1194.
Finding Aid: Partial inventory, 1954.
Location: Archivio di Stato di Roma.

5.1.99.3 Ufficio del bollo, registro, ipoteche e tasse riunite

[DATABASE ID: VATV20207-A]
Inclusive Dates: 1816–1871.
Bulk: 1,986 registri, 35 vols., and 3 rubrice.
Reference: D'Angiolini, p. 1194.
Finding Aid: List, 1954.
Location: Archivio di Stato di Roma.

5.1.100 Direzione generale del debito pubblico

[DATABASE ID: VATV660-A]

This office was established in 1816 with responsibility for the public debt of the Papal States. In 1822 a Cassa di ammortizzazione was established, and in 1832 a Consiglio di liquidazione del debito pubblico, both closely related to the direzione. Part of the responsibility of these agencies was transferred from the Computisteria generale and the Secretary of State. In 1832 the direzione and the cassa became part of the Consiglio di finanza. In 1847 the direzione became dependent on the tesoriere generale, and later in that year on the Ministero delle finanze.

RECORDS. Records of the office consist of the following series.

5.1.100.1 Direzione generale del debito pubblico

[DATABASE ID: VATV20150-A]
Inclusive Dates: 1810–1880 (bulk 1816–1870).
Bulk: 3,175 buste, 146 cassette, 541 registri, 283 vols., 162 protocolli, and 57 rubrice.
References: D'Angiolini, pp. 1172–1173; Lodolini (1960), pp. 195–196.
Finding Aid: Printed inventory, 1992.
Location: Archivio di Stato di Roma.

5.1.101 Direzione generale delle carceri, case di condanne e luoghi di pena

[DATABASE ID: VATV846-A]

This office was established in 1847 as a dependency of the Ministero dell'interno. Prisons were previously the responsibility of the Congregatio Sacra Consulta, and before the reforms of early 1847 of the tesoriere generale. The Direzione generale was responsible for prisons of the Papal States except in Rome (which were the responsibility of the Ministero di polizia).

RECORDS. Records of the office consist of the following series.

5.1.101.1 Direzione generale delle carceri, case di condanna, e luoghi di pena

[DATABASE ID: VATV20132-A]
Inclusive Dates: 1804–1871 (bulk 1847–1870).
Bulk: 589 buste, 419 registri, rubrice, and protocolli.
Reference: D'Angiolini, p. 1155.
Finding Aid: Summary inventory, 1970.
Location: Archivio di Stato di Roma.

5.1.102 Direzione generale delle dogane

[DATABASE ID: VATV723-A]

This office was established in 1828 to combine responsibility for customs previously split between the tesoriere generale and Computisteria generale. The direzione was responsible for customs in all the Papal States and for consumption taxes in Rome and the four legations. In 1832 the direzione became a direzione generale of the tesoriere, and in 1847 a direzione generale of the Ministero delle finanze. At that time its name was changed to Direzione generale delle dogane e dazi di consumo. In 1850 responsibility for direct taxes was transferred from the Direzione generale delle proprietà camerali and it was renamed the Direzione generale delle dogane, dazi diretti e indiretti.

Among the offices dependent on the Direzione generale delle dogane were the Amministrazione delle saline di Cervia e di Comacchio, Sovrintendenza dei piroscafi, and Truppa di finanza.

RECORDS. Records of the office consist of the following series.

5.1.102.1 Direzione generale delle dogane, dazi di consumo, e diritti uniti

[DATABASE ID: VATV20145-A]
Inclusive Dates: 1762–1870 (bulk 1828–1870).
Bulk: 2,368 buste, mazzi, vols., and registri.
References: D'Angiolini, pp. 1170–1171; Lodolini (1960), p. 196.
Finding Aid: Inventory, in part analytical, in part summary.
Location: Archivio di Stato di Roma.

5.1.103 Direzione generale delle poste
[DATABASE ID: VATV717-A]

After the restoration of 1814 this office was established as the Amministrazione delle poste, dependent on the tesoriere generale. In 1848 it became a direzione generale of the Ministero delle finanze.

RECORDS. Records of the office consist of the following series.

5.1.103.1 Amministrazione poi Direzione generale delle poste
[DATABASE ID: VATV20151-A]
Inclusive Dates: 1814–1872.
Bulk: 239 buste, 267 registri, protocolli, and rubricelle.
References: D'Angiolini, p. 1174; Lodolini (1960), p. 208.
Finding Aid: Inventory (in part summary, in part analytical), 1970.
Location: Archivio di Stato di Roma.

5.1.104 Direzione generale delle proprietà camerali
[DATABASE ID: VATV732-A]

This office was established in 1850 from the Direzione generale dei dazi diretti e delle proprietà camerali when responsibility for direct taxes was transferred from that office to the Direzione generale delle dogane.

RECORDS. Records of the office consist of the following series.

5.1.104.1 Direzione generale dei dazi diretti e delle proprietà camerali poi Direzione generale delle proprietà camerali
[DATABASE ID: VATV20144-A]
Inclusive Dates: 1848–1870.
Bulk: 1,274 buste, 182 vols., 44 protocolli, and 21 indici dei protocolli.
References: D'Angiolini, p. 1170; Lodolini (1960), p. 199.
Finding Aid: Summary inventory.
Location: Archivio di Stato di Roma.

5.1.105 Direzione generale di polizia
[DATABASE ID: VATV733-A]

This agency was established in 1816 as a central authority for police in Rome, dependent on the secretary of state and later on the segreteria per gli affari di Stato interni. The governor of Rome was the director. Among the groups dependent on the direzione were the carabinieri; later the gendarmeria, and the bersaglieri. In 1833 the agency's jurisdiction was extended to the delegations and to the legation of Velletri. Its responsibility was expanded to include statistics and the construction industry. In 1847 the governor of Rome lost his judicial competence but the direzione remained under his control. Later in 1847 the Ministero di polizia took over responsibility for police, but in 1850 the direzione was reestablished.

Among the offices dependent on the Direzione generale di polizia was the Commissione delle recupere.

In addition to the records listed below, series listed with other agencies relate directly to this agency and should be consulted. See Papal States miscellaneous series *Miscellanea del periodo costituzionale* and *Miscellanea di carte politiche e riservate*.

RECORDS. Records of the agency consist of the following series.

5.1.105.1 Direzione generale di polizia
[DATABASE ID: VATV10258-A]
Inclusive Dates: 1814–1860.
Bulk: 16 linear m.
Organization: Collection appears to be organized regionally by towns and areas.
Scope: Records subtitled Carceri and Cause politiche.
Location: Archivio Segreto Vaticano.

5.1.105.2 Direzione generale di polizia
[DATABASE ID: VATV20133-A]
Inclusive Dates: 1816–1870.
Bulk: 3,420 buste and 2,159 registri.
Organization: Protocollo ordinario, 1816–1870, 2,529 buste, 1,737 protocolli (with gaps), 234 rubricelle (with gaps), and 40 registri; —Protocollo segreto, 1835–1870, 727 buste, 47 rubriche alfabetiche, 50 registri, and 51 protocolli; —Commissione delle recupere, 1849–1850, 9 buste; —Polizia, ordine pubblico, 1818–1870, 48 buste; —Polizia, personale, 1820–1848, 50 buste; —Carte Randi, 1820–1870, 57 buste.
References: D'Angiolini, pp. 1156–1158; Lodolini (1960), pp. 208–209.
Finding Aids: Summary inventories for almost all the series.
Location: Archivio di Stato di Roma.

5.1.106 Esercito. Divisione, Prima. Uditorato militare
[DATABASE ID: VATV889-A]

This agency was the military tribunal of the first instance for the Prima divisione, headquartered in Rome.

RECORDS. Records of the agency consist of the following series.

5.1.106.2 Uditorato militare della prima divisione (di Roma)
[DATABASE ID: VATV20254-A]
Inclusive Dates: 1831–1870.
Bulk: 52 buste, 5 rubrice, and 3 protocolli.
References: D'Angiolini, p. 1204; Lodolini (1960), p. 203.
Finding Aid: Inventory.
Location: Archivio di Stato di Roma.

5.1.107 Giudice delle mercedi
[DATABASE ID: VATV769-A]

This agency was established in 1629 as a tribunal concerned with the payment of rural workers. Suppressed in 1809, its jurisdiction transferred to the justice of the peace of Rome. In 1814 it was reestablished. In 1831 it was combined with the Tribunale civile del senatore, and when that tribunal was suppressed in 1847, it was taken over by the Tribunale civile di Roma.

RECORDS. Records of the agency consist of the following series.

5.1.107.1 Giudice delle mercedi
[DATABASE ID: VATV20225-A]
Inclusive Dates: 1831–1870.
Bulk: 5 vols.
References: D'Angiolini, pp. 1196–1197; Lodolini (1960), pp. 120–121.
Finding Aid: Inventory, 1971.
Location: Archivio di Stato di Roma.

5.1.108 Giunta di Stato
[DATABASE ID: VATV637-A]

The giunta was a provisional regime established after the fall of the Roman republic in September 1799. Its responsibility ended with the return of the new pope, Pius VII, in June 1800.

RECORDS. Records of the agency consist of the following series.

5.1.108.1 Giunta di Stato
[DATABASE ID: VATV20106-A]
Inclusive Dates: 1799–1800.
Bulk: 236 fascicoli.
References: D'Angiolini, p. 1141; Lodolini (1960), pp. 184–185.
Finding Aids: Inventory.
Location: Archivio di Stato di Roma.

5.1.109 Guardia civica di Roma
[DATABASE ID: VATV636-A]

The guardia was established as a civil militia in 1796 by Pius VI in response to French threats. It was intended to maintain order and strengthen the regular troops. In 1815 it was reestablished by the secretary of state. Alternative names include Milizia civile and Truppa civica di Roma.

RECORDS. Records of the agency consist of the following series.

5.1.109.1 Guardia civica di Roma
[DATABASE ID: VATV20197-A]
Inclusive Dates: 1813–1847 (bulk 1815–1847).
Bulk: 33 buste.
Reference: D'Angiolini, pp. 1192–1193.
Finding Aids: Summary inventory, 1920.
Location: Archivio di Stato di Roma.

5.1.109.2 Truppa civica di Roma, IV reggimento
[DATABASE ID: VATV20056-A]
Inclusive Dates: 1796–1798.
Bulk: 3 buste and 4 vols.
References: D'Angiolini, p. 1126; Lodolini (1960), p. 183.
Finding Aid: Inventory.
Location: Archivio di Stato di Roma.

5.1.110 Guardia civica scelta
[DATABASE ID: VATV122-A]

In 1851 this group was united with the Milizia Urbana by Pius IX to form the Palatine Guard of Honor.

RECORDS. No records for this group were located.

5.1.111 Impresa dei lotti
[DATABASE ID: VATV728-A]

Public lotteries began in the Papal States in the seventeenth century. In 1848 administration of the lotteries became a direzione generale of the Ministero delle finanze.

RECORDS. Records of the agency consist of the following series.

5.1.111.1 Impresa e amministrazione generale dei lotti poi Direzione generale dei lotti
[DATABASE ID: VATV20054-A]
Inclusive Dates: 1756–1870.
Bulk: 764 buste and 182 registri.
References: D'Angiolini, pp. 1123–1125; Lodolini (1960), p. 197.
Finding Aid: List, 1970.
Location: Archivio di Stato di Roma.

5.1.112 Magistrato centrale di sanità e polizia marittima di Civitavecchia
[DATABASE ID: VATV890-A]

Originally known as the Ispettorato di sanità marittima e polizia dei porti di Civitavecchia, this office was responsible for maritime, harbor, and sanitary matters for the entire Tyrrhenian Sea coast of the Papal States. The apostolic delegate in Civitavecchia was president of the Magistrato centrale.

RECORDS. Records of the agency consist of the following series.

5.1.112.1 Ispettorato di sanità marittima e polizia dei porti di Civitavecchia poi Magistrato centrale di sanità e polizia marittima di Civitavecchia
[DATABASE ID: VATV20212-A]
Inclusive Dates: 1819–1870.
Bulk: 90 buste.
Reference: D'Angiolini, p. 1195.
Finding Aid: Summary inventory.
Location: Archivio di Stato di Roma.

5.1.113 Milizia urbana
[DATABASE ID: VATV121-A]

In 1851 this group was joined with the Guardia civica scelta to form the Palatine Guard of Honor.

RECORDS. No records for this group were located.

5.1.114 Ministero dei lavori pubblici
[DATABASE ID: VATV799-A]

Established in 1847, this office received responsibilities transferred from the Camerlengato and the Prefettura d'acque e strade The minister was a member of the Consiglio dei ministri. In 1850 the office was united with the Ministero dei commercio, belle arti, industria, e agricoltura to form the Ministero dei lavori pubblici, commercio, e belle arti.

RECORDS. Records of the agency consist of the following series.

5.1.114.1 Prefettura generale di acque e strade poi Ministero dei lavori pubblici
[DATABASE ID: VATV20175-A]
Inclusive Dates: 1834–1866 (bulk 1834–1855).
Bulk: 847 buste, registri, protocolli, and rubrice.
Reference: D'Angiolini, pp. 1183–1185.
Finding Aid: Partial summary inventories.
Location: Archivio di Stato di Roma.

5.1.115 Ministero dei lavori pubblici, commercio, e belle arti
[DATABASE ID: VATV712-A]

In 1850 the Ministero dei lavori pubblici was combined with the Ministero de commercio, belle arti, industria, e agricoltura to form the Ministero dei lavori pubblici, commercio, e belle arti. Its responsibilities were transferred from the Camerlengato and Prefettura d'acque e strade. The minister was a member of the Consiglio dei ministri. An alternate name for this agency is Ministero de commercio, agricoltura, industria, belle arti, e lavori pubblici.

Among the offices dependent on this ministry were the Commissariato generale delle ferrovie and the Direzione dei telegrafi.

RECORDS. Records of the agency consist of the following series.

5.1.115.1 Ministero del commercio, belle arti, industria, agricoltura, e lavori pubblici
[DATABASE ID: VATV20176-A]
Inclusive Dates: 1826–1873 (bulk 1855–1870).
Bulk: 651 buste, 140 registri, 89 protocolli, and 18 rubrice.
References: D'Angiolini, pp. 1185–1186; Lodolini (1960), pp. 204–205.
Finding Aids: Summary inventory; particular inventories of individual series, 1965 and 1983.
Location: Archivio di Stato di Roma.

5.1.116 Ministero del commercio, belle arti, industria, e agricoltura
[DATABASE ID: VATV797-A]

This office was established in 1847 and took over most of the responsibilities of the Camerlengato. The minister was a member of the Consiglio dei ministri. In 1850 the office was joined to the Ministero dei lavori pubblici and became the Ministero dei lavori pubblici, commercio, e belle arti.

RECORDS. No records for this office were located, but series listed with other agencies relate directly to this agency and should be consulted. See Papal States miscellaneous series *Miscellanea del periodo costituzionale, 1846–1849,* and Papal States, Ministero dei lavori pubblici, commercio e belle arti series *Ministero del commercio, belle arti, industria, agricoltura e lavori pubblici.*

5.1.117 Ministero dell'estero
[DATABASE ID: VATV795-A]

Established in 1847, this office was held by the secretary of state, who as minister was a member of the Consiglio dei ministri.

RECORDS. See Secretariatus Status in the section "Roman Curia: Offices."

5.1.118 Ministero dell'interno
[DATABASE ID: VATV705-A]

Established in 1847, this office combined responsibilities previously held by the Segreteria per gli affari di Stato interni and the Congregazione del buon governo. The ministry supervised the internal administration of the Papal States, including responsibility for local government, records, hospitals, almshouses, food supply, forests, health, and census. It also took powers from the Sacra Consulta, including responsibility for prisons (except the prisons of Rome). The minister was a member of the Consiglio dei ministri. In 1848 responsibility for food supply was transferred to the Ministero dei commercio. The office took responsibility for the maintenance of public order from the Ministero di polizia from 1848 until the Direzione generale di polizia was reestablished in 1850. In 1853 responsibility for the administration of justice was transferred from the Ministero di grazia e giustizia. Among the offices dependent on this ministry were the Commissione mista pel brigantaggio, Direzione generale degli archivi, and Direzione generale delle carceri, case di condanne, e luoghi di pena.

In addition to the records listed below, series listed with other agencies relate directly to this agency and should be consulted. See Papal States miscellaneous series *Miscellanea del periodo costituzionale* and *Miscellanea di carte politiche e riservate.*

RECORDS. Records of the agency consist of the following series.

5.1.118.1 Amministrazione delle carceri di Roma
[DATABASE ID: VATV20203-A]
Inclusive Dates: 1853–1871.
Bulk: 529 cassette.
Reference: D'Angiolini, p. 1193.
Finding Aid: Summary inventory, 1970.
Location: Archivio di Stato di Roma.

5.1.118.2 Carcere dei minori di Santa Balbina
[DATABASE ID: VATV20205-A]
Inclusive Dates: 1845 and 1853–1896.
Bulk: 46 buste and 22 registri.
Reference: D'Angiolini, p. 1194.
Finding Aid: Summary inventory, 1970.
Location: Archivio di Stato di Roma.

5.1.118.3 Case di detenzione, di pena e correzione
[DATABASE ID: VATV20206-A]
Inclusive Dates: 1817–1895.
Bulk: 203 buste, 205 registri, and protocolli.
Organization: Casa di detenzione alle Terme diocleziane, 1817–1891; —Casa di pena famminile di villa Altieri, 1871–1895; —Casa di correzione di S. Michele a Ripa, 1855–1894; —Castel Sant'Angelo, 1817–1850.
Reference: D'Angiolini, p. 1194.
Finding Aid: Summary inventory, 1970.
Location: Archivio di Stato di Roma.

5.1.118.4 Segreteria per gli affari di Stato interni poi Ministero dell'interno
[DATABASE ID: VATV20130-A]
Inclusive Dates: 1827–1870 (bulk 1833–1870).
Bulk: 2,417 buste, 696 registri, 378 protocolli, and 379 rubricelle.
Organization: Protocollo ordinario, 1827–1870 (bulk 1833–1870), 2,228 buste, 696 registri, 377 protocolli and 379 rubricelle; —Casermaggio estero, 1831–1870, 161 buste; —Protocollo riservato, 1849–1870, 28 buste and 1 protocollo.
References: D'Angiolini, pp. 1153–1154; Lodolini (1960), pp. 200–201.
Finding Aids: Various inventories.
Location: Archivio di Stato di Roma.

5.1.119 Ministero dell'istruzione pubblica
[DATABASE ID: VATV796-A]

This ministry was established in 1847 from the Congregazione degli studi, and given responsibility for all teaching that was not the responsibility of the ecclesiastical authorities. The minister was a member of the Consiglio dei ministri. The ministry's jurisdiction extended to schools, colleges, libraries, and scientific academies. The ministry was abolished in 1849 and its duties absorbed by a reestablished Congregazione degli studi.

RECORDS. No records for this ministry could be located, but series listed with another agency relate directly to this agency and should be consulted. See Congregatio Studiorum series *Congregazione degli studi.*

5.1.120 Ministero delle armi
[DATABASE ID: VATV707-A]

This ministry was established in 1847 from the Presidenza delle armi and was given responsibility for armies, armories, fortresses, military schools and hospitals. The minister was a member of the Consiglio dei ministri.

In addition to the records listed below, series listed with another agency relate directly to this agency and should be consulted. See Papal States miscellaneous series *Miscellanea del periodo costituzionale.*

RECORDS. Records of the agency consist of the following series.

5.1.120.1 Ministero delle armi
[DATABASE ID: VATV20187-A]
Inclusive Dates: 1801–1880 (bulk 1848–1870).
Bulk: 3,155 buste, 1,811 protocolli, rubrice, and registri di matricole.
References: D'Angiolini, pp. 1189–1190; Lodolini (1960), pp. 202–203.
Finding Aids: Summary inventory; There is also an alphabetical rubric of buste for 1518 and 1519 as well as a partial printed inventory.
Location: Archivio di Stato di Roma.

5.1.120.2 Miscellanea dei volontari delle campagne 1848–1849
[DATABASE ID: VATV20188-A]
Inclusive Dates: 1848–1849.
Bulk: 209 buste and 1 registro.
References: D'Angiolini, p. 1190; Lodolini (1960), pp. 212–213.
Finding Aids: Inventory. There are also alphabetical indexes and rubrics as well as a printed summary inventory.
Location: Archivio di Stato di Roma.

5.1.121 Ministero delle finanze
[DATABASE ID: VATV720-A]

This ministry was established in 1847, with responsibilities formerly held by the tesoriere. The minister was a member of the Consiglio dei ministri. The ministry was comprised of five active direzioni: Dazi diretti e proprietà camerali, Dogane e dazi di consumo, Bollo e registro, Lotti, and Poste; and one passive direzione: Direzione generale del debito pubblico. The Direzione del tesoro was also subordinate. Responsibility for mines was transferred from the Camerlengato. Responsibility for the mint was transferred from the Presidenza della zecca.

Among the offices dependent on this ministry was the Commissione di liquidazione dei crediti a tutto giugno 1849.

RECORDS. Records of the agency consist of the following series.

5.1.121.1 Ministero delle finanze
[DATABASE ID: VATV20143-A]
Inclusive Dates: 1847–1870.
Bulk: 194 buste and 142 registri.
Organization: Protocollo generale o della segreteria, 1848–1870, 150 buste and 142 protocolli; —Rendiconti annuali con le rispettive fedi originali di deposito delle amministrazioni camerali, 1847–1869, 44 buste.
References: D'Angiolini, pp. 1169–1170; Lodolini (1960), pp. 192–193.
Finding Aid: Partial summary inventory.
Location: Archivio di Stato di Roma.

5.1.122 Ministero di grazia e giustizia
[DATABASE ID: VATV716-A]

Established in 1847 from the Auditor Camerae, this ministry was given responsibility for the administration of justice and supervision of courts. The minister was a member of the Consiglio dei ministri. In 1853 the ministry was suppressed and its competence transferred to the Ministero dell'interno.

RECORDS. Records of the agency consist of the following series.

5.1.122.1 Ministero di grazia e giustizia
[DATABASE ID: VATV20136-A]
Inclusive Dates: 1834–1867 (bulk 1848–1853).
Bulk: 397 buste, 31 vols., 34 protocolli, 2 registri, and 44 rubrice alfabetiche.
References: D'Angiolini, pp. 1159–1160; Lodolini (1960), p. 207.
Finding Aid: Summary inventory.
Location: Archivio di Stato di Roma.

5.1.123 Ministero di polizia
[DATABASE ID: VATV798-A]

Established in 1847, this ministry had responsibility for the maintenance of public order and for the prisons of Rome. The minister was a member of the Consiglio dei ministri. The ministry was suppressed in 1848 and the major part of its competence transferred to the Ministero dell'interno. Some responsibilities were also transferred to the Ministero del commercio, belle arti, industria, e agricoltura.

RECORDS. No records for this ministry were located, but series listed with another agency relate directly to this agency and should be consulted. See Papal States, Direzione generale di polizia series *Direzione generale di polizia.*

5.1.124 Notai del consolato dei fiorentini
[DATABASE ID: VATV894-A]

Leo X (1513–1521) established a private tribunal composed of the Florentine consul and two consiglieri.

The tribunal was abolished by Innocent XII (1691–1700), but the office of the notai remained.

In addition to the records listed below, series listed with another agency relate directly to this agency and should be consulted. See Papal States miscellaneous series *Testamenti segreti.*

RECORDS. Records of the agency consist of the following series.

5.1.124.1 Notai del consolato dei fiorentini
[DATABASE ID: VATV20377-A]
Inclusive Dates: 1562–1893.
Bulk: 467 vols., 5 vols. protesti, 11 repertori, and 1 rubricella.
Scope: Sixteenth century, 14 vols.; —Seventeenth century, 157 vols.; —Eighteenth century, 109 vols.; —Nineteenth century, 187 vols.
Reference: D'Angiolini, p. 1216.
Finding Aid: There is a printed list of notai.
Location: Archivio di Stato di Roma.

5.1.125 Notai del tribunale del governatore
[DATABASE ID: VATV747-A]

Established in 1617, these were notaries of the criminal chancery of the Tribunale del governatore. The office was suppressed in 1849.

RECORDS. Records of the agency consist of the following series.

5.1.125.1 Notai del tribunale criminale del governatore
[DATABASE ID: VATV20077-A]
Inclusive Dates: 1617–1849.
Bulk: 182 vols. and 1 protesti registro.
Scope: Seventeenth century, 32 vols.; —Eighteenth century, 94 vols.; —Nineteenth century, 56 vols.
References: D'Angiolini, p. 1135; Lodolini (1960), p. 60.
Finding Aids: Summary inventory. There is also an alphabetical index of notai and a printed list of notai.
Location: Archivio di Stato di Roma.

5.1.126 Notai del tribunale dell'agricoltura
[DATABASE ID: VATV748-A]

Established in 1602, the office was suppressed in 1845. See the agency history of the Tribunale dell'agricoltura.

RECORDS. Records of the agency consist of the following series.

5.1.126.1 Notai del tribunale dell'agricoltura
[DATABASE ID: VATV20085-A]
Inclusive Dates: 1602–1845.
Bulk: 317 vols.
Scope: Seventeenth century, 88 vols.; —Eighteenth century, 193 vols.; —Nineteenth century, 36 vols.
References: D'Angiolini, p. 1137; Lodolini (1960), p. 60.

Finding Aids: Inventory, 1983. There is also an alphabetical index of notai and a printed list of notai.
Location: Archivio di Stato di Roma.

5.1.127 Notai del tribunale dell'auditor camerae
[DATABASE ID: VATV742-A]

This office was established in 1487. The number of notaries varied: ten notaries from 1566 to 1692; five notaries from 1693 to 1820; then the number declined, to one in 1871, when the office was suppressed. See the agency history for the Tribunale dell'auditor camerae.

RECORDS. Records of the agency consist of the following series.

5.1.127.1 Notai del tribunale dell'auditor camerae
[DATABASE ID: VATV20065-A]
Inclusive Dates: 1487–1871.
Bulk: 7,316 vols.
Scope: These are for the most part Istrumenti (7,235 vols.). They subdivide as follows: Fifteenth century, 1 vol.; —Sixteenth century, 1,403 vols.; —Seventeenth century, 4,166 vols.; —Eighteenth century, 1,413 vols.; —Nineteenth century, 252 vols. There are also Testamenti (81 vols.). These subdivide as follows: Sixteenth century, 3 vols.; —Sixteenth–seventeenth century, 14 vols.; —Seventeenth century, 59 vols.; —Eighteenth century, 5 vols.
References: D'Angiolini, p. 1129; Lodolini (1960), p. 59.
Finding Aids: Summary inventory. There is also an alphabetical index of notai, an inventory of wills and donations, and a printed list of notai.
Location: Archivio di Stato di Roma.

5.1.128 Notai del tribunale delle ripe
[DATABASE ID: VATV745-A]

The office was established in 1555 and was suppressed in 1820. See the agency history for the Tribunale delle ripe.

RECORDS. Records of the agency consist of the following series.

5.1.128.1 Notai del tribunale delle ripe
[DATABASE ID: VATV20044-A]
Inclusive Dates: 1555–1835.
Bulk: 269 vols.
Organization: Curia di Ripetta, 1555–1820, 159 vols.; —Curia di Ripagrande, 1629–1835, 110 vols.
Scope: Curia di Ripetta volumes subdivide as follows: Sixteenth century, 10 vols.; —Seventeenth century, 58 vols.; —Eighteenth century, 73 vols.; —Nineteenth century, 18 vols. Curia di Ripagrande subdivide as follows: Seventeenth century, 30 vols.; —Eighteenth century, 49 vols.; —Nineteenth century, 31 vols.
References: D'Angiolini, pp. 1105–1106; Lodolini (1960), p. 59.
Finding Aids: Various inventories, 1979.
Location: Archivio di Stato di Roma.

5.1.129 Notai del tribunale delle strade
[DATABASE ID: VATV746-A]

This office was established in 1554 and was suppressed in 1833. An alternate name is Notai di acque e strade. See also the agency history of the Tribunale delle strade.

RECORDS. Records of the agency consist of the following series.

5.1.129.1 Notai del tribunale delle strade
[DATABASE ID: VATV20041-A]
Inclusive Dates: 1553–1833.
Bulk: 247 vols.
Scope: Sixteenth century, 30 vols.; —Seventeenth century, 93 vols.; —Eighteenth century, 77 vols.; —Nineteenth century, 47 vols.
References: D'Angiolini, pp. 1103–1104; Lodolini (1960), p. 60.
Finding Aids: There is an old summary inventory and an old index of names of notai. There is also a summary inventory, 1975, with index of names of notai as well as a printed list of notai.
Location: Archivio di Stato di Roma.

5.1.130 Notaro maggiore della camera capitolina
[DATABASE ID: VATV896-A]

Established in 1778 with the division of the office of Protonotaro del senatore, the office was continued after the end of the Papal States as the Notaro maggiore presso al municipio romano.

In addition to the records listed below, series listed with another agency relate directly to this agency and should be consulted. See Papal States miscellaneous series *Testamenti segreti.*

RECORDS. Records of the agency consist of the following series.

5.1.130.1 Notaro maggiore della camera capitolina
[DATABASE ID: VATV20379-A]
Inclusive Dates: 1755–1890.
Bulk: 134 vols., 4 buste, and 16 registri.
Reference: D'Angiolini, p. 1216.
Finding Aids: Inventory, 1979. There is also a printed list of notai.
Location: Archivio di Stato di Roma.

5.1.131 Prefettura degli archivi
[DATABASE ID: VATV801-A]

Established in 1588, the prefetto was a chierico di camera. In 1822 the office became a presidenza, with responsibility for mortgages added.

RECORDS. Records of the agency consist of the following series.

5.1.131.1 Prefettura degli archivi
[DATABASE ID: VATV20046-A]
Inclusive Dates: 1705–1825.
Bulk: 49 buste and 118 registri in 20 buste.
References: D'Angiolini, pp. 1110–1111; Lodolini (1960), pp. 62–64.
Finding Aids: Summary inventory of administrative acts and list (1970) of judicial acts.
Location: Archivio di Stato di Roma.

5.1.132 Prefettura dell'annona
[DATABASE ID: VATV800-A]

This office was established by Julius II (1503–1513) to provide for the importation of grain, fix the price of grain, and purchase grain for resale to bakers. The prefetto was a chierico di camera. Several temporary congregations with similar names had parallel responsibility at different times. In 1828 the prefettura was united with the Presidenza della grascia to form the Presidenza dell'annona e grascia.

RECORDS. No records for this office were located, but series listed with another agency relate directly to this agency and should be consulted. See Papal States, Presidenza dell'annona e grascia series *Presidenze e Deputazioni dell'annona e della grascia.*

5.1.133 Prefettura dell'ergastolo di Corneto
[DATABASE ID: VATV40063-A]

No history of this agency could be found.

RECORDS. Records of the agency consist of the following series.

5.1.133.1 [Archivio]
[DATABASE ID: VATV10262-A]
Inclusive Dates: 1572–1871.
Bulk: 45 linear m.
Organization: Subseries are as follows: Ergastolo di Corneto (Regolamenti, visite e relazioni), 1752–1849, 1 busta; — Registro generale dei condannati, 1814–1870, 1 vol.; —Tabelle dei detenuti, 1814–1847, 1 busta; —Specchi dei detenuti, 1822–1843, 1 busta; —Carteggio relativo ai detenuti, 1832–1869, 1 busta; —Posizioni personali dei detenuti, 1814–1869, 11 buste; —Contabilit . . . e carteggio relativo, 1821–1871, 24 buste; —Rendiconti della prefettura dell'Ergastolo di Corneto al Ministero dell'Interno, 1866–1867, 1 busta; —Atti Civilia, 1572–1870, about 200 vols. (in 1728 becomes Atti Civilia-Curiae Episcopalis), most volumes indexed by name; —Liber Matrimoniorum, 1631–1651, 1 vol.; —Processus, ca.1630–1659, 1 linear m.; —Introitus, 1779, 1 vol.; — Miscellaneous buste, 15 linear m.
Reference: Fink p. 134.
Finding Aids: ASV Indice 1123 provides a brief listing of the initial subseries Ergastolo di Corneto. Entries indicate the current segnatura, the inclusive dates, and the general nature of the volume or buste (posizioni, regolamenti, contabilità).

Note: The title for this series was supplied by the project staff. The series has no offical designation by the ASV.
Location: Archivio Segreto Vaticano.

5.1.134 Prefettura di Castel Sant'Angelo
[DATABASE ID: VATV803-A]

The prefetto was a chierico di camera.

RECORDS. No records for this office were located, but series listed with another agency relate directly to this agency and should be consulted. See Papal States, Presidenza delle armi series *Soldatesche e galere.*

5.1.135 Prefettura generale di acque e strade
[DATABASE ID: VATV663-A]

This office was established in 1833 from the Congregazione delle acque and the Presidenza delle strade, with responsibility for roads, navigation, ports, and public works in general. In 1847 the prefetto became a member of the Consiglio dei ministri, and responsibility for the port of Rome was transferred from the tesoriere generale. Later in 1847 the prefettura was transformed into the Ministero dei lavori pubblici.

RECORDS. No records for this office were located, but series listed with another agency relate directly to this agency and should be consulted. See Papal States, Ministero dei lavori pubblici series *Prefettura generale di acque e strade poi Ministero dei lavori pubblici.*

5.1.136 Presidenza degli acquedotti urbani
[DATABASE ID: VATV610-A]

The office existed as early as the 1500s for the administration of the Roman aqueducts. The presidente was a chierico di camera. The presidenza was abolished during the French period (1809–1814) when the municipality of Rome had responsibility for the aqueducts. The presidenza was reestablished in 1814.

RECORDS. Records of the agency consist of the following series.

5.1.136.1 Presidenza degli acquedotti urbani
[DATABASE ID: VATV20039-A]
Inclusive Dates: 1557–1870.
Bulk: 87 buste.
References: D'Angiolini, p. 1103; Lodolini (1960), p. 153.
Finding Aid: Summary inventory.
Location: Archivio di Stato di Roma.

5.1.137 Presidenza degli archivi
[DATABASE ID: VATV844-A]

This office was established in 1822 from the Prefettura degli archivi but was given added responsibility for mortgages. In 1832 mortgages were transferred to the direzione generale del bollo e registro. In 1848, with the institution of the ministerial system, the presidenza became a direzione generale dependent on the Ministero dell'interno.

RECORDS. No records for this office were located, but series listed with another agency relate directly to this agency and should be consulted. See Papal States, Direzione generale degli archivi series *Presidenza poi Direzione generale degli archivi.*

5.1.138 Presidenza dell'annona e grascia
[DATABASE ID: VATV613-A]

Leo XII established this office in 1828 from a combination of the Prefettura dell'annona and the Presidenza della grascia, with responsibility for regulation of the trade in grain, meat, oil, and other provisions. In 1847 its responsibilities were transferred to the municipality of Rome, to the Ministero dell'interno, and to the Ministero del commercio.

RECORDS. Records of the agency consist of the following series.

5.1.138.1 Presidenze e Deputazioni dell'annona e della grascia
[DATABASE ID: VATV20049-A]
Inclusive Dates: 1571–1860.
Bulk: 1,401 buste, 1,217 registri, 3 vols., and 4 rubrice.
References: D'Angiolini, pp. 1106–1109; Lodolini (1960), pp. 156–162.
Finding Aid: Summary inventory.
Location: Archivio di Stato di Roma.

5.1.139 Presidenza della grascia
[DATABASE ID: VATV805-A]

This office existed by 1599, with responsibility for oil, for procuring cattle for slaughter, and for other provisions. The presidente was a chierico di camera. In 1828 the presidenza was combined with the Prefettura dell'annona to form the Presidenza dell'annona e grascia.

RECORDS. No records for this office were located, but series listed with another agency relate directly to this agency and should be consulted. See Papal States, Presidenza dell'annona e grascia series *Presidenze e Deputazioni dell'annona e della grascia.*

5.1.140 Presidenza della zecca
[DATABASE ID: VATV777-A]

This office existed as early as the sixteenth century, in charge of the mint. The presidente della zecca was a chierico di camera. The presidenza was confirmed in 1828 by Leo XII. In 1847 the mint became the responsibility of the Ministero delle finanze, and the presi-

denza ceased to exist.

In addition to the records listed below, series listed with another agency relate directly to this agency and should be consulted. See Miscellaneous official series *Miscellaneorum armarium VIII.*

RECORDS. Records of the agency consist of the following series.

5.1.140.1 Presidenza della zecca
[DATABASE ID: VATV20053-A]
Inclusive Dates: 1749–1881 (bulk 1749–1870).
Bulk: 295 buste and 77 registri and fascicoli.
Reference: D'Angiolini, pp. 1122–1123.
Location: Archivio di Stato di Roma.

5.1.140.2 Zecca di Roma
[DATABASE ID: VATV20209-A]
Inclusive Dates: 1749–1870.
Bulk: ca. 300 buste and cassette.
References: D'Angiolini, p. 1194; Lodolini (1960), p. 165.
Location: Archivio di Stato di Roma.

5.1.141 Presidenza delle armi
[DATABASE ID: VATV661-A]

This office was established in 1828 by Leo XII from the Congregazione militare. The presidente delle armi was a chierico di camera. In 1847 the presidente became a member of Consiglio dei ministri, and responsibility for armories was transferred from the tesoriere generale. Later in 1847 the presidenza was transformed into the Ministero delle armi.

RECORDS. Records of the office consist of the following series.

5.1.141.1 Epoca napoleonica: Presidenza delle armi
[DATABASE ID: VATV40018-A]
Inclusive Dates: 1840–1845.
Bulk: 14 vols.
Note: This series was cited in Natalini et al., p. 274, but not seen by project staff in 1990.
Location: Archivio Segreto Vaticano.

5.1.141.2 Presidenza delle armi
[DATABASE ID: VATV20186-A]
Inclusive Dates: 1828–1847.
Bulk: 1,060 buste.
Reference: D'Angiolini, p. 1189.
Finding Aid: Summary inventory.
Location: Archivio di Stato di Roma.

5.1.141.3 Soldatesche e galere
[DATABASE ID: VATV20013-A]
Inclusive Dates: 1431–1841.
Bulk: 774 buste and 41 registri.
References: D'Angiolini, pp. 1079–1080; Lodolini (1960), p. 80.
Finding Aid: Inventory, 1912.
Location: Archivio di Stato di Roma.

5.1.142 Presidenza delle carceri
[DATABASE ID: VATV806-A]

This office was in existence by 1548. The presidente was a chierico di camera.

RECORDS. No records were located for this office.

5.1.143 Presidenza delle dogane
[DATABASE ID: VATV807-A]

The presidente was a chierico di camera.

RECORDS. No records were located for this office.

5.1.144 Presidenza delle ripe
[DATABASE ID: VATV614-A]

This office was in existence by 1545, with administrative and judicial control over the Roman ports and the Tiber. The presidente delle ripe was a chierico di camera. The duties of the office were defined by Benedict XII in 1725. In 1828 Leo XII transferred the presidenza's administrative function to the tesoriere generale, and the office became a section of the Tesorierato. In 1847 the office became part of the Prefettura generale di acque e strade.

RECORDS. Records of the office consist of the following series.

5.1.144.1 Presidenza delle ripe
[DATABASE ID: VATV20042-A]
Inclusive Dates: 1703–1849.
Bulk: 73 buste and registri.
References: D'Angiolini, pp. 1104–1105; Lodolini (1960), pp. 162–164.
Finding Aid: Inventory, 1979.
Location: Archivio di Stato di Roma.

5.1.145 Presidenza delle strade
[DATABASE ID: VATV611-A]

This office was in existence before 1549, with administrative and judicial responsibility for roads. The presidente was a chierico di camera. In 1800 its responsibilities were transferred in great part to the Congregazione del buon governo. In 1816 its contentious jurisdiction ceased. Its name was changed in 1828 to Presidenza delle strade, acque e ripe, when responsibility for ports and navigation was added to its renewed responsibility for roads. In 1833 the presidenza was replaced by the Prefettura generale di acque e strade. This office is also known as Congregazione delle strade. Among the offices dependent on this presidenza was the Consiglio d'arte.

RECORDS. Records of the office consist of the following series.

5.1.145.1 Presidenza delle strade
[DATABASE ID: VATV20037-A]
Inclusive Dates: 1467–1833.
Bulk: 287 registri, 301 filze and 331 pacchi.
References: D'Angiolini, pp. 1100–1101; Lodolini (1960), pp. 153–156.
Finding Aids: Summary inventory.
Location: Archivio di Stato di Roma.

5.1.146 Presidenze regionarie di polizia
[DATABASE ID: VATV704-A]

This office was established in 1816 by the secretary of state to provide police protection in Rome. The presidenze were also responsible for the census.

RECORDS. Records of the office consist of the following series.

5.1.146.1 Presidenze regionarie di polizia
[DATABASE ID: VATV20198-A]
Inclusive Dates: 1847–1849.
Bulk: 56 buste.
References: D'Angiolini, p. 1193; Lodolini (1960), p. 214.
Finding Aids: Summary inventory.
Location: Archivio di Stato di Roma.

5.1.147 Procuratore del fisco
[DATABASE ID: VATV808-A]

This was at one time an office of the Camera.

RECORDS. No records for this office were located.

5.1.148 Sacro monte della pietà di Roma
[DATABASE ID: VATV891-A]

Founded by Giovanni Maltei da Calvi as a charitable institution and approved by Paul III in 1539, the Monte di pietà also served as a bank. It was managed by a confraternity known as S. Maria del sacro monte di pietà. In 1743 Benedict XIV placed the Monte di pietà in charge of the Depositeria della Camera apostolica and the tesoriere segreta. In 1855 the Monte took responsibilities formerly held by the Depositeria urbana.

In addition to the records listed below, series listed with another agency relate directly to this agency and should be consulted. See Papal States, Congregazione economica series *Luoghi pii.*

RECORDS. Records of the agency consist of the following series.

5.1.148.1 Monte di pietà
[DATABASE ID: VATV20374-A]
Inclusive Dates: 1585–1873.
Bulk: 728 registri, 491 buste, and 469 rubbricelle.
Organization: Depositi: libri mastri, 1585–1871; — Rubricelle dei depositi, 1641–1871; —Mandati cedole e giu-

stificazioni di pagamento, 1703–1709 and 1800–1873; —Ruoli di giubilazione, 1821–1834.
> *References:* D'Angiolini, p. 1225; Lodolini (1960), p. 104.
> *Finding Aid:* Inventory.
> *Location:* Archivio di Stato di Roma.

5.1.149 Segretaria per gli affari di Stato interni
[DATABASE ID: VATV810-A]

Gregory XVI (1831–1846), finding it a burden for one secretary of state to handle both internal (Papal States) and external affairs, directed a chirograph (Feb. 20, 1833) to the secretary of state instituting the Segreteria per gli affari di Stato interni. The task of the new secretariat was defined as "the organ of communication for the various ministers and dicasteries of the State of all the orders relative to internal affairs." This change was of short duration. On August 1, 1846, Pius IX (1846–1878) suppressed the new office, and though retaining the two divisions of the secretariat, reunited the two offices once again under one person.

In 1847 the internal section of the secretariat became the Ministero dell'interno, with responsibilities combined from this office and the Congregazione del buon governo.

Among the offices dependent on the secretary was the Direzione generale di polizia.

RECORDS. See "Secretariatus Status," listed among the offices of the Roman Curia, and Papal States, Ministero dell'interno series *Segreteria per gli affari di Stato interni poi Ministero dell'interno.*

5.1.150 Sovrintendenza dei piroscafi
[DATABASE ID: VATV724-A]

This office was active in the 1800s, with responsibility for the papal fleet. It was dependent on the Direzione generale delle dogane. In 1856 the navy was united with finance and postal steamers in this office.

RECORDS. Records of the office consist of the following series.

5.1.150.1 Sovrintendenza dei piroscafi
[DATABASE ID: VATV20146-A]
Inclusive Dates: 1820–1870.
Bulk: 80 buste.
References: D'Angiolini, pp. 1171–1172; Lodolini (1960), pp. 199–200.
Finding Aid: Summary inventory, 1914.
Location: Archivio di Stato di Roma.

5.1.151 Tesorierato generale della Camera apostolica
[DATABASE ID: VATV651-A]

In the thirteenth century, the office of thesaurarius was established with responsibility for control over the income derived from the temporal possessions of the church and other tribute accruing to the papal treasury. The office's functions were definitively set forth by Benedict XIV in 1742. It was responsible for a wide array of functions, including lotteries, jails, fortresses, ecclesiastical examinations, customs, ports, navigation, and administration of the city of Terracina. In 1800 the tesoriere became dependent on the camerlengo. Beginning in 1815 the office was responsible for all revenue and property, along with salt and tobacco, prisons and jails, banks, ports, arsenals, naval stores, and fortresses. Responsibility for ports and navigation was transferred to the Presidenza delle strade, acque e ripe, and responsibility for customs to the Direzione generale delle dogane in 1828. In 1832 the duties of the computisteria generale were added to the tesoriere's responsibility, and administration of revenues was divided among three direzioni generali: delle tasse diretti, delle dogane, and del bollo e registro. After 1832 the tesoriere was assisted by the Consiglio di finanza and Consiglio fiscale.

In 1847 the tesoriere became a member of the Consiglio dei ministri, while the office's duties were reduced: the tesoriere's judicial function was ended; responsibility for prisons was transferred to the Sacra Consulta; responsibility for armories to the Presidenza delle armi; responsibility for the port of Rome to the Prefettura delle acque e strade, and responsibility for the government of Porto and Fiumicino to the Presidenza delle Comarca. At the same time the Direzione generale del debito pubblico was made dependent on the tesoriere. After the loss of the Papal States in 1870 the position was not occupied.

Among the other offices dependent on the tesoriere in the nineteenth century were the Amministrazione dei boschi e delle foreste, Commissione dei crediti camerali arretrati, Congregazione del censo, and Direzione generale delle poste.

RECORDS. Records of the agency consist of the following series.

5.1.151.1 [Archivio]
[DATABASE ID: VATV10126-A]
Inclusive Dates: 1654–1658, 1670–1860 (bulk 1670–1788).
Bulk: 21 linear m.
Organization: 242 numbered vols. and 3 appendices. Subseries include: 1. Diverse, 1654–1658; —2. Registro, 1670–1788; —3. [Lettere di . . .] Umbria, Bologna, [etc.] Diverse, 1670–1788; —4. Patrimoni diverse, Marc(h)a diverse.

Diverse, 1654–1658 is alphabetical. Registro, Patrimoni diverse, and Marc(h)a diverse are chronological. [Lettere di . . .] is arranged geographically by town and chronologically.

Note: The title for this series was supplied by the project staff. There is no official ASV designation for this series.

Scope: This series contains incoming requests and outgoing responses. The tie between these is difficult to make at times. Selected registers contain indices that lead to letters in the

Registro and [Lettere di . . .] series. This series was originally interspersed with the Commissariato delle armi, Registro di lettere series.

Finding Aids: ASV Indice 195A primarily provides access to the Commissariato delle armi, Registro di lettere series. However, this indice does note which volumes are now part of this Tesoriere generale series and the full title and inclusive dates of those volumes. There is also a loose sheet in the front of this index that lists Tesoriere generale and Registro di lettere volumes with their old and new numbers and series designation.

ASV Indice 1122 provides access to the series through three methods: by volume, by date, and by geography. The first section of the index lists each volume, the full title and name of the tesoriere, inclusive dates, and alphabetical or geographical notes to materials included in each volume. The second section lists the volumes alphabetically and then chronologically in two groups: vols. 1–36 (solely alphabetical are given) and vols. 37–242 (where dioceses are listed, i.e., Bologna, Campagna, etc.). The third section is the only section in which the three "Appendice," called here the *Carte Tosti,* are listed. The appendices are organized into files and a general summation of material in each file is given.

Location: Archivio Segreto Vaticano.

5.1.151.2 Carteggio del tesoriere generale
[DATABASE ID: VATV20012-A]
Inclusive Dates: 1552–1816.
Bulk: 502 vols., registri, and mazzi.
References: D'Angiolini, p. 1080; Lodolini (1960), pp. 173–175.
Finding Aid: Inventory, 1983.
Location: Archivio di Stato di Roma.

5.1.151.3 Tesorierato generale della Camera apostolica
[DATABASE ID: VATV20142-A]
Inclusive Dates: 1814–1847.
Bulk: 1,726 buste, vols., and registri.
Organization: Protocollo generale o della segreteria, 1814–1847, 546 buste and several protocolli and registri; — Amministrazione I, 1837–1848, 310 buste and 77 registri; — Amministrazione III, 1829–1847 (bulk 1836–1847), 57 buste and 52 registri; —Amministrazione IV, 1837–1847, 130 buste and 58 registri; —Amministrazione V, 1828–1847, 394 buste and 43 registri; —Ruoli degli impiegati, 1836–1847, 59 buste and vols.
References: D'Angiolini, pp. 1166–1169; Lodolini (1960), pp. 173–175.
Finding Aids: There are partial summary inventories and lists for almost all of the series.
Location: Archivio di Stato di Roma.

5.1.151.4 Uditore del tesoriere
[DATABASE ID: VATV20241-A]
Inclusive Dates: 1818–1831.
Bulk: 29 buste and 25 registri.
Reference: D'Angiolini, p. 1200.
Finding Aid: Inventory, 1970.
Location: Archivio di Stato di Roma.

5.1.152 Tipografia camerale
[DATABASE ID: VATV868-A]

This office served as a printing agency of the Papal States.

RECORDS. Records of the office consist of the following series.

5.1.152.1 Tipografia camerale
[DATABASE ID: VATV20032-A]
Inclusive Dates: 1698–1871 (bulk 1773–1871).
Bulk: 227 buste.
References: D'Angiolini, pp. 1093–1094; Lodolini (1960), pp. 89–90.
Finding Aids: Inventory, 1876, accompanied by indexes.
Location: Archivio di Stato di Roma.

5.1.153 Tipografia vaticana
[DATABASE ID: VATV751-A]

This office served as a printing agency of the Papal States.

RECORDS. No records for this office could be located.

5.1.154 Tribunale civile di Roma
[DATABASE ID: VATV683-A]

Established in 1847, this tribunal was formerly known as Tribunale dell'auditor camerae. Also in 1847, the tribunal took over the civil jurisdiction of the Tribunale del senatore and the Giudice del mercedi.

RECORDS. Records of the agency conist of the following series.

5.1.154.1 Congregazione civile dell'auditor camerae poi Tribunale civile di Roma
[DATABASE ID: VATV20228-A]
Inclusive Dates: 1831–1871.
Bulk: 2,581 buste, 701 vols., 64 protocolli, and 53 rubrice.
Reference: D'Angiolini, p. 1197.
Finding Aid: Inventory.
Location: Archivio di Stato di Roma.

5.1.154.2 Presidenza del tribunale civile di Roma
[DATABASE ID: VATV20229-A]
Inclusive Dates: 1850–1870.
Bulk: 68 fascicoli and 16 buste.
References: D'Angiolini, p. 1197; Lodolini (1960), p. 208.
Finding Aid: Inventory, 1970.
Location: Archivio di Stato di Roma.

5.1.155 Tribunale criminale
[DATABASE ID: VATV622-A]

This tribunal was active in the sixteenth through nineteenth centuries.

RECORDS. No records for this tribunal were located.

5.1.156 Tribunale criminale dei bersaglieri
[DATABASE ID: VATV837-A]

The bersaglieri were established in 1833, dependent on the governor of Rome. In 1848 they were united with the carabinieri.

RECORDS. Records of the agency consist of the following series.

5.1.156.1 Tribunale criminale dei bersaglieri
[DATABASE ID: VATV20235-A]
Inclusive Dates: 1836–1842.
Bulk: 254 fascicoli, 1 registro, and 1 rubrica.
Reference: D'Angiolini, pp. 1198–1199.
Finding Aid: Inventory, 1970.
Location: Archivio di Stato di Roma.

5.1.157 Tribunale criminale del camerlengo
[DATABASE ID: VATV627-A]

This tribunal of the Camera was suppressed in 1809. See the agency history of the Camerlengato.

RECORDS. Records of the agency consist of the following series.

5.1.157.1 Tribunale criminale del camerlengo e del tesoriere
[DATABASE ID: VATV20024-A]
Inclusive Dates: 1645–1809 and 1814–1835.
Bulk: 781 buste.
Organization: Subseries include: Acqua, 1744–1822; —Agricoltura, 1673–1835; —Annona, 1725–1835; —Antichita, 1684–1835; —Armi e marina, 1686–1835; —Arte salutare e sanitarie, 1752–1835; —Basilica vaticana, 1827–1835; —Caccia e pesca, 1736–1831; —Carta, cera e stracci, 1677–1835; —Carte da giuoco, 1729–1835; —Depositeria, 1718–1835; —Dogana, 1738–1830; —Drappi, 1817–1829; —Forzati, 1717–1826; —Frodi, 1665–1825; —Lotti, 1677–1805; —Macinato, 1678–1835; —Monete, 1709–1807; —Monte di pietà, 1713–1829; —Neve e ghiaccio, 1806–1834; —Nitri e polveri, 1700–1835; —Ori e argenti, 1755–1835; —Personale, 1648–1835; —Pescheria, 1753–1833; —Pesi e misure, 1713–1834; —Piazza Navona, 1759–1835; —Poste, 1700–1835; —Privative, 1712–1835; —Sali e tabacchi, 1669–1835; —Sapienza, 1824–1834; —Sensali, 1818–1834; —Strade, tassa dei cavalli, 1645–1835; —Truppa di finanza, 1765–1835.
Reference: D'Angiolini p. 1090.
Finding Aids: There is a general list as well as an inventory (1956) for the items Acqua, Agricoltura, Annona.
Location: Archivio di Stato di Roma.

5.1.158 Tribunale criminale del tesoriere
[DATABASE ID: VATV626-A]

This tribunal of the Camera was suppressed in 1809. See the agency history for the Tesorierato.

RECORDS. No records could be located for this tribunal, but series listed with another agency relate directly to this agency and should be consulted. See Papal States, Tribunale crimi-nale del camerlengo series *Tribunale criminale del camerlengo e del tesoriere.*

5.1.159 Tribunale criminale di Roma
[DATABASE ID: VATV811-A]

In 1847 the Tribunale del governo became the Tribunale criminale di Roma, assuming responsibilities from the Tribunale del uditore di camera and the Tribunale del senatore.

RECORDS. Records of the agency consist of the following series.

5.1.159.1 Tribunale criminale della Camera apostolica poi Tribunale criminale di Roma
[DATABASE ID: VATV20245-A]
Inclusive Dates: 1835–1847 and 1848–1862.
Bulk: 1,191 fascicoli and 11 registri.
Reference: D'Angiolini, p. 1201.
Finding Aid: Inventory, 1970.
Location: Archivio di Stato di Roma.

5.1.159.2 Tribunale del governo di Roma poi Tribunale criminale di Roma
[DATABASE ID: VATV20231-A]
Inclusive Dates: 1814–1870.
Bulk: 2,691 buste, 284 registri, 21 buste, and vols., 380 protocolli, and 31 rubrice.
Reference: D'Angiolini, p. 1198.
Finding Aid: Partial inventory, 1971.
Location: Archivio di Stato di Roma.

5.1.160 Tribunale criminale pontificio
[DATABASE ID: VATV737-A]

This tribunal was active in the nineteenth century.

RECORDS. No records for this tribunal were located.

5.1.161 Tribunale dei conservatori
[DATABASE ID: VATV860-A]

The conservatori were representatives of the noble families of Rome, who watched over aqueducts, antiquities, statues, and the city walls. They punished merchants for cheating on weights and prices and granted the rights of Roman citizenship. As a tribunal, they had civil and criminal jurisdiction over matters in their competence as well as for appeals from the consuls of art and agriculture. The tribunal was suppressed in 1847.

RECORDS. Records of the agency consist of the following series.

5.1.161.1 Tribunale dei conservatori
[DATABASE ID: VATV20068-A]
Inclusive Dates: 1564–1837.
Bulk: 61 vols.
Reference: D'Angiolini, p. 1131.

Finding Aid: Inventory, 1970.
Location: Archivio di Stato di Roma.

5.1.161.2 Università di arti e mestieri
  [DATABASE ID: VATV20069-A]
  Inclusive Dates: 1541–1801.
  Bulk: 68 vols.
  Reference: D'Angiolini, p. 1132.
  Finding Aids: Inventory, 1970.
  Location: Archivio di Stato di Roma.

5.1.162 Tribunale dei maestri giustizieri
  [DATABASE ID: VATV861-A]

The origins of this tribunal are unclear, but it existed at least by 1513. It was made up of arbitrators who settled small cases between neighbors, relating to hedges, ditches, cane thickets, fruit, and streams. The tribunal was suppressed in 1801.

RECORDS. Records of the agency consist of the following series.

5.1.162.1 Tribunale dei maestri giustizieri
  [DATABASE ID: VATV20071-A]
  Inclusive Dates: 1546–1792.
  Bulk: 17 registri, 2 filze, and 1 busta.
  References: D'Angiolini, p. 1132; Lodolini (1960), p. 118.
  Finding Aid: Inventory, 1970 and 1980.
  Location: Archivio di Stato di Roma.

5.1.163 Tribunale del cardinale decano del sacro collegio
  [DATABASE ID: VATV862-A]

Traditionally the cardinal dean of the sacred college served as governor of the diocese of Ostia and Velletri, with civil and criminal jurisdiction over the region. In 1810 the diocese and the tribunal were abolished by the French government. The tribunal was reestablished in 1814 but was finally abolished in 1832.

RECORDS. Records of the agency consist of the following series.

5.1.163.1 Tribunale del cardinale decano del sacro collegio
  [DATABASE ID: VATV20086-A]
  Inclusive Dates: 1661–1809 and 1814–1831.
  Bulk: 35 vols. and 15 buste.
  Reference: D'Angiolini, pp. 1137, 1199.
  Finding Aid: Inventory, 1970.
  Location: Archivio di Stato di Roma.

5.1.164 Tribunale del cardinale vicario
  [DATABASE ID: VATV765-A]

This tribunal had civil and criminal jurisdiction over the clergy, laity, and holy places of Rome and its district. After 1550 it also had private jurisdiction over

the Jews of Rome. It was suppressed during the French regime, 1809–1814, reformed in 1831, and finally suppressed in 1863.

In addition to the records listed below, series listed with another agency relate directly to this agency and should be consulted. See Papal States miscellaneous series *Testamenti segreti.*

RECORDS. Records of the agency consist of the following series.

5.1.164.1 [Archivio]
  [DATABASE ID: VATV10285-A]
  Inclusive Dates: 1620–1863.
  Bulk: 1 linear m. (8 buste).
  Organization: Buste are not in chronological order.
  Note: The title for this series was supplied by the project staff. There is no official ASV designation for this series.
  Location: Archivio Segreto Vaticano.

5.1.164.2 Notai della curia del cardinale vicario
  [DATABASE ID: VATV20083-A]
  Inclusive Dates: 1508–1892.
  Bulk: 3,234 vols., 30 repertorii, 4 registri and fascicoli, 1 rubricella.
  Organization: Ufficio 1. 1508–1883, 800 vols., 10 repertorii and 1 fascicolo di protesti; —Ufficio 2. 1528–1885, 863 vols., 8 repertorii, 2 registri di protesti and 1 rubricella; —Ufficio 3. 1528–1873, 770 vols.; —Ufficio 4. 1589–1892, 801 vols. and 12 repertorii.
  Scope: Ufficio 1: Sixteenth century, 53 vols.; —Seventeenth century, 278 vols.; —Eighteenth century, 344 vols.; —Nineteenth century, 125 vols.
  Ufficio 2: Sixteenth century, 57 vols.; —Seventeenth century, 279 vols.; —Eighteenth century, 443 vols.; —Nineteenth century, 84 vols.
  Ufficio 3: Sixteenth century, 47 vols.; —Seventeenth century, 314 vols.; —Eighteenth century, 320 vols.; —Nineteenth century, 89 vols.
  Ufficio 4: Sixteenth century, 5 vols.; —Seventeenth century, 300 vols.; —Eighteenth century, 298 vols.; —Nineteenth century, 198 vols.
  Reference: D'Angiolini, p. 1136.
  Finding Aid: Printed list of notai.
  Location: Archivio di Stato di Roma.

5.1.164.3 Tribunale del cardinale vicario o del vicariato di Roma
  [DATABASE ID: VATV20082-A]
  Inclusive Dates: [15—], 1620–1809 and 1814–1902.
  Bulk: 100 vols., 241 buste, and 127 registri.
  References: D'Angiolini, pp. 1136, 1199; Lodolini (1960), p. 117.
  Finding Aids: Index, 1922; inventory, 1939.
  Location: Archivio di Stato di Roma.

5.1.165 Tribunale del governatore
  [DATABASE ID: VATV621-A]

This tribunal was established in 1435 with civil and criminal jurisdiction for Rome and its district. It was suppressed in 1809 and reestablished in 1814 as the Tribunale del governo di Roma. See the agency history for the governatore.

In addition to the records listed below, series listed with another agency relate directly to this agency and should be consulted. See Papal States miscellaneous series *Testamenti segreti*.

RECORDS. Records of the agency consist of the following series.

5.1.165.1 Curia di Borgo
[DATABASE ID: VATV20080-A]
Inclusive Dates: 1480–1631, 1665–1808, and 1814–1817.
Bulk: 111 vols.
Reference: D'Angiolini, p. 1135.
Finding Aid: Inventory, 1970.
Location: Archivio di Stato di Roma.

5.1.165.2 Notai della curia di Borgo
[DATABASE ID: VATV20081-A]
Inclusive Dates: 1566–1883.
Bulk: 406 vols., 1 repertorio, and 1 rubrica.
Reference: D'Angiolini, p. 1136.
Finding Aid: Summary inventory. There is also a partial inventory of proceedings, 1836 to 1883, and a printed list of notai.
Location: Archivio di Stato di Roma.

5.1.165.3 Notai della curia di governo
DATABASE ID: VATV20079-A]
Inclusive Dates: 1551–1884.
Bulk: 304 vols., 1 protesti registro, 4 repertorii, and 2 rubrice.
Scope: Sixteenth century, 1 vol.; —Seventeenth century, 53 vols.; —Eighteenth century, 122 vols.; —Nineteenth century, 128 vols.
Reference: D'Angiolini, p. 1135.
Finding Aid: Printed list of notai.
Location: Archivio di Stato di Roma.

5.1.165.4 Tribunale civile del governatore
[DATABASE ID: VATV20078-A]
Inclusive Dates: 1621–1809.
Bulk: 235 vols. and 344 buste.
References: D'Angiolini, p. 1135; Lodolini (1960), p. 117.
Finding Aid: Inventory, 1970.
Location: Archivio di Stato di Roma.

5.1.165.5 Tribunale criminale del governatore
[DATABASE ID: VATV20073-A]
Inclusive Dates: 1505–1814.
Bulk: 3,548 vols., 3,485 registri, 189 buste.
Organization: Processi, 1505–1809, 3,548 vols.; —Investigazioni, 1519–1809, 1,209 registri; —Costituti, 1513–1697, 906 registri; —Testimoni, 1545–1719, 112 registri; —Relazioni dei birri, 1589–1743, 52 registri; —Querelari, 1660–1776, 46 registri; —Visite dei notai e deposizioni, 1547–1693, 93 registri; —Fideiussioni, 1521–1797, 136 registri; —Registrazioni e manuali d'atti, 1516–1809, 672 registri; —Visite dei chirurghi, 1535–1798, 209 registri; —Sentenze

originali e sentenze delle mercedi, 1533–1794, 12 buste; —Sentenze, 1550–1809, 44 registri; —Lettere, 1662–1792, 6 registri.
References: D'Angiolini, pp. 1133–1134; Lodolini (1960), p. 117.
Finding Aids: Summary inventory. There are also partial inventories and lists.
Location: Archivio di Stato di Roma.

5.1.166 Tribunale del governo di Roma
[DATABASE ID: VATV812-A]

This tribunal was established in 1814 as a criminal court for Rome and Comarca. Before it was suppressed by the French in 1809, this tribunal was called the Tribunale del governatore. In 1847, in a reform of Pius IX, this tribunal assumed responsibility for criminal matters from the Tribunale dell'auditor camerae and the Tribunale del senatore, and its name was changed to the Tribunale criminale di Roma. See also the agency history for the governatore.

In addition to the records listed below, series listed with another agency relate directly to this agency and should be consulted. See Papal States, Tribunale criminale di Roma series *Tribunale del governo di Roma poi Tribunale criminale di Roma*.

RECORDS. Records of the agency consist of the following series.

5.1.166.1 Tribunale civile del governo di Roma
[DATABASE ID: VATV20234-A]
Inclusive Dates: 1814–1816.
Bulk: 20 buste and 7 vols.
Reference: D'Angiolini, p. 1198.
Finding Aid: Inventory, 1970.
Location: Archivio di Stato di Roma.

5.1.166.2 Tribunale del governo di Roma
[DATABASE ID: VATV360-A]
Inclusive Dates: [18—].
Bulk: 236 items.
References: Fink, p. 57; Boyle, p. 99.
Note: This series was not located by the project staff, 1989–1990.
Location: Archivio Segreto Vaticano.

5.1.167 Tribunale del senatore
[DATABASE ID: VATV623-A]

The senator at one time was the chief legislative, judicial, and executive authority in the commune of Rome. In his role as a tribunal the senator had both civil and criminal jurisdiction. In the sixteenth century the tribunal's authority was limited by the camerlengo and the governor. In 1580 the tribunal was divided into separate civil and criminal judgeships. Later, responsibility for streets passed to the Tribunale delle strade. Benedict

XIV reduced the competence of the tribunal in 1744 to hearing minor cases. The Roman republic of 1798–1799 suppressed the tribunal, but it was reestablished in 1800. It was again suppressed during the French regime, 1809–1814, and was again reestablished.

The Giudice del mercedi was combined with the Tribunale del senatore in 1831. In 1832 the tribunal was again restricted to minor cases. In 1847 the tribunal was abolished, its criminal jurisdiction passing to the Tribunale criminale di Roma and its civil jurisdiction to the Tribunale civile di Roma.

RECORDS. Records of the agency consist of the following series.

5.1.167.1 Banchieri ebrei
[DATABASE ID: VATV20072-A]
Inclusive Dates: 1585–1691.
Bulk: 89 vols.
Reference: D'Angiolini, p. 1132.
Finding Aids: Summary inventories, 1936 and 1970.
Location: Archivio di Stato di Roma.

5.1.167.2 Confraternità avanti a giudici deputati
[DATABASE ID: VATV20070-A]
Inclusive Dates: 1571–1815.
Bulk: 20 vols. and 5 buste.
Reference: D'Angiolini, p. 1132.
Finding Aid: Inventory, 1970.
Location: Archivio di Stato di Roma.

5.1.167.3 Tribunale civile del senatore
[DATABASE ID: VATV20066-A]
Inclusive Dates: 1494–1809 and 1814–1847.
Bulk: 3,237 vols., 354 buste, 332 filze, 56 registri, and 1 cassetta.
References: D'Angiolini, pp. 1131, 1196; Lodolini (1960), p. 117.
Finding Aids: Inventories, 1936 and 1970.
Location: Archivio di Stato di Roma.

5.1.167.4 Tribunale criminale del senatore
[DATABASE ID: VATV20067-A]
Inclusive Dates: 1454–1809 and 1814–1847.
Bulk: 1,149 vols., 940 registri, and 9 rubriche.
References: D'Angiolini, pp. 1131, 1196; Lodolini (1960), p. 117.
Finding Aid: Inventory.
Location: Archivio di Stato di Roma.

5.1.168 Tribunale dell'agricoltura
[DATABASE ID: VATV625-A]

This tribunal was responsible for hearing controversies relating to agriculture in Rome and its district. It was suppressed during the French regime, 1809–1814. In 1818 its competence was redefined. It was suppressed in 1824.

RECORDS. Records of the agency consist of the following series.

5.1.168.1 Tribunale dell'agricoltura
[DATABASE ID: VATV20084-A]
Inclusive Dates: 1616–1809 and 1814–1824.
Bulk: 146 vols., 67 buste, and 7 registri.
References: D'Angiolini, pp. 1137, 1199; Lodolini (1960), pp. 120–121.
Finding Aid: Inventory, 1938.
Location: Archivio di Stato di Roma.

5.1.169 Tribunale dell'annona e della deputazione annonaria
[DATABASE ID: VATV843-A]

This tribunal was established in 1814 and was responsible for disputes relating to the grain trade. The tribunal was suppressed in 1824.

RECORDS. Records of the agency consist of the following series.

5.1.169.1 Tribunale dell'annona e della deputazione annonaria
[DATABASE ID: VATV20174-A]
Inclusive Dates: 1818–1824.
Bulk: 12 registri, 6 buste, and 1 vol.
Reference: D'Angiolini, p. 1182.
Finding Aid: Inventory.
Location: Archivio di Stato di Roma.

5.1.170 Tribunale dell'auditor camerae
[DATABASE ID: VATV681-A]

This tribunal was responsible for all cases concerning the financial administration of the Curia. In 1800 responsibility for appeals of criminal cases from diocesan curias was transferred to the Congregation of Bishops and Regulars. In 1831 the Tribunale dell'uditore del camerlengo and the Tribunale dell'uditore del tesoriere were suppressed and their competence passed to this tribunal. In 1847, in a reform of Pius IX, the criminal jurisdiction of this tribunal was transferred to the Tribunale del governo, which then became the Tribunale criminale di Roma. At the same time the Tribunal dell'auditor camerae was renamed the Tribunale civile di Roma. See the agency history of the Auditor Camerae.

In addition to the records listed below, series listed with another agency relate directly to this agency and should be consulted. See Papal States, Tribunale civile di Roma series *Congregazione civile dell'auditor camerae poi Tribunale civile di Roma*, and Papal States, Tribunale criminale di Roma series *Tribunale criminale della Camera apostolica poi Tribunale criminale di Roma*.

RECORDS. Records of the agency consist of the following series.

5.1.170.1 Tribunale civile dell'auditor camerae
[DATABASE ID: VATV20063-A]
Inclusive Dates: 1540–1809 and 1814–1831.
Bulk: 2,610 vols., 2,784 filze, and 274 registri.
References: D'Angiolini, pp. 1129, 1197; Lodolini (1960), p. 109.
Finding Aid: Summary inventory, 1970.
Location: Archivio di Stato di Roma.

5.1.170.2 Tribunale criminale dell'auditor camerae
[DATABASE ID: VATV20064-A]
Inclusive Dates: 1567–1803 and 1815–1846.
Bulk: 55 vols., 283 filze, 22 registri, and 2 registri di indici.
Reference: D'Angiolini, pp. 1129, 1197.
Finding Aid: Summary inventory, 1970.
Location: Archivio di Stato di Roma.

5.1.171 Tribunale della Camera apostolica
[DATABASE ID: VATV866-A]

This tribunal was a court of first instance. Its composition was stabilized by Sixtus V, comprising the camerlengo, tesoriere and twelve chierici. In 1800 its responsibility was increased, when it took over the duties of the Congregazione per la revisione dei conti and the Congregazione camerale. It was suppressed in 1809 by the French regime but was reestablished in 1814 when the pope's power was restored. In 1817 the tribunal ceased to exist as a court of first instance. As an appeals court, the tribunal was known as the Tribunale della piena camera. See the agency history for the Camera.

RECORDS. Records of the agency consist of the following series.

5.1.171.1 Tribunale collegiale della Camera apostolica
[DATABASE ID: VATV20242-A]
Inclusive Dates: 1818–1824.
Bulk: 19 buste and 17 registri.
Reference: D'Angiolini, p. 1200.
Finding Aid: Inventory, 1970.
Location: Archivio di Stato di Roma.

5.1.171.2 Tribunale della Camera apostolica (di prima istanza e di piena camera)
[DATABASE ID: VATV20023-A]
Inclusive Dates: 1440, 1510–1809, and 1814–1817.
Bulk: 1,261 vols. and 868 buste.
Organization: Memorie, 1721–1769, 4 buste; —Congregazione della piena camera, 1677–1766, 61 vols.; —Sentenze del tribunale della piena camera, 1672–1788, 4 buste.
Reference: D'Angiolini, pp. 1089–1090.
Finding Aid: Inventory, 1970.
Location: Archivio di Stato di Roma.

5.1.172 Tribunale della piena camera
[DATABASE ID: VATV762-A]

This tribunal was established in 1379. It evolved into the highest court of the Papal States, with appelate juris-

diction. The tribunal was made up of the chierici di camera, who all joined together in this tribunal to decide the most important questions. In 1824 added responsibility was assumed from the Tribunale collegiale della Camera apostolica. See the agency history for the Camera.

In addition to the records listed below, series listed with another agency relate directly to this agency and should be consulted. See Papal States, Tribunale della Camera apostolica series *Tribunale della Camera apostolica (di prima istanza e di piena camera)*.

RECORDS. Records of the agency consist of the following series.

5.1.172.1 Tribunale della piena camera
[DATABASE ID: VATV20243-A]
Inclusive Dates: 1818–1871.
Bulk: 13 buste and 9 registri, 3,655 fascicoli, 1 busta, 2 protocolli, and 3 rubriche.
References: D'Angiolini, p. 1200; Lodolini (1960), p. 110.
Finding Aid: Inventory, 1970.
Location: Archivio di Stato di Roma.

5.1.173 Tribunale della piena camera per la revisione dei conti
[DATABASE ID: VATV654-A]

Established in 1816, this office was made up of the chierici di camera, with responsibility for examining budgets. In 1828 it was suppressed and replaced by the Congregazione di revisione dei conti. See the agency history for the Camera.

RECORDS. Records of the agency consist of the following series.

5.1.173.1 Tribunale della piena camera per la revisione dei conti
[DATABASE ID: VATV20244-A]
Inclusive Dates: 1814–1826.
Bulk: 10 buste.
References: D'Angiolini, p. 1201; Lodolini (1960), p. 182.
Finding Aid: Inventory.
Location: Archivio di Stato di Roma.

5.1.174 Tribunale delle acque e strade
[DATABASE ID: VATV814-A]

This tribunal was established in 1514 and suppressed in 1833.

RECORDS. No records for this office were located.

5.1.175 Tribunale delle ripe
[DATABASE ID: VATV813-A]

This tribunal predates the establishment of the Presidenza delle ripe. A camerlengo delle ripe was appointed by Alexander VI in 1498 to judge suits related to river traffic. With the establishment of the presidenza in the sixteenth century, the judicial responsibility was reorganized. The presidenza delegated responsibility to the camerlengo di Ripa and to the judge of the Ripetta. (The Ripa and Ripetta were the two ports of Rome.) Both judges had civil and criminal jurisdiction. The office was suppressed by the French in 1809 and reestablished in 1814. In 1816 the judge of the Ripetta was suppressed. The contentious jurisdiction of the assessor of the ripe was suppressed in 1824 and its responsibility transferred to the Tribunale di commercio.

RECORDS. Records of the agency consist of the following series.

5.1.175.1 Tribunale delle ripe
[DATABASE ID: VATV20043-A]
Inclusive Dates: 1594–1824.
Bulk: 316 vols., 56 buste, and 2 registri.
Organization: Curia di Ripetta, 1594–1817, 204 vols., 55 buste, and 2 registri; —Curia di Ripagrande, 1629–1824. 112 vols. and 1 busta.
Reference: D'Angiolini, p. 1105.
Finding Aid: Inventory, 1979.
Location: Archivio di Stato di Roma.

5.1.176 Tribunale delle strade
[DATABASE ID: VATV612-A]

This tribunal was the judicial arm of the Presidenza delle strade. It had contentious jurisdiction over questions related to roads. It was suppressed by the French in 1809, reestablished in 1814, and finally suppressed in 1816.

RECORDS. Records of the agency consist of the following series.

5.1.176.1 Tribunale delle strade
[DATABASE ID: VATV20040-A]
Inclusive Dates: 1524–1817.
Bulk: 266 vols., 78 filze, and 13 registri.
Reference: D'Angiolini, p. 1103.
Finding Aid: Summary inventory, 1938.
Location: Archivio di Stato di Roma.

5.1.177 Tribunale di appello di Roma
[DATABASE ID: VATV738-A]

This tribunal was active in the nineteenth century.

RECORDS. No records for this tribunal were located.

5.1.178 Tribunale di commercio di Roma
[DATABASE ID: VATV687-A]

Established in 1824 to deal with commercial disputes, this tribunal took responsibility from the Tribunale delle ripe.

RECORDS. Records of the agency consist of the following series.

5.1.178.1 Tribunale di commercio di Roma
[DATABASE ID: VATV20230-A]
Inclusive Dates: 1825–1871.
Bulk: 236 vols. and 58 buste.
References: D'Angiolini, pp. 1197–1198; Lodolini (1960), p. 109.
Finding Aid: Inventory, 1970.
Location: Archivio di Stato di Roma.

5.1.179 Tribunale di Rieti e Spoleto
[DATABASE ID: VATV739-A]

This tribunal was active in the nineteenth century.

RECORDS. No records for this tribunal were located.

5.1.180 Tribunale supremo della sacra consulta penale
[DATABASE ID: VATV675-A]

This tribunal was active in the nineteenth century.

RECORDS. No records for this tribunal were located.

5.1.181 Tribunale supremo della sacra consulta politico
[DATABASE ID: VATV674-A]

This tribunal was active in the nineteenth century.

RECORDS. No records for this tribunal were located.

5.1.182 Truppa di finanza
[DATABASE ID: VATV849-A]

This office was a dependency of the Direzione generale delle dogane.

RECORDS. Records of the agency consist of the following series.

5.1.182.1 Truppa di finanza
[DATABASE ID: VATV20148-A]
Inclusive Dates: 1822–1870.
Bulk: 34 buste and 69 registri.
Reference: D'Angiolini, p. 1172.
Finding Aid: Summary inventory of buste.
Location: Archivio di Stato di Roma.

5.1.183 Truppe di finanza. Ispettorato
[DATABASE ID: VATV729-A]

This office was established in 1857.

RECORDS. No records for this office were located.

5.1.184 Uditorato generale militare
[DATABASE ID: VATV710-A]

This office was active in the nineteenth century as an appeals tribunal for the military.

RECORDS. Records of the agency consist of the following series.

5.1.184.1 Uditorato generale militare
[DATABASE ID: VATV20256-A]
Inclusive Dates: 1814–1870.
Bulk: 1,642 buste, 91 rubrice, and protocolli.
References: D'Angiolini, p. 1204; Lodolini (1960), p. 203.
Finding Aid: Summary inventory of buste.
Location: Archivio di Stato di Roma.

MISCELLANEOUS RECORDS FOR WHICH NO CREATING AGENCY COULD BE DETERMINED

These are record groups that could not be assigned to any specific agency or office within the structure of the Papal States as determined by the project staff, yet clearly originated from that division of the administration of the Holy See.

5.1.185 Cancelleria del censo di Roma: Catasti
[DATABASE ID: VATV20385-A]
Inclusive Dates: 1777–1891.
Bulk: 459 pacchi and registri.
Reference: D'Angiolini, p. 1221.
Finding Aid: Inventory, 1976.
Location: Archivio di Stato di Roma.

5.1.186 Cancelleria del censo di Subiaco: Catasti
[DATABASE ID: VATV20386-A]
Inclusive Dates: 1672, 1735–1867.
Bulk: 27 registri.
Reference: D'Angiolini, p. 1221.
Finding Aid: Inventory by place.
Location: Archivio di Stato di Roma.

5.1.187 Cancelleria del censo di Tivoli: Catasti
[DATABASE ID: VATV20387-A]
Inclusive Dates: 1734, 1772–1883.
Bulk: 428 registri.
Reference: D'Angiolini, p. 1220.
Finding Aid: Inventory by place.
Location: Archivio di Stato di Roma.

5.1.188 Collezione prima dei catasti
[DATABASE ID: VATV20383-A]
Inclusive Dates: 1360, 1440–1470, 1531–1842.
Bulk: 236 registri and 6 pacchi.
Reference: D'Angiolini, p. 1220.
Finding Aid: Inventory in alphabetical order by locality.
Location: Archivio di Stato di Roma.

5.1.189 Collezione seconda dei catasti
[DATABASE ID: VATV20384-A]
Inclusive Dates: 1521–1876.
Bulk: 3,543 registri and buste.

Reference: D'Angiolini, p. 1221.
Finding Aid: Inventory by locality, with alphabetical rubric.
Location: Archivio di Stato di Roma.

5.1.190 Governatorato—Ufficio verifiche
[DATABASE ID: VATV40007-A]
Inclusive Dates: [18—]–[18—].
Bulk: 18 buste.
Note: This series was cited in Natalini et al., p. 272, but not seen by project staff in 1990.
Location: Archivio Segreto Vaticano.

5.1.191 Governo provvisorio dello Stato Pontificio
[DATABASE ID: VATV40020-A]
Inclusive Dates: [18—]–[18—].
Bulk: 20 buste.
Note: This series was cited in Natalini et al., p. 274, but not seen by project staff in 1990.
Location: Archivio Segreto Vaticano.

5.1.192 Miscellanea del periodo costituzionale
[DATABASE ID: VATV20191-A]
Inclusive Dates: 1846–1849.
Bulk: 41 buste and 2 registri.
Scope: This series includes records of the Sacra consulta, Consiglio dei ministri, Alto consiglio, Consiglio dei deputati, Ministero dell'interno, Ministero delle armi, Ministero del commercio, belle arti, industria e agricoltura, Direzione generale di polizia, and Congregazione speciale di sanità.
Reference: D'Angiolini, p. 1191.
Finding Aid: Partial inventory (in part summary).
Location: Archivio di Stato di Roma.

5.1.193 Miscellanea della statistica
[DATABASE ID: VATV20183-A]
Inclusive Dates: 1785–1872.
Bulk: 66 buste.
Reference: D'Angiolini, p. 1187.
Finding Aid: Inventory, 1952.
Location: Archivio di Stato di Roma.

5.1.194 Miscellanea di carte politiche e riservate
[DATABASE ID: VATV20252-A]
Inclusive Dates: [15—]–1900.
Bulk: 5,662 fascicoli.
Scope: This series includes records of the Sacra Consulta, Ministero dell'interno, and Direzione generale di polizia.
Reference: D'Angiolini, p. 1203.
Finding Aid: Chronological card index by names of persons, places, and subjects (incomplete).
Location: Archivio di Stato di Roma.

5.1.195 Miscellanea notarile
[DATABASE ID: VATV20388-A]
Inclusive Dates: 1391, 1449–1450, 1486–1745.
Bulk: 41 vols.
Reference: D'Angiolini, p. 1220.
Finding Aid: Inventory.
Location: Archivio di Stato di Roma.

5.1.196 [Miscellaneous SF/484]
[DATABASE ID: VATV10166-A]
Inclusive Dates: 1479–1899.
Bulk: 9 linear m.
Scope: Material in this series includes: 1. (All'Ill.mo et Ecc.mo Signor V. Alexander Ruspoli, Principe di Cervetri, Marchese di Riano, e Conte dell'Insigne Terre di Vignanello) "Nota lo stato de al presente si osserua e tiene nell'Insigne Terra di Vignanello, diocesi di Civita Castellana, e nella Provincia di Viterbo compilossi dalla ch.me. del Cardinal Stefano e Pro Pavolo Hardini Conti e Consig. di essa Terra nel Pontificato di Sisto IV l'anno 1479; e confermato poi dal Conte Girolamo de Marsciano del tenore infrascritto" (copy); —2. Essendo stati noi sottoscritti computisti deputati da MonSig. Illmo. e Rmo. Enea Silvio Piccolomini governatore di Roma a formare il Conto della cassa della Segretaria de Brevi ritenuta ed esercitata dal Sig. Abb. Gio. Fiori Sostituto della medicina da November 1544 a tutto si ni Marzo 1564, come dal decreto di nostra Deputazione manato si 10 Agosto corrente, ed inserto nel Piocesso Criminale . . . Ci siamo portati nella detta Segretaria con la permissione dell'Emo.e. Rmo. Sig. Card. Antonelli Segretaria ci sono stati consegnati si seguenti librie scritture (copy); —3. Bilancio registers, [16—]; —4. Printed books of Legge pontificie, legge penale, formularies, protocols, etc., [18—].
The series title was assigned by the project staff based on the location of the material in 1990.
Location: Archivio Segreto Vaticano.

5.1.197 Notai dei distretti riuniti di Roma e Velletri
[DATABASE ID: VATV20389-A]
Inclusive Dates: 1830–1899.
Bulk: 569 vols., 58 repertorii, 23 indici, 13 fascicoli, and 36 atti sciolti.
Organization: Albano (Albano Laziale) e Castelgandolfo, 1868–1899, 34 vols. istrumenti, 1 vol. testamenti, 2 repertorii, and 1 indice; —Anticoli Corrado e Arsoli, 1862–1890, 13 vols. istrumenti and testamenti and 2 repertorii; —Bracciano, 1848–1879, 27 vols. istrumenti, 2 vols. testamenti, 2 repertorii, and 1 indice; —Castelnuovo di Porto, 1844–1882, 19 vols. istrumenti, 4 vols. testamenti and 2 repertorii; —Cave, 1863–1877, 2 vols. istrumenti, 1 vol. testamenti, and 2 repertorii; —Cerreto (Cerreto Laziale), 1858–1877, 2 vols. and 1 repertorio; —Cisterna (Cisterna di Latina), 1846–1877, 9 vols., 2 repertorii, and 2 indici; —Civitavecchia, 1862–1882, 25 vols., 3 repertorii, and 2 indici; —Cori, 1872–1895, 11 vols., 3 repertorii, and 1 indice; —Genzano (Genzano di Roma), 1847–1888. 28 vols. istrumenti, 2 vols. testamenti, 2 repertorii, and 2 indici; —Marino, 1855–1897, 37 vols., 4 repertorii, and 1 indice; —Montecelio, 1872–1877, 2 vols. and 36 atti sciolti; —Monterosi, 1867–1895, 14 vols., 2 repertorii, and 2 indici; —Monterotondo, 1856–1885, 27 vols., 2 repertorii, and 1 indice; —Moricone, 1861–1889, 34 vols., 2 repertorii, 2 indici, and 1 fascicolo; —Norma, 1864–1886, 1 vol. and 1 repertorio; —Olevano (Olevano Romano), 1840–1877, 7 vols. and 1 repertorio; —Palestrina, 1830–1877, 37 vols., 2 repertorii, and 2 indici; —Sezze, 1865–1899, 32 vols., 3 repertorii, and 1 indice; —Terracina, 1857–1884, 16 vols. and 2 repertorii; —Tivoli, 1843–1890, 85 vols., 6 repertorii, and 1 indice; —Tolfa, 1865–1898, 12 vols., 2 repertorii, and 1 indice; —Valmontone, 1869–1876, 4 vols. and 2 repertorii; —Velletri,

1842–1888, 43 vols., 2 repertorii, and 2 indici; —Vicovaro, 1835–1889, 8 vols. and 2 repertorii; —Zagarolo, 1840–1887, 30 vols., 4 repertorii, and 1 indice.
Reference: D'Angiolini, p. 1218.
Finding Aid: Alphabetical list by notaio.
Location: Archivio di Stato di Roma.

5.1.198 Particolare dei disordini (nello Stato Pontificio)
[DATABASE ID: VATV40001-A]
Inclusive Dates: 1814–1815.
Bulk: 21 buste.
Note: This series was cited in Natalini et al., p. 270, but not seen by project staff in 1990.
Location: Archivio Segreto Vaticano.

5.1.199 Testamenti segreti
[DATABASE ID: VATV20390-A]
Inclusive Dates: [16—]–[18—].
Bulk: 118 buste (11,427 testamenti).
Scope: This series includes testamenti of the Notai capitolini, Notai della curia del cardinale vicario, Notai della curia di governo, Notai della curia di borgo, Notai del consolato dei fiorentini, Notai della fabbrica di S. Pietro, and Notaro maggiore della camera capitolina.
References: D'Angiolini, p. 1217; Lodolini (1960), pp. 61–62.
Location: Archivio di Stato di Roma.

5.2 TERRITORY UNDER FRENCH OCCUPATION, 1809–1814

In 1809 the pope was deposed as the ruler of the Papal States by the French under Napoleon. The area called the Marches was annexed by the Kingdom of Italy and the remaining area of the Papal States was annexed by France. The old agencies of government were abolished and a French administration was instituted. In 1814 the pope's rule over the Papal States was restored, and the French administrative agencies were abolished.

There is a limited amount of information on the structure of the government of the Papal States during this period. Therefore, in this section no individual agency histories are provided. When something is known about a particular agency, that information is included in the scope note for the particular series. This occupation affected other agencies of the Holy See as well. See, in particular, entries for the Secretariatus Status listed in the section "Roman Curia: Offices."

Information for the series listed in this section was taken from the section "Archivio di Stato di Roma," by Edvige Aleandri Barletta and Carla Lodolini Tupputi, in *Guida generale degli Archivi di Stato Italiani*, edited by Piero D'Angiolini and Claudio Pavone (Rome, 1986) and *L'Archivio di Stato di Roma: Epitome di una guida degli archivi dell'amministrazione centrale dello Stato Pontificio*, by Armando Lodolini (Rome, 1960).

RECORDS. Records of the territorial administration consist of the following series.

5.2.1 Amministrazione del debito pubblico
[DATABASE ID: VATV20110-A]
Inclusive Dates: 1809–1814.
Bulk: 61 vols., 195 buste, 44 registri, and 1 rubricella.
Reference: D'Angiolini, p. 1146.
Location: Archivio di Stato di Roma.

5.2.2 Atti dello stato civile napoleonico
[DATABASE ID: VATV20376-A]
Inclusive Dates: 1565–1849 (bulk 1810–1814).
Bulk: 64 filze, 21 registri, and 5 buste.
Scope: The office of Stato civile was established in 1809 as a registry office. In 1814 it was abolished by the papal government. Responsibility for registering births, marriages, and deaths was then returned to the church parishes.
Reference: D'Angiolini, pp. 1221–1222.
Finding Aid: Inventory, 1971.
Location: Archivio di Stato di Roma.

5.2.3 Commissione militare permanente nella XXX divisione militare
[DATABASE ID: VATV20127-A]
Inclusive Dates: 1809–1814.
Bulk: 26 buste and 1 rubrica.
Scope: This was a commission established to combat banditry.
Reference: D'Angiolini, p. 1148.
Finding Aid: List, with alphabetical index of posizioni.
Location: Archivio di Stato di Roma.

5.2.4 Commissione per gli abbellimenti di Roma
[DATABASE ID: VATV20114-A]
Inclusive Dates: 1810–1817 and 1830–1832.
Bulk: 6 registri, 3 vols., and 1 busta.
References: D'Angiolini, p. 1147; Lodolini (1960), p. 189.
Finding Aid: Inventory.
Location: Archivio di Stato di Roma.

5.2.5 Consulta straordinaria per gli Stati romani
[DATABASE ID: VATV20107-A]
Inclusive Dates: 1809–1810.
Bulk: 40 buste, 25 registri, and 1 vol.
Scope: This office was established in 1809 to take possession of Rome, Lazio, and Umbria for the French imperial government and to provide for the reorganization of the government of the territory.
References: D'Angiolini, p. 1145; Lodolini (1960), p. 187.
Finding Aid: Inventory, 1984.
Location: Archivio di Stato di Roma.

5.2.6 Corte di appello poi Corte imperiale
[DATABSE ID: VATV20125-A]
Inclusive Dates: 1809–1814.
Bulk: 13 registri, 1 vol., and 1 busta.
Scope: This court was established in 1809 during the French regime. This office was also known as the Corte imperiale and was abolished in 1814.
References: D'Angiolini, p. 1148; Lodolini (1960), p. 188.
Finding Aid: Inventory, 1971.
Location: Archivio di Stato di Roma.

5.2.7 Corte di giustizia criminale
[DATABASE ID: VATV20126-A]
Inclusive Dates: 1809–1814.
Bulk: 291 buste and 40 registri.
References: D'Angiolini, p. 1148; Lodolini (1960), p. 188.
Finding Aid: Inventory, 1971.
Location: Archivio di Stato di Roma.

5.2.8 Dipartimenti del Musone, del Metauro e del Tronto
[DATABASE ID: VATV20111-A]
Inclusive Dates: 1808–1827.
Bulk: 221 registri.
Reference: D'Angiolini, p. 1146.
Finding Aid: Partial inventory, 1947 (non rispondente).
Location: Archivio di Stato di Roma.

5.2.9 Direzione generale di polizia
[DATABASE ID: VATV20109-A]
Inclusive Dates: 1809–1814.
Bulk: 81 fascicoli and 14 registri.
Reference: D'Angiolini, pp. 1145–1146.
Finding Aid: Inventory, 1971.
Location: Archivio di Stato di Roma.

5.2.10 Giudicature di pace di Albano (Albano Laziale)
[DATABASE ID: VATV20118-A]
Inclusive Dates: 1809–1813.
Bulk: 5 vols.
Reference: D'Angiolini, p. 1148.
Finding Aid: List, 1970.
Location: Archivio di Stato di Roma.

5.2.11 Giudicature di pace di Bracciano
[DATABASE ID: VATV20119-A]
Inclusive Dates: 1809–1814.
Bulk: 9 buste.
Reference: D'Angiolini, p. 1148.
Finding Aid: List, 1970.
Location: Archivio di Stato di Roma.

5.2.12 Giudicature di pace di Civitavecchia
[DATABASE ID: VATV20120-A]
Inclusive Dates: 1809–1814.
Bulk: 3 buste.
Reference: D'Angiolini, p. 1148.
Finding Aid: List, 1970.
Location: Archivio di Stato di Roma.

5.2.13 Giudicature di pace di Marino
[DATABASE ID: VATV20121-A]
Inclusive Dates: 1809–1813.
Bulk: 3 vols.
Reference: D'Angiolini, p. 1148.
Finding Aid: List, 1970.
Location: Archivio di Stato di Roma.

5.2.14 Giudicature di pace di Olevano (Olevano Romano)
[DATABASE ID: VATV20122-A]
Inclusive Dates: 1810.
Bulk: 1 vol.
Reference: D'Angiolini, p. 1148.

Finding Aid: List.
Location: Archivio di Stato di Roma.

5.2.15 Guidicature di pace di Roma

[DATABASE ID: VATV20117-A]
Inclusive Dates: 1808–1814.
Bulk: 52 buste.
Reference: D'Angiolini, p. 1148.
Finding Aid: Inventory, 1971.
Location: Archivio di Stato di Roma.

5.2.16 Miscellanea del governo francese

[DATABASE ID: VATV20108-A]
Inclusive Dates: 1809–1814.
Bulk: 127 buste.
References: D'Angiolini, p. 1145; Lodolini (1960), pp. 186–187.
Finding Aid: Inventory, 1984.
Location: Archivio di Stato di Roma.

5.2.17 Municipalità di Roma

[DATABASE ID: VATV20116-A]
Inclusive Dates: 1810–1814.
Bulk: 6 vols.
References: D'Angiolini, p. 1147; Lodolini (1960), p. 188.
Finding Aid: Summary inventory.
Location: Archivio di Stato di Roma.

5.2.18 Tribunale di commercio di Roma

[DATABASE ID: VATV20124-A]
Inclusive Dates: 1810–1814.
Bulk: 8 buste.
Scope: This office was established in 1809 as a civil court. It was abolished in 1814.
References: D'Angiolini, p. 1148; Lodolini (1960), p. 188.
Finding Aid: Inventory, 1971.
Location: Archivio di Stato di Roma.

5.2.19 Tribunale di prima istanza di Roma

[DATABASE ID: VATV20123-A]
Inclusive Dates: 1809–1814.
Bulk: 57 registri, 159 buste, 8 fascicoli, and 17 vols.
References: D'Angiolini, p. 1148; Lodolini (1960), p. 188.
Finding Aid: Inventory, 1971.
Location: Archivio di Stato di Roma.

5.2.20 Ufficio di conservazione delle ipoteche di Roma

[DATABASE ID: VATV20112]
Inclusive Dates: 1809–1816.
Bulk: 38 registri.
Scope: This office was established in 1809 as a tribunal for matters relating to mortgages.
Reference: D'Angiolini, pp. 1146–1147.
Finding Aid: Inventory.
Location: Archivio di Stato di Roma.

5.2.21 Ufficio di conservazione delle ipoteche di Tivoli

[DATABASE ID: VATV20113-A]
Inclusive Dates: 1809–1816.
Bulk: 14 registri.

Scope: This office was established in 1809 as a tribunal for matters relating to mortgages.
Reference: D'Angiolini, p. 1147.
Finding Aid: Inventory.
Location: Archivio di Stato di Roma.

5.3 LOCAL ADMINISTRATIONS

As the Papal States grew during the Middle Ages and the Renaissance, it took over many small regions that had been governed in many different ways. Governors or rectors were appointed at the local level. Cardinal legates were appointed to administer the most important provinces, called legations; and delegates, usually bishops, were appointed to lesser areas, called delegations. The number and identity of legations and delegations were modified many times.

Under Sixtus V (1585–1590) there were four legations—Umbria, Campagna, Marches, and the Patrimony of St. Peter—and one delegation—Bologna. Under Clement XI (1700–1721) four legations covered the northern part of the country—Bologna, Ferrara, Romagna, and Urbino—while eight delegations covered the remaining territory.

After 1849, four legations—Bologna, Urbino, Perugia, and Velletri—along with the presidency of Rome and Comarca, covered the entire state, with delegations serving as subprovinces under the legations.

The government of Rome was separate from the structure of legations and delegations. From the time of Gregory XIII (1572–1585) the district surrounding Rome was called the Comarca, and was governed by the Congregazione del buon governo. Many of the offices of the Papal States were specifically organized to administer aspects of the government of Rome, for instance the Presidenza delle ripe administered the ports of Rome and the Tiber River. By the eighteenth century, and sometimes earlier, the vice-camerlengo of the Camera Apostolica served as governor of Rome.

A Roman republic was established on February 15, 1798, when Pius VI was deposed as head of state. Territorially it comprised the Papal States less Pessaro and the four legations in the north, which were annexed to the Cisalpine Republic. The authority of the republic ended on September 29, 1799, and papal rule was restored.

In 1827 the Comarca (not including the city of Rome) was made a presidency, governed by a president. In 1847 Rome was added to its jurisdiction, and it was renamed presidency of Rome and Comarca.

In November 1848 the pope fled Rome, and a few months later a second Roman republic was proclaimed. The republic ruled for only a short time, and the pope's authority was restored in 1850.

Records of individual local governments are found in the Archivio Segreto Vaticano and in the Archivio di

Stato di Roma. They are described separately below. Note that there may be more than one series listed for a particular local administration.

Records described from the Archivio Segreto Vaticano were surveyed on site as a part of the Vatican Archives Project. Information on records in the Archivio di Stato di Roma was taken from the section "Archivio di Stato di Roma," by Edvige Aleandri Barletta and Carla Lodolini Tupputi, in *Guida generale degli Archivi di Stato Italiani*, edited by Piero D'Angiolini and Claudio Pavone (Rome, 1986), and *L'Archivio di Stato di Roma: Epitome di una guida degli archivi dell'amministrazione centrale dello Stato Pontificio*, by Armando Lodolini (Rome, 1960). According to the listings in these guides, the record series for several local administrations go beyond 1870. Those are so noted in the listings below. Researchers should be aware that all the holdings of the Archivio di Stato listed in this guide are open for research.

5.3.1 Albano Laziale

RECORDS. Records of the administration consist of the following series.

5.3.1.1 Atti dei notai di Albano (Albano Laziale)
[DATABASE ID: VATV20391-A]
Inclusive Dates: 1537–1878.
Bulk: 532 vols. and 3 atti sciolti.
Organization: Rogiti originali, 1537–1878, 401 vols.; —Copie, 1645–1878, 131 vols.; —Testamenti segreti, 1755, 1763, and 1849, 3 documents.
Scope: Rogiti originali: Sixteenth century, 12 vols.; —Seventeenth century, 180 vols.; —Eighteenth century, 153 vols.; —Nineteenth century, 56 vols.
Copies: Seventeenth century, 5 vols.; —Eighteenth century, 84 vols.; —Nineteenth century, 42 vols.
Reference: D'Angiolini, p. 1218.
Location: Archivio di Stato di Roma.

5.3.1.2 Governatori di Albano (Albano Laziale)
[DATABASE ID: VATV20087-A]
Inclusive Dates: 1569–1809.
Bulk: 195 vols. and 5 buste.
Reference: D'Angiolini, p. 1138.
Finding Aid: List, 1970.
Location: Archivio di Stato di Roma

5.3.1.3 Governi de Albano (Albano Laziale)
[DATABASE ID: VATV20214-A]
Inclusive Dates: 1814–1870.
Bulk: 434 buste, 67 registri, and 178 vols.
Reference: D'Angiolini, p. 1196.
Finding Aid: List, 1970.
Location: Archivio di Stato di Roma.

5.3.2 Anguillara Sabazia

RECORDS. Records of the administration consist of the following series.

5.3.2.1 Atti dei notai di Anguillara (Anguillara Sabazia)
[DATABASE ID: VATV20392-A]
Inclusive Dates: [15—]–[18—].
Bulk: 91 vols., buste and registri.
Reference: D'Angiolini, p. 1218.
Location: Archivio di Stato di Roma.

5.3.3 Arsoli

RECORDS. Records of the administration consist of the following series.

5.3.3.1 Atti dei notai di Arsoli
[DATABASE ID: VATV20393-A]
Inclusive Dates: [15—]–[18—].
Bulk: ca. 580 vols.
Reference: D'Angiolini, p. 1218.
Location: Archivio di Stato di Roma.

5.3.4 Bracciano

RECORDS. Records of the administration consist of the following series.

5.3.4.1 Atti dei notai di Bracciano
[DATABASE ID: VATV20394-A]
Inclusive Dates: 1558–1918 (bulk 1558–1848 and 1861).
Bulk: 353 vols.
Scope: Sixteenth century, 32 vols.; —Seventeenth century, 188 vols.; —Eighteenth century, 74 vols.; —Nineteenth century, 21 vols.
Reference: D'Angiolini, p. 1218.
Finding Aid: Inventory, 1978.
Location: Archivio di Stato di Roma.

5.3.4.2 Governi baronali di Bracciano
[DATABASE ID: VATV20091-A]
Inclusive Dates: 1606–1808.
Bulk: 474 buste.
Reference: D'Angiolini, p. 1138.
Finding Aid: List, 1970.
Location: Archivio di Stato di Roma.

5.3.4.3 Governi baronali di Bracciano
[DATABASE ID: VATV20221-A]
Inclusive Dates: 1814–1870.
Bulks: 182 buste.
Reference: D'Angiolini, p. 1196.
Finding Aid: List, 1970.
Location: Archivio di Stato di Roma.

5.3.5 Campagnano di Roma

RECORDS. Records of the administration consist of the following series.

5.3.5.1 Atti dei notai di Campagnano (Campagnano di Roma)

[DATABASE ID: VATV20395-A]
Inclusive Dates: 1517–1867.
Bulk: 285 vols., 9 repertorii and 5 registri.
Scope: Sixteenth century, 19 vols.; —Seventeenth century, 129 vols.; —Eighteenth century, 100 vols.; —Nineteenth century, 51 vols.
Reference: D'Angiolini, p. 1219.
Finding Aid: Inventory and alphabetical index of notai.
Location: Archivio di Stato di Roma.

5.3.5.2 Governatori di Campagnano (Campagnano di Roma)

[DATABASE ID: VATV20088-A]
Inclusive Dates: 1585–1809.
Bulk: 176 buste.
Reference: D'Angiolini, p. 1138.
Finding Aid: Inventory, 1970.
Location: Archivio di Stato di Roma.

5.3.5.3 Governi di Campagnano di Roma

[DATABASE ID: VATV20215-A]
Inclusive Dates: 1814–1870.
Bulk: 588 buste.
Reference: D'Angiolini, p. 1196.
Finding Aid: Inventory, 1970.
Location: Archivio di Stato di Roma.

5.3.6 Carpineto Romano

RECORDS. Records of the administration consist of the following series.

5.3.6.1 Atti dei notai di Carpineto (Carpineto Romano)

[DATABASE ID: VATV20396-A]
Inclusive Dates: 1493–1887.
Bulk: 288 vols. and 564 fascicoli.
Scope: Fifteenth century, 3 vols.; —Sixteenth century, 64 vols. and 17 fascicoli; —Seventeenth century, 116 and 198 respectively; —Eighteenth century, 65 and 310; —Nineteenth century, 40 and 39.
Reference: D'Angiolini, p. 1219.
Finding Aids: There is a chronological list and an alphabetical index by notai.
Location: Archivio di Stato di Roma.

5.3.6.2 Governi baronali di Carpineto Romano

[DATABASE ID: VATV20092-A]
Inclusive Dates: 1521–1809.
Bulk: 63 buste.
Reference: D'Angiolini, p. 1138.
Finding Aid: List, 1970.
Location: Archivio di Stato di Roma.

5.3.6.3 Governi baronali di Carpineto Romano

[DATABASE ID: VATV20222-A]
Inclusive Dates: 1815–1856.
Bulk: 7 buste.
Reference: D'Angiolini, p. 1196.
Finding Aid: List, 1970.
Location: Archivio di Stato di Roma.

5.3.7 Castel Gandolfo

RECORDS. Records of the administration consist of the following series.

5.3.7.1 Atti dei notai di Castel Gandolfo

[DATABASE ID: VATV20397-A]
Inclusive Dates: 1607–1868.
Bulk: 112 vols., buste, and registri.
Reference: D'Angiolini, p. 1219.
Finding Aid: List of payments, 1979.
Location: Archivio di Stato di Roma.

5.3.7.2 Curia vescovile di Castel Gandolfo: cause del tribunale civile

[DATABASE ID: VATV40005-A]
Inclusive Dates: 1779–1831.
Bulk: 34 vols.
Note: This series was cited in Natalini et al., p. 270, but not seen by project staff in 1990.
Location: Archivio Segreto Vaticano.

5.3.8 Castel Madama

RECORDS. Records of the administration consist of the following series.

5.3.8.1 Atti dei notai di Castel Madama

[DATABASE ID: VATV20398-A]
Inclusive Dates: 1535–1895.
Bulk: 206 vols., buste, and registri.
Reference: D'Angiolini, p. 1219.
Finding Aid: Inventory, 1977.
Location: Archivio di Stato di Roma.

5.3.9 Castelnuovo di Porto

RECORDS. Records of the administration consist of the following series.

5.3.9.1 Atti dei notai di Castelnuovo di Porto

[DATABASE ID: VATV20399-A]
Inclusive Dates: 1402–1870.
Bulk: 160 buste, vols., and registri.
Reference: D'Angiolini, p. 1219.
Finding Aid: Summary inventory.
Location: Archivio di Stato di Roma.

5.3.9.2 Governi di Castelnuovo di Porto

[DATABASE ID: VATV20216-A]
Inclusive Dates: 1801–1870.
Bulk: 508 buste and 96 registri.
Reference: D'Angiolini, p. 1196.
Finding Aid: Inventory, 1958.
Location: Archivio di Stato di Roma.

5.3.10 Civitavecchia (Delegazione)

RECORDS. Records of the adminstration consist of the following series.

5.3.10.1 Delegazione apostolica di Civitavecchia
[DATABASE ID: VATV20199-A]
Inclusive Dates: 1814–1870.
Bulk: 989 buste and 124 registri.
References: D'Angiolini, p. 1193; Lodolini (1960), p. 219.
Finding Aid: Inventory.
Location: Archivio di Stato di Roma.

5.3.10.2 Direzione provinciale di polizia di Civitavecchia
[DATABASE ID: VATV20200-A]
Inclusive Dates: 1846–1870.
Bulk: 154 buste.
References: D'Angiolini, p. 1193; Lodolini (1960), p. 220.
Finding Aid: List.
Location: Archivio di Stato di Roma.

5.3.10.3 Governo e Tribunale civile e criminale di Civitavecchia
[DATABASE ID: VATV20213-A]
Inclusive Dates: 1570–1871.
Bulk: 955 buste.
Reference: D'Angiolini, pp. 1195–1196.
Finding Aid: List, 1970.
Location: Archivio di Stato di Roma.

5.3.11 Corneto

RECORDS. Records of the administration consist of the following series.

5.3.11.1 Curia vescovile di Corneto: cause del tribunale civile
[DATABASE ID: VATV40006-A]
Inclusive Dates: 1572–1880.
Bulk: 180 buste and 205 vols.
Note: This series was cited in Natalini et al., p. 270, but not seen by project staff in 1990.
Location: Archivio Segreto Vaticano.

5.3.12 Fiano Romano

RECORDS. Records of the administration consist of the following series.

5.3.12.1 Atti dei notai di Fiano (Fiano Romano)
[DATABASE ID: VATV 20400-A]
Inclusive Dates: 1574–1818.
Bulk: 58 vols. and 1 registro.
Reference: D'Angiolini, p. 1219.
Location: Archivio di Stato di Roma.

5.3.13 Frascati

RECORDS. Records of the administration consist of the following series.

5.3.13.1 Atti dei notai di Frascati
[DATABASE ID: VATV20401-A]
Inclusive Dates: 1477, 1506–1910.
Bulk: about 900 vols. and registri.

Organization: Rogiti originali, 1506–1857, 542 vols.; —Appendice, 1477 and 1558–1910, 121 vols.; —Copie, 1664–1870, 229 vols.; —Repertori e rubricelle.
Scope: Rogiti originali and Appendice: Sixteenth century, 35 vols.; —Seventeenth century, 201 vols.; —Eighteenth century, 215 vols.; —Nineteenth century, 157 vols. Copie: Seventeenth century, 30 vols.; —Eighteenth century, 102 vols.; —Nineteenth century, 97 vols.
Reference: D'Angiolini, p. 1219.
Finding Aids: There is a chronological list and an alphabetical list of notai and of localities.
Location: Archivio di Stato di Roma.

5.3.13.2 Governi di Frascati
[DATABASE ID: VATV20217-A]
Inclusive Dates: 1792–1865 (bulk 1803–1865).
Bulk: 7 buste.
Reference: D'Angiolini, p. 1196.
Finding Aid: Inventory, 1979.
Location: Archivio di Stato di Roma.

5.3.14 Genazzano

RECORDS. Records of the administration consist of the following series.

5.3.14.1 Atti dei notai di Genazzano
[DATABASE ID: VATV20402-A]
Inclusive Dates: 1505–1878.
Bulk: 482 buste and registri.
Reference: D'Angiolini, p. 1219.
Finding Aid: Inventory, 1980.
Location: Archivio di Stato di Roma.

5.3.15 Manziana

RECORDS. Records of the administration consist of the following series.

5.3.15.1 Atti dei notai di Manziana
[DATABASE ID: VATV20403-A]
Inclusive Dates: 1535–1895.
Bulk: 62 vols., buste, and registri.
Reference: D'Angiolini, p. 1219.
Location: Archivio di Stato di Roma.

5.3.16 Marino

RECORDS. Records of the administration consist of the following series.

5.3.16.1 Governatori di Marino
[DATABASE ID: VATV20089-A]
Inclusive Dates: 1606–1809.
Bulk: 218 vols., 26 buste, and 1 registro.
Reference: D'Angiolini, p. 1138.
Finding Aid: List, 1970.
Location: Archivio di Stato di Roma.

5.3.16.2 Governi di Marino
[DATABASE ID: VATV20218-A]
Inclusive Dates: 1814–1870.
Bulk: 269 buste, 48 registri, and 4 vols.
Reference: D'Angiolini, p. 1196.
Finding Aid: List, 1970.
Location: Archivio di Stato di Roma.

5.3.17 Monterotondo

RECORDS. Records of the adminstration consist of the following series.

5.3.17.1 Atti dei notai di Monterotondo
[DATABASE ID: VATV20404-A]
Inclusive Dates: 1443–1855.
Bulk: 433 buste and registri.
Reference: D'Angiolini, p. 1220.
Location: Archivio di Stato di Roma.

5.3.17.2 Governi di Monterotondo
[DATABASE ID: VATV20219-A]
Inclusive Dates: 1828–1870.
Bulk: 28 buste.
Reference: D'Angiolini, p. 1196.
Finding Aid: Inventory, 1963.
Location: Archivio di Stato di Roma.

5.3.18 Morlupo

RECORDS. Records of the administration consist of the following series.

5.3.18.1 Atti dei notai di Morlupo
[DATABASE ID: VATV20405-A]
Inclusive Dates: 1562–1824.
Bulk: 84 vols., 13 registri, 1 busta, and 2 rubricelle.
Reference: D'Angiolini, p. 1220.
Finding Aid: Summary inventory, 1980.
Location: Archivio di Stato di Roma.

5.3.19 Nettuno e Porto d'Anzio

RECORDS. Records of the administration consist of the following series.

5.3.19.1 Vicegoverno di Nettuno e Porto d'Anzio
[DATABASE ID: VATV20220-A]
Inclusive Dates: 1821–1870.
Bulk: 147 buste.
Reference: D'Angiolini, p. 1196.
Finding Aid: List, 1970.
Location: Archivio di Stato di Roma.

5.3.20 Olevano Romano

RECORDS. Records of the adminstration consist of the following series.

5.3.20.1 Atti dei notai di Olevano (Olevano Romano), Roiate e Civitella
[DATABASE ID: VATV20406-A]
Inclusive Dates: 1496–1870 (bulk 1496–1828).
Bulk: 284 vols. and registri.
Reference: D'Angiolini, p. 1220.
Finding Aid: Inventory, 1978.
Location: Archivio di Stato di Roma.

5.3.20.2 Governatori di Olevano (Olevano Romano)
[DATABASE ID: VATV20090-A]
Inclusive Dates: [15—]–1800.
Bulk: 102 buste and vols.
Reference: D'Angiolini, p. 1138.
Location: Archivio di Stato di Roma.

5.3.21 Palestrina

RECORDS. Records of the administration consist of the following series.

5.3.21.1 Atti dei notai di Palestrina
[DATABASE ID: VATV20407-A]
Inclusive Dates: 1480–1938.
Bulk: about 600 buste, vols., and registri.
Organization: Originali e copie, 1480–1843; —Copie, 1818–1938.
Reference: D'Angiolini, p. 1220.
Location: Archivio di Stato di Roma.

5.3.22 Paliano

RECORDS. Records of the administration consist of the following series.

5.3.22.1 Governi baronali di Paliano, dei principi Colonna
[DATABASE ID: VATV20093-A]
Inclusive Dates: [15—]–[18—].
Bulk: 25 sacchi.
Reference: D'Angiolini, p. 1138.
Location: Archivio di Stato di Roma.

5.3.23 Palombara Sabina

RECORDS. Records of the administration consist of the following series.

5.3.23.1 Atti dei notai di Palombara Sabina
[DATABASE ID: VATV20408-A]
Inclusive Dates: [15—]–[18—].
Bulk: 730 buste, vols., and registri.
Reference: D'Angiolini, p. 1220.
Location: Archivio di Stato di Roma.

5.3.24 Roma e Comarca

RECORDS. Records of the administration consist of the following series.

5.3.24.1 Notai della presidenza di Roma e Comarca

[DATABASE ID: VATV20196-A]
Inclusive Dates: 1832–1870.
Bulk: 11 vols. and 1 rubricella.
References: D'Angiolini, p. 1192; Lodolini (1960), p. 60.
Finding Aids: There is a chronological inventory and a printed list of notai.
Location: Archivio di Stato di Roma.

5.3.24.2 Presidenza di Comarca poi Presidenza di Roma e Comarca

[DATABASE ID: VATV20195-A]
Inclusive Dates: 1828–1870.
Bulk: 2,242 buste and 116 registri.
References: D'Angiolini, p. 1192; Lodolini (1960), pp. 217–219.
Finding Aid: Summary inventory.
Location: Archivio di Stato di Roma.

5.3.25 Rome: Repubblica Romana (1798–1799)

RECORDS. Records of the administration consist of the following series.

5.3.25.1 Alta pretura, Sezione civile

[DATABASE ID: VATV20101-A]
Inclusive Dates: 1798.
Bulk: 16 filze, 6 buste, 4 registri and 2 vols.
References: D'Angiolini, p. 1140; Lodolini (1960), p. 188.
Finding Aid: Printed inventory.
Location: Archivio di Stato di Roma.

5.3.25.2 Giudici provvisori

[DATABASE ID: VATV20097-A]
Inclusive Dates: 1798.
Bulk: 1 filza.
Reference: D'Angiolini, p. 1139.
Finding Aid: Printed inventory.
Location: Archivio di Stato di Roma.

5.3.25.3 Preture di Roma

[DATABASE ID: VATV20099-A]
Inclusive Dates: 1798–1799.
Bulk: 31 vols.
Reference: D'Angiolini, pp. 1139–1140.
Finding Aid: Printed inventory.
Location: Archivio di Stato di Roma.

5.3.25.4 Repubblica romana

[DATABASE ID: VATV20096-A]
Inclusive Dates: 1798–1799.
Bulk: 63 buste and 280 fascicoli.
Organization: Senato, 1 fascicolo; —Consolato, 21 fascicoli; —Ministero di giustizia e polizia, 4 fascicoli; —Ministero dell'interno, 8 fascicoli; —Ministero delle finanze, 200 fascicoli; —Ministero della guerra, marina e affari esteri, 5 fascicoli; —Grande questura, 31 fascicoli; —Grande contabilità, 1 fascicolo; —Comitato di guerra e finanze: dipartimento di guerra e dipartimento di finanza, 3 fascicoli; —Comitato provvisorio di governo: dipartimento di guerra, comitato militare, dipartimento di finanza, amministrazione del diritto di regi-

stratura bollo e demanio nazionale, dipartimento dell'interno, 6 fascicoli.
References: D'Angiolini, p. 1139; Lodolini (1960), p. 183.
Finding Aid: Inventory, 1984.
Location: Archivio di Stato di Roma.

5.3.25.5 Repubblica Romana

[DATABASE ID: VATV10196-A]
Inclusive Dates: ca. 1798–1867.
Bulk: 14 linear m.
Organization: 1. Repubblica Romana, 1798–[1805], 11 vols.; —2. I Dovere de' cittadini verso la patria e degli impiegati mumicipale, 1824; —3. Censura di grazia, 1850–1851; —4. Registro di arrivo, 1852; —5. Rubricella, 1849; —6. Pontificio instituto statistico-agrario, [ca. 18—], 4 buste; —7. Gruppi di carte diverse (printed); —8. Miscellaneous buste and boxes, [17—]–[18—], 33 buste and boxes; —9. Consulado Pontificio, 1816–1860, 13 vols. (includes Registri di atti di Nascita, 1816, 1821); —10. Documents sobre la espedicion a Italia, 1849, 2 vols.; —11. Correspondenza dal Cardinale Antonelli, 1867; —12. Ragguaglio delle cose operate dal ministero del commercio, 1859–1864 (printed); —13. Censo: Dispositione legislative, 1817–1834 (printed); —14. Rubricelle, 1848; —15. Petitions (mostly blank); —16. Opinamenti conformi; —17. Indice della Biblioteca drammatica del teatro Graziani; —18. Regolamento Administrivo, 1830; —19. Riflessioni, 1794; —20. Milizia Pontificia, [ca. 18—]; —21. Biglietti, ecc., 1817–1819 [vol. no. 7(I), 7(II), 88–95]; —22. Repubblica Romana, 1848–1850, 24 boxes.
Location: Archivio Segreto Vaticano.

5.3.25.6 Tribunale civile del dipartimento del Tevere

[DATABASE ID: VATV20100-A]
Inclusive Dates: 1798–1799.
Bulk: 10 vols.
References: D'Angiolini, p. 1140; Lodolini (1960), p. 188.
Finding Aid: Printed inventory.
Location: Archivio di Stato di Roma.

5.3.25.7 Tribunale temporaneo di appello

[DATABASE ID: VATV20098-A]
Inclusive Dates: 1798–1799.
Bulk: 2 filze and 2 vols.
References: D'Angiolini, p. 1139; Lodolini (1960), p. 188.
Finding Aid: Printed inventory.
Location: Archivio di Stato di Roma.

5.3.26 Rome: Repubblica Romana (1849)

RECORDS. Records of the administration consist of the following series.

5.3.26.1 Miscellanea della repubblica romana

[DATABASE ID: VATV20192-A]
Inclusive Dates: 1849.
Bulk: 99 buste and 1 registro.
References: D'Angiolini, p. 1191; Lodolini (1960), p. 212.
Finding Aid: Partial summary inventory; list.
Location: Archivio di Stato di Roma.

5.3.26.2 Tribunale di appello e Tribunale supremo della repubblica romana
[DATABASE ID: VATV20253-A]
Inclusive Dates: 1849.
Bulk: 8 buste and 1 vol.
Reference: D'Angiolini, p. 1203.
Finding Aid: List, 1970.
Location: Archivio di Stato di Roma.

5.3.27 Sacrofano

RECORDS. Records of the administration consist of the following series.

5.3.27.1 Atti dei notai di Sacrofano
[DATABASE ID: VATV20410-A]
Inclusive Dates: 1535–1895.
Bulk: 35 vols., 3 registri, and 3 buste.
Scope: Sixteenth century, 1 vol. and 1 busta di copie; —Seventeenth century, 17 vols. and 2 buste di copie; —Eighteenth century, 16 vols. and 3 registri; —Nineteenth century, 1 vol.
Reference: D'Angiolini, p. 1220.
Finding Aid: Inventory, 1978.
Location: Archivio di Stato di Roma.

5.3.27.2 Governi baronali di Scrofano (Sacrofano)
[DATABASE ID: VATV20095-A]
Inclusive Dates: 1591–1816.
Bulk: 145 registri and buste and 13 rubricelle.
Organization: Atti civili, 1591–1816, 108 registri and 1 busta; —Atti criminali, 1594–1782, 33 registri and 3 buste.
Reference: D'Angiolini, p. 1138.
Finding Aid: Inventory, 1977.
Location: Archivio di Stato di Roma.

5.3.28 Sant'Oreste

RECORDS. Records of the administration consist of the following series.

5.3.28.1 Atti dei notai di Sant'Oreste
[DATABASE ID: VATV20409-A]
Inclusive Dates: [14—]–[19—].

Bulk: 180 buste, vols. and registri.
Reference: D'Angiolini, p. 1220.
Location: Archivio di Stato di Roma.

5.3.28.2 Governi baronali di Sant'Oreste
[DATABASE ID: VATV20094-A]
Inclusive Dates: [15—]–[18—].
Bulk: about 200 pezzi.
Reference: D'Angiolini, p. 1138.
Location: Archivio di Stato di Roma.

5.3.29 Torrita Tiberina

RECORDS. Records of the administration consist of the following series.

5.3.29.1 Atti dei notai di Torrita (Torrita Tiberina)
[DATABASE ID: VATV20411-A]
Inclusive Dates: 1507–1816.
Bulk: 48 vols., 17 buste, and 7 registri.
Reference: D'Angiolini, p. 1219.
Location: Archivio di Stato di Roma.

5.3.30 Velletri (Legazione)

RECORDS. Records of the adminstration consist of the following series.

5.3.30.1 Direzione provinciale di polizia di Velletri
[DATABASE ID: VATV20202-A]
Inclusive Dates: 1814–1870.
Bulk: 59 registri.
References: D'Angiolini, p. 1193; Lodolini (1960), p. 220.
Finding Aid: List.
Location: Archivio di Stato di Roma.

5.3.30.2 Legazione apostolica di Velletri
[DATABASE ID: VATV20201-A]
Inclusive Dates: 1832–1870.
Bulk: 479 buste.
References: D'Angiolini, p. 1193; Lodolini (1960), p. 219.
Finding Aid: Inventory, 1929.
Location: Archivio di Stato di Roma.

PART 6

Permanent Commissions

PAPAL COMMISSIONS AS SUCH ARE AN ADMINISTRATIVE CONCEPT dating from the nineteenth century. However, in earlier times some congregations were on occasion referred to as commissions. For the period from the start of the nineteenth century, there are basically two types of commissions: higher-ranking groups composed entirely of cardinals, and lower-ranking groups composed of lesser officials, headed by a cardinal. The lower-ranking commissions have usually been attached to a congregation. This guide does not distinguish between the two types of commissions.

6.1 Abbazia di S. Girolamo per la revisione ed emendazione della "Volgata"
[DATABASE ID: VATV074-A]

This group was established in 1933, replacing the Pontifical Commission for the Revision and Emendation of the Vulgate. Its purpose is to restore, as far as possible, the original readings of the Vulgate text and to prepare a critical edition.

RECORDS. This agency existed entirely after 1922.

6.2 Commissio ad Codicis Canones Authentice Interpretandos
[DATABASE ID: VATV072-A]

After the publication of the 1917 Code of Canon Law, Benedict XV replaced the Pontificia Commissio pro Ecclesiae Legibus in Unum Redigendis (established by Pius X) with a new commission to interpret authentically the norms of the code.

Reference. See motu proprio *Cum iuris canonici Codicem* (Sept. 15, 1917), in *Acta Apostolicae Sedis* 9 (1917): 483–484: "Consilium seu Commissionem uti vocant, constituimus, cui uni ius erit Codices canones authentice interpretandi, audita tamen, in rebus maioris momenti, sacra ea Congregatione cuius propria res sit, quae consilio disceptanda proponitur."

RECORDS. No records for this commission were located.

6.3 Commissio Pontificia pro Unione Ecclesiarum Dissidentum
[DATABASE ID: VATV460-A]

This commission was established on March 19, 1895, by Leo XIII to further Christian unity. In 1908 it was attached to the Congregatio de Propaganda Fide.

RECORDS. No records for this commission were located. See listings for the Propaganda Fide.

6.4 Commissione araldica per la corte pontificia
[DATABASE ID: VATV089-A]

This commission was established in 1915.

RECORDS. No records for this commission were located.

6.5 Commissione cardinalizia per il santuario di Pompei
[DATABASE ID: VATV085-A]

This commission was established by Leo XIII (1878–1903) to oversee the pontifical sanctuary of the Blessed Virgin of the Rosary in Pompei.

RECORDS. No records for this commission were located.

6.6 Commissione cardinalizia per gli studi storici
[DATABASE ID: VATV077-A]

After the Vatican Archives were opened to scholars, this commission was established in 1883 by Leo XIII to promote the study of history. Its function was continued by Pius XII in 1954 through the Pontifical Commission of Historical Sciences.

RECORDS. No records for this commission were located.

6.7 Commissione della visita apostolica
[DATABASE ID: VATV469-A]

The *Normae peculiare* was published on September 29, 1908, three months after the publication of the constitution *Sapienti consilio* and was appended to it. This was the authority for the appointment of this commission to take the place of the Congregatio Visitationis Apostolicae with all its rights and functions. The competence of this commission included making an annual visitation of the churches of Rome, inquiring into the fulfillment of the endowed masses and other pious foundations, and examining the financial condition of the churches and institutions of the city. The functions of this commission, limited as they are to the city of Rome, are altogether distinct from those of the Consistorial Congregation, which has the competence for directing apostolic visitations in other parts of the Catholic world.

RECORDS. No records for this commission were located.

6.8 Commissione permanente per la tutela dei monumenti storici ed artistici della Santa Sede
[DATABASE ID: VATV088-A]

This commmission was established in 1923.

RECORDS. This commission functioned entirely after 1922.

6.9 Opera della preservazione della fede
[DATABASE ID: VATV087-A]

Established in 1902 by Leo XIII, this commission was replaced in 1930 by the Pontifical Work for the Preservation of the Faith and for the Erection of New Churches in Rome (alternate English name: Commission for the Preservation of the Faith in Rome).

RECORDS. No records for this commission were located.

6.10 Pontifical Commission for the Administration of Peter's Pence
[DATABASE ID: VATV467-A]

This commission was established by Leo XIII (1978–1903) to administer alms given for the temporal support of the pope and the work of the Holy See.

RECORDS. No records for this commission were located.

6.11 Pontifical Commission for the General Restoration of the Liturgy
[DATABASE ID: VATV142-A]

This commission was established by Pius XII in 1948 to revise the Roman Missal, the Breviary, and the Roman Pontifical.

RECORDS. This commission was established after 1922.

6.12 Pontificia Commissio ad Redigendum Codicem Iuris Canonici Orientalis
[DATABASE ID VATV073-A]

Established by Pius XI in 1935 to draw up a code of oriental canon law, this commission succeeded a commission appointed in 1929 to draw up a schema for the code (alternate English name: Pontifical Commission for the Redaction of the Code of Oriental Canon Law [CICO]).

RECORDS. This commission was established after 1922.

6.13 Pontificia Commissio de Sacra Archeologia
[DATABASE ID: VATV079-A]

This commission was established by Pius IX in 1852 to preserve and provide for study of early Christian cemeteries, monuments, and basilicas in and around Rome. In 1925 it was given pontifical rank and its powers were widened. Under the Lateran Treaty its authority was extended throughout Italy. The activities of the Pontifical Roman Academy of Archaeology and the Pontifical Institute of Christian Archaeology are coordinated with those of the commission.

RECORDS. No records of the commission were located

6.14 Pontificia Commissio pro Ecclesiae Legibus in Unum Redigendis
[DATABASE ID: VATV148-A]

This commission was set up by Pius X with his motu proprio *Arduum sane* (Mar. 19, 1904) to prepare a code of canon law (cf. *Acta Sanctae Sedis*, 36:549). The document reads: "Consilium, sive, ut aiunt, Commissionem Pontificiam constituimus, quam penes erit totius negotii moderatio et cura, eaque constabit ex nonnullis SRE Cardinalibus, a Pontifice nominatim designandis."

No specific title was given in the document. It is referred to in many references in various ways: "Ex Commissione Codificatrice" (*Acta Sanctae Sedis*, Index [1910]); "Commissio Cardinalitia Codificatorum" (plus consultors and collaborators) (Beste, p. 39). However, *Acta Sanctae Sedis* 37:131 gives a letter of Cardinal Gasparri, then an archbishop, informing the cardinals of the above action and the letter is signed officially:

Petrum Gasparri, Arch. Caesareensem, Secretarium Pontificae Commissionis pro Ecclesiae Legibus in Unum Redigendis.

The commission was headed by the secretary of the Congregatio pro Negotiis Ecclesiasticis Extraordinariis. The commission worked until the code was completed in 1916. The code was promulgated in 1917 and took effect in 1918. After the publication of the code, this commission was replaced by a new one, the Pontificia Commissio ad Codicis Canones Authentice Interpretandos.

RECORDS. Records of the commission consist of the following series.

6.14.1 Archivio della codificazione del diritto canonico: Codex juris canonici
[DATABASE ID: VATV10021-A]
Inclusive Dates: 1904–1917.
Bulk: 14 linear m.
Organization: 97 numbered boxes plus miscellaneous duplicate materials. The collection is organized along the same schema as the 1917 Code of Canon Law.

Subseries and box numbers are : 1–3. Praeliminaria varia; — 4–5. Postulata episcoporum in ordinem digesta a P. Klumpfer; —7–9. Studi preparatori alla codificazione del diritto canonico (lib. I–III); —10–11. Liber I, Normae generales, Voti; — 12. Liber I, Schemi del lib. I; —13. Liber I, Verbali delle Consulte parziali e generali; —14–18. Liber II, De Personis, Voti; —19–25. Liber II, Schemi; —26–27. Liber II, Verbali delle Consulte parziali e Congregazioni particolari; —28. Liber II, Verbali delle Consulte parziali; —29–30. Liber II, Verbali delle congregazioni particolari; —31–42. Liber III, De Rebus. Voti; —43–51. Liber III, Schemi; —52–60. Liber II, Verbali delle Consulte (de Sacramentis, de Ordine, de Matrimonio, etc.); —61–65. Liber IV, De Processibus, Voti; —66–71. Liber IV, Schemi; —72–74. Liber IV, Verbali delle Consulte; —75–77. Liber V, De Delictis et Poenis, Voti; —78–79. Liber V, Schemi; —80–82. Liber V, Verbali delle Consulte; —83–85. Animadversiones episcoporum in Codex Juris Canonici (CJC); —86–87. Bozze del CJC (con note manoscritte del Cardinal P. Gasparri; —88–89. Schema completo del CJC; —90. Cose varie per la promulgazione del CJC; —91–97. Pontificia Commissio ad Codicis Canones.

Note: Vols. 1, 2, 5, 7–9, 13, 25–30, 52–59, 72–74, 80–81, 86–87, and 96–97 are available on microfilm.

Finding Aids: ASV Indice 1164 provides a detailed inventory of the entire collection. The index lists each box and the major categories of information contained therein. The copy in the index room is a much-reduced photocopy of the original, which is shelved in the stacks with this series, before box 1.

Location: Archivio Segreto Vaticano.

6.15 Pontificia Commissione antipreparatoria per il concilio ecumenico
[DATABASE ID: VATV091-A]

This commission was established in 1959 to prepare for the Second Vatican Council. Its work was completed in 1960.

RECORDS. This commmission was created after 1922.

6.16 Pontificia Commissione per gli archivi ecclesiastici d'Italia
[DATABASE ID: VATV078-A]

This commission was established by Pius XII in 1955 to provide assistance and collaboration in the preservation and administration of local archives.

RECORDS. This commission was created after 1922.

6.17 Pontificia Commissione per l'America latina
[DATABASE ID: VATV084-A]

This commission was established by Pius XII in 1958 to study the problems of Catholic life in Latin America. The commission follows and sustains the activity of the Latin American Episcopal Council.

RECORDS. This commission was created after 1922.

6.18 Pontificia Commissione per la cinematografia
[DATABASE ID: VATV082-A]

This commission was established by Pius XII in 1952, as successor to the Pontifical Commission for Educational and Religious Motion Pictures, to study problems in the motion picture world that have some connection with faith and morals. In 1954 the commission's competence was widened and it was renamed the Pontifical Commission for Motion Pictures, Radio, and Television (alternate English name: Pontifical Commission for Cinematography).

RECORDS. This commission was created after 1922.

6.19 Pontificia commissione per la cinematografia didattica e religiosa
[DATABASE ID: VATV083-A]

This commission was established in 1948 to study motion picture productions intended as illustrations in the teaching of Christian doctrine. In 1952 it was transformed into the Pontifical Motion Picture Commission (alternate name: Pontifical Commission for Educational and Religious Cinematography).

RECORDS. This commission was created after 1922.

6.20 Pontificia Commissione per la cinematografia, la radio e la televisione
[DATABASE ID: VATV081-A]

Pius XII established this commission in 1954 as a broadening of the responsibility of the Pontifical Motion Picture Commission. In 1959 (motu proprio *Boni Pastoris*, Feb. 22) John XXIII affiliated the commission with the Secretariatus Status. Paul VI (motu proprio *In*

fructibus, Apr. 2, 1964) extended the scope of the commission to include the press and changed its name to the Pontifical Commission for the Media of Social Communications.

RECORDS. This commission was created after 1922.

6.21 Pontificia Commissione per la revisione ed emendazione della Volgata
[DATABASE ID: VATV075-A]

With a letter of Cardinal Mariano Rampola del Tindero (Nov. 21, 1907), Pius X instituted a commission of study for the preparation of a critical edition of the Vulgate, assigning the task to the Benedictines. With motu proprio *Consilium* (Nov. 23, 1914) Benedict XV gave the commission the new name of Pontifical Commission for the Revision of the Vulgate. It was replaced in 1933 by the Abbey of St. Jerome for the Revision and Emendation of the Vulgate.

RECORDS. No records were located for this commission.

6.22 Pontificia Commissione per la Russia
[DATABASE ID: VATV021-A]

Pius XI established this commission on June 20, 1925, as part of the Congregatio pro Ecclesia Orientalis with responsibility for the clergy and faithful in Russia belonging to the Latin rite. It was made independent on April 6, 1930. On December 21, 1934, the commission came under the control of the Congregatio pro Negotiis Ecclesiasticis Extraordinariis.

RECORDS. This commission was created after 1922.

6.23 Pontificia Opera di assistenza
[DATABASE ID: VATV090-A]

This commission was established in 1953 to carry on relief and social welfare activities in Italy.

RECORDS. This commission was created after 1922.

6.24 Pontificia Opera per la preservazione della fede e per la provvista di nuove chiese in Roma
[DATABASE ID: VATV086-A]

This commission was established in 1930 to safeguard the faith in the diocese of Rome, to erect and endow new churches in that diocese, and to negotiate with civil authorities in cases involving the expropriation of sacred buildings in Rome. It replaced the Society for the Preservation of the Faith.

RECORDS. This commission was established after 1922.

6.25 Pontificio Comitato di scienze storiche
[DATABASE ID: VATV076-A]

This commission was established by Pius XII in 1954 as a continuation of the Cardinalitial Commission for Historical Studies. It represents the Holy See in the Comité international des sciences historiques, with a view to collaborating in the development of historical sciences through international cooperation.

RECORDS. This commission was created after 1922.

6.26 Pontificio Commissio de Re Biblica
[DATABASE ID: VATV071-A]

Leo XIII established this commission in 1902 to promote the progress of biblical studies and to see that these studies are kept free of error (alternate English name: Pontifical Commission for Biblical Studies).

RECORDS. No records for this commission were located.

6.27 Pontificium Consilium Centrale pro Arte Sacra in Italia
[DATABASE ID: VATV080-A]

This commission was established in 1924 to promote Christian art and to direct the restoration of churches.

RECORDS. Records of the commission consist of the following series.

6.27.1 [Archivio]
[DATABASE ID: VATV10492-A]
Inclusive Dates: 1939–1960.
Bulk: 213 linear m.
Reference: Natalini et al., p. 269.
Location: Archivio Segreto Vaticano.

6.28 Sala stampa della Santa Sede
[DATABASE ID: VATV40065-A]

No history was prepared for this agency.

RECORDS. Records of the agency consist of the following series.

6.28.1 Sala stampa della Santa Sede
[DATABASE ID: VATV40008-A]
Inclusive Dates: 1931–1972.
Bulk: 112 buste.
Reference: Natalini et al., p. 270.
Location: Archivio Segreto Vaticano.

PART 7

Miscellaneous Official Materials and Separate Collections

THIS SECTION OF THE GUIDE PRESENTS A VARIETY OF HISTORICAL documents that are found in the Archivio Segreto Vaticano, the Archives of the Propaganda Fide, the Archives of the Fabbrica di San Pietro, and the Archives Nationales, Paris. The common thread in these materials is simply that the project staff could not clearly assign these to any of the specific bureaucratic offices identified in the previous sections of the guide. That does not mean that the records described here are of relative less importance.

Among the records in this section are those contained in the *Archivum Arcis*, which are among the most important in the ASV. Because this series is for the most part pre-1588 the specific documents in this important series do not match specific offices and is listed in this section.

For the most part, however, this section consists of two types of material, miscellaneous official material and separate collections. The miscellaneous official material is found in a variety of places. Some is found in a series of cabinets. However, because the material in these cabinets (or armaria) are so well known, the individual items stored therein have taken on a permanent sort of identification even though some of this material might logically be placed elsewhere in the ASV.

There are also several separate collections that have come to the archives for a variety of reasons. The individual and family papers have come in large part because the activities of specific individuals and families have been sufficiently intertwined with the activities of the papacy that it made sense to choose the ASV as a repository. It is in these cases that one finds official material blended in with family papers. Some of these collections contain official material that family members, upon completion of a period of service to the Holy See, chose to take with them as they departed office.

This section also contains descriptions of records from a variety of institutions. The reasons why records of various confraternities, religious orders, monasteries, convents and churches have come to these archives are much less clear.

The documents in this section are presented in the following groupings:

Miscellaneous Official Materials
 1. Archivum Arcis
 2. Miscellaneous Armaria of the ASV
 3. Original Armaria of the ASV
 4. Miscellaneous Series

Separate Collections
 5. Individual and Family Papers
 6. Archconfraternities and Confraternities
 7. Religious Orders

8. Monasteries, Convents, Abbeys, and Churches
9. Miscellaneous Manuscripts
10. Spogli Cardinali

References. The following sources were used in the preparation of the individual histories and biographies that introduce the various separate collections in this section of the guide. D. Ameyden, *La storia delle famiglie romane*, con note ed aggiunte de A. Bertini (Rome, 1910–1914). R. G. Asch and A. M. Burke, eds., *Princes, Patronage, and the Nobility: The Court at the Beginning of the Modern Age, c. 1450–1650* (London, 1991). C. F. Black, *Italian Confraternities in the Sixteenth Century* (Cambridge, 1989). P. Boutry, "Nobiltà romana e curia nell'età della restaurazione," in *Signori, patrizi, cavalieri in Italia nell età moderna*, edited by M. A. Visceglia (Bari, 1992). *Catholic Encyclopedia* (New York, 1907–1922). F. L. Cross, ed., *Oxford Dictionary of the Christian Church*, 3d ed., edited by E. A. Livingstone (Oxford, 1997). *Dizionario biografico degli italiani* (Rome, 1960–). *Dizionario degli istituti di perfezione* (Rome, 1974–1988). M. Eliade, ed., *Encyclopedia of Religion* (New York, 1987–1988). *Enciclopedia cattolica* (Vatican City, 1949–1954). *Enciclopedia italiana di scienze, lettere ed arti* (Rome, 1929–1939). E. E. Y. Hales, *Revolution and Papacy, 1796–1846* (New York, 1960). P. Litta, *Famiglie celebri italiane*, 2d ser. (Naples, 1902–1923). P. K. Meagher, T. C. O'Brien, and C. M. Aherne, *Encyclopedic Dictionary of Religion* (Washington, D.C., 1979). A. Mercati et al., eds., *Dizionario ecclesiastico* (Turin, 1953–). G. Moroni, *Dizionario di erudizione storico-ecclesiastica* (Venice, 1840–1861). *New Catholic Encyclopedia* (New York, 1967–1979). E. W. Quinn, *Archconfraternities, Archsodalities, and Primary Unions: With a Supplement on the Archconfraternity of Christian Mothers* (Washington, D.C., 1962). V. Spreti, ed., *Enciclopedia storico-nobiliare italiana* (Milan, 1928–1936). P. E. Visconti, *Città e famiglie nobili e celebri dello Stato pontificio* (Rome, 1847).

7.1
ARCHIVUM ARCIS

7.1.1 Archivum Arcis (often referred to as AA)

[DATABASE ID: VATV194-A]

Inclusive Dates: 567–1823?.

Bulk: 6,720 numbered items.

Organization: The items of the series are assigned numbers. Materials are physically separated by composition (e.g. paper, paper with lead seals, paper with wax seals, parchment, parchment with lead seals, volumes, etc.). Because of the physical separation of materials described above, this collection has been divided into two sets of armaria designated AA Arm. A–M and AA Arm. I–XVIII.

Scope: Boyle describes this complex series as records of papal privileges, deeds to land, and related documents of royal and imperial relations with the papacy, including royal letters and privileges, diplomata of emperors; it also includes acts of homages to popes, authentications of councils by bishops, lists of bishops. MacFarlane notes that the series includes original incoming letters to various departments of the Curia, transcripts of very early documents now lost, papal bulls, and some cameral material. Boyle notes that the papacy from the thirteenth century kept documents of this nature separately. Sixtus IV (1471–1484) assembled the collection in Castel S. Angelo. Upon the arrest of Pius VI (1775–1799) by the forces of Napoleon in 1798, the collection was transferred to the Vatican Archives.

Note: Nos. 1, 2, 9, 18, 25, 47, 255, 294–296, 435 B–C, 563, 612, 620 (1), 623, 651, 658, 659, 670, 720, 737–739, 798, 803–805, 808, 810, 954, 1009, 1251–1257, 1586, 1602, 1711, 1815, 2137, 2174, 2190, 2604, 2655, 3323, 3485, 3530, 3674, 3837–3838, 3848, 3913, 4082, 4991, 5079, 5120, 5122–5123, 5125, 5215, 5245–5248, 5251–5261, 5615, 5623, 6190 B, 6428, 6461, 6468, 6492, and 6721 of AA Arm. I–XVIII; AA Arm. B, vol. 20; AA Arm. C, vol. 1063; and AA Arm. E, vol. 129 are available on microfilm.

References: Boyle, pp. 58–60; Fink, pp. 146–148; Pásztor (1970), pp. 21–24; Pásztor (1983), pp. 99–101; MacFarlane, p. 91.

O. Sforza and M. V. Zacchero, ASV *Archivum Arcis Armario B3, 7 Giugno 1590, Libro di tutta la spesa fatta da N.S. Sisto V alla Colonna Antonina e Traiana* (Rome, 1984) [this title was noted but not verified by project staff]. This is an edition of one volume (*Archivum Arcis* Armario B3). It is very readable and contains illustrations and photocopies from the original volume.

T. Freudenberger, *Augustinus Steuchus aus Gubbio, Augustinerchorherr und päpstlicher Bibliothekar (1497–1548) und sein literarisches Lebenswerk* (Münster, 1953). L. Lopetegui, "San Francisco de Borja y el plan misional de san Pío V. Primeros pasos de una Congregación de Propaganda Fide," *Archivum historicum Societatis Iesu* 11 (1942): 1–26. D. Mansilla, *La documentación española del archivo del Castel S. Angelo (395–1498)* (Rome, 1958). D. Mansilla, "La reorganización eclesiástica española del siglo XVI," *Anthologica annua* 4 (1956): 97–238. A. L. Martin, ed., *Correspondance du nonce en France, Fabio Mirto Frangipani 1568–1572 et 1586–1587, Nonce extraordinaire en 1574, 1575–1576 et 1578* (Rome, 1984). A. Martini, *I sigilli d'oro dell'Archivio segreto*

vaticano (Milan, 1984). A. Mercati, "Schedario Garampi, Registri Vaticani, Registri Lateranensi, Rationes Camerae, Inventario del Fondo Concistoriale," vol. 1 of *Sussidi per la consultazione dell'Archivio Vaticano*, (Rome, 1926) G. Mollat, "Lettres communes Jean XXII (1316–1334): Analysées d'après les registres dits d'Avignon et du Vatican," forms part of *Bibliothèque des Écoles françaises d'Athènes et de Rome*, 3d ser., *Registres et lettres des papes du XIVe siècle* (Paris, 1904–1947). P. Sella, *Le bolle d'oro dell'Archivio Vaticano* (Vatican City, 1934). J. Haller et al., ed., *Repertorium Germanicum: Regesten aus den päpstlichen Archiven zur Geschichte des Deutschen Reichs und seiner Territorien im XIV. und XV. Jahrhundert: Pontifikat Eugens IV. (1431–1447)* (Berlin, 1897), calendars items concerning Germany in this series.

Finding Aids: ASV Indici 56–57, by G. B. Confalonieri, present the organization of the *Archivum Arcis* prior to about 1910, when the records were arranged into Armaria superiora (A–M) and Armaria inferiora (I–XVIII). Within each armarium, items were given a capsula or folio number as well as an item number. Many works including that of Confalonieri cite this former classification, which must be translated into the current volume number. If a researcher has an old Arm. Cap. number, the first step is to verify that this is the correct citation through ASV Indici 56–57. The second step is to locate the current volume number in ASV Indice 1074.

Fondo Confalonieri 86 covers much of the same ground as Indice 57 (AA Arm. A–M). According to Pásztor (1970) [see above], this volume may provide more detailed access points to Arm. A–B.

ASV Indice 1074 is a concordance between the former and current volume numbers of items in *Archivum Arcis*, Armaria I–XVIII, nos. 1–6720. By taking the former number from Indici 56–57, one can determine the new volume number through this concordance.

ASV Indice 691, sections 2 and 3, is a listing of materials according to their new numbers with notes on their composition or physical state.

ASV Indice 1001 serves as an alphabetical index to AA Arm. C–F. Msgr. Charles Burns of the ASV stated that this indice and Indici 1002–1012, described below, are transcriptions of other earlier indici.

ASV Indici 1002–1012 (A–D) provide detailed summaries of the contents of AA Arm. I–XVIII. These indici are organized by the new numbers that were assigned to items in this collection early in the twentieth century. Indice 1012 also provides an alphabetical index to entries pertaining to item numbers 1–6720 in Indici 1002–1012.

There are other ASV Indici that may pertain in some way to the AA Arm. At this point these have not been analyzed. They are: ASV Indici 10–11, 17–25, 29–41, 44–47, 49–50, 57 (ff. 16–25), 59–64, 68–70, 149, and 694–699. Pásztor (1970) states that Indici 69–70 are chronological indexes to the AA Arm I–XVIII and were compiled by G. Garampi. Indice 69 covers the period to 1539 and Indice 70 spans 1540–1808.

In the ASV Sala degli Indici, see the index card file under the stairs. These are transcriptions from the indici within some *Archivum Arcis* volumes and older indexes to the collections. Little attempt was made to check information with the actual materials. While there is much good information here, old errors are also perpetuated.

ASV Indice 124, "Primo Sbozzo di Inventario di tutti i libri che sono nell'Archivio Segreto Vaticano," by Giovanni Bissaiga in 1672, provides more descriptive and accurate volume titles for select volumes in some series including AA Arm. I–XVIII, no. 952 on folio 290v.

Location: Archivio Segreto Vaticano.

7.2
MISCELLANEOUS ARMARIA OF THE ASV
[DATABASE ID: VATV152-A]

This is an old and well-known miscellany of material in the ASV. In total it constitutes 120.7 linear meters and covers the dates 1330–1851. This miscellany originally consisted of fifteen series comprising twenty-five hundred volumes titled *Miscellaneorum armarium I* (etc.). Now series IV and V are combined. Many volumes from this series have been transferred to the Vatican Library. The series includes a wide array of records from many offices and individuals. Each of the fourteen *Miscellaneorum armaria* is described separately immediately following this entry in the guide.

For the most part this series contains documents pertaining to political and ecclesiastical history of the sixteenth to nineteenth century, including: correspondence, documentation of practice or norms of procedure, regulations of congregations or other curial offices, records concerning the oversight of religious orders, instructions, reports, literary works, historical, political and theological writings, diaries, bulls, and edicts. (Most of the literary works have been transferred to the Vatican Library; see Index 315 [5–6] in the index room adjacent to the Sala dei manoscritti in the Vatican Library.) Much of the material originated in departments or offices of the Curia, notably the Secretariatus Status, the Congregatio super Statu Regularium, the Congregatio Negotiis et Consultationibus Episcoporum et Regularium Praeposita, the Congregatio Iurisdictionis et Immunitatis Ecclesiasticae, the Congregazione dei confini, the Congregatio de Propaganda Fide, and the offices of the vice-chancellor and chamberlain of the Cancellaria Apostolica, who handled consistorial business. Some material also came from private archives or holdings, most of which concerns the activities of curial departments, such as the papers of Cardinal Ceva in *Misc. Arm. III*, 31–50 or the correspondence with nuncios in *Misc. Arm. II*, 131.

ASV Indice 213, "Indice di libri de Msgr. Ciampini alcune de quale sono stati comprati da Il. Sg.le. Clemente XI e posti nell'studi . . . e fuori sono stati segnali con la lett. 'C' e posti in diversi luoghi secundo le materie nelle quali trattavano," includes a list of volumes from this series that were added to the Vatican Archives in the period 1700–1721. The detailed description of each *Misc. arm.* includes a list of volumes taken from this source.

References. Fink, pp. 97–99; Boyle, pp. 71–72; Pásztor (1970), pp. 200–204; Pásztor (1983), pp. 186–189.

B. Barbiche, ed., *Correspondance du nonce en France, Innocenzo del Bufalo, évêque de Camerino, 1601–1604* (Rome, 1964). C. Binder, "Il magistero del Sacro Pallazzo Apostolico del cardinale di Torquemada," *Memorie domenicane*, n.s., 30 (1954): 3–24. A. Fraccacreta, "Notizie sul monastero benedettino di S. Maria in Campo Marzio," *L'Urbe* (Rome) 4, fasc. 4 (1939): 24–34. J. Lestocquoy, ed., *Correspondance des nonces en France: Lenzi et Gualterio, Légation du Cardinal Trivultio (1557–1561)* (Rome, 1977). J. Lestocquoy, ed., *Correspondance du nonce en France: Prospero Santa Croce (1552–1554)* (Rome, 1972). A. Mercati, "Briciole della corrispondenza di Antonio Vallisneri il Seniore: Con appendice alle lettere di scienziati dall'Archivio segreto vaticano," *Commentationes Pontificia academia scientiarium* 7 (1943): 783–881. A. Mercati, "Per la storia letteraria di Reggio Emilia," *Atti e memorie della Deputazione di storia patria per le antiche provincie modenesi*, ser. 5, 12 (1919): 37–117. L. Oliger, ed., "Breve compendio de los ritos idolatricos de Nueva Espana, auctore Bernardino de Sahagun O.F.M," *Antonianum* 17 (1942): 3–38, 133–174. E. Olmos y Canalda, *Reivindicación de Alejandro VI*, 3d ed. (Valencia, 1953). A. Rota, "Michelangelo e il Monte della Fede," *Archivi* (Rome), ser. 2, 4 (1937): 27–60. R. Toupin, ed., *Correspondance du nonce en France, Giovanni Battista Castelli (1581–1583)* (Rome, 1967). M. Vanti, *Mons. Bernardino Cirillo, commendatore e maestro generale dell'ord. di S. Spirito (1556–1575)* (Rome, 1936). M. Vanti, *S. Giacomo degl'Incurabili di Roma nel Cinquecento: Dalle compagnie del Divino Amore a San Camillo de Lellis* (Rome, 1938).

J. Haller et al., eds., *Repertorium Germanicum: Regesten aus den päpstlichen Archiven zur Geschichte des deutschen Reichs und seiner Territorien im XIV. und XV. Jahrhundert: Pontifikat Eugens IV. (1431–1447)* (Berlin, 1897) calendars items concerning Germany in this series.

Although focused on sources pertaining to America, C. R. Fish, *Guide to the Materials for American History in Roman and other Italian Archives* (Washington, D.C., 1911, pp. 45–51), provides useful details regarding the contents of this series.

Finding Aids. ASV Indice 1029-I provides volume-level description for the entire *Misc. arm.* series. It also lists the identification number for each volume transferred from the series to the Vatican Library (usually a number beginning "Vat. Lat."), identifies each missing volume, and provides notes about further finding aids available for several parts of the series. Indice 1029-II is a subject index to Indice 1029-I. It is not comprehensive, however, and at best indexes only Indice 1029-I, not the records themselves.

ASV Indice 136, by De Pretis, is similar to 1029-I, but contains briefer descriptions of the volumes.

Schedario Melampo, located in the ASV Sala degli Indici, consists of individual slips of paper bound in small volumes or *blocchetti*. This schedario contains information similar to that located in ASV Indice 136 for *Misc. arm. I–XIII*. For *Misc. arm. XIV* and *XV*, however, Schedario Melampo is much more detailed, providing almost a complete calendar of the series.

The *Schedario Garampi* includes an index to some of the material in this series. Garampi's chronological index (ASV Indici 168–173) also includes entries for materials in this series.

ASV Indice 1107 (formerly Indice 40) provides a listing of materials from this as well as other series that have been transferred from the Vatican Archives to the Vatican Library. This concordance indicates the former Vatican Archives volume numbers and the current Vatican Library volume numbers.

7.2.1 Miscellaneorum armarium I

[DATABASE ID: VATV470-A]

Inclusive Dates: 1542–1771 (scattered dates).

Bulk: 11 linear m. (226 numbered vols.).

Scope: This series consists chiefly of Secretariatus Status correspondence relating to nuncios, legati a latere, and other cardinals. It includes some published materials. Volumes relating to political affairs in Germany, France, Spain, Portugal, Savoy, and Parma predominate, with a few volumes also relating to Hungary, England, Ireland, Flanders, Holland, Sweden, Denmark, Poland, Switzerland, Malta, Avignon, China, and many of the Italian states.

A few volumes relating to the Anglican schism [Vat. Lat. 11710–11711], Venice, and Parma, have been transferred from this series to the Vatican Library. They are now identified as Vat. Lat. 11710–11712 and 12925.

Misc. arm. I, vol. 220 is now part of the *Fondo Garampi*.

ASV Indice 213, "Indice di libri de Msgr. Ciampini alcune de quale sono stati comprati da Il. Sg.le. Clemente XI e posti nell'studi . . . e fuori sono stati segnali con la lett. 'C' e posti in diversi luoghi secundo le materie nelle quali trattavano," indicates that *Misc. arm. I*, vols. 13–14, 51, 76–77, and 80 were added to the Vatican Archives between 1700 and 1721.

Note: Vol. 12 is available on microfilm.

Reference: Boyle, p. 71.

Finding Aids: ASV Indice 1029-I is a volume-level description; Indice 1029-II is an alphabetically arranged index (names, regions, agency, etc.).

ASV Indice 136, by De Pretis, is similar to 1029-I but contains briefer descriptions of the volumes.

ASV Indice 124, "Primo Sbozzo di Inventario di tutti i libri che sono nell'Archivio Segreto Vaticano," by Giovanni Bissaiga (1672), gives an early description of select volume titles on folios 307v–308r and 339r.

Schedario Melampo, located in the Sala degli Indici, consists of individual slips of paper bound in small volumes or *blocchetti*. This schedario contains information similar to that located in ASV Indice 136 for *Misc. arm. I–XIII*.

The *Schedario Garampi* includes an index to some of the

material in this series. Garampi's chronological index (ASV Indici 168–173) also includes entries for materials in this series.

ASV Indice 1107 (formerly Indice 40) provides a listing of materials from this as well as other series that have been transferred from the Vatican Archives to the Vatican Library. This concordance indicates the former Vatican Archives volume numbers and the current Vatican Library volume numbers.

Location: Archivio Segreto Vaticano, Biblioteca Apostolica Vaticana.

7.2.2 Miscellaneorum armarium II

[DATABASE ID: VATV471-A]

Inclusive Dates: 1555–1729 (scattered dates).

Bulk: 10.5 linear m. (182 numbered vols.).

Scope: The major portion of this series is titled Politicorum varia (vols. 1–140), and contains political correspondence of the Secretariatus Status relating to relations with Germany, Poland, Venice, Spain, France, the Ottoman Empire, Persia, Russia, and Ethiopia.

Several volumes from this series, including some of the politicorum varia and some personal manuscripts, have been transferred to the Vatican Library. They are now identified as Vat. Lat. 11713–11723.

ASV Indice 213, "Indice di libri de Msgr. Ciampini alcune de quale sono stati comprati da Il. Sg.le. Clemente XI e posti nell'studi . . . e fuori sono stati segnali con la lett. 'C' e posti in diversi luoghi secundo le materie nelle quali trattavano," indicates that *Misc. arm. II*, vols. 143–145 were added to the Vatican Archives between 1700 and 1721.

Note: Vols. 92 and 115 are available on microfilm.

Reference: Boyle, p. 72.

Finding Aids: ASV Indice 1029-I is a volume-level description; Indice 1029-II is an alphabetically arranged index (by name, region, etc.).

ASV Indice 110, "Index librorum 112 Diversorum scripturarum confecta Rmo. Dmo. Felice Contelorio et unitorum per me Joannen Bissaigham & fuit compactus an 1694" (ff. 3–47), provides an item-level description of "Politicorum varia" in volumes 1 through 108A. Entries proceed volume by volume, giving a summary of the business (e.g., "Conditiones a Confessionibus exhibita 1558, fol. 126"), and note folios on which "politicorum varia" is located. At times this is a very analytical inventory, at other times only a few folios in a volume are summarized. The comprehensiveness of this index has not been determined.

ASV Indice 136, by De Pretis, is similar to ASV Indice 1029-I but contains briefer descriptions of the volumes.

Schedario Melampo, located in the ASV Sala degli Indici, consists of individual slips of paper bound in small volumes or *blocchetti*. This schedario contains information similar to that located in ASV Indice 136 for *Misc. arm. I–XIII*.

The *Schedario Garampi* includes an index to some of the material in this series. Garampi's chronological index (ASV Indici 168–173) also includes entries for materials in this series.

ASV Indice 1107 (formerly Indice 40) provides a listing of materials from this as well as other series that have been transferred from the Vatican Archives to the Vatican Library. This concordance indicates the former Vatican Archives volume numbers and the current Vatican Library volume numbers.

ASV Indice 124, "Primo Sbozzo di Inventario di tutti i libri che sono nell'Archivio Segreto Vaticano," by Giovanni Bissaiga (1672), provides an early description of some volume titles. *Misc. arm. II* volumes are listed on folios 279r, 291r, and 368r–376r.

Location: Archivio Segreto Vaticano, Biblioteca Apostolica Vaticana.

7.2.3 Miscellaneorum armarium III

[DATABASE ID: VATV472-A]

Inclusive Dates: 1565–1804 (scattered dates).

Bulk: 4.8 linear m. (about 90 vols.).

Scope: This series originally consisted of approximately 307 volumes. At the present time only about 90 of them remain in the series. These remaining volumes consist primarily (but not entirely) of records of the Secretariatus Status, relating to relations with Portugal, France, Spain, England, Poland, Germany, and several of the Italian states. Also included are volumes of letters of Venetian ambassadors in Rome (vols. 24–30), a history of the Holy Office (vol. 250), scattered records of the Rota (vol. 269 and 284), some briefs (vols. 270–273) and the personal manuscripts of Cardinal Francesco Adriano Ceva (vols. 31–50), which include diplomatic correspondence.

About 150 volumes from this series have been transferred to the Vatican Library, including many biographical and genealogical works, commentaries on ancient authors, political, scientific, and religious works. A further 50 volumes are missing from the series. The volumes transferred are now identified as Vat. Lat. 7703–7705, 7707, 7775–7776, 7817, 11724–11865, 12926–12929, 14328, and 14330, and Racc. Gen. Misc. II.70, Stor. II.274–276, III.43A, and V.5786, Class. Ital. IV.731, and Teol. V.1292(1–2).

ASV Indice 213, "Indice di libri de Msgr. Ciampini alcune de quale sono stati comprati da Il. Sg.le. Clemente XI e posti nell'studi . . . e fuori sono stati segnali con la lett. 'C' e posti in diversi luoghi secundo le materie nelle quali trattavano" indicates that *Misc. arm. III*, vols. 24–25, 28–30, 60–62, 64, 67–69, 75, 79–80, 81–83, 90, 98, 112, 122, 124–125, and 139 were added to the Vatican Archives between 1700 and 1721.

Note: Vol. 72 is available on microfilm.

References: Boyle, p. 72.

Finding Aids: ASV Indice 1029-I provides volume-level description. Indice 1029-II is an alphabetically arranged index.

ASV Indice 2, "Indici di diverse materie, Tom. 2" (ff. 493–534), contains the "Indice di scritture scielte e cauate dalli Regti. che gia erano del Card. Ceva." This provides some descriptive information on *Misc. arm. III*, vols 31–56; these appear to be partial contents listings to parts of these volumes.

ASV Indice 218, "Indice di Diversi Librarie di Manoscritti" (ff. 2–64), provides calendars of the Ceva manuscripts (vols. 31–50). Indice 218 includes a calendar (to vols. 31–47 only) and an alphabetical index (through letter C only). These do not duplicate each other or the Indice 2 calendars.

ASV Indice 136, by De Pretis, is similar to ASV Indice 1029-I but contains briefer descriptions of the volumes.

Schedario Melampo, located in the ASV Sala degli Indici, consists of individual slips of paper bound in small volumes or *blocchetti*. This schedario contains information similar to that located in ASV Indice 136 for *Misc. arm. I–XIII*.

The *Schedario Garampi* includes an index to some of the material in this series. Garampi's chronological index (ASV Indici 168–173) also includes entries for materials in this series.

ASV Indice 1107 (formerly Indice 40) provides a listing of materials from this as well as other series that have been transferred from the Vatican Archives to the Vatican Library. This concordance indicates the former Vatican Archives volume numbers and the current Vatican Library volume numbers.

ASV Indice 124, "Primo Sbozzo di Inventario di tutti i libri che sono nell'Archivio Segreto Vaticano," by Giovanni Bissaiga (1672), provides an early description of some volume titles in *Misc. arm. III* on folios 278r, 301r–303r, and 340r.

Location: Archivio Segreto Vaticano, Biblioteca Apostolica Vaticana.

7.2.4 Miscellaneorum armaria IV–V

[DATABASE ID: VATV473-A]

Inclusive Dates: 1568–1851.

Bulk: 30.6 linear m. (376 numbered vols.).

Organization: Misc. arm. IV–V comprises one numbered sequence of volumes. *Misc. arm IV* includes vols. 1–90, and *Misc. arm. V* includes vols. 91–376. The series contains several distinct subseries as well as many miscellaneous volumes. The major subseries include: Editti [alphabetical by subject], vols. 50–74; —Editti [with no apparent internal order, also known as Libri], vols. 75–93; —Bandi and editti [by date, 1720–1834], vols. 106–202; —Collezione Ottoboniana [also known as Bandi verdi], vols. 203–258; —Bandi [by date, 1706–1735], vols. 259–278; —Editti e bandi del tribunale della grascia, vols. 279–280; —Stampa diversa [by date, 1773–1777], vols. 281–286; —Collezione de publiche disposizioni [by date, 1800–1809, 1814–1833], vols. 287–314; —Leggi, regoli, ed altri carte pubbliche [1563–1846, bulk 1817–1846], vols. 315–345; —Relating to the Monte [a fragment of a much larger series], vols. 347–350; —Relating to the Tribunale delle strade, vol. 351.

Scope: This series is also referred to as *Bandi*. This is primarily a collection of public notices, proclamations, edicts, and miscellaneous published items. Most of the items in this series have been published as *Regesti di bandi, editti, notificazioni e provvedimenti diversi relativi alla città di Roma ed allo Stato pontificio* (Rome, 1920–1958).

Vols. 30, 33, and 68 are available on microfilm.

Reference: Boyle, p. 72.

Finding Aids: Indice 1029-I provides volume-level description; Indice 1029-II is an alphabetically arranged index. Indice 1030 provides detailed listing of contents of numbered volumes 76–93. An unnumbered index (36 units bound into 18 vols. of blocchetti) of information slips provides a calendar for each item in volumes 1–36 (date, name, author, data, oggetto, inizio, sottoscrizione, ufficio, destinatario, osservazioni).

ASV Indici 150–151 are subject indices to the Collezione Ottoboniana (also known as the Bandi verdi).

ASV Indice 136, by De Pretis, is similar to ASV Indice 1029-I but contains briefer descriptions of the volumes.

Schedario Melampo, located in the Sala degli Indici, consists of individual slips of paper bound in small volumes or *blocchetti*. This schedario contains information similar to that located in ASV Indice 136 for *Misc. arm. I–XIII*.

The *Schedario Garampi* includes an index to some of the material in this series. Garampi's chronological index (ASV Indici 168–173) also includes entries for materials in this series.

Location: Archivio Segreto Vaticano.

7.2.5 Miscellaneorum armarium VI

[DATABASE ID: VATV475-A]

Inclusive Dates: 1538–1702 (scattered dates).

Bulk: .3 linear m. (6 vols.).

Scope: This series is also referred to as *Visite a chiese di Roma*. It contains papers relating to miscellaneous churches and religious orders. One volume (vol. 39) relates to churches in Asia, Africa, and the Near East. The series originally contained about 174 volumes, of which about 20 are missing. About 150 volumes from this series have been transferred to the Vatican Library, including 28 volumes of the papers of Giovanni Antonio Bruti (now Vat. Lat. 11869–11896), papers relating to miscellaneous churches and religious orders, and genealogical works. The volumes transferred are now identified as Vat. Lat. 7779, 7783, 7787–7790, 7803, 7808–7814, 7831–7834, 7836–7843, 7845–7846, 7848–7849, 7857, and 11869–11984, and Racc. Gen. Stor. IV.1776–1777, V.1363, and VI.194(2), and Vite V.1030.

Two volumes (formerly vols. 40–41), relating to churches in Asia, Africa, Russia, and the Near East, have been transferred to the archives of the Congregatio de Propaganda Fide.

ASV Indice 213, "Indice di libri de Msgr. Ciampini alcune de quale sono stati comprati da Il. Sg.le. Clemente XI e posti nell'studi . . . e fuori sono stati segnali con la lett. 'C' e posti in diversi luoghi secundo le materie nelle quali trattavano," indicates that *Misc. arm. VI*, vols. 33, 35, 37, 42, and 73 were added to the Vatican Archives between 1700 and 1721.

Reference: Boyle, p. 72.

Finding Aids: ASV Indice 1029-I provides volume-level description. Indice 1029-II is an alphabetically arranged index.

ASV Indice 136, by De Pretis, is similar to ASV Indice 1029 I but contains briefer descriptions of the volumes.

ASV Indice 124, "Primo Sbozzo di Inventario di tutti i libri che sono nell'Archivio Segreto Vaticano," by Giovanni Bissaiga (1672), provides an early description of select volumes in *Misc. arm. VI* on folio 363v.

Schedario Melampo, located in the ASV Sala degli Indici, consists of individual slips of paper bound in small volumes or *blocchetti*. This schedario contains information similar to that located in ASV Indice 136 for *Misc. arm. I–XIII*.

The *Schedario Garampi* includes an index to some of the material in this series. Garampi's chronological index (ASV Indici 168–173) also includes entries for materials in this series.

ASV Indice 1107 (formerly Indice 40) provides a listing of materials from this as well as other series that have been transferred from the Vatican Archives to the Vatican Library. This concordance indicates the former Vatican Archives volume numbers and the current Vatican Library volume numbers.

Location: Archivio Segreto Vaticano, Biblioteca Apostolica Vaticana.

7.2.6 Miscellaneorum armarium VII

[DATABASE ID: VATV476-A]

Inclusive Dates: 1569–1778.

Bulk: 8.5 linear m. (includes 139 numbered vols.).

Scope: This series contains (chiefly but not exclusively) records of visitations of churches, colleges, and other institutions in Rome and its vicinity. Among other material included are a 1701 visitation of the Holy Office (vol. 85) and an instructio of the Congregation of the Council (vol. 104).

The records of apostolic visits offer fascinating views into the life of monasteries, oratories, parish churches, and the churches of cardinals, bishops and religious orders. As sources for the state of parishes and diocese, visits have much in common with the "relations ad limina" and the acts of local synods (see S. Congregatio Concilii). The contents of visits vary widely and depend greatly on how the cardinal or commissioner conducting the visit approached his job. Some were rather dry bureaucrats, who have left us simply lists of the location and condition of doors, windows and liturgical furnishings inside a church; from him we may also learn what the priest reported as his age, his income, or the number of students studying catechism with him. Others render their point of view in strong autobiographical tones, allowing us to see them as they shake a broken door, or traipse around a neighborhood interrogating residents in an effort to track down the parish priest. While some are mainly concerned with administrative or sacramental affairs, others display a keen concern for the physical setting, describing altarpieces, the condition and subject of frescoes, and details pertaining to all aspects of decoration and architecture. Music, musical instruments, and theatrical activities are important to some. Others emphasize economic matters. Finally, attitudes may range from the sternly disciplinary to the magnanimous and protective. Many visits combine to some degree various of the above features. The visitor's point of view can be as revealing as the observations recorded.

A number of volumes from this series have been transferred to the Vatican Library, including, among others, papers of Felice Contelori (now Vat. Lat. 11995–12006) and volumes relating to churches of Rome.

Reference: Boyle, p. 72.

Finding Aids: ASV Indice 1029-I provides volume-level description. Indice 1029-II is an alphabetically arranged index.

For a guide to the records of Roman visitations in this and other series, see S. Pagano, "Le visite apostoliche a Roma nei secoli XVI–XIX," *Ricerche per la storia religiosa di Roma* 4 (1980): 317–464. This volume is shelved as no. XII 16 in the ASV Index Room.

ASV Indice 136, by De Pretis, is similar to ASV Indice 1029-I but contains briefer descriptions of the volumes.

ASV Indice 124, "Primo Sbozzo di Inventario di tutti i libri che sono nell'Archivio Segreto Vaticano," by Giovanni Bissaiga (1672), provides an early description of select volume titles in *Misc. arm. VII* on folio 188r.

Schedario Melampo, located in the ASV Sala degli Indici, consists of individual slips of paper bound in small volumes or *blocchetti*. This schedario contains information similar to that located in ASV Indice 136 for *Misc. arm. I–XIII*.

The *Schedario Garampi* includes an index to some of the material in this series. Garampi's chronological index (ASV Indici 168–173) also includes entries for materials in this series.

ASV Indice 1107 (formerly Indice 40) provides a listing of materials from this as well as other series that have been transferred from the Vatican Archives to the Vatican Library. This concordance indicates the former Vatican Archives volume numbers and the current Vatican Library volume numbers.

Location: Archivio Segreto Vaticano, Biblioteca Apostolica Vaticana.

7.2.7 Miscellaneorum armarium VIII

[DATABASE ID: VATV477-A]

Inclusive Dates: 1554–1734 (scattered dates).

Bulk: 10.7 linear m. (includes 102 numbered vols.).

Scope: This series consists chiefly of records of congregations concerned with the regulation and reformation of religious orders, including the Congregatio Status Regularium, Congregatio super Statu Regularium, and Congregatio Episcoporum et Regularium. It also includes some records of the Congregatio Avenionis (vols. 86–88), Congregatio Palatinatus (vols. 89–91), and Congregazione sopra la zecca (vol. 102).

A few miscellaneous volumes from this series have been transferred to the Vatican Library. They are now identified as Vat. Lat. 12007–12009.

ASV Indice 213, "Indice di libri de Msgr. Ciampini alcune de quale sonostati comprati da Il. Sg.le. Clemente XI e posti nell'studi . . . e fuori sono stati segnali con la lett. 'C' e posti in diversi luoghi secundo le materie nelle quali trattavano," indicates that *Misc. arm. VIII*, vols. 58, 60, and 79 were added to the Vatican Archives between 1700 and 1721.

Note: Vol. 79 is available on microfilm.

Reference: Boyle, p. 72.

Finding Aids: ASV Indice 1029-I provides volume-level description. Indice 1029-II is an alphabetically arranged index.

ASV Indice 136, by De Pretis, is similar to ASV Indice 1029-I but contains briefer descriptions of the volumes.

Schedario Melampo, located in the ASV Sala degli Indici, consists of individual slips of paper bound in small volumes or *blocchetti*. This schedario contains information similar to that located in ASV Indice 136 for *Misc. arm. I–XIII*.

The Schedario Garampi includes an index to some of the material in this series. Garampi's chronological index (ASV Indici 168–173) also includes entries for materials in this series.

ASV Indice 1107 (formerly Indice 40) provides a listing of materials from this as well as other series that have been transferred from the Vatican Archives to the Vatican Library. This concordance indicates the former Vatican Archives volume numbers and the current Vatican Library volume numbers.

Location: Archivio Segreto Vaticano, Biblioteca Apostolica Vaticana.

7.2.8 Miscellaneorum armarium IX

[DATABASE ID: VATV478-A]

Inclusive Dates: 1609–1795 (scattered dates).

Bulk: 9 linear m. (includes 124 numbered vols.).

Scope: Much of this series consists of records of the Congregazione dei confini, relating to the Papal States. Vols. 11–19 include "Colettanea per città, terre e luoghi." The series also includes many volumes of Processi, including legal proceedings of the Sacra Consulta (vol. 50) and Congregatio Lauretana (vol. 85). The series is supposed to contain records of the Congregatio Immunitatis (vols. 1–10), but of these volumes all but vol. 10 are missing.

A few miscellaneous volumes have been transferred from this series to the Vatican Library. They are now identified as Vat. Lat. 12010–12013.

Reference: Boyle, p. 72.

Finding Aids: ASV Indice 1029-I provides volume-level description. Indice 1029-II is an alphabetically arranged index to Indice 1029-I.

ASV Indice 136, by De Pretis, is similar to ASV Indice 1029-I but contains briefer descriptions of the volumes.

Schedario Melampo, located in the ASV Sala degli Indici, consists of individual slips of paper bound in small volumes or *blocchetti*. This schedario contains information similar to that located in ASV Indice 136 for *Misc. arm. I–XIII*.

The Schedario Garampi includes an index to some of the material in this series. Garampi's chronological index (ASV Indici 168–173) also includes entries for materials in this series.

ASV Indice 1107 (formerly Indice 40) provides a listing of materials from this as well as other series that have been transferred from the Vatican Archives to the Vatican Library. This concordance indicates the former Vatican Archives volume numbers and the current Vatican Library volume numbers.

Location: Archivio Segreto Vaticano, Biblioteca Apostolica Vaticana.

7.2.9 Miscellaneorum armarium X

[DATABASE ID: VATV479-A]

Inclusive Dates: 1535–1805 (scattered dates).

Bulk: 10.2 linear m. (ca. 130 vols.).

Summary: About 60 volumes are missing from this series, including records of the Holy Office, Propaganda Fide, and Congregation of the Council. The volumes present include chiefly processi against cardinals and others, including Galileo (vol. 204) and Giordano Bruno (vol. 205). [A photocopy of the Galileo processus is available for use. The Bruno processus is reserved. Inquire at the desk about these volumes.] Informationes of the Congregation of the Council are found in vols. 130–133.

About 60 volumes from this series have been transferred to the Vatican Library, including biographies and works relating to saints, religious texts, diary and declarations of the Council of Trent (now Vat. Lat. 12078–12079), and scattered records of a number of congregations and offices, including the Holy Office (now Vat. Lat. 12014–12017), Congregatio de Auxiliis (now Vat. Lat. 12032–12037), Propaganda Fide (now Vat. Lat. 12073), Penitentiary (now Vat. Lat. 12076–12077), and Congregatio Concilii (now Vat. Lat. 12081). The volumes transferred are now identified as Vat. Lat. 7755, 7781, and 12014–12087, and Racc. Gen. Storia III.581, Teolog. II.199, and Vite III.378 and IV.1125.

Vol. 184 has been transferred to *Armarium LX*, where it is now vol. 27.

Note: Vols. 204 and 205 are available on microfilm.

Reference: Boyle, p. 72.

Finding Aids: ASV Indice 1029-I provides volume-level description. Indice 1029-II is an alphabetically arranged index to Indice 1029-I.

ASV Indice 136, by De Pretis, is similar to ASV Indice 1029-I but contains briefer descriptions of the volumes.

ASV Indice 124, "Primo Sbozzo di Inventario di tutti i libri che sono nell'Archivio Segreto Vaticano," by Giovanni Bissaiga (1672), provides an early description of the volume titles for select volumes of *Misc. arm. X* on folios 304r, 307r, and 340r.

Schedario Melampo, located in the ASV Sala degli Indici,

consists of individual slips of paper bound in small volumes or *blocchetti*. This schedario contains information similar to that located in ASV Indice 136 for *Misc. arm. I–XIII*.

The *Schedario Garampi* includes an index to some of the material in this series. Garampi's chronological index (ASV Indici 168–173) also includes entries for materials in this series.

ASV Indice 1107 (formerly Indice 40) provides a listing of materials from this as well as other series that have been transferred from the Vatican Archives to the Vatican Library. This concordance indicates the former Vatican Archives volume numbers and the current Vatican Library volume numbers.

Location: Archivio Segreto Vaticano, Biblioteca Apostolica Vaticana.

7.2.10 Miscellaneorum armarium XI

[DATABASE ID: VATV480-A]

Inclusive Dates: ca. 1330–1814 (scattered dates).

Bulk: 2.1 linear m. (about 50 vols.).

Scope: Most of the volumes originally in this series are no longer found here. Among the remaining volumes are scattered cameral records (vols. 84–85A), papers relating to reforms of offices (vols. 88–92), oaths of fidelity of cardinals (vols. 137–140 and 195A–197A; these are very small volumes), and an evaluation of the office of uditore della camera (vol. 211).

Vol. 18 is reserved. Ask at the desk for information about access. About 170 volumes from this series have been transferred to the Vatican Library. Many of them relate to papal elections, including records of conclaves (now Vat. Lat. 12176–12191 and 12250–12251). Also included are lives of popes and cardinals and papers relating to Italian politics. The volumes transferred are now identified as Vat. Lat. 12088–12252 and 12933–12934, Reg. Lat. 2112, and Racc. Gen. Stor. III.5791, IV.1778, and V.1365.

Vol. 59 has been transferred to *Archivum Arcis* I–XVIII, where it is now no. 412.

ASV Indice 213, "Indice di libri de Msgr. Ciampini alcune de quale sono stati comprati da Il. Sg.le. Clemente XI e posti nell'studi . . . e fuori sono stati segnali con la lett. 'C' e posti in diversi luoghi secundo le materie nelle quali trattavano," indicates that *Misc. arm. XI*, vols. 58, 80, 83–85, 98, 103–104, 106–109, 112, 118, 124, 148, 154, 156–158, 160–167, 183, and 185 were added to the Vatican Archives between 1700 and 1721.

Note: Vol. 93A is available on microfilm.

Reference: Boyle, p. 72.

Finding Aids: ASV Indice 1029-I provides volume-level description. Indice 1029-II is an alphabetically arranged index to Indice 1029-I.

ASV Indice 136, by De Pretis, is similar to ASV Indice 1029 I but contains briefer descriptions of the volumes.

Schedario Melampo, located in the ASV Sala degli Indici, consists of individual slips of paper bound in small volumes or *blocchetti*. This schedario contains information similar to that located in ASV Indice 136 for *Misc. arm. I–XIII*.

The *Schedario Garampi* includes an index to some of the material in this series. Garampi's chronological index (ASV Indici 168–173) also includes entries for materials in this series.

ASV Indice 1107 (formerly Indice 40) provides a listing of materials from this as well as other series that have been transferred from the Vatican Archives to the Vatican Library. This concordance indicates the former Vatican Archives volume numbers and the current Vatican Library volume numbers.

ASV Indice 124, "Primo Sbozzo di Inventario di tutti i libri che sono nell'Archivio Segreto Vaticano," by Giovanni Bissaiga (1672), provides an early description and listing of some volume titles from *Misc. arm. XI* on folios 179r, 237v, 245v, 340rv, 346r, and 352v.

Location: Archivio Segreto Vaticano, Biblioteca Apostolica Vaticana.

7.2.11 Miscellaneorum armarium XII

[DATABASE ID: VATV481-A]

Inclusive Dates: ca. 1463–ca. 1801.

Bulk: 2 linear m.

Scope: This series originally included about 225 volumes. Only about 35 are now in the series. The volumes present contain consistorial records including acta, propositiones, and cedole.

About 150 volumes from this series have been transferred to the Vatican Library. These volumes include, among other items, diaries of Burchardi, De Grassis, Martinelli, Firmani, Mucanti, Alaleonis, Sarvanti, Bona, and others, as well as an index to many of the diaries. The volumes transferred are identified by the library as Vat. Lat. 12253–12399.

About 35 volumes from this series have been transferred to the *Fondo Concistoriale* in the Archivio Segreto Vaticano. They contain consistorial records similar to the records remaining in this series. The volumes transferred are now identified as Cong. Consistorialis series *Acta misc.*, vols. 18–22, 29–53, 55, 57, 60, 63, and 66; and *Acta camera*, vol. 43.

ASV Indice 213, "Indice di libri de Msgr. Ciampini alcune de quale sono stati comprati da Il. Sg.le. Clemente XI e posti nell'studi . . . e fuori sono stati segnali con la lett. 'C' e posti in diversi luoghi secundo le materie nelle quali trattavano" indicates that *Misc. arm. XII*, vols. 152, 179, and 180 were added to the Vatican Archives between 1700 and 1721.

References: Boyle, p. 72.

Finding Aids: ASV Indice 1029-I provides volume-level description. Indice 1029-II is an alphabetically arranged index to Indice 1029-I.

ASV Indice 136, by De Pretis, is similar to ASV Indice 1029-I but contains briefer descriptions of the volumes.

ASV Indice 124, "Primo Sbozzo di Inventario di tutti i libri che sono nell'Archivio Segreto Vaticano," by Giovanni Bissaiga (1672), provides an early description of selected volume titles in *Misc. arm. XII* on folios 342r–343v and 347v.

Schedario Melampo, located in the ASV Sala degli Indici, consists of individual slips of paper bound in small volumes or *blocchetti*. This schedario contains information similar to that located in ASV Indice 136 for *Misc. arm. I–XIII*.

The *Schedario Garampi* includes an index to some of the material in this series. Garampi's chronological index (ASV Indici 168–173) also includes entries for materials in this series.

ASV Indice 1107 (formerly Indice 40) provides a listing of materials from this as well as other series that have been transferred from the Vatican Archives to the Vatican Library. This concordance indicates the former Vatican Archives volume numbers and the current Vatican Library volume numbers.

Location: Archivio Segreto Vaticano, Biblioteca Apostolica Vaticana.

7.2.12 Miscellaneorum armarium XIII

[DATABASE ID: VATV482-A]

Inclusive Dates: 1405–1806.

Bulk: 7 linear m.

Scope: This series originally contained about 160 volumes. About 70 remain in the series. The remaining volumes include records of the Congregatio Consistorialis (vols. 45–49, 52, 74–81, 89A, and 93–96; Praeconia consistorialis, vols. 71–73A; Acta consistorialia, vols. 150–152), as well as matrimonial dispensations (vols. 38–41), Congregatio Concilii records (vol. 42), and other records.

About 90 volumes from this series have been transferred to the Vatican Library, and are now identified as Vat. Lat. 12400–12483. The volumes transferred include diaries, including Paridis de Grassis diaries (Vat. Lat. 12411–12420), records relating to ceremonials, consistorial records, and the Fondo Piccolomini, papers of Francesco Maria Piccolomini, bishop of Pirgi and Pienza (Vat. Lat. 12434–12473; the library does not identify these volumes as a fondo).

A few volumes have been transferred to other series in the Archivio Segreto Vaticano: vol. 69 to Secretaria Brevia series *Sec. Brev.* 4531A; vol. 97 to Rota Romana series *Decisiones,* vol. 161; vol. 146 to Congregatio Consistoriales series *Proc. Consistoriales,* vol. 207A.9.

References: Boyle, p. 72. F. Combaluzier, "Sacrés épiscopaux à Rome de 1565 à 1662: Analyse intégrale du Ms. 'Miscellanea XIII, 33' des Archives Vaticanes," *Sacris Erudiri* 18 (1967–1968): 120–305.

Finding Aids: ASV Indice 1029-I provides volume-level description. Indice 1029-II is an alphabetically arranged index to Indice 1029-I.

ASV Indice 136, by De Pretis, is similar to ASV Indice 1029 I but contains briefer descriptions of the volumes.

Schedario Melampo, located in the ASV Sala degli Indici, consists of individual slips of paper bound in small volumes or *blocchetti.* This schedario contains information similar to that located in ASV Indice 136 for *Misc. arm. I–XIII.*

The *Schedario Garampi* includes an index to some of the material in this series. Garampi's chronological index (ASV Indici 168–173) also includes entries for materials in this series.

ASV Indice 1107 (formerly Indice 40) provides a listing of materials from this as well as other series that have been transferred from the Vatican Archives to the Vatican Library. This concordance indicates the former Vatican Archives volume numbers and the current Vatican Library volume numbers.

ASV Indice 124, "Primo Sbozzo di Inventario di tutti i libri che sono nell'Archivio Segreto Vaticano," by Giovanni Bissaiga (1672), provides an early description of select volume titles from *Misc. arm. XIII* on folio 341rv.

Location: Archivio Segreto Vaticano, Biblioteca Apostolica Vaticana.

7.2.13 Miscellaneorum armarium XIV

[DATABASE ID: VATV483-A]

Inclusive Dates: 1587–1841.

Bulk: 6 vols.

Scope: This series originally contained 6 volumes. They have all been transferred from the ASV to the Vatican Library. The volumes transferred from this series to the Vatican Library are now identified as Vat. Lat. 12484–12490. (Vol. 4 is Vat.

Lat 12487 and 12488.) They include miscellaneous correspondence and other papers.

Reference: Boyle, p. 72.

Finding Aids: The Schedario Melampo, in the Vatican Archives Index Room, includes a detailed listing, almost a complete calendar, of the contents of this series.

Location: Biblioteca Apostolica Vaticana.

7.2.14 Miscellaneorum armarium XV

[DATABASE ID: VATV484-A]

Inclusive Dates: 1429–1799 (scattered dates).

Bulk: 8 linear m.

Scope: This series originally contained about 240 numbered volumes, though in some cases several volumes constituted a single number. A number of volumes have been transferred to the Vatican Library. The volumes remaining include papers relating to cardinals and the Sacred College, the maggiordomo (vol. 20), the economic state of the Camera (vol. 21), political papers of nuncios and legates (vols. 60–108), and papers relating to relations with France (vols. 205–207 and 213–217).

Vols. 158–182 of this series make up the Fondo Visconti, which includes papers collected by P. E. Visconti, covering the period of the sixteenth-nineteenth centuries. About half of the volumes have been transferred to the Vatican Library, where they are identified as Vat. Lat. 12541–12553 (they are not identified as a fondo in the library).

About 90 other volumes from this series have been transferred to the Vatican Library. They are now identified as Vat. Lat. 12491–12493, 12496–12566, and 12568–12569; Reg. Lat. 2108–2111 and 2113–2119; and Racc. Gen. Filos. III.41, Lett. Ital. IV.732, and Storia III.826. Among the volumes transferred are documents left by Cardinal Mazarin (Vat. Lat. 12492), letters of Cola di Rienzo (Vat. Lat. 12503), papers relating to the kingdom of the Congo (Vat. Lat. 12516), and conclave records (Vat. Lat. 12518–12539 and 12554).

Note: Vol. 159 is available on microfilm.

Reference: Boyle, p. 72.

Finding Aids: ASV Indice 1029-I provides volume-level description. Indice 1029-II is an alphabetically arranged index.

ASV Indice 1107 (formerly Indice 40) provides a listing of materials from this as well as other series that have been transferred from the Vatican Archives to the Vatican Library. This concordance indicates the former Vatican Archives volume numbers and the current Vatican Library volume numbers.

Schedario Melampo, located in the Sala degli Indici, consists of individual slips of paper bound in small volumes or *blocchetti.* This schedario contains information similar to that located in ASV Indice 136 for *Misc. arm. I–XIII.* For *Misc. Arm. XIV* and *XV,* however, Schedario Melampo is much more detailed, providing an almost complete calendar of the series.

Misc. arm. XV, vol. 98, indexes vols. 89–97 (titled Relazioni diverse) of this series. Vol. 98 also indexes volumes once part of this subseries (originally 22 vols.), but now lost.

ASV Indice 136, by De Pretis, is similar to ASV Indice 1029-I but contains briefer descriptions of the volumes.

The *Schedario Garampi* includes an index to some of the material in this series. Garampi's chronological index (ASV Indici 168–173) also includes entries for materials in this series.

ASV Indice 124, "Primo Sbozzo di Inventario di tutti i libri che sono nell'Archivio Segreto Vaticano," by Giovanni Bissaiga (1672), provides an early description of select volume titles in *Misc. arm.* XV on folio 189r.

Location: Archivio Segreto Vaticano, Biblioteca Apostolica Vaticana.

7.3
ORIGINAL ARMARIA OF THE ASV

The armaria in this section are part of a set of cabinets (armaria) that contain the earliest material in the ASV. In most cases the material in each armarium can be assigned to a specific agency and is described in this guide in the section for that agency. The four armaria listed here could not be assigned to any one bureaucratic division of the Holy See or particular division of this guide. For a complete listing of the original armaria, with references to their location in this guide, see Appendix 2.

7.3.1 Armarium XXXIX

[DATABASE ID: VATV10216-A]

Inclusive Dates: 1198 (copy)–1556.

Bulk: 6 linear m. (63 vols.).

Organization: Volumes 1–15, 17–36, and 40–65 are Registra brevium, 1198–1556 (some sixteenth century copies) — Other volumes are: 16. Registrum brevium (ad principes) Sixti IV, 1483.; —16a. Registrum brevium (ad principes) Sixti IV, 1484.; —16b. copy of vol. 16.; —16c. copy of vol. 16a with a sworn statement by the copier, Giuseppe Enghien, 1741; —16d. fotocopie, Exemplar Codex Verlanus, add. 25 May 1940.; —37–38. Indults?; —39. Brevia licentiarum per locandis seu arendandis bonis ecclesiasticis a Leone PP. X concess: ab anno 1517 usque ad annum 1521 inclusive; —51a, 54a/b. Poenitentiaria-Supplicationes originales. For vol. 10, the original is in Sala Cimeli and a photocopy is in the cabinet behind the desk.

Scope: MacFarlane notes that these volumes begin with the copies of briefs sent out under Martin V and end in 1565. They contain a good deal of interesting material of an ecclesiastical nature that called for the notice or assistance of the crown, besides requests and information of a more diplomatic nature. Much of the earliest-dated material is made up of sixteenth-century copies. Unfortunately the series has suffered considerable losses, and vols. 4–10 and 12–21 are all that remain for the fifteenth century.

Note: Vols. 7, 8, and 42 are available on microfilm.

References: Boyle, pp. 63–64; Pásztor (1970), pp. 16–17; Pásztor (1983), p. 95; MacFarlane, p. 84.

K. A. Fink, "Die ältesten Breven und Brevenregister," *Quellen und Forschungen aus italienischen Archiven und Bibliotheken* 25 (1933–1934): 292–307. K. A. Fink, "Die politische Korrespondenz Martins V. nach den Brevenregistern," *Quellen und Forschungen aus Italienischen Archiven und Bibliotheken* 26 (1935–1936): 172–244. T. Frenz, "Armarium XX–XIX vol. 11 im Vatikanischen Archiv: Ein Formelbuch für Breven aus der Zeit Julius II," in *Römische Kurie, kirchliche Finanzen, vatikanisches Archiv: Studien zu Ehren von Hermann Hoberg* (Rome, 1979), pp. 197–213. G. Gualdo, "Il

'Liber brevium de curia anni septimi' di Paolo II: Contributo allo studio del breve pontificio," in *Mélanges Eugène Tisserant* (Vatican City, 1964), vol. 4, pp. 301–345. F. R. Hausmann, "Armarium 39, Tomus 10 des Archivio Segreto Vaticano," *Quellen und Forschungen aus italienischen Archiven und Bibliotheken* 50 (1971): 112–180. G. Lang, "Studien zu Brevenregistern und Brevenkonzepten des 15. Jahrhunderts aus dem vatikanischen Archiv," *Publikationen des Österreichisches historisches Institut in Rom* 4 (1938): 131–147. C. M. de Witte, "Notes sur les plus anciens registres de brefs," *Bulletin de l'Institut historique Belge de Rome* 31 (1958): 153–168.

Finding Aids: ASV Indice 133-II, ff. 176–178 verso, briefly lists summary titles of each volume. The index (compiled by Petrus De Pretis after 1741) is basically informative but often fails to note copies. The index also uses terms such as *regestrum* and *brevia* too inclusively and does not clearly note items that do not fit the basic thematic focus of each armarium, or which items are clearly from other offices. Therefore, entries in this index do not reflect the exact titles of volumes. The recently typed footnotes are also sometimes inaccurate.

ASV Indice 114, by Felice Contelori, provides excerpts from *Arm. XXXIX*, vol. 18 on page 30.

ASV Indice 124, "Primo Sbozzo di Inventario di tutti i libri che sono nell'Archivio Segreto Vaticanom," by Giovanni Bissaiga (1672), provides more descriptive and accurate volume titles for some armarium volumes. Select *Armarium XXXIX* volumes are listed on folios 187v, 191v, 207v, 256v–261v, 263v–264r, 270v, 292r, and 377v. The exact titles listed in Indice 124 are sometimes provided in a footnote in ASV Indice 133, so researchers can see exactly how generic the titles in ASV Indice 133 are.

Location: Archivio Segreto Vaticano.

7.3.2 Armarium LII

[DATABASE ID: VATV374-A]

Inclusive Dates: 1552–1602 and undated.

Bulk: 65 vols.

Scope: MacFarlane notes that this armarium contains signatures, judgments, audiences, and visitations of commissioners-general to the Holy See, and is mostly a collection of sixteenth–seventeenth-century reports, instructions and sentences of commissioners-general of the Holy See. The signatures are represented in volumes 1–16, 40, and 41 and date between 1552 and 1652. Vols. 17–22 are the reports, some of them political, of Cardinal Santorio from 1566 to 1602.

Note: Vols. 32, 33, 34, 35, 36, 37, 55 are available on microfilm.

References: Fink, pp. 32–33; Boyle, p. 39; Pásztor (1970), pp. 19–20; MacFarlane, p. 35.

A. Mercati, "Schedario Garampi, Registri Vaticani, Registri Lateranensi, Rationes Camerae, Inventario del Fondo Concistoriale," vol. 1 of *Sussidi per la consultazione dell'Archivio Vaticano*, (Rome, 1926), p. 42. L. Pásztor, "Contributo di un fondo miscelaneo all'archivistica e alla storia: L'Arm. LII dell'Archivio Segreto Vaticano," *Annali della Scuola speciale per Archivisti e Bibliotecari dell'Università di Roma* 6 (1966): 1–31.

Finding Aids: ASV Indice 133, ff. 224r–226v, briefly lists summary titles of each volume. The index (compiled by Petrus De Pretis after 1741) is basically informative but often fails to note copies. The index also uses terms such as *regestrum* and *brevia* too inclusively and does not clearly note items that do not fit the basic thematic focus of each armarium, or which items are clearly from other offices.

ASV Indice 114, by Felice Contelori, provides selected excerpts from various volumes in *Armarium LII* on p. 620.

Location: Archivio Segreto Vaticano.

7.3.3 Armarium LIII

[DATABASE ID: VATV375-A]
Inclusive Dates: ca. 1200–1500.
Bulk: 79 vols.
Organization: Volume enumeration and titles are: 1. Supplicationes Gregory XIII; —2. Supplicationes Sixtus V; —3. Supplicationes Gregory XIV; —4. Supplicationes Clement VIII; —5. Supplicationes a Urban VIII; —6. Minute supplicationum, 1644–1666; —7. Minute supplicationum, 1684–1695; —8. Formularium bullarum; —9. Formularium bullarum; —10. Formularium bullarum; —11. Formularium expeditionum; —12. Formularium expeditionum; —13. Formularium expeditionum; —14. Formule benefici moderne; —15. Supplicationum formularium; —16. Supplicationum formularium; —17. Supplicationum formularium; —18. Formularium liber et decretorum; —19. (Cancelleria Apostolica) Formularium; —20. (Cancelleria Apostolica) Formularium; —21. (Roman Curia) Supplicationes originales; —22. Extraordinarum bullarum; —23. Minute officiorum, 1639–1640; —24. Minute bullarum; —25. Absolutiones et dispensationes (lost); —26. Absolutiones; —27. Confirmationes; —28. Coadjutorie; —29. Ecclesie divers; —30. Eul. . . . prioratus; —31. (Camera Apostolica) Bullarum expeditiarum; —32. Erectiones; —33. Erectiones et uniones; —34. Erectiones, suppressiones, et uniones; —35. Miscellanea bullarum et brevia; —36. Uniones; —37. Pensiones et res. . . . fructus; —38. Pensiones et resc. . . . fructus; —39. Provisiones; —40. Provisiones; —41. Provisiones, resignationes, cessiones; —42. Provisiones beneficiales: Urbis; —43. Indulgentiarum; —44. Indulgentiarum; —45. Resignationes; —46. Per obitum resignationes et reservationes; —47. (Cancelleria Apostolica) Miscellanea; —48. (Cancelleria Apostolica and Dataria Apostolica) Miscellanea; —49. (Dataria Apostolica) Miscellanea; —50. Expeditionum bullarum (lost); —51. (Cancelleria Apostolica) Practica; —52. (Cancelleria Apostolica) Regulae, Cardinale Pamphili (lost); —53. Taxae scriptorum apostolicorum; —54. Comput. super solutionum . . .; —55. (Dataria Apostolica) Componenda (lost); —56. Quittenza iustitie maioris et minoris (lost); —57. Office. An. 1625–1626; —58. (Cancelleria Apostolica) Entrata dell'officio di costode (lost); —59. Repertorium divers. mater.; —60. Repertorium rerum beneficialium (lost); —61. Repertorium rerum civilium (lost); —62. Index notabilium ant. can . . . ; —63. Benefici e pensioni di Monsignor Sacieri; —64. Solutiones, quindenni, 1656–1669; —65. not determined; —66. (Dataria Apostolica) Restrictivae supplicationum; —67. (Cancellaria Apostolica) Notabilia; —68. (Dataria Apostolica) Observationes beneficiales; —69. Significan. seu excommunicationum, 1635–1649 plus insert 1325; —70. Collecta bullarum et formularium littararum apostolicarum; —71. Formularium supplicationum; —72. . . . in Expeditiones bullarum formularium . . . ; —73. Formulae diversarum bullarium; —74. Formularium supplicationum; —75. (Cancelleria Apostolica) Notabilia; —76. Notae et formularia pro supplicationibus; —77. Bullarum Leo

X, Clement VII, Paul III, et Paul IV; —78. Confirmationes divers.; —79. Ex. diversarum bullarum.

Scope: These volumes of formularies of the Papal Chancery and Datary and transcriptions are invaluable for the history of the papal curia. MacFarlane cites volume 8 as a useful example; it is well indexed and gives formularies for visitations, reservations, absolutions, confirmations, nominations, and many other types of papal letter, all in a clear legible hand.

References: Fink, p. 33; Boyle, p. 39; MacFarlane, p. 35. P. M. Baumgarten, *Von der apostolischen Kanzlei: Untersuchungen über die päpstliche Tabellionen und die Vizekanzler der heiligen Römischen Kirche im XIII. XIV. und XV. Jahrhundert* (Cologne, 1908). W. von. Hofmann, *Forschungen zur Geschichte der kurialen Behörden vom Schisma bis zur Reformation* (Rome, 1914).

Finding Aids: ASV Indice 133, ff. 228r–230v, briefly lists summary titles of each volume. The index (compiled by Petrus De Pretis after 1741) is basically informative but often fails to note copies. The index also uses terms such as *regestrum* and *brevia* too inclusively and does not clearly note items that do not fit the basic thematic focus of each armarium, or which items are clearly from other offices.

ASV Indice 213, "Indice di libri de Msgr. Ciampini alcune de quale sono stati comprati da Il. Sg.le. Clemente XI e posti nell'studi . . . e fuori sono stati segnali con la lett. 'C' e posti in diversi luoghi secundo le materie nelle quali trattavano," includes *Arm. LIII*, vols. 12–14, 16, 22, 27, 28, 31–33, 36–39, 41–44, 46, 51, 53, 55, 57, 65, 72, and 77 in a donation that took place between 1700 and 1721. The description of these volumes in Indice 213 is fuller than the description in ASV Indice 133.

Location: Archivio Segreto Vaticano.

7.3.4 Armarium LIV

[DATABASE ID: VATV376-A]
Inclusive Dates: Not determined.
Bulk: 35 vols.
Scope: MacFarlane notes that the contents of this armarium are of fundamental importance for the history of the Great Schism, 1378–1418. Vols. 14–39 are the chancery copies of the actual depositions taken down from the supporters of both Urban VI and Clement VII for the Spanish kings within the first few years of the outbreak of the schism, and many of them are vivid eyewitness accounts of the disputed election of April 8, 1378. Vols. 40–48 are later copies of depositions, besides several short tracts on papal power occasioned by the schism, which take the controversy into the Conciliar period and beyond to Luther. The contents of these so-called Libri de Schismate (vols. 14–48) have been admirably described by M. Seidlmayer, and the whole series has been extensively drawn upon by historians of the Great Schism.

According to Boyle, this armarium originally contained forty-eight volumes. Among the thirty-five volumes now in *Armarium LIV*, there is the Thesaurus historicus (ca. 1750) of Cornelius Margarini (vols. 1–13). There is also material relating to Martin Luther.

References: Fink, p. 33; Boyle, pp. 39–40; MacFarlane, pp. 35–36. M. Seidlmayer, "Die spanischen 'Libri de Schismate' des vatikanischen Archivs," in *Gesammelte Aufsätze zur Kulturgeschichte Spaniens* (Münster, 1940), vol. 8, pp. 199–262.

Finding Aids: ASV Indice 133, ff. 196r–198v, briefly lists summary titles of each volume. The index (compiled by Petrus De Pretis after 1741) is basically informative but often fails to note copies. The index also uses terms such as *regestrum* and *brevia* too inclusively and does not clearly note items that do not fit the basic thematic focus of each armarium, or which items are clearly from other offices.

There is an inventory of the thesaurus on file cards (15 bound volumes) in ASV Index Room. This series was not consulted by project staff in 1990.

Location: Archivio Segreto Vaticano.

7.4
MISCELLANEOUS SERIES

These are official records series that simply did not fit anywhere else. Either the records could not be associated with a particular office, the office itself was not part of the central Vatican administration, or the office was part of a more recent configuration of the organization of the Holy See. The *Instrumenta miscellanea* listed here are of particular importance.

7.4.1 Amministrazione del Patrimonio della Sede Apostolica

7.4.1.1 [Archivio]

[DATABASE ID: VATV30012-A]
Inclusive Dates: 1936–1979.
Bulk: 28 linear m.
Note: L'Attività della Santa Sede (1990) reports that 28 meters of màterials from the amministrazione dating from 1936–1979 entered the archives in December 1989.
Location: Archivio Segreto Vaticano.

7.4.2 Anno giubilare della redenzione: Comitato centrale

7.4.2.1 Comitato centrale

[DATABASE ID: VATV10241-A]
Inclusive Dates: 1983–1984.
Bulk: 10 linear m.
References: Natalini et al., p. 265.
Location: Archivio Segreto Vaticano.

7.4.3 Concilium Romanum

7.4.3.1 [Archivio]

[DATABASE ID: VATV10393-A]
Inclusive Dates: 1472–1726.
Bulk: 1 linear m. (14 buste).
Scope: This series consists of material concerning the Roman Council celebrated at the Lateran in 1725. Vol. 1 contains the decrees of the council. Vol. 6 is a "Historia Concillium Romanum" containing notes by Mercati.

Vols. 2–4 and 15–16 were formerly part of the series *Archivum Arcis.*

Finding Aids: ASV Indice 1006 (f. 1) lists several items that roughly correspond to the selected volumes in this series (e.g., 2–4).
Note: This series does not have an official ASV designation. The title was supplied by project staff.
Location: Archivio Segreto Vaticano.

7.4.4 Diocese of Pistoia and Prato: Synod, 1786

7.4.4.1 Carte del Sinodo di Pistoia

[DATABASE ID: VATV40031-A]
Inclusive Dates: 1786–1794.
Bulk: 48 buste.
Note: This series was cited in Natalini et al., p. 269, but not seen by project staff in 1990.
Location: Archivio Segreto Vaticano.

7.4.5 Diocese of Rome

7.4.5.1 Archivio del vicariato

[DATABASE ID: VATV299-A]
Inclusive Dates: 1570–[19—?].
Bulk: Extent undetermined.
Scope: These are parochial registers and the like of the diocese of Rome. Boyle notes that these had been in the charge of the ASV but housed in the Braccio di Carlo Magno in St. Peter's Basilica. In 1964 the collection was transferred to the newly established Vicariate Archives at St. John Lateran.
References: Fink, p. 144; Boyle, p. 95. *Attività della S. Sede* (1964), pp. 696–697.
Location: Vicariate Archives, St. John Lateran, Rome.

7.4.6 Opera di soccorso per le chiese rovinate dalla guerra

7.4.6.1 L'Opera di soccorso per le chiese rovinate dalla guerra

[DATABASE ID: VATV10309-A]
Inclusive Dates: 1919–1927.
Bulk: 12 linear m.
Organization: Although some buste bear numbers, the series is unorganized and items are not numerically arranged.
Scope: This series contains information on repairing and rebuilding Catholic parishes in Italy after World War I. The records document the actual rebuilding as well as the efforts to raise money to finance the rebuilding. The series contains numerous photographs and negatives of parishes and works of art.
Location: Archivio Segreto Vaticano.

7.4.7 Pontificio consiglio per la promozione dell'unità de cristiani

7.4.7.1 [Archivio]

[DATABASE ID: VATV30011-A]
Inclusive Dates: 1960–1975.
Bulk: 52 linear m.
Note: According to L'Attività della Santa Sede (1991), these materials were transferred to the ASV in June 1991.
Location: Archivio Segreto Vaticano.

7.4.8 Ufficio pontificio costruzioni parrocchiali

7.4.8.1 Case parrocchiali
[DATABASE ID: VATV10308-A]
Inclusive Dates: ca. 1927–1939.
Bulk: 36 linear m.
Location: Archivio Segreto Vaticano.

7.4.9 Vatican Council I: 1869–1870

7.4.9.1 Concilio Vaticano I
[DATABASE ID: VATV10494-A]
Inclusive Dates: ca. 1862–1879.
Bulk: Extent not determined.
Scope: This is a collection in several locations in the ASV that contains a variety of documentation relating to the council. These are not the official records of the council but rather an assemblage of documentation accumulated by various participants and brought together in the ASV. There are both manuscript material and printed items. Records contain material from various commissions of the council (acta, decreta, etc.) including the Commission for Ecclesiastical Discipline, the Commission for the Oriental Church and Mission, and the Commission on Dogma, among others. There are also records of the sessions of the council and personal notations and records of various participants. ASV Indice 1172 gives a full account of the origins and diversity of what constitutes this series.
Finding Aids: ASV Indice 1172 I and II provides a very detailed description of this series. Prepared in 1995 by Giuseppe M. Croce, the indice is divided into three parts. The first part (pp. 1–191) describes manuscript material. The second part (pp. 192–484) describes printed atti, protocolli, and vota of the commissions. The third part (pp. 485–861) describes a variety of materials including "stenografie originali," "observationes," speeches, sermons, pamphlets, newspaper and journal articles, and the like. At the end of this indice there are two specific indexes. The first (pp. 862–863) is an index to journals, magazines, and newspapers appearing in the collection. The second (pp. 864–910) is an index of names and places.
Location: Archivio Segreto Vaticano.

7.4.10 Vescovo dell'esercito e dell'armata

7.4.10.1 Prospetto dell'operato del clero e del laicato cattolico in Italia durante la guerra
[DATABASE ID: VATV10457-A]
Inclusive Dates: 1918.
Bulk: 2 linear m. (25 scatole).
Organization: Nos. 1–24 are alphabetical by diocese. No. 25 is labeled "Ordini o congregazioni religiose."
Scope: This is a survey of institutions concerning the participants in relief work during the war and the type and extent of the work. Some of the surveys were returned with addenda materials that include institutional manuals or historical notes.
Location: Archivio Segreto Vaticano.

Agency not determined

7.4.11 Archives du Vatican (Bulles et brefs)
[DATABASE ID: VATV40050-A]
Dates: 861–1815.
Bulk: Full extent not determined.
Organization: There is a considerable amount of material from the Vatican Archives that remained in Paris as a result of the move of the entire archives to Paris in 1807 (see introduction). This material is clearly identified through the various inventories in the Archives Nationales, mostly under the designation "L" in the section for the Ancien Regime. However, there is some material in other sections. As in the Archives Nationales, this material is divided in this guide into several series, each of which is listed separately in this guide: *Registres financiers* (L24–L52) [described in the records of the Camera Apostolica]; —*Registres de copies de bulles* (L53–L84) [described in this section]; —*Répertoires de la Congrégation des Évêques et de Réguliers* (L84–L161) [described in the records of the Congregatio Negotiis et consultationibus Episcoporum et Regularium Praeposita]; —*Miscellaneous* (L164–L167B) [described in this section]; —[*Archives Nationales, Miscellaneous*]; —*Inventaires* (L372–L400) [described in the "Separate Collections: Miscellaneous Manuscripts" section of this guide]. Note that the series [*Archives Nationales, Miscellaneous*] is a designation for material located in sections of the Archives Nationales other than that designated "L." Note also that the series *Inventaires* consists of inventories of Vatican Archives materials prepared by French archivists during the time all the records of the ASV were in the custody of the Archives Nationales.
Reference: Favier, *Fonds,* vol. 1, pp 310–314, 330.
Location: Archives Nationales, Paris.

7.4.12 [Archives Nationales, Miscellaneous]
[DATABASE ID: VATV40051-A]
Dates: 1494–1808.
Bulk: not determined.
Organization: Over the years since the bulk of the papal registers were classified by Delaborde, several registers of papal origin have been discovered in the Archives Nationales. This entry in the guide simply notes those located by the project staff. They are: LL 1–5. Bulls and briefs, 1514–1621; —K1334 nos. 15–36, Propaganda Fide, 1798–1808; —M879–884 (contents not clear); —MM852, MM853, MM880–892, Diaria Urbis, 1494–1512 (MM852), Regarding the Church in Spain, 57 items (MM853), Relating to religious houses including the Augustinians and Servites, 1600s–1780 (MM880–892).
References: Favier, *Fonds,* vol. 1, p. 330; Favier, *Inventaires,* p. 106.
Finding Aids: For LL1–5, see Archives Nationales finding aid L/19, which gives a brief listing for each number. For K1334 nos. 15–36, see Archives Nationales finding aid K/18, which gives a brief indication of the dates and contents of the material. For M879–884, see Archives Nationales finding aid M/19, which gives a general description of this material but does not list specific box numbers. For MM852, MM853, and MM880–892, see Archives Nationales finding aid M/26, which gives a brief listing for each MM box. Archives Nationales finding aid M/25 is better for box MM853.
Location: Archives Nationales, Paris.

7.4.13 Bandi sciolti

[DATABASE ID: VATV303-A]

Inclusive Dates: 1425–1904.

Bulk: 80 items.

Scope: This collection includes unbound paper placards that communicate papal decisions, regulations, and announcements, mostly regarding Rome and the Papal States. However the collection is quite varied and one finds here also encyclicals and canonization pronouncements, together with published decisions regarding minting of coins, other kinds of economic controls, oversight of ecclesiastical buildings, street maintenance, and the like. Most of the bandi regarding Rome have been published.

References: Fink, p. 127; Boyle, p. 95. *Regesti di bandi, editti, notificazioni e provvedimenti diversi relativi alla Città di Roma ed allo Stato Pontificio* (Rome, 1920–1958).

Finding Aids: See ASV Indice 1079.

Location: Archivio Segreto Vaticano.

7.4.14 Bullarium generale

[DATABASE ID: VATV306-A]

Inclusive Dates: 1165–1552 (bulk 1282–1425).

Bulk: 219 items.

Organization: There are two subseries: Bullarium generale, I (nos. 1–111), which covers Alexander III–Clement VI; — Bullarium generale, II (nos. 1–108), covers primarily Innocent VI to Martin V; however, at the end of this series there is a bull from Julius II, a notarial document from 1552, several letters from Benedict XII (1337), and an item from John XXII (1327).

Scope: These are original bulls (and other material).

References: Fink, pp. 150–151; Boyle, p. 96.

Finding Aids: A. Mercati, "Il 'Bullarium generale' dell'Archivio Segreto Vaticano," in *Sussidi per la consultazione dell'Archivio Vaticano* (Vatican City, 1947), vol. 3, pp. v–xiv, 1–58. Mercati has compiled an item-by-item calendar of the entire collection. This calendar dates and identifies the bull, gives a contents summary and/or explanatory notes, and provides a detailed physical description of each item. Mercati also cites other works that publish or mention each item.

Location: Archivio Segreto Vatican.

7.4.15 Immacolata concezione

[DATABASE ID: VATV166-A]

Inclusive Dates: ca. 1615–1855.

Bulk: 3 linear m. (about 88 vols. and buste).

Scope: This series includes: "Breve esposizione degli atti, 1855" (1 vol.); —"Episcoporum sententiae"; —"Voti sull'Immacolata Concezione . . . emessi da varii consultori, 1852" (3 vols.); —Poetry and letters concerning the Immaculate Conception.

Location: Archivio Segreto Vaticano.

7.4.16 Instrumenta Melfiensia

[DATABASE ID: VATV347-A]

Inclusive Dates: 1102–1694.

Bulk: 53 items.

Reference: Boyle, p. 98.

Scope: Not inspected, 1989–1990.

Location: Archivio Segreto Vaticano.

7.4.17 Instrumenta miscellanea

[DATABASE ID: VATV193-A]

Inclusive Dates: 819–1921.

Bulk: 7,916 items.

Organization: The order in this series·is never chronological: the first seven thousand items are more chronological than later donations, but the chronological blocchetti index removes this problem if one is looking for items within a certain period. See the index note concerning some minor aberrations in this index. The last item on which the actual donation date is mentioned is no. 7909 in 1982. At the time of Garampi, the collection numbered only 4,106 items.

Nos. 6636, 6637, and 6686 were formerly part of *Fondo Certosini*. These documents date from 1450, 1541, and 1436, respectively.

Scope: Boyle notes that these records are primarily cameral in origin and were originally located in Castel S. Angelo. This series covers a wide range of subject matter, and a great number of them are cameral in content. There are original procurations, obligations and payments made by bishops and abbots, inquests, accounts of the papal household and of collectors, as well as the correspondence of Cameral officials. MacFarlane notes that bulls and notarial instruments are also included, so that the collection, or at least the indices to it, is one all scholars should examine, whatever their interests.

Note: Nos. 1–4, 6–8, 10–11, 14–17, 19–26, 98, 241, 244, 440, 701, 854, 922, 923, 951, 955–956, 960, 961A, 997, 998, 1027, 1030, 1049, 1056, 1074–1076, 1098, 1104, 1110, 1133, 1158, 1207, 1211–1212, 1270, 1276–1278, 1280, 1281, 1532, 1802, 1814, 2556, 4108, 4299, 4707, 4594, 4780, 5181, 5211, 5270, 5439, 5540, 6459, 6650, 6660, 7187, 7288, 7469, and 7506 are available on microfilm.

References: Boyle, p. 57; Fink, pp. 148–149; Pásztor (1970), pp. 204–206; MacFarlane, pp. 91–92.

B. Barbiche, ed., *Correspondance du nonce en France, Innocenzo del Bufalo, évêque de Camerino, 1601–1604* (Rome, 1964). G. Battelli, "Due frammenti dei registri membranacei di Clemente VI," *Bullettino dell'Archivio paleografico italiano,* n.s., 2–3, pt. 1 (1956–1957): 69–76 [this article concerns I.M. 6755 and BAV Ottob. Lat. 2546]. U. Berlière, "Inventaire des 'Instrumenta Miscellanea' des Archives Vaticanes au point de vue de nos anciens diocèses," *Bulletin de l'Institut historique Belge de Rome* 4 (1924): 5–162; 7 (1927): 117–138 [this article is continued by Lefèvre, see below]. C. Burns, "Sources of British and Irish History in the Instrumenta Miscellanea of the Vatican Archives," *Archivum Historiae Pontificiae* 9 (1971): 7–141. R. J. Dodd, "Vatican Archives: Instrumenta Miscellanea: Documents of Irish Interest," *Archivium hibernicum* 14 (1956): 229–253. H. Gilles, "Les auditeurs de Rote au temps de Clément VII et Benoît XIII, 1378–1417: Notes biographiques," *Mélanges d'archéologie et d'histoire* 67 (1955): 321–337. P. Lefèvre. "Inventaire des 'Instrumenta Miscellanea' des Archives Vaticanes au point de vue de nos anciens diocèses, Deuxième supplément," *Bulletin de l'Institut historique Belge de Rome* 9 (1929): 323–340 [Lefèvre is a continuation of Berlière, see above]. G. Mantese, *Pietro Tamburini e il giansenismo bresciano* (Brescia, 1942). A. Mercati, "Dagli 'Instrumenta Miscellanea' dell'Archivio segreto vaticano," *Quellen und Forschungen aus italienischen Archiven und Bibliotheken* 27 (1936–1937): 135–177. A. Mercati, "Favori di Paolo III musici (G. Archadelt, J. Barry, B. Crotti, F. da Milano)," *Note d'ar-*

chivio per la storia musicale 10 (1933): 109–115. A. Mercati, "Le pergamene di Melfi all'Archivio Segreto Vaticano," in *Miscellanea Giovanni Mercati* (Vatican City, 1946), vol. 5, pp. 263–323. A. Mercati, *Reggiani in relazione col Tiziano* (Rome, 1944). M. Milian Boix, *El fondo "Instrumenta Miscellanea" del Archivo Vaticano: Documentos referentes a España (853–1782)* (Rome, 1969). G. Mollat, "Jean de Cardaillac, un prélat réformateur du clergé au XIVe siecle," *Revue d'histoire ecclésiastique* 48 (1953): 74–121. A. M. Sweet, "The Apostolic See and the Heads of English Religious Houses," *Speculum* 28 (1953): 468–484.

Finding Aids: ASV Indice 1056 provides brief chronological calendars as well as geographic/subject indices to the *Instrumenta miscellanea*, nos. 1–7453. The index actually includes two chronological indexes: the first beginning on page 1 and the second, comprising later acquisitions, commencing on page 112 verso. Entries in the chronological sections include date or inclusive dates, item number, and a note of the primarily geographic locality, but occasionally the office (Camera), person (Cardinal Delphin), or religious order that figures prominently in the item. There are also two geographic/subject indices that correspond to the two chronological listings. These begin on pages 151 and 193. While primarily geographic, these indices also indicate papal offices and cardinals who figure prominently or created certain items.

The ASV also has two series of blocchetti (Blochetti II) or schedarii (file card size) indices that calendar the *Instrumenta miscellanea* in greater depth. One schedario is organized numerically (33 blocchetti) and the other is organized chronologically (40 blochetti). Both include all the *Instrumenta miscellanea* (nos. 1–7916). These are useful not only because they provide the only listing of the entire series, but also because the blocchetti give full titles of items in the *Instrumenta*, date, and occasionally informative annotations. Researchers should note that there some minor aberrations in the chronological index. Blochetti 23 and 24 and blochetti 33 and 34 calendar items out of chronological order. Blochetti 24 notes items as late as the nineteenth century; blochetti 34 notes items in the seventeenth century.

ASV Indice 147 calendars approximately the first three thousand items of the series in their pre-twentieth century order. The index gives the old number, date, exact title or title summary. Sometimes the new number is indicated in pencil.

ASV Indice 691, part 1, is the least informative index to the series. The first section of this index lists nos. 1–4111 in numerical order with occasional conservation notes or a note to the type of material (pergam., stampate, etc.).

ASV Indice 124, "Primo Sbozzo di Inventario di tutti i libri che sono nell'Archivio Segreto Vaticano," by Giovanni Bissaiga (1672), provides more descriptive and accurate volume titles for select volumes in some series including *Instrumenta miscellanea*, no. 202, on folio 311v.

Citation: This series is cited as I.M. or Instr. Misc.
Location: Archivio Segreto Vaticano.

7.4.18 Instrumenta pactensia
[DATABASE ID: VATV348-A]
Inclusive Dates: 1171–1447.
Bulk: 3 items.
Reference: Boyle, p. 98.

This series was not inspected by project staff in 1990.
Location: Archivio Segreto Vaticano.

7.4.19 Miscellanea diplomatica
[DATABASE ID: VATV351-A]
Inclusive Dates: 1077–1906.
Bulk: 108 items.
Reference: Boyle, p. 98.
Location: Archivio Segreto Vaticano.

7.4.20 Miscellaneous (L164–L167B)
[DATABASE ID: VATV40055-A]
Date: [14—]–1705.
Bulk: Not determined.
Organization: These are in two groups. Fragments of registers from the Camera Apostolica and the Camera Urbis (fifteenth and seventeenth century) (L164–L166); —Minutes de bulles en rouleaux de papier (1693–1705) (L167a–L167b).
Scope: The rolled documents apparently pertain to the possessions of the Abby of St. Sophie.
References: Favier, *Fonds*, vol. 1, p. 312; Favier, *Inventaires*, p. 100.
Finding Aids: Archives Nationales finding aid L/2 contains a list of these box numbers with inclusive dates.
Location: Archives Nationales, Paris.

7.4.21 Piante e carte geografiche
[DATABASE ID: VATV358-A]
Inclusive Dates: Unknown.
Bulk: Extent undetermined.
Reference: Boyle, p. 99.
Finding Aids: Indice 1059.
This series was not seen by project staff in 1990.
Location: Archivio Segreto Vaticano.

7.4.22 Prigioneri di guerra
[DATABASE ID: VATV10263-A]
Inclusive Dates: 1915–1918.
Bulk: 44 linear m.
Organization: This series is divided into two subseries: correspondence to the pope requesting information regarding prisoners (37 m.); and registers of prisoners from the camps (7 m.).
Scope: This series primarily contains letters (supplications to the pope) from predominently Italian, French, and English family members and friends seeking information on soldiers. The registers are from the actual prisoner of war camps and list Italian detainees.
Reference: Fink, p. 140.
Location: Archivio Segreto Vaticano.

7.4.23 Prigionieri guerra
[DATABASE ID: VATV10493-A]
Inclusive Dates: 1939–1945.
Bulk: Amount not determined.
Reference: Natalini et al., p. 273.
Location: Archivio Segreto Vaticano.

7.4.24 Registres de copies de bulles (L53–L84)
[DATABASE ID: VATV40057-A]
Inclusive Dates: 1572–1584, 1623–1644.
Bulk: about 3.6 linear m.

Organization: These divide into two subseries as identified by the archivist H. Delaborde: Registres de Grégoire XIII, 1572–1584, 51 vols., which are contained in Archives Nationales boxes numbered L53–L68; —Registres de Urbain VIII, 1623–1644, 132 vols., which are contained in Archives Nationales boxes numbered L69–L84.

Scope: In *Inventario dei Registri vaticani* (Vatican City, 1981), p. 304, Martino Giusti places these registers among those Vatican Registers that deal with the Camera Apostolica.

References: Favrier, *Fonds*, vol. 1, p. 311; Favier, *Inventaires*, p. 100.

Finding Aids: Archives Nationales finding aid L/2 provides a simple list of each L number in the series as prepared by Delaborde. There is only indication of inclusive dates of the contents of each box.

Archives Nationales microfilm 246mi contains an analytic inventory of this series as prepared by Martin-Chabot. Part 1 of this inventory contains a detailed description of each of the registers in this series.

Location: Archives Nationales, Paris.

7.5
INDIVIDUAL AND FAMILY PAPERS

The interrelationship between the principal families of Italy and the Holy See is as enduring as it is complex. Like all of the evolving courts of Europe, the Holy See was also dependent on a designated patrician population, which held enormous influence on the shape of the economy and of the general policies of the pope, the Papal States, and, consequently, the church as a whole.

The composition of the Italian nobility was highly heterogeneous. Before the unification of the Italian peninsula in the nineteenth century, the various sovereigns who ruled over different parts of the Italian territory all bestowed titles of nobility. This held true also for the emperors of the Holy Roman Empire, the kings of Spain and of the Two Sicilies, the grand dukes of Tuscany, the dukes of Parma, and still others, including the patriarchs of cities such as Florence, Genoa, and Venice.

The popes were temporal sovereigns of the relatively extensive Papal States and, as such, recognized some existing titles and bestowed new ones. As Rome emerged as a major city in the late Middle Ages and as capital of the states of the church, the nobility of the city emerged in two classes: (1) nobles descended from feudatories who had received a fief from the reigning pope; and (2) common nobles whose nobility issued from the appointment to some office in the papal court. The popes also granted titles of nobility and continued to do so even after the *de facto* extinction of the temporal sovereignty over these states. Many cities maintained a *libro d'oro*, which recorded the names of all the families officially registered as members of Roman noble families. The *Libro d'oro del Campidoglio* of Rome was damaged by revolutionaries (1848), but the inventory of its contents

had been included in the constitution of Benedict XIV (*Urbem Romam*, Jan. 4, 1746). The document attempted to clear up the confusion that had been introduced into the various degrees of Roman citizenship and to stabilize accurately limitations within which the ranks of patricians and nobles would be distinguished from the other citizens and inhabitants of Rome. The document also prescribed the order and defined the number of noble families written on the tablets of the Roman Senate in the Campidoglio, and outlined the method that the conservators of Rome should use in adding other families to the list. Among these families, Benedict hoped "there would always be families of the Roman Pontiffs." To the above provisions he added the two lists of family names that had been registered in the Roman *Libro d'oro*: 181 family names of patricians and 60 family and first names of conscripted Romans. He also enumerated a list of favors and privileges that the Secretariat could confer on the families either exclusively or in concurrence with the Datary. It should be noted, however, that some families from outside of Italy were also admitted to Roman nobility.

On May 2, 1853, Pius IX directed a chirograph to Cardinal Altieri, president of Rome and Comarca, referring to the provisions decreed by Benedict XIV in his *Urbem Romam*. The letter stated that because of the changes that had taken place since 1746 some modifications of Benedict's norms were necessary to make them easier to apply to current needs. Pius also ordered the renovation of the *Libro d'oro* under the care of a special heraldic congregation composed of senators of Rome, four noble conservators, and four investigators (voters). The restored *libro* now in the Campidoglio has been closed to registrations since 1870.

When the unification of Italy was concluded with the occupation of Rome by the Piedmontese troops in 1870, the House of Savoy attempted to amalgamate the various nobilities. The project failed both politically and juridically. Many noble families remained faithful to the dethroned dynasties from which they had received their titles. Particularly, a considerable number of the Roman aristocracy, maintaining tradition, continued to figure officially in Vatican solemnities. They refused to recognize Rome's annexation to Italy, rejected any rapprochement with the new civil authorities, and closed their salons as a sign of protest. To this protesting nobility was given the name "Black Nobility."

The Lateran Treaty of February 11, 1929, assured the Roman nobility of a special status since it recognized the pope's right to grant new titles and accepted those conferred previously by the Holy See. Article 42 of the treaty specified that "Italy would admit by royal decree the recognition of titles of nobility conferred by the supreme pontiff, including those granted after 1870 and those conferred in the future."

The Vatican Archives and the Vatican Library are

repositories for collections of papers for many of the most prominent families in central Italy. These collections were received by the Vatican generally in recognition of the fact that so many members of these families held positions of prominence in the administration of the Holy See. Each collection listed in this section is prefaced by a general history of the particular family. However, time did not permit members of the project staff to conduct extensive research in these collections or in the bibliography that arises from these collections. As a result the precise relationship between the particular papers in Vatican collections to the family history prepared by the project staff was not determined. The family histories are included in this guide simply to provide a general sense of why these collections may now be found in these particular repositories.

Since time did not permit extensive research into the collections, information on the histories of the particular families was gathered from a variety of general sources on Italian history and on the history of the Holy See. The principal sources used in the preparation of the family histories that appear in this section are listed among the references noted in the introduction to Part 7 of this guide.

7.5.1 Aiuti, Attilio

7.5.1.1 Carte Aiuti

[DATABASE ID: VATV40024-A]
Inclusive Dates: 1852–1903.
Bulk: 2 buste.
Note: This series was cited in Natalini et al., p. 269, but not seen by project staff in 1990.
Location: Archivio Segreto Vaticano.

7.5.2 Alexander VIII

Descended from a noble Venetian family, Pietro Vito Ottoboni (1610–1691) was the son of Marco Ottoboni, chancellor of the Republic of Venice. At the age of seventeen Pietro earned a doctorate in civil and canon law at the University of Padua, and at twenty entered the curial service in Rome. In 1630 he became a judge of the Rota. Innocent X named him a cardinal in 1652. He was given the bishopric of Brescia in 1654 but in 1664 returned to Rome, where he became a prominent member of the Roman Curia. He was elected pope in 1689, taking the name Alexander VIII.

As pope, in contrast to Innocent XI his austere predecessor, Alexander made extensive use of nepotism. He appointed his grandnephew, Pietro, cardinal nephew, and his nephew, Giambattista, secretary of state, bestowing on them and other relatives gainful benefices.

He reduced taxes in the papal states and decreased the cost of food imports. He negotiated a reconciliation with Louis XIV, who in 1690 gave back Avignon and Venaissin, seized during the reign of Innocent XI (1676–1689). Alexander's recruitment of troops for the aid of Venice in the Turkish wars, however, met with great resentment. Because of his interest in a favorable Stuart restoration in England, Alexander established a commission to study English affairs. He condemned thirty-one Jansenist propositions (Denzinger, 2301–2313, 2315). In the bull *Inter multiplices* (Aug. 4, 1690), promulgated just two days before his death (1691), he declared the four Articles of the Assembly of the French Clergy (1682) null and void.

A connoisseur of letters himself, he was noted for his patronage of the Vatican Library, his purchase of the valuable manuscripts ("Reginenses") and other collections of Queen Christina of Sweden (1626–1689), who, after her abdication and public reception into the Catholic church (1655), had settled in Rome.

7.5.2.1 Fondo Ottoboni

[DATABASE ID: VATV10274-A]
Inclusive Dates: ca. 1641–1670.
Bulk: 2 linear m. (19 vols.).
Organization: Volume titles and enumeration are as follows: 1. Lettere originali scritte da diversi al cardinale Ottoboni, poi Alessandro VIII, dal 1664 al 1666; —2. idem. 1 gennaio a tutto giugno del 1667; —3. idem. 1 luglio a tutto dicembre del 1667; —4. idem. 1668; —5. idem. 1 gennaio a tutto giugno del 1669; —6. idem. 1 luglio a tutto dicembre del 1669; —7. idem. 1670; —8. Lettere scritte dal Mazzoli di Brescia al Sig. Cardle. Ottoboni sopra interessi particolari nelli anni 1667 e 1668; —9. Lettere originale de' ministri del re di Spagna a Theodoro Ameyden, dal 1640 al 1642; —10. Lettere originali di diverse persone nominate nell'indice prefisso allo stesso Ameyden, 1641 e 1642; —11. Lettere originale de' ministri del re di Spagna al detto Ameyden, del 1643; —12. idem. de ministri al Ameyden del 1644; —13. Lettere communi all' Ameyden, del 1644; —14. Lettere originali de'ministri del re di Spagna, del 1645 e 1646; —15. Lettere originali di diverse persone al Ameyden, del 1645 e 1646; —16. Lettere originali de' ministri del re di Spagna all'Ameyden, del 1647 e 1648; —17. Lettere originale di diverse persone al Ameyden, del 1647 e 1648; —18. Lettere originale de' ministri del re di Spagna al Ameyden, del 1649 e 1651; —19. Lettere communi all'Ameyden, del 1649 e 1650.

Scope: Fondo Ottoboni was formerly part of a Diverse series, thus the note in most of the volumes "Catalogato a nunziature diverse." The history and the interrelationship between the *Fondo Ottoboni* and other fondi including the *Fondo Card. Bernardino Spada*, the *Nunziature diverse*, and the *Fondo Favoriti-Casoni* is best examined by Pásztor (cf. below). What follows is a concordance between the present *Fondo Ottoboni* (FO) volume numbers and the former Diverse (D) volume numbers: FO 1 = D 242; FO 2 = D 245; FO 3 = D 246; FO 4 = D 247; FO 5 = D 248; FO 6 = D 249; FO 7 = D 250; FO 9 = D 367; FO 10 = D 368; FO 11 = D 169; F 12 = D 170; FO 13 = D 171; FO 14 = D 172; FO 15 = D 173; FO 16 = D 174; FO 17 = D 175; FO 18 = D 177; FO 19 = D 176. Most volumes contain internal indices to correspondents.

Fondo Ottoboni (vols. 1–6 and 8–19) entered the ASV as part of the eredità-Passionei in 1761–1763.

Reference: G. Gualdo, "Archivi di famiglie romane nell'Archivio vaticano," *Archivio della Società romana di storia patria* 104 (1981): 147–158.

Finding Aids: L. Pásztor, "Per la storia dell'Archivio Segreto Vaticano nei secoli XVII–XVIII," *Archivio della Società romana di storia patria* 91 (1968): 157–249. An index to volumes 1–7 and 9–19 can be extracted from pages 225–226 (vols. 1–7) and pages 217–218 (vols. 9–19). This brief listing of volumes with their current volume numbers is reproduced above in a different format. This article is more important for the provenance and history of the *Fondo Ottoboni* and related fondi.

ASV Indice to the SS. *Lettere diverse*, which is available behind the desk in the main ASV reading room, lists the *Fondo Ottoboni* in its former designation as a part of the *Lettere diverse*. This listing is not as complete as the one provided above nor does it indicate the current volume numbers. This is not an official ASV finding aid and must be used in consultation with ASV staff.

Location: Archivio Segreto Vaticano.

7.5.3 Barberini Family

A celebrated noble Roman family of Tuscan origin, the Barberini showed great leadership in the governance of the church and in the enhancement of the city of Rome in the seventeenth century. The Barberini were not popular in their native Florence nor in Rome, where they eventually settled. They reached the peak of their power when Maffeo was elected pope as Urban VIII in 1623.

Originally the family lived in Ancona and was known by the name Tafani. After acquiring wealth by trade, however, they changed the name to Barberini, derived from the Castle Barberini (first called Castellini) in the Val d'Elsa not far from Siena. By the end of the fourteenth century they had established themselves in Florence as a wealthy merchant family.

Under the pontificate of Paul III (1534–1549), Antonio Barberini went to Rome. In 1555 he summoned his two nephews, Francesco (1528–1600) and Raffaelo, to join him. Francesco, the real founder of the Barberini dynasty, and Raffaelo accumulated the wealth and trade advantages that became the base of Barberini power and influence. Francesco first entered the Roman Curia and became protonotary apostolic and referendary to both Signaturas, but he soon dedicated himself to diplomatic activity, fulfilling important foreign missions. When he died in 1600 he left his patrimony to his nephew Maffeo, whose education he supported and whose preparation for a career in the Roman Curia he encouraged.

Well educated and talented, Maffeo, after obtaining a doctorate from the University of Pisa in 1589, returned to Rome where he took on many delicate tasks under the pontificates of Clement VIII (1592–1605) and Leo XI (1605). Paul V named him a cardinal (1606), bishop of Spoleto (1608), legate in Bologna (1611), and prefect of the Signatura in 1617. He was elected pope in 1623, taking the name Urban VIII.

After a few years this election resulted in increased power and wealth for the Barberini family. Urban VIII enriched his own relatives, including two sisters in a Carmelite convent in Florence, with honors and benefits. Urban named his brother Carlo governor of Borgo and a general of the church. He named another brother (Antonio, 1569–1646, a Capuchin) and two nephews (Francesco, 1597–1679, and Antonio, 1607–1671) cardinals and advanced other relatives to influential places. Francesco built the Barberini Palace on the slope of the Quirinal at the Quattro Fontane with the cooperation of Maderno, Borromini, Bernini, and a corps of celebrated painters, among them Pietro da Cortona. This residence was endowed with a gallery of paintings and tapestries as well as a theater noted for memorable performances, among the most famous, those in 1656 in honor of Queen Christina of Sweden. In 1627 Francesco founded the Biblioteca Barberiniana containing the famous collection of manuscripts and rare books that Leo XIII acquired for the Vatican in 1902.

The wholesale way in which the Barberini plundered the ancient monuments of Rome to build their palaces gave rise to the saying: "Quod non fecerunt barbari, fecerunt Barberini" (What the barbarians did not do, the Barberini did). The Colosseum proved a convenient quarry for marble and the dome of the Pantheon a good source for metal. The Palazzo Barberini and the baldacchino in St. Peter's by Bernini are among the many monuments that can be recognized by the Barberini coat of arms with its emblem of three bees.

In the early seventeenth century the duchy of Castro, then possessed by the Farnesi, was enormously in debt. When the Barberini took steps to acquire it, Odoardo Farnese refused to comply. This refusal created a conflict that degenerated quickly into a long war. Venice, Florence, and Modena formed a coalition in aid of the Farnesi. After long negotiations, the treaty of Venice (Mar. 31, 1644) brought the conflict to a close. Odoardo recovered the duchy of Castro. At the same time he was reconciled with the Holy See.

The prestige of the Barberini suffered a great blow in 1644 when Urban VIII died. The new pontiff, Innocent X (1644–1655), was not hostile but accused the Barberini of having profited from their administration of the Apostolic Camera; the nephews were forced to flee Italy and take refuge in France. Confronted with the possibility of a war and a possible schism, Innocent X condescended to restore the confiscated goods to the Barberini and permitted them to return to Rome. The marriage between Maffeo Barberini, son of Taddeo, and Olimpia Giustiniani, niece of Innocent X, was the seal of approval. From then on the Barberini ceased to interfere with Italian politics.

7.5.3.1 Fondo Barberini

[DATABASE ID: VATV40064-A]
Inclusive Dates: 1300–1650.
Bulk: 3,250 vols.
Scope: This is a large and important collection that is particularly important for the history of politics and diplomacy in the seventeenth century. The collection of the Barberini family is considerable, comprising printed works, manuscripts, and archives. The portion of the collection known as the Archivio Barberini is the section of the collection that is considered the family archives. It contains a variety of materials including correspondence and financial records.
References: Boyle, p. 74; Pásztor (1970), p. 597. A. Pasture, "Inventaire de la Bibliothèque Barberini, à la Bibliothèque Vaticane, au point de vue de l'histoire des Pays-Bas," *Bulletin de l'Institut historique belge de Rome* 3 (1924): 43–157. C. Giblin, "Vatican Library: MSS. Barberini Latini," *Archivium hibernicum* 18 (1955): 67–144. L. E. Halkin, *Les sources de l'histoire de la Belgique aux Archives et à la Bibliothèque Vaticanes: État des collections et répertoire bibliographique* (Brussels, 1951).
Finding Aids: The principal indexes for the Archivio Barberini are all found under the number 382 in the Vatican Library. There are eight volumes in all. The first volume is a summary and select inventory. Vols. 2–8 are a set of detailed inventories of the papers. They list each item and give current segnatura. There are extensive indexes and catalogues for other parts of the collection as well.

Also useful is M. A. Lavin, *Seventeenth-Century Barberini Documents and Inventories of Art* (New York, 1975). This work cites important documents in the collection relating to seventeenth-century art. It is assigned index number 106 in the Vatican Library.
Location: Biblioteca Apostolica Vaticana.

7.5.4 Baumgarten, Paul Maria

7.5.4.1 Carte Baumgarten

[DATABASE ID: VATV40025-A]
Inclusive Dates: 1856–1937.
Bulk: 5 buste.
Note: This series was cited in Natalini et al., p. 269, but not seen by project staff in 1990.
Location: Archivio Segreto Vaticano.

7.5.5 Belli, Luigi

The ancient Belli family originated in Avigliana, then were found in Torino, and later in Racconigi. The first records of the family are from the fourteenth century. Among their noted members was Lieutenant General Simon, wounded at Sommacampagna (1848), created count by royal decree of 1903 with right of transmitting his title to his nephew Carlo. Carlo, the last of the family, died in 1926, with no male heir. The precise relationship between this family and the series listed was not determined.

7.5.5.1 Archivio dello studio Belli

[DATABASE ID: VATV10095-A]
Inclusive Dates: 1779–1826.
Bulk: 1.5 linear m. (12 boxes).
Organization: The initial four boxes are alphabetical (A–S) and unnumbered. The final eight boxes are numbered 1–8. Box 7 contains "Fabbriceria della parrocchiale di Sant'Alessandro in Colonna, 1870" and "Note e istruzione a Paolo Villadicani" (Archbishop of Messina). Box 8 contains information on Portugal, China, and India.
References: Pásztor (1970), pp. 238–239; Pásztor (1983), pp. 204–205.
Finding Aids: ASV Indice 1165, "Indice delle materie beneficiali, indulti ed altre grazie e concessioni a favore delle Corti Portogallo e Brasile," acts as an index to ten boxes of this collection. Pages 2–30v contain an itemized inventory of the material that can be located in the four alphabetical unnumbered boxes (A–S). This section also lists documents between the letters T and Z, which are no longer found in this collection. A handwritten copy of the corresponding inventory pages also appears at the beginning of each of the four unnumbered alphabetical boxes. Additionally, Indice 1165 (pp. 35–37) contains an inventory of the "provisiones" in numbered boxes 1–6.
Location: Archivio Segreto Vaticano.

7.5.6 Benedict XIII (of Avignon)

Pedro de Luna was born about 1328 at Illueca, Aragón, of one of the rich and noble families of the area. He obtained his doctorate and lectured in canon law at Montpellier. Gregory XI named him a cardinal in 1375. He supported the election of Urban VI but once convinced that the election was invalid gave his full support to Clement VII of Avignon. When Clement VII died, the cardinals hoped that the Great Schism might be ended if the Avignon cardinals refrained from electing a successor. When the cardinals met in conclave on September 26, 1394, all twenty-one of them took an oath to work for the elimination of the schism, each agreeing, if elected, to abdicate if and when the majority judged it proper.

They unanimously chose Pedro de Luna, cardinal deacon of Santa Maria in Cosmedin, who had opposed the oath and had taken it reluctantly. He accepted the office and took the name Benedict XIII. As pope, Benedict refused to take specific steps to end the schism and refused his own resignation as a means to the end. After he lost the support of France (1408), the Councils of Pisa (1409) and Constance (1417) deposed him. The election of Martin V (Oddo Colonna) as pope healed the schism though Benedict still refused to accept his deposition. He died on May 23, 1423.

7.5.6.1 Bullarum Benedicti XIII

[DATABASE ID: VATV304-A]
Inclusive Dates: 1394–1413.
Bulk: 2 linear m. (11 boxes or 210 numbered units).

Organization: These are divided into two series: Series I, October 13, 1394–May 14, 1403 (6 boxes or 112 nos.); —Series II, May 19, 1407–April 17, 1413 (5 boxes or 98 nos.).

Finding Aids: ASV Blocchetti Indici 23 and 24 calendar the entire collection. Entries include the date and place of origin of each document, an indication of the diplomatic nature of the document or the type of business, a summary of each item, and physical details (dimensions, the presence of a seal, etc.). There is usually a note as to whether the item is a copy or an original.

Location: Archivio Segreto Vaticano.

7.5.7 Benedict XIV

Prospero Lorenzo Lambertini was born in Bologna on March 31, 1675, of a noble but impoverished family. He received his early education from private tutors but at the age of thirteen (1688) was sent to the Collegium Clementinum in Rome. There he studied for four years concentrating on law and theology, making himself thoroughly familiar with the church fathers, the decrees of the councils, and the pronouncements of the popes. In 1694 he received a doctorate in law and theology from the University of Rome.

He began his public career as an assistant to an auditor of the Rota. He subsequently held the offices of consistorial advocate (1701), promoter of the faith (1708), and assessor at the Congregation of Rites (1712). In 1718 he became secretary of the Congregation of the Council. Named titular bishop of Theodosia in 1725, he was appointed to the archbishopric of Ancona in 1727. Named a cardinal in 1728 (reserved *in petto* from Dec. 9, 1726), he was transferred to the see of Bologna (1731) and elected to the papacy in 1740.

Benedict's previous experience had prepared him for the task he then assumed. He was a man of broad theological, legal, and medical learning and was experienced in church government and administration. Not satisfied with mere condemnation of error, he began in the first years of his pontificate to issue encyclical letters in order to apply the doctrine of the church to the problems of his age, fully aware of the need to integrate the divergent cultures of scientific and religious thought.

Shortly after assuming office he established a curial congregation to select worthy bishops, reminded ordinaries of their duties, emphasized the importance of the formation of priests, improved living conditions in the papal states, and restored major and minor churches. In matters unconcerned with dogma he was known to be extremely conciliatory. This is evident in his handling of several issues including: the negotiations with the monarchs of Europe, the crisis between the French bishops and the Parlement, the difficult question of mixed marriages, and the legislation relating to the Index of Prohibited Books.

His *De servorum Dei beatificatione et beatorum can-*

onizatione (1734–1738) grew out of his practical experience as promoter of the faith and is still the classic reference on beatifications and canonizations although there have been a few moderate revisions in recent years. His extensive work on diocesan synods, *De synodo dioecesana*, was based on his experience in Ancona and Bologna. He carried on a correspondence with scholars throughout the world. More than 760 of his letters are extant.

To encourage historical studies he founded a number of academies in Rome, enlarged the Vatican Library, and initiated the compilation of a detailed catalog of its manuscripts. He gave his wholehearted approval for the appointment of two women as professors at the University of Bologna and established chairs of chemistry, mathematics, and experimental physics at the Sapienza.

A few weeks before his death (May 3, 1758), he appointed Cardinal Saldanha to investigate the charges made against the Jesuits in Portugal. Saldanha did not receive the brief until after Benedict's death. Nevertheless, exceeding the powers conveyed to him, he pronounced judgment on the Jesuits before the elevation of Benedict's successor, thus leaving a major problem for the latter.

7.5.7.1 Fondo Benedetto XIV: Bolle e costitutiones
[DATABASE ID: VATV10096-A]

Inclusive Dates: 1598–1758 (bulk 1750–1758).

Bulk: 2 linear m. (33 numbered vols.).

Organization: Topical. Material is chronological within each topic. Vol. 1 is missing.

Scope: These include records of committees formed by Benedict XIV on a variety of topics including: reform of the breviary, reduction of feast days, martyrology, Greek and Eastern rites. The records are important for the study of liturgy, feasts, and the like. The series also contains rough drafts of encyclicals and printed copies of the acts of the Consistory, motu proprios, and bulls. These papers were acquired by the ASV about 1758 (cf. L. Pásztor, "Per la storia dell'Archivio Segreto Vaticano nei secoli XVII–XVIII," *Archivio della Società romana di storia patria* 91 [1968]: 157–249).

References: Fink, p. 129; Pásztor (1970), pp. 212–213; Boyle, p. 96 (identifies this series as *Bullae concistoriales Benedicti XIV*).

Finding Aids: ASV Indice 1062, by G. Marx, provides a brief, descriptive calendar/inventory of each document in vols. 1–28 of *Fondo Benedetto XIV*.

In the soffitone (V/1) there is a one-drawer schedario entitled "Per titolo" that serves as a partial index to materials regarding religious orders (ca. fifteenth–nineteenth century) in *Fondo Benedetto XIV: Bolle e costitutiones* as well as a number of other indexed and unindexed series in the ASV. Entries are brief and indicate the religious order, a short reference to the business, the fondo, and current volume number.

Citation: This series is usually cited as *Fondo Benedetto XIV.*

Location: Archivio Segreto Vaticano.

7.5.8 Benedict XV

See Secretariatus Status series *Spogli SS. Benedetto XV*, 1914–1922.

7.5.9 Beni Family

The family probably originated in Gubbio. In 1761 a certain Antonio obtained nobility of Tolentino for himself and his descendants. The Heraldic Consultation declared the family worthy to receive the title of nobile di Tolentino because of the official election of the nobles for the descendants of Antonio in 1761. The precise connection between this series and this family was not determined.

7.5.9.1 Archivio Beni

[DATABASE ID: VATV291-A]
Inclusive Dates: 1297–1916.
Bulk: 4.5 linear m. (163 numbered buste and 126 cataloged pergamene, also about 100 uncataloged pergamene).
Organization: The series is divided into two major sections: the 163 buste and the pergamene. The 163 volumes, buste, and so forth contain some pergamene and copies of medieval documents as well as several treatises of Paolo Beni (1552–1625) on physics, Aristotle, history, and the like. The index is good for scope and content information. Vol. 1 is an account book (introitus, exitus), ca. 1360; vol. 20 is original and copies of materials of an Augustinian monastery, S. Maria di Val di Ponte in Perugia (sixteenth–seventeenth century); vol. 61. concerns canonization (seventeenth century).
Note: Vols. 36, 118, 123, 125, 126, 128, and 129 are available on microfilm.
Reference: Fink, pp. 126–127.
Finding Aids: ASV Indice 1127, "Inventario dell'Archivio della famiglia dei conti Beni di Gubbio," by M. Giusti, provides detailed descriptions of the contents of each busta of the series. Entries indicate the titles or type of material (istrumenti, breve, sentenze, processi, cause), the inclusive dates, whether the material is original or has been copied, the existence of an internal index, and physical details (binding, pagination). ASV Blocchetti Indice 2 calendars the 126 items in the *Archivio Beni* "Pergamene." This calendar, with corrections, proceeds item by item providing location, date, a detailed summary of the subject and persons concerned, a classification of the item (bull, brief, etc.), and physical information.
Location: Archivio Segreto Vatican.

7.5.10 Benigni, Umberto

7.5.10.1 Fondo Benigni

[DATABASE ID: VATV30010-A]
Inclusive Dates: 1879–1925.
Bulk: 59 buste (nn. 1–9647).
Note: The family gave the papers to Pio Cenci, archivist of the ASV, in 1934, shortly after Benigni's death. More was added to the collection by the Maestro di Casa dei Sacri Palazzi Apostolici in early 1935.
Reference: G. Pizzorusso, "Le Fonds Benigni aux Archives

Secretes du Vatican," *Annali Accademici Canadesi* 8 (1992): 107–111. Pizzorusso provides a brief introduction (citing Pagano as his source) and then proceeds to cite documents of Canadian interest. This article shows the types of materials available for consultation in the fondo.
Finding Aids: S. Pagano, "Il fondo di Mons. Umberto Benigni dell'Archivio Segreto Vaticano. Inventario," *Ricerche per la storia religiosa di Roma* 8 (1990): 347–402. Pagano's work is a published guide to the collection. He provides a lengthy introduction to the provenance and formation of the fondo, descriptive notes, and a busta-by-busta summary of the contents. Pagano also provides three indexes at the end of his inventory: I. Quotidiani e periodici, II. Nomi di persona e di luogo, III. Materie. The personal name index also indexes roles or positions, for example, Maestro di Casa.
Location: Archivio Segreto Vaticano.

7.5.11 Benincasa Family

Ven. Orsola Benincasa, mystic and foundress of the Suore Teatine dell'Immacolata Concezione, was born in Naples in 1547 and died there in 1623. The family came from Tuscany but did not have any relationship with the family of St. Catherine of Siena. In 1579, when refused admission to the Capuchinesses, she retired to a hermitage on nearby Monte Sant'Elmo. In 1582 she went to Rome accompanied by her nephew saying that it had been revealed to her that she should go to the pope to exhort him to take action in reforming the church. After hearing her message, Gregory XIII had her examined by a commission of nine prelates and theologians among whom were Cardinals Giulio Santori and Antonio Carafa, the general of the Jesuits Claudio Acquaviva, and St. Philip Neri in whose respectful custody she was placed. St. Philip, however, remained unconvinced. After several months of severe tests she was released and sent back to Naples without anything being achieved. After returning to Monte Sant'Elmo she founded the Congregazione delle Teatine in 1583, a religious congregation of simple vows, to which she added in 1617 a branch dedicated to the contemplative life. Their rules were approved by Gregory XV in 1623. Venerable Orsola died in 1618. The "heroicity" of her virtue was proclaimed by Pius VI in 1793. The precise relationship between the *Fondo Benincasa* and the families cited was not determined.

7.5.11.1 Fondo Benincasa

[DATABASE ID: VATV320-A]
Inclusive Dates: 1605–1797.
Bulk: 2 linear m. (34 numbered vols.).
Organization: Subseries, volume numbers, and titles include: 1. Lettere di Flavio Rosario, Eligio Cellesi, Giovanni Francesco Torre, Angelo Bondi, 1645–1681; —2. Lettere di Francesco e Niccola Sabbioni, Giovanni Tarquinio Gallucci, Carlo Liberati, Giacomo Magliabecchi, Luca Gabrielli, e Filippo Buttari Caccianemici, 1654–1719; —3. Lettere tra i Benincasa, 1654–1689; —4. Lettere di Giovanni F. Macozzi,

Nicolo Benedetti, Isidoro Benedetti, Carlo Vespignani, Giovanni Francesco Fantoni, Giovanni Battista Ricci, Malatesta (abbate) Olivieri; —5. Lettere di Giovanni Bazzani, Giovanni Battista e Paolo Vittorio Boschetti, Antonio Zini, Giovanni Battista Galantari, Padre Domenico Bonandrini, F. Cesare di San Marco, Padre Andrea Benincasa; —6. Lettere di Guilio Ceruti, Giovanni Battista e Quintiliano Valenti, Gasparo Morcaccioni, Antonio Alfieri, Giovanni Battista Leonori, 1695–1730; —7–9. Lettere di cardinali, 1656–1787; —10. Lettere di Card. Borgia, 1789; —11. Lettere di Gian Battista Neel, 1748–1778; —12–15. Lettere da Roma, 1757–1768; —16. Reg. di lettere di Luciano Benincasa a Clarice d'Aste Paraciani; Lettere di Clarice d'Aste Paraciani, Angelo Paraciani, Filippo Carandini, Luca Giovannini, 1762–1773; —17. Lettere di Paolo Massei, Luigi Paffetti, Claudio Neel, 1736–1795; —18–23. Lettere de commissari delle armi, 1645–1730; —24–26. Lettere di Nunziato N. Baldocci, 1648–1670; —27. Lettere di Tomaso e Iacopo Betti, 1648–1658; —28. Lettere di Leone e Giovane Betti, 1650–1671; —29. Lettere di Giovanni e Pietro Baldocci, 1652–1669; —30. Lettere di Francesco Cozzi, 1652–1673; —31. Lettere di mons. Tesoriere al depositario della Reverenda Camera Apostolica e commisario di guerra in Ancona, 1793–1797; —32. Cassa della depositeria camerale d'Ancona, 1793–1797; —33. Giornale delle spese di Francesco Neri, 1605–1611; —34. Processo avanti il commissario della Rev. Fabbrica, 1660.

References: Fink, p. 127; Boyle, p. 96.

Finding Aids: ASV Indice 1026 (pp. 299–303) provides a detailed listing of correspondents in *Fondo Benincasa*. Entries proceed volume by volume, indicating the writer and recipient(s), inclusive dates, and folio numbers. The subject of the correspondence is not usually indicated.

Location: Archivio Segreto Vaticano.

7.5.12 Berzi, Angelo

Angelo Berzi was a Bergamese theologian born in Chiuduno in 1815. He completed his studies at the seminary in Bergamo, was ordained a priest, then taught philosophy. His system of philosophical, theological, and mystical views provoked violent reactions and sent him successively to Bergamo, Cremona, and Brescia.

On March 5, 1855, the Holy Office condemned his teaching as a mixture of mysticism and monistic interpretation of revelation, completely personal and at variance with traditional teaching. Suspended for five months, he returned to the family home in Chiuduno. There he spent the next twenty-eight years in solitude, prayer, and uninterrupted study until his death in 1884, leaving some eighty of his unedited works unpublished.

7.5.12.1 Carte Berzi

[DATABASE ID: VATV10067-A]

Inclusive Dates: 1842–1943 (bulk 1842–1869).

Bulk: 3.5 linear m. (33 boxes).

Organization: Subseries include: I. Scritti autobiografici di Don Angelo Berzi; —II. Fonti storiche Berziste; —III. Trattati intorno alla scienza teologica; —IV. Scritti su Gesu Cristo; —V. Scritti sull'Eucaristia; —VI. Scritti su Maria Immacolata; —VII. Trattatelli teologici; —VIII. Opere scritturistiche e patristiche; —IX. Scritti sulla mistica; —X. Scritti di direzione spirituale; —XI. Testi di lezioni e prediche; —XII. Poesie di Don Angelo Berzi; —XIII. Epistolario e carteggio; —XIV. Scritti di Don Angelo Berzi o relativi a personaggi del movimento Berzista; —XV. Scritti minori; —XVI. Pubblicazioni di vari autori.

Scope: This series contains the writings of Don Angelo Berzi on spirituality and theology. Both manuscript and published versions of selected works are present as well as copious notes. The final box contains a biography of Berzi published in 1943. The collection was acquired by the ASV in 1976.

Reference: Natalini et al., p. 269.

Finding Aids: O. Cavalleri, "Le Carte Berzi dell'Archivio segreto vaticano," *Commentari dell'Ateneo di Brescia* (1982): 129–155. Cavalleri has compiled and published a detailed index to the entire *Carte Berzi*. Cavalleri's index provides a brief introduction to the collection and then proceeds subseries by subseries (cf. above), describing the contents of the major sections or "positions" within each subseries. This published inventory enables researchers to gain a global understanding of the *Carte Berzi* as well as to request specific items in the collection.

Location: Archivio Segreto Vaticano.

7.5.13 Bolognetti Family

According to tradition the Bolognetti family originated in Umbria but moved to Bologna where they were of modest means. Many of their descendants were members of the armed forces, among them Colonel Carlo Bolognetti, commissioner general of the ecclesiastical forces in Avignon. Among the family members was Giovanni, a famous jurist. There were also two cardinals and many prelates.

Alberto Bolognetti was born in Bologna in 1536. He obtained great fame in law, in which field he was designated laureate in 1562. Under the sponsorship of Cardinal Paleotto he continued his studies and taught at Salerno for nine years. In 1576 Gregory XIII called him to Rome and sent him as nuncio to Florence in the company of Duke Francesco I. In 1578 he was sent to the nunciature for Venice and the next year was given the bishopric of Massa and Polonia. In 1581 the pope recalled him and appointed him nuncio to Spain and then to Poland. As nuncio his letters and instructions contributed to the implementation of the decrees of the Council of Trent.

In 1583 Gregory XIII named him a cardinal. He died at Villac in Carinthia in 1585 while returning to Rome for the election of the new pope (Sixtus V). He was buried in the family tomb in the Church of Santa Maria dei Servi in Bologna. He published a number of works on civil law.

Mario Bolognetti was one of the counts of Vicovaro where he was born in 1690. From his earliest years he had dedicated himself to service to the Holy See. Innocent XIII (1721–1724) named him an apostolic protonotary and then promoted him to the Apostolic Camera. Benedict XIV named him to the College of Cardinals on September 9, 1743. In 1750 Mario was appointed to the legation of Ravenna. He held successively various positions in the Roman congregations. He died at Rome in 1756 at the age of sixty-six and was buried in Rome.

The house of Bolognetti came to an end in 1775 with the death of Giacomo, who was survived by a daughter who married Count Virginio Cenci. Count Virginio transmitted to his own son, Alessandro, the maternal name with which he was inscribed among the patrician Romans and conscripted with "senatus consulto" on June 12, 1838. The Bolognetti have two chapels and many tombs in Bologna, Pavia, and Rome, all of which have inscriptions in memory of the various members of the family. Between 1647 and 1761 four members of the family were named cardinals. The precise relationship between the *Fondo Bolognetti* and the family was not determined.

7.5.13.1 Fondo Bolognetti

[DATABASE ID: VATV321-A]

Inclusive Dates: 1528 (copy)–1798.

Bulk: 18 linear m. (346 numbered vols.).

Organization: Subseries (volume titles) have been reconstructed from the numbered volumes as follows: 1–4. Tassoni, Alessandro, "Annali dall'anno 1 della nascita di Cristo al 1400"; —5–7. Lettere dell'Emo. Sig. Card, Mazzarini, 1647–1649; —8, 36, 43–44, 147, 150, 172. Card. Carlo Carafa; —9, 56–57, 65–66, 86, 102, 129–132, 134–137, 163, 236. Spagna, 1549–1701; —10, 24–25, 39–40, 75, 158–160, Relazioni di Corti, 1535–1628; —12. Rossi, "Istoria del sacco di Roma"; —14, 59, 145, 188. Francia, 1687–1690; —15–18, 58, 60–61, 63, 87–89, 99–101, 106–108, 115–118, 122, 127–128, 138–140, 164–176, 199–203, 213–215, 217, 211–223, 235, 237, 243, 249–250, 253, 256–257, 260, 263, 266–270, 275, 282, 290–292, 296, 302–303, 305–307, 309, 311, 315, 320, Diversi, 1663–1692; —19. Remedie per cavalli; —20–21, 242, 273–274. Conclavi; —22–23. Lettere di Antonio Arrulio; —26–27, 33–34, 38, 53–54, 144, 314. Relazioni diverse, 1636–1697; —28. Investiture di papi; —29. Tragedie del Card. Delfino; —30. Lettere di Lorenzo Magalotti; —31. Opere accademiche del Marchese Santinelli; —32, 48. Corte di Roma; —35, 241. Polonia; —41. Elogia pontificum et cardinalium defunctorum di Teodoro Amayden; —13, 45–47, 51–52, 226–234, 246–247, 319. Papi (Successi, elezioni, notabili, etc.); —55. Historia di Ravenna, 1638; —62, 141–142, 182. Republica di Venetia; —64, 129, 179, 244. Napoli; —67–70, 240. Diario di Roma, 1700–1703; —71–74. Diaria Alexandri VI; —77–80. Giornale, 1692–1695; —81. Compendio d'istorie; —82–84. Opere di Clemente IX; —85. Governo di Roma e casi diversi; —90. Morale cavate da Aristotile; —91. "Tolleide e Scorneide" (sonnets); —92. Giustizie; —93. Negozie diversi; —94–95. Lettere del Card. Polo; —96, 180–181. Vite diverse; —97–98. Lettere di Urbano VII; —109–111, 178. Firenze; —112. Capitolo de frati; —113–114. Le vere massime della politica; —119–120. Lettere diverse; —123, 207, 224, 287. Vite diverse (de Cardinali); —124–126. Cina; —133. Bologna. Historia; —143. Missioni; —146. Lettere di Mons. Varese; —148. Lettere del Card. Panciroli; —149. Lettere di Mons. Ubaldini; —150–153. Segretaria di Stato; —154, 329. Concilio di Trento, "Materie ecclesiastiche" accurante Th. Rhymer; —156–157. Istruzioni, 1621–1666; —161–162. La Buchereide del Conte Lorenze Magalotti; —177. Regalia; —183. Corsi; —184. Acque; —185–187, 208, 210, 225. Ceremonia; —190–195. Storia di Castro; —196–198, 204–205. Sicilia; —206. Governo del Card. Altieri; —211. Commedie del Faginoli; —212. Commentar. Tursellini; —216. Commedie diverse; —219. Conservat. urbis; —220. Cronaca di Viterbo; —238. Osservazioni su i due libri del Card. Tamasi, "Codices sacramentorum" e "Antiqui libri missarum," 1723; —239. Legazioni del card. de Medic in Francia; —245. Asia, Africa, America; —254. Poesie di Bruqueres (canonico Michele); —255. Ugonotti; —258. Lettere del card. de Noailles; —259. Re de Navarra; —260. Mons. Bichi (Portogallo); —262. L'interesse innocente, politica civile, considerazioni politica religiose; —265. Vita di suor Veronica Giuliani; —271. Istoria di Spoleti; —276. Istruzioni ai Monarchi; —277. Il Ricciardetto di Forteguerri; —278. Successi del cardinal Corscia; —283. Parma e Piacenza; —284. Sardegna; —285. Ethiopia ed Egitto; —288. Scritture e documenti del Madruzza (Lorenzo); —289. Sordi. Carattere per ben goveruare; —293–295. Lorenzini. Opere; —297. Fulvii, Carduli; —298–300. Cocco. "Scienza de sovrani; —301. Gigli. Poesie inedite; —304, 322–325. Gesuiti; —308. Disegni di porte e fenestre; —310. Vita de Donna Olimpia; —312. Notizie delle famiglie sovrane d'Europa; —313. Notizie e privilegi de 4 maggior Patriarchi; —316–318, 331–337. Miscellanee manoscritti; —321. Modena contro la Camera Apostolica; —326. Psalmi et alia; —328. Piccini. Geografiche antiche; —330. De exorcista Elvacensi; —338. Miscellanee comuni; —339–343. Miscellanee; —344–346. Scritture diverse.

Scope: These are copies of documents largely without any citation to the source. Materials relate to much more than French and Italian churches as stated by Boyle. There is actually a much smaller portion of material concerning churches in general and a considerable amount concerning the church politically, especially relations with Spain and France.

According to a description of microfilm held by the University of Notre Dame (U.S.A.), vols. 3, 4, 19, and 108 of this series relate to the English colonization of Maryland and contain correspondence of Gregorio Panzani, the secret agent of Urban VIII in England, along with a handwritten copy of his diary (1634–1636).

Notes: The collection was acquired by the Holy See in 1810. Vols. 3, 4, 19, 108, 143, 245, and 277 are available on microfilm.

References: Pásztor (1983), pp. 205–206; Fink, pp. 127–128; Boyle, p. 97. G. Gualdo, "Archivi di famiglie romane nell'Archivio vaticano," *Archivio della Società romana di storia patria* 104 (1981): 147–158.

Finding Aids: ASV Indice 1049, compiled by Angelo Mercati (1929–1930), is a detailed synopsis of the contents of each volume now existing in the *Fondo Bolognetti*. Each entry provides the general title of the volume followed by an indication of the major writers, recipients, subjects, geographic locations, and sometimes dates that are located in the volume. The entries are dense, particularly those in the subseries entitled "Diverse . . ."; thus, a careful reading is necessary to get the most out of this index.

ASV Indice 142 (formerly vol. 347 of this series) is an alphabetical subject index to the *Fondo Bolognetti*. Although a researcher may begin here, the index is not complete and a thorough reading of Indice 1049 will still be necessary. This index lists personal names, geographic locations, types of documents (breve, inventario, istruzioni, etc.), subjects (such as "ceremonies" as well as specific types of ceremonies: funerals, investitures), and the current volume numbers. As in most subject indexes the choice of subjects is subjective and a researcher cannot always guess the exact term or methodology employed by the indexer. For example, in this index most of the cardinals are indexed under "Cardinal" and may not be listed under their surnames. Others, such as Francesco delle Rovere, are listed under their given names and not their surnames.

ASV Indice 136 (pp. 74–78v), by De Pretis, is an 1878 listing of brief volume titles.

Location: Archivio Segreto Vaticano.

7.5.14 Boncompagni Family

The house of Boncompagni had its origin in Umbria but moved to Bologna in the thirteenth century where the family was comfortable but not wealthy. Many of their descendants were members of the armed forces. The foundations of its fortune were laid by Cardinal Ugo Boncompagni who was elected pope in 1572 under the name of Gregory XIII.

From this pontiff, whose name was immortalized by his reformation of the calendar, the family is directly descended through a natural son of Gregory's named Giacomo who married a Sforza di Santa Fiora. Gregory gave Giacomo the titles duke of Sora and d'Arpino and marquis of Vignola and enriched him accordingly. Perhaps no other family enjoyed the fruits of nepotism to the extent of the Boncompagni. Through carefully arranged alliances with the heiresses of three other papal families, the Boncampagni were able to accumulate significant wealth.

Giacomo married Ippolita Ludovisi who brought as her dowry the great wealth of Gregory XV (Ludovisi) while the pope's brother Niccolò by three marriages accumulated immense riches in his house. Niccolò's first wife, Isabella Gesualdi, brought with her the princedom of Venosa. His second wife was a Mendoza who brought him the principality of Piombino with almost sovereign sway over that small state. The third was Constance Pamphili, daughter of the notorious Olimpia Maldaichini, sister-in-law of Innocent X (Pamphili) who had great influence over the pope and in Rome.

The state of Piombino, already mentioned as having been acquired through the Mendoza marriage, had been inherited by that family from the d'Arpini, originally a peasant family, but with ambitions "above the plow" that raised them in 1392 to the condition of independent rulers. Their authority was transmitted to their descendants of the other houses already mentioned.

The principate of Piombino remained with the Boncompagni up to the Napoleonic invasion. They did not return the patrimonial rights until the Congress of Vienna (1815) with the conclusion of a settlement in money from part of the grand duchy of Tuscany in which Piombino was incorporated. In the eighteenth century Pietro Gregorio Boncompagno married Maria Francesca, last of the Ottoboni family, adding her name to the line. By remaining faithful to Spain the Boncompagni did not play an important part in the political policies of their time.

Notwithstanding its former great wealth the Boncompagni family became comparatively poor. Its once famous estate within the walls of Rome was divided into innumerable villas, and the great though modern palace of the family was taken over as a residence for the queen mother. The precise relationship between the series listed below and the family was not determined.

7.5.14.1 Archivio Boncompagni

[DATABASE ID: VATV293-A]

Inclusive Dates: 871–ca. 1900.

Bulk: 288 linear m.

Organization: Part of the archivio was originally organized according to armaria, mazzi, sections, and document numbers. These have been partially replaced by protocol numbers 1–about 1000. The former volume numbers are still visible, although the order has been changed. Subseries include: Bolle; —Breve; —Investiture, ommaggi, privilegi; —Feudi; —Fiscali feudali; —Sora (Stato di . . .); —Tenuta; —Carte varie; —Familie Ludovisi; —Istromenti; —Piombino (Stato di . . .); —Processi (criminali e civili); —Regno (Stato di . . .); —Firenze; —Vignola; —Eredità; —Libri Mastri; —Registri di lettere; —Indici.

Scope: This is a family archive of wide ranging and facinating variety. Some buste contain pergamene originals and copies that are quite ancient, for example, busta 270 with "Scritture diplomatiche del Monastero di S. Maria in Elce" dating from 871 to 1192; and busta 272, "Bolle e Breve Pontifici riguardanti il Monastero di S. Maria in Elce," from the years 1102–1603. Some of the pergamene documents have been removed from their buste and are archived separately in the internal Sala dei Pergamene.

Note: There is a related collection entitled *Archivio Boncompagni-Ottoboni* located in the archives of the Vicariato di Roma. In the Biblioteca Apostolica Vaticana there is a Boncompagni Codice. Vols. 20–24 of the Congregatio de Propaganda Fide series *Fondo Consalvi*, "Pianoamministrativo del Cardinal Boncompagni," about 1780–1790 (re Bologna), are now in the Archivio Segreto Vaticano. The internal, unnumbered index volume for the *Fondo Consalvi* provides a description of these items on pages 60–72. This collection was acquired by the ASV from 1947–1953. Charles Burns (1991) states that it came to the ASV in 1948. Vols. 289–290, 325, and 333A are available on microfilm.

References: Boyle, p. 95; Fink, p. 129; Pásztor (1970), pp. 598–599. G. Gualdo, "Archivi di famiglie romane nell'Archivio vaticano," *Archivio della Società romana di storia patria* 104 (1981): 147–158.

Finding Aids: The ASV Boncompagni schedario consists of twenty-two file drawers of cards in the Sala d'Indici. The Boncompagni schedario is a detailed, alphabetical calendar of approximately half of the *Archivio Boncompagni*. This alphabetical list includes types of documents (bolle, breve, etc.), persons (both personal names and offices), and geographic locations. Entries for each document summarize the business, usually date the item, and provide the current Protocolli and item numbers. The schedario covers many of the same sections as ASV Indice 730.

ASV Indice 730, "Rubricelle generale dell'Archivio dell'Eccellentissima Casa Boncompagni accresciuto e riordinato l'anno 1782," is a detailed index to types of material (bolle, breve, benefici, istromenti, inventori, testamenti, etc.) that can be located throughout a large part of the collection. Much (it cannot be determined if all) of the *Archivio Boncompagni* treated here is also calendared in the Boncompagni schedario (cf. above). Indice 730 proceeds alphabetically through the types of documents and lists those falling under each category. Entries usually include the year, a brief description of the document and the location. Entries are grouped by location, armadio, mazzo, parte, and numero. Occasionally a Protocollo number has been annotated in pencil. The Protocollo represents the current volume number. If no Protocollo number has been written in pencil by an item desired, the document probably is still extant in the *Archivio Boncompagni*, but a search throughout the collection will be required.

ASV Indice 729, "Indice dell'Archivio Boncompagni-Ludovisi," covers the sections of the *Archivio Boncompagni* dealing with the Stato di Sora and the Archivio Ludovisi, the Stato di Piombino, the Archivio Boncompagni-Ludovisi, and the Archivio del Marchesato di Vignola. This index provides several alphabetical lists to types of material (atti, bolle, feudi, istromenti) with very brief annotations contained in the different sections of the *Archivio Boncompagni*. Although material exists for all of these sections, the former volume numbers in this index could not be translated into current call numbers.

ASV Indice 728, "Rubrica dell'Archivio dell'Eccma. Casa Boncompagni-Ottoboni," is another alphabetical list of types of documents, persons, places, and events in the *Archivio Boncompagni-Ottoboni* currently housed in the Vicariato di Roma at St. John Lateran in Rome.

At the end of the *Archivio Boncompagni* there are a number of internal indices to the collection entitled "Indice per materie," "Indice alphabetica," "Indice dell'Archivio Boncompagni Ludovisi," and so forth, all of which refer to buste/items using the former volume numbers. Documents listed here are still extant in the *Archivio Boncompagni* as the former volume numbers are still visible. However, a careful search of the stacks is required.

G. L. Masetti Zannini, "L'Archivio privato del cardinale Ignazio Boncompagni-Ludovisi," *Bolletino del Museo del Risorgimento* 7 (1962): 199–210. Masetti Zannini provides a general introduction to the *Archivio Boncompagni* and Cardinal Ignazio Boncompagni as well as bibliographies on the Boncompagni family and Bologna during the eighteenth and nineteenth centuries. Masetti Zannini's primary purpose in this article, however, is the compilation of a chronological list of documents in the *Archivio Boncompagni* that deal with the personal life of Cardinal Ignazio Boncompagni Ludovisi, his early education, and the legation of Bologna. Items are cited by their current volume numbers.

Location: Archivio Segreto Vaticano.

7.5.15 Borghese Family

Of Sienese origin, the Borghese family first appears in the records in 1238. The Borghese were especially prominent during the period of the Renaissance. Marcantonio Borghese, a juriconsult who became a member of the papal court in the sixteenth century, established the family in Rome when one of his sons, Camillo, became pope under the name of Paul V, the source of the family's prominence. Yet, notwithstanding the high position attained by this house and its royal alliances, the family, in its native Siena, was little more than what the name implies, "bourgeois." Another son, Francesco, was commander of the papal troops. The pope secured important titles of nobility for his nephew Marcantonio and raised another nephew, Scipione, to the cardinalate.

Marcantonio's son Paolo married Olimpia, the heiress of the important family of the Aldobrandini. Paolo's son Giovanni Battista was ambassador of Philip V to Rome, and Giovanni Battista's son Marcantonio Borghese was for a time viceroy of Naples. A later Marcantonio was a noted collector. Camillo Filippo Ludovisi Borghese married Marie Paulina Bonaparte, sister of Napoleon I (1803), and sold to the latter much of the Borghese collection of Italian art.

The family was always noted for its loyalty to the Holy See from which its wealth and honors came. No less than eight princedoms, six dukedoms, and seven marquisates are found in the head branch alone, not to mention other titles that are born by descendants through maternal inheritance. In most cases the Borghese have married nobility, particularly the old nobility of Austria-Hungary. They have in this way transmitted to their children eligibility for the coveted Knighthood of Malta for which the sons of a woman of non-noble birth were disqualified.

Paul V enriched the members of his family by bestowing upon them extensive and valuable lands. The great Borghese Palace in Rome, the home of valuable art collections, which was itself a work of art, was followed by many marine and country villas. The Borghese also seized the Cenci property when it was confiscated because of the Cenci family scandal of patricide. The dramatic story of Beatrice Cenci's life has been a favorite theme of poetry and art. The Cenci property included the historic estate later known as the Villa Borghese. The precise relationship between the series listed below and these particular members of the family was not determined.

7.5.15.1 Archivio Borghese
[DATABASE ID: VATV292-A]
Inclusive Dates: 1576–1925.
Bulk: 1,120 linear m. (8,690 numbered items and a few unnumbered items).

Organization: Subseries include: Acquatraversa; —Acqua; —Aguzzano; —Alienazioni; —Ammune e contabilita; —Archivio; —Atti di familia; —Atti di ultima volanta; —Boccone; —Bomarzo; —Brevi, bolle, chirographi, motupropri; —Campo del Fico, Tufello; —Canemorto (Orvinio); —Capitolo di S. Maria, Regina coeli; —Capocotta e Campo Ascolano; —Capella Paolina; —Capella Borghese; —Carroeto; —Casa calda; —Casal Ferratella; —Castel Aricone; —Castel Campanile; —Castel Chiodato; —Castellone; —Castel vecchio; —Castiglion del Lago; —Cervellatta; —Ciccognola; —Cisterna; —Civitella; —Collalto; —Collelungo; —Collepiccolo (Colle di Tora); —Colonna; —Concordie e quietanze; —Crediti fruttiferi, censi e canoni; —Cretone; —Csarni e fedi di testimoni; —Fabbricati in Roma; —Feudi e tenute; —Fiano Romano; —Finocchio; —Fontana candida; —Frascati; —Frasso Sabino; —Galleria e museo e scavi nelle tenute; —Giuliano; —Innominate; —Inventari; —Instituti di credito (società diverse); —Jus patronato, Cappellanie, Doti; —Le Case; —Licenza; —Lucedio; —Mandati di Procura; —Marche e Civitanova; —Marco Simone; —Mastroddo; —Mentana; —Miscellanea; —Molara; —Montecompatri; —Montefortino (Artena); —Monte Percile; —Monte Porzio; —Monticelli; —Montorio in valle; —Moricone; —Morlupo; —Morolo e Castel Orciano; —Nettuno Anzio; —Norma; —Olevano —Olevano tenuta; —Orcianello; —Ordini di pagamento; —Palo; —Palombara; —Pantano; —Perugia; —Petescia; —Pietraforte; —Poggio Moiano; —Poggio nativo; —Polline; —Porareccina; —Pozzaglia; —Prattica; —Rignano; —Roccagiovane; —Roccapriora; —Roma; —Rossano; —Rustica; —Salviati-Borghese (Patrimonio); —S. Angelo; —S. Nicola Acquaviva; —S. Polo; —S. Vita; —Scarpa; —Scorano; —Sgurgola; —Stabia (Faleria); —Stazzano; —Storta; —Stracciano; —Sulmono; —Tagliente e Torre; —Tarquinia e Pian d'Arcione; —Testa di lepre; —Titoli d'acquisto; —Titoli di credito; —Titoli onorifici e privilegi; —Tor di Quinto; —Tor Forame; —Tor Madonna; —Torre e Tor Tagliente; —Torrecchia; —Torrenova; —Torrespaccata; —Toscana (Beni in); —Tufello; —Valchetta; —Vallinfreda; —Valmontone; —Vigne e Terreni; —Villa al Gianicolo; —Villa Pinciana; —Ville Tusculane; —Violata e Violatella; —Vivaro; —Indici; —Piante; —Filza libri mastri; —Casa Borghese; —Ordini pagati dal cassiere; —Eredità; —Villa, galleria e museo (1886–1892); —Libri di istromenti, catasti, ecc.; —Processi criminali; —Abbadie; —Artisti varii; —Guardaroba; —Congregazioni; —Salviati; —Scritture diverse e mandati; —Filza mandati, Santo Spirito. The collection was acquired by the ASV in May 1931.

References: Fink, p. 128; Boyle, p.95. G. Gualdo, "Archivi di famiglie romane nell'Archivio vaticano," *Archivio della Società romana di storia patria* 104 (1981): 147–158. C. Erdmann, "Unbekannte Briefe des Kardinals Farnese an den Nuntius Bertano (1549)," *Quellen und Forschungen aus Italienischen Archiven und Bibliotheken* 21 (1929–30): 293–304.

Finding Aids: ASV Indice 727 provides a good overview of the collection through a complete listing of all items in this series. Entries include the current volume number, inclusive dates, former volume identification data (e.g., tome and lettere designations), and selected notes. This index gives good access to researchers seeking information on a specific subject (e.g., Galleria Borghese), although researchers should carefully peruse this entire index when searching for information. This index contains the most detailed access to materials after

no. 1165 in this collection. For items 1–1164, ASV. Indici 888–896 (cf. below) provide the best access, although Indice 727 must still be consulted to locate current volume numbers.

ASV Indice 727A, "Archivio Borghese 8606–8622," by C. De Domenicis and F. Di Giovanni, provides detailed access to items encompassing the numbers stated, 8606–8622 (olim cartelle A1, BII, CIII, and V–IX). This group of materials is largely maps. Information in this calendar includes item number, description, physical notes (e.g., disegno a penna colorato), and size.

ASV Indici 888–897 (formerly *Archivio Borghese* nos. 1165–1174) provide detailed access to nos. 1–1164 in this series. Indici 888–897 calendar most of the items in the buste and volumes listed above (Acquatraversa-Vivaro). These calendars include: date, type of document (e.g., breve, certificato, istromento, elenco, affito, perizie, lettere, chirografo, etc.), a description of the item, and the former tome and document number. The subseries name and tome and document number must then be taken to ASV Indice 727 to locate the current volume number and request the desired item.

Location: Archivio Segreto Vaticano.

7.5.15.2 Fondo Borghese
[DATABASE ID: VATV159-A]

Inclusive Dates: 1376(copy)–1827 (bulk 1580–1750).

Bulk: 106 linear m.

Organization: There are six series that overlap in dates, types of materials, and contents. They are divided as follows (numerical designation provided by project staff): 1. 977 item numbers (1376 (copy)–1624); —2. 521 item numbers (1485–1765); —3. 132 item numbers (1579–1624); —4. 308 item numbers (1547–1792); —5. items numbered 19–36, 40–50, 52, 62, 64, 66 (ca. 1734–1789); —6. Carte Borghese (120 packets) 1423 (copy)–1827. The Carte Borghese is often referred to as "Casa Borghese."

Scope: This large collection (once a part of the Secretariat of State correspondence between 1592 and 1621) was acquired from the Borghese family for the Vatican Archives by Leo XIII in 1891. According to Charles Burns (1991), Leo XIII purchased the *Fondo Borghese* (e.g., the diplomatic materials relating to Clement VII and Paul V, which had been gathered by the Prussian Historical Institute). See also ASV Indici 193, "Inventario dell'Archivio Borghese donato all'archivio Vaticano dall'Istituto Storico Prussiano."

This collection has proved a rich source for the political and religious history of Europe during the critical pontificates of Clement VIII, Leo XI, and Paul V (himself a Borghese).

Most volumes contain internal indexes. It is important to note associated records: Vat. Greco. 2594–2600 in the Biblioteca Apostolica Vaticana. These were formerly identified in the ASV as *Fondo Borghese* IV, vols. 28, 108, 109, 123, 137, 205, and 206, respectively.

Note: Vol. 175; Series I, vols. 9, 380, 425 bis, 581, 696A, 697A, 700, 732; Series II, vols. 59, 68, 187, 449, 517; Series III, vols. 9C, 10D, 12C, 18, 67A, 68A, 84D, 372, 475; Series IV, vols. 91, 100, 102, 118, 120, 137, 140, 733; and Series V, vol. 103 are available on microfilm.

References: Fink, pp. 100–101; Pásztor (1970), pp. 213–216; Pásztor (1983), pp. 197–199; Boyle, p. 74; MacFarlane, pp. 88–89.

D. Conway, "Guide to Documents of Irish and British Interest in the Fondo Borghese," *Archivium hibernicum* 23 (1960): 1–147; 24 (1961): 31–102. Conway's articles demonstrate the range of material that can be located in the Fondo and also serve as the best location guide for records concerning the nunciatures of Spain, and the like.

G. Gualdo, "Archivi di famiglie romane nell'Archivio vaticano," *Archivio della Società romana di storia patria* 104 (1981): 147–158. A. Pasture, "Inventaire du fonds Borghèse au point de vue de l'histoire des Pays–Bas," *Bulletin de la Commission royale d'histoire de Belgique* 79 (1910): 1–217. B. Barbiche, ed., *Correspondance du nonce en France, Innocenzo del Bufalo, évêque de Camerino, 1601–1604* (Rome, 1964). I. Cloulas, ed., *Correspondance du nonce en France, Anselmo Dandino (1578–1581)* (Rome, 1970). J. Hagan, "Some Papers Relating to the Nine Years' War," *Archivium hibernicum* 2 (1913): 274–320. P. Hurtubise and R. Toupin, *Correspondance du nonce en France, Antonio Maria Salviati 1572–1578* (Rome, 1975). Z. Kristen, *Epistulae et Acta Johannis Stephani Ferrerii, 1604–1607* (Prague, 1944–). J. Lestocquoy, ed., *Correspondance des nonces en France: Dandino, Della Torre et Trivultio, 1546–1551 avec des documents relatifs a la rupture des relations diplomatiques, 1551–1552* (Rome, 1966). J. Lestocquoy, ed., *Correspondance du nonce en France: Prospero Santa Croce (1552–1554)* (Rome, 1972). M. Linhartová, *Epistulae et Acta Antonii Caetani, 1607–1611* (Prague, 1932–1940). A. O. Meyer, "Die Prager Nuntiatur des Giovanni Stefano Ferreri und die Wiener Nuntiatur des Giacomo Serra (1603–1606)," vol. 3 of *Nuntiaturberichte aus Deutschland nebst ergänzenden Actenstücken. Vierte Abteilung, siebzehntes Jahrhundert* (Berlin, 1913). H. de Schepper and G. Parker, "The Formation of Government Policy in the Catholic Netherlands under 'the Archdukes,' 1596–1621," *English Historical Review* 91 (1976): 241–254.

N. Mosconi, *La Nunziatura di Praga di Cesare Speciano, 1592–1598: Nelle carte inedite vaticane e ambrosiane* (Brescia, 1966–). Volume 2 reprints documents from SS. *Nunz. Germania* 15 and Separate Collections Family series *Fondo Borghese,* tome 109, volume 4. There is a good biography of Speciano in volume 1 and an introduction to his diplomatic work and the times.

A. Levinson, "Polnisch-Preussisches aus der Biblioteca Borghese im Vatikanischen Archiv," *Zeitschrift des westpreussischen Geschichtsvereins* 47: 1–27; 48: 85–158 [this title was noted but not verified by project staff]. Levinson's articles provide excerpts of documents concerning Prussia in the *Fondo Borghese.* There is an introduction discussing the importance of the fondo for Prussian history.

Finding Aids: ASV Indice 192 is an alphabetical subject listing of materials in the initial four series of the *Fondo Borghese.* This is the best index with which to begin to investigate the contents of this fondo. Entries point to items and include a detailed description of each item cited, including inclusive dates, type of business, selected notes (e.g., copy), and the current volume number. Indice 192 lists both personal and corporate names, subjects (e.g., chiesa, politica), offices (e.g., arcivescovo, magistrato), and geographical references (Ferrara, Francia, fiume, mare, etc.). Pasted into the beginning of Indice 192 is a specialized index that cites pontifical ceremonies in the first four series of this collection.

ASV Indice 193 is a busta-by-busta listing of materials in the initial four series of the *Fondo Borghese.* This index is dense as

the buste are generally described in detail. Entries include the current volume number, the type of material (e.g., letter, brief, avvisi) or exact title of the document, inclusive dates, pagination, and some additional notes (e.g., copy).

ASV Indice 1052 provides access to the letters in the final (unnumbered, sixth) subseries, entitled "Carte Borghese" by this index. Entries are organized by packet and list the general contents of each grouping of letters in each packet, the inclusive dates, and a brief description. These descriptions vary considerably in depth, for example, letters can be lumped together and simply designated "lettere francesi" or more adequately described as "Lettere di Teresa Borghese e Adriano Carafa suo marito, 1722–1737."

ASV Indice 199 is a subject-based index to the *Fondo Borghese,* primarily series I. This index is not very reliable. Annotations in pencil lead researchers to the current volume numbers of several items listed in Indice 199. Other references can be located by requesting an item by the volume number cited in Indice 199. Most of the volume numbers cited in Indice 199, however, do not correspond to the present volume numbers and therefore Indice 199 should be considered a last resort.

Location: Archivio Segreto Vaticano.

7.5.15.3 Instrumenta Burghesiana

[DATABASE ID: VATV346-A]
Inclusive Dates: 1322–1721.
Bulk: 178 items.
Scope: Papers related to Borghese family.
References: Fink, p. 151; Boyle, p. 98. G. Gualdo, "Archivi di famiglie romane nell'Archivio vaticano," *Archivio della Società romana di storia patria* 104 (1981): 147–158.
Finding Aids: ASV Blocchetti Indice 4 is a chronological calendar to the entire series. Entries indicate the date and place of origin of the document and provide a summary of each item. A brief one-to three-word description of the type of business or diplomatic identification of the document (bolle, breve, etc.) is often included along with a physical description (dimensions, presence of a seal, etc.).
Location: Archivio Segreto Vaticano.

7.5.16 Brancadori, Ludovico

7.5.16.1 Collezione Brancadori

[DATABASE ID: VATV314-A]
Inclusive Dates: 1760–1850 (bulk 1831–1849).
Bulk: 1 linear m. (20 vols.).
Summary: Collections of L. Brancadori relating to the Papal. States.
References: Fink, pp. 128–129; Boyle, p. 96. E. Michel, "La raccolta storica Brancadori dell'Archivio Vaticano," *Rassegna storica del Risorgimento* 23 (1936): 1428–1430.
Finding Aids: ASV Indice 1126 contains two busta-by-busta listings with detailed contents notes. The listings have some slight differences. One of these lists is more complete in the sense that it points to a greater number of documents in each busta. Finally, depending on the entry, one of these lists may treat a given document in more depth.
Location: Archivio Segreto Vaticano.

7.5.17 Canosa Family

7.5.17.1 Carte Canosa

[DATABASE ID: VATV307-A]

Inclusive Dates: 1821–1837.

Bulk: .5 linear m. (4 buste).

Scope: Canosa family is of Pesaro.

Reference: Boyle, p. 18.

Finding Aids: The Secretarius Status series *Rubricelle* is not an index to this series, but one can find out more about the Canosas by looking in the SS. *Rubricelle* during this period under Pesaro. The actual *Carte Canosa* seem to have a lot of personal requests to "Principe Canosa" in them.

Location: Archivio Segreto Vaticano.

7.5.18 Carafa Family

The Carafa family (sometimes spelled Caraffa) of Italy flourished for many centuries in Naples. Some say that the family is descended from the royal family in Polonia or from a cavalier of the house of Caracciolo who, discovering a plot against the life of Otto I (crowned emperor in 936), with his own death generously saved the life of his sovereign. Those guarding the victim of the cavalier exclaimed with affection, "O cara fe," from which, it is said, the name Carafa was given to the family. Others tell rather different tales.

The family is divided into branches, that of Bilancia and that of Carafa (of the thorns). The first is of the duchy of Andria, the other of the princes of the Belvedere. There were also Caraffa of the Serra, and to this branch belonged Cardinal Filippo, the first Carafa to be elevated to the College of Cardinals (1378). The family was celebrated for the number of cardinals, archbishops, viceroys of Naples, warriors, and scientists it produced.

Cardinal Filippo Carafa was archdeacon of the Cathedral of Bologna but died in 1389 during the pestilence in that city. Cardinal Oliviero Carafa, conte di Montalona (born in 1430), took part in four conclaves, and died in Rome in 1511. Cardinal Gianvicenzo, nephew of Oliviero, was a noble Neapolitan patrician. Giovanni Pietro (Gianpietro), the most illustrious of this distinguished Neapolitan family, was brought into close contact with the Roman Curia by his uncle, Oliviero. Gianpietro (1476–1559) was bishop of Chieti (Theate) (1504–1524) and in 1520 sat on the commission at Rome appointed to deal with the problems raised by Martin Luther. In 1524 he resigned that bishopric to found, with St. John Cajetan, the Theatine order. In 1536 he became archbishop of Naples and was named a cardinal. In 1555 he was elected pope taking the name of Paul IV.

Other members of the branches of the family include: Carlo (1517–1561), a cardinal and nephew of Paul IV; Antonio (1538–1591), a cardinal; Alfonso, cardinal librarian; Vincenzo (1585–1649), seventh general of the

Society of Jesus; Pierluigi (1581–1655), cardinal; Carlo (1611–1680), legate to Bologna; Fortunato (1631–1697); Pierluigi (1676–1755); and Francesco di Traietto (1722—1818). The precise relationship between the series listed below and the family was not determined.

7.5.18.1 Fondo Carafa

[DATABASE ID: VATV10296-A]

Inclusive Dates: ca. 1720–1934 (bulk 1720–1799).

Bulk: 5 linear m.

Organization: Subseries include: Filza (di giustificazione, di pagamenti, di div liste, etc.); —Rincontro di Banco di Santo Spirito, 1742–1750, 1 vol.; —Rincontro di Monte di Pietà, ca. 1720–1750; —Registro de mandati, ca. 1730–1750; —Hered., 1755–1799; —Saldo di conte, 1729–1736; —Libro di istromenti, ca. 1720–1790; —Archivio Monte Carafe, ca. 1850–1934, 3 buste.

Location: Archivio Segreto Vaticano.

7.5.19 Carinci, Alfonso

7.5.19.1 Fondo Carinci

[DATABASE ID: VATV322-A]

Inclusive Dates: 1420–1909.

Bulk: 91 items.

Scope: Items were donated to the ASV by Mons. Alfonso Carinci in no less than five donations. The following donations are documented in ASV Blocchetti Indici 5: *Fondo Carinci,* nos. 1–43, December 31, 1930; —nos. 44–83, October 27, 1941; —no. 84, September 3, 1941; —nos. 85 and 86, May 26, 1944.

References: Fink, p. 151; Boyle, p. 97.

Finding Aids: ASV Blocchetti Indici 5 calendars the entire collection. Entries indicate the date and place of origin of the document, a brief description of the type of business, a summary of the item, and physical details (dimensions, presence of a seal, etc.).

Location: Archivio Segreto Vaticano.

7.5.20 Carpegna Family

The family Carpegna di Gabrielli, descended in 962 from Armileone Carpineo, obtained from the emperor Ottone the donation of twenty-four castelli in Montefeltro. In 1140 the family divided into three branches: the first of which flourished well; the second died out after three generations; the third had its origin at Montefeltro from which the dukes of Urbino descended. In 1223 Raniero and Ugo bought the castle of Miratorio and in the sixteenth century Giovanni came into possession of the marchesato of Rosina, in the Valley of the Tiber.

In 1463 the family divided into two separate branches. From one of these branches two cardinals emerged, Ulderico in 1633 and Gasparo in 1670. Ulderico was appointed bishop of Gubbio in 1630, of Todi in 1638, of Albano in 1666, and Frascati in 1671 followed by Palestrina, Sabina, and Porto. He died in

1679. Gasparo di Carpegna, titular archbishop of Nicea and a datario under Clement X, collected a famous library and a museum of Christian antiquities. He became bishop of Sabina, vicar of Rome, and vice-chancellor of the church. He died in 1714. The Cardegna family gave the cardinal's papers and other materials to the Vatican Archives in 1753.

The family died out with Count Francesco Maria, who with his will of September 25, 1747, named his nephew Antonio Gabrielli, son of Laura di Carpegna and Mario marchese Gabrielli, as heir, with the obligation of assuming the title of count of Carpegna. The counts of Carpegna then became Gabrielli and inherited in 1865 the property and titles of the Falconieri princes. Dante has subtly memorialized the "greatness of soul" of an early ancestor with his reference to "Guido di Carpigna" in his La divina commedia (Purg., canto xiv, 98).

7.5.20.1 Fondo Carpegna

[DATABASE ID: VATV323-A]

Inclusive Dates: 1523–1706.

Bulk: 10 linear m. (237 numbered vols.).

Organization: Subseries can be reconstituted as indicated by the following groupings of volume numbers: 1–17, 25–26, 37–40, 55 (there are three volumes designated 55)–57, 59–65, 77–81, 83–90, 217. Varia, 1603–1701; —19–23, 30. Dataria Apostolica, 1669–1675; —27–28. Varia indulta, 1523–1681; —29. Officia Romanae Curiae, 1668–1673; —31–34, 52–54, 76, 151. Congregation. particulares Immunitat., 1630–1699; —45, 47–48. Congregation. super Regularibus, 1687–1697; —49–51, 75, 98. Congregation. particulares variae, 1680–1703; —55–55bis, 96, 205–206. Propaganda Fide, 1663–1706; —67. Januen. Profess., 1702; —69–70, 82, 224–225. Sinensibus, 1693–1697; —71. Messerani, 1692–1704; —73. Congregatio dei Riti; —74. Super Codice Leopoldi, 1702–1706; —91. Acta Consistorialia, 1655–1660; —100. Scritture per la dispensa di Malta, 1633; —114–115. Lettere di Mons. Calini, 1561–1563 (re the Council of Trent); —116, 118, 227. Spagna; —122. Chaine, 1662–1665; —128. De Electione Regis Poloniae, 1695–1698; —133. Gonzalez Synopsis; —152. S. Congregatio Indulgentiarum et Reliquiarum, 1670–1680; —154. Investiture divorsorum pontificum; —159. Lettere di raguaglio scritta ad un nobilo veneziano ecclesiastico; —160 Lettere diverse al Cav. Cassiano dal Pozzi; —163. Massime edicisioni su materie canoniche ed ecclesiastiche astratte da opera del Card. Albizzi; —164. Congregazione del Sant'Officio a Napoli, 1601–1633; —166, 173. S. Officii; —167. Patentati, 1580–1680; —168–169, 171–172. Gravami espressi nel libro dato per i christiani discendenti da sangue hebreo nel regno di Portogallo; —170. S. Congregationis universalis Inquisitionis; —193. Indulta diversa; —200. Nunziatura di Spagna, 1627–1628; —202. Legazione d'Inghilterra, 1571; —203. Breve descrizione delle 17 provincie avvero Paesi Bassi; —208. Raggioni della Sede Apostolica nel regno di Napoli; —210–216. Trattato delle regalia; —219. Compendium decretorum; —228–229. Istoria del pontificato di Alessandro VII; —230. Baviera, Congregationis Benedict., 1680–1687; —231–237. Visitatio Apostolica, Inventarii Sabina.

Vol. 65 (according to Pásztor cf. below) is related to and a possible index to the *Fondo Pio*.

Scope: These are the records and papers of Cardinal Gaspero Carpegna. They consist of originals and copies. Occasionally individual volumes in this collection contain internal indices. Vol. 233 is visitations by Paleotti. The collection was acquired by the ASV in 1753. Volumes 114, 115, and 160 were acquired by the ASV in 1761 and 1763. For detailed provenance information on these volumes see Pásztor article cited below.

References: Boyle, p. 97; Fink, p. 130; Pásztor (1970), pp. 217–218, 223–224; Pásztor (1983), pp. 199–200, 203. G. Gualdo, "Archivi di famiglie romane nell'Archivio vaticano," *Archivio della Società romana di storia patria* 104 (1981): 147–158. L. Pásztor, "Per la storia dell'Archivio Segreto Vaticano nei secoli XVII–XVIII," *Archivio della Società romana di storia patria* 91 (1968): 157–249. Pásztor discusses the provenance of three volumes now in this series and their interrelationships with other series in the ASV and the Biblioteca Apostolica Vaticana.

Finding Aids: ASV Indice 1050, compiled by Angelo Mercati (1930), provides a detailed volume-by-volume synopsis of the entire collection as it exists today. Indice 1050 proceeds volume by volume, giving the general title and then extracting information from documents contained therein. Significant persons, places, and events are listed, as well as the subject and types of documents (indultum, decreta, memoriali), and sometimes dates.

ASV Indice 140 and 141 are alphabetic subject indici to the initial eighty-five volumes of the *Fondo Carpegna*. As in all subject indici, desired items can be difficult to locate, depending on the methodology of the indexer. Indici 140 and 141 list personal names, geographic locations, types of documents and business (bulla, beneficia, dispensatio, manifesto, etc.), and the (former) tome number and folio. Folio numbers in both indici generally refer to the written folio number, not the later stamped numeral. In the beginning of Indice 140, there is a concordanza between the former tome numbers used in Indice 140 and the current volume numbers. Indice 141 provides better access to materials regarding the Roman Curia (Congregations) than 140, but documents cited in tomes "var. 20–23" could not be located by the project staff using Indice 140 and 141.

Note that there are three volumes in the *Fondo Carpegna* designated as vol. 55. They are: 55 ter., 55, and 55 bis. Indici 141 lists documents from vol. 55 ter.

Location: Archivio Segreto Vaticano.

7.5.21 Castellani, Giovanni Battista

The Castellani is an ancient and noble Roman family name, but with uncertain origin. Ludovico Monaldeschi in his diary (1327) commented on the entrance of a "Ludovico the Bavarian" (Bavaro) into Rome and called him one of the "Castellani." Shortly after, a Pietro Castellani was appointed an officer by the Roman people in the war against outlaws.

Of this family there were conservators: Castellano (1383), Cecco (1429), Mariano (1507), Corinzio (1571), and Lorenzo (1605). There is little information later than that of Amayden but the name Castellani was highly respected in Rome. The family was not included in Benedict XIV's *Urbem Romam* (Jan. 4, 1746), which lists the families officially registered as aristocracy at the time. The precise relationship of the series listed and the family was not determined.

7.5.21.1 Fondo Castellani

[DATABASE ID: VATV324-A]

Inclusive Dates: 1848–1849.

Bulk: .5 linear m. (19 items).

Organization: The series is divided into two sections: 1. Volumes I–V, registers of letters; —2. Sezioni A–N, copies of the letters registers, protocolli, and other miscellaneous materials.

Scope: Sezione C contains the actual copies of most of the letters registered in volumes I–V. The collection was acquired by the Holy See in 1908.

Reference: Boyle, p. 97.

Finding Aids: A volume entitled "Elenco degli Atti e documenti della legazione di Venezia a Roma" begins this series. This "Elenco" indexes Sezione A–N of the *Fondo Castellani*. Although the numerical order of items in Sezioni A–N has not always been maintained, the numbers indicated by the "Elenco" are still visible in the actual buste and valid.

Sezione B contains two protocol volumes that are located at the end of the collection. These provide some insight into the range of issues confronted by the legation but are not useful for locating materials within the *Fondo Castellani*.

Location: Archivio Segreto Vaticano.

7.5.22 Cerretti, Bonaventura

7.5.22.1 Carte Cerretti

[DATABASE ID: VATV40026-A]

Inclusive Dates: 1917–1932.

Bulk: 1 busta.

Note: This series was cited in Natalini et al., p. 269, but not seen by project staff in 1990.

Location: Archivio Segreto Vaticano.

7.5.23 Chigi Family

The Chigi family originiated in Siena, Italy, in the eleventh century. There, as highly successful bankers, they acquired the castle of Macereto and the title of counts dell'Ardengesca. In 1200 Ranuzio was lord of the castle; Anselmo in 1248. The latter was one of fifty Sienese nobles elected by the city to assist Emperor Frederick II in the war of Parma, in which Anselmo distiniguished himself. Chigi, the son of Anselmo, inherited from his father not only his authority and privileges but also his love of Italy, and it was his name that was preserved by the descendants. The Chigi were frequently charged with tasks for their city, especially those that brought them into contact with the papal court. They acquired nobility in 1377 and were distinguished

later by having two or perhaps three of their members beatified during the pontificate of Fabio Chigi, who became Alexander VII in 1655.

From Agostino the Elder the various branches of the family descended: Chigi-Albani; the Chigi Camollia, later the ChigiSaracini; the Chigi di Città, or of Siena; the Chigi of Rome; the Chigi of Viterbo, later the Chigi-Montoro and the Montoro-Patrizi; and the Chigi-Zondadari.

Mariano (1439–1504), the most prominent of Agostino's sons, was the founder of a banking house in Siena and on occasion was sent as an ambassador of Siena to the court of Pope Alexander VI and to the republic of Venice. He became, however, a dedicated humanist and patron of the arts. In 1473–1474 he reconstructed the palazzo on via del Casato di Sotto in Siena and in 1502 commissioned Pietro Perugino, best known as Raphael's teacher, to do the *Crocefisso con vari Santi* in the church of S. Agostino in Siena.

Of the sons of Mariano, Agostino the Magnificent (1464–1520) was the most outstandiing. As the representative of his father's banking house, he established himself in Rome, set up his own company in partnership with Francesco Tomasi, and quickly opened negotiations with the Spannocchi. From his bank in Rome he had relations with commerce throughout Europe. He financed Cesare Borgia in war, the Medici in exile, Leo X in munificence. Pope Julius II adopted Agostino and his brother Sigismondo into his own Della Rovere family. But the honors given him by this pope, as formerly by Alexander VI, were as nothing compared with the favors Leo X bestowed on him.

After the death of Agostino little was left of the riches he had accumulated. His brother Sigismondo (1479–1525) had built the Villa delle Volte and had enlarged and embellished the paternal palazzo in Siena. Mario, his son, spent a great deal of the inhrerited patrimony. From him was born Flavio (1548–1611), father of Fabio, the future Alexander VII (1655–1667).

Fabio Chigi was born in 1599 in Siena where he studied philosophy, law, and theology. In 1626 he began an ecclesiastical career in Rome. After being inquisitor (1639) and apostolic delegate to Malta, he became papal nuncio at Cologne (1639–1651), where he represented the pope at the negotiations leading to the peace of Westphalia (1648). In 1651 he became secretary of state and in 1652 was created cardinal and named bishop of Imola. In 1655, after an eighty-day conclave, he was elected pope and and duly enthroned as Alexander VII. He began his pontificate as an enemy of nepotism, even forbidding his relatives to visit Rome, but under pressure from his advisors, who feared a weakening of the papal position through the absence of the family, he began to call his relatives to Rome and to enrich them with offices, palaces, and estates.

As a theologian he held strong anti-Jansenist views. In this he was supported by Louis XIV, but political disputes arose beween them. Louis thereupon seized Avignon and Venaissin, and the pope had to accept the humiliating treaty of Pisa (1664). A friend of the Jesuits, Alexander obtained the readmission of the order to the republic of Venice. He delighted in the company of scholars and writers, enriched the Roman University and the Vatican Library, and was a generous patron of art. It was he also who commissioned Bernini to build the two semicircular colonnades to enclose the piazza of St. Peter's.

7.5.23.1 Fondo Chigi

[DATABASE ID: VATV40066-A]
Inclusive Dates: ca. 1600–1700.
Bulk: 3,916 vols.
Scope: These volumes are principally the papers of Fabio Chigi, later Alexander VII (1655–1667), though the correspondence of other members of the Chigi family, two of whom were cardinals, is included. The material chiefly concerns the political history of Europe in the seventeenth century, though some of it deals with earlier periods.
Note: The Chigi library was one of the great glories of the Chigi family. Fabio Chigi began the collection in his own palace in Rome but later, as Alexander VII, took advantage of his office to expand it. The Chigi cardinals, especially Flavio the Elder, continued to add to the collection. In 1918 the Italian government purchased the library together with the Chigi palazzo but in 1923 ceded the library to the Holy See, where it was incorporated into the Vatican Apostolic Library.
References: Boyle, p. 74; Fink, p. 102; MacFarlane, p. 90. L. P. Gachard, "La bibliotheque des princes Chigi, à Rome," *Compte rendu des séances de la Commission Royale d'Histoire,* 3d ser., 10 (1869): 219–244. M. Albert, *Nuntius Fabio Chigi und die Anfänge des Jansenismus, 1639–1651: Ein römischer Diplomat in theologischen Auseinandersetzungen* (Rome, 1988).
Finding Aids: The principal inventories for the Archivio Chigi (family papers) are all found under the numbers 191 and 389 in the Vatican Library. It is best to begin in the 389 section with vol. 7, which is a shelf listing of all the segnature in the collection. Vols. 1–34 in the 191 section provide a detailed listing of segnature 4111 to 23101 in the collection. This is the Inventario Baronci. Vol. 8 in the 389 section lists segnature 24900 to 25306 (for the most part prints and views). There is a note that "le segnature del n. 23102 al n. 24899 sono da considerarsi vuote." Vols. 9–10 in the 389 section index the correspondence in the collection by author. Vols. 1–6 in the 389 section are an inventory of the Chigi Library. There are other indexes that list the Chigi manuscript collection.
Location: Biblioteca Apostolica Vaticana.

7.5.24 Cibo Family

This noble family originated in Greece but in the fourth century migrated to Genoa, Italy, where they further expanded into a variety of locations. They became prominent in the first half of the fifteenth century

in the person of Arano who was in the service of the Aragonese of Naples and a public official in Rome (1455). His son Giovanni Battista became pope (1484–1492), taking the name Innocent VIII. Maurizio (d. 1490), brother of the pope, did not participate in public affairs. Innocenzo (1491–1500) was made a cardinal in 1513, archbishop of Turin (1516), and bishop of Marseille (1517). Giambattista (1508–1550) was also bishop of Marseille; Alderamo (1613–1700) was created a cardinal in 1645, and became a papal legate and secretary of state. Camillo (1681–1743) was appointed patriarch of Jerusalem (1718) and cardinal (1729).

Of the sons that Innocent had before taking orders, Francesghetto married Maddalena, daughter of Lorenzo de' Medici, entering in this way into the area of Medici politics. Lorenzo (1500–1549), son of Franceschetto, was commander general of the pontifical state and was for some time at the court of France. Alderamo was cardinal secretary of state (1676–1689) to Innocent IX and restored many churches, among them the ornate chapel of Santa Maria del Popolo in Rome. Camillo, named a cardinal in 1729, renounced his rights to the duchy of Massa and Carrara in favor of his brother Alderamo III in order to carry on his ecclesiastical career. Maria Teresa, niece of Camillo, was the last descendant. The precise relationship of the series listed below and the family was not determined.

7.5.24.1 Fondo Cibo

[DATABASE ID: VATV328-A]
Inclusive Dates: 1619–1737.
Bulk: 3 linear m. (26 buste).
Organization: This series has two major divisions: materials concerning the career of Cardinal Camillo Cibo: Buste 1–4, 7, 22, 23; —materials concerning the Cibo family: Buste 5, 6, 8–21, 24–26.
Busta titles include: 1. Originali de libri della vita dell'E.mo. Card. Camillo Cybo; —2. Originali del libro del Maggiordomato colle scritture autentiche in esso nominate; —3–4. Diverse e varie scritture appartenenti a diverse cariche esercitate dal Cardinal Cibo; —5. Processi civili e criminali; —6. Decisioni, sentenze, decreti, editti, fedi, esami, informazioni, deliti, inventari; —7. Scritture diverse tra le quali vene sono alcune originali e d'importanza appartenenti alla carica di maggiordomo; —8. Documenti autentici portati nel libro che descrive le differenze tra il monastero di S. Filippo e quello delle Turchine; —9. Interessi altrui; —10–11. Aiello; —12–13. Padullo; —14–18. Ferentillo; —19. Monte Luca e Cavalcata; —20. Gran Priorate di Malta; —21. Scritture diverse e testimenti; —22–23. Bolle e breve; —24–26. Lettere.
Scope: According to Boyle, this series consists of the papers of Cardinal Camillo Cibo, mainly relating to the business of the Congregation of Bishops and Regulars.
Note that there are several related collections: the *Archivio Card. Camillo Cybo* located in the Archivio di Stato di Roma; *Fondo Gesuitico,* mss. 85–104, located in the collections of the Biblioteca Nazionale Vittorio Emmanuele di Roma; and material in the Archivio di Stato di Modena.

References: Boyle, p. 97; Fink, p. 130. G. Gualdo, "Archivi di famiglie romane nell'Archivio vaticano," *Archivio della Società romana di storia patria* 104 (1981): 147–158.

Finding Aids: ASV Indice 1080, by Guidi, is an inventory of the twenty-six buste in *Fondo Cibo,* as it is currently comprised in the ASV. This inventory lists the titles of the buste and provides some contents notes. The former armaria and protocollo numbers are given alongside the current volume numbers as well as other annotations, such as if the material is indexed in Indice 214. At the end of the list of buste, Guidi has also compiled a concordanza between the the former volume numbers referred to in Indice 214 and the current buste numbers, which is essential when using Indice 214. He also lists the buste in the Archivio di Stato di Roma.

L. Sandri, "Il cardinale Camillo Cybo ed il suo archivio (1681–1743)," *Archivi (Rome),* ser. 2, 6 (1939): 63–82. Sandri's article serves a number of purposes. First, it provides a historical introduction to the life and work of Cardinal Camillo Cibo and an indication of the contents of the Cibo Archives. The article then inventories the archival materials of Cardinal Cibo and the Cibo family in the ASV, the Archivio di Stato di Roma, and the Biblioteca Nazionale Vittorio Emmanuele di Roma. Sandri's inventory for the ASV material is similar to Guidi's in ASV Indice 1080. Entries give busta titles and the current and former volume numbers.

ASV Indici 214–216 contain an inventory of the entire Cibo family archives, thus presenting researchers with tantalizing detailed descriptions of materials not in the ASV. These indici also do not include materials concerning the ecclesiastical career of Cardinal Cibo. Indice 215 inventories Armaria A from the Cibo Archives, none of which material is in the ASV. Indice 216 describes the contents of Armaria B, a small part of which, for example, select items from Protocolli IX–XVI, is contained in the ASV's *Fondo Cibo.* After locating the Protocollo number in Armaria B, refer to Indice 1080 to see what buste currently contain material from that armaria and protocollo number. Indice 214 describes the contents of Armaria C and D in the Cibo Family Archives. Only select materials from Armaria C are now in the ASV. The concordanza at the end of the busta listing in Indice 1080 leads researchers from Indice 214 to any extant materials in the current *Fondo Cibo.*

Location: Archivio Segreto Vaticano.

7.5.25 Clement XI

Giovanni Francesco Albani was born of a noble Umbrian family and educated at the Roman College, where he became sufficiently proficient in the classics that he was admitted to the exclusive Accademia founded in Rome by Queen Christina of Sweden. After studying philosophy and law, he entered the curial service and advanced rapidly at the papal court. At the age of twenty-eight he governed successively Rieti, Sabina, and Orvieto. In all his assignments he was well received.

Recalled to Rome, he became vicar of St. Peter's and on the death of Giovanni Cardinal Slusio (1687) succeeded to the position of secretary of papal briefs. In 1690 he was named cardinal and exercised great influence under Alexander VIII and Innocent XII; he drafted

the latter's constitution *Romanum decet pontificem* (Jun. 22, 1692) outlawing nepotism. Ordained to the priesthood in September 1700, he was elected pope at the forty-six-day conclave that followed, a candidate supported by the *zelanti,* that is, the cardinals who wanted a nonpolitical pope with the interests of the church at heart. His qualifications overbalanced the objection that he was only fifty-one years of age.

An ecclesiastic of austere habits, he accepted the papacy with reluctance. In spite of his administrative duties he remained a scholar throughout his life, striving always to enlarge the collections of the Vatican Library, one of the most important additions to the collection being the manuscripts (mostly Syriac) collected at his urging by the Orientalist and librarian Joseph Simeon Assemani (1687–1768). He also endeavored to preserve the cultural treasures of Rome by prohibiting the exportation of ancient objects.

The historian Christopher M. S. Johns (1993) notes: "during the first quarter of the eighteenth century Clement XI redirected papal art patronage away from the glorification of an individual pontiff, which typified the art campaigns of his predecessors, to that of the institution itself . . . [i.e.] the papacy as a spiritual and cultural entity. At the center of his policy was the restoration of several early Christian basilicas, a program deeply informed by the contemporary Paleo-Christian revival in sacred sciences and popular piety. Seeking to represent the image of Rome and the papacy to an increasingly well-educated and secularized Europe, Clement XI thus prepared the way for the creation of a museum-like city that still serves as the spiritual and cultural capital of the classical tradition."

He had less success in the political arena. Owen Chadwick notes that "more calamities happened to the papacy during this pontificate than under any pope since the reformation." Much of his reign was given over to the War of the Spanish Succession (1701–1714), which quickly demonstrated his own and the papacy's ineffectiveness.

During his pontificate Jansenism was condemned by his constitution *Vineam Domini Sabaoth* (Jul. 16, 1705), and his famous bull *Unigenitus Dei Filius* (Sept. 8, 1713). His constitution *Ex illa die* (Mar. 19, 1715) reiterated the 1704 ruling against the use by missionaries of Chinese rites on the pretext that they were primarily civic acts. This prohibition was finally lifted by Pius XII in 1939.

7.5.25.1 Fondo Albani
[DATABASE ID: VATV162-A]
Inclusive Dates: ca. 1500–1721.
Bulk: 15 linear m. (268 numbered vols.).
Organization: Subseries, volume titles, and enumeration includes: 1–13. Governo spirituale pontificio; —14. Ministri e uffici; —15. Camera Apostolica; —16. Governo economico;

—17. Distretto di Roma, Sabino, Lazio, e Galere; —18. Campagna e Maritima; —19. Patrimonio Castro, Marche; —20. Urbino, Montefeltro, e San Marino; —21–22. Bologna; —23–24. Ferrara e Ravenna; —25–28. Stato pontificio d'Italia; —29–39. Comacchio; —40. Avignone; —41–44. Parma e Piacenza; —45–56. Napoli; —57–76. Sicilia; —77. Sicilia, Malta, Sardegna, e Corsica; —78. Genova; —79. Genova, Venezia, Toscana, Mantova, Ginevra, Grigioni, e Svizzera; —80. Milano; —81–86. Savoja e Piedmonte; —87–108. Spagna; —109–112. Cardinale Alberoni; —113–114. Portogallo; —115–162. Francia (includes: Caso di Conscienza, costituzione *Vineam Dignitatis*, costituzione *Unigenitus*, costituzione *Pastoralis*); —163–168. Anglia, Hibernia, e Scozia; —169–185. Germania; —186–188. Lorena (Codice Leopoldino); —189–191. Missioni Settentrionali e Recesso d'Ildesio, 1628–1720; —192. Tratto di Riswik; —193–196. Polonia; —197. Ungheria e Transilvania; —198–205. Miscellanea di Europa, 1691–1721; —206. Lettere di Principe; —207–209. Lettere di Cardinale; —210–219. Guerra contro il Turco; —220–222. Greci, Marioni, e Rito Greco; —223. Gerusalemme, Palastina, con altri luoghi dell'Asia sogetti al Turco (Siria, Maroniti, Armenia, Armeni, Giorgia, e Persia); —224–264. Indie Orientali e Cina; —265. Affrica, America, ed Indie Occidentali; —266. Memorie del pontificio di Clem. XI; —267–268. Indice delle scritture di Papa Clement XI.

Scope: The collection is miscellaneous, but appears carefully ordered according to themes or subjects, which relate to the activities, projects, interests, or political vision of Clement XI. Most of the material dates from the late seventeenth and early eighteenth century (ca. 1690–1720). Collected here are various kinds of documents: avvisi, apostolic visits, bandi, memoriali, even entire books bound into the present volumes. *Albani* 3 is dedicated to Rome and the regulation of public mores. *Albani* 56 ff. 305–453 is a very nice collection of letters written in a lively diarist's style, demonstrating a special interest on the part of the writer in religious events, cult and ceremonies in Naples (e.g., processions of holy blood, heretics, etc.). Folios 465ff make up a small dossier regarding baptism of infidels or catecumeni. The entire volume appears to be a rich source for religious and political events in late seventeenth- and early eighteenth-century Naples. *Albani* 224–264 are dedicated to "Indie Orientali e Cina," and are followed by volumes dedicated to Africa and America. *Albani* 259 is a miscellany concerning China; 264 contains works by the famous Jesuit missionary to China, Matteo Ricci.

Note: Fondo Albani vols. 223 and 265 were transferred to the Archivio della Propaganda Fide. The *Fondo Albani* was acquired by the Holy See in 1751. The collection was formerly called, at various points in time, *Bibliotheca Albani* and *Miscellanea Clementis XI*.

References: Boyle, p. 96; Pásztor (1972), pp. 210–211.

G. Gualdo, "Archivi di famiglie romane nell'Archivio vaticano," *Archivio della Società romana di storia patria* 104 (1981): 147–158. C. Giblin, "Material Relative to Ireland in the Albani Collection of MSS in the Vatican Archives," *Irish Ecclesiastical Record*, 5th ser., 102 (1964): 389–396. C. Giblin, "Miscellaneous Papers," *Archivium hibernicum* 16 (1951): 62–98. H. Hager and S. S. Munshower, eds., *Projects and Monuments in the Period of the Roman Baroque* (University Park, Pa., 1984). C. M. S. Johns, "The Art Patronage of Pope Clement XI Albani and the Paleochristian Revival in Early

Eighteenth Century Rome" (Ph.D. diss., University of Delaware, 1985). C. M. S. Johns, *Papal Art and Cultural Politics: Rome in the Age of Clement XI* (Cambridge, 1993). T. A. Marder, "The Porto di Ripetta in Rome," *Journal of the Society of Architectural Historians* 39 (1980): 28–56. T. A. Marder, "Specchi's High Altar for the Pantheon and the Statues by Cametti and Moderati," *Burlington Magazine* 122 (1980): 30–40. G. Moroni, "Clement XI, Papa CCLIII," in *Dizionario di erudizione storico-ecclesiastica* (Venice, 1842), vol. 14, pp. 59–70.

Finding Aids: ASV Indici 143–144 (which are virtually identical to volumes 267 and 268 within the series) calendar a large percentage of the materials in volumes 1–265. Indici 143–144 proceed volume by volume providing detailed descriptions and summarizing the contents of most documents. Entries indicate the type of document (breve, viglietti, relazione, etc.), the writer and/or recipient, the subject, and frequently, the date. Whether a given item is a copy or an original is not consistently noted. Page numbers are not indicated, but documents are listed in the indici in the order in which they appear.

C. Burns, "Pope Clement XI and the British Isles: The Inventory of Fondo Albani 163–168," in *Ecclesiae Memoria: Miscellanea in onore del R.P. Josef Metzler, O.M.I., prefetto del Archivio Segreto Vaticano*, edited by W. Henkel (Rome, 1991), pp. 41–85. Burns provides a good introduction to the materials under consideration and a history of the *Fondo Albani* as a whole. He provides a short list of the volumes under consideration and then a detailed analysis of the contents of these volumes, which concern the British Isles. The analysis proceeds volume by volume. Pertinent folios are noted with the documents and a two- to three-line description of each one is given. If a researcher is interested in the history of the British Isles, this article is good for locating items in this collection.

Location: Archivio Segreto Vaticano.

7.5.26 Colette, Saint

Colette Boylet (or Boëllet, 1381–1447) was born at Corbie, France, of parents advanced in age who, convinced that she had been born through the intercession of St. Nicholas of Bari, named her Colette, the diminutive of Nicolette. Her father, Robert Boylet, was a carpenter at the abbey of Corbie; her mother, Catherine Moyen, was a religious woman who marveled at the devotion of her daughter and her secret attendance at the canonical hours at the abbey.

In 1399 both of Colette's parents died and she was placed under the guardianship of the Benedictine abbot Raoul de Roye. Feeling that she was called to the religious life, Colette successively joined the Beguines, the Benedictines, and the Urbanist Poor Clares of Moncel. Later on she took the habit of the Franciscan Third Order, but from 1402 until 1406 she lived as a recluse in Corbie near the parish church.

Convinced that she was called to reform the Poor Clares, she sought and received permission from Benedict XIII, of Avignon, to devote herself to this work. Benedict received her into the Second Order of St.

Francis, dispensed her from a novitiate, and appointed her abbess general. In 1408, with the aid of Henri de la Baume, she began the work of restoring the primitive Rule of St. Clare. She reformed many of the existing convents of the Urbanist Clares in her lifetime and established some twenty new ones. She was beatified in 1740 and canonized in 1807.

7.5.26.1 Fondo S. Coleta

[DATABASE ID: VATV341-A]

Inclusive Dates: 1442–1632.

Bulk: 22 items.

Scope: The collection seems to be French in origin, put together for the canonization of Colette. There are testimonies to miracles and to the history of her life. A few documents deal with the life of the sisters in general. Nos. 21 and 22 were formerly considered part of the Apostolic Nunciature for Venice series *Archivio della Cancelleria della Nunziatura di Venezia.* They respectively bore volume numbers 15651 and 15652.

Reference: Boyle, p. 98.

Finding Aids: ASV Blocchetti Indice 14 (second section) calendars the entire collection. Entries indicate the date and place of the document and provide a summary of each item and some physical description.

Location: Archivio Segreto Vaticano.

7.5.27 Colonna Family

The Colonna were a powerful Roman family that played an important role in papal and European politics from the Middle Ages to the twentieth century. Originally, it has been said, the family descended from the counts of Tusculum, taking their name from the castle of Colonna located on the Alban hills of Italy. Others give the Trajan Column (Colonna Traiana) as the source of the family name.

The Colonnas made their first appearance in recorded history in the person of Petrus de Columna (1064–1118?), landowner of Colonna, Monte Pazio, and claimant of Palestrina. With the destruction of Tusculum by the Romans (1191), the name of the ancient counts disappeared, but that of Colonna remained.

From the beginning, the policy of the Colonna family was anti-papal. Politically they were mostly Ghibelline and pro-imperial, maintaining toward the popes a quasi-independent attitude. They were in perpetual feud with their neighbors, especially with the rival house of Orsini. In spite of this attitude members of the family were often appointed by pontiffs to high offices in the church and state. Rarely were they without at least one representative in the College of Cardinals, and in 1417, at one of the most critical moments in the history of the church, the election to the papacy of Oddo Colonna as Martin V effectively ended the Great Schism.

Oddo Colonna (1368–1431) was born at Gennazano, studied law at Perugia, became protonotary apostolic under Urban VI, and was named a cardinal by Innocent VII (1404–1406). On November 11, 1417, he was elected pope, taking the name Martin after the saint of the day of his election. He had to wait in Florence before he could enter Rome, but in September 1420 he finally made the entrance that was so crucial for the future of the papacy and the Papal States. His first move was to address the restoration of the prestige of the papacy, which had suffered so grievously during the schism. He strove to restore papal power, maintaining troop concentrations to secure that power. Though Martin had been a supporter of the Council of Pisa (1409) and its conciliarism, he successfully opposed any overly strict limitation on papal power.

There were many learned members in the Colonna family. Giles (d. 1316) was an Augustinian who studied under St. Thomas Aquinas and became the general of the order in 1292. Agapito (d. 1380), nuncio to Emperor Charles IV and peace envoy to Castile and Portugal, was named a cardinal in 1378 along with his brother Stefano (d. 1379). Oddo (later Martin V) became a cardinal in 1405. In 1426 Martin V named his nephew Prospero a cardinal but withheld the announcement until 1430.

Vittoria Colonna, daughter of Fabrizio and Agnese di Montefeltro, was born in Castello di Marino in 1492 and died in Rome in 1547. She was noted for her gift of attracting the literati of her day, among them Michelangelo, who dedicated some of his lyrics to her.

At the age of four Vittoria was promised in marriage to Ferdinando Francesco d'Avalos, son of the marquis of Pescara, the marriage to take place when they both reached the age of seventeen; they were married in 1509. In 1525, after the death of her husband from wounds received in battle, Vittoria retired to Ischia for a short time and wrote many verses of which he was the inspiration. Soon, however, she began to take an active part in the spiritual reform movement in which many were involved at that time. Between 1541 and 1544 she was in touch with Cardinal Reginald Pole, who had a great influence on her life.

In 1501 Cesare Borgia defeated the Colonna; confiscations and exile followed. Julius II (1503–1513) tried to reconcile the Colonna family by restoring their palace and other possessions, marrying his niece to a Colonna, and bestowing on the head of the family the honor of being the "prince in attendance at the papal throne." These concessions, however, did not placate Pompeo Colonna (d. 1532), a nephew of Prospero, who had been chosen to represent the family in the church. Leo X named him a cardinal in 1517, but this did not stop Pompeo, Vespacciano, and Ascanio Colonna (d. 1559) from attempting to lay siege to the Vatican in 1526.

Marc Antonio II (d. 1584), Ascanio's son, fought the last battle against the papacy (1556). Less than thirteen years later (1570) Pius V asked him to command the papal fleet in the war against the Turks. Later when Don Juan of Austria became the general of the expedition, Marc Antonio was his lieutenant. The latter's part in the battle of Lepanto (1571) made him a hero.

The large number of Colonna cardinals named after 1562 indicates the high favor the family enjoyed with the papacy after that time. During the 462 years of enmity (1100–1562), eleven Colonna cardinals had been named; in only 241 years of good relations after 1562, twelve Colonna cardinals were named. The precise relationship between the series listed and the family was not determined.

7.5.27.1 Archivio Colonna

[DATABASE ID: VATV294-A]

Inclusive Dates: 1631–1855.

Bulk: 14 linear m. (103 numbered and 1 unnumbered busta entitled "Casa Colonna").

Scope: The collection appears to be largely different types of financial records, including some dealings with Monte di Pietà. The 1631 records are in busta 99 and list payments to "officiali" and "donne," among other groups. The latest records are copies of earlier documents by Sig. Coppi, who did research in the archivio in 1855. The final unnumbered "Casa Colonna" buste is a 1647 inventory of a guardaroba. Buste numbers 104 and 105 as cited by Boyle could not be located in 1990.

References: Fink, p. 131; Boyle, p. 95. G. Gualdo, "Archivi di famiglie romane nell'Archivio vaticano," *Archivio della Società romana di storia patria* 104 (1981): 147–158.

Location: Archivio Segreto Vaticano.

7.5.28 Confalonieri, Giovanni Battista

The ancient Milanese house of the Confalonieri had the privilege of accompanying the archbishops of Milan on their entrance into the city for their installation. There were many branches including the counts of Agliate and the counts of Colnago as well as feudal lords of other territories. The line that was registered with the Roman nobility was, however, that of Piacenza.

Giovanni Battista began his career as a canon in Velletri in the service of Cardinal Gesualdo, bishop of Velletri. From 1585 to 1592 Giovanni was secretary to Cardinal Montalto, nephew of Sixtus V, and an assistant to Fabio Biondo, both of whom he accompanied to the legation in Portugal. In 1596 he returned from Lisbon to Rome, where he remained for a while, leaving again in 1597 for Spain. There he stayed until 1600 as secretary of the nuncio, Camillo Caetani. He was still in Madrid when Cardinal Gesualdo engaged him again, but when he returned from Madrid to Rome he remained there for just a short time. In 1601, renouncing his (canonship) position in Velletri, he returned to

Rome and functioned again as an agent for various bishops from Portugal.

In two years (1609–1611) during the pontificate of Paul V, he was part-time segreteria segreta working with the nuncios of Portugal, Vienna, Graz, Colonia, and Polonia. He was also involved with matters relative to the Levante and Persia.

In August 1626 Giovanni was appointed prefect of the archives of the Castel S. Angelo, where from 1638 he had as assistant Carlo Cartari. He died in 1648.

7.5.28.1 Fondo Confalonieri

[DATABASE ID: VATV327-A]

Inclusive Dates: 1351 (copy)–1636.

Bulk: 4 linear m. (89 vols.).

Scope: These are the records of G. Confalonieri, prefect of archives of Castel S. Angelo. The collection includes copies and original documents concerning various aspects of the church. These represent a variety of congregations (Concilio, Inquisizione), nunciatures (Germania, Francia), genealogies of principi, letters to principi, and so forth. Volumes 1 and 3 were acquired by the ASV in 1761–1763 and were formerly part of a Diversorum series. Vol. 86 is an index to *Archivum Arcis*, Arm. A–M, and is similar to ASV Indice 57.

Note: Vols. 45 and 60 are available on microfilm.

References: Boyle, p. 97; Fink, p. 132; Pásztor (1970), pp. 219–220; Pásztor (1983), pp. 200–202. G. Gualdo, "Archivi di famiglie romane nell'Archivio vaticano," *Archivio della Società romana di storia patria* 104 (1981): 147–158. L. Pásztor, "Per la storia dell'Archivio Segreto Vaticano nei secoli XVII–XVIII," *Archivio della Società romana di storia patria* 91 (1968): 157–249. Pásztor discusses the provenance of two volumes of this series and their interrelationship with other series in the ASV and the Biblioteca Apostolica Vaticana.

Finding Aids: ASV Indice 1051 calendars documents that can be found in each volume of the series. Indice 1051 indicates the type of document (breve, minute), a brief synopsis of the subject or correspondents, and its original date. Whether the item is a copy is not consistently noted.

ASV Indice 194 (pp. 1–2v) briefly lists each volume in this series.

Location: Archivio Segreto Vaticano.

7.5.29 Consalvi, Ercole

Ercole Consalvi (1757–1824), cardinal and statesman, was born in Rome but came from a noble family of Toscanella. His ancestors belonged to the noble line of the Brunacci in Pisa but one of them settled in Toscanella in the seventeenth century. Ercole's grandfather, Gregorio Brunacci, inherited a large fortune on condition of taking the name and arms of the Consalvi family. In this way Gregorio Brunacci became Marchese Gregorio Consalvi with residence in Rome.

From 1771 until 1776 Consalvi attended the seminary in Frascati, where he won the admiration and protection of Henry Stuart, duke of York, who was the cardinal bishop of Frascati. Returning to Rome he entered the Accademia Ecclesiastica and became a deacon but was never ordained a priest. An intelligent man, he quickly moved into a curial career.

In 1783 Pius VI named him a private chamberlain. A number of curial positions followed; in 1792 he obtained nomination as an auditor of the Rota. After the death of Pius VI (1799) the cardinals assembled in Venice for the conclave and Consalvi was chosen as secretary by an almost unanimous vote. Cardinal Chiaramonti, elected as Pius VII (1800–1823), soon appointed Consalvi as prosecretary of state; consequently Consalvi accompanied the pope to Rome where Consalvi was definitively appointed secretary of state.

During his first years in that office Consalvi was only moderately successful in his efforts to restore the Papal States. His main achievement was the short-lived 1801 concordat with France which made possible the reestablishment of the church in France after the revolution. Although Napoleon later managed to obtain his dismissal from office and force his retirement to Reims, Consalvi was not intimidated. On Napoleon's abdication in 1814, Consalvi was immediately reappointed as secretary of state and represented the pope at the Congress of Vienna in 1815. It was there that he obtained the restoration of the Papal States, the reorganization of which occupied the last years of his life.

7.5.29.1 Fondo Consalvi

[DATABASE ID: VATV20275-A]

Inclusive Dates: ca. 1755–1823.

Bulk: 5 linear m. (37 items).

Organization: The *Fondo Consalvi* consists of items numbered 1–36. The unnumbered thirty-seventh item is an index, which is described below. Nos. 27–28, 30, and 35 are missing.

Scope: This is a collection of papers of Secretary of State Cardinal Ercole Consalvi, who was later (1824) prefect of the Congregation de Propaganda Fide. According to Kowalsky-Metzler, the collection includes documents concerning the Consalvi family history, the literary activity of the cardinal, and some of his activities in the Roman Curia. The curial records concern the Rota, the Concilio, the Tribunale della Segnatura di Giustizia, S. Offizio, Lauretana, and the Propaganda Fide. There is information about land holdings, income, and bequests, as well as information on music, poetry, agriculture, public administration, and legal proceedings (civil and criminal).

The final busta, which is not listed in the index described below, contains printed materials. The books and pamphlets are largely eighteenth- and nineteenth-century religious devotional literature. The other part of the busta is comprised of secular newspapers, principally the *Journal de l'empire,* 1813–1814. The most interesting items in this busta, however, are at the end. These are two indexes to the library of Cardinal Consalvi entitled "Indice de Libri che compongono la Libreria dell. Eminenti e Rmo. Signor Cardinal Consalvi divisa nelle Seguenti Materie, cioe = Istorici Sacri, Profani . . . Rettorici . . . Poetici Italiani e Latini . . . Teologi . . . Filosofi, Fisici, e Mattematici . . . Antiquari, Impressioni ed Ogetti di Belle Arti . . . Miscellanea, o siano Opere Risguar-

danti diverse Materie . . . Giureconsulti Canonici e Civili . . . Ascetica Sacri e Vite. de SSnti." and "Indice di libri legali, Storici, Poefici, Moralie, e Filosof esistenti nella libbreria di Mons. Illmo. e Rmo. Hercole Consalvi."

Vols. 20–24, "Piano amministrativo del Cardinal Boncompagni," about 1780–1790 (re Bologna), are now in the Archivio Segreto Vaticano. The index noted below provides a detailed description of these items.

Reference: Kowalsky-Metzler (1988), pp. 80–82.

Finding Aids: An unnumbered internal index to the *Fondo Consalvi* entitled "Descrizione delle Carte appartenenti alla Cha. Mema. dell. Emo. Sig. Cardinale Ercole Consalvi ed archiviazione fatta a diligenza e premure di Sua Eccellenza Sig. Conte Francesco Saverio Parisani, Erede fiduciario ed amministratore della Eredità del lo dato porporato" is a detailed index to buste 1–35 of the *Fondo Consalvi.* This "Descrizione" initially provides an overview of items in buste 1–35. Then, the documents in the buste are itemized, providing detailed contents information and access to the collection. The index lists page numbers in the overview and then goes on to indicate fascicoli and item numbers in the detailed description. The fascicoli and number designations in the more detailed description are the best means of locating items in the series; however, items within the buste viewed were not in the exact order indicated by the index. Parts of individual fascicoli appeared to have been moved around. A researcher should be careful. It is best to work through the *Fondo Consalvi* with the index, but researchers should be prepared to hunt through the buste to find individual items.

Location: Historical Archives of the Congregation for the Evangelization of Peoples (Propaganda Fide).

7.5.30 Degola, Eustachio

Eustachio Degola was born in Genoa in 1761 and died there in 1826. Educated at the school of Molinelli, he combined the anti-Roman aversion of Fra' Paolo Sarpi (to whom he dedicated an apologetic work) with the spirituality of Port-Royal. Ordained a priest, he was the last and most original figure of Italian Jansenism.

Among his various friendships was that of Alessandro Manzoni. Degola was an apostle for the conversion of Calvinists. After the conversion of the family Geymuller (1805–1808), he contributed to the conversion of Enrichetta Manzoni Blondel (1810) and Adele Sellon, marchesa di Cavour. In 1820 he assisted Ottavio Assarotti (1753–1829) in founding in Genoa an institute for deaf-mutes. His papers are a valuable source of information on the ecclesiastical controversies of his time.

7.5.30.1 Carte Degola

[DATABASE ID: VATV10065-A]

Inclusive Dates: 1789–1812.

Bulk: .5 linear m. (5 boxes).

Scope: Carte Degola contains two types of materials, letters to Degola, organized by correspondent, and Degola's writings. The contents of the letters and writings seem to deal primarily with spirituality.

Location: Archivio Segreto Vaticano.

7.5.31 Della Valle–Del Bufalo Family

7.5.31.1 Archivio Della Valle–Del Bufalo
[DATABASE ID: VATV296-A]
Inclusive Dates: 1327–1881.
Bulk: 20 linear m.
Organization: 285 buste and vols. Subseries include: Financial and Estate records; —Lettere diverse; —Familia (carte, eredità, etc.); —Patrimonio; —Instrumenti; —Legazione del Messico presso la Santa Sede, 1839–1853. There is also some pergamene.
Note: The collection was acquired by the ASV in 1947 and 1948. Vol. 129 is available on microfilm.
References: Boyle, p. 95; Fink, p. 134; Pásztor (1970), p. 241. G. Gualdo, "Archivi di famiglie romane nell'Archivio vaticano," *Archivio della Società romana di storia patria* 104 (1981): 147–158.
Finding Aids: ASV Indice 1075 provides a busta-by-busta listing of the entire collection. Entries include the principal type of material in each busta, inclusive dates, former volume number, and occasionally other annotations.
Della Valle–Del Bufalo no. 227 is a very detailed inventory of certain sections of this fondo, which primarily concern the property holdings of the families (e.g., tomes or buste 1–104, but largely 75–95). Busta 227 is organized by property (Castel Malnome, Palazzo S. Andrea, Canoni al Pantano, Luoghi di Monte, etc.) and then provides a chronological list of documents regarding each property. Entries give the date, a brief synopsis of the contents, sometimes writers or recipients, and the current tome (busta) and page numbers.
Location: Archivio Segreto Vaticano.

7.5.32 Dengel, Ignaz Philipp

Dengel was head of the Austrian Institute in Rome.

7.5.32.1 Carte Dengel
[DATABASE ID: VATV10264-A]
Inclusive Dates: 1567 (copy)–1928.
Bulk: 2 linear m. (17 items).
Scope: This collection contains primarily Dengel's research notes on various topics, such as the Rota. There are large quantities of notes from the nunciatures for Germany and Spain and genealogical information on the Biglia family. Notes are from collections in the ASV as well as in other archival repositories.
Reference: Natalini et al., p. 269.
Location: Archivio Segreto Vaticano.

7.5.33 Fantuzzi, Gaetano

The Fantuzzi family originated as Elefantuzzi (Elephantutius) in Bologna. Gaetano, the son of Count Giacomo Fantuzzi and Laura Gottifredi, was born in 1708 at Gualdo near Ravenna. After studies in the humanities and philosophy at the college in Modena, Gaetano studied law at the University of Pisa under the direction of Professor Averani. In 1730 he went to Rome, where he was quickly noticed for his juridical and poetic talents.

He entered the studio of Monsignor Peralta, auditor of the Spanish Rota, where he became the secretary. In 1738 he himself was named auditor of the Rota.

Benedict XIV appointed him regent of the Penitentiary and consultor to the Congregation of Rites. In 1758 Clement XIII named him a cardinal. He became prefect of the Congregation of Immunity and was a member of eight other congregations. In 1771 he was designated as protector of his native Ravenna. He participated in the conclaves of Clement XIV and Pius VI. At the time of the first he was momentarily a candidate of Cardinal Rezzonico. Upon his death in 1778 his collection of paintings was transported back to the family villa in Gualdo.

7.5.33.1 Miscellanea Fantuzzi
[DATABASE ID: VATV10265-A]
Inclusive Dates: 1643–1778.
Bulk: 2 linear m.
Organization: 46 vols. Volume numbers with contents groupings are as follows: 1. Biglietti, 1762–1777; —2. Varie memorie e biglietti, 1754–1770; —3–5. Lettere, 1759–1778; —6–10. Affari esteri, 1763–1778; —11–12. Vari stati esteri, 1763–1777; —13–14. Annona di Roma, 1764–1776; —15. Annona di Roma, Stato Att. e Pass., 1724–1749; —16. S. Cong. Firmana, 1740; —17–24. S. Cong. Immunità, 1761–1778; —25. Cong. particolari, 1751–1778; —26. Cong. varie; —27–29. Penitenzeria, 1643–1747; —33–34, 37, 39–40, 42–43. Rota Romana, ca. 1745–1768; —44. Voti particolari, memorie, 1778; —45–46. Miscellanea e varia, ca. 1759–1765. Vols. 30, 35–36, and 41 were missing in 1990.
Scope: The *Miscellanea Fantuzzi* contains materials (copies and originals) collected by Cardinal Gaetano Fantuzzi in his various ecclesiastical positions.
Location: Archivio Segreto Vaticano.

7.5.34 Farnese Family

Authorities do not agree on the origin of this noble Roman family. It is generally believed that in the eleventh or twelfth century the family took its name from its fief of Castrum Farneti, then called Farnese. Up to the fourteenth century the Farnese were small feudalists at the service of various cities, particularly Viterbo and Orvieto. The oldest sources on the family indicate that in 1154 a Prudenzio Farnese received Adrian IV into the town of Orvieto. A Pietro defended the city against Henry VI, and another Pietro went to the aid of Florence when it was threatened by Henry VII. Guido was bishop of Orvieto in 1303 and in 1309 consecrated the Duomo.

Ranuccio the elder (d. 1460) transferred the Farnese residence to Rome, where he was made senator in 1417 and given benefices by Martin V and Eugene IV. His sons entered into the Roman aristocracy through marriage. Gabriele married Isabella Orsini and Pier-Luigi married Giovannella Caetani di Sermoneta. A son of

Gabriele Ranuccio died in the battle of Fornovo. Laura, a daughter of Giulia, married Niccolò della Rovere, nephew of Julius II.

Alessandro Farnese (1468–1549) received a humanist education at Rome and Florence. After his ordination in 1519 he reorganized his private life and became identified with the reform party in the Roman Curia. He was elected pope in 1534 and took the name Paul III. A true Renaissance pope, he restored the University of Rome, enriched the Vatican Library, and exploited the talents of artists, notably Michelangelo, whom he commissioned to complete the Last Judgment in the Sistine Chapel. He made great efforts to establish the Farnese family among the powerful houses of Italy. His pontificate was marked by a number of important events. He excommunicated Henry VIII of England (1538); approved the establishment of the Society of Jesus (1540); and convened the Council of Trent (1545) for which his far-reaching report on the state of the church (constitution *Regimini militantis ecclesiae*, Sept. 29, 1540) formed the basis.

Antonio Farnese (1679–1731), duke of Parma and Piacenza, was the last of the Farnese line. On Antonio's death in 1731 his niece Elisabetta Farnese, wife of Philip V, king of Spain, obtained the agreement of England and France to the succession of her son Charles to the duchy. In 1738, however, Charles relinquished the title to Parma and Piacenza upon receiving the crown of the Two Sicilies. In 1748 Philip, younger brother of Charles, became duke of Parma and Piacenza.

7.5.34.1 Carte Farnesiane
[DATABASE ID: VATV158-A]
Inclusive Dates: 1475–1762 (bulk 1542–1569).
Bulk: 1.5 linear m. (21 vols. and 1 unnumbered busta).
Scope: MacFarlane notes that this is a fragment of the Farnese family archives, which were first established in Parma in the late sixteenth century and later transferred to Naples. This part of them came into the Vatican Archives in the late nineteenth century and consists of correspondence dealing with the diplomatic relations between the Holy See and other European powers in the sixteenth and seventeenth centuries. The series begins in essence in 1545 within the pontificate of Paul III (1534–1549) who, before his elevation, had been Cardinal Alessandro Farnese. As would be expected, the whole collection is a mine of information on the Council of Trent and the period immediately following it.
References: Fink, pp. 99–100; Boyle, pp. 73, 96; Pásztor (1970), pp. 220–221; MacFarlane, p. 89. G. Gualdo, "Archivi di famiglie romane nell'Archivio vaticano," *Archivio della Società romana di storia patria* 104 (1981): 147–158. G. Drei, *Gli archivi Farnesiani, loro formazione e vicende* (Parma, 1930) [this title was noted but not verified by project staff]. S. Ehses, "Die Carte Farnesiane des Vatikanischen Archivs," *Römische Quartalschrift für christliche Altertumskunde und für Kirchengeschichte* 28 (1914): 41–47. R. Filangieri di Candida, "Perdita e ricuperi del diplomatico Farnesiano," in *Miscellanea archivistica Angelo Mercati* (Vatican City, 1952), pp. 269–279. J.

Lestocquoy, ed., *Correspondance du nonce en France: Prospero Santa Croce (1552–1554)* (Rome, 1972).
Finding Aids: ASV Indice 1067 calendars vols. 1–19 of the *Carte Farnesiane* in great detail and provides a summary of vols. 20, 21, and 22 (the unnumbered final busta). The calendar indicates volume, document number, date, and folio number(s) and gives a brief synopsis of the business and/or writers.
Location: Archivio Segreto Vaticano.

7.5.35 Favoriti, Agostini

Agostini Favoriti (d. 1682) was secretary of the College of Cardinals (1658–1659).

7.5.35.1 Fondo Favoriti-Casoni
[DATABASE ID: VATV308-A]
Inclusive Dates: 1643–1698.
Bulk: 4.5 linear m. (35 vols. and/or buste and about 20 boxes).
Organization: Titles and volumes or buste with the current numbering in nuovi locali are: 1. Registro di lettere latine e volgari di monsignor Favoriti a diversi a nome proprio e del cardinale Chigi, dal 1660 al 1663 (i.e., 1666); —2. Idem, del 1664 al 1665; —3. Idem, dal 1666; —4. Registro di lettere latine e volgari di monsignor Favoriti a nome proprio e del cardinale Rospigliosi, dal 1667 al 1669; —5. Registro di lettere latine di monsignor Favoriti per cardinale Altieri, dal 1670 al 1675; —6. Registro di lettere latine per la segretaria di Stato di Clemente X, dal 1670 al 1676; —7. Registro di lettere latine di monsignor Favoriti e monsignor Casoni per la segretaria di Stato. dal 1678 al 1689; —8. Idem, dal 1678 al 1688; —9. Registro di lettere proprie di monsignori Favoriti e Casoni dal 1668 febraio all'ottobre 1689;—12. Registri di lettere, 1677 e 1678; —14. Minute di lettere, 1681 e 1682; —17. "Giornale" [Registri di lettere], 1684, 1687, 1688; —18. [Minute], 1698; —19. Lettere (copies and originals), 1653–1673; —20. Idem, 1676–1682; —21. Idem, 1683–1687; —22. Idem, 1677–1679; —23. Lettere (copies?), 1643–1678; —24. Idem, 1661–1690; —25. Lettere A–H (organized alphabetically, many from religious orders), ca. 1646–1685; —26. Lettere (copies and originals), 1545 (copy)–1679; —27. Lettere e minute, ca. 1664–1667; —28. Lettere L–W, ca. 1623–1670; —29. Copie lettere, memorie, and materials concerning theological questions, ca. 1650–1705; —35. Note, memoriali, etc., ca. 1661–1680.
Note: Vols. 10–11, 15–16, and 30–34 are missing.
Scope: See Pásztor article for information on the careers of Favoriti and Casoni. Casoni inherited the position and the archives of Favoriti and it was turned over to the ASV after Casoni's death. The archives was acquired by the ASV in 1761–1763. For a detailed account of the provenance see Pásztor below. This series is also referred to as *Carte Favoriti-Casoni.*
Reference: Boyle, p. 96.
Finding Aids: L. Pásztor, "Per la storia dell'Archivio Segreto Vaticano nei secoli XVII–XVIII," *Archivio della Società romana di storia patria* 91 (1968): 157–249. The inventory, reproduced above, of items 1–9 appears on page 176 or can be extracted from pages 223, 225–226, 228, 230, and 233. This is an accurate albeit brief listing of these volumes. The description of vols. 10–35 in the footnote on pages 169–170 provides a general overview of the materials that may be found in the *Fondo Favoriti-Casoni*, but is not an accurate inventory. Not

only have the volume numbers been changed, but the contents of the buste have been reorganized (cf. above the contents of buste 12, 14, 17, 23).

The ASV Indici to the Secretarius Status series *Lettere diverse*, which is available behind the desk in the main ASV reading room contains a partial listing of *Fondo Favoriti-Casoni* in its former identification as part of the *Lettere diverse*. This listing is not as complete as that provided above and does not indicate the current volume numbers. This is not an official finding aid and must be used in consultation with the ASV staff.

Location: Archivio Segreto Vatican.

7.5.36 Felix V (Antipope)

Amadeus VIII of Savoy was born at Chambéry in 1383 and died at Geneva in 1451. He was the son of Amadeus VII, whom he succeeded as count of Savoy in 1391. He was created duke of Savoy in 1416. In 1434, deeply affected by the deaths of his wife (1422) and eldest son (1431), he withdrew to the chateau of Ripaille, where he founded and governed an order of knights-hermits of St. Maurice. After the deposition of Eugene IV at the Council of Basel in 1439, Amadeus VIII was elected in his place. Since the election was carried out by one cardinal and thirty-two electors nominated by a commission, it was considered irregular. Since Amadeus was a deeply spiritual person he accepted this election with reservations. He abdicated as duke on January 6, 1440, and after ordination and consecration was crowned as Felix V at Basel on June 24 of that year.

He failed to receive the support of those who had elected him and ultimately found the position burdensome. After reaching an accomodation with the legitimately elected pope, Nicholas V, Amadeus solemnly abdicated in 1449 as the last of the antipopes. Nicholas appointed him cardinal bishop of Santa Sabina with a substantial pension.

7.5.36.1 Bollario di Felice V

[DATABASE ID: VATV10212-A]

Inclusive Dates: 1440–1448(copies).

Bulk: .25 linear m. (6 buste and vols.).

Organization: Buste/volumes are entitled: 1. "Bollario di Felice V–Amedeo VIII"; —2. "Bolle di Felice V per la diocesi di Torino"; —3. "Dal bollario di Felice V pp.: Bolle riguardanti l'Italia"; —4. "Dal bollario di Felice V pp.: Bolle riguardante l'Italia"; —5. "Registro del bollario di pp. Felice V"; —6. "Bollario di Felice V: Registro cronologico."

Scope: These are transcriptions of eight volumes of the bulls of Felix V in the Archivio di Stato di Torino. Rev. Angelo Fascano transcribed the bulls between 1928 and 1932.

The series title of the originals is *Bollario di Felice V. Archivio di Stato di Torino*, located in the Archivio di Corte, Museo Storico, Turin, Italy.

Finding Aids: ASV Indice 1111 (II) provides volume-by-volume descriptions of these transcriptions and indicates the

manner in which they relate to the original volumes. Some information on the original manuscripts is also included.

This material is usually cited as *Bull. Felice V*.

Location: Archivio Segreto Vaticano.

7.5.37 Filonardi Family

Ennio Filonardi, from Bauco of Veruli in Campagna, was an auditor of the Rota, datario of Paul III, and cardinal. These positions place his residence in Rome around the year 1530, in the region of S. Eustachio where the Filonardi continued to live. He was also bishop of Forli, governor of Imola, vice legate of Bologna, then nuncio in Switzerland. Paul III named him a cardinal in 1536. He became bishop of Alba and of Sorrento and died in 1549 at the age of eighty-three.

Filippo Filonardi, bishop of Aquino and a nephew of Cardinal Ennio, was created a cardinal in 1611. He died in 1619. The precise relationship of the series listed below to this family was not determined.

7.5.37.1 Casa Filonardi

[DATABASE ID: VATV20483-A]

Inclusive Dates: Unknown.

Bulk: 27 scatole.

Location: Historical Archives of the Congregation for the Evangelization of Peoples, or Propaganda Fide.

7.5.38 Finy, Francesco

7.5.38.1 Fondo Finy

[DATABASE ID: VATV330-A]

Inclusive Dates: 1231(copy)–1740 (bulk 1661–1729).

Bulk: 1 linear m. (36 vols.).

Organization: Subseries and volume numbers are as follows: 1, 6, 26. Ordinis praedicatorum; —2, 16, 23. De Regularibus; —3. Ecclesiae Lipontinae; —4. Orazioni e componimenti; —5. Cardinalibus; —7. Episcopis; —8. Epistol. pastoral; —9. Erudizione profane; —10. De Sanctis. et Viris Illustr.; —11. Politica seculare; —12, 19. Sacris ritibus; —13. M.Lercari; —14. Dogmatica; —15. Cocionator; —17. De Scriptor. et Censur. Libr.; —18. De Conf. ecclesiae et altare; —20. Erud. ecclesiae; —21. Theolog. moral.; —22,25. Iuris canonici; —24. Cler. ordin.; —27, 32. Ecclesiae Caesenaten; —28. Concil. Rom.; —29. Indulgentiae; —30. Constitut. Apostolicae; —31. Imolen.; —33. Caesenat. censur.; —34. Mons. Orario Fortunato, vescovadi di Nardo, in Lib. I, II, III, Re et in Cantic.; —35. M. L. Crispini, Lettere; —36. Cardinalibus, conclavi, et Card. Coscia.

Scope: This collection contains original documents as well as copies. The collection was donated to Pius XI by the chapter of the Cathedral in Gravina in Puglia in 1929.

References: Fink, p. 135; Boyle, p. 97; Pásztor (1983), p. 202.

Finding Aids: ASV Indice 1053 calendars most of the *Fondo Finy*. The detailed entries include indications of the volume and folio, a brief synopsis of the business and correspondents/writer(s), and the date. The *Fondo Finy* is organized by large subject categories, as noted in the organization section above. However, researchers looking for materials on the Dominicans should begin with the Ordinis Praedicatorum and de Regularibus volumes, but should not end their search with these tomes. For example, a careful reading of the calendared entries in Indice 1053 for other volumes will yield more information on the Dominicans in other locations.

Location: Archivio Segreto Vaticano.

7.5.39 Garampi, Giuseppe

Giuseppe Garampi (1725–1792) was born in Rimini of a noble family; early in life, inspired by the work of Ludovico Muratori, he developed a passion for historical studies. In Rome he belonged to the Academy of Church History founded by Benedict XIV, who assigned him to the papal archives in 1749 (the year of his ordination) and appointed him prefect in 1751. During these years Garampi began his vast and valuable *Schedario Garampi* (listed and described among the series descriptions that follow), an incomplete project comprising 124 volumes that he and his assistants compiled from the Vatican Archives between 1751 and 1772.

From 1761 to 1762 he traveled through Germany, Switzerland, Holland, and France. He was nuncio to Germany for Clement XIII and to Poland for Clement XIV. Wherever he was he studied the history of the church, worked for the improvement of religion and scholarship, and acquired books for his library. He built up a magnificent collection of his own that was later divided between the Vatican and the Gambalunga Library in Rimini. He was raised to the cardinalate in 1785, was archbishop of Montefiascone and also of Corneto (now Tarquinia), and served as the director of the German College in Rome.

7.5.39.1 Collectanea miscellanea
[DATABASE ID: VATV10266-A]
Inclusive Dates: 471 (copy)–1703.
Bulk: .5 linear m.
Organization: 8 pacchi that contain positiones numbered 1–673 (3. contains nos. 266–357; —8. contains nos. 621–673).
Finding Aids: ASV Blocchetti Indici 15–16 calendar Garampi's entire *Collectanea miscellanea* numerically. Entries indicate the item number, original date and place, type of document, synopsis of the business, and sometimes the location of the original or where the item has been published.

ASV Blocchetti Indici 17–18 are photocopies of Blocchetti Indici 15–16, but are organized chronologically. Pencil annotations in Blocchetti Indici 15–16 are not legible in Blocchetti Indici 17–18, so Blocchetti Indici 15–16 should be consulted for the most complete information.

Location: Archivio Segreto Vaticano.

7.5.39.2 Collezione Garampi
[DATABASE ID: VATV10267-A]
Inclusive Dates: 686(copy)–1748.
Bulk: 3 linear m. (26 numbered boxes).
Organization: Subseries (box titles) are as follows: 1. Disertat. varie; —2. Excerpta ex chartis Archivorum Urbis; —3.

Chronica. Anconit. Civ. Castelli. Favent.o gall. Soract. Tuelert. Viterb. Urbevet.; —4. Studia Gen. Curria Rom et Urbis; —5. Ursinorum genealogia; —7. Croniche di Broglio; —8, 9, 13, 16, 19, 21, 23–26. Codex diplomatic.; —11. Acta SS Cyri et Ioh Callixti PP II Opera Descript. Terre S. Soltanien Epi. Relatio; —12. Disertat et notitiae ex. Arch. Pontif.; —15. Constitut. ex Saluta Ecclarum.; —17. Excerpta ex. Biblioth. Urbis; —18. Apendix ad Cod. Diplom.; —22. Excerpta ex codd MSS et Archivis Pontificiis. Boxes 6, 10, 14, and 18 are missing.

Scope: Garampi often cites the original place where a copied document was found, such as the Biblioteca Chigi, now located in the BAV. The contents of the boxes appear to be unorganized. Many of the items in the boxes are just being used as file dividers for additional *Schedario Garampi* pieces of paper.

Location: Archivio Segreto Vaticano.

7.5.39.3 Cronologico
[DATABASE ID: VATV10248-A]
Inclusive Dates: 1550–1721.
Bulk: 1 linear m. (17 vols.).
Scope: This collection forms ASV Indici 168–184 in the ASV Sala d'Indici and should not be confused with the Cronologico section of the *Schedario Garampi*, described as a separate series among the series of Garampi listed in this guide. These index primarily later and different sources than the *Schedario*, primarily secondary antiquarian sources, but also some primary sources, such as the apostolic visits, selected *Armaria* series, and *Registra Vaticana*.
Reference: Pásztor (1970), pp. 12–13.
Location: Archivio Segreto Vaticano.

7.5.39.4 Fondo Garampi
[DATABASE ID: VATV332-A]
Inclusive Dates: ca. 814 (copy)–1797 (bulk 1666–1791).
Bulk: 18 linear m.
Organization: 305 vols., followed by one unnumbered busta, miscellaneous buste numbered 1–29, and 17 unnumbered buste.
Scope: According to Boyle, this is a collection of documents of, or copied by, Garampi. This series includes Adversariorum (vols. 134–138), research notes of Garampi, and a limited number of original documents. Vols. 37–39 deal with the Capitolo di S. Pietro and the Reverenda Fabbrica.
Note: Vols. 7, 23, 52, and Add. 55–56 are available on microfilm.
References: Fink, pp. 135–136; Boyle, p. 97.
Finding Aids: ASV Indice 157 lists vols. 1–305 of the *Fondo Garampi* and provides detailed access to vols. 1–264. Entries for the first 264 vols. calendar select items in each busta and indicate the type of document (bolle, lettere in cifre, diario, inventario, etc.), a brief synopsis of the subject, the writer and recipient (if applicable), and the date. Whether the item is an original or a copy is not consistently noted.

ASV Indice 1068 is a register of letters in vols. 272–300 of the *Fondo Garampi*. Entries list writer, recipient, date and place the letter was written, volume, and folio. At the end of Indice 1068 there is another list that indicates which buste or parts of buste in *Fondo Garampi* have been lost.

ASV Indice 231, "Rubricella delli Tomi tre di Minute di

Brevi a Principi di Paolo V e Gregorio XV," contains a note by Mercati that "questo volume fu trovato dall' Emo. Garampi nello spoglio delle sue carte rimasse alla cifra e fra consegnato . . . 1786." This is not an index to any apparent series and there is no other indication that it came from this series. However its nature is like many of the volumes found here. The book is organized by type of business.

P. Carucci and R. Santoro, eds., "Le fonti archivistiche," vol. 1 of *La Rivoluzione Francese (1787–1799): Repertorio delle fonti archivistiche e delle fonti a stampa conservate in Italia e nella Città del Vaticano*, (Rome, 1991). This work identifies series in the ASV that pertain to the French Revolution found in *Fondo Garampi* (vols. 95, 154, 159, 179, 214, and 264). Entries list the volume number, identify the total number of folios in a volume, provide the formal or a supplied title, summarize the materials in the volume concerning the French Revolution, and note the inclusive dates. At times, individual items are identified and described.
Location: Archivio Segreto Vaticano.

7.5.39.5 Schedario Garampi
[DATABASE ID: VATV10002-A]
Inclusive Dates: 1584–1908.
Bulk: 14 linear m. (135 vols.).
Scope: This great source forms ASV Indici 158–167, 445–556, 670–681 and is located in the ASV Sala degli Indici. Major divisions of the series include: Indici 538–549, [Registro cronologico]; —Indici 158–167, Indice alfabetico delle principali materie contenute nel registro cronologico delle Miscellanee dell'Archivio Segreto Vaticano; —Indici 445–537, 550–556, 670–681, [Registro alfabetico].

Boyle notes that this index was compiled by Garampi when he was serving as prefect of the Vatican Archives from 1751 to 1772. During this time he and his assistants assembled citations to individual documents on more than one and a half million slips of paper, which were then pasted into the large volumes that constitute the series. As Boyle points out, this series is sometimes difficult to use because Garampi used his own set of sigla. Users of the *Schedario* should consult A. Mercati's work, "Schedario Garampi, Registri Vaticani, Registri Lateranensi, Rationes Camerae, Inventario del Fondo Concistoriale," vol. 1 of *Sussidi per la consultazione dell'Archivio Vaticano* (Rome, 1926). Mercati, in that work, attempts to make sense of the older sigla. Boyle recommends that users consult the copy of Mercati's work that is on the shelves of the ASV Sala degli Indici, because that copy has later additional notes by Mercati penciled in the margins.

Major divisions of the ASV indici that constitute the Registro alfabetico include: Indici 445–474, Benefici (with benefices listed in alphabetical order); —Indici 475–511, Vescovi (a chronological listing then arranged by diocese; within each diocese bishops are listed alphabetically); —Indici 512–534, Miscellanea I (alphabetical by diocese); —Indici 535–537, Abbates (alphabetical by diocese and monastery); —Indici 538–549, Cronologico (chronological indexes); —Indice 550, Papi (alphabetical); —Indice 551, Cardinali (alphabetical); —Indici 552–554, Uffici (curial officials); —Indici 554–556, Chiese di Roma (alphabetical order by name);—Indici 670–681, Miscellanea II (alphabetical).
References: Pásztor (1970), pp. 11–13; Boyle, pp. 33–34.
Location: Archivio Segreto Vaticano.

7.5.40 Garroni, Ignazio

7.5.40.1 Carte Garroni
[DATABASE ID: VATV40027-A]
Inclusive Dates: 1900–1905.
Bulk: 1 buste.
Note: This series was cited in Natalini et al., p. 269, but not seen by project staff in 1990.
Location: Archivio Segreto Vaticano.

7.5.41 Gioazzini, Filippo

7.5.41.1 Archivio legale Gioazzini
[DATABASE ID: VATV10269-A]
Inclusive Dates: 1691(copy)–1883.
Bulk: 13 linear m. (883 items).
Scope: Copies (printed and written) and originals of various legal decisions and positions of interest to Gioazzini. There appears to be some of Gioazzini's own work in the collection also.
Reference: Fink, p. 136.
Location: Archivio Segreto Vaticano.

7.5.42 Gramiccia, Pietro

7.5.42.1 Fondo e collezione Gramiccia-Pagliucchi
[DATABASE ID: VATV10270-A]
Inclusive Dates: ca. 1820–1856.
Bulk: .5 linear m. (17 buste).
Scope: This collection was donated to the ASV in 1936. See the listing for *Carte Pagliuchi* among the listing of family collections.
Location: Archivio Segreto Vaticano.

7.5.43 Gregory XVI

Bartolomeo Alberto Cappellari was born of a noble family at Belluno (Lombardy) in 1765. At the age of eighteen he joined the Camaldolese order (1783), entering the Monastery of S. Michele in Murano and taking the name Mauro. After ordination in 1787 he became professor of philosophy and science for five years, then went to Rome (1795) to assist the order's procurator general. He was elected abbot of the Monastery of S. Gregorio al Celio (1805) and procurator general of the Camaldolese order (1807). Forced to leave Rome after Pius VII's arrest by Napoleon, he taught at Murano and Padua but returned to Rome in 1814. He was named vicar-general of the Camaldolese in 1823 and cardinal in 1826. Professor of theology, consultor to several Roman congregations, and prefect of the Congregation for the Propagation of the Faith were but a few of the positions he held. In March 1830 he helped draft the address of Pius VIII to the German bishops on mixed marriages. In 1830, in a conclave in which Spain exercised its veto to exclude Cardinal Giustiniani, he was elected pope, taking the name Gregory XVI.

In his opposition to naturalistic liberalism, Gregory failed to dissociate it sufficiently from political liberalism and therefore was in the position of trying to block an inevitable development. He disapproved of the separation of church and state, worked to suppress all revolutionary movements, and urged support for monarchical regimes. His *Mirari vos* (Aug. 15, 1832), forerunner of the Syllabus of Errors of Pius IX (1864), was provoked by the political situation in Italy, the increasing influence of Lamennais among Catholic liberals, and the continued conservative presence of Metternich.

Personally interested in rebuilding the missions, he increased missionary personnel. Gregory eliminated the patronato and padroado privilege of Spain and Portugal, set up guidelines for missionaries, encouraged the development of native clergy, called on religious orders to staff the missions, and condemned slavery. He named residential bishops for Latin America and despite Spanish opposition favored national emancipation of the Latin American republics.

He opened the Museum of Etruscan Antiquities and the Egyptian Museum in the Vatican and continued the reconstruction of the the the Basilica of St. Peter. His private secretary, Gaetano Moroni, began at this time his still useful *Dizionario di erudizione storico-ecclesiastica* (1840–1861, 103 vols. in 53 actual vols., plus 6 index vols.), which is especially good for coverage of this period. Gregory died suddenly in 1846.

7.5.43.1 Archivio particolare
[DATABASE ID: VATV10197-A]
Inclusive Dates: 1831–1845.
Bulk: 2.5 linear m. (24 numbered boxes and buste).
Organization: Subseries include: Prefettura delle acque e strade; —Congregazione delle revisione; —Bolletini sanitari; —Rivoluzione del 1831.
Scope: Material in this series relate primarily to the Papal States.
Citation: This series is usually cited as *Gregorio XVI. Archivio particolari.*
Location: Archivio Segreto Vaticano.

7.5.44 Kanzler, Hermann

Hermann Kanzler (1822–1888), German general of the pontifical army, was born in Weingarten, Baden. He did his licentiate studies at Mannheim and then entered the military college of Karlsruhe. In 1841, however, he renounced his military career and dedicated himself to the study of languages and travel. In 1845 he placed himself at the service of the pope and offered to help organize a pontifical army. In the same year he was admitted to service of the Holy See in Bologna. Prepared in military science and equipped with good organizational skills, he, along with his regiment, earned a special commendation from General Durando. Kanzler was promoted to lieutenant in 1849 and to captain a few

months later. By 1859 he had been promoted to the rank of colonel; six years later he was made a general.

7.5.44.1 Carte Kanzler-Vannutelli
[DATABASE ID: VATV309-A]
Inclusive Dates: ca. 1839–1872.
Bulk: 8 linear m. (about 75 buste).
Organization: Collezione A, numbered 1–61; —Collezione B, numbered I–XV.
Scope: The collection is unorganized and the series do not appear to be very distinct. The Protocolli registers at the end are really "letterbooks" and may be the best place to begin research.
References: Fink, pp. 136–137; Boyle, p. 96.
Location: Archivio Segreto Vaticano.

7.5.45 Leo XIII

See Secretariatus Status series *Miscellanea Leo XIII*, [18—]–[19—], and *Spogli di Leone XIII*, 1878–1903.

7.5.46 Macchi, Vincenzo

Vincenzo Macchi (1770–1860) was born at Capodimonte in the diocese of Montefiasconi and died at Rome. He was assigned to the nunciature for Lisbon when the French invaded Portugal in 1808, but Macchi, following the court, left for Brazil. Between 1808 and 1817 Macchi was internuncio and apostolic delegate in Portugal. In 1818 he was appointed nuncio to Switzerland and in 1819 transferred to Paris, where he remained until 1827. He was named a cardinal in 1826. When he returned from France he assumed the tasks of legate to Ravenna (1828–1830), president of the Congregation for the Revision of Accounts and Public Administration (1832–1835), prefect of the Congregation of the Council, and many other positions within the Roman Curia.

Pius IX (1846–1878) in the first years of his pontificate named Vincenzo a member of a commission to examine certain affairs of state. On the death of Cardinal Micara (1847) he was made bishop of Ostia and Velletri and deacon of the College of Cardinals. He interested himself in the restoration of a famous castle, restored the cathedral, and made other improvements in his diocese. His sepulcher is at the Church of SS. Giovanni e Paolo.

7.5.46.1 Carte Macchi
[DATABASE ID: VATV310-A]
Inclusive Dates: 1742–1877 (bulk 1825–1860).
Bulk: 3.5 linear m. (21 boxes and buste).
Organization: Materials within the containers are numbered as posizioni 1–75.
Scope: This collection was acquired by the ASV in 1919. Eight volumes were transferred to the *Archivio della Nun-*

ziatura in Francia (as listed in the section on nunciatures in this guide) and are currently vols. 1–8 in that series.

References: Pásztor (1970), pp. 221–222; Fink, p. 137; Boyle, p. 96. G. Gualdo, "Archivi di famiglie romane nell'Archivio vaticano," *Archivio della Società romana di storia patria* 104 (1981): 147–158.

Finding Aids: O. Cavalleri, *Le Carte Macchi dell'Archivio segreto vaticano: Inventario* (Vatican City, 1979). This detailed book calendars the entire *Carte Macchi* collection as well as the initial eight volumes of the *Archivio della Nunziatura in Francia* (formerly part of the *Carte Macchi*), for which Macchi served as nuncio. This calendar provides a brief introduction to the series and then proceeds volume by volume, explicating each document. Entries include the current volume number and foliation, the title of the volume, and inclusive dates of the volume. The entries then list each document in the volume, current folio numbers, type of document (lettera, bolle, breve, conto, inventario, relazioni, etc.), a synopsis of the business, correspondents (if applicable), and the date.

Location: Archivio Segreto Vaticano.

7.5.47 Mazio, Raffaele

7.5.47.1 Carte Mazio
[DATABASE ID: VATV10271-A]
Inclusive Dates: 1803–1828.
Bulk: 2 linear m. (58 buste).
Organization: Subseries, titles, and busta numbers are: 1. Germania in generale, 1814–1817; —2–5. Austria, 1806–1809, 1816–1824; —6–10. Baviera, 1806–1909, 1816–1824; —11–13. Wuerttemberg, 1807–1809, 1815–1818; —14. Hannover, 1815–1825; —15. Sassonia, 1809, 1821; —16–17. Ratisbona e Costanza, 1803–1808; 1816–1825; —18. Prussia, 1817–1825; —19–20. Principi protestanti uniti della Confederazione Germanica, 1814–1823; —22. Svizzera, 1808; 1818–1825; —23. Olanda, 1816–1817; —24–33. Belgio, 1814–1827; —Inghilterra, 1814–1828; —34. Francia, 1801, 1805, 1815–1818; —35–39. Spagna, 1816–1822; —40. Portogallo, 1816–1825; —41. America (del sud), 1819–1824; —42–43. Piemonte, 1816–1828; —44. Napoli, 1816–1828; —45. Parma, 1816–1818; —46. Firenze, 1824–1825; —47–54. Lucca, 1817–1826; —55. Miscellanea, 1805–1809, 1815–1826; —56. Appendice, 1806, 1816–1828(?); —57–58. Duplicati.
Scope: The introduction to Indice 1137 by Lajos Pásztor is very good for scope and contents information. Pásztor also wrote an article on the collection that expands on his work in Indice 1137. This makes the article a better source for information on the contents of the series. The article is cited among the finding aids below.
Carte Mazio 55 (Misc. 2,10) was formerly identified as Secretariatus Epistolae ad Principes et Optimates series *Epistolae ad principes* 231 and Secretariatus Status series *Epoca napoleonica: Francia* 21/31, respectively. *Carte Mazio* 34 (Francia 2,7,5,6) was formerly identified as *Epoca napoleonica: Francia* 1/8, 17/19, 18/12, 18/17, respectively. *Carte Mazio* 55 (Misc. 1,4) was formerly identified as Secretariatus Status series *Epoca napoleonica: Italia* 1/6 and 18, respectively.
Note: Parts 26–28 and 33 are available on microfilm.
Reference: L. Pásztor, "La Congregazione degli affari eccle-

siastici straordinari tra il 1814 e il 1850," *Archivum historiae pontificiae* 6 (1968): 191–318.

Finding Aids: ASV Indice 1137 provides a general introduction to the series and a detailed busta-by-busta listing of the entire collection. Entries proceed document by document (position by position) and indicate the title of each document and inclusive dates. Indice 1137 contains frequent annotations, particularly regarding the provenance of some parts of the collection.

L. Pásztor, "Il card. Raffaele Mazio e il suo archivio," in *Studi in onore di Leopoldo Sandri* (Rome, 1983), pp. 707–734. Pásztor's article is a more amplified version of his Indice 1137. In addition to reproducing Indice 1137, Pásztor has added biographical information on Cardinal Raffaele Mazio, bibliographic references, and other useful notes for understanding the collection.

Location: Archivio Segreto Vaticano.

7.5.48 Mazzei, Gennaro

7.5.48.1 Archivio Mazzei
[DATABASE ID: VATV10272-A]
Inclusive Dates: 1808–1842.
Bulk: 2 linear m. (18 buste).
Reference: Fink, p. 137.
Location: Archivio Segreto Vaticano.

7.5.49 Mencacci, Paolo

Publicist and fervent Catholic, Paolo Mencacci (1828–1897) was the founder of the Circolo di S. Pietro and of Gioventi Cattolica. He was also the author of a number of books on the papacy and related topics.

7.5.49.1 Fondo Mencacci
[DATABASE ID: VATV335-A]
Inclusive Dates: 1792–1870.
Bulk: .3 linear m. (7 buste).
Scope: The collection consists primarily of letters of P. Mencacci relating especially to last years of the Papal States and to Pius VII and Napoleon.
References: Fink, p. 137; Boyle, p. 97. E. Michel, "La raccolta storica Mencacci dell'Archivio Vaticano," *Rassegna storica del Risorgimento* 22.2 (1935): 389–395.
Finding Aids: ASV Indice 1126 provides two virtually identical copies of a synopsis of the materials contained in each busta. Each copy of the synopsis is at the end of an index to the *Collezione Brancadori* and can be difficult to locate as the pages are unnumbered.
Location: Archivio Segreto Vaticano.

7.5.50 Odescalchi di Palo Family

7.5.50.1 Carte Odescalchi di Palo
[DATABASE ID: VATV40028-A]
Inclusive Dates: [18—]–[18—].
Bulk: 4 buste.
Note: This series was cited in Natalini et al., p. 269, but not seen by project staff in 1990.
Location: Archivio Segreto Vaticano.

7.5.51 Origo Family

The Origo family were of the nobility of Trevi. The relationship of this collection to specific family members was not determined.

7.5.51.1 Fondo Origo

[DATABASE ID: VATV10273-A]
Inclusive Dates: ca. 1574–1918.
Bulk: 8 linear m.
Organization: Although some buste are numbered, there is no semblance of numerical order to the fondo.
Scope: This is a curious collection. The second buste (marked no. 84) contains what appear to be bulls and/or briefs. Halfway through the collection no. 187 (numbers do not mean anything) is "cedere dell Sr. Agostino Maria Gavoti."
Reference: Fink, pp. 138–139.
Location: Archivio Segreto Vaticano.

7.5.52 Pagliuchi, Pio

7.5.52.1 Carte Pagliuchi

[DATABASE ID: VATV40029-A]
Inclusive Dates: 1824–1860.
Bulk: 4 buste.
Note: This series was cited in Natalini et al., p. 269, but not seen by project staff in 1990. See *Fondo e collezione Gramiccia-Pagliucchi* among the listing of family collections.
Location: Archivio Segreto Vaticano.

7.5.53 Parisani, Torquato

Torquato Parisani (or Parisiani), S.J., a missionary, was born in Acoli Piceno in 1612 and died in 1688. He entered the Society of Jesus in 1640 and was a fellow disciple of Paolo Segneri, the famous Jesuit preacher. Torquato obtained permission to go to the missions, sailed from Lisbon, traveled through India (1644), and disembarked at Goa. In 1647 his superiors assigned him to Ethiopia but unable to penetrate the country because of religious persecution, he remained on the island of Suakin (Sudan) for several years. In 1649 he returned to Goa, where he taught philosophy and theology. He died in 1688. The precise relationship between this series and Father Parisani was not determined.

7.5.53.1 Parisiani

[DATABASE ID: VATV20536-A]
Inclusive Dates: Not determined.
Bulk: Extent undetermined.
Location: Historical Archives of the Congregation for the Evangelization of Peoples, or Propaganda Fide.

7.5.54 Pasolini-Zanelli Family

7.5.54.1 Carte Pasolini-Zanelli

[DATABASE ID: VATV336-A]
Inclusive Dates: 1786–1814.
Bulk: 1 linear m. (23 buste).

Scope: According to Boyle these are "Papers relating to family of Leo XII," but they seem to be more appropriately characterized as related to the secretary of state. Germano Gualdo says that they came from the contessa Silvia Baroni, widow of Pasolini-Zanelli. She was a descendent of Tiberio Troni, a secretary of Cardinal Annibale Della Genga (later Leo XII) and an uditore di nunziatura. In 1920 the contessa donated the material of T. Troni, containing the spogli of Cardinal Della Genga to the ASV. The collection was acquired by the ASV in 1920 (carte dell'eredità Troni e spoglia del card. Della Genga) and 1931. Note that Boyle refers to this series as *Fondo Pasolini-Zanelli*.
References: Boyle, p. 98; Fink, p. 139. G. Gualdo, "Archivi di famiglie romane nell'Archivio vaticano," *Archivio della Società romana di storia patria* 104 (1981): 147–158.
Finding Aids: Indice 1088 provides a detailed busta-by-busta listing of the entire series. Entries summarize the major business of each busta, indicate the writer and recipient, if known, and list inclusive dates.
Location: Archivio Segreto Vaticano.

7.5.55 Patrizi Family

The original Patrizi family has been extinct since 1736, but the name has been carried on twice through the maternal side.

Cardinal Costantino Patrizi (1798–1876) was born at Siena, the son of Giovanni, who was a hereditary standard bearer of the church and a senator of Rome. Costantino was ordained a priest in 1821. Under Pius VII he was named a domestic prelate and appointed a referendary of the Apostolic Signatura. Leo XII inscribed him among the auditors of the Rota. Gregory XVI appointed him his major domo. In the consistory of 1834 Gregory also named him a cardinal *in petto* but did not publish the fact until 1836. In 1841 Costantino became vice-general of Rome. In the consistory held by Pius IX at Gaeta in 1849, he was selected for the suburban see of Albano. He moved successively to Porto and S. Rufina (1860), then to prefect of the Congregation of Ceremonies and Rites and then to secretary of the Congregation of the Holy Office. In 1870 he became dean of the College of Cardinals. He officiated as procurator for Carlo Cardinal Odescalchi in the consistory of 1838 when the cardinal abandoned his "purple" in order to work with the missions. He was legate of Pius IX to Paris for the baptism of Prince Eugene, son of Napoleon III (1856).

Francesco (1413–1494) was bishop of Gaeta, governor of Foligno, and friend of Enea Silvio Piccolomini (Pius II, 1458–1464). A later Francesco (1529–1597), a philosopher, was born at Cherso del Quernaro and died in Rome. Following his uncle's wishes he joined the Venetian naval fleet. Not satisfied there he went to Padua to study medicine, relinquishing his attraction for letters and philosophy. Francesco Saverio, S.J. (1797–1881), an exegete, was born in Rome. Francesco entered the Society of Jesus (1814) and eventually became a professor of Hebrew and biblical exegesis in the Roman College and also at Louvain. The precise relationship between the series listed below and specific family members was not determined.

7.5.55.1 Archivio Patrizi-Montoro

[DATABASE ID: VATV297-A]

Inclusive Dates: 1216–1904 (bulk 1650–1800).

Bulk: 220 linear m. (1751 buste and 558 vols.).

Organization: The following schema reproduces in outline the various subseries of the *Archivio Patrizi*, which in fact consists primarily of the records of the Patrizi, Montoro, Chigi, and Naro families, as well as, passim, other prominent Roman families with whom they shared marriage and property alliances. The letters used below to designate the subseries are also the letters to use when requesting materials. An Italian version of this outline is included with a collection of specialized and diverse indexes (known as ASV Indice 54* "retro sala") at the circulation desk in the main reading room (the indice is not a formal finding aid and must be used in consultation with the archives staff).

A. Archivio Montoro, 1219–1848. 399 buste. Lineage records, bulls, briefs, notarial documents, authorizations for payment, judicial acts, accounts received for "castello di Montoro," inventories, day books, testaments, financial records of the Poggi-Chigi-Montoro family, receipts, primogeniture records, letters of the family Poggi, legal suits of the Montoro family, and the like.

B. Archivio della famiglia Patrizi, [ca. 14—]–[18—]. 469 buste. Pontifical bulls and briefs, notarial documents, inventories, maps and plans, financial records, letters, poetry, primogeniture records, journals, and the like.

C. Archivio Naro, [ca. 12—]–[18—]. 609 buste. Genealogical information, originals and copies of notarial documents (wills, long-term rents, donations, dowries, sales); notarial documents concerning the Porcari family (1453–1731); notarial and financial records from the Frangipani family (seventeenth–eighteenth century); records of the Macchiavelli family (seventeenth–eighteenth century); matrimonial, dowry, inheritance, property, and Rota records of the Carpegna family (eighteenth–nineteenth century); documents concerning the inheritance of Flaminia Ricci (seventeenth–eighteenth century); documents concerning the properties and descendants of Lucrezia Naro de Nobili and information on the genealogy of the Nobili family (sixteenth–eighteenth century); and inheritance of Prudenza Capizzucchi-Naro-Ruspoli (eighteenth century). Properties of the Nobili family at Monte Alfino, Montepulciano, and elsewhere (fourteenth–eighteenth century); records concerning the Chapel of St. John the Baptist at Santa Maria sopra della Minerva, Rome (sixteenth–eighteenth century); chaplaincy in Gesù, Rome (seventeenth–nineteenth century); pious endowments, relics, offices, notarial documents, records of every sort pertaining to members of prominent Roman families. In addition to the families named above, records cover the Orsini, Capponi, Capranica, and others.

D. Collection of documents organized by N. Castelli, archivist for the Naro-Patrizi family, [14—]–[18—]. 9 vols. Includes an appendix containing information on various states (Austria, Poland, Genoa, Spain).

E. Archivio Naro, [14—]–[18—]. 251 buste. Inheritance, financial, primogeniture records, as well as records documenting transactions with Monte di Pietà (seventeenth–eighteenth century), Banco di Santo Spirito (seventeenth century), and payments to artists (eighteenth century).

F. Judicial decisions of sacred congregations, [16—]. 5 vols.

G. Patrizi correspondence, 1865–1904. 14 buste.

H. Receipts, [18—]. 121 buste.

I. Montoro family, [15—]–[16—]. 12 vols. Various records.

L. Household account books, 1744–1856. 20 vols.

M. Account books of tax collector of Rome, 1739–1852. 13 vols.

N. Castel Giuliano. Account books, 1755–1799. 7 vols.

O. Payments due from Castel Giuliano and Sasso, 1752–1837. 7 vols.

P. Castel Giuliano and Sasso. Warehouses, 1754–1792. 3 vols.

Q. Castel Giuliano. Account books of "dispense," 1754–1792. 25 vols.

R. Workers of the "selleria," 1747–1787. 3 vols.

S. Financial records for country estates, 1746–1799. 4 vols.

T. Account books, 1712–1732. 6 vols.

U. Payment authorizations, 1745–1839. 15 vols.; — Register of payments of the cashier from the Banco di Santo Spirito, 1840–1858. 5 vols.

Z. Lists of those provided for by Marchese Patrizi, 1739–1843. 14 vols.

AA. Livestock records, 1745–1774. 4 vols.

BB. Administration books re Virginia Patrizi and Portia Patrizi.

CC. Copybooks of letters of the Patrizi family (including those regarding Porzia Patrizi and the Naro patrimony), 1789–1846. 8 vols.

DD. Records of Masses, [17—]. 10 vols.

EE. State of the Patrizi family, 1739–1792. 38 vols.

FF. Accounts paid of the post office, 1732–1748. 6 vols.

GG. Financial records concerning the dependents of the Montoro feudal estate, 1635–1784. 19 vols.

HH. Account books of the Montoro family, 1751–1784. 9 vols.

II. Account books of the administrator of the Montoro estate, 1732–1780. 9 vols.

LL. Employees of Castel Giuliano, 1751–1792. 21 vols.; — Misc. household records (inventories, journals, etc.), [14—]–[18—]. 298 vols.

The collection was acquired by the ASV in 1946.

Note: Vol. 28A is available on microfilm.

References: Fink, p. 139; Boyle, p. 95. G. Gualdo, "Archivi di famiglie romane nell'Archivio vaticano," *Archivio della Società romana di storia patria* 104 (1981): 147–158.

Finding Aids: ASV Indici 723 and 724, "Indici di tutte le materie esistenti nell'Archivio dell'Ecc.ma. Casa Chigi-Montoro: Rubricella, 1806" (parte primo and parte secunda, respectively). The materials of the Poggi-Chigi-Montoro families, indexed in these volumes, form subseries A. The subseries of the *Archivio Patrizi* are given in the schema given above and in the Indice 54* (retro Sala), "Archivio Patrizi-Inventari" (cf. below). Indici 723 and 724 are descriptive inventories of records scattered throughout subseries A. The descriptions are presented according to various themes—taxes, specific properties, chapels, family members—and give a reference to the volume and page number within *Archivio Patrizi*, subseries A. Each indice is prefaced with a useful internal alphabetical index (to persons, places, etc.). Researchers should look for information on all of the major families included in this collection in all indices.

ASV Indice 725 is titled "Rubricellone di tutte le materie esistente nell'Archivio dell'Ill.mo. Casa Patrizi composto sotto gli auspizi dell'Ill.mo. Sig. Marchese Francesco Patrizi da Filippo Maria Magni archivista" (1794, with nineteenth-century additions). This indice is organized thematically in the same manner as Indici 723 and 724 above.

ASV Indice 726 is titled "Rubricellone Generale di tutte le materie esistenti nell'Archivio dell'Ill.ma. Famiglia Naro composto sotto gli auspici dell'Ill.mo. Sig. Marchese Franceco Patrizi, già Naro da Filippo Maria Magni" (1793, with nineteenth-century additions). There are clear descriptions of records pertaining to numerous branches of the Naro Family, related by marriage and economic interests to many other prominent Roman families (primarily fifteenth–eighteenth century). The divisions of this index reflect a primary interest in family and property. Indice 726 itself has an alphabetical index. To request materials from this section of the Naro Archivio, use the call numbers noted here that reflect a previous organization still operative. However these call numbers must be prefixed with *Archivio Patrizi*, subseries "C" (cf. above in the organizational note). Researchers should look for information on all of the major families represented in this collection in all of the indices.

ASV Indice 54*, "Archivio Patrizi-Inventari" (retro sala), available at the circulation desk in the main reading room, contains the organizational schema in Italian, translated into English above, as well as a number of specialized and diverse indici. (The indice is not a formal finding aid and must be used in consultation with the archives staff.) Among the loose fascicules found here are some that simply reproduce sections from Indici 723–726, list lost volumes, or provide an alternative means of approaching the material. Though all the fascicles contained in Indice 54* (retro sala) are not of equal value, some provide a useful and expedient complement to Indici 723–726.

Location: Archivio Segreto Vaticano.

7.5.56 Piastrelli, Luigi

7.5.56.1 Carte Piastrelli

[DATABASE ID: VATV30000-A]

Inclusive Dates: 1907–1911.

Bulk: 4 buste.

Organization: Chronological. Busta titles are as follows: 1. Lettere, 1907; —2. Lettere, 1908; —3. Lettere, 1909; —4. Stampati (Giornali e riviste), 1907–1909.

Finding Aids: ASV Indice 1167, "Carte Luigi Piastrelli: Elenco delle lettere autografe e dei documenti riguardanti il moviemento modernista," was compiled by Luigi Piastrelli himself. The index is organized according to the buste and there are three separate types of indices to buste 1–3. The first section, "Elenco dei mittenti delle lettere numerate in ordine della data di arrivo," is an alphabetical listing by the name of the correspondent with a number corresponding to the letter by that person in the busta. The second section, "Argomenti trat-

tati nella corrispondenza numerata," indexes this series by name (e.g., Baldini), title, (e.g., Archivescovo di Perugia), or event (e.g., Mostra Arte Umbra). The third section is a calendar of letters in chronological order, organized by number (num.), date (data), author (autore), and subject (argomento). The subject given here provides a brief description of the letter and is greatly amplified from the brief argomenti provided in the second section, above. The section of indice 1167 that provides access to the fourth busta is organized similarly to that indexing the first three buste. There are three sections: (1) "Elenco dei giornali e reviste," which gives the name of the journal and the item number in the busta; (2) "Titoli della corrispondenze pubblicate sui giornali citati nell'elenco," which provides the title of the article and the journal number in the buste; and (3) a calendar that provides the number (num.), title (titolo del giornale), city (Proven), date (data), and brief subject (argomento).

Location: Archivio Segreto Vaticano.

7.5.57 Pio, Carlo

The Pio da Carpi family is famous in the history of Italy, involving many lines connected to well-known family names forming somewhat of a consortium. In the ninth and tenth centuries they had vast possessions especially in Parmigiano, Reggiano, and Modena. In the twelfth century Bernardo was the founder or head of one branch. From him were derived many lines that died out: the marquises of Trent (1747); the princes Pio di Savoia extinct in 1776 and called di Savoia from their founder Alberto (1455–1531) who, for favors rendered, had received from Duke Ludovico for himself and his descendants the privilege of assuming name, title, and arms of Savoia.

Carlo Pio (1622–1689), after having served in the pontifical army, was taken prisoner by the Florentines and transferred to Rome. Chosen to be a member of the staff in the Apostolic Camera, he later became general treasurer (some say through bribery). In 1654 Innocent X named him cardinal and legate of Urbino. The following year he was elected bishop of Ferrara. In 1682 he returned to Rome, where he was appointed prefect of the Congregazione del Buon Governo and in 1683 named bishop of Sabina.

7.5.57.1 Fondo Pio

[DATABASE ID: VATV337-A]

Inclusive Dates: 1216(copy)–1681 (bulk 1523–1681).

Bulk: 13 linear m. (292 vols.).

Organization: Subseries include: Gruppi particolari (Conclavi, ceremoniale, etc.); —Colonia; —Fiandra; —Firenze; —Francia; — Genova; —Germania; —Inghilterra; —Malta; —Napoli; —Polonia; —Portogallo; —Savoia; —Spagna; —Svizzera; —Venezia; —Avignone; —Bologna; —Ferrara; —Romagna; —Urbino; —Lettere Diverse.

Scope: This collection includes Secretariat of State material including records relating to nunciatures for Colonia (1578–1624), Fiandra (1529–1641), Firenze (1561–1641), Francia l(1541–1681), Genova (1557–1667), Germania (1539–1681), Inghilterra (1526–1677), Malta (1605–1667), Napoli (1552–1681), Polonia (1592–1639), Portogallo (1579–1668), Savoia (1579–1639), Spagna (1560–1680), Svizzera (1579–1621), Venezia (1579–1665); legations of Avignone (1579–1663), Bologna (1607–1651), Ferrara (1472–1655), Romagna (1534–1672), Urbino (1570–1628); Lettere diversi (1523–1681). Also according to Boyle, the collection includes Gruppi particolari, reports of conclaves (1305–1680).

Most of the fondo originally belonged to Cardinal Carlo Pio di Savoia, then was acquired in 1753 by Benedict XIV. Volumes 37, 48, 50, 54, 57, 61, 64, 69, 70, 71, 101, 127–129, 133, 135, 142–146, 154, 158, 167–169, 174, 177, 182, 189, and 248 were acquired by the ASV in 1761 and 1763. For detailed provenance information cf. Pásztor's article cited below.

Note: Vols. 58, 107, 114–115, and 156 are available on microfilm.

References: Fink, pp. 139–140; Pásztor (1970), pp. 223–224; Pásztor (1983), p. 203; Boyle, p. 98. G. Gualdo, "Archivi di famiglie romane nell'Archivio vaticano," *Archivio della Società romana di storia patria* 104 (1981): 147–158. L. Pásztor, "Per la storia dell'Archivio Segreto Vaticano nei secoli XVII–XVIII," *Archivio della Società romana di storia patria* 91 (1968): 157–249. Pásztor discusses the provenance of thirty-three volumes now in this series and their interrelationships with other series in the ASV and the Biblioteca Apostolica Vaticana. A brief listing for each of these thirty-three volumes can be extracted from this article.

J. Lestocquoy, ed., *Correspondance des nonces en France: Dandino, Della Torre et Trivulti, 1546–1551 avec des documents relatifs a la rupture des relations diplomatiques, 1551–1552* (Rome, 1966). J. Lestocquoy, ed., *Correspondance du nonce en France: Prospero Santa Croce (1552–1554)* (Rome, 1972).

Finding Aids: ASV Indice 1091, by P. Savio, provides a detailed inventory of documents in each volume. Entries indicate the current and former volume numbers, the type of document, and the folio. The content/subject of the documents is usually apparent from the title. Inclusive dates are often noted. Beginning on page 67 of Indice 1091, there is a geographic/subject index to the *Fondo Pio* that provides chronological listings.

ASV Indice 704, compiled in 1915 by M. Ugolini, is organized in the same manner as the first section of Indice 1091 and provides a detailed inventory of documents in each volume. In general, Indice 704 is not as complete as Indice 1091, but it occasionally provides a detail that is omitted from Indice 1091. Indice 704 also has an internal index primarily to geographic locations and important persons mentioned in the index.

ASV Indici 218 (pp. 152–194) and 219 (pp. 101–121v) and *Fondo Carpegna* (in the ASV and listed separately), vol. 65 (pp. 193–212v), are virtually identical lists to (primarily) types of documents (acta concistoriale, bolle, breve, canonizazione, discorsi, dialoghi, historie, viaggi, vite, etc.) represented in the *Fondo Pio.* Although one should not assume that these lists are complete, if one is seeking a specific item, these lists may be the quickest means of locating documents by type. The former volume numbers are given in Indici 218 and 219 and *Fondo Carpegna* 65, so researchers must still turn to Indice 1091 to locate the current volume numbers.

Location: Archivio Segreto Vaticano.

7.5.58 Pistolesi Family

7.5.58.1 Carte Pistolesi
[DATABASE ID: VATV311-A]
Inclusive Dates: not determined.
Bulk: Extent undetermined.
Reference: Boyle, p. 96.
Note: Not located by project staff in 1990.
Location: Archivio Segreto Vaticano.

7.5.59 Pius IX

Giovanni Maria Mastai-Ferretti (1792–1878) was born in Senigallia (Ancona). His family, which belonged to the lower nobility of Lombardy, was noted for its moderate reform tendencies. The future pope studied at the Piarist College of Volterra until he had what was probably an epileptic attack. After completing his studies at the Roman College his ill health seemed to be an obstacle to his entering the priesthood, but eventually after the intervention of Pius VII he was ordained (1819) at the age of twenty-seven.

His first years as a priest were spent at Ricovero di Tata Giovanni, an orphanage in Rome. In 1823 Pius VII sent him with the apostolic delegation to Chile, and while there he visited Peru and Colombia. In 1825 he was back in Rome in charge of the hospice of San Michele. In 1827 he was named archbishop of Spoleto, transferred to the see of Imola (1832), and created a cardinal in 1840. His mild but firm handling of the revolutionary disturbances and his episcopal administration at Imola showed him capable of handling the liberal advocates of the area. He remained at Imola until his election as pope (June 16, 1846). He took the name Pius in honor of Pius VII, his benefactor and predecessor in the see of Imola.

An enlightened conservative rather than a liberal by conviction, he began his pontificate by granting a general amnesty to all political prisoners and exiles. The pope's lack of political ability precipitated a crisis. Besieged in the Quirinal after the assassination of the papal minister, Count Pellegrino Rossi, the pope fled to Gaeta (1848), and Mazzini took over the rule of Rome.

When Pius returned to Rome (1850), his attitude was completely changed. He no longer made any attempts to introduce liberal reforms. He rapidly became more firmly convinced of the connection between the principles of the French Revolution and the destruction of traditional values. By 1864 the progressive liberal of 1847 had become "the symbol of European reaction."

In 1860 Cavour capitalized on the opportunity to hasten Italian unification, but French military aid made it possible for the pope to retain Rome and its environs for another decade. In 1870 when the French troops were recalled because of the Franco-Prussian War, the Italian troops moved in and occupied Rome, ending the temporal power of the pope. When Pius subsequently rejected the Law of Guarantees (1871), he became a voluntary prisoner of the Vatican.

The publication of the encyclical *Quanta cura* (Dec. 8, 1864), a general condemnation of modern errors, followed by the compilation of the Syllabus of Errors were efforts of Pius IX to denounce socialism and the conception of religion and society held by the liberals. The definition of the dogma of the Immaculate Conception (1854) and the convocation of the First Vatican Council (1869–1870), which defined papal primacy and infallibility, aroused widespread antagonism. The Kulturkampf in Germany, the religious situation in Austria, difficulties in Latin America, and the expulsion of the papal nuncio from Switzerland testified to the reaction toward the increased centralization of authority in the church. Through it all, however, Pius IX maintained an inexplicable charity for his adversaries that nothing ever corrupted.

In addition to the records listed below, see the Secretariatus Status series *Pio IX* and *Stampe Pio IX*.

7.5.59.1 Archivio particolare Pio IX: Corrispondenza con sovrani e particolari

[DATABASE ID: VATV298-A]

Inclusive Dates: ca. 1846–1874.

Bulk: 1 linear m. (8 boxes).

Organization: The material is organized in the 8 boxes according to geographic locations as follows: I. Austria, Baden, Baviera, Belgio, Brasile, Danimarca; —II. Francia; —III. Hanover, Inghilterra, Messico; —IV. Napoli, Parma, Piacenza; —V. Portogallo, Prussia, Russia, Sardegna, Sassonia, Svezia e Norvegia, Svizzera, Wurtemburg; —VI. Spagna; —VII. Toscana e Lucca, Stato Pontificio; —VIII. Autografi di minute di lettere di Sua Santità.

References: Fink, p. 140; Boyle, p. 97; Pásztor (1970), pp. 224–228; Pásztor (1983), pp. 203–204. G. Martina, "Nel centenario della morte di Massimiliano D'Asburgo: La corrispondenza tra Pio IX e Massimiliano," *Archivum Historiae Pontificiae* 5 (1967): 373–391.

Finding Aids: ASV Indice 1131, "Archivio Particolari Pio IX, lettere ai sovrani, ecc.," indexes this entire series. Entries proceed alphabetically by geographical name. Within each geographical division, letters to the "sovrani" and "particolari" are categorized separately, in two roughly chronological lists. Each letter is treated individually. Entries include the date and current number of the letter, the writer or recipient, and a summary of the letter or response.

Location: Archivio Segreto Vaticano.

7.5.59.2 Archivio particolare Pio IX: Oggetti vari

[DATABASE ID: VATV354-A]

Inclusive Dates: ca. 1846–1878.

Bulk: 6 linear m. (35 boxes divided into 2,187 cassetta numbers).

Organization: Cassette are not equal to boxes.

Notes: The following cassette are missing: 10, 13, 15, 16, 19–25, 51, 60, 85, 127, 128, 237, 243, 244, 278, 290, 304, 322, 323, 362, 371, 501, 555, 606, 690, 883, 896, 926–932,

977, 983, 1029, 1064, 1091, 1096, 1109, 1112, 1119, 1162, 1171, 1195, 1234, 1301, 1350, 1425, 1468, 1516, 1540–1559, 1760, 1764, 1808, 1814, 1878, 1905, 1922, 1935, 1942, 1957, 1982, 2000, 2127, 2137, 2167, 2170, 2172, 2175, 2181. Fasc. 465 is available on microfilm.

References: Fink, p. 140; Boyle, p. 97; Pásztor (1970), pp. 224–228.

Finding Aids: ASV Indice 1132 is an alphabetical index to personal names, geographic locations, the Roman Curia, religious orders, and subjects that can be found in the *Archivio particolari: Oggetti vari*. Entries lead to individual documents; however, items can be hard to locate in Indice 1132. Reading through the entire volume and exploring different access points is the best way to approach Indice 1132.

Location: Archivio Segreto Vaticano.

7.5.59.3 Fondo particolare Pio IX

[DATABASE ID: VATV338-A]

Inclusive Dates: 1725–1878.

Bulk: 7 linear m. (39 boxes organized according to cassette).

Organization: (One cassetta = 1 box). Cassette categories and titles are: 1. Miscellanea in lingua spagnola, 1725–1835; —2. Carte Casa Mastai Ferretti, 1792–1845; —3. Sermoni e scritti varii di Mgr. Andrea Mastei Ferretti, vescovo di Pesaro, 1788–1820; —4. Sermoni e scritti varii di Mgr. Andrea Mastai Ferretti, 1793–1822; —5. Lettere di varii a Giovanni Maria Mastai Ferretti, 1818–1832; —6. Ospizio Apostolico di S. Michele a Ripa, 1825–1846; —7. Lettere a Giovanni Maria Mastai Ferretti di Spoleto e Imola, 1826–1842; —8. I moti del Trentuno e il vescovado Mastai a Spoleto, 1831–1847; —9. Prediche, 1820–1831; —10. Prediche (Spoleto e Imola), 1827–1846; —11. Lettere e documenti varii di Casa Mastai Ferretti e varie inerenti al vescovado imolese, 1832–1846; —12. Vescovato di Spoleto ed Imola, 1829–1838; —13. Prelatura ercolani, 1825–1844; —14. Prelatura ercolani, 1826–1877; —15. Prelatura ercolani, 1828–1846; —16. Scala Santa (lavori di restauro), 1851–1854; —17. Senigallia, 1852–1876; —18. Ospizio dell'Immacolata Concezione, 1854–1861; —19. Vigna Pia, 1847–1851 ; Eredità Gismondi, 1875–1877; —20. Varie di carattere amministrativo, 1848–1873; —21. Cattedrale di Imola, 1847–1852; —22. Varie, 1847–1850; —23. Progetti e lavori diversi, 1846–1876 (includes information on Sistine Chapel) ; Sottoscrizioni pro Garcia Moreno, 1876; —24. Lavori diversi, 1861–1865; —25. Finanze pontificie, 1815–1856; —26. Varie amministrative, 1847–1870; —27. Varie amministrative, 1851–1876; —28. Beneficenza, 1855–1877; —29. Rendiconti (spese e sussidi) del Card. Antonelli, 1848–1852; —30. Rendiconti filippani (affari privati di Pio IX), 1846–1849; —31. Rendiconti filippani, 1850–1853; —32. Rendiconti filippani, 1854–1859; —33. Rendiconti filippani, 1856–1871; —34. Rendiconti del maestro dei sacri palazzi (G. Spagna), 1866–1877; —35. Rendiconti varii, 1854–1865; —36. Suppliche per arredi sacri, 1873–1877; —37. Rendiconti di Mgr. Cenni (Caudatario pontificio); —38. Rendiconti di Mgr. Cenni, 1868–1878; —39. Varie, 1854–1861.

References: Fink, p. 140; Boyle, p. 98; Pásztor (1970), pp. 228–229.

Finding Aids: ASV Indice 1133 proceeds cassetta by cassetta (box by box) with brief contents notes. Some of the entries are detailed and inventory each item in a box, others are contents summaries. The basic cassetta categories are listed above. An earlier index to these same materials has been bound into the back of Indice 1133. This older inventory describes the materials differently and can give more conplete details for certain items.

Location: Archivio Segreto Vaticano.

7.5.60 Pius X

See Secretariatus Status series *Autografi di SS. Pio X* (1903–1913), *Miscellanea Pio X* (1903–1914), *Particolari Pio X* (1904–1914), and *Spogli di SS. Pio X* (1903–1914).

7.5.61 Pius XI

7.5.61.1 Carte Pio XI
[DATABASE ID: VATV40030-A]
Inclusive Dates: 1890–1939.
Bulk: 2 buste.
Note: This series was cited in Natalini et al., p. 269, but not seen by project staff in 1990.
Location: Archivio Segreto Vaticano.

7.5.62 Ronconi, Filippo

Filippo Ronconi (d. 1751) was prefect of the Vatican Archives.

7.5.62.1 Fondo Ronconi
[DATABASE ID: VATV339-A]
Inclusive Dates: 1487(copy)–1827 (bulk 1642–1714).
Bulk: 1.5 linear m. (23 vols.).
Scope: This is a collection of documents copied from the ASV. The collection was acquired by the ASV about 1751. The extent to which this collection provides copies of originals subsequently lost was not determined.
References: Fink, p. 141; Pásztor (1970), p. 230; Boyle, p. 98.
Finding Aids: Indice 1060 is a busta-by-busta listing of the entire collection. Entries list the title of each volume, which also serves as an indication of the major subject of the busta. Dates, major individuals, geographic areas are also usually noted.
Location: Archivio Segreto Vaticano.

7.5.63 Rospigliosi Family

The Rospigliosi originated in Lombardy but in the thirteenth century they moved to Pistoia. Numerous members of the family served the church in ecclesiastical, military, and diplomatic careers. At the beginning of the fifteenth century a Giovanni was a captain in the military in the service of Martin V (1417–1431). Giovanni Battista, after having fought for the French, was named admiral by Pius V (1566–1572) in 1566. When Giulio, born at Pistoia in 1600, was elected pope with the name of Clement IX, Camillo, his brother, became

general of the church. Giacomo (d. 1684) was named cardinal nephew in 1667 and appointed internuncio to Brussels, legate to Avignon and Ferrara, and ambassador to Louis XIV. Clement X created Felice (d. 1688) a cardinal in 1667.

Giovanni Battista (1646–1722), the pope's nephew, became prince of the Roman Empire. By marrying Maria Camilla Pallavicini, niece of Cardinal Lazzaro Sforza Pallavicini, last of his branch, Giovanni acquired a fortune and the ducal fief of Zagarolo; later the title of prince was included in the family honors. Giulio Cesare (1781–1859) acquired the titles of Margherita Colonna Gioeni. Of their children, Clemente was the founder of the Gioeni branch, and Francesco of that of the Pallavicini.

7.5.63.1 Archivio Rospigliosi
[DATABASE ID: VATV10282-A]
Inclusive Dates: 1660–1915.
Bulk: 191 linear m. (2,125 items).
Scope: The collection was acquired by the ASV in May 1931.
References: G. Gualdo, "Archivi di famiglie romane nell'Archivio vaticano," *Archivio della Società romana di storia patria* 104 (1981): 147–158. G. C. Rospigliosi and L. Andreani, ed., *Libro a di richordi d'Antonio di Toddeo Rospiglioxi (1459–1498)* (Pisa, 1909).
Finding Aids: ASV Indice 1128 is a volume-by-volume inventory of the entire *Archivio Rospigliosi*. Entries indicate the current volume number, inclusive date(s), pagination (if applicable), and a descriptive title of the tome or busta. A list of Libri Mastri is at the end of the indice.

Archivio Rospigliosi nos. 1–4 and 6 are identified as indices to the *Archivio Rospigliosi* in ASV Indice 1128. These indici provide various means of approach to the collection. However, they refer to former volume numbers and there is no concordanza to the current volume numbers. These indici are currently useful only as historical reminders of the full extent of the *Archivio Rospigliosi* or as tantalizing clues to what may be in the ASV *Archivio Rospigliosi*.
Location: Archivio Segreto Vaticano.

7.5.63.2 Archivio Rospigliosi-Gioeni
[DATABASE ID: VATV10058-A]
Inclusive Dates: 1343(copy)–1826.
Bulk: 76 linear m. (239 numbered vols. and 36 linear m. of unnumbered vols.).
References: Fink, p. 136. G. Gualdo, "Archivi di famiglie romane nell'Archivio vaticano," *Archivio della Società romana di storia patria* 104 (1981): 147–158.
Location: Archivio Segreto Vaticano.

7.5.64 Ruspoli Family

The original family of Ruspoli died out in the male branch in the seventeenth century when Vittoria Ruspoli, the last of her house, married Sforza Marescotti. Their eldest son Francesco adopted his mother's family name. He purchased the fief of Cerveteri from the Orsini and obtained for it the title of prince in 1712. The Ruspoli claimed Siena as their original location; the Marescotti came from Bologna.

Two of the family by the name of Bartolomeo earned distinction: one was named a cardinal (1750); the other became Grand Master of the Order of Malta (1800). Gregory XVI conferred on the head of the house the honorary title of Master of the Sacred Hospice. (See the history for the Papal Court, Famiglia della Santità de Nostra Signore series *Magister Sacri Hospitii*.) A second branch of the Ruspoli is represented by the duke d'Alcudia in Spain, of which country he is a grandee. A third branch, resident like the first in Rome, obtained the title of prince di Poggio Suasa in 1880.

7.5.64.1 Archivio Ruspoli-Marescotti

[DATABASE ID: VATV10275-A]

Inclusive Dates: ca. 1390–1904.

Bulk: 295 linear m.

Organization: Only the first subseries is numbered and systematically described. Subseries include: Famiglia Conti (Archivio, including conti e ricevute), 1–740; —Famiglia Conti (Lettere-buste), 1–83; —Famiglia conti (Registri-mandati), 1–77; —Famiglia Conti (Registri-mandati), 1–77; —Famiglia conti (Vignanello: Giustificazione/Libro mastro), 1–93; —Famiglia Conti (Riano: Giustificazione/Libro mastro), 1–168; —Famiglia Conti (Giustificazione-Libro mastro della spese), 1–6; —Famiglia Conti (Giustificazione famiglia), 1–64; —Famiglia Conti (Giustificazione Libro mastro-Roma), 1–382; —Famiglia Conti (Giustificazione Libro mastro Cerveteri), 2–158; —Famiglia Conti (Filza Libro mastro, Anni 1822–1903); —Famiglia Conti (Vignanello, spese, ecc.); —Famiglia Conti (Cerveteri-Carte varie); —Copie lettere (1878–1896), 1–24; —Famiglia Conti (Libri cassa, processi, cause civili); —Ruspoli-Marescotti (Mastri volumi), 1–23, 1–7; —Rubricelle Libri mastri, 1–16; —Rubricelle lettere A–Z, 10 vols.; —Cassette con schede.

Scope: This is an interesting collection with information on several notable Roman families, from the fourteenth to the nineteenth century. Busta 653, for example, contains testaments (pergamene) from 1390 (in Trastevere), a number of these are by women.

References: Fink, p. 141. G. Gualdo, "Archivi di famiglie romane nell'Archivio vaticano," *Archivio della Società romana di storia patria* 104 (1981): 147–158. U. Kirkendale, "The Ruspoli Documents on Handel," *Journal of the American Musicological Society* 20 (1967): 222–273, 517–518. A. Campitelli, "La Rocca ed il Borgo di Vignanello dai Farnese ai Ruspoli," in *La dimensione europea dei Farnese*, edited by B. de Groof and E. Galdieri (Brussels, 1993), pp. 115–153.

Finding Aids: ASV Indice 719 is a busta-by-busta, document-by-document inventory of numbers 1–724 of part of the initial subseries, Famiglia Conti. Entries provide a date, brief description of each document, and the division, armadio, tome, and fascicoli number. Depending on the item requested, all of this information may be essential or simply the tome number. Indice 719 begins with an internal alphabetical index to types of documents, persons, and places, but it is supplanted by ASV Indici 720–722 and the "Descrizione Generale degli Archivi" within the collection itself.

ASV Indici 720–722 are alphabetical/subject indices to a large portion of the first subseries, Famiglia Conti. These alphabetical indici list property holdings, persons, geographic locations, types of transactions (affitti, vendita, etc.), and some types of documents (bolle, istromenti, etc.). Entries indicate the date, a brief description of the document or busta, and the location (e.g., A.i.Prot.no.10). Full citations to materials should be copied.

ASV Blocchetti Indice 22 is a detailed and descriptive calendar of documents from "Sovrani" in the initial subseries of the *Archivio Ruspoli-Marescotti* (Famiglia Conti), buste 202–203, dating from 1678 to 1780.

Researchers should note that all of the indexes described thus far only pertain to the first subseries, Famiglia Conti, and that there are hundreds of volumes in the other subseries outlined above. If desired items are not found in the initial subseries, researchers should begin to request a series of volumes at the very end of all the *Archivio Ruspoli*. At the end of the archivio (sez. M, before *Fondo Salviati*), there is an entire area devoted to various indici and rubricelle.

In this last section of shelving are various contents listings, schede, and indexes that have been executed by different family members and archivists. In some cases, these could point one toward a specific part of the unindexed collection and in other cases these are useful for indicating the former contents of the collection. For example, one finds pergamene indexed that no longer appear in the collection. However, the brief but informative descriptions provide evidence of transactions and important events in the family's history. For example, one of the items, "Misure del Catasto di Poli e Guardagnolo," provides schematic drawings of the boundaries of land holdings in Poli, Guardagnolo, and other places that indicate who owned the adjacent lands.

Another item in this last section is the "Descrizione Generale degli Archivio," which notes inside that it is the "Rubricellone di tutte le scritture dell'Archivio dell'Eccellentissima Casa Ruspoli fatto e composto dal Signor Cesare Giuseppe Bianchi Archivista l'anno MDCCXVII." This large volume begins with an index of all the material registered in the rubricelle from the different sections of the archivio. However, there is another index within this volume to specific types of material (testamenti, codicilli, donazioni, etc.) beginning on folio 141. This index also appears to index the initial section of the archivio, Famiglia conti. Some items in this index are also in ASV Indici 719–722. Other items, however, are only listed in one or the other of these indexes. For example, ASV Indici 719–722 primarily index the Famiglia Marescotti materials in "Armario A," whereas this "Descrizione" indexes Marescotti materials throughout the collection.

Also on the last shelving unit containing the *Archivio Ruspoli* is a "Cassette con Schede," an alphabetical listing of subjects, persons, dates, type of business or form of document, and dates. This is of little use as a finding aid because few volume numbers are provided; however, as with the other rubricelle, it offers concise descriptions of materials that are or were in the collection at one time and provides evidence of transactions and events. It has not been determined which parts of the collection these index.

Another interesting group of contents listings on the shelf is a group of ten volumes of rubricelle. The volumes bear the following designations (A, B, C, D, E, F, G, H, I, J–Z). The set A–H are the same size and shape. The last two volumes I and J–Z are different in appearance. It has not been determined which parts of the collection these index.

Location: Archivio Segreto Vaticano.

7.5.65 Sala, Giuseppe Antonio

Giuseppe Sala (1762–1839) was born in Rome and died there. He was a member of the delegation seated in Rome during the absence of Pius VI. Pius VII (1800–1823) sent him to Paris in 1801 as secretary of the legation of Cardinal Caprara and he proved to be a zealous, objective, and loyal informer for Pius VII of the events taking place during the pope's imprisonment at Savona (1809–1814).

Sala returned to Rome and was appointed secretary of the new apostolic delegation for the second French occupation. With the restoration he began the publication of his *Piano di riforma* in which he proposed as a remedial principle the laicization of the public tasks. This was interrupted, however, by Consalvi, legate to the Congress of Vienna.

After 1815 Sala was secretary for many commissions and committees. He also involved himself in working with the hospitals of the city. Gregory XVI raised him to the cardinalate in 1831 and named him prefect for the Congregation for the Index and then for the Congregation of Bishops and Regulars. Among his unedited writings he left a copy of his *Piano di riforma*, which gives an objective account of the events of the years 1798 and 1799. See G. A. Sala, *Piano di riforma umiliato a Pio VII*, edited by G. Cugnoni (Tolentino, 1907).

7.5.65.1 Riforma

[DATABASE ID: VATV10169-A]
Inclusive Dates: 1800–1823.
Bulk: 6 linear m. (51 buste [50 numbered and 1 unnumbered]).
Organization: Subseries titles with their current buste numbers are: 1. Manoscritto del piano di riforma, umiliato a Sua Santità Pio VII subito dopo la Sua elezione, da G.A. Sala, 1800.; —2–6. Minute, ristretti, intimi di Congregazione, 1813–1820; —7–8. Varie di congregazione, 1814–1818; —9–18. Posizioni con numero, 1817–1821; —19. Aquapendente, 1814–1815, Agostiniani, 1813–1818, Alatri, 1814, Albano, 1816, Alcantarini; —20. Amelia, 1814–1820, Anagni, 1815, Ancona, 1818–1820, Ascoli, 1815–1821, Assisi, 1815–1817; —21. Bagnorea, 1814–1816, Barnabiti, 1816–1822, Basiliani, 1814–1816, Benedettini, Benefratelli, 1814, Benevento, 1815–1816, 1819, Bertinoro, 1818, Bologna, 1818–1819, 1821, Bolsene (see Orvieto); —22. Cagli, 1814–1817, 1821, Camaldolesi, 1814–1815, Camerino, 1814–1815, 1817, 1820–1821, Canonici Regolari di S.S. Salvatore, 1814, 1817, 1820, 1823, Cappuccini, 1814–1818, 1820, Carmelitani, 1815–1817, Cascia, 1814, Cassinesi, 1814; —23. Celestini, 1815–1818, Certosini, 1814, Cervia, 1814, 1816, 1818, Chierici minori, 1814–1815, 1817, Cingoli, 1818–1820, Cisterciensi, 1814–1815, 1817, 1825, Città di Castello, 1814, 1816,

Città delle Pieve, 1814–1815; —24. Conventuali, 1814–1819, Corneto, 1814–1818; —25. Domenicani, 1816, Dottrinari, 1814–1819; —26. Fabriano, 1814–1817, Faenza, 1820–1821, Fano, 1814, 1818, 1821, Farfa, 1814–1818, 1820–1821; —27. Ferentino, 1814–1818, Fermo, 1814, Ferrara, 1817–1821, Filippini, 1817–1821; —28. Foligno, 1815–1818, Forli, 1815, 1817–1821, Forlimpopoli, 1818, 1821, Fossombrone, 1814, 1815, 1817, 1820–1821, Francescani, Frascati, 1814–1816, 1822; —29. Girolamini del Beato Pietro di Pisa, 1814–1816, 1822, Gubbio, 1814–1817, 1821, Iesi, 1815, 1817–1821, Imola, 1818 1821, Liguoriani, Loreto, 1818, 1820–1821; —30. Macerata, Tolentino, 1815–1818, 1821, Matelica (see Fabriano), Mercenar, Mercenari Scalzi (Mercedari), 1815, Minimi, 1815–1816, Ministri degli infermi, 1815, Minori conventuali, 1815, Minori osservanti, 1814–1816, 1819, Minori riformati, 1814–1815, Missioni (Congregazione delle missioni), 1814–1816; —31. Montalto, 1821, Montefeltro, 1814–1817, 1820, 1821, Montefiascone, 1815–1816, Montemilone, [182–]; —32. Narni, 1820, Nepi (see Sutri), Nocera, 1815–1818 1821; —33. Olivetani, 1815–1818, Orte (see Orvieto), Orvieto, 1814–1817, 1819, 1820; —34. Palestrina, 1816, Paolotte, 1814, Passionisti, Pergola, 1817–1821, Perugia, 1814–1818; —35. Pesaro, 1814–1817, 1821, 1822, Piemonte, 1815, Pii operai, 1814, Piperno (see also Terracina), 1816, 1821, Pisa, 1815, Pistola, 1814, Pontedorvo, 1815–1816, Predicatori, 1815; —36. Ravenna, 1815, 1817–1819, 1821, Recanati (see Loreto), Rieti, Rimini, 1815–1816, Ripatransone, 1817–1820; —37. Roma, 1814–1820; —38. Sabina, 1815–1816, San Angelo in Vado (see Urbania), San Severino, 1816–1818, Sarsina, 1818, Segni, 1814–1816, Serviti, 1814–1817, 1822, Silvestrini, 1815–1816; —39. Siena, 1816, Sinigaglia, 1815–1819, 1821, 1822, Scolopi, 1814–1817, Scuole pie, 1814, Somaschi, 1815; —40. Spoleto, 1814–1818; —41. Spoleto, Subiaco, 1814–1818, Sutri, 1815, 1816, 1818–1819; —42. Testini, 1814, Tebe, 1814, Terni, 1815–1816, 1819, Terracine and Sezze and Piperno, 1814–1821; —43. Ter'Ordine di S. Francesco, 1814–1816, 1822, Tivoli, 1814–1818, Todi, 1814, 1816, 1817, Tolentino (see also Macerata), 1817, 1819, Treia, 1818, 1820, Trinitari, 1814–1816, 1818; —44. Urbania and San Angelo in Vado, 1815–1818, Urbino, 1814–1816, 1819; —45. Vallambrosani, 1816, Velletri, 1814, 1815, 1817, 1820, Verginiani, 1814–1815, Veroli, 1814–1816, 1817, Viterbo, 1815–1818, Volterre, 1814; —46. Duplicati in stampa del piano di riforma, Articoli I–XIII; —47. Duplicati in stampa del piano di riforma, Articoli XIV–XVI; —48. Duplicati di ristretti per l'EM.mi. Card. Arezzo-Di Pietro, Mons. Governatore; —49. Duplicati di ristretti per l'Em.mi. Card. Litta-Pacca-Somalglia; —50. Dotazione del clero, Ripristinazione di monasteri, 1800, 1813–1824; —51. Riforma dei tribunale, 1800.

Finding Aids: ASV Indice 1124 briefly lists the contents of each busta and its inclusive dates. The series is primarily arranged by location and religious congregation. The first part of the index is essentially reproduced in the organizational note above. After the initial listing of all buste, the second part of this index (pp. 4–7) concentrates on the Posizioni (buste 9–18) and presents an alphabetical listing of locations and religious congregations along with their respective buste and posizioni numbers. Pages 7r (bottom) and 7v have informative notes concerning this series.

There is also an undesignated document on this series available at the desk in the ASV main reading room. This is not an official ASV finding aid and must be used in consultation with the ASV staff. Information here conflicts with information in Indice 1124 concerning busta 50.

Citation: This collection is usually cited as *Riforma.*

Location: Archivio Segreto Vaticano.

7.5.66 Salviati Family

The Salviati were a celebrated Florentine family dedicated to service of the church, with many cardinals and other prominent persons among the members of their various branches. Some say that originally the name may have been Caponsacchi. Most of the members of the family and their descendants of the sixteenth century lived in Rome, were born there, and died there.

Among the better known are Francesco (d. 1478), cardinal and archbishop of Pisa; Giovanni (1490–1553), cardinal and nephew of Leo X and cousin of Clement VII; Bernardo (1482–1568), cardinal and brother of Giovanni; Anton Maria (1537–1602), cardinal and nephew of Bernardo and Giovanni; and Alamanno (1669–1733), cardinal, nuncio to France (1707), and prefect of Signatura Iustitiae (1731). Gregorio Salviati (Rome, 1722–1794) was auditor of the Apostolic Camera. Pius VI named him a cardinal in 1777.

Scipione Salviato, eminent Catholic layman, was born in Paris in 1823 and died in Rome in 1892. He was son of Prince Francesco Borghese and Princess Adele de La Rochefoucauld and nephew of Cardinal Gregorio Salviati. Scipione inherited from his uncle his name and ducal title. An impressive Catholic layman, he finished his education in Rome and then joined the civic guard. During the turbulent times of Giuseppe Mazzini's (1805–1872) agitations of the Italian republican underground, Scipione went abroad but returned after the restoration of the pontifical government. By special request of Pius IX he succeeded Giovanni Acquaderni as president of the group organized to work with the Catholics of Rome.

7.5.66.1 Carte Salviati

[DATABASE ID: VATV10276-A]

Inclusive Dates: 1601–1799 (bulk 1711–1799).

Bulk: 8 linear m. (82 pacchi).

Scope: Pacchi 62 has information, about 1777, on the "carica di Uditore della Camera."

References: G. Gualdo, "Archivi di famiglie romane nell'Archivio vaticano," *Archivio della Società romana di storia patria* 104 (1981): 147–158. P. Hurtubise, *Une famille-témion, les Salviati* (Vatican City, 1985).

Finding Aids: ASV Indice 1052 provides a pacco-by-pacco inventory of the entire collection. Entries give a brief description of the documents in each pacco and inclusive dates.

Location: Archivio Segreto Vaticano.

7.5.66.2 Fondo Salviati

[DATABASE ID: VATV340-A]

Inclusive Dates: 1604–1784.

Bulk: 10 linear m. (83 buste).

Organization: Subseries, buste titles, and enumeration are: 1–32. Inquisizione di Malta; —33–78. Vicelegazione di Avignone; —79–83. Casa Salviati e miscellanea.

Scope: These are primarily the papers of Gregorio Salviati (1722–1794).

References: Fink, p. 141; Boyle, p. 98. G. Gualdo, "Archivi di famiglie romane nell'Archivio vaticano," *Archivio della Società romana di storia patria* 104 (1981): 147–158. P. Hurtubise, *Une famille-témion, les Salviati* (Vatican City, 1985). P. Hurtubise and R. Toupin, *Correspondance du nonce en France, Antonio Maria Salviati 1572–1578* (Rome, 1975).

Finding Aids: ASV Indice 1026 (pp. 278–289) provides a detailed busta-by-busta listing of nos. 1–81 in the *Fondo Salviati.* Entries provide a brief indication of the type of documents that can be found in each busta, inclusive dates, and occasionally a contents note.

Location: Archivio Segreto Vaticano.

7.5.67 Santacroce Family

The Santacroce, a noble Roman family whose name is now extinct, was formerly mentioned as the oldest in the thirteenth century in the registers of Innocent IV (1243–1254). Its members were named princes by Clement XI (1700–1721). Many of them distinguished themselves by their service to the church. Prospero (1513–1589) was successively a consistorial lawyer of the Rota, bishop of Chissamo, and nuncio in Germany to Charles V (1548). Recalled in 1550 he was nuncio in France (1552–1554), in Spain (1560), and again in France (1561–1566). He was created a cardinal (1564) and became administrator of the archbishopric of Arles.

Antonio (1498–1541), was archbishop of Seleucia and nuncio to Poland, then archbishop of Chieti (1531) and of Urbino (1563). Marcello (d. 1674) was a prefect of the Signatura, then bishop of Tivoli and cardinal. Pietro was governor of the Castel S. Angelo at the beginning of the seventeenth century and at the service of the church under Leo X. The family died out with an Antonio in the nineteenth century.

7.5.67.1 Archivio Santacroce

[DATABASE ID: VATV10277-A]

Inclusive Dates: ca. 1595–1884.

Bulk: 6.5 linear m. (53 pacchi).

Scope: Note that there is an Archivio Santacroce (1200–1837) in the Archivio di Stato di Roma.

References: Fink, p. 142. G. Gualdo, "Archivi di famiglie romane nell'Archivio vaticano," *Archivio della Società romana di storia patria* 104 (1981): 147–158.

Location: Archivio Segreto Vaticano.

7.5.68 Santini Family

7.5.68.1 Fondo Santini

[DATABASE ID: VATV343-A]

Inclusive Dates: 1505–1899.

Bulk: 13 linear m. (235 items).

Scope: These are primarily Datary records, originally belonging to Giuseppe Santini, and are useful for information on the Datary and Chancery. Item no. 198 is a 1505 Regolae Cancellariae; item no. 202 contains information on Datary offices (1605). There are several formularies. There are also "Carte relative a monasteri italiani," which are primarily eighteenth century. ASV Indice 213, "Indice di libri de Msgr. Ciampini alcune de quale sono stati comprati da Il. Sg.le. Clemente XI e posti nell'studi . . . e fuori sono stati segnali con la lett. "C" e posti in diversi luoghi secundo le materie nelle quali trattavano," includes *Fondo Santini* nos. 7, 152, 167, 196, and 205 as a part of this donation that took place between 1700 and 1721.

Note: Fondo Santini v. XIII (pp. 14–16) contains a list of entries referring to Oxford from a lost Cancelleria Apostolica series *Registra Lateranensia* volume of Eugene IV.

References: Fink, p. 142; Pásztor (1970), pp. 230–231; Boyle, p. 98. G. Gualdo, "Archivi di famiglie romane nell'Archivio vaticano," *Archivio della Società romana di storia patria* 104 (1981): 147–158. P. Hurtubise and R. Toupin, *Correspondance du nonce en France, Antonio Maria Salviati 1572–1578* (Rome, 1975).

Finding Aids: ASV Indice 1066 is an inventory of the contents of each busta in the series. Entries include the type of volume or documents in the busta and sometimes the inclusive dates and/or contents notes.

Within the *Fondo Santini*, nos. 116 and 117 respectively index the "Minutarum" volumes 68–88 and 89–115. These indices are organized alphabetically by type of minute (e.g. dispensatio, confirmatio, listis, indultum, nova privileg., etc).

Location: Archivio Segreto Vaticano.

7.5.69 Savelli Family

The Savelli were an ancient and powerful Roman family whose history is closely connected with the history of Rome and of the church of the medieval period. They were supportive of the Guelphs and hostile to the Colonna family. They cooperated when they were struggling with Boniface VIII (1294–1303) but parted ways after the conflict was over. The first of the family on record was an Aimerico, father of Cardinal Cencio Savelli who became pope in 1218 under the name of Honorius III. It was with him that the fortune of the family began. At the same time, there was another Cardinal Cencio Savelli who died in 1218. The relationship between the series listed below and specific family members was not determined.

7.5.69.1 Fondo Savelli

[DATABASE ID: VATV10278-A]

Inclusive Dates: ca. 1586–1650.

Bulk: 10 linear m.

Organization: Subseries include: Constitutorum; —Investigationum liber; —Liber querelarium; —Attorum criminali; —Liber sententiarum; —Criminalia; —Rubricelle.

Reference: Fink, p. 133.

Location: Archivio Segreto Vaticano.

7.5.70 Scaramucci Family

The family appears to have been involved with the Amministrazione dei Beni.

7.5.70.1 Fondo Scaramucci

[DATABASE ID: VATV10280-A]

Inclusive Dates: 1811–1874.

Bulk: 3 linear m. (23 pacchi).

Reference: Fink, p. 143.

Location: Archivio Segreto Vaticano.

7.5.71 Serafini, A.

7.5.71.1 Fondo Serafini

[DATABASE ID: VATV10369-A]

Inclusive Dates: 1832–1963.

Bulk: 14 boxes.

Organization: Subseries are: Manoscritti (7 boxes); —Manoscritti varie (1 box); —Bozze (6 boxes).

Scope: This collection consists mostly of copies (but a few original published items) of documents regarding the pontificate of Pius IX gathered perhaps for a history or biography. The one box (the only one that does not concern the biography of Pius IX), Manoscritti varie, is entitled "Commissione mista per la Revisione degli schemi sulla libertà e tolleranza religiosa."

Reference: Natalini et al., p. 269.

Location: Archivio Segreto Vaticano.

7.5.72 Soderini, Clement

7.5.72.1 Soderini, Clement

[DATABASE ID: VATV10279-A]

Inclusive Dates: ca. 1910–1920.

Bulk: 11 linear m.

Scope: Among the items in this collection are a typed manuscript of a history of Soderini and the papacy during his career, a series of scrapbooks (of primarily newpaper articles) documenting World War I, and note cards, presumably for writing the biography or a commissioned autobiography. The origins of this material and the purposes for which the collection was assembled are not clear.

Reference: Natalini et al., p. 269.

Location: Archivio Segreto Vaticano.

7.5.73 Spada Family

The Spada collections in the ASV are of two family members.

1. Bernardino Spada was born in Ravenna in 1594 and died in Rome in 1661. Bernardino studied law and the humanities in Ravenna. Paul V named him apostolic secretary and appointed him a referendary.

Gregory XV assigned him to a variety of tasks, and finally Urban VIII made him bishop *in partibus* of Amiata and nuncio to Paris; he received the purple in 1626. During the pestilence of 1630 he showed great charity in helping those in need.

2. Giuseppe (Rome, 1796–1867), a Dominican, wrote a number of books. It was his opinion that the Roman "revolution" was the work not of Romans but of foreigners.

7.5.73.1 Fondo card. Bernardino Spada

[DATABASE ID: VATV10281-A]

Inclusive Dates: 1610–1661.

Bulk: 3 linear m. (25 vols.).

Organization: Volumes are: 1. Lettere originali di papa Innocenzo X e di papa Alessandro VII e di altri al card. Spada dal 1642 al 1661; —2. Lettere originali di casa d'Austria, imperadore, re di Francia, Spagna, loro ministri, al card. Spada, dal 1642 al 1661; —3. Lettere senza tempo a parenti, cardinali, re e duchi, principi del card. Spada, 1624–61; —4. Lettere originali di principi di Mantova, Mirandola, Parma, Savoia, Lorena, Baviera al card. Spada dal 1624 al 1661; —5. Lettere originali de' principi di Modena, scritte al card. Spada, dal 1624 al 1661; —6. Lettere originali de' principi di Toscana al card. Spada, dal 1624 al 1661; —7. Lettere originali del card. di S. Onofrio Barberini al card. Spada, dal 1624 al 1631; —8. Lettere originali del card. Antonio Barberini al card. Spada dal 1626 al 1659; —9. Lettere originali di D. Carlo Barberini al card. Spada, dal 1625 al 1630; —10. Lettere originali di D. Taddeo Barberini al card. Spada, dal 1625 al 1647; —11. Lettere del card. Magallotti al card. Spada, dal 1622 al 1636; —12. Lettere originali del Ludovisi, con alcune scritture in fine al card. Spada, dal 1622 al 1661; —13. Lettere originali del Card. spada, scritte a varie persone, dal 1610 al 1627; —14. Idem, 1629; —15. Idem, 1630 e 1631; —16. Idem, 1632 al 1634; —17. Idem, 1640 al 1644; —18. Idem, 1645 al 1654; —19. Idem, 1655 al 1659; —20. Lettere originali del card. Spada, scritte a varie persone, dal 1660 al 1661; —21. Lettere originali del card. Francesco Barberini al card. Spada e ad altri, degli anni 1630, 1631, fino al 1642; —22. Lettere originali del card. Barberino al card. Spada e del card. Spada al cardinale detto, de seguenti anni: 1643–1652, 1654, 1656, 1657, 1661; —23. Raccolta in registro di lettere del card. Bernardino Spada scritte a diversi dal 1626 al 1635; —24. Idem, 1636 al 1661; —25. Lettere senza tempo.

Scope: These are the papers of Bernardino Spada. They were formerly part of a Diversorum series derived from the eredità Passionei. In addition to the *Fondo card. Bernardino Spada*, the Secretarius Status series *Nunziature diverse*, the *Fondo Ottoboni*, and part of the *Fondo Favoriti-Casoni* are derived from the Diversorum. (cf. Pásztor below). *Fondo card. Bernardino Spada* entered the ASV as part of the eredità Passionei (cf. Pásztor below) in 1761–1763.

Finding Aids: L. Pásztor, "Per la storia dell'Archivio Segreto Vaticano nei secoli XVII–XVIII," *Archivio della Società romana di storia patria* 91 (1968): 157–249. An index to volumes 1–25 appears in a footnote on pages 191–192. A listing of the entire fondo can also be extracted from pages 213–216. The brief listing of volume titles with their current volume numbers is reproduced above, as there is no other index to the *Fondo*

card. Bernardino Spada. This article is especially important for the provenance and history of the *Fondo card. Bernardino Spada* and related series.

Location: Archivio Segreto Vaticano.

7.5.73.2 Fondo Spada

[DATABASE ID: VATV315-A]

Inclusive Dates: 1770–1851.

Bulk: 20 linear m. (418 vols.).

Organization: There is an additional 5 linear m. of material that was located in the Soffitone of the ASV in 1990.

Scope: These are the papers of Giuseppe Spada (1796–1867). According to Boyle some of the papers related to the Roman republic of 1849. In some ways the collection appears like someone's private library. Vols. 411–418 are a later donation and vastly different in character. These later volumes have to do with Conclavi as well as and nuncios in Germany and Lucerne. Much of this material comes from Giuseppe Evangelisti, cifrista pontificale.

References: Fink, p. 143; Boyle, p. 96. E. Michel, "La raccolta storica Spada dell'Archivio Vaticano," *Rassegna storica del Risorgimento* 12 (1925): 177–181. G. Gualdo, "Archivi di famiglie romane nell'Archivio vaticano," *Archivio della Società romana di storia patria* 104 (1981): 147–158. Gualdo has good information on vols. 1–410. Boyle and Gualdo identify this series as *Collezione Spada*.

Finding Aids: ASV Indici 706 (I–II) provide access to the entire *Fondo Spada* (except material in the Soffitone). Indice 706 (I) treats volumes 1–199 in detail with a few notes to higher volume numbers. In the first section of Indice 706 (I), entries list the volume titles, inclusive dates of the material or publication date, and occasionally more specific contents information. Other sections of Indice 706 (I) provide access to certain types of materials in the *Fondo Spada* (e.g., "Atti officiali," "Commissioni provisoria municipale," "Documenti storici colla data," "Documenti storici senza data," "Giornale," "Inviti scrri," "Legge, disposizioni, e regolamente," "Miscellanee politiche," "Motu proprii," "Opere storico politiche," "Proclami, Induzzi, Proglaini, Presidi, Circoli, municipi ordini, etc.," "Stampe litografie pubblicate in Roma"). Indice 706 (II) lists the titles of volumes and publication dates for volumes 200–418.

Location: Archivio Segreto Vaticano.

7.5.74 Sperelli, Sperello

7.5.74.1 Carte Sperelli

[DATABASE ID: VATV10097-A]

Inclusive Dates: 1700–1710.

Bulk: 10 linear m. (96 vols.).

Organization: Six subseries, volume numbers and titles are as follows: 1. Congregatio del concilio, 1701–1710, vols. 1–34; —2. Episcolarum et regularum (Visita), 1700–1710, vols. 35–75; —3. Immunitatus (Visitationes), 1702–1709, vols. 76–87; —4. Visitationis (Congregationis Sacrae Visitationis Apostolicae), 1702–1710, vols. 88–90; —5. Congregationes deputatae (Sacre Congregatione particulari), 1702–1708, vols. 91–94; —6. Propositiones ecclesiarum (also Praeconium) [to Consistory], 1701–1709, vols. 95–96.

Scope: This is a collection of material dealing with the Congregatio Concilii. It contains primarily printed positions and decisions as well as some written petitions.

Reference: Pásztor (1970), p. 148 (n. 2). Pásztor identifies this series as SS. *Spogli, Sperelli* (20 vols.).

Location: Archivio Segreto Vaticano.

7.5.75 Steffani, Agostino

Agostino Steffani (1654–1728) was born at Castel-franco and was an Italian composer, diplomat, and ecclesiastic. At age twelve Count Tattenbach, who had heard him sing at St. Mark's in Venice, brought him to Munich to study. He remained there for two years and obtained the position of court musician; he was soon promoted to director and court organist. In 1673 he went to Rome for one year in order to perfect himself in his profession. In 1688 he left Munich and was attached as musician to the court of Hanover where he resided with the philosopher Leibnitz.

In 1680 he was ordained and also produced his first opera. The Holy See made him an apostolic protonotary for north Germany, and in recognition of his services in Hanover the pope appointed him bishop of Spiga in Asia Minor. He was later appointed ambassador to Brussels. His merits as a musician were solemnly recognized in London by the Academy of Ancient Music, which elected him honorary life-president (1724).

7.5.75.1 Fondo Spiga

[DATABASE ID: VATV20274-A]

Inclusive Dates: 1686–1728.

Bulk: 5 linear m. (86 vols.).

Organization: Subseries volume contents designations and numbers include: vols. 59–65. Lettere, 1704–1729; —vols. 66–75. Roma, 1723–1727; —vols. 76–85. Diversi paesi, 1723–1727; —vol. 86. Pfalz.

Scope: This is a collection of the papers of Bishop Agostino Steffani, titular bishop of Spiga and vicar apostolic of Upper and Lower Saxony from 1705 to 1728. The papers relate primarily to the ecclesiastical history of Germany.

Reference: Kowalsky-Metzler (1988), p. 80.

Location: Historical Archives of the Congregation for the Evangelization of Peoples, or Propaganda Fide.

7.5.76 Theiner, Augustin

Augustin Theiner (1804–1874) was a priest of the Oratory and a student of canon law and history. After studying at Breslau and Halle he received a scholarship from the Prussian government that enabled him to do research throughout Europe. While in Paris he met Lamennais and Moehler who persuaded him to concentrate on ecclesiastical studies. Soon after this, he was ordained a priest and became a member of the Oratory of St. Philip Neri in Rome. Before and during the First Vatican Council (1869–1870) he was in close connection with the opponents of infallibility.

He was an avid historian and made use of the resources of the Vatican Archives. However, because he abused his position in the archives by communicating to Cardinal Hohenlohe the order of business of the Council of Trent that had been kept secret, he was deprived by order of Pius IX of his particular privileges. After his death two volumes were published entitled *Acta genuina SS. oecumenici Concilii Tridentini: sub Paulo III. Julio III. et Pio IV. . . .* (Zagreb, 1874).

7.5.76.1 Carte Theiner

[DATABASE ID: VATV312-A]

Inclusive Dates: 1216 (copy)–1874.

Bulk: 2 linear m. (16 numbered boxes).

Organization: Subseries, box numbers, and titles include: 1–4. Correspondence (organized alphabetically); —5–6. Trascrizioni riguardanti il Concilio di Trento; —11 and 14. Trascrizioni riguardanti la Cina (includes material dealing with Card. de Tournon), ca. 1693–1720; —15–16. Copies of papal documents.

The initial four boxes contain the following: 1. A–F (1177 fol.); —2. G–L (966 fol.); —3. M–R (1067 fol.); —4. S–Z (fol. 1–738), Lettere di scriventi non identificati (fol. 739–836), Lettere non indirizzate al Theiner e non accluse a lettere a lui destinate (fol. 839–896), Lettere e minute di Theiner, 1844–1874 (fol. 897–915), Miscellanea (fol. 916–987) a. Note d'archivio (fol. 917–943), b. Carte d'archivio, fra cui due lettere di Ercole Consalvi del 1806 (fol. 944–954), c. Stampati (fol. 955–977), d. Varia (fol. 978–986), e. Supplemento: Lettere di Giovanni Battista De Negri e Antonino Isaia (sp.)(fol. 988–995), f. Certificato di maturità del Regio Ginnasio Cattolico di Breslau per August Theiner, 1823 VIII 15, Copia authentica (fol. 997–998).

Reference: Boyle, p. 96. Augustin Theiner, ed. *Codex diplomaticus domini temporalis S. Sedis* (Rome, 1861–1862).

Finding Aids: ASV Indici 121* (not in the numerical sequence of indici in the Sala degli Indici) is available at the desk in the ASV main reading room. This is not a formal finding aid and must be used in consultation with the ASV staff. Indici 121* provides a general introduction and a brief overview of the contents of the initial four boxes, which has been reproduced above.

Location: Archivio Segreto Vaticano.

7.5.77 Tosi, Gioacchino

7.5.77.1 Archivio Tosi

[DATABASE ID: VATV10240-A]

Inclusive Dates: 1788–1836.

Bulk: 4 linear m. (57 buste).

Organization: Subseries, buste titles, and numbers are: 1. Posizioni delle cause di Mons. Tosi Vescovo di Anagni risultati delle Congregazione degli Em.mi. Cardinali Congregazioni Disordini, 1814–1815; —2. Atti delle cause, 1814–1815; —3. Protocollo del registro degli atti delle cause; —4. Riflessioni e schiarimenti sopra l'affare di Mons. Tosi; —5. Lettere con relazioni; —6. Posizioni a stampe distribuite ai membri della Cong.ne particolari, 1814; —7–9. Allegati a stampe, 1814; —10. Riflessioni e schiarimenti, 1814; —11. Riflessioni e sommario (stampe), 1814; —12. Ritrattazioni originali di Mons.

Tosi, 1814–1816; —13. Voti dei consultori, 1815; —14. Carteggio di Mons. Tosi con diversi cardinali, vescovi, e prelati di curia, 1806–1809; —15. Biglietti di congressi, nomina del vescovo di Ferertino ad amministrare la diocesi di Anagni. Registro di lettere di Mons. Bonazzoli, 1810–1814, 1817, 1823; —16. Supplice e memoriali pro e contro Mons. Tosi, 1814–1823; —17. Suppliche e lettere di Mons. Tosi al Papa e al Seg. rio di Stato, 1814; —18. Pastorali di Mons. Tosi, 1802–1814; —19. Raccolte di editti e pastorali di Mons. Tosi, 1804–1814; —20. Lettere e pastorali di Mons. Tosi, 1804–1814; —21. Commentario de Rebus Gestis; —22. Sommario della causa di Mons. Tosi, 1823; —23. Carte diverse circa la causa di Mons. Tosi; —24. Biglietti di Pio VII e lettere di Cardinali a Mons. Tosi, 1800–1829; —25. Lettere diverse a Mons. Tosi, 1799–1828; —26. Lettere di personaggi a Mons. Tosi, 1789–1829; —27. Lettere dei Gesuiti, Bartolomeo Montosi ed altri a Mons. Tosi molte di P. Giuseppe Pignatelli; —28. Lettere editti e pastorali di Mons. Tosi, 1802–1806; —29. Lettere diverse di Mons. Tosi al suo Vicario, 1804–1814; —30. Raccolta di lettere sull'affare del canonico Spolverini già vice gerente di Anagni, 1806–1807; —31. Lettere di Mons. Frisoni Angelo, segretario di Mons. Tosi, 1806–1807; —32–36. Lettere di diversi a Mons. Tosi, 1814–1836; —37–40. Lettere di Suor Ignazia Marescotti a Mons. Tosi, 1799–1825; —41. Costituzioni e regole di monache, 1813–1825; —42–43. Lettere diverse di monache a Mons. Tosi, 1804–1822; —44. Posizioni di affari diversi, 1801–1816; —45. Documenti diversi (molti si riferiscono a fatti dell'epoca Napoleonica); —46. Carte riguardanti la causa . . . e carte diverse di Mons. Tosi, 1814–1816; —47. Diverse a Mons. Tosi, 1815; —48–50. Manoscritti vari, autografi di Mons. Tosi; —51–52. Prediche e manoscritti di Mons. Tosi; —53. Omelia, cenni e discorsi per predicare l'Avvento; —54. Carte varie; —55. Registro di lettere latine, epoca in cui Mons. Tosi era segretario delle L.L., 1801–1804; —56. Scritture varie (diretto naturale e pubblico); —57. Duplicati di stampe.

Finding Aids: A brief listing of the contents of each busta is available at the desk in the main ASV reading room. This is not a formal finding aid and must be used in consultation with the ASV staff. This list has been largely reproduced in the organizational note above.

Location: Archivio Segreto Vaticano.

7.5.78 Ubaldini Family

Ottaviano Ubaldini was born in Tuscany about 1210 and died in 1273. He was proposed for the bishopric of Bologna but was too young to receive it. He was, however, appointed administrator. Innocent IV named him a cardinal in 1244, then legate in Lombardy where he used the full strength of the church against Frederick II and Manfredi. Dante alludes to him in his *La divina commedia* (*Inf.* X, 120).

Roberto Ubaldini was born at Florence in 1580 and died in Rome in 1635. He was a nephew and secretary of state of Leo XI (1605) and master of the Apostolic Camera under Paul V (1605–1621). He became bishop of Montepulciano (1606) and nuncio in France, where he endeavored to calm the religious struggle by implementing the decrees of the Council of Trent and working to maintain peace with Spain. He was made a cardinal in 1615 and legate to Bologna in 1623 but in 1632 fell into disgrace with Urban VIII because of his political bias against Spain. The precise relationship of the series listed below and specific family members was not determined.

7.5.78.1 Archivio Ubaldini

[DATABASE ID: VATV457-A]

Inclusive Dates: 1187(copy)–1752 (bulk 1514–1752).

Bulk: 1.5 linear m. (49 numbered vols. and 3 unnumbered bundles).

Scope: This collection consists of material relating to the Urbino legation as well as portions of the archives of the Ubaldini family. In the last unnumbered bundle there is a Registro di supliche from 1574. The 1187 document is in vol. 49.

References: Fink, p. 89; Boyle, pp. 76–77.

Finding Aids: Indice 1023 (pp. 148–151) includes list of volume titles, brief description of contents, inclusive dates, and selected annotations (foliation, dimensions). On pages 235–238, a chronological index to the *Archivio Ubaldini* is presented.

Citation: This collection is usually cited as SS. *Arch. Ubaldini.*

Location: Archivio Segreto Vaticano.

7.5.79 Zarlatti, Francesco

Francesco Zarlatti was maestro di casa for Lord Clifford. Antonio Zarlatti was the esattore of the Odescalchis.

7.5.79.1 Archivio Zarlatti

[DATABASE ID: VATV10283-A]

Inclusive Dates: ca. 1811–1883.

Bulk: 9 linear m. (223 pacchi).

Scope:. In this collection there are financial records concerning the Odescalchi family, Augusto Foscolo (patriarch of Jerusalem), and Scipione Conestabile.

References: Fink, p. 145. G. Gualdo, "Archivi di famiglie romane nell'Archivio vaticano," *Archivio della Società romana di storia patria* 104 (1981): 147–158.

Location: Archivio Segreto Vaticao.

7.6 ARCHCONFRATERNITIES AND CONFRATERNITIES

7.6.1 Arciconfraternità della Pietà dei Carcerati in S. Giovanni della Pigna (Rome)

This confraternity was founded in 1575 (or 1578?) by the Jesuit Giovanni Tagliere for assisting prisoners and expediting the settlement of their cases. It was approved by Gregory XIII (constitution *Pii Patris*, Jun. 28, 1579). In 1582 the confraternity was assigned to the Church of

S. Giovanni della Pigna (so called because it was located in the area by that name).

Sixtus X, a great admirer of the confraternity's work, confirmed its institution and gave it a regular income to help it obtain the release of prisoners at Christmas and Easter and to help the poor who could not pay their debts. He also freed the archconfraternity from a large census debt and with the constitution *Ex debito* (Jul. 1, 1589) allowed it to free a convict from the death penalty in the Papal States on the Monday after the first Sunday of Lent. Since the latter privilege awarded by some pontiffs led to crimes being unpunished, Innocent X (1644) abolished the practice. But such abolitions did not prevent the archconfraternity from the free exercise of its zeal in visiting prisons, seeking justice for the causes of those without means, giving food to the poor, and alms to released prisoners. It also distributed rosaries and spiritual books, preached the Gospel, administered the sacrament of penance, and watched over the *carceri segrete* (secret prisons) and prisoners condemned to the galleys. In 1775 its statutes were printed in Rome under the title *Nuovi statuti della ven. Arciconfraternità della Pietà de' Carcerati.*

7.6.1.1 Archivio dell' Arciconfraternità della Pietà dei Carcerati in S. Giovanni della Pigna

[DATABASE ID: VATV302-A]

Inclusive Dates: 1505–1872.

Bulk: 20 linear m. (260 numbered volumes, plus Libri mastri separately numbered 1–11).

Organization: Subseries, volume numbers, and contents designations include: vols. 1–34, Istromenti, 1572–1781 (some volumes indexed); —vol. 35, Actorum, 1556–1653; —vols. 36–39, Interessi diversi, 1505–1739; —vols. 40–44, Conti, 1556–1702; —vols. 45–107, Giustificazione, 1703–1888; —vols. 108–110, Bilancio, posizioni, procure, 1776–ca. 1850; —vols. 111–113, Congregazione, 1579–1829; —vols. 134–169, Camerlengato, 1584–1657; —vols. 170–181, 187–206, 222–223, Rincontro, ca. 1550–1809; —vol. 182, Rubrica scarcerazione, 1592; —vols. 184–185, Visite per la scarcerazione, 1606–1702; —vol. 186, Libretti scarcerazione, 1711–1719; —vols. 213–253, Registro di mandate, saldo di conti, entrate ed uscita, libri mastri, etc., 1592–1868; —vol. 254 Ordini di pagamento/Registro degli ordini, 1832–1868; —vols. 255–259, Noti, [18—]; —vol. 260, Descrizione dei libri protocolli fascicoli, e filze esistenti nell'Archivio della Ven. Arciconfraternità della Pietà dei Carcerati in S. Giovanni della Pigna. Vols. 1–11. Libri mastri, 1627–1870 (separately numbered 1–11; with separate Rubricelle).

Scope: The earliest item (1505) is in vol. 36; other early items are (1516) in vol. 37, p. 249, a testament of Achille Caravaggio; and one item regarding S. Cosma in Damaso is in vol. 36, p. 69 (1529). Researchers should be warned that the dates on the outside of the buste and the like should be taken with a grain of salt. Neither of the dates on the spines of vols. 36 and 37 above indicate that these early items would be enclosed. Libri mastri vol. 11 is a detailed summary of letters "Registri di lettere," 1757–1768.

References: Fink, p. 126; Boyle, p. 95.

Finding Aids: ASV Indice 703 is an alphabetical index to types of documents (bolle, breve, etc.), persons, churches, other organizations, and selected subjects that can be found in the Carcerati. The volume numbers given in this index refer to the former volume numbers, which are still visible on most of the buste. The current volume numbers can be located by consulting "Catagoria prima" of the "Descrizione dei libri protocolli fascicoli, e filze esistenti nell'Archivio della Ven. Arciconfraternità della Pietà dei Carcerati in S. Giovanni della Pigna" (cf. below). Researchers looking for types of documents in Indice 703 should be careful. Although there is only one listing under Testamenti, there are a number of testaments throughout the Carcerati. Most of the testaments are listed under personal name in Indice 703.

"Descrizione dei libri protocolli fascicoli, e filze esistenti nell'Archivio della Ven. Arciconfraternità della Pietà dei Carcerati in S. Giovanni della Pigna" is vol. 260 of the Carcerati series. This volume is divided into two sections. The "Catagoria prima" is an inventory of all the buste and volumes in the Carcerati (ca. late nineteenth century?). Someone at the ASV has annotated this list in pencil creating a valuable concordanza between the former and current volume numbers. The second section, "Catagoria seconda," is a "descrizione e transunto degli istromenti, testamenti, atti privati, ed altre carte alligate nei Tomi 50. 51. 52. e 53. pertanti il titolo Interesse diverse." Olim. 50–53 respectively bear the current volume numbers 36–39. This section calendars each document in these tomes indicating the date and the notary and providing a detailed description of the document.

"Rubricelle degli istrumenti esistenti nell'Archivio della Ven. Arcità. della Pietà dei Carcerati," olim. vol. 48 (which has not been given a new volume number), is located in the stacks between vols. 34 and 35. This volume says that it is an index to olim. vols. 45 and 46, but it is actually an index to olim. vols. 46 and 47 (currently vols. 33 and 34). This rubricelle provides more detailed access to vols. 33 and 34 than the other indices. This rubricelle also contains a "Catalogo degli atti notarili esistente nell'Archivio Urbano risguardanti la Ven. Arcità. della Pietà."

Location: Archivio Segreto Vaticano.

7.6.2 Arciconfraternità del Gonfalone (Rome)

The Arciconfraternità del Gonfalone, probably a derivative of the ascetic movement promoted by Ranieri Fassani, was founded in 1264 at S. Maria Maggiore in Rome by twelve noble standard-bearers (gonfalonieri) as the Compagnia dei Raccomandati della SS. Vergine. St. Bonaventure (ca. 1217–1274), then inquisitor general and later superior general of the Franciscan Order, sponsored their formation and received them into spiritual communion with the Franciscans. Their way of life, or rule, was drawn up, and a habit designed (white with a red cross on the right shoulder). The chapel of the Madonna della Pietà in the basilica of S. Maria Maggiore was assigned as their station. Their purpose was defined as the ransom of captives.

From the beginning, with the approval of Clement IV (1265), the members of the confraternity called themselves the raccomandati della SS. Vergine. In 1354 during the turbulence in Rome because of the death of Cola di Rienzo, the members of the Raccomandati della SS. Vergine rose in opposition to the violence of the Roman lords whom they perceived as oppressive. They unanimously elected as the vicar of the pope Giovanni Cerone, a popular older Roman who was also a governor of the Campidoglio. He gave the society the name of Gonfalone since it was under the standard of liberty, country, and justice that they had helped restore liberty to the city of Rome. It was on this occasion that the Roman pontiffs assigned the raccomandati to the Church of SS. Pietro e Paolo. The members of the Gonfalone also had the care of the miraculous statue of the Madonna preserved at Santa Maria Maggiore.

Gregory XIII raised the confraternity of the Gonfalone to an archconfraternity and gave it the task of redeeming slaves. With his constitution of October 12, 1576, he granted many indulgences for reciting the rosary by these brothers according to the prescriptions of St. Bonaventure and to other prayers as noted in their statutes. Sixtus V granted these privileges only to the congregations established in the colleges of the Jesuits (constitution *Cum benigna*, April 1, 1586). This collection was acquired by the ASV in 1950 and 1957.

7.6.2.1 Archivio della Arciconfraternità del Gonfalone

[DATABASE ID: VATV301-A]

Inclusive Dates: 1267–1897.

Bulk: 112 linear m. (1403 numbered buste, vols., and boxes, plus 2 linear m. of unnumbered materials).

Organization: Subseries with contents designations and buste numbers include: 1–24. [Antichita] Mazzi A–Z, 1351–1765; —25–41. [Antichita] Mazzi I–XVII, 1339–1720; —42–45. Statuti, 1584–1735; —46–70. Decreti, 1528–1857; —71–88. Congregazioni o congressi, 1578–1889; —89–102. Libri di puntature dei fratelli, 1797–1893; —103–107. Libri di anniversari, 1470–1564; —108–249. Entrata e uscita del camerlengo, 1479–1629; —250–402. Libri dell'esattore, 1507–1876; —403–443. Registri dei mandati, 1544–1858; —444–505. Computisteria, 1496–1798; —506–699. Giustificazioni, 1550–1891; —700–734. "Instrumenta", 1447–1887; —735–768. Catasti, 1483–ca. 1700; —769–785. Libri mastri, 1696–1876; —786–789. Libri di salariati, 1526–1671; —790–813. Rendiconti diversi di banche e monti, 1630–1695; —814–859. Case e botteghe, ca. 1400–1876; —860–868. Stato dei fondi urbani, ca. 1600–1891; —869–876. Oratorio del Gonfalone e chiesa di S. Lucia, 1685–1868; —877–1024. Registri di messe, litanie e obblighi liturgici, 1690–1890; —1025–1037. Spese per la cera, 1660–1878; —1038–1088. Cappellanie, 1594, 1839–1874; —1089–1096. Anni Santi, 1550, 1650–1725; —1097–1113. Pia casa del rifugio, 1671–1891; —1114–1172. Doti e matrimoni di zitelle, 1495–1886; —1138–1172. Opera pia del riscatto degli schiavi, 1526–1858; —1173–1189. Cause giudiziarie diverse, 1563–ca. 1800; —1090–1217. Miscellanea, ca. 1457–1890; —1218–1227. Inventari, 1480–1757; —1228–1231. Rubricelle, 1726–1856; —1232–1243. Confraternite aggregate, 1560–ca. 1702; —1244–1253. Eredità Carpegna, 1714–1834; —1254–1269. Eredità Díaz, 1612–1798; —1270–

1275. Eredità Gasparri Ferretti, 1840–1890; —1276–1342. Eredità Ghirlandari, 1336–1889; —1343–1382. Eredità Rustici Castellani, 1565–1798; —1383–1402. Eredità Scapucci, 1563–1772; —1403. Prestiti d'archivio, 1889–1891.

References: Fink, p. 126. L. Ruggeri, *L'Archiconfraternità del Gonfalone: Memorie* (Rome, 1866). This is the basic historical study to date on the Gonfalone. Ruggeri cites the Gonfalone by its former volume numbers and therefore the concordanza between the former and current volume numbers in Pagano (cf. below) is essential for locating documents identified by Ruggeri. S. Pagano and G. Barone, "Archconfraternità del Gonfalone," *Ricerche per la storia religiosa di Roma* 6 (1985): 215–219, provides a brief historical introduction to the collection.

G. Barone and A. M. Piazzoni, "Le più antiche carte dell'Archivio del Gonfalone (1267–1486)," in *Le chiavi della memoria: Miscellanea in occasione del I centenario della Scuola vaticana di paleografia, diplomatica e archivistica,* (Vatican City, 1984), pp. 17–105. S. Bono, "L'Arciconfraternità del Gonfalone di Roma e il riscatto degli schiavi dai musulmani," *Capitolium* (Sept. 1957): 3–7. S. Bono, "Genovesi schiavi in Algeri barbaresca," *Bollettino ligustico per la storia e la cultura regionale* 3 (1953): 67–72. S. Bono, "La missione dei Cappuccini ad Algeri per il rescatto degli schiavi cristiani nel 1585," *Collectanea Franciscana* 25 (1955): 149–163, 279–304.

Le confraternite Romane: Esperienza religiosa, società, commitenza artistica: Colloquio della Fondazione Caetani, roma, 14–15 maggio 1982, edited by L. Fiorani (Rome, 1984), is devoted to confraternities in Rome. In particular, three articles concern the Gonfalone: A. Cavallaro, "Antoniazzo Romano e le confraternità del Quattrocento a Roma," 335–365 (art history); A. Esposito, "Le 'confraternite' del Gonfalone (secoli XIV–XV)," 91–136 (social history); and A. Serra, "Funzioni e finanze delle confraternite romane tra il 1624 e il 1797," 261–292 (economic history). V. De Bartholomaeis, *Le origini della poesia drammatica italiana,* 2d ed. (Turin, 1952) deals with theater history. K. Oberhuber, "Jacopo Bertoia im Oratorium von S. Lucia del Gonfalone in Rom," *Römische historische Mitteilungen* 3 (1958–60): 239–254. M. Vattasso, *Per la storia del dramma sacro in Italia* (Rome, 1903).

Finding Aids: S. Pagano, *L'Archivio dell'Arciconfraternita del Gonfalone: Cenni storici e inventario* (Vatican City, 1990). Pagano's published index provides detailed access to the *Archivio Gonfalone* and supersedes ASV Indici 700 (cf. below). This index includes a lengthy introduction to the history of the Gonfalone and its archives, bibliographies on confraternities in Rome and scholarly use of the *Archivio Gonfalone,* a concordanza between the former and current volume numbers, a chronological prospectus and a prospectus to the subseries (cf. above), as well as internal indices to soggetti, persons and places, and Gonfalone officials (notaries). Most important, Pagano proceeds through the collection busta by busta describing the contents of each busta (persons and business involved, inclusive dates, etc.), and often listing all items in certain buste (e.g., istromenti) individually. The descriptions of items in quotation marks are taken directly from ASV Indice 700. Pagano indicates both the document number and folio, since many of the mazzi have continuous numeration and are cited by researchers by both the document number and folio. Pagano's index represents an extraordinary effort to make the *Archivio Gonfalone* more accessible to researchers. There are caveats in using the index, however. Researchers should study this entire volume to familiarize themselves with Pagano's detailed presentation of the Gonfalone. The extensive internal indices, which do not overlap, are invaluable, but tricky to use. Indices to personal and place names, soggetti, and notaries exist and should be considered comprehensive but not totally complete (e.g., information on Eredità Rustici Castellani appears in no. 730/80 but not in the internal index). Because of the nature of the categorization of materials these indexes have to be used carefully. For example, if one is looking for information on Santa Cecilia in Trastevere one must first look in the special section of the name and place index dealing with Rome. From there, one can consult the list of churches (which will not reveal any references to Santa Cecilia), or the list of convents and monasteries (which will be fruitful).

ASV Indice 700, "Rubricella degli atti e documenti della ven. archiconfraternita del SS.mo Gonfalone di Roma, compilata da Giovanni de Regis nell'anno 1877," indexes six volumes of the Istromenti, current volume numbers 729–734. Indice 700 contains two sections, an A–Z internal index and then a description of documents, primarily regarding the eighteenth and nineteenth centuries, according to categories (e.g., istromenti, legati, case, etc.). Generally the exact descriptions from this index are transcribed by Pagano (cf. above). Very occasionally, however, Indice 700 provides more amplified information (e.g., no. 730/1, Crivelli testament is summarized in Indice 700). Documents are presented in chronological order within each category.

Location: Archivio Segreto Vaticano.

7.6.3 Arciconfraternità del Santissimo Sacramento, Immacolata Concezione, Beata Vergine della Cintura, Santi Martiri Trifono, Respicio, Ninfa e San Camillo de Lellis

This archconfraternity was the result of a merger approved by Pius VII in 1802 of two separate archconfraternities. The first and older of the two, called Arciconfraternità del Santissimo Sacramento, Beata Vergine della Cintura (o Maria Santissima della Cintura), dei Santi martiri Trifone, Respicio e Ninfa, was established in the old church of San Trifone in the via della Scrofa. That church traditionally preserved relics of Saint Tryphon and his company of martyrs. On April 7, 1571, Pius V approved the establishment of a confraternity. When the old church of San Trifone was demolished, the confraternity was transferred to the Church of S. Agostino. By bull *Onerosa summi pastoralis* (Nov. 13, 1734), Clement XII established the confraternity at San Salvatore in Primicerio near Piazza Fiammetta.

The second, the Arciconfraternità del SS.mo Sacramento, Immacolata Concezione, S. Camillo de Lellis, was established at the Church of Sante Simone e Giuda ai Coronari during the pontificate of Benedict XIV (1740–1758). Financial pressures led it to propose a merger with the confraternity of S. Trifone. The merged group was established at the Church of S. Salvatore in

Primicerio. The group continued until sometime between 1928 and 1942 (documentation not clear).

7.6.3.1 Arciconfraternità del Santissimo Sacramento, Immacolata Concezione, Beata Vergine della Cintura, Santi Martiri Trifono, Respicio, Ninfa e San Camillo de Lellis
[DATABASE ID: VATV40023-A]
Inclusive Dates: 1632–1921.
Bulk: 10 linear m. (134 buste and volumes).
Organization: The series is divided into three subseries: Arciconfraternità del Santissimo Sacramento, Beata Vergine della Cintura, Santi Martiri Trifono, Respicio e Ninfa 1632–1834; —Confraternità del Santissimo Sacramento, Immacolata Concezione e San Camillo de Lellis 1758–1803; —Arciconfraternità del Santissimo Sacramento, Immacolata Concezione, Beata Vergine dell Cintura, Santi Martiri Trifone, Respicio, Ninfa e San Camillo de Lellis, 1802–1923.
Scope: The series contains mostly financial information for each organization. There is some membership information, correspondence, and printed items.
Reference: Natalini et al., p. 267.
Finding Aids: ASV Index 1171 prepared by Francesca di Giovanni contains a detailed inventory of the series with some indication of the dates and contents of each volume or buste. In addition, it provides an index of names in the series.
Location: Archivio Segreto Vaticano.

7.6.4 Arciconfraternità del SS. Crocifisso in S. Marcello (Rome)

This confraternity had its origin in a special devotion that referred to a crucifix in the Church of S. Marcello. The crucifix had been recovered intact after a fire had destroyed the church. Many people began to venerate the image in a distinctive way. In 1522, when Rome was attacked by a contagious disease, some devout people instituted a society of persons who carried the crucifix in procession to the Basilica of St. Peter, begging pardon of the Lord for their faults. This society was eventually called the Arciconfraternità del SS. Crocifisso.

In 1523 Clement VII confirmed the statutes of the oratory of the archconfraternity and Julius III (1550) granted it the privilege of freeing every year a prisoner condemned to death, a privilege no longer enjoyed by the society. Legend has it that among those who benefited from such a concession was the celebrated Bernardo Cenci, a young boy of fifteen who, along with his sister Beatrice, was accused of parricide. After three days Bernardo was set free from prison and death but with the condition that each year he would pay twenty-five scudi to the Arciconfraternità della Santissima Trinità. It was later demonstrated by the celebrated jurist Farinaccio that Bernardo was innocent.

On the day of the Epiphany the archconfraternity gives clothing, dinner, and alms to three poor people in honor of the Most Holy Trinity. It has its station a little distance from the Church of S. Marcello, built by Cardinal Alessandro and Ranuccio Farnese, the façade of which was designed by Vignola. The statutes of the archconfraternity were published in Urbino in 1771.

7.6.4.1 Archivio della Arciconfraternità del SS. Crocifisso in S. Marcello

[DATABASE ID: VATV300-A]

Inclusive Dates: 1400–1890.

Bulk: 89 linear m.

Organization: Subseries include: A–XI. Libri dei camerlenghi (and misc. financial records), 1529–1890; —B–XIX. Carte delle vertenze per la amministrazione delle rendite del Monastero delle Cappuccinie in Monte Cavallo, 1583–[18—];—G. Appuntature dei Fratelli, 1721–1858; —H–XVII. Libro de decreti della S. Visita di S. Marcello, 1753–1760; —I–V. Istrumenti, 1400–1621; —Manuale actorum, 1619–1626; —Sodisfazione di Messe, 1705–1842; —Q. Oblighi di Messe, 1852–1875; —Q–R. Doti. (The alphanumeric system for the subseries is taken directly from the collection itself.)

Scope: The earliest document (1400) in Istrumenti volume I–V/4.

Note: A portion is available on microfilm.

References: Fink, p. 133; Boyle, p.95.

Finding Aids: ASV Indice 702 provides a general inventory in the form of an alphabetical list of types of documents, personal names, other organizations, and the like to most of the SS. *Crocifisso* series and calendars three istrumenti volumes I–V/2–4. Indice 702 organizes the SS. *Crocifisso in S. Marcello* materials according to an alphabetical and numerical schema by which the records can still be identified. However, the records are not as well organized as indicated by Indice 702, and the material requested may be difficult to locate. Finally, not all the materials in this series fall within this alphanumeric schema and are therefore not mentioned in Indice 702.

Location: Archivio Segreto Vaticano.

7.6.5 Arciconfraternità del Sacramento

This archconfraternity probably had its origin in the Compagnia del SS. Sacramento instituted in the Church of S. Maria sopra Minerva by a society of citizens and Roman curials under the direction of the Dominican Tommaso Stella. The purpose of the religious union was to promote devotion to the Holy Eucharist, visits to the Blessed Sacrament, care for the decoration of churches and altars, and vigilance over places where the Blessed Sacrament was reserved and from which it was carried with reverence to the infirm. The constitution of Paul III (*Dominus noster*, Nov. 30, 1539) confirmed the institute, enriched it with indulgences, and decreed that all confraternities in existence with the same aim or name be automatically affiliated with the Confraternity of the Blessed Sacrament of the Minerva.

On November 3, 1606, Paul V granted it many other privileges and indulgences and established it as an archconfraternity. It is believed to be the first dedicated to Corpus Christi and to have drawn others to it to honor the sacrament. Many cardinals participate in the annual procession, which is held the Friday morning within the octave of the feast of Corpus Christi. The ceremony is conducted with great dignity as the procession makes its way to the patriarchal churches and basilicas of Rome. The archconfraternity distributes many alms. The form of its logo is a chalice with two angels upholding the host.

Almost contemporary with the compagnia founded at the Minerva (1539) was the compagnia of the sacrament founded by Giacomo Hercolano at St. Peter's Basilica. Approved in 1540 by Paul III it was given the name Arciconfraternità del SS. Corpo di Cristo. The first location of the society was in an oratory in the atrium of the basilica where members gathered to conduct meetings and to hear talks by one of the canons. Later, at the request of Paul III, the center was moved to the chapel of SS. Simon and Jude in St. Peter's, which was converted to an oratory through the work of Antonio da Sangallo, Antonio Labacco, and Perin del Vaga. The new chapel was consecrated on March 19, 1548. At the beginning of the seventeenth century the society established itself in the Church of S. Caterina de porticu S. Petri and more recently in the Church of SS. Michele e Magno.

At the head of this confraternity were the cardinal protector and primicerio, five deputies, and a camerlengo; these constituted the board or major advisers; there were also many minor officials. In 1586 the members began to wear the red robe with the emblem of the society. The members' main activities were: the solemn accompaniment of the viaticum for the infirm; annual liberation of a prisoner condemned to the gallows; distribution of subsidies to the poor; and in particular the exposition of the Blessed Sacrament on Quinquagesima Sunday at the time of the carnival. During the Holy Years the society assisted pilgrims, supported a hospice for poor Spanish pilgrims (instituted in cooperation with the Spanish priest Cristoforo Cabrera in Borgo Pio), and took care of the burial of the dead. There is an actual statute of the archconfraternity (Mar. 10, 1924) that reaffirms, in substance, the original objective of the confraternity. Along with its other duties, the association also cares for the chapel that, since the time of Paul III, it maintains in St. Peter's.

7.6.5.1 Archivio della Arciconfraternità del Sacramento

[DATABASE ID: VATV177-A]

Inclusive Dates: 1692–1880.

Bulk: 10 linear m.

Summary: These records appear to be mainly financial records, that is, proveditore de morti; giustificazione; eredità Madalena Stampa, 1818; 1692 item is a financial ledger entitled "Principia il libro dell'appuntature."

Location: Archivio Segreto Vaticano.

7.6.5.2 Archivio della Arciconfraternità del SS.mo Sacramento

[DATABASE ID: VATV40037-A]

Inclusive Dates: 1645–post 1922.

Bulk: 230 registri, volumi e mazzi, plus 7 scatole of miscellaneous material.

Organization: These materials are organized into six subseries:

1. Atti ufficiali: Decreti de congregazione, 1545–1817 (5 vols.); Cataloghi dei fratelli, 1541–1816 (5); Procure e lettere di compagnie aggregate, sec. XVI–XIX (3); Congregazioni e congressi, 1818–1903 (3); Sacra visita, 1904.

2. Chiesa: Processioni e morti, 1546–1826 (10); Messe per defunti, 1745–1790 (2); Legati pii; Indugenze 1613.

3. Patrimonio: Instrumenti, 1545–1793 (11); Restauri e vendite di case di borgo Pio e Vittorio, in via della Vite; Stato attivo e passivo delle eredità, 1819–1823; Inventari delle scritture, 1627, 1671.

4. Amministrazione e contabilità: Mandati, 1573–1815 (89); Mandati e giustificazioni, 1687—sec. XX (33); Libri mastri, 1610–1871 (6); Rubricella del libro mastro; Filza del libro mastro, 1892–1895; Entrate e uscite, 1547–1816 (53); Introito e esito del camerlengo, 1802–1849 (2); Inventari dei mobili, 1627–1671 (3); Bilanci, 1821–1915; Vertenze; Corrispondenza.

5. Assistenza: Registro dei denari ricevuti dagli osti per le elemosine, 1789–1817; Libro delle zitelle dotate, 1655; Rubricella delle doti conferite, sec. XIX; Libro delle pellegrine che dalla priora saranno ricettate nell'ospizio, 1661–1672.

6. Varie: Rubricella d'archivio, s.d. (fine sec. XVII–sec. XVIII con altre scritture ottocentesche); Fogli stampati dalla Repubblica Romana, 1798, 1846.

Location: Archivio della Reverenda Fabbrica di S. Pietro.

7.6.6 Confraternità di S. Giovanni Decollato

[DATABASE ID: VATV888-A]

This group was established in 1488. In the Papal States, the confraternity was related to the Tribunale del governatore (to 1809), the Tribunale del governo di Roma (1814–1847), and the Tribunale criminale di Roma (1847–1870).

7.6.6.1 Confraternità di S. Giovanni Decollato

[DATABASE ID: VATV20076-A]

Inclusive Dates: 1497–1870.

Bulk: 36 registri and 4 fascicoli.

Organization: Giornale del provveditore, 24 registri; —Ultime volontà dichiarate al cappellano, 11 registri; —Interessi dei carcerati, 4 fascicoli; —Ordini ricevuti dai vari tribunali per l'esecuzione delle sentenze, 1 registro.

References: D'Angiolini, p. 1134; Lodolini (1960), p. 122.

Finding Aids: Inventory (1971), and alphabetical calendar of executed men (nineteenth century).

Location: Archivio di Stato di Roma.

7.7
RELIGIOUS ORDERS

[DATABASE ID: VATV10324-A]

This is a collection of material occupying in total about 30 linear meters in the ASV. Holdings for each order are described separately in this section of the guide. However, the material is often referred to as a single entity titled *Ordini religiosi*. It is difficult to determine the exact origin of these series. Many contain lists of the religious houses for the various congregations represented and/or books of decisions pertaining to the careers and activities of members of the orders and the maintenance of their property holdings. Entries in this section are alphabetical by the English form of the name of the order, which is not always the most commonly used form.

There can be three separate or perhaps combined hypotheses to the origin of these records. First, these materials may have originally been part of the Generalate Archives of these congregations that were taken to Paris by Napoleon and then returned to the Vatican on the assumption that they would be returned to the individual congregations (cf. J. T. Minisci. "Il fondo 'Basiliani' dell'Archivio segreto vaticano," *Bollettino della Badia Greca di Grottaferrata* n.s. 6 [1952]: 65–85). Another hypothesis is that these records are part of the missing volumes of the Congregatio sullo Stato Religiosi cited by Boaga in his *La soppressione innocenziana dei piccoli conventi in Italia* (Rome, 1971). The records of these congregations generally begin in the early sixteenth century and many appear to be concerned with the locations and size of religious houses, and some, as the Barnabiti, directly deal with the suppression of monasteries (although the letters in that case are to the secretary of state). A third possibility is that they were assembled in the course of a judicial or regulatory process by a congregation or office. In any case, the project staff did not have sufficient time to explore the records listed or the relevant bibliography to determine answers to these questions. The introductions to the various orders are provided simply as a context for understanding in a general way the likely origin of the material.

Reference. Fink, pp. 138, 151.

7.7.1 Antonines

Antonines is the popular name given to several communities claiming the patronage of St. Antony of Egypt (ca. 251–ca. 354), among them the Maronites (founded 1695; approved 1732) who without sufficient historical evidence trace continuity with the original disciples of St. Antony in the desert. The Hospital Brothers of St. Antony, founded by Gaston de Dauphiné (1095), did not survive beyond the French Revolution. The so-called rule of St. Antony is dated after the latter's death but is based on authentic and apocryphal writings of St. Antony.

7.7.1.1 Antoniani

[DATABASE ID: VATV10326-A]

Inclusive Dates: 1641–1791.

Bulk: .1 linear m. (1 busta).

Organization: Monastero di S. Antonio di Vienna, Bolle

d'Innocenzo X e Urbano VIII; —Bolla di soppressione dell'Ordine Ospitalario detto degli Antoniani tanto in Francia, quanto in Piedmonte, in Napoli, ed in altri luoghi, 1791; —Memorie, 1726–1789 (Turin, S. Marcellin).

Location: Archivio Segreto Vaticano.

7.7.2 Apostolic Clerics of St. Jerome

Originally a lay congregation founded about 1366 in Siena, Italy, by Bl. John Colombini and approved by Urban V in 1367. In the beginning the members followed the Benedictine rule, but in 1426 Bl. John of Tossignano composed their constitutions based on the rule of St. Augustine. Their particular dedication was to the works of mercy, especially the care of the sick. Frequent use of the name "Jesus" at the beginning and end of their sermons led to their being called "Jesuati" (Gesuati). In 1499, with the approval of Alexander VI, they changed their name to Apostolic Clerics of St. Jerome. They took only minor orders until 1606 when Paul V granted permission for some of their members to pursue higher studies and to be ordained. In 1668 Clement IX's bull (*Romanus Pontifex*) dissolved the congregation because of their small numbers and because many of their members had lost the original spirit of the order. About 1367 Catherine, Colombini's cousin, established the Poor Jesuatesses of the Visitation of the Blessed Virgin Mary, a contemplative order following the rule of St. Augustine. The congregation survived in Italy until 1872.

7.7.2.1 Gesuati

[DATABASE ID: VATV10346-A]

Inclusive Dates: ca. 1400–1800.

Bulk: .05 linear m. (1 busta).

Scope: The earliest materials of the ordini religiosi are here, dating back to at least 1488.

Location: Archivio Segreto Vaticano.

7.7.3 Augustinians

The Augustinians, formerly called Hermits of St. Augustine, trace their lineage to Augustine (354–430), bishop of Hippo and Doctor of the Church. In 1256 a number of groups were canonically organized as a mendicant religious order dedicated not only to community life in prayer, meditation, and solitude, but also to the active apostolate in the towns. Its constitutions, newly revised in 1968, are based on the rule and writings of Augustine. Historical linkage with Augustine has never been established, but the order follows his rule, and its tradition has been characterized by constant study of and devotion to St. Augustine.

7.7.3.1 Fondo Agostiniani: Pergamene

[DATABASE ID: VATV318-A]

Inclusive Dates: 1287–1762.

Bulk: 188 items.

Organization: This collection divides into two series: I. 1258–1762 (items numbered 1–157); —II. 1491–1682 (items numbered 158–188).

References: Pásztor (1970), pp. 232–233; Fink, pp. 138, 151; Boyle, p. 96.

Note: This collection is usually cited by its subseries: *Fondo Agostiniani* I, and *Fondo Agostiniani* II.

Location: Archivio Segreto Vaticano.

7.7.3.2 Fondo Agostiniani III: Pacchi

[DATABASE ID: VATV10325-A]

Inclusive Dates: ca. 1500–1771.

Bulk: .5 linear m. (9 pacchi).

Scope: This is a miscellany of materials dealing with everything from the involvement of the Augustinians in trying to convert the king of England in 1652 to a list (by Garampi) of bulls (in the RV?) dealing with the Augustinians.

Reference: Pásztor (1970), pp. 232–233.

Finding Aids: ASV Blocchetti Indice 1 (after item 188) contains a partial and outdated index to the initial five pacchi. Blocchetti 1 gives brief summaries of documents that were in the Agostiniani about 1930. Although the blocchetti can be used today, two caveats apply: (1) not all the items in pacchi 1–5 are noted and (2) some items listed in the blocchetti are no longer in the pacchi.

Note: This collection is usually cited as *Fondo Agostiniani* III.

Location: Archivio Segreto Vaticano.

7.7.4 Augustinians. Provincia di Lombardia

7.7.4.1 Agostiniani Osservanti di Lombardia

[DATABASE ID: VATV10330-A]

Inclusive Dates: 1671–1782.

Bulk: .3 linear m. (6 vols.).

Organization: Volume titles include: Decreta P. Francisci Marie Curani de Cremona, Viar. Gen. Cong. Lomb., 1671–1677; —Decreta, 1725–1734; —Liber secret, 1759–1771 (sequuntur decreta sub regimine R.P. Augustini Bazani di Taurino S.T.L.E. Vic. Gen. elect 16 april 1758); —Liber decretorum, 1743–1750; —Directorio, 1782; —Filiationes Conventium Nostre Congregationes Observantie Lombardie.

Scope: The largest section of this series is four volumes of Liber decretorum. These contain decisions pertaining to the careers and activities of members of the order and to the maintenance of the property of the congregation. All volumes except the Liber decretorium, 1743–1750, are identified as concerning the Lombard congregation. This volume says that it was given to the archive of the congregation in Rome. The Directorio is for the procuratòr general of the order and lists who is annually paid, when, and in what congregations and curial institutions around Rome.

Location: Archivio Segreto Vaticano.

7.7.4.2 Procuratore generale

[DATABASE ID: VATV10412-A]

Inclusive Dates: 1472 (copy)–1743.

Bulk: 1 linear m.

Organization: Volume titles include: 1. "Cartularium ordinis sive Congregationis Fratrum Heremitarum Sancti

Agostini provincie Lombardie de Observantia ab anno 1472 usque ad anno 1695"; —2. includes "Acta definitorii capituli Generalis celebrati in conventu S. Maria Misericordiae [Bologna] anno 1628."

Scope: All volumes appear to be from the congregation (office of the procurator general). Volume 1 says it is a copy of a book of supplications made by Guilliotus of Torino, procurialis general of the Augustinians of Lombardy. (The original book was done by L. Grifus, under Egidius of Viterbo.) However, volume 1 appears to be part Guilliotus's copy and part earlier copies. Volume 1 also appears to include a register of successful responses to supplications. The procurator general also acted as a ponente for the supplications of the Augustinians of Lombardy and others, for example, nuns. The other volumes contain much of a similar variety of material, including supplications, original bulls and briefs, acta from the chapter meetings, verification that Masses were celebrated, faculties to reform convents, and so forth for convents all over Italy.

Location: Archivio Segreto Vaticano.

7.7.5 Barnabites

The Barnabites are a religious order founded in Milan in 1530 by St. Antonio Maria Zaccaria. Formally known as the Clerks Regular of St. Paul, they were popularly called Barnabites from their church of St. Barnabas in Milan. They are committed to parish ministry, education of the young, preaching, and missions to the unbaptized.

7.7.5.1 Barnabiti

[DATABASE ID: VATV10327-A]
Inclusive Dates: 1743–1796.
Bulk: .05 linear m. (1 busta).
Scope: Material includes a letter regarding the finances of the Barnabiti college in Perugia, an inventory of the Chiesa del Gesù (Perugia), and letters from Lucerne to the Secretario di Stato concerning Giacomo Verdel.
Location: Archivio Segreto Vaticano.

7.7.6 Benedictines

Benedictines carry on a tradition that stems from the origin of the Christian monastic movement in the third century. St. Benedict (ca. 480–ca. 550) was born at Nursia and educated at Rome. About the year 500, the condition of contemporary society led him to withdraw to a cave at nearby Subiaco where a community gradually grew up around him. In 525 he moved with a small band of monks to Monte Cassino where he remained until his death. It was here (ca. 540) that he drew up his plan for the reform of monasticism and composed a rule for his monks, mostly laymen. This rule, which reflected contemporary practice, was for almost two centuries merely one of several from which abbots could choose. Meanwhile, the rule found its way to monasteries in England, Gaul, and elsewhere, becoming the

rule of choice for monasteries of Europe from the ninth century onward.

The fifteenth century saw the beginning of a new form of Benedictine life, that is, the congregation, which gave rise to more regular life in their monasteries. All the houses of Italy and Sicily eventually joined the congregation, which with the accession of Monte Cassino in 1504 called itself the Cassinese Congregation. The reform movement that followed spread to the formation of many other confederations.

The bond joining Benedictine monks has been in the main a spiritual rather than an organizational one. The Order of St. Benedict signifies not a centralized institute but a confederation of congregations of monks and nuns following the rule of Benedict. Each monastery is autonomous with no juridical ties to the rest of the confederation.

7.7.6.1 Benedettini

[DATABASE ID: VATV10328-A]
Inclusive Dates: 1708–1800.
Bulk: .3 linear m. (3 buste).
Scope: The collection contains many historical notes on the Benedictines dating back to Martin V, particularly regarding privileges. There are also printed materials regarding the order in Cluny.
Location: Archivio Segreto Vaticano.

7.7.6.2 Cassinensi

[DATABASE ID: VATV10335-A]
Inclusive Dates: 1628–1792.
Bulk: .05 linear m. (1 busta).
Scope: This collection concerns houses in Ferrara, Venice, and Subiaco, but mainly correspondence of the generalate in Rome, acts of the chapter from 1688 to 1760, and "Practica solita farsi nel Capitolo Genle. della Congregazion Casinense a tenore della Sa. Regola e Costituzioni Apostoliche."
Location: Archivio Segreto Vaticano.

7.7.7 Bethlehemites

The name *Bethlehemites* has been applied to several orders of religious at different times. One order of men and women following the rule of St. Augustine was dedicated to hospital work. Their priory in London (ca. 1247), known as the hospital of St. Mary of Bethlehem, housed mentally ill patients. After the dissolution of the monasteries under Henry VIII, the hospital became a royal foundation for the mentally ill. A few other houses of this order are known to have been established in Scotland, Italy, and France. A military order dedicated to Our Lady of Bethlehem was established at Cambridge in 1257. Pius II also founded a military order dedicated to Mary of Bethlehem for the defense of the island of Lemnos against the Turks after the fall of Constantinople in 1453. Another order of Bethlehemites or Belemites (also called Hospitallers) was founded by Pedro de

Betancourt about 1650 in Guatemala for the purpose of caring for the sick, working with prisoners, and educating poor children. The order was suppressed by the government in 1820.

7.7.7.1 Fondo Betlemiti

[DATABASE ID: VATV40034-A]

Inclusive Dates: [16—]–[18—].

Bulk: 59 buste and vols.

Note: This series was cited in Natalini et al., p. 271, but not seen by project staff in 1994.

Location: Archivio Segreto Vaticano.

7.7.8 Brothers Hospitallers of St. John of God

This Order of Charity for the Service of the Sick, or Brothers Hospitallers, was founded by St. John of God (1495–1550), a Portuguese soldier and shepherd. The order, whose members are for the most part laymen, developed out of St. John's work for the sick. In 1572 Pius V formally approved the order, which adopted the Augustinian rule. The spirit of the congregation is summed up in its motto, "Caritas."

7.7.8.1 Benefratelli

[DATABASE ID: VATV10331-A]

Inclusive Dates: 1731–1807.

Bulk: .05 linear m. (1 busta).

Scope: These records are original supplications to the pope concerning privileges relating to the provinces of Baviera and Fabriano.

Location: Archivio Segreto Vaticano.

7.7.9 Camaldolites

The Camaldolites are a religious order founded about 1012 by St. Romuald, a Benedictine, at Camaldoli (Campus Maldoli) near Arezzo. As part of the monastic reform movement of the tenth and eleventh centuries, Romuald intended to combine the eremetic or hermit-like life with the cenobitic or communal life of Western monasteries, notably the Benedictine. In the beginning its ideal was to have a minimum of communal ties, but in 1102 a monastery was founded at Fontebuono with ordinary cenobitic regulations. Romuald left no written rule and even today practice differs in the various congregations.

7.7.9.1 Camaldolesi

[DATABASE ID: VATV10332-A]

Inclusive Dates: 1684–1776.

Bulk: .05 linear m. (1 busta).

Scope: These records are primarily financial records, "Libretti delle ricevute," between 1684 and 1690, of the Abbot Aureliano Franchi. There is also a minute of a letter concerning the "nuovo consenso."

Location: Archivio Segreto Vaticano.

7.7.10 Canons Regular of Our Savior

The congregation of Ssmo Salvatore, also called Congregatio Renana, was so called from the Church of S. Salvatore in Bologna to which, in the middle of the fourteenth century, the Canons Regular of S. Maria di Reno were transferred. At the beginning of the twelfth century this latter order was located on the little stream of Reno within the territory of Bologna. However, the foundation of this congregation was the work of Stefano Agazzari, prior of the recently founded Canons Regular of S. Ambrogio in Gubbio. In 1418 Agazzari obtained permission from Pope Martin V to unite the Canons of S. Ambrogio with those of S. Salvatore. The following year the Congregation of Ssmo Salvatore was formed. Many other canons regular joined the congregation in succeeding years. The congregation was suppressed in 1810 but restored during the years 1814–1819. A decree of 1823 joined the restored congregation to that of the Lateran under name Canons Regular of the Most Holy Savior of the Lateran (Canonici Regolari della Congregazione del Ssmo Salvatore Lateranense). It later became a part of the Confederation of the Canons Regular of St. Augustine.

7.7.10.1 Canonici Regolari S. Salvatoris

[DATABASE ID: VATV10329-A]

Inclusive Dates: 1532 (published copy)–1733.

Bulk: .1 linear m. (2 vols.).

Organization: Printed titles are: 1. Privilegi (pub. 1730) containing privileges dating from December 23, 1532, of the Renana Congregatio; —2. Bullarum (pub. 1733).

Location: Archivio Segreto Vaticano.

7.7.11 Capuchins

Parallel to the general "conventual community" was a small but significant part of the Franciscan community that resisted many of the implications of clericalization. This group held on to the more itinerant and rigorous lifestyle associated with the hermitages and the "observant" movement of renewal that arose around 1330 (observers of the rule of St. Francis). From this latter movement the Capuchins were formed.

On May 29, 1517, Leo X issued his bull *Ite et vos* marking an official division of the Friars Minor into two distinct and autonomous groups: Conventuals, OFM/Conv., and Observants, OFM. Leo XIII's bull *Felicitate quadam* (1898) eventually reunited the various reform groups of the previous years (Recollects, Reformed, Discalced) with the Observants.

7.7.11.1 Cappuccini

[DATABASE ID: VATV10334-A]

Inclusive Dates: 1605–1805.

Bulk: .1 linear m. (1 busta).

Scope: This collection contains information on various

provinces including Rome, Genova, Sicily (1578–ca. 1700), Firenze, Andalusia (1616–1726), Castillia (1740–1774), a 1758 published defense of P. Eusebio, and a "Series Capitulorum Generalium Ordinis Capuccinorum pro Superibribus Generalibus (1529–1847)."

Reference: Fink, p. 138.
Location: Archivio Segreto Vaticano.

7.7.12 Carmelites

The Order of Our Lady of Mount Carmel was founded in Palestine around 1154 by St. Berthold (d. about 1195) but it has claimed (without authentic documentation) continuity with hermits settled on Mount Carmel in earlier times, and even to be a direct descendant of Elijah and the "sons of the prophets" (cf. 2 *Kgs.* 2). The primitive rule as laid down in 1209 by Albert of Vercelli, Latin patriarch of Jerusalem, was one of extreme asceticism and solitude. Honorius III approved the definitive rule in 1226. The main concerns of the order are contemplation, missionary work, and theology.

7.7.12.1 Carmeletani

[DATABASE ID: VATV10338-A]
Inclusive Dates: ca. 1500–1800.
Bulk: .1 linear m. (1 busta).
Scope: The collection includes information sent to the Cong. statu regulari and Cong. delle Riforma in the sixteenth century from the Carmeletani in Mantova, also information on houses in Parma, Venice, France, Spain. There are some copies and originals of bulls, briefs (indulgentiae), and the like, as well as a list of houses/members in Italy, 1668–1670.

Located separately were the following other Carmelite materials: four books from the Procura generale—volume 1, 1718–1721, contains formulas for different (frequently used) procedures in various congregations at the end; vol. 2, 1721–1724; vol. 3, 1724–1728; vol. 4, 1740–1743. "Registrum omnium actorum factorum et jurium productorum pro parte et instantia . . . Carmelitanorum . . . cum Margharita Laurent Griffone . . . notarii archivii," 1720–1723.

Location: Archivio Segreto Vaticano.

7.7.13 Carthusians

A religious order of great austerity dedicated exclusively to the contemplative life, the Carthusians were founded by St. Bruno in 1084 in the Chartreuse mountains, a branch of the French Alps. Remaining for the most part in their private cells and dedicated to silence, the Carthusians follow a life similar to that of the early desert monks of Egypt and Syria while actually living together in a monastery and adopting much of the spirit of the rule of St. Benedict. The rule of the Carthusians was approved in 1176 and has received slight alteration since that time. The work of the Carthusians consists of reading, prayer, the labor of their hands, and the writing of books. The Carthusians reached their peak of obser-

vance and influence in the fifteenth century. Since then their members have maintained their monastic spirit intact, despite revolutions, wars, and suppression.

7.7.13.1 Certosini

[DATABASE ID: VATV10361-A]
Inclusive Dates: 1749.
Bulk: 1 document.
Location: Archivio Segreto Vaticano.

7.7.13.2 Fondo Certosini

[DATABASE ID: VATV326-A]
Inclusive Dates: 1374–1688.
Bulk: 27 items.
Scope: Three documents from 1450, 1541, and 1436 are now identified as *Instrumenta miscellanea* nos. 6636 (1450), 6637 (1541), and 6686 (1436).

References: Fink, pp. 138, 151; Boyle, p. 97.
Finding Aids: ASV Blocchetti Indice 8 calendars the entire *Fondo Certosini.* Entries indicate the date and place of the original document, whether the item is a copy or an original, and physical details (dimensions, the presence of a seal, etc.). A summary of each item is also provided.

Location: Archivio Segreto Vaticano.

7.7.14 Celestines

A branch of the Benedictines, called also Hermits of St. Damian or Hermits of Morrone, founded by the hermit Pietro del Morrone (later Pope Celestine V). Pietro became a monk in 1235 and spent several years in seclusion on Monte Morrone. His asceticism attracted several companions. After approval by Urban IV in 1264, they adopted the Benedictine rule. Noted for the severity of their lifestyle they were again approved by Gregory X in 1274 and by Pietro when he became pope. The women's community developed alongside the men's and flowered in the sixteenth and seventeenth centuries. At the height of the group, more than 150 men's and women's monasteries were operating, primarily in Italy and France. In Italy the group centered around Naples, where they received special graces from the Casa d'Angiò. The Celestines declined rapidly after the suppression of some religious groups and confiscation of property held by religious in late eighteenth-century France and the later suppression of religious groups in Italy during the Napoleonic period.

The only remnants of the Celestine tradition are two main monasteries for Celestine women, San Basilio in Aquila, founded in 1320, and San Ruggero in Barletta, which had Benedictine origins in the tenth and eleventh centuries but became Celestine in 1544. These two monasteries joined with the monasteries of Castellana Grotte in Bari and Castel Ritaldi in Perugia in 1971 to form a federation that carries on Celestine spirituality.

The Celestines are not to be confused with some of the Franciscan spirituals who derived their name from the special protection given them by Celestine V. When Celestine resigned in 1294, his successor, Boniface VIII, revoked the privileges that had been given to the Franciscan Celestines.

7.7.14.1 Celestini
[DATABASE ID: VATV10360-A]
Inclusive Dates: 1698 (copy)–1782.
Bulk: .02 linear m. (1 busta).
Scope: This is a group of letters addressed to the secretary of state trying to expedite a brief, all dealing with a request to conduct elections in secret(?) during the chapter meeting.
Location: Archivio Segreto Vaticano.

7.7.14.2 Fondo Celestini
[DATABASE ID: VATV325-A]
Inclusive Dates: 1267–1762.
Bulk: 343 items.
References: Fink, pp. 138, 151; Boyle, p. 97.
Finding Aids: ASV Blocchetti Indici 6 and 7 are a two-volume schedario that calendars the entire series. Entries proceed in chronological order and include the date and place of the document, an initial brief summary of the business (donatio, oblatio, acquisitio, etc.), and a summary of the document. Entries are not in numerical order as indicated on the spine. The current volume number is the stamped number cited in the calendar. The calendar also refers to (numbers followed by an asterisk) a "Regesto copiosa di documenti Celestini," where many of these pergamene have been reproduced. The "Regesto copiosa" could not be located as of 1990.
Location: Archivio Segreto Vaticano.

7.7.14.3 Fondo Celestini: Procura generale
[DATABASE ID: VATV10418-A]
Inclusive Dates: 752(copy)–1801.
Bulk: 3 linear m. (25 vols.).
Organization: Volume titles/contents include: Bullae (copies), 3 vols.; —Procura generale, 2 vols.; —Reg. expeditiones, 1639–1648, 1 vol.; —Pro monasteriis Vici, Beneventi ac Vitulani, 1 vol.; —Pro monasteriis Capuae, Caselucis ac Iserniae, 1 vol.; —Processum, 1 vol.; —Bullae constitutiones, 1 vol.; —Sulla osservanza, 1 vol.; —De Rebus Gallicis Coelestinis, 1 vol.; —Visitationes non Gallie, 1618, 1 vol., indexed internally (contains carte sciolte, 1794); —Acta congregationis, 1794–1801, 1 vol.; —Aquila, 1 vol.; —Pro Collemadio, 1 vol.; —Collegio, 1 vol.; —Pro Lucerna, 1 vol.; —Norcia, 1 vol.; —Pro Nursia a Cassio, 1 vol.; —Pro monast. novi, 1 vol.; —Salta. 1 vol.; —Pro S. Eusebio de Urbe, 2 vol.; —Pro Abbatia Sancti Spiritus de Murrone, 1 vol.
Location: Archivio Segreto Vaticano.

7.7.15 Cistercians

On March 21, 1098, the Benedictine abbot Robert of Molesme led twenty-one of his monks to Citeaux, near Dijon, to establish a new monastery where they hoped to follow Benedict of Nursia's rule for monasteries in all its fullness. The monks of Molesme obtained a papal command for the return of Robert to their monastery. The new community of Citeaux continued until 1109 under the leadership of Alberic, who introduced the idea of lay brothers being accepted as full members of the monastic family. Stephen Harding, who followed Alberic as head of the community, welcomed Bernard of Fontaines (later of Clairvaux) who entered the order in 1112 with thirty of his relatives. Before Bernard died in 1153, he had not only founded the great Abbey of Clairvaux but personally sent forth men to found sixty-five other houses. The order offers a life of poverty, simplicity, and solitude under the guidance of the rule of St. Benedict.

7.7.15.1 Cistercensi
[DATABASE ID: VATV10337-A]
Inclusive Dates: 1621(printed copy)–1809.
Bulk: .05 linear m. (1 busta).
Scope: This collection contains a packet of documents: "Documenti su gli affari dell'ordine Cisterciense" (printed), breve to the order and letters from the order regarding houses in Spain, France (Amiens), Tuscany, Naples, Ferrara, and on Torcello.
Location: Archivio Segreto Vaticano.

7.7.16 Clerks Regular of Somaschi

The Clerks Regular of Somaschi are an order of clerks regular in solemn vows who follow the rule of St. Augustine. They were founded in 1532 by St. Jerome Emiliani at Somasca in northern Italy to work among the poor and afflicted and to care for orphans. The founder, who remained a layman, died in Somasca in 1537. In the beginning the order was called the Society of Servants of the Poor and its membership included both clerics and laymen. In 1540 Paul III approved the society; in 1547 Paul IV united it with the Theatines but the union lasted only until 1555. An attempt was made also to unite it with the Jesuits but without success. On December 6, 1568, Pius V promoted the society to a religious order; gave it its present title; and extended its activities to work in seminaries, colleges, academies, and parishes.

7.7.16.1 Somaschi
[DATABASE ID: VATV10362-A]
Inclusive Dates: ca. 1500–1800.
Bulk: 2.5 linear m. (18 buste).
Scope: Busta 1 has material addressed to S. Cong. Regularum and later buste also have material so addressed. Busta 2 seems right out of the order's archive.
Reference: Fink, pp. 138, 151.
Location: Archivio Segreto Vaticano.

7.7.17 Conventuals

This branch of the Franciscan order favored the accumulation and common holding of property. Their members followed a mitigated rule in contrast with the friars of the older tradition (Observants) who rejected property altogether. The policy was approved by John XXII in 1322. Leo X's bull *Ite et vos* (May 29, 1517) marked the definite separation of the Conventuals and the Observants. All the reform communities were united in one order with the name Friars Minor of the Observance, while the others assumed the name Friars Minor Conventual.

7.7.17.1 Minori Conventuali

[DATABASE ID: VATV10344-A]
Inclusive Dates: 1586 (copy)–1790.
Bulk: .2 linear m. (3 buste).
Scope: "A" includes a packet of instructions and practica dealing with customs (eighteenth cent.). "B" has information regarding the 1770 constitution "dei cordiglieri riuniti ai conventuali" and earlier materials, some with their seal; "Minori conventuali di Roma e altrove" containing 1731 information concerning the testament of Francesco Antonio Amilcari (who also turned up in the Minori Riformati file); an account of work done at S. Cosma; a group of letters regarding P. Cristoforo Mascaro on Minorca, 1775; a packet containing information on the Visitatori della Provincia d'Italia about 1625; and material regarding the convents in Assisi, SS. Apostoli in Rome, the Collegio di S. Bonaventura, the Church of S. Sebastian in Sibenico, and the Conventuali in Bagnacavallo.
Location: Archivio Segreto Vaticano.

7.7.18 Crozier Fathers

The Canons Regular of the Order of the Holy Cross, commonly known as Crosier Fathers, were founded, according to tradition, by Theodore of Celles about 1210. The name *Crosier* is derived from the French *croisés* (Lat., *crucisignati*); the English medieval rendering of the word was Crutched (crossed) Friars from the crusader's cross worn on the scapular of the friars. Their work is accomplished mainly through missions, retreats, and education.

7.7.18.1 Crociferi

[DATABASE ID: VATV10336-A]
Inclusive Dates: 1572–1702.
Bulk: .05 linear m. (1 busta).
Scope: This primarily concerns the order in Germany (Rheni).
Location: Archivio Segreto Vaticano.

7.7.19 Dominicans

[DATABASE ID: VATV329-A]

In a broad sense *Dominican* refers to a family of friars (clerical and nonclerical), cloistered nuns, professed sisters in apostolic congregations, and laity, all of whom consider St. Dominic de Guzmán as their founder and inspiration. In the narrower sense *Dominicans* refers to the Order of Friars Preachers founded by St. Dominic de Guzmán in 1216. Honorius III gave formal sanction to their work on December 22, 1216, and on January 17, 1217, approved their title and preaching mission. The Dominicans were the first religious to abandon manual labor in favor of intellectual work. It is also the only religious order in the church that has received explicitly as its mission the ministry of preaching. The members maintain a balance of apostolic work and contemplative community living and are committed to lifelong study.

7.7.19.1 Domenicani

[DATABASE ID: VATV10353-A]
Inclusive Dates: 1303(copy), 1851.
Bulk: 1 vol. with insert.
Scope: The contents of the volume are: "Index alphabeticus conventuum et monasteriorum ordinis fratrum praedicatorum ex notitia eiusdem ordinis a Bernardo Guidonis anno 1303 composita editaque ab Echardo, Tom.1. Scriptor Ord. Praed. pag.IV." ("coenobia et monasteria quibus annus adscriptus non est, fere omnia ante annum 1303 fuerunt constituta"); — "Programmata a S. studiorum congregatione proposita ad eorum periclitandam doctrinam qui majoribus excolendis disciplinis aditum sibi patere cupiunt," 1851.
Location: Archivio Segreto Vaticano.

7.7.19.2 Fondo Domenicani I: Pergamene

[DATABASE ID: VATV10322-A]
Inclusive Dates: 1207–1765.
Bulk: 466 items.
References: Fink, pp. 138, 151; Pásztor (1970), pp. 234–235; Boyle, p. 97.
Finding Aids: ASV Blocchetti Indici 9–10 are a chronological calendar of the entire *Fondo Domenicani I.* Blocchetti 9 and 10 indicate the place and date (day, month, year) of the item and the type of business (bulla, licentia, confirmatio statuta et privilegia, etc.). They also provide a synopsis of each item, a physical description of the item, and note if it was published (at the time Blocchetti 9 and 10 were compiled). The spines of Blocchetti 9 and 10 contain erroneous designations of which item numbers are described in each blocchetto.
Location: Archivio Segreto Vaticano.

7.7.19.3 Fondo Domenicani II: Pacchi e volumi

[DATABASE ID: VATV10321-A]
Inclusive Dates: 1216(copy)–ca. 1850.
Bulk: 4 linear m. (42 numbered buste).
Scope: These are primarily copies but some are originals.
References: Fink, pp. 138, 151; Pásztor (1970), pp. 234–235; Boyle, p. 97.
Finding Aids: ASV Indice 1149, compiled by P. Tommaso Droetto, O.P., provides a brief introduction and inventory of each busta in the *Fondo Domenicani.* Indice 1149 proceeds busta by busta, indicating the major types of documents and business contained therein, inclusive dates, and if the material is an original, copy, or printed.
Location: Archivio Segreto Vaticano.

7.7.20 Franciscans

Franciscan describes all those men and women of the Franciscan first, second, and third (regular and secular) orders. Members of the first order include Friars Minor, Friars Minor Conventual, and Friars Minor Capuchin. All three branches of the Franciscan first order follow the rule of St. Francis of Assisi (1181–1226), which was approved by Honorius III with his so-called *regula bullata* of November 29, 1223. The distinctions among the three groups in their efforts to live, reform, and revitalize the charism of Francis varied in different historical periods. The distinguishing mark of the order is its insistence on complete poverty not only for individual members but also corporately for the order as a whole. This ideal proved unworkable if taken literally. Thus two schools of thought developed: those who insisted on interpretation according to the letter of the rule; and those (the majority) who took a more moderate view in accordance with the requirements of the times. In the following centuries many reform parties sprang up. In 1897, however, Leo XIII regrouped the different branches of the Franciscans.

7.7.20.1 Fondo Francescani
[DATABASE ID: VATV331-A]
Inclusive Dates: 1464–1758.
Bulk: .5 linear m. (15 items).
Organization: Item titles/contents include: 1. Registrum vicarii generalis, 1464–1468 (pergamene); —2. "Pro RR monialibus Sti. Cosmati et D. Christophoro Lellino con RR PP Sti. Franci. ad Ripa"; —3. Libro di conti (entrata ed uscita) del panificio dei minori osserv. della provincia di Basilicata, 1682–1701; —4. Libro quarto de dubbii sopra la regola del Serafino P.S. Francesco; —5. Tabula et constitutiones per celebris Capitoli Generalis, 1700; —6. [re: Recollects in Belgium and Flanders], 1664–1725; —7. Includes: Ad vitam regularum et statuta ordinis, 1709–1752; Epistolae Provincial. Alicitae, 1746–1758; Collegia Missionarum ad S. Bartholomanem in Insula, [17—]; —8. "Copie d'une histoire de Sainte Colette," 1494; —9. [missing]; —10. Convento San Francesco, 1573–1659; —11. Novitiorum Professionum Sancti Antonii Tiburis, 1659–1696; —12. Includes: "Haec statuta provincialia in capitulo provinciali die 2 junii 1754 in conventu nostro argentinensi ad S. Andrea Apost.," 1766; "Affare del gran'convento de Cordoliers di Parigi"(Regolae), 1726; "De sanctitate vitae et miraculis serui Dei F. Petri Regalati auctoris. regularis observ. S. Francisci in Hispania relatio ad sanctissimum D.N. Urbanum VIII," (printed) 1630; —13. [Letters], 1715–1797; —14. [Correspondence with secretary of state and Penitenziaria, 1732–1804, and Third Order Regulars of St. Francis in France], "Varie lettere riguardante la celebrazione del capitolo Provle. a Parprignani e Marsiglia," 1756–1757; —15. Legati, ca. 1516–1750 (18th century list) and varie [1—]–1646.
Reference: Fink, pp. 138, 151.
Location: Archivio Segreto Vaticano.

7.7.21 Hieronymites
[DATABASE ID: VATV334-A]

The name *Hieronymites* is given to various congregations of the fourteenth and fifteenth centuries in Spain and Italy. The Spanish congregation of the Hermits of

St. Jerome was organized by Pedro Fernández Pecha (d. 1374), the royal chamberlain. On October 18, 1373 Gregory XI confirmed and approved the Hermits as a congregation. The Spanish Hermits were highly influential in the spiritual and cultural work of the church. During the following centuries they devoted themselves to the Divine Office, the liturgical apostolate, and to works of charity for strangers, but along with other religious orders they were suppressed in 1835. In 1907, however, they began to reestablish themselves in Segovia and now have a headquarters in Cáceres, Spain.

7.7.21.1 Fondo Girolamini: Parte I, Carte
[DATABASE ID: VATV10319-A]
Inclusive Dates: 1426–1944.
Bulk: 8 linear m. (194 numbered buste and three unnumbered buste).
Organization: Subseries/items titles/contents include: 1–6. SS. Rituum Congregatio, re: Nicolai a Furca Palena, Pietro Gambacorta, Marco Marconi; —7–8. Registro degli atti del P. generale, 1783–1886; —24. Rubricelle dei nomi dei religiosi, [18—]–[19—]; —38, 42. Eredità; —39–41, 43, 85–112. Registri di Messe, ca. 1837–1919; —50–60. Museo Tassiano; —61. Libro delle Compagnia del Rosario nella chiesa di S. Onofrio, ca. 1621–1843; —62. Liber mortuorum ecclesiae ac. monasterii S. Honuphrii Urbis, ca. 1590–1749; —63. Libro dei morti, sepolti nella chiesa di S. Onofrio, ca. 1755–1850; —124–134. Libri di conventi Girolamini, ca. 1825–1910; —182. Quaderni contenenti il diario ed altri scritti spirituali di Suor Maria Giovanna Galli; —Unnumbered buste contain financial records, primarily eighteenth and nineteenth centuries, but also "Contratti," ca. 1426.
Scope: Sez. V (Congregazioni Religiosi Soppresse), Girolamini in S. Francesco a Monte Mario is located in the Archivio di Stato di Roma. Vat.Lat. 13104 (Bl. Pietro Gambacorta et Romitani di S. Girolamo, 1421–1530) is located in the Biblioteca Apostolica Vaticana. Buste 1–193 were acquired by the ASV in 1945. Busta 194 was acquired by the ASV in 1970.
References: Fink, p. 136; Boyle, p.97; Natalini et al., p. 271.
Finding Aids: ASV Indice 1054, compiled by G. Gullette (1949), contains an introduction to the history of the order and the material transferred from its archives to the ASV. Indice 1054 also provides descriptions of buste 1–194, which indicate the type of material, the subject, and the inclusive dates.
Location: Archivio Segreto Vaticano.

7.7.21.2 Fondo Girolamini: Parte II, Pergamene
[DATABASE ID: VATV10320-A]
Inclusive Dates: 1422–1863.
Bulk: 66 items.
Scope: These are originals and early copies. Many of the fifteenth-century wills are from Urbino. See also Sez. VI (Collezione di Pergamene), *Girolamini in S. Onofrio* in the Archivio di Stato di Roma; and Sez. VI (Collezione di Pergamene), *Girolamini in S. Alessio* in the Archivio di Stato di Roma. The collection was acquired by the ASV in 1945.
Finding Aids: ASV Indice 1054 provides a general introduction to the Girolamini and their archives. Indice 1054 also contains a detailed calendar of the entire pergamene collec-

tion, including the type of document (istromenti, bolle, breve), a contents summary, annotations (e.g., original or copy), and date.

Location: Archivio Segreto Vaticano.

7.7.22 Jesuits

In 1534 Ignatius of Loyola, a Basque and former soldier, met in Paris with six companions to take a private vow of poverty and one to place themselves at the disposition of the pope. On September 27, 1540, Paul III issued the bull *Regimini militantis ecclesiae,* canonically establishing the Society of Jesus. The constitutions of the society were drawn up by Ignatius who submitted his work for approval in 1550. Along with working toward the spiritual benefits of its members, the aim of the order was twofold: to foster reform in the church and to undertake missionary work, especially in the recently discovered parts of the world. The members undertook a variety of tasks arising from the Reformation crisis, but their work soon began to consist mainly in teaching, giving the spiritual exercises, and in administering the sacraments. In 1551 they opened the Roman College, later to be called the Gregorian University. In 1773 Clement XIV (under pressure from the Bourbons and Jansenists) suppressed the order. An inconsistent policy of promulgation and enforcement led to much confusion. Pius VII restored the society in 1814. Today the Jesuits are responsible for numerous institutions in Rome (including the Vatican Radio Station) and for schools and academic centers around the world.

7.7.22.1 Fondo Gesuiti

[DATABASE ID: VATV333-A]

Inclusive Dates: 1545–1826.

Bulk: 2.5 linear m. (61 buste).

Organization: Subseries and selected busta titles include: 1. Carte relative alla riforma dei PP. gesuiti, 1758; —2–4. Carte relative all'affare dei gesuiti del Portugallo, 1758–1760; —5–6. Lettere di vescovi di Spagna, Germania, Polonia, Francia, Ibernia e Italia scritte alla Santità di N.S. papa Clemente XIII in raccomandazione dei gesuiti all'occasione della compagnia di Gesù, 1765; —7. Due lettere anomine intorno alla bolla di nuova conferma dell'istituto de gesuiti "Apostolicum pascendi Dominici munus," 1765; —8–9. Lettere dell'episcopato di Spagna al re cattolico, 1769; —10. Ordinanze e procedimenti riguardanti i gesuiti di Spagna, 1766–1768; —11. Nota dei gesuiti indiani, francesi, e portughesi giunti in vari tempi in Roma fino al giorno 24 gennaio 1760, con l'indicazione dell'alloggio; —12. Querele contro i gesuiti, 1765–1775; —13. Ristretti di processi fatti dai re cattolici Filippo II e Filippo IV contro i gesuiti, estratti dall'Archivio del Palazzo di Spagna nel 1770; —14. Fogli periodici contro i gesuiti spacciati dall'abate Bensi, 1771–1773; —15–21. Atti della congregazione "Intorno alla soppressione dei gesuiti" 1773; —22–24. Atti e carte diverse della congregazione per la soppressione della compagnia di Gesù, 1773–1778; —25–29. Rapporti del Maschio della real fortezza di Castel Sant'Angelo, 1773–1775; —30. Carte della

congr. per la soppr. della comp. di Gesù relative al processo di Valentano, 1774; —31–33. Atti criminali della congr. per la soppressione della comp. di Gesù, 1774; —42. Carte relative al Collegio Germanico, 1691–1808; —43. Carte relative alla consegna del Collegio Romano alla compagnia di Gesù, 1824; —45. Bolle, breve, memoriali, 1545.

Scope: This miscellaneous collection appears to have been collected by someone in the Vatican and is not a part of the Jesuit archives that has been alienated. It does mainly concern the suppression of the Jesuits.

Busta 49 is not atypical. Entitled "Lettere Diverse, 1612–1826," this packet contains complaints, laments, requests, and controversies, mostly presented by Jesuit communities or individuals to or collected by the prior general. The bulk of the documents are from the seventeenth century. These varied documents come from all over Europe and from "the Indies" as well as one item, a copy of an eighteenth-century letter, regarding Jesuits in China; they are written in Latin, French, Italian, and Spanish. There are many petitions, some by men wishing to transfer to another order or house, and one, addressed to the pope, requesting reinstatement into the Jesuit Order. Problems with other religious orders emerge often among these papers, and also matters concerning nuns. One document concerns the censorship of one Jesuit's allegedly antipapal work published in German. The earliest document, dated May 22, 1612, is a letter (or copy of a letter) by the "martire Padre Scotto Benedettino" to Jesuits in England.

References: Fink, p. 138; Pásztor (1970), pp. 236–237; Boyle, p. 97.

Finding Aids: ASV Indice 1077 provides the current volume numbers, a brief description of the contents, and the inclusive dates of buste 1–59. Two earlier (ca. eighteenth–nineteenth century) inventories have been pasted into the back of this index. Although they no longer indicate the correct volume numbers, they do provide a historical glimpse of the *Fondo Gesuiti,* some parts of which are not extant in the Fondo today.

Location: Archivio Segreto Vaticano.

7.7.22.2 Gesuiti

[DATABASE ID: VATV10347-A]

Inclusive Dates: ca. 1759.

Bulk: .05 linear m. (1 busta).

Scope: All this material deals with the Jesuits in Portugal, ca. 1759.

Location: Archivio Segreto Vaticano.

7.7.23 Mercedarians

Mercedarians is the popular name for the Order of Our Lady of Mercy, derived from the Spanish word *merced* (mercy). Members have been known also as the Knights of St. Eulalia and Nolascans. Pius XI bestowed the name by which the institute has since been known officially: Order of the Blessed Virgin Mary for the Ransom of Captives. St. Peter Nolasco founded the order in 1218 with the twofold purpose of tending the sick and rescuing Christians who had been taken prisoners by the Moors. The Mercedarians owed their rule to St. Raymond of Peñafort (1175–1275). In addition to the usual three vows, a fourth was added pledging them to offer themselves as hostages, if needed, for the redemption of captives.

7.7.23.1 Mercedari

[DATABASE ID: VATV10341-A]

Inclusive Dates: 1670–1747.

Bulk: .05 linear m. (1 busta).

Scope: This collection includes "Examen parenetico de un papal del P.F. Cosme de Alcaniz antes lector de theologia y aora guardian del convento de los PP. Capuchinos de la ciudad de Huefa."

Location: Archivio Segreto Vaticano.

7.7.24 Minims

The Minims are a mendicant order founded in 1435 by S. Francesco di Paola at Paola (Calabria). The first rule, confirmed by Alexander VI in 1493, was based on that of St. Francis of Assisi; the second, and more independent one, by the same pope in 1501. As the name indicates, they aimed to practice humility as their chief virtue, regarding themselves as the least (*minimi*) of all religious. Their apostolate is in parish work, preaching, and teaching.

7.7.24.1 Minimi

[DATABASE ID: VATV10340-A]

Inclusive Dates: 1699–1860.

Bulk: .05 linear m. (1 busta).

Scope: These are supplications (including one asking for an Apostolic Visit).

Location: Archivio Segreto Vaticano.

7.7.25 Ministers of the Sick

Camillians is the popular name of the Order of St. Camillus, whose official name is Order of Clerics Regular, Servants of the Sick. The congregation was founded in Rome about 1582 by St. Camillus de Lellis, approved by the pope in 1586, and elevated to an order with the privileges of the mendicants by Gregory XIV in 1591. To the usual three vows of religion a fourth was added, that of serving the sick, including the victims of the plagues. This vow is still made by all members of the order.

7.7.25.1 Ministri degli Infermi

[DATABASE ID: VATV10339-A]

Inclusive Dates: 1685–1824.

Bulk: 3 letters.

Scope: One letter may be a request for a brief to help stabilize the order in Naples and Sicily.

Location: Archivio Segreto Vaticano.

7.7.26 Olivetans

Giovanni Tolomei (St. Bernard Ptolomei) founded a branch of the Benedictine order at Monte Oliveto, near

Siena, in 1319. This group received papal confirmation in 1344 but joined the Benedictine Federation in 1960 under their title of Order of Our Lady of Mount Olivet.

7.7.26.1 Olivetani

[DATABASE ID: VATV10350-A]

Inclusive Dates: 1531–1802.

Bulk: .05 linear m. (1 busta).

Scope: The collection includes: 1. a 1535(?) account of problems relating to statutes(?) at the convent in Naples(?) with a 1540 inventory of the sacristy; — 2. a Memoria per l'udienza a dell'Emo. Sig. Card. Seg. di Stato concerning the convent in Todi, about 1800, and "Libro della famiglie e monasteri della Cogne. del Monte Oliveto nell' anno 1642 con i nomi dei monaci."

Location: Archivio Segreto Vaticano.

7.7.27 Oratorians

The original Oratory grew out of the community of priests that had gathered around St. Philip Neri (1515–1595), son of a Florentine notary, who went to Rome in 1533. In 1548 he became the cofounder of the Confraternity of the Most Holy Trinity for the care of pilgrims and convalescents, which in the year of the Jubilee (1575) assisted 145,000 people. From these activities the Congregation of the Oratory was born, probably so called from the room at San Girolamo where their meetings were held. St. Philip's Oratory is a congregation of secular priests living in community without vows, those with private means supporting themselves. Their chief task is to lead men to God through prayer, popular preaching, and the sacraments. They lay stress not only on liturgy but also on attractive services, and especially on good music. The modern "oratorio" grew out of the *laudi spirituali* sung in their devotional exercises, many of which were composed by Palestrina. The individual oratories, or houses, were independent until 1942 when they were consolidated into a confederation. They received papal approval in 1612 and were confirmed in 1942.

7.7.27.1 Filippini

[DATABASE ID: VATV10345-A]

Inclusive Dates: 1628–1805.

Bulk: .05 linear m. (1 busta).

Scope: This collection includes "Contributioni fatte da molti divoti religiosi dell'ordine de Servi di Maria per il trionfo di S. Filippo Benitii propagatore di detto ordini, canonizzato dal Gran Pontefice Clemente X a 12 Aprile dell'anno 1671" (published in Perugia, 1676), correspondence to different congregations and a supplication.

Location: Archivio Segreto Vaticano.

7.7.28 Order of St. Basil the Great

This order arises out of the monastic movement founded in the fourth century by St. Basil the Great in

Neocaesarea in Pontus. Repelled by the excess of self-denial of existing monastic orders, Basil encouraged a balance between complete austerity on the one hand and works and charitable acts on the other. His rules were known to St. Benedict. Basilian monasticism spread from Greece to Italy in the west and Russia in the east. By the eighth and ninth centuries there were a number of established Basilian communities in both areas. After the schism between Eastern and Western churches, the Basilian monasteries that remained loyal to Rome were for the most part in Italy.

7.7.28.1 Fondo Basiliani

[DATABASE ID: VATV319-A]

Inclusive Dates: Bulk 1508–1772.

Bulk: 2 linear m. (80 numbered buste and 3 unnumbered vols.).

Organization: Subseries include: Bolle e privilegi; —Capitoli e diete; —Registri di affari dell'ordine; —Visite a chiese e monasteri; —Carte di singoli monasteri; —Processi; —Miscellanea.

Unnumbered volume titles are: "Regestum omnium previsionum factarum a revmo. Pre. S.T.M. D.Petro Menniti Abbate Generali totis ordinis A.P.N. Basilii Magni," 1696–1718; —"Liber in quo continentur instrumenta publica separationum mensarum conventualium ab abbatialibus omnium monasteriorum Italie Ordinis S. Basilii Magni authoritate Apostolica factarum" (D. Petro Menniti, abbate) ca. 1600–1730; —Registro di monastero di S. Filareto di Mileto(?), 1733–1739.

Scope: The collection was acquired by the ASV after 1815 (cf. Minisci below).

Note: Vols. 1 and 23 are available on microfilm.

References: Fink, pp. 138, 151; Boyle, p. 96.

Finding Aids: See J. T. Minisci, "Il fondo 'Basiliani' dell'Archivio segreto vaticano," *Bollettino della Badia Greca di Grottaferrata*, n.s. 6 (1952): 65–85. Minisci has compiled a descriptive inventory of *Fondo Basiliani* nos. 1–80 according to the categories (e.g., subseries presented above). Minisci identifies the major documents and volumes, generally notes inclusive dates, and provides useful annotations. The copy in the ASV Sala d'Indici is further annotated with the current volume numbers.

Location: Archivio Segreto Vaticano.

7.7.29 Passionists

This religious institute, officially called the Congregation of the Passion of Our Lord Jesus Christ, was founded in Italy in 1720 by Paolo Francesco Danai (St. Paul of the Cross, 1694–1775). Their rule and constitutions were approved by Benedict XIV in 1741 and 1746. Clement XIV's bull *Supremi Apostolatus* (November 16, 1769) gave final approval to the institute and conferred the privileges of the old orders on the new congregation. The members take the traditional vows as well as a spiritual vow to promote the memory of the Passion in today's world. They are noted for their missions and retreats.

7.7.29.1 Passionisti

[DATABASE ID: VATV10355-A]

Inclusive Dates: 1787–1822.

Bulk: .02 linear m. (1 busta).

Scope: These are letters regarding the communities in Spoleto and Corneto.

Location: Archivio Segreto Vaticano.

7.7.30 Pauline Fathers (Order of St. Paul the First Hermit)

The Pauline Fathers took their name from the hermit St. Paul of Thebes, who lived in Egypt during the third or fourth century. An order of priests and brothers, it originated in 1250 with the union of a monastery in Patach, Hungary, and another in Pisilia, Hungary, that had been established by Eusebius of Esztergom (d. 1270). The order received papal approval in 1308 and followed a strict observance of the rule of St. Augustine. In the sixteenth and seventeenth centuries the Reformation and the Turkish invasions caused the order a serious decline, but a notable revival occurred at the end of the seventeenth century and a major expansion took place. Guillaume Collier established the order in France and Paul V gave it formal approval in 1620. The French group, known familiarly as the Brothers of Death, oriented their asceticism toward a constant concern with death. The order was contemplative until the sixteenth century when the Holy See assigned it to charitable, educational, and parochial works. In 1788 Emperor Joseph suppressed the houses in his Hapsburg states. The Portuguese and French houses did not survive the French Revolutionary period, but the two monasteries at Kraków and Czestochowa have survived.

7.7.30.1 Paolini

[DATABASE ID: VATV10349-A]

Inclusive Dates: ca. 1770.

Bulk: 2 documents (1 busta).

Scope: The documents are: 1. Notizie relative l'Ordine Equestre di S. Paolo estrate dal libro intitolato Catalogo degli Ordini Equestre Militari del Padre Bonanni Gesuita (this volume may relate to the Paolini, a military order of knights); —2. Litterae Apostolicae (Clementi XIV) quibus Paulo Eszterhazii priori generali ordinis monachorum A. Pauli primae Eremite, 1770.

Location: Archivio Segreto Vaticano.

7.7.31 Piarists

An order of clerics regular (also known as the Scolopi) for the education of the young, the name *Piarist* comes from the last word of their Latin name (Clerici Regulares Scholarum Piarum). A Spanish diocesan priest, Joseph Calasanctius (canonized in 1767), opened a school in Rome in 1597. Clement VIII encouraged and financially assisted the new institution. Paul V recognized the group's foundation as a formal religious congregation in 1617. Their work continued to develop, but free education for the poor was an idea that was suspect at the time. The founder's friendship with Galileo and his use of the great scientist as a teacher in his schools contributed to internal dissension and external attacks on the work of the order. In 1646 Innocent X reduced the order to a simple federation of independent religious houses. It was only in 1656, after the founder's death, that Alexander VII partially reestablished the Piarists as a congregation of simple vows. Clement IX completely reinstituted the order in 1669.

7.7.31.1 Fondo Scolopi

[DATABASE ID: VATV344-A]
Inclusive Dates: 1614–1774.
Bulk: 101 items.
Scope: Fondo Scolopi, nos. 95–101, was formerly identified as *Fondo Veneto I* (Archivio della Cancellaria della Nunziatura Veneta or ACNV), nos. 15719–15725.
References: Fink, p. 138; Boyle, p. 98.
Finding Aids: ASV Blocchetti Indice 13 calendars the entire collection. Entries include the following information for each item: the date and place or origin, a brief description of the business or type of document, a contextual summary, physical information (dimensions, presence of a seal, etc.), and whether the item is an original or a copy.
Location: Archivio Segreto Vaticano.

7.7.31.2 Scolopi

[DATABASE ID: VATV10358-A]
Inclusive Dates: 1607–1803.
Bulk: .3 linear m. (6 items).
Scope: The collection includes: Regulae communes, ordo et ritus ordine da tenersi per la celebrazione de capitolo generale, 1637; —Bullae, 1609–1803; —Varie bullar., 1607–1686 (register with brief entries); —Regestrum litterarum patentium et testimonialium, 1659–1665; —Supplications, etc.; —Regestra generalia, 1692–1697 (organized by type of document, e.g., literae obedientiales, dispensationes).
Location: Archivio Segreto Vaticano.

7.7.32 Premonstratensians

The Premonstratensians were founded by St. Norbert of Xanten at Prémontré, France, in 1120. The founder intended the order to blend the contemplative with the active religious life. Norbertine life is intensely liturgical with particular attention given to the liturgy of the eucharist. Through Norbert's friendship with St. Bernard of Clairvaux the life also shows distinct Cistercian influences. The order suffered severely during the French Revolution and had become nearly extinct in the early nineteenth century. Since then, the order has become especially strong in Belgium.

7.7.32.1 Premonstratensi

[DATABASE ID: VATV10348-A]
Inclusive Dates: 1704–1729.
Bulk: .05 linear m. (1 busta).

Scope: These materials concern problems between the bishop of Toul and the abbot of Estival and financial records from the Collegium S. Norberti in Rome.
Location: Archivio Segreto Vaticano.

7.7.33 Riformati

The early history of the Recollects and the Riformati is not easy to unravel. The origin of both groups is closely connected with the houses of recollection that had been a feature of Franciscan life from the beginning. Francesco da Jesi (1469–1549) and Bernardino d'Asti (1484–1554) are usually claimed as the founders of the Reformed. In 1532 Clement VII allowed these two friars to organize some Italian houses of recollection under the jurisdiction of the Observant provincial. In 1570 Gregory XIII released these houses from the authority of the Observant Provincials, and in 1595 they were allowed to adopt their own constitutions. In 1621 Gregory XV granted them their own vice general and general chapter, which gave them complete autonomy. In 1897 Leo XIII with his constitution *Felicitate quadam* decreed that in the future the official name of the Friars Minor would be Order of Friars Minor, with no added designations. This was confirmed by Pius X in 1909.

7.7.33.1 Minori Riformati

[DATABASE ID: VATV10343-A]
Inclusive Dates: 1471 (copy)–1758.
Bulk: .1 linear m. (1 busta).
Scope: This collection includes materials dealing with the eredità of Sisra. Marta Amilehari (also spelled Amilcari) in the 1730s, a decision book (1655) from S. Cosmato in Rome, letters from French houses, and a visita(?) to the house in Paris in 1624–1625.
Location: Archivio Segreto Vaticano.

7.7.34 Servites

In 1233 seven wealthy Florentine city councillors left their native city to retire outside the gate of Balla in an area known as Cafaggio for a life of poverty and penance. There was at first no thought of founding an order but only a desire for a life in the spirit of the primitive church. These men are known collectively as the Seven Founders of the Servites and were canonized by Leo XIII in 1888. In 1240 the bishop of Florence approved the community under the name Servants of St. Mary, selected because St. Mary was the name of their oratory. They adopted the rule of St. Augustine with some additions from the Dominican constitutions. In 1256 Alexander IV approved them as an order of friars living in corporate poverty. The bull of Benedict XI reconfirmed the approval in 1304.

7.7.34.1 Fondo Serviti

[DATABASE ID: VATV10242-A]

Inclusive Dates: 1613–1809.

Bulk: 1 linear m. (32 buste).

Organization: Busta titles are: 1. Decreti di visita, 1672–1677; —2. Spese per la festa e ottavario di S. Filippo, 1671–1683; —3. Miscellanea Palombella, [1—]–1764; —4. Lettere di rimessa per la canonizzazione di S. Filippo, 1670–1672; —5. Rescritti, 1655–1689; —6. Vicenza: causa tra il convento di S. Maria e il Capitolo, 1613–1614; —7. Registro di lettere del Priore generale Poggi, 1700–1702; —8. Mantova e Mirandola, 1652–1675; —9. Provincia di Mantova, 1633–1639; —10. Confraternità dei Sette Dolori, 1774–1809; —11. Cathalogus scriptorum del Palombella (tomo II), 1749; —12. Indice dei Tomi, [1—]–1767; —13. Priori generali, 1675–1807; —14. Capitoli generali, 1646–1780; —15. Studi, 1679–1805; —16. Spogli originali per la canonizzazione di S. Filippo, 1668–1678; —17. Collette originali per la canonizzazione di S. Filippo, 1670–1673; —18. Province diverse, [17—?]–1802; —19. Toscana, 1600–1809; —20. Romana, 1649–1809; —21. Romagna, 1681–[17—]; —22. Lombardia, 1773–1803; —23. Marca Trevisana e Veneta, 1594–1789; —24. Mantova e Marca Anconitana, 1759–1803; —25. Piemente, 1769–1797; —26. Napoli, 1615–1797; —27. Corsica, 1718–1796; —28. Germania, 1617–1791; —29. Spagna, 1756–1787; —30. Portogallo, 1744–1755; —31. Conti diversi, 1670–1678; —32. Entrata e uscita per la canonizzazione di S. Filippo, 1670–1678.

Reference: Pásztor (1970), pp. 237–238.

Finding Aids: The brief list of busta titles (bearing their current volume numbers) in this series, reproduced above, is available at the desk in the main ASV reading room. The list is not a formal finding aid and must be used in consultation with the archives staff.

Location: Archivio Segreto Vaticano.

7.7.35 Theatines

This religious order was founded in Rome in 1524 by Gaetano da Thiene of Vicenza (St. Cajetan) and Gian Pietro Caraffa (later Pope Paul IV). Clement VII had allowed Gian Pietro to resign his bishopric of Chieti so that he and Gaetano could found a congregation of clerks regular dedicated to restoring the apostolic way of life. They were officially approved as Clerks Regular of Divine Providence. From Caraffa's former diocese of Chieti (Theate) they acquired the popular name of Teatini. The congregaion rejected all benefices and devoted themselves to the service of the poor and the sick. The congregation played an important part in the Counter-Reformation.

7.7.35.1 Teatini

[DATABASE ID: VATV10352-A]

Inclusive Dates: 1611–1772.

Bulk: .05 linear m. (1 busta).

Location: Archivio Segreto Vaticano.

7.7.36 Third Order Regular of St. Francis

The Third Order Regular of St. Francis of Penance traces its foundation to the Third Order Secular begun by St. Francis of Assisi in 1221 for people living in the world and desirous of Christian perfection. In time many of these tertiaries left their homes to live either in hermitages or in common, bound by traditional religious vows. The first official approval was given by Nicholas V (Jul. 20, 1447) in the apostolic letter *Pastoralis officii* with the recommendation that the tertiaries constitute themselves as a mendicant order.

7.7.36.1 Francescani osservanti

[DATABASE ID: VATV10333-A]

Inclusive Dates: 1728–1780.

Bulk: .05 linear m. (1 vol.).

Scope: This is a chronicle concerning the decisions, events, and activities in the lives of the members and the maintenance of the properties of the "tertii ordinis S. Francisci de Poenitentia Regularis Observantis, quae in Conventu SS. Cosmae et Damiani de Urbe . . . 1728–1780."

Location: Archivio Segreto Vaticano.

7.7.37 Trappists

Since the early nineteenth century *Trappists* has been the popular name for the main branch of the Cistercians of the Strict Observance who were centered at the Abbey of La Grande Trappe in France until the restoration of Citeaux as the motherhouse in 1892. The reform was originally introduced by Armand de Rancé, godson of Richelieu, who was at an early age provided with a number of benefices, including that of commendatory abbot of La Trappe. In 1662 he resigned all his benefices except that of La Trappe, which he kept for his Cistercian reform. To the existing rules of the reformed Cistercians he ordered more stringent regulations, including his total prohibition of study. For a while in the nineteenth century there were three varieties of strict observance in force. In 1892 Leo XIII was unsuccessful in trying to unite these Cistercian groups but finally recognized two separate groups called the Order of Citeaux and the Cistercian Order of the Strict Observance (Trappists). The most important change in recent years has been the abolition of lay brothers as a separate class, the encouragement of study, and participation in ecumenical activities.

7.7.37.1 Trappisti

[DATABASE ID: VATV10354-A]

Inclusive Dates: 1800–1801.

Bulk: .05 linear m. (1 busta).

Scope: According to the cover, this busta contains "Parere, voti, etc. della Congregazione degli Affari Ecclesiastici circa la professione di alcune novizie (Svizzera e Russia)."

Location: Archivio Segreto Vaticano.

7.7.38 Trinitarians

The order was founded in 1198 at Cerfroid, in the diocese of Meaux, by St. John of Matha (d. 1213) and

St. Felix of Valois (d. 1212). Because of the lack of records early Trinitarian history is unclear. Recent critics have questioned the existence of St. Felix of Valois. The order is dedicated primarily to promoting devotion to the Holy Trinity. Originally its unique apostolate was the redemption of Christians held captive by the Muslims. When slavery was abolished, the Trinitarians became engaged in education, nursing, and pastoral work.

7.7.38.1 Trinitari
[DATABASE ID: VATV10359-A]
Inclusive Dates: 1651–1765.
Bulk: .05 linear m. (1 busta).
Scope: There are only three items, all printed: 1. Octauum capitulum generale reverendissini patris AC domini D. Ludovici maioris, AC generalis ministri totius ordinis Sanctissimae Trinitatis, & redemptionis capitiuorum, 1651 (contains marginal annotations); —2. Capitulum generale electionis reverendissimi patris Guillelmi LeFebure, sacrae facultatis Parisiensis Doctoris Theologi . . . , 1749; —3. Capitulum generale electionis reverendissimi patris ac domini Francisci-Mauritii Pichault . . . , 1765.
Location: Archivio Segreto Vaticano.

7.7.39 Vincentians

The congregation is a community of priests and brothers founded by St. Vincent de Paul in Paris in 1625. They and the Daughters of Charity of St. Vincent de Paul (founded 1633) constitute the "double family" of St. Vincent under one superior general. The aims of the congregation are the preaching of missions to the poor; training of ecclesiastics; foreign missions; and administering and promoting Catholic education. The community was formally confirmed by Urban VIII in 1632 and came to be known as Lazarists, from the priory of St.-Lazare, which was Vincent's headquarters in Paris. Vincentian vows are simple but private.

7.7.39.1 Lazzaristi
[DATABASE ID: VATV10342-A]
Inclusive Dates: 1724–1762.
Bulk: .05 linear m. (1 busta).
Scope: This busta includes a "Memorie delle Missioni" that contains reports from religious houses in Italy (largely near Rome) and a few in France.
Location: Archivio Segreto Vaticano.

7.8
MONASTERIES, CONVENTS, ABBEYS, AND CHURCHES

In addition to the churches and monasteries listed in this section, users of this guide should be aware that there is a substantial amount of records from suppressed monasteries located in the Apostolic Nunciature for

Venice series *Fondo Veneto I* and *Fondo Veneto II* and in *Fondo Toscano*.

7.8.1 Basilica di S. Maria in Cosmedin (Rome)

7.8.1.1 Archivio della Basilica di S. Maria in Cosmedin
[DATABASE ID: VATV40071-A]
Inclusive Dates: 1561–1890.
Bulk: 228 vols. and miscellaneous buste.
Scope: The series contains primarily parish records incuding financial records. There are printed volumes as well.
Finding Aids: An inventory of the collection can be found in the Vatican Library under the number 383.
Location: Biblioteca Apostolica Vaticana.

7.8.2 Chiesa di S. Lorenzo in Damaso (Rome)

7.8.2.1 Archivio della Basilica di S. Lorenzo in Damaso
[DATABASE ID: VATV295-A]
Inclusive Dates: 1436–1880.
Bulk: 1241 items.
References: Fink, p. 126; Boyle, p. 95.
Location: This series has been deaccessioned from the Archivio Segreto Vaticano.

7.8.3 Monastero dei SS. Gregorio e Siro di Bologna

7.8.3.1 Archivio del Monastero dei SS. Gregorio e Siro di Bologna
[DATABASE ID: VATV353-A]
Inclusive Dates: Unknown.
Bulk: 186 items.
Scope: Boyle notes that this collection includes four original briefs addressed to Eugene IV.
References: Fink, p. 151; Boyle, p. 99. A. Mercati, "Dall'Archivio dei SS. Gregorio e Siro di Bologna: Lettere ad Eugenio IV ivi smarrite," in *Sussidi per la consultazione dell'Archivio Vaticano* (Vatican City, 1947), vol. 3, pp. 77–91.
Finding Aids: ASV Indice 155, "Repertorio in forma dopia per Cognomi," is an alphabetical index to personal names, place names (including churches and monasteries), and organizations. Entries provide the name, a summary of the document, the folio, libro, and item numbers.
Location: Archivio Segreto Vaticano.

7.8.4 Monastero di Clarisse di S. Francesco (Todi)

7.8.4.1 Instrumenta Tudertina
[DATABASE ID: VATV350-A]
Inclusive Dates: 1051–1511.
Bulk: 29 items.
Scope: Note that item no. 29 concerns the substitution of one religious order (Conventuali) for another (Domenicani) in the Church of the Annunziata Conventuali, Monte S. Leucio.
Note: There is also a collection Monastero di S. Francesco in the Archivio Communale di Todi and a "Compendio delle scritture antiche e moderne del Monastero di S. Francesco di Todi" located in the Archivio Vescovile di Todi.

Reference: Fink, p. 151.

Finding Aids: ASV Blocchetti Indice 21 calendars the entire collection. Entries include the date and place of origin of the document, a one-to three-word indication of the type of business or diplomatic category of document (bull, brief), a summary of each item, a note as to whether the item is a copy or an original, and physical information (dimensions, etc.). The calendar also notes if a document had been published or summarized in a publication at the time Blocchetii Indice 21 was compiled.

Location: Archivio Segreto Vaticano.

7.8.5 Monastero di S. Ambrogio (Rome)

7.8.5.1 Archivio del Monastero di S. Ambrogio
[DATABASE ID: VATV10245-A]
Inclusive Dates: 1786–1880.
Bulk: .5 linear m. (6 buste).
Organization: Buste enumerations, titles/contents include: 1. Fedi di Battesimo, cresima, accettazione delle sorelle e rescritti per la diminuzione delle date; Posizione del sig. Azzurri per la casa del fattore; Visite apostolica; Sanatoria dei V.V. Regolari; Vendita fatta del Governo Francese, 1812; Erogazione di due legati, 1857; Obbligazione del signor Azzurri e dell'ebreo Giuseppe Gonzaghi; Posizione del legate Monetti; —2. Conti di Artisti, 1850; Posizione della Casa B.S. Agata, Istromenti dote Milza, Posizione giardino della Penna; Istromenti diversi censi; Obbligazione diversi doti; Cessioni dell'acqua; Istanze per riavere al monastero; S.S. Relique; —3. Riparti d'introito ed esito, 1834–1856; Rendiconti copie anno, 1841–1856; Bilanci redatti dalle monache, 1834–1860; —4. Giustificazioni, pagamenti fatti 1861–1865; Bilancio, 1844–1869; —5. Giustificazioni, pagamenti, fatti, 1866–1871; —6. Giustificazioni, pagamenti, 1872–1880.
Reference: Fink, p. 138.
Location: Archivio Segreto Vaticano.

7.8.6 Monastero di S. Caterina da Siena (Rome)

7.8.6.1 Archivio del Monastero de S. Caterina da Siena
[DATABASE ID: VATV10311-A]
Inclusive Dates: 1372(copy)–1800.
Bulk: 1 linear m. (12 vols.).
Organization: Volume enumeration and titles or contents designations are as follows: 1. Libro di istrumenti, luglio 1607–ottobre 1615; —2. Catasto, 1642; —3. Libro del monastero, 1668–1672; —4. Instrumenti, 1654–1683; —5. Libro delle congregationi, 1703–1748; —6. Registro dei mandati, 1766–1781; —7. Catasto, 1677; —8. Instrumenti, 1768–1788; —9. Instrumenti di canoni, 1589–1645; —10 and 12. "Compendio per modo d'indice di tutte le scritture, contratti, liti, e sentenze ed altri interessi quali si trovano registrati nell'Archivio del S. Monastero di S. Caterina da Siena dell'Ordine di S. Domeenico di Roma con due indici in fine, uno delle materie e l'altro de cognome di quelle persone colle quali ha avuto interesse il d(etto) Monastero fatto nell'anni 1756–1757 e 1758 in tempo del Priorato dell'Ill(ustriss)ma Sig.la Sor M(aria) Costanza Bolognetti e del camarlengato dell'Ill(ustrissi)ma Sig.la Sor M(aria) Ottavia Anguillara (copied and noted documents

date from 1556); —11. Indice di scritture e catasto di case, 1372(copy)–1800. Compiled after 1758.
Scope: These are largely eighteenth-century registers copying earlier documents. Vol. 10 is organized alphabetically by theme, "Aceso" (by which they accepted houses), "Acqua," "Acquisto," and so forth. This index gives a brief summary of documents extant in the archive between 1756 and 1758. There are many seventeenth-century documents noted, but documents noted here do date from 1556 onward. Vol. 10 is virtually equal to vol. 12. A quick survey of vol. 11 indicated that a September 2, 1372, record of a deposit by Giacoma, the widow of Giovanni Pucci Berentino, is the earliest registered document in this series.
Reference: Fink, p. 138.
Location: Archivio Segreto Vaticano.

7.8.7 Monastero di S. Galla (Rome)

7.8.7.1 Archivio del Monastero di S. Galla
[DATABASE ID: VATV356-A]
Inclusive Dates: 1583–1934.
Bulk: 23 linear m.
Organization: Subseries are: Filza di giustificazioni, 1609–1922; —Contratti, 1887–[post-1922]; —Libri d'istromenti, ca. 1720–1820; —Libri di Messe, 1767–1867; —Libri mastri; —"Istromenti" (scatole), 1686 (copy)– ca. 1915.
Scope: The collection was acquired by the ASV in January 1936.
Reference: Fink, p. 139.
Finding Aids: ASV Indice 1130 contains a brief listing of parts of the Ospizio di Santa Galla collection, principally, the Filza di Giustificatzioni and the Istromenti in boxes (numbered 1–108). The list of Istromenti is particularly brief, and in this case the term should be applied broadly. This section of Indice 1130 does not usually indicate inclusive dates.
Location: Archivio Segreto Vaticano.

7.8.8 Monastero di S. Maria dell'Umiltà (Rome)

7.8.8.1 Istromenti del Monastero di S. Maria dell'Umiltà
[DATABASE ID: VATV10246-A]
Inclusive Dates: 1680–1808.
Bulk: .2 linear m. (3 vols.).
Organization: Volume titles and enumeration are: 1. Libro d'istromenti, 1680–1711; —2. Libro d'istromenti, 1748–1768; —3. Libro d'istromenti, 1769–1808.
Reference: Fink, p. 138.
Location: Archivio Segreto Vaticano.

7.8.9 Monastero di S. Maria Maddalena (Rome)

7.8.9.1 Archivio del Monastero di S. Maria Maddalena
[DATABASE ID: VATV10244-A]
Inclusive Dates: 1649–1827.
Bulk: .4 linear m. (5 vols.).
Organization: Volume enumeration and titles are as follows: 1. Catasto di tutti li beni de venerabile Monasterio di Santa Maria Maddalena a Monte Cauallo di Roma, 1649–1651; —2–5. Istromenti, 1672–1831.

Reference: Fink, p. 138.
Location: Archivio Segreto Vaticano.

7.8.10 Monastero S. Caterina (Perugia)

7.8.10.1 Instrumenta Perusina
[DATABASE ID: VATV349-A]
Inclusive Dates: 1214–1774.
Bulk: 232 items.
References: Fink, p. 151; Boyle, p. 98. A. Pantoni, "Santa Caterina di Perugia," *Benedictina* 5 (1951): 233–262; 6 (1952): 238–262.
Finding Aids: ASV Indice 1115.
Location: Archivio Segreto Vaticano.

7.8.11 Monastero S. Silvestro de Nonantola (Nonantola)

7.8.11.1 Monasterium S. Silvestri de Nonantula
[DATABASE ID: VATV10452-A]
Inclusive Dates: 802 (copy)–1780.
Bulk: 440 items.
Note: Related records are Ottob. Lat. no. 2359 and Vat. Lat. no. 5501 in the Biblioteca Apostolica Vaticana and Manoscritto no. 2248 (S. Salvatore 567) in the Biblioteca Università di Bologna.
Note: Nos. 1–440 are available on microfilm.
References: Fink, p. 151; Boyle, p. 99. G. Gullotta, *Gli antichi cataloghi e i codici della'Abbazia di Nonantola* (Vatican City, 1955). A. Mercati, "Una notiziola sul giureconsulto Pillio," *Atti e memorie della Deputazione di storia patria per le antiche provincie modenesi,* ser. 8, 4 (1952): 34–35. G. Gullotta, "Sul registro dei documenti nonantolani dell'Archivio Segreto Vaticano e sugli antichi cataloghi e i codici nonantolani," *Atti e memorie della Deputazione di storia patria per le antiche provincie modenesi* ser. 8, 5 (1953): 147–156. This volume contains a series of articoli concerning S. Silvestro in Nonantola.
Finding Aids: ASV Indice 1093, compiled by Mons. Giuseppe Gullotta, inventories each item in the collection. Entries include the place and date of origin and a brief indication of contents. Later annotations have been added that identify some of the copies.
Location: Archivio Segreto Vaticano.

7.8.12 Monastero S. Trifone

7.8.12.1 Fondo S. Trifone
[DATABASE ID: VATV342-A]
Inclusive Dates: 1006–1188.
Bulk: 8 items.
References: Fink, p. 151; Boyle, p. 98.
Finding Aids: ASV Blocchetti Indice 14 calendars each item. Entries include the following information for each item: the date and a detailed summary. The place of origin, a brief indication of the type of document, and presence of a seal are noted. Some later annotations have been made regarding citations of an item.
Location: Archivio Segreto Vaticano.

7.8.13 Pantheon (Rome)

7.8.13.1 Archivio della Chiesa de S. Maria ad Martyres detta della Rotonda o Pantheon
[DATABASE ID: VATV40070-A]
Inclusive Dates: 1591–1862.
Bulk: Extent undetermined.
Scope: This series contains primarily financial records and pious bequests. The archives also contains manuscripts dated 1216–1732, bulls, and other documents.
Finding Aids: An inventory of the collection by segnatura number can be found in the Vatican Library under the number 384.
Location: Biblioteca Apostolica Vaticana.

7.8.14 San Clemente (church, Rome)

7.8.14.1 S. Clemente
[DATABASE ID: VATV20537-A]
Inclusive Dates: Unknown.
Bulk: Extent undetermined.
Location: Historical Archives of the Congregation for the Evangelization of Peoples (Propaganda Fide).

7.8.15 S. Marta (convent, Rome)

7.8.15.1 Archivio di S. Marta
[DATABASE ID: VATV10323-A]
Inclusive Dates: 1506–1827.
Bulk: 27 linear m. (233 numbered items plus 12 unnumbered vols.).
Organization: Subseries are divided among the items as follows: 1–48, 50–82. Filze di giustificazioni, 1546–1810; —49, 111–121. Istromenti, 1527 (49), 1622–1785 (111–121); —83. Filze di conti dell'artisti, 1756–1787; —84–85. Patente, 1650; —87, 122. Libri dell'eredità; —94–99. Libri di spese per la fabbrica, 1604–1669; —100–104. Libri d'educande, 1664–1785; —107–110. Libri delle congregazione, 1591–1827; —123. Registro della licenza ottenuta dalle RR Monache . . . per la celebrazione delle messe del Santissimo Rosario, 1677, 1712; —130–150. Rincontro, 1605–1725; —154–161. Commestibile, 1674–1761; —164–175. Entrata e uscita, 1506–1777; —Libri mastri; —200–216. Scritture di interesse diverse, ca. 1528–1800; —219–223. Perusina; —229. Licenze, 1750; —Rubricelle di libri mastri. 11 vols.; —Catasti, 1650–1667. 1 vol.
References: Fink, p. 138; Boyle, p. 99 (Boyle calls this an ospizio).
Finding Aids: In scatole 140 of the *Archivio di S. Marta* there are two inventories (marked no. 88 and no. 89. These are the first and second books of an "Inventario di libri e scritture di S. Marta," 1607. While these inventories do not aid researchers in locating items within the Archivio today, these books do give an overall picture of the scope of materials that might be contained in the Archivio and they provide a historical glimpse into the Archivio.
Location: Archivio Segreto Vaticano.

7.8.16 Santa Maria delle Grazie (church, Rome)

7.8.16.1 Archivio del S. Maria delle Grazie
[DATABASE ID: VATV10243-A]
Inclusive Dates: ca. 1608–1927.
Bulk: 5.5 linear m. (46 items).
Scope: Santa Maria delle Grazie is a parish church in Rome.
See also Corporazioni maschili, Congregazione dei Padri della
Penitenza detta degli Scalzetti in Santa Maria delle Grazie a
Porta Angelica (1761–1838), located in the Archivio di Stato di
Roma. The collection was acquired by the ASV in 1939.
Finding Aids: ASV Indice 60*, available at the desk in the
main ASV reading room, provides an overall inventory of this
collection. The indice is not a formal finding aid and must be
used in consultation with the archives staff. Entries proceed
busta-by-busta listing the inclusive dates and summarizing the
contents.
Location: Archivio Segreto Vaticano.

7.8.17 S. Maria in Regola (abbey)

7.8.17.1 Abbazia di S. Maria in Regola
[DATABASE ID: VATV20478-A]
Inclusive Dates: Unknown.
Bulk: 41 scatole.
Location: Historical Archives of the Congregation for the
Evangelization of Peoples (Propaganda Fide).

7.8.17.2 Lettere
[DATABASE ID: VATV20546-A]
Inclusive Dates: Unknown.
Bulk: Extent undetermined.
Location: Historical Archives of the Congregation for the
Evangelization of Peoples (Propaganda Fide).

7.8.18 SS. Domenico e Sisto (monastery, Rome)

7.8.18.1 Fondo del Monastero di SS. Domenico e Sisto
[DATABASE ID: VATV355-A]
Inclusive Dates: 1389–1867.
Bulk: 16 linear m.
Organization: Subseries include: Instrumenti, 1507–1824;
—Registro dei mandati, 1619–1794; —Entrata et uscita, 1596–
1807; —Libro per la Madre Priora, 1654–1660; —Libro di
ricevute, 1604; —Fattore, entrata et uscita, giornale, strac-
ciafoglio, 1552–1674; —Libro mastro, 1715–1795; —Ruolo
con dicte di Provisione, 1734–1757; —Ruolo di salariati, 1758;
—Spese della Camerlenga, 1596–1667; —Borsaria, 1605–
1615; —Scritture a stampa duplicate; —Debiti, crediti, etc.,
1715–1790; —Patenti, 1688–1696; —Libro delle memorie, ordini, decreti e risoluzioni delle Congregazioni del Monastero di
SS. Domenico e Sisto, 1662; —Rincontro del Monastero con il
Sacro Monte della Pietà, 1619–1801; —Idem, Atti dall'anno
1794; —Conti e spese, piante di casali, 1746–1780; —Libro
d'appigionamenti e spigionamenti di case, 1725; —Rincontro
del Sacro Monte della Pietà e del Banco di Santo Spirito, 1715–
1780; —Registro de depositi e dell'ordini che si spediscono dalla
R. M. Priora di SS. Domenico e Sisto a Monte Magnanapoli di
Roma, 1880–1896; —Registro delle franchigie dall'anno 1732;
—Libro dove si scrivono li vitti delle Signore Educande, 1720;

—Spese, 1431–1816; —Affitti, pigione, quietanze, fruttiferi,
etc., 1641–1785; —Elemosine e entrate, 1566–1584; —Rice-
vuto di varii legatari della q. Brigida Masi che lascio erede il
Monastero di SS. Domenico e Sisto, 1608–1640; —Giustificazioni (di tesoreria, dei mandati, del giornal dal libro mastro,
del libro mastro), 1689–1867; —Lettere, 1700–1800; —Libro
congressi, 1840–1842; —Registro delle fede, 1802; —Castello
di Prassede, Giornale dell'introito ed esito, 1717–1724; —
Romana census, 1670; —Toscanella; —Cause contro . . . ,
ca. 1500–1800; —Magistrale, 1625–1724; —Icenze di vestizi-
oni, professioni ed altri particolari, 1716–1766; —Rubricelle;
—Testamento e codicillo di Catta.r ta q. Antonio Batta Alber-
toni, 1487; —Censi.
Note: This fondo was being processed in 1990 and was difficult to consult.
References: Fink, p. 138; Boyle, p. 99.
Finding Aids: An unnumbered inventory to this collection
by Guia Verdesi and Virginia Bernardini is available at the desk
in the main ASV reading room. This is not an official ASV
finding aid and must be used in consultation with ASV staff.
This inventory lists individual volumes in this fondo according
to their physical location on the shelves (as of 1989). Although
volumes tend to be grouped by type, the entire inventory
should be read carefully for stray volumes of each type or single
volumes. Entries in the index usually include the nature of the
business in the volume, and inclusive dates. Occasionally personal names or geographic locations of the extensive holdings
are listed.
S. Pagano, *L'Archivio del Convento dei SS. Domenico e
Sisto di Roma: Cenni storici e inventario* (Vatican City, 1994).
This is an extensive index of this series. Pagano provides a
summary of each busta in the series. He also provides a schema
for considering the diverse collection as a single chronological
unit. There is a name and place index. The introduction contains an excellent history of the convent and its work.
Location: Archivio Segreto Vaticano.

7.8.18.2 SS. Domenico e Sisto: Pergamene
[DATABASE ID: VATV068-A]
Inclusive Dates: May 26, 1196–1567.
Bulk: .3 linear m. (2 buste).
Organization: Busta 1: numbered 1–60; busta 2: unnumbered.
Note: Additional SS. Domenico e Sisto pergamene can be
found in other archives. See Corporazioni religiose soppresse,
S. Domenico, Miscellanea, no. 66, "Liber privilegiorum,
Registrum notabilium rerum ac negotiorum monasterii Sancti
Sixti de Urbe" (Archivio di Stato di Perugia). Bullaire, L. 248
(Archives Nationales, Paris). Annuali del venerando monastero
di SS. Domenico e Sisto . . . (Archivio Generale dei Predi-
catori). Archivio dei notai capitolani, vol. 329 (Archivio di
Stato di Roma). Vat. Lat. 11392 (Biblioteca Apostolica Vati-
cana). Archivio del capitolo di S. Pietro in Vaticano, capse 36,
62, 74 (Biblioteca Apostolica Vaticana). Archivio di S. Maria
in Via Lata, Varia I (Biblioteca Apostolica Vaticana). Codici
Chigiani E.V. 144 and E.VI. 187 (Biblioteca Apostolica Vaticana). Docc. nn. 1, 43, 99, 108 (Archivio del convento della
Madonna del Rosario).
Finding Aids: Cristina Carbonetti Venditelli, ed., *Le più
antiche carte del convento di San Sisto in Roma (905–1300)*
(Rome, 1987).
Location: Archivio Segreto Vaticano.

7.8.19 SS. Vincenzo e Anastasio (abbey, Rome)

7.8.19.1 Archivio

[DATABASE ID: VATV10317-A]
Inclusive Dates: 1539–1915.
Bulk: 57 linear m. (523 numbered buste[51 linear m.] and 6 linear m. misc.).
Organization: The *Archivio* is divided into six subseries: A. Commune a tutta l'abbazia, 1602–1911, 95 buste and 7 appendice; —B. Monterosa, 1596–1876, 206 buste; —C. Ponzano, 1539–1913, 123 buste; —D. S. Oreste, 1570–1915, 99 buste; —[between B and C]. E. Libri di Messe (di Cappellani diverse), ca. 1679–1837 ; Legati liberati, 1761–1840, 2 linear m.; — F. Miscellanea, 4 linear m.
Reference: Fink, p. 125.
Finding Aids: ASV Indice 1129 provides detailed access to the numbered buste in the four major subseries (A–D). Entries proceed busta by busta and indicate the types of material (visitations, matrimonialia, atti, etc.) contained in the busta and the inclusive dates. Occasionally, each document in the busta is described individually.
No. C–123 in this series, "Indice delle materie contenute nei vari protocolli esistenti nella Cancelleria Abbaziale di Ponzano . . . 1867," is no longer a useful index for locating items in this collection. However, it does reflect the contents of the *Archivio* at one point in time. No. C–123 also contains an 1847 inventory of objects and papers in the Cancelleria.
Note: An alternate name is Tre Fontane.
Location: Archivio Segreto Vaticano.

7.9
MISCELLANEOUS MANUSCRIPTS

7.9.1 Collegio Ginnasi della Sapienza (Rome)

7.9.1.1 Archivio Collegio Ginnasi

[DATABASE ID: VATV10268-A]
Inclusive Dates: 1640–1868.
Bulk: 4 linear m.
Scope: The archive contains mainly financial records, but there are lists of students and some indications of the curriculum and student life.
Location: Archivio Segreto Vaticano.

7.9.2 Kingdom of the Two Sicilies: Incaricato d'Affari (Tuscany)

7.9.2.1 Incaricato d'Affari di Napoli presso la corte di Firenze

[DATABASE ID: VATV40036-A]
Inclusive Dates: 1816–1848.
Bulk: 155 buste.
Note: This series was cited in Natalini et al., p. 272, but not seen by project staff in 1990.
Finding Aids: ASV Indice 1119.
Location: Archivio Segreto Vaticano.

7.9.3 Ordine equestre del santo sepolcro di Gerusalemme

7.9.3.1 Verbale della consulta

[DATABASE ID: VATV10239-A]
Inclusive Dates: [1978?].
Bulk: .3 linear m. (1 buste).
Summary: Description on buste: "Corrispondenza, biglietti, ecc. de S.E. Cav. Gr. Cr. Conte Francesco Canuti Castelvetri, Governatore Generale del Ordine. . . ."
Location: Archivio Segreto Vaticano.

7.9.4 Ospizio de'Convertendi (Rome)

7.9.4.1 Archivio

[DATABASE ID: VATV10318-A]
Inclusive Dates: 1653–1895.
Bulk: 50 linear m.
Organization: Subseries are numbered separately and numbers all overlap. Subseries include: Filza di giustificazioni, 1675–1820; —Giustificazioni di spese, pagamenti, etc., 1731–1769; —Filza di memoriali, di elemosinaria, 1753–1797; —Eredità; —Fogli dove sono notati gl'ospiti ricevuti e spese . . . , 1689–1749; —Registri di mandati, 1703–1764; —Entrata ed uscita, 1703–1764; —Ricevute, 1649–1693; —Giustificazioni del libri mastri, 1823–1885; —Giornale (spese cibarie quotidiane), 1672–1796, 1804–1857; —Libri di messe, 1680–1696, 1705–1798, 1733–1883; —Registri d'ospite tedeschi, 1773–1833; —Registri generale d'ospite, 1673–1895; —Istromenti, 1675–1732; —Visite, 1748–1761.
Reference: Fink, p. 133.
Location: Archivio Segreto Vaticano.

7.9.5 S. Apollinare (seminary, Rome)

7.9.5.1 [Archivio]

[DATABASE ID: VATV10310-A]
Inclusive Dates: 1851–1857.
Bulk: 21 vols.
Organization: Volume titles and numbers are: 1. Seminario Romano (Lavori murari), 1851–1855; —2. Seminario Pio provinciale; —3. Scuole e biblioteca; —4. Chiesa; —5. Segreteria e tribunale vicariato; —6. Botteghe e farmacia; —7. Addizionali; —8–10. Vie delle fratte, 1856–1857; —11. Caldararo, 1851–1853; —12. Chiavaro, 1851–1853; —13. Falegname, 1851–1853; —14. Lavagnaro, 1852–1853; —15. Imbiancatore, 1851–1853; —16. Scalpelino, 1851–1853; —17. Stagnaro; —18. Vernicaro, 1851–1853; —19–20. Giustificazioni dei mandati, no.1–617, 1851–1855; —21. Bollettario, 1851–1855.
Note: This collection has no official ASV designation. The title was supplied by the project staff.
Location: Archivio Segreto Vaticano.

Agency Not Determined

7.9.6 Catalogus universalis nundinis franco-furtensibus autumnalibus

[DATABASE ID: VATV10351-A]
Inclusive Dates: 1655, 1657–1658.
Bulk: 1 vol.

Scope: This contains two booksellers' catalogs bound together—Merianus of Frankfurt-am-Main: "Catalogus omnium librorum qui in officina haeredum matthaei meriani, bibliopolae et sculptoris Moeno-Francofurtani, eorum impendio impressi, & maximam partem aere ornati venerunt," 1657; and Kinchius of Cologne: "Catalogus librorum officinae Coloniensis Ioannis Antonii Kinchii Iunioris Ciuis & bibliopolae Coloniensis praeter alios externae & diversae editionis omni Facultate libros apud eum praestantes Coloniae Francofurti, et Lipsie qui hoc elenchonon continentur" (with written annotations).

Each catalog contains many of the same categories of books, including: Libri theologici theologorum catholicorum, Libri iuridici, Libri medici et chymici, Libri politici, historici et geographici, Libri philosophici et artium humaniorum, Libri poetici et ad rem metricam pertinentes, Libri musici, Libri peregrini idiomatis, and Libri futuris nundinis prodituri.

Location: Archivio Segreto Vaticano.

7.9.7 Chiese collegiate di Roma

[DATABASE ID: VATV40032-A]
Inclusive Dates: 1737–1850.
Bulk: 4 buste.
Organization: S. Croce in Gerusalemme; —S. Giovanni Battista dei Genovesi; —S. Lorenzo in Damaso; —S. Pietro in Vaticano (Fabbrica).
Note: This series was cited in Natalini et al., p. 269, but not seen by project staff in 1990.
Location: Archivio Segreto Vaticano.

7.9.8 [Expedition of Commodore Matthew Perry]

[DATABASE ID: VATV30014-A]
Inclusive Dates: 1853.
Bulk: 1 item.
L'Attivita della Santa Sede reports that a Japanese manuscript describing the expedition of Commodore Matthew Perry to Japan was given to the ASV by Kei Kikuchi.
Location: Archivio Segreto Vaticano.

7.9.9 Famiglie nobili

[DATABASE ID: VATV40033-A]
Inclusive Dates: [16—]–[17—].
Bulk: 14 buste.
Organization: Aldobrandini di Roma; —Varano di Camerino e Ferrara.
Note: This series was cited in Natalini et al., p. 270, but not seen by project staff in 1990.
Location: Archivio Segreto Vaticano.

7.9.10 Fondo Culto

[DATABASE ID: VATV40035-A]
Inclusive Dates: 1879–1931.
Bulk: 53 buste and 114 vols.
Note: This series was cited in Natalini et al., p. 271, but not seen by project staff in 1990.
Location: Archivio Segreto Vaticano.

7.9.11 Inventaires (1810–1815) des archives du Vatican et d'autres archives italiennes (L372–L400)

[DATABASE ID: VATV40054-A]
Inclusive Dates: 1810–1815.
Bulk: about 3.5 linear m.

Organization: Boxes L372–L399 contain inventories of material received from the Vatican. Box L400 contains inventories of material received from Sardinia, Naples, and Milan.
Scope: With the exception of L400, this is a collection of inventories prepared by French archivists when the contents of the Archivio Segreto Vaticano were removed to Paris at the order of Napoleon. Since many documents were lost in the process of returning the archives to the Vatican, these inventories are particularly valuable as a source for what in fact was later lost. In some cases extensive analysis was done on particular series so that the inventories do contain some copies of and extracts from the original material.
Reference: Favier, *Fonds,* vol. 1, p. 314.
Finding Aids: The Favier guide as noted in the reference above contains a brief listing of some of the contents of this series. Archives Nationales finding aid L/2 provides a listing for each item in this series along with a general indication of its subject matter.
Location: Archives Nationales, Paris.

7.9.12 [Miscellanea SF/457]

[DATABASE ID: VATV10363-A]
Inclusive Dates: ca. 1667–1830.
Bulk: .5 linear m.
Scope: This a a mix of material, two bound volumes (of supplications?) from both men's and women's congregations, an apologia from a monastery in Classe, and so forth. The loose material contains a 1667 "Inventario delli mobili di Sant'Angelo Rosaro" in Foligno. Anyone trying to find anything about any religious order in this period may want to at least browse through the volumes.
Reference: Fink, p. 151.
Note: This is a true miscellany and does not have an official designation in the ASV. The title was supplied by the project staff, based on the location of the material in 1990.
Location: Archivio Segreto Vaticano.

7.9.13 Prelatura Valdina

[DATABASE ID: VATV10394-A]
Inclusive Dates: ca. 1855–1881.
Bulk: .5 linear m. (6 boxes).
Scope: In 1990 this material was physically located among the records in the middle of the Bishops and Regulars but does not seem to have anything to do with that congregation. There are references to this material in the standard sources. The collection includes a Mass book, 1865–1888; "Note di carte ed effetti alla Prelatura Valdina che sono state consegnate al Sottos. Procuratore da S.E. Roma Sig. Cardinale . . . Protettore della Prelature" (this is not an index to the unorganized boxes); and the "testamento e codicilli del Principi D. Giovanni Valdina, principe di Valdina e Marchese della Rocca" (1688) [printed copy?].
Location: Archivio Segreto Vaticano.

7.10
SPOGLI CARDINALI

[DATABASE ID: VATV10187-A]

The Spogli Cardinali of the Archivio Segreto Vaticano are collections of papers considered personal by individual cardinals but deposited in the ASV. These are not official records of the Roman Curia. However, because these cardinals have, for the most part, held positions of the highest rank within the Vatican, the collections are very complementary to the official records.

The Spogli are a large and diverse group of papers. Although it is difficult to characterize major subjects in the collection, there are several areas of strength in the collection as a whole. The bulk of the Spogli dates from 1780 to 1900. Major themes include penal and judicial reform in Italy and the Papal States (nineteenth century), the Napoleonic invasion of Rome, the Austrian invasions of Rome, and various apostolic delegations and legations.

At the time of this survey, the Spogli represented collections of assorted materials from 206 (primarily) cardinals, but also from some minutanti (in the Secretariat of State), and from several archivists of the Secretariat of State. Records in the buste seem to be very wide ranging, from notes concerning their positions in the Roman Curia to minute books of letters in their role as archbishops of sees.

This guide simply presents a sense of the contents of the collection. There is some disagreement as to the relationship of these papers to the Vatican Archives proper. Boyle puts the Spogli with the Collegio dei Cardinali, but Pásztor seems to make an equally convincing argument for placement within the Secretariatus Status.

Please note that in some cases the biographical information of the particular cardinal or official could not be determined. In other cases only minimal information could be found. Also in many cases the precise inclusive dates of the documents were not available. Project staff did not have the time to consult each of the Spogli to determine the earliest and latest documents. In any case, all the individual Spogli are listed with varying degrees of supporting information.

References. Boyle, p. 83; Fink, p. 66; Pásztor (1970), p. 112; Pásztor (1983), pp. 144–147.

Finding Aid. A single finding aid exists for all the collections noted in this section. The five-volume alphabetical inventory of the entire collection is available at the desk in the main ASV reading room. (The indice is not a formal finding aid and must be used in consultation with the archives staff.) This index provides a brief biography of each contributor of Spogli to this collection, and contents summaries of each Spogli busta. The inventory was the source for biographical sketches in this guide when no other source is indicated. In no case is there more biographical information in the inventory than is provided in this guide. Some copies of these inventories and the biographical information have been placed in the actual buste (inside covers).

ASV Indice 1143 (formerly Indice 85) provides only the last names of persons in this collection and the number of buste from each individual. It does not provide any sense of the contents or richness of this series.

7.10.1 Spoglio del Charles Januarius Acton
[DATABASE ID: VATV10451-A]
Inclusive Dates: 1835–1849.
Bulk: 7 buste.
Biography: Charles Januarius Acton was born in Naples on March 6, 1803 and died there on June 23, 1847. He became a cardinal on February 18, 1839. Acton served as a member of the following congregations: Visita Apostolica, Concistoriale, Vescovi e Regolari, Concilio, Immunità, Propaganda Fide, Indice, Riti, Disciplina Regolare, Indulgenze e Sacre Reliquie, Affari Ecclesiastici Straordinari, Speciale per la riedificazione della Basilica di S. Paolo. He was a protector of the Nobile Accademia Ecclesiastica, Ordine dei Minori Cappuccini, Monaci Benedettini Cassinesi, PP. della Penitenza in S. Maria delle Grazie a Porta Angelica, Ordine Premonstratense, Monastero di S. Susanna alle Terme Diocleziane, Collegio Inglese, SS. Bartolomeo ed Alessandro della Nazione Bergamasca, Arciconfraternite del SS. Sacramento in S. Lorenzo in Lucina, Madonna del Buon Consiglio, SS. Celso e Giuliano in S. Maria del Soccorso, Madonna del Carmine alle tre Cannelle, Confraternità del Gonfalone e del SSmo. Rosario unite nella Chiesa di S. Maria in Monticelli, SS. Vincenzo ed Anastasio alla Regola, Comune di Genazzano, Compagnia del Buon Consiglio in Urbania, Confraternità delle Sacre Stimmate eretta in Velletri.
Location: Archivio Segreto Vaticano.

7.10.2 Spogli Andrea Aiuti
[DATABASE ID: VATV10555-A]
Inclusive Dates: [18—?]–[19—?].
Bulk: 7 buste.
Biography: Andrea Aiuti was born on June 17, 1849, in Rome. He completed his studies at the Seminary of St. Apollinare. His posts included aggiunto in the Congregazione del Concilio, secretary of the internunciature and chargé d'affaires in Rio de Janeiro, and apostolic delegate in India. He was elevated to archbishop in 1887. In 1891 he was recalled to Rome to work in the Propaganda Fide. After a short stay Aiuti was appointed apostolic nuncio to Munich in 1893 and then to Lisbon in 1896. He was made a cardinal on June 22, 1903. He died in Rome on April 28, 1905. He was a member of the following congregations: Concilio, Cerimoniale, Affari Ecclesiastici Straordinari, and Lauretana. Aiuti was also a member of the Commissione Cardinalizia per l'esame dei visitatori apostolici in Italia and protector of the Confraternità del Sacramento a S. Lorenzo in Lucina and the Società di Mutuo Soccorso San Gioacchino.
Scope: The buste consist of a variety of materials including some relating to missions in India.
Location: Archivio Segreto Vaticano.

7.10.3 Spoglio del Giuseppe Albani
[DATABASE ID: VATV10556-A]
Inclusive Dates: [17—?]–[18—?].
Bulk: 7 buste.
Biography: Giuseppe Albani was born in Rome on September 13, 1750, and died in Pesaro on December 3, 1834. He was sent by the papacy to Vienna in 1784 to foster better relations.

After he became cardinal on February 23, 1801, Albani became protector of the emperor of Austria (1803). Other posts he held included secretary of state, prefect of the Congregazione di Buon Governo, pro-secretary of the Congregazione dei Brevi, legate to Bologna, and cardinal librarian of the Holy Roman Church. When he died he was legate to Pesaro and Urbino.

Reference: Enciclopedia cattolica, vol. 1 (Vatican City, 1948).

Location: Archivio Segreto Vaticano.

7.10.4 Spoglio del Giuseppe Alberghini

[DATABASE ID: VATV10557-A]

Inclusive Dates: [17—?]–[18—?].

Bulk: 2 buste.

Organization: Materials are divided into three sections: Congregazione di Revisione; —S. Congregazione dei Vescovi e Regolari: Processi; —Arciginnasio della Sapienza: Biblioteca Alessandrina (Ammistrazione, cattedre e professori; Collegio Avvocati; Consistoriali; Collegio dei Medici; Congregazione della Purificazione di Maria Vergine; Opere della Biblioteca; Orto botanico; Regolamento; Stampatori di Roma).

Biography: Giuseppe Alberghini was born on September 18, 1770. He was raised to the rank of cardinal April 6, 1835. Algerghini served as librarian of the Sapienza (Alessandrina), Avvocato Consistoriale, and Assessor of the S. Uffizio. He died on September 30, 1847. He was a member of the following congregations: S. Uffizio, Visita Apostolica, Vescovi e Regolari, Propaganda Fide, Esami dei Vescovi in Sacri Canoni, Economica, Fabbrica, Buon Governo, Acque, and Speciale per la riedificazione Basilica di S. Paolo.

Reference: G. Moroni, *Dizionario di erudizione storico-ecclesiastica*, vol. 3 (Venice, 1840).

Location: Archivio Segreto Vaticano.

7.10.5 Spoglio del Luigi Amat di San Filippo e Sorso

[DATABASE ID: VATV30007-A]

Inclusive Dates: [17—?]–[18—?].

Biography: Luigi Amat di San Filipo e Sorso was born on June 20, 1796, in Cagliari, and died in Rome on March 30, 1878. He was protected by Cardinal Consalvi and was part of the nunziatures in Naples (1826) and Madrid (1833–1835). Amat di San Filippo became a cardinal in 1837. He also served as bishop of Palestrina (1852), bishop of Porto e S. Ruffino (1870), and Ostia and Velletri (1877).

Location: Archivio Segreto Vaticano.

7.10.6 Spoglio del Giacomo Antonelli

[DATABASE ID: VATV10559-A]

Inclusive Dates: [18—]–[18—].

Bulk: 6 buste.

Biography: Giacomo Cardinal Antonelli was born on April 12, 1806, in Sonnino, near Terracina (Latium), Italy, of a middle-class family that prospered through government farm contracts and land reconstruction. The family was later enobled by Gregory XVI. The family remained faithful to the pontiff during the French occupation and with the help of a Dominican prelate obtained a family prelature.

Giacomo studied at the Roman Seminary and at the Sapienza but never proceeded beyond the diaconate to which he was ordained in 1840. In the offices he held under Gregory XVI

he apparently demonstrated intelligence and rare gifts of administrative and executive ability. Support from Cardinals Luigi Lambruschini, papal secretary of state (1836–1846), and the Camaldolese Giacinto Zurla, confessor of Gregory XVI and prefect of studies at the Collegio Urbino, opened the way for Giacomo to a successful career that included many papal posts (e.g., referendario of the Segnatura; assessor of the criminal tribunal in Rome; apostolic delegate to Orvieto, Viterbo, and Macerata; protesoriere della Camera; tesoriere della Camera; sostituto del Cardinal Mattei; and a number of other diplomatic posts). He was elevated to the cardinalate by Pius IX in 1847. He first became pro-secretary of state in 1848 and then secretary of state in 1852, a post he held until his death at the Vatican on November 6, 1876.

Giacomo Antonelli helped formulate and administer the liberal reform of Pius IX who selected him to be premier of the first constitutional ministry of the Papal States. Antonelli arranged the temporary papal residence at Gaeta (1848), when violence arose in the Papal States. He became head of the papal government in exile. His diplomacy was extremely important in the resistance of the papacy to Italian national unification. He reduced dependence on Austria but after 1859 looked to France to protect the States of the Church. He opposed the calling of the First Vatican Council lest it adversely affect relations with France and advised the pope to drop the infallibility question. Nicknamed the "Red Pope," he became the virtual temporal ruler of Rome until 1870. A statesman rather than a prelate, he was praised by his friends but regarded as unscrupulous by his enemies.

Through his efforts the invasion of Rome in 1870 took place with a minimum of violence. He advised Pius IX to remain in Rome and successfully rearranged the papal finances in accord with the reduction of papal temporal sovereignty.

Location: Archivio Segreto Vaticano.

7.10.7 Spoglio del Antonio Antonucci

[DATABASE ID: VATV10558-A]

Inclusive Dates: [18—]–[18—].

Bulk: 1 busta.

Biography: Antonio Antonucci was born in Subiaco on September 17, 1789. He was bishop of Ancona, chargé d'affaires and vice superior of the mission in Holland. He became a cardinal on March 15, 1858, and died in Ancona on January 29, 1879.

Location: Archivio Segreto Vaticano.

7.10.8 Spoglio del Tommaso Arezzo

[DATABASE ID: VATV30008-A]

Inclusive Dates: 1813–1830.

Bulk: 2 buste.

Biography: Tommaso Arezzo was born on December 17, 1756 in Ortobello and died on February 3, 1833, in Rome. His father was the marchese Orazio, brigadier general in the Neapolitan army and colonel of the Farnese regiment. His mother, Marianna Fitzgerald and Brown, was born in Ireland of the family of the dukes of Linster. Prepared for diplomatic service, Orazio was called to Rome by Pius VII (1800–1823) and sent on various diplomatic missions. His ecclesiastical career included postings as vice-legato in Bologna and governor of Fermo, Perugia, and Macerata and service as part of the papal diplomatic missions in Germany and Russia. The deaths of his father and brother left him with a large patrimony but on his ordination in 1801 he renounced his title as head of the family in favor of Giuseppe and returned to Rome. During the Napoleonic occupation of Rome, Arezzo was exiled to Bastia where he remained for five years. After the reestablishment of papal power in 1814, Arezzo became pro-commissario of the Santo Offizio and a member of the Congregazione per la Riforma. On March 8, 1816, he was made cardinal and apostolic delegate to Ferrara. He also served as bishop suburbicario of Sabina and in 1830 became vice-cancelliere della S. Romana Chiesa e Commendatario di S. Lorenzo in Damaso. He also served in the following congregations: Concistoriale, Vescovi e Regolari, Propaganda Fide, and Indulgenza e Sacra Reliquie. He was protector of the Oblate convittrici del Bambino Gesù di Roma, the Congregazione del B. Pier da Pisa, dell'Arciconfraternità di S. Caterina della Nazione Senese, della Città di Lugo.

Scope: Materials in the first busta deal with Arezzo's service as legate to Ferrara. The second busta contains autographed, signed letters to Arezzo as legate by Cardinal Consalvi.

Location: Archivio Segreto Vaticano.

7.10.9 Spoglio del Luigi Armellini
[DATABASE ID: VATV10561-A]

Inclusive Dates: [17—?]–[18—?].

Bulk: 4 buste.

Biography: Luigi Armelli served as primo minutante della Segretario di Stato.

References: G. Barluzzi, *Elogio storico del cavaliere Luigi Armellini* (Rome, 1842). P. Castellano, *Elogio funebre del cavaliere Luigi Armellini primo minutante della Segreteria di Stato, morto in Napoli il 17 Aprile 1842* (Loreto, 1842).

Location: Archivio Segreto Vaticano.

7.10.10 Spoglio del Bartolomeo Artibani
[DATABASE ID: VATV10562-A]

Inclusive Dates: 1873–1908.

Bulk: 1 busta.

Biography: Bartolomeo Artibani served as minutante to the secretary of state from 1873 to 1908.

Scope: The busta (actually a fascicolo) contains telegrams in code, drafts of letters, and letters addressed to the pope.

Location: Archivio Segreto Vaticano.

7.10.11 Spogli Fabio Maria Asquini
[DATABASE ID: VATV10563-A]

Inclusive Dates: [18—]–[18—].

Bulk: 1 busta.

Biography: Fabio Maria Asquini was born in Fagagna on August 14, 1802, and died in Rome in December 1878. He became a cardinal on January 22, 1844. His ecclesiastical career spanned many decades and included posts in the following congregations: S. Romana ed Universale Inquisizione, Vescovi e Regolari, Concilio, speciale per la revisione dei Concili provinciali, Ceremoniale, Fabbrica, Speciale per la Riedificazione della Basilica di S. Paolo, Indulgenze e Reliquie, Immunità, and the Cong. dei Brevi. He was protector of the Congregazione Benedettina di Monte Vergine, dell'Instituto delle Figlie della Carità dette Cannosiane, del Monastero de S. Caterina de'Funari, dell'arciconfraternità dei SS. Bartolomeo ed Alessandro della Nazione Bergamasca, della Confraternita

del SSmo Sagramento in Fagagna, and dell'Accademia Teologica nell'Università Romana.

Scope: The contents of the busta include information on the nunciature for Naples and affairs in Ferrara and Ancona.

Reference: K. Eubel, *Hierarchia catholica medii et recentioris aevi, sive Summorum pontificum, S.R.E. cardinalium, ecclesiarum antistitum*, vol. 7 (Münster, 1913–1978).

Location: Archivio Segreto Vaticano.

7.10.12 Spoglio del Carlo Autilio
[DATABASE ID: VATV10564-A]

Inclusive Dates: ca. 1849–1852.

Bulk: 1 busta.

Biography: Carlo Autilio was vicario generale of Mons. Girolamo dei Marchesi D'Andrea (later Cardinal D'Andrea) and inspector of the mail in Naples.

Scope: The busta contains miscellaneous letters regarding administrative matters.

Location: Archivio Segreto Vaticano.

7.10.13 Spoglio del Giovanni Barberi
[DATABASE ID: VATV10565-A]

Inclusive Dates: 1812–1821.

Bulk: 1 busta.

Biography: Giovanni Barberi held several important financial posts in the papacy including procurator general for the Camera. He is noted for helping to restore financial matters after the reestablishment of the Papal States in 1814.

Scope: Materials in the busta concern financial matters of the papacy, payments to papal employees, criminal cases, and the supposed flight of Napoleon from Saint Helena.

Reference: G. Moroni, *Dizionario di erudizione storico-ecclesiastica*, (Venice, 1840), vol. 30, p. 157; vol. 53, p. 136; vol. 74, p. 323; and vol. 103, p. 485.

Location: Archivio Segreto Vaticano.

7.10.14 Spoglio del Lorenzo Barili
[DATABASE ID: VATV10566-A]

Inclusive Dates: [18—]–[18—].

Bulk: 1 busta.

Biography: Lorenzo Barili was born on December 1, 1801, in Ancona and died in Rome on March 8, 1875. His ecclesiastical career began in Ancona. In November 1845 he became cameriere d'onore of the uditore in the nunciature for Lisbon. In 1851 he received the title of domestic prelate (monsignor) and was appointed internuncio of New Granada (Bogot, Colombia). In 1857 Barili became apostolic nuncio in Spain. He was created a cardinal March 13, 1868, and participated in the First Vatican Council. When he died, he was a member of the following congregations: Concistoriale, Riti, Indice, Affari Ecclesiastici Straordinari, and Studi. He was protector of the Congregazione Benedettina Camaldolese.

Scope: The contents of this busta reflect Barili's ecclesiastical career. Materials concern the nunciatures for New Granada (Colombia) and Spain; and the congregations of Indulgenze, Indice, Concilio, Vescovi e Regolari, and Affari Ecclesiastici Straordinari.

Reference: G. Moroni, *Dizionario di erudizione storico-ecclesiastica* (Venice, 1840).

Location: Archivio Segreto Vaticano.

7.10.15 Spoglio del Giuseppe Luigi Bartoli
[DATABASE ID: VATV10567-A]
Inclusive Dates: ca. 1827–1852.
Bulk: 12 buste.
Organization: Busta 1, Legazione di Velletri; —Busta 2, Codici e procedure criminali; —Buste 3–7, Miscellanea; —Busta 8, Congressi (1833) and Materie fiscali (1827–1833); —Buste 9–10, Materie fiscali (1833–1839); —Buste 11–12, Avvocato fiscale (1832–1852).
Biography: Giuseppe Luigi Bartoli served as advocate general of financial matters for the Camera.
Scope: Papers concern Bartoli's involvement in financial matters, legal reform, and the diplomatic legation in Velletri.
Reference: G. Moroni, *Dizionario di erudizione storico-ecclesiastica* (Venice, 1840), vol. 90, p. 33.
Location: Archivio Segreto Vaticano.

7.10.16 Spoglio del Domenico Bartolini
[DATABASE ID: VATV10568-A]
Inclusive Dates: [18—]–[18—].
Bulk: 1 busta.
Biography: Domenico Bartolini was born on May 16, 1813, in Rome, and died in Florence on October 2, 1887. He was a biographer and author of historical works.
Location: Archivio Segreto Vaticano.

7.10.17 Spoglio del Gaetano Bedini
[DATABASE ID:VATV10569-A]
Inclusive Dates: 1845–1852.
Bulk: 5 buste.
Biography: Gaetano Bedini was born in Senigallia on May 15, 1806, and died in Viterbo on September 6, 1864. He served as the commissario pontificio straordinario di Bologna from 1849 to 1851. After that post, Bedini became the apostolic nuncio in Brazil, secretary of the Congregatio de Propaganda Fide (1854–1861), and archbishop of Viterbo and bishop of Toscanella. He became a cardinal on September 27, 1861.
Scope: This collection primarily concerns Bedini's work as Commissario Straordinario di Bologna. The first four buste are primarily made up of correspondence with prelates and other functionaries written in order to carry out these responsibilities. The end of busta 4 and all of busta 5, however, concern Bedini's other positions. These two buste include materials dealing with Bedini's work as internuncio and then as nuncio in Brazil, correspondence with American bishops, his work as secretary at the Propaganda Fide including an apostolic visit to the United States in 1854, and correspondence written during his tenure as Archbishop-Bishop of Viterbo and Toscanella.
Location: Archivio Segreto Vaticano.

7.10.18 Spoglio del Carlo di Conti Belgrado
[DATABASE ID: VATV10570-A]
Inclusive Dates: 1846–1858.
Bulk: 1 busta.
Biography: Carlo di Conti Belgrado was born on May 2, 1809, and became a bishop on September 28, 1855. Between 1845 and 1847, he served as apostolic delegate in Perugia. Conti Belgrado then served as bishop of Ascoli from 1855 to 1860.
Scope: This collection focuses on Belgrado's work as apostolic delegate in Perugia and as bishop of Ascoli.
Location: Archivio Segreto Vaticano.

7.10.19 Spoglio del Giuseppe Berardi
DATABASE ID: VATV10571-A]
Inclusive Dates: 1849–1878.
Bulk: 4 buste.
Biography: Giuseppe Berardi was born in Ceccano (Frosinone) on September 28, 1810, and died in Rome on April 6, 1878. He served the papacy in several different capacities. Beginning in 1849, Berardi was commissario straordinario pontificio di marittima e campagna as well as vice-legate to Velletri. Later, he became, successively, sostituto della segretario di stato and segretario delle cifre. Berardi became a cardinal on March 13, 1868. He was a member of the following congregations at the time of his death: Bishops and Regulars, Council, Disciplina Regolare, Affari Ecclesiastici Straordinari, and Studi. He was also a protector of various religious orders.
Scope: The contents of the four buste center around Berardi's work in the secretary of state's office. The materials deal with the reestablishment of the Papal States, particularly with issues regarding administration, finance, and security (police and military). There are also some materials that deal with the Kingdom of Naples both before and after the fall of the king (1852–1861).
References: G. Moroni, *Dizionario di erudizione storico-ecclesiastica* (Venice, 1840); and *Gerarchia cattolica* (Rome, 1877–1879).
Location: Archivio Segreto Vaticano.

7.10.20 Spoglio del Tommaso Bernetti
DATABASE ID: VATV10572-A]
Inclusive Dates: [17—]–[18—].
Bulk: 1 busta.
Biography: Tommaso Bernetti was born in Fermo on December 29, 1779, and died there on March 21, 1852. Bernetti, a nephew of Cardinal Brancadoro, served the papacy from the early days of his ecclesiastical career. On June 27, 1827, he became a cardinal and was soon after nominated as legate to Ravenna. Due to ill health, however, he returned to Rome and in 1828, he began to work in the offices of the secretary of state. He was elevated to the dignity of vice-chancellor of the church in 1844.
Scope: The contents of the busta include materials dealing with the secretary of state, various congregations and papal offices, and the papal military and police forces.
Reference: *Enciclopedia cattolica*, vol. 2 (Vatican City, 1948).
Location: Archivio Segreto Vaticano.

7.10.21 Spoglio del Francesco Bertazzoli
DATABASE ID: VATV10573-A]
Inclusive Dates: [17—]–[18—].
Bulk: 1 busta.
Biography: Francesco Bertazzoli was born in Lugo on May 1, 1754, and died in Rome on April 7, 1830. He studied theology in Bologna and was a favorite of Pope Pius VII. He was nominated bishop of Montalto, canon of S. Maria Maggiore, and elemosiniere segreto, and became cardinal on March 10, 1823.
Scope: The spoglio del Bertazzoli contains a codice of penal procedure and materials concerning Turin.
Reference: *Enciclopedia cattolica*, vol. 2 (Vatican City, 1948).
Location: Archivio Segreto Vaticano.

7.10.22 Spoglio del Angelo Bianchi
DATABASE ID: VATV10574-A]
Inclusive Dates: [18—]–[18—].
Bulk: 3 buste.
Biography: Bianchi was born on November 19, 1817, in Rome and died on January 22, 1897. He served as maestro delle Ceremonie Pontificie and chargé d'affaires in Switzerland. In 1874 he was designated segretario of the Congregation for Bishops and Regulars, a post that he left to become apostolic nuncio for Madrid. In 1882 he became cardinal and in 1889 served as pro-datarius.
Scope: The contents of the buste mirror Bianchi's ecclesiastical career. The first busta contains material regarding the nunciatures of Holland, Munich, Lucerne, and Spain. The second busta contains congratulations on his rise to cardinal and the third busta contains materials concerning his role as pro-datarius and as a member of various congregations.
Location: Archivio Segreto Vaticano.

7.10.23 Spoglio del Luigi Bilio
[DATABASE ID: VATV10575-A]
Inclusive Dates: 1849–1878.
Bulk: 2 buste.
Biography: Luigi Bilio was born in Alessandria in the Piedmont on March 25, 1826, and died in Rome on January 30, 1884. He was a member of the Barnabites. He was nominated consultor for the Congregazione della Curia Romana and on April 22, 1866, created cardinal. He served as penitenziere maggiore and secretary of the S. Romana ed Universalis Inquisizione. He also served in the following congregations: Immunità, Propaganda Fide, Affari di Rito Orientale, Indice, Sacri Riti, Indulgenze e Sacre Reliquie, Affari Ecclesiastici Straordinari, and Studi. He is considered the principal author of the "Sillabo" of Pius IX. Bilio was also president of the Commissione dogmatica and president general for the First Vatican Council.
Scope: The first busta contains materials concerning the First Vatican Council, including a document on papal infallibility. It also has some items dealing with the S. Romana ed Universalis Inquisizione, the Congregazione dei Vescovi e Regolari, the Propaganda Fide, and a number of monasteries for which he was protector. The second busta contains private and official correspondence from a variety of individuals—cardinals, prelates, priests, and the laity.
References: G. Moroni, *Dizionario di erudizione storico-ecclesiastica* (Venice, 1840). E. Campana, *Il Concilio Vaticano* (Lugano, 1926–). E. Cecconi, *Storia del Concilio ecumenico Vaticano serilta sui documenti originali* (Rome, 1873–1879).
Location: Archivio Segreto Vaticano.

7.10.24 Spoglio del Giuseppe Andrea Bizzarri
[DATABASE ID: VATV10576-A]
Inclusive Dates: [18—]–[18—].
Bulk: 5 buste.
Biography: Giuseppe Andrea Bizzarri was born on May 11, 1802, in Paliano, and died March 16, 1863. He served as canonico liberiano, protonotario apostolica, and prefect of the S.C. Vescovi e Regolari and of the S.C. Disciplina Regolare. In 1855 he was appointed chargé d'affaires between the pope and the king of the Two Sicilies.

Scope: The contents of the buste mirror Bizzarri's ecclesiastical career. Busta 1 contains materials on the congregations for bishops and regulars and Propaganda Fide. Busta 2 is a miscellany of materials on various congregations and other matters. Busta 3 contains various pontifical documents of Pius VI, Pius VII, Pius VIII, Pius IX, Benedict XIV, Gregory XVI, and Leo XII. Busta 4 also deals with various matters, and busta 5 concerns the Kingdom of the Two Sicilies.
Location: Archivio Segreto Vaticano.

7.10.25 Spoglio del Pier Filippo Boatti
[DATABASE ID: VATV10577-A]
Inclusive Dates: [17—?]–[18—?].
Bulk: 1 busta.
Biography: Pier Filippo Boatti was minutante della Segreterio dei Confini.
Scope: The single busta contains miscellaneous papers and materials regarding the military.
Location: Archivio Segreto Vaticano.

7.10.26 Spoglio del Gabriele Boccali
[DATABASE ID: VATV10578-A]
Inclusive Dates: 1879–1882.
Bulk: 1 busta.
Biography: Boccali was uditore di Sua Santità.
Scope: This is a collection of letters sent to Leo XIII by laypersons and ecclesiastics.
Location: Archivio Segreto Vaticano.

7.10.27 Spoglio del Giuseppe Bofondi
[DATABASE ID: VATV10579-A]
Inclusive Dates: 1825–1867.
Bulk: 9 buste.
Biography: Giuseppe Bofondi was born on October 24, 1795, in Forlì. He was a distinguished student in the field of jurisprudence and served as uditore of the S. Rota between 1820 and 1842. At that point, he was appointed decano of the Rota, a post that he held until 1847. Bofondi became a cardinal on December 21, 1846, the same year in which he became prolegato straordinario of Ravenna. In 1848 he moved to a post in the offices of the secretary of state. Bofondi was protector of the Collegio Capranica and an apostolic visitor of the hospitals S. Lucia and Brefotrofio in Narni.
Scope: The contents of the buste are largely financial records. Several buste do concern Bofondi's work in the Rota, as legate to Ravenna, as apostolic visitor to the hospitals of S. Lucia and Brefotrofio, and in the offices of the secretary of state. A small amount of material concerns Bofondi's role as protector of the Collegio Capranica and regarding the office of president of the Censo.
References: *Enciclopedia cattolica* (Vatican City, 1948). G. Moroni, *Dizionario di erudizione storico-ecclesiastica* (Venice, 1840).
Location: Archivio Segreto Vaticano.

7.10.28 Spoglio del Giacomo Luigi Brignole
[DATABASE ID: VATV10580-A]
Inclusive Dates: 1830–1833.
Bulk: 2 buste.
Biography: Giacomo Brignole was born on May 8, 1797, in Genoa and died on June 23, 1853. His ecclesiastical service

included the roles of nuncio to Florence, vice-commissario pontificio straordinario and pro-legate to Bologna, tesoriere generale of the Camera, prefect of the S. Congregazione dell'Indice, president of the Commissione speciale per la riforma delle carceri e luoghi di pena, and presidente of the Consulta di stato per le finanze. He became a cardinal on January 20, 1834.

Scope: The materials in busta 1 primarily concern papal military and police matters. Busta 2 mostly concerns Brignole's role as vice-commissario of Bologna, although there are some materials that deal with his role as nuncio to Florence.

Location: Archivio Segreto Vaticano.

7.10.29 Spoglio del Camillo Caccia Dominioni

[DATABASE ID: VATV10581-A]
Inclusive Dates: ca. 1877–1946.
Bulk: 1 busta.
Biography: Camillo Caccia Dominioni was born on February 7, 1877, in Milan and died in Rome on November 22, 1946. He was ordained September 23, 1899, and became a cardinal on December 16, 1935.
Scope: The busta contains materials regarding the veto of the cardinal of Cracow in the conclave for the election of Pius X: "un discorso manoscritto del Card. Alimonda, lettere e documenti esibiti dal generale Nobile, in relazione alla sua impresa al Polo con il dirigibile 'Italia,'" and "verbale dell'apposizione dei sigilli."
Location: Archivio Segreto Vaticano.

7.10.30 Spoglio del Giovanni Caccia Piatti

[DATABASE ID: VATV10582-A]
Inclusive Dates: [17—?]–[18—?].
Bulk: 1 busta.
Biography: Giovanni Caccia Piatti was born on March 8, 1751, in Novara and died on September 15, 1833. He served as apostolic delegate to Pesaro, uditore generale of the Camera, prefect of the Segnatura, and was appointed to the Congregazione dei Riti, Cerimonie, Consulta, and delle Acque. Caccia Piatti was a protector of various religous orders and of the city of Pesaro and the terra of Orciano.
Scope: The busta contains minutes of letters written during Caccia Piatti's time as legate to Pesaro and materials regarding customs (*dogane*) and finances of the Consulta.
Location: Archivio Segreto Vaticano.

7.10.31 Spoglio del Antonio Maria Cagiano de Azevedo

[DATABASE ID: VATV10584-A]
Inclusive Dates: 1832–1867.
Bulk: 6 buste.
Biography: Antonio Maria Cagiano de Azevado was born in Santopadre on December 14, 1797, and died in Rome on January 13, 1867. His ecclesiastical career was diverse. He served as avvocato concistoriale, apostolic delegate to Perugia and Spoleto (1832–1835), pro-legato pontificio of Ferrara (1835–1836), secretary of the Consulta and uditore of the Camera (after 1836). He became a cardinal on January 22, 1844, and then bishop of Senigallia (1844–1848).
Scope: The most important documents in the buste regard the political, administrative, and religious situation in Perugia, Spoleto, and Ferrara, during Cagiano de Azevedo's tenure as

apostolic delegate. Other materials concern the Consulta, reform of the penal code, the diocese of Senigallia, and affairs regarding the religious communities and civil organizations of which he was a protector.
Reference: G. Moroni, *Dizionario di erudizione storico-ecclesiastica* (Venice, 1840).
Location: Archivio Segreto Vaticano.

7.10.32 Spoglio del Lorenzo Caleppi

[DATABASE ID: VATV10583-A]
Inclusive Dates: [17—?]–[18—?].
Bulk: 3 buste.
Biography: Lorenzo Caleppi was born on April 29, 1741, in Cervia, Italy, and died on January 10, 1847, in Rio de Janeiro. He began his studies at the College of Nobles at Ravenna but transferred to Rome to study jurisprudence. He began his prelature career as auditor of the nunciature when Giuseppe Garampi, appointed nuncio to Warsaw (1772), took Lorenzo with him. Always accompanying Garampi, Lorenzo held the same office in Vienna from 1776 until 1785 when Pius V selected him to present the red biretta to Garampi on the latter's appointment as cardinal. In June 1786, Lorenzo was invited to Naples to assist in concluding a concordat with that court. Pius VI called on him for special tasks includiing working with the Oeuvre Pie de l'Hospitalité, through which several thousand French émigrés, including priests, were enabled to live at the expense of the papal treasury at the time of the French Revolution. In 1797 he was a member of the delegation that signed the treaty of Tolentino.

In 1801 he succeeded Bartholomeo Pacca as nuncio to Lisbon and in 1808 he followed the royal family to Rio de Janeiro in Brazil, where he won the esteem and gratitude of John VI. Caleppi maintained the Portuguese nunciature for Brazil until 1816. Pius VII named him a cardinal (1816), the first in the Americas. He died at Rio de Janeiro on January 10, 1817.
Scope: The contents of the buste include a manuscript of a book, *Memorie intorno alla vita del Cardinal Lorenzo Caleppi*, written by Camillo Luigi de Rossi, who was Caleppi's secretary from 1795 until his death. This was published as a book in Rome in 1845 by the Propaganda Fide and is available at the Vatican Library.

In addition to the *Memorie* the buste contain materials primarily relating to the nunciatures for Portugal. There are some small, surprising, groups of records, however, including "Eredità Garampi" and a "Memoire Justicative de la conduite tenue par l'abbé Zacchi pendant les sept ans qu'il a été chargé de l'education de S.A. le Prince Joseph Wenzel de Liechtenstein."
Note: Pásztor (1970), pp. 216–217, refers to a "carte Caleppi," which he lists as having 7 buste. This latter series may or may not be the same as the Spogli.
Location: Archivio Segreto Vaticano.

7.10.33 Spoglio del Paolo Campa

[DATABASE ID: VATV10585-A]
Inclusive Dates: [17—?]–[18—?].
Bulk: 1 busta.
Biography: Paolo Campa served as archivist for the office of the secretary of state.
Location: Archivio Segreto Vaticano.

7.10.34 Spoglio del Giovanni Pietro Campana

[DATABASE ID: VATV10586-A]

Inclusive Dates: [18—]–[18—].

Bulk: 1 busta.

Biography: Campana was known in nineteenth-century Rome for his knowledge of archeology and of the ancient world.

Location: Archivio Segreto Vaticano.

7.10.35 Spoglio del Giovanni Battista Cannella

[DATABASE ID: VATV10587-A]

Inclusive Dates: [18—]–[18—].

Bulk: 3 buste.

Biography: Giovanni Battista Cannella was born in L'Aquila and died in Rome on March 27, 1859. He served as revisore of the Commissioni, apostolic delegate to Orvieto, sostituto for the segreteria per gli Affari di Stato Interni (1846), and segretario of the S.C. Affari Ecclesiastici Straordinari (1853).

Scope: The contents of the buste are supplications, avvisi, notificazioni, circolari, and other miscellaneous materials concerning various congregations. There is one group of materials concerning Jews in Rome.

Location: Archivio Segreto Vaticano.

7.10.36 Spoglio del Francesco Capaccini

[DATABASE ID: VATV10588-A]

Inclusive Dates: 1806–1844.

Bulk: 3 buste.

Biography: Francesco Capaccini was born in Rome on August 14, 1784, and died there on June 15, 1845. His ecclesiastical career included minutante for the secretary of state; sostituto for the secretary of briefs (1815); legate to Holland and Munich (1828); sostituto for the secretary of state (1831); diplomatic missions to Vienna, Berlin and Bonn (1837), and to the Netherlands (1841); apostolic delegate to Lisbon (1842–1844); and uditore for the Camera (1844). He became a cardinal on July 22, 1844, shortly before his death.

Scope: The spoglio contains records of Capaccini's service in the offices of the segretario dei brevi, dei memoriali, and di stato. Some materials exist concerning his diplomatic missions to Holland and his work as apostolic delegate to Lisbon.

According to the index, an addition of materials has been made to the third busta, "un pacco di documenti, attinenti il Congresso di Vienna e altre pratiche di competenza della Segreteria di Stato, rinvenute nello spoglio di Mons. Achille Maria Ricci."

References: G. Moroni, *Dizionario di erudizione storico-ecclesiastica* (Venice, 1840). *Enciclopedia cattolica*, vol. 3 (Vatican City, 1948).

Location: Archivio Segreto Vaticano.

7.10.37 Spoglio del Annibale Capalti

[DATABASE ID: VATV10589-A]

Inclusive Dates: 1849–1878.

Bulk: 1 busta.

Biography: Annibale Capalti was born in Rome on January 21, 1811, and died in 1877. He became a cardinal in 1868. He served as amministratore generale, abate commendatario and ordinary of SS. Vincenzo e Anastasio alle Tre Fontane, and first secretary and then prefect of the S.C. degli Studi. He was a founder of the Società asili d'infanzia.

Scope: The busta contains materials regarding the S.C. degli Studi, the Consiglio di Stato, the civil code, and other miscellaneous items.

Location: Archivio Segreto Vaticano.

7.10.38 Spoglio del Mauro Cappellari

[DATABASE ID: VATV10591-A]

Inclusive Dates: [18—]–[18—].

Bulk: 1 busta.

Scope: Materials addressed to Pope Gregory XVI when he was prefect of the Propaganda Fide.

Location: Archivio Segreto Vaticano.

7.10.39 Spoglio del Benedetto Cappelletti

[DATABASE ID: VATV10590-A]

Inclusive Dates: 1814–1845.

Bulk: 7 buste.

Biography: Benedetto Cappelletti was born in Rieti on November 2, 1764, and died on May 16, 1834. He was educated by Benedictine monks. His ecclesiastical career included service as referendario of the Segnatura; pronotario and ponente of the S.C. del Buon Governo; and pontifical delegate to Viterbo, Macerata, and Urbino-Pesaro. Cappelletti also served as governor of Rome, director general of the police, and after he became a cardinal on September 30, 1831, bishop of Rieti.

Scope: The strength of the materials lies in the documents concerning the legations of Viterbo, Macerata, and Urbino-Pesaro, and those dealing with Cappelletti's work as governor of Rome, "Bollettini politici-Amministrativi."

References: G. Moroni, *Dizionario di erudizione storico-ecclesiastica* (Venice, 1840), vol. 9, p. 168. *Enciclopedia cattolica* (Vatican City, 1948).

Location: Archivio Segreto Vaticano.

7.10.40 Spoglio del Caracciolo

[DATABASE ID: VATV10592-A]

Inclusive Dates: 1819.

Bulk: 1 busta.

Location: Archivio Segreto Vaticano.

7.10.41 Spoglio del Giuseppe Cardoni

[DATABASE ID: VATV10593-A]

Inclusive Dates: [18—]–[18—].

Bulk: 1 busta.

Biography: Giuseppe Cardoni was born on February 28, 1802, in Balangero (Torino). He was bishop of Loreto and Recanati, and president of the Accademia pontificia dei nobili ecclesiastici.

Scope: The contents of the busta include information on the Papal States, various apostolic delegations, congregations, and offices. Several items concern ecclesiastical studies and practices. There are briefs and printed works in this collection.

Location: Archivio Segreto Vaticano.

7.10.42 Spoglio del Nicola Carenzi

[DATABASE ID: VATV10594-A]

Inclusive Dates: [17—?]–[18—?].

Bulk: 1 busta.

Biography: Carenzi was minutante of the office of the secretary of state.

Scope: Materials in the busta concern the following car-

dinals: Albani, de Bayane, Braschi, Caprara, Carandini, Crivelli, De Rohan, De Zelada, Della Porta, Doria, Erschine, Mattei, Pignatelli, Ranuzzi, Rinuccini, Roverella, Saluzzo, Scotti, Valenti, and Vincenti. There is also information on the Società di Assicurazione.
Location: Archivio Segreto Vaticano.

7.10.43 Spoglio del Castruccio Castracane
[DATABASE ID: VATV10595-A]
Inclusive Dates: [18—]–[18—].
Bulk: 1 busta.
Biography: Castruccio Castracane became a cardinal in 1833. He also served as bishop of Palestrina and penitenziere maggiore. He died in Rome in 1852.
Location: Archivio Segreto Vaticano.

7.10.44 Spoglio del Prospero Caterini
[DATABASE ID: VATV10596-A]
Inclusive Dates: 1860–1874.
Bulk: 1 busta.
Biography: Prospero Caterini was born in Orano on October 15, 1795, and died in Rome on October 28, 1881. He became a cardinal on March 7, 1853. He served as prefect of the Concilio for many years. During the First Vatican Council he was president of the Commissione della Disciplina Ecclesiastica. Caterini also participated in the Congregazioni Cardinalizie per la Revisione dei Concili Provinciali, della Immunità and della S. Romana ed Universale Inquisizione. He was a protector of various societies and an apostolic visitor to the Ordine dei Fate Bene Fratelli.
Scope: Materials in the busta primarily concern the Concilio, but there are a few documents concerning the apostolic visit to the Ordine dei Fate Bene Fratelli, 1860–1861.
Reference: G. Moroni, *Dizionario di erudizione storico-ecclesiastica* (Venice, 1840).
Location: Archivio Segreto Vaticano.

7.10.45 Spoglio del Federico Amadori Cattani
[DATABASE ID: VATV10597-A]
Inclusive Dates: [18—?]–[19—?].
Bulk: 1 busta.
Biography: Federico Amadori Cattani was born in Marradi on April 17, 1856, and died in Rome on April 11, 1943. He served as secretary for the Supremo Tribunale della Segnatura Apostolica and Auditor Sanctissimi (1924). He was dean of the Rota and a member of the Congregazioni dei Sacramenti and dal Concilio. He became a cardinal in 1935.
Scope: Materials in the busta concern various religious communities, offices, and persons.
Location: Archivio Segreto Vaticano.

7.10.46 Spoglio del Francesco Guido-Bono Cavalchini
[DATABASE ID: VATV10598-A]
Inclusive Dates: [17—]–[18—].
Bulk: 1 busta.
Biography: Francesco Guido-Bono Cavalchini was born in Tortona on December 4, 1755, and died in Rome on December 5, 1828. He served in the Camera, the Consulta, and in various posts concerning the Papal States, including governor of Rome. He became a cardinal August 14, 1807. He was arrested during the French occupation of Rome but was re-

stored as governor in 1814. He was a member of the Congregazione del Buon Governo.
Scope: Materials in the busta relate to the Congregazione del Buon Governo.
Reference: G. Moroni, *Dizionario di erudizione storico-ecclesiastica* (Venice, 1840), vol. 11, pp. 5–6.
Location: Archivio Segreto Vaticano.

7.10.47 Spoglio del Bonaventura Cerretti
[DATABASE ID: VATV10599-A]
Inclusive Dates: 1914–1921.
Bulk: 1 busta.
Biography: Bonaventura Cerretti was born in Bardano di Orvieto on June 17, 1872, and died in Rome on May 8, 1933. He was ordained in 1895 and entered the office of the secretary of state. Cerretti served as part of the apostolic delegations in Mexico and the United States and was apostolic delegate in Australia (1914). From 1917 to 1921, he served as secretary for the S. Congregazione per gli Affari Ecclesiastici Straordinari. Then, Cerretti became apostolic nuncio to Paris (1921–1925). In 1925 he became a cardinal. At the same time he became bishop of Velletri.
Scope: Materials in the busta concern the apostolic delegation in Australia and the nunciature for Paris, the Congregazione per gli Affari Ecclesiastici Straordinari (particularly concerning matters in the United States), and various religious orders. There is miscellaneous additional correspondence.
Reference: *Enciclopedia cattolica* (Vatican City, 1948), vol. 3, p. 1326.
Location: Archivio Segreto Vaticano.

7.10.48 Spoglio del Flavio Chigi
[DATABASE ID: VATV10600-A]
Inclusive Dates: [18—]–[18—].
Bulk: 1 busta.
Biography: Flavio Chigi was born in Rome on May 31, 1810, and died there on February 15, 1885. His ecclesiastical career included posts as nuncio to Munich (1850–1851) and Paris (1861–1873). He was protector of the church, archconfraternity, and college of Piceni in Rome; as well as protector of the archconfraternities del SS. Sacramento al Laterno, degli Agonizzanti, and del SS.mo Crocifisso in S. Marcello. He was also a protector of the Insigne Cappella Corsini in S. Giovanni in Laterano and archpriest of the Patriarcale Arcibasilica Lateranense. Chigi was segreteria dei memoriali di sua santita.
Scope: The busta includes materials relating to the nunciature of Paris, the Arciconfraternità de'Piceni, and the Arcipretura della Basilica Lateranense.
Location: Archivio Segreto Vaticano.

7.10.49 Spoglio del Luigi Ciacchi
[DATABASE ID: VATV10601-A]
Inclusive Dates: ca. 1832–1850.
Bulk: 2 buste.
Biography: Luigi Ciacchi was born on August 16, 1788, in Pesaro, and died in Rome on December 17, 1865. His ecclesiastical service included postings as prolegate for the province of Bologna and apostolic delegate in Macerata. He also led the papal police force. He became a cardinal in 1838.
Scope: Materials in the two buste concern the Commissione

Governativa di Stato, 1850; the apostolic delegation in Macerata; the priory of S. Salvatore; and other miscellaneous papers, some relating to Cardinal Bernetti (secretary of state, 1832–1834).

Reference: Enciclopedia cattolica (Vatican City, 1948).
Location: Archivio Segreto Vaticano.

7.10.50 Spoglio del Tommaso Ciampi

[DATABASE ID: VATV10602-A]
Inclusive Dates: [17—?]–[18—?].
Bulk: 1 busta.
Biography: Tommaso Ciampi served as archivist for the office of the secretary of state.
Location: Archivio Segreto Vaticano.

7.10.51 Spoglio del Luigi Ciani

[DATABASE ID: VATV10603-A]
Inclusive Dates: [17—?]–[19—?].
Bulk: 1 busta.
Biography: Luigi Ciani served as archivist for the office of the secretary of state.
Location: Archivio Segreto Vaticano.

7.10.52 Spoglio del Nicola Paracciani Clarelli

[DATABASE ID: VATV10604-A]
Inclusive Dates: [18—]–[18—].
Bulk: 4 buste.
Biography: Nicola Paracciani Clarelli was born in Rieti on April 12, 1799, and died in Vico Equense on July 7, 1872. He served as bishop of Montefiascone e Corneto and as a member of the apostolic delegation in Portugal (1820). He became a cardinal in 1844. Clarelli also assumed the roles of chierico di Camera and tesoriere generale of the Camera; and secretary of the S. Congregazione delle Acque, dei Brevi, and delle Congregazione Cardinalizia di Consulta. He was prefect of the S. Congregazione dei Vescovi e Regolari (1860), of the Disciplina Regolari, and of the Rev. Fabbrica di S. Pietro. He was president of the Commissione dei Sussidi, of the Pubblica Beneficienza, and of the Istituto Sordo-muti.
Scope: The collection mirrors Clarelli's ecclesiastical life. There appears to be little in the four buste concerning many of the roles he had. There are materials that concern his work in Portugal, his service with the Consulta, the Congregazione delle Acque, the Congregazione dei Vescovi e Regolari, the Segreteria dei Brevi, the Fabbrica di San Pietro, the Congregazione Cardinalizia ad referendum Brefotrofio di S. Spirito, the Camera, and other offices and congregations of the Holy See.
Location: Archivio Segreto Vaticano.

7.10.53 Spoglio del Ercole Consalvi

[DATABASE ID: VATV10605-A]
Inclusive Dates: 1813–1823.
Bulk: 2 buste.
Biography: Ercole Consalvi was born in Rome on June 8, 1757, and died in Anzio on January 24, 1824. Consalvi came from a noble family of Toscanella. His ancestors belonged to the noble line of the Brunacci in Pisa but one of them settled in Toscanella in the seventeenth century. The grandfather of Er-

cole, Gregorio Brunacci, inherited a large fortune on condition of taking the name and arms of the Consalvi family. In this way Gregorio Brunacci became Marchese Gregorio Consalvi with residence in Rome.

From 1771 until 1776 Consalvi attended the seminary in Frascati where he won the admiration and protection of Henry Stuart, duke of York, who was the cardinal bishop of Frascati. While in Frascati, he served successively as ponente al Buon Governo, volante di Segnatura, assessore della Segreteria di Stato, and uditore di Rota. Returning to Rome he entered the Accademia Ecclesiastica and on May 20, 1800, became a cardinal deacon but was never ordained a priest. He quickly moved into a curial career.

In 1783 Pius VI named him a private chamberlain. A number of curial positions followed; in 1792 he obtained nomination as an auditor of the Rota. After the death of Pius VI (1799), the cardinals assembled in Venice for the conclave and Consalvi was chosen as secretary by an almost unanimous vote. Cardinal Chiaramonti, elected as Pius VII (1800–1823), soon appointed Consalvi as pro-secretary of state; consequently, Consalvi accompanied the pope to Rome where Consalvi was definitively appointed secretary of state.

During his first years in that office Consalvi was only moderately successful in his efforts to restore the Papal States. His main achievement was the short-lived 1801 Concordat with France which made possible the reestablishment of the church in France after the Revolution. Napoleon later managed to obtain his dismissal from office and force his retirement to Reims. Consalvi was not intimidated. On Napoleon's abdication in 1814, Consalvi was immediately reappointed as secretary of state and represented the pope at the Congress of Vienna in 1815. It was there that he secured the restoration of the Papal States, the reorganization of which occupied the last years of his life.

Scope: The buste are not very well described. The first busta appears to contain miscellaneous papers and memoria concerning pontifical functionaries, finances, customs, and the police. The second busta has information on the Congress of Vienna and German ecclesiastical affairs.
References: G. Moroni, *Dizionario di erudizione storicoecclesiastica*, vol. 17, (Venice, 1840). *Enciclopedia cattolica* (Vatican City, 1948), vol. 4, p. 3945.
Location: Archivio Segreto Vaticano.

7.10.54 Spoglio del Mariano Cordovani

[DATABASE ID: VATV10606-A]
Inclusive Dates: 1949–1950.
Bulk: 1 busta.
Biography: Mariano Cordovani was Maestro del Sacro Palazzo Apostolico from 1936 to 1950. He was a member of the Dominican order.
Location: Archivio Segreto Vaticano.

7.10.55 Spoglio del Cosimo Corsi

[DATABASE ID: VATV10607-A]
Inclusive Dates: [17—?]–[18—?].
Bulk: 1 busta.
Biography: Cosimo Corsi was born in Florence in 1798 and served as uditore and then dean of the Rota until 1841.
Location: Archivio Segreto Vaticano.

7.10.56 Spoglio del Carlo Cremonesi

[DATABASE ID: VATV10608-A]
Inclusive Dates: [18—?]–[19—?].
Bulk: 1 busta.
Biography: Carlo Cremonesi was born on November 4, 1866, and died in Vatican City on November 25, 1943. He became a cardinal in 1935 and was president of the Amministrazione per le Opera di Religione.
Scope: The busta contains information on various offices, personnel, and a naval project.
Location: Archivio Segreto Vaticano.

7.10.57 Spoglio del Carlo Cristofori

[DATABASE ID: VATV10609-A]
Inclusive Dates: [18—]–[18—].
Bulk: 1 busta.
Biography: Carlo Cristofori was born in Viterbo on January 5, 1813, and died in Rome on January 30, 1891. He became a cardinal July 27, 1885, and served as reggente of the Penitenzieria and prefect of the S. Congregazione Indulgenze e Reliquie.
Scope: Materials in the busta concern the S. Congregazione Concistoriale and various Roman organizations.
Location: Archivio Segreto Vaticano.

7.10.58 Spoglio del Wlodimiro Czacki

[DATABASE ID: VATV10610-A]
Inclusive Dates: ca. 1870–1885.
Bulk: 1 busta.
Biography: Wlodimiro Czacki was born in Poryck, Poland, on April 16, 1834, and died in Rome on March 8, 1888. He became a cardinal on September 25, 1882, and served as secretary of the Congregazione degli Affari Ecclesiastici Straordinari. Materials in the busta are diverse. The papers include information on the relationship between the church and the Italian state; the nunciature for Paris, Poland, the Monastero del Divino Amore in Nazzano; the University of Lille; and correspondence with various papal offices.
Location: Archivio Segreto Vaticano.

7.10.59 Spoglio del Ercole Dandini

[DATABASE ID: VATV10611-A]
Inclusive Dates: [17—?]–[18—?].
Bulk: 1 busta.
Biography: Ercole Dandini was born on July 25, 1759, and died on July 22, 1840. He served as cameriere d'onore and ablegato to Viterbo. He was created a cardinal in 1823 and served as economo and then secretary of the Fabbrica di San Pietro, prefect of the Congregazione del Buon Governo and visitatore apostolico dell'Arciospedale e Pio Istituto di S. Spirito in Sassia.
Scope: Materials in the busta concern the congregations of Buon Governo and Economica.
Reference: G. Moroni, *Dizionario di erudizione storico-ecclesiastica* (Venice, 1840).
Location: Archivio Segreto Vaticano.

7.10.60 Spoglio del Girolamo D'Andrea

[DATABASE ID: VATV10612-A]
Inclusive Dates: 1838–1868.
Bulk: 17 buste.
Biography: Girolamo D'Andrea was born on April 12, 1812, in Naples and died in Rome on April 14, 1868. He served as nuncio for Switzerland, commissario pontificio straordinario in Umbria, and as bishop of Sabina. D'Andrea became a cardinal on March 15, 1852.
Scope: The contents of the buste mirror D'Andrea's ecclesiastical career. The buste include materials concerning the nunciature for Switzerland and particularly the commissario pontificio straordinario in Umbria, and Sabina. Other documents deal with various Roman tribunals and the congregations of the Indice and Cerimoniale. Issues that appear in later buste include the government of the abbey in Subiaco, regulations in seminaries and instructions for sacred visits, and the administration of the diocese of Sabina.
Location: Archivio Segreto Vaticano.

7.10.61 Spoglio del Pietro Giuseppe D'Avella y Navarro

[DATABASE ID: VATV10613-A]
Inclusive Dates: ca. 1831–1851.
Bulk: 3 buste.
Biography: Pietro Giuseppe D'Avella y Navarro was born in Barcelona in 1775 and died circa 1853. He was dean and then uditore of the Rota and apostolic visitor to the Convento dei PP. Trinitari in Via Condotti.
Scope: The contents of the buste deal with D'Avella y Navarro's service in the Rota and as apostolic visitor to the Convento of the PP. Trinitari in Via Condotti. Some materials also deal with Spain and the Abbey of San Paolo.
Location: Archivio Segreto Vaticano.

7.10.62 Spoglio del Emanuale De Gregorio

[DATABASE ID: VATV10614-A]
Inclusive Dates: [17—?]–[18—?].
Bulk: 3 buste.
Biography: Emanuale De Gregorio was born in Naples on December 18, 1758, and died in Rome on November 7, 1839. He became a cardinal in 1816.
Scope: The contents of the buste are miscellaneous. Some materials, however, do deal with the Penitentiary and the Concilio.
Location: Archivio Segreto Vaticano.

7.10.63 Spoglio del Annibale Sermattei Della Genga

[DATABASE ID: VATV10620-A]
Inclusive Dates: [17—?]–[18—?].
Bulk: 2 buste.
Biography: Annibale Sermattei Della Genga was born on August 22, 1760, and died on February 10, 1829. He became Pope Leo XII on September 28, 1823. He studied at Osimo and in Rome and was ordained in 1783. He served successively as nuncio to Lucerne, Cologne, and Munich. Della Genga became a cardinal on March 8, 1816, then bishop of Senigallia; in 1820 he became vicar of Rome.
Scope: Materials primarily concern the nunciatures for Germany. There are also some other miscellaneous personal papers in the collection. The materials were acquired through the family of Pope Leo XII. They initially were photocopied, but later purchased in 1931.
Reference: *Enciclopedia cattolica* (Vatican City, 1948), vol. 7, pp. 1156–1157.
Location: Archivio Segreto Vaticano.

7.10.64 Spoglio del Giulio Maria Della Somaglia

[DATABASE ID: VATV10621-A]

Inclusive Dates: 1801–1828.

Bulk: 2 buste.

Biography: Giulio Maria Della Somaglio was born on July 29, 1744, in Piacenza of a noble Italian family and died on April 2, 1830. In 1774 he became secretary of the Congregation of Indulgences and Relics and in 1784 of the Congregation of Rites. He was named a cardinal in June 1795, and during the French occupation of Rome he was imprisoned. He attended the conclave at Venice (1800). He was one of thirteen cardinals, out of twenty-seven invited, who refused to attend the marriage of Napoleon I and Archduchess Marie Louise of Austria. As a result he and other cardinals were deprived of their benefices and exiled. After Napoleon's abdication, Della Somaglia governed Rome until the return of Pius VII in June of 1815. He was bishop of Frascati (1814), secretary of the Holy Office (1814), bishop of Ostia and Velletri (1820), dean of the College of Cardinals, and vice cancelliere and sommista of the Camera. Leo XII appointed him secretary of state in 1823, a position he held until 1828.

Scope: Materials in the buste mirror Della Somaglia's ecclesiastical career. They include primarily materials from the Congregazione Economica, but also contain information on the Vicario di Roma, the Camera, the College of Cardinals, Sant'Uffizio, secretary of state, and the Basilica of S. Paolo (Rome).

Location: Archivio Segreto Vaticano.

7.10.65 Spoglio del Francesco Salesio Della Volpe

[DATABASE ID: VATV10622-A]

Inclusive Dates: ca. 1903.

Bulk: 1 busta.

Biography: Francesco Della Volpe was born on December 24, 1844, in Ravenna and died in Rome on November 5, 1916. He was created a cardinal in 1899 and served as camerlengo of the Camera, arcicancelliere dell'Università Romana, and prefect of the Index.

Scope: The busta contains materials regarding the conclave of 1903.

Location: Archivio Segreto Vaticano.

7.10.66 Spoglio del Antonino De Luca

[DATABASE ID: VATV10615-A]

Inclusive Dates: [18—]–[18—].

Bulk: 3 buste.

Biography: Antonino De Luca was born in Bronte on October 28, 1805, and died in Rome on December 28, 1883. He became a cardinal March 16, 1863. His major posts included bishop of Palestrina and Aversa, nuncio for Baveria (1854–1856), nuncio for Vienna (1856–1863), vice-cancelliere of the Camera (1878–1883), sommista delle Lettere Apostoliche (1878–1883), commendatario di San Lorenzo in Damaso (1878–1883), and prefect of the Congregazione degli Studi (1879–1883) and of the Indice (1867–1877). He was a member of the following congregations: Inquisizione, Vescovi e Regolari, Propaganda Fide, Rito Orientali, Indice, Cerimoniale, Disciplina Regolare, and Affari Ecclesiastici Straordinari. De Luca was a protector of the Ordine del Minore Conventuali, Congregazione di S. Suplizio di Francia, Istituto Nazionale Teutonico in S. Maria dell'Anima, Congr. delle Suore di No-stra Signora di Nazaret, Figlie del S. Cuore di Maria di Francia, Istituto Bavarese delle povere Suore delle Scuole di Nostra Signora, Religiose Spedaliere, Fate-bene sorelle di Milano, Sovrano Militare Ordine Gerosolimitano, Pontificia Accademia de'Nobili Ecclesiastici, Arciconfraternità del Gonfalone in S. Lucia, Confraternità del SSmo. Rosario eretta in S. Pietro di Poli, Pia Società di S. Cecilia in Germania, and the Comune di Palombara.

Scope: The contents of the buste concern De Luca's tenure as nuncio in Vienna and Bavaria, his work as bishop of Aversa, and as prefect of the Indice. Miscellaneous papers also reflect his service as member of other congregations and as a protector.

Reference: Gerarchia cattolica (Rome, 1883).

Location: Archivio Segreto Vaticano.

7.10.67 Spoglio del Francesco De Medici

[DATABASE ID: VATV10616-A]

Inclusive Dates: 1843–1856.

Bulk: 1 busta.

Biography: Francesco De Medici was born in Naples on November 8, 1808, and died in Rome on October 11, 1857. He became cardinal deacon on June 16, 1856, and was Maggiordomo di Sua Santità. The busta contains materials regarding De Medici's position as maggiordomo, particularly relating to a trip to the provinces made by Gregorio XVI in 1843.

Location: Archivio Segreto Vaticano.

7.10.68 Spoglio del Gaetano De Ruggero

[DATABASE ID: VATV10618-A]

Inclusive Dates: [18—]–[18—].

Bulk: 1 busta.

Biography: Gaetano De Ruggero was born in Naples on June 12, 1816, and died in Rome on October 9, 1896. He was created cardinal deacon on May 5, 1889. He served as Segreterio dei Brevi and gran cancelliere degli Ordine Equestri Pontifici. Materials contained in the busta concern a cause between DeRuggero and the Ordine dei SS. Maurizio e Lazzaro and the confiscation of ecclesiastical properties.

Location: Archivio Segreto Vaticano.

7.10.69 Spoglio del Pietro De Silvestri

[DATABASE ID: VATV10619-A]

Inclusive Dates: [18—]–[18—].

Bulk: 1 busta.

Biography: Pietro De Silvestri was born in Rovigo on February 13, 1805, and died in Rome on November 19, 1875. He became a cardinal on March 15, 1858. De Silvestri was a member of the following congregations: Visita Apostolica, Vescovi e Regolari, Concilio, Disciplina Regolare, and Fabbrica. He was protector of the Università dei Periti Patenti Rigattieri, Archconfraternities of SS. Angeli Custodi, S. Francesco di Paola alla Suburra, S. Michele Arcangelo ai Corridori, and S. Pietro erected in the Chiesa di San Antonio Abate in Udina. Other protectorates included: Romana Curia in S. Lucia della Tinta, Gesù Nazareno in S. Elena ai Cesarini, Congregazione degli Illirici in S. Girolamo, Orfanotrofio Guglielmi in Terni, Monasteries of SSma Incarnazione del Divin Verbo in Rome, SSmo. Bambino Gesù in Palestrina, and Opere Pie Barberini.

Scope: Materials in the busta concern the First Vatican Council among other topics.

Reference: Gerarchia cattolica (Rome, 1875).
Location: Archivio Segreto Vaticano.

7.10.70 Spoglio del Camillo Di Pietro
[DATABASE ID: VATV10624-A]
Inclusive Dates: ca. 1840–1869.
Bulk: 8 buste.
Biography: Camillo Di Pietro, cardinal, was born on January 10, 1806, in Rome and died there on March 6, 1884. He was a nephew of Michele Di Pietro who was named cardinal during the pontificate of Pius VII. He studied at the Roman seminary and held a public theological disputation (dialectical debate) in the presence of Leo XII. In 1829 he was named a judge of the Consulta, then governor of Orvieto, and finally an auditor of the Rota in 1835. He was a member of the Commissioni Speciali Cardinalizie that investigated the powers of the judiciary. He became titular archbishop of Berito and nuncio to Naples and Lisbon. In Portugal he was successful in obtaining for the church notable concessions regarding the Portuguese territory of India.

Pius IX appointed him a cardinal in the consistory of 1853 but it was *in pectore* and not announced until 1856. On September 20, 1867, he chose to take the sede suburbicaria of Albano and then the sede di Porto e S. Rufina. He played a significant role in the conclave of 1878, which resulted in the election of Leo XIII (1878–1903). The new pontiff, in gratitude, named him the successor in the office of camerlengo. On the death of Cardinal Amat (1878), Di Pietro became bishop of Ostia and dean of the College of Cardinals. He also served as arcicancelliere della Università Romana, prefect of the Cong. Cerimoniale, and dean of the College of Cardinals.
Scope: The buste represent a range of subjects. The largest group concerns the patrimony of the Di Pietro family and a dispute between the Di Pietro family and the duke of Caetani. Other materials deal with the Commissione del Consiglio di Stato, the Signatura, the Concilio, the Commissione Speciale della S. C. del Censo, the Uditore Sanctissimi, and a case between the commune of Rocca di Papa and Prince Andrea Colonna.
References: G. Moroni, *Dizionario di erudizione storico-ecclesiastica* (Venice, 1840). *Enciclopedia cattolica* (Vatican City, 1948), vol. 4, p. 1683.
Location: Archivio Segreto Vaticano.

7.10.71 Spoglio del Michele Di Pietro
[DATABASE ID: VATV10623-A]
Inclusive Dates: 1802–1818.
Bulk: 1 busta.
Biography: Michele Di Pietro, cardinal, was born in Albano on January 18, 1747, and died in Rome on July 2, 1821. He received his doctorate at Rome, taught in the Roman College, was appointed secretary for various commissions, and with his friend Cardinal Gerdil was named to the commission charged with studying the decisions of the Synod of Pistoia. He was appointed as apostolic delegate to the governor of Rome (1798) during the imprisonment of Pius VI and was patriarch of Jerusalem (1800); in 1801 he was named a cardinal. Imprisoned by Napoleon (1811) he was freed for the negotiations at Fontainbleau and was one of those who advised Pius VII to revoke the pseudo-agreements of the concordat. On his return to Rome he became bishop of Albano (1820). He was prefect of

the Indice, the penitenziere maggiore, and a member of various congregations.
Scope: The busta contains materials regarding the Pentientiary, various requests for indults and dispensations, miscellaneous drafts of letters, and several letters signed by Cardinal Ercole Consalvi.
References: G. Moroni, *Dizionario di erudizione storico-ecclesiastica* (Venice, 1840). *Enciclopedia cattolica* (Vatican City, 1948), vol. 4, p. 1683.
Location: Archivio Segreto Vaticano.

7.10.72 Spoglio del Giuseppe Evangelisti
[DATABASE ID: VATV10625-A]
Inclusive Dates: ca. 1824–1841.
Bulk: 1 busta.
Biography: Giuseppe Evangelisti was cifrista of the office of the secretary of state.
Scope: Materials in the busta include notes concerning various cardinals and prelates and an edition of *Cracas*.
Location: Archivio Segreto Vaticano.

7.10.73 Spoglio del Marco Evangelisti
[DATABASE ID: VATV10626-A]
Inclusive Dates: 1848–1853.
Bulk: 1 busta.
Biography: Marco Evangelisti was an employee in the office of the secretary of state (1848–1856).
Scope: Materials in the busta relate to Evangelisti's work in the secretary of state's office. Subjects include reform of the penal code, minutes from papal audiences, and reform of the civil code and the judicial system.
Location: Archivio Segreto Vaticano.

7.10.74 Spoglio del Giovan Francesco Falzacappa
[DATABASE ID: VATV10627-A]
Inclusive Dates: 1871, 1878.
Bulk: 1 busta.
Biography: Giovan Francesco Falzacappa was born in Corneto on April 7, 1767, and died in Rome on November 18, 1840.
Scope: The busta contains two letters, one from 1871 and the other from 1878. Neither appears to pertain to Cardinal Falzacappa.
Location: Archivio Segreto Vaticano.

7.10.75 Spoglio del Girolamo Feliciangeli
[DATABASE ID: VATV10628-A]
Inclusive Dates: 1820–1830.
Bulk: 1 busta.
Biography: Girolamo Feliciangeli was secretary of the nunciature for Munich, Bavaria.
Scope: Materials in the busta concern the nunciature for Munich. This busta was lost on April 21, 1980.
Location: Archivio Segreto Vaticano.

7.10.76 Spoglio del Gabriele Ferretti
[DATABASE ID: VATV10629-A]
Inclusive Dates: ca. 1830–1860.
Bulk: 3 buste.
Biography: Gabriele Ferretti was born on January 31, 1795, in Ancona and died in Rome on September 31, 1860. He

became a cardinal on November 30, 1838. He was bishop of Sabina and perpetual abate of S. Maria in Farfa. Ferretti also served as commendario dei SS. Vincenzo ed Anastasio alle Tre Fontane, gran priore commendatario in Roma del Sacro Ordine Militare Gerosolimitano, penitenziere maggiore, and apostolic visitor of Luoghi pii dei Catecumeni.

Scope: A major section of the busta contains materials dealing with the Ospedale di S. Lucia in Narni, including an apostolic visit there by Ferretti. The other materials in the buste are miscellaneous.

Location: Archivio Segreto Vaticano.

7.10.77 Spoglio del Innocenzo Ferrieri

[DATABASE ID: VATV10630-A]

Inclusive Dates: [18—]–[18—].

Bulk: 1 busta.

Biography: Innocenzo Ferrieri was born in Fano on September 11, 1810, and died in Rome on January 13, 1887. He served as chargé d'affaires for the Netherlands, pontifical ambassador to Constantinople, and apostolic nuncio to Naples. He was protector for the Frati Ospitalieri called the Concettini, the monastery of S. Cecilia, and the Accademia Teologica. He was also camerlengo for the S. Collegio, prefect for the Congregazione dei Vescovi e Regolari and the Disciplina Regolare.

Scope: The busta contains materials concerning Ferrieri's work as prefect of the Congregazione dei Vescovi e Regolari and camerlengo of the College of Cardinals.

Location: Archivio Segreto Vaticano.

7.10.78 Spoglio del Giuseppe Fesch

[DATABASE ID: VATV10632-A]

Inclusive Dates: [17—?]–[18—?].

Bulk: 1 busta.

Biography: Giuseppe Fesch was born on January 3, 1763, in Ajaccio (Corsica) and died in Rome on May 13, 1839. Through his mother's second marriage, he was uncle to Napoleon Bonaparte. Fesch studied in the seminary in Aix en Provence and became a priest in 1785. In 1802, he became archbishop of Lyon and in 1803 he became a cardinal. At that time Fesch also became ambassador from France to the Holy See. Fesch was perpetual director of the Arciconfraternità degli Amanti di Gesù e Maria, called the Via Crucis. He was protector for the archconfaternities of Santa Maria dell'Orazione (called della Morte) and of Santissima Assunta in S. Maria dei Miracoli; the Collegio Ghislieri; the Congregazione Basiliane del Santissimo Salvatore e di S. Giovanni in Soairo dei Greci Melchiti; the Monache Passioniste di Corneto; the Venerabile Compagnia di S. Lorenzo in Lucina; the monastero di Fognano; and the Diocese of Faenza.

Scope: The contents of the buste include correspondence from various offices, congregations, and protectorates, as well as some materials dealing with the Bonaparte family.

Reference: Enciclopedia cattolica (Vatican City, 1948).

Location: Archivio Segreto Vaticano.

7.10.79 Spoglio del Adriano Fieschi

[DATABASE ID: VATV10631-A]

Inclusive Dates: ca. 1831–1858.

Bulk: 3 buste.

Biography: Adriano Fieschi was born in Genoa on March 7, 1788, and died in Rome on February 6, 1858. His ecclesiasti-

cal career centered around the office of the secretary of state. Fieschi was vice-legato to Bologna and apostolic delegate to Perugia and Spoleto. He became a cardinal on June 23, 1834. Between 1847 and 1857 he was legate to the province of Pesaro and Urbino. He was a member of the Concilio, Immunità, and Riti.

Scope: Materials in the buste center around Fieschi's different posts in the office of the secretary of state, particularly the apostolic delegation in Perugia, the legation in Pesaro and Urbino, the legation in Bologna, and various matters concerning the Governo Pontificio. There is a bit of material concerning benefices at the Basilica of S. Maria ad Martyres.

Location: Archivio Segreto Vaticano.

7.10.80 Spoglio del Raffaele Fornari

[DATABASE ID: VATV10633-A]

Inclusive Dates: [17—?]–[18—?].

Bulk: 1 busta.

Biography: Raffaele Fornari was born in Rome on January 23, 1788, and died there June 15, 1854. He became a cardinal on December 21, 1846. Fornari was prefect of the Congregazione degli Studi and a member of the following congregations: Inquisizione, Vescovi e Regolari, Concilio, Immunità, Indice, Affari Ecclesiastici Straordinari, Propaganda Fide, and Esame dei Vescovi in Sagra Teologia e in Sacri Canoni. He was a protector of the Società di S. Vincenzo de'Paoli, the Accademia Teologica of Rome University, the Ordine dei Carmellitani Calzati e Scalzi, Minori Cappuccini, Congregazione Benedittina di Francia, L'Ordine Premostratese, l'Opera Pia Spontini in Majolati, and the cities of Vetralia and Cento.

The materials mainly concern the city of Vetralla.

Reference: Notizie (Rome, 1854).

Location: Archivio Segreto Vaticano.

7.10.81 Spogli Alessandro Franchi

[DATABASE ID: VATV10634-A]

Inclusive Dates: [18—]–[18—].

Bulk: 3 buste.

Biography: Alessandro Franchi was born on June 25, 1819, in Rome and died there on July 31, 1878. His ecclesiastical career centered around work in the office of the secretary of state, and included service as chargé d'affaires ad interim in Spain, internuncio to the Tuscan court, secretary for the Congregazione per gli Affari Ecclesiastici Straordinari, apostolic nuncio for Spain, extraordinary ambassador to Constantinople, and secretary of state. He became a cardinal on December 22, 1873. Franchi also served as prefect of Sacri Palazzi Apostolici, the Propaganda Fide, and the Congregazione Lauretana. He was a member of the following congregations: Inquisizione, Concili, Vescovi e Regolari, Propaganda, Propaganda per gli affari orientali, Indulgenze e Sacre Reliquie, Affari Ecclesiastici Straordinari, and Studi.

Franchi was also protector of the following groups: Istituto di N.S. delle Missioni, Opera Apostolica per le Missioni estere affidata alle Suore di S. Giuseppe dell'Apparizione, Istituto delle Suore di S. Giuseppe dell'Apparizione, Istituto delle Suore di S. Giuseppe di Cluny, Istituto di S. Giuseppe di Chambery, Istituto delle Suore di Carità di Montreal nel Canada, Confraternita del Divino Amore unità alla Confraternità di S. Francesco di Paola alle Fratte, Arciconfraternità delle

S. Stimmate di Firenze, and the Università Cattolica Laval a Quebec.

Scope: The contents of the buste include information on Franchi's role in the apostolic delegation in Spain, as ambassador to Constantinople, internuncio to Tuscany, and as prefect for the Propaganda Fide. There is limited information on his work as protector for pious organizations and as apostolic visitor to the Luoghi Pii dei Catecumeni.

References: Gerarchia cattolica (Rome, 1878). *Enciclopedia cattolica* (Vatican City, 1948).

Location: Archivio Segreto Vaticano.

7.10.82 Spoglio del Giovanni Battista Franzelin

[DATABASE ID: VATV10635-A]

Inclusive Dates: [18—]–[18—].

Bulk: 1 busta.

Biography: Johannes Baptist Franzelin was born in Altino on April 15, 1816, and died in Rome on February 11, 1886. He became a Jesuit priest and a celebrated theologian. Franzelin became a cardinal on April 3, 1876.

Scope: The busta contains information concerning the constitution of the monks of the Benedettini Cassinesi della primitiva osservanza.

Location: Archivio Segreto Vaticano.

7.10.83 Spoglio del Filippo Frassinelli

[DATABASE ID: VATV10636-A]

Inclusive Dates: [17—?]–[19—?].

Bulk: 2 buste.

Biography: Filippo Frassinelli was aggiunto in the office of the secretary of state.

Scope: The materials in the buste refer to the reform of the papal military.

Location: Archivio Segreto Vaticano.

7.10.84 Spoglio del Luigi Frezza

[DATABASE ID: VATV10637-A]

Inclusive Dates: [17—?]–[18—?].

Bulk: 1 busta.

Biography: Luigi Frezza was born in Città Lavinia on May 27, 1783, and died in Rome on October 15, 1837. He became a cardinal on June 23, 1834. Frezza was consultore della Propaganda Fide, secretary of the Consistory and of the Congregazione per gli Affari Ecclesiastici Straordinari. He was a member of the Indice.

Scope: Materials in the busta concern the Congregazione per gli Affari Ecclesiastici Straordinari and deceased cardinals (the defunto porporato).

Reference: Notizie (Rome, 1837).

Location: Archivio Segreto Vaticano.

7.10.85 Spogli Andrea Frühwirth

[DATABASE ID: VATV10638-A]

Inclusive Dates: [18—?]–[19—?].

Bulk: 1 busta.

Biography: Andreas Frühwirth was born in S. Anna (Styria) on August 21, 1845, and died in Rome on February 9, 1933. He served as nuncio to Bavaria. In 1915 he became cardinal. He served as penitenziere maggiore and cancelliere of the Camera.

Scope: The materials in the busta are largely of a personal nature: photographs, a register of Mass intentions, and academic diplomas.

Location: Archivio Segreto Vaticano.

7.10.86 Spogli Giulio Gabrielli

[DATABASE ID: VATV10639-A]

Inclusive Dates: 1814–1821.

Bulk: 1 busta.

Biography: Giulio Gabrielli was born on July 20, 1748, in Rome and died in Albano on September 16, 1822. He was a cardinal and also was abate commendatario for several communities: S. Paolo in Valdiponti in Perugia, S. Giovanni dell' Eremo di Città della Pieve, and SS. Vito e S. Pancrazio di Todi. Gabrielli served as prodatario di Sua Santità. He was a member of the following congregations: Uffizio, Concistoriale, Concilio, Residenza de'Vescovi, Propaganda, Esame de'Vescovi in Sagri Canonici, Buon Governo, and Affari Ecclesiastici. He was protector of the Augustinians, Congregazione dei Sacerdoti di S. Lucia de Ginnasi, and the following monasteries: di S. Lucia (Pieve), S. Lucia (Perugia), S. Maria in Betlam (Foligno). He was also a protector of the conservatorio delle Mendicanti, Collegio Ghislieri, Confraternità di S. Caterina (Assisi), and of the cities of Assisi, Nepi, Gualdo di Nocera, Cascia, Otricoli, Toscanella, and Massa di Todi.

Scope: The materials in the busta concern Gabrielli's work in the congregation of the Affari Ecclesiastici Straordinari, particularly relations with England, France, and Spain. Other materials concern the nomination of Modesto Farina as bishop of Padua and legal issues surrounding the bishop of Città di Castello.

Reference: Notizie (Rome, 1822).

Location: Archivio Segreto Vaticano.

7.10.87 Spoglio del Luigi Galimberti

[DATABASE ID: VATV10640-A]

Inclusive Dates: [18—]–[18—].

Bulk: 2 buste.

Biography: Luigi Galimberti was born on April 25, 1836, in Rome and died on May 7, 1896. He was secretary for the Congregazione per gli Affari Ecclesiastici Straordinari and apostolic nuncio to Vienna. Galimberti became a cardinal on January 16, 1893, and served as prefect of the Vatican Archives.

Scope: The records in the buste include archival and printed materials from the following congregations: Concistoriale, Indice, and Lauretana. Materials also include items dealing with religious teaching in Belgium and the competence of the Congregazione per gli Affari Ecclesiastici Straordinari.

Location: Archivio Segreto Vaticano.

7.10.88 Spoglio del Pietro Francesco Galleffi

[DATABASE ID: VATV10641-A]

Inclusive Dates: 1830–1841.

Bulk: 1 busta.

Biography: Pietro Francesco Galleffi was born on October 27, 1770, and died in Rome on June 18, 1837. He completed his studies in Rome and became a cameriere segreti participanti of Pope Pius VII. He served as economo and later prefect of the Fabbrica, and co-visitor of the hospital of S. Spirito in 1800. On July 12, 1803, he became a cardinal. Galleffi then became abate commendario of Subiaco and prefect of the Congregazione della Disciplina Regolare. He was exiled during the Napoleonic wars and upon the return of the pope to Rome in 1814, he became secretary of memoriali and in 1820 archpriest of the Basilica Vaticano and bishop of Albano. He also served as subdean of the S. Collegio and bishop of Porto and Civitavecchia (1830), camerlengo della S.R. Chiesa, and arcicancelliere dell'Università Romana.

Galleffi was a member of the following congregations: Uffizio, Concistoriale, Disciplina Regolare, Indulgenze e Sacre Reliquie, Esame dei Vescovi in Sacri Canoni, Economica, Studi, Speciale per la riedificazione della Basilica di S. Pietro. He was protector of these religous communities: Minori osservanti e riformati; Minore conventuali; Terz'Ordine di S. Francesco; Camaldolese; Chierici Regolari minori; Santissimo Salvatore; S. Brigida and the Chiesa di'Neofiti alla Madonna de Monti; Conservatorio Pio and conservatorio di S. Eufemia; the monasteries of S. Urbino, S. Susanna alle Terme Diocleziano, Sette dolori, S. Chiara (Montecastrillo), the archconfraternities of Santissima Trinità de Pellegrini e Convalescenti, S. Maria del Carmine alle Tre Cannelle, the Chiesa della Madonna Santissima di Loreto dei Fornari, S. Giuliano (Banchi), Ospizio di Cofti, S. Stefano di Mori (Rome), Chiesa Nazionale de SS. Venanzio ad Ansuino de Camerinese, Madonna (Quercia), Confraternità di S. Emidio (Trastevere), Chiesa di S. Giuseppe de Falegnami al Foro Romano, and the Arciconfraternità del Santissimo rosario.

Scope: Materials in the busta concern the Fabbrica, the Segreterio dei Memoriali, the Basilica Vaticana, and the Camera.

Reference: Enciclopedia cattolica (Vatican City, 1948).

Location: Archivio Segreto Vaticano.

17.10.89 Spogli Antonio Domenico Gamberini

[DATABASE ID: VATV10642-A]

Inclusive Dates: ca. 1830–1841.

Bulk: 1 busta.

Biography: Antonio Gamberini was born on October 31, 1760, and died on April 25, 1841. He was noted for his juridical and theological learning as well as his pastoral activities. He was uditore of Rome and secretary of the Concilio. He served as bishop of Orvieto. On December 15, 1828, he was named cardinal. In 1839 he was given the suburbicarian see of Sabina. Gamberini was a principal collaborator of Pope Gregory XVI and had the title *segretario di stato per gli affari interni.*

Scope: The busta contains a miscellaneous group of materials, some concerning advocates in the Consistory and traffic on the Tiber.

Reference: Enciclopedia cattolica (Vatican City, 1948). *Notizie* (Rome).

Location: Archivio Segreto Vaticano.

7.10.90 Spoglio del Enrico Gasparri

[DATABASE ID: VATV10643-A]

Inclusive Dates: 1914.

Bulk: 1 busta.

Biography: Enrico Gasparri was born in Ussita on July 25, 1871, and died on May 20, 1946. He was apostolic delegate to Chile, bishop of Velletri, subdean of the College of Cardinals, and prefect of the Signatura Apostolica. He became a cardinal on December 14, 1925.

Scope: The busta contains materials regarding a request for the title of conte by S. J. Martinelli of Rio de Janeiro in 1914.

Location: Archivio Segreto Vaticano.

7.10.91 Spoglio del Francesco Aidan Gasquet

[DATABASE ID: VATV10644-A]

Inclusive Dates: 1917.

Bulk: 1 busta.

Biography: Francis Aidan Gasquet was born in London on October 5, 1846, and died in Rome on April 5, 1929. He entered the Benedictine novitiate in 1865. In 1896 he was nominated to the Commissione Pontificia per la Questione della Validità delle Ordinazioni Anglicane and in 1900 became the resident abbot of the Bendictine order in England. He was also head of a commission to revise the Vulgate Bible. He became a cardinal in 1914 and was nominated as librarian and archivist of the S. R. Chiesa in 1919.

Scope: The collection is a single item, "Opuscolo biografico ed illustrativo scritto nel cinquantenario della professione monastica, 1917."

Location: Archivio Segreto Vaticano.

7.10.92 Spoglio del Francesco Gaude

[DATABASE ID: VATV10645-A]

Inclusive Dates: 1850–1860.

Bulk: 3 buste.

Biography: Francesco Gaude was born in Cambiano on April 5, 1809, and died in Rome on December 14, 1860. He was a member of the Dominican order and became cardinal on December 17, 1855.

Scope: Materials in the buste include documents dealing with two cities for which Gaude was protector, Tolentino and Morlupo, and with the Collegio dei Commercianti. There is also some published material relating to reform of the University of Rome (1858–1859).

Location: Archivio Segreto Vaticano.

7.10.93 Spoglio del Ludovico Gazzoli

[DATABASE ID: VATV10646-A]

Inclusive Dates: 1822–1858.

Bulk: 2 buste.

Biography: Ludovico Gazzoli was born in Terni on May 5, 1774, and died on February 12, 1858. He was apostolic delegate to the province Pesaro-Urbino. He became a cardinal on September 30, 1831. He served as president of the Congregazione del Buon Governo.

Scope: Materials in the buste concern the apostolic delegation in Pesaro-Urbino, the Congregazione del Buon Governo, published works concerning the case of Conte Pellegrino Rossi vs. Card. G. Antonelli and the reform of various aspects of pontifical administration. Additional published materials concern the civil and economic natures of the competencies of the Segnatura, Rota, and Buon Governo.

Location: Archivio Segreto Vaticano.

7.10.94 Spoglio del Pietro Giannelli

[DATABASE ID: VATV10647-A]

Inclusive Dates: [18—]–[18—].

Bulk: 1 busta.

Biography: Pietro Giannelli was born in Termi on August 11, 1807, and died in Rome on November 5, 1881. He became a cardinal in 1875. He was apostolic nuncio to Naples and secretary of the Concilio. Giannelli was a member of the following congregations: Inquisizione, Vescovi e Regolari, Indulgenze e Sacre Reliquie, and Affari Ecclesiastici Straordinari. He was protector of the Arciconfraternità di S. Girolamo della carità, the Oblate Convittrici del SSmo. Bambino Gesù, and the Monastery of S. Giacomo alla Longara.

Scope: The busta contains correspondence regarding the nunciature of Naples and the union between the Kingdom of the Two Sicilies and the Kingdom of Italy. It also contains various documents regarding the Concilio and other congregations.

Reference: Gerarchia cattolica (Rome, 1881).

Location: Archivio Segreto Vaticano.

7.10.95 Spoglio del Angelo Giansanti
[DATABASE ID: VATV10648-A]

Inclusive Dates: 1861–1864.

Bulk: 1 busta.

Biography: Very little information is available for Angel Giansanti. The inventory to the Spogli notes only the following: "Avvocato concistoriale del fisco e della Camera." The records are letters concerning juridical matters dating between 1861 and 1864.

Location: Archivio Segreto Vaticano.

7.10.96 Spoglio del Eugenio Giordani
[DATABASE ID: VATV10649-A]

Inclusive Dates: 1840.

Bulk: 1 busta.

Scope: No information could be found for Eugenio Giordani. The busta contains only a brief letter dated November 23, 1840.

Location: Archivio Segreto Vaticano.

7.10.97 Spoglio del Giacomo Giustiniani
[DATABASE ID: VATV10650-A]

Inclusive Dates: 1830–1843.

Bulk: 1 busta.

Biography: Giacomo Giustiniani was born on December 29, 1769, and died February 24, 1843. He was successively vicelegato of Ravenna (1794), governor of Perugia (1795), presidente della Giunta di Stato di Roma, and pro-governor of Rome (1814). He was nuncio to Spain between 1817 and 1826. Giustiniani became a cardinal on October 2, 1826, and was bishop of Imola until 1832. He served as camerlengo of the S. R. Chiesa, prefect of the Fabbrica and the Indice, and segretario dei Memoriali.

Scope: Materials in the busta include invitations from the secretary of state to be part of the Congregazione Cardinalizie per riforme varie attinenti la civile ed ecclesiastica amministrazione, and miscellaneous manuscript and published materials concerning the dicastry.

Location: Archivio Segreto Vaticano.

7.10.98 Spoglio del Pasquale Tommaso Gizzi
[DATABASE ID: VATV10651-A]

Inclusive Dates: [17—?]–[18—?].

Bulk: 1 busta.

Biography: Pasquale Tommaso Gizzi was born on September 22, 1787, and died on July 3, 1849, in Lenola. He studied

civil and canon law at the Sapienza and became a lawyer in 1819. He was uditore for the nuncio in Switzerland and in 1827 became internuncio. He was successively chargé d'affaires in Turin (1829–1835), apostolic delegate to Ancona (1837–1839), internuncio to Belgium (1839–1841), and nuncio to Turin (1841–1844). Gizzi became a cardinal on July 12, 1841. He was legate to Forlì between 1844 and 1846. In 1846 he became secretary of state.

Scope: Materials in the busta concern the nunciature for Turin, the legation in Forlì, and Gizzi's work in the office of the secretary of state.

Reference: Enciclopedia cattolica (Vatican City, 1948).

Location: Archivio Segreto Vaticano.

7.10.99 Spoglio del Eustachio Gonella
[DATABASE ID: VATV10652-A]

Inclusive Dates: 1848–1870.

Bulk: 1 busta.

Biography: Eustachio Gonella was born in Turin on September 9, 1811, and died in Rome on April 15, 1870. He was apostolic delegate to Viterbo and apostolic nuncio in Belgium. Gonella became a cardinal on March 13, 1868. He was later bishop of Viterbo and Toscanella.

Scope: Materials in the buste include letters from the period Gonella was apostolic delegate to Viterbo, nuncio to Belgium, and bishop of Viterbo.

Location: Archivio Segreto Vaticano.

7.10.100 Spoglio del Gennaro Granito Pignatelli di Belmonte
[DATABASE ID: VATV10653-A]

Inclusive Dates: [18—?]–[19—?].

Bulk: 1 busta.

Biography: Gennaro Granito Pignatelli de Belmonte was born in Naples on April 10, 1851, and died on February 16, 1948. He was apostolic nuncio in Belgium. He became a cardinal on November 27, 1911, and received the suburbicarian dioceses of Albano and Ostia. He was prefect of the Congregazione Cerimoniale.

Location: Archivio Segreto Vaticano.

7.10.101 Spoglio del Domenico Guidi
[DATABASE ID: VATV10654-A]

Inclusive Dates: 1830–1865.

Bulk: 2 buste.

Biography: Domenico Guidi was minutante for the secretary of state.

Scope: Materials primarily relate to Guidi's work in the office of the secretary of state. Some documents, however, pertain to the First Vatican Council.

Location: Archivio Segreto Vaticano.

7.10.102 Spoglio del Giuseppe Hergenrother
[DATABASE ID: VATV10655-A]

Inclusive Dates: 1879–1890.

Bulk: 2 buste.

Biography: Joseph Hergenrother was born in Würzburg on September 17, 1824, and died on October 3, 1890. He was a professor of history in the faculty of theology. He became a cardinal on May 12, 1879, and served as prefect of the Vatican Archives from 1879 to 1890.

Scope: The materials concern the Archivio Segreto Vaticano and the Biblioteca Apostolica Vaticana, and include requests for permission to use the facilities and reform of the rules of use.

Location: Archivio Segreto Vaticano.

7.10.103 Spoglio del Filippo Invernizzi

[DATABASE ID: VATV10656-A]

Inclusive Dates: 1826–1828.

Bulk: 1 busta.

Biography: Filippo Invernizzi was dean of the avvocati concistoriali and presided over various special commissions concerning judicial matters in the Papal States.

Scope: The materials are solely financial records from Invernizzi's time as president of the Commissione Speciale di Ravenna (1826–1828).

Location: Archivio Segreto Vaticano.

7.10.104 Spoglio del Giovanni Janni

[DATABASE ID: VATV10658-A]

Inclusive Dates: 1833–1850.

Bulk: 1 busta.

Biography: Giovanni Janni worked in the office of Uditore di Sua Santità during the pontificates of Gregory XVI and Pius IX.

Location: Archivio Segreto Vaticano.

7.10.105 Spoglio del Domenico Jorio

[DATABASE ID: VATV10657-A]

Inclusive Dates: [18—?]–[19—?].

Bulk: 1 busta.

Biography: Domenico Jorio was born in S. Stefano on October 7, 1867, and died in Rome on October 21, 1954. He served in the Datary, presiding over the sezione matrimoniale. He became a cardinal on December 16, 1935, and was prefect of the Congregazione per la Disciplina Regolari, and a member of the following congregations: de Propaganda Fide, Orientale, Concilio, Uffizio, Seminari e Università, and the Signatura Apostolica.

Location: Archivio Segreto Vaticano.

7.10.106 Spoglio del Luigi Lambruschini

[DATABASE ID: VATV10659-A]

Inclusive Dates: 1831–1851.

Bulk: 2 buste.

Biography: Luigi Lambruschini was born on May 16, 1776, in Sestri Levante and died in Rome on May 12, 1854. He was a Barnabite and served as an examiner of bishops, consultor to the Inquisizione, and secretary for the Congregazione per gli Affari Ecclesiastici Straordinari. In 1819 he became bishop of Genoa, then nuncio to Paris (1827–1831). In 1831 he became a cardinal. Lambruschini was prefect of the Congregazione degli Studi, Segretario dei Brevi, bibliotecario of the S.R. Chiesa, bishop suburbicario di Porto e S. Rufino and of Civitavecchia, and a subdean of the College of Cardinals.

Scope: The materials include a manuscript of Lambruschini's *Memorie storiche*, which was published by Pirri in 1934. The manuscript version includes notes by Lambruschini. Other records concern the secretary of state, the legation in Velletri, and the construction of streets.

Additional materials concerning Luigi Lambruschini can be found in the fondo "Carteggio Lambruschini" at the archives of the Barnabites in Rome.

Location: Archivio Segreto Vaticano.

7.10.107 Spoglio del Giorgio Lana

[DATABASE ID: VATV10660-A]

Inclusive Dates: 1859–1860.

Bulk: 1 busta.

Biography: Giorgio Lana was a captain in the Genio, "con mansione direttive."

Scope: The materials in the busta are financial records and correspondence related to the Genio.

Location: Archivio Segreto Vaticano.

7.10.108 Spoglio del Vincenzo La Puma

[DATABASE ID: VATV10661-A]

Inclusive Dates: [18—?]–[19—?].

Bulk: 1 busta.

Biography: Vincenzo La Puma was born in Palermo on January 22, 1874, and died in Rome on November 4, 1943. He became cardinal on December 16, 1935, and served as prefect of the Congregazione dei Religiosi.

Scope: The busta contains a few personal letters.

Location: Archivio Segreto Vaticano.

7.10.109 Spoglio del Egidio Lari

[DATABASE ID: VATV10662-A]

Inclusive Dates: ca. 1931–1944.

Bulk: 9 fascicoli.

Biography: Egidio Lari was born in Borgo a Buggiano on March 8, 1882, and died in Rome on November 17, 1965. He was apostolic delegate in Persia (1931–1936) and nuncio to Bolivia (1939–1944).

Location: Archivio Segreto Vaticano.

7.10.110 Spoglio del Pietro Lasagni

[DATABASE ID: VATV10663-A]

Inclusive Dates: 1833–1850.

Bulk: 1 busta.

Biography: Pietro Lasagni was born in Caprarola on June 15, 1814, and died in Rome on April 19, 1885. He served as secretary of the Congregazione dei Vescovi e Regolari and the Conclave. He became a cardinal on December 13, 1880. He later became Segretario dei Memoriali.

Scope: Materials in the busta concern the religious orders for which he was protector, the Opera della S. Infanzia, and reform of the Cerimoniale, particularly the nomination of new bishops.

Location: Archivio Segreto Vaticano.

7.10.111 Spoglio dei Fratelli Lattanzi

[DATABASE ID: VATV10664-A]

Inclusive Dates: ca. 1850–1899.

Bulk: 4 buste.

Biography: The Lattanzi brothers were a diverse group. Domenico Lattanzi was a priest and canon in Rome who taught at Collegio Romano and Lorenzo was a lawyer at the ufficio di Sostituto Luogotenente Criminale del Tribunale del Vicariato di Roma.

Scope: The buste contain papers regarding private, family, professional, and financial matters pertaining to Fr. Domenico, Avv. Lorenzo, Francesco, Luigi, and Settimio Lattanzi. Topics include the restoration of the family palazzo, the patrimony of the Lattanzi, the activities of the Sostituto Luogotenente Criminale del Tribunale del Vicariato, and in letters and philosophical writings by Domenico Lattanzi.

Location: Archivio Segreto Vaticano.

7.10.112 Spoglio del Carlo Laurenzi

[DATABASE ID: VATV10665-A]
Inclusive Dates: ca. 1867–1884.
Bulk: 2 buste.
Biography: Carlo Laurenzi was born in Perugia on January 12, 1821, and died in Rome in 1893. He served as uditore di Sua Santità. He became cardinal priest on December 13, 1880, in pectore. He was a member of the following congregations: Studi, Affari Ecclesiastici Straordinari, Riti, Inquisizione, and Vescovi e Regolare.
Scope: The materials in the buste include records of the apostolic delegation in Albano and Velletri (1867–1869) during a cholera outbreak, printed and manuscript materials concerning the Papal States, information on primary schools in Rome under ecclesiastical authority (1878), printed materials concerning Catholic schools, the institute "Angelo Mai" in Rome, seminaries, the Amministrazione dei Beni della Santa Sede, the Datary, and the secretary of state.
Location: Archivio Segreto Vaticano.

7.10.113 Spoglio del Luigi Lavitrano

[DATABASE ID: VATV10666-A]
Inclusive Dates: [18—?]–[19—?].
Bulk: 3 buste.
Biography: Luigi Lavitrano was born in Forio on March 7, 1874, and died on August 2, 1950. He became a cardinal on December 16, 1929. Lavitrano was archbishop of Palermo and prefect of the Congregazione per Religiosi. He was a member of the following congregations: Chiese Orientali, Sacramenti, Concistoriale, and Concilio.
Location: Archivio Segreto Vaticano.

7.10.114 Spoglio del Francesco Leggeri

[DATABASE ID: VATV10667-A]
Inclusive Dates: 1828–1846.
Bulk: 7 buste.
Biography: Francesco Leggeri was procuratore generale del fisco and of the Reverenda Camera Apostolica from 1828 to 1846.
Scope: The contents of the buste include minutes of letters explaining processes, competences, and judicial matters.
Location: Archivio Segreto Vaticano.

7.10.115 Spoglio del Lorenzo Litta

[DATABASE ID: VATV10668-A]
Inclusive Dates: [17—?]–[18—?].
Bulk: 1 busta.
Biography: Lorenzo Litta was born in Milan on February 23, 1756, and died in Sabina on May 1, 1820. He studied at the Collegio Clementino in Rome and was ordained in 1789. On June 23, 1793, he was posted to the apostolic nunciature in

Poland. From there, he served as extraordinary ambassador to St. Petersburg. He became a cardinal in 1801 and was sent to France. He returned to Rome in 1809 and became cardinal-bishop of Sabina and prefect of the Propaganda Fide. Litta was also prefect of other congregations including Residenza de'Vescovi, Correzione de' Libri della Chiesa Orientale, Spirituale del Collegio, and Stamperia di Propaganda Fide. In addition, he was a member of the following congregations: Offizio, Vescovi e Regolari, Concilio, Immunità, Propaganda, Cina e Indie Orientali, Riti, Esame de Vescovi, Consulta, Acque, Economica, Affari Ecclesiastici Straordinari, and Studi.

Litta was protector of the following organizations: PP. Chierici Regolari delle Scuole Pie, Collegio Nazareno, Congregazione de' PP. Filippini di Norcia, Congregazione Basiliana di S. Giovanni in Soairode' Greci Melchiti, Monaci Armeni in S. Gregorio Illuminatore, Maestre Pie, religiosi non Claustrali, Compagnia di S. Orsola (Tours), Ordine di S. Giorgio di Dio(Benefratelli), la Sapienza, the Nobile Accademia Ecclesiastica, Arciconfraternità di S. Maria del Gonfalone, SS. Nome di Maria, S. Trifone, Capitolo della insigne Collegiata Parrochiale, chiesa di S. Paolo Naufrago (Valetta), Gozo (Malta), Civitavecchia, the Confraternita dell'Adorazione perpetua del SS. Sagramento di Posi, the city of Norcia, the terre di Monticelli, Palombara e Monte Rotondo, and the Veneranda Arciconfraternità della Dottrina Cristiana in S. Maria del Pianto. He was protector of the following monasteries: Camaldolesi, Passioniste di Corneto, S. Francesco di Paola alla Suburra, and the church and monastery of S. Caterina de Funari; and these conservatories: S. Croce (la Scalette), S. Pasquale, and the Assunta.
Scope: Materials in the busta primarily concern the Propaganda Fide. Records concerning a few other congregations and offices are also present.
References: Enciclopedia cattolica (Vatican City, 1948). *Notizie* (Rome, 1819).
Location: Archivio Segreto Vaticano.

7.10.116 Spoglio del Benedetto Lorenzelli

[DATABASE ID: VATV10669-A]
Inclusive Dates: [18—?]–[19—].
Bulk: 11 buste.
Biography: Benedetto Lorenzelli was born in Badi on May 11, 1853, and died in Bucciano on September 15, 1915. He served as internuncio to the Netherlands and Luxemburg, beginning May 30, 1893. He then became nuncio to Bavaria (October 10, 1896), and later nuncio to France (May 8, 1899). He became archbishop of Lucca (November 14, 1904) and was named cardinal on April 15, 1907. Lorenzelli was prefect of the Congregazione degli Studi and a member of the following congregations: Propaganda, Affari di Rito Orientale, Indice, Riti, Affari Ecclesiastici Straordinari, and the Commissione per gli Studi Biblici.
Scope: Materials in the eleven buste concern the nunciatures for France, Bavaria, and the Netherlands, and the following offices and congregations: Secretariat of State, Congregazione degli Studi, Propaganda Fide, Riti, Commissione per gli Studi Biblici, and the diplomatic corps. Much of the contents of the buste is miscellaneous correspondence and published materials.
Location: Archivio Segreto Vaticano.

7.10.117 Spoglio del Angelo Luchini
[DATABASE ID: VATV10670-A]
Inclusive Dates: 1860–1870.
Bulk: 4 buste.
Biography: Angelo Luchini was the primary sostituto commissario of the Reverenda Camera Apostolica from 1862 to 1880.
Scope: The materials in the buste concern Luchini's work in the Camera. Most of the materials deal with the Ministero delle Finanze and several subsections including the Direzione Generale del Debito, Segreteria Generale, Computisteria Generale, Direzione Generale delle Proprietà Camerali e Dazi Diretti (1861–1870), and Direzione Generale dei Lotti (1860–1870). There are also some materials concerning a legal case between the Camera and the Tribunale Civile di Rome.
Location: Archivio Segreto Vaticano.

7.10.118 Spoglio del Gaetano Ludovici
[DATABASE ID: VATV10671-A]
Inclusive Dates: 1827–1834.
Bulk: 1 busta.
Biography: Gaetano Ludovici was scrittore in the Penitenzieria.
Scope: The busta includes miscellaneous materials from 1827–1834.
Location: Archivio Segreto Vaticano.

7.10.119 Spoglio del Vincenzo Macchi
[DATABASE ID: VATV10672-A]
Inclusive Dates: 1808–1860.
Bulk: 4 buste.
Biography: Vincenzo Macchi was born at Capodimonte in the diocese of Montefiascone on August 31, 1770, and died on September 30, 1860, in Rome. He was assigned to the nunciature for Lisbon when the French invaded Portugal in 1808, but Macchi, following the court, left for Brazil. Between 1808 and 1817 Macchi was internuncio and apostolic delegate in Portugal. In 1818 he was appointed nuncio to Switzerland and in 1819 transferred to Paris where he remained until 1827. He was named a cardinal in 1826. When he returned from France he assumed the tasks of legate to Ravenna (1828–1830), president of the Congregation for the Revision of Accounts and Public Administration (1832–1835), prefect of the Congregation of the Council, the signatura, Dataria, and the Segreterio dei Brevi; and many other positions within the Roman Curia. From 1830 to 1840, with some interruptions, he was commissario straordinario and legate to Bologna.
Pius IX (1846–1878) in the first years of his pontificate named Vincenzo a member of a commission to examine certain affairs of state. On the death of Cardinal Micara (1847) he was made bishop of Ostia and Velletri and dean of the College of Cardinals. He interested himself in the restoration of a famous castle, restored the cathedral, and made other improvements in his diocese. His sepulchre is at the church of SS. Giovanni e Paolo.
Scope: Materials in the buste concern the legations in Bologna and Velletri, the papal goverment in Ravenna, and a record by Macchi concerning the nunciature for Lisbon during the Napoleonic invasion. Researchers interested in the activities and career of Cardinal Vincenzo Macchi should also consult the series: Carte Macchi, also in the ASV. In this guide see

the entry for Vincenzo Macchi in the section "Miscellaneous Official Materials and Separate Collections: Individual and Family Papers."
Location: Archivio Segreto Vaticano.

7.10.120 Spoglio del Luigi Maglione
[DATABASE ID: VATV10673-A]
Inclusive Dates: ca. 1939.
Bulk: 1 busta.
Biography: Luigi Maglione was born in Casoria on March 2, 1877, and died there on April 22, 1944. He became a cardinal on December 16, 1935. He was secretary of state during the pontificate of Pius XII.
Location: Archivio Segreto Vaticano.

7.10.121 Spoglio del Riccardo Magnanensi
[DATABASE ID: VATV10674-A]
Inclusive Dates: [18—?]–[19—?].
Bulk: 1 busta.
Biography: Riccardo Magnanensi was Segretario dell'Ufficio del Maestro di Camera.
Scope: Materials in the busta include documents concerning the Magnanensi family, the Istituto Volta, and other various administrative matters.
Location: Archivio Segreto Vaticano.

7.10.122 Spoglio del Angelo Mai
[DATABASE ID: VATV10675-A]
Inclusive Dates: 1838–1839.
Bulk: 1 busta (9 items).
Biography: Angelo Mai was born in Schilpario on March 7, 1782, and died in Albano on September 9, 1854. A Jesuit, he served as scrittore of the Biblioteca Ambrosiana and prefect of the Biblioteca Apostolica Vaticana. He became a cardinal on February 12, 1838.
Scope: The busta contains nine items, all signed by Secretary of State Cardinal Luigi Lambruschini appointing Mai to the following congregations: Vescovi e Regolari, Propaganda Fide, Studi, Chiesa Orientali, Promovendi all'Episcopato, Cina, and Affari Ecclesiastici Straordinari.
Location: Archivio Segreto Vaticano.

7.10.123 Spoglio del Pietro Marini
[DATABASE ID: VATV10676-A]
Inclusive Dates: 1828–1863.
Bulk: 3 buste.
Biography: Pietro Marini was born in Rome on October 5, 1794, and died there on August 9, 1863. He distinguished himself in the field of jurisprudence where he soon became prelate uditore of the Rota. He became a cardinal deacon on December 21, 1846, and was legate to Forlì. Marini also served as prefect of the Signatura and was a member of other tribunals, both civil and ecclesiastical. He was a member of the following congregations: Censo, Studi, Indice, Indulgenze, Reliquie, Visita Apostolica, Vescovi e Regolari, Concilio, Propaganda, and Chiesa Orientali.
Scope: Materials in the buste concern many aspects of Marini's service: legation in Forlì, judicial and financial reform particularly through a Commissione Cardinalizie and in Mon-

talto di Castro, Commissione dei Sussidi, the Signatura, the Camera, and the Consiglio di Stato.

Location: Archivio Segreto Vaticano.

7.10.124 Spogli Francesco Marmaggi

[DATABASE ID: VATV10677-A]

Inclusive Dates: [18—?]–[19—?].

Bulk: 1 busta.

Biography: Francesco Marmaggi was born in Rome on August 31, 1876, and died there on November 3, 1946. He became a cardinal on December 16, 1935. Marmaggi served as prefect of the Concilio.

Location: Archivio Segreto Vaticano.

7.10.125 Spoglio del Giuseppe Marozzo

[DATABASE ID: VATV10678-A]

Inclusive Dates: ca. 1802–1804.

Bulk: 1 busta.

Biography: Giuseppe Marozzo was apostolic nuncio to the Court of Florence (1802–1804).

Scope: Materials in the busta are miscellaneous; a few pertain to judicial or historical matters.

Location: Archivio Segreto Vaticano.

7.10.126 Spoglio del Pacifico Massella

[DATABASE ID: VATV10679-A]

Inclusive Dates: 1913–1922.

Bulk: 1 busta.

Biography: Pacifico Masella was Segretario delle Lettere Latine (1913–1922).

Scope: Records in the busta pertain to Masella's work as secretary in the office of Lettere Latine.

Location: Archivio Segreto Vaticano.

7.10.127 Spoglio del Massimo Massimi

[DATABASE ID: VATV10680-A]

Inclusive Dates: [18—?]–[19—?].

Bulk: 1 busta.

Biography: Massimo Massimi was born in Rome on April 10, 1877, and died on March 6, 1954. He served as prelate and dean of the Rota. Massimi became a cardinal on December 16, 1939. He was prefect of the Segnatura.

Scope: Documents in the busta include ponenze from the secretary of state and the Concilio.

Location: Archivio Segreto Vaticano.

7.10.128 Spogli Mario Mattei

[DATABASE ID: VATV10681-A]

Inclusive Dates: ca. 1820–1870.

Bulk: 4 buste.

Biography: Mario Mattei was born in Pergola on September 6, 1792, and died on October 7, 1870. He became a cardinal July 2, 1832. He served in the Tesorierato generale and in the internal affairs section of the office of the secretary of state. Mattei was also pro-datario, prefect of the Congregazione Cerimoniale, archpriest of the Patriarchal Basilica of Saint Peter, and prefect of the Fabbrica. He was appointed bishop of Ostia and Velletri and dean of the College of Cardinals. Mattei was a member of the following congregations: Inquisizione, Visita Apostolica, Vescovi e Regolari, Concilio, and Censo.

Scope: Records in the four buste pertain to the Congregatio

de Buon Governo, the Tesorerato generale, the Segretario di Stato per gli Affari Interni, the Censo, the Datary, the Concilio, and the administration of the Capitolo di S. Pietro.

Location: Archivio Segreto Vaticano.

7.10.129 Spoglio del Antonio Matteucci

[DATABASE ID: VATV10682-A]

Inclusive Dates: 1831–1854.

Bulk: 1 busta.

Biography: Antonio Matteucci was born in Fermo on March 15, 1802, and died on July 9, 1866. He spent many years in the Ufficio di Giudice of the Fabbrica. Matteucci became a cardinal on June 22, 1866.

Scope: Materials in the busta include a rubricelle of Matteucci's archives at the time of his death. Other materials concern the Fabbrica and a few letters refer to Cardinal Mattei in the Segretario di Stato per gli Affari Interni.

Location: Archivio Segreto Vaticano.

7.10.130 Spoglio del Carlo Mauri

[DATABASE ID: VATV10683-A]

Inclusive Dates: ca. 1816–1823.

Bulk: 1 busta.

Biography: Carlo Mauri was sostituto in the office of the secretary of state.

Scope: The busta contains miscellaneous personal letters and a printed piece entitled "Observations sur la promesse d'enseigner quatre articles," dated 1818.

Location: Archivio Segreto Vaticano.

7.10.131 Spoglio del Raffaele Mazio

[DATABASE ID: VATV10684-A]

Inclusive Dates: ca. 1815–1827.

Bulk: 1 busta.

Biography: Raffaele Mazio was born in Rome on October 24, 1765, and died on February 4, 1832. He was successively secretary for the Congregazione Ceremoniale, a participant with Cardinal Consalvi in the Congress of Vienna, assessor of the Inquisizione, and segreterio delle Lettere Latine. Mazio became a cardinal on March 15, 1830.

Scope: Records concern Mazio's work in the Segretaria delle Lettere Latine, questions concerning monasteries and the Capitolo in Lucca, concerns over the dioceses of Piedmont after the fall of Napoleon, correspondence about religious affairs in the Netherlands, and a letter from Maestricht (Netherlands) dated May 20, 1815, describing military movements prior to the battle of Waterloo.

Note: Researchers interested in the activities and career of Cardinal Raffaele Mazio should also consult Individual and Family Papers series *Mazio, Raffaele (Carte Mazio)*.

Location: Archivio Segreto Vaticano.

7.10.132 Spoglio del Federico De Mérode

[DATABASE ID: VATV10617-A]

Inclusive Dates: 1865.

Bulk: 1 busta.

Biography: Frederic de Mérode was born in Brussels on March 20, 1820, and died in Rome on July 10, 1874. After serving in the Belgian military he became a priest and transferred to Rome as a military chaplain for the papal military. He was cameriere segreto partecipante e ministero delle Armi from

1860 to 1865. On October 6, 1865, he was nominated ele-mosiniere pontificio.

Scope: The materials in the busta concern Mérode's tenure as ministro delle Armi in 1865.

Reference: Enciclopedia cattolica (Vatican City, 1948), vol. 8, p. 734.

Location: Archivio Segreto Vaticano.

7.10.133 Spoglio del Raffaele Merry del Val
[DATABASE ID: VATV10685-A]
Inclusive Dates: ca. 1890–1906.
Bulk: 1 busta.
Biography: Raphael Merry del Val was born in London on October 10, 1865, and died in Rome on February 26, 1930. He was president of the Pontificia Accademia dei Nobili Ecclesiastici. Merry del Val became a cardinal and was nominated secretary of state by Pius X on November 9, 1904. Later, he also became secretary of the Holy Office.
Scope: Materials in the busta pertain to the Capitolo della Chiesa di Monte Santo, the Direzione Generale dell'Azione Cattolica Italiana, and the office of the secretery of state.
Location: Archivio Segreto Vaticano.

7.10.134 Spoglio del Teodolfo Mertel
[DATABASE ID: VATV10686-A]
Inclusive Dates: 1846–1899.
Bulk: 55 buste.
Biography: Teodolfo Mertel was born in Allumiere on February 6, 1806, and died on July 9, 1899. He received a degree in law in Rome and served as uditore of the Rota and later as president of the Tribunale Civile di Roma (1843). In 1848 Mertel became secretary of the Commissione Cardinalizia di Redigere lo Statuto di Pio IX. After the return of Pius IX from Gaeta, Mertel served in the ministry of Grazia e Giustizia and then in the Ministero dell'Interno. In February 1858 he was created cardinal deacon. Pius IX named Mertel vice-cancelliere and executor of his will. Mertel was also involved in the preparations for the revisions of canon law in 1917. He was a member of the following congregations: Concilio, Propaganda Fide, Vescovi e Regolari, Censo, Visita Apostolica, and Fabbrica; and he was president of the Consiglio di Stato. He was a protector of many religious institutes.
Scope: The buste contain ponenze from the Concilio (1858–1895), the Propaganda Fide (1854–1899), the Congregazione dei Vescovi e Regolari (1858–1895), the Cancelleria (1878–1899), and the Fabbrica (1860). The materials from the Propaganda include information on a concordat with Portugal (1864) and synods in Albania (1877–1879), Alexandria, and Leopoli (Lwow, 1891–1899). Records also pertain to the Censo, the Camera, the Rota, and the Segnatura.

Other materials concern the Papal States and various civil offices such as the Ministero dell'Interno, the Consiglio dei Ministri, the Alto Consilio, and the Ministero delle Finanze. The buste also contain a number of civil and criminal cases and discussions of judicial reform. One group of items of particular interest concerns the construction of railroads in the Papal States (1846–1857). Mertel's records also deal with parish, confraternity, and religious community life in Rome.
Reference: Pásztor (1983) pp. 145–146.
Location: Archivio Segreto Vaticano.

7.10.135 Spoglio del Giuseppe Mezzofanti
[DATABASE ID: VATV10687-A]
Inclusive Dates: 1833–1848.
Bulk: 1 busta.
Biography: Giuseppe Mezzofanti was born in Bologna on September 19, 1774, and died in Rome on March 12, 1849. He became a cardinal on February 12, 1838. Mezzofanti served as prefect of the Congregazione della Correzione dei Libri, the Chiesa Orientale, and Studi.
Scope: Materials pertain to the Biblioteca Apostolica Vaticana and the Congregazione degli Studi.
Location: Archivio Segreto Vaticano.

7.10.136 Spoglio del Ludovico Micara
[DATABASE ID: VATV10688-A]
Inclusive Dates: 1739–1846.
Bulk: 1 busta.
Biography: Ludovico Micara was born in Frascati on October 12, 1775, and died in Rome on May 24, 1847. He was a member of the Capuchins. Micara became a cardinal on March 13, 1826. He was bishop of Ostia and Velletri and dean of the College of Cardinals. Later, Micara also served as legate to Velletri. His nephew, Clemente Micara, was also a cardinal. Micara was prefect of the S.C. Cerimoniale e dei Riti and president of the Camera.
Scope: Materials in the buste include judicial matters from the Rota, the Consulta, and other tribunals. There are also some published circular letters from the secretary of state to legates in the provinces and a "Regola e Testamento del serafico Padre S. Francesco," dated 1739.
Location: Archivio Segreto Vaticano.

7.10.137 Spoglio del Giuseppe Mignone
[DATABASE ID: VATV10689-A]
Inclusive Dates: 1907–1942.
Bulk: 2 buste.
Biography: Giuseppe Mignone was cameriere segreto partecipante for Benedict XV (1917–1920) and elemosiniere segreto for Pius XI.
Scope: The majority of the materials concern the diocese of Bologna during the tenure of Cardinal Giacomo della Chiesa (Benedict XV) as archbishop. There is also a letter from 1920 signed by Monsignor Achille Ratti, apostolic nuncio to Warsaw.
Location: Archivio Segreto Vaticano.

7.10.138 Spogli Luigi Misciatelli
[DATABASE ID: VATV10690-A]
Inclusive Dates: ca. 1914–1922.
Bulk: 1 busta.
Biography: Luigi Misciatelli was vice-prefect of the Sacri Palazzi Apostolici during the pontificate of Benedict XV.
Scope: Materials in the busta include a report on the pontifical police, various letters asking favors of the pope, and a letter autographed by Benedict XV concerning an earthquake in Avezzano.
Location: Archivio Segreto Vaticano.

7.10.139 Spoglio del Mario Mocenni
[DATABASE ID: VATV10692-A]
Inclusive Dates: ca. 1879–1890.
Bulk: 4 buste.

Biography: Mario Mocenni was born in Montefiasconi on January 22, 1823, and died in Rome on November 14, 1904. For many years he served as sostituto for the secretary of state. Mocenni became a cardinal on January 16, 1893, and was bishop suburbicario of Sabina and perpetual abate of Farfa. He was a member of the following congregations: Vescovi e Regolari, Riti, Fabbrica, and Studi.

Scope: Materials in the buste concern the Secretariat of State and the Congregation of Bishops and Regulars. One interesting item in the Secretariat of State documents is a controversy among Monsignor Bonomelli, bishop of Cremona; Cardinal Ferrari, archbishop of Milan; and the journalist David Albertario. Other materials in the buste relate to the suburbicario of Sabina and various religious institutes for which Mocenni was protector, including the Augustinian monastery of S. Marta; the Roman churches of SS. Carlo e Ambrogio al Corso, San Francesco a Ripa, San Bernardino da Siena, SS. Stimmate, Santa Maria in Cosmedin, San Giovanni in Laterano, the church and confraternity of Santa Maria dei Miracoli; and the Ursuline Oblates and the Oblates of the Tor de' Specchi.

Location: Archivio Segreto Vaticano.

7.10.140 Spoglio del Raffaele Monaco La Valletta

[DATABASE ID: VATV10694-A]

Inclusive Dates: [18—]–[18—].

Bulk: 1 busta.

Biography: Raffaele Monaco La Valletta was born in L'Aquila on February 23, 1827, and died in Rome on July 14, 1890. He became a cardinal on March 13, 1868, and was cardinal vicar of Rome and the penitenziere maggiore. He also served as prefect of the Congregazione Cerimoniale, as bishop of Ostia and Velletri, and as a dean of the College of Cardinals.

Scope: The few items in the busta are of a historical and judicial nature.

Location: Archivio Segreto Vaticano.

7.10.141 Spoglio del Terenziano Moreschi

[DATABASE ID: VATV10691-A]

Inclusive Dates: 1841–1855.

Bulk: 1 busta.

Biography: Terenziano Moreschi was minutante of the secretary of state during the pontificate of Pius IX.

Scope: Materials pertain to Moreschi's work in the office of the secretary of state and are largely requests for pontifical graces.

Location: Archivio Segreto Vaticano.

7.10.142 Spogli Francesco Nardi

[DATABASE ID: VATV10695-A]

Inclusive Dates: [18—]–[18—].

Bulk: 1 busta.

Biography: Francesco Nardi was born in Vazzola-Ceneda on June 18, 1808.

Scope: The busta contains personal letters and some financial records.

Location: Archivio Segreto Vaticano.

7.10.143 Spoglio del Ignazio Nasalli

[DATABASE ID: VATV10693-A]

Inclusive Dates: ca. 1824.

Bulk: 1 busta.

Biography: Ignazio Nasalli was born on October 7, 1750, in Parma and died on December 2, 1831. He was apostolic nuncio to the Netherlands and Switzerland.

Scope: The busta contains materials comprised mostly of biglietti from 1824 when Naselli was in Switzerland.

Reference: G. de Marchi, *Le nunziature apostoliche dal 1800 al 1956* (Rome, 1957).

Location: Archivio Segreto Vaticano.

7.10.144 Spoglio del Lorenzo Nina

[DATABASE ID: VATV10696-A]

Inclusive Dates: [18—]–[18—].

Bulk: 1 busta.

Biography: Lorenzo Nina was born in Recanti on May 12, 1812, and died on July 25, 1885. He was created cardinal on March 12, 1877. He was secretary of state for Leo XIII and then served as prefect of the Concilio. He was a member of the following congregations: Affari Ecclesiastici Straordinari, Propaganda Fide, Orientale, and the Inquisizione.

Scope: Materials in the busta relate to his work in the office of the secretary of state and with the Amministrazione Pontificia. In particular there are some materials regarding the restoration of the Palazzo Betocchi di Anagni, an inquest into twelve *luoghi pii*, and the Monastery of S. Croce in Santa Francesca Romana.

Location: Archivio Segreto Vaticano.

7.10.145 Spoglio del Carlo Odescalchi

[DATABASE ID: VATV10697-A]

Inclusive Dates: ca. 1835.

Bulk: 1 busta.

Biography: Carlo Odescalchi was born on March 5, 1786. He became a cardinal on March 10, 1823, and was vicar general of Sua Santità for the diocese of Rome. He renounced his post as cardinal and became a Jesuit.

Scope: Materials in the busta relate to various questions concerning the basilica of Santa Maria Maggiore and the church of Santa Prassede in Rome.

Location: Archivio Segreto Vaticano.

7.10.146 Spoglio del Luigi Oreglia di S. Stefano

[DATABASE ID: VATV10698-A]

Inclusive Dates: [18—?]–[19—?].

Bulk: 1 busta.

Biography: Luigi Oreglia di S. Stefano was born in Bene Vagienna on July 9, 1828, and died on December 7, 1913. In 1866 he was named apostolic nuncio to Belgium. He became apostolic nuncio to Portugal in 1868. In 1873 Oreglia di S. Stefano became a cardinal. He was then bishop of the suburbicaria of Palestrina and later of Porto e S. Rufina. In 1896 he became the dean of the College of Cardinals and took the see of Ostia and Velletri. He was prefect of the congregations of Indulgenze and Reliquie and the Cerimoniale. He also served as camerlengo of the Camera and arcicancelliere of the University of Rome. He was a member of the following congregations: Concistoriale, Bishops and Regulars, Propaganda Fide, Orientale, Affari Ecclesiastici Straordinari, and Studi.

Scope: Materials in the busta concern Oreglia di S. Stefano's appointments in the congregations of Indulgences and Relics and in the Propaganda Fide. There are also some materials relating to religious institutes for which he was a protector, particularly the monastery of the Capuchin nuns in Rome and the Ospizio di S. Maria degli Angeli.

Location: Archivio Segreto Vaticano.

7.10.147 Spoglio del Anton-Maria Orioli

[DATABASE ID: VATV10699-A]

Inclusive Dates: 1847.

Bulk: 1 busta.

Biography: Anton-Maria Orioli was born in Bagnacavallo on December 10, 1778, and died in Rome on February 20, 1852. He entered the order of the Minori Conventuali. He became a cardinal on February 12, 1838. He was prefect of the Congregation of Bishops and Regulars.

Scope: Materials in the busta primarily refer to the request of the citizens of Terni to return their bishop Monsignor Tizzani. Other letters refer to the competences of the Congregation of the Bishops and Regulars.

Location: Archivio Segreto Vaticano.

7.10.148 Spoglio del Bartolomeo Pacca

[DATABASE ID:VATV10700-A

Inclusive Dates: 1808–1842.

Bulk: 9 buste.

Biography: Bartolomeo Pacca was born in Benevento on December 25, 1756, and died in Rome on April 19, 1844. In 1785 he was named nuncio to Cologne. He later served as nuncio to Portugal. In 1795 he became a cardinal. When the French entered Rome in 1808–1809, he accompanied Pope Pius VII to prison in France. After the fall of Napoleon, he became pro-secretary of state. Pacca served as camerlengo of the Sacra Romana Chiesa, segreterio of the Holy Office, and prefect of the Congregazione Cerimoniale and Pro-Datary.

Scope: Materials in the nine buste include records of religious problems in Germany in the nineteenth century in which Ludwig Pastor made an intercession; Pacca's recollections of the Napoleonic period and its aftermath in two volumes entitled *Memorie storiche del primo Ministero* (1808–1809 and 1814–1815); records regarding the offices of pro-segretario di stato and camerlengo; and documents concerning the competence of the Consistory. A final section of the buste contains family papers and personal materials.

Location: Archivio Segreto Vaticano.

7.10.149 Spoglio del Tiberio Pacca

[DATABASE ID: VATV10701-A]

Inclusive Dates: 1809–1820.

Bulk: 5 buste.

Biography: Tiberio Pacca was born on August 31, 1786, and died in Naples on June 29, 1837. He was a nephew of Cardinal Bartholomeo Pacca and also followed the pope into exile during the Napoleonic invasion. Pacca was apostolic delegate in Romagna and in Civitavecchia. He also served as governor of Rome and camerlengo of the Sacra Romana Chiesa.

Scope: Materials in the five buste concern Pacca's exile in France and Fenestrelle, letters relating to the apostolic delegations in Romagne and Civitavecchia and the Commissione Pontificia in Milan. Additional items pertain to Pacca's tenure as governor of Rome and vice-camerlengo.

Location: Archivio Segreto Vaticano.

7.10.150 Spoglio del Antonio Pallotta

[DATABASE ID: VATV10702-A]

Inclusive Dates: 1816–1834.

Bulk: 2 buste.

Biography: Antonio Pallotta was born in Ferrara on February 23, 1770, and died in Monte Cassiano (Macerata) on July 19, 1834. He began his ecclesiastical career in 1796 and became referendario of the Segnatura. In 1816 Pallotta became uditore generale of the Camera. He was made a cardinal on March 10, 1823. He also served as legate a latere in the provinces of Campagna and Marittima where he assisted in judicial matters.

Scope: Materials in the buste touch on various aspects of Pallotta's ecclesiastical career. There are records from the Camera, the secretary of state, and the legation in Campagna and Marittima. Many of the records concerning the legation deal with the establishment of justice and ridding the area of brigands.

Location: Archivio Segreto Vaticano.

7.10.151 Spoglio del Luigi Pallotti

[DATABASE ID: VATV10703-A]

Inclusive Dates: 1853–1881.

Bulk: 1 busta.

Biography: Luigi Pallotti was born in Albano Laziale on March 3, 1829, and died in Rome in 1890. He was secretary for the Congregazione per gli Affari Ecclesiastici Straordinari and the Congregazione degli Studi. He also served as prefect of the Segnatura. Pallotti became a cardinal on May 23, 1887.

Scope: The busta includes materials dealing with the office of the secretary of state, including the religious congregation of S. Vincenzo de Paoli in Spain, and political notices concerning the death of Giuseppe Garibaldi. Materials from the Congregazione degli Studi include the Catholic University of Malta, and the Università dell'Apollinare and the Seminary in Rome.

Location: Archivio Segreto Vaticano.

7.10.152 Spoglio del Luigi Paolucci de Calboli

[DATABASE ID: VATV10704-A]

Inclusive Dates: 1830–1851.

Bulk: 1 busta.

Biography: Luigi Paolucci de Calboli was apostolic delegate in Forlì from 1830 to 1851.

Scope: Materials in the buste concern the apostolic delegation in Forlì.

Location: Archivio Segreto Vaticano.

7.10.153 Spoglio del Domenico Passionei

[DATABASE ID: VATV10705-A]

Inclusive Dates: [16—?]–[17—?].

Bulk: 2 buste.

Biography: Domenico Passionei was born in Fossombrone on December 2, 1682, and died in Camaldoli on July 5, 1761. He served as nuncio for Switzerland and Vienna. He became a cardinal on June 23, 1738, and was secretary of briefs.

Scope: The buste contain letters written to Cardinal Passionei.

Location: Archivio Segreto Vaticano.

7.10.154 Spoglio del Costantino Patrizi
[DATABASE ID: VATV10706-A]
Inclusive Dates: 1826–1860.
Bulk: 2 buste (busta 1 and busta speciale).
Biography: Costantino Patrizi was born in Siena on September 4, 1788, and died on December 17, 1876. The son of Giovanni who was a hereditary standard bearer of the Holy Roman Church and a senator of Rome, Costantino was ordained a priest in 1821. Under Pius VII he was named a domestic prelate and appointed a referendary of the apostolic Signatura; Leo XII inscribed him among the auditors of the Rota; Gregory XVI appointed him his major domo. In the consistory of 1834 Gregory also named him a cardinal *in pectore* but did not publish the fact until 1836. In 1841 Costantino became vice general of Rome. In the consistory held by Pius IX at Gaeta in 1849, he was selected for the suburban see of Albano. He moved successively to Porto and S. Rufina (1860), then to prefect of the Congregation of Ceremonies and Rites, then to secretary of the Congregation of the Holy Office. In 1870 he became dean of the College of Cardinals. He officiated as procurator for Carlo Cardinal Odescalchi in the consistory of 1838 when the cardinal abandoned his "purple" in order to work with the missions. He was legate of Pius IX to Paris for the baptism of Prince Eugene, son of Napoleon III (1856).
Scope: The first busta contains materials dating from 1839–1842 when Patrizi was prefect of the Bishops and Regulars and includes a part of a holograph of a testament of Cardinal Gioacchino Pecci (later Leo XIII) from the period when he was archbishop of Perugia. The *busta speciale* contains various bulls and diplomas. For example, there is a bull (1828) conferring the Abbey of SS. Vincenzo and Anastasio alle Tre Fontane, a diploma nominating Patrizi as a regent of the Penitentiary, and a bull appointing him bishop.
Note: See also Patrizi family collection in the Archivio Segreto Vaticano.
Location: Archivio Segreto Vaticano.

7.10.155 Spoglio del Carlo Maria Pedicini
[DATABASE ID: VATV10707-A]
Inclusive Dates: 1816–1823.
Bulk: 2 buste.
Biography: Carlo Maria Pedicini was born in Benevento on November 2, 1769, and died in Rome on November 19, 1843. He became a cardinal on March 10, 1823. Over the years he served as prefect of the Riti and Immunità, pro-segretario dei memoriale, vice-cancelliere of the Sacra Romana Chiesa, and bishop of Porto and S. Rufino, and Civitavecchia.
Scope: Materials in the buste concern the Riti, Immunità, and Pedicini's work as vice-cancelliere of the Sacra Romana Chiesa. One entire busta concerns the falsification of rescritti and the competence of the segreteria dei memoriali.
Location: Archivio Segreto Vaticano.

7.10.156 Spogli Francesco Pentini
[DATABASE ID: VATV10709-A]
Inclusive Dates: [184-?]–[186-?].
Bulk: 3 buste.
Biography: Francesco Pentini was born in Rome on December 11, 1797, and died there on December 17, 1869. He was well versed in the law and served as referendario of the Segnatura. Pentini also had a long tenure with the Camera and held the office of ministero dell'Interno for some years both before and after the establishment of the Roman Republic in 1848. He became a cardinal on March 26, 1863.
Scope: The contents of the buste include materials pertaining to the ministero dell'Interno (1847–1856) and published works regarding court cases against the Roman Republic, political conspiracies, and the Papal States.
Location: Archivio Segreto Vaticano.

7.10.157 Spoglio del Girolamo Petri
[DATABASE ID: VATV10708-A]
Inclusive Dates: ca. 1848.
Bulk: 1 busta.
Biography: Girolamo Petri was minutante of the secretary of state during the pontificate of Pius IX.
Scope: Materials in the busta include records regarding Petri's work as minutante for the secretary of state. There is also some printed material from the period and a bronze commemorative medallion of the battle of Vincenze of June 10, 1848.
Location: Archivio Segreto Vaticano.

7.10.158 Spoglio del Adeodato Giovanni Piazza
[DATABASE ID: VATV10710-A]
Inclusive Dates: [18—?]–[19—?].
Bulk: 2 buste.
Biography: Adeodato Giovanni Piazza was born in Vigo di Cadore on September 30, 1884, and died in Rome on November 30, 1957. He was a member of the Discalced Carmelites. Piazza became a cardinal on December 13, 1937, and was bishop suburbicario of Sabina and Poggio Mirteto. He also served as secretary of the Consistoriale.
Scope: Materials in the buste include ponenze from the following congregations: Council, Religious, Propaganda Fide, Consistory, Riti, Discipline of the Sacraments, and the Holy Office.
Location: Archivio Segreto Vaticano.

7.10.159 Spoglio del Enrico Piccoli
[DATABASE ID: VATV10711-A]
Inclusive Dates: [184-?]–[187-?].
Bulk: 1 busta.
Biography: Enrico Piccoli was under-archivist for the office of the secretary of state during the pontificate of Pius IX (1846–1878).
Scope: Materials in the busta pertain to the office of the secretary of state and include a long letter from Cardinal Gioacchino Pecci, archbishop of Perugia, and congratulatory letters to Cardinal Antonelli.
Location: Archivio Segreto Vaticano.

7.10.160 Spoglio del Giovanni Pierantozzi
[DATABASE ID: VATV10712-A]
Inclusive Dates: ca. 1870.
Bulk: 1 busta.
Biography: Giovanni Pierantozzi was a minutante in the office of the secretary of state during the pontificates of Pius IX (1846–1878) and Leo XIII (1878–1903). He died in 1909.
Scope: Materials in the busta pertain to Pierantozzi's work in the office of the secretary of state. Of particular interest is a minute of a letter written by Pius IX to General Kanzler on

September 19, 1870, concerning the resistance at the front and the troops from the Piedmont.
Location: Archivio Segreto Vaticano.

7.10.161 Spoglio del Giuseppe Pinchetti Sanmarchi
[DATABASE ID: VATV10713-A]
Inclusive Dates: 1903–1922.
Bulk: 1 busta.
Biography: Giuseppe Pinchetti Sanmarchi was a prelate in Rome and later canon of S. Maria Maggiore.
Scope: Materials in busta are photocopies of letters used in a biography of Pinchetti Sanmarchi.
Location: Archivio Segreto Vaticano.

7.10.162 Spoglio del Paolo Polidori
[DATABASE ID: VATV10714-A]
Inclusive Dates: ca. 1820–1847.
Bulk: 3 buste.
Biography: Paolo Polidori was born in Jesi on January 4, 1778, and died in Rome on April 23, 1847. He was sostituto in the office of the secretary of state and secretary for the Consistory. He became a cardinal on June 23, 1834, and was prefect of the Concilio and the Congregazione della Disciplina Regolare.
Scope: Materials in the three buste pertain to Polidori's work as sostituto for the secretary of state and secretary of the Consistory. A limited number of documents concern the Concilio and Congregazione della Disciplina Regolare.
Location: Archivio Segreto Vaticano.

7.10.163 Spoglio del Angelo Quaglia
[DATABASE ID: VATV10715-A]
Inclusive Dates: [18—]–[18—].
Bulk: 1 busta.
Biography: Angelo Quaglia was born in Corneto on August 28, 1802, and died in Rome on April 28, 1872. He studied law and was prelato uditore of the Rota. He became a cardinal on September 27, 1861. Quaglia was prefect of the Congregation for Bishops and Regulars.
Scope: The busta contains materials pertaining to Quaglia as uditore of the Rota and prefect of the Bishops and Regulars. It also includes information on restoration projects at the Istituto S. Michele and the Lateran Palace.
Location: Archivio Segreto Vaticano.

7.10.164 Spoglio del Mariano Rampolla del Tindaro
[DATABASE ID: VATV10717-A]
Inclusive Dates: 1878–1902.
Bulk: 5 buste.
Biography: Mariano Rampolla del Tindaro was born in Polizzi (Sicily) on August 17, 1843, and died in Rome on December 16, 1913. In 1882 he was named apostolic nuncio to Spain. He assisted in the mediation of Leo XIII between Spain and Germany concerning the Caroline Islands. Rampolla del Tindaro became a cardinal on May 27, 1887, and secretary of state until the death of Leo XIII (1903). Among other posts, Rampolla was vicar-apostolic of the Belgian Congo.
Scope: The materials in the buste pertain to the period when Rampolla del Tindaro was secretary of state (1887–1903). Documents pertain to North and South America; the Austro-Hungarian Empire; Belgium and Holland; religious instruction in secondary schools; and other issues in France, Germany (especially the Kulturkampf, 1878–1885), England, Ireland, Spain, Portugal, Switzerland; Eastern Rite churches; Italian politics; and religious life in Italy.
Reference: Pásztor (1983) pp. 146–147.
Location: Archivio Segreto Vaticano.

7.10.165 Spoglio del Lorenzo Randi
[DATABASE ID: VATV10716-A]
Inclusive Dates: ca. 1859–1872.
Bulk: 2 buste.
Biography: Lorenzo Randi was born in Bagnacavallo on July 18, 1818, and died in Rome on December 20, 1887. He entered the prelature and was commissario straordinario and apostolic delegate in the Marche. Randi also served as vice-camerlengo, governor of Rome, and director general of the police. He became a cardinal on March 15, 1875.
Scope: The two buste contain political correspondence regarding the situation in the Marche between 1859 and 1868, information pertaining to the papal police (1870–1871), and various other letters and requests.
Location: Archivio Segreto Vaticano.

7.10.166 Spoglio del Carlo Augusto di Reisach
[DATABASE ID: VATV10718-A]
Inclusive Dates: [18—]–[18—].
Bulk: 2 buste.
Biography: Karl August von Reisach was born in Roth (Bavaria) on July 6, 1800, and died in Rome on December 29, 1869. He was archbishop of Munich and Freising. He became a cardinal on December 17, 1855. Reisach served as prefect of the Congregazione degli Studi and became bishop suburbacario of Sabina and of the Abbey of S. Maria di Farfa.
Location: Archivio Segreto Vaticano.

7.10.167 Spoglio del Achille Maria Ricci
[DATABASE ID: VATV10719-A]
Inclusive Dates: ca. 1818–1861.
Bulk: 12 buste.
Biography: Achille Maria Ricci was born in Naples. In 1835 he was prelato abbreviatore and later uditore of the Camerlengo. He was apostolic delegate to Camerino, Civitavecchia, Ancona, Ravenna, and Velletri. He also served as commendatore di S. Spirito and president of the Commissione degli Ospedali di Roma.
Scope: Records in the buste are largely of a political nature. They pertain to political affairs in Germany, Poland, Spain, and other countries. Among these documents are copies of correspondence between Napoleon and Pius VI. Other materials in the buste pertain to the apostolic delegations in Ancona, Velletri (specifically the Neapolitan war 1860–1861), Camerino, the siege of Gaeta in 1861, Civitavecchia, and particularly Ravenna. A limited number of documents concern the office of the uditore of the Camerlengo.
Note: Some of the materials from the Spoglio del Achille Maria Ricci have been transferred to the Secretary of State series and can now be located in the following posizioni: A. 1818 R. 171 Tit. 9 Hannover Ministry; A 1822 R. 171 Tit. 9 Hannover Ministry; A. 1823 R. 171 Tit. 9 Hannover Ministry, A. 1824 R. 171 Tit. 9 Hannover Ministry, A. 1825 R. 171

Tit. 9 Hannover Ministry; and A. 1829 R. Tit. 9 Hannover Ministry.

Location: Archivio Segreto Vaticano.

7.10.168 Spogli Nicola Riganti

[DATABASE ID: VATV10720-A]

Inclusive Dates: [18—]–[18—].

Bulk: 1 busta.

Biography: Nicola Riganti was an official in the Consulta at the beginning of the nineteenth century.

Scope: The busta contains a few personal and official letters.

Location: Archivio Segreto Vaticano.

7.10.169 Spoglio del Agostino Rivarola

[DATABASE ID: VATV10721-A]

Inclusive Dates: 1814–1842.

Bulk: 8 buste.

Biography: Agostino Rivarola was born in Genoa on March 14, 1788, and died in Rome on November 7, 1842. He was apostolic delegate to Perugia and then Macerata. In 1814 he became president of the Commissione di Stato and aided in the reestablishmnent of papal power after the fall of Napoleon. From 1824 to 1826 he was legate a latere in Romagna for the repression of insurrections. Rivarola became a cardinal on October 1, 1817, and after 1828 became prefect of the Congregazione delle Acque e Strade.

Scope: The eight buste contain materials regarding Rivarola's various work in the church. Documents pertain to the Commissione di Stato, the legations in Ravenna and Romagna, and the Congregazione delle Acque e Strade. There are a number of police inquests against conspirators in Ravenna and Romagna. Unique items in the collection include a letter from the czar of Russia in 1824 requesting the reestablishment of the Jesuits, and materials regarding various religious orders for which Rivarola was protector including the Augustinians and the Ordine della Penitenza.

Location: Archivio Segreto Vaticano.

7.10.170 Spoglio del Roberto Roberti

[DATABASE ID: VATV10722-A]

Inclusive Dates: 1843–1864.

Bulk: 8 buste.

Biography: Roberto Roberti was born in San Giusto on December 23, 1788, and died in Rome on November 6, 1867. He was apostolic delegate to Perugia, sostituto for the Segreteria di Stato per gli Affari Interni, and uditore generale of the Camera. He became a cardinal on September 30, 1850. He was segreterio dei memoriali.

Scope: Most of the buste contain miscellaneous uncatalogued letters of a personal and official nature. The first several buste, however, do contain materials pertaining to the apostolic delegation in Perugia, the Segreteria di Stato per gli Affari Interni and the Camera.

Location: Archivio Segreto Vaticano.

7.10.171 Spoglio del Raffaello Rossi

[DATABASE ID: VATV10723-A]

Inclusive Dates: 1930–1945.

Bulk: 3 buste.

Biography: Raffaello Rossi was born in Pisa on October 28, 1876, and died on September 17, 1948. He entered the Discalced Carmelites and was ordained in 1901. He became bishop of Volterra on April 22, 1920. Rossi became a cardinal on June 30, 1930. He was secretary for the Congregazione Concistoriale from 1931 to 1948.

Location: Archivio Segreto Vaticano.

7.10.172 Spoglio del Luigi Ruffo Scilla

[DATABASE ID: VATV10724-A]

Inclusive Dates: [18—]–[18—].

Bulk: 1 busta.

Biography: Luigi Ruffo Scilla was born in Palermo on April 16, 1840, and died on May 29, 1895. He became a cardinal on December 14, 1891.

Scope: Materials in the busta pertain to personal interests.

Location: Archivio Segreto Vaticano.

7.10.173 Spoglio del Giovanni Rufini

[DATABASE ID:VATV10725-A]

Inclusive Dates: ca. 1832.

Bulk: 1 busta.

Biography: Giovanni Rufini was consultant to the office of the secretary of state. The busta contains a letter Rufini wrote as a consultant to the office of the secretary of state concerning legal issues and a draft of Cardinal Lambruschini's response. There is a penciled-in note on the information sheet on Rufini in the index to see a busta at the end of the fondo. There is no indication in the index that such a busta exists.

Location: Archivio Segreto Vaticano.

7.10.174 Spoglio del Giovanni Rusconi

[DATABASE ID: VATV10726-A]

Inclusive Dates: ca. 1837–1858.

Bulk: 2 buste.

Biography: Giovanni Rusconi was vice-president of the Consulta di Stato per la Finanza during the pontificate of Pius IX. He also served in the Camera and was *in commenda* to the Abbey of SS. Gregorio e Siro in Bologna. Rusconi also served as apostolic delegate to Ancona.

Scope: Materials in the two buste concern the office of the Consulta di Stato per le Finanze (1856–1857), the apostolic delegation in Ancona (1846–1847), and the Abbazia dei SS. Gregorio e Siro in Bologna (1817, 1856–1858). There are also some miscellaneous materials in the buste concerning legal matters, the papal railroad, and the Tiber.

Location: Archivio Segreto Vaticano.

7.10.175 Spoglio del Francesco Sabatucci

[DATABASE ID: VATV10727-A]

Inclusive Dates: ca. 1841.

Bulk: 1 busta.

Biography: Francesco Sabatucci was minutante for the secretary of state during the pontificate of Gregory XVI. Under Pius IX he was segretario del consiglio dei ministri.

Scope: Materials in the busta concern a journey of Gregory XVI throughout the Papal States in 1841, an autographed letter of Leo XIII when he was apostolic delegate in Perugia, and letters from Sabatucci concerning administrative reform.

Location: Archivio Segreto Vaticano.

7.10.176 Spogli Carlo Sacconi
[DATABASE ID: VATV10728-A]
Inclusive Dates: [18—]–[18—].
Bulk: 1 busta.
Biography: Carlo Sacconi was born in Montalto on May 9, 1808, and died on February 25, 1889. He was apostolic nuncio in Paris, prodatario, and prefect of the Congregazione Cerimoniale. He became a cardinal on September 27, 1861, and was bishop of Ostia and Velletri.
Scope: The busta contains miscellaneous published materials, including court cases.
Location: Archivio Segreto Vaticano.

7.10.177 Spoglio del Giuseppe Antonio Sala
[DATABASE ID: VATV10729-A]
Inclusive Dates: [17—?]–[18—?].
Bulk: 5 buste.
Biography: Giuseppe Sala was born in Rome on October 27, 1762, and died there on June 23, 1839. He was a member of the delegation seated in Rome during the absence of Pius VI, assisting with the Napoleonic Concordat. Pius VII (1800–1823) sent him to Paris as secretary of the legation of Cardinal Caprara (1801); he proved to be a zealous, objective, and loyal informer for Pius VII of the events taking place during the pope's imprisonment at Savona (1809–1814).

Sala returned to Rome and was appointed secretary of the new apostolic delegation for the second French occupation. With the restoration he began the publication of his *Piano di riforma* in which he proposed as a remedial principle the laicization of the public tasks. This was interrupted, however, by Consalvi, legate to the Congress of Vienna.

After 1815 Sala was secretary for many commissions and committees as well as for the following congregations: Riforma, Affari Ecclesiastici, Riti, and Concilio. He also aided in improving papal relations with the Piedmont He also involved himself in working with the hospitals of the city. Gregory XVI raised him to the cardinalate on September 30, 1831, and named him prefect for the Congregation for the Index and then for the Congregation of Bishops and Regulars. Among his unedited writings he left a copy of his *Piano di reforma*, which gives an objective account of the events of the years 1798 and 1799.

Scope: Materials in the buste contain information from the Congregazione per gli Affari Ecclesiastici (particularly regarding the Kingdom of the Two Sicilies and the Piedmont), letters pertaining to the Napoleonic period, correspondence regarding the congregations of the Index, Riti, Cardinalizie di Stato, and the Bishops and Regulars. Other items are a letter from Don Gioacchino Pedrilli and material regarding various jubilee years.
Location: Archivio Segreto Vaticano.

7.10.178 Spoglio del Alessandro di Sanmarzano
[DATABASE ID: VATV10730-A]
Inclusive Dates: 1836–1838.
Bulk: 1 busta.
Biography: Alessandro di Sanmarzano was first assessor and vice-president of the Tribunale Criminale del Governo di Roma during the pontificate of Gregory XVI.
Scope: The busta contains materials related to various legal processes and sentencing.
Location: Archivio Segreto Vaticano.

7.10.179 Spoglio del Loreto Santucci
[DATABASE ID: VATV10731-A]
Inclusive Dates: 1815–1841.
Bulk: 2 buste.
Biography: Loreto Santucci was a minutante in the office of the secretary of state. The two buste contain minutes of various letters drafted by Santucci as part of his duties in that office.
Location: Archivio Segreto Vaticano.

7.10.180 Spoglio del Vincenzo Santucci
[DATABASE ID: VATV10732-A]
Inclusive Dates: 1829–1863.
Bulk: 2 buste.
Biography: Vincenzo Santucci was born in Gorga on February 18, 1796, and died on August 19, 1861. He served as chargé d'affaires in the nunciature for Turin, sostituto for the secretary of state, and in 1847, secretary for the Congregazione per gli Affari Ecclesiastici Straordinari. Santucci became a cardinal on March 7, 1853, and became prefect of the Congregazione degli Studi.
Scope: Materials in the two buste include letters pertaining to the office of the secretary of state, the Riti, and the Consistory. There are also various printed materials regarding the political situation and judicial matters in Rome and the Papal States. One group of documents also concerns an apostolic visit to the Ministri degli Infermi in 1853.
Location: Archivio Segreto Vaticano.

7.10.181 Spoglio del Enea Sbarretti
[DATABASE ID: VATV10733-A]
Inclusive Dates: ca. 1850.
Bulk: 1 busta.
Biography: Enea Sbarretti was born in Spoleto on January 27, 1808, and died in Rome on May 1, 1884. He was a renowned scholar in ecclesiastical law. He became a cardinal on March 12, 1877; he was prefect of the congregations Economica and Propaganda Fide, and president of the Camera degli Spogli.
Scope: Materials in the busta include supplications of a judicial nature and various letters and printed materials.
Location: Archivio Segreto Vaticano.

7.10.182 Spoglio del Placido Maria Schiaffino
[DATABASE ID: VATV10734-A]
Inclusive Dates: [18—]–[18—].
Bulk: 1 busta.
Biography: Placido Maria Schiaffino was born in Genoa on September 9, 1829, and died in Rome on September 23, 1889. He became cardinal on July 27, 1885. He was bibliotecario and apostolic administrator of the abbey in Subiaco.
Scope: Materials in the busta pertain to the Vatican Library, the abbey in Subiaco, and miscellaneous matters.
Location: Archivio Segreto Vaticano.

7.10.183 Spoglio del Enrico Sibilia
[DATABASE ID: VATV10735-A]
Inclusive Dates: [18—?]–[19—?].
Bulk: 1 busta.
Biography: Enrico Sibilia was born in Anagni on March 17, 1861, and died on August 4, 1948. He was uditore of the Rota and an apostolic nuncio to Chile (1908–1914) and Austria

(1922–1935). Sibilia became a cardinal on December 16, 1935, and was bishop of Sabina and Poggio Mireto.

Scope: The busta contains printed cases from the Rota and personal letters.

Location: Archivio Segreto Vaticano.

7.10.184 Spoglio del Demetrio Silvagni-Loreni

[DATABASE ID: VATV10736-A]

Inclusive Dates: 1829–1863.

Bulk: 6 buste.

Biography: Demetrio Silvagni-Loreni was luogotenente of the Tribunale Criminale del Camerlengato, assessor of the Direzione Generale di Polizia, and a judge of the Supremo Tribunale della Consulta during the pontificates of Gregory XVI and Pius IX.

Scope: Materials in the six buste pertain to various criminal cases (particularly against conspirators and in Perugia, Montalto di Castro, and Senigallia), the papal stand against secret societies, and administrative reform of the Camerlengato and the Tesorierato. The buste also contain a number of miscellaneous records of a personal and official nature.

Location: Archivio Segreto Vaticano.

7.10.185 Spogli Giovanni Simeoni

[DATABASE ID: VATV10737-A]

Inclusive Dates: [18—]–[18—].

Bulk: 2 buste.

Biography: Giovanni Simeoni was born in Paliano on July 23, 1816, and died on January 14, 1892. He was a nuncio in Spain. Simeoni became cardinal on September 12, 1875. He succeeded Cardinal Antonelli as secretary of state and was later prefect of the Propaganda Fide.

Scope: The two buste contain miscellaneous manuscript and printed personal and official materials including some pertaining to the Propaganda Fide.

Location: Archivio Segreto Vaticano.

7.10.186 Spoglio del Lorenzo Simonetti

[DATABASE ID: VATV10738-A]

Inclusive Dates: ca. 1849–1856.

Bulk: 1 busta.

Biography: Lorenzo Simonetti was born in Rome and died there on January 9, 1855. He was successively secretary of the Congregazione degli Studi and assessor of the Inquisizione. He became a cardinal on November 24, 1845, and became segretario dei memoriali.

Scope: Materials in the busta pertain to the segretario dei memoriali, the Concilio, and other offices and congregations. There are also some original briefs and miscellaneous family papers.

Location: Archivio Segreto Vaticano.

7.10.187 Spogli Giovanni Soglia

[DATABASE ID: VATV10739-A]

Inclusive Dates: 1848–1856.

Bulk: 1 busta.

Biography: Giovanni Soglia was born in Casola Valsenio on October 11, 1779, and died in 1856. He became a cardinal on February 18, 1839. Soglia served in the office of the secretary of state and was bishop of Osimo and Cingoli.

Scope: Materials in the busta concern Soglia's work in the office of the secretary of state and as bishop of Osimo e Cingoli.

Location: Archivio Segreto Vaticano.

7.10.188 Spoglio del Giuseppe Spina

[DATABASE ID: VATV10740-A]

Inclusive Dates: 1800–1822.

Bulk: 1 busta.

Biography: Giuseppe Spina was born in Sarzana on March 12, 1756, and died on October 13, 1828. He was archbishop of Genoa and prefect of the Signatura di Giustizia.

Scope: Materials in the busta are diverse. There is a group of letters written from Paris during the Napoleonic exile of Pope Pius VI from Rome. Other records pertain to the archdiocese of Genoa and the apostolic delegation in Bologna.

Location: Archivio Segreto Vaticano.

7.10.189 Spoglio del Ugo Spinola

[DATABASE ID: VATV10741-A]

Inclusive Dates: 1819–1860.

Bulk: 6 buste.

Biography: Ugo Spinola was born in Genoa on June 29, 1791, and died in Rome on January 23, 1858. He was apostolic delegate to Perugia, Macerata, and then Tolentino. Spinola became a cardinal on July 12, 1832. He served as commissario straordinario a Bologna (1833–1835) and then as pro-datario.

Scope: Materials in the six buste pertain to the apostolic delegations in Perugia, Tolentino, Macerata, and Camerino. Records also concern legal and financial reform as part of larger administrative reforms in the Papal States. A few items concern the commissario straordinario di Bologna; the Congregazione di Revisione dei Conti; and various cities and religious houses for which Spinola served as protector, including Forlì, San Leo, Poli, Terni (orphanage, which contains an apostolic visit from 1836 to 1840), and the Suore di S. Anna di Torino and the church and ospizio di S. Giuliano dei Fiamminghi.

Location: Archivio Segreto Vaticano.

7.10.190 Spogli Talbot

[DATABASE ID: VATV10742-A]

Inclusive Dates: 1861.

Bulk: 1 busta.

Biography: This collection likely relates to Monsignor George Talbot, the younger son of Lord Talbot. He was received into the church in 1847, and later ordained by (then) Bishop Wiseman. Talbot's position in the Vatican was unique. He was not only chamberlain to Pius IX but a close friend and his constant attendant. This gave Talbot unusual influence in Rome which was considered by many to be unwarranted. Talbot also remained a close friend of Cardinal Manning. In 1869 Talbot was removed from the Vatican to an asylum where he died in 1886.

Scope: Materials include a brief report from France (1861).

Location: Archivio Segreto Vaticano.

7.10.191 Spoglio del Camillo Tarquini

[DATABASE ID: VATV10743-A]

Inclusive Dates: [18—]–[18—].

Bulk: 1 busta.

Biography: Camillo Tarquini was born in Marta on September 27, 1810, and died in Rome on February 15, 1874. He distinguished himself as a legal scholar in canon law, taught at the Collegio Romano, and was a consultor to various congregations. He became a cardinal on December 22, 1873.

Scope: Materials in the busta include various printed materials concerning the Holy Office, the Index, the concordat of 1801, and other matters. This series includes material relating to the competency of the Holy Office and the Index.

Location: Archivio Segreto Vaticano.

7.10.192 Spoglio del Federico Tedeschini
[DATABASE ID:VATV10744-A]
Inclusive Dates: 1914–1959.
Bulk: 25 buste.
Biography: Federico Tedeschini was born in Antrodoco on October 12, 1873, and died on November 2, 1959. He served as cancelliere dei Brevi and sostituto for the office of the Secretary of State (1914–1921). After that he was named apostolic nuncio in Spain, where he remained until 1935. Tedeschini became a cardinal on March 13, 1933. He was bishop of Frascati, archpriest of the Basilica of S. Pietro, prefect of the Fabbrica, datario, and a protector of many religious institutes and a member of many congregations.
Scope: Material in the buste reflects Tedeschini's ecclesiastical career. Some items pertain to the office of sostituto of the secretary of state, the apostolic nunciature for Spain, the Congregazione dei Seminari ed Università degli Studi, the Riti, the Concilio, the Datary, the Congregazione per gli Affari Ecclesiastici Straordinari, the Rota, the Amministrazione dei Beni della S. Sede, the Segnatura, the revision of the Code of Canon Law, the basilicas of S. Pietro and S. Paolo, and various religious institutes including the Oeuvre de St. Paul Apostolat par la presse.
Location: Archivio Segreto Vaticano.

7.10.193 Spoglio del Francesco Tiberi
[DATABASE ID: VATV10745-A]
Inclusive Dates: ca. 1837–1838.
Bulk: 1 busta.
Biography: Francesco Tiberi was born in Rieti on January 4, 1775, and died on October 29, 1839. He became a cardinal on September 30, 1831. He also served as prefect of the Segnatura di Grazia.
Scope: Materials in the busta concern legal reform and Tiberi as protector of the city of Rieti.
Location: Archivio Segreto Vaticano.

7.10.194 Spoglio del Bernardo Tirabassi
[DATABASE ID: VATV10746-A]
Inclusive Dates: ca. 1841.
Bulk: 1 busta.
Biography: Bernardo Tirabassi was a minutante in the office of the secretary of state.
Scope: Materials in the busta include letters from Monsignor Carlo Sacconi to Canonico Tirabassi for the nunciature for Torino (1841).
Location: Archivio Segreto Vaticano.

7.10.195 Spoglio del Giulio Tonti
[DATABASE ID: VATV10747-A]
Inclusive Dates: [18—?]–[19—?].
Bulk: 1 busta.

Biography: Giulio Tonti was born in Rome on December 9, 1844, and died on December 11, 1918. He became a cardinal on December 6, 1915, and was prefect of the Congregazione dei Religiosi.
Scope: Materials in the busta are primarily personal letters to various people in Portugal (in Portuguese).
Location: Archivio Segreto Vaticano.

7.10.196 Spoglio del Antonio Tosti
[DATABASE ID: VATV10748-A]
Inclusive Dates: ca. 1823–1844.
Bulk: 4 buste.
Biography: Antonio Tosti was born in Rome on October 4, 1776, and died there on March 20, 1866. He was chargé d'affaires for the Holy See in Turin and later tesoriere generale. He became a cardinal on February 12, 1838. In 1854, Tosti was nominated librarian of the Holy Roman Church.
Scope: Materials in the four buste pertain to the Camera, the tesoriere generale, Tosti's work as chargé d'affaires in Turin, the Ospizio Apostolico San Michele, the archconfraternity of SSmo. Nome di Maria, the English College in Rome, the restoration of the Basilica of San Paolo, the ministero delle Armi, Acque, e Strade, and various other criminal cases, protectorates, and congregations.
Reference: Enciclopedia cattolica (Vatican City, 1948).
Location: Archivio Segreto Vaticano.

7.10.197 Spogli Tiberio Trani
[DATABASE ID: VATV10749-A]
Inclusive Dates: ca. 1849–1850.
Bulk: 1 busta.
Biography: Tiberio Trani was director of customs during the pontificate of Pius IX.
Scope: Materials in the busta concern various financial and personal matters of Trani.
Location: Archivio Segreto Vaticano.

7.10.198 Spoglio del Luigi Tripepi
[DATABASE ID: VATV10750-A]
Inclusive Dates: ca. 1883.
Bulk: 1 busta.
Biography: Luigi Tripepi was born in Cardeto on June 21, 1836, and died on December 29, 1906. He became a cardinal on August 15, 1901. Tripepi was prefect of the Congregazione delle Indulgenze e Reliquie and sostituto for the office of the secretary of state.
Scope: Materials in the busta relate primarily to the Commissione Cardinalizie per gli studi storici. Other items include Tripepi's will and the legal case surrounding his estate.
Location: Archivio Segreto Vaticano.

7.10.199 Spoglio del Giuseppe Ugolini
[DATABASE ID: VATV10751-A]
Inclusive Dates: 1816–1867.
Bulk: 4 buste.
Biography: Giuseppe Ugolini was born in Macerata on January 9, 1783, and died in Rome on December 19, 1867. He served successively as apostolic delegate to Frosinone, prosegretario di Propaganda Fide, presidente delle Armi, and giudice della Commissione Speciale Deputata per le Cause Poli-

tiche. Ugolini was nominated cardinal on February 12, 1838. He was a member of the Censo.

Scope: Materials in the four buste pertain to the Propaganda Fide, the apostolic delegation in Frosinone (particularly regarding brigands), the legation in Turin, various political conspiracies, the Censo, and persecution of the Catholic Church in Russia and Poland.

Location: Archivio Segreto Vaticano.

7.10.200 Spoglio del Silvio Valenti Gonzaga
[DATABASE ID: VATV10760-A]
Inclusive Dates: 1744–1747.
Bulk: 1 busta.
Biography: Silvio Valenti Gonzaga was secretary of state under Pope Benedict XIV.
Scope: The busta contains letters of a private nature regarding France during the years 1744–1747.
Location: Archivio Segreto Vaticano.

7.10.201 Spoglio del Luigi Vannicelli Casoni
[DATABASE ID: VATV10752-A]
Inclusive Dates: 1835–1877.
Bulk: 9 buste.
Biography: Luigi Vannicelli Casoni was born in Amelia on April 16, 1801, and died in Rome on April 21, 1877. He was vice-commissario delle Quattro Legazioni and later governor of Rome. Vannicelli Casoni became a cardinal in 1842. He served as vice-camerlengo, legate to Bologna, and president of the Censo. In 1850 he was elected archbishop of Ferrara and in 1870, pro-datario. He continued to act as archbishop after becoming pro-datario.
Scope: Materials in the nine buste contain information on many of the public administrative and judicial reform movements in nineteenth-century Italy. They also contain information on the Quattro Legazioni (including Bologna and Forlì), the office of vice-camerlengo, the Censo, and other congregations. The records also document the offices of the governor of Rome, the Direzione Generale di Polizia, and the inundation of the Po River in 1872.
Location: Archivio Segreto Vaticano.

7.10.202 Spoglio del Carlo Giovanni Villani
[DATABASE ID: VATV10753-A]
Inclusive Dates: 1850–1858.
Bulk: 2 buste.
Biography: Carlo Giovanni Villani was consigliere di stato during the pontificate of Pius IX.
Scope: The buste contain materials from the office of the Consiglio di Stato (1850–1858).
Location: Archivio Segreto Vaticano.

7.10.203 Spoglio del Clemente Villecourt
[DATABASE ID: VATV10754-A]
Inclusive Dates: ca. 1787–1867.
Bulk: 2 buste.
Biography: Clement Villecourt was born in Lyons, France, on October 9, 1787, and died in Rome in 1867. He was bishop of La Rochelle (1836–1855). He became a cardinal on December 17, 1855. He was a member of the following congregations: Bishops and Regulars, the Council, the Index, and Rites. He also was a protector of various religious societies.

Scope: Materials in the buste pertain to the congregations of the Index, the Holy Office, the Rota, and the Secretariat of State, as well as the diocese of La Rochelle.
References: G. Moroni, *Dizionario di erudizione storico-ecclesiastica* (Venice, 1840). *Notizie* (Rome).
Location: Archivio Segreto Vaticano.

7.10.204 Spoglio del Salvatore Vitelleschi
[DATABASE ID: VATV10755-A]
Inclusive Dates: ca. 1870–1875.
Bulk: 1 busta.
Biography: Salvatore Vitelleschi was born in Rome on July 21, 1818, and died on October 17, 1875. He was secretary for the Congregation of Bishops and Regulars. He became a cardinal on September 17, 1875.
Scope: The busta contains materials concerning various reform movements within the papal administration in the nineteenth century and some documents relating to the Congregation of Bishops and Regulars.
Location: Archivio Segreto Vaticano.

7.10.205 Spoglio del Carlo Vizzardelli
[DATABASE ID: VATV10756-A]
Inclusive Dates: 1832–1849.
Bulk: 1 busta.
Biography: Carlo Vizzardelli was born in Monte S. Giovanni on July 21, 1791, and died May 24, 1851. He was secretary for Lettere Latine and then secretary for the Congregazione per gli Affari Ecclesiastici Straordinari. He became a cardinal on January 20, 1848. He served as prefect of the Congregazione degli Studi and followed Pope Pius to Gaeta in 1848–1849.
Scope: Materials in the busta pertain to the Segreteria delle Lettere Latine, and the congregations of the Affari Ecclesiastici Straordinari and Studi.
Location: Archivio Segreto Vaticano.

7.10.206 Spoglio del Alberto Zama
[DATABASE ID: VATV10757-A]
Inclusive Dates: 1893.
Bulk: 1 busta.
Biography: Alberto Zama was sotto-archivista for the office of the secretary of state.
Scope: The collection consists mainly of letters received by Zama regarding the payment of fees.
Location: Archivio Segreto Vaticano.

7.10.207 Spoglio del Carlo Zen
[DATABASE ID: VATV10758-A]
Inclusive Dates: 1817–1818.
Bulk: 1 busta.
Biography: Carlo Zen was apostolic nuncio in Switzerland.
Scope: The busta contains letters from bishops in Switzerland during the years 1817–1818.
Location: Archivio Segreto Vaticano.

7.10.208 Spoglio del Placido Zurla
[DATABASE ID: VATV10759-A]
Inclusive Dates: 1825–1838.
Bulk: 3 buste.
Biography: Placido Zurla was born in Segnano on April 2,

1769, and died on October 20, 1834. He was a member of the Camaldolese order. He became a cardinal on May 16, 1823. He served as vicar general for the diocese of Rome under the pontificate of Gregory XVI. He was also prefect of the Congregazione della Residenza dei Vescovi and Studi.

Scope: Materials in the buste pertain to the secretary of state, vicariato of Rome, conspiracies (particularly concerning the police and a group of former Augustinians), the Congregazione per gli Affari Ecclesiastici Straordinari, the German College in Rome, and religious and sanitation assistance during the years of cholera (1836 and 1837).

Location: Archivio Segreto Vaticano.

Vatican City and Palatine Offices and Administration

THE STATE OF VATICAN CITY WAS ESTABLISHED AS A SOVEREIGN state in the Lateran Treaty of 1929 for the purpose of assuring the independence of the popes. The state has a government separate from the administration of the Catholic Church, but because of the state's tiny size, the government is not extensive.

The chief governing body of the Vatican City is the Pontificia commissione per lo Stato della Città del Vaticano (described below). The governor of the state administers the Vatican City, aided by a central council made up of the directors of the central offices—the Secretariat, Direzione generale dei monumenti, musei e gallerie pontificie (described below), and technical services. The justice system includes a tribunal of first instance, court of appeals (the Rota Romana, described in the section "Roman Curia: Tribunals" of this guide), court of cassation, and supreme tribunal (the Signatura Apostolica, also described in the Tribunals section). The military includes the Guardie nobili pontificia and Guardia palatina d'onore, both largely ceremonial, and the Guardia svizzera pontificia and Gendarmeria pontificia (all four described in the section "Papal Court: Famiglia della santità della Nostro Signore" of this guide).

Records created after 1922 are currently closed to research in the Archivio Segreto Vaticano. As a result, no records of the state of Vatican City are described in this guide, and agency histories are not included for all offices.

The Palatine Administration includes offices for which the pope has authority in his role as bishop of Rome, rather than as head of the Catholic church. It includes a diverse group of offices, with no common history. Although many of these offices were founded prior to 1922, records for their adminstration are not generally accessible.

What follows is a list of agencies attached to the Vatican City State and to the Palatine Administration as found in the *Annuario pontificio* of 1960, the eve of the Second Vatican Council. The purpose of this list is to simply identify offices, many of which are well known but that do not appear in other sections of this guide.

A. OFFICES OF THE VATICAN CITY STATE

Direzione generale dei monumenti, musei e gallerie pontificie
[DATABASE ID: VATV213-A]

This is the official title for the adminstration of the Vatican Museums. As artistic collections organized in appropriate buildings and accessible to the public, the museums originated under Clement XIV (1769–1775) and Pius VI (1775–1800). The museums were under the Prefecture of the Sacred Apostolic Palaces until 1929, when they came under the jurisdiction of the Governor of the State of Vatican City.

The archives of the Vatican Museums remain within the office of the director.

Fondo assistenza sanitaria
[DATABASE ID: VATV133-A]

This office was established in 1953 and has been administered under the supervision of the Pontifical Commission for the State of Vatican City and or the Cardinalitial Commission for the Administration of the Properties of the Holy See.

Pontificia commissione per lo Stato della Città del Vaticano
[DATABASE ID: VATV146-A]

This office was established by Pius XII in 1939 to govern the State of Vatican City, under powers delegated from the Pope.

B. OFFICES OF THE PALATINE ADMINISTRATION

Archivio vaticano
[DATABASE ID: VATV212-A]

Archives of the Church were kept from the earliest times in the Scrinium Sanctai Romanae Ecclesiae. A central archives was established by Paul V in 1611, to serve the administrative needs of the curia. The name Archivio segreto vaticano was applied later.

The archives of the Archivio segreto vaticano remain within the office of the prefect.

Biblioteca apostolica vaticana
[DATABASE ID: VATV135-A]

The Scrinium of the Roman Church existed from the fourth century, functioning as both library and archives. In the sixth century it was under the primicerius notariorum. By the end of the eighth century it was headed by the bibliothecarius, who also served as the chancellor. This library was lost in the thirteenth century. New collections were transferred to Avignon with the papal court, and were left there when the popes returned to Rome. The present library was founded by Nicholas V in about 1450. Until Leo X (1513–1522) appointed the first cardinal librarian (another source says first appointed 1548) the library was under the cardinal camerlengo. Until 1588 the library was known as the Libreria Palatina. In the early seventeenth century archival holdings were removed to the Archivio vaticano.

The archives of the Biblioteca apostolica vaticana remain within the office of the prefect. See C. M. Grafinger, *Beiträge zur Geschichte der Biblioteca Vaticana* (Vatican City, 1996).

Amministrazione dei beni della Santa Sede
[DATABASE ID: VATV129-A]

This office was established in 1926 by the merger of the Administrative Offices of the Prefettura dei Sacri palazzi apostolici and of the Sezione dei dicastri ecclesiastici.

Amministrazione speciale della Santa Sede
[DATABASE ID: VATV132-A]

This office was established in 1929 to administer the funds paid by the Italian government to the Holy See in implementation of the Lateran Treaty.

Nuntius
[DATABASE ID: VATV145-A]

This title was held by two separate offices: one, established in 1948, headed by a layman; the other headed by an ecclesiastic.

Prefettura dei Sacri palazzi apostolici
[DATABASE ID: VATV130-A]

After the dissolution of the Papal States Pius IX entrusted the administration of all the temporalities and goods of the Holy See to the Prefect of the Apostolic Palace (chirograph, Dec. 18, 1876). These duties were formerly performed by the praefectus palatii apostolici (the major-domo, part of the Famiglia della santità di Nostro Signore). Through actions of 1880, 1883, and 1891, administration of the patrimony of the Holy See was turned over to a commission of cardinals. In 1926 the office was merged with the Sezione dei dicastri ecclesiastici to form the Amministrazione dei beni della Santa Sede.

Sezione dei dicastri ecclesiastici
[DATABASE ID: VATV131-A]

The exact date when this office was established is not known. In 1926 it merged with the administrative offices of the Prefettura dei Sacri palazzi apostolici to form the Amministrazione dei beni della Santa Sede.

The Original Armaria of the Archivio Segreto Vaticano

THE ORIGINAL ARMARIA ARE A SET OF SEVENTY-FOUR CABINETS that constitute the earliest material in the ASV. Although they are often referred to as a single unit, they contain materials generated or collected by a number of agencies of the Holy See. Where possible the armaria are listed in this guide under the agency most responsible for their contents. Four armaria could not be assigned to a single agency, and are listed in the section "Miscellaneous official materials" of the guide. What follows is a listing of all of the original armaria, with notations as to where they may be found in the guide.

Armaria I–XXVIII
See Cancellaria Apostolica series *Registra Vaticana*,
872 (ca. 1070 copy)–1605.

Armarium XXIX
See Camera Apostolica series *Armarium XXIX*, diversa
cameralia, 1389–1555.

Armarium XXX
See Camera Apostolica series *Armarium XXX*, diversa
cameralia, 1550–1578.

Armarium XXI
See Camera Apostolica series *Armarium XXXI*,
872–1605.

Armarium XXXII
See Camera Apostolica series *Armarium XXXII*,
[12—]–[15—].

Armarium XXXIII
See Camera Apostolica series *Armarium XXXIII*,
quindennia, 1419–1766.

Armarium XXXIV
See Camera Apostolica series *Armarium XXXIV*,
instrumenta cameralia, 1313–1826.

Armarium XXXV
See Camera Apostolica series *Armarium XXXV*,
[11—]–[15—].

Armarium XXXVI
See Camera Apostolica series *Armarium XXXVI*,
informationes camerales, 1335–1700.

Armarium XXXVII
See Camera Apostolica series *Armarium XXXVII*,
informationes camerales, ca. 1500–1700.

Armarium XXXVIII
See Segreteria dei brevi series *Armarium XXXVIII*,
1508–1734.

Armarium XXXIX
See Miscellaneous official series *Armarium XXXIX*,
1198 (copy)–1556.

Armaria XL–XLI
See Secretaria Apostolica series *Armaria XL–XLI*,
minutae brevium, 1478–1554.

Armaria XLII–XLIII
See Segreteria dei brevi series *Armaria XLII–XLIII*,
minutae brevium, 1555–1656.

Armaria XLIV–XLV
See Secretaria Apostolica series *Armaria XLIV–XLV*,
brevia ad principes et alios viros, 1513–1730.

Armarium XLVI
See Secretariatus Status series *Armarium XLVI*.

Armarium XLVII
See Secretariatus Status series *Armarium XLVII*.

Armarium XLVIII
See Secretariatus Status series *Armarium XLVIII*.

Armarium XLIX
See Secretariatus Status series *Armarium XLIX*.

Armaria L–LI
See Camera Apostolica series *Armaria L–LI*, 872–1590.

Armarium LII
See Miscellaneous official series *Armarium LII*,
1552–1602 and undated.

Armarium LIII
See Miscellaneous official series *Armarium LIII*,
ca. 1200–1500.

Armarium LIV
See Miscellaneous official series *Armarium LIV*.

Armaria LV–LVI
These cabinets are empty.

Armarium LVII
See Camera Apostolica series *Fondo camerale*,
1274–1564, of which this series forms a part.

Armaria LVIII–LIX
These cabinets are empty.

Armarium LX
See Secretariatus Status series *Armarium LX*.

Armarium LXI
See Secretariatus Status series *Armarium LXI*.

Armaria LXII–LXIII
See Secretariatus Status series *Armaria LXII–LXIII*,
1537–1588.

Armarium LXIV
See Secretariatus Status series *Armarium LXIV*,
ca. 1520–1630.

Armaria LXV–LXXIV
See Camera Apostolica series *Fondo camerale*,
1274–1564, of which this series forms a part.

APPENDIX 3

Inventory of Numbered Indici in the Archivio Segreto Vaticano Index Room

WHAT FOLLOWS IS A NUMERICAL LIST OF THE NUMBERED INDICI IN the ASV Index Room as found by project staff in 1996. Following the main list is a listing of the blocchetti indici, a series of card files and files of paper slips also found in the Index Room. Indice numbers preceded by the symbol • are not noted in the description of any records in this guide.

NOTES ON THE INDICI OF THE ASV

The history of the indici is as vast and complex as the Archivio Segreto Vaticano (ASV) itself. However, the indici have evolved and are still evolving. Researchers using the numbered indici should be aware of the principal ways in which all the indici have changed over the years.

A user normally begins using the ASV by visiting the Index Room of the archives, so it is essential that he or she understand the origins and different methodologies used in compiling the various indici. There are three categories of finding aids that together are known as the numbered indici to the collections.

First, there are the modern indici that have been prepared over the past eighty or so years. These are modern access tools to some of the major series in the archives. They resemble modern provenance-based finding aids found in all major archives. Those in the ASV reflect extraordinary scholarship on the part of the archivists and are exceptionally valuable tools. These are with a few exceptions numbered above 1000.

Second, there are indici that were, for the most part, prepared prior to the opening of the archives for research in 1881. These fall into two subcategories. (A) There is an interesting collection of summary registers and inventories that were selected by the ASV staff from the stacks and placed in the Index Room to serve users as indici to the collections. In most cases these particular indici were prepared at the same time as the records themselves and were designed for administrative retrieval of particular records series. These can be much more difficult to use than the modern indici, written in diverse hands and often of unpredictable format. Because there have been many changes in the archives over the years, most notably the losses during the Napoleonic era, many of these older indici are inaccurate with regard to the current contents and organization of the record series they purport to describe. However, these may provide the only evidence of documents that no longer exist. (B) There are some early inventories of documents prepared by early archivists. Particularly important are those that list the contents of the original cabinets or armaria of the ASV. These indici are numbered 1 through 924.

Third, there are a variety of specialized indici that are not provenance-based but rather reflect the interests or the energies of a particular archivist in relation to particular documents or subjects. The most important of these is the *Schedario Garampi*, prepared in the late eighteenth century by Giuseppe Garampi (see in this guide the section "Separate collections, Individual and family papers: Garampi, Giuseppe"), which presents a sometimes chronological listing of selected documents in the *Miscellaneorum armaria* of the archives. There are many others as well. These specialized indici rarely indicate indexing criteria nor do they indicate if they cover all or part of a series. These indici are found within numbers 1 through 924.

The numbered indici are fluid. New numbers are added regularly and others are retired. Finally, users should be aware that the strategy or methodology by which the indici are compiled is often difficult to determine. Many indici (particularly the older) appear to be complete, but upon inspection index only a certain type of document or only cover part of the series. Methodology is rarely stated. Because of our unique access to the stacks, we have been able to point out many of these methodological approaches in the finding aids section of the series descriptions. Therefore, best use of this list can be made in conjunction with the series descriptions.

Users should note that the indici have been renumbered and reordered several times. Thus, if one is using older sources, such as Fink or even Boyle, discrepancies between the text and the current numbering system may cause some confusion.

There are several other places in addition to the Index Room to search for finding aids both inside and outside the ASV. For example, proper administrative practice required the development of inventories and indexes to record series. These access tools were created at the same time as the documents themselves. Some of these are located in the Index Room. Many more are located in the stacks as part of the records series to which they pertain and are not considered by the ASV to be official indici. These particular indexes and inventories were created to facilitate administrative retrieval. They can range from chronological listing of items received to an alphabetical listing by correspondent or diocese. The protocol books for the Congregation of Bishops and Regulars and those for the *Fondo moderno* of the Secretariat of State are examples. (These are in the Index Room but are not part of the numbered indici.) Therefore a careful examination of all the resources on both levels of the Index Room is beneficial.

Some reserved indici are held at the reference desk of the ASV. These are older indici that have been replaced by newer indici, indici deemed too rough for proper research, and indici to collections that cross the 1922 closure date. The older indici that have technically been replaced by newer indici can be useful. Often, they contain unique information (and perhaps a slightly different indexing methodology than the newer indice) that can provide helpful research clues. In general, however, there are more retrieval problems using these indici, so caution is suggested. These indici may be requested at the reference desk.

Users should also be aware of a myriad of published works in many languages that can be used as access tools. These include publications of some actual indici, in-depth studies of records series in the archives such as Katterbach on the supplications, Hoberg on the Rota, or Pásztor on the *Fondo moderno*. Second, there are the major national guides that highlight documents in a variety of series that cover a specific country, done under a variety of auspices. These point to specific material of a particular national interest. Third, there are many editions of particular documents or sets of documents. These are directed in some cases toward analysis and publication of specific items or more general descriptions of major documents relating to a particular subject area. Some of these items are in the Index Room of the ASV or in a separate room in the ASV devoted to related printed works.

Inventories prepared by French archivists when the contents of the Archivio Segreto

Vaticano were removed to Paris at the order of Napoleon are held by the Archives Nationales of Paris. They are described in this guide as Miscellaneous series: *Inventaires (1810–1815) des archives du Vatican et d'autres archives italiennes (L372–L400)*.

All of these different types of indici: numbered and unnumbered indici in the Index Room, published indici, indici remaining in the ASV stacks, and those indici reserved behind the desk, are listed with their corresponding series descriptions in this guide.

References. U. Berlière, "Aux Archives vaticanes." *Revue Bénédictine* 20 (1903): 132–173. L. E. Boyle, *A Survey of the Vatican Archives and of its Medieval Holdings* (Toronto, 1972). K. A. Fink, *Das Vatikanische Archiv: Einführung in die Bestände und ihre Erforschung* (Rome, 1951). M. Giusti, *Studi sui registri di bolle papali* (Vatican City, 1968). G. Gualdo, *Sussidi per la consultazione dell'Archivio Vaticano*, new ed. (Vatican City, 1989). L. Guérard, *Petite introduction aux inventaires des archives du Vatican* (Rome, 1901). A. Mercati, *Schedario Garampi, Registri Vaticani, Registri Lateranensi, Rationes Camerae, Inventario del Fondo Concistoriale*, vol. 1 of *Sussidi per la consultazione dell'Archivio Vaticano* (Rome, 1926).

1-2. Indici di diverse materie fragmenta

• 3. Index generalis diversorum

• 4. Inve. Bon Bon VIII [dorso], capitula inventar di nomina rubricum [internal] [formerly Arm. 56, vol. 45]

• 5. Invent. Bonor. Greg. XII [dorso] [formerly Arm. 56, no. 46]

• 6. Inventario di Leone X [dorso] [formerly Arm. 56, no. 47]

• 7. Armar. IX Ord. II. Inventarium scriptorum que inventa sunt in studio Gregorii Papae XIII notatum subindicis diversorum. Volume VIII. The index also contains several parts with different indici including: Diverse robbe della Guardarobba Si. No. 8 and Tutti libri sotto scritti lo stati consegnati al Card. sa Sixto in pui molte et . . . fu . . . di Sa. Martino 1565

• 8-9. Arm. IX Ord. II. Inventarium scripturarum existentium in Guardarobba Sanctissimi adnotatum sub indicis diversorum, Volumine IX

• 10. Indicum diversorum [spine] Arm. IX Ord. II. Inventarium scripturarum existentium in Arce Sti. Angeli, Volum. VI Anagnin

• 11. Index scripturarum existentium in Castel Sti. Angeli Urbis in Camera Thesaurarii

• 12. Dupplicatus Index scripturarum quae fuercint olim e civiatae Anagnina asportatae, Volumen VII

13-15. Indici by Domenico Ranaldi

• 13. Armar. Ord. Primum inventarium Dmi. Dominici Raynaldi cum aliis fragmentis indicum sub volumine XII [cover] Index alphabeticus praecipriarum uocrim et capitum quae in hoc Volumine XII. Indicum diversorum continentur inter haec habentur inventaria diversa una cumprima divisione et distribution scriptorum facta ad armaria et capsulas in [ferrious?] Archivi Arcis S. Angeli per D. Domini cum Raynaldum olim eiusdem archivi custodem litera. A. Paginam primam litera uero B. Paginam secundam indicat. [title page]

• 14. Indicum diversorum [spine] Armar. IX Ord. II. Indices duarum classium scriptorum, vol. III.

• 15. Indicum diversorum [spine] Armar. IX Ord. II. Indicum scriptorum Pauli Papae. III et ecclesia Ravennae Volume V

• 16. Index archivi Ravennaten ecclesiae [AA Arm. I–XVIII 4946]

• 17. B. Volumen secundum additorum ad capsulam VIII. Armar. XV. Summaria scriptorum ex archivio Ravennae desumptorum [ΛΛ Arm. I–XVIII 4946]

• 18. Nota delli libri et scritture e all giornata di . . . nell'Archivio di Castello . . . da N.S. Clem. VIII

• 19. Indicum frammenti [spine] Armar. IX Ord. II. Inventarium scriptorum et framentorum notabilium adnotatum sub indicis diversorii Volumine XI [cover], by M. Lonigo [This is a group of different indici which have been bound together]

• 20. Indicum diversorum [spine] Armar. IX Ord. II. Inventarum scriptorum quae in XVI armarus inferioribus Archivi Arcis S. Angelicorum capsulis asseruabantur eo tempore . . . Inventarium fuit absolutum quod adnotatur . . . Indicum diversorum Volumine XIII

21-29. Indici by Silvio de Paoli

• 21, part 1. Index MM—Inventario di Castello [spine]

• 21, part 2. Index divers. et . . . • Castri. S. Angeli [dorso]

• 22. Index divers. Arch. Castri. S. Angeli [dorso]

• 23. Index divers. ex Arch. Cast. S. Ang. [spine] [formerly Arm. 56, vol. 29]

• 24. Index divers. ex Cast. St. Angeli HH [spine] [formerly Arm. 56, vol. 30]

• 25-28. Series scripturarum quae in Archivio Arcis S. Angeli continentur iussa SS.mi D.N. Pauli Pape Quinti A Silvio de Paulis disposita. Anno MDCX [formerly Arm. 56, vol. 27]

• 29. Indicum diversorum [spine] Index verborum quae in scriptorum serie Archivi Arcis Hadrienae continentur

30-41. Indici by Michele Lonigo

• 30-31. Leonici vicariatus & infeudatione [spine]

Indicis locupletissimi vicariatum ac infeudationum civitatum, terrarum, et castrorum quae reperiuntur descriptae in libris investituar. Archivi Castri Sti. Angeli Alma Urbis.

Est autem presens index non modo libris investiturarum archici dicti castri, verum et libris antiquis Archivii Camerae Apostolicae accommodatus.

Ex incipit Pars haec prima [secunda] a littera A. extenditurque ad L. [M. extenditurque a Z.] inclusive.

Michaelis Leonici clerici Esten. Illsmi. et Rmi. D.D. Bartholomai tituli Sanctae Mariae in Porticu S. R. Ecca. Presbi. Cardlis. Ceru nuncupati, familiaris domesti. Labore et diligentia in uneim congestus.

Ad Sanctissm. Patrem et Beatm. Dnum. Hrum. D. Paulis V Ste. Rom. e Unlis. Ecca. Pont. Maximum [title page]

• 32-33. Same as 30-31.

• 34. Index Archivii Castri S. Angeli, Michael Leonici [spine] [title page the same as Indici 30 and 32]

34 (old number). Index of cameral material in Registra Avenionensia, by P. Sella [at reference desk]

• 35-36. Same as Indice 30-31 or 32-33.

• 37-38. Index copiosissimus rerum & materiarum oium. quae continentur in libris Archivii Castri Sancti. Angeli, quos uersa pagina docet Michaelis Leonici Clerici Esten. Illsmi. et Rmi. D.D. Bartholomai tituli Sanctae Mariae in Porticu S. R. Ecca. Presbi. Cardlis. Ceru nuncupati, familiaris studio et diligentia in unum congestus.

• 39. Same as 37 and 38

• 40. Index cononum & tributor. Quae Romanae ecclie. soluunt.

• 41. Index locupletissimus nominum omnium civitatum, terrarum, castrorum, et locorum di guibus agitur in decem prioribus libris inuestitur. qui reperiuntur in Archivio Castri S. Angeli Alma. Urbis. Per Michael Leonicum Clericum Esten. in ordine digestus. Ad sanctissimum Patrem et Beatissm. Dominum Paulum Quintum Pontifm. Maxm.

• 42. Index diversorum [spine] In hoc volum. III continentur fragmenta repertorii literarum Julii Papae Secundi, Leonis Papae Decimi, Adriani Sexti, Clementis Septimi, Pauli Terti. Fragmenta classium doctorum theologium. Nota da libri dati al pre toledo. Quidam index alphabeticus. Libellus subtitolo sequenti. Nota delle scritture pervenute in man mia per met-tere nell' Archivio di Castello. Si crede e [Eesia?] di mano dello bo:me: dels Nicolo Alemanni [title page]

43–59. Indici by Giovanni Batista Confalonieri
• 43. Joannis Baptistae Confalonerii sacerdotis Romani Sacrae theologia ac philosophia doctoris prothonotarii apostolici custodis Archivi Arcis Sancti Angeli et decanitrium visitatorum Monasterii Monialium S. Susanna. Eminmus. & Rmus. D. Cardinalis Lantes protector heremitarum port & angelicae nuncupator facemo bene adesso che hauemo tempo in Anno 1624. Hospitii & ecclesiae curum mihi dedit [title page]
• 44. Index diversor. Ca. S. Angeli [spine]
• 45. Armar. IX Ord. II (4) [cover] In hoc voluminum continentur inventarium in summam redactum armarionum inferiorum Archivi Arcis Sancti Angeli [title page]
• 46. Inventarum armar. super. [spine] In hoc volume continentur inventarium scriptorum quae asservantur in armariis superioribus Archivi Arcis Sancti Angeli quod fuit recognitum in eodum archivio per pradatos congregationis hac de causa a Smi. D.N. Urbano Papa 8o institutae vigore et iuxta ten orem litterarum in forma brevis subdat. Romae apud S. Petr. sub Annulo Piscatoris XVII Januarii MDCXXIII pontificatus sui anno primo.
Caeterum litterae eadem servantur armario inferiori XV capsula XVI eiusdem archivi [title page]
• 47. Liber receptorum accommodatorum diversorum ad directionem et conservationem Archivi Castri Sancti Angeli a Joanne Baptista Confaloneris . . . 1626 [title page]
• 48. Joannis Baptiste Confalonerii . . . custodis Archivi Arcis S. Angeli . . . 1624 [title page]
• 49. Inventarium armar. Super. [spine] Scriptorum in charta pergamena olim (v.b. traditur) ab Avenionentibus ad Romanum Pontificem missionum quae anno salutis 1621 è Biblioteca Vaticana ad Archivum Arcis sancti Angeli . . . 1611 [title page]
• 50–52. Summarii scriptorum quae in Archivio Arcis Hadrianae continentur [cover] Pars [Prima-Tertia] inventorii [spine]. [See also Indice 56 for Pars Quarto]
• 53–54. Minutarum IV part seu append. inventarii armariorum XVIII Arch. Arcis S. Angeli cura Joh. Baptae Confalonieri . . . 1626
• 55. [Loose sheets, no real title page, looks like it is the rough notes towards an index]
56. Inventarium additorum [spine] Direttorio per li custodi che faranno dell'Archivio di Castel S. Angelo sopra dell'uso dell'inventarii & indici che si conservano nell'Armario IX Ord. II [title page] Pars quarta siue appendix ad ceteras tres partes mense Januarii anno Domini MDCXXIX [f. 14r, see also ASV Indici 50–52 for parts 1–3] [ff. 3r–10r contains a list of AA indices, project staff could not match any of these to those in the Index Room.] Prepared in 1628 by G. B. Confalonieri.
57. Inventarium [spine] Summarii scriptorum quae in armariis superioribus Archivi Arcis Sancti Angeli asservantur. Liber unicus [title page] Prepared in 1628 by G. B. Confalonieri.
• 58. Index dell'appendice dell'Arch. di Cast. delle collectanee del Lonigo [spine] Joannes Baptista Confalonieri [f. 1] [May 1629]
• 59. Recogno. facta in visitatione de anno 1632 [spine] In hoc volumine notantur scripta recognita & collata cuiis quae

continentur in quarta parte inventarii Archivi Arcis S. Angeli siue in accessione scriptorum illorum quae [hactenus?] praetermissa a Joanne Baptista Confalonierio eiusde, archivi custode observata, et animaduersa propriis arculis quantum fieri potuit fuerunt reposita [title page]

• 60. Diarium Arch. Arcis S. Angeli a car. cartario elabor [spine], by G. Garampi [1638]

61–64. Indici by Carlo Cartari
• 61. Index C . . . [spine] Sommarii curti da me Carlo Cartari alle scritture dell'Archivio di Castello . . . [f. 4]
• 62. Rubrica indici charta [spine]
• 63–64. Indice dell'Archivo. di Castel S. Angelo [tied by ASV in the Indice degl'Indici]

• 65. [No indice located with this number]

66–70. Indici by Giuseppe Garampi
• 66–67. Indici dell'Archivi di Castelli [spine]
   66. [AA Arm. 1–3326]
   67. [AA Arm. 3326–6517]
• 68. Index litterar. pontif. et imperial. quae in Archivo Castri S. Angeli asservantus Joh. XII ad Clem X.
• 69–70. Indice cronologica dell'Archivio di Castel S. Angelo, by G. Garampi [tied by ASV in the Indice degl'Indici]
   69. [364–1539]
   70. [1539–1808]

---

71. Rubricelle di varii papi da Gregorio X a Giulio II [formerly Arm. 50, no. 40A]. [Arm. 35, vols. 3–5 on ff. 20–74; RV 7 rub. beginning on f. 75; RV 682–768, 772–866, 886–925, volume list beginning on f. 179; and RV 1700 (rub) beginning on f. 231.]
• 72. Indices univ. librorum arc. rubric. LX, RRR, compiled by F. Contelori, 17th century,
• 73. Rubricelle regist. sert. et alia
• 74. Excerpta ex diversis libris Camerae usque ad A. 1547 pro censibus infeudationibus et aliis iuribus S.R.E. (ff. 4–157). Inventarium bullarum et scripturarum olim in Bibla. Vata. secreta existen. (ff. 165–195). Index in librum censualem Patrimonii B. Petri olim in Archo. Camere ubi recensentur omnia loca quo tenentur solvere sal Focaticum (ff. 197–199v). Index litterarum arm. I Gregorii XI (ff. 203–215). Censuale S.R.E. ex Cencio camerario (ff. 223 ss.)
• 75. Index aliquorum librorum seu registrorum (Léon X–1609)
• 76. Index generalis super omnilius libris bibliothecae Illmi et Rmi camerarii divisus in provinciis
• 77. Armarii IX, Ordine II, Indices D. Dominici Raynaldi, eorum quae in Archivio Vaticano continentur—Volumen I

78–96. Indici by Michele Lonigo
• 78. De temporali dominio et sprituali iurisdictione Sedis Apostolicae in insula et regno Siciliae (1609)
• 79. Same as 78
• 80–81. Lucubrationum Cameralium (1611)
• 82. De auctoritate Summi Pontificis circa Statum Romani Imperii

• 83. Jura, silicet, Sedis Apostolice in ducatibus Urbini et Montisferetri (1613)

• 84. Praxim previlegiorum Sedis Apostolice, in eam partem que temporalia dominia ejusdem Sedis concernit (1614)

• 85. Lucubrat.

• 86. Eccles. Collectan.

• 87. Fragmentorum seu collectaneorum Michaelis Leonici, volumen VII

• 88. Mot. seu memor. Mic. Leon.

• 89. Jura Sedis Apostolice in regno Anglie

• 90. Jura Sedis Apostolice in regno Aragonie

• 91. Jura diversa ad probandam posessionem et proprietatem Sedis Apostolice in civitatibus, terris et castris infeudatis et nondum devolutis

• 92. Jura Sedis Apostolice in civitate Comachi

• 93. Epistolae ad divers.

• 94. Beneventan. turbate jurisdictionis varia

• 95. Indice delle lettere di Napoli dell'illmo et revermo Sr. card. Rusticucci, anni 1570, 1571, 1585 to 1587

• 96. Index epist. ad reges

• 97. Armarii IX. Ordine II. Summarii et indicis scriptorum civitatum, castrorum, terrarum et locorum. Volum. II

• 98. Summarium diversorum actorum sub diversis pontificibus ad Cameram Ap. pertinentium

99–116. Indici by Felice Contelori
[according to Gualdo]

99–105. Historia cameralis

• 106. Repertorium de electione Romani Pontificis

• 107. Genealogia familiae Comitum Romanorum, quae am primariis nobilitatis Romanae principibus affinitates indicantur e probatis eunta documentis [BAV Vat. Lat. 12612]

• 108. De comitissae Mathildis genere et donatione partes duae [BAV Vat. Lat. 12613]

• 109. Excerpta ex historicis pro genere materno et materno [sic] Mathildis [BAV Vat. Lat. 12614]

110. Index librorum 112 diversorum scripturarum confecta Rmo. Dmo. Felice Contelorio et unitorum per me Joannen Bissaigham & fuit compactus an 1694 [formerly Arm. 58, vol. 41]

111–114. F. Contelori's exerpts of documents. [formerly Arm. 58, vols. 37–40]

112. [Includes summaries of Reg. Lat. of Martin V, f. 276–345]

• 115. Copie exerpta et lucubrationibus Contelori, seu indicis lit. A. a pag. 599 usque ad 642. [formerly Arm. 58, vol. 36]

• 116. Copie ut supra ex lucubrationibus Contelorii, seu indicis lit. A, vol. III [formerly indice 41]

• 117. Centoflorenus Constantius—Cameralia 1650. [formerly Arm 58, vol. 21]

• 118. Index libri cameralia inscripti per Centoflorenum [formerly Arm. 58, vol. 23]

• 119. Copie praecedentis indicis [formerly Arm. 58, vol. 24]

• 120. Primo sbozzo dell' Archivio Vaticano dettato da Costanzo Centofiorini

• 121. Centofiori. Indici delle materie, che si contengono ne' registri o libri dell' Archivio Vat. (illegible marginal note indicates that this is copy of something n. 122) [formerly Arm. 58, vol. 22)

• 122. Centofiori. 1646 Copy of 121.

• 123. Camppius Antonius. Tractatus de rebus Camerae Apostolicae [formerly Arm. 58, vol. 42]

124–132. Indici by Giovanni Bissaiga

124. Primo sbozzo d'inventario di tutti i libri che sono nell'Archivio Secreto Vaticano [by Giovanni Bissaiga, 1672] [formerly Arm. 56, vol. 54]

125. Copy of 124, 1673 [formerly Arm. 56, vol. 36]

126. Indice de libri di Mons. Contilori segnati a tergo A . . . V con l'indice di diverse bolle stampate [1673]

127. Bissaiga Giovanni. Quinterni di note giornaliere [formerly Indice 40]

• 128–131. Bissaiga. Memorie

    128. 1685–1687. [formerly Indice 43]

    129. 1687–1688 [formerly Indice 42]

    130. 1688 [formerly Indice 44]

    131. 1689–1690 [formerly Indice 45]

• 132. Indice delle memorie del Bissaiga fatto da Io. de Giuliis [formerly Arm. 56, vol. 52]

133–136. Indici by Pietro Donnino de Pretis

133. De Pretis Petrus Dominus. Inventarium Archivii Secreti Vaticani. This is an inventory by volume of the armaria, I–LXXIV of the original Archivio Segreto Vaticano. [formerly Indice 118]

134. De Pretis . . . 1731, Inventario delle nunziature. [formerly Indice 119]

135. Continuatione dell'inventario della nunciatura di Germania [formerly Indice 121]

136. De Pretis Dominio. Inventario degli armadi delle miscellanee. (I, i, 1901)

---

137. Index iurum sanctae et apostol. Rom. eccle. euisq. rev. cam. in civitatibus terris aliisq. sibi subiectis locis in secretiori Vaticano charthophylacio asseruatorum Iulio Monterentio et Fel. e Contilor. o olim eiusden Camerae Commissarrio Generalibus accurantibus Pars. Prima complectens, civites, terras, alias, loca &c., 1734

138. Indice generale delle scritture di Monsig.r de Rossi fatte per servitio della Rev. Camera dall'anno 1644 fino al 1673 le quali si conservano in Archivio Vaticano in 16 volumi, ne quali si principia dal 1673 andando in dietro. Quali Indice per maggior regola si è fatto con ordine retrogrado [formerly Arm. 36, Tom. 48]

• 139. Indici dei regg. bollari di Greg. XIII e Sisto V dell'Archivio della Segreteria dei brevi

140–141. Fondo Carpegna

142. Fondo Bolognetti

143–144. Fondo Albani

• 145. Indice delle scritture d'Avignone che hora stanno nella sala sopra l'Archivio Secreto nell'palazzo Apostolico di S. Pietro in Vaticano. 1671

• 146. Liber cerimoniarum Curiae Romanae. Modus servendi in domo cardinalium [BAV Borghese Lat. 390]

147. Instrumenta miscellanea

• 148. Index diariorum magistrorum caeremoniarum opere et cura Joannis Bissaigha et Constantii Centofloreni [BAV Vat. Lat. 12326]

• 149. Rubricella per materie delli bandi che si conservano nell'Archivio Apostolico di Castel S. Angelo

150–151. Subject indices to the Collezione Ottoboniana (also known as the Bandi verdi).

• 152. Indice di una collezione di bandi che non e nell'ASV

• 153. Indice di bandi

• 154. Index diplomatum et bullarum que continentur in tribus tomis. Platine asservatis in Arm. III. Ord. II. tum etiam rerum que continentur in libro qui inscribitur "Memorialium" Arm. IV. caps. III.

155. Repertorio in forma dopia per Cognomi [Index SS. Gregorio e Siro]

• 156. Indice de tomi e de mazzi di carte che si mandano al sig. Canonico Giuseppe Garampi nella sede vacante dopo la morte della S.Ma. di PP. Benedetto XI8 da conservarsi nell'Archivio Segreto Vaticano [traces of some volumes in extant series.]

157. Elenco delle Casse della Ch. Me. del Cardinal Garampi [Fondo Garampi]

158–167. Indice alfabetico delle principali materie contenute nel registro cronologico delle Miscellanee dell'Archivio Vaticano, by G. Garampi [Some citations to volumes in current series, Armarii particularly]

• 168–184. Registro cronologico dell'Archivio Segreto

    168. 1550–1559
    169. 1560–1569
    170. 1570–1579
    171. 1580–1589
    172. 1590–1599
    173. 1600–1609
    174. 1610–1619
    175. 1620–1629
    176. 1630–1639
    177. 1640–1649
    178. 1650–1659
    179. 1660–1669
    180. 1670–1679
    181. 1680–1689 [formerly Indice 81]
    182. 1690–1699 [formerly Indice 82]
    183. 1700–1709 [formerly Indice 83]
    184. 1710–1719, 1720, 1721. [formerly Indice 84]

• 185. Repertorio cronologico di lettere scritte dai papi ai principi e vescovi edite dal 30 novembre 1700 fino al 1.o ottobre 1767. [formerly Indice 85]

186–189. Index rerum praecipue ecclesiasticarum regni Poloniae, 1776. [formerly Indice 103] [These have been removed from the Index Room and are now identified as Archivio della Nunziatura Apostolica di Polonia, vols. 2–5]

    186. Vol. 1, Tome 1 Litt. A ad D
    187. Vol. 1, Tome 2 Litt. E ad L
    188. Vol. 2, Tome 1 Litt. L ad R
    189. Vol. 2, Tome 2 Litt. R ad Z

190–191. Index rerum praecipue ecclesiasticarum regni Poloniae, copy of Indici 186–189

    190. Vol. 1, Litt. A ad L
    191. Vol. 2, Litt. M ad Z

192. Fondo Borghese = Schedario fatto dall' Archivista di Casa Borghese Sig. Passerini, e legato nell' Archivio Vaticano. Lettere A–Z

193. Inventario dell'Archivio Borghese donato all'Archivio Vaticano dall' Istituto Storico Prussiano

194. Inventario dei manoscritti di Gio. Battista Confalonieri della Serie 3.a della bulle e dei bandi collocati nella Camera, che mette alla biblioteca di consultazione 1425–1854, degli avvisi 1605–1707, e della concordanza dei numeri dei libri Introitus et Exitus ossia del numero vecchio col nuovo. 1900

195. Inventarium supplicationum Datariae Apostolicae a Clement PP. VI ad Pium PP. VII–1900

195A. 1902 Inventario dei 984 volumi del Commissariato della armi. 1904 Inventarium voluminum brevium Datariae Apostolicae quae in Archivio Apostolico Vaticano reposa sunt mense Maii 1904

• 196. Index anonymus [formerly Arm. 56, vol. 20] [Vat. Lat. 12675]

• 197. Archivi terrae asprae sabinen epitaomae [formerly Indice 95] [Vat. Lat. 12676]

• 198. Index librorum manuscriptorum qui in bibliotheca Emmi. et Revmi. D. Palatii Cardlis. de Alteris S.R.E. Camerarii servantur per ordinam alphabeticum digestus ab Abbate Fagnano eisdem bibliothecae custode [formerly Arm. 56, vol. 15] [Vat. Lat. 12677]

199. Ripartimento di manoscritti dell'Emmi. Sigr. Cardle. Scipione Borghese [formerly Arm. 56, vol. 14]

• 200. Indice delle materie, che si contengono in diversi tomi di MM. in folgio esistenti nella libraria dell' Eccmo. Sig. Principe Chigi. [formerly Arm. 56, vol. 7] [Vat. Lat. 12618]

• 201. Nominum et cognominum quae in codicibus manuscriptis (Bibliothecae Chigianae) continentur index generalis a Vincentio Mannaiono ordinatus et conscriptus [formerly Arm. 56, vol. 4] [Vat. Lat. 12619]

• 202. Index brevis auctoram tantammmodo a Vincentio Mannaiono conscriptus. [formerly Arm. 56, vol. 5] [Vat. Lat. 12620]

• 203. Inventarium manuscriptum Vincentii Mannaoini notandum, quod non concordat cum hudierno codicum ordine. [formerly Arm. 56, vol. 6] [Vat. Lat. 12621]

• 204. Inventario manoscritto della fe. me: dell' Emo. Sig. Cardinal Flavio Chigi [formerly Arm. 56, vol. 9] [Vat. Lat. 12622]

• 205. Exemplar praecidentis [formerly Arm. 56, vol. 10] [Vat. Lat. 12623]

• 206. Inventarium librorum glo. me: Sigismundi Chigii S.R.E. Cardinalis confectum de mandato Excmi. Principis D. Augusti Chigii anno millesimo septingentesimo sexto [formerly Arm. 56, vol. 11] [Vat. Lat. 12624]

• 207. Index manuscriptorum, quae in bibliotheca Chigiana asserrantar [formerly Arm. 56, vol. 12] [Vat. Lat. 12625]

• 208. Index archivi Chigianii [formerly Arm. 56, vol. 13] [Vat. Lat. 12627]

• 209. Indice di quanto si contiene in un manoscritto della libraria Chigiana di scritture che Papa Alessandro VII tenera appresso di se col titolo Napoli e Spagna [Vat. Lat. 12628]

• 210. Index bibliotecae illustrissimi ac Revmi. Domini Joannis Ciampini. Materiai. [formerly Arm. 56, vol. 62] [Vat. Lat. 12629]

• 211. Index librorum bibliothecae Illmi. ac. Revmi. Joannes Ciampini. Nomina. [formerly Arm. 56, vol. 17] [Vat. Lat. 12630]

• 212. Index bibliothecae Illmi. ac Revmi. Dni. Joannes Ciampini. Cognomina. [formerly Arm. 56, vol. 18] [Vat. Lat. 12631]

213. Index di libri di Mons. Ciampini, alcune de quale

sono stati comprati da Il. Sg.le Clemente XI, e posti nell'studi . . . e fuori sono stati segnali con la lett. C. e posti in diversi luoghi secundo le materie delle quali trattavono. [formerly Arm. 56, vol. 19]

214. Rubricellone di tutte le scritture istromenti testamenti ed altro che attualmente si conservano nell'archivio domestico dell'Emo. e Revmo. Sig. Card. Camillo Cybo poste in ordinanza co' suoi ristretti distintamente secondo le loro materie e serie de tempi da Matteo Gioia l'anno MDCCXXXVII [formerly Arm. 56, vol. 19]

215. Rubricellone delle scritture appartenenti alla serenissa. casa Cybo messe in ordinanza con suoi ristretti e serie dei tempi.

216. Rubricellone delle scritture appartenenti al palazzo e villa ed altri effetti in Castel Gandolfo, e di tutte le giustificazioni per l'alienarioni fatte d'alcuni capitali soggetti al fideicomso. e primogenitura della Serenissa. casa Cybo in luogo dei quali restano surrogati il pal[?u]rrino, villa ed effetti sudetti. Tutto in ordine con susi. Ristretti secondo la serie de loro tempi.

•217. Indice de' manoscritti che sono nella libraria dell' Emo Sigr. Card. Lorenzo Cortini l'anno 1706 [formerly Arm. 56, vol. 16] [Vat. Lat. 12631]

218. Indici di diverse librarie di manoscritti [formerly Arm. 56, vol. 22]

Indici Card. Ceva, ff. 2 (de Libri); ff. 54 (de Manoscritti) ora Misc. Arm. III 31–47

Indici Abbte. Gaii, ff. 76

Indici Card. Sigismondo Chigi, ff. 106

Indici Collegio Capranica, ff. 114

Indici Casa Mattei, ff. 140

Indici Card. Pio, ff. 150 (a copy of ASV Indice 219, ff. 101–)

Indici Archivio della Basilica Vaticana, ff. 199

Indici Archivio della SS. Nunziature, ff. 216

Nota delli libri et scritture migliori ritrovate nel Archivio della Nunziatura di Roma da Sig. Card. Vervallo fra la scritture di Urbano [by Lonigo]

Indici Camillo Tolomei, ff. 232

219. Index manuscriptorum codicum bibliothecae Serenissme [formerly Arm. 56, vol. 53]

Reginae Christinae Sveciae

Emi. Cardinalis Pio

Bibliothecae Ambrosianae Mediolami

Bibliothecae Barberini

Bibliothecae Casinensis

Librorum orientalium in folio Illmi Xri. Comitto Marsilii

Bibliothecae Slusianae

•219A. Inventario di tutti li libri, conti e scritture che si trovano nell'Archivio della Rev. Camera Apostolica in palazzo per tutto questo di 21 d'agosto 1631 da Ridolfo [GS] cilandaria. [formerly Arm. 56, vol. 37] [A large section concerns fabbriche. This is an index to books which authorize payments with a note about what the books cover, e.g., f. 203 Un libro in foglio coperti di corame conti delle fabbriche che fatta in Roma dell'anno 1542.]

•220. Inventario dei libri, che si sono trovati nell'Archivio della Tesoreria della Camera Apostolica fatto da mettieronno. da Tarano notaro dell'Auditore della Camera consegnati a me Vincentio Renzi tanto in nome mio come di m. Cesare Fontana 1562.

•221. Ristretto delle materie contenute nel presente inventario de'libri conti e scritture esistenti nell'Archivio della Computisteria Generale della Revda. Camera Apostolica nel Palazzo Vaticano fatto coll'authorità di Mons. Illmo. e Revmo. Gio: Fransceso Banchieri Tesoriere generale di N. Sre. l'anno 1747. Avuto dall'eredità del sudetto Emo. Banchieri l'anno 1763. [formerly Indice 89]

•222. Copia del precedente ristretto—Avuto dall'eredità del Emo. Banchieri nel 1763. [formerly Arm. 56, vol. 60] [Avuto della eredità del sud. Emo. Banchieri 9 bre 1763] [This is a bella copia of 221 and much easier to read.]

223. Inventario delle materie dell'Archivio Camerale— Diversorum [formerly Indice 57] [già v. ora il codice 195A]

•224. Inventario dell'Archivio della Città di Terracina, che si conserva nella sagrestia di S. Cesario formato nel giugno dell'anno MDCCLXXXI. con copie o ristretto di parecchi documenti del medesimo archivio con un inventario in fine dell'archivio della catedrale, e copia e ristretto di alcuni monumenti. I monumenti già stampati dal Contalori historia Terracinae per le varianti, che si sono incontrate, sono state correrre a margine della stampa annessa alla presente raccolta. To. 1 [formerly Indice 90] [Vat. Lat. 12632]

•225. Contalore Dominicus Antonius. De historia Terracincen. Libri Quinque. 1706. [formerly Indice 91] [Vat. Lat. 12633]

•226. Pergamene e carte originali levate dall'Archivio di Terracina nell'estate dell'anno 1781. [formerly Indice 94] [Vat. Lat. 12634]

227. Inventarium omnium et singulorum privilegiorum, litterarum, diplomatum et monumentorum quaecumque in Archivio Regni in Avce. Cracov. continentur per Commissarios a Sac. Reg. Maiestate et Republica ad revidendum et connotandum omnes scripturas in eodem Archivio existentes deputato confectum Anno Domini MDCLXXXII, et repositum in Archivio Molis Hadrianae die 20 Martii 1713 a Dominico Rivera. [formerly Indice 102]

•228. Raccolta di notizie spettante alle famiglie Romane estratte dai libri e registri dell'Archivio Capitolino. [formerly Arm. 56, vol. 42] [Vat. Lat. 12635]

•229. Index Anonimus partis praccedentetis voluminis instrumentorum Archivi Capitolini. [formerly Arm. 56, vol. 43] [Vat. Lat. 12636]

•230. Inventario delli libri della regina di Svetiae stima fatta dei medesimi, et alcuni fogli d'osservzioni in ordine a detti libri et alla compra della libraria. [formerly Arm. 56, vol. 3] [Vat. Lat. 12637]

231. Rubricella delli tomi tre di minute di Brevi a Principi di Paolo V e Gregorio XV. [Questo volume fu trovato dall'Emo. Garampi nello spoglio delle sue carte rimasse alla cifra e fra consegnato a Callisto . . . 1786. [Organized by type of business.]

•232–233. Inventaire de l'Archiv Apostolique d'Avignon. Pio VI Pontifice Maximo Principe Optimo i[m?]bente Lazaro Opizio S.R.E. Card. Pallavincino status administro moderante Jacobo Filomarino pro legato mandatis suffragante subversa huius tabularii documenta in ordinem restituit Carolus Bondacca auditor Anno MDCCLXXX.

232. To. 1 A–D.

233. To. 2 E–Z.

•234–236. Exemplar praecedentis sub n. 233

234. To. 1. A–C

235. To. 2. D–Z
236. To. 3. E–Z
•236A. Caleppi Lorenzo—Catalogo degli emigranti francesi 1793. Passate al fondo Emigranti no. 50.
•237. Index cronologicus [Indice cronologico di diplomi imperiali e bolle pontificie edite ed inedite concedute a diversi paesi d'Italia, sopra tutto ad Arezzo ed a Siena. Essi cominciano dall'anno 702 fino al 1750. [formerly Indice 86] [Arezzo—Archivio Capitolare]
•238–239. Index Bibliothecae Spada.
238. Tome 1. A–L [Vat. Lat. 12638]
239. Tome 2. M–Z [Vat. Lat. 12639]

240–288. Indexes to the Vatican registers

240. Repertorium bullarium Joannis VIII et Gregorii VII. John VIII (RV 1) and Gregory VII (RV 2), by Michele Lonigo, 1614 [formerly Arm. 50, vol. 1]
•241. Gregory VII [?]
242–243. Index prosopographicus et geographicus in epistolas Innocentii PP. III, cura et aere. Iosephi Garampi confectus. Innocent III (RV 4, 5, 7, 7A, 8) [formerly Indice 125–126]
244–251. Index locorum et personarum, quae in iscriptionibus litterarum Honorii III [. . . Bonifatii VIII] Summorum Pontificum occurrunt. Collegit, reconsuit, et alphabetice disposuit Josephus Comes Garampius. Honorius III (RV 9–13), Gregory IX (RV 14–20), Innocent IV (RV 21–23), Alexander IV (RV 24–25), Urban IV (RV 26–29), Clement IV (RV 30–36), Gregory X (RV 37), John XXI (RV 38), Nicholas III (RV 39–40), Martin IV (RV 41–42), Honorius IV (RV 43), Nicholas IV (RV 44–46), Boniface VIII (RV 47–50).
252. Indice alfabetico dello sole chiese o monasteri e persone, contenute in 8 tomi (indici 244–251), riguardanti i Registri Vaticani n. 9–50, by G. Garampi.
253. Innocent III (RV 4, 7), Honorius III (RV 10–11), Gregory IX (RV 14, 16–20).
254. Notes regarding extant and lost parts of the Vatican registers of Innocent III, Honorius III, Gregory IX, Innocent IV, Alexander IV, Urban IV and Clement IV.
255. Repertorium bullarum Honorii III, prepared by Michele Lonigo, 1604. Honorius III (RV 9–13)
256. Index bullarum. Gregory IX (RV 14–20)
257. Rubricellarum liberi Urbani IIII, Clementis IIII, Nicolai III, Martini IIII, Nicolai IIII, Bonifatii VIII, Clementis V. Urban IV (RV 28–29), Clement IV (RV 30, 32), Nicholas III (RV 40), Martin IV (RV 41), Nicholas IV (RV 45), Boniface VIII (RV 47–50), Clement V (RV 53, 61)
258. Repertorium bullarum Alexander IV, prepared by Michele Lonigo, 1614. Alexandri IV (RV 24–25)
259. Repertorium bullarum Gregorii X et Joannis XXI, prepared by Michele Lonigo, 1614. Gregory X (RV 37), John XXI (RV 38)
260. Fragmente rubricellarum seu indicum bullarum scriptorum et beneficiorum collatorum. Urban IV (RV 28), John XXII (RV 77, 104, 106), Clement VI (153, 156) and RA 21, 43, 117, 136, 182, 197, 201, 202.
261. Rubricellarum liber. Joannis XXII. John XXII (RV 110, 113, 116, 117)
262. Indici dei Registri Vaticani. Benedict XII (RV 123, 125, 130, 131, 133–136)
263. Indici dei Registri Vaticani. Clement VI (RV 137–146)

264. Rubricellae bullarum a Clemente VI usque ad Martinum quintum. Clement VI (RV 242), Innocent VI (RV 242), Boniface IX (RV 313, 315, 316, 319, 320), Innocent VII (RV 333, 334), Gregory XII (RV 335–338), John XXIII (of Pisa) (RV 343, 345, 346), Martin V (RV 352, 356); and Diversa Cameralia 2 (Arm. 29, vol. 2); Arm. 34, vol. 4; Cod. Ottob. Lat. 2548A
265. Rubricae registri litterarum apostolicarum secretarum tam patentium quam clausarum sanctissimi patris et domini nostri domini Innocentii papae VI quae per eius cameram transiverunt (p. 2) and Rubricae registri litterarum secretarum et commissionum sanctissimi in Christo patris et domini nostri domini Urbani PP. V (p. 194). Innocent VI (RV 235–240), Urban V (RV 245–250)
266. Gregorii . . . Rubricae litterarum secretarum missarum per reverendissimos patres dominos sanctae romanae ecclesiae cardinales apostolica sede vacante per obitum felicis recordationis domini Urbani papae quinti. Gregory XI (RV 263, 264, 266, 267, 269–271)
•267. Card for this number indicates: Vedi: Reg Suppl. Rubr. N. I
268. Index diversarum bullarum et privilegiorum et aliorum iurium pro sancta Romana Ecclesia, exerpta ex registri. Innocent III through Pius IV
269. Rubricae tertii libri litterarum apostolicarum de curia domini Martini Papae V. Martin V (RV 353), Eugene IV (RV 365, 374–376)
270. Rubrica. Nicholas V (RV 385–402)
271. Fragmentary indexes relating to RV volumes of Innocent III (RV 5, 7, 8), Honorius III (RV 9–13), Gregory IX (RV 14–16, 18–20), Innocent IV (RV 21–23), Alexander IV (RV 24–25), Urban IV (28–29), Clement IV (RV 32), Gregory X (RV 37), John XXI (RV 38), Nicholas III (RV 39–40), Martin IV (RV 41), Honorius IV (RV 43), Nicholas IV (RV 44–46), Boniface VIII (RV 47–50), John XXII (RV 109), Benedict XII (RV 130–136), Nicholas V (RV 385–402); also Diversa Cameralia Arm. 29, vol. 6
272. Rubricelle librorum S.d.n. Pii pp. II litterarum apostolicarum . . . Pius II (RV 498–499, 501–511)
273. Rubricella seu index bullarum Pauli PP. II. Paul II (RV 524–540, 542–545)
274. Rubricelle libri. Sixtus IV (RV 551–652, 654)
275. Rubricelle libri. Innocent VIII (RV 698–717, 720–738, 740–768), Julius II (RV 932, 934)
276. Rubricelle libri. Alexander VI (RV 772–866),
277. Rubricelle libri. Pius III (RV 885), Julius II (RV 885–888, 890–927, 935, 936, 939–944, 951–983)
278. Rubricelle libri. Leo X (RV 991–1192, 1213–1214).
279–280. Leonis X bullae secretae . . . Leo X (RV 1193–1204)
281. Rubricelle . . . Adrian VI (RV 1215–1236), Clement VII (RV 1238–1434)
282. Rubricelle . . . Paul III (RV 1454–1684)
283. Rubricelle . . . Julius III (RV 1724–1782, 1790)
284. Rubricelle . . . Paul IV (RV 1805–1849)
285. Rubricelle . . . Pius IV (RV 1855–1917)
286. Rubricelle . . . Pius V (RV 1935–1998)
287. Indice de'libri delle bolle delli Secretarii Apostolici, messi nell'Archivio Vaticano sino a Pio V, conminciando da Sisto papa quarto [Sixtus IV (RV 660–667), Innocent VIII (RV 682–690), Alexander VI (RV 879–883), Julius II (RV 985–

988), Leo X (RV 1205–1208), Adrian VI (RV 1237), Clement VII (RV 1442–1453), Paul III (RV 1700–1720), Julius III (RV 1796–1802), Paul IV (RV 1853–1854), Pius IV (RV 1918–1922), Pius V (RV 2002–2003)]

288. Rubricelle . . . Paul III (RV 1693–1698), Julius III (RV 1791–1795), Paul IV (RV 1850–1852), Pius IV (RV 1923–1934), Pius V (RV 2004–2017); also Diversa Cameralia volumes in Armarii 29, 30, and 34; and the Fondo Consistoriale-Acta Miscellanea 60.

•289. Indice di tutte le gratie concesse nel pontificato di Gregorio XIII dall'anno 1572 fino al 1582 et in due anni del pontificato di Sisto V Cioe nel 1585–1586.

290–319. Index Brevium

290. Clem. VII index brevium, ab anno 1523 ad 1528. [Corrispondenza degli anni e dei tomi (o parti di essi, citati in questo indice 290 con i numeri dell'Arm. 40, Minute dei Brevi]

291. Clemente VII, index brevium ab anno 1528 ad 1530 [Corrispondenza degli tomi 18 a 31 dell' Arm. 40]

292. Clem. VII index brevium, ab anno 1531 ad 1534, Tom. III [Arm. 40, vols. 32–48]

293. Clem. VII expeditiones secreti brev.

294. Index brev. Clement VII, ab an 1526 ad 1536.

295–297. Paul III index brev. [Arm. 40, vols. 49–53; Arm. 41, vols. 1–46]

298. Index brev. matrim. 1534–1550 [Arm. 41, vols. 51–54]

299. Rubricella brevium indulgentiarum ab an: 1535 [sic. 1534] ad 1566. [Julius III, Paolo IV, Pio IV, Pio V: Minutae brevium indulgentiarum] [Arm 41, vols. 47–49; Arm. 42, vols. 2–3]

300–303. Paul III brevium summar. ind.
   300. 1534–1537.
   301. 1538–1541
   302. 1542–1545
   303. 1546–1549. Tom. IV

304. Index brevium Paul III. [Arm. 40, vol. 49]

304A. Index [Arm. 41, vols. 5, 6, 7, 8]

305. Index brev. Julii III, ab an 1550 usque ad 1554 [Arm. 41, vols. 55–72] Index brevium . . . Julii ac suarum epistolarum brevia indulgentiarum et dispensationum matrimonialium sunt in distincti voluminii disposita loco de cii alium indice in separatum . . . [Arm. 41, vols. 55–72.]

306. Index brev. Julii III, ab an: 1550 usque ad 1555

307. Index brevium Pauli PP. IV 13 Maii 1555 usque ad 18 Augusti 1559 [Arm. 42, vols. 6–12]

308. Paul IV index brev.

309. Index brevium Pio PP. IV, ab an: 1559 usque ad 1565 [Arm. 42, vols. 13–23]

310. Pii IV Brevium summar. index ab anno 1560 ad 65

311. Index brevium Sancti Pii V existentium in Archivio Secreto Vaticano assumptabus fuit ad apostolicam seden die 7 Jan. 1566 translatus autum ad angelica 7 Maii 1572. [Arm. 42, vols. 25–27]

312. [now Reg. Vat. 2020]

313. Index brevium Gregorii XIII existentium in Archivio Secreto Vaticano creatus fuit pontifex di 13 Maii 1572 . . . die 10 Aprilii 1585. [Arm. 42, vols. 28–46]

314. Index brevium Sixti PP. V existentium in Archivio Secreto Vaticano ab anno 1585 ad 1590 creatus fuit pontifex die

24 Aprilii 1585 . . . die 27 Augusti 1590. [Arm. 42, vol. 47]

315. Index brevii Sixti 1585 & 1586 [Sec. Brev. 113–122]

•316. Index brevium Leonis Papa XI et Pauli V per alphabeticum diocesium ad materiarum ordinem dispositus in quo nomina indultaniorum atque argumenta materiarum expressa sunta studio ac labore Philippi Antonis Ronconis tabularis secretior aplici. Vaticani Prefect. [Arm. 42, vols. 52–57]

317. Index brevium Urbani Pape VIII per alphabeticum diocesium ac materiarum ordinum dispostus in quo nomina indultandorum atque argumenta materiarum plene expressa sunt studio ac labore Philippi Antonii Ronconis tabularii secretior aplici. Vaticani Prefecti. [Arm. 38, vols. 10–16A; Arm. 42, vols. 58–63; Arm. 43, vols. 1–10]

•318–319. Rerum et negotiorum Sanctae Apostolicae Sedis a Pio IV ad Innocentium XII, sive ab anno 1560 ad 1700, synopsis ex regestis brevium . . . Iosepho Garampio . . . Clementis PP. XIII anno pontificatus VIII.

319A. Concordata numeri rubricellarum [= Schedario Garampi] Regestorum Lateranensium seu verterio cum novo numero, 1903

320–430. Rubricellae and summaries of Lateran registers, 1389–1799

320. Summarium quarundam bullarum Pontificatus Bonifatii Nnoni, Fair copy (1618) of Ranaldi's Summarium (BAV Vat. lat. 6952) of letters of Boniface IX

321. Another copy, by F. Contelori, of Ranaldi's Summarium

322. Summary by G. B. Confalonieri, 1618, of letters of Gregory XII [very fragile]

323. Summary by G. B. Confalonieri of letters of Alexander V (of Pisa)

324. Fair copy (1618) of Ranaldi's Summarium (BAV Vat. lat. 6952) of letters of Innocent VII and John XXIII (of Pisa)

324A. Summary by G. B. Confalonieri of volumes of Gregory XII, Alexander V (of Pisa), and John XXIII (of Pisa)

325–326. Summary of letters of Calixtus III

327. Summary of the volumes relating to Calixtus III (pp. 1–194) and Julius III (pp. 195–394)

328–329. Pius II
   328. Years 1–2
   329. Years 3–6

330–331. Paul II, alphabetical, A–O only

332–335. Sixtus IV
   332. Years 1–3
   333. Years 4–6
   334. Years 10–11
   335. Years 12–13

336–338. Innocent VIII
   336. Years 1–2
   337. Years 5–6
   338. Years 7–8

339–343. Alexander VI
   339. Years 1–3
   340. Years 4–5
   341. Years 6–7
   342. Years 8–9
   343. Years 10–12

344. Pius III, Julius II

345–348. Julius II

345. Rubricelle
346. Years 1–2
347. Years 3–4
348. Years 5–6
349. Julius II, years 7–9 (pp. 1–374), Pius III (pp. 375–378)
350–354. Leo X
350. Year 1
351. Yeas 2–3
352. Years 4–5
353. Years 6–7
354. Years 8–9
355. Leo X (pp. 6–136), Adrian VI (pp. 137–231)
356. Adrian VI
357–365. Clement VII
366–370. Paul III
•371. [This is now Camera Apostolica series *Rubricellae*, vol. 8]
372. Paul IV
373. Paul IV (pp. 1–48), Pius IV (pp. 49–84), Gregory XV (pp. 85–316)
374. Pius IV
375–377. Gregory XIII, Summary of letters
378. Gregory XIII, Rubricelle
379–381. Clement VIII, Rubricelle
379. Years 1–3
380. Years 4–7
381. Years 8–12
382. See Indice 744
383–385. Paul V
383. Years 5–7
384. Years 8–10
385. Years 14–16
386. Gregory XV
387–395. Urban VIII
387. Years 1–4
388. Years 5–8
389. Years 9–12
390. Years 13–16
391. Years 17–21
392–395. Rubricelle
396–398. Innocent X
396. Years 1–3
397. Years 4–6
398. Years 7–11
399. See Indice 745
400–401. Alexander VII
400. Years 1–3
401. Years 4–13
402. Clement IX
403. Clement X
404. Innocent XII
405. See Indice 746
406–415. Benedict XIV
406–410. Epitome litterarum beneficialium
406. Years 1–3
407. Years 4–7
408. Years 8–11
409. Years 12–14
410. Years 15–18
411–415. Epitome litterarum matrimonialium
411. Years 1–3

412. Years 4–7
413. Years 8–11
414. Years 12–14
415. Years 15–18
416–419. Clement XIII
416. Years 1–3
417. Years 4–6
418. Years 7–9
419. Years 10–11
420. See Indice 747
421–423. Clement XIV
421–422. Epitome litterarum beneficialium
423. Epitome litterarum matrimonialium
424–430. Pius VI

431–436. Summaries of the Registra supplicationum
431. Rubricelle del libro primo del pontificato di Nostro Signore PP. Pio Settimo dell'anno VIII
432. Rubricelle [beneficiorum] annorum 1806, 1807, 1808 scilicet annorum septimi et octavi Pii Pape Septimi
433. Rubricelle secretorum . . . Pii PP. VII lib. sexto
434. Rubricelle [beneficiorum] anni 1803 anni quarti Pii PP. VII
435. Liber secundus anni XV Ssmi. Dni. Nri. Pii PP. VII
436. Rubricelle [beneficiorum] 1806 anni primi Dni. Nri. Pii PP. VII

437–444. Materials related to preparation of Orbis Christianus
•437–440. Apparatus ad universalem episcopatuum Orbis Christiani notitiam, ordine alphabetico digestus
•441. Index episcoporum Orbis Christiani
•442. Patriarchatus, archiepiscopatus et episcopatus in partibus infidelium, ordine alphabetico diposit
•443. Orbis Christianus. Fragmenta
•444. Indicum fragmenta

445–556. Schedario Garampi
445–537. [Registro alfabetico] vols. 1–94 (of Schedario)
445–474. Benefici (with benefices listed in alphabetical order) vols. 1–30
475–511. Vescovi (a chronological listing then arranged by diocese. Within each diocese bishops are listed alphabetically) vols. 31–67
512–534A. Miscellanea I (alphabetical by diocese) vols. 68–91
535–537. Abbates (alphabetical by diocese and monastery) vols. 92–94
538–549. [Registro cronologico] vols. 95–106
550–556. [Registro alfabetico] vols. 107–113
550. Papi (alphabetical) vol. 107
551. Cardinali (alphabetical) vol. 108
552–554. Uffici (curial officials) vols. 109–111
555–556. Chiese di Roma (alphabetical order by name) vols. 112–113

557–641. Index bullarum (Calendar of Avignon registers), made by P. de Montroy at Avignon, 1718–1732. Alphabetical, diocese by diocese.

642–669. Indice dell'Archivio Apostolico di Avignone (Calendar of Avignon registers), made by J. de Martin at Avignon, 1711. Each volume is calendared in turn, pontificate by pontificate, item by item.

670–681. Miscellanea II of Garampi's Schedario, vols. 114–125 of Schedario

682–683. [This is now Camera Apostolica series *Rubricellae*, vols. 37–38]

684. [This is now Camera Apostolica series *Taxae*, vol. 31]

685. Lateran registers; Registri communis literarum apostolicarum, Calisto III, Libri de perduti, compiled by E. Ranuzzi (May 1918)

686. Inventario e descrizione dell'Archivio Segreto della S. Congregazione de confini, an inventory compiled in 1839 [formerly Indice 107]

•687. Collectio historica ecclesiae Romanae a saec. V ad XVIII. [A scrapbook of various citations compiled in the 1920's. Mercati's notes seem to suggest that the book and a companion volume are particularly useful for finding material on other archives in the Vatican and for ASV material which has passed to the Vatican Library.]

•688. Index to bulls and briefs from Pius V to Gregory XIII

•689. Index to bulls and briefs from Sixtus V to Clement XII

690. Indice di brevi pontifici relativi a ordini religiose dei Registra Lateranensia da Martino V a Paolo IV (1417–1621), by Gaetano Marini [Giusti notes "non si tratta de breve ma di bolle"]

691. An inventory of I. Instrumenta miscellanea; II. Documenti de Castel S. Angelo Armar. I–XVIII; III. Documenti de Castel S. Angelo Armar. B, C, D, E, F.

This appears to be an inventory conducted in 1921 to determine the physical state of the documents in these series.

•692. Indicum diversorum volum. XXVIII. Index investiturarum Tom. Ius

•693. Indicum diversorum vol. XXIX. Index investiturarum Tom. II

•694–697. Indice dell Archivio di Castello

694. Index to Arm. I–Arm. IV

695. Index to Arm. V–Arm. XI

696. Index to Arm. XII–Arm. XIV

697. Index to Arm. VIII–Arm. XVI

•698–699. Index to Arm. I–XII

700. Rubricella degli atti e documenti della ven. Archiconfraternità di SS.mo Gonfalone di Roma, compilata da Giovanni de Regis nell'anno 1877

701. Protocollo delle cause ventilate in Sacra Rota dal 1800 a tutto il mese de settembre 1870

702. Confraternità del Crocifisso (S. Marcello) Catalogo dettagliato dei singoli atti contenuti nei protocolli segnati PP–QQ–RR. Rubricello prepared in 1886.

Also brief contents list to the holdings.

703. Indice della Confraternità S.M. della pietà dei carcerati. Indice analitico

704. Inventario del Fondo Pio esistente all'Archivio Vaticano 15 dicembre 1915, by M. Ugolini

705. Inventarium Regestorum Lateranensium seu de Dataria in Tabularium Vaticanum jussu Leonis XIII, prepared ca. 1900 by Pietro Wenzel

706–1 and 2 (2 vols). Inventory of Fondo Spada

707–712. Index actorum Sacra Congregationis Consistorialis

707. Dioceses, 1593–1806

708. Dioceses, 1700–1868

709. Dioceses, 1869–1906

710. Materiae, 1627–1806

711. Materiae, 1700–1869

712. Materiae, 1869–1906

713. Index decretorum: Index generalis actorum Sacrae Congregationis Consistorialis, 1700–1823

714–715. Sacra Congregazione Concistoriale: Ricorsi e cause concistoriali non risoluti (ossia Affari pendenti)

714. 1818–1847

715. 1848–1875

716–718. Registro dei concistori

716. 1800–1824

717. 1825–1847

718. 1848–1875

719. Indice dell'Archivio del Eccma Casa Ruspoli (1871)

720–722. Indice alfabetico Archivio Ruspoli

723–724. Indici di tutte le materie esistenti nell'Archivio dell Ecc.ma Casa Chigi-Montoro, 1806

725. Rubricellone di tutte le materie esistenti nell'archivio dell'Ill.ma Casa Patrizi composto sotto gli auspici del Ill.mo Sig. Marchese Francesco Patrizi da Fillippo Maria Magni archivista dell'indeto popolo Romano, l'anno 1794

726. Rubricellone generale di tutte le materie esistenti nell'archivio dell'Ill.ma. Famiglia Naro composto sotto gli auspici dell'Ill.mo. Sig. Marchese Francesco Patrizi, già Naro da Filippo Maria Magni (1793, with 19th century additions)

727. Archivio Borghese inventario, 1931

727A. Archivio Borghese 8606–8622, by C. De Domenicis and F. Di Giovanni. Questi numeri comprendono piante, disegni, stampe, imagini varie, un tempo raccolti in cartelle

728. Rubrica dell'archivio dell'Ecc.ma Casa Boncompagni-Ottoboni (The fondo Boncompagni Ottoboni described in this index is located in the Archivio Storico del Vicariato di Roma.)

729. Indice dell'Archivio Boncompagni-Ludovisi (a brief alphabetic index)

730. Rubricelle generale dell'archivio dell'Eccellentissima Casa Boncompagni accresciuto e riordinato L'anno MDCCLXXXII

731–885. Chronological indexes, of the Segreteria dei Brevi, 1198–1879 [740–885 formerly Indici 10–150]

740. Cedul. Consist. Martin V–Clement VIII

886–887. Protocol book, Vigilanza

886. 1826–1828

887. 1828–1829

888–897. Archivio Borghese—General index

898. Collogione dell'ordine di S. Gregorio Magno civile e militare. Diviso in quattro classi, 1831–1869

899–900. Registri dei cavalieri dello Speron d'Oro fatti per breve prima della reforma ordinata dal Sommo Pontifice Gregorio XVI, 1834–1867

901. Sec Brev. Speron d'Oro Indice, 1847–50

902–903. Sec Brev. Equestre Ordine Piano Aldegendo

902. Protocollo, 1847–1868

903. Indice, 1847–1867

904. Curia Romana: Ricerche d'archivio (Sec. Brev.)

905–909. Vescovadi: Ricerche d'archivio (Sec. Brev.)

910–920. Fondo storico della S. Congregezione del Concilio—Posiziones: Rilevazione, 1568–1592, by D. Troiani

921–924. Rilevazione, Posiziones 49–75, by D. Troiani (70–75 by P. Caiazza)

925–1000. [No indici with these numbers]

1001–1012. Calendar (1910–1927) by V. Nardoni, etc., of the archives of Castel S. Angelo (Archivum Arcis or AA).

1013–1035. Calendars of Secretariat of State (SS.) holdings

1013–1014. SS. Cardinali

    1013. Volume listing

    1014. Alphabetical inventory

1015–1016. Vescovi e prelati

    1015. Volume listing

    1016. Alphabetical inventory

1017–1018. Principi

1019–1021. Particolari

1022. Soldati

1023. Legations of Avignon, Bologna, Ferrara, Romagna, Urbino, Archivio Ubaldini, by P. Savio

1024. Nunciatures of Florence, Genoa, Corsica, Malta, Naples, Savoy, Venice (and its Archivio)

    1024–I. Volume listing

    1024–II. Chronological inventory

1025. Nunciatures of France, Portugal, Spain

1026. Fiandra, Paci, Nunz. diverse, Avvisi, Memoriali-Biglietti, Emigrati della rivoluzione francese, Fondo Salviati, Benincasa, by P. Savio

1027. Nunciatures of Germany, Cologne

1028. Nunciature of Switzerland

    1029. Misc. Arm. I–XV

    1029–I. Inventory

1029–II. Index

1030. Misc. Arm. IV–V (Bandi): Inventory.

1031. Interni, 1822–1833

1032. Esteri, 1815–1850

1033. Interni–Esteri, 1814–1822

1034. Prontuario per la consultazione dei protocolli dell'archivio della Segreteria di Stato, 1816–1851

1035. Prontuario per la consultazione delle rubricelle dell'archivio della Segreteria di Stato, 1816–1860

1036. Inventory of Fondo camerale: Obligationes et solutiones, Introitus et exitus, Collectoriae, Obligationes communes, Obligationes particulares, cameral parts of Avignon registers.

1037. Indice alfabetico per diocese dell'Indice 282, Paolo III (Vatican registers, vols. 1454–1684)

1038. Alphabetical list of dioceses in Indice 283 (Vatican registers, vols. 1724–1782, Julius III, 1550–1555)

1039–1040. Inventory of Lateran registers, by M. H. Laurent

    1039. 1–1127 (1389–1503)

    1040. 1128–2467 (1503–1892)

1041. Inventory of Lateran briefs 1–883 (1490–1807)

1042. Index by diocese of Minutae brevium (1523–1599)

1043. Index by diocese of Annatae (1421–1797) [3 vols.]

1044. Index by diocese of Resignationes (1457–1594)

1045. Index of Processus consistoriales (1563–1906)

1046. Inventory of Processus datariae (1622–1900)

1047. Index of processes of Congregation of Rites (1588–1920)

1048. Inventory of Secretarius Camerae (1470–1796)

1049. Fondo Bolgnetti, by A. Mercati

1050. Fondo Carpegna, by A. Mercati

1051. Fondo Confalonieri

1052. Fondo Borghese, Carte Salviati

1053. Fondo Finy

1054. Fondo Girolamini, by G. Gullette

1055. Archives of Nunciature of Vienna

    1055–I. 1607–1890 (vols. 1–641)

    1055–II. Processi canonici dei vescovati e delle abbazie ca. 1600–ca. 1900

    1055–III. Indice dei processi dei vescovi e degli abbati 1582–1879.

    1055–IV. Inventarium . . . in archivio hujus apostolicae nuntiaturae existentium

    1055A. Archivio Nunziatura di Vienna, vols. 483–549, 1874–1880, Inventario by Ines Bassani and Aldo Martini

1056. Instrumenta miscellanea [Chronological and alphabetical in 2 sections]

1057. Manualia actorum et citationum, Rota Romana (1464–1800)

1058. Archivio dello Scrittore segreto (1734–1906)

1059. Piante e carte geografiche

1060. Fondo Ronconi

1061. Registers of Abbreviatori di curia (1735–1906)

1062. Fondo Benedetto XIV, by G. Marx

1063. Congregation of Sacro Palazzo Apostolico

1064. Archives of protonotaries apostolic

1065. Memoriali (Supplications) (1636–1796)

1066. Fondo Santini

1067. Carte Farnesiane

1068. Fondo Garampi (vols. 272–300).

1069. Inventory of Epistolae ad principes (1560–1914)

1070. Archivio della Nunziatura Apostolica di Lucerna (1617–1922)

1071. SS. Inghilterra, Baviera, Cardinali, Vescovi e prelati, Principi, Particolari

1072. Positiones of Rota (1627–1660), by H. Hoberg

1073. Diaria of Rota (1566–1870), by H. Hoberg

1074. Archivio di Castel S. Angelo (Armaria inferiora), Concordanza fra l'antica e la nuova segnatura (A.A. Arm. I–XVIII, 1–6720)

1075. Archivio Della Valle-Del Bufalo

1076. Congregazione del Buon Governo, by H. Hoberg

1077. Fondo Gesuiti

1078. Visite ospedale Roma

1079. Bandi sciolti

1080. Fondo Cibo

1081–1086 Archives of various nunciatures

1081. The Hague (L'Aja), 1802–1879

1082. Brussels (Bruxelles) and Netherlands, 1879–1899

1083. Cologne (Colonia)

1084. Florence (Firenze)

1085. Naples (Napoli)

1086. Paris (Parigi), 1819–1850

1087. Missioni, by H. Hoberg

1088. Carte Pasolini-Zanelli

1089. SS. Esteri (1851–1922)
  1089–I. 1851–1877
  1089–II. 1878–1913
  1089–III. 1914–1922
1090. Archives of Nunciature of Madrid (1623–1921)
1091. Fondo Pio, by P. Savio
1092. Positiones of Rota (1627–1870), by H. Hoberg
1093. Archives of S. Silvestro, Nonantola (802–1780), by G. Gollotta
1094. Rota (Processus actorum), by H. Hoberg
1095. Rota (Decisiones), by H. Hoberg
1096. Monaco (Archivio della Nunziatura)
1097. Rota (Iura Diversa), by H. Hoberg
1098–1099. Sec. Brev. (Inventario-prospetto della serie Sec. Brev.), by P. Guidi and C. Natalini
  1098. 1554–1846 [formerly Indice 35]
  1099. 1831–1878
1100. Sec. Brev. (index to Indici 731–885)
1101. Registri Avenionensia (Prospectus)
1102. Vescovi e regolari (Praeposita registra), by H. Hoberg
1103. Vescovi e regolari (Rubricellae), by H. Hoberg
1104 (1). Vescovi e regolari (Positiones, 1573–1908), by C. Burns
1104 (2). Vescovi e regolari (Positiones, Archivio Segreto, 1727–1908)
1105. Vescovi e regolari (Decreta, 1656–1906)
1106. Rota (Processus actorum, analytic index 1–100), by H. Hoberg
1107. Voll. passati alla Biblioteca Vaticana [formerly Indice 40]
1108. Rota (Miscellanea 1–28), by H. Hoberg
1109. Rota (Serie minori), by H. Hoberg
1110. Segretario di Stato (Manual to rubriche system)
1111. Felice V (Bollario)
1112. Fondo dell'Archivio di Stato di Roma [formerly Indice 41]
1113. Dataria Apostolica (Registra contradictorum, Expeditiones, Missis, Misc.) [withdrawn]
1114. Fondo Veneto II (MSS Monasteri soppressi)
1115. Instrumenta Perusina nn. 1–232
1116. Indulgenze e SS. Reliquie (Congregazione)
1117. Visita Apostolica (Congregazione)
1118. Quattro legazione (Segretario di Stato, Archivio del Commissariato straordinario . . .)
1119. Napoli (Incaricato d'Affari di Napoli presso la corte di Firenza)
1120. Segretaria di Stato (Concilio centrale di censura e sussidi, 1871–1878)
1121. Cedularum et Rotulorum (Cardinali)
1122. Tesoriere generale (Camera Apostolica)
1123. Ergastolo di Corneto (1752–1871)
1124. Riforma (Congregazione)
1125. Epoca Napoleonica (Biglietti)
1126. Collezione Brancadori, Fondo Mencacci
1127. Inventario dell'archivio della famiglia dei conti Beni di Gubbio, by M. Giusti
1128. Rospigliosi (Archivio)
1129. SS. Vincenzo e Anastasio (Tre Fontane)
1130. Ospizio di S. Galla
1131–1133. Pio IX (Archivio Particolare)
  1131. Archivio particolare Pio IX, lettere ai sovrani, ecc.

1132. Archivio particolare Pio IX, oggetti vari
  1133. Fondo particolare
1134. Alessandro VI ed i Borgia (Schedario Garampi)
1135. Segretaria di Stato (Epoca Napoleonica, Baviera, Francia, Italia)
• 1136. Chiese in partibus
1137. Mazio, Raffaele Cardinale (Carte)
1138. Rota (Miscellanea, Appendix), by H. Hoberg
1139. Segretaria di Stato (Visita apostolica nel Messico)
1140. Visita ad limina (Concilio—Relationes)
1141. Torino (Archivio della Nunziatura . . .)
1142. Luoghi pii di Roma (Congregazione economica), by S. Pagano
1143. Cardinali (S.S.—Spogli)
1144. Visita Apostolica (Congregazione, 1700–1825)
1145. Visita Apostolica (Congregazione, inventario), by S. Pagano
1146. Epistolae ad principes (Positiones et minutae, 1823–1969)
1147–1147A. Riti (Congregazione) (Processus beatification and canonization), by Y. Beaudoin
  1147. 1588–1982
  1147A. 1982–1994
1148. Epistolae Latinae
1149. Domenicani (Fondo), by T. Droetto
1150. Lauretano (Fondo)
1151. Segretaria di Stato (Registri bullarum, già Coadiutorie e commende)
1152. Peru (Archivio Della Nunziatura . . . , 1862–1921)
1153. Brasile (Archivio della Nunziatura . . . 1808–1920), by C. Lopez
1154. Concilio (Congregazione, Visite Apostoliche, 1571–1803), by G. Roselli
1155. Segretaria di Stato (Archivi delle Nunziature) Messico (1904–1921)
1156–1157. America Centrale (Archivio della Nunziatura)
  1156. 1908–1922
  1157. 1922–1932
1158. Armaria LXI (list of vols.) [additional copy at reference desk]
1159. Segretaria di Stato (Archivi delle Nunziature) Argentina (1900–1922)
1160. Bolivia (Archivio della Nunciatura . . . 1864–1932), by C. Lopez
1161. Lisbona (Archivio della Nunziatura . . . 1580–1917)
1162. Bruxelles (Archivio della Nunziatura, 1904–1922)
1163. Canada (Archivio della Nunziatura . . . 1899–1921), by C. De Domenicis
1164. Codificazione diritto canonico
1165. Archivio dello Studio Belli. Indice delle materie beneficiali, indulti ed altre grazie e concessioni a favore delle corti Portogallo e Brasile
• 1166. Fondo Veneto II (MSS Monasteri soppressi) [at reference desk]
1167. Carte Luigi Piastrelli: Elenco delle lettere autografe e dei documenti riguardanti il movimento modernista, compiled by Luigi Piastrelli
1168. Inventario dell'Archivio della Nunziatura (già Delegazione) Apostolica degli Stati Uniti d'America, 1893–1921, v. 1 (sez. I–IX Duluth), by Claudio Dominicis (1991)

1169. Congregatio Consistorialis: Relationes

1170. Armaria XXIX–XXX, Camera Apostolica, Diversa Cameralia, voll. 1–251, Inventario sommario, by F. Di Giovanni and G. Roselli

1171. Arciconfraternità del Santissimo Sacramento, Immacolata Concezione, Beata Vergine della Cintura, Santi Martiri Trifono, Respicio, Ninfa, e San Camillo de Lellis

1172. Concilio Vaticano I, by G. Croce

1173. Archivio Storico della Sacra Congregazione del Concilio. Inventario sommario

1174. Riti (Processus)

Blocchetti of the ASV

Blocchetti I. 1–33. Instrumenta miscellanea numerical
Blocchetti II. 1–40. Instrumenta miscellanea chronological
Blocchetti III.

    1–62. Fondo Veneto I

    63–65. Fondo Toscano

Blocchetti IV.

    • I–IV. De Schismate (Arm. LIV, t. XIV)

    • I–XII. Cornelii Margarini, thesauri historici sacrae et politicae veritatis inventarium (Arm. LIV, t. I–XII)

Blocchetti V.

    • 1–2. Schedario Melampo

    • 1–36. Bandi (Misc. Arm. IV–V)

Blocchetti VI.

    1. Fondo Agostiniani III

    2. Archivio Beni pergamene

    3. Schede dei brevi originali, Cartella A. I. nn. 1–192 (a. 1503–1734) and Schede dei brevi originali, Cartella B. II. nn. 193–311 (a. 1741–1836)

    4. Instrumenta Burghesiana

    5. Fondo Carinci

    6–7. Fondo Celestini

    8. Fondo Certosini

    9–10. Fondo Domenicani I

    11. Congregazione economica

    • 12. Miscellanea diplomatica

    13. Fondo Scolopi

    14. Fondo S. Coleta, Fondo S. Trifone

    15–16. Calendar of Garampi's Collectanea miscellanea

    17–18. Photocopies of Blocchetti Indici 15–16, arranged chronologically

    • 19–20. Pubblicazioni citate in forma abbreviato nelle schede Garampi

    21. Instrumenta Tudertina

    22. Archivio Ruspoli-Marescotti

    23–24. Bullarum Benedicti XIII

The following numbered indici have appeared in reference works or have been seen by project staff, but are not currently found in the ASV Index Room.

    • 2*. According to Gualdo, 2* is an index relating to the Schedario Garampi

    54*. Archivio Patrizi—Inventari [at reference desk]

    60*. Archivio del S. Maria delle Grazie [at reference desk]

    72*. Minuta de l'inventario dell'Archivio della Cancelleria della Nunziatura Veneta dal 1500 al 1899, compiled in the early twentieth century by P. Cenci [at reference desk]

    121*. Carte Theiner [at reference desk]

Bibliography

THIS BIBLIOGRAPHY BEGAN WITH THE BIBLIOGRAPHY DEVELOPED by Leonard Boyle for his *Survey of the Vatican Archives and Its Medieval Holdings* (Toronto, 1972), and was expanded to include titles that were used in the preparation of this guide, titles that are known to be useful in understanding the various series described in the guide, titles that provide examples of records found in the series, and general introductions and earlier guides to the archives. It makes no claim to be a comprehensive bibliography of works relating to the Vatican Archives, or works that have used the archives.

A more extensive bibliography is found in the *Bibliografia dell'Archivio Vaticano* (Vatican City, 1962–), edited by G. Battelli. This is a compilation of scholarly works based on the holdings of the ASV, divided according to specific ASV records series. Though it is very thorough it is not complete.

For the most part, editions of documents are entered in this bibliography under their editors, rather than under the authors of the original documents. The works of each author and editor are brought together under one name, usually their actual name, not the latinized or italianized form that appears on some of their publications.

A few titles listed in this bibliography were seen by project staff at one point of the project or another but they are no longer accessible to us and we have not been able to verify them in standard bibliographical sources. These titles are noted as being unverified.

This bibliography was assembled in a separate database, using Pro-Cite database management software. Individual titles were then inserted from Pro-Cite into the principal database that forms the central portion of this guide.

Abate, P. "Lettere 'secretae' d'Innocenzo IV e altri documenti in una raccolta inedita del secolo XIII (Regesto)." *Miscellanea Franciscana* 55 (1955): 317–324.

Abbott, T. K. *A Catalogue of the Manuscripts in the Library of Trinity College Dublin.* Dublin, 1900.

Accioly, H. *Os primeiros núncios no Brasil.* Sao Paulo, 1949.

Acht, P. "Der Recipe-Vermerk auf den Urkunden Papst Bonifaz' VIII." *Zeitschrift für bayerische Landesgeschichte* 18 (1955): 243–255.

Acht, P. "Drei Fälschungen von Papsturkunden des 13. Jahrhunderts." *Bullettino dell'Archivio paleografico italiano,* n.s. 2–3, pt. 2 (1956–1957): 33–57.

Acht, P. "Kanzleitkorrekturen auf Papsturkunden des 13. und 14. Jahrhunderts." *Folio diplomatica* 1 (1971). (This title was noted but not verified by project staff.)

800 Jahre Franz von Assisi: Franziskanische Kunst und Kultur des Mittelalters. Vienna, 1982.

Acta legationis cardinalis Gentilis, 1307–1311. Budapest, 1885.

Afzelius, A., et al., eds. *Diplomatarium Danicum.* Raekke 2. Copenhagen, 1938–1960.

Albe, E. "Les religieuses Hospitalières de l'Ordre de Saint-Jean de Jérusalem au diocèse de Cahors." *Revue d'histoire de l'Église de France* 27 (1941): 180–220.

Alberigo, G. *Cardinalato e collegialità: studi sull'ecclesiologia tra l'XI e il XIV secolo.* Florence, 1969.

Albert, M. *Nuntius Fabio Chigi und die Anfänge des Jansenismus, 1639–1651: Ein Römischer Diplomat in theologischen Auseinandersetzungen.* Rome, 1988.

Albizzi, F. *Risposta all'historia della sacra Inquisitione composta già dal R.P. Paolo Servita*. 2d ed. Rome, 1680(?).

Alessandri, L., and F. Pennacchi. "Bullarium pontificium quod exstat in archivo sacri conventus S. Francisci Assisiensis (nunc apud publicam Bibliothecam Assisii), 1220–1832." *Archivum Franciscanum Historicum* 8 (1915): 592–617; 10 (1917): 185–219; 11 (1918): 206–250, 442–490; 12 (1919): 132–186, 471–543; 13 (1920): 136–180, 508–585.

Amabile, L. *Il Santo Officio della Inquisizione in Napoli: Narrazione con molti documenti inediti*. Città Di Castello, 1892.

Ambrosini, M. L., and M. Willis. *The Secret Archives of the Vatican*. Boston, 1969.

Ameyden, D. *La storia delle famiglie romane*. Con note ed aggiunte de A. Bertini. Rome, 1910–1914.

Anaissi, T. *Bullarium Maronitarum: Complectens bullas, brevia, epistolas, constitutiones aliaque documenta a Romanis pontificibus ad patriarchas Antiochenos Syro-Maronitarum missa, ex tabulario secreto S. Sedis, bibliotheca Vaticana, bullariis variis etc. excerpta et juxta temporis seriem disposita*. Rome, 1911.

Analecta vaticano-belgica. Rome, 1906–.

Ancel, R. "La Secretairie pontificale sous Paul IV." *Revue des questions historiques* 79 (1906): 408–470.

Ancel, R. "Étude critique sur quelques recueils d'Avvisi: Contribution a l'histoire du journalisme en Italie." *Mélanges d'archéologie et d'histoire* 28 (1908): 115–139.

Ancel, R. *Nonciatures de France: Nonciatures de Paul IV avec le derniere annee de Jules III et Marcel II*. Paris, 1909–1911.

Annuario pontificio. Rome [etc.], 1716–.

Anstruther, G. "Cardinal Howard and the English Court." *Archivum Fratrum Praedicatorum* 28 (1958): 315–361.

Antonelli, F. "L'archivio della S. Congregazione dei Riti." In *Il libro e le biblioteche: Atti del primo Congresso bibliografico francescano internazionale, 20–27 febbraio 1949*, vol. 2, pp. 61–76. Rome, 1950.

Antonelli, F. "S. C. dei Riti." In *Enciclopedia cattolica*, vol. 4, pp. 330–333. Vatican City, 1950.

Antonelli, F. "L'archivio della S. Congregazione dei Riti." In *Relazioni del X Congresso internazionale di scienze storiche* (Rome, 1955), vol. 7, pp. 99–100. Florence, 1955.

Antonelli, M. *Alcuni banchetti politici a Montefiascone nel secolo decimoquarto*. Rome, 1901.

Araldi, L. *L'Italia nobile*. Bologna, 1972.

Archivi e archivistica a Roma dopo l'unità: Genesi storica, ordinamenti, interrelazioni: Atti del convegno, Roma, 12–14 marzo 1990. Rome, 1994.

"Archivio Segreto del Vaticano, Archivio della Sacra Congregazione del Concilio, Relazioni dei vescovi dopo le visite ad limina: Venezia." (This title was noted but not verified by project staff.)

Arciconfraternità della Pietà de' Carcerati. *Nuovi statuti della ven. Arciconfraternità della Pietà de' Carcerati, eretta nella Chiesa di S. Giovanni della pigna*. Rome, 1775.

Arndt, W. F., and M. Tangl. *Schrifttafeln zur Erlernung der lateinischen Palaeographie*. 4. erweiterte Aufl. Berlin, 1904–1929.

Asch, R. G., and A. M. Birke, eds. *Princes, Patronage, and the Nobility: The Court at the Beginning of the Modern Age, c. 1450–1650*. London, 1991.

Attività della Santa Sede. Rome, 1941–.

Aubert, R., et al. *The Church between Revolution and Restoration*. Translated by P. Becker. New York, 1981.

Audard, E. "L'histoire religieuse de la Révolution française aux Archives Vaticanes." *Revue d'histoire de l'Église de France* 4 (1913): 516–535, 625–639.

Auvray, L. *Les registres de Grégoire IX: Recueil des bulles de ce pape publiées ou analysées d'après les manuscrits originaux au Vatican*. Vol. 9 of *Bibliothèque des Écoles françaises d'Athènes et de Rome*. 2d ser., *Registres des papes du XIIIe siècle*. Paris, 1896–1955.

Baart, P. A. *The Roman Court, or, A Treatise on the Cardinals, Roman Congregations . . . of the Holy Roman Church*. 4th ed. New York, 1899.

Bååth, L. M., ed. *Acta cameralia*. Vol. 1 of *Acta pontificum Suecia: Auspiciis archivi regni Sueciae*. Stockholm, 1936–1937.

Bååth, L. M. "L'inventaire de la Chambre apostolique de 1440." In *Miscellanea archivistica Angelo Mercati*, pp. 135–157. Vatican City, 1952.

Bacci, A. "Segreteria dei brevi ai principi." In *Enciclopedia cattolica*, vol. 11, pp. 247–248. Vatican City, 1953.

Baethgen, F. "Quellen und Untersuchungen zur Geschichte der päpstlichen Hof- und Finanzverwaltung unter Bonifaz VIII." *Quellen und Forschungen aus italienischen Archiven und Bibliotheken* 20 (1928–29): 114–237.

Baix, F. "De la valeur historique des actes pontificaux de collation des bénéfices." In *Hommage à Dom Ursmer Berlière*, pp. 57–66. Brussels, 1931.

Baix, F., and A. Uyttebrouck, eds. *La Chambre apostolique et les 'Libri annatarum' de Martin V (1417–1431)*. Vol. 14 of *Analecta vaticano-belgica: Documents relatifs aux anciens diocèses de Cambrai, Liège, Thérouanne et Tournai*. Rome, 1942–1960.

Baluze, É., ed. *Epistolarum Innocentii III romani pontificis libris undecim: Accedunt gesta ejusdem Innocentii et prima collectio decretalium composita a Rainerio diacono Pomposiano*. Paris, 1682.

Baluze, É. *Vitae paparum Avenionensium*. Edited by G. Mollat. Paris, 1914–1927.

Bangen, J. H. *Die Römische Curie, ihre gegenwärtige Zusammensetzung und ihr Geschäftsgang*. Münster, 1854.

Barbiche, B., ed. *Correspondance du nonce en France, Innocenzo del Bufalo, évêque de Camerino, 1601–1604*. Vol. 4 of *Acta nuntiaturae gallicae*. Rome, 1964.

Barbiche, B. "Les 'scriptores' de la chancellerie apostolique sous le pontificat de Boniface VIII (1295–1305)." *Bibliothèque de l'École des Chartes* 128 (1970): 114–187.

Barbiche, B. "Diplomatique et histoire sociale: Les 'scriptores' de la Chancellerie apostolique au XIIIe siècle." *Annali della Scuola speciale per archivisti e bibliotecari dell'Università di Roma* 12 (1972): 117–129.

Barbiche, B., ed. *Les actes pontificaux originaux des Archives Nationales de Paris*. Vatican City, 1975–1982.

Barbiche, B. "Le personnel de la chancellerie pontificale au XIIIe et XIVe siècles." In *Prosopographie et genèse de l'état moderne*, edited by F. Autrand, pp. 117–130. Paris, 1986.

Barbiche, B. "Les registres du cardinal Flavio Orsini légat a latere en France en 1572–1573." *Archivum Historiae Pontificiae* 31 (1993): 265–273.

Barletta, E. A., and C. L. Tupputi. "Archivio di Stato di Roma." In *Guida generale degli Archivi di Stato Italiani*, edited by P. D'Angiolini and C. Pavone, vol. 3, pp. 1023–1279. Rome, 1986.

Barone, G., and A. M. Piazzoni. "Le più antiche carte dell'Archivio del Gonfalone (1267–1486)." In Le chiavi della memoria: Miscellanea in occasione del I centenario della Scuola vaticana di paleografia, diplomatica e archivistica, pp. 17–105. Vatican City, 1984.

Baronio, C. Annales ecclesiastici. Edited by A. Theiner. Rome, 1856.

Barozzi, N., and G. Berchet, eds. Relazioni degli stati europei lette al Senato dagli ambasciatori veneti nel seculo decimosettimo. Venice, 1856–1878.

Barraclough, G. "The Making of a Bishop in the Middle Ages: The Part of the Pope in Law and Fact." Catholic Historical Review 19 (1933): 275–319.

Barraclough, G. "The Chancery Ordinance of Nicholas III: A Study of the Sources." Quellen und Forschungen aus italienischen Archiven und Bibliotheken 25 (1933–1934): 192–250.

Barraclough, G. Public Notaries and the Papal Curia: A Calendar and a Study of a Formularium Notariorum Curie from the Early Years of the Fourteenth Century. London, 1934.

Barraclough, G. "Audientia litterarum contradictarum." In Dictionnaire de droit canonique, edited by R. Naz, vol. 1, pp. 1387–1399. Paris, 1935.

Barraclough, G. "Formulare für Suppliken aus der ersten Hälfte des 13. Jahrhunderts." Archiv für katholisches Kirchenrecht 115 (1935): 435–463.

Barraclough, G. Papal Provisions: Aspects of Church History, Constitutional, Legal and Administrative, in the Later Middle Ages. Oxford, 1935.

Barraclough, G. "The Executors of Papal Provisions in the Canonical Theory of the 13th and 14th centuries." In Acta Congressus iuridici internationalis VII saeculo a decretalibus Gregorii IX ed XIV a Codice Iustiniano promulgatis: Romae 12–17 novembris 1934, vol. 3, pp. 109–150. Rome, 1936.

Barraclough, G. "Ordo judiciarius qui in romana curia consuevit communiter observari." Jus pontificium 17 (1937): 111–130, 209–217.

Barraclough, G. "Corrector litterarum apostolicarum." In Dictionnaire de droit canonique, edited by R. Naz, vol. 3, pp. 681–689. Paris, 1942.

Barraclough, G. "Minutes of Papal Letters (1316–1317)." In Miscellanea archivistica Angelo Mercati, pp. 109–127. Vatican City, 1952.

Barraclough, G. "The English Royal Chancery and the Papal Chancery in the Reign of Henry III." Mitteilungen des Instituts für österreichische Geschichtsforschung 62 (1954): 365–378.

Bartoloni, F. "Additiones Kehrianae." Quellen und Forschungen aus italienischen Archiven und Bibliotheken 34 (1954): 31–64.

Bartoloni, F. "Suppliche pontificie dei secoli XIII e XIV." Bullettino dell'Istituto storico italiano per il medio evo e Archivio muratoriano 67 (1955): 1–187.

Bartoloni, F. "Per un censimento dei documenti pontifici da Innocenzo III a Martino V (escluso)." In Atti del Convegno di studi delle fonti del medioevo europeo in occasione del 70 della fondazione dell'Instituto storico italiano, Roma, 14–18 aprile 1953, vol. 2, pp. 3–22. Rome, 1957.

Bassani, A. I. "Le fonti dell'Archivio Segreto Vaticano per una storia ecclesiastica della repubblica e del regno d'Italia." In Vita religiosa e cultura in Lombardia e nel Veneto nell'età napoleonica, by F. Agostino et al., pp. 363–393. Rome, 1990.

Basso, M. I privilegi e le consuetudini della Rev.da Fabbrica di San Pietro in Vaticano. Rome, 1987–1988.

Battelli, G. "Una supplica originale 'per fiat' di Urbano V: Contributo alla storia della Cancellaria pontificia nel secolo XIV." In Scritti di paleografia e diplomatica in onore di Vincenzo Federici, pp. 275–292. Florence, 1944.

Battelli, G., ed. Latium. Vol. 10 of Rationes decimarum Italiae nei secoli XIII e XIV, edited by P. Guidi and P. Sella. Vatican City, 1946.

Battelli, G. "Archivi ecclesiastici: Speciali provvidenze della Santa Sede per la conservazione degli archivi ecclesiastici." In Enciclopedia cattolica, vol. 1, p. 1832. Vatican City, 1948.

Battelli, G. Lezioni di paleografia. 3d ed. Vatican City, 1949.

Battelli, G. "Liber diurnus romanorum pontificum." In Enciclopedia cattolica, vol. 7, pp. 1262–1267. Vatican City, 1951.

Battelli, G. "Epistula circa il prestito del materiale conservato negli archivi ecclesiastici in Italia." Monitor ecclesiasticus 78 (1953): 205–208.

Battelli, G. "Registri pontifici." In Enciclopedia cattolica, vol. 10, pp. 656–660. Vatican City, 1953.

Battelli, G. "La scuola di archivistica presso l'Archivio Segreto Vaticano." Archivum 3 (1953): 45–49.

Battelli, G. Adnotationes ad "Statuto della Scuola Vaticana di Paleografia e Diplomatica eretta presso l'Archivio Vaticano". Rome, 1954.

Battelli, G. "I transunti di Lione nel 1245." Mitteilungen des Instituts für österreichische Geschichtsforschung 62 (1954): 336–364.

Battelli, G. "Archivio Vaticano." In Enciclopedia cattolica, vol. 12, pp. 1131–1135. Vatican City, 1955.

Battelli, G. "Le ricerche storiche nell'Archivio Vaticano." In Relazioni del X Congresso internazionale di scienze storiche, Rome, 1955, vol. 1, pp. 451–477. Florence, 1955.

Battelli, G. "Due frammenti dei registri membranacei di Clemente VI." Bullettino dell'Archivio paleografico italiano, n.s. 2–3, pt. 1 (1956–1957): 69–76.

Battelli, G. "La Bibliografia dell'Archivio vaticano." Rivista di storia della chiesa in Italia 14 (1960): 135–137.

Battelli, G. "Il censimento dei documenti pontifici dal 1198 al 1417." Rivista di storia della chiesa in Italia 14 (1960): 138–140.

Battelli, G. "Aspetti giuridici ed esigenze scientifiche nella fotografia dei fondi." Archiva ecclesiae 3–4 (1960–1961): 58–81.

Battelli, G. "Mezzi bibliografici d'informazione e di studio presso l'Archivio Vaticano." Rassegna degli Archivi di Stato 22 (1962): 25–32.

Battelli, G. "Archivi, biblioteche e musei: Compiti comuni e zone d'interferenza." Archiva ecclesiae 5–6 (1962–1963): 20–40.

Battelli, G, ed. Bibliografia dell'Archivio Vaticano. Vatican City, 1962–.

Battelli, G. "'Membra disiecta' di registri pontifici dei secoli XIII e XIV." In *Mélanges Eugène Tisserant*, vol. 4, pp. 1–34. Vatican City, 1964.

Battelli, G. *Acta pontificum*. 2d ed. Vatican City, 1965.

Battelli, G. "Per una diplomatica dei nunzi pontifici: Un frammento di registro dell'anno 1404." In *Miscellanea in memoria di Giorgio Cencetti*, pp. 539–554. Turin, 1973.

Battelli, G. "'Gratiae rotulares' originali di Benedetto XIII antipapa." In *Römische Kurie, kirchliche Finanzen, vatikanisches Archiv: Studien zu Ehren von Hermann Hoberg*, vol. 1, pp. 57–64. Rome, 1979.

Battelli, G. "Documento pontificio (sec. XIII–XIV)." *Boletin de la Sociedad Castellonense de cultura* 58 (1982): 571–627.

Battistella, A. *Il S. Officio e la riforma religiosa in Friuli: Appunti storici documentati*. Udine, 1895.

Batzer, E. *Zur Kenntnis der Formularsammlung des Richards von Pofi*. Heidelberg, 1910.

Baudrillart, A., et al. *Dictionnaire d'histoire et de géographie ecclésiastiques*. Paris, 1912–1988.

Bauer, C. "Studi per la storia delle finanze papali durante il pontificato di Sisto IV." *Archivio della Società romana di storia patria* 50 (1927): 319–400.

Baumgarten, P. M. *Untersuchungen und Urkunden über die Camera Collegii Cardinalium für die Zeit von 1295 bis 1437*. Leipzig, 1898.

Baumgarten, P. M. *Aus Kanzlei und Kammer: Erörterungen zur kurialen Hof- und Verwaltungsgeschichte im XIII. XIV. und XV. Jahrhundert: Bullatores, Taxatores domorum, Cursores*. Freiburg, 1907.

Baumgarten, P. M. "Das päpstliche Siegelamt beim Tode und nach Neuwahl des Papstes." *Römische Quartalschrift für christliche Altertumskunde und für Kirchengeschichte* 21 (1907): 32–47.

Baumgarten, P. M. *Von der apostolischen Kanzlei: Untersuchungen über die päpstliche Tabellionen und die Vizekanzler der heiligen Römischen Kirche im XIII. XIV. und XV. Jahrhundert*. Cologne, 1908.

Baumgarten, P. M. "Die Entwicklung der neuzeitlichen Bullenschrift." *Römische Quartalschrift für christliche Altertumskunde und für Kirchengeschichte* 23.2 (1909): 16–34.

Baumgarten, P. M. "Der Ersatz eines zerbrochenen Bullenstempels unter Innocenz IV." *Römische Quartalschrift für christliche Altertumskunde und für Kirchengeschichte* 23.2 (1909): 114–116.

Baumgarten, P. M. "Institutes, Roman Historical." In *Catholic Encyclopedia*, vol. 3, pp. 61–65. New York, 1910.

Baumgarten, P. M. "Registrierungsnotizen auf Originalen und in den Registerbänden des 14. und 15. Jahrhunderts." *Römische Quartalschrift für christliche Altertumskunde und für Kirchengeschichte* 26.2 (1912): 144–152.

Baumgarten, P. M. "Vatican Archives." In *Catholic Encyclopedia*, vol. 15, pp. 286–290. New York, 1912.

Baumgarten, P. M. "Neueste Ausstattung der apostolischen Breven." *Römische Quartalschrift für christliche Altertumskunde und für Kirchengeschichte* 27 (1913): 43*–44*.

Baumgarten, P. M. "Über einige päpstliche Kanzleibeamte des XIII. und XIV. Jahrhunderts." In *Kirchengeschichtliche Festgabe Anton de Waal*, pp. 37–102. Freiburg, 1913.

Baumgarten, P. M. "Die transsumierende Tätigkeit der apostolischen Kanzlei." *Römische Quartalschrift für christliche Altertumskunde und für Kirchengeschichte* 28 (1914): 215–219.

Baumgarten, P. M., and G. Battelli, eds. *Schedario Baumgarten: Descrizione diplomatica di bolle e brevi originali da Innocenzo III a Pio IX*. Vatican City, 1965–1966.

Bauwens, L. "Analytisch Inventaris der Diversa Cameralia van het Vaticaans Archief (1500–1549)." *Bulletin de l'Institut historique Belge de Rome* 28 (1953): 31–50.

Beckmann, J. *La Congregation de la Propagation de la Foi face a la politique internationale*. Schöneck-Beckenried, 1963.

Beggiao, D. *La visita pastorale di Clemente VIII (1592–1600): Aspetti di riforma post-tridentina a Roma*. Rome, 1978.

Bell, H. E. "The Proposed Continuation of the Calendars of Roman State Papers Relating to English Affairs." 1939. (This title was noted but not verified by project staff.)

Bell, H. I. "A List of Original Papal Bulls and Briefs in the Department of Manuscripts of the British Museum." *English Historical Review* 36 (1921): 393–419, 556–583.

Benedictines. *Bullarium Casinense, seu Constitutiones summorum pontificum, imperatorum, regum, principum et decreta sacrarum congregationum pro congregatione Casinensi*. Venice, 1650.

Benedictines of Monte Cassino, eds. *Regestum Clementis Papae V: Ex Vaticanis archetypis sanctissimi domini nostri Leonis XIII pontificis maximi iussu et munificenta nunc primum editum*. Rome, 1885–1888.

Benoît, F. "Les archives de la Sacrée-Congrégation d'Avignon au Vatican (1693–1790)." *Mémoires de l'Académie de Vaucluse* 23 (1923): 1–28.

Benoit, M. "Inventaire des principales séries de documents intéressant le Canada, sous le pontificat de Léon XIII (1878–1903), dans les archives de la Sacrée Congrégation 'De Propaganda Fide' à Rome." (This is a computer printout found in the Archives of the Propaganda Fide.)

Berger, É., ed. *Les registres d'Innocent IV: Publiées ou analysés d'après les manuscrits originaux du Vatican et de la Bibliothèque nationale*. Vol. 1 of *Bibliothèque des Écoles françaises d'Athènes et de Rome*. 2d ser., *Registres des papes du XIIIe siècle*. Paris, 1884–1920.

Berlière, U. "Aux Archives vaticanes." *Revue Bénédictine* 20 (1903): 132–173.

Berlière, U. *Inventaire analytique des Libri obligationum et solutionum des Archives Vaticanes au point de vue des anciens diocèses de Cambrai, Liège, Thérouanne et Tournai*. Rome, 1904.

Berlière, U. *Inventaire analytique des Diversa Cameralia des Archives Vaticanes (1389–1500) au point de vue des anciens diocèses de Cambrai, Liège, Thérouanne et Tournai*. Rome, 1906.

Berlière, U., ed. *Suppliques de Clément VI (1342–1352): Textes et analyses*. Vol. 1 of *Analecta vaticano-belgica: Documents relatifs aux anciens diocèses de Cambrai, Liège, Thérouanne et Tournai*. Rome, 1906.

Berlière, U. "Épaves d'archives pontificales du XIVe siècle: Le ms. 775 de Rhiems." *Revue Bénédictine* 24 (1907): 456–478; 25 (1908): 19–47.

Berlière, U., ed. *Suppliques d'Innocent VI (1352–1362): Textes et analyses*. Vol. 5 of *Analecta vaticano-belgica: Documents relatifs aux anciens diocèses de Cambrai, Liège, Thérouanne et Tournai*. Rome, 1911.

Berlière, U. "Inventaire des 'Instrumenta Miscellanea' des Archives Vaticanes au point de vue de nos anciens diocèses." *Bulletin de l'Institut historique Belge de Rome* 4 (1924): 5–162; 7 (1927): 117–138.

Berlière, U., ed. *Les collectories pontificales dans les anciens diocèses de Cambrai, Thérouanne et Tournai au XIVe siècle.* Vol. 10 of *Analecta vaticano-belgica: Documents relatifs aux anciens diocèses de Cambrai, Liège, Thérouanne et Tournai.* Rome, 1929.

Bernouilli, J., ed. *Acta pontificum Helvetica: Quellen schweizerischer Geschichte aus dem päpstlichen Archiv in Rom.* Vol. 1, *1198–1268.* Basel, 1891.

Berthold, O. *Kaiser, Volk und Avignon: Ausgewählte Quellen zur antikurialen Bewegung in Deutschland in der ersten Hälfte des 14. Jahrhunderts.* Berlin, 1960.

Bertier de Sauvigny, G. A. de. "L'histoire religieuse de la Restauration (1814–1830) aux Archives du Vatican." *Revue d'histoire de l'Église de France* 38 (1952): 77–89.

Biaudet, H. *Les nonciatures apostoliques permanentes jusqu'en 1648.* Helsinki, 1910.

Bignami Odier, J. "Guide au Dept. des manuscrits de la bibliothèque du Vatican." *Mélanges d'archéologie et d'histoire* 51 (1934): 205–239.

Bignami Odier, J. *Premières recherches sur le Fonds Ottoboni.* Vatican City, 1966.

Bignami Odier, J., and J. Ruysschaert. *La Bibliothèque Vaticane de Sixte IV à Pie XI: Recherches sur l'histoire des collections de manuscrits.* Vatican City, 1973.

Binder, C. "Il magistero del Sacro Pallazzo Apostolico del cardinale di Torquemada." *Memorie domenicane,* n.s. 30 (1954): 3–24.

Bizzarri, G. A. *Collectanea in usum Secretariae Sacrae Congregationis Episcoporum et Regularium.* Rome, 1885.

Black, C. F. "Perugia and Papal Absolutism in the Sixteenth Century." *English Historical Review* 96 (1981): 509–539.

Black, C. F. *Italian Confraternities in the Sixteenth Century.* Cambridge, 1989.

Blaul, O. *Studien zum Register Gregors VII (Teildruck).* Strasbourg, 1911.

Blet, P., ed. *Girolamo Ragazzoni évêque de Bergame, nonce en France: Correspondance de sa nonciature, 1583–1586.* Vol. 2 of *Acta nuntiaturae gallicae.* Rome, 1962.

Blet, P., ed. *Correspondance du nonce en France Ranuccio Scotti, 1639–1641.* Vol. 5 of *Acta nuntiaturae gallicae.* Rome, 1965.

Blet, P. *Histoire de la représentation diplomatique du Saint Siège: Des origines à l'aube du XIXe siècle.* 2d ed. Vatican City, 1982.

Bliss, W. H., ed. *Calendar of Entries in the Papal Registers Relating to Great Britain and Ireland: Calendar of Petitions to the Pope, A.D. 1342–1419.* London, 1896.

Bliss, W. H., C. Johnson, and J. A. Twemlow, eds. *Calendar of Entries in the Papal Registers Relating to Great Britain and Ireland: Calendar of Papal Letters.* London, 1893–.

Blumenthal, U. "Bemerkungen zum Register Papst Paschalis II." *Quellen und Forschungen aus italienischen Archiven und Bibliotheken* 66 (1986): 1–19.

Boaga, E. *La soppressione innocenziana dei piccoli conventi in Italia.* Rome, 1971.

Bock, F. "Die Geheimschrift in der Kanzlei Johanns XXII: Eine diplomatische Studie." *Römische Quartalschrift für christliche Altertumskunde und für Kirchengeschichte* 42 (1934): 279–303.

Bock F. "Studien zum politischen Inquisitionsprozess Johanns XXII." *Quellen und Forschungen aus italienischen Archiven und Bibliotheken* 26 (1935–1936): 21–142; 27 (1936–1937): 109–134.

Bock, F. "Kaisertum, Kurie und Nationastaat im Beginn des 14. Jahrhunderts." *Römische Quartalschrift für christliche Altertumskunde und für Kirchengeschichte* 44 (1936): 105–122, 169–220.

Bock, F. "Mittelalterliche Kaiserurkunden im alten Urbinater Archiv." *Quellen und Forschungen aus italienischen Archiven und Bibliotheken* 27 (1936–1937): 251–263.

Bock, F. "Über Registrierung von Sekretbriefen (Studien zu den Sekretregistern Johanns XXII)." *Quellen und Forschungen aus italienischen Archiven und Bibliotheken* 28 (1937–1938): 147–234.

Bock, F. "Über Registrierung von Sekretbriefen (Studien zu den Sekretregistern Benedikts XII)." *Quellen und Forschungen aus italienischen Archiven und Bibliotheken* 29 (1938–1939): 41–88.

Bock, F. "Studien zur Registrierung der politischen Briefe und der allgemeinen Verwaltungssachen Johanns XXII." *Quellen und Forschungen aus italienischen Archiven und Bibliotheken* 30 (1940): 137–188.

Bock, F. "Einführung in das Registerwesen des Avignonesischen Papsttums." *Quellen und Forschungen aus italienischen Archiven und Bibliotheken* 31 (1941): 1–107.

Bock, F. "Roma al tempo di Roberto d'Angiò." *Archivio della R. Deputazione romana di storia patria,* n.s. 8 (1942): 163–208.

Bock, F. "Annotationes zum Register Gregors VII." *Studi Gregoriani per la storia di Gregorio VII e della riforma gregoriana* 1 (1947): 281–306.

Bock, F. "Die erste urkundlich greifbare Ordnung des päpstlichen Archivs." *Mitteilungen des Instituts für österreichische Geschichtsforschung* 62 (1954): 317–335.

Bock, F. "Osservazioni sulle lettere 'executorie' papali della seconda metà del secolo XIII." *Rivista di storia della chiesa in Italia* 8 (1954): 185–206.

Bock, F. "Studien zu den Originalregistern Innocenz III (Reg. Vat. 4–7A)." *Archivalische Zeitschrift* 50–51 (1955): 329–364.

Bock F. "Studien zu den Registern Innocenz IV." *Archivalische Zeitschrift* 52 (1956): 11–48.

Bock, F. "Originale und Registereintrage zur Zeit Honorius III." *Bullettino dell'Archivio paleografico italiano,* n.s. 2–3, pt. 1 (1956–1957): 99–116.

Bock, F. "Kodifizierung und Registrierung in der spätmittelalterlichen kurialen Verwaltung." *Archivalische Zeitschrift* 56 (1960): 11–75.

Bock, F. "Bemerkungen zu den ältesten Papstregistern und zum 'Liber Diurnus Romanorum Pontificum.'" *Archivalische Zeitschrift* 57 (1961): 11–51.

Bock, F. "Päpstliche Sekretregister und Kammerregister: Ueberblick und Ergänzung früherer Studien zum Registerwesen des Spätmittelalters." *Archivalische Zeitschrift* 59 (1963): 30–58.

Böhmer, J. F. "Päpste und Reichssachsen." In *Regesta Imperii.* Part 5, *Die Regesten des Kaiserreichs . . . 1198–1272,* vol. 3, pp. 1055–1579. Innsbruck, 1892–1894.

Bonenfant, P. "Rapport au Comité Directeur de l'Institut historique Belge de Rome sur les publications à faire pour le XVe siècle." *Bulletin de l'Institut historique Belge de Rome* 28 (1953): 357–366.

Bonnet, C., and C. Jourdain-Annequin, eds. *Héraclès: d'Une rive à l'autre de la Mediterranée: Bilan et perspectives: Actes de la Table Ronde de Rome, Academia Belgica-École française de Rome, 15–16 septembre 1989, à l'occasion du Cinquantenaire de l'Academia Belgica, en hommage à Franz Cumont, son premier président.* Brussels, 1992.

Bonnici, A. "Il fondo 'Malta' della Segreteria di Stato nell'Archivio Segreto Vaticano." *Melita Historica* 10 (1992): 375–411.

Bono, S. "Genovesi schiavi in Algeri barbaresca." *Bollettino ligustico per la storia e la cultura regionale* 3 (1953): 67–72.

Bono, S. "La missione dei Cappuccini ad Algeri per il riscatto degli schiavi cristiani nel 1585." *Collectanea Franciscana* 25 (1955): 149–163, 279–304.

Bono, S. "L'Arciconfraternità del Gonfalone di Roma e il riscatto degli schiavi dai musulmani." *Capitolium* (Sept. 1957): 3–7.

Borino, G. B. "Note Gregoriane per la storia di Gregorio VII e della Riforma Gregoriana: Può il Reg. Vat. 2 (Registro di Gregorio VII) essere il registro della cancelleria?" *Studi Gregoriani per la storia di Gregorio VII e della riforma gregoriana* 5 (1956): 391–402; 6 (1959–61): 363–389.

Borsting, H. *Das Provinciale Romanum mit besonderer Berucksichtigung seiner handschriftlichen Ueberlieferung.* Lengerich, 1937.

Boshof, E., and H. Wolter. *Rechtsgeschichtlich-diplomatische Studien zu frümittelalterlichen Papsturkunden.* Cologne, 1976.

Bossányi, A. *Regesta supplicationum: A pápai Kérvénykönyvek magyar vonatkozású okmányai: Avignoni korszak.* Budapest, 1916–1918.

Bouard, A. de. *Manuel de diplomatique française et pontificale.* Paris, 1929–1952.

Bouix, D. *Tractatus de Curia Romana seu de cardinalibus, romanis congregationibus, legatis, nuntiis, vicariis, et protonotariis apostolicis.* Paris, 1859.

Bourgin, G. *La France et Rome de 1788 à 1797: Regestes des dépêches du cardinal secrétaire d'état tirées du fonds des "Vescovi" des archives secrètes du Vatican.* Paris, 1909.

Bourmont, A. de. "Fonds des canonisations." *Analecta Bollandiana* 5 (1886): 147–161.

Bourty, P. "Nobilità romana e curia nell'età della Restaurazione." In *Signori, patrizi, cavalieri in Italia nell'età moderna*, by M. A. Visceglia, pp. 390–422. Bari, 1992.

Bovicella, G. B. *La pieta trionfante su le distrutte grandezze del gentilismo nella magnifica fondazione dell'insigne basilica di S. Lorenzo in Damaso di Roma, con la serie istorica di tutte le sue chiese figliali, degli uffizi della Cancelleria apostolica e de' cancellieri dells S.R.C.* Rome, 1729.

Boyce, G. K. "Documents of Pope Leo X in the Morgan Library." *Catholic Historical Review* 35 (1949–1950): 163–175.

Boyle, L. E. "The Constitution 'Cum ex eo' of Boniface VIII: Education of Parochial Clergy." *Mediaeval Studies* 24 (1962): 263–302.

Boyle, L. E. "Review of O. Hageneder and A. Haidacher, edd., Die Register Innocenz' III., I, Band 1, Pontifikatsjahr 1198–1199: Texte, Graz-Cologne, 1964." *Speculum* 42 (1967): 153–162.

Boyle, L. E. A *Survey of the Vatican Archives and of its Medieval Holdings.* Toronto, 1972.

Brackmann, A. "Papsturkunden des östlichen Deutschlands (Berlin, Stettin, Magdeburg, Zerbst, Dresden, Meissen, Leipzig, Zeitz)." *Nachrichten der königlichen Gesellschaft der Wissenschaften zu Göttingen. Philologisch-historische Klasse* (1902): 193–223.

Brackmann, A. "Papsturkunden der Schweiz (Basel, . . . Aarau)." *Nachrichten der königlichen Gesellschaft der Wissenschaften zu Göttingen. Philologisch-historische Klasse* (1904): 417–517.

Brackmann, A. "Papsturkunden des Nordens, Nord- und Mittel-Deutschlands (Stockholm, Uppsala, Copenhagen, Hanover, Hildesheim, . . . Meiningen)." *Nachrichten der königlichen Gesellschaft der Wissenschaften zu Göttingen. Philologisch-historische Klasse* (1904): 1–45.

Brackmann, A., ed. *Provincia Salisburgensis et episcopatus Tridentinus.* Vol. 1 of *Germania Pontificia, sive Repertorium privilegiorum et litterarum a Romanis pontificibus ante annum MCLXXXXVIII Germaniae ecclesiis, monasteriis, civitatibus singulisque personis concessorum.* Berlin, 1910.

Brackmann, A. *Papsturkunden.* Leipzig, 1914.

Brackmann, A., ed. *Provincia Maguntinensis.* Vols. 2–3 of *Germania Pontificia, sive Repertorium privilegiorum et litterarum a Romanis pontificibus ante annum MCLXXXVIII Germaniae ecclesiis, monasteriis, civitatibus singulisque personis concessorum.* Berlin, 1923–1935.

Brady, W. M. *The Episcopal Succession in England, Scotland and Ireland, A. D. 1400–1875: With Appointments to Monasteries and Extracts from Consistorial Acts Taken from mss. in Public and Private Libraries in Rome, Florence, Bologna, Ravenna and Paris.* Rome, 1876–1877.

Brentano, R. *Two Churches: England and Italy in the Thirteenth Century.* Princeton, 1968.

Bréquigny, L. G. O. F. de, and F. J. G. de La Porte du Theil, eds. *Diplomata, chartae, epistolae et alia documenta ad res Francicas spectantia: Pars altera, tomus primus Innocentii III epistolas . . . exhibens.* Paris, 1791.

Bresslau, H. *Handbuch der Urkundenlehre für Deutschland und Italien.* Berlin, 1958–1968.

Bridges, S. F. "A Breton adventurer in Naples." *Papers of the British School at Rome* 19 (n.s. 6) (1951): 154–159.

Briegleb, P., and A. Laret-Kayser. *Documents relatifs au Grand Schisme.* Vol. 6, *Suppliques de Benoît XIII (1394–1422).* Vols. 26–27 of *Analecta vaticano-belgica: Documents relatifs aux anciens diocèses de Cambrai, Liège, Thérouanne et Tournai.* Brussels, 1973.

Broderick, J. F. "The Sacred College of Cardinals: Size and Geographical Composition (1099–1986)." *Archivum Historiae Pontificiae* 25 (1987): 7–47.

Brom, G. *Bullarium Trajectense: Romanorum Pontificum diplomata quotquot olim usque ad Urbanum papam VI (an. 1378) in veterem episcopatum Trajectensem destinata reperiuntur.* The Hague, 1891–1896.

Brom, G. *Archivalia in Italië belangrijk voor de geschiedenis van Nederland.* The Hague, 1908–1914.

Brom, G. *Guide aux archives du Vatican.* 2d ed. Rome, 1911.

Brosius, D. "Breven und Briefe Papst Pius' II." *Römische*

Quartalschrift für christliche Altertumskunde und für Kirchengeschichte 70 (1975): 180–224.

Brouette, E., ed. *Les 'Libri annatarum' pour les pontificats d'Eugène IV à Alexander VI*, vol. 4, *Pontificats d'Innocent VIII et d'Alexander VI, 1484–1503*. Vol. 24 of *Analecta vaticano-belgica: Documents relatifs aux anciens diocèses de Cambrai, Liège, Thérouanne et Tournai*. Rome, 1963.

Brulez, W. *Correspondance de Richard Pauli-Stravius (1634–1642)*. Vol. 10 of *Analecta vaticano-belgica*. Ser. 2, section A, *Nonciature de Flandre*. Brussels, 1955.

Brulez, W. *Correspondence de Martino Alfieri (1634–1639)*. Vol. 1 of *Analecta vaticano-belgica*. Ser. 2, section B, *Nonciature de Cologne*. Brussels, 1956.

Bues, A. *Nuntiatur Giovanni Dolfins, 1573–1574*. Vol. 7 of *Nuntiaturberichte aus Deutschland nebst ergänzenden Actenstücken. Dritte Abteilung, 1572–1585*. Tübingen, 1990.

Bulferetti, L. "Lettere inedite di giansenisti bresciani." *Atti dell'Accademia delle scienze di Torino. Classe di scienze morali, storiche e filologiche* 84.2 (1949–1950): 67–108.

Bullard, M. M. *Filippo Strozzi and the Medici: Favor and Finance in Sixteenth-Century Florence and Rome*. Cambridge, 1980.

Bullarium Sacri Ordinis Cluniacensis: Complectens plurima privilegia per summos Pontifices tum ipsi Cluniacensi Abbatae, tum ei subditis Monasteriis hactenus concessa. Lyons, 1680.

Buonamici, F. M. *De claris pontificiarum epistolarum scriptoribus ad Benedictum XIV Pont. Max. liber*. Rome, 1753.

Buonocore, M. *Bibliografia dei fondi manoscritti della Biblioteca vaticana (1968–1980)*. Vatican City, 1986.

Burchard, J. *Liber notarum ab anno 1483 usque ad annum 1506*. Edited by E. Celani. Città di Castello, 1907–1914.

Burchi, P. *Catalogus processuum beatificationis et canonizationis qui in tabulariis et bibliothecis urbis asservantur*. Rome, 1965.

Burger, H. "Beiträge zur Geschichte der äusseren Merkmale der Papsturkunden im späteren Mittelalter." *Archiv für Urkundenforschung* 12 (1931–1932): 206–243.

Burns, C. "New Light on the 'Bulla' of the Council of Basle." *Innes Review* 15 (1964): 92–95.

Burns, C. "Sources of British and Irish History in the Instrumenta Miscellanea of the Vatican Archives." *Archivum Historiae Pontificiae* 9 (1971): 7–141.

Burns, C. "A Calendar of Scottish Documents in the Missioni Collection of the Vatican Archives." *Innes Review* 24 (1973): 51–68.

Burns, C. "Vatican Sources and the Honorary Papal Chaplains of the Fourteenth Century." In *Römische Kurie, kirchliche Finanzen, vatikanisches Archiv: Studien zu Ehren von Hermann Hoberg*, vol. 1, pp. 65–95. Rome, 1979.

Burns, C. "Additions to the 'Fondo Missioni' Handlist." *Innes Review* 33 (1982): 31–43.

Burns, C. "Pope Clement XI and the British Isles: The Inventory of Fondo Albani 163–168." In *Ecclesiae Memoria: Miscellanea in onore del R.P. Josef Metzler OMI, prefetto del Archivio segreto vaticano*, edited by W. Henkel, pp. 41–85. Rome, 1991.

Burrus, E. J. "Research Opportunities in Italian Archives and Manuscript Collections for Students of Hispanic American History." *Hispanic American Historical Review* 39 (1959): 428–463.

Buschbell, G. *Reformation und Inquisition in Italien: Um die Mitte des XVI. Jahrhunderts*. Paderborn, 1910.

Cabrol, F. et al., eds. *Dictionnaire d'archéologie chrétienne et de liturgie*. Paris, 1907–1953.

Caenegem, R. C. van, and F. L. Ganshof. *Kurze Quellenkunde des westeuropäischen Mittelalters: Eine typologische, historische und bibliographische Einführung*. Göttingen, 1964.

Caiazza, P. "L'archivio storico della Sacra Congregazione del Concilio: Primi appunti per un problema di riordinamento." *Ricerche di storia sociale e religiosa* 42 (1992): 7–24.

Cameron, A. I. *The Apostolic Camera and Scottish Benefices, 1418–1488*. Edinburgh, 1934.

Cameron, A. I. "Vatican Archives, 1073–1560." In *An Introductory Survey of the Sources and Literature of Scots Laws*, pp. 274–281. Edinburgh, 1936.

Cameron, A. I., ed. *Calendar of Scottish Supplications to Rome, 1423–1428*. Edinburgh, 1956.

Campeau, L. *La première mission d'Acadie, 1602–1616*. Rome, 1967.

Campeau, L. *La première mission des Jesuites en Nouvelle-France, 1611–1613, et les commencements du Collège de Québec, 1626–1670*. Montréal, 1972.

Campeau, L. *Établissement à Québec, 1616–1634*. Rome, 1979.

Campitelli, A. "La Rocca ed il Borgo di Vignanello dai Farnese ai Ruspoli." In *La dimensione europea dei Farnese*, edited by B. de Groof and E. Galdieri, pp. 115–153. Brussels, 1993.

Capasso, R. "Un contributo allo studio delle suppliche pontificie nel secolo XIII." *Bullettino dell'Archivio paleografico italiano*, n.s. 2–3, pt. 1 (1956–1957): 169–173.

Caravale, M., and A. Caracciolo. *Lo Stato pontificio da Martino V a Pio IX*. Turin, 1978.

Cárcel Ortí, V. "Los despachos de la nunciatura de Madrid (1847–1857)." *Archivum Historiae Pontificiae* 13 (1975): 311–400; 14 (1976): 265–356.

Cárcel Ortí, V. "El archivo del nuncio en España, Giacomo Giustiniani (1817–1827)." *Escritos del Vedat* 6 (1976): 265–300.

Cárcel Ortí, V, ed. *Correspondencia diplomatica del Nuncio Tiberi (1827–1834)*. Pamplona, 1976.

Cárcel Ortí, V. "El archivo de la nunciatura de Madrid desde 1868 hasta 1875." *Archivum Historiae Pontificiae* 15 (1977): 363–376.

Cárcel Ortí, V. "El archivo del nuncio Barili (1857–1868)." *Archivum Historiae Pontificiae* 17 (1979): 289–355.

Cárcel Ortí, V. "El archivo de Pietro Gravina, Nuncio en España (1803–1817)." *Escritos del Vedat* 9 (1979): 303–320.

Cárcel Ortí, V. "El archivo del nuncio Simeoni y del encargado de negocios Rampolla (1875–1877)." *Scriptorium Victoriense* 26 (1979): 338–352; 27 (1980): 102–110, 199–233.

Cárcel Ortí, V. "El archivo de los nuncios de Leon XIII en Espana. 1, Nunciatura de Cattani (1877–1879)." *Italica* 16 (1982): 237–264.

Cárcel Ortí, V. "La correspondance diplomatique des nonces apostoliques dans l'Espagne du XIXe siècle." *Revue d'histoire diplomatique* 96 (1982): 320–334.

Cárcel Ortí, V, ed. *Correspondencia diplomatica del Nuncio Amat (1833–1840)*. Pamplona, 1982.

Cárcel Ortí, V. "El archivo de los nuncios de Leon XIII en Espana. 2, Nunciatura de Bianchi (1879–1883)." *Italica* 17 (1984): 231–262.

Cárcel Ortí, V. "El archivo del nuncio Mariano Rampolla (1883–1887)." *Hispania sacra* 39 (1987): 747–788.

Cárcel Ortí, V. "El archivo del nuncio Angelo di Pietro (1887–1893)." *Hispania sacra* 41 (1989): 183–226.

Cárcel Ortí, V. "El archivo del nuncio Serafino Cretoni (1893–1896)." *Hispania sacra* 42 (1990): 537–572.

Cárcel Ortí, V. "El archivo del nuncio Giuseppe Francia-Nava di Bontife (1896–1899)." *Hispania sacra* 44 (1992): 459–485.

Cardauns, L. *Nuntiaturen Morones und Poggios, Legationen Farneses und Cervinis, 1539–1540.* Vol. 5 of *Nuntiaturberichte aus Deutschland nebst ergänzenden Actenstücken. Erste Abteilung, 1533–1559.* Berlin, 1909.

Cardauns, L. *Gesandtschaft Campegios, Nuntiaturen Morones und Poggios 1540–1541.* Vol. 6 of *Nuntiaturberichte aus Deutschland nebst ergänzenden Actenstücken. Erste Abteilung, 1533–1559.* Berlin, 1910.

Cardauns, L. *Berichte vom Regensburger und Speierer Reichstag, 1541–1542, Nuntiaturen Verallos und Poggios, Sendungen Farneses und Sfondratos, 1541–1544.* Vol. 7 of *Nuntiaturberichte aus Deutschland nebst ergänzenden Actenstücken. Erste Abteilung, 1533–1559.* Berlin, 1912.

Cardella, L. *Memorie storiche de'cardinali della Santa Romana Chiesa.* Rome, 1792–1797.

Carga, G. "Informatione del secretario et secreteria di Nostro Signore e di tutte gli offitii che da quella dipendono." In *Monumenta Vaticana historiam ecclesiasticam saeculi XVI illustrantia,* by H. Laemmer, pp. 457–468. Freiburg, 1861.

Carocci, S., et al., eds. *Bibliografia dell'Archivio Centrale dello Stato, 1953–1978.* Rome, 1986.

Carolus Barre, L. "Le cardinal de Dormans chancelier de France, principal conseiller de Charles V, d'après son testament et les archives du Vatican." *Mélanges d'archëologie et d'histoire* 52 (1935): 315–365.

Carucci, P., and R. Santoro, eds. *Le fonti archivistiche.* Vol. 1 of *La Rivoluzione Francese (1787–1799): Repertorio delle fonti archivistiche e delle fonti a stampa conservate in Italia e nella Città del Vaticano.* Rome, 1991.

Carusi, E. *Dispacci e lettere di Giacomo Gherardi, nunzio pontificio a Firenze e Milano (11 settembre 1487–10 ottobre 1490).* Rome, 1909.

Casamassima, E. *Trattati di scrittura del Cinquecento italiano.* Milan, 1966.

Casey, T. F. *The Sacred Congregation de Propaganda Fide and the Revision of the First Provincial Council of Baltimore (1829–1830).* Rome, 1957.

Caspar, E. L. E. "Studien zum Register Gregors VII." *Neues Archiv der Gesellschaft für ältere deutsche Geschichtskunde* 38 (1913): 145–226.

Caspar, E. L. E., ed. *Das Register Gregors VII.* Berlin, 1920–1923.

Caspar, E. L. E., ed. "Fragmenta registri Iohannis VIII papae." In *Epistolae karolini aevi,* vol. 5, pp. 273–312. Berlin, 1928.

Caspar, E. L. E., ed. "Fragmenta registri Stephani V papae." In *Epistolae karolini aevi,* vol. 5, pp. 334–353. Berlin, 1928.

Caspar, E. L. E. "Johannis VIII papae epistolae dubiae." In *Epistolae karolini aevi,* vol. 5, pp. 330–333. Berlin, 1928.

Caspar, E. L. E. "Registrum Iohannis VIII papae." In *Epistolae karolini aevi,* vol. 5, pp. 1–272. Berlin, 1928.

Caspar, E. L. E., and G. Laehr. "Epistolae ad res Orientales spectantes." In *Epistolae karolini aevi,* vol. 5, pp. 371–384. Berlin, 1928.

Caspar, E. L. E., and G. Laehr. "Johannis VIII papae epistolae passim collectae." In *Epistolae karolini aevi,* vol. 5, pp. 313–329. Berlin, 1928.

Catholic Church. *Codex iuris canonici Pii X Pontificis Maximi iussu digestus, Benedicti Papae XV auctoriatate promulgatus.* Rome, 1917.

Catholic Church. Congregatio Concilii. *Thesaurus resolutionum Sacrae Congregationis Concilii.* Rome, 1739–1963.

Catholic Church. Congregatio de Propaganda Fide. *Collectanea constitutionum, decretorum, indultorum ac instructionum Sanctae Sedis: Ad usum operariorum apostolicorum Societatis Missionum ad Exteros.* Rev. ed. Hong Kong, 1905.

Catholic Church. Congregatio de Propaganda Fide. *Iuris pontificii de Propaganda Fide: Pars prima complectens bullas brevia acta S.S. a congregationis institutione ad praesens* [and] *Pars secunda complectens decreta instructiones encyclicas literas etc. ab eadem congregatione lata.* Rome, 1888–1909.

Catholic Church. Congregatio pro Causis Sanctorum. *Miscellanea in occasione del IV centenario della Congregazione per le cause dei santi (1588–1988).* Vatican City, 1988.

Catholic Encyclopedia. New York, 1907–1922.

Cau, A. "Tre lettere pontificie inedite del sec. XIII: Contributo alla diplomatica pontificia." *Ricerche medievali* 3 (1968): 33–45.

Cauchie, A. "De la création d'une école belge à Rome." In *Compte rendu des travaux du dixième congrès tenu à Tournai du 5 au 8 août 1895, Congrès de la Fédération archéologique et historique de Belgique,* pp. 739–802. Tournai, 1896.

Cauchie, A., and R. Maere. *Recueil des instructions générales aux nonces de Flandre (1596–1635).* Brussels, 1904.

Cavallaro, A. "Antoniazzo Romano e le confraternità del Quattrocento a Roma." In *Le confraternite Romane: Esperienza religiosa, società, commitenza artistica: Colloquio della Fondazione Caetani, Roma, 14–15 maggio 1982,* edited by L. Fiorani, pp. 335–365. Rome, 1984.

Cavalleri, O. *Le Carte Macchi dell'Archivio segreto vaticano: Inventario.* Vatican City, 1979.

Cavalleri, O. "Le Carte Berzi dell'Archivio segreto vaticano." *Commentari dell'Ateneo di Brescia* (1982): 129–155.

Cavalleri, O. *L'Archivio di Mons. Achille Ratti Visitatore Apostolico e Nunzio a Varsavia (1918–1921): Inventario.* Vatican City, 1990.

Célier, L. "Appunti sul libro di note di un abbreviatore di parco maggiore." *Archivio della Società romana di storia patria* 30 (1907): 243–248.

Célier, L. *Les dataires du XVe siècle et les origines de la Daterie apostolique.* Paris, 1910.

Celse, M. von. *Apparatus ad historiam Sveo-Gothicam.* Stockholm, 1782.

Cenci, P. "L'archivio della cancelleria della Nunziatura Veneta." In *Miscellanea Francesco Ehrle*, vol. 5, pp. 273–330. Rome, 1924.

Cerasoli, F., and C. Cipolla. *Innocenzo VI e casa Savoia: Documenti dell'archivio vaticano*. Turin, 1900.

Cerchiari, E. *Capellani Papae et Apostolicae Sedis Auditores causarum sacri palatii apostolici seu Sacra Romana Rota, ab origine ad diem usque 20 Septembris 1870: Relatio historica-iuridica SSMO D.N. Benedicto Papae XV dicata. . . .* Rome, 1919–1921.

Ceresa, M. *Bibliografia dei Fondi Manoscritti della Biblioteca Vaticana (1981–1985)*. Vatican City, 1991.

Chaix de Lavarène, L. A. C., ed. *Monumenta pontificia arverniae decurrentibus IX°, X°, XI°, XII° saeculis: Correspondance diplomatique des papes concernant l'Auvergne, depuis le pontificat de Nicolas Ier jusqu'à celui d'Innocent III*. Clermont-Ferrand, 1880.

Chamard, F. "Les bulles de plomb des lettres pontificales." *Revue des questions historiques* 34 (1883): 609–616.

Chambers, D. S. *Cardinal Bainbridge in the Court of Rome, 1509 to 1514*. Oxford, 1965.

Cheney, C. R. *The Study of the Mediaeval Papal Chancery*. Glasgow, 1966.

Cheney, C. R., and M. Cheney. *The Letters of Pope Innocent III (1198–1216) Concerning England and Wales: A Calendar with an Appendix of Texts*. Oxford, 1967.

Cheney, C. R., and W. H. Semple. *Selected Letters of Pope Innocent III Concerning England (1198–1216)*. London, 1953.

Cherubini, P. *Mandati della Reverenda Camera Apostolica (1418–1802)*. Rome, 1988.

Chevalier, U. *Répertoire des sources historiques du Moyen Age*. Paris, 1894–1907.

Chiappafreddo, F. "L'Archivio della Sacra Congregazione del Concilio." In *La sacra Congregazione del Concilio: Quarto centenario della fondazione, 1564–1964, studi e ricerche*, pp. 395–422. Vatican City, 1964.

Choupin, L. *Valeur des décisions doctrinales et disciplinaires du Saint-Siege*. Paris, 1907.

Choupin, L. "La constitution 'Sapienti consilio' de Pie X et la réorganisation de la curie romaine." *Études* 117 (1908): 308–320, 642–658.

Christensen, C. A., ed. *Diplomatarium Danicum*. Raekke 3. Copenhagen, 1958–.

Ciampini, G. G. *De Abbreviatorum de parco maiori, sive Assistentium S.R.E. vicecancellario in litterarum apostolicarum expeditionibus antiquo statu, illorumve in collegium erectione, munere, dignitate, praerogativis ac privilegiis dissertatio historica*. Rome, 1691.

Ciampini, G. G. *Abbreviatoris de Curia Compendiaria Notitia*. Rome, 1696.

Cicerchia, E., and A. M. de Strobel. "Documenti inediti dell'Archivio segreto vaticano sui restauri delle Stanze di Raffaello e della Cappella sistina nel settecento." *Bollettino—Monumenti, musei e gallerie pontificie* 6 (1986): 105–152.

Ciprotti, P. "Cancelleria apostolica." In *Enciclopedia del diritto*, vol. 5, pp. 1070–1071. Varese, 1959.

Claeys–Bouvaert, F. "Brief." In *Dictionnaire de droit canonique*, edited by R. Naz, vol. 2, pp. 1060–1062. Paris, 1937.

Classen, P. *Kaiserreskript und Königsurkunde: Diplomatische Studien zum Problem der Kontinuität zwischen Altertum und Mittelalter*. Thessalonike, 1977.

Clercq, C. de. "Le fonds dit de canonisations à la Bibliothèque Nationale de Paris." *Revue de droit canonique* 4 (1954): 76–90.

Clergeac, A. "Inventaire analytique et chronologique de la Série des Archives du Vatican, dite 'Lettere di Vescovi.'" *Annales de St.-Louis-des-Français* 10 (1906): 215–268, 319–375, 419–470.

Clergeac, A. *La curie et les bénéficiers consistoriaux: Étude sur les communs et menus services, 1300–1600*. Paris, 1911.

Cloulas, I., ed. *Correspondance du nonce en France, Anselmo Dandino (1578–1581)*. Vol. 8 of *Acta nuntiaturae gallicae*. Rome, 1970.

Cobban, A. B. "Edward II, John XXII and the University of Cambridge." *Bulletin of the John Rylands Library* 47 (1964): 49–78.

Codignola, L. *Guide des documents relatifs à l'Amérique du Nord française et anglaise dans les archives de la Sacrée Congrégation de la Propaganda à Rome, 1622–1799*. Ottawa, 1990.

Codignola, L. *Vatican, Archives of the Sacred Congregation "de Propaganda Fide" 1622–1799*. Ottawa, 1990.

Codignola, L. *Calendar of Documents relating to Canada in the Archives of the Sacred Congregation "de Propaganda Fide" in Rome, 1800–1830*. Ottawa, 1993. (This is a limited edition found in the Archives of the Propaganda Fide.)

Codignola, L. *Calendar of Documents relating to Canada in the Archives of the Sacred Congregation "de Propaganda Fide" in Rome, 1831–1846*. Forthcoming.

Coleman, W. J. *The First Apostolic Delegation in Rio de Janeiro and its Influence in Spanish America: A Study in Papal Policy, 1830–1840*. Washington, D.C., 1950.

Colker, M. L. *Trinity College Library Dublin: Descriptive Catalogue of the Mediaeval and Renaissance Latin Manuscripts*. Aldershot, 1991.

Collura, P. "Addizioni e correzioni al Potthasat relative alla Sicilia tratte dai tabulari delle chiese vescovili dell'isola." *Annali della Scuola speciale per archivisti e bibliotecari dell'Università di Roma* 12 (1972): 166–192.

Combaluzier, F. "Sacrés épiscopaux à Rome de 1565 à 1662: Analyse intégrale du Ms. 'Miscellanea XIII, 33' des Archives Vaticanes." *Sacris Eruditi* 18 (1967–1968): 120–305.

Comyns, J. J. *Papal and Episcopal Administration of Church Property: An Historical Synopsis and Commentary*. Washington, D.C., 1942.

Conti, O. P. *Origine, fasti e privilegi degli avvocati concistoriali: Memorie storiche*. Rome, 1898.

"Convegno di studio su Roma punto d'incontro e di nuove aperture alla cultura europea dal 1870 al 1914: Relazioni e comunicazioni, nel vol. Il Centenario della Società." *Archivio della Società romana di storia patria* 100 (1979): 29–204.

Conway, D. "Guide to Documents of Irish and British Interest in the Fondo Borghese." *Archivium hibernicum* 23 (1960): 1–147; 24 (1961): 31–102.

Corbo, A. M. "Martino V, Eugenio IV e la ricostituzione dell'archivio papale dopo Costanza." *Rassegna degli Archivi di Stato* 28 (1968): 36–66.

Cornaro, A., et al. *Der Schriftverkehr zwischen dem päpst-*

lichen Staatssekretariat und dem Nuntius am Kaiserhof Antonio Eugenio Visconti, 1764–1774. Vienna, 1970.

Corvisieri, C. "Compendio dei processi del Santo Uffizio di Roma (da Paolo III a Paolo IV)." *Archivio della Società romana di storia patria* 3 (1879): 261–290, 449–471.

Cosma, R. "Due nuovi registri di brevi di Sisto IV." *Archivio della Società romana di storia patria* 103 (1980): 305–312.

Costantini, C. "Ricerche d'archivio sull'istruzione 'de clero indigena:' Emanata dalla S.C. de Propaganda Fide il 23 novembre 1845." In *Miscellanea Pietro Fumasoni-Biondi*, vol. 1, pp. 1–78. Rome, 1947.

Costello, M. A. "Obligationes pro annatis diocesis Dublinensis, 1421–1520." *Archivium hibernicum* 2 (1913): 1–72.

Costello, M. A., and D. Buckley, eds. "Obligationes pro annatis diocesis Cloynensis, 1413–1526." *Archivium hibernicum* 24 (1961): 1–30.

Costello, M. A., and T. J. Clohosey, eds. "Obligationes pro annatis diocesis Ossoriensis, 1413–1531." *Archivium hibernicum* 20 (1957): 1–37.

Costello, M. A., and A. Coleman, eds. *Ulster.* Vol. 1 of *De Annatis Hiberniae: A Calendar of the First Fruits' Fees Levied on Papal Appointments to Benefices in Ireland A.D. 1400 to 1535. . . .* Dundalk, 1909.

Costello, M. A., and P. K. Egan, eds. "Obligationes pro annatis diocesis Clonfertensis, 1420–1531." *Archivium hibernicum* 21 (1958): 52–74.

Costello, M. A., and D. F. Gleeson, eds. "Obligationes pro annatis diocesis Laoniensis, 1421–1535." *Archivium hibernicum* 10 (1943): 1–103.

Costello, M. A., and G. Mac Niocaill, eds. "Obligationes pro annatis diocesis Elphinensis, 1426–1548." *Archivium hibernicum* 22 (1959): 1–27.

Costello, M. A., and M. Moloney, eds. "Obligationes pro annatis diocesis Limiricensis, 1421–1519." *Archivium hibernicum* 10 (1943): 104–162.

Costello, M. A., and J. O'Connell, eds. "Obligationes pro annatis diocesis Ardfertensis, 1421–1517." *Archivium hibernicum* 21 (1958): 1–51.

Costello, M. A., and J. F. O'Doherty, eds. "Obligationes pro annatis provinciae Tuamensis, 1413–1548." *Archivium hibernicum* 26 (1963): 56–117.

Costello, M. A., and P. Power, eds. "Obligationes pro annatis diocesis Lismorensis, 1426–1529." *Archivium hibernicum* 12 (1946): 15–61.

Costello, M. A., and P. Power, eds. "Obligationes pro annatis diocesis Waterfordensis, 1421–1507." *Archivium hibernicum* 12 (1946): 1–14.

Costello, M. A., and J. Ranson, eds. "Obligationes pro annatis diocesis Fernensis, 1413–1524." *Archivium hibernicum* 18 (1955): 1–15.

Costello, M. A., L. Ryan, and W. Skehan, eds. "Obligationes pro annatis diocesis Cassellensis, 1433–1534." *Archivium hibernicum* 28 (1966): 1–32.

Costello, M. A., L. Ryan, and W. Skehan, eds. "Obligationes pro annatis diocesis Imelacensis, 1429–1444." *Archivium hibernicum* 28 (1966): 33–44.

Coulon, A., and S. Clémencet, eds. *Lettres secrètes et curiales du pape Jean XXII 1316–1334 relatives à la France.* Vol. 1 of *Bibliothèque des Écoles françaises d'Athènes et de Rome.*

3d ser., *Registres et lettres des papes du XIVe siècle.* Paris, 1900–.

Cowan, I. B. "The Vatican Archives: A Report on Pre-reformation Scottish Material." *Scottish Historical Review* 48 (1969): 227–242.

Cowdrey, H. E. J. *The Epistolae Vagantes of Pope Gregory VII.* Oxford, 1972.

Crehan, J. "Saint Ignatius and Cardinal Pole." *Archivum historicum Societatis Iesu* 25 (1956): 72–98.

Creytens, R. "La giurisprudenza della sacra Congregazione del Concilio nella questione della clausura delle monache (1564–1576)." In *La sacra Congregazione del Concilio: Quarto centenario della fondazione, 1564–1964, studi e ricerche,* pp. 563–597. Vatican City, 1964.

Criscuolo, V. *I Cappuccini e la Congregazione romana dei vescovi e regolari.* Rome, 1989–.

Cross, F. L., ed. *The Oxford Dictionary of the Christian Church.* 3d ed. Edited by E. A. Livingstone. Oxford, 1997.

Crovella, H. "De Libro Visitationum Sacrorum Liminum." In *La sacra Congregazione del Concilio: Quarto centenario della fondazione, 1564–1964, studi e ricerche,* pp. 423–446. Vatican City, 1964.

Crump, C. G. "The Arrest of Roger Mortimer and Queen Isabel." *English Historical Review* 26 (1911): 331–332.

Cuarterón y Fernandez, C. *Spiegazione e traduzione dei XIV Quadri relativi alle isole di Salibaboo, Talaor, Sanguey, Nanuse, Mindanao, Celebes, Borneo, Bahalatolis, Tambisan, Sulu, Toolyan, e Labuan presenti alla Sacra Congregazione de Propaganda Fide.* Rome, 1855.

Cugnoni, G. *Documenti chigiani concernenti Felice Peretti, Sisto V, come privato e come pontefice.* Rome, 1882.

Curschmann, F. *Die älteren Papsturkunden des Erzbistums Hamburg: Eine diplomatische Untersuchung.* Hamburg, 1909.

Dainville-Barbiche, S. de, ed. *Correspondance du nonce en France, Fabrizio Spada, 1674–1675.* Vol. 15 of *Acta nuntiaturae gallicae.* Rome, 1982.

Daly, L. W. "Early Alphabetical Indices in the Vatican Archives." *Traditio* 19 (1963): 483–485.

D'Amico, J. F. *Renaissance Humanism in Papal Rome: Humanists and Churchmen on the Eve of the Reformation.* Baltimore, 1991.

Dante, E. "Catalogo dell'Archivio della Prefettura delle Ceremonie Apostoliche." 1956. (This title was noted but not verified by project staff.)

Daumet, G., ed. *Lettres closes, patentes et curiales [du pape Benoît XII] se rapportant à la France: Publiées ou analysées d'après les registres du Vatican.* Vol. 2 of *Bibliothèque des Écoles françaises d'Athènes et de Rome.* 3d ser., *Registres et lettres des papes du XIVe siècle.* Rome, 1899–1920.

Davidsohn, R. "Process wegen Fälschung einer päpstlichen Bulle, 1216." *Neues Archiv der Gesellschaft für ältere Deutsche Geschichtskunde* 19 (1894): 232–235.

Davies, C. S. L. "Bishop John Morton, the Holy See, and the Accession of Henry VII." *English Historical Review* 102 (1987): 2–30.

De Bartholomaeis, V. *Le origini della poesia drammatica italiana.* 2d ed. Turin, 1952.

Debevec, A. *United States Documents in the Propaganda Fide Archives: A Calendar.* 2d ser. Washington, D.C., 1966–. (This title was noted but not verified by project staff.)

De Biasio, L. "Note storiche sul Santo Officio di Aquileia e Concordia." (This title was noted but not verified by project staff.)

Decreta authentica Sacrae Congregationis Indulgentiis Sacrisque Reliquiis Praepositae, ab anno 1668 ad annum 1882. Regensburg, 1883.

Deeley, A. "Papal Provisions and Rights of Royal Patronage in the Early 14th Century." English Historical Review 43 (1928): 497–527.

Deeters, W. "Ein Breve des Papstes Nikolaus V. an den oströmischen Kaiser von 1453." Quellen und Forschungen aus italienischen Archiven und Bibliotheken 48 (1968): 365–368.

Deeters, W. "Über das Repertorium Germanicum als Geschichtsquelle: Versuch einer methodischen Anleitung." Blätter für Deutsche Landesgeschichte 105 (1969): 27–43.

De Feo, I. Sisto V, un grande papa tra Rinascimento e barocco. Milan, 1987.

Delehaye, H. Les lettres d'indulgence collectives. Brussels, 1928.

Delisle, L. V. "Mémoire sur les actes d'Innocent III." Bibliothèque de l'École des Chartes 19 (1858): 1–73.

Delisle, L. V. "Lettres inédites d'Innocent III." Bibliothèque de l'École des Chartes 34 (1873): 397–419.

Delisle, L. V. "Les registres d'Innocent III." Bibliothèque de l'École des Chartes 46 (1885): 84–94.

Delisle, L. V. "Les 'litterae tonsae' à la chancellerie romaine au XIIIe siècle." Bibliothèque de l'École des Chartes 62 (1901): 256–263.

Dell'Aquila-Visconti, G. Del prelato abbreviatore de Curia sinossi istorica e catalogo cronologico dal 1382 al 1870. Rome, 1870.

Delorme, F. M., and A. L. Tautu, eds. Acta Clementis pp. V (1305–1314) e registris Vaticanis aliisque fontibus. Vatican City, 1955.

Del Re, N. "I cardinali prefetti della sacra Congregazione del Concilio dalle origini ad oggi (1564–1964)." In La sacra Congregazione del Concilio: Quarto centenario della fondazione, 1564–1964, studi e ricerche, pp. 265–307. Vatican City, 1964.

Del Re, N. La curia romana: lineamenti storico-giuridici. 3d ed. Rome, 1970.

Del Re, N. "Sisto V e la sua opera di riorganizzazione del governo centrale della Chiesa e dello Stato." Idea 36.1 (1980): 41–53.

De Luca, G. B. Eminentissimi ac reverendissimi domini Joannis Baptistae de Luca, S.R.E. cardinalis et., relatio Curiae Romanae, in qua ominium congregationum, trubunalium aliarumque iurisdictionum Urbis status ac praxis dilucide describitur . . . Prodit nunc primum in Germania. Cologne, 1683.

Delumeau, J. Vie économique et sociale de Rome dans la seconde moitié du XVIe siècle. Paris, 1957–1959.

De Marchi, G. Le nunziature apostoliche dal 1800 al 1956. Rome, 1957.

Demoulin, L. Correspondance de Vincenzo Montalto, Administrateur de la nonciature de Flandre. Vol. 14 of Analecta vaticano-belgica. Ser. 2, section A, Nonciature de Flandre. Brussels, 1985.

Dengel, I. P. Die politische und kirchliche Tätigkeit des Monsignor Josef Garampi in Deutschland, 1761–1763: Geheime Sendung zum geplanten Friedenskongress in Augsburg und Visitation des Reichsstiftes Salem. Rome, 1905.

Dengel, I. P. Nuntius Biglia 1565–1566 (Juni): Commendone als Legat auf dem Reichstag zu Augsburg 1566. Vol. 5 of Nuntiaturberichte aus Deutschland nebst ergänzenden Actenstücken. Zweite Abteilung, 1560–1572. Vienna, 1926.

Dengel, I. P. Nuntius Biglia 1566–1569: Commendone als Legat 1568–1569. Vol. 6 of Nuntiaturberichte aus Deutschland nebst ergänzenden Actenstücken. Zweite Abteilung, 1560–1572. Vienna, 1939.

Dengel, I. P., and H. Kramer. Nuntius Biglia 1570 (Jänner) bis 1571 (April). Vol. 7 of Nuntiaturberichte aus Deutschland nebst ergänzenden Actenstücken. Zweite Abteilung, 1560–1572. Graz, 1952.

Denifle, H. "Die päpstlichen Registerbände des 13. Jahrhunderts und das Inventar derselben vom J. 1339." Archiv für Literatur- und Kirchengeschichte des Mittelalters 2 (1886): 1–105.

Denifle, H. La désolation des églises, monastères et hôpitaux en France pendant la guerre de cent ans. Paris, 1897–1899.

Denifle, H., and G. Palmieri, eds. Specimina palaeographica ex Vaticani tabularii romanorum pontificum registris selecta et photographica arte ad unguem expressa, ab Innocentio III ad Urbanum V. Rome, 1888.

Denzinger, H. Enchiridion symbolorum. 36th ed. Barcinone, 1976.

Denzler, G. Die Propagandakongregation in Rom und die Kirche in Deutschland im ersten Jahrzehnt nach dem Westfälischen Frieden: Mit Edition der Kongregationsprotokolle zu deutschen Angelegenheiten 1649–1657. Paderborn, 1969.

Dephoff, J. Zum Urkunden- und Kazleiwesen des Konzils von Basel. Hildesheim, 1930.

Déprez, E. "Recueil de documents pontificaux conservés dans diverses archives d'Italie (XIIIe et XIVe siecles)." Quellen und Forschungen aus italienischen Archiven und Bibliotheken 3 (1900): 103–128, 255–307.

Déprez, E. Clément VI (1342–1352): Lettres closes, patentes et curiales se rapportant à la France. Vol. 3 of Bibliothèque des Écoles françaises d'Athènes et de Rome. 3d ser., Registres et lettres des papes du XIVe siècle. Paris, 1910–1961.

Déprez, E., ed. Innocent VI: Lettres closes, patentes et curiales se rapportant à la France: publiées ou analysées d'après les registres du Vatican. Vol. 4 of Bibliothèque des Écoles françaises d'Athènes et de Rome. 3d ser., Registres et lettres des papes du XIVe siècle. Rome, 1909–.

Déprez, E., and G. Mollat. Lettres closes, patentes et curiales intéressant les pays autres que la France [Clément VI]. Vol. 3 of Bibliothèque des Écoles françaises d'Athènes et de Rome. 3d ser., Registres et lettres des papes du XIVe siècle. Paris, 1960–1961.

Derkenne, P., and P. Gemis. Inventaire analytique de documents relatifs à l'histoire du diocèse de Liège sous le régime des nonces de Cologne: Marco Galli (1659–1666). Vol. 8 of Analecta vaticano-belgica. Ser. 2, section B, Nonciature de Cologne. Brussels, 1993.

Despy, G., ed. Lettres d'Innocent VI (1352–1362): Textes e analyses. Vol. 17 of Analecta vaticano-belgica: Documents relatifs aux anciens diocèses de Cambrai, Liège, Thérouanne et Tournai. Brussels, 1953.

Dessart, H., L. E. Halkin, and J. Hoyoux. Inventaire analytique de documents relatifs à l'histoire du diocèse de Liège sous le régime des nonces de Cologne. Vols. 2–7 of Analecta vaticano-belgica. Ser. 2, section B, Nonciature de Cologne. Brussels, 1957–1991.

De Stefani, L. La nunziatura di Francia del Cardinale Guido Bentivoglio: Lettere a Scipione Borghese. Florence, 1863–1870.

Diaz, F. Francesco Buonvisi: Nunziatura a Colonia. Rome, 1959.

Diaz, F., and N. Carranza. Francesco Buonvisi: Nunziatura a Varsavia. Rome, 1965.

Diaz de Cerio Ruiz, F. Regesto de la correspondencia de los obispos de España en el siglo XIX con los nuncios, segun el Fondo de la Nunciatura de Madrid en el Archivo Vaticano (1791–1903). Vatican City, 1984.

Diaz de Cerio Ruiz, F. Indice-catalogo del Fondo de la Nunciatura de Madrid en el Archivo Vaticano (1794–1899). Rome, 1993.

Di Capua, F. Il ritmo prosaico nella lettere dei papi e nei documenti della Cancelleria romana dal IV al XIV secolo. Rome, 1937–.

Di Capua, F. Fonti ed esempi per lo studio dello "Stilus Curiae Romanae" medioevale. Rome, 1941.

Diederich, T. "Prolegomena zu einer neuen Siegel-Typologie." Archiv für Diplomatik, Schriftengeschichte, Siegel- und Wappenkunde 29 (1983): 242–284.

Diekamp, W. "Zum päpstlichen Urkundenwesen des XI., XII. und der ersten Hälfte des XIII. Jahrhunderts." Mitteilungen des Instituts für österreichische Geschichtsforschung 3 (1882): 565–627.

Diekamp, W. "Zum päpstlichen Urkundenwesen von Alexander IV. bis Johann XXII. (1254–1334)." Mitteilungen des Instituts für österreichische Geschichtsforschung 4 (1883): 497–540.

Diener, H. "Rubrizellen zu Kanzleiregistern Johanns XXIII. und Martins V." Quellen und Forschungen aus italienischen Archiven und Bibliotheken 39 (1959): 117–172.

Diener, H. "Ein Formularbuch aus der Kanzlei der Päpste Eugen IV. und Nicolaus V." Quellen und Forschungen aus italienischen Archiven und Bibliotheken 42–43 (1963): 370–411.

Diener, H. "Zur Persönlichkeit des Johannes de Segovia: Ein Beitrag zur Methode der Auswertung päpstlicher Register des späten Mittelalters." Quellen und Forschungen aus italienischen Archiven und Bibliotheken 44 (1964): 289–365.

Diener, H. "Die grossen Registerserien im Vatikanischen Archiv (1378–1523): Hinweise und Hilfsmittel zu ihrer Benutzung und Auswertung." Quellen und Forschungen aus italienischen Archiven und Bibliotheken 51 (1972): 305–368.

Diener, H. "Verlorene Kanzleiregister de Päpste Bonifaz IX., Innozenz VII., Alexander V. und Johannes XXIII. (1389–1415)." In Römische Kurie, kirchliche Finanzen, vatikanisches Archiv: Studien zu Ehren von Hermann Hoberg, pp. 107–133. Rome, 1979.

Diener, H. "Das Vatikanische Archiv." In Il libro del centenario: L'Archivio segreto vaticano a un secolo dalla sua apertura, 1880/81–1980/81, pp. 55–75. Vatican City, 1982.

Diener, H. "Lo Schedario Garampi." In L'Archivio segreto vaticano e le ricerche storici: Città del Vaticano, 4–5 giugno 1981, by P. Vian, pp. 181–191. Rome, 1983.

Diener, H. "Materialien aus dem Vatikanischen Archiv: Die Registerserien des Spätmittelalters als Quelle." In Bericht über den sechzehnten österreichischen Historikertag in Krems/Donau veranstaltet . . . in der Zeit vom 3. bis 7. September 1984, pp. 387–397. Vienna, 1985.

Digard, G. A. L., et al. Les registres de Boniface VIII: Recueil des bulles de ce pape publiées ou analysées d'après les manuscrits originaux des Archives du Vatican. Vol. 4 of Bibliothèque des Écoles françaises d'Athènes et de Rome. 2d ser., Registres des papes du XIIIe siècle. Paris, 1884–1939.

Dittrich, F. Nuntiaturberichte Giovanni Morones vom Deutschen Königshofe, 1539, 1540. Paderborn, 1892.

Dizionario biografico degli italiani. Rome, 1960–.

Dizionario degli istituti di perfezione. Rome, 1974–1988.

Dlugopolski, E., ed. Acta Bonifacii papae IX. Kraków, 1939–.

Dobson, R. B., ed. The Church, Politics and Patronage in the Fifteenth Century. Gloucester, 1984.

Dodd, R. J. "Vatican Archives: Instrumenta Miscellanea: Documents of Irish Interest." Archivium hibernicum 14 (1956): 229–253.

Donkin, E. M. "A Collective Letter of Indulgence for an English Beneficiary." Scriptorium 17 (1963): 316–323.

Donnay, F. Inventaire analytique de documents relatifs à l'histoire du diocèse de Liège sous le régime des nonces de Cologne: Giuseppe-Maria Sanfelice (1652–1659). Vol. 7 of Analecta vaticano-belgica. Ser. 2, section B, Nonciature de Cologne. Brussels, 1991.

Donnelly, A. "The Per Obitum Volumes in the Archivio Vaticano." Archivium hibernicum 1 (1912): 28–38.

D'Onofrio, C. Castel S. Angelo e Borgo tra Roma e Papato. Rome, 1978.

Dorez, L., and J. Guiraud. Les registres d'Urbain IV (1261–1264): Recueil des bulles de ce pape publiées ou analysées d'après les manuscrits originaux du Vatican. Vol. 13 of Bibliothèque des Écoles françaises d'Athènes et de Rome. 2d ser., Registres des papes du XIIIe siècle. Paris, 1899–1929.

Drei, G. Gli archivi Farnesiani, loro formazione e vicende. Parma, 1930. (This title was noted but not verified by project staff.)

Dubrulle, H. Bullaire de la province de Reims sous le pontificat de Pie II. Lille, 1905.

Dubrulle, H. Suppliques du pontificat de Martin V. (1417–1431). Dunkirk, 1922.

Dubrulle, H. Les registres d'Urbain V (1362–1363): Recueil des bulles de ce pape publiées ou analysées d'après les manuscrits originaux du Vatican. Forms part of Bibliothèque des Écoles françaises d'Athènes et de Rome. 3d ser., Registres et lettres des papes du XIVe siècle. Paris, 1926.

Duca, S., P. Simeon, and S. Familia, eds. Enchiridion archivorum ecclesiasticorum: Documenta potiora Sanctae Sedis de Archivis ecclesiasticis a Concilio Tridentino usque ad nostros dies. Vatican City, 1966.

Duchesne, L. Le Liber pontificalis: Texte, introduction et commentaire. Paris, 1886–1957.

Dudík, B. Iter Romanum: Im Auftrag des hohen maehrischen Landesausschusses in den Jahren 1852 und 1853 unternommen und veroffentlicht. Vienna, 1855.

Dudík, B. Auszüge für Mährens allgemeine Geschichte aus dem Regesten der Päpste Benedikt XII., Clemens VI. Brünn, 1885.

Duíchev, I. Prepiskata na Papa Inokentija III s Búlgaritie: Innocentii PP. III epistolae ad Bulgariae historiam spectantes. Sofia, 1942.

Dunning, P. J. "Pope Innocent III and the Irish Kings." Journal of Ecclesiastical History 8 (1957): 17–32.

Dunning, P. J. "The Letters of Innocent III as a Source for Irish History." Proceedings of the Irish Catholic Historical Committee (1958): 1–10.

Dunning, P. J. "The Letters of Innocent III to Ireland." Traditio 18 (1962): 229–253.

Durand de Maillane, P. T. Dictionnaire de droit canonique et de pratique beneficiale: Confere avec les maximes et la jurisprudence de France. 2d ed. Lyons, 1770.

Edwards, R. D. "The Kings of England and Papal Provisions in Fifteenth-Century Ireland." In Medieval Studies Presented to Aubrey Gwynn, 265–280. Dublin, 1961.

Ehrenberg, H. Italienische Beiträge zur Geschichte der Provinz Ostpreussen: Im Auftrage des Provinzial-Ausschusses der Provinz Ostpreussen in italienischen Handschriften-Sammlungen, vornehmlich dem vatikanischen Archive gesammelt. Königsberg, 1895.

Ehrle, F. "Zur Geschichte des Schatzes, der Bibliothek und des Archivs der Päpste im vierzehnten Jahrhundert." Archiv für Literatur- und Kirchengeschichte des Mittelalters 1 (1885): 1–48, 228–364.

Ehrle, F. "Die Übertragung des letzten Restes des päpstlichen Archivs von Avignon nach Rom." Historisches Jahrbuch 11 (1890): 727–729.

Ehrle, F. Martin De Alpartils Cronica Actitatorum temporibus Domini Benedicti XIII. Paderborn, 1906.

Ehrle, F. "Die Frangipani und der Untergang des Archivs und der Bibliothek der Päpste am Anfang des 13. Jahrhunderts." In Mélanges offerts a Emile Chatelain, pp. 448–483. Paris, 1910.

Ehrle, F. Biblioteca ed Archivio Vaticana: Biblioteche diverse. Vol. 5 of Miscellanea Francesco Ehrle. Rome, 1924.

Ehrle, F. Paleografico e diplomatica. Vol. 4 of Miscellanea Francesco Ehrle. Rome, 1924.

Ehrle, F. Per la storia di Roma e dei papi. Vol. 2 of Miscellanea Francesco Ehrle. Rome, 1924.

Ehses, S. "Clemens VII. und Karl V. zu Bologna (1533)." Römische Quartalschrift für christliche Altertumskunde und für Kirchengeschichte 5 (1891): 299–307.

Ehses, S. "Das Dispensbreve Julius II. für die Ehe Heinrichs VIII. mit Katharina von Aragonien." Römische Quartalschrift für christliche Altertumskunde und für Kirchengeschichte 7 (1893): 180–198.

Ehses, S. Römische Dokumente zur Geschichte der Ehescheidung Heinrichs VIII. von England 1527–1534. Paderborn, 1893.

Ehses, S. Ottavio Mirto Frangipani in Köln, 1587–1590. Vol. 2 of Nuntiaturberichte aus Deutschland nebst ergänzenden Actenstücken, 1585 (1584)–(1592). Erste Abteilung. Paderborn, 1899.

Ehses, S. "Die Carte Farnesiane des Vatikanischen Archivs." Römische Quartalschrift für christliche Altertumskunde und für Kirchengeschichte 28 (1914): 41–47.

Ehses, S., and A. Meister. Bonomi in Köln, Santorio in der Schweiz, die strassburger Wirren. Vol. 1 of Nuntiaturberichte aus Deutschland nebst ergänzenden Actenstücken, 1585 (1584)–(1592). Erste Abteilung. Paderborn, 1895.

Eliade, M., ed. Encyclopedia of Religion. New York, 1987.

Elias, H. J. "La nonciature de Guido Bentivoglio, archevêque de Rhodes, à Bruxelles (1607–1615)." Bulletin de l'Institut historique Belge de Rome 8 (1928): 273–281.

Ellemunter, A. Antonio Eugenio Visconti und die Anfänge des Josephinismus: Eine Untersuchung über das theresianische Staatskirchentum unter besonderer Beruchsichtigung der Nuntiaturberichte, 1767–1774. Graz, 1963.

Elliott-Binns, L. E. The History of the Decline and Fall of the Medieval Papacy. London, 1934.

Ellis, J. T. Cardinal Consalvi and Anglo-papal Relations, 1814–1824. Washington, D.C., 1942.

Elze, R. "Die päpstliche Kapelle im 12. und 13. Jahrhundert." Zeitschrift der Savigny-Stiftung für Rechtsgeschichte. Kanonistische Abteilung 36 (1950): 145–204.

Elze, R. "Das 'Sacrum Palatium Lateranense'." Studi Gregoriani per la storia di Gregorio VII e della riforma gregoriana 4 (1952): 27–54.

Elze, R. "Der Liber Censuum des Cencius (Cod. Vat. Lat. 8486) von 1192 bis 1228: Zur Ueberlieferung des Kaiserkrönungsordo Cencius II." Bullettino dell'Archivio paleografico italiano, n.s. 2–3, pt. 1 (1956–1957): 251–270.

Enciclopedia cattolica. Vatican City, 1948–1954.

Enciclopedia italiana di scienze, lettere ed arti. Rome, 1929–1939.

Engel, W. Vatikanische Quellen zur Geschichte des Bistums Würzburg im XIV. und XV. Jahrhundert. Würzburg, 1948.

Era, A. "Il giureconsulto Gironi Pau (+ Hieronymus Pauli) e la sua 'Practica cancillariae (!) apostolicae.'" In Studi di storia e diritto in onore di Carlo Calisse, vol. 3, pp. 367–402. Milan, 1939–1940.

Erben, W. Die Kaiser- und Königsurkunden des Mittelalters in Deutschland, Frankreich und Italien. Munich, 1907.

Erben, W. "Bemalte Bittschriften und Ablassurkunden." Archiv für Urkundenforschung 8 (1923): 160–188.

Erben, W. "Kaiserbullen und Papstbullen." In Festschrift Albert Brackmann, edited by L. Santifaller, pp. 148–167. Weimar, 1931.

Erdmann, C. Papsturkunden in Portugal. Berlin, 1927.

Erdmann, C. "Unbekannte Briefe des Kardinals Farnese an den Nuntius Bertano (1549)." Quellen und Forschungen aus italienischen Archiven und Bibliotheken 21 (1929–1930): 293–304.

Erdmann, C. "Zu den sekretregistern Johannes XXII." Quellen und Forschungen aus italienischen Archiven und Bibliotheken 29 (1938–1939): 233–248.

Erler, G. "Ein Band des Supplikenregisters Bonifactius' IX, in dem königlichen Bibliothek zu Eichstatt." Historisches Jahrbuch 8 (1887): 487–495.

Erler, G. Der Liber Cancellariae Apostolicae vom Jahre 1380 und der Stilus palatii abbreviatus. Leipzig, 1888.

Erth, N. "Diktatoren frühmittelalterlicher Papstbriefe." Archiv für Urkundenforschung 15 (1938): 56–132.

Espinosa, I. F. de. Crónica de los colegios de Propaganda Fide de la Nueva España. New ed. Washington, D.C., 1964.

Esposito, A. "Le 'confraternite' del Gonfalone (secoli XIV–XV)." In Le confraternite Romane: Esperienza religiosa, società, commitenza artistica: Colloquio della Fondazione Caetani, Roma, 14–15 maggio 1982, edited by L. Fiorani, pp. 91–136. Rome, 1984.

Essen, L. Van der, and A. Louant. Correspondance d'Ottavio Mirto Frangipani, premier nonce de Flandre (1596–1606).

Vol. 1–3 of *Analecta vaticano-belgica*. Ser. 2, section A, *Nonciature de Flandre*. Rome, 1924–1942.

Eubel, K. "Der Registerband des Cardinal Grosspönitentiars Bentevenga." *Archiv für katholisches Kirchenrecht* 64 (1890): 3–69.

Eubel, K. "Der Registerband des Gegenpapstes Nikolaus V." *Archivalische Zeitschrift* 4 (1893): 123–212.

Eubel, K. *Die avignonesische Obedienz der Mendikanten-Orden: Sowie der Orden der Mercedarier und Trinitarier zur zeit des grossen Schismas*. Paderborn, 1900.

Eubel, K. "Elenchus Romanorum pontificum epistolarum quae in archivo sacri conventus Assisiensis O. Min. Conv. exstant." *Archivum Franciscanum Historicum* 1 (1908): 601–616; 2 (1909): 108–122.

Eubel, K. *Hierarchia catholica medii et recentioris aevi, sive Summorum pontificum, S.R.E. cardinalium, ecclesiarum antistitum series*. Münster, 1913–1978.

Ewald, P. "Registrum Anacleti II antipapae." *Neues Archiv der Gesellschaft für ältere Deutsche Geschichtskunde* 3 (1878): 164–168.

Ewald, P., and L. M. Hartmann, eds. *Gregorii I papae registrum epistolarum*. Berlin, 1887–1889.

Ewald, W. "Studien zur Ausgabe des Registers Gregors I." *Neues Archiv der Gesellschaft für ältere Deutsche Geschichtskunde* 3 (1878): 433–625.

Fabian, F. *Prunkbittschriften an den Papst*. Graz, 1931.

Fabre, P., and L. Duchesne. *Le Liber censuum de l'Église romaine*. Paris, 1889–1952.

Fabri de Peiresc, N. C. *Correspondance de Peiresc avec plusieurs missionaires et religieux de l'ordre des Capucins, 1631–1637*. Paris, 1891.

Fairbank, A. J., and B. Wolpe. *Renaissance Handwriting: An Anthology of Italic Scripts*. London, 1960.

Falcone, P. "La nunziatura di Malta dell'Archivio segreto sella S. Sede." *Archivio storico di Malta* 5 (1934): 172–267.

Fallani, G., and M. Escobar, eds. *Vaticano*. Florence, 1946.

Fanfani, A. *Storia del lavoro in Italia dalla fine del secolo XV agli inizi del XVIII*. Milan, 1943.

Fanta, A., F. Kaltenbrunner, and E. von Ottenthal, eds. *Actenstücke zur Geschichte des Deutschen Reiches unter den Königen Rudolf I. und Albrecht I*. Vienna, 1889.

Farber, K. M. "Der Brevensekretär Cesare Glorierio: Ein Beitrag zur Geschichte der kurialen Sekretariate in der zweiten Hälfte des 16. Jahrhunderts." *Quellen und Forschungen aus italienischen Archiven und Bibliotheken* 67 (1987): 198–220.

Fasano Guarini, E., ed. *Potere e società negli stati regionali italiani fra '500 e '600*. Bologna, 1978.

Favier, J. "'Introitus et Exitus' sous Clément VII et Benoît XIII: Problèmes de diplomatique et d'interpretation." *Bullettino dell'Archivio paleografico italiano*, n.s. 2–3, pt. 1 (1956–1957): 285–294.

Favier, J. *Les finances pontificales à l'époque du Grand Schisme d'Occident, 1378–1409*. Paris, 1966.

Favier, J., ed. *Les Archives Nationales: État général des fonds*. Paris, 1978–.

Fawtier, R. "Documents négligés sur l'activité de la Chancellerie apostolique à la fin du XIIIe siècle: Le registre 46A et les comptes de la chambre sous Boniface VIII." *Mélanges d'archëologie et d'histoire* 52 (1935): 244–272.

Fawtier, R. "Introduction." In *Les registres de Boniface VIII*, by G. A. L. Digard et al., vol. 4, pp. v–cvi. Paris, 1939.

Fawtier, R. "Un grand achèvement de l'École française de Rome: La publication des Registres des papes du XIIIe siècle." *Mélanges d'archëologie et d'histoire* 71 (1960): i–xiii.

Fayen, A., ed. *Lettres de Jean XXII (1316–1334): Textes et analyses*. Vol. 2–3 of *Analecta vaticano-belgica: Documents relatifs aux anciens diocèses de Cambrai, Liège, Thérouanne et Tournai*. Rome, 1908–.

Fedele, P. "La Commission internationale pour la bibliographie des Archives du Vatican." *Bulletin of the International Committee of Historical Sciences* 2 (1939): 224–235.

Fedele, P. "L'Uffiziolo di Madonna rilegato da Benvenuto Cellini," *Mélanges d'archéologie et d'histoire* 29 (1909): 329–339.

Fedeli, C. *I documenti pontifici riguardanti l'Università di Pisa*. Pisa, 1908.

Federici, V. *La scrittura delle cancellerie italiane dal secolo XII al XVII*. Rome, 1934.

Feigl, H. "Die Überlieferung der Register Papst Innocenz III." *Mitteilungen des Instituts für österreichische Geschichtsforschung* 65 (1957): 242–295.

Feigl, H. "Die Registrierung der Privilegien unter Papst Innocenz III." *Mitteilungen des Instituts für österreichische Geschichtsforschung* 68 (1960): 114–127.

Feldkamp, M. F. *Die kölner Nuntiatur und ihr Archiv: Eine behördengeschichtliche und quellenkundliche Untersuchung*. Vol. 1 of *Studien und Texte zur Geschichte der kölner Nuntiatur*. Vatican City, 1993.

Feldkamp, M. F. *Dokumente und Materialien über Jurisdiktion, Nuntiatursprengel, Haushalt, Zerimoniell und Verwaltung der kölner Nuntiatur (1584–1794)*. Vol. 2 of *Studien und Texte zur Geschichte der kölner Nuntiatur*. Vatican City, 1993.

Feldkamp, M. F. *Inventar des Fonds 'Archivio della Nunziatura di Colonia' im vatikanischen Archiv*. Vol. 3 of *Studien und Texte zur Geschichte der kölner Nuntiatur*. Vatican City, 1995.

Felici, G. *La Reverenda Camera Apostolica: Studio storico-giuridico*. Rome, 1940.

Fenicchia, V. "Documenti trasferiti dall'Archivio vescovile di Anagni all'Archivio di Castel S. Angelo nel 1578." In *Mélanges Eugène Tisserant*, vol. 4, pp. 189–204. Vatican City, 1964.

Fenning, H. "John Kent's Report on the State of the Irish Mission, 1742." *Archivium hibernicum* 28 (1966): 59–102.

Fenning, H. "A Guide to Eighteenth-Century Reports on Irish Dioceses in the Archives of Propaganda Fide." *Collectanea hibernica*, no. 11 (1968): 19–35.

Fenning, H. "The Dominicans and the Propaganda Fide, 1622–1668: A Catalogue of the First Series of the SOCG Volumes 1 to 30." *Archivum Fratrum Praedicatorum* 41 (1971): 241–323.

Fenning, H. "Documents of Irish Interest in the Fondo Missioni of the Vatican Archives." In *Miscellanea in onore di Monsignor Martino Giusti*, vol. 1, pp. 191–254. Vatican City, 1978.

Fichtenau, H. *Arenga: Spätantike und Mittelalter im Spiegel von Urkundenformeln*. Graz, 1957.

Fierens, A., ed. *Lettres de Benoît XII (1334–1342): Textes et analyses*. Vol. 4 of *Analecta vaticano-belgica: Documents* relatifs aux anciens diocèses de Cambrai, Liège, Thérouanne et Tournai. Rome, 1910.

Fierens, A., ed. Suppliques d'Urbain V (1362–1370): Textes et analyses. Vol. 7 of Analecta vaticano-belgica: Documents relatifs aux anciens diocèses de Cambrai, Liège, Thérouanne et Tournai. Rome, 1914.

Fierens, A., and C. Tihon. Lettres d'Urbain V (1362–1370): Textes et Analyses. Vols. 9 and 15 of Analecta vaticano-belgica: Documents relatifs aux anciens diocèses de Cambrai, Liège, Thérouanne et Tournai. Brussels, 1928–1932.

Filangieri di Candida, R. "Perdita e ricuperi del diplomatico Farnesiano." In Miscellanea archivistica Angelo Mercati, pp. 269–279. Vatican City, 1952.

Fink, K. A. "Die ältesten Breven und Brevenregister." Quellen und Forschungen aus italienischen Archiven und Bibliotheken 25 (1933–1934): 292–307.

Fink, K. A. "Zur Geschichte des päpstlichen Referendariats." Analecta sacra tarraconensia 10 (1934): 75–100.

Fink, K. A. "Untersuchungen über die päpstlichen Breven des 15. Jahrhunderts." Römische Quartalschrift für christliche Altertumskunde und für Kirchengeschichte 43 (1935): 55–86.

Fink, K. A. "Die politische Korrespondenz Martins V. nach den Brevenregistern." Quellen und Forschungen aus italienischen Archiven und Bibliotheken 26 (1935–1936): 172–244.

Fink, K. A. "Zu den Brevia Lateranensia des Vatikanischen Archivs." Quellen und Forschungen aus italienischen Archiven und Bibliotheken 32 (1942): 260–266.

Fink, K. A., ed. Martin V., 1417–1431. Berlin, 1943–1958.

Fink, K. A. Das Vatikanische Archiv: Einführung in die Bestände und ihre Erforschung. Rome, 1951.

Fink, K. A. "Poggio-Autographen kurialer Herkunft." In Miscellanea archivistica Angelo Mercati, pp. 129–133. Vatican City, 1952.

Fink, K. A. "Neue Wege zur Erschliessung des Vatikanischen Archivs." In Vitae et Veritati: Festgabe für Karl Adam, pp. 187–203. Düsseldorf, 1956.

Fink, K. A. "Arengen spätmittelalterlicher Papsturkunden." In Mélanges Eugène Tisserant, vol. 4, pp. 205–227. Vatican City, 1964.

Fink, K. A. "Urkundenwesen, Päpstlicher." In Lexikon für Theologie und Kirche, edited by J. Höfer and K. Rahner, vol. 10, pp. 560–563. 2d ed. Freiburg, 1965.

Fink, K. A. "Vatican Archives." In New Catholic Encyclopedia, vol. 14, pp. 551–555. New York, 1967.

Fink, K. A. "L'origine dei brevi apostolici." Annali della Scuola speciale per archivisti e bibliotecari dell'Università di Roma 11 (1971): 75–81.

Fink, K. A. "Das Archiv der Sacra Poenitentiaria Apostolica." Zeitschrift für Kirchengeschichte 83 (1972): 88–92.

Fink, K. A. Chiesa e papato nel medioevo. Bologna, 1987.

Finke, H., ed. Die Papsturkunden Westfalens bis zum Jahre 1378. Münster, 1888–.

Finke, H., ed. Acta Concilii Constanciensis. Münster, 1896–1928.

Finke, H. Aus den Tagen Bonifaz VIII: Funde und Forschungen. Münster, 1902.

Fiorani, L., ed. Storiografia e archivi delle confraternite romane. Rome, 1985.

Fischer, K. von, and F. A. Gallo, eds. Italian Sacred and Ceremonial Music. Monaco, 1987.

Fish, C. R. Guide to the Materials for American History in Roman and Other Italian Archives. Washington, D.C., 1911.

Flanagan, U. G. "Papal Letters of the 15th Century as a Source for Irish History." Proceedings of the Irish Catholic Historical Committee (1959): 11–15.

Flanagan, U. G. "Papal Provisions in Ireland, 1307–1378." In Historical Studies III: Papers Read before the Fourth Irish Conference of Historians, pp. 92–103. London, 1961.

Fliniaux, A. "Contribution à l'histoire des sources de droit canonique: Les anciennes collections des 'Decisiones Rotae Romanae.'" Revue historique de droit français et étranger, 4th ser. 4 (1925): 61–93, 382–410.

Foerster, H. P. Mittelalterliche Buch- und Urkundenschriften auf 50 Tafeln. Bern, 1946.

Foerster, H. P. Urkundenlesebuch für den akademischen Gebrauch. Bern, 1947.

Foerster, H. P. "Der Liber Diurnus-Fragmente in der Kanonessammlung des Kardinals Deusdedit." In Lebendiges Mittelalter: Festgabe für Wolfgang Stammler, pp. 44–55. Fribourg, 1958.

Foerster, H. P. Liber diurnus romanorum pontificum. Bern, 1958.

Fogarty, G. P. The Vatican and the American Hierarchy from 1870 to 1965. Stuttgart, 1982.

Le fonctionnement administratif de la papauté d'Avignon: Aux origines de l'état moderne. Rome, 1990.

Fonti medioevali e problematica storiografica: Atti del Congresso internazionale tenuto in occasione del 90° anniversario della fondazione dell'Istituto storico italiano (1883–1973): Roma, 22–27 ottobre 1973. Rome, 1976–1977.

Fonzi, F. Nunziature di Savoia. Rome, 1960.

Förstemann, J. Novae constitutiones audientiae litterarum contradictarum in Curia Romana promulgatae A.D. 1375. Leipzig, 1897.

Fournier, E. "Abréviateurs." In Dictionnaire de droit canonique, edited by R. Naz, vol. 1, pp. 98–106. Paris, 1935.

Fraccacreta, A. "Notizie sul monastero benedettino di S. Maria in Campo Marzio." L'Urbe (Rome) 4, fasc. 4 (1939): 24–34.

Fraikin, J. Bulles inédites relatives à diverses églises d'Italie. Rome, 1900.

Fraikin, J. Nonciatures de Clément VII. Vol. 1, Depuis la bataille de Pavie jusqu'au rappel d'Acciaiuoli, 25 février 1525–juin 1527. Paris, 1906.

Fraknoi, V., ed. Bullae, 1389–1404 [Bonifatii IX]. Budapest, 1888–1889.

Fraknoi, V. Mathiae Corvini Hungariae regis epistolae ad romanos pontifices datae et ab eis acceptae, 1458–1490. Budapest, 1891.

Fraknoi, V., ed. Monumenta Romana episcopatus Vesprimiensis: Munificentia Caroli L.B. Hornig Episcopi Vesprimiensis. Budapest, 1896–1907.

François, M. "Les sources de l'histoire religieuse de la France au Vatican." Revue d'histoire de l'Église de France 19 (1933): 305–346.

Frenz, T. "Das Eindringen humanistischer Schriftformen in die Urkunden und Akten der päpstlichen Kurie im 15. Jahrhundert." Archiv für Diplomatik, Schriftengeschichte,

Siegel- und Wappenkunde 19 (1973): 287–418; 20 (1974): 384–506.

Frenz, T. "Die 'computi' in der Serie der Brevia Lateranensia im Vatikanischen Archiv." *Quellen und Forschungen aus italienischen Archiven und Bibliotheken* 55–56 (1976): 251–275.

Frenz, T. "Randbemerkungen zu den Supplikenregistern Calixts III." *Quellen und Forschungen aus italienischen Archiven und Bibliotheken* 55–56 (1976): 410–420.

Frenz, T. "Zum Problem der Reduzierung der Zahl der päpstlichen Kanzleischreiber nach dem Konzil von Konstanz." In *Grundwissenschaften und Geschichte: Festschrift für Peter Acht*, pp. 256–273. Kallmünz, 1976.

Frenz, T. "Zur äusseren Form der Papsturkunden 1230–1530." *Archiv für Diplomatik, Schriftengeschichte, Siegel- und Wappenkunde* 22 (1976): 347–375.

Frenz, T. "Die verlorenen Brevenregister 1421–1527." *Quellen und Forschungen aus italienischen Archiven und Bibliotheken* 57 (1977): 354–365.

Frenz, T. "Die Grundung des Abbreviatorenkollegs durch Pius II. und Sixtus IV." In *Miscellanea in onore di Monsignor Martino Giusti*, vol. 1, pp. 297–329. Vatican City, 1978.

Frenz, T. "Littera Sancti Petri: Zur Schrift der neuzeitlichen Papsturkunden 1550–1878." *Archiv für Diplomatik, Schriftengeschichte, Siegel- und Wappenkunde* 24 (1978): 443–515.

Frenz, T. "Armarium XXXIX vol. 11 im Vatikanischen Archiv: Ein Formelbuch für Breven aus der Zeit Julius' II." In *Römische Kurie, kirchliche Finanzen, vatikanisches Archiv: Studien zu Ehren von Hermann Hoberg*, pp. 197–213. Rome, 1979.

Frenz, T. "Abbreviator." In *Lexikon des Mittelalters*, vol. 1, pp. 16–17. Munich, 1980.

Frenz, T. "Anulus piscatoris." In *Lexikon des Mittelalters*, vol. 1, p. 739. Munich, 1980.

Frenz, T. "Auscultator." In *Lexikon des Mittelalters*, vol. 1, pp. 1247–1248. Munich, 1980.

Frenz, T. "Breve." In *Lexikon des Mittelalters*, vol. 2, pp. 636–638. Munich, 1982.

Frenz, T. "Päpstliche Bulle (Siegel und Urkunden)." In *Lexikon des Mittelalters*, vol. 2, p. 934. Munich, 1982.

Frenz, T. *Die Kanzlei der Päpste der Hochrenaissance (1471–1527)*. Tübingen, 1986.

Frenz, T. *I documenti pontifici nel medioevo e nell'eta moderna*. Translated by S. Pagano. Vatican City, 1989.

Freüdenberger, T. *Augustinus Steuchus aus Gubbio, Augustinerchorher und päpstlicher Bibliothekar (1497–1548) und sein literarisches Lebenswerk*. Münster, 1953.

Frey, K. "Studien zu Michelagniolo Buonarroti und zur Kunst seiner Zeit [Part 3]." *Jahrbuch der königlich preuszischen Kunstsammlungen* 30 (1909), Beiheft: 103–180.

Friedensburg, W. *Nuntiaturen des Vergerio, 1533–1536*. Vol. 1 of *Nuntiaturberichte aus Deutschland nebst ergänzenden Actenstücken. Erste Abteilung, 1533–1559*. Gotha, 1892.

Friedensburg, W. *Nuntiatur des Morone, 1536–1538*. Vol. 2 of *Nuntiaturberichte aus Deutschland nebst ergänzenden Actenstücken. Erste Abteilung, 1533–1559*. Gotha, 1892.

Friedensburg, W. *Legation Aleanders, 1538–1539*. Vols. 3–4 of *Nuntiaturberichte aus Deutschland nebst ergänzenden Actenstücken. Erste Abteilung, 1533–1559*. Gotha, 1893.

Friedensburg, W. *Nuntiatur des Verallo*. Vols. 8–9 of *Nuntiaturberichte aus Deutschland nebst ergänzenden Actenstücken. Erste Abteilung, 1533–1559*. Gotha, 1898–1899.

Friedensburg, W. *Legation des Kardinals Sfondrato, 1547–1548*. Vol. 10 of *Nuntiaturberichte aus Deutschland nebst ergänzenden Actenstücken. Erste Abteilung, 1533–1559*. Berlin, 1910.

Friedensburg, W. *Nuntiaturen des Bischofs Pietro Bertano von Fano, 1548–1549*. Vol. 11 of *Nuntiaturberichte aus Deutschland nebst ergänzenden Actenstücken. Erste Abteilung, 1533–1559*. Berlin, 1910.

Friedländer, I. F. *Die päpstlichen Legaten in Deutschland und Italien am Ende des XII. Jahrhunderts (1181–1198)*. Berlin, 1928.

Frutaz, A. P. *La sezione storica della Sacra Congregazione dei Riti: Origini e metodo di lavoro*. 2d ed. Vatican City, 1964.

Fuhrmann, H. "Die Fälschungen im Mittelalter: Überlegungen zum mittelalterlichen Wahrheitsbegriff." *Historische Zeitschrift* 197 (1963): 529–601.

Fumi, L. "L'Inquisizione romana e lo Stato di Milano: Saggio di ricerche nell'Archivio di Stato." *Archivio storico lombardo*, 4th ser. 37, no. 13 (1910) (This title was noted but not verified by project staff.)

Fürst, C. G. *Cardinalis: Prolegomena zu einer Rechtsgeschichte des römischen Kardinalskollegiums*. Munich, 1967.

Fürst, C. G. "'Statim ordinetur episcopus': Die Papsturkunden 'sub bulla dimidi' Innozenz III. und der Beginn der päpstlichen Gewalt." In *Ex aequo et bono: Willibald M. Plochl zum 70. Geburtstag*, pp. 45–65. Innsbruck, 1977.

Gabotto, F. *Le bolle pontificie dei registri Vaticani relative ad Ivrea*. Vol. 2 of *Le carte dell'Archivio vescovile d'Ivrea fino al 1313*. Pinerolo, 1900.

Gachard, L. P. "Les archives du Vatican." *Bulletin de la Commission royale d'histoire de Belgique* 1 (1874): 211–386.

Gachard, L. P. "La bibliotheque des princes Chigi, à Rome." *Compte rendu des séances de la Commission Royale d'Histoire*, 3d ser. 10 (1869): 219–244.

Gaeta, F., et al., eds. *Nunziature di Venezia*. Rome, 1958–.

Galavotti, P., ed. *Index ac Status Causarum*. Vatican City, 1988.

Ganzer, K. *Papsttum und Bistumsbesetzungen in der Zeit von Gregor IX. bis Bonifaz VIII: Ein Beitrag zur Geschichte der päpstlichen Reservationen*. Cologne, 1968.

Garnier, J. *Liber diurnus romanorum pontificum: Ex antiquissimo codice ms. nunc primum in lucern editus*. Paris, 1680.

Garofalo, S. *Il cardinale Carlo Confalonieri (1893–1986)*. Rome, 1993.

Gasnault, P. "Quatre suppliques inédites adressées à Jean XXII." *Bullettino dell'Archivio paleografico italiano*, n.s. 2–3, pt. 1 (1956–1957): 317–323.

Gasnault, P. "Suppliques en matière de justice au XIVe siècle." *Bibliothèque de l'École des Chartes* 115 (1957): 43–57.

Gasnault, P. "Notes et documents sur la Chambre Apostolique a l'époque d'Urbain V." *Mélanges d'archéologie e d'histoire* 70 (1958): 367–394.

Gasnault, P. "Une supplique originale de l'Abbaye de Cluny approuvée par Martin V." *Revue Mabillon* 51 (1961): 325–328.

Gasnault, P. "Contribution a l'histoire des registres de lettres secretes d'Innocent VI." *Annali della Scuola speciale per archivisti e bibliotecari dell'Università di Roma* 12 (1972): 77–97.

Gasnault, P. "Trois lettres secrètes sur papier de Clément VII (Robert de Genève) et une supplique originale signée par ce pape." In *Palaeographica, diplomatica et archivistica: Studi in onore di Guilio Battelli*, vol. 2, pp. 337–351. Rome, 1979.

Gasnault, P. "La transmission des lettres pontificales au XIIIe et au XIVe siecle." In *Histoire comparee de l'administration (IVe–XVIIIe siecles): Actes du XIVe Colloque historique franco-allemand Tours, 27 mars–1er avril 1977*, pp. 81–87. Munich, 1980.

Gasnault, P., and M. H. Laurent. *Lettres secrètes et curiales [Innocent VI]: Publiées ou analysées d'apres les registres des Archives vaticanes.* Vol. 4 of *Bibliothèque des Écoles françaises d'Athènes et de Rome.* 3d ser., *Registres et lettres des papes du XIVe siècle.* Paris, 1959–.

Gasparolo, F., ed. "Costituzione dell'Archivio Vaticano e suo primo indice sotto il pontificato di Paolo V: Manoscritto inedito de Michele Lonigo." *Studi e documenti di storia e diritto* 8 (1887): 3–64.

Gasparrini Leporace, T. *Le suppliche di Clemente VI.* Rome, 1948–.

Gasparrini Leporace, T. "Una supplica originale per 'fiat' del papa Giovanni XXII." *Bullettino dell'Istituto storico italiano per il medio evo e Archivio muratoriano* 75 (1963): 247–257.

Gassó, P. M., and C. M. Batllè. *Epistolae quae supersunt [Pelagius I].* Montserrat, 1956.

Gastout, M. *Documents relatifs au Grand Schisme*, vol. 7, *Suppliques et lettres d'Urbain VI (1378–1389) et de Boniface IX (cinq premières années, 1389–1394).* Vol. 29 of *Analecta vaticano-belgica: Documents relatifs aux anciens diocèses de Cambrai, Liège, Thérouanne et Tournai.* Brussels, 1976.

Gay, J., and S. Vitte. *Les registres de Nicolas III (1277–1280): Recueil des bulles de ce pape, publiées ou analysées d'après les manuscrits originaux du Vatican.* Vol. 14 of *Bibliothèque des Écoles françaises d'Athènes et de Rome.* 2d ser., *Registres des papes du XIIIe siècle.* Paris, 1898–1938.

Gelmi, G. "La Segreteria di Stato sotto Benedetto XIV, 1740–1758." Ph.D. diss., Pontifical Gregorian University, 1975.

Giblin, C. "Miscellaneous Papers." *Archivium hibernicum* 16 (1951): 62–98.

Giblin, C. "Vatican Library: MSS Barberini Latini." *Archivium hibernicum* 18 (1955): 67–144.

Giblin, C. "The Processus Datariae and the Appointment of Irish Bishops in the Seventeenth Century." In *Father Luke Wadding Commemorative Volume*, pp. 508–616. Dublin, 1957.

Giblin, C. *Irish Franciscan Mission to Scotland, 1619–1646: Documents from Roman Archives.* Dublin, 1964.

Giblin, C. "Material Relative to Ireland in the Albani Collection of MSS in the Vatican Archives." *Irish Ecclesiastical Record*, 5th ser. 102 (1964): 389–396.

Giblin, C. "A Congregatio Particularis on Ireland, at Propaganda Fide, May 1671." *Collectanea hibernica*, nos. 18–19 (1976–1977): 19–39.

Gieysztor, A. "Une bulle de Pascal II retrouvée." *Bullettino dell'Archivio paleografico italiano*, n.s. 2–3, pt. 1 (1956–1957): 361–365.

Gilles, H. "Les auditeurs de Rote au temps de Clément VII et Benoît XIII, 1378–1417: Notes biographiques." *Mélanges d'archëologie et d'histoire* 67 (1955): 321–337.

Girgensohn, D. "Territoriale Sammlungen." In *Neuere Editionen mittelalterlichen Königs- und Papsturkunden: eine Uebersicht*, by L. Santifaller and D. Girgensohn, pp. 43–56. Graz, 1958.

Giry, A. *Manuel de diplomatique: Diplomes et chartes, chronologie technique, elements critiques et parties constitutives de la teneur des chartes, les chancelleries, les actes prives.* Paris, 1894.

Giusti, M. "I registri vaticani e le loro provenienze." In *Miscellanea archivistica Angelo Mercati*, pp. 383–459. Vatican City, 1952.

Giusti, M. "I registri vaticani e la loro continuazione." *La Bibliofilia (Florence)* 60 (1958): 130–140.

Giusti, M. "Note sui registri Lateranensi." In *Mélanges Eugène Tisserant*, vol. 4, pp. 229–249. Vatican City, 1964.

Giusti, M. *Studi sui registri di bolle papali.* Vatican City, 1968.

Giusti, M. "L'Archivio Segreto Vaticano." In *Il Vaticano e Roma cristiana*, pp. 335–353, 507–508. Vatican City, 1975.

Giusti, M. "Materiale documentario degli archivi papali rimasto nell'Archivio nazionale di Parigi dopo il loro ritorno a Roma negli anni 1814–1817." In *Römische Kurie, kirchliche Finanzen, vatikanisches Archiv: Studien zu Ehren von Hermann Hoberg*, vol. 1, pp. 263–274. Rome, 1979.

Giusti, M. *Inventario dei Registri vaticani.* Vatican City, 1981.

Giusti, M., and P. Guidi, eds. *Tuscia. 2, Le decime degli anni 1295–1304.* Vol. 7 of *Rationes decimarum Italiae nei secoli XIII e XIV*, edited by P. Guidi and P. Sella. Vatican City, 1942.

Glasschröder, F. X. "Vatikanisches Archiv." In *Lexikon für Theologie und Kirche*, edited by M. Buchberger, vol. 1, pp. 619–620. 2d ed. Freiburg, 1930.

Glénisson, J. "Documenti dell'Archivio Vaticano relativi alla collettoria di Sicilia, 1372–1375." *Rivista di storia della chiesa in Italia* 2 (1948): 225–262.

Goetting, H. "Die Gandersheimer Originalsupplik an Papst Paschalis II." *Niedersächsisches Jahrbuch fur Landesgeschichte* 21 (1949): 93–122.

Goetz, H. *Nuntiatur des Girolamo Martinengo (1550–1554).* Vol. 16 of *Nuntiaturberichte aus Deutschland nebst ergänzenden Actenstücken. Erste Abteilung, 1533–1559.* Tübingen, 1965.

Goetz, H. *Nuntiatur Delfinos, Legation Morones, Sendung Lippomanos (1554–1556).* Vol. 17 of *Nuntiaturberichte aus Deutschland nebst ergänzenden Actenstücken. Erste Abteilung, 1533–1559.* Tübingen, 1970.

Goetz, H. "Die Nuntiaturberichte des 16. Jahrhunderts als Komplementärquelle zur Geschichtsschreibung." *Quellen und Forschungen aus italienischen Archiven und Bibliotheken* 53 (1973): 214–226.

Goetz, H. *Nuntiatur Giovanni Delfinos, 1572–1573.* Vol. 6 of *Nuntiaturberichte aus Deutschland nebst ergänzenden Actenstücken. Dritte Abteilung, 1572–1585.* Tübingen, 1982.

Goetz, H. *Life in the Middle Ages, from the Seventh to the Thirteenth Century.* Translated by A. Wimmer. Notre Dame, Ind., 1993.

Goldinger, W. "Österreich und die Eröffnung des Vatikanischen Archivs." *Archivalische Zeitschrift* 47 (1951): 23–52.

Göller, E. "Zur Geschichte der päpstlichen Poenitentiarie unter Clemens VI." *Römische Quartalschrift für christliche Altertumskunde und für Kirchengeschichte* 17 (1903): 413–417.

Göller, E. "Mitteilungen und Untersuchungen über das päpstliche Register- und Kanzleiwesen im 14. Jahrhundert, besonders unter Johann XXII. und Benedikt XII." *Quellen und Forschungen aus italienischen Archiven und Bibliotheken* 6 (1903): 272–315; 7 (1904): 42–90.

Göller, E. "Der Liber Taxarum der päpstlichen Kammer: Eine Studie über seine Entstehung und Anlage." *Quellen und Forschungen aus italienischen Archiven und Bibliotheken* 8 (1905): 113–173, 305–343.

Göller, E. "Die Kommentatoren der päpstlichen Kanzleiregeln vom Ende des 15. bis zum Beginn des 17. Jahrhunderts." *Archiv für katholisches Kirchenrecht* 85 (1905): 441–460; 86 (1906): 20–34, 259–265.

Göller, E. "Inventarium instrumentorum Camerae apostolicae: Verzeichnis der Schuldurkunden des päpstlichen Kammerarchivs aus der Zeit Urbans V." *Römische Quartalschrift für christliche Altertumskunde und für Kirchengeschichte* 23 (1909): 65–109.

Göller, E, ed. *Die Einnahmen der apostolischen Kammer unter Johann XXII.* Vol. 1 of *Vatikanische Quellen zur Geschichte des päpstlichen Hof- und Finanzverwaltung 1316–1378.* Paderborn, 1910.

Göller, E. *Die päpstliche Pönitentiarie von ihren Ursprung bis zu ihrer Umgestaltung unter Pius V.* Rome, 1907–1911.

Göller, E. "Das alte Archiv der päpstlichen Pönitentiarie." In *Kirchengeschichtliche Festgabe Anton de Waal,* pp. 1–19. Freiburg, 1913.

Göller, E, ed. *Clemens VII. von Avignon, 1378–1394.* Berlin, 1916.

Göller, E. *Die Grundlagen des päpstlichen Benefizialwesens und die Praxis der Stellenbesetzung zur Zeit des grossen Schismas.* Berlin, 1916.

Göller, E, ed. *Die Einnahmen der apostolischen Kammer unter Benedikt XII.* Vol. 4 of *Vatikanische Quellen zur Geschichte des päpstlichen Hof- und Finanzverwaltung 1316–1378.* Paderborn, 1920.

Göller, E. "Die neue Bestände der Camera Apostolica im päpstlichen Geheimarchiv." *Römische Quartalschrift für christliche Altertumskunde und für Kirchengeschichte* 30 (1922): 38–53.

Göller, E. "Untersuchungen über das Inventar des Finanzarchivs der Renaissancepäpste." In *Miscellanea Francesco Ehrle,* vol. 5, pp. 227–250. Rome, 1924.

Göller, E. "Aus der Camera Apostolica der Schismapäpste." *Römische Quartalschrift für christliche Altertumskunde und für Kirchengeschichte* 32 (1924): 82–147; 33 (1925): 72–110.

Göller, E. "Hadrian VI. und der Aemterkauf an der päpstlichen Kurie." In *Abhandlungen aus dem Gebiete der mittleren und neueren Geschichte und ihrer Hilfswissenschaften: Eine Festgabe zum siebzigsten Geburtstag Geh. Rat Prof. Dr. Heinrich Finke,* pp. 375–407. Münster, 1925.

Göller, E. "Die Kubikulare im Dienste der päpstlichen Hofverwaltung vom 12. bis 15. Jahrhundert." In *Papsttum und Kaisertum: Forschungen zur politischen Geschichte und*

Geisteskultur des Mittelalters Paul Kehr zum 65. Geburtstag dargebracht, pp. 621–647. Munich, 1926.

Gomes, L. *Commentaria R.P.D. Ludovici Gomes . . . in regulas cancellariae iudiciales quae usu quotidiano in curia & torgo saepe versantur.* Paris, 1543.

Goñi Gaztambide, J. "El fiscalismo pontificio en España en tiempo di Juan XXII." *Anthologica annua* 14 (1966): 65–99.

Goñi Gaztambide, J. "Juan XXII y la provision de los obispados españoles." *Archivum Historiae Pontificiae* 4 (1966): 25–58.

González, J. *Dilucidum ac perutile glossema, seu commentatio ad regulam octavan Cancellariae, de reservatione mensium at alternativa episcoparum. . . .* Rome, 1604.

González de la Calle, P. U., and A. Huarte y Echenique. *Constituciones y bulas complementarias dadas a la universidad de Salamanca por el pontífice Benedicto XIII, Pedro de Luna.* Ed. paleográfica con prólogo y notas. Zaragoza, 1932.

Gottlob, A. "Das Vatikanische Archiv." *Historisches Jahrbuch* 6 (1885): 271–284.

Gottlob, A. *Aus der Camera apostolica des 15. Jahrhunderts: Ein Beitrag zur Geschichte des päpstlichen Finanzwesens und des endenden Mittelalters.* Innsbruck, 1889.

Gottlob, A. *Die päpstlichen Kreuzzugs-steuern im XIII. Jahrhunderts: Ihre rechtliche Grundlage, politische Geschichte und technische Verwaltung.* Heiligenstadt, 1892.

Gottlob, A. *Die Servitientaxe im 13. Jahrhundert: Eine Studie zur Geschichte des päpstlichen Geburhenwesens.* Stuttgart, 1903.

Grafinger, C. M. *Beiträge zur Geschichte der Biblioteca Vaticana.* Vatican City, 1996.

Gramatica, L., and G. Galbiati. *Il codice ambrosiano del Liber Diurnus Romanorum Pontificum.* Milan, 1921.

Grandjean, C. A. *Le registre de Benoît XI: Recueil des bulles de ce pape publiées ou analysées d'après le manuscrit original des Archives du Vatican.* Vol. 2 of *Bibliothèque des Écoles françaises d'Athènes et de Rome.* 2d ser., *Registres des papes du XIIIe siècle.* Paris, 1883–.

Grange, H. *Sommaires des lettres pontificales concernant le Gard (anciens diocèses de Nimes, d'Uzès et parties d'Avignon et d'Arles), émanant des Papes d'Avignon, XIVme siècle.* Nîmes, 1911–.

Gras, P. "Une bulle de plomb du pape Jean XV (995)." *Bibliothèque de l'École des Chartes* 122 (1964): 252–256.

Grasse, J. G. T., F. Benedict, and H. Plechl. *Orbis Latinus: Lexikon lateinischer geographischer Namem: Handausgabe.* Braunschweig, 1971.

Grat, F. *Étude sur le motu proprio, des origines au début du XVIe siècle.* Melun, 1945.

Great Britain. Public Record Office. *Lists of Diplomatic Documents, Scottish Documents and Papal Bulls Preserved in the Public Record Office.* London, 1923.

Greipl, E. J. "Die Bestände des Archivs der Münchner Nuntiatur in der Zeit von 1877 bis 1904." *Römische Quartalschrift für christliche Altertumskunde und Kirchengeschichte* 78 (1983): 192–269.

Grendler, P. F. *The Roman Inquisition and the Venetian Press, 1540–1605.* Princeton, 1977.

Griffi, P. *Il De Officio Collectoris in Regno Angliae.* Edited by M. Monaco. Rome, 1973.

Grimaldi, F., and A. Mordenti, eds. *Guida degli archivi lauretani.* Rome, 1985–1986.

Grisar, J. "Le biblioteche e gli archivi dei dicasteri della Curia romana." In *Il libro e le biblioteche: Atti del primo Congresso bibliografico francescano internazionale, 20–27 febbraio 1949*, vol. 2, pp. 33–60. Rome, 1950.

Groof, B. de, and E. Galdieri, eds. *La dimensione europea dei Farnese.* Brussels, 1993.

Gross, H. *Rome in the Age of Enlightenment: The Post-Tridentine Syndrome and the Ancien Regime.* Cambridge, 1990.

Gualdo, G. "Il 'Liber brevium de curia anni septimi' di Paolo II: Contributo allo studio del breve pontificio." In *Mélanges Eugène Tisserant*, vol. 4, pp. 301–345. Vatican City, 1964.

Gualdo, G. "Lo 'Schedario Baumgarten' e gli studi di diplomatica pontificia." *Rivista di storia della chiesa in Italia* 20 (1966): 71–81.

Gualdo, G. "L'Archivio Segreto Vaticano." *L'Osservatore della domenica*(1969): 46–49, 51–52.

Gualdo, G. "I brevi 'sub plumbo'." *Annali della Scuola speciale per archivisti e bibliotecari dell'Università di Roma* 11 (1971): 82–121.

Gualdo, G. "Die Geheimarchive des Vatikans." In *Die Kunstschätze des Vatikans: Architektur, Malerei, Plastik*, pp. 157–160, 375–376. 2d ed. Freiburg, 1975.

Gualdo, G. "Archivi di famiglie romane nell'Archivio vaticano." *Archivio della Società romana di storia patria* 104 (1981): 147–158.

Gualdo, G. "'Litterae ante coronationem' agli inizi del '400." *Atti dell'Istituto Veneto di scienze, lettere ed arti* 140 (1981–1982): 175–198; 289–306.

Gualdo, G. "Documenti dell'Archivio vaticano per la storia delle Marche nell'èta di Sisto V (1585–1590)." *Studia picena* 50.1–2 (1985): 27–51.

Gualdo, G. *Sussidi per la consultazione dell'Archivio Vaticano.* New ed. Vatican City, 1989.

Gualteruzzi, T. T. *Venerabilis collegii secretariorum apostolicorum privilegia, et iura diversa, undique in unum collecta. . . .* Rome, 1587.

Guérard, L. *Documents pontificaux sur la Gascogne, d'après les archives du Vatican: Pontificat de Jean XXII (1316–1334).* Paris, 1896–1903.

Guérard, L. *Petite introduction aux inventaires des archives du Vatican.* Rome, 1901.

Guerello, F. *Lettere di Innocenzo IV dai cartolari notarili genovesi.* Rome, 1961.

Guidi, P., ed. *Tuscia. 1, La decima degli anni 1274–1280.* Vol. 1 of *Rationes decimarum Italiae nei secoli XIII e XIV*, edited by P. Guidi and P. Sella. Vatican City, 1932.

Guidi, P. *Inventari di libri nelle serie dell'Archivio Vaticano, 1287–1459.* Vatican City, 1948.

Guidi, P., and P. Sella, eds. *Rationes decimarum Italiae nei secoli XIII e XIV.* Vatican City, 1932–1952.

Guilday, P. "The Sacred Congregation de Propaganda Fide (1622–1922)." *Catholic Historical Review* 6 (1920–1921): 478–494.

Guillemain, B. "Le personnel de la cour de Clement V." *Mélanges d'archéologie et d'histoire* 63 (1951): 140–181.

Guillemain, B. *La politique bénéficiale du pape Benoît XII, 1334–1342.* Paris, 1952.

Guillemain, B. *La cour pontificale d'Avignon (1309–1376): Étude d'une société.* Paris, 1962.

Guillemain, B. *Les recettes et les dépenses de la Chambre apo-*
stolique pour la quatrième année du pontificat de Clément V (1308–1309): Introitus et exitus 75. Rome, 1978.

Guiraud, J. *Les registres de Grégoire X (1272–1276): Recueil des bulles de ce pape publiées ou analysées d'après les manuscrits originaux des Archives du Vatican.* Vol. 12 of *Bibliothèque des Écoles françaises d'Athènes et de Rome.* 2d ser., *Registres des papes du XIIIe siècle.* Paris, 1892–.

Guiraud, J., and E. Cadier. *Les registres de Grégoire X (1272–1276) et de Jean XXI (1276–1277): Recueil des bulles de ces papes: Tables publiées ou analysées d'après le manuscrit des Archives du Vatican.* Vol. 12 of *Bibliothèque des Écoles françaises d'Athènes et de Rome.* 2d ser., *Registres des papes du XIIIe siècle.* Paris, 1960.

Gullota, G. "Sul regesto dei documenti nonantolani dell'Archivio segreto vaticano e sugli antichi cataloghi e i codici nonantolani." *Atti e memorie della Deputazione di storia patria per le antiche provincie modenesi*, 8th ser. 5 (1953): 147–156.

Gullotta, G. *Gli antichi cataloghi e i codici della'Abbazia di Nonantola.* Vatican City, 1955.

Gundlach, W., ed. "Codex Carolinus." In *Epistolae merowingici et karolini aevi*, vol. 1, pp. 469–657. Berlin, 1892.

Gundlach, W., ed. "Epistolae aevi merowingici collectae." In *Epistolae merowingici et karolini aevi*, vol. 1, pp. 434–468. Berlin, 1892.

Gundlach, W., ed. "Epistolae arelatenses genuinae." In *Epistolae merowingici et karolini aevi*, vol. 1, pp. 1–83. Berlin, 1892.

Gundlach, W., ed. "Epistolae langobardicae collectae." In *Epistolae merowingici et karolini aevi*, vol. 1, pp. 691–715. Berlin, 1892.

Gundlach, W., ed. "Epistolae viennenses spuriae." In *Epistolae merowingici et karolini aevi*, vol. 1, pp. 84–109. Berlin, 1892.

Hackenberg, A. "Zu den ersten Verhandlungen der S. Congregatio Cardinalium Concilii Tridentini Interpretum (1564–1568)." In *Festschrift zum elfhundertjahrigen Jubiläum des Deutschen Campo Santo in Rom.* Freiburg, 1897.

Hagan, J. "Some Papers Relating to the Nine Years' War." *Archivium hibernicum* 2 (1913): 274–320.

Hagan, J. "Miscellanea Vaticano-Hibernica, 1580–1631." *Archivium hibernicum* 3 (1914): 227–565.

Hagan, J. "Miscellanea Vaticano-Hibernica, 1420–1631." *Archivium hibernicum* 4 (1915): 215–318.

Hagan, J. "Miscellanea Vaticano-Hibernica." *Archivium hibernicum* 6 (1917): 94–115.

Hagan, J. "Miscellanea Vaticano-Hibernica, 1572–1585." *Archivium hibernicum* 7 (1918–1922): 67–356.

Hageneder, O. "Die äusseren Merkmale der Originalregister Innocenz III." *Mitteilungen des Instituts für österreichische Geschichtsforschung* 65 (1957): 296–339.

Hageneder, O. "Das Sonne-Mond-Gleichnis bei Innozenz III: Versuch einer Teil weisen Neuinterpretation." *Mitteilungen des Instituts für österreichische Geschichtsforschung* 65 (1957): 340–368.

Hageneder, O. "Quellenkritisches zu den Originalregistern Innozenz III." *Mitteilungen des Instituts für österreichische Geschichtsforschung* 68 (1960): 128–239.

Hageneder, O. "Über 'Expeditionsbündel' in Registrum Vaticanum 4." *Römische historische Mitteilungen* 12 (1970): 111–124.

Hageneder, O. "Die päpstlichen Register des 13. und 14. Jahrhunderts." *Annali della Scuola speciale per archivisti e bibliotecari dell'Università di Roma* 12 (1972): 45–76.

Hageneder, O., and A. Haidacher, eds. *Die Register Innocenz III.* Graz, 1964.

Hager, H., and S. S. Munshower, eds. *Projects and Monuments in the Period of the Roman Baroque.* University Park, Pa., 1984.

Haidacher, A. "Beiträge zur Kenntnis der verlorenen Registerbände Innozenz' III." *Römische historische Mitteilungen* 4 (1960–1961): 36–62.

Haidacher, A. *Geschichte der Päpste in Bildern.* Heidelberg, 1965.

Haine, A. *Synopsis S.R.E. Cardinalium Congregationum.* Louvain, 1857.

Hales, E. E. Y. *Revolution and Papacy, 1796–1846.* New York, 1960.

Halkin, L. E. *Les sources de l'histoire de la Belgique aux Archives et à la Bibliothèque Vaticanes: État des collections et répertoire bibliographique.* Brussels, 1951.

Halkin, L. E. "Les Archives des nonciatures: Rapport au comité directeur de l'Institut historique Belge de Rome." *Bulletin de l'Institut historique Belge de Rome* 33 (1961): 649–700.

Halkin, L. E. *Les Archives des nonciatures.* Brussels, 1968.

Haller, J. "Die Verteilung der Servitia Minuta und die Obligation der Prälaten im 13. und 14. Jahrhundert." *Quellen und Forschungen aus italienischen Archiven und Bibliotheken* 1 (1898): 281–295.

Haller, J. "Zwei Aufzeichnungen über die Beamten der Curie im 13. und 14. Jahrhundert." *Quellen und Forschungen aus italienischen Archiven und Bibliotheken* 1 (1898): 1–38.

Haller, J. "Die Ausfertigung der Provisionen: Ein Beitrag zur Diplomatik der Papsturkunden des 14. und 15. Jahrhunderts." *Quellen und Forschungen aus italienischen Archiven und Bibliotheken* 2 (1899): 1–40.

Haller, J. *Piero da Monte, ein Gelehrter und päpstlicher Beamter des 15. Jahrhunderts: Seine Briefsammlung.* Rome, 1941.

Haller, J., et al., eds. *Repertorium Germanicum: Regesten aus den päpstlichen Archiven zur Geschichte des deutschen Reichs und seiner Territorien im XIV. und XV. Jahrhundert: Pontifikat Eugens IV. (1431–1447).* Berlin, 1897.

Hallman, B. M. *Italian Cardinals, Reform, and the Church as Property.* Berkeley, 1985.

Halphen, L. *Études sur l'administration de Rome au moyen-âge (751–1252).* Paris, 1907.

Halushchynskyi, T. T. *Acta Innocentii pp. III (1198–1216) e registris Vaticanis aliisque eruit.* Vatican City, 1944.

Halushchynskyi, T. T., and A. H. Velykyi. *Epistolae metropolitarum, archiepiscoporum et episcoporum.* Rome, 1956–1980.

Hammermayer, L. "Grundlinien der Entwicklung des päpstlichen Staatssekretariats von Paul V. bis Innozenz X., 1605–1655." *Römische Quartalschrift für christliche Altertumskunde und für Kirchengeschichte* 55 (1960): 157–202.

Hampe, K., ed. "Epistolae selectae pontificum romanorum Carolo Magno et Ludowico Pio regnantibus scriptae." In *Epistolae karolini aevi*, vol. 3, pp. 1–84. Berlin, 1899.

Hampe, K., ed. "Leonis III. papae Epistolae selectae." In *Epistolae karolini aevi*, vol. 3, pp. 85–104. Berlin, 1899.

Hampe, K. "Aus verlorenen Registerbänden der Päpste Innozenz III. und Innozenz IV." *Mitteilungen des Instituts für österreichische Geschichtsforschung* 23 (1902): 545–567; 24 (1903): 198–237.

Hanquet, K., ed. *Documents relatifs au Grand Schisme.* Vol. 1, *Suppliques de Clément VII (1378–1379).* Vol. 8 of *Analecta vaticano-belgica: Documents relatifs aux anciens diocèses de Cambrai, Liège, Thérouanne et Tournai.* Brussels, 1924.

Hanquet, K., and U. Berlière, eds. *Documents relatifs au Grand Schisme,* vol. 2, *Lettres de Clément VII (1378–1379).* Vol. 12 of *Analecta vaticano-belgica: Documents relatifs aux anciens diocèses de Cambrai, Liège, Thérouanne et Tournai.* Rome, 1930.

Hansen, J. *Der Kampf um Köln, 1576–1584.* Vol. 1 of *Nuntiaturberichte aus Deutschland nebst ergänzenden Actenstücken. Dritte Abteilung, 1572–1585.* Berlin, 1892.

Hansen, J. *Der Reichstag zu Regensburg 1576: Der Pacificationstag zu Köln 1579: Der Reichstag zu Augsburg 1582.* Vol. 2 of *Nuntiaturberichte aus Deutschland nebst ergänzenden Actenstücken. Dritte Abteilung, 1572–1585.* Berlin, 1894.

Hartmann, H. "Beiträge zum Urkundenwesen des Reformpapsttums. 1, Ueber die Entwicklung der Rota." *Archiv für Urkundenforschung* 16 (1939): 385–412.

Hartmann, L. M. "Die Entstehungszeit des Liber Diurnus." *Mitteilungen des Instituts für österreichische Geschichtsforschung* 13 (1892): 239–254.

Haskins, C. H. "The Vatican Archives." *American Historical Review* 2 (1896–1897): 40–58.

Haskins, C. H. "The Sources for the History of the Papal Penitentiary." *American Journal of Theology* 9 (1905): 421–450.

Haskins, C. H. "Two Roman Formularies in Philadelphia." In *Miscellanea Francesco Ehrle,* vol. 4, pp. 275–286. Rome, 1924.

Haubst, R. "Der Reformentwurf Pius des Zweiten." *Römische Quartalschrift für christliche Altertumskunde und für Kirchengeschichte* 49 (1954): 188–242.

Hausmann, F. R. "Armarium 39, Tomus 10 des Archivio Segreto Vaticano." *Quellen und Forschungen aus italienischen Archiven und Bibliotheken* 50 (1971): 112–180.

Hausmann, F. R. "Ein Sammelband über Papst Pius II." *Quellen und Forschungen aus italienischen Archiven und Bibliotheken* 50 (1971): 462–474.

Hauviller, E. *Analecta Argentinensia: Vatikanische Akten und Regesten zur Geschichte des Bistums Strassburg im XIV. Jahrhundert (Johann XXII., 1316–1334), und Beiträge zur Reichs- und Bistumsgeschichte.* Strasbourg, 1900.

Hayez, A., ed. *Gregoire XI, 1370–1378: Lettres communes analysées d'apres les registres dits d'Avignon ed du Vatican.* Vol. 6 bis of *Bibliothèque des Écoles françaises d'Athènes et de Rome.* 3d ser., *Registres et lettres des papes du XIVe siècle.* Rome, 1992–.

Hayez, A., et al. "De la supplique à la lettre: Le parcours des grâces en Cour de Rome sous Urbain V (1362–1366)." In *Le fonctionnement administratif de la papauté d'Avignon: Aux origines de l'état moderne,* pp. 171–205. Rome, 1990.

Heckel, R. von. "Das päpstliche und sicilische Registerwesen: in vergleichender Darstellung, mit besonderer Berücksichtigung der Ursprünge." *Archiv für Urkundenforschung* 1 (1908): 371–511.

Heckel, R. von. "Die Organisation der kurialen Behörden und ihr Geschäftsgang." In *Magister Heinrich der Poet in Würzburg und die römische Kurie*, by H. Grauert, pp. 206–229, 487–493. Munich, 1912.

Heckel, R. von. "Untersuchungen zu den Registern Innocenz' III." *Historisches Jahrbuch* 40 (1920): 1–43.

Heckel, R. von. "Das Aufkommen der ständigen Prokuratoren an der päpstlichen Kurie im 13. Jahrhundert." In *Miscellanea Francesco Ehrle*, vol. 2, pp. 290–321. Rome, 1924.

Heckel, R. von. "Eine Kanzleianweisung über die schriftmassige Ausstattung der Papsturkunden aus dem 13. Jahrhundert in Durantis Speculum iudiciale." In *Festschrift für Georg Leidinger zum 60. Gerburtztag an 30. Dezember 1930*, pp. 109–118. Munich, 1930.

Heckel, R. von. "Beiträge zur Kenntnis des Geschäftsgangs in der päpstlichen Kanzlei im 13. Jahrhundert." In *Festschrift Albert Brackmann*, edited by L. Santifaller, pp. 434–460. Weimar, 1931.

Heckel, R. von. "Die Verordnung Innocenz' III. über die absolute Ordination und die Forma 'Cum secundum apostolum.'" *Historisches Jahrbuch* 55 (1935): 277–304.

Heckel, R. von. "Studien über die Kanzleiordnung Innozenz' III." *Historisches Jahrbuch* 57 (1937): 258–289.

Heigl, P. "Zum Register Johanns VIII." *Mitteilungen des Instituts für österreichische Geschichtsforschung* 32 (1911): 618–622.

Heller, E., ed. *Die Ars Dictandi des Thomas von Capua.* Heidelberg, 1929.

Heller, E. "Der kuriale Geschäftsgang in den Briefen des Thomas v. Capua." *Archiv für Urkundenforschung* 14 (1936): 198–318.

Henggeler, R. "Die mittelalterlichen Papsturkunden im Stiftsarchiv Einsiedeln." In *Miscellanea archivistica Angelo Mercati*, pp. 201–225. Vatican City, 1952.

Henkel, W. "Das Inventar des 'Fondo Concili' im Archiv der Konzilskongregation." *Annuarium Historiae Conciliorum* 15 (1983): 430–451.

Herde, P. "Der Zeugenzwang in den päpstlichen Delegationsreskripten des Mittelalters." *Traditio* 18 (1962): 255–288.

Herde, P. "Marinus von Eboli: 'Super revocatoriis' und 'de confirmationibus:' Zwei Abhandlungen des Vizekanzlers Innocenz IV. über das päpstliche Urkundenwesen." *Quellen und Forschungen aus italienischen Archiven und Bibliotheken* 42–43 (1963): 119–264.

Herde, P. "Papal Formularies for Letters of Justice (13th–16th Centuries): Their Development and Significance for Medieval Canon Law." In *Proceedings of the Second International Congress of Medieval Canon Law*, edited by S. Kuttner and J. J. Ryan, pp. 321–346. Vatican City, 1965.

Herde, P. *Beiträge zum päpstlichen Kanzlei- und Urkundenwesen im dreizehnten Jahrhundert.* Kallmünz, 1967.

Herde, P. "Ein Formelbuch Gerhards von Parma mit Urkunden des Auditor Litterarum Contradictarum aus dem Jahre 1277." *Archiv für Diplomatik, Schriftengeschichte, Siegel- und Wappenkunde* 13 (1967): 225–312.

Herde, P. *Audientia litterarum contradictarum: Untersuchungen über die päpstlichen Justizbriefe und die päpstliche Delegationsgerichtsbarkeit vom 13. bis zum Beginn des 16. Jahrhunderts.* Tübingen, 1970.

Herde, P. "Zur Audientia litterarum contradictarum und zur 'Reskripttechnik'." *Archivalische Zeitschrift* 69 (1973): 54–90.

Herde, P. "Die 'Registra Contradictarum' des Vatikanichen Archivs (1575–1799)." In *Palaeographica, diplomatica et archivistica: Studi in onore di Guilio Battelli*, vol. 2, pp. 407–444. Rome, 1979.

Herde, P. "Cautio (littera conventionalis)." In *Lexikon des Mittelalters*, vol. 2, p. 1587. Munich, 1983.

Herde, P. "Formel, -sammlung, -bucher. 2, Päpstliche Kurie." In *Lexikon des Mittelalters*, vol. 4, p. 647. Munich, 1987.

Hergenröther, J., ed. *Leonis X pontificis maximi regesta: E tabularii Vaticani manuscriptis voluminibus aliisque monumentis.* Freiburg, 1884–1891.

Hernáez, F. J. *Colección de bulas, breves y otros documentos relativos a la Iglesia de América y Filipinas, dipuesta, anotada e ilustrada.* Brussels, 1879.

Heywood, J. C. *Documenta selecta e tabulario secreto vaticano quae romanorum pontificum erga Americae populos curam ac studia . . . testantur phototypia descripta.* Rome, 1893.

Hildebrand, H. *Livonica, vornähmlich aus dem 13. Jahrhundert im vatikanischen Archiv.* Riga, 1887.

Hill, R. R. *American Missions in European Archives.* Mexico City, 1951.

Hilling, N. *Procedure at the Roman Curia: A Concise and Practical Handbook.* New York, 1907.

Hilling, N. *Die römische Rota und das Bistum Hildesheim am Ausgange des Mittelalters (1464–1513): Hildesheimische Prozessakten aus dem Archiv der Rota zum Rom.* Münster, 1908.

Hilpert, H. *Kaiser- und Papstbriefe in den "Chronica majora" des Matthaeus Paris.* Stuttgart, 1981.

Hinojosa y Naveros, R. de. *Los despachos de la diplomacia pontificia en España: Memoria de una missión oficial en el Archivo Secreto de la Santa Sede.* Madrid, 1896.

Hirsch-Gereuth, U. A. von, ed. "Epistolae selectae Sergii II, Leonis IV, Benedicti III, pontificum romanum." In *Epistolae karolini aevi*, vol. 3, pp. 581–614. Berlin, 1899.

Hoberg, H. *Die Inventare des päpstlichen Schatzes in Avignon, 1314–1376.* Vatican City, 1944.

Hoberg, H. "Die Servitientaxen der Bistümer im 14. Jahrhundert." *Quellen und Forschungen aus italienischen Archiven und Bibliotheken* 33 (1944): 101–135.

Hoberg, H. *Taxae pro communibus serviitiis, ex libris obligationum ab anno 1295 usque ad annum 1455 confectis.* Vatican City, 1949.

Hoberg, H. "Die Amtsdaten der Rotarichter in den Protokollbüchern der Rotonotare von 1464 bis 1566." *Römische Quartalschrift für christliche Altertumskunde und für Kirchengeschichte* 48 (1953): 43–78.

Hoberg, H. "Die Antrittsdaten der Rotarichter von 1566 bis 1675." *Römische Quartalschrift für christliche Altertumskunde und für Kirchengeschichte* 48 (1953): 211–224.

Hoberg, H. "Die Protokollbücher der Rotonotare von 1464 bis 1517." *Zeitschrift der Savigny-Stiftung für Rechtsgeschichte. Kanonistische Abteilung* 39 (1953): 177–227.

Hoberg, H. "Der Amtsantritt des Rotarichters Antonio Albergati (1649)." *Römische Quartalschrift für christliche Altertumskunde und für Kirchengeschichte* 49 (1954): 112–122.

Hoberg, H. "Die 'Admissiones' des Archivs der Rota." *Archivalische Zeitschrift* 50–51 (1955): 391–408.

Hoberg, H. "Das älteste Inventar der liturgischen Geräte und Paramente des Rotakollegs (1430)." *Quellen und Forschungen aus italienischen Archiven und Bibliotheken* 35 (1955): 275–281.

Hoberg, H. "Die diarien der Rotarichter." *Römische Quartalschrift für christliche Altertumskunde und für Kirchengeschichte* 50 (1955): 44–68.

Hoberg, H., ed. *Die Einnahmenregister des päpstlichen Thesaurars.* Vol. 1 of *Die Einnahmen der apostolischen Kammer unter Innocenz VI.* Paderborn, 1955.

Hoberg, H. "Der Informativprozess des Rotarichters Dominikus Jacobazzi (1492)." *Römische Quartalschrift für christliche Altertumskunde und für Kirchengeschichte* 51 (1956): 228–235.

Hoberg, H. "Register von Rotaprozessen des 14. Jahrhundert im Vatikanischen Archiv." *Römische Quartalschrift für christliche Altertumskunde und für Kirchengeschichte* 51 (1956): 54–69.

Hoberg, H. "Der Informationsprozess über die Qualifikation des Rotarichters Antonio Corsetti (1500)." In *Mélanges Eugène Tisserant*, vol. 4, pp. 389–406. Vatican City, 1964.

Hoberg, H. "Vatikanische Archiv." In *Lexikon für Theologie und Kirche*, edited by J. Höfer and K. Rahner, vol. 12, pp. 635–636. 2d ed. Freiburg, 1964.

Hoberg, H. "Die ältesten Informativprozesse über die Qualifikation neuernannter Rotarichter (1492–1547)." In *Reformata Reformanda: Festgabe für Hubert Jedin zum 17 Juni 1965*, edited by E. Iserloh and K. Repgen, pp. 129–141. Münster, 1965.

Hoberg, H. "Der Fonds Missioni des Vatikanisches Archivs." *Euntes Docete* 21 (1968): 91–107.

Hoberg, H. "Die Tätigkeit der Rota am Vorabend der Glaubensspaltung." In *Miscellanea in onore di Monsignor Martino Giusti*, vol. 2, pp. 1–32. Vatican City, 1978.

Hoberg, H. "Das Vatikanische Archiv als Geschichtsquelle." *Römische Quartalschrift für christliche Altertumskunde und für Kirchengeschichte* 74 (1979): 1–15.

Hoberg, H. "Das Vatikanische Archiv seit 1950." *Römische Quartalschrift für christliche Altertumskunde und für Kirchengeschichte* 77 (1982): 146–156.

Hoberg, H. "Passauer Prozesse in den ältesten im Vatikanischen Archiv erhaltenen Protokollbüchern der Rotanotare (1464–1482)." In *Ecclesia Peregrinans: Josef Lenzenweger zum 70 Geburtstag*, edited by K. Amon et al., pp. 153–158. Vienna, 1986.

Hoberg, H. "Grössere Publikationen aus dem Vatikanischen Archiv seit 1950." *Römische Quartalschrift für christliche Altertumskunde und für Kirchengeschichte* 82 (1987): 122–134.

Hoberg, H. "Aggiunte recenti al Fondo 'Missioni' dell'Archivio vaticano." In *Ecclesiae Memoria: Miscellanea in onore del R.P. Josef Metzler OMI, prefetto dell'Archivio segreto vaticano*, edited by W. Henkel. Rome, 1991.

Hoberg, H. *Inventario dell'Archivio della Sacra Romana Rota (sec. XIV–XIX).* Vatican City, 1994.

Hoffman, G. *Epistolae pontificiae ad Concilium Florentinum spectantes.* Rome, 1940–1946.

Hoffmann, H. "Zum Register und zu den Briefen Papst Gregors VII." *Deutsches Archiv für Erforschung des Mittelalters* 32 (1976): 86–130.

Hoffmann, H. L. *De Archivo Secreto Vaticano qua centrali: Tractatus investigans ac decidere intendens quaestionem an Archivum secretum vaticanum sit revera centrale.* Rome, 1962.

Hofmann, W. von. *Forschungen zur Geschichte der kurialen Behörden vom Schisma bis zur Reformation.* Rome, 1914.

Holter, K. "Illuminierte Ablassbriefe aus Avignon fur die Welser Stadpfarrkirche." *Jahrbuch des Musealvereines Wels* 9 (1962–1963): 65–81.

Holtzmann, W. *Papsturkunden in England.* Berlin, 1930–1952.

Holtzmann, W. "Die Register Papst Alexanders III. in die Händen der Kanonisten." *Quellen und Forschungen aus italienischen Archiven und Bibliotheken* 30 (1940): 13–87.

Holtzmann, W. "Über eine Ausgabe der päpstlichen Dekretalen des 12. Jahrhunderts." *Nachrichten der Akademie der Wissenschaften in Göttingen. Philologisch-historische Klasse* (1945): 15–36.

Holtzmann, W. "Paolo Kehr e le ricerche archivistiche per l'Italia Pontificia." In *Miscellanea archivistica Angelo Mercati*, pp. 43–49. Vatican City, 1952.

Holtzmann, W. "Paolo Kehr e le ricerche archivistiche per l'Italia Pontificia." In *Miscellanea archivistica Angelo Mercati*, pp. 43–49. Vatican City, 1952.

Holtzmann, W. *Das Deutsche historische Institut in Rom.* Cologne, 1955.

Holtzmann, W. *Beiträge zur Reichs- und Papstgeschichte des höhen Mittelalters.* Bonn, 1957.

Holtzmann, W. "Kanonistische Ergänzungen zur Italia Pontificia." *Quellen und Forschungen aus italienischen Archiven und Bibliotheken* 37 (1957): 55–102; 38 (1958): 67–175.

Holtzmann, W. "Nachträge zu den Papsturkunden Italiens X." *Nachrichten der Akademie der Wissenschaften in Göttingen. Philologisch-historische Klasse* 8 (1962): 205–247.

Holtzmann, W., and E. W. Kemp. *Papal Decretals Relating to the Diocese of Lincoln in the Twelfth Century.* Hereford, 1954.

Hone, N. "Documents of the Apostolic Chancery." *Month* 81 (1894) (This title was noted but not verified by project staff.)

Huizing, P., and K. Walf, eds. *The Roman Curia and the Communion of Churches.* New York, 1979.

Humphrey, W. *Urbs et Orbis, or, The Pope as Bishop and as Pontiff.* London, 1899.

Hurtubise, P. *Une famille-témion, les Salviati.* Vatican City, 1985.

Hurtubise, P., and R. Toupin. *Correspondance du nonce en France, Antonio Maria Salviati 1572–1578.* Vols. 12–13 of *Acta nuntiaturae gallicae.* Rome, 1975.

Huyben, J. "Een verloren gewaand handschrift van den 'Liber diurnus Romanorum Pontificum'." In *Miscellanea historica in honorem Alberti De Meyer*, pp. 255–265. Louvain, 1946.

Ilardi, V. "Fifteenth-century Diplomatic Documents in Western European Archives and Libraries (1450–1494)." *Studies in the Renaissance* 9 (1962): 64–112.

Ilgen, T. *Sphragistik: Heraldik deutsche Munzgeschichte.* Leipzig, 1912.

Illibato, A. *Il "Liber Visitationis" di Francesco Carafa nella diocesi di Napoli (1542–1543).* Rome, 1983.

"L'immagine dell'Olanda e delle Fiandre nella letteratura italiana: Het beeld van Italië in de literatuur van Nederland en Vlaanderen." *Bulletin de l'Institut historique Belge de Rome* 61 (1991) (This title was noted but not verified by project staff.)

Inguanez, M. "Le bolle pontificie di S. Spirito del Morrone conservate nell'archivio di Montecassino (1157–1698)." *Gli Archivi italiani* 5 (1918): 111–132, 158–176.

Inguanez, M., L. Mattei-Cerasoli, and P. Sella, eds. *Campania*. Vol. 6 of *Rationes decimarum Italiae nei secoli XIII e XIV*, edited by P. Guidi and P. Sella. Vatican City, 1942.

L'institution ecclesiale a la fin du Moyen Age. Rome, 1984. (This title was noted but not verified by project staff.)

Ioly Zorattini, P. C., ed. *Processi del S. Uffizio di Venezia contro ebrei e giudaizzanti*. Florence, 1980–.

Italy. Archivio Centrale dello Stato. *Bibliografia le fonti documentarie nelle pubblicazioni dal 1979 al 1985*. Rome, 1992.

Jackowski, L. "Die päpstlichen Kanzleiregeln und ihre Bedeutung fur Deutschland." *Archiv für katholisches Kirchenrecht* 90 (1910): 3–47, 197–235, 432–463.

Jacqueline, B. "Actes de la S.C. 'de Propaganda Fide' concernant la province de Normandie (1622–1658)." *Cahiers Leopold Delisle* 17, fasc. 1–2 (1968): 3–21.

Jacqueline, B. "L'organisation interne du dicastère missionaire après 350 ans." In *Sacrae Congregationis de Propaganda Fide Memoria Rerum: 350 anni a servizio delle missioni*, edited by J. Metzler. Rome, 1972.

Jadin, L. "Procès d'information pour la nomination des évêques et abbés des Pays-Bas, de Liége et de Franche-Comté d'après les Archives de la Congrégation Consistoriale. 1re partie, 1564–1637." *Bulletin de l'Institut historique Belge de Rome* 8 (1928): 5–263.

Jadin, L. "Procès d'information pour la nomination des évêques et abbés des Pays-Bas, de Liége et de Franche-Comté d'après les archives de la Daterie, 1631–1775." *Bulletin de l'Institut historique Belge de Rome* 11 (1931): 347–389.

Jaffé, P. *Regesta pontificum romanorum ab condita ecclesia ad annum post Christum natum MCXCVIII*. Leipzig, 1885–1888.

Jaitner, L. *Nuntius Pietro Francesco Montoro (1621 Juli–1624 Oktober)*. Vol. 6 of *Nuntiaturberichte aus Deutschland nebst ergänzenden Actenstücken, Die Kölner Nuntiatur*. Munich, 1977.

Jansen, M. "Zur päpstlichen Urkunden- und Taxwesen um die Wende des 14. und 15. Jahrhunderts." In *Festgabe Karl Theodor von Heigel zur Vollendung seines sechzigsten Lebensjahres gewidmet*, pp. 146–159. Munich, 1903.

Janssen, W. *Die päpstlichen Legaten in Frankreich vom Schisma Anaklets II. bis zum Tode Coelestins III. (1130–1198)*. Cologne, 1961.

Jedin, H. *Geschichte des Konzils von Trient*. Freiburg, 1949–.

Jedin, H. *Chiesa della fede, chiesa della storia: Saggi scelti*. Brescia, 1972.

Jedin, H. "Nuntiaturberichte und Durchführung des Konzils von Trient: Hinweise und Fragen." *Quellen und Forschungen aus italienischen Archiven und Bibliotheken* 53 (1973): 180–213.

Jennings, B. "Ireland and the Propaganda Fide, 1672–6." *Archivium hibernicum* 17 (1955): 16–66; 18 (1956): 1–60.

Jennings, B. "Acta S. Congregationis de Propaganda Fide, 1622–1650 (Irlanda)." *Archivium hibernicum* 22 (1959): 28–139.

Jensen, O. "The 'Denarius Sancti Petri' in England." *Transactions of the Royal Historical Society*, n.s. 15 (1901): 171–247.

Jensovsky, B. *Acta Urbani* V, 1362–1370. Prague, 1944–1954.

Johns, C. M. S. "The Art Patronage of Pope Clement XI Albani and the Paleochristian Revival in Early Eighteenth Century Rome." Ph.D. diss., University of Delaware, 1985.

Johns, C. M. S. *Papal Art and Cultural Politics: Rome in the Age of Clement XI*. Cambridge, 1993.

Jones, F. M. "Documents Concerning the Collegium Pastorale Hibernicum of Louvain, 1624." *Archivium hibernicum* 16 (1951): 40–61.

Jones, F. M. "Papal Briefs to Father Mansoni, Papal Nuncio to Ireland." *Archivium hibernicum* 17 (1953): 51–68.

Jonghe, É. de, and T. Simar. *Archives congolaises*. Brussels, 1919.

Jordan, E. *Les registres de Clément IV (1265–1268): Recueil des bulles de ce pape publiées ou analysées d'après les manuscrits originaux des Archives du Vatican*. Vol. 11 of *Bibliothèque des Écoles françaises d'Athènes et de Rome*. 2d ser., *Registres des papes du XIIIe siècle*. Paris, 1893–1945.

Jordan, K. "Die päpstliche Verwaltung im Zeitalter Gregors VII." *Studi Gregoriani per la storia di Gregorio VII e della riforma gregoriana* 1 (1947): 111–135.

Jordan, K. *Die Entstehung der römische Kurie: Ein Versuch*. Darmstadt, 1962.

Jordao, L. M. *Bullarium patronatus Portugalliae regum in ecclesiis Africae, Asiae atque Oceaniae: Bullas, brevia, epistolas, decreta actaque Sanctae Sedis ab Alexandro III ad hoc usque tempus amplectens*. Lisbon, 1868–1873.

Just, L. "Die Quellen zur Geschichte der kölner Nuntiatur in Archiv und Bibliothek des Vatikans." *Quellen und Forschungen aus italienischen Archiven und Bibliotheken* 29 (1938–1939): 249–296.

Kallfelz, H. "Fragmente eines Suppliken-Rotulus aus der 2. Hälfte des 14. Jahrhunderts im Archiv der Marktgemeinde Burgstadt am Main." *Wurzburger Diozesangeschichtsblätter* 42 (1980): 159–174.

Kaltenbrunner, F. "Papsturkunden in Italien." *Sitzungsberichte der kaiserlichen Akademie der Wissenschaften zu Wien. Philosophisch-historische Klasse* 94 (1879): 627–705.

Kaltenbrunner, F. "Bemerkungen über die äusseren Merkmale der Papsturkunden des 12. Jahrhunderts." *Mitteilungen des Instituts für österreichische Geschichtsforschung* 1 (1880): 373–410.

Kaltenbrunner, F. "Römische Studien: Die päpstlichen Register des 13. Jahrhunderts." *Mitteilungen des Instituts für österreichische Geschichtsforschung* 5 (1884): 213–294.

Karttunen, L. *Les nonciatures apostoliques permanentes de 1650 à 1800*. Helsinki, 1912.

Katterbach, B. "Päpstliche Suppliken mit der Klausel der sola Signatura." *Römische Quartalschrift für christliche Altertumskunde und für Kirchengeschichte* 31 (1923): 185–196.

Katterbach, B. *Specimina supplicationum ex registris Vaticanis*. Rome, 1927.

Katterbach, B. "Archivio e archivistica." In *Enciclopedia italiana*, vol. 4, pp. 83–88. Rome, 1929.

Katterbach, B. "Archivio Vaticano." In *Enciclopedia italiana*, vol. 4, pp. 88–90. Rome, 1929.

Katterbach, B. *Referendarii utriusque signaturae a Martino V ad Clementem IX et praelati Signaturae supplicationum a Martino V ad Leonem XIII.* Vol. 2 of *Sussidi per la consultazione dell'Archivio Vaticano.* Vatican City, 1931.

Katterbach, B. *Inventario dei registri delle suppliche.* Vatican City, 1932.

Katterbach, B., and W. M. Peitz. "Die Unterschriften der Päpste und Kardinäle in den 'Bullae maiores' vom 11. bis 14. Jahrhundert." In *Miscellanea Francesco Ehrle*, vol. 4, pp. 177–274. Rome, 1924.

Katterbach, B., A. Pelzer, and C. Tarouca da Silva. *Codices latini saeculi XIII.* Rome, 1929.

Katterbach, B., and C. Tarouca da Silva. *Epistolae et instrumenta Saeculi XIII.* Vatican City, 1930.

Kehr, P. F. "Bemerkungen zu den päpstlichen Supplikenregistern des 14. Jahrhunderts." *Mitteilungen des Instituts für österreichische Geschichtsforschung* 8 (1887): 84–102.

Kehr, P. F. "Papsturkunden in Venedig." *Nachrichten der königlichen Gesellschaft der Wissenschaften zu Göttingen. Philologisch-historische Klasse* (1896): 277–308.

Kehr, P. F. "Über den Plan einer kritischen Ausgabe der Papsturkunden bis Innocenz III." *Nachrichten der königlichen Gesellschaft der Wissenschaften zu Göttingen. Philologisch-historische Klasse* (1896): 72–86.

Kehr, P. F. "Papsturkunden in Padova, Ferrara und Bologna, nebst einem Nachtrag über die Papsturkunden in Venedig." *Nachrichten der königlichen Gesellschaft der Wissenschaften zu Göttingen. Philologisch-historische Klasse* (1897): 349–389.

Kehr, P. F. "Papsturkunden in Pisa, Lucca und Ravenna." *Nachrichten der königlichen Gesellschaft der Wissenschaften zu Göttingen. Philologisch-historische Klasse* (1897): 175–216.

Kehr, P. F. "Papsturkunden in Reggio nell'Emilia." *Nachrichten der königlichen Gesellschaft der Wissenschaften zu Göttingen. Philologisch-historische Klasse* (1897): 223–233.

Kehr, P. F. "Papsturkunden in Umbrien." *Nachrichten der königlichen Gesellschaft der Wissenschaften zu Göttingen. Philologisch-historische Klasse* (1898): 349–396.

Kehr, P. F. *Le bolle pontificie anteriori al 1198 . . . che si conservano nell'archivio di Montecassino.* Montecassino, 1899.

Kehr, P. F. "Le bolle pontificie che si conservano negli archivi Senesi." *Bullettino Senese di storia patria* 6 (1899): 51–102.

Kehr, P. F. "Papsturkunden in Sizilien." *Nachrichten der königlichen Gesellschaft der Wissenschaften zu Göttingen. Philologisch-historische Klasse* (1899): 283–334.

Kehr, P. F. "Über die Papsturkunden für S. Maria de Valle Josaphat." *Nachrichten der königlichen Gesellschaft der Wissenschaften zu Göttingen. Philologisch-historische Klasse* (1899): 338–368.

Kehr, P. F. "Diplomatische Miszellen. 3, Zu Heubert von Silva Candida." *Nachrichten der königlichen Gesellschaft der Wissenschaften zu Göttingen. Philologisch-historische Klasse* (1900): 103–109.

Kehr, P. F. "Papsturkunden in Campanien." *Nachrichten der königlichen Gesellschaft der Wissenschaften zu Göttingen. Philologisch-historische Klasse* (1900): 286–344.

Kehr, P. F. "Papsturkunden in Rom." *Nachrichten der königlichen Gesellschaft der Wissenschaften zu Göttingen. Philologisch-historische Klasse* (1900): 111–197, 360–434; (1901) 239–271; (1903) 1–161.

Kehr, P. F. "Papsturkunden in Salerno, La Cava und Neapel." *Nachrichten der königlichen Gesellschaft der Wissenschaften zu Göttingen. Philologisch-historische Klasse* (1900): 198–269.

Kehr, P. F. "Diplomatische Miszellen. 4, Die Scheden des Panvinius." *Nachrichten der königlichen Gesellschaft der Wissenschaften zu Göttingen. Philologisch-historische Klasse* (1901): 1–27.

Kehr, P. F. "Papsturkunden im ehemaligen Patrimonium und südlichen Toscana." *Nachrichten der königlichen Gesellschaft der Wissenschaften zu Göttingen. Philologisch-historische Klasse* (1901): 196–228.

Kehr, P. F. "Scrinium und Palatium: Zur Geschichte des päpstlichen Kanzleiwesens im XI. Jahrhundert." *Mitteilungen des Instituts für österreichische Geschichtsforschung*, Erganzungsband 6 (1901): 70–112.

Kehr, P. F. "Ältere Papsturkunden in den päpstlichen Registern von Innocenz III. bis Paul III." *Nachrichten der königlichen Gesellschaft der Wissenschaften zu Göttingen. Philologisch-historische Klasse* (1902): 393–558.

Kehr, P. F. "Papsturkunden in der Lombardei." *Nachrichten der königlichen Gesellschaft der Wissenschaften zu Göttingen. Philologisch-historische Klasse* (1902): 130–167.

Kehr, P. F. "Papsturkunden in Ligurien." *Nachrichten der königlichen Gesellschaft der Wissenschaften zu Göttingen. Philologisch-historische Klasse* (1902): 169–192.

Kehr, P. F. "Papsturkunden in Mailand." *Nachrichten der königlichen Gesellschaft der Wissenschaften zu Göttingen. Philologisch-historische Klasse* (1902): 67–129.

Kehr, P. F. "Le bolle pontificie che si conservano nell'archivio diplomatico di Firenze." *Archivio storico italiano*, 5th ser. 32 (1903): 1–18.

Kehr, P. F. "Nachträge zu den römischen Berichten." *Nachrichten der königlichen Gesellschaft der Wissenschaften zu Göttingen. Philologisch-historische Klasse* (1903): 505–591.

Kehr, P. F. "Papsturkunden im westlichen Toscana." *Nachrichten der königlichen Gesellschaft der Wissenschaften zu Göttingen. Philologisch-historische Klasse* (1903): 592–641.

Kehr, P. F. "Die Minuten von Passignano: Eine diplomatische Miszelle (mit Faksimile)." *Quellen und Forschungen aus italienischen Archiven und Bibliotheken* 7 (1904): 8–41, 375.

Kehr, P. F. "Papsturkunden im östlichen Toscana." *Nachrichten der königlichen Gesellschaft der Wissenschaften zu Göttingen. Philologisch-historische Klasse* (1904): 139–203.

Kehr, P. F. "Nachträge zu den Papsturkunden Italiens." *Nachrichten der königlichen Gesellschaft der Wissenschaften zu Göttingen. Philologisch-historische Klasse* (1905): 321–380; (1908) 223–304; (1909) 435–517; (1910) 229–288; (1911) 267–335; (1912) 321–383, 414–480; (1914) 52–92; (1924) 156–193.

Kehr, P. F., ed. *Italia pontificia, sive Repertorium privilegiorum et litterarum a Romanis pontificibus ante annum MCLXXXXVIII Italiae ecclesiis, monasteriis, civitatibus singulisque personis concessorum, Roma.* Berlin, 1906–.

Kehr, P. F. "Anzeige von regesta pontificum romanorum,

Germania pontificia II, 1." *Deutsche Literaturzeitung* 45 (1924): 1128–1134.

Kehr, P. F. *Die ältesten Papsturkunden Spaniens*. Berlin, 1926.

Kehr, P. F. *Papsturkunden in Spanien: Vorarbeiten zur Hispania Pontificia*. Berlin, 1926–1928.

Kehr, P. F. "Über die Sammlung und Herausgabe der älteren Papsturkunden bis Innozenz III (1198)." *Sitzungsberichte der Preussischen Akademie der Wissenschaften. Philosophisch-historische Klasse* 10 (1934): 83–92.

Kehr, P. F., and W. Holtzmann, eds. *Italia pontificia, sive Repertorium privilegiorum et litterarum a Romanis pontificibus ante annum MCLXXXXVIII Italiae ecclesiis, monasteriis, civitatibus singulisque personis concessorum*. Berlin, 1961–1965.

Kelly, J. N. D. *Oxford Dictionary of Popes*. Oxford, 1986.

Kempf, F. *Die Register Innocenz III: Eine paläographisch-diplomatische Untersuchung*. Rome, 1945.

Kempf, F., ed. *Regestum Innocentii III papae super negotio Romani Imperii*. Rome, 1947.

Kempf, F. *Papsttum und Kaisertum bei Innocenz III: die geistigen und rechtlichen Grundlagen seiner Thronstreitpolitik*. Rome, 1954.

Kempf, F. "Zu den Originalregistern Innocenz III." *Quellen und Forschungen aus italienischen Archiven und Bibliotheken* 36 (1956): 86–137.

Kenneally, F. *United States Documents in the Propaganda Fide Archives: A Calendar*. Washington, D.C., 1966–.

Kern, L. "Une supplique adressée au pape Paul III (1534–1549) par un groupe de Valaisans." In *Études d'histoire ecclésiastique et de diplomatique*. Lausanne, 1973.

Kiewning, H. *Nuntiatur des Pallotto, 1628–1630*. Vols. 1–2 of *Nuntiaturberichte aus Deutschland nebst ergänzenden Actenstücken. Vierte Abteilung, siebzehntes Jahrhundert*. Berlin, 1895–1897.

Kirkendale, U. "The Ruspoli Documents on Handel." *Journal of the American Musicological Society* 20 (1967): 222–273, 517–518.

Kirsch, J. P. "Andreas Sapiti, ein englischer Prokurator an der Kurie im 14. Jahrhundert." *Historisches Jahrbuch* 14 (1893): 582–603.

Kirsch, J. P. "Ein Formelbuch der päpstlichen Kanzlei aus der Mitte des 14. Jahrhunderts." *Historisches Jahrbuch* 14 (1893): 814–820.

Kirsch, J. P. *Die päpstlichen Kollectorien in Deutschland während des XIV. Jahrhunderts*. Paderborn, 1894.

Kirsch, J. P. *Die Rückkehr der Päpste Urban V. und Gregor XI. von Avignon nach Rom: Auszüge aus den Kameralregistern des vatikanischen Archivs*. Paderborn, 1898.

Kirsch, J. P. *Die päpstlichen Annaten in Deutschland während des XIV. Jahrhunderts*. Paderborn, 1903–.

Klewitz, H. W. "Die Entstehung des Kardinalskollegiums." *Zeitschrift der Savigny-Stiftung für Rechtsgeschichte. Kanonistische Abteilung* 25 (1936): 115–221.

Klewitz, H. W. "Das 'Privilegienregister' Gregors VII." *Archiv für Urkundenforschung* 16 (1939): 413–424.

Klicman, L. *Acta Clementis VI, pontificis romani, 1342–1352*. Prague, 1903.

Klinkenborg, M. "Papsturkunden in Brescia und Bergamo." *Nachrichten der königlichen Gesellschaft der Wissenschaften zu Göttingen. Philologisch-historische Klasse* (1897): 263–282.

Klinkenborg, M. "Papsturkunden in Nonantola, Modena und Verona." *Nachrichten der königlichen Gesellschaft der Wissenschaften zu Göttingen. Philologisch-historische Klasse* (1897): 234–262.

Klinkenborg, M. "Papsturkunden im Principato, in der Basilicata und in Calabrien." *Nachrichten der königlichen Gesellschaft der Wissenschaften zu Göttingen. Philologisch-historische Klasse* (1898): 335–348.

Klinkenborg, M., and L. Schiaparelli. "Papsturkunden in den Abruzzen und am Monte Gargano." *Nachrichten der königlichen Gesellschaft der Wissenschaften zu Göttingen. Philologisch-historische Klasse* (1898): 290–334.

Klinkenborg, M., and L. Schiaparelli. "Papsturkunden in der Romagna und den Marken." *Nachrichten der königlichen Gesellschaft der Wissenschaften zu Göttingen. Philologisch-historische Klasse* (1898): 6–44.

Knöpfler, J. "Papsturkunden des 12., 13. und 14. Jahrhunderts aus dem germanischen Nationalmuseum in Nürnberg, mit einer historischen Skizze des venetianischen Klosters Brondolo." *Historisches Jahrbuch* 24 (1903): 307–318, 763–785.

Kollmann, I., ed. *Acta Sacrae Congregationis de Propaganda Fide res gestas bohemicas illustrantia*. Prague, 1923–1955.

Kopczynski, M. *Die Arengen der Papsturkunden nach ihrer Bedeutung und Verwandung bis zu Gregor VII*. Bottrop, 1936.

Korzeniowski, J. *Excerpta ex libris manuscriptis archivi consistorialis Romani, 1409–1590*. Kraków, 1890.

Kowalsky, N. *Inventario dell'Archivio storico della S. Congregazione de Propaganda Fide*. Schöneck-Beckenried, 1961.

Kowalsky, N., and J. Metzler. *Inventory of the Historical Archives of the Congregation for the Evangelization of Peoples or "de Propaganda Fide."* 3d enl. ed. Rome, 1988.

Krarup, A., ed. *Bullarium Danicum: Pavelige aktstykker vedrorende Danmark, 1198–1316*. Copenhagen, 1932.

Kraus, A. "Das päpstliche Staatssekretariat im Jahre 1623: Eine Denkschrift des ausscheidenden Sostituto an den neuernannten Staatssekretär." *Römische Quartalschrift für christliche Altertumskunde und für Kirchengeschichte* 52 (1957): 93–122.

Kraus, A. "Zur Geschichte des päpstlichen Staatssekretariats: Quellenlage und Methode." *Jahresbericht der Görres-Gesellschaft* (1957): 5–16.

Kraus, A. "Die Aufgaben eines Sekretärs zur Zeit Urbans VIII (1623)." *Römische Quartalschrift für christliche Altertumskunde und für Kirchengeschichte* 53 (1958): 89–92.

Kraus, A. "Die Sekretäre Pius II: Ein Beitrag zur Entwicklungsgeschichte des päpstlichen Sekretariats." *Römische Quartalschrift für christliche Altertumskunde und für Kirchengeschichte* 53 (1958): 28–50.

Kraus, A. "Secretarius und Sekretariat: Der Ursprung der Institution des Staatssekretariats und ihr Einfluss auf die Entwicklung moderner Regierungsformen in Europa." *Römische Quartalschrift für christliche Altertumskunde und für Kirchengeschichte* 55 (1960): 43–84.

Kraus, A. *Das päpstliche Staatssekretariat unter Urban VIII., 1623–1644*. Rome, 1964.

Kreuzer, G. *Die Honoriusfrage im Mittelalter und in der Neuzeit*. Stuttgart, 1975.

Kristeller, P. O. *Iter Italicum: A Finding List of Uncatalogued or Incompletely Catalogued Humanistic Manuscripts of the*

Renaissance in Italian and Other Libraries. London, 1963–1992.

Kristen, Z. Epistulae et Acta Johannis Stephani Ferrerii, 1604–1607. Prague, 1944–.

Krofta, K. Acta Urbani VI et Bonifatii IX pontificum romanorum. Prague, 1903.

Kühne, U., ed. Alexander V., Johann XXIII., Konstanzer Konzil, 1409–1417. Berlin, 1935.

Künzle, P. "Del cosidetto 'Titulus Archivorum' di Papa Damaso." Rivista di storia della chiesa in Italia 7 (1953): 1–26.

Kupke, G. Nuntiaturen des Pietro Bertano und Pietro Camaiani, 1550–1552. Vol. 12 of Nuntiaturberichte aus Deutschland nebst ergänzenden Actenstücken. Erste Abteilung, 1533–1559. Berlin, 1901.

Kuttner, S. "Cardinalis: The History of a Canonical Concept." Traditio 3 (1945): 129–214.

Laehr, G. "Formosi papae [891–896] Epistolae quotquot ad res Germanicas spectant." In Epistolae karolini aevi, vol. 5, pp. 366–370. Berlin, 1928.

Laehr, G. "Stephani V Epistolae passim collectae quotquot ad res Germanicas spectant." In Epistolae karolini aevi, vol. 5, pp. 354–365. Berlin, 1928.

Laemmer, H. Monumenta Vaticana historiam ecclesiasticam saeculi XVI illustrantia, ex tabulariis Sanctae Sedis apostolicae secretis. Freiburg, 1861.

Lafitau, P. F. La vie de Clement XI, souverain pontife. Padua, 1752.

Lambert, H. Correspondance d'Andrea Mangelli internonce aux Pay-bas (1652–1655). Vol. 15 of Analecta vaticano-belgica. Ser. 2, section A, Nonciature de Flandre. Brussels, 1993.

Lang, A. Beiträge zur Kirchengeschichte der Steiermark und ihrer Nachbarländer aus römischen Archiven. Graz, 1903.

Lang, A. Die Urkunden über die Beziehungen der päpstlichen Kurie zur Provinz und Diözese Salzburg in der Avignonischen Zeit, 1316–1378. Graz, 1903–1906.

Lang, G. "Studien zu Brevenregistern und Brevenkonzepten des 15. Jahrhunderts aus dem vatikanischen Archiv." Publikationen des Österreichisches historisches Institut in Rom 4 (1938): 131–147.

Lang, G. "Stephanus de Fonte und Symon de Vares: Zwei Supplikenregistratoren unter Innozenz VI." Quellen und Forschungen aus italienischen Archiven und Bibliotheken 33 (1944): 259–268.

Langlois, E. Les registres de Nicolas IV: Recueil des bulles de ce pape publiées ou analysées d'après le manuscrit original des Archives du Vatican. Vol. 5 of Bibliothèque des Écoles françaises d'Athènes et de Rome. 2d ser., Registres des papes du XIIIe siècle. Paris, 1886–1905.

Lanhers, Y., et al. Tables des registres de Clément V, publiés par les Bénédictins. Forms part of Bibliothèque des Écoles françaises d'Athènes et de Rome. 3d ser., Registres et lettres des papes du XIVe siècle. Paris, 1948–1957.

Largiadèr, A. "Zum Problem der Papsturkunden des Spätmittelalters." Bullettino dell'Archivio paleografico italiano, n.s. 2–3, pt. 2 (1956–1957): 13–25.

Largiadèr, A. Die Papsturkunden des Staatsarchivs Zürich von Innozenz III. bis Martin V.: Ein Beitrag zum Censimentum Helveticum. Zürich, 1963.

Largiadèr, A. Die Papsturkunden der Schweiz von Innozenz III. bis Martin V., ohne Zürich: Ein Beitrag zum Censimentum Helveticum. Zürich, 1968–.

La Roncière, C. B. de, et al. Les registres d'Alexandre IV: Recueil des bulles de ce Pape, publiées ou analysées d'après les manuscrits originaux des Archives du Vatican. Vol. 15 of Bibliothèque des Écoles françaises d'Athènes et de Rome. 2d ser., Registres des papes du XIIIe siècle. Paris, 1902–1959.

Larraona, A., and S. Goyeneche. "De SS. Congregationum, Tribunalium et Officiorum constitutione et interna ordinatione post const. 'Sapienti Consilio'." In Romana Curia a Beato Pio X, Sapienti Consilio reformata. Rome, 1951.

Laufs, M. Politik und Recht bei Innozenz III: Kaiserprivilegien, Thronstreitregister und Egerer Goldbulle in der Reichs- und Rekuperationspolitik Papst Innozenz' III. Cologne, 1980.

Laurent, M. "Guillaume des Rosières et la bibliothèque pontificale à l'époque de Clément VI." In Mélanges Auguste Pelzer, pp. 579–604. Louvain, 1947.

Laurent, M. Le culte de S. Louis d'Anjou a Marseille au XIVe siècle: Les documents de Louis Antoine de Ruffi suivis d'un choix de lettres de cet érudit. Rome, 1954.

Laurent, M. "Trois nouveaux rôles de suppliques 'per fiat' présentés à des papes du XIVe siècle (Vat. lat. 14400)." Mélanges d'archëologie et d'histoire 66 (1954): 219–239.

Laurent, M. "Une supplique de Pierre de Gambacorta présentée par Ludovico Barbo à Eugène IV." Bullettino dell'Archivio paleografico italiano, n.s. 2–3, pt. 2 (1956–1957): 27–32.

Laurent, M., P. Gasnault, and M. Hayez. Lettres communes analysées d'après les registres dits d'Avignon et du Vatican [Urbain V]. Vol. 5 bis of Bibliothèque des Écoles françaises d'Athènes et de Rome. 3d ser., Registres et lettres des papes du XIVe siècle. Paris, 1954–.

Lavin, M. A. Seventeenth-Century Barberini Documents and Inventories of Art. New York, 1975.

Lazarus, P. Das Basler Konzil: Seine Berufung und Leitung, seine Gliederung und seine Behördenorganisation. Berlin, 1912.

Lea, H. C. A Formulary of the Papal Penitentiary in the Thirteenth Century. Philadelphia, 1892.

Lea, H. C. The Inquisition in the Spanish Dependencies: Sicily, Naples, Sardinia, Milan, the Canaries, Mexico, Peru, New Granada. London, 1908.

Lecacheux, P. "Un formulaire de la Pénitencerie Apostolique au temps du cardinal Albornoz (1357–1358)." Mélanges d'archëologie et d'histoire 18 (1898): 37–49.

Lecacheux, P., and G. Mollat, eds. Lettres secrètes et curiales du pape Urbain V (1362–1370) se rapportant à la France: Publ. ou analysées d'apres les registres du Vatican [puis] d'Avignon et du Vatican. Vol. 5 of Bibliothèque des Écoles françaises d'Athènes et de Rome. 3d ser., Registres et lettres des papes du XIVe siècle. Paris, 1902–1955.

Leccisotti, T. D. Documenti Vaticani per la storia di Montecassino: Pontificato di Urbano V. Montecassino, 1952.

Leccisotti, T. D. "Nonantola e i possedimenti cassinesi nel ducato di Persiceta." Atti e memorie della Deputazione di storia patria per le antiche provincie modenesi, 8th ser. 5 (1953): 176–181.

Leccisotti, T. D. "Note in margine all'edizione dei regesti di Clemente V." In Mélanges Eugène Tisserant, vol. 5, pp. 15–45. Vatican City, 1964.

Leccisotti, T. D., and C. Taberelli. *Le carte dell'archivio di S. Pietro di Perugia*. Milan, 1956.

Leclercq, H. "Chancellerie apostolique." In *Dictionnaire d'archéologie chrétienne et de liturgie*, vol. 3, pt. 1, pp. 175–207. Paris, 1907.

Lee, E. *Sixtus IV and Men of Letters*. Rome, 1978.

Lefebvre, C. "Rote romaine." In *Dictionnaire de droit canonique*, edited by R. Naz, vol. 7, pp. 742–771. Paris, 1960–1961.

Lefebvre, C. "La S. Congrégation du Concile et le Tribunal de la S. Rote Romaine à la fin du XVIe siècle." In *La sacra Congregazione del Concilio: Quarto centenario della fondazione, 1564–1964, studi e ricerche*, pp. 163–177. Vatican City, 1964.

Lefebvre, C. "Les origines et la rôle du Cardinalat au moyen âge." *Apollinaris* 41 (1968): 59–70.

Lefèvre, P. "Inventaire des 'Instrumenta Miscellanea' des Archives Vaticanes au point de vue de nos anciens diocèses, Deuxième supplément." *Bulletin de l'Institut historique Belge de Rome* 9 (1929): 323–340.

Leflon, J., and A. Latreille. "Répertoire des fonds napoléoniens aux Archives Vaticanes." *Revue historique* 203 (1950): 59–63.

Legros, H. M., and E. Kerchner. "Lettres d'indulgences de la cour de Rome au XVe siècle." *Revue des études historiques* 92 (1933): 543–556.

Leiss, A. *Aus 1200 Jahren: Das Bayerische Hauptstaatsarchiv zeigt seine Schatze*. Munich, 1979.

Lemmens, L. *Hierarchia latina orientis, 1622–1922*. Rome, 1923–1924.

Lenzenweger, J. "Konkordanzen." In *Acta Pataviensia Austriaca*. Vol. 1, *Klemens VI (1342–1352)*, pp. 43–176. Vienna, 1974.

Leonard, E. *Histoire de Jeanne Ire, reine de Naples, comtesse de Provence (1343–1382)*. Monaco, 1932–1936.

Le Pelletier, J. *Instruction tres-facile et necessaire pour obtenir en cour de Rome toutes sortes d'expeditions de benefices, dispenses de mariages et autres, les scavoir lire, leur prix, les mettre a execution, et de qui a Paris on est oblige de se servir pour les obtenir*. 6th ed. Paris, 1686.

Lerche, O. "Die Privilegierung der deutschen Kirche durch Papsturkunden bis auf Gregor VII.: Ein Beitrag zur Geschichte des päpstlichen Formelwesens." *Archiv für Urkundenforschung* 3 (1911): 125–232.

Lesellier, J. "Notaires et archives de la Curie romaine (1507–1525): Les notaires français à Rome." *Mélanges d'archéologie et d'histoire* 50 (1933): 250–275.

Lestocquoy, J, ed. *Correspondance des nonces en France: Carpi et Ferrerio 1535–1540, et légations de Carpi et de Farnèse*. Vol. 1 of *Acta nuntiaturae gallicae*. Rome, 1961.

Lestocquoy, J. *Correspondance des nonces en France, Capodiferro, Dandino et Guidiccione, 1541–1546: Légations des cardinaux Farnèse et Sadolet et missions d'Ardinghello, de Grimani et de Hieronimo da Correggio*. Vol. 3 of *Acta nuntiaturae gallicae*. Rome, 1963.

Lestocquoy, J., ed. *Correspondance des nonces en France: Dandino, Della Torre et Trivultio, 1546–1551 avec des documents relatifs a la rupture des relations diplomatiques, 1551–1552*. Vol. 6 of *Acta nuntiaturae gallicae*. Rome, 1966.

Lestocquoy, J., ed. *Correspondance du nonce en France: Prospero Santa Croce (1552–1554)*. Vol. 9 of *Acta nuntiaturae gallicae*. Rome, 1972.

Lestocquoy, J., ed. *Correspondance des nonces en France: Lenzi et Gualterio, Légation du Cardinal Trivultio (1557–1561)*. Vol. 14 of *Acta nuntiaturae gallicae*. Rome, 1977.

Leturia, P. de. "El Archivio de la S. Congregación de Negocios Eclesiásticos Extraordinarios y la encíclica de León XII sobre la revolución hispano-americana." In *Miscellanea archivistica Angelo Mercati*, pp. 169–199. Vatican City, 1952.

Levi, G. "Il tomo I dei Regesti Vaticani (lettere di Giovanni VIII)." *Archivio della Società romana di storia patria* 4 (1881): 161–194.

Levinson, A. "Polnisch-Preussisches aus der Biblioteca Borghese im Vatikanischen Archiv." *Zeitschrift des westpreussischen Geschichtsvereins* 47: 1–27; 48: 85–158. (This title was noted but not verified by project staff.)

Liber confraternitatis Sancti Spiritus de Urbe, 1446–1523. Budapest, 1889.

Il libro del centenario: L'Archivio segreto vaticano a un secolo dalla sua apertura, 1880/81–1980/81. Vatican City, 1982.

Likhachev, N. P. *Pis'mo papy Piia V k tsariu Ivanu Groznomu v sviazi s vroprosom o papskikh breve: Etiud po diplomatikie*. St. Petersburg, 1906.

Lindsay, E. R., and A. I. Cameron, eds. *Calendar of Scottish Supplications to Rome, 1418–1422*. Edinburgh, 1934.

Linhartová, M. *Epistulae et Acta Antonii Caetani, 1607–1611*. Prague, 1932–1940.

Litta, P. *Famiglie celebri italiane*. 2d ser. Naples, 1902–1915.

Litva, F. "L'attività finanziaria della Dataria durante il periodo tridentino." *Archivum Historiae Pontificiae* 5 (1967): 79–174.

Llorca, B. *Bulario pontificio de la inquisición española en su período constitucional (1478–1525)*. Rome, 1949.

Lodolini, A. *L'archivio di Stato in Roma e l'archivio del Regno d'Italia: Indice generale storico descrittivo de analitico, con il concorso dei funzionari*. Rome, 1932.

Lodolini, A. *L'archivio di Stato di Roma: Epitome d'una guida degli archivi dell'amministrazione dello Stato Pontificio*. Rome, 1960.

Lodolini, E. "Il consolato pontificio in Brasile (1831–1846) e il consolato Brasiliano nello Stato Pontificio (1847–1857)." *Rassegna storica del Risorgimento* 68 (1981): 303–324.

Loenertz, R. "Les missions dominicaines en Orient et la Société des Frères Pérégrinants." *Archivum Fratrum Praedicatorum* 2 (1932): 1–83; 3 (1933): 5–55; 4 (1934): 1–48.

Logoz, R. C. "Zwei Miszellen zur Geschichte der päpstlichen Register im Mittelalter." *Archivum Historiae Pontificiae* 9 (1971): 401–410.

Logoz, R. C. *Clément VII (Robert de Genève): Sa chancellerie et le clergé romand au début du grand schisme (1378–1394)*. Lausanne, 1974.

Lohrmann, D. "Berard von Neapel, ein päpstlicher Notar und Vertrauter Karls von Anjou." In *Adel und Kirche: Gerd Tellenbach zum 65. Geburtstag, dargebracht von Freunden und Schülern*, pp. 477–498. Freiburg, 1968.

Lohrmann, D. *Das Register Papst Johannes VIII. (872–883): Neue Studien zur Abschrift Reg. Vat. 1, zum verlorenen Originalregister und zum Diktat der Briefe*. Tübingen, 1968.

Lopetegui, L. "San Francisco de Borja y el plan misional de san Pío V: Primeros pasos de una Congregación de Propaganda Fide." *Archivum historicum Societatis Iesu* 11 (1942): 1–26.

López-Velarde López, B. *Expansión geográfica franciscana en el hoy norte central y oriental de México*. Mexico City, 1964.

Löwenfeld, S., ed. *Epistolae pontificum Romanorum ineditae*. Leipzig, 1885.

Löwenfeld, S. "Papsturkunden in Italien: Ein Nachtrag." *Sitzungsberichte der kaiserlichen Akademie der Wissenschaften zu Wien. Philosophisch-historische Klasse* 97 (1880): 55–68.

Loye, J. de. *Les archives de la Chambre apostolique au XIVe siècle. 1re partie, Inventaire*. Paris, 1899.

Lück, D. "Die Kölner Erzbischofe Hermann II. und Anno II. als Erzkanzler der Römischen Kirche." *Archiv für Diplomatik, Schriftengeschichte, Siegel- und Wappenkunde* 16 (1970): 1–50.

Lukács, L. *The Vatican and Hungary, 1846–1878: Reports and Correspondence on Hungary of the Apostolic Nuncios in Vienna*. Budapest, 1981.

Lunt, W. E. *Papal Revenues in the Middle Ages*. New York, 1934.

Lunt, W. E. *Financial Relations of the Papacy with England*. Cambridge, Mass., 1939–1962.

Lunt, W. E. *Accounts rendered by Papal Collectors in England, 1317–1378*. Philadelphia, 1968.

Lutz, G. "Glaubwürdigkeit und Gehalt von Nuntiaturberichten." *Quellen und Forschungen aus italienischen Archiven und Bibliotheken* 53 (1973): 227–275.

Lutz, H. *Nuntiaturen des Pietro Camaiani und Achille de Grassi, Legation des Girolamo Dandino (1552–1553)*. Vol. 13 of *Nuntiaturberichte aus Deutschland nebst ergänzenden Actenstücken. Erste Abteilung, 1533–1559*. Tübingen, 1959.

Lutz, H. "Nuntiaturberichte aus Deutschland: Vergangenheit und Zukunft einer 'klassischen' Editionsreihe." *Quellen und Forschungen aus italienischen Archiven und Bibliotheken* 45 (1965): 274–324.

Lutz, H. *Nuntiatur des Girolamo Muzzarelli, Sendung des Antonio Agustin, Legation des Scipione Rebiba (1554–1556)*. Vol. 14 of *Nuntiaturberichte aus Deutschland nebst ergänzenden Actenstücken. Erste Abteilung, 1533–1559*. Tübingen, 1971.

Lutz, H. "Die Bedeutung der Nuntiaturberichte für die europäische Geschichtsforschung und Geschichtsschreibung." *Quellen und Forschungen aus italienischen Archiven und Bibliotheken* 53 (1973): 152–167.

Lutz, H. *Friedenslegation des Reginald Pole zu Kaiser Karl V. und König Heinrich II (1553–1556)*. Vol. 15 of *Nuntiaturberichte aus Deutschland nebst ergänzenden Actenstücken. Erste Abteilung, 1533–1559*. Tübingen, 1981.

Lux, K. *Constitutionum apostolicarum de generali beneficiorum reservatione, collectio et interpretatio ab a. 1265 usque ad a. 1378 emissarum, tam intra quam extra corpus iuris exstantium*. Bresslau, 1904.

Mabillon, J., and M. Germain. *Museum Italicum, seu Collectio veterum scriptorum ex bibliothecis italicis*. Paris, 1687.

Macfarlane, L. "An English Account of the Election of Urban VI (1378)." *Bulletin of the Institute of Historical Research* 26 (1953): 75–85.

Macfarlane, L. "The Vatican Archives: With Special Reference to Sources for British Medieval History." *Archives* 4 (1959): 29–44, 84–101.

Macfarlane, L. "The Vatican Library and Archives: Opportunities for English-speaking Students." *Wiseman Review* 488 (1961): 128–141.

MacFinn, E. "Scríbhinní i gCartlainn an Vatican: Tuarascbháil." *Analecta hibernica* 16 (1946): 1–280.

Magnino, L. *Pontificia nipponica: Le relazioni tra la Santa Sede e il Giappone attraverso i documenti pontifici*. Rome, 1947–1948.

Maier, A. "Der Handschriftentransport von Avignon nach Rom im Jahr 1566." In *Mélanges Eugène Tisserant*, vol. 7, pp. 9–27. Vatican City, 1964.

Maillard-Luyparert, M. *Documents relatifs au Grand Schisme*. Vol. 8, *Lettres d'Innocent VII (1404–1406)*. Vol. 32 of *Analecta vaticano-belgica: Documents relatifs aux anciens diocèses de Cambrai, Liège, Thérouanne et Tournai*. Brussels, 1987.

Majic, T. "Die apostolische Pönitentiarie im 14. Jahrhundert." *Römische Quartalschrift für christliche Altertumskunde und für Kirchengeschichte* 50 (1955): 129–177.

Major, K. "Original Papal Documents in the Bodleian Library." *Bodleian Library Record* 3 (1950–1951): 242–256.

Mann, H. K. *The Lives of the Popes in the Early Middle Ages*. London, 1902–1932.

Mansilla, D. "La documentación pontificia del archivo de la catedral de Burgos." *Hispania sacra* 1 (1948): 141–162, 427–438.

Mansilla, D. *La documentación pontificia hasta Innozencio III, 965–1216*. Rome, 1955.

Mansilla, D. "La reorganización eclesiástica española del siglo XVI." *Anthologica annua* 4 (1956): 97–238.

Mansilla, D. *La documentación española del archivo del Castel S. Angelo (395–1498)*. Rome, 1958.

Mansilla, D. *La documentación pontificia de Honorio III (1216–1227)*. Rome, 1965.

Mantese, G. *Pietro Tamburini e il giansenismo bresciano*. Brescia, 1942.

Marchal, G. P. "Supplikenregister als codicologisches Problem: Die Supplikenregister des Basler Konzils." *Basler Zeitschrift für Geschichte und Altertumskunde* 74 (1974): 201–235.

Marder, T. A. "The Porto di Ripetta in Rome." *Journal of the Society of Architectural Historians* 39 (1980): 28–56.

Marder, T. A. "Specchi's High Altar for the Pantheon and the Statues by Cametti and Moderati." *Burlington Magazine* 122 (1980): 30–40.

Marini, G., ed. "Memorie istoriche degli Archivi della Santa Sede." In *Memorie istoriche degli Archivi della S. Sede e della Bibl. Ottoboniana ora riunita alla Vaticana*, pp. 5–39. Rome, 1825.

Marini, M. "Memorie storiche dell'occupazione e restituzione degli Archivi della Santa Sede." In *Regestum Clementis Papae V*, edited by Benedictines of Monte Cassino, vol. 1, pp. ccxxviii–cccxxv. Rome, 1885.

Marques, J. M. *Indices del Archivo de la Nunciatura de Madrid*. Rome, 1976–.

Marquis, A. "Le collège des correcteurs et scripteurs d'archives: Contribution à l'étude des charges vénales de la Curie Romaine." In *Römische Kurie, kirchliche Finanzen, vatikanisches Archiv: Studien zu Ehren von Hermann Hoberg*, pp. 459–471. Rome, 1979.

Martin, A. L., ed. *Correspondance du nonce en France, Fabio*

Mirto Frangipani 1568–1572 et 1586–1587, Nonce extraordinaire en 1574, 1575–1576 et 1578. Vol. 15 of *Acta nuntiaturae gallicae.* Rome, 1984.

Martin, J. *Conciles et bullaire du diocèse de Lyon, des origines à la réunion du Lyonnais à la France en 1312.* Lyons, 1905.

Martin, M. *The Roman Curia as it Now Exists: An Account of its Departments, Sacred Congregations, Tribunals, Offices, Competence of Each, Mode of Procedure, How to Hold Communication with, the Latest Legislation.* New York, 1913.

Martina, G. "Nel centenario della morte di Massimiliano D'Asburgo: La corrispondenza tra Pio IX e Massimiliano." *Archivum Historiae Pontificiae* 5 (1967): 373–391.

Martínez, A. V. *Documentos pontificios de Galicia (1088–1341). I, Relación de bulas, breves, epistolas.* La Coruña, 1941.

Martini, A. *I sigilli d'oro dell'Archivio segreto vaticano.* Milan, 1984.

Masetti Zannini, G. L. *Abiti e novizie nel monastero di Santa Maria delle Vergini (1656–1662).* (This title was noted but not verified by project staff.)

Masetti Zannini, G. L. "Sisto V, I 'Vescovi e Regolari' e le Indie Occidentali." In *Sisto V.* Vol. 1, *Roma e Lazio.* (This title was noted but not verified by project staff.)

Masetti Zannini, G. L. "L'Archivio privato del cardinale Ignazio Boncompagni-Ludovisi." *Bolletino del Museo del Risorgimento* 7 (1962): 199–210.

Masetti Zannini, G. L. "Cesare Baronio a sua madre (Lettere inedite)." *Oratorium* 1 (1970): 29–42.

Masetti Zannini, G. L. "Veronica Franco a Roma una pellegrina 'tra mille'." *Strenna dei romanisti* (1982) (This title was noted but not verified by project staff.)

Masetti Zannini, G. L. "Lavori, fioretti e rappresentazioni nel monastero di San Gugliolmo (1624–1659)." *Strenna storica bolognese* 33 (1983): 162–173.

Masetti Zannini, G. L. "Il Cardinale Baronio e la musica nei monasteri femminili." *Atti del convegno internazionale di studi* (1984). (This title was noted but not verified by project staff.)

Masetti Zannini, G. L. "Donna Mariana de Leyva dal Monastero di Soncino a quello di Monza." *Studia borromaica* 4 (1990). (This title was noted but not verified by project staff.)

Masetti Zannini, G. L. "'Gusto et genio' di Leonora Campeggi Contrari (dai suoi cartegi 1536–1575)." *Strenna storica bolognese* (1990). (This title was noted but not verified by project staff.)

Masetti Zannini, G. L. "Canto profano e musica sacra femminile del settecento Romano." *Strenna dei romanisti* (1991). (This title was noted but not verified by project staff.)

Masetti Zannini, G. L. "Suavita di canto" e "Purita di cuore" aspetti della musica nei monasteri femminili Romani. Florence, 1993. (This title was noted but not verified by project staff.)

Mas Latrie, L. de. "Les éléments de la diplomatique pontificale." *Revue des questions historiques* 39 (1886): 415–541; 41 (1887): 382–435.

Mas Latrie, L. de. *Trésor de chronologie d'histoire et de géographie, pour l'etude et l'emploi des documents du moyen âge.* Paris, 1889.

Mayr-Adlwang, M. "Über Expensenrechnungen für päpstl. Provisionsbullen des 15. Jahrhunderts." *Mitteilungen des Instituts für österreichische Geschichtsforschung* 17 (1896): 71–108.

Mazzoleni, J. *Esempi di scritture cancelleresche, curiali e minuscole.* Naples, 1972.

McManamon, J. M. "The Ideal Renaissance Pope: Funeral Oratory from the Papal Court." *Archivum Historiae Pontificiae* 14 (1976): 9–70.

McManus, F. R. *The Congregation of Sacred Rites.* Washington, D.C., 1954.

McNulty, J., ed. *Thomas Sotheron v. Cockersand Abbey: A Suit as to the Advowson of Mitton Church, 1369–70 (Vatican Archives. Collectoriae 417A).* Manchester, 1939.

McReavy, L. L. "The Reorganization of the Roman Curia." *Clergy Review* 53 (1968): 306–313.

Meagher, P. K., T. C. O'Brien, and C. M. Aherne, eds. *Encyclopedic Dictionary of Religion.* Washington, D.C., 1979.

Meerbeeck, L. van. *Correspondance des nonces Gesualdo, Morra, Sanseverino, avec la Secrétairerie d'Etat pontificale, 1615–1621.* Vol. 4 of *Analecta vaticano-belgica.* Ser. 2, section A, *Nonciature de Flandre.* Brussels, 1937.

Meerbeeck, L. van. *Correspondance du Nonce Fabio de Lagonissa, archevêque de Conza, 1627–1634.* Vol. 11 of *Analecta vaticano-belgica.* Ser. 2, section A, *Nonciature de Flandre.* Brussels, 1966.

Meerbeeck, L. van. *Correspondance du nonce Decio Carafa, archeveque de Damas (1606–1607).* Vol. 13 of *Analecta vaticano-belgica.* Ser. 2, section A, *Nonciature de Flandre.* Brussels, 1979.

Meester, B. de. *Correspondance du nonce Giovanni-Francesco Guidi di Bagno (1621–1627).* Vols. 5–6 of *Analecta vaticano-belgica.* Ser. 2, section A, *Nonciature de Flandre.* Brussels, 1938.

Meinardus, O. "Formelsammlungen und Handbücher aus den Bureaus der päpstlichen Verwaltung des 15. Jahrhunderts in Hannover." *Neues Archiv der Gesellschaft für ältere Deutsche Geschichtskunde* 10 (1885): 35–79.

Meinert, H., J. Ramackers, and D. Lohrmann. *Papsturkunden in Frankreich.* Neue Folge. Berlin, 1932–.

Meister, A. *Die Geheimschrift im Dienste der päpstlichen Kurie von ihren Anfängen bis zum Ende des XVI. Jahrhunderts.* Paderborn, 1906.

Mejer, O. "Die heutige römische Curie: Ihre Behörden und ihr Geschäftsgang." *Zeitschrift für das Recht und die Politik der Kirche* 1 (1844): 71–108.

Melampo, A. "Attorno alle bolle papali da Pasquale I a Pio X." *Miscellanea di storia e cultura ecclesiastica* 3 (1905): 555–565.

Melampo, G., and V. Ranuzzi. *Saggio bibliografico dei lavori eseguiti nell'Archivio Vaticano.* Rome, 1909.

Menis, G. C., ed. *1000 processi dell'Inquisizione in Friuli (1551–1647).* 2d ed. Udine, 1985.

Menzer, A. "Die Jahresmerkmale in den Datierung der Papsturkunden bis zum Ausgang des 11. Jahrhunderts." *Römische Quartalschrift für christliche Altertumskunde und für Kirchengeschichte* 40 (1932): 27–103.

Mercati, A. "Per la storia letteraria di Reggio Emilia." *Atti e memorie della Deputazione di storia patria per le antiche provincie modenesi,* 5th ser. 12 (1919): 37–117.

Mercati, A. *Raccolta di concordati su materie ecclesiastiche tra la Santa Sede e le autorità civili.* Rome, 1919.

Mercati, A. *Monumenta Vaticana veterem diocesim Co-*

lumbensem (Quilon) et eiusdem episcopum Iordanum Catalani ord. praed. respicientia. Rome, 1923.

Mercati, A. *Schedario Garampi, Registri Vaticani, Registri Lateranensi, Rationes Camerae, Inventario del Fondo Concistoriale.* Vol. 1 of *Sussidi per la consultazione dell'Archivio Vaticano.* Rome, 1926.

Mercati, A. "Episodi piratici del secolo XVI da 'indulgentiae pro captivis'." *Archivio della Società romana di storia patria* 52 (1929): 453–470.

Mercati, A. "Favori di Paolo III musici (G. Archadelt, J. Barry, B. Crotti, F. da Milano)." *Note d'archivio per la storia musicale* 10 (1933): 109–115.

Mercati, A. "Schema della disposizione dei fondi nell'Archivio Vaticano." *Bulletin of the International Committee of Historical Sciences* 5 (1933): 909–912.

Mercati, A. "Cité du Vatican." In *Guide international des archives—Europe,* pp. 369–386. Paris, 1934.

Mercati, A. *La provenienza di alcuni oggetti delle collezioni vaticane.* Vatican City, 1936.

Mercati, A. "Dagli 'Instrumenta Miscellanea' dell'Archivio segreto vaticano." *Quellen und Forschungen aus italienischen Archiven und Bibliotheken* 27 (1936–1937): 135–177.

Mercati, A. *Il sommario del processo di Giordano Bruno: Con appendice di documenti sull'eresia e l'Inquisizione a Modena nel secolo XVI.* Vatican City, 1942.

Mercati, A. "Briciole della corrispondenza di Antonio Vallisneri il Seniore: Con appendice alle lettere di scienziati dall'Archivio segreto vaticano." *Commentationes Pontificia academia scientiarium* 7 (1943): 783–881.

Mercati, A. *Reggiani in relazione col Tiziano.* Rome, 1944.

Mercati, A. "La Biblioteca Apostolica e l'Archivio Segreto Vaticano." In *Vaticano,* edited by G. Fallani and M. Escobar, pp. 469–493. Florence, 1946.

Mercati, A. "Le pergamene di Melfi all'Archivio Segreto Vaticano." In *Miscellanea Giovanni Mercati,* vol. 5, pp. 263–323. Vatican City, 1946.

Mercati, A. "Il 'Bullarium generale' dell'Archivio Segreto Vaticano." In *Sussidi per la consultazione dell'Archivio Vaticano,* vol. 3, pp. v–xiv, 1–58. Vatican City, 1947.

Mercati, A. "Dall'Archivio dei SS. Gregorio e Siro di Bologna: Lettere ad Eugenio IV ivi smarrite." In *Sussidi per la consultazione dell'Archivio Vaticano,* vol. 3, pp. 77–91. Vatican City, 1947.

Mercati, A. "Supplementi al registro dell'antipapa Niccolò V." In *Sussidi per la consultazione dell'Archivio Vaticano,* vol. 3, pp. 59–76. Vatican City, 1947.

Mercati, A. "Documenti dall'Archivio Segreto Vaticano." In *Miscellanea Pio Paschini: Studi di storia ecclesiastica,* vol. 2, pp. 1–37. Rome, 1949.

Mercati, A. "Complementi al 'Bullarium Franciscanum'." *Archivum Franciscanum Historicum* 43 (1950): 161–180, 335–359.

Mercati, A. *Dall'Archivio Vaticano: I. Una corrispondenza fra curiali della prima metà del Quattrocento. II. Diari di concistori del Pontificato di Adriano VI.* Vatican City, 1951.

Mercati, A. *Miscellanea archivistica Angelo Mercati.* Vatican City, 1952.

Mercati, A. "Una notiziola sul giureconsulto Pillio." *Atti e memorie della Deputazione di storia patria per le antiche provincie modenesi,* 8th ser. 4 (1952): 34–35.

Mercati, A., E. Nasalli-Rocca, and P. Sella, eds. *Aemilia: Le decime dei secoli XIII–XIV.* Vol. 2 of *Rationes decimarum Italiae nei secoli XIII e XIV,* edited by P. Guidi and P. Sella. Vatican City, 1933.

Mercati, A., A. Pelzer, and A. M. Bozzone. *Dizionario ecclesiastico.* Turin, 1954–1958.

Mercati, G. *Miscellanea Giovanni Mercati.* Vatican City, 1946.

Mercati, G. *Note per la storia di alcune biblioteche romane nei secoli XVI–XIX.* Vatican City, 1952.

Merlini-Nolfi, M. *Rescripta authentica Sacrae Congregationis Indulgentiis SS.que Reliquiis praepositae ab a. 1668 ad a. 1882.* Regensburg, 1882.

Metzler, J. "Indici dell'Archivio storico della S. C. de Propaganda Fide." *Euntes Docete* 21 (1968): 109–130.

Metzler, J., ed. *Compendio di storia della Sacra Congregazione per l'evangelizzazione dei popoli o "De Propaganda Fide" 1622–1972.* Rome, 1973.

Metzler, J. "Das Vatikanarchiv eine quelle missionsgeschichtlicher Forschung." *Zeitschrift für Missionswissenschaft und Religionswissenschaft* 2–3 (1986): 266–270.

Metzler, J. "The Vatican Archives and their Missionary Holdings." *Mission Studies* 7.1 (1990): 108–117.

Metzler, J.; ed. *America pontificia primi saeculi evangelizationis 1493–1592: Documenta pontificia ex registris et minutis praesertim in Archivo Secreto Vaticano existentibus.* Vatican City, 1991.

Metzler, J. "The Legacy of Pius XI." *International Bulletin for Missionary Studies* 17.2 (1993): 62–65.

Meyer, A. O. *Die prager Nuntiatur des Giovanni Stefano Ferreri und die wiener Nuntiatur des Giacomo Serra (1603–1606).* Vol. 3 of *Nuntiaturberichte aus Deutschland nebst ergänzenden Actenstücken. Vierte Abteilung, siebzehntes Jahrhundert.* Berlin, 1913.

Meysztowicz, W. *Repertorium bibliographicum pro rebus polonicis Archivi secreti vaticani.* Vatican City, 1943.

Meysztowicz, W. *De Archivo Nuntiaturae Varsaviensis quod nunc in Archivo secreto vaticano Servatur.* Vatican City, 1944.

Miccio, S. "Vita di Don Pietro di Toledo, Marchese di Villafranca." *Archivio storico italiano* 9 (1846): 1–144.

Michael-Schweder, I. *Die Schrift auf den päpstlichen Siegeln des Mittelalters.* Graz, 1926.

Michaud, M. "Chambre apostolique." In *Dictionnaire de droit canonique,* edited by R. Naz, vol. 3, pp. 388–431. Paris, 1942.

Michel, E. "La raccolta storica Spada dell'Archivio Vaticano." *Rassegna storica del Risorgimento* 12 (1925): 177–181.

Michel, E. "La raccolta storica Mencacci dell'Archivio Vaticano." *Rassegna storica del Risorgimento* 22.2 (1935): 389–395.

Michel, E. "La raccolta storica Brancadori dell'Archivio Vaticano." *Rassegna storica del Risorgimento* 23 (1936): 1428–1430.

Migne, J. P. *Patrologiae cursus completus . . . Series latina in qua prodeunt patres, doctores scriptoresque Ecclesiae Latinae a Tertulliano ad Innocentium III.* Paris, 1844–1864.

Milian Boix, M. *El fondo "Instrumenta Miscellanea" del Archivo Vaticano: Documentos referentes a España (853–1782).* Rome, 1969.

Millares Carlo, A. *Documentos pontificios en papiro de archivos catalanes*. Madrid, 1918.

Miller, M. "Das römische Tagebuch des Ulmer Stadtammans Konrad Locher aus der Zeit des Papstes Innocenz VIII." *Historisches Jahrbuch* 60 (1940): 270–300.

Millett, B. "The Archives of the Congregation de Propaganda Fide." *Proceedings of the Irish Catholic Historical Committee* (1956): 20–27.

Millett, B. "Calendar of Volume 1 (1625–1668) of the Scritture Riferite nei Congressi, Irlanda, in Propaganda Archives." *Collectanea hibernica*, nos. 6–7 (1963–1964): 18–211.

Millett, B. "Catalogue of Volume 294 of the Scritture Originali Riferite nelle Congregazione Generali in Propaganda Archives." *Collectanea hibernica*, no. 8 (1965): 7–37.

Millett, B. "Catalogue of Irish Materials in Fourteen Volumes of the Scritture Originali Riferite nelle Congregazioni Generali in Propaganda Archives." *Collectanea hibernica*, no. 10 (1967): 7–59.

Millett, B. "Catalogue of Irish Material in Vols. 129–131 of the Scritture Originali Riferite nelle Congregazioni Generali in Propaganda Archives." *Collectanea hibernica*, no. 11 (1968): 7–18.

Millett, B. "Catalogue of Irish Material in Vols. 132–139 of the Scritture Originali Riferite nelle Congregazioni Generali in Propaganda Archives." *Collectanea hibernica*, no. 12 (1969): 7–44.

Millett, B. "Catalogue of Irish Material in Vols. 140–143 of the Scritture Originali Riferite nelle Congregazioni Generali in Propaganda Archives." *Collectanea hibernica*, no. 13 (1970): 21–60.

Millett, B. "Calendar of Volume 2 (1669–71) of the Scritture Riferite nei Congressi, Irlanda, in Propaganda Archives." *Collectanea hibernica*, no. 16 (1973): 7–47; no. 17 (1974–1975): 17–68.

Millett, B. "Calendar of Volume 3 (1672–5) of the Scritture Riferite nei Congressi, Irlanda, in Propaganda Archives." *Collectanea hibernica*, nos. 18–19 (1976–1977): 40–71; nos. 21–22 (1979–1980): 7–81.

Millett, B. "Calendar of Irish Material in Vols. 12 and 13 (ff. 1–200) of Fondo di Vienna in Propaganda Archives." *Collectanea hibernica*, no. 24 (1982): 45–80.

Millett, B. "Calendar of Volume 13 of the Fondo di Vienna in Propaganda Archives: Part 2, ff. 201–401." *Collectanea hibernica*, no. 25 (1983): 30–62.

Millett, B. "Catalogue of Irish Material in Vols. 370 and 371 of the Scritture Riferite Originali nelle Congregazioni Generali in Propaganda Archives." *Collectanea hibernica*, nos. 27–28 (1985–1986): 44–85.

Minisci, J. T. "Il fondo 'Basiliani' dell'Archivio segreto vaticano." *Bollettino della Badia Greca di Grottaferrata*, n.s. 6 (1952): 65–85.

Miquel Rosell, F. J. *Regesta de letras pontificias del Archivo de la Corona de Aragón, Sección Cancellaria Real (Pergamenos)*. Madrid, 1948.

Mirot, L., and H. Jassemin, ed. *Lettres secrètes et curiales du pape Grégoire XI [1370–1378] relatives à la France: Extraites des registres du Vatican*. Vol. 7 of *Bibliothèque des Écoles françaises d'Athènes et de Rome*. 3d ser., *Registres et lettres des papes du XIVe siècle*. Paris, 1935–1957.

Mistruzzi di Frisinga, C. *La nobilità dello Stato pontificio*. Rome, 1963.

Móe, E. van. "Suppliques originales adressées a Jean XII, Clément VI et Innocent VI." *Bibliothèque de l'École des Chartes* 92 (1931): 253–276.

Mohler, L. *Die Kardinäle Jakob und Peter Colonna: Ein Beitrag zur Geschichte des Zeitalters Bonifaz' VIII*. Paderborn, 1914.

Mohler, L., ed. *Kardinal Bessarion als Theologe, Humanist und Staatsmann: Funde und Forschungen*. Paderborn, 1923.

Mohler, L., ed. *Die Einnahmen der apostolischen Kammer unter Klemens VI*. Vol. 5 of *Vatikanische Quellen zur Geschichte des päpstlichen Hof- und Finanzverwaltung 1316–1378*. Paderborn, 1931.

Mollat, G. *Lettres communes Jean XXII (1316–1334): Analysées d'après les registres dits d'Avignon et du Vatican*. Vol. 1 bis of *Bibliothèque des Écoles françaises d'Athènes et de Rome*. 3d ser., *Registres et lettres des papes du XIVe siècle*. Paris, 1904–1947.

Mollat, G. *La collation des bénéfices ecclésiastiques sous les papes d'Avignon (1305–1378)*. Paris, 1921.

Mollat, G. "A propos du droit de dépouille." *Revue d'histoire ecclésiastique* 29 (1933): 316–343.

Mollat, G. "Contribution à l'histoire de l'administration judiciaire de l'Église romaine au XIVe siècle." *Revue d'histoire ecclésiastique* 32 (1936): 877–928.

Mollat, G. "Bénéfices ecclésiastiques en Occident." In *Dictionnaire de droit canonique*, edited by R. Naz, vol. 2, pp. 406–449. Paris, 1937.

Mollat, G. "Contribution à l'histoire de la Chambre apostolique au XIVe siècle." *Revue d'histoire ecclésiastique* 45 (1950): 82–94.

Mollat, G. "Contribution à l'histoire du Sacré Collège de Clément V à Eugène IV." *Revue d'histoire ecclésiastique* 46 (1951): 22–112, 566–594.

Mollat, G. "Jean de Cardaillac, un prélat réformateur du clergé au XIVe siecle." *Revue d'histoire ecclésiastique* 48 (1953): 74–121.

Mollat, G. "Correspondance de Clément VI par cédules." *Bullettino dell'Archivio paleografico italiano*, n.s. 2–3, pt. 2 (1956–1957): 175–178.

Mollat, G. "La juridiction d'un prieuré au XIVe siècle." *Revue d'histoire ecclésiastique* 52 (1957): 491–498.

Mollat, G. "Le Saint-Siège et la France sous le pontificat de Clément VI (1342–1352)." *Revue d'histoire ecclésiastique* 55 (1960): 5–24.

Mollat, G. "Registres pontificaux." In *Dictionnaire de droit canonique*, edited by R. Naz, vol. 7, pp. 536–538. Paris, 1960–1961.

Mollat, G. *Les papes d'Avignon, 1305–1378*. 10th ed. Paris, 1964.

Mollat, G. *Lettres secrètes et curiales du pape Grégoire XI (1370–1378) intéressant les pays autres que la France: Publiées ou analysées d'apres les registres du Vatican*. Forms part of *Bibliothèque des Écoles françaises d'Athènes et de Rome*. 3d ser., *Registres et lettres des papes du XIVe siècle*. Paris, 1962–1965.

Moltesen, L. J., ed. *Acta pontificum Danica: Pavelige aktstykker vedrorende Danmark, 1316–1536*. Copenhagen, 1904–1943.

Mommsen, T. "Die Papstbriefe bei Beda." *Neues Archiv der Gesellschaft für ältere Deutsche Geschichtskunde* 17 (1892): 387–396.

Monachino, V., et al., eds. *Guida degli archivi diocesani d'Italia*. Rome, 1990–.

Monaco, M. "Le finanze pontificie al tempo di Clemente VII." *Studi romani* 6 (1958): 278–296.

Monaco, M. *La situazione della reverenda Camera Apostolica nell'anno 1525: Ricerche d'archivio: Un contributo alla storia delle finanze pontificie*. Rome, 1960.

Monson, C. *Disembodied Voices: Music and Culture in an Early Modern Italian Convent*. Berkeley, 1995.

Mooney, C. "Letters of Pope Innocent IV Relating to Ireland." *Collectanea hibernica*, no. 2 (1959): 1–12.

Moran, C. "Les archives du Saint-Siège, importantes sources de l'histoire politico-religieuse du Canada." *Culture* (Ottawa) 7 (1946): 151–176.

Morghen, R. "Ricerche sulla formazione del registro di Gregorio VII." *Bullettino dell'Istituto storico italiano per il medio evo e Archivio muratoriano* 73 (1961): 1–40.

Moroni, G. "Archivi della Santa Sede." In *Dizionario di erudizione storico-ecclesiastica*, vol. 2, pp. 277–288. Venice, 1840.

Moroni, G. "Clement XI, Papa CCLIII." In *Dizionario di erudizione storico-ecclesiastica*, vol. 14, pp. 59–70. Venice, 1842.

Moroni, G. *Dizionario di erudizione storico-ecclesiastica*. Venice, 1840–1861.

Mosconi, N. *La Nunziatura di Spagna di Cesare Speciano, 1586–1588: Su documenti inediti dell'Archivio segreto vaticano*. 2d ed. Brescia, 1961.

Mosconi, N. *La Nunziatura di Praga di Cesare Speciano, 1592–1598: Nelle carte inedite vaticane e ambrosiane*. Brescia, 1966–.

Motsch, J., ed. *Balduin von Luxemburg, Erzbischof von Trier, Kurfurst des Reiches 1285–1354: Festschrift aus Anlass des 700. Geburtsjahres*. Mainz, 1985.

Motzki, A. *Urkunden zur Caminer Bistumsgeschichte, auf Grund der Avignonesischen Supplikenregister*. Stettin, 1913.

Motzki, A. *Avignonesische Quellen zur Geschichte des Ordenlandes (1342–1366)*. Braunsberg, 1914.

Müller, G. *Legation Lorenzo Campeggios, 1530–1531, und Nuntiatur Girolamo Aleandros, 1531*. Ergänzungsband 1 of *Nuntiaturberichte aus Deutschland nebst ergänzenden Actenstücken. Erste Abteilung, 1533–1559*. Tübingen, 1963.

Müller, G. *Legation Lorenzo Campeggios, 1532, und Nuntiatur Girolamo Aleandros, 1532*. Ergänzungsband 2 of *Nuntiaturberichte aus Deutschland nebst ergänzenden Actenstücken. Erste Abteilung, 1533–1559*. Tübingen, 1969.

Müller, G. *Die römische Kurie und die Reformation, 1523–1534: Kirche und Politik während des Pontifikats Clemens' VII*. Gütersloh, 1969.

Müller, G. "Die Bedeutung der Nuntiaturberichte für die Kirchengeschichte." *Quellen und Forschungen aus italienischen Archiven und Bibliotheken* 53 (1973): 168–179.

Murray, A. *Pope Gregory VII and His Letters*. New York, 1966.

Muzzioli, G. *Rotulo originale di suppliche per "fiat" di Benedetto XIII antipapa*. Rome, 1947. (This title was noted but not verified by project staff.)

Nádas, J. "Further Notes on Magister Antonius Dictus Zacharias de Teramo." *Studi musicali* 15 (1986): 167–182.

Nanni, L., ed. *Leo X–Pius IV (1513–1565)*. Vol. 1 of *Epistolae ad principes*. Vatican City, 1992.

Nanni, L., ed. *S. Pius V–Gregorius XIII: 1566–1585*. Vol. 2 of *Epistolae ad principes*. Vatican City, 1994.

Natalini, T., S. Pagano, and A. Martini, eds. *Archivio segreto vaticano*. Florence, 1991.

Naz, R., ed. *Dictionnaire de droit canonique, contenant tous les termes du droit canonique, avec un sommaire de l'histoire et des institutons et de l'état actuel de la discipline*. 7 vols. Paris, 1935–1965.

Naz, R. "Moto proprio." In *Dictionnaire de droit canonique*, vol. 6, p. 957. Paris, 1954–1957.

Naz, R. "Secrétaire d'État." In *Dictionnaire de droit canonique*, vol. 7, pp. 899–900. Paris, 1958–1965.

Naz, R. "Secrétairerie d'État." In *Dictionnaire de droit canonique*, vol. 7, pp. 901–904. Paris, 1958–1965.

Nebbiai Dalla Guarda, D. *I documenti per la storia delle biblioteche medievali (Secoli IX–XV)*. Rome, 1992.

Nélis, H. "L'application en Belgique de la règle de chancellerie apostolique: 'De idiomate beneficiatorum' aux XIVe et XVe siècles." *Bulletin de l'Institut historique Belge de Rome* 2 (1922): 129–141.

Nélis, H. *Documents relatifs au Grand Schisme*. Vol. 3, *Suppliques et lettres de Clement VII (1379–1394)*. Vol. 13 of *Analecta vaticano-belgica: Documents relatifs aux anciens diocèses de Cambrai, Liège, Thérouanne et Tournai*. Brussels, 1934.

Neveu, B., ed. *Correspondance du nonce en France, Angelo Ranuzzi 1683–1689*. Vol. 10–11 of *Acta nuntiaturae gallicae*. Rome, 1973.

Neveu, B. "Episcopus et Princeps Urbis: Innocent XI réformateur de Rome d'après des documents inédits (1676–1689)." In *Römische Kurie, kirchliche Finanzen, vatikanisches Archiv: Studien zu Ehren von Hermann Hoberg*, pp. 597–633. Rome, 1979.

New Catholic Encyclopedia. New York, 1967–1979.

Nicolio, G. *Un inventaire des Archives de la Propagande, milieu du XVIIe Siècle (fra Girolamo Nicolio, augustin, 14 avril 1662, son Journal historique des missions d'Afrique, d'Amerique et d'Asie)*. Edited by F. Combaluzier. Schöneck-Beckenried, 1947.

Nielsen, H. *Ein päpstliches Formelbuch aus der Zeit des grossen abendländischen Schismas*. Copenhagen, 1979.

Norberg, D. L. *In registrum Gregorii Magni studia critica*. Uppsala, 1937–1939.

Norberg, D. L. *Critical and Exegetical Notes on the Letters of St. Gregory the Great*. Stockholm, 1982.

Nostitz-Rieneck, R. von. "Zum päpstlichen Brief- und Urkundenwesen der ältesten Zeit." In *Festgaben zu Ehren Max Budinger's von seinen Freunden und Schulern*, pp. 151–168. Innsbruck, 1898.

Novák, J. B. *Acta Innocentii VI pontificis romani, 1352–1362*. Prague, 1907.

Nubola, C., and A. Turchini, eds. *Visite pastorali ed elaborazione dei dati: Esperienze e metodi*. Bologna, 1993.

Nuntiaturberichte aus Deutschland nebst ergänzenden Actenstücken. Erste Abteilung, 1533–1559. Gotha, 1892–.

Nuntiaturberichte aus Deutschland nebst ergänzenden Ac-

tenstücken. Zweite Abteilung, 1560–1572. Vienna, 1897–1967.

Nuntiaturberichte aus Deutschland nebst ergänzenden Actenstücken. Dritte Abteilung, 1572–1585. Turin, 1972–.

Nuntiaturberichte aus Deutschland nebst ergänzenden Actenstücken. Vierte Abteilung, siebzehntes Jahrhundert. Berlin, 1895–1913.

Nuntiaturberichte aus Deutschland nebst ergänzenden Actenstücken, 1585 (1584)–1592. Paderborn, 1895–1919.

Nüske, G. F. "Untersuchungen über das Personal der päpstlichen Kanzlei 1254–1304." *Archiv für Diplomatik, Schriftengeschichte, Siegel- und Wappenkunde* 20 (1974): 39–240; 21 (1975): 249–431.

Nyberg, T. "Der Geschäftsgang bei der Ausfertigung der Grünungsdokumente des Birgittenkloster Altomünster durch die römischen Kurie." *Archivum Historiae Pontificiae* 9 (1971): 209–248.

Oberhuber, K. "Jacopo Bertoia im Oratorium von S. Lucia del Gonfalone in Rom." *Römische historische Mitteilungen* 3 (1958–1960): 239–254.

Odoardi, G. "La hierarchia catholica." *Miscellanea Franciscana* 53 (1953): 90–115.

Olarra Garmendia, J., and M. L. Larramendi de Olarra. *Indices de la correspondencia entre la Nunciatura en España y la Santa Sede durante el reinado de Felipe II.* Madrid, 1948–1949.

Olarra Garmendia, J., and M. L. Larramendi de Olarra. *Correspondencia entre la Nunciatura en España y la Santa Sede: Reinado de Felipe III (1598–1621).* Rome, 1960–1967.

Oliger, L., ed. "Breve compendio de los ritos idolatricos de Nueva Espana, auctore Bernardino de Sahagun O.F.M." *Antonianium* 17 (1942): 3–38, 133–174.

Olivier-Martin, F. *Les registres de Martin IV (1281–1285): Recueil des bulles de ce pape publiées ou analysées d'après les manuscrits originaux des Archives du Vatican.* Vol. 16 of *Bibliothèque des Écoles françaises d'Athènes et de Rome.* 2d ser., *Registres des papes du XIIIe siècle.* Paris, 1901–1935.

Olmos y Canalda, E. *Reivindicación de Alejandro VI.* 3d ed. Valencia, 1953.

O'Malley, J. W. *The First Jesuits.* Cambridge, Mass., 1993.

Opitz, G. "Über Registrierung von Sekretbriefen: Studien zu den Sekretregistern Clemens VI." *Quellen und Forschungen aus italienischen Archiven und Bibliotheken* 29 (1938–1939): 89–134.

Opitz, G. "Die Sekretäre Franciscus de Sancto Maximo und Johannes de Sancto Martino: Bemerkungen zur Früzeit des päpstlichen Sekretariats." *Quellen und Forschungen aus italienischen Archiven und Bibliotheken* 30 (1940): 189–206.

Opitz, G. "Die Sekretärexpedition unter Urban V. und Gregor XI." *Quellen und Forschungen aus italienischen Archiven und Bibliotheken* 33 (1944): 158–198.

Ortolan, T. M. "Cour romaine." In *Dictionnaire de théologie catholique*, vol. 3, pt. 2, pp. 1931–1983. Paris, 1923.

O'Sullivan, M. D. "Italian Merchant Bankers and the Collection of Papal Revenue in Ireland in the 13th Century." *Galway Archeological Association Journal* 22 (1946–1947): 132–163. (This title was noted but not verified by project staff.)

Ottenthal, E. von. "Die Bullenregister Martin V. und Eugen IV." *Mitteilungen des Instituts für österreichische Geschichtsforschung*, Erganzungsband 1 (1885): 401–589.

Ottenthal, E. von. "Römische Berichte. 4, Bemerkungen über päpstliche Cameralregister des 15. Jahrhunderts." *Mitteilungen des Instituts für österreichische Geschichtsforschung* 6 (1885): 615–626.

Ottenthal, E. von. *Regulae cancellariae apostolicae: Die päpstlichen Kanzleiregeln von Johannes XXII. bis Nikolaus V.* Innsbruck, 1888.

Pace, V. "Cultura dell'Europa medievale nella Roma di Innocenzo III: Le illustrazioni marginali del Registro Vaticano 4." *Römisches Jahrbuch für Kunstgeschichte* 22 (1985): 45–61.

Paez, P. *Historia Aethiopiae.* Vols. 2–3 of *Rerum aethiopicarum scriptores occidentales inediti a saeculo XVI ad XIX*, edited by C. Beccari. Rome, 1905–1906.

Pagano, S. "Le visite apostoliche a Roma nei secoli XVI–XIX: Repertorio delle fonti." *Ricerche per la storia religiosa di Roma* 4 (1980): 317–464.

Pagano, S., ed. *I documenti del processo di Galileo Galilei.* Vatican City, 1984.

Pagano, S. *L'Archivio dell'Arciconfraternita del Gonfalone: Cenni storici e inventario.* Vatican City, 1990.

Pagano, S. "Il fondo di Mons. Umberto Benigni dell'Archivio Segreto Vaticano: Inventario." *Ricerche per la storia religiosa di Roma* 8 (1990): 347–402.

Pagano, S. *L'Archivio del Convento dei SS. Domenico e Sisto di Roma: Cenni storici e inventario.* Vatican City, 1994.

Pagano, S., and G. Barone. "Archconfraternità del Gonfalone." *Ricerche per la storia religiosa di Roma* 6 (1985): 215–219.

Pagano, S., and C. Ranieri. *Nuovi documenti su Vittoria Colonna e Reginald Pole.* Vatican City, 1989.

Palazzini, G. "I poteri straordinari del segretario della S. Congregazione del Concilio dal 1798 al 1801." In *La sacra Congregazione del Concilio: Quarto centenario della fondazione, 1564–1964, studi e ricerche* pp. 383–392. Vatican City, 1964.

Palazzini, P. "L'atto di consegna dell'Archivio della S. Congregazione del Concilio nella 1626 tra i due segretari: Fagnani e Paolucci." In *Miscellanea Antonio Piolanti*, vol. 2, pp. 239–257. Rome, 1963.

Pallottini, S. *Collectio Omnium Conclusionum ed Resolutionum quae in Causis Propositis apud Sacram Congregationem Cardinalium S. Concilii Tridentini Interpretum Prodierunt, ab eius Institutione Anno MDLXIV ad Annum MDCCCLX.* Rome, 1867–1893.

Palmieri, G. "Prolegomena." In *Regestum Clementis Papae V*, edited by Benedictines of Monte Cassino, vol. 1, pp. xiii–xcii. Rome, 1885.

Palmieri, G. *Introiti ed esiti di Papa Niccolò III 1279–1280: Antichissimo documento di lingua italiano tratto dall'Archivio Vaticano corredato di due pagine in eliotipia degl'indici alfabetici geografico e onomastico e di copiose note.* Rome, 1889.

Palmieri, G., ed. *Viaggio in Germania, Baviera, Svizzera, Olanda, e Francia compiuto negli anni 1761–1763: Diario del Cardinal Giuseppe Garampi.* Rome, 1889.

Palmieri, G. *De archivo Sacrae Congregationis Caeremonialis.* Rome, 1893.

Palumbo, P. F. *Lo scisma del MCXXX: I precedenti, la vicenda roman e le ripercussioni europee della lotta tra Anacleto II e*

Innocenzo II: Col regesto degli atti di Anacleto II. Rome, 1942.

Palumbo, P. F. "La cancelleria di Anacleto II." *Studi salentini* 17 (1964): 5–52.

Pantoni, A. "Santa Caterina di Perugia." *Benedictina* 5 (1951): 233–262; 6 (1952): 238–262.

Paoli, C. *Grundriss zu Vorlesungen ueber lateinische Palaeographie und Urkundenlehre.* Innsbruck, 1889–1900.

Papa, G. "Il cardinale Antonio Carafa, prefetto della S. Congregazione del Concilio." In *La sacra Congregazione del Concilio: Quarto centenario della fondazione, 1564–1964, studi e ricerche*, 309–338. Vatican City, 1964.

Paquay, J. *Documents pontificaux concernant le diocèse de Liège.* Liège, 1936. (This title was noted but not verified by project staff.)

Paravicini Bagliani, A. "Il 'Registrum causarum' di Ottaviano Ubaldini e l'amministrazione della giustizia alla Curia Romana nel secolo XIII." In *Römische Kurie, kirchliche Finanzen, vatikanisches Archiv: Studien zu Ehren von Hermann Hoberg*, pp. 635–657. Rome, 1979.

Paravicini Bagliani, A., and A. Vauchez, eds. *Poteri carismatici e informali: chiesa e societa medioevali.* Palermo, 1992.

Parisella, A. "'Iber Litterarum' Sacrae Congregationis Concilii." In *La sacra Congregazione del Concilio: Quarto centenario della fondazione, 1564–1964, studi e ricerche*, pp. 447–476. Vatican City, 1964.

Partner, P. "Camera Papae: Problems of Papal Finance in the late Middle Ages." *Journal of Ecclesiastical History* 4 (1953): 55–68.

Partner, P. *The Papal State under Martin V: The Administration and Government of the Temporal Power in the early 15th Century.* London, 1958.

Partner, P. "The 'Budget' of the Roman Church in the Renaissance Period." In *Italian Renaissance Studies: A Tribute to the Late Cecilia M. Ady*, edited by E. F. Jacob, pp. 256–278. London, 1960.

Partner, P. *Renaissance Rome, 1500–1559: A Portrait of a Society.* Berkeley, 1976.

Partner, P. "Papal Financial Policy in the Renaissance and Counter-Reformation." *Past and Present*, no. 88 (1980): 17–62.

Partner, P. *The Pope's Men: The Papal Civil Service in the Renaissance.* Oxford, 1990.

Paschini, P. *Venezia e l'Inquisizione romana da Giulio III a Pio IV.* Padua, 1959.

Pastor, L. von. *The History of the Popes from the Close of the Middle Ages.* Translated and edited by F. I. Antrobus et al. London, 1891–1953.

Pasture, A. "Inventaire du fonds Borghèse au point de vue de l'histoire des Pays-Bas." *Bulletin de la Commission royale d'histoire de Belgique* 79 (1910): 1–217.

Pasture, A. "Inventaire de la Bibliothèque Barberini, à la Bibliothèque Vaticane, au point de vue de l'histoire des Pays-Bas." *Bulletin de l'Institut historique Belge de Rome* 3 (1924): 43–157.

Pásztor, E. "Il processo di Andrea da Gagliano (1337–1338)." *Archivum Franciscanum Historicum* 48 (1955): 252–297.

Pásztor, E. "Una raccolta di sermoni di Giovanni XXII." *Bullettino dell'Archivio paleografico italiano*, n.s. 2–3, pt. 2 (1956–1957): 265–289.

Pásztor, E. "Au sujet d'une source des "Vitae Paparum Avenionensium" de Baluze provenant des Archives Vaticanes." *Revue d'histoire ecclésiastique* 54 (1959): 507–512.

Pásztor, E. "Contributo alla storia dei registri pontifici del secolo XIII." *Bullettino dell'Archivio paleografico italiano*, 3d ser. 1 (1962): 37–83.

Pásztor, E. "Studi e problemi relativi ai registri di Innocenzo III." *Annali della Scuola speciale per archivisti e bibliotecari dell'Università di Roma* 2 (1962): 289–304.

Pásztor, E. "Ricostruzione parziale di un registro pontificio deperdito del secolo XIII." In *Mélanges Eugène Tisserant*, vol. 5, pp. 199–207. Vatican City, 1964.

Pásztor, E. "Per la storia dei registri pontifici nel duecento." *Archivum Historiae Pontificiae* 6 (1968): 71–112.

Pásztor, E. "Studi sui registri di bolle papali." *Annali della Scuola speciale per archivisti e bibliotecari dell'Università di Roma* 9 (1969): 187–196.

Pásztor, E. "Il Registro Vaticano 42." *Annali della Scuola speciale per archivisti e bibliotecari dell'Università di Roma* 10 (1970): 25–103.

Pásztor, E. "I registri camerali di lettere pontificie del secolo XIII." *Archivum Historiae Pontificiae* 11 (1973): 7–83.

Pásztor, E. "La Curia Romana." In *Le istituzioni ecclesiastiche della "societas christiana" dei secoli XI–XII: Papato, cardinalato ed episcopato*, pp. 490–504. Milan, 1974.

Pásztor, E. "Per la storia dell'amministrazione dello Stato pontificio sotto Martino IV." In *Miscellanea in onore di Monsignor Martino Giusti*, vol. 2, pp. 181–194. Vatican City, 1978.

Pásztor, E. "La Curia Romana all'inizio dello scisma d'occidente." In *Genèse et débuts du Grand Schisme d'Occident*, pp. 31–43. Paris, 1980.

Pásztor, E. "Funzione politico-culturale di una struttura della chiesa: Il cardinalato." In *Aspetti culturali della società italiana nel periodo del papato avignonese*, pp. 199–226. Todi, 1981.

Pásztor, E. "Lettere di Urbano IV 'super negotio Regni Siciliae'." In *Aus Kirche und Reich: Studien zu Theologie, Politik und Recht im Mittelalter: Festschrift für Friedrich Kempf zu seinem fünfundziebzigsten Geburtstag und fünfzigjahren Doktorjubiläum*, edited by H. Mordek, pp. 383–395. Sigmaringen, 1983.

Pásztor, L. "Per la storia della Segreteria di Stato nell'Ottocento: La riforma del 1816." In *Mélanges Eugène Tisserant*, vol. 5, pp. 209–272. Vatican City, 1964.

Pásztor, L. "Archivio Segreto Vaticano." *Archivum* 15 (1965): 305–310.

Pásztor, L. "Contributo di un fondo miscellaneo all'archivistica e alla storia: L'Arm. LII dell'Archivio Segreto Vaticano." *Annali della Scuola speciale per archivisti e bibliotecari dell'Università di Roma* 6 (1966): 1–31.

Pásztor, L. "La Segretaria di Stato di Pio IX durante il triennio 1848–1850." *Annali della Fondazione italiana per la storia amministrativa* 3 (1966): 308–365.

Pásztor, L. "Il Sostituto del Concistoro e il suo archivio." *Archivum Historiae Pontificiae* 5 (1967): 355–372.

Pásztor, L. "La Congregazione degli affari ecclesiastici straordinari tra il 1814 e il 1850." *Archivum Historiae Pontificiae* 6 (1968): 191–318.

Pásztor, L. "Per la storia dell'Archivio Segreto Vaticano nei secoli XVII–XVIII." *Archivio della Società romana di storia patria* 91 (1968): 157–249.

Pásztor, L. "L'histoire de la curie romaine, problème d'histoire de l'Église." *Revue d'histoire ecclésiastique* 64 (1969): 353–366.

Pásztor, L. "L'Archivio della Segretaria di Stato tra il 1833 e il 1847." *Annali della Scuola speciale per archivisti e bibliotecari dell'Università di Roma* 10 (1970): 104–148.

Pásztor, L. *Guida delle fonti per la storia dell'America Latina negli archivi della Santa Sede e negli archivi ecclesiastici d'Italia.* Vatican City, 1970.

Pásztor, L. *La Curia Romana: Problemi e ricerche per la sua storia nell'età moderna e contemporanea.* 2d enlarged ed. Rome, 1971.

Pásztor, L. "Le cedole concistoriali." *Archivum Historiae Pontificiae* 11 (1973): 209–268.

Pásztor, L. "La classificazione delle carte della Segreteria di Stato tra il 1833 e il 1847." In *Miscellanea in memoria di Giorgio Cencetti,* pp. 639–663. Turin, 1973.

Pásztor, L. "La Segreteria di Stato di Gregorio XVI, 1833–1846." *Archivum Historiae Pontificiae* 15 (1977): 295–332.

Pásztor, L. "Per la storia degli Archivi della Curia Romana nell'epoca moderna: Gli archivi delle Segreterie dei Brevi ai Principi e delle Lettere Latine." In *Römische Kurie, kirchliche Finanzen, vatikanisches Archiv: Studien zu Ehren von Hermann Hoberg,* pp. 659–686. Rome, 1979.

Pásztor, L. "Per la storia dell'Archivio Segreto Vaticano nei secoli XIX–XX: La carica di Archivista della Santa Sede, 1870–1920: La prefettura di Francesco Rosi Bernardini, 1877–1879." *Archivum Historiae Pontificiae* 17 (1979): 367–423.

Pásztor, L. "Governo di Bologna nel secolo XVIII nei fondi dell'Archivio segreto vaticano." In *Famiglie senatorie e istituzioni cittadine a Bologna nel settecento: Atti del I Colloquio, Bologna, 2–3 febbraio 1980,* pp. 173–177. Bologna, 1980.

Pásztor, L. "L'Archivio della Segreteria di Stato di Pio IX durante il triennio 1848–1850." *Annali della Scuola speciale per archivisti e bibliotecari dell'Università di Roma* 21–22 (1981–1982): 54–148.

Pásztor, L. "Il card. Raffaele Mazio e il suo archivio." In *Studi in onore di Leopoldo Sandri,* pp. 707–734. Rome, 1983.

Pásztor, L. *Guida delle fonti per la storia dell'Africa a Sud del Sahara negli Archivi della Santa Sede e negli Archivi ecclesiastici d'Italia.* Zug, 1983.

Paulhart, H. "Papsturkunden in Oberösterreich: Originale spätmittelalterlicher Papsturkunden in Oberösterreichischen Archiven aus der Zeit 1198–1417." *Mitteilungen des oberösterreichischen Landesarchivs* 8 (1964): 160–172.

Paulus, N. *Practica Cancellariae Apostolicae cum stylo et formis in Romana Curia usitatis.* Lyon, 1549.

Paye-Bourgeois, J., ed. *Documents relatifs au Grand Schisme.* Vol. 4, *Lettres de Benoît XIII (1394–1422),* Part 1 (1394–1395). Vol. 31 of *Analecta vaticano-belgica: Documents relatifs aux anciens diocèses de Cambrai, Liège, Thérouanne et Tournai.* Brussels, 1983.

Peball, K. "Zu den kanonistischen Randziechnen im Register Papst Innozenz III." *Römische historische Mitteilungen* 1 (1956–1957): 77–105.

Pecchiai, P. "Le carte del fondo 'Corsica' nell'Archivio vaticano." *Archivio storico di Corsica* 9.4 (1933): 3–7.

Peitz, W. M. *Das Register Gregors I: Beitrage zur Kenntnis des päpstlichen Kanzlei- und Registerwesens bis auf Gregor VII.* Freiburg, 1917.

Peitz, W. M. *Liber Diurnus: Beiträge zur Kenntnis der ältesten päpstlichen Kanzlei vor Gregor dem Grossen.* Vienna, 1918.

Peitz, W. M. *Regestum dni. Innocentii tertii pp. super negotio Romani Imperii (Reg. Vat. 6).* Rome, 1927.

Peitz, W. M. *Liber Diurnus: Methodisches zur Diurnusforschung.* Rome, 1940.

Pellicia, G. *La preparazione ed ammissione dei chierici ai santi ordini nella Roma del sec. XVI.* Rome, 1946.

Perard-Castel, F. *Traite de l'usage et pratique de la cour de Rome, pour l'expedition des signatures et provisions des benefices de France.* New ed. Paris, 1717.

Perels, E. "Die Briefe Papst Nikolaus' I." *Neues Archiv der Gesellschaft für ältere Deutsche Geschichtskunde* 37 (1912): 538–586; 39 (1914): 43–153.

Perels, E., ed. "Epistolae variorum ad divorium Lotharii II regis pertinentes." In *Epistolae karolini aevi,* vol. 4, pp. 207–240. Berlin, 1925.

Perels, E., ed. "Hadriani II. papae epistolae." In *Epistolae karolini aevi,* vol. 4, pp. 691–765. Berlin, 1925.

Perels, E., ed. "Nicolas I. papae epistolae." In *Epistolae karolini aevi,* vol. 4, pp. 257–690. Berlin, 1925.

Peri, V. "Progetti e rimostranze: Documenti per la storia dell'Archivio Segreto Vaticano dall'erezione alla metà del XVIII secolo." *Archivum Historiae Pontificiae* 19 (1981): 191–237.

Perrin, C. E. "La cour pontificale d'Avignon (1309–1376)." *Revue historique* 232 (1964): 361–378.

Perugini, A. "Segreteria delle lettere latine." In *Enciclopedia cattolica,* vol. 11, p. 248. Vatican City, 1953.

Petra, V. *De Sacra Poenitentiaria Apostolica.* Rome, 1712.

Petra, V. *Commentaria ad constitutiones apostolicas, seu bullas singulas summorum pontificum in Bullario Romano contentas, secundum collectionem Cherubini.* Venice, 1729.

Petrucci, A. *Breve storia della scrittura latina.* New ed. Rome, 1992.

Petrucci, A. "Note di diplomatica pontificia. 1, Un privilegio solenne di Innocenzo III; 2, I capitoli di Innocenzo VIII per Perugia; 3, L'origine dei brevi pontifici e gli antichi eruditi." *Archivio della Società romana di storia patria* 89 (1966): 47–85.

Pfaff, V. "Die Einnahmen der römischen Kurie am Ende des 12. Jahrhunderts." *Vierteljahrschrift für Sozial- und Wirtschaftgeschichte* 40 (1953): 97–118.

Pfaff, V. "Der Liber Censuum von 1192 (Die im Jahre 1192/93 der Kurie Zinspflichtigen)." *Vierteljahrschrift für Sozial- und Wirtschaftgeschichte* 44 (1957): 78–96, 105–120, 220–242, 325–351.

Pflugk-Harttung, J. von, ed. *Acta pontificum romanorum inedita.* Tübingen, 1881–1888.

Pflugk-Harttung, J. von. "Das Komma auf päpstlichen Urkunden." *Mitteilungen des Instituts für österreichische Geschichtsforschung* 5 (1884): 434–440.

Pflugk-Harttung, J. von. *Specimina selecta chartarum pontificum romanorum.* Stuttgart, 1885–1887.

Pflugk-Harttung, J. von. "Die Schreiber der päpstlichen Kanzlei bis auf Innocenz II (1130)." *Römische Quartalschrift für christliche Altertumskunde und für Kirchengeschichte* 1 (1887): 212–230.

Pflugk-Harttung, J. von. "Die Liniirung der älteren Papst-bullen." *Römische Quartalschrift für christliche Altertums-kunde und für Kirchengeschichte* 2 (1888): 368–381.

Pflugk-Harttung, J. von. *Die Bullen der Päpste bis zum Ende des zwölften Jahrhunderts.* Gotha, 1901.

Pflugk-Harttung, J. von. "Papsturkunden auf Marmor." *Quellen und Forschungen aus italienischen Archiven und Bibliotheken* 4 (1902): 167–183; 5 (1903): 130.

Pflugk-Harttung, J. von. "Über Münzen und Siegel der älteren Päpste." *Quellen und Forschungen aus italienischen Archiven und Bibliotheken* 5 (1903): 1–18.

Philippi, F. "Zur Technik der Siegelbullen." *Archiv für Urkundenforschung* 5 (1914): 289–298.

Piazzoni, A. M., and P. Vian. *Manoscritti vaticani latini 14666–15203: Catalogo sommario.* Vatican City, 1989.

Piccialuti, M. *La carità come metodo di governo: Istituzioni caritative a Roma dal pontificato di Innocenzo XII a quello di Benedetto XIV.* Turin, 1994.

Piccolomini, P. "Corrispondenza tra la corte di Roma e L'Inquisizione di Malta durante la guerra di Candia (1645–1669)." *Archivio storico italiano,* 5th ser. 41 (1908): 45–127; 45 (1910): 303–355; 46 (1910): 3–52; 49 (1912): 34–80, 322–354.

Pietramellara, G. *Il libro d'oro del Campidoglio.* Rome, 1893–1897.

Pitra, J. B. *Analecta novissima spicilegii solesmensis, altera continuatio.* Paris, 1885–1888.

Pitz, E. *Papstreskript und Kaiserreskript im Mittelalter.* Tübingen, 1971.

Pitz, E. *Supplikensignatur und Briefexpedition an der römischen Kurie im Pontifikat Papst Callixts III.* Tübingen, 1972.

Pivec, K., and H. Heimpel. "Neue Forschungen zu Dietrich von Niem." *Nachrichten der Akademie der Wissenschaften in Göttingen. Philologisch-historische Klasse,* no. 4 (1951).

Pizzorusso, G. "Le 'Lettere di Stato': Una fonte documentaria dell'Archivio della Congregazione 'de Propaganda Fide' di particolari interesse canadese (1893–1908)." *Annali accademici canadesi* 5 (1989): 101–114.

Pizzorusso, G. "Donato Sbarretti, delegato apostolico a Ottawa e la difficile organizzazione del Concilio plenario canadese (1909)." *Annali accademici canadesi* 6 (1990): 77–88.

Pizzorusso, G. "Archives du College Urbain de Propaganda Fide." *Annali accademici canadesi* 7 (1991): 94–97.

Pizzorusso, G. "Le Fonds Benigni aux Archives Secretes du Vatican." *Annali accademici canadesi* 8 (1992): 107–111.

Pizzorusso, G. "Un diplomat du Vatican en Amerique: Donato Sbarretti a Washington, le Havane et Ottawa (1893–1910)." *Annali accademici canadesi* 9 (1993): 5–33.

Pizzorusso, G. *Inventaire des documents d'intérêt canadien dans les archives de la Congrégation de "Propaganda Fide,"* 1904–1914. Rome, 1993.

Planchart, A. E. "Guillaume Du Fay's Benefices and His Relationship to the Court of Burgundy." *Early Music History* 8 (1988): 117–171.

Planchart, A. E. "The Early Career of Guillaume Du Fay." *Journal of the American Musicological Society* 46 (1993): 341–368.

Poggiani, G. *Julii Pogiani Sunensis: Epistolae et orationes.* Edited by A. M. Graziani. Rome, 1756–1762.

Polidoro, P. *De vita et rebus gestis Clementis undecimi Pontificis Maximi.* Urbino, 1727.

Pontificum romanorum diplomata papyracea quae supersunt in tabulariis Hispaniae, Italiae, Germaniae. Rome, 1928.

Poole, R. L. *Lectures on the History of the Papal Chancery down to the Time of Innocent III.* Cambridge, 1915.

Poole, R. L. *Studies in Chronology and History.* Oxford, 1934.

Posner, E. M. "Das Register Gregors I." *Neues Archiv der Gesellschaft für ältere Deutsche Geschichtskunde* 41 (1922): 245–315.

Post, R. R. *Supplieken gericht aan de pausen Clemens VI, Innocentius VI en Urbanus V, 1342–1366.* Utrecht, 1936–1937.

Potthast, A. *Regesta pontificum romanorum inde ab A. post Christum natum MCXCVIII ad A. MCCCIV.* Berlin, 1874–1875.

Pou y Marti, J. M. *Archivo de la embajada de España cerca de la Santa Sede: Indice analitico de los codices de la biblioteca contigua al archivo.* Rome, 1925.

Pratesi, A. "Problemi e prospettive del censimento dei documenti pontifici." *Annali della Scuola speciale per archivisti e bibliotecari dell'Università di Roma* 12 (1972): 108–116.

Pressutti, P., ed. *Regesta Honorii papae III, iussu et munificentia Leonis XIII pontificis maximi ex vaticanis archetypis aliisque fontibus.* Rome, 1888–1895.

Prinzivalli, A. *Resolutiones, seu decreta authentica Sacrae Congregationis Indulgentiis Sacrisque Reliquiis praepositae ab anno 1668 ad annum 1861.* Rome, 1862.

Prodi, P. *Il cardinale Gabriele Paleotti (1522–1597).* Rome, 1959–1967.

Prodi, P. *Lo sviluppo dell'assolutismo nello stato pontificio (secoli XV–XVI).* Bologna, 1968–.

Prodi, P. *The Papal Prince: One Body and Two Souls: The Papal Monarchy in Early Modern Europe.* Translated by S. Haskins. Cambridge, 1987.

Prokes, J. *Husitika vatikanské knihovny v Rime.* Prague, 1928.

Prou, M. *Les registres d'Honorius IV: publiées d'après le manuscrit des Archives du Vatican.* Vol. 7 of *Bibliothèque des Écoles françaises d'Athènes et de Rome.* 2d ser., *Registres des papes du XIIIe siècle.* Paris, 1888.

Ptasnik, J. *Acta Camerae Apostolicae, 1207–1344.* Kraków, 1913.

Ptasnik, J. *Acta Camerae Apostolicae, 1344–1374.* Kraków, 1913.

Ptasnik, J. *Analecta Vaticana 1202–1366.* Kraków, 1914.

Pullan, B. S. *The Jews of Europe and the Inquisition of Venice, 1550–1670.* Oxford, 1983.

Quinn, E. W. *Archconfraternities, Archsodalities, and Primary Unions: With a Supplement on the Archconfraternity of Christian Mothers.* Washington, D.C., 1962.

Rabikauskas, P. "Papstname und Ordnungszahl: Über die Anfänge des Brauches, gleichnamige Päpste durch eine Ordnungszahl zu unterscheiden." *Römische Quartalschrift für christliche Altertumskunde und für Kirchengeschichte* 51 (1956): 1–15.

Rabikauskas, P. *Die römische Kuriale in der päpstlichen Kanzlei.* Rome, 1958.

Rabikauskas, P. "Zur fehlenden und unvollständigen Skriptumzeile in den Papstprivilegien des 10. und 11. Jahrhunderts." In *Saggi storici intorno al papato,* 91–116. Rome, 1959.

Rabikauskas, P. "Kanzlei, Päpstliche." In *Lexikon für Theologie und Kirche*, edited by J. Höfer and K. Rahner, vol. 5, pp. 1313–1315. 2d ed. Freiburg, 1960.

Rabikauskas, P. "De significatione verborum 'bulla,' 'breve.'" *Periodica de re morali, canonica, liturgica* 55 (1966): 85–92.

Rabikauskas, P. "'Annus incarnationis' et 'Annus pontificatus' nei privilegi di Innocenzo III." *Archivio della Società romana di storia patria* 91 (1968): 45–55.

Rabikauskas, P. *Relationes status dioecesium in magno ducatu Lithuanie*. Rome, 1971–1978.

Rabikauskas, P. "Cancellaria apostolica (In eius memoriam: saec. XI– die 31 martii 1973)." *Periodica de re morali, canonica, liturgica* 63 (1974): 243–273.

Rabikauskas, P. *Diplomatica generalis: Praelectionum lineamenta*. 4th ed. Rome, 1976. (This title was noted but not verified by project staff.)

Rabikauskas, P. *Diplomatica pontificia: Praelectionum lineamenta*. 5th ed. Rome, 1994.

Rabil, A., ed. and trans. *Knowledge, Goodness, and Power: The Debate over Nobility among Quattrocento Italian Humanists*. Binghamton, N.Y., 1991.

Radocsay, D. "Über einige illuminierte Urkunden." *Acta historiae artium Academiae scientiarum Hungaricae* 17 (1971): 31–61.

Rainer, J. *Nuntius G. Delfino und Kardinallegat G.F. Commendone, 1571–1572*. Vol. 8 of *Nuntiaturberichte aus Deutschland nebst ergänzenden Actenstücken. Zweite Abteilung, 1560–1572*. Graz, 1967.

Rainer, J. "Bartholomäus Portia als Nuntius bei Erzherzog Ferdinand II. von Tirol 1573/74." In *Neue Beitrage zur geschichtlichen Landeskunde Tirols: Festschrift für Univ. Prof. Dr. Franz Huter anlässlich der Vollendung des 70. Lebensjahres*, edited by E. Troger and G. Zwanowitz, vol. 2, pp. 347–360. Innsbruck, 1969.

Rainer, J. "Anfänge einer Universität Klagenfurt im 17. Jahrhundert." In *Die Landeshauptstadt Klagenfurt: Aus ihrer Vergangenheit und Gegenwart*, edited by G. Moro, vol. 1, pp. 310–332. Klagenfurt, 1970.

Rainer, J., ed. *Nuntiatur des Germanico Malaspina, Sendung des Antonio Possevino 1580–1582*. Vienna, 1973.

Rainer, J. "Nuntiaturberichte: Forschungsstand und Forschungsprobleme." *Innsbrucker historische Studien* 9 (1986): 69–90.

Ramacciotti, A. *Gli archivi della Reverenda Camera Apostolica, con inventario analitico-descrittivo dei registri camerali conservati nell'Archivio di Stato di Roma nel Fondo Camerale Primo*. Rome, 1961.

Ramackers, J. *Papsturkunden in den Niederlanden, Belgien, Luxemburg, Holland und Französisch-Flandern*. Berlin, 1933–1934.

Ramackers, J. "La minute d'un mandement d'Alexandre III a l'archevêque Bertrand de Bordeaux (1162–1173)." *Le Moyen Age, revue d'histoire et de philologie* 44 (1934): 96–98.

Ramackers, J. "Zwei unbekannte Briefe Urbans II: Zugleich ein Beitrag zum Problem der Register dieses Papstes." *Quellen und Forschungen aus italienischen Archiven und Bibliotheken* 26 (1935–1936): 268–276.

Ramsden, E. H. "Further Evidence on a Problem Picture." *Burlington Magazine* 107 (1965): 185–192.

Raponi, N. "Recenti edizioni di Nunziature pontificie e le 'Nunziature d'Italia'." *Rassegna degli Archivi di Stato* 25 (1965): 245–266.

Raquez, O. "La Congrégation pour la correction des livres de l'Église orientale (1719–1862)." In *Sacrae Congregationis de Propaganda Fide Memoria Rerum: 350 anni a servizio delle missioni*, edited by J. Metzler, vol. 2, pp. 514–534. Rome, 1973.

Rationes collectorum pontificiorum in Hungaria, 1281–1375. Budapest, 1875.

Regesti di bandi, editti, notificazioni e provvedimenti diversi relativi alla città di Roma ed allo Stato pontificio. Rome, 1920–1958.

Regolamento dell'Archivio Vaticano. Rome, 1927.

Reichenberger, R. *Germanico Malaspina und Filippo Sega (Giovanni Andrea Caligari in Graz)*. Erste Hälfte of *Nuntiaturberichte aus Deutschland nebst ergänzenden Actenstücken, 1585 (1584)–(1592)*. Zweite Abteilung, *Die Nuntiatur am Kaiserhofe*. Paderborn, 1905.

Reimers, H. *Oldenburgische Papsturkunden (1246–1500)*. Oldenburg, 1907.

Reimers, H. *Friesische Papsturkunden: aus den vatikanischen Archiven zu Rom*. Leeuwarden, 1908.

Reinhard, W. "Katholische Reform und Gegenreformation in der Kölner Nuntiatur 1584–1621: Aufgabe und erste Ergebnisse eines Editionsunternehmens der Görres-Gesellschaft (Nuntiaturberichte aus Deutschland. Die Kölner Nuntiatur I–V)." *Römische Quartalschrift für christliche Altertumskunde und für Kirchengeschichte* 66 (1971): 8–65.

Reinhard, W. *Nuntius Antonio Albergati (1610 Mai–1614 Mai)*. Vol. 5 of *Nuntiaturberichte aus Deutschland nebst ergänzenden Actenstücken, Die Kölner Nuntiatur*. Munich, 1972–.

Reinhard, W. *Papstfinanz und Nepotismus unter Paul V. (1605–1621): Studien und Quellen zur Struktur und zu quantitativen Aspekten des päpstlichen Herrschaftssystems*. Stuttgart, 1974.

Relève alphabetique des noms de personnes et de lieux: Contenus dans les registres de suppliques d'Urbain V. Rome, 1991–. (This title was noted but not verified by project staff.)

Renouard, Y. "Achats et paiements de draps flamands par les premiers papes d'Avignon." *Mélanges d'archéologie et d'histoire* 52 (1935): 273–313.

Renouard, Y. "Les minutes d'Innocent VI aux archives du Vatican." *Archivi (Rome)*, 2d ser. 2 (1935): 14–26.

Renouard, Y. "Comment les papes d'Avignon expédiaient leur courrier." *Revue historique* 180 (1937): 1–29.

Renouard, Y. "Le compagnie commerciali fiorentine del Trecento." *Archivio storico italiano* 96 (1938): 41–68, 163–179.

Renouard, Y. *Les relations des Papes d'Avignon et des compagnies commerciales et bancaires de 1316 à 1378*. Paris, 1941.

Renouard, Y. "Intérêt et importance des Archives Vaticanes pour l'histoire économique du Moyen Age, spécialement du XIVe siècle." In *Miscellanea archivistica Angelo Mercati*, pp. 21–41. Vatican City, 1952.

Renouard, Y. *La Papauté à Avignon*. Paris, 1954.

Renouard, Y. "Eđouard II et Clément V d'après les rôles gascons." *Annales du Midi* 67 (1955): 119–141.

Renouard, Y. *Études d'histoire médiévale*. Paris, 1968.

Renouard, Y. *The Avignon Papacy, 1305–1403*. Translated by D. Bethell. London, 1970.

Repertorium der diplomatischen Vertreter aller Länder seit dem Westfalischen Frieden (1648). Oldenburg, 1936–1965.

Repertorium Fontium Historiae Medii Aevi: primum ab Augusto Potthast digestum, nun cura collegii historicorum e pluribus nationibus emendatum et auctum. Rome, 1962–.

Repertorium Germanicum: Verzeichnis der in den päpstlichen Registern und Kameralakten vorkommenden Personen, Kirchen und Orte des deutschen Reiches, seiner Diözesen und Territorien, vom Beginn des Schismas bis zur Reformation. Berlin, 1916–.

Repgen, K. "Zur Diplomatik der Nuntiaturberichte: Dienstvorschrift für das Abfassen von Avvisi aus dem Jahre 1639." *Römische Quartalschrift für christliche Altertumskunde und für Kirchengeschichte* 49 (1954): 123–126.

Rest, J. "Illuminierte Ablassurkunden aus Rom und Avignon aus der Zeit von 1282–1364." In *Abhandlungen aus dem Gebiete der mittleren und neueren Geschichte und ihrer Hilfswissenschaften: Eine Festgabe zum siebzigsten Geburtstdg Geh. Rat Prof. Dr. Heinrich Finke,* pp. 147–168. Münster, 1925.

Reusens, E. H. J. *Elements de paleographie.* Louvain, 1899.

Richard, P. "La légation Aldobrandini et le traité de Lyon (septembre 1600–mars 1601): La diplomatie pontificale, ses agents au temps de Clément VIII." *Revue d'histoire et de littérature religieuses* 7 (1902): 481–509; 8 (1903): 25–48, 133–151.

Richard, P. "Origines de la nonciature de France: Nonces résidants avant Léon X (1456–1511)." *Revue des questions historiques* 78 (1905): 103–147.

Richard, P. "Origines de la nonciature de France: Débuts de la représentation permanent sous Léon X (1513–1521)." *Revue des questions historiques* 80 (1906): 112–180.

Richard, P. "Origines des nonciatures permanentes: La représentation pontificale au XVe siècle (1450–1513)." *Revue d'histoire ecclésiastique* 7 (1906): 52–70, 317–338.

Richard, P. "Origine et développement de la secrétairerie de l'État apostolique, 1417–1823." *Revue d'histoire ecclésiastique* 11 (1910): 56–72, 505–529, 728–754.

Rieder, K. *Römische Quellen zur Konstanzer Bistumsgeschichte zur Zeit der Päpste in Avignon, 1305–1378.* Innsbruck, 1908.

Riezler, S. *Vatikanische Akten zur deutschen Geschichte in der Zeit Kaiser Ludwigs des Bayern.* Innsbruck, 1891.

Riganti, G. B. *Commentaria in regulas, constitutiones et ordinationes Cancellariae Apostolicae.* Rome, 1744–1747.

Rigg, J. M., ed. *Calendar of State Papers Relating to English Affairs, Preserved Principally at Rome in the Vatican Archives and Library.* London, 1916–1926.

Ripa, M. *Storia della fondazione della Congregazione e del Collegio dei Cinese: Sotto il titolo della sagra famiglia di G. C.* Naples, 1832–.

Ritzler, R. "Intorno al 'Liber Diurnus'." *Miscellanea Franciscana* 42 (1942): 77–82.

Ritzler, R. "Die archivalischen Quellen der 'Hierarchia catholica.'" In *Miscellanea archivistica Angelo Mercati,* pp. 51–74. Vatican City, 1952.

Ritzler, R. "Bischöfliche Informativprozesse im Archiv der Datarie." *Römische Quartalschrift für christliche Altertumskunde und für Kirchengeschichte* 50 (1955): 95–101.

Ritzler, R. "Procesos informativos de los obispos de España y sus dominios en el Archivo Vaticano." *Anthologica annua* 4 (1956): 465–498.

Ritzler, R. "Die bischöflichen Informativprozesse in den 'Processus Consistoriales' im Archiv des Kardinalskollegs bis 1907." *Römische historische Mitteilungen* 2 (1957–1958): 204–220.

Ritzler, R. "Per la storia dell'Archivio del Sacro Collegio." In *Mélanges Eugène Tisserant,* vol. 5, pp. 300–338. Vatican City, 1964.

Ritzler, R. "Die Verschleppung der päpstlichen Archiv nach Paris unter Napoleon I. und deren Rückführung nach Rom in den Jahren 1815 bis 1817." *Römische historische Mitteilungen* 6–7 (1964): 144–190.

Rius Serra, J., ed. *Rationes decimarum Hispaniae (1279–1280).* Barcelona, 1946–1947.

Robert, U. *Bullaire du Pape Calixte II, 1119–1124: Essai de Restitution.* Paris, 1891.

Robinson, I. S. *The Papacy 1073–1198: Continuity and Innovation.* Cambridge, 1990.

Robres Lluch, R., and V. Castell Maiques. "La visita 'ad limina' durante el Pontificado de Sixto V (1585–1590): Datos para una estadistica general: Su complimiento en Iberoamerica." *Anthologica annua* 7 (1959): 147–213.

Rockinger, L. Ritter von, ed. *Briefsteller und Formelbücher des elften bis vierzehnten Jahrhunderts.* Munich, 1863.

Rodenberg, C. *Epistolae saeculi XIII e regestis pontificum selectae.* Berlin, 1883–1894.

Rodrigues Valencia, V. "La diócesis de Buenos Aires y la Santa Sede en los últimos años del patronato español." *Anthologica annua* 9 (1961): 817–833.

Rogers, J. F. "Les bénéfices en Angleterre." In *Dictionnaire de droit canonique,* edited by R. Naz, vol. 2, pp. 658–670. Paris, 1937.

Romana beatificationis et canonizationes . . . Innocentii Papae XI. Vatican City, 1943. (This title was noted but not verified by project staff.)

Romita, F. "Le origini della sacra Congregazione del Concilio." In *La sacra Congregazione del Concilio: Quarto centenario della fondazione, 1564–1964, studi e ricerche,* pp. 13–50. Vatican City, 1964.

Rosa, E. "I 'semenzar' del sacerdozio e la Sacra Congregazione dei Seminari e delle Università degli Studi." *Civiltà cattolica* 85 (1934): 588–597.

Rospigliosi, G. C., and L. Andreani, eds. *Libro A di richordi d'Antonio di Taddeo Rospigliosi (1459–1498).* Pisa, 1909.

Rosshirt, J. K. "Von den päpstlichen Kanzleiregeln." *Archiv für katholisches Kirchenrecht* 3 (1858): 373–395.

Rossini, G. "Alcune carte nonantolane nella Biblioteca comunale di Faenza." *Atti e memorie della Deputazione di storia patria per le antiche provincie modenesi,* 8th ser. 5 (1953): 157–171.

Rota, A. "Michelangelo e il Monte della Fede." *Archivi (Rome),* 2d ser. 4 (1937): 27–60.

Rouet de Journal, M. J. *Nonciatures de Russie d'après les documents authentiques.* Rome, 1922–.

Rouquette, J. B., and A. Villemagne. *Bullaire de l'église de Maguelone.* Montpellier, 1911–1914.

Roziere, E. de. *Liber diurnus, ou Recueil des formules usitees par la chancellerie pontificale du Ve au XIe siecle, publie d'apres le manuscrit des archives du Vatican.* Paris, 1869.

Ruggeri, L. *L'Archiconfraternità del Gonfalone: Memorie.* Rome, 1866.

Ruggiero, M. G. P. *L'archivo della computisteria generale della Camera Apostolica dopo la riforma di Benedetto XIV (1744): Ipotesi di ricerca.* Rome, 1981. (This title was noted but not verified by project staff.)

Ruggiero, M. G. P. *La Reverenda Camera Apostolica e i suoi archivi (secoli XV–XVIII).* Rome, 1987.

La sacra Congregazione del Concilio: Quarto centenario della fondazione, 1564–1964, studi e ricerche. Vatican City, 1964.

La Sacra Congregazione per le Chiese orientali nel cinquantesimo della fondazione (1917–1967). Grottaferrata, 1969.

Sägmüller, J. B. *Die Thätigkeit und Stellung der Cardinäle bis Papst Bonifaz VIII.* Freiburg, 1896.

"Le Saint-Office." *La Vie intellectuelle* 24 (1953): 137–152.

Sala, G. A. *Piano di riforma umiliato a Pio VII.* Edited by G. Cugnoni. Tolentino, 1907.

Salmon, P. *Analecta liturgica: Extraits des manuscrits liturgiques de la Bibliotheque Vaticane: Contribution a l'histoire de la priere chretienne.* Vatican City, 1974.

Salomon, R. G. "Eine russische Publikation zur päpstlichen Diplomatik." *Neues Archiv der Gesellschaft für ältere Deutsche Geschichtskunde* 32 (1906): 459–475.

Samaran, C., and G. Mollat. *La fiscalité pontificale en France au XIVe siècle: Période d'Avignon et du Grand Schisme d'Occident.* Paris, 1905.

Sambin, P. *Un formulario di lettere vescovili del secolo XIV.* Padua, 1961.

Sambin, P. *Lettere inedite di Innocenzo IV.* Padua, 1961.

Sandri, L. "Il cardinale Camillo Cybo ed il suo archivio (1681–1743)." *Archivi (Rome),* 2d ser. 6 (1939): 63–82.

Sandri, L. "Note sui registri delle 'Rationes decimarum' dell'Archivio di Stato di Roma." In *Mélanges Eugène Tisserant,* vol. 5, pp. 338–359. Vatican City, 1964.

Sanfilippo, M. "La Santa Sede, il Canada e la delegazione apostolica ad Ottawa." *Annali accademici canadesi* 2 (1986): 112–119.

Sanfilippo, M. *Inventaire des documents d'intérêt canadien dans l'Archivio segreto vaticano sous le pontificat de Leon XIII, 1878–1903: Délégation apostolique du Canada, Délégation apostolique des États Unis, Epistolae ad principes et Epistolae latinae, et autres series mineures.* Rome, 1987. (This title was noted but not verified by project staff.)

Sanfilippo, M. "Fonti Vaticane per la storia canadese: La delegazione apostolica in Canada, 1899–1910." *Annali accademici canadesi* 3–4 (1988): 63–79.

Sanfilippo, M. "Monsignor Pisani e il Canada." *Annali accademici canadesi* 6 (1990): 61–75.

Sansterre, J. "La date des formules 60–63 du 'Liber Diurnus.'" *Byzantion* 48 (1978): 226–243.

Santarem, M. F. de Barros e Sousa, Visconde de, L. A. Rebello da Silva, and J. J. da Silva Mendes Leal. *Relaçoes politicas e diplomaticas entre Portugal e la Curia de Roma.* Secçao 17, vols. 9–13 of *Quadro elementar das relaçoes politicas e diplomaticas de Portugal com as diversas potencias do mundo.* Lisbon, 1864–1876.

Santifaller, L. "Die Verwendung des Liber Diurnus in den Privilegien der Päpste von den Anfängen bis zum Ende des 11. Jahrhunderts." *Mitteilungen des Instituts für österreichische Geschichtsforschung* 49 (1935): 225–366.

Santifaller, L. "Beiträge zur Geschichte der Kontextschlussformeln der Papsturkunde." *Historisches Jahrbuch* 57 (1937): 233–257.

Santifaller, L. *Die Abkürzungen in den ältesten Papsturkunden (788–1002).* Weimar, 1939.

Santifaller, L. "Saggio di un elenco dei funzionari, impiegati e scrittori della cancellaria pontificia dall'inizio all'anno 1099." *Bullettino dell'Istituto storico italiano per il medio evo e Archivio muratoriano* 56 (1940): 1–858.

Santifaller, L, ed. *1100 Jahre österreichische und europäische Geschichte: in Urkunden und Dokumenten des Haus-, Hof- und Staatsarchivs.* Vienna, 1949.

Santifaller, L. "Über die Titel in den Adressen der Papsturkunden von den Anfängen bis zum Ende des 11. Jahrhunderts." *Zgodovinski Casopis* 6–7 (1952–1953): 246–258.

Santifaller, L. *Beiträge zur Geschichte der Beschreibstoffe im Mittelalter, mit besonderer Berücksichtigung der päpstlichen Kanzlei.* Graz, 1953.

Santifaller, L., ed. "Studien und Vorarbeiten zur Edition der Register Papst Innozenz III." *Mitteilungen des Instituts für österreichische Geschichtsforschung* 65 (1957): 237–241.

Santifaller, L., et al. *Quellen und Forschungen zum Urkunden- und Kanzleiwesen Papst Gregors VII.* Vatican City, 1957–.

Santifaller, L. "Über die Verbal-Invokation in den älteren Papsturkunden." *Römische historische Mitteilungen* 3 (1958–1960): 18–113.

Santifaller, L. "Der 'Censimento' der spätmittelalterlichen Papsturkunden." *Mitteilungen des Instituts für österreichische Geschichtsforschung* 72 (1964): 122–134.

Santifaller, L. "Übersicht über die Verleihung päpstlicher Privilegien für deutsche Klöster bis zum Jahre 1099." In *Zur Geschichte des ottonisch-salischen Reichskirchensystems,* pp. 68–77. 2d ed. Vienna, 1964.

Santifaller, L. "Über die Neugestaltung der äusseren Form der Papstprivilegien unter Leo IX." In *Festschrift Hermann Wiesflecker zum sechzigsten Geburtstag,* edited by A. Novotny and O. Pickl, pp. 29–38. Graz, 1973.

Santifaller, L. *Liber Diurnus: Studien und Forschungen.* Stuttgart, 1976.

Santifaller, L., and D. Girgensohn. *Neuere Editionen mittelalterlichen Königs- und Papsturkunden: eine Uebersicht.* Graz, 1958.

Santini, P. *De referendariorum ac signaturae historico-iuridica evolutione.* Rome, 1951.

Santos Abranches, J. dos. *Summa do bullario Portuguez.* Coimbra, 1895.

Santosuosso, A. "Religious Orthodoxy, Dissent and Suppression in Venice in the 1540s." *Church History* 42 (1973): 476–485.

Santy, F. *Belgie in het Vaticaans Archief: Nuntiatuur te Brussel 1875–1904: Regestenlijst.* Vol. 8 of *Analecta vaticano-belgica.* Ser. 2, section C, *Nonciature de Bruxelles.* Louvain, 1989.

Sauerland, H. V. *Vatikanische Urkunden und Regesten zur Geschichte Lothringens.* Metz, 1901–1905.

Sauerland, H. V. *Urkunden und Regesten zur Geschichte der Rheinlande aus dem Vatikanischen Archiv.* Bonn, 1902–.

Savio, P. *De Actis Nuntiaturae Poloniae quae partem Archivi Secretariatus Status constituunt.* Vatican City, 1947.

Sayers, J. E. "Canterbury Proctors at the Court of the Audientia Litterarum Contradictarum." *Traditio* 22 (1966): 311–345.

Sayers, J. E. *Original Papal Documents in the Lambeth Palace Library: A Catalogue.* London, 1967.

Sbrana, C. "Un ignorato fondo di storia economica romana: Il Fondo Quarantotti." *Cahiers internationaux d'histoire économique et sociale* 1 (1972): 370–376.

Scalia, G. "Gli 'archiva' di papa Damaso e le biblioteche di papa Ilaro." *Studi medievali,* 3d ser. 18 (1977): 39–63.

Scano, D. *Codice diplomatico delle relazioni fra la Santa Sede e la Sardegna.* Cagliari, 1940–1941.

Schadelbauer, K., and O. Fritz. "Der Schnurkanal bei Siegelbullen im Röntgenbild." *Archiv für Urkundenforschung* 10 (1926–1928): 226–327.

Schäfer, K. H., ed. *Die Ausgaben der apostolischen Kammer unter Johann XXII., nebst den Jahresbilanzen von 1316–1375.* Vol. 2 of *Vatikanische Quellen zur Geschichte des päpstlichen Hof- und Finanzverwaltung 1316–1378.* Paderborn, 1911.

Schäfer, K. H. *Deutsche Ritter und Edelknechte in Italien während des 14. Jahrhunderts.* Paderborn, 1911–1940.

Schäfer, K. H., ed. *Die Ausgaben der apostolischen Kammer unter Benedikt XII., Klemens VI. und Innocenz VI. (1335–1362).* Vol. 3 of *Vatikanische Quellen zur Geschichte des päpstlichen Hof- und Finanzverwaltung 1316–1378.* Paderborn, 1914.

Schäfer, K. H., ed. *Die Ausgaben der apostolischen Kammer unter den Päpsten Urban V. und Gregor XI., (1362–1378), nebst Nachträgen und einem Glossar für alle drei Ausgabenbände.* Vol. 6 of *Vatikanische Quellen zur Geschichte des päpstlichen Hof- und Finanzverwaltung 1316–1378.* Paderborn, 1937.

Schaller, H. M. "Die Kanzlei Friedrichs II: Ihr Personal und ihr Sprachstil II." *Archiv für Diplomatik, Schriftengeschichte, Siegel- und Wappenkunde* 4 (1958): 264–327.

Schamoni, W. *Inventarium Processuum Beatificationis et Canonizationis Bibliothecae Nationalis Parisiensis Provenientium ex Archivis S. Rituum Congregationis Typis Mandatorum inter Annos 1662–1809.* Hildesheim, 1983.

Schellhass, K. *Die süddeutsche Nuntiatur des Grafen Bartholomäus von Portia.* Vols. 3–5 of *Nuntiaturberichte aus Deutschland nebst ergänzenden Actenstücken. Dritte Abteilung, 1572–1585.* Berlin, 1896–1909.

Schepper, H. de, and G. Parker. "The Formation of Government Policy in the Catholic Netherlands under 'the Archdukes,' 1596–1621." *English Historical Review* 91 (1976): 241–254.

Schiaparelli, L. "Papsturkunden in Apulien." *Nachrichten der königlichen Gesellschaft der Wissenschaften zu Göttingen. Philologisch-historische Klasse* (1898): 237–289.

Schiaparelli, L. "Papsturkunden in Benevent und der Capitanata." *Nachrichten der königlichen Gesellschaft der Wissenschaft zu Göttingen. Philologisch-historische Klasse* (1898): 45–97.

Schiaparelli, L. "Papsturkunden in Friaul." *Nachrichten der königlichen Gesellschaft der Wissenschaften zu Göttingen. Philologisch-historische Klasse* (1899): 251–282.

Schiaparelli, L. "Papsturkunden in Malta." *Nachrichten der königlichen Gesellschaft der Wissenschaften zu Göttingen. Philologisch-historische Klasse* (1899): 369–409.

Schiaparelli, L. "Papsturkunden in Venetien." *Nachrichten der königlichen Gesellschaft der Wissenschaften zu Göttingen. Philologisch-historische Klasse* (1899): 197–249.

Schiaparelli, L. "Papsturkunden in Parma und Piacenza." *Nachrichten der königlichen Gesellschaft der Wissenschaften zu Göttingen. Philologisch-historische Klasse* (1900): 1–75.

Schiaparelli, L. "Papsturkunden in Piemont." *Nachrichten der königlichen Gesellschaft der Wissenschaften zu Göttingen. Philologisch-historische Klasse* (1901): 117–170.

Schiaparelli, L. "Papsturkunden in Turin." *Nachrichten der königlichen Gesellschaft der Wissenschaften zu Göttingen. Philologisch-historische Klasse* (1901): 57–115.

Schieffer, R. "Tomus Gregorii papae: Bemerkungen zur Diskussion um das Register Gregors VII." *Archiv für Diplomatik, Schriftengeschichte, Siegel- und Wappenkunde* 17 (1971): 169–184.

Schieffer, T. "Der Stand des göttinger Papsturkundenwerkes." *Annali della Scuola speciale per archivisti e bibliotecari dell'Università di Roma* 12 (1972): 193–205.

Schillmann, F. "Ein päpstliche Formelbuch des XIV. Jahrhunderts." *Zeitschrift für Kirchengeschichte* 21 (1910): 283–300.

Schillmann, F. *Die Formularsammlung des Marinus von Eboli.* Rome, 1929–.

Schlecht, J. *Andrea Zamometic und der Basler Konzilsversuch vom Jahre 1482.* Paderborn, 1903.

Schlecht, J., and T. J. Scherg, eds. *Bavarica aus dem Vatikan, 1461–1491.* Munich, 1932.

Schmidt, K. G., and P. F. Kehr. *Päpstliche Urkunden und Regesten aus den Jahren 1295–1378: Die Gebiete der heutigen Provinz Sachsen und deren Umlande betreffend.* Halle, 1886–1889.

Schmidt, R. "Die Kanzleivermerke auf der Stiftungsbulle fur die Universität Rostock vom Jahre 1419." *Archiv für Diplomatik, Schriftengeschichte, Siegel- und Wappenkunde* 21 (1975): 432–449.

Schmitz, L. "Die Libri Formatarum Camerae Apostolicae." *Römische Quartalschrift für christliche Altertumskunde und für Kirchengeschichte* 8 (1894): 451–472.

Schmitz-Kallenberg, L. "Papsturkunden." Pt. 2 of *Urkundenlehre,* by R. Thommen, pp. 56–116. Leipzig, 1913.

Schmitz-Kallenberg, L. *Practica Cancellariae Apostolicae Saeculi XV Exeuntis: Ein Handbuch für den Verkehr mit der päpstlichen Kanzlei.* Münster, 1904.

Schneider, F. E. "Zur Entstehungsgeschichte der römischen Rota als Kollegialgericht." In *Kirchengeschichtliche Festgabe Anton de Waal,* pp. 20–36. Freiburg, 1913.

Schneider, F. E. *Die römische Rota: Nach geltendem Recht auf geschichtlicher Grundlage.* Paderborn, 1914–.

Schneider, F. E. "Über den Ursprung und die Bedeutung des Namens Rota als Bezeichnung für den obersten päpstlichen Gerichtshof." *Römische Quartalschrift für christliche Altertumskunde und für Kirchengeschichte* 41 (1933): 29–43.

Schneider, J. *Rescripta authentica Sacrae Congregationis Indulgentiis Sacrisque Reliquiis Praepositae, necnon Summaria Indulgentiarum.* Regensburg, 1885.

Schreiber, G. "Das päpstliche Staatssekretariat." *Historisches Jahrbuch* 79 (1960): 175–198.

Schulte, A. *Die Fugger im Rom, 1495–1523.* Leipzig, 1904.

Schütte, L. *Vatikanische Aktenstücke zur italienischen Legation des Duranti und Pilifort der Jahre 1305–1306.* Leobschütz, 1909.

Schwalm, J. *Das Formelbuch des Heinrich Bucglant: An die päpstliche Kurie in Avignon: Gerichtete Suppliken aus der ersten Hälfte des 14. Jahrjunderts.* Hamburg, 1910.

Schwarz, B. *Die Organisation kurialer Schreiberkollegien von ihrer Entstehung bis zur Mitte des 15. Jahrhunderts.* Tübingen, 1972.

Schwarz, B. "Der Corrector litterarum apostolicarum: Entwicklung des Korrektorenamtes in der päpstlichen Kanzlei von Innozenz III. bis Martin V." *Quellen und Forschungen aus italienischen Archiven und Bibliotheken* 54 (1974): 122–191.

Schwarz, B. "Abbreviature Officium est Assistere Vicecancellario in Expeditione Litterarum Apostolicarum: Zur Entwicklung des Abbreviatorenamtes vom Grossen Schisma bis zur Gründung des Vakabilistenkollegs der Abbreviatoren durch Pius II." In *Römische Kurie, kirchliche Finanzen, vatikanisches Archiv: Studien zu Ehren von Hermann Hoberg*, pp. 789–823. Rome, 1979.

Schwarz, B. "Die Abbreviatoren unter Eugen IV: Päpstliches Reservationsrecht, Konkordatspolitik, und kuriale Aemterorganisation." *Quellen und Forschungen aus italienischen Archiven und Bibliotheken* 60 (1980): 200–274.

Schwarz, B. "Ämterkäuflichkeit eine Institution des Absolutismus und ihre mittelalterlichen Wurzeln." In *Staat und Gesellschaft in Mittelalter und Früher Neuzeit: Gedenkschrift für Joachim Leuschner*, pp. 176–196. Göttingen, 1983.

Schwarz, W. E. *Die Nuntiatur-Korrespondenz Kaspar Groppers nebst verwandten Aktenstücken, 1573–1576.* Paderborn, 1898.

Schweizer, J. *Antonio Puteo in Prag, 1587–1589.* Vol. 2 of *Nuntiaturberichte aus Deutschland nebst ergänzenden Actenstücken, 1585 (1584)–(1592). Zweite Abteilung, Die Nuntiatur am Kaiserhofe.* Paderborn, 1912.

Schweizer, J. *Die Nuntien in Prag: Alfonso Visconte 1589–1591, Camillo Caetano 1591–1592.* Vol. 3 of *Nuntiaturberichte aus Deutschland nebst ergänzenden Actenstücken, 1585 (1584)–(1592). Zweite Abteilung, Die Nuntiatur am Kaiserhofe.* Paderborn, 1919.

Sciambra, M., G. Valentini, and I. Parrino. *Il Liber Brevium di Callisto III: La Crociata, L'Albania e Skanderbeg: Descrizione, introduzione, edizione in regesta e parzialmente integra, e indici.* Palermo, 1968.

Sebastiani, M. L. "Per la diplomatica dei registri di Eugenio IV." *Le chiavi della memoria: Miscellanea in occasione del I centenario della Scuola vaticana di paleografia, diplomatica e archivistica*, pp. 551–564. Vatican City, 1984.

Seidlmayer, M. "Die spanischen 'Libri de Schismate' des vatikanischen Archivs." In *Gesammelte Aufsätze zur Kulturgeschichte Spaniens*, vol. 8, pp. 199–262. Münster, 1940.

Sella, P., ed. *Aprutium-Molisium: Le decime dei secoli XIII–XIV.* Vol. 3 of *Rationes decimarum Italiae nei secoli XIII e XIV*, edited by P. Guidi and P. Sella. Vatican City, 1936.

Sella, P. *Le bolle d'oro dell'Archivio Vaticano.* Vatican City, 1934.

Sella, P. *I sigilli dell'Archivio Vaticano.* Vatican City, 1937–.

Sella, P., ed. *Sicilia.* Vol. 8 of *Rationes decimarum Italiae nei secoli XIII e XIV*, edited by P. Guidi and P. Sella. Vatican City, 1944.

Sella, P., ed. *Sardinia.* Vol. 9 of *Rationes decimarum Italiae nei secoli XIII e XIV*, edited by P. Guidi and P. Sella. Vatican City, 1945.

Sella, P., ed. *Marchia.* Vol. 11 of *Rationes decimarum Italiae nei secoli XIII e XIV*, edited by P. Guidi and P. Sella. Vatican City, 1950.

Sella, P., ed. *Umbria.* Vol. 12 of *Rationes decimarum Italiae nei secoli XIII e XIV*, edited by P. Guidi and P. Sella. Vatican City, 1952.

Sella, P., and G. Vale, eds. *Venetiae-Histria-Dalmatia.* Vol. 5 of *Rationes decimarum Italiae nei secoli XIII e XIV*, edited by P. Guidi and P. Sella. Vatican City, 1941.

Semmler, J. "Beiträge zum Aufbau des päpstlichen Staatssekretariats unter Paul V. (1605–1621)." *Römische Quartalschrift für christliche Altertumskunde und für Kirchengeschichte* 54 (1959): 40–80.

Semmler, J. *Das päpstliche Staatssekretariat in den Pontifikaten Pauls V. und Gregors XV., 1605–1623.* Rome, 1969.

Seppelt, F. X., ed. *Monumenta Coelestiniana: Quellen zur Geschichte des Päpstes Coelestin V.* Paderborn, 1921.

Serafini, A. "Le origini della pontificia Segretaria di Stato e la 'Sapienti consilio' del Pio X." *Apollinaris* 25 (1952): 165–239.

Serra, A. "Funzioni e finanze delle confraternite romane tra il 1624 e il 1797." In *Le confraternite Romane: Esperienza religiosa, società, commitenza artistica: Colloquio della Fondazione Caetani, Roma, 14–15 maggio 1982*, edited by L. Fiorani, pp. 261–292. Rome, 1984.

Serra Estelles, J. *Los registros de suplicas y letras pontificias de Clemente VII de Aviñon (1378–1394): Estudio diplomatico.* Rome, 1988.

Serrano, L., ed. *Correspondencia diplomatica entre España y la Santa Sede durante el pontificado di S. Pio V.* Madrid, 1914.

Sforza, G. "Riflessi della Controriforma nella Repubblica di Venezia." *Archivio storico italiano* 93.1 (1935): 5–34, 189–216; 93.2 (1935): 25–52, 173–186.

Sforza, O., and M. V. Zacchero. *ASV Archivum Arcis Armario B3, 7 Giugno 1590, Libro di tutta la spesa fatta da N.S. Sisto V alla Colonna Antonina e Traiana.* Rome, 1984. (This title was noted but not verified by project staff.)

Sheehy, M. P. *Pontificia Hibernica: Medieval Papal Chancery Documents Concerning Ireland, 640–1261.* Dublin, 1962–1965.

Sheptyts'kyi, A. *Monumenta Ucrainae historica.* Rome, 1964–.

Siete Iglesias, A. de Vargas-Zúñiga y Montero de Espinosa, marqués de, and B. Cuartero y Huerta. *Bulas y documentos pontificios (590–1670): Cartas y documentos del reino de Aragón (1213–1516).* Vol. 1 of *Indice de la colección de don Luis de Salazar y Castro.* Madrid, 1949.

Simon, A. *Correspondance du nonce Fornari (1838–1843).* Vol. 1 of *Analecta vaticano-belgica.* Ser. 2, section C, *Nonciature de Bruxelles.* Brussels, 1956.

Simon, A. "Archives de la nonciature a Bruxelles (Rome)." *Cahiers (Centre interuniversitaire d'histoire contemporaine)* 3 (1957): 23–36.

Simon, A. *Documents relatifs a la nonciature de Bruxelles (1834–1838).* Vol. 2 of *Analecta vaticano-belgica.* Ser. 2, section C, *Nonciature de Bruxelles.* Brussels, 1958.

Simon, A. *Lettres de Pecci (1834–1846).* Vol. 3 of *Analecta vaticano-belgica.* Ser. 2, section C, *Nonciature de Bruxelles.* Brussels, 1959.

Simon, A. *Instructions aux nonces de Bruxelles, 1835–1889.* Vol. 4 of *Analecta vaticano-belgica.* Ser. 2, section C, *Nonciature de Bruxelles.* Brussels, 1961.

Soenen, M. *Documents relatifs au Grand Schisme.* Vol. 9, *Lettres de Gregoire XII, 1406–1415.* Vol. 30 of *Analecta vaticano-belgica: Documents relatifs aux anciens diocèses de Cambrai, Liège, Thérouanne et Tournai.* Brussels, 1976.

Sorge, G. *Il "Padroado" regio e la S. Congregazione "de Propaganda Fide" nei secoli XIV–XVII.* Bologna, 1985.

Sorge, G. *Matteo de Castro (1594–1677): Profilo di una figura emblematica del conflitto giurisdizionale tra Goa e Roma nel secolo XVII.* Bologna, 1986.

Sousa Costa, A. D. de. *Súplicas dos pontificados de Clemente VI, Inocéncio VI e Urbano V.* Rome, 1968.

Spinelli, G. "Regestro del volume I (1649–1713) della serie 'Congressi,' dell'Archivio storico della Sacra Congregazione 'de Propaganda Fide,' Roma." Ph.D. diss., Università degli studi di Pisa, 1986–1987. (This title was noted but not verified by project staff.)

Spreti, V. *Enciclopedia storico-nobiliare italiana.* Milan, 1928–1936.

Stacul, P. *Il cardinale Pileo da Prata.* Rome, 1957.

Stangler, G. *Matthias Corvinus und die Renaissance in Ungarn 1458–1541.* Vienna, 1982.

Starr, P. "Music and Music Patronage at the Papal Court, 1447–1464." Ph.D. diss., Yale University, 1987.

Starzer, A., and O. Redlich, eds. *Eine Wiener Briefsammlung zur Geschichte des Deutschen Reiches und der österreichischen Länder in der zweiten Hälfte des XIII. Jahrhunderts.* Vienna, 1894.

Steen, W. van der. *Belgie in het Vaticaans Archief: Congregatie voor Buitengewone Kerkelijke Aangelegenheden, 1878–1903: Regestenlijst.* Vol. 7 of *Analecta vaticano-belgica.* Ser. 2, section C, *Nonciature de Bruxelles.* Louvain, 1989.

Steen, W. van der, and K. Meerts. *Belgie in het Vaticaans Archief: Staatssecretariaat (rubriek 256), 1878–1903: Regestenlijst.* Vol. 6 of *Analecta vaticano-belgica.* Ser. 2, section C, *Nonciature de Bruxelles.* Louvain, 1989.

Steinacker, H. "Das Register Papst Johanns VIII." In *Homenatge a Antoni Rubiò i Lluch: Miscellania d'estudis literaris, històrics i lingüistics,* vol. 1, pp. 479–505. Barcelona, 1936.

Steinherz, S. *Die Nuntien Hosius und Delfino, 1560–1561.* Vol. 1 of *Nuntiaturberichte aus Deutschland nebst ergänzenden Actenstücken. Zweite Abteilung, 1560–1572.* Vienna, 1897.

Steinherz, S. *Nuntius Delfino 1562–1565.* Vols. 3–4 of *Nuntiaturberichte aus Deutschland nebst ergänzenden Actenstücken. Zweite Abteilung, 1560–1572.* Vienna, 1903–1914.

Stella, A., and A. Bolognetti, eds. *Chiesa e Stato nelle relazione dei nunzi pontifici a Venezia: Ricerche sul giurisdizionalismo veneziano dal XVI al XVIII secolo.* Vatican City, 1964.

Stelzer, W. "Beiträge zur Geschichte der Kurienprokuratoren im 13. Jahrhundert." *Archivum Historiae Pontificiae* 8 (1970): 113–138.

Stickler, A. M. *Historia iuris canonici latini: Institutiones academicae. I, Historia fontium.* Turin, 1950.

Stloukal, K. *Acta Gregorii XI, pontificis romani.* Prague, 1949–1953.

Stock, L. F. *Consular Relations between the United States and the Papal States: Instructions and Despatches.* Washington, D.C., 1945.

Storm, G. *Afgifter fra den Norske kirkeprovins til det Apostoliske Kammer of Kardinalkollegiet, 1311–1523.* Christiania, 1897.

Storm, G. *Regesta Norvegica: Kronologisk fortegnelse over dokumenter vedkommende norge, nordmaend og den norske kirkeprovins.* Christiania, 1898.

Strnad, A. A. *Die Register Innocenz' III.* Graz, 1968–.

Stroll, M. "The Twelfth-century Apse Mosaic in San Clemente in Rome and its Enigmatic Inscription." *Storia e civiltà* 4 (1988). (This title was noted but not verified by project staff.)

Strong, E. "Istituti stranieri a Roma: Cenni storici." *Annales institutorum* 1 (1929): 15–60.

Summers, N. "Vatican City." In *Guide to the Diplomatic Archives of Western Europe,* pp. 290–300. Philadelphia, 1959.

Sweet, A. M. "The Apostolic See and the Heads of English Religious Houses." *Speculum* 28 (1953): 468–484.

Sydow, J. "Untersuchungen zur kurialen Verwaltungsgeschichte im Zeitalter des Reformpapsttums." *Deutsches Archiv für Erforschung des Mittelalters* 11 (1954): 18–73.

Tacchi Venturi, P. "Diario consistoriale di Giulio Antonio Santori, cardinale di S. Severina." *Studi e documenti di storia e diritto* 23 (1902): 297–347; 24 (1903): 73–142, 205–272; 25 (1904): 89–135.

Taccone-Galucci, D. *Regesti dei romani pontifici per le chiese della Calabria.* Rome, 1902.

Tallone, A. *Le bolle pontificie degli archivi Piemontesi.* Pinerolo, 1900.

Tamburini, F. "L'Archivio delle Penitenzieria Apostolica e il primo registro delle suppliche (1410–1411)." Ph.D. diss., Pontifical Lateran University, 1969.

Tamburini, F. "Il primo registro di suppliche dell'Archivio della Sacra Penitenzieria Apostolica (1410–1411)." *Rivista di storia della chiesa in Italia* 23 (1969): 384–427.

Tamburini, F. "Un registro di bolle di Sisto IV nell'Archivio della Penitenzieria Apostolica." In *Palaeographica, Diplomatica et Archivistica: Studi in onore di Giulio Battelli,* vol. 2, pp. 375–405. Rome, 1979.

Tangl, G. *Das Register Innozenz' III. über die Reichsfrage 1198–1209.* Leipzig, 1923.

Tangl, G. *Studien zum Register Innozenz' III.* Weimar, 1929.

Tangl, G. "Ein verschollenes Originalregister Innozenz' III." *Quellen und Forschungen aus italienischen Archiven und Bibliotheken* 26 (1935–1936): 1–20; 27 (1936–1937): 264–267.

Tangl, M. "Das Taxwesen der päpstlichen Kanzlei vom 13. bis zur Mitte des 15. Jahrhunderts." *Mitteilungen des Instituts für österreichische Geschichtsforschung* 13 (1892): 1–106.

Tangl, M. *Die päpstlichen Kanzleiordnungen von 1200–1500.* Innsbruck, 1894.

Tangl, M. *Das Mittelalter in Quellenkunde und Diplomatik: Ausgewählte Schriften.* Berlin, 1966.

Tarouca, C. da Silva. "Die Quellen der Briefsammlungen Papst Leos des Grossen." In *Papsttum und Kaisertum: Forschungen zur politischen Geschichte und Geisteskultur des*

Mittelalters Paul Kehr zum 65. Geburtstag dargebracht, 23–47. Munich, 1926.

Tarouca, C. da Silva. "Nuovi studi sulle antiche lettere dei papi." *Gregorianum* 12 (1931): 3–56, 349–425, 547–598.

Tarouca, C. da Silva. *Epistularum romanorum pontificium ad vicarios per Illyricum aliosque episcopos collectio Thessalonicensis, ad fidem codicis Vat. lat. 5751*. Rome, 1937.

Tautu, A. L., ed. *Acta romanorum pontificum a S. Clemente I (an.c. 90) ad Coelestinum III (1198)*. Vatican City, 1943.

Tautu, A. L., ed. *Acta Honorii III (1216–1227) et Gregorii IX (1227–1241) e registris Vaticanis aliisque fontibus*. Rome, 1950.

Tautu, A. L., ed. *Acta Ioannis XXII (1317–1334) e registribus Vaticanis aliisque fontibus*. Vatican City, 1952.

Tautu, A. L.. *Acta Urbani IV, Clementis IV, Gregorii X (1261–1276) e registris Vaticanis aliisque fontibus*. Vatican City, 1953.

Tautu, A. L., ed. *Acta Benedicti XII, 1334–1342, e regestis Vaticanis aliisque fontibus*. Vatican City, 1958.

Tautu, A. L., ed. *Acta Clementis VI (1342–1352) e regestis Vaticanis aliisque fontibus*. Vatican City, 1960.

Tautu, A. L., ed. *Acta Innocentii pp. VI (1352–1362) e regestis Vaticanis aliisque fontibus*. Vatican City, 1961.

Tautu, A. L., ed. *Acta Urbani PP. V (1362–1370) e regestis Vaticanis aliisque fontibus*. Vatican City, 1964.

Tautu, A. L., ed. *Acta Gregorii P.P. XI (1370–1378) e regestis Vaticanis aliisque fontibus*. Vatican City, 1966.

Tautu, A. L., ed. *Acta Urbani P.P. VI (1378–1379), Bonifacii P.P. IX (1389–1404), Innocentii P.P. VII (1404–1406), et Gregorii P.P. XII (1406–1415) e regestis vaticanis ed lateranensibus aliisque fontibus*. Rome, 1970.

Tautu, A. L., ed. *Acta pseudopontificum Clementis VII (1378–1394), Benedicti XIII (1394–1417), Alexandri V (1409–1410), et Johannis XXIII (1406–1417) e regestis Avenionensibus, Vaticanis, Lateranensibus et supplicationum*. Rome, 1971.

Tautu, A. L., and F. M. Delorme, eds. *Acta romanorum pontificum ab Innocentio V ad Benedictum XI (1276–1304) e regestis Vaticanis aliisque fontibus*. Vatican City, 1954.

Tedeschi, J. "A 'Queer Story': The Inquisitorial Manuscripts." In *Treasures of the Library, Trinity College Dublin*, edited by P. Fox, pp. 67–74. Dublin, 1986.

Teige, J. "Beiträge zum päpstlichen Kanzleiwesen des 13. und 14. Jahrhunderts." *Mitteilungen des Instituts für österreichische Geschichtsforschung* 17 (1896): 408–440.

Teige, J.. *Beiträge zur Geschichte der Audientia litterarum contradictarum*. Prague, 1897.

Tellenbach, G. "Beiträge zur kuriale Verwaltungsgeschichte im 14. Jahrhundert." *Quellen und Forschungen aus italienischen Archiven und Bibliotheken* 24 (1932–1933): 150–187.

Tellenbach, G., ed. *Urban VI., Bonifaz IX., Innozenz VII. und Gregor XII., 1378–1415*. Berlin, 1933–1961.

"Terzo centenario della Sacra Congregazione de Propaganda Fide." *Civiltà cattolica* 73.2 (1922): 519–530; 73.3 (1922): 8–18.

Tessier, G. "Diplomatique." In *L'Histoire et ses méthodes*, by C. Samaran, pp. 633–676. Paris, 1961.

Tessier, G. *La diplomatique*. 2d ed. Paris, 1962.

Tessier, G. "Note sur un manuel à l'usage d'un officier de la Cour pontificale (XIIIe siècle)." In *Études d'histoire du droit canonique dédiées à Gabriel Le Bras*, vol. 1, pp. 357–371. Paris, 1965.

Theiner, A. *Documents inédits relatifs aux affaires religieuses de la France 1790 a 1800*. Paris, 1857–1858.

Theiner, A. *Vetera monumenta historica Hungariam sacram illustrantia, maximam partem nondum edita ex tabulariis vaticanis*. Rome, 1859–1860.

Theiner, A. *Vetera monumenta Poloniae et Lithuaniae gentiumque finitimarum historiam illustrantia, maximam partem nondum edita ex tabulariis vaticanis*. Rome, 1860–1864.

Theiner, A. *Codex diplomaticus dominii temporalis S. Sedis: Recueil de documents pour servir à l'histoire du gouvernement temporal des états du Saint-Siège, extraits des archives du Vatican*. Rome, 1861–1862.

Theiner, A. *Vetera monumenta Slavorum meridionalium historiam illustrantia, maximam partem nondum edita ex tabulariis vaticanis*. Rome, 1863–1875.

Theiner, A. *Vetera monumenta Hibernorum et Scotorum historiam illustrantia, quae ex Vaticani, Neapolis ac Florentiae tabulariis: Ab Honorio PP. III usque ad Paulum PP. III, 1216–1547*. Rome, 1864.

Theiner, A. *Monumenta spectantia ad unionem ecclesiarum Graecae et Romanae maiorem partem e santioribus vaticani tabularis*. Vienna, 1872.

Theiner, A. *Acta genuina SS. oecumenici Concilii Tridentini: sub Paulo III. Julio III. et Pio IV. . . .* Zagreb, 1874.

Thiel, A. *Epistolae romanorum pontificum genuinae et quae ad eos scriptae sunt A.S. Hilaro usque ad Pelagium II.* Braunsberg, 1868.

Thielens, J. *La correspondance de Vincenzo Santini internonce aux Pays-Bas, 1713–1721*. Vol. 12 of *Analecta vaticano-belgica*. Ser. 2, section A, *Nonciature de Flandre*. Brussels, 1969.

Thompson, J. W. "The Papal Registers." *Church Quarterly Review* 127 (1938): 37–75.

Tihon, C. "Les expectatives 'in forma pauperum,' particulièrement au XIVe siècle." *Bulletin de l'Institut historique Belge de Rome* 5 (1925): 51–118.

Tihon, C. "Grâces et faveurs accordées par le cardinal Carlo Caraffa pendant sa légation à Bruxelles (1557–1558)." *Bulletin de l'Institut historique Belge de Rome* 27 (1952): 269–291.

Tihon, C. "Suppliques originales adressées au cardinal-légat C. Caraffa (1557–1558)." In *Miscellanea archivistica Angelo Mercati*, pp. 159–168. Vatican City, 1952.

Tihon, C., ed. *Lettres de Grégoire XI (1371–1378)*. Vols. 11, 20, 25, and 28 of *Analecta vaticano-belgica: Documents relatifs aux anciens diocèses de Cambrai, Liège, Thérouanne et Tournai*. Brussels, 1958–1975.

Tillmann, H. "Zum Regestum super negotio Romani imperii Innocenz' III." *Quellen und Forschungen aus italienischen Archiven und Bibliotheken* 23 (1931–1932): 53–79.

Tisserant, E. *Archives Vaticanes, Histoire ecclésiastique*. Vols. 4–5 of *Mélanges Eugène Tisserant*. Vatican City, 1964.

Tisserant, E. *Bibliothèque Vaticane*. Vols. 6–7 of *Mélanges Eugène Tisserant*. Vatican City, 1964.

Tits-Dieuaide, M., ed. *Documents relatifs au Grand Schisme*. Vol. 5, *Lettres de Benoît XIII (1394–1422)*, Part 2 (1395–1422). Vol. 19 of *Analecta vaticano-belgica: Documents relatifs aux anciens diocèses de Cambrai, Liège, Thérouanne et Tournai.* Brussels, 1960.

Tjäder, J. O. "Le origini della scrittura curiale romana." *Bullettino dell'Archivio paleografico italiano,* 3d ser. 2–3 (1963–1964): 7–54.

Tondelli, L. "Una bolla ignorata di Innocenzo IV a Nonantola." *Atti e memorie della Deputazione di storia patria per le antiche provincie modenesi,* 8th ser. 5 (1953): 172–175.

Toupin, R., ed. *Correspondance du nonce en France, Giovanni Battista Castelli (1581–1583).* Vol. 7 of *Acta nuntiaturae gallicae.* Rome, 1967.

Trenchs Odena, J. "La Cámara Apostolica y sus documentos." *Boletín de la Sociedad Castellonense de cultura* 58 (1982): 629–652.

Trenchs Odena, J. "La Penitenciaria Apostolica: Documentos y registros." *Boletín de la Sociedad Castellonense de cultura* 58 (1982): 653–692.

Tromp, S. "De manuscriptis acta et declarationes antiquas S. Congregationis Concilii Tridentini continentibus." *Gregorianum* 38 (1957): 481–502; 39 (1958): 93–129.

Tüchle, H. *Acta S.C. de Propaganda Fide Germaniam spectantia: Die Protokolle der Propaganda-Kongregation zu deutschen Angelegenheiten 1622–1649.* Paderborn, 1962.

Tüchle, H. *Die Protokolle der Propagandakongregation zu deutschen Angelegenheiten 1657–1667 diasporasorge unter Alexander VII.* Paderborn, 1972.

Ugolino, M. *La nuova Biblioteca Leonina nel Vaticano.* Rome, 1893.

Ullmann, W. "On the Heuristic Value of Medieval Chancery Products, with Special References to Papal Documents." *Annali della Fondazione italiana per la storia amministrativa* 1 (1964): 117–134.

Ullmann, W. "A Decision of the Rota Romana on the Benefit of Clergy in England." In *Collectanea Stephan Kuttner,* vol. 3, pp. 457–489. Bologna, 1967.

Vacant, A., and E. Mangenot, eds. *Dictionnaire de théologie catholique.* Paris, 1908–1949.

Valk, J. P. de. "Het archief van de Haagse nuntiatuur, 1802–1879." *Jaarboek van het Katholiek Documentatie* 7 (1977): 119–153.

Valk, J. P. de. *Lettres de Francesco Capaccini: Agent diplomatique et internonce du Saint-Siège au Royaume Uni del Pays Bas, 1828–1831.* Vol. 5 of *Analecta vaticano-belgica.* Ser. 2, section C, *Nonciature de Bruxelles.* Brussels, 1983.

Valk, J. P. de. *Inventaris van Romeinse Archivalia Betreffende het Verenigd Koninkrijk der Nederlanden 1813–1831.* Vols. 9–10 of *Analecta vaticano-belgica.* Ser. 2, section C, *Nonciature de Bruxelles.* Brussels, 1991.

Van Isacker, P., and U. Berlière, eds. *Lettres de Clément VI (1342–1352).* Vol. 6 of *Analecta vaticano-belgica: Documents relatifs aux anciens diocèses de Cambrai, Liège, Thérouanne et Tournai.* Rome, 1924–.

Vanti, M. *Mons. Bernardino Cirillo, commendatore e maestro generale dell'ord. di S. Spirito (1556–1575).* Rome, 1936.

Vanti, M. *S. Giacomo degl'Incurabili di Roma nel Cinquecento: Dalle compagnie del Divino Amore a San Camillo de Lellis.* Rome, 1938.

Vanyo, T. "Das Archiv der Konsistorialkongregation." In *Leo Santifaller Festschrift,* pp. 151–179. Vienna, 1950.

Varsányi, G. I. "De competentia et procedura Sacrae Congregationis Concilii ab origine ad haec usque nostra tempora."

In *La sacra Congregazione del Concilio: Quarto centenario della fondazione, 1564–1964, studi e ricerche,* pp. 51–161. Vatican City, 1964.

Vattasso, M. *Per la storia del dramma sacro in Italia.* Rome, 1903.

Vattasso, M., and E. Carusi. *Codices vaticani latini: Codices 10301–10700.* Rome, 1920.

Vaucelle, E. *Catalogue des lettres de Nicolas V concernant la province ecclésiastique de Tours d'après les registres des Archives Vaticanes.* Paris, 1908.

Vehse, O. "Die älteren Papsturkunden der grossen Karthause zu Farneta." In *Festschrift Albert Brackmann,* edited by L. Santifaller, pp. 422–433. Weimar, 1931.

Velykyi, A. H. S. *Josaphat Hieromartyr: Documenta romana beatificationis et canonizationis.* Rome, 1952–.

Velykyi, A. H. *Documenta pontificum romanorum historiam Ucrainae illustrantia (1075–1953).* Rome, 1953–1954.

Velykyi, A. H. *Acta S.C. de Propaganda Fide Ecclesiam Catholicam Ucrainae et Bielarusjae spectantia.* Rome, 1953–1955.

Velykyi, A. H. *Litterae S.C. de Propaganda Fide ecclesiam catholicam Ucrainae et Bielarusjae spectantes.* Rome, 1954–1957.

Velykyi, A. H. *Congregationes particulares Ecclesiam Catholicam Ucrainae et Bielarusjae spectantes.* Rome, 1956–1957.

Velykyi, A. H. *Litterae nuntiorum apostolicorum historiam Ucrainae illustrantes (1550–1850).* Rome, 1959–.

Venditelli, C. C. *Le più antiche carte del convento di San Sisto in Roma (905–1300).* Rome, 1987.

Vendola, D., ed. *Apulia, Lucania, Calabria.* Vol. 4 of *Rationes decimarum Italiae nei secoli XIII e XIV,* edited by P. Guidi and P. Sella. Vatican City, 1939.

Vendola, D. *Documenti tratti dai Registri Vaticani (da Innocenzo III a Nicola IV).* Trani, 1940.

Vestri, O. *In Romanae aulae actionum, et iudiciorum mores.* Venice, 1573.

Vian, P. *L'Archivio Segreto Vaticano e le ricerche storiche: Città del Vaticano, 4–5 giugno 1981.* Rome, 1983.

Vidal, J. M. *Benoît XII (1334–1342): Lettres communes analysées d'après les registres dits d'Avignon et du Vatican.* Vol. 2 bis of *Bibliothèque des Écoles françaises d'Athènes et de Rome.* 3d ser., *Registres et lettres des papes du XIVe siècle.* Paris, 1903–1911.

Vidal, J. M. *Bullaire de l'inquisition française au XIVe siècle et jusqu'a la fin du grand schisme.* Paris, 1913.

Vidal, J. M., and G. Mollat. *Benoît XII (1334–1342): Lettres closes et patentes intéressant les pays autres que la France.* Vol. 2 bis of *Bibliothèque des Écoles françaises d'Athènes et de Rome.* 3d ser., *Registres et lettres des papes du XIVe siècle.* Paris, 1913–1950.

Villani, P., D. Veneruso, and M. Bettoni. *Nunziature di Napoli.* Rome, 1962–.

Visconti, P. E. *Città e famiglie nobili e celebri dello Stato pontificio.* Rome, 1847.

Volpini, R. "Additiones Kehrianae." *Rivista di storia della chiesa in Italia* 22 (1968): 313–424; 23 (1969): 313–361.

Wagner, W. "Die Bestände des Archivio della Nunziatura Vienna bis 1792." *Römische historische Mitteilungen* 2 (1957–58): 82–203.

Wahrmund, L. *Quellen zur Geschichte des römisch-kanonischen Prozesses im Mittelalter.* Innsbruck, 1905–.

Waley, D. P. "A Register of Boniface VIII's Chamberlain." *Journal of Ecclesiastical History* 8 (1957): 141–152.

Wandruszka, A. *Nuntius Commendone 1560 (Dezember)–1562 (März).* Vol. 2 of *Nuntiaturberichte aus Deutschland nebst ergänzenden Actenstücken. Zweite Abteilung, 1560–1572.* Graz, 1953.

Watt, D. E. R. "Sources for Scottish History of the Fourteenth Century in the Archives of the Vatican." *Scottish Historical Review* 32 (1953): 101–122.

Watt, D. E. R. "University Clerks and Rolls of Petitions for Benefices." *Speculum* 34 (1959): 213–229.

Watt, D. E. R. "University Graduates in Scottish Benefices before 1410." *Records of the Scottish Church History Society* 15 (1965): 77–88.

Watt, J. A. "Negotiations between Edward II and John XXII Concerning Ireland." *Irish Historical Studies* 10 (1956): 1–20.

Watt, J. A. "The Papacy and Episcopal Appointments in 13th Century Ireland." *Proceedings of the Irish Catholic Historical Committee* (1959): 1–9.

Weakland, J. E. "Administration and Fiscal Centralization under Pope John XXII (1316–1334)." *Catholic Historical Review* 54 (1968): 39–54, 285–310.

Weber, C. *Die ältesten päpstlichen Staatshandbücher: Elenchus Congregationum, Tribunalium et Collegiorum Urbis, 1629–1714.* Rome, 1991.

Weber, C., ed. *Legati e governatori dello Stato pontificio (1550–1809).* Rome, 1994.

Weber, F. J. "The Secret Vatican Archives." *American Archivist* 27 (1964): 63–66.

Weber, F. J. "Roman Archives of Propaganda Fide." *Records of the American Catholic Historical Society of Philadelphia* 76 (1965): 245–248.

Weiss, S., and J. Rainer. *Nuntiatur des Germanico Malaspina und des Giovanni Andrea Caligari 1582–1587.* Vienna, 1981.

Werunsky, E. "Bemerkung über die im Vatikanischen Archiv befindlichen Register Clemens VI. und Innozenz VI." *Mitteilungen des Instituts für österreichische Geschichtsforschung* 6 (1885): 140–155.

Werunsky, E. *Excerpta ex registris Clementis VI. et Innocentii VI. summorum pontificum historiam S. R. Imperii sub regimine Karoli IV. illustrantia.* Innsbruck, 1885.

White, J. M. *The Diocesan Seminary in the United States: A History from the 1780's to the Present.* Notre Dame, Ind., 1989.

Wiederhold, W. "Papsturkunden in Florenz." *Nachrichten der königlichen Gesellschaft der Wissenschaften zu Göttingen. Philologisch-historische Klasse* (1901): 306–325.

Wiederhold, W. *Papsturkunden in Frankreich: Reiseberichte zur Gallia pontificia.* Berlin, 1906–1913.

Wijnhoven, J. *Nuntius Pier Luigi Carafa (1624 Juni–1627 August).* Vol. 7 of *Nuntiaturberichte aus Deutschland nebst ergänzenden Actenstücken, Die Kölner Nuntiatur.* Paderborn, 1980.

Williman, D. "Letters of Etienne Cambarou, Camerarius Apostolicus (1347–1361)." *Archivum Historiae Pontificiae* 15 (1977): 195–215.

Williman, D. "The Camerary and the Schism." In *Genèse et débuts du Grand Schisme d'Occident,* pp. 65–71. Paris, 1980.

Williman, D. "Summary Justice in the Avignonese Camera." In *Proceedings of the Sixth International Congress of Medieval Canon Law,* edited by S. Kuttner and K. Pennington, pp. 437–449. Vatican City, 1985.

Williman, D. *The Right of Spoil of the Popes of Avignon 1316–1415.* Philadelphia, 1988.

Williman, D. *Calendar of the Letters of Arnaud Aubert, Cameraris Apostolicus, 1361–1371.* Toronto, 1992.

Wirz, C. *Akten über die diplomatischen Beziehungen der römische Curie zu der Schweiz, 1512–1552.* Basel, 1895.

Wirz, C. *Bullen und Breven aus italienischen Archiven, 1116–1623.* Basel, 1902.

Wirz, C. *Regesten zur Schweizergeschichte aus den päpstlichen Archiven, 1447–1513.* Bern, 1911–1918.

Witte, C. M. de. "Notes sur les plus anciens registres de brefs." *Bulletin de l'Institut historique Belge de Rome* 31 (1958): 153–168.

Witte, C. M. de, ed. *La correspondance des premiers nonces permanents au Portugal, 1532–1553.* Lisbon, 1980–1986.

Wittstadt, K. *Nuntius Atilio Amalteo (1606 September–1607 September).* Vol. 4 of *Nuntiaturberichte aus Deutschland nebst ergänzenden Actenstücken, Die Kölner Nuntiatur.* Munich, 1975.

Wojtyska, H. D., ed. *Acta Nuntiaturae Polonae.* Rome, 1990–.

Wright, C. W. *Music and Ceremony at Notre Dame of Paris, 500–1500.* Cambridge, 1989.

Wyngaert, A. van den, G. Mensaert, and F. Margiotti. *Sinica Franciscana: Itinera et relationes Fratrum Minorum saeculi XIII et XIV.* Florence, 1929–.

Zacour, N. P. *Talleyrand: The Cardinal of Périgord, 1301–1364.* Philadelphia, 1960.

Zimmermann, H. "Papstregesten, 911–1024." In *Regesta Imperii.* Part 2, *Die Regesten des Kaiserreichs, sächsisches Haus, 919–1024,* by J. F. Böhmer. Vienna, 1969.

Zöllner, W. *Die Papsturkunden des Staatsarchivs Magdeburg von Innozenz III. bis zu Martin V.* Halle, 1966–.

Index of Agency Names

THIS INDEX INCLUDES THE NAMES OF ALL AGENCIES WITH SEPARATE entries in the text. It does not include agencies that are mentioned in the text but do not have separate entries. For most of the agencies of the Curia, the index includes alternative forms of names in Latin, English, and Italian. Most other names are presented in Italian only. For all agency names, the index presents inverted forms of the names alphabetized under significant words in the name. Note that the index is arranged using letter-by-letter (rather than word-by-word) alphabetization.

Index of Series Titles

THIS INDEX INCLUDES THE TITLES OF ALL RECORDS SERIES described in the text. It also includes titles inverted so they are alphabetized by the names of persons, places, or organizations mentioned in the titles. Common abbreviations of titles are also listed. Titles in brackets were assigned by project staff.

Castelnuovo di Porto, Atti dei notai di, 5.3.9.1

Castelnuovo di Porto, Governi di, 5.3.9.2

Castracane, Castruccio, Spoglio del, 7.10.43

Catalogus universalis nundinis franco-furtensibus autumnalibus, 7.9.6

Caterini, Prospero, Spoglio del, 7.10.44

Cattani, Federico Amadori, Spoglio del, 7.10.45

Causae criminales, 5.1.38.1

Cause, 3.3.2.2

[Cause], 3.1.15.5

Cause, posizioni e lettere, 2.2.1.3

Cause e posizione: Stampati, 2.2.1.2

Cavalchini, Francesco Guido-Bono, Spoglio del, 7.10.46

Cavalieri: Lista del fruttato dei signori cavalieri . . . per il mese . . . , 3.2.7.9

Cecoslovacchia, Archivio della Nunziatura di, 4.25.1

Cedulae et controcedulae, 3.1.3.12

Cedularum et rotulorum, 3.1.3.13

Celestini, 7.7.14.1

Cerretti, Bonaventura, Spoglio del, 7.10.47

Cerretti, Carte, 7.5.22.1

Certificati, 2.2.23.2

Certosini, 7.7.13.1

Cervia e di Comacchio, Amministrazione delle saline di, 5.1.6.1

Chiese collegiate di Roma, 7.9.7

Chigi, Flavio, Spoglio del, 7.10.48

Chigi, Fondo, 7.5.23.1

Chile, Archivio della Nunziatura Apostolica in, 4.18.1

Ciacchi, Luigi, Spoglio del, 7.10.49

Ciampi, Tommaso, Spoglio del, 7.10.50

Ciani, Luigi, Spoglio del, 7.10.51

Cibo, Fondo, 7.5.24.1

Cina, Archivio dell' Internunziatura in, 4.19.1

Circolari, 3.1.15.6

Cistercensi, 7.7.15.1

Civitavecchia, Delegazione apostolica di, 5.3.10.1

Civitavecchia, Direzione provinciale di polizia di, 5.3.10.2

Civitavecchia, Giudicature di pace di, 5.2.12

Civitavecchia, Governo e Tribunale civile e criminale di, 5.3.10.3

Civitella, Atti dei notai di Olevano (Olevano Romano), Roiate e, 5.3.20.1

Clarelli, Nicola Paracciani, Spoglio del, 7.10.52

[Clement XI], Fondo Albani, 7.5.25.1

CLO, 3.1.32.1

Coadiutorie e commende, Registri "Bullarum" già, 3.2.14.118

Coleta, Fondo S., 7.5.26.1

Collectanea, 3.1.15.7

Collectanea miscellanea, 7.5.39.1

Collectoriae, 3.2.3.22

Collectoriali, 4.90.2

Collegi, 3.2.14.36

Collegio dei mazzieri, 2.1.6.1

Collegio dei notai capitolini, 5.1.16.1

Collegio dei protonotarii apostolici, 2.1.8.1

Collegio Urbano, 3.1.6.45

Collezione bolle e breve apostolici, 3.1.3.14

Collezione Brancadori, 7.5.16.1

Collezione delle assegne, 3.2.3.23

Collezione di rescritti: Ponenza, 3.1.15.8

Collezione d'istruzioni, circolari e decreti a stampa, 3.1.6.5

Collezione Garampi, 7.5.39.2

Collezione prima dei catasti, 5.1.188

Collezione seconda dei catasti, 5.1.189

Colonia, Archivio della Nunziatura di Colonia, 4.20.1

Colonia, Nunziatura de, 3.2.14.89

Colonna, Archivio, 7.5.27.1

Colonna, Governi baronali di Paliano, dei principi, 5.3.22.1

Comacchio, Amministrazione delle saline di Cervia e di, 5.1.6.1

Comarca, Notai della presidenza di Roma e, 5.3.24.1

Comarca, Presidenza di, poi Presidenza di Roma e Comarca, 5.3.24.2

Comitato centrale, 7.4.2.1

Commissariato generale della Camera apostolica, 5.1.19.1

Commissariato generale delle ferrovie, 5.1.20.1

Commissariato straordinario delle quattro legazione, 3.2.14.37

Commissario generale della Camera apostolica, 5.1.19.2

Commissione consultiva per il miglioramento della finanza pubblica, 5.1.21.1

Commissione consultiva per la deviazione dell'Aniene, 5.1.5.2

Commissione dei crediti camerali arretrati, 5.1.22.1

Commissione deputata per il recupero dei beni e diritti ecclesiastici in Faenza, 5.1.24.1

Commissione di liquidazione dei crediti a tutto giugno 1849, 5.1.25.1

Commissione di revisione dei conti consuntivi anteriori al 1850, 5.1.26.1

Commissione di revisione dei crediti verso la Francia, 5.1.27.1

Commissione francese per la liquidazione dei crediti dello Stato Pontificio verso la Francia, 5.1.32.1

Commissione militare permanente nella XXX divisione militare, 5.2.3

Commissione per gli abbellimenti di Roma, 5.2.4

Commissione per la conservazione delle chiese di Roma, 5.1.31.1

Commissione per la revisione dei contratti non compiuti sotto il Regno italico, 5.1.33.1

Commissione per la riedificazione della basilica di S. Paolo, 5.1.76.1

Commissione pontificia di liquidazione dei crediti insinuati in tempo utile contro la Francia, 5.1.34.1

Commissiones, 3.3.2.3

Commissione speciale per la repressione del brigantaggio, 5.1.35.1

Commissioni soccorse, 3.2.14.38

Compositiones, 3.2.7.10

Computa officiorum, 3.2.7.11

Computisteria, 2.2.23.3

Computisteria generale della Camera apostolica, 5.1.36.1, 5.1.36.2

Computisteria mandati estinti dei pagamenti sul conto corrente, 1.4

Concessioni generali, 3.3.1.1

Concilia provincialia, 3.1.2.2

Concilio Vaticano I, 7.4.9.1

Concistori: Propositiones, 3.1.3.15

Conclavi, 1.5

Conclavi: Historical studies, 1.6

Confalonieri, Fondo, 7.5.28.1

Confini, 3.2.14.39

Confraternità avanti a giudici deputati, 5.1.167.2

Confraternità di S. Giovanni Decollato, 7.6.6.1

Congregatio Particularis de rebus Sinarum et Indiarum Orientalium, 3.1.6.6

Congregatio super Correctione Librorum Ecclesiae Orientalis, 3.1.32.1

Congregazione ad referendum, 5.1.48.1

Congregazione camerale, 5.1.49.1

Congregazione camerale pel contenzioso amministrativo, 5.1.50.1

Congregazione camerale per la revisione generale dei titoli relativi a privilegi ed esenzioni, 5.1.49.2

Congregazione civile dell'auditor camerae poi Tribunale civile di Roma, 5.1.154.1

Congregazione criminale, 5.1.52.1

Congregazione degli spogli, 3.1.42.1

Direzione generale del bollo, registro, ipoteche, e tasse riunite, Amministrazione poi, 5.1.99.1

Direzione generale del debito pubblico, 5.1.100.1

Direzione generale delle carceri, case di condanna, e luoghi di pena, 5.1.101.1

Direzione generale delle dogane, dazi di consumo, e diritti uniti, 5.1.102.1

Direzione generale delle poste, Amministrazione poi, 5.1.103.1

Direzione generale delle proprietà camerali, Direzione generale dei dazi diretti e delle proprietà camerali poi, 5.1.104.1

Direzione generale di polizia, 5.1.105.1, 5.1.105.2, 5.2.9

Direzione provinciale di polizia di Civitavecchia, 5.3.10.2

Direzione provinciale di polizia di Velletri, 5.3.30.1

Dispense dei decreti, 3.1.40.2

Dispense matrimoniali, 3.2.7.17

Diversorum, 3.2.10.3

Divisioni, 3.2.3.26

Domanda di autografi pontifici, 3.2.14.45

Domande, 3.2.14.46

Domenicani, 7.7.19.1

Doni, 3.2.14.47

Doni arredamenti sacri, 3.2.14.48

Doti, 3.2.11.8

Dubia extra congregationum generalem resoluta, 3.1.12.3

Egitto e l'Arabia, Archivio della Delegazione Apostolica per l', 4.31.1

Elemosinarum, 3.2.7.18

Emigrati della rivoluzione francese, 3.2.14.49

Entrata ed uscita delle mezze annate, pensioni e quindenni, 3.2.7.19

Entrata et uscita de quindenni, 3.2.3.27

Epistolae Latinae, 3.2.13.1

Epoca napoleonica: Baviera, 3.2.14.50

Epoca napoleonica, Biglietti, 3.2.14.30

Epoca napoleonica: Cardinali e governo, 3.2.14.51

Epoca napoleonica: Francia, 3.2.14.52

Epoca napoleonica: Governatori, 3.2.14.53

Epoca napoleonica: Italia, 3.2.14.54

Epoca napoleonica: Presidenza delle armi, 5.1.141.1

Epoca napoleonica: Vescovi e governo, 3.2.14.55

Equatore, Archivio della Nunziatura Apostolica in, 4.29.1

Eredità, 3.1.6.46

Esercizi, 3.2.11.9

Esteri, 3.2.14.56, 3.2.14.57

Estonia, Archivio della Nunziatura d', 4.34.1

Estremo Oriente, Archivio della procura della congregazione nell', 3.1.6.2

Evangelisti, Giuseppe, Spoglio del, 7.10.72

Evangelisti, Marco, Spoglio del, 7.10.73

[Expedition of Commodore Matthew Perry], 7.9.8

Expeditiones, 3.2.7.20

Facoltà straordinarie, 3.1.6.12

Faenza, Commissione deputata per il recupero dei beni e diritti ecclesiastici in, 5.1.24.1

Falzacappa, Giovan Francesco, Spoglio del, 7.10.74

Famiglie nobili, 7.9.9

Fantuzzi, Miscellanea, 7.5.33.1

Farnesiane, Carte, 7.5.34.1

Favoriti-Casoni, Fondo, 7.5.35.1

Felice V, Bollario di, 7.5.36.1

Feliciangeli, Girolamo, Spoglio del, 7.10.75

Ferrara, Legazione di, 3.2.14.67

Ferretti, Gabriele, Spoglio del, 7.10.76

Ferrieri, Innocenzo, Spoglio del, 7.10.77

Fesch, Giuseppe, Spoglio del, 7.10.78

Feudi del Piedmonte, 3.1.15.10

Fiandra, Nunziatura di, 3.2.14.91

Fiano (Fiano Romano), Atti dei notai di, 5.3.12.1

Fieschi, Adriano, Spoglio del, 7.10.79

Filippine, Archivio della Nunziatura Apostolica nelle, 4.77.1

Filippini, 7.7.27.1

Filonardi, Casa, 7.5.37.1

Finy, Fondo, 7.5.38.1

Firenze, Archivio della Nunziatura di, 4.96.1

Firenze, Incaricato d'Affari di Napoli presso la corte di, 7.9.2.1

Firenze, Nunziatura di, 3.2.14.92

Firme questione romana, 3.2.14.58

Fogli d'udienza, 3.1.12.4

Fondo Agostiniani: Pergamene, 7.7.3.1

Fondo Agostiniani III: Pacchi, 7.7.3.2

Fondo Albani, 7.5.25.1

Fondo Barberini, 7.5.3.1

Fondo Basiliani, 7.7.28.1

Fondo Benedetto XIV: Bolle e costitutiones, 7.5.7.1

Fondo Benigni, 7.5.10.1

Fondo Benincasa, 7.5.11.1

Fondo Betlemiti, 7.7.7.1

Fondo Bolognetti, 7.5.13.1

Fondo Borghese, 7.5.15.2

Fondo camerale, 3.2.3.28

Fondo Carafa, 7.5.18.1

Fondo card. Bernardino Spada, 7.5.73.1

Fondo Carinci, 7.5.19.1

Fondo Carpegna, 7.5.20.1

Fondo Castellani, 7.5.21.1

Fondo Celestini, 7.7.14.2

Fondo Celestini: Procura generale, 7.7.14.3

Fondo Certosini, 7.7.13.2

Fondo Chigi, 7.5.23.1

Fondo Cibo, 7.5.24.1

Fondo concistoriale, 3.1.3.19

Fondo Confalonieri, 7.5.28.1

Fondo Consalvi, 7.5.29.1

Fondo Culto, 7.9.10

Fondo dell'Archivio di Stato di Roma, 3.2.3.29

Fondo del Monastero di SS. Domenico e Sisto, 7.8.18.1

Fondo di Vienna, 3.1.6.13

Fondo Domenicani I: Pergamene, 7.7.19.2

Fondo Domenicani II: Pacchi e volumi, 7.7.19.3

Fondo e collezione Gramiccia-Pagliucchi, 7.5.42.1

Fondo Favoriti-Casoni, 7.5.35.1

Fondo Finy, 7.5.38.1

Fondo Francescani, 7.7.20.1

Fondo Garampi, 7.5.39.4

Fondo Gesuiti, 7.7.22.1

Fondo Girolamini: Parte I, carte, 7.7.21.1

Fondo Girolamini: Parte II, pergamene, 7.7.21.2

Fondo Lauretano, 3.1.14.1

Fondo Mencacci, 7.5.49.1

Fondo moderno, 3.2.14.59

Fondo Origo, 7.5.51.1

Fondo Ottoboni, 7.5.2.1

Fondo particolare Pio IX, 7.5.59.3

Fondo Pio, 7.5.57.1

Fondo Ronconi, 7.5.62.1

Fondo S. Coleta, 7.5.26.1

Fondo S. Trifone, 7.8.12.1

Fondo Salviati, 7.5.66.2

Fondo Santini, 7.5.68.1

Fondo Savelli, 7.5.69.1

Fondo Scaramucci, 7.5.70.1

Fondo Scolopi, 7.7.31.1

Fondo Serafini, 7.5.71.1

Fondo Serviti, 7.7.34.1

Fondo Spada, 7.5.73.2

Fondo Spiga, 7.5.75.1

Fondo Toscano, 4.100.7

Fondo Veneto I, 4.100.1

Chronological Index

SERIES CONTAINING RECORDS CREATED FROM 1401 TO 1500

SERIES CONTAINING RECORDS CREATED FROM 1501 TO 1600

SERIES CONTAINING RECORDS CREATED FROM 1601 TO 1700

SERIES CONTAINING RECORDS CREATED FROM 1701 TO 1800

SERIES CONTAINING RECORDS CREATED FROM 1801 TO 1900

7.10.43	Spoglio del Castruccio Castracane	7.10.107	Spoglio del Giorgio Lana
7.10.44	Spoglio del Prospero Caterini	7.10.108	Spoglio del Vincenzo La Puma
7.10.45	Spoglio del Federico Amadori Cattani	7.10.110	Spoglio del Pietro Lasagni
7.10.46	Spoglio del Francesco Guido–Bono Cavalchini	7.10.111	Spoglio dei Fratelli Lattanzi
7.10.48	Spoglio del Flavio Chigi	7.10.112	Spoglio del Carlo Laurenzi
7.10.49	Spoglio del Luigi Ciacchi	7.10.113	Spoglio del Luigi Lavitrano
7.10.50	Spoglio del Tommaso Ciampi	7.10.114	Spoglio del Francesco Leggeri
7.10.51	Spoglio del Luigi Ciani	7.10.115	Spoglio del Lorenzo Litta
7.10.52	Spoglio del Nicola Paracciani Clarelli	7.10.116	Spoglio del Benedetto Lorenzelli
7.10.53	Spoglio del Ercole Consalvi	7.10.117	Spoglio del Angelo Luchini
7.10.55	Spoglio del Cosimo Corsi	7.10.118	Spoglio del Gaetano Ludovici
7.10.56	Spoglio del Carlo Cremonesi	7.10.119	Spoglio del Vincenzo Macchi
7.10.57	Spoglio del Carlo Cristofori	7.10.121	Spoglio del Riccardo Magnanensi
7.10.58	Spoglio del Wlodimiro Czacki	7.10.122	Spoglio del Angelo Mai
7.10.59	Spoglio del Ercole Dandini	7.10.123	Spoglio del Pietro Marini
7.10.60	Spoglio del Girolamo D'Andrea	7.10.124	Spogli Francesco Marmaggi
7.10.61	Spoglio del Pietro Giuseppe D'Avella y Navarro	7.10.125	Spoglio del Giuseppe Marozzo
		7.10.127	Spoglio del Massimo Massimi
7.10.62	Spoglio del Emanuale De Gregorio	7.10.128	Spogli Mario Mattei
7.10.63	Spoglio del Annibale Sermattei Della Genga	7.10.129	Spoglio del Antonio Matteucci
7.10.64	Spoglio del Giulio Maria Della Somaglia	7.10.130	Spoglio del Carlo Mauri
7.10.66	Spoglio del Antonino De Luca	7.10.131	Spoglio del Raffaele Mazio
7.10.67	Spoglio del Francesco De Medici	7.10.132	Spoglio del Federico De Merode
7.10.68	Spoglio del Gaetano De Ruggero	7.10.133	Spoglio del Raffaele Merry del Val
7.10.69	Spoglio del Pietro De Silvestri	7.10.134	Spoglio del Teodolfo Mertel
7.10.70	Spoglio del Camillo Di Pietro	7.10.135	Spoglio del Giuseppe Mezzofanti
7.10.71	Spoglio del Michele Di Pietro	7.10.136	Spoglio del Ludovico Micara
7.10.72	Spoglio del Giuseppe Evangelisti	7.10.139	Spoglio del Mario Mocenni
7.10.73	Spoglio del Marco Evangelisti	7.10.140	Spoglio del Raffaele Monaco La Valletta
7.10.74	Spoglio del Giovan Francesco Falzacappa	7.10.141	Spoglio del Terenziano Moreschi
7.10.75	Spoglio del Girolamo Feliciangeli	7.10.142	Spogli Francesco Nardi
7.10.76	Spoglio del Gabriele Ferretti	7.10.143	Spoglio del Ignazio Nasalli
7.10.77	Spoglio del Innocenzo Ferrieri	7.10.144	Spoglio del Lorenzo Nina
7.10.78	Spoglio del Giuseppe Fesch	7.10.145	Spoglio del Carlo Odescalchi
7.10.79	Spoglio del Adriano Fieschi	7.10.146	Spoglio del Luigi Oreglia di S. Stefano
7.10.80	Spoglio del Raffaele Fornari	7.10.147	Spoglio del Anton-Maria Orioli
7.10.81	Spogli Alessandro Franchi	7.10.148	Spoglio del Bartolomeo Pacca
7.10.82	Spoglio del Giovanni Battista Franzelin	7.10.149	Spoglio del Tiberio Pacca
7.10.83	Spoglio del Filippo Frassinelli	7.10.150	Spoglio del Antonio Pallotta
7.10.84	Spoglio del Luigi Frezza	7.10.151	Spoglio del Luigi Pallotti
7.10.85	Spogli Andrea Frühwirth	7.10.152	Spoglio del Luigi Paolucci de Calboli
7.10.86	Spogli Giulio Gabrielli	7.10.154	Spoglio del Costantino Patrizi
7.10.87	Spoglio del Luigi Galimberti	7.10.155	Spoglio del Carlo Maria Pedicini
7.10.88	Spoglio del Pietro Francesco Galleffi	7.10.156	Spogli Francesco Pentini
7.10.89	Spogli Antonio Domenico Gamberini	7.10.157	Spoglio del Girolamo Petri
7.10.92	Spoglio del Francesco Gaude	7.10.158	Spoglio del Adeodato Giovanni Piazza
7.10.93	Spoglio del Ludovico Gazzoli	7.10.159	Spoglio del Enrico Piccoli
7.10.94	Spoglio del Pietro Giannelli	7.10.160	Spoglio del Giovanni Pierantozzi
7.10.95	Spoglio del Angelo Giansanti	7.10.162	Spoglio del Paolo Polidori
7.10.96	Spoglio del Eugenio Giordani	7.10.163	Spoglio del Angelo Quaglia
7.10.97	Spoglio del Giacomo Giustiniani	7.10.164	Spoglio del Mariano Rampolla del Tindaro
7.10.98	Spoglio del Pasquale Tommaso Gizzi	7.10.165	Spoglio del Lorenzo Randi
7.10.99	Spoglio del Eustachio Gonella	7.10.166	Spoglio del Carlo Augusto di Reisach
7.10.100	Spoglio del Gennaro Granito Pignatelli di Belmonte	7.10.167	Spoglio del Achille Maria Ricci
		7.10.168	Spogli Nicola Riganti
7.10.101	Spoglio del Domenico Guidi	7.10.169	Spoglio del Agostino Rivarola
7.10.102	Spoglio del Giuseppe Hergenrother	7.10.170	Spoglio del Roberto Roberti
7.10.103	Spoglio del Filippo Invernizzi	7.10.172	Spoglio del Luigi Ruffo Scilla
7.10.104	Spoglio del Giovanni Janni	7.10.173	Spoglio del Giovanni Rufini
7.10.105	Spoglio del Domenico Jorio	7.10.174	Spoglio del Giovanni Rusconi
7.10.106	Spoglio del Luigi Lambruschini	7.10.175	Spoglio del Francesco Sabatucci

SERIES CONTAINING RECORDS CREATED BEGINNING 1901

RECORD SERIES NOT REPRESENTED IN THE CHRONOLOGICAL INDEX

Because inclusive dates were not identified for these series, they have not been included in the chronological index.

AGENCIES NOT REPRESENTED IN THE CHRONOLOGICAL INDEX

These agencies are represented in this volume by agency histories only. No records were identified for them, although related records are found in many cases under other headings.